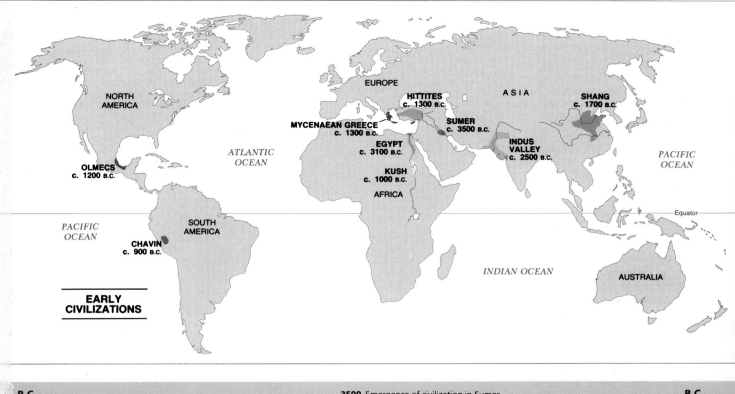

EARLY
CIVILIZATIONS

Map labels:
NORTH AMERICA
ATLANTIC OCEAN
PACIFIC OCEAN
SOUTH AMERICA
OLMECS c. 1200 B.C.
CHAVIN c. 900 B.C.
EUROPE
HITTITES c. 1300 B.C.
MYCENAEAN GREECE c. 1300 B.C.
EGYPT c. 3100 B.C.
KUSH c. 1000 B.C.
AFRICA
SUMER c. 3500 B.C.
INDUS VALLEY c. 2500 B.C.
ASIA
SHANG c. 1700 B.C.
PACIFIC OCEAN
INDIAN OCEAN
AUSTRALIA
Equator

Time Line

B.C.					B.C.
			3500 Emergence of civilization in Sumer		
28,000 Paleolithic (Old Stone) Age (to 10,000 B.C.)			3000 Bronze Age (to 1200 B.C.)		1700 Shang Dynasty in China
				2050 Middle Kingdom in Egypt	1250 Destruction of Troy
30,000	**5000**	**4000**	**3000**	**2000**	**1000**
	7000 Neolithic (New Stone) Age (to 3000 B.C.)			2370 Akkadian Empire in Sumer	1122 Chou Dynasty in China
				2500 Rise of civilization in Indus valley	
	10,000 Mesolithic Age (to 7000 B.C.)		2700 Old Kingdom in Egypt— Pyramid Age		1760 Babylonian Empire

This map, like the others that follow, is designed to show historical relationships from a global perspective. More precisely, it delineates the major societies that coexisted within a specific time frame and engaged in cultural exchanges.

As the Time Line above makes clear, societal evolution has been *accelerating*. After hundreds of thousands of years, the food-gathering Paleolithic Age yields to the Mesolithic, followed relatively quickly by

the food-producing Neolithic Age. Next comes the first of four riverine civilizations, which evolved independently. Great urban societies on the Tigris-Euphrates and Nile were linked by the Fertile Crescent, and cultural exchanges also took place with the Indus Valley civilization. Developing along the Huang Ho, China was geographically most distant from the other civilizations, so that cultural exchanges with civilizations to the west were minimal.

During the second millenium B.C. Indo-European tribes migrated into India (Indo-Aryans), Anatolia (Hittites), and the Mediterranean (Greeks, Romans). Civilizations also evolved in the Americas, but much later and independently. A similar evolutionary sequence—food gathering, food producing, and urban civilizations—occurred, it too marked by increasing societal complexity.

What has happened to the four riverbank civilizations shown in the preceding map? Chinese society has expanded to the Yangtse River. The Indus Valley civilization has disappeared, but numerous Indo-Aryan states have now arisen in the Ganges plain. Land in the Tigris-Euphrates valleys have been annexed by the Persians, who also control a declining Egyptian civilization.

The Mediterranean lands have become much more significant. Phoenician cities flourish on the east coast and Carthage in North Africa. Especially important are Athens and other city-states in Greece, about to enter into a deadly struggle with expansionist Persia. In Italy are two more Indo-European peoples: the Etruscans and a still small but virile city-state, the newly created Republic of Rome.

Iron-making techniques have spread into sub-Sahara Africa. An iron-age culture existed at Nok, while in the upper Nile valley flourished the kingdom of Kush. Stone-age peoples still inhabit most of the New World. During the Formative period of Mesoamerican culture (to A.D. 150) the Olmecs are prominent in the Gulf Coast plain of Mexico, while early Mayan villages are developing in the lowlands.

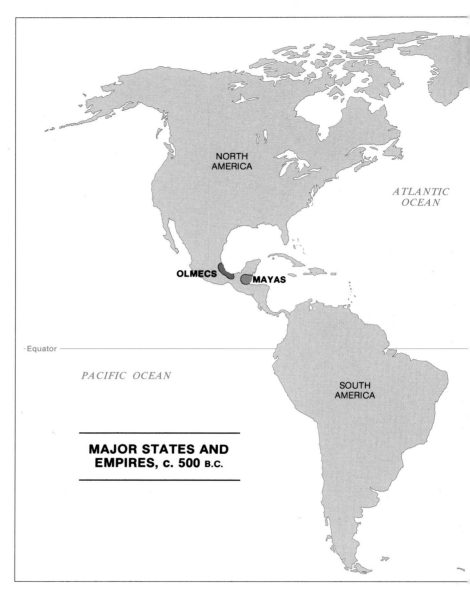

MAJOR STATES AND EMPIRES, c. 500 B.C.

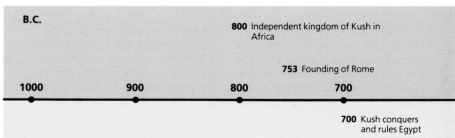

B.C.

800 Independent kingdom of Kush in Africa

753 Founding of Rome

| 1000 | 900 | 800 | 700 |

700 Kush conquers and rules Egypt

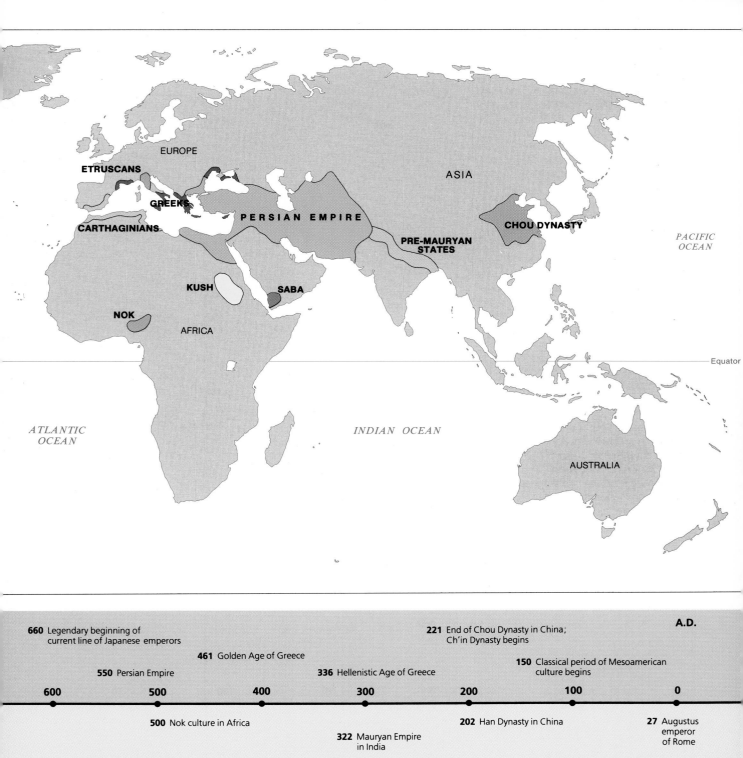

EUROPE

ETRUSCANS

GREEKS

CARTHAGINIANS

ASIA

PERSIAN EMPIRE

CHOU DYNASTY

PRE-MAURYAN STATES

PACIFIC OCEAN

KUSH

SABA

NOK

AFRICA

Equator

ATLANTIC OCEAN

INDIAN OCEAN

AUSTRALIA

							A.D.

660 Legendary beginning of current line of Japanese emperors

221 End of Chou Dynasty in China; Ch'in Dynasty begins

461 Golden Age of Greece

150 Classical period of Mesoamerican culture begins

550 Persian Empire

336 Hellenistic Age of Greece

600	500	400	300	200	100	0

500 Nok culture in Africa

202 Han Dynasty in China

27 Augustus emperor of Rome

322 Mauryan Empire in India

509 Beginning of Roman Republic

331 Empire of Alexander the Great

100 Rule by Yamato clan in Japan

The most prominent development in this era is the growth of
the Roman world-state, by A.D. 200
at the height of its power and
prosperity. Its diverse lands and peoples surround the entire Mediterranean Sea, extending from Britain to
Mesopotamia and from the Baltic
Sea well into Africa. Rome's most
dangerous rival, the Parthian Empire, lies immediately to Rome's
east. Parthian nomads had wrested
a large portion of the old Persian
Empire and for several hundred
years managed to withstand Roman
power. East of Parthia is the Kushan
Empire, which stretches to the Indus
River. To the east of the Kushan
Empire lie the far-flung territories of
the Han Dynasty in China. The
suzerainty and dynamic economy of
the Han stretch southward well into
Southeast Asia. Tenuous trade
routes commercially unite the vast
Eurasian landmass. The silk route
stretches overland across Parthian
and Kushan territory, while sea
routes link the Roman world with
India, Ceylon, Southeast Asia, and
China. In Africa Axum has supplanted the kingdom of Kush, while in
the New World Mesoamerican civilizations are now well established in
Central America and in the Central
Andes of South America.

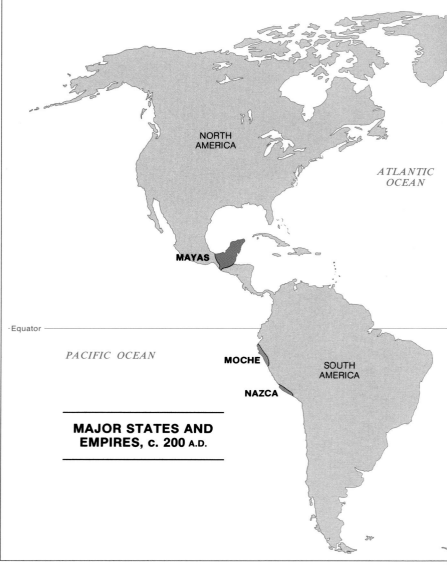

**MAJOR STATES AND
EMPIRES, c. 200 A.D.**

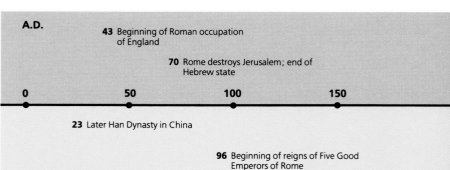

A.D.

43 Beginning of Roman occupation
of England

70 Rome destroys Jerusalem; end of
Hebrew state

0   50   100   150

23 Later Han Dynasty in China

96 Beginning of reigns of Five Good
Emperors of Rome

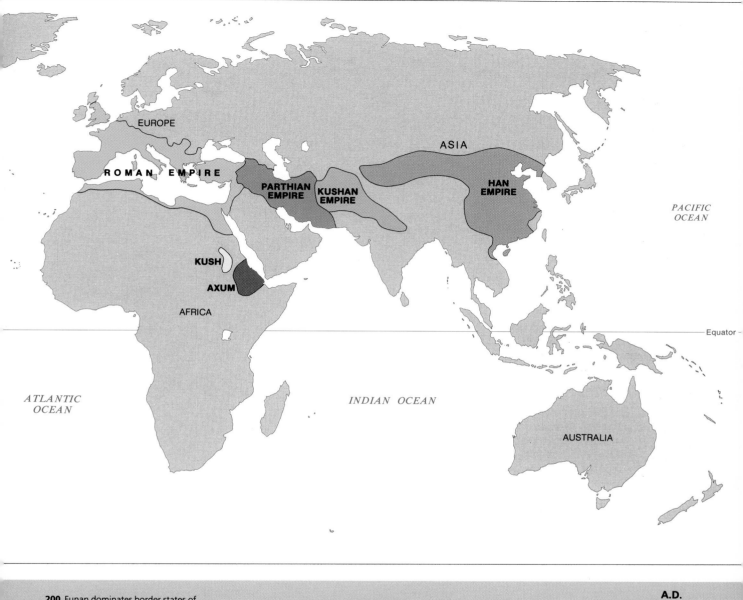

EUROPE

ASIA

ROMAN EMPIRE

PARTHIAN
EMPIRE

KUSHAN
EMPIRE

HAN
EMPIRE

PACIFIC
OCEAN

KUSH

AXUM

AFRICA

Equator

ATLANTIC
OCEAN

INDIAN OCEAN

AUSTRALIA

A.D.

200 Funan dominates border states of
Southeast Asia

330 Founding of Constantinople

476 Traditional date of
fall of Roman Empire

220 Fall of Later Han Dynasty in China
Collapse of Kushan state in India

378 Visigoths defeat Romans at Battle
of Adrianople

| 200 | 250 | 300 | 350 | 400 | 450 | 500 |

320 Chandra Gupta I establishes
Gupta Empire in India

481 Clovis I becomes
ruler of small
Frankish kingdom

300 Rise of Ghana in Africa

395 Theodosius I divides Roman
Empire between his two sons

The global map has altered markedly during the past 600 years. The western portion of the Roman world-state has disappeared, while the eastern part is now the Byzantine Empire. In what was Roman Gaul, Charlemagne has just created the new but unstable Carolingian Empire. Flanking the Byzantine Empire to the north is another unstable coalition, one formed by Bulgarian warbands. The area between the Black and Caspian seas is the domain of the Khazars, a steppe people notable for facilitating trade between East and West.

The most spectacular changes in the world map have been wrought by the triumph of Islam. The Abbasid Caliphate dominates the Middle East, and new Muslim kingdoms have appeared in North Africa and Spain. The most notable state in Africa is Ghana on the upper Niger. In the New World, Mayan civilization has reached its apogee, while in the Peruvian highlands have arisen the kingdoms of Huari and Tiahuanaco.

In northern India are numerous states, including the Rashtrakuta, Pratihara, and Pala kingdoms. China is now ruled by the T'ang, one of the greatest dynasties in its history. Chinese influence has extended eastward to the flourishing independent states in Korea and Japan.

MAJOR STATES AND EMPIRES, c. 800 A.D.

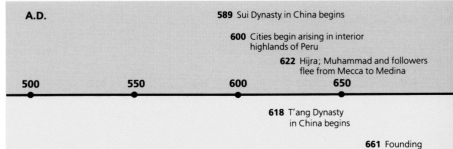

A.D.

589 Sui Dynasty in China begins

600 Cities begin arising in interior highlands of Peru

622 Hijra; Muhammad and followers flee from Mecca to Medina

500   550   600   650

618 T'ang Dynasty in China begins

661 Founding of Umayyad Dynasty

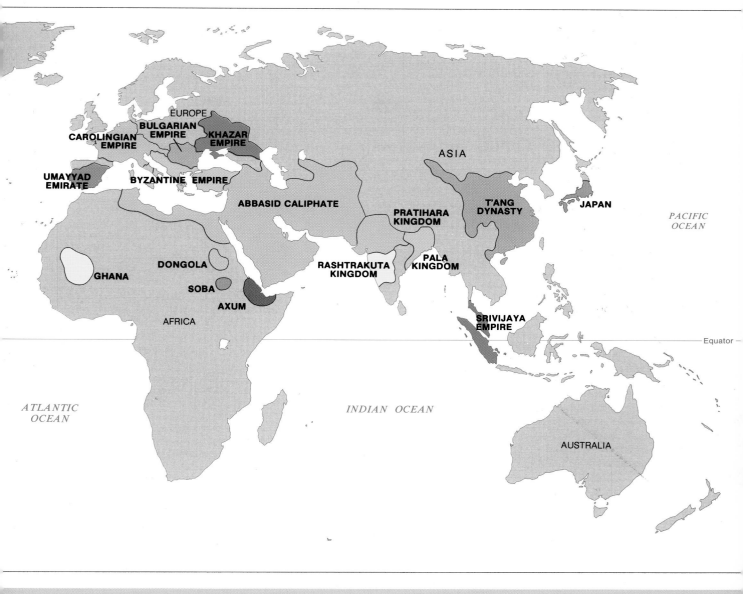

EUROPE

CAROLINGIAN EMPIRE

BULGARIAN EMPIRE

KHAZAR EMPIRE

UMAYYAD EMIRATE

BYZANTINE EMPIRE

ASIA

T'ANG DYNASTY

JAPAN

PACIFIC OCEAN

ABBASID CALIPHATE

PRATIHARA KINGDOM

GHANA

DONGOLA

SOBA

AXUM

AFRICA

RASHTRAKUTA KINGDOM

PALA KINGDOM

SRIVIJAYA EMPIRE

Equator

ATLANTIC OCEAN

INDIAN OCEAN

AUSTRALIA

711 Muslim forces from North Africa invade Spain

900 Toltecs create new power in Valley of Mexico

A.D.

794 Heian period in Japan begins

960 Sung Dynasty in China begins

700　　750　　800　　850　　900　　950　　1000

800 Charlemagne crowned emperor; peak of power of Frankish state and Carolingian Empire

910 *Reconquista*; Christians begin reclaiming Spain from Muslims

750 Beginning of Abbasid Dynasty; high tide of Islamic power and civilization

907 Last T'ang emperor deposed

The Islamic world now straddles North Africa while its grasp of Eurasian territory reaches from the Iberian Peninsula eastward into India, where in 1206 Muslim forces penetrated the Punjab and established the Delhi Sultanate. In Southeast Asia the Khmer Empire is the dominant state and the kingdom of Srivijaya is the chief power in the Indonesian archipelago.

The central and northern portions of Eurasia are about to be engulfed by the Mongols, a warlike, nomadic people from the Asian interior. The Mongols eventually conquered China, overwhelmed the Muslim states in central Asia, invaded Europe, and for a time threatened the West.

The European powers of this era included the Holy Roman Empire and the new nation-states of France and England, which will come to dominate Western politics. At the beginning of the thirteenth century, Ghana fell to Mali, a new African Islamic kingdom that reached from the Atlantic to the upper Niger. The Aztecs of Mesoamerica migrated to the valley of Mexico, where they will create a powerful empire, as will the Incas, who by 1250 had conquered Tiahuanaco and other mountain tribes in the Peruvian Andes.

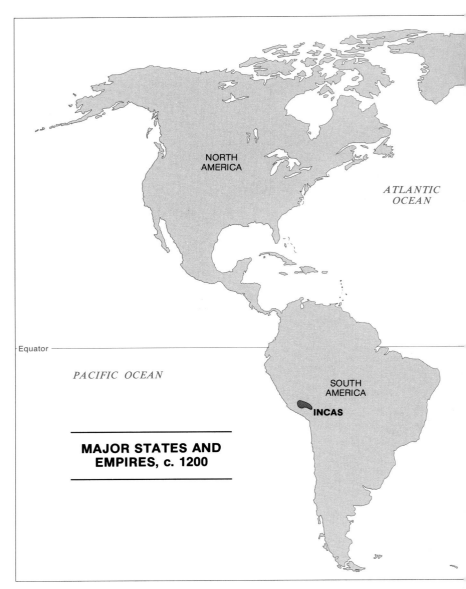

MAJOR STATES AND EMPIRES, c. 1200

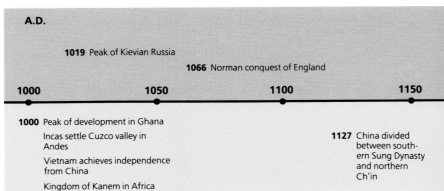

A.D.

1019 Peak of Kievian Russia

1066 Norman conquest of England

| 1000 | 1050 | 1100 | 1150 |

1000 Peak of development in Ghana

Incas settle Cuzco valley in Andes

Vietnam achieves independence from China

Kingdom of Kanem in Africa

1127 China divided between southern Sung Dynasty and northern Ch'in

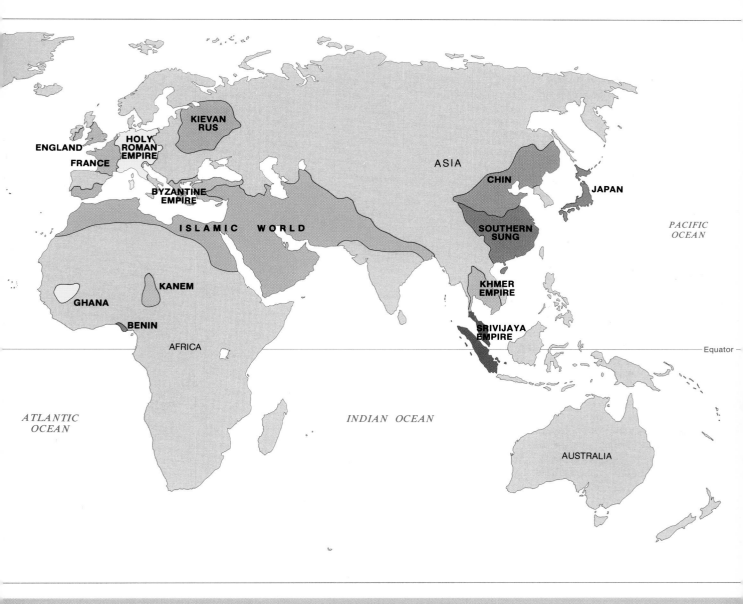

ENGLAND
FRANCE
HOLY ROMAN EMPIRE
KIEVAN RUS
BYZANTINE EMPIRE
ISLAMIC WORLD
ASIA
CHIN
JAPAN
SOUTHERN SUNG
KHMER EMPIRE
SRIVIJAYA EMPIRE
PACIFIC OCEAN
GHANA
KANEM
BENIN
AFRICA
Equator
ATLANTIC OCEAN
INDIAN OCEAN
AUSTRALIA

1185 Kamakura shogunate in Japan

1281 Japan stops Mongol invasion

A.D.

1200 Peak of Khmer Empire in Southeast Asia
Kingdom of Benin in Africa

1336 Ashikaga shogunate in Japan

1392 Yi Song-gye founds Yi Dynasty in Korea

| 1200 | 1250 | 1300 | 1350 | 1400 |

1206 Delhi Sultanate established
Mongol leader Temujin recognized as Genghis Khan

1300 Aztec confederacy in Mexico

1368 Ming Dynasty established in China

1275 Marco Polo at court of Kublai Khan

1348 Black Death sweeps Europe

1215 Magna Carta

Between the fourteenth and seventeenth centuries, Asian superiority gradually waned before the rising technical and commercial strength of the West. This shift was largely due to the European's discovery of the New World and their opening of sea lanes to all continents. But in 1500 Europe was far from dominant.

China has been reunited under the Ming and will expand into Mongolia and Annam (Vietnam). Torn by civil war, Japan will be reunited and also invade Korea. The weak Delhi Sultanate is about to be invaded by Babur, who will lay the foundation for the luxurious Mughul Empire in India.

Important new actors on the political stage include the Ottomans, whose empire will eventually touch three continents. The expanding Duchy of Moscow is paving the way for Russia's vast Eurasian empire. Explorers from Spain and Portugal are creating overseas colonial empires for the Iberian powers.

The African kingdoms of the era are the Bantu states of Zimbabwe in the southern highlands, Kongo near the Congo estuary, Benin in what is now Nigeria, and Songhai in the western Sudan. In the New World, the Aztecs in Mexico and the Incas in South America are flourishing, unaware of their impending destruction at the hands of the Spanish *conquistadores.*

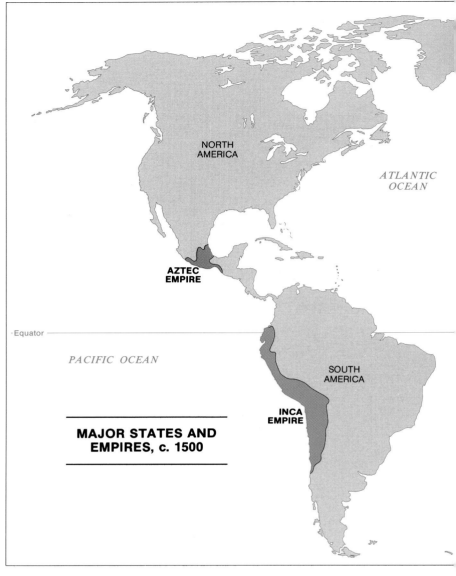

MAJOR STATES AND EMPIRES, c. 1500

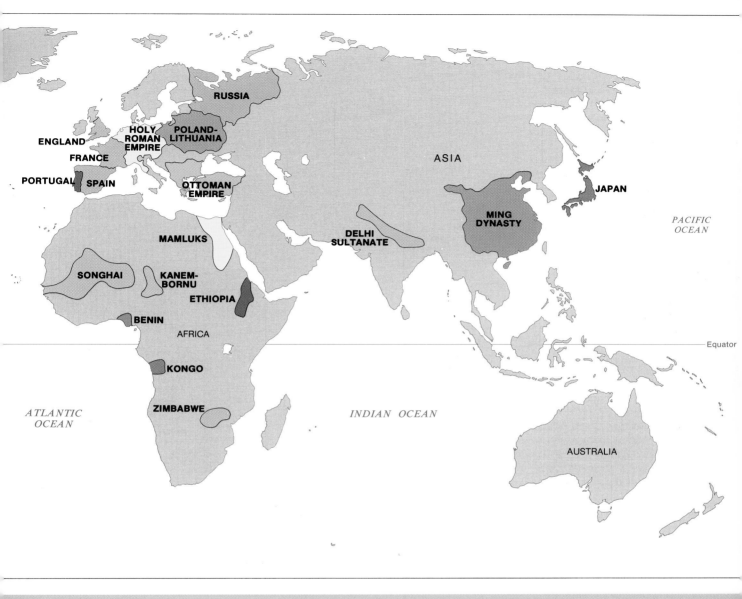

ENGLAND

HOLY
ROMAN
EMPIRE

FRANCE

PORTUGAL

SPAIN

RUSSIA

POLAND-
LITHUANIA

OTTOMAN
EMPIRE

ASIA

JAPAN

MING
DYNASTY

PACIFIC
OCEAN

MAMLUKS

DELHI
SULTANATE

SONGHAI

KANEM-
BORNU

ETHIOPIA

BENIN

AFRICA

Equator

KONGO

ATLANTIC
OCEAN

ZIMBABWE

INDIAN OCEAN

AUSTRALIA

1527 Beginning of Mughul Empire in
India

1588 Spanish Armada defeated

A.D.

1603 Tokugawa shogunate in Japan

1531 Pizzaro conquers Peru

1644 Manchus invade Ming China;
establish Ch'ing Dynasty

1550   **1600**   **1650**   **1700**

1517 Luther issues ninety-five theses

1519 Cortés arrives in Mexico

1520 Ottoman power peaks under
Suleiman the Magnificent
(1520-66)

1613 Michael Romanov establishes
Romanov Dynasty in Russia

1688 Glorious Revolution
in England

1628 Mughul Empire reaches height
under Shah Jahan (1628–58)

1637 Japan expels all Europeans

When we contrast this map with its predecessors, we see a marked expansion of "civilized" areas at the expense of vestigial primitive societies. This map further demonstrates cartographically European dominance at the beginning of the nineteenth century. The economic dynamics set in motion by the Industrial Revolution created in Europe an insatiable appetite for raw materials and opened vast new markets for finished good.

The British Empire now stretches over five continents with British colonial settlements in northern North America, Africa (Cape Colony), Asia (India), and Australia. In 1800 Napoleon's victories establish French rule over Egypt, and in 1830 France will invade Algeria in northern Africa. The Netherlands is spreading its control in Southeast Asia, and Spain rules the Philippines. Meanwhile, Russia has consolidated its control over northern Eurasia.

Isolated by choice from the West are Japan under the Tokugawa Shogunate and China ruled by the Ch'ing (Manchu) Dynasty. A number of independent states still dot Africa, but unexplored lands remain in much of the African interior as well as in Australia, in the northern latitudes of North America, and in South America, including the Amazon basin.

MAJOR WORLD STATES AND COLONIAL POSSESSIONS, 1800

- France
- Great Britain
- Batavian Republic (The Netherlands)
- Portugal
- Spain
- Other independent states

1700 Age of Reason; Industrial Revolution begins in England

1757 Battle of Plassey begins domination of India by British East India Company

| 1700 | 1725 | 1750 | 1775 |

1775 American Revolution begins

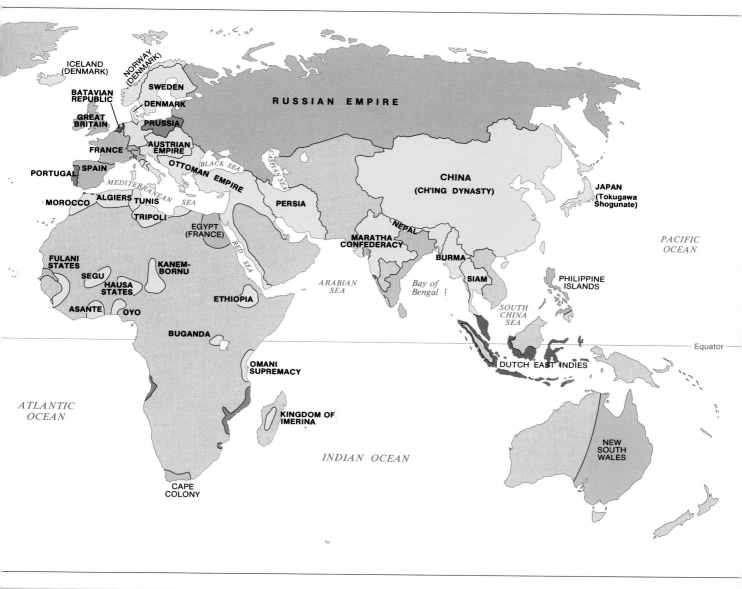

ICELAND
(DENMARK)

NORWAY (DENMARK)

SWEDEN

BATAVIAN
REPUBLIC

DENMARK

GREAT
BRITAIN

PRUSSIA

FRANCE

AUSTRIAN
EMPIRE

RUSSIAN EMPIRE

PORTUGAL

SPAIN

OTTOMAN EMPIRE

BLACK SEA

CASPIAN SEA

CHINA
(CH'ING DYNASTY)

JAPAN
(Tokugawa
Shogunate)

MOROCCO

ALGIERS

TUNIS

MEDITERRANEAN SEA

PERSIA

PACIFIC
OCEAN

TRIPOLI

EGYPT
(FRANCE)

RED SEA

NEPAL

MARATHA
CONFEDERACY

FULANI
STATES

KANEM-
BORNU

BURMA

SEGU

HAUSA
STATES

ARABIAN
SEA

Bay of
Bengal

SIAM

PHILIPPINE
ISLANDS

ASANTE

OYO

ETHIOPIA

SOUTH
CHINA
SEA

BUGANDA

Equator

OMANI
SUPREMACY

DUTCH EAST INDIES

ATLANTIC
OCEAN

KINGDOM OF
IMERINA

NEW
SOUTH
WALES

INDIAN OCEAN

CAPE
COLONY

1788 First English colony
in Australia

1829 Greece achieves independence
from Turkey

1898 Spanish-American
War

1789 French Revolution begins;
U.S. Constitution adopted

1822 Brazil achieves
independence

1859 Darwin publishes
Origin of Species

1894 Sino-Japanese
War begins

1800   **1825**   **1850**   **1875**   **1900**

1804 Napoleon declares
himself emperor

1830 July Revolution in Paris
enthrones Louis Philippe

1885 French gain control over
Indochina

1815 Napoleon defeated,
exiled to St. Helena

1848 *Communist Manifesto*
published

1899 Boer War
begins

1854 Japan opens ports to the West

Events of the nineteenth century further increased European hegemony over the world. The map of Africa shows the most notable effects. In 1870 only 10 percent of the continent was under direct European control. By 1900 most independent African states have disappeared, and the major European nations have divided the continent among themselves as they go about expanding their colonial empires.

In the Western Hemisphere, Canada has confederated and Latin America has thrown off Spanish and Portuguese rule to evolve into a collection of independent states. The United States, on the verge of becoming a great power, has begun acquiring a colonial empire, annexing both Alaska and the Philippines.

An emergent Eastern power is Japan, which annexed Formosa in 1895 and Korea in 1910. The Western powers and Japan have taken advantage of China's internal weakness to wrest both trading ports and economic concessions. Elsewhere in Asia, the Dutch, German, French, and British still claim colonial possessions.

Several important geopolitical coalitions exist among the nations of Europe; these are the military alliances that will precipitate World War I.

MAJOR WORLD STATES AND COLONIAL POSSESSIONS, 1900

- Belgium
- France
- German Empire
- Great Britain
- Italy
- The Netherlands
- Portugal
- Spain
- United States
- Other independent states

1900 U.S. emerges as most powerful nation in Western Hemisphere; Boxer Rebellion in China

1914 Panama Canal opened; Francis Ferdinand of Austria assassinated; World War I begins

1900   1905   1910   1915

1901 Commonwealth of Australia formed

1909 Union of South Africa formed

1917 Russian Revolution; U.S. enters World War I

1918 Armistice ends World War I

GREENLAND
(DENMARK)

ICELAND
(DENMARK)

SWEDEN

THE NETHERLANDS
GREAT
BRITAIN
GERMAN
EMPIRE
DENMARK

BELGIUM
AUSTRIA-
HUNGARY

FRANCE

PORTUGAL SPAIN
ITALY

MOROCCO

TRIPOLI

EGYPT

FRENCH WEST AFRICA

ANGLO-
EGYPTIAN
SUDAN

LIBERIA

ETHIOPIA

BELGIAN
CONGO

BRITISH
EAST AFRICA

GERMAN
EAST
AFRICA

ANGOLA

GERMAN
SOUTHWEST
AFRICA

MOZAMBIQUE

UNION
OF
SOUTH AFRICA

ATLANTIC
OCEAN

MEDITERRANEAN SEA

GREECE

BLACK SEA

OTTOMAN
EMPIRE

CASPIAN SEA

RUSSIAN EMPIRE

MANCHURIA

PERSIA

AFGHANISTAN

ARABIA

RED SEA

ARABIAN
SEA

INDIA

BURMA

CHINA

KOREA

JAPAN

PACIFIC
OCEAN

TAIWAN
(JAPAN)

SIAM

FRENCH
INDOCHINA

Bay of
Bengal

SOUTH
CHINA
SEA

PHILIPPINE
ISLANDS

PACIFIC ISLANDS
(GERMAN, 1899)

Equator

DUTCH EAST INDIES

INDIAN OCEAN

MADAGASCAR

AUSTRALIA

NEW
ZEALAND

1922 Union of Soviet Socialist Republics established; Mussolini
marches on Rome

1933 Hitler becomes dictator of
Germany

1929 Stock market crash in U.S.;
worldwide depression

1939 Germany invades Poland; World
War II begins

1920   **1925**   **1930**   **1935**   **1940**   **1945**   **1950**

1927 Stalin takes power in Russia;
Chiang Kai-shek purges Communists from China

1936 Mussolini conquers Ethiopia;
Spanish civil war begins

1945 Germany surrenders; Hiroshima, Nagasaki bombed, Japan
surrenders; World War II ends

1919 Paris Peace Conference;
League of Nations created;
Third Communist International
(Comintern) formed

1931 Spain becomes republic;
Japan invades Manchuria

1941 Japanese attack Pearl Harbor;
U.S. enters World War II

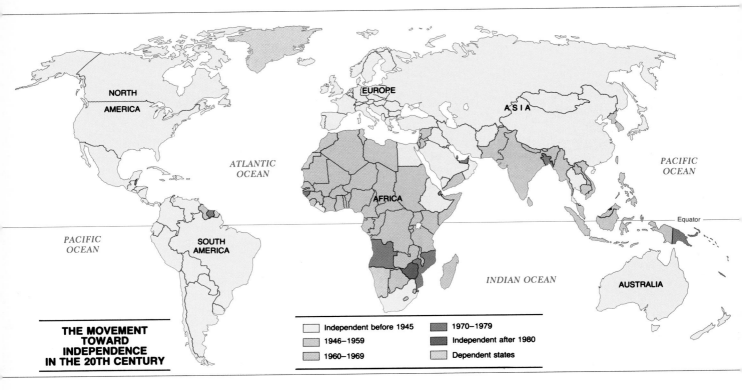

THE MOVEMENT
TOWARD
INDEPENDENCE
IN THE 20TH CENTURY

Independent before 1945		1970–1979	
1946–1959		Independent after 1980	
1960–1969		Dependent states	

The twentieth century has been called "The Age of Global Civilization"—a characterization compatible with the astronauts' pictures showing an indivisible sphere swimming in space. A global economy links the nations of the world, and daily we are made aware of shared dangers to our planetary environment.

The most striking geopolitical development of the twentieth century has been the liquidation of empires, replaced by scores of new independent nation-states. This occurrence is most evident in Africa, but the twentieth century has also seen the emergence of new nations in Asia, India, the Far East, and South America. Today there are more states—about 180—than ever before in history.

In the bipolar world of the twentieth century, competing ideologies, racial tensions, and disparities between rich and poor lands are some of the conditions bedeviling international relations. As the twenty-first century nears, humankind is slowly acquiring a new self-awareness: of interrelatedness among all its members, and no less with other forms of life compromising the ecology of the planet.

Civilization
Past & Present

Seventh Edition

T. WALTER WALLBANK
Emeritus, University of Southern California

ALASTAIR M. TAYLOR
Emeritus, Queen's University

NELS M. BAILKEY
Emeritus, Tulane University

GEORGE F. JEWSBURY
Oklahoma State University

CLYDE J. LEWIS
Emeritus, Eastern Kentucky University

NEIL J. HACKETT
Director, Oklahoma State University—Kyoto, Japan

HarperCollinsPublishers

Executive Editor: Bruce Borland
Development Editor: Betty Slack
Project Coordination, Text and Cover Design: PC&F, Inc.
Cover Photo: Blaeu Wall Map, The British Library
Photo Researcher: Sandy Schneider
Production Manager: Michael Weinstein
Compositor: PC&F, Inc.
Printer and Binder: Von Hoffmann Press
Cover Printer: The Lehigh Press, Inc.

Civilization Past & Present, Seventh Edition

Library of Congress Cataloging-in-Publication Data

Civilization, past & present / T. Walter Wallbank . . . [et al.]. — 7th
   ed.
        p.   cm.
      Includes bibliographical references and indexes.
      ISBN 0-673-38867-0 (student edition)
      ISBN 0-673-46618-3 (teacher edition)
      1. Civilization.   I. Wallbank, T. Walter (Thomas Walter), 1901–
.   II. Title: Civilization, past & present.
   CB69.C564   1991
   909 — dc20   91-25406
                                                          CIP

91 92 93 94 9 8 7 6 5 4 3 2 1

Brief Contents

*Each chapter ends with a Conclusion, Suggestions for Reading, and Notes.

Maps

Retrospective/Prospective, 1942–1992

*Of making many books there is no end; and much study is
a weariness of the flesh.*

Ecclesiastes 12:12

Authors and publishers can attest to the truth of the first part of this maxim; students will wholeheartedly endorse the second part! But this essay is about the making of only one book and how it came to chronicle historical events on a global scale. *Civilization Past & Present* was the first American college text to undertake the challenge to record the evolution of humanity from earliest times to the present. Today, half a century and seven editions later, its mission continues.

Genesis

A half century ago, when the book was conceived, the world was at war. The year 1940 witnessed the Nazi conquest of Western Europe and the Battle of Britain, while 1941 was marked by Hitler's invasion of Soviet Russia and Japan's attack on Pearl Harbor, immediately followed by the spread of war throughout the Pacific. By 1942, millions of Americans were in uniform, and shipyards and factories were turning out a vast armada of ships, planes, and tanks. Hollywood continued to produce movies, many with war themes; radio brought Jack Benny's jokes and Bing Crosby's songs into city apartments and country farmhouses; and college students across the country danced to the music of Glenn Miller and Artie Shaw. Television was still in the experimental stage, and the electronic computer had yet to be invented.

Conflict and carnage continued until, by 1945, the United States and its allies had destroyed Hitler's Berlin bunker, annihilated Hiroshima, and marked the end of history's most lethal war by creating the United Nations. On every continent people longed and worked for a new era of peace and prosperity in a world which would never again be the same.

This book grew out of a survey course offered at the University of Southern California. That course's purpose was to offer all students, whether in arts or commerce or engineering, a clearer idea of how the world in which they lived came to be. The textbook was planned when the totalitarian governments in Europe and Asia were bent on conquest, yet the majority of Americans still endeavored to insulate themselves from participating in, or accepting the consequences of, world events. Many believed it possible to rely on the geographical protection of oceans, on the Monroe Doctrine, and the tradition of "no foreign entanglements." This widespread attitude was reflected in the limitation of most college survey courses to Western culture.

In the face of such historical egocentrism, the authors believed that the United States was about to embark on a new role of world leadership, one which would require having an informed citizenry for its successful execution. To become so informed, students needed to learn about the great culture systems of the world, their historical antecedents, and those current trends and problems which were shaping the course of contemporary world affairs. To meet this need, the authors of *Civilization Past & Present* undertook to describe the significant factors in the evolution not only of Western civilization but also of the Middle East, Africa, South Asia, China, Japan, and Latin America. It was a large challenge, and the result proved to be innovative and unique.

Basic Approach and Structure

It has been said that the most difficult task in writing any book is conceiving and structuring the table of contents. What should be included? What must be left out? How should the parts be arranged so that they are coherent and make sense and also move logically from the beginning to the conclusion of the book? If these questions confront every author, then how daunting—if not madly presumptuous—the challenge becomes when authors attempt to cope with global history from Stone Age to contemporary times, and to do so within the confines of a single volume.

From the beginning, a holistic approach was applied to the structure and contents of *Civilization Past & Present*. More particularly, in order to minimize the authors' inevitable cultural bias (from having been born into and conditioned by the knowledge, values, and behavior of a Western society), they adopted from social anthropologists the concept of the "universal culture pattern." According to this principle (discussed in more detail in the Prologue), all members of the human species in every generation and every society share a fundamental commonality: to satisfy certain basic needs. How a given society responds to these needs determines its individual culture pattern. The universal culture pattern offers a useful analytical device for studying the interconnected components of societies and for understanding and appreciating the unique contributions of each. Throughout seven editions of *Civilization Past & Present*, the authors have utilized this approach, with excellent results.

The evolution of humankind has followed a particular sequence in historical geography. Stone Age peoples lived in small and scattered communities. Next arose archaic civilizations along the banks of major rivers, whose waters were utilized for irrigation and farming. Movement and activities in these riverine systems occurred in essentially one-dimensional space. Classical civilizations, such as those of Greece and Rome, grew up along the shores of seas and expanded into the hinterland. This conquest of two-dimensional space was expanded in early modern times across oceans and then to the exploration and control of entire continental regions. In this century, our species' geographical reach has soared vertically into space, linking all peoples in a "global village" and enabling humans to set foot on the moon. The authors of *Civilization Past & Present* used this anthropogeographical sequence as another guiding principle in structuring a logical and coherent format for the text.

From the beginning, a comprehensive map program has been an integral part of the text's focus on historical geography. The first edition included nearly 150 maps prepared by R. M. Chapin, Jr., who had developed at *Time* magazine his skill in dramatizing historical movements in spatial perspective. Later editions featured two-color maps distributed throughout the text; an atlas of full-color reference maps, accompanied by explanatory notes; and a series of full-color maps on the development of civilization, with timelines and explanatory text.

Special features have long been noteworthy additions to *Civilization Past & Present*. For example, the fourth edition included a series of Frontier Essays, written by eminent scholars to supplement the narrative with discussions of revolutionary discoveries of past events and to show the nature and trends of historical scholarship. In later editions appeared Historical Critiques, a second series of essays, also written by noted specialists. These Critiques dealt with such topics as the birth of history in the West, the historical method in China and India, the question of whether there had been an "Industrial Revolution," and a review of reinterpretations of history and society throughout the twentieth century.

Three kinds of Profiles have appeared in various editions of *Civilization Past & Present*. The first set of Profiles provided an in-depth focus on the human side of history. For example, one of these essays, which described the unraveling of the hoax concerning Piltdown Man as the evolutionary "missing link," demonstrated the age-old danger of attempting to fit "facts" into preconceived theories. In an account of the fate of Native Americans, another Profile dealt with the origins and consequences of the most massive uprooting of one population by another in modern times.

The fifth edition introduced Family Profiles, each one describing living conditions in different historical eras. The Family Profiles offered insights into the lives of a working-class Roman family, an upper-class family in Sung China, an Aztec family, English families in the 16th and 17th centuries, a Parisian family in 1815 and its descendants in 1914, a Jewish family in Nazi Germany, two generations of an Indian family in the 1930s and in the present, and an upper-middle class family in contemporary Venezuela.

To focus attention on the unique role played by human actors on the world stage, the sixth edition offered biographical Profiles of fascinating men and women. Hatshepsut, Diogenes, Saint Augustine, Empress Wu, Babur the Tiger, Petrarch, Catherine the Great, Sir Isaac Newton, Beethoven, Emmeline Pankhurst, Shaka the Zulu, Charlie Chaplin, and Anwar el-Sadat were some of the subjects of these Profiles. The current edition of the text features excerpts from primary source documents, allowing students to experience at first hand the voices and records of the past.

Integral to the book's format are the suggestions for reading at the end of each chapter; the chronological tables, which show the sequence of events discussed in the text and their relationship across a global spectrum; and the general index, which also provides a pronunciation guide to the names and places referred to throughout the text. Last but far from least, the authors and editors have always taken special interest—and pride—in the text's illustration program. The first edition included more than 350 photographs, drawings, and diagrams, placed directly in relation to the textual discussions they reinforced visually. In later editions, inserts of full-color art reproductions appeared throughout the text. These works of art were carefully selected to illustrate some facet of the universal culture pattern and, together with the accompanying commentary, constituted a capsule history of world art.

Focusing on the Past

Why should we give thought to focusing on the past which, after all, can never return? The answer can be simply put: because history provides a means for profiting from human experience. As the philosopher George Santayana reminds us: "Those who cannot remember the past are condemned to repeat it." To remain ignorant of our antecedents is akin to opening a novel at random, say to page 199, and then attempting to make sense of the plot without having any idea of what has gone before.

Civilization Past & Present approaches the study of history from a dual perspective: the past as past, and the past as prologue. In terms of the first perspective, it seeks to understand humanity's previous experiences—failures and triumphs alike—in their own right and to be enriched by that knowledge. It is like vacationing in Rome. The experience of walking through the ruins of the Forum and the Colosseum or looking in awe upon Michelangelo's frescoes in the Sistine Chapel is immeasurably enhanced by some understanding of how and why Rome came to be called the "Eternal City."

According to the Greek philosopher Heraclitus, change is the one constant in life. Hence, like other historians, the authors of this book recognize that although the past is indeed past, our knowledge and understanding of it can never be static. From one edition to the next, *Civilization Past & Present* has taken account of new discoveries as well as of fresh interpretations of the past. In this regard, the book brought a new global focus to bear on the interactions of the major civilizations of India, China, and Rome to show that a meaningful exchange of commerce and ideas between East and West took place for centuries in classical times and again a thousand years later. Moreover, history needs to be reviewed at frequent intervals, not only to reflect new knowledge but also to relate it to the needs and aspirations of the present. For example, in the third edition, the intense interest of the newly independent African history. This coverage has been revised and expanded again in subsequent editions in the light of new research.

Focusing on the Present

The perspective of past as prologue has meant that the text has focused as needed on contemporary concerns. This book's half century of exisitence coincides with the occurrence of many of the most momentous events in world history. Just as the nature and tempo of these events underwent change, so successive editions kept pace with the shifts and assessed their significance. For example, the first edition, published in 1942, allocated some 40 pages to the events leading up to World War II and the conflagration itself, while the second edition, appearing in 1949, shortened the treatment of that conflict to focus more attention on postwar domestic conditions and international issues.

Editions of *Civilization Past & Present* published in the 1950s and 1960s reflected the outbreak and evolution of the Cold War, as the world became polarized into two ideological blocs and alliances, directed by two superpowers, each armed with the most lethal weapons in history. As a direct consequence of the Cold War, thousands of people died in two "hot" wars in Korea and Vietnam. The editions published in the 1960s and 1970s attested that the Cold War with its ever-constant threat of a nuclear holocaust remained uppermost in the minds of people everywhere. President Kennedy was echoing the thoughts of many Americans when he stated: "This is a dangerous and uncertain world . . . . No one expects our lives to be easy—not in this decade, not in this century." Nor, he might have added, should we expect our times to be devoid of surprises and sudden changes in world events. As this latest edition makes abundantly clear, the political and economical upheavals of 1989–1990 sent shock waves through the Soviet Union and Eastern Europe, and in their wake collapsed decades-old ideological structures and military alliances. The Cold War that had polarized entire continents and cost trillions of dollars in wasted resources and lost economic opportunities had come to an end, and the world was moving into a new era—one that would still be uncertain but militarily, perhaps, less dangerous.

Focusing on the Golden Anniversary Edition

In its continuing concern about contemporary issues, *Civilization Past & Present* has undertaken to identify and analyze what its authors consider the major problems confronting humanity for both today and tomorrow. Currently, one of these problems, the widespread and accelerating deterioration of the global environment, has become a matter of concern for many Americans. Yet it is interesting to note that when the second edition appeared in 1949—more than four decades ago—the text had already drawn attention to the "ecological dilemma." The text opened its discussion by pointing out that

> *statistics portend the swift approach of a problem so vast in its complexity as to be potentially more tragic than any existing political or ideological conflict. For an understanding of this problem we must leave the tense conference room of foreign ministers and the semicircular table of the Security Council, and visit the quiet office of the ecologist—a scientist who studies the relations between organisms, including human beings, and their environment.*

This scientist warned that the population is increasing by leaps and bounds at the very time natural resources are dwindling at an ever-accelerating speed. The fate of every human being depends on the use or misuse of four major elements: water, soil, plants, and animals. There is a natural balance among these elements; should it be destroyed nature can swiftly wreak destruction on all forms of life—and turn wheat lands into dust bowls. Back in 1949, the ecologist was already describing the earth as a "plundered planet." In the 1990s, the ecologist's concerns have become even more pressing.

In 1949 the text suggested that at its current rate of growth, "the world's population may well exceed the 3,000,000,000 mark by the end of the century." This demographic projection underestimated the prospect by virtually 100 percent. After some three million years, the planet's human population amounted to about 1.7 billion in A.D.

1900. Within one century, it will have increased almost fourfold—and the end is not yet in sight. Furthermore, the overwhelming proportion of that increase is occurring in developing nations, which are struggling to obtain the technology and resources to support their burgeoning populations. What can—what will—the rich nations do to assist them?

The ecological dilemma and unchecked population growth were but two problems identified in the text back in 1949. Others included mass illiteracy, hunger, and disease in the developing nations; atomic energy and its promise of abundant peacetime power coupled with its perils of destruction and radiation (as the disaster at Chernobyl would demonstrate decades later); the dynamics of nationalism and the politics of new nations, all too often accompanied by the erosion or outright destruction of individual rights; and the struggle over those rights, manifested in the strife caused by racial bondage in South Africa. Technology's promises and problems have long been a focus of the text, in discussions of the revolution in communications, the impact of automation on the economy, and the individual in mass society.

Focusing on the Future

The world's problems will not disappear of their own accord but will continue, and in many cases intensify, to the end of the century and beyond. As a result of the end of the Cold War, today's students can be resonably certain they will not be consumed in a nuclear holocaust. Given the exciting prospects suggested by science and technology, they will have little cause to be bored to death. But humanity's sojourn on this planet will be undoubtedly very different. All peoples and all nations are becoming progressively interdependent; rich and poor, Western and non-Western, societies can expect to find themselves in mutual win-win, or perhaps lose-lose, situations. In short, we are fast becoming a "global village" and in so becoming are attesting as well to the validity of the underlying thesis which motivated the authors of *Civilization Past & Present* in the late 1930s to accept the challenge to write a world history.

It should be refreshing to learn that even in an age which by our standards seems calm and contented, that valiant old warrior, the Duke of Wellington, viewed the future with such foreboding that when he lay on his deathbed in 1854, he declared, "I thank God that I am spared the ruin that is gathering around us." History teaches us that men and women have never yet given up their struggle not only to survive but also to improve human existence. All through the killing days of World War II and the wrenching upheavals of the succeeding decades, the authors and editors of *Civilization Past & Present* remained optimistic about the outcome, their optimism tempered with realism. Now as American society moves toward a new century, with its myriad promises and perils alike, they continue to remain realistically optimistic.

Alastair M. Taylor
Emeritus, Queen's University

Originally published in 1942, *Civilization Past & Present* was the first text of its kind. Its objective was to present a survey of world cultural history, treating the development and growth of civilization not as a unique European experience but as a global one through which all the great culture systems have interacted to produce the present-day world. It attempted to include all the elements of history—social, economic, political, religious, aesthetic, legal, and technological.

The purposes of *Civilization Past & Present*, as envisaged in the first edition five decades ago, have even more relevance today. A knowledge of Western civilization is an essential aim of education, but this alone is no longer adequate. With the accelerating tempo of developments in communication and technology, every day each part of the world is brought into closer contact with the other parts; the world is now truly a "global village." Perhaps the most significant happening in our time is the political and cultural reemergence of the world's non-Western peoples. They have played an important role in world affairs, and in the future their role will be even more important. Hence, these people, their cultures, and their civilizations must be known and understood.

New to the Seventh Edition

The Seventh Edition maintains the various strengths that have made *Civilization Past & Present* a widely popular introductory textbook. The authors have sought to profit from the many helpful suggestions that have come from users and reviewers, to utilize the latest historical scholarship, and to extend the historical narrative to the present day. While the seventh edition retains the basic organization and approach of its predecessors, all chapters have been reviewed and revised in the light of new developments. The number of chapters has been reduced from 39 to 37 as several chapters have been condensed and combined. Many chapters have been completely rewritten, and there are some new chapters. Chapter 6, new to this edition, describes the beginning, spread, and zenith of Islamic civilization and culture. Chapter 7, another new chapter, examines the Byzantine Empire and the early history of Eastern Europe and Russia.

Chapters 9, 10, and 11 have been thoroughly revised to integrate better the social, political, economic, cultural, and intellectual history of the European Middle Ages. Better integration of topics was also the goal for revision of chapters 23, 24, and 25, which examine the Napoleonic and Industrial Revolutions; the revolutions of the mid-nineteenth century, their ideological underpinnings, and the cultural responses to them; and European domestic politics of the late nineteenth century to the brink of World War I. Chapters 35, 36, and 37, which cover the period since the end of World War II, have also been thoroughly revised to reflect the shift from a world of East and West—Soviet and American—spheres to a new bipolarism of North and South, the spheres of the industrialized and the industrializing nations. Finally, the Epilogue uses the recent Persian Gulf War to examine the past both as past and as prologue to the future.

Features

This text has been developed with the dual purpose of helping students acquire a solid knowledge of past events and, equally important, of helping them think more constructively about the significance of those events for the difficult times in which we now live. Several features assist students toward achievement of those goals.

The Maps

Two-color maps are distributed liberally throughout the text. Some are designed to make clear the nature of a single distinctive event or discussed in the text; others illustrate larger trends. Thirty-two new maps have been added throughout the text to provide a geographical framework for the material presented. The series of full-color maps (including timelines and narrative) at the front of the text presents a comparative view of major world states and empires over the centuries from the Stone Age to the present. The narrative provides brief descriptions of the various empires, while the accompanying timeline highlights significant events of the era. The fourteen full-color maps at the back of the text constitute an atlas of historical reference maps. The notes preceding the Historical Atlas describe the principal features and significance of each of the reference maps.

The Color Plates

Nine inserts of full-color art reproductions appear throughout the text. The works of art have been carefully selected to illustrate some facet of a cultural pattern discussed in the text. These reproductions, with the accompanying commentary, constitute a capsule history of world art.

The Document Excerpts

Each chapter includes one or more excerpts from documents of the era under discussion. The excerpts have been selected from a variety of documents—political, economic, legal, intellectual, popular—to show students the kinds of materials historians use to understand and interpret the past. Reading the excerpts will permit students to experience at first hand the voices and records of the past.

Suggestions for Reading

Each chapter ends with an annotated bibliography listing special historical studies, biographies, reputable historical fiction, and some collections of source materials. The works listed are intended to provide students with ample sources from which to prepare special reports or with which to improve their understanding of a particular subject.

The Chronological Tables

At the end of the book are chronological tables showing the sequence of events discussed in the text. These tables are intended to show the relationship among events in various parts of the world over periods of time.

The Pronunciation Key

In the general index, the correct pronunciation is given for most proper names. Thus, students will find it easy, as well as helpful, to look up the correct pronunciation of the names and places referred to in the text. The index also provides pronunciation guides for many unusual, difficult, or foreign words.

The pedagogical features of the Seventh Edition, along with the text narrative, are intended to provide the reader with an understanding of the contribution of past eras to the shaping of subsequent events and to illuminate the manner in which the study of global history affords insights into the genesis, nature, and direction of our civilization. As we approach the end of the twentieth century, the need for this kind of historical perspective has never been greater.

Supplements

The following supplements are available for use in conjunction with this book:

For the Student

Studying Civilization, in two volumes, prepared by David G. Egler, Sterling J. Kernek, and Charles O'Brien, of Western Illinois University. Volume I covers chapters 1 through 18. Volume II covers chapters 17 through 37. The study guides include chapter overviews, lists of chapter themes and concepts, and many varied exercises, including multiple-choice questions and map quizzes.

Mapping World Civilization: Student Activities is a free map workbook for students by Gerald Danzer, University of Illinois, Chicago. It features numerous map skill exercises written to enhance students' basic geographical literacy. The exercises provide ample opportunities for interpreting maps and analyzing cartographic materials as historical documents. The instructor is entitled to one free copy of *Mapping World Civilization: Student Activities* for each copy of the text purchased from HarperCollins.

SuperShell II Computerized Tutorial is an interactive program for computer-assisted learning, prepared by Paul A. Bishoff, Oklahoma State University. It features multiple-choice, true-false, and completion quizzes, comprehensive chapter outlines, flash cards for key terms and concepts, and diagnostic feedback capabilities. This tutorial is available for IBM computers.

Timelink: World History Computerized Atlas by William Hamblin, Brigham Young University. This is a highly graphic, Hypercard-based computerized atlas and historical geography tutorial for the Macintosh.

For the Instructor

Instructor's Resource Manual by George Jewsbury, Oklahoma State University. This unique instructor's manual offers a multi-resource presentation for each chapter, including chapter outlines and suggestions for integrating a variety of conceptual hooks into class lectures, including art, music, literature, quotations, and media resouces. The manual is shrinkwrapped with a free music cassette.

Experiencing World Music is a 60-minute audio cassette containing over 20 selections of important music from a wide range of times and cultures. Selections range between 1 and 4 minutes in length. Commentaries about the pieces and suggestions for using them in lectures, prepared by Evan Tonsing, Oklahoma State University, and Jane Adas, Rutgers, are included in the *Instructor's Resource Manual*. Western pieces include short selections from the medieval period to the present. Non-western pieces include short selections from China, India, Japan, Iran, Africa, Turkey, and other countries. The audiocassette comes shrinkwrapped with the *Instructor's Resource Manual*.

Test Bank by George Jewsbury, Oklahoma State University. A total of 2000 questions, including 50 multiple-choice questions and 5 essay questions per text chapter. Each test item is referenced by topic, type, and text page number. *Test Bank* is available in print and computerized format.

TestMaster Computerized Testing System is a test-generation software package available for the IBM and Macintosh. It allows users to add, delete, edit, and print test items. The system is available free to adopters.

World History Through Maps and Views prepared by Gerald Danzer, University of Illinois, Chicago, winner of the AHA's James Harvey Robinson Award for his work in the development of map transparencies. This set of 100 four-color transparencies from selected sources is bound in a three-ring binder and is available free to adopters. It also contains an introduction on teaching history with maps and a detailed commentary on each transparency. The collection includes cartographic and pictorial maps, views and photos, urban plans, building diagrams, classic maps, and works of art.

Map transparencies is a set of 48 two- and four-color transparencies of basic maps designed to be used in teaching world civilization courses.

The HarperCollins World Civilization Media Program offers a wide variety of media enhancements, including videos and historical newsreels. This program is useful for teaching world civilization courses. It is offered to qualified adopters of HarperCollins world civilization texts.

Grades is a grade-keeping and classroom-management software program that maintains data for up to 200 students.

Acknowledgments

To the following reviewers who gave generously of their time and knowledge to provide thoughtful evaluations and many helpful suggestions for the revision of the text, the authors express their gratitude.

Jay Pascal Anglin
University of Southern Mississippi

Joel Berlatsky
Wilkes College

Jackie R. Booker
Kent State University

Darwin F. Bostwick
Old Dominion University

Robert F. Brinson, Jr.
Santa Fe Community College

Robert H. Buchanan
Adams State College

James O. Catron, Jr.
North Florida Junior College

William H. Cobb
East Carolina University

J. L. Collins
Allan Hancock College

Lawrence J. Daly
Bowling Green State University

John D. Fair
Auburn University at Montgomery

Nels W. Forde
University of Nebraska

Joseph T. Fuhrmann
Murray State University

Jeffrey S. Hamilton
Old Dominion University

J. Drew Harrington
Western Kentucky University

Conrad C. Holcomb, Jr.
Surry Community College

Michael L. Krenn
University of Miami

Caroline T. Marshall
James Madison University

Norman Pollock
Old Dominion University

J. Graham Provan
Millikin University

George B. Pruden, Jr.
Armstrong State College

John D. Ramsbottom
Northeast Missouri State University

Ruth Richard
College of Lake County

Hugh I. Rodgers
Columbus College

Patrick J. Rollins
Old Dominion University

Barry T. Ryan
Westmont College

Louis E. Schmier
Valdosta State College

Barbara G. Sniffen
University of Wisconsin-Oshkosh

Lawrence Squeri
East Stroudsburg University

Gordon L. Teffeteller
Valdosta State College

Malcolm R. Thorp
Brigham Young University

Helen M. Tierney
University of Wisconsin-Platteville

David L. White
Appalachian State University

John R. Willertz
Saginaw Valley State University

Perspective on Humanity

If the time span of our planet—now estimated at some 5 billion years—were telescoped into a single year, the first eight months would be devoid of any life. The next two months would be taken up with plant and very primitive animal forms, and not until well into December would any mammals appear. In this "year," members of *Homo erectus*, our ancient predecessors, would mount the global stage only between 10 and 11 p.m. on December 31. And how has the human species spent that brief allotment? Most of it— the equivalent of more than half a million years—has been given over to making tools out of stone. The revolutionary changeover from food-hunting nomads to farmers who raised grain and domesticated animals would occur in the last sixty seconds. And into that final minute would be crowded all of humanity's other accomplishments: the use of metal; the creation of civilizations; the mastery of the oceans; and the harnessing of steam, then gas, electricity, oil, and, finally, in our lifetime, nuclear energy. Brief though it has been, humanity's time on the globe reveals a rich tapestry of science, industry, religion, and art. This accumulated experience of the human species is available for study. We call it *history*.

Past and Present

As we read and learn about early societies and their members, we discover them to be very different from us and the world in which we live. And yet, we are linked by more than curiosity to our ancient predecessors. Why? Because we are of the same species, and we share a fundamental commonality that connects present with past: the human-environment nexus. It is the dynamic interplay of environmental factors and human activities that accounts for the terrestrial process known as history. The biological continuity of our species, coupled with humanity's unflagging inventiveness, have enabled each generation to build on the experiences and contributions of its forebears—so that continuity and change in human affairs proceed together.

The Universal Culture Pattern

In the interplay of men and women with their environment and fellow beings, certain fundamental needs are always present. Six needs, common to people at all times and in all places, form the basis of a "universal culture pattern" and deserve to be enumerated.

1. *The need to make a living.* Men and women must have food, shelter, clothing, and the means to provide for their offsprings' survival.

2. *The need for law and order.* From earliest times, communities have had to keep peace among their members, defend themselves against external attack, and protect community assets.

3. *The need for social organization.* For people to make a living, raise families, and maintain law and order, a social structure is essential. Views about the relative importance of the group and the individual within it may vary with any such social structure.

4. *The need for knowledge and learning.* Since earliest times, humankind has transmitted knowledge acquired through experience, first orally and then by means of writing systems. As societies grow more complex, there is increasing need to preserve knowledge and transmit it through education to as many people as possible.

5. *The need for self-expression.* People have responded creatively to their environment even before the days when they decorated the walls of Paleolithic caves with paintings of the animals they hunted. The arts appear to have a lineage as old as human experience.

6. *The need for religious expression.* Equally old is humanity's attempt to answer the "why" of its existence. What primitive peoples considered supernatural in their environment could often, at a later time, be explained by science in terms of natural phenomena. Yet today, no less than in archaic times, men and women continue to search for answers to the ultimate questions of existence.

Culture Change and Culture Lag

When people in a group behave similarly and share the same institutions and ways of life, they can be said to have a common *culture*. Throughout this text we shall be looking at a number of different cultures, some of which are designated as *civilizations*. (If all tribes or societies have culture, then civilization is a particular *kind* of culture.) "A culture is the way of life of a human group; it includes all the learned and standardized forms of behavior which one uses and others in one's group expect and recognize. . . . Civilization is that kind of culture which includes the use of writing, the presence of cities and of wide political organization, and the development of occupational specialization."[1]

Cultures are never wholly static or wholly isolated. A particular culture may have an individuality that sets it off sharply from other cultures, but invariably it has been influenced by external contacts. Such contacts may be either peaceful or warlike, and they meet with varying degrees of acceptance. Through these contacts occurs the process of culture *diffusion*. Geography, too, has profoundly influenced the development of cultures, although we should not exaggerate its importance. Environmental influences tend to become less marked as people gain technological skill and mastery over the land. The domestication of animals and cereals, for example, took place in both the old and new worlds, but the animals and grains were different because of dissimilar ecological factors. Invention is another important source of culture change, although it is not clear to what extent external physical contact is required in the process of invention. Perhaps it may be possible for men and women in different times and places to hit on similar solutions to the challenges posed by their respective environments—resulting in the phenomenon known as *parallel invention.*

Some parts of a culture pattern change more rapidly than others, so that one institution sometimes becomes outmoded in relation to others in a society. When different parts of a society fail to mesh harmoniously, the condition is often called *culture lag.* Numerous examples of this lag could be cited: the exploitation of child laborers during the nineteenth century, the failure to allow women to vote until this century, and the tragedy of hunger in the midst of plenty.

Past and Present as Prologue

What can the past and present—as history—suggest to us for tomorrow's world? In the first place, changes in the physical and social environments will probably accelerate as a result of continued technological innovation. These changes can result in increased disequilibrium and tensions among the various segments comprising the universal culture pattern—in other words, in increased culture lag.

Has the past anything to tell the future about the consequences of cultural disequilibrium—anything that we might profitably utilize in present-day planning for the decades ahead? Because our planet and its resources are finite, at some point our society must expect to shift progressively from exponential growth toward an overall global equilibrium. By that term, we mean the setting of maximal levels on the number of humans who can inhabit this planet with an assured minimal standard of life and on the exploitation of the earth's resources required to provide that standard. Otherwise, environmental disaster on an unprecedented scale could result in the decades ahead. Past and present conjoin to alert us to the need to engage in new forms of planning for the years ahead and also to the need to rethink our existing social goals and value systems. We need as long and as accurate a perspective as possible to make realistic analyses and to take the proper actions to improve our quality of life.

The "How" of History

History is the record of the past actions of humankind, based on surviving evidence. History shows that all patterns and problems in human affairs are the products of a complex process of growth. By throwing light on that process, history provides a means for profiting from human experience.

History as a Science

There is more than one way to treat the past. In dealing with the American Revolution, for example, the historian may describe its events in narrative form or, instead, analyze its general causes and compare its stages with the patterns of revolutions in other countries. Unlike the scientist who attempts to verify hypotheses by repeating experiments under controlled conditions in the laboratory and to classify phenomena in a general group or category, the historian has to pay special attention to the *uniqueness* of data, because each event takes place at a particular time and in a particular place. And since that time is now past, conclusions cannot be verified by duplicating the circumstances in which the event occurred.

Nevertheless, historians insist that history be written as scientifically as possible and that evidence be analyzed with the same objective attitude employed by the scientist examining natural phenomena. This scientific spirit requires historians to handle evidence according to established rules of historical analysis, to recognize biases and attempt to eliminate their effects, and to draw only such conclusions as the evidence seems to warrant.

The Historical Method

To meet these requirements, historians have evolved the "historical method." The first step is the search for *sources*, which may be material remains, oral traditions, pictorial data, or written records. From the source the historian must infer the facts. This process has two parts. *External criticism* tests the genuineness of the source.

In *internal criticism* the historian evaluates the source to ascertain the author's meaning and the accuracy of the work.

The final step in the historical method is *synthesis*. Here the historian must determine which factors in a given situation are most relevant to the purpose at hand, since obviously not everything that occurred can be included. This delicate process of selection underscores the role that subjectivity plays in the writing of history. Furthermore, the more complex the events involved, the more crucial becomes the historian's judgment.[2]

Periodization

Can we really categorize history as "ancient," "medieval," or "modern"? Clearly, what is "modern" in the twentieth century could conceivably be considered "medieval" in the twenty-fifth century, and eventually "ancient" in the thirty-fifth century A.D. Yet not to break up the account would be akin to reading this book without the benefit of parts, chapters, paragraphs, or even separate sentences. Like time itself, history would then become a ceaseless flow of consciousness and events. To simplify the task and to manage materials more easily, the historian divides time into periods. The divisions chosen and the lines drawn reveal the distinctive way in which the historian regards the past—namely, in terms of patterns that seem logical and meaningful.

The "Why" of History

The historian seeks to describe not only *what* has happened and *how* it happened, but also *why* society undergoes change. Any search of this kind raises a number of fundamental questions: the roles of Providence, the individual, and the group in history; the extent to which events are unique or, conversely, can fit into patterns; and the problem of progress in human affairs. The answers vary with different philosophical views of the universe and the human role therein.

Those who hold the teleological view see in history the guidance of a Divine Will, directing human destinies according to a cosmic purpose. Other thinkers have exalted the role of the individual in the historical process—such as Thomas Carlyle, who contended that major figures chiefly determined the course of human events. Opponents of Carlyle's thesis often contend that history is determined by "forces" and "laws" and by the actions of entire societies. Sociologists approach history primarily by analyzing the origins, institutions, and functions of groups. Economists tend to look at the historical record from the standpoint of group action and especially the impact of economic forces.

To Karl Marx irresistible economic forces governed human beings and determined the trend of events. Marx contended that the shift from one economic stage to another—such as the shift from feudalism to capitalism—is attained by upheavals, or revolutions, which occur because the class controlling the methods of production eventually resists further progress in order to maintain its vested interests.

Numerous other attempts have been made to explain societal processes according to a set of principles. Oswald Spengler maintained that civilizations were like organisms; each grew with the "superb aimlessness" of a flower and passed through a cycle of spring, summer, autumn, and winter. Charles Darwin's evolutionary hypothesis made a strong impact on nineteenth-century thought and gave rise to the concept that the principle of "survival of the fittest" must also apply to human societies. This line of thought—known as Social Darwinism—raises social and ethical questions of major importance.

Does history obey impersonal laws and forces so that its course is inevitable? Or, at the other extreme, since every event is a unique act, is history simply the record of unforeseen and unrelated episodes? Can this apparent dilemma be avoided? We believe it can. Although all events are, in various respects, unique, they also contain elements that invite comparison. The comparitive approach permits us to seek relationships between historical phenomena and to group them into movements or patterns or civilizations. We eschew any "theory" of history, preferring to see merit in a number of basic concepts. These include the effects of physical environment on social organization and institutions; the roles played by economic, political, and religious factors; and the impact exerted by men and women occupying key positions in various societies.

The Challenge of History

Progress and growth is a continuous factor. It depends on, and contributes to, the maintenance of peace and security, the peaceful settlement of international disputes, and worldwide improvement in economic and social standards. Surely an indispensable step toward solving contemporary humanity's dilemma—technology without the requisite control and power without commensurate wisdom—must be a better understanding of how the world and its people came to be what they are today. Only by understanding the past can we assess both the perils and the opportunities of the present—and move courageously and compassionately into the future.

Notes

1. David G. Mandelbaum, "Concepts of Civilization and Culture," *Encyclopaedia Britannica*, 1967 ed., vol. 5, p. 831A.
2. See P. Gardiner, *The Nature of Historical Explanation* (London: Oxford University Press, 1952), p. 98.

Chapter 1

Along the Banks of Rivers

The Civilizations of the Ancient Near East

Paleoanthropologists estimate that between three and four million years ago, ancestors of the human race appeared on earth, naked in a world of enemies. The skills necessary for survival were mastered over many hundreds of thousands of years. Agriculture and the ways of life it engendered were the most important achievements. The first farmers scattered kernels of grain on the earth and waited patiently for harvest time. Wild beasts were tamed as work animals or kept for their meat and hides. Because their fields and flocks could supply most of their wants, a settled life in villages became possible; people were no longer compelled to move on endlessly in search of food, as their food-gathering ancestors had done for countless generations.

It was along the banks of great rivers that villages first grew into towns and cities. In early Egyptian picture writing a town is shown as a cross within a circle—the intersection of two pathways enclosed by a wall. The symbol is an appropriate one, for in the history of the human race the town —⊗— marks the spot where civilization as we know it began.

Within the towns the business of living took new turns. While the majority still farmed, there were now more craftsmen turning out specialized wares, merchants trading for metals and other needed raw materials, priests conducting religious ceremonies, and administrators planning and supervising the necessary cooperative effort for the common good. Specialization allowed leisure time for intellectual and artistic pursuits that enriched the lives of the participants and developed a cultural heritage.

A culture can endure only if the knowledge necessary for its survival is passed on from generation to generation. Early peoples relied on information transmitted by word of mouth. But as cultures became increasingly complex, methods for keeping records were needed and systems of writing were created. To most authorities, the development of writing is a prerequisite to civilization.

The four earliest civilizations—Mesopotamian, Egyptian, Indian, and Chinese—arose between c. 3100 B.C. and c. 1500 B.C., in each case in the valley of a great river system. In this chapter we shall trace the progress of civilization, including the earliest advances in technology and creation of writing systems, in Mesopotamia and Egypt. In chapter 4 we shall examine the stirrings of civilization in India and in China.

The Development of the Human Race

Did God create humanity "in His own image," or was our species itself the product of physical change and adaptation no less than the rocks, plants, and animals of this planet? This question—so basic in nineteenth-century thought that it caused anguish and bitter controversy among theologians and scientists alike—came to the fore when Sir Charles Lyell's *Principles of Geology* (1830) provided evidence that the earth was the product of a tremendously long period of change.

Evolution: A Major Theory

The issue of human evolution became critical with the appearance of Charles Darwin's two treatises, *The Origin of Species* (1859) and *Descent of Man* (1871). The controversy surrounding the theory of human evolution has raged on into the twentieth century, although with decreasing intensity as more fossil evidence has come to light. Of course, the fossil record can probably never be complete, and paleontologists have only skeletal remains (usually partial ones) to analyze. The evidence for evolution appears overwhelming, but the theory by no means precludes the presence of a guiding intelligence ultimately responsible for a progressive development of organic life from simple to more complex forms, culminating in the intelligence and creativity of our own species.

Evolution of the Hominids

Who the ancestors of early humans were and when and where tools were first made are much debated questions in scholarly circles. According to the theory of evolution, a crucial development occurred when the ape family became differentiated into the tree-dwelling apes and the ground-dwelling types known as *hominids* ("prehumans" or "protohumans"). The remains of Australopithecines ("Southern Apes"), the earliest known hominids, were first discovered in South Africa in 1924 (see map, p. 3). *Australopithecus* had an erect posture but an apelike brain.

Since World War II, and especially during the 1970s, our knowledge of the hominids and their relation to the genus *Homo* ("man") has been rapidly growing. The dominant present view is that Australopithecus was succeeded by three species of the genus *Homo: Homo habilis, Homo erectus,* and *Homo sapiens.* (A genus contains one or more species. The genus name is capitalized and precedes the species name, which is not capitalized.)

Three major sites in East Africa have produced a remarkable collection of Australopithecine fossils. Between 1972 and 1977, an expedition led by C. D. Johanson worked at Hadar in Ethiopia. The Hadar collection comprises at least thirty-five individuals, with one female skeleton—named Lucy after the Beatles' song

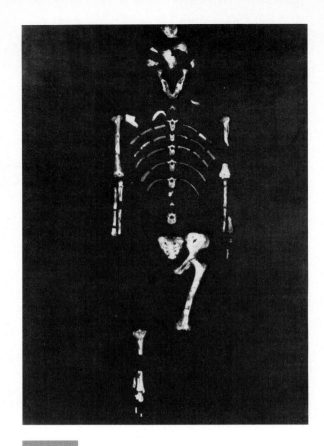

"Lucy," dating from more than three million years ago, is the oldest known Australopithecine and one of the most complete and best-preserved finds from the period.

"Lucy in the Sky with Diamonds"—nearly 40 percent complete and between 3.0 and 3.5 million years ago.

During this period, too, the British anthropologist Mary D. Leakey discovered at Laetoli, in northern Tanzania, the fossil jaws and teeth of eight adults and three children, between 3.35 and 3.75 million years old. Subsequently, she uncovered fifty-seven footprints made by two individuals—the oldest known marks of human-like creatures on earth.

Meanwhile, in 1972 at a site on the east side of Lake Rudolph, Kenya, Mary Leakey's son Richard had made yet another major discovery. Of special interest was his discovery of a skull (labeled KNM-ER 1470), probably 2.9 million years old. Leakey's claim that 1470 is a representative of the genus *Homo* has been challenged.

STONE AGE ENVIRONMENTS

- Land exposed during the Pleistocene Epoch
----- Area covered by glaciers
• Australopithecus
○ Homo habilis
+ Homo erectus
× Homo sapiens

The find made earlier (1964) by his father, L. S. B. Leakey, however, has been generally accepted as the earliest representative of our own genus, *Homo.*

L. S. B. Leakey had made his discovery at Olduvai Gorge, in Tanzania, at a site some 1.75 million years old. *Homo habilis* ("skillful man"), as Leakey named his find, was about four feet tall, walked erect, and had a well-developed opposable thumb. Significantly, these fossil remains were found in association with crude tools. With the advent of a hominid capable of making tools, Leakey felt confident in assigning his find to the genus *Homo.*

The first evidence of the more advanced group known as *Homo erectus* was discovered in Java in 1891. Peking man and other members of this group, whose earliest fossils are about 1.5 million years old, have been discovered in Asia, Africa, and Europe. *Homo erectus* had a brain size larger than *Homo habilis* but smaller than our own. The members of *Homo erectus* were about five feet tall, had heavy brows, and a receding forehead. They developed the ability to control and use fire, a major step in mastering the environment and setting humans apart from the rest of the natural world. They also perfected the first major standardized all-purpose tool, the hand ax, made by striking flakes from a flint stone that had been hardened in fire to make it flake easily. Its cutting edge was as effective as steel in cutting meat. The hand ax remained a favored tool for over a million years, long after the extinction of *Homo erectus* about 300,000 years ago and the gradual emergence of *Homo sapiens.*

From about 100,00 to 40,000 years ago, just before and during the early part of the last glaciation of the Ice Age, the Neanderthals were the principal inhabitants of Europe and adjacent parts of Asia and Africa. Somewhat taller than five feet, Neanderthals had sloping foreheads with prominent brow ridges and thickset bodies. They invented tools of advanced design, were able hunters, and adapted to extreme cold by using fire, wearing clothes, and living in caves.

Despite a brain capacity averaging slightly larger than our own, Neanderthals were long considered to be brutish, dimwitted, slouching creatures—the stereotypical "cave man" of modern cartoonists. Recent reconstructions of the fossil evidence, however, have determined that Neanderthals are a subspecies of *Homo sapiens* and deserve the label *Homo sapiens neanderthalensis.* "If he could be reincarnated and placed in a New York subway—provided he was bathed, shaved, and dressed in modern clothing—it is doubtful whether he would attract any more attention than some of its other denizens."[1]

The culminating phase of the development of the genus *Homo* occurred some 40,000 years ago when the Cro-Magnons, a subspecies of *Homo sapiens* called *Homo sapiens sapiens,* replaced *Homo sapiens neanderthalensis* in Europe. What happened to the Neanderthals can only be conjectured.

Named after the locality in southern France where their bones were first unearthed in 1868, Cro-Magnon skeletons are virtually indistinguishable from human skeletons of today. Skillfully made flint and bone tools and polychrome paintings found on the walls of caves reflect an advanced culture. By 20,000 B.C. Cro-Magnon and other representatives of *Homo sapiens sapiens* inhabited Europe, Asia, Africa, and Australia, and had moved across the Bering Strait to America. Today, *Homo sapiens sapiens* is the only existing species of the genus *Homo.*

Paleolithic Culture

Benjamin Franklin is credited with first defining the human being as a "tool-making animal." The making and using of tools is the first evidence of the human ability to use reason to solve problems. Since the use of stone implements was the most distinctive feature of early human culture, (Anthropologists use the term *culture* for a primitive people's way of life.) this first cultural stage is known as the Paleolithic or Old Stone Age. It was a food-collecting stage, characterized by hunting, fishing, and the collecting of wild fruits, nuts, and berries.

Much of our knowledge of Paleolithic culture comes from groups that have survived into modern times—Indians in the rain forests of Brazil, for example. Labor was divided according to sex. Men hunted, fished, and protected the group. Women gathered wild plants, fruits, and nuts, and prepared the food for eating, they processed animal hides and wood into household objects, and cared for the children. Men and women shared such tasks as building dwellings, making ornaments and tools, and training children for adult life.

To withstand the cold, late Paleolithic peoples made garments from skins and erected buildings in areas where natural caves did not exist. The reindeer and mammoth hunters of what is today Czechoslovakia and Russia lived in tents and huts made of hides and brush or in communal houses partially sunk into the ground with mammoth's ribs for roof supports. There is evidence that they used coal for fuel.

One of the highest achievements of late Paleolithic culture was art. Animated, realistic paintings of bison, reindeer, primitive horses, and other animals, colored in shades of black, red, yellow, and brown, have been found in more than a hundred Cro-Magnon caves in Spain and France, dating from about 28,000 to 10,000 B.C. Cave art rivals that of civilized artists not only stylistically but also as an expression of significant human experience. It represents the Paleolithic response to complete dependence on an abundance of game animals and success in hunting them. By drawing pictures of food animals—sometimes shown pregnant or pierced by spears and arrows—the artists may have believed that they could wield a mystical power over the spirits of the animals to ensure the animals' multiplication and human mastery over them. Like the religious art of civilized peoples, the magico-religious basis of Paleolithic art in no way detracts from its esthetic qualities as true art. Paleolithic artists also modeled in clay and chiseled pictures on rock and bone.

Mesolithic Culture

With the final retreat of the glaciers about 10,000 B.C., Europe became covered with dense forests. Because of their highly specialized adaptation to cold weather, the reindeer moved north while the hairy mammoth and other animals hunted by late Paleolithic peoples became extinct. Humans, however, adjusted to postglacial conditions by developing new cultures called Mesolithic or Transitional. Many of these Mesolithic groups lived along the coast, fishing and gathering shellfish. Others lived inland, where they made bows and arrows for hunting and devised skis, sleds, and dugout canoes. Our Mesolithic forebears also domesticated the dog.

The Neolithic Revolution

While the Mesolithic peoples of Europe were adjusting to the postglacial environment by developing new food-gathering techniques, something of far greater consequence—a shift from food gathering to food producing—was taking place in the Near East (now generally called the Middle East). Here, on the hilly flanks of the mountains bordering the Fertile Crescent (see map below) there was sufficient rainfall to nourish wild forms of wheat and barley and to provide grass for wild sheep, goats, and pigs. By 7000 B.C., people in this region had domesticated these grains and animals and were living in villages near their herds and fields. (At about the same time, yams were domesticated in Southeast Asia; and the cultivation of rice in China dates back to about 6500 B.C.) This momentous change, the most far-reaching breakthrough in the relationship of people to their environment, ushered in the Neolithic or New Stone Age.

One of the oldest Neolithic village sites to be excavated is Jarmo in northern Iraq. The 150 people of the village lived in twenty mud-walled

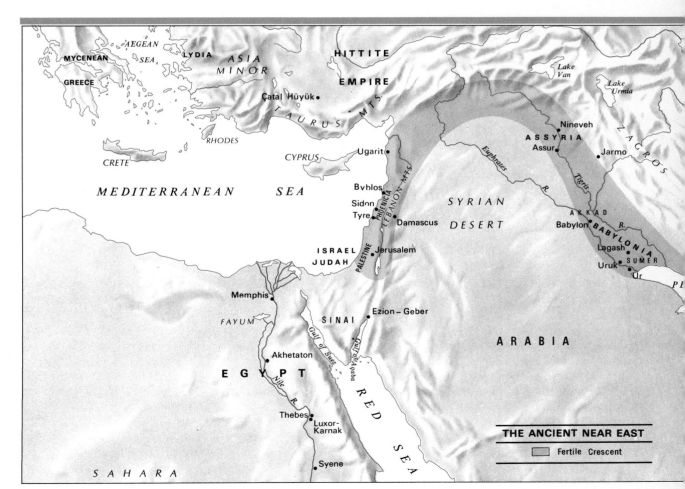

THE ANCIENT NEAR EAST

Fertile Crescent

houses, reaped their grain with stone sickles, stored their food in stone bowls, and possessed domesticated goats, sheep, and dogs. The later levels of settlement contain evidence of domesticated pigs and clay pottery. Since many tools were made of obsidian, a volcanic rock from beds 300 miles away, a primitive form of commerce must have existed.

The best preserved early village so far uncovered by Çatal Hüyük in southern Turkey, excavated in 1961. The large, 32-acre site, first occupied shortly before 6000 B.C, contains some of the most advanced features of Neolithic culture: pottery, woven textiles, mudbrick houses, shrines honoring a mother goddess, and plastered walls decorated with murals and carved reliefs.

It is generally thought that because of their earlier role as gatherers of wild foods, women were responsible for the invention of agriculture. As long as the ground was prepared by hoeing rather than by plowing, women remained the cultivators. They also invented and performed the making of pots from clay, and the spinning and weaving of textiles from cultivated flax and animal wool.

The Neolithic revolution spread to the Balkan Peninsula by 5000 B.C., Egypt and central Europe by 4000 B.C., and Britain and northwest India by 3000 B.C. The Neolithic cultures of Middle America and the Andes are independent developments, and a possible relationship between China and the Near East is now doubted.

Primitive Society

The organization of a primitive society may be as complex as our own. Rules regarding the role of parents, treatment of children, punishment of the evildoer, conduct of business, worship of the gods, and conventions of eating and recreation have existed for thousands of years, along with methods to compel the individual to do "the correct thing."

How can we know about those features of early culture that are not apparent from the remains of tools and other objects? The myths of primitive people throw light on their beliefs and customs. Defined as "the result of the working of a naive imagination upon the facts of experience," myths are invented to explain natural phenomena—thunder, for example—as the action of gods. In describing the daily life of the gods, myth makers describe what is familiar in their own lives.

Forms of Social Organization

Among all peoples, the basic social unit appears to be the elementary family group—parents and their offspring. Anthropologists do not know for certain what marriage customs were prevalent in the earliest societies, but monogamy was probably most common. Other social groupings found in primitive societies include the extended family, the clan, and the tribe.

The extended family is an individual family together with a circle of related persons who usually trace their descent through their mothers and are bound together by mutual loyalty. The extended family strengthens the elementary unit in obtaining food and in protecting its members against other groups. Land is communally owned but allocated to separate families. Weapons, tools, and utensils are individually owned.

A clan is a group of extended families whose members believe that they have a common ancestor. A clan is patrilineal if its members trace their relationship through the male line and matrilineal if through the female. Many primitive peoples identify their clans by a totem—an animal or other natural object that is revered. Totemism exists today in military insignia and the emblems of fraternal organizations.

A tribe comprises a number of clans, both related and unrelated. It is a community characterized by a common speech or distinctive dialect, common cultural heritage, specific inhabited territory, and tribal chief. Group loyalty is strong, often accompanied by contempt for the people and customs of other tribes.

Collective Responsibility in Law and Government

No community, however small and primitive, can exist and hold together unless rules regarding the relations between members are recognized as binding upon all. Such rules crystallize into precedent or custom, and the origin of these customary laws may be attributed to the gods. Later, under the conditions of an urban civilization in which life is much more complicated, a new kind of law, made by humans and called legislation, emerges to deal with new problems for which the old customary laws have no specific remedy.

In primitive societies correct behavior consists in not violating custom. The close relationships that exist in extended families and clans encourage conformity. Justice in a primitive group maintains equilibrium. Theft disturbs economic equilibrium, and justice is achieved by a settlement between the injured person and the thief. The victim is satisfied and the thief is not punished. Murder and wounding are also private matters to be avenged by the next of kin on the principle of "an eye for an eye." On the other hand, certain acts, such as treason, witchcraft, and incest, are considered dangerous to the whole group and require punishment by the entire community. Clan members who get into trouble too often may be outlawed from the clan or executed.

As a general rule, government in primitive societies is of a democratic character. The older tribal members—the council of elders—play a dominant role in decision making because of their greater experience and knowledge of the group's customs and lore. Serious decisions, such as going to war or electing a chief, require the consent of a general assembly of all adult males. The elected chief of the tribe is pledged to rule in accordance with custom and in consultation with the council of elders. Due to the strong element of representation present, this early form of government has been called "primitive democracy."[2]

Religion, Magic, and Science

Religion is a strong force in the lives of primitive people. One form of early religious belief is animism, the belief that all things in nature—wind, stones, trees, animals, and humans—are inhabited by spirits. Many spirits became objects of reverence, with the human being's own spirit being one of the first. Neanderthal people placed food and implements alongside their carefully buried dead, an indication that they believed in

an afterlife and held their ancestors in awe. We know also that late Paleolithic people revered the spirits of the animals they hunted for food as well as the spirit of fertility upon which both human and animal life depended. This led to totemism and to the worship of a fertility goddess—the Mother Goddess—who is known to us from many carved and modeled female figures with exaggerated sexual features.

At Çatal Hüyük, thirty-three representations of the Mother Goddess have been found, but only eight of a god. The latter represented the son of the goddess, or her consort. The relative scarcity of representations of gods, together with evidence that the cult of the goddess was administered by priestesses rather than priests, supports the view that women occupied a central position in Neolithic society.

The *Venus of Willendorf* is a female fertility figurine from Vienna dating from 15,000–10,000 B.C.

Closely associated with primitive religion is the practice of magic. In addition to revering the spirits, primitive people wanted to compel the spirits to favor them. They employed magic to ward off droughts, famines, floods, and plagues. There may have been an element of magic in the paintings of primitive peoples, who may have believed that through their paintings they could wield power over the spirits of animals.

Traditionally, magic has been regarded as diametrically opposed to science. Magic claims supernatural powers over natural forces, whereas science rejects any such determinism and studies natural phenomena by open-ended methods in its search for general laws. Yet, as scholars are increasingly recognizing, both primitive people and scientists believe that nature is orderly and that what is immediately apprehended by the senses can be systematically classified. The great contributions of Stone Age men and women—domestication of plants and animals, invention of tools, pottery, and weaving—involved centuries of methodical observation and oft-repeated experiments, few of which could have yielded immediate results. Early people must therefore be credited with a desire for knowledge for its own sake.

Further indications of this desire have been provided by studies of the large stone monuments (megaliths) constructed by the Neolithic peoples. The megalithic complex of Stonehenge in England has traditionally been considered a religious structure. However, the astronomer Gerald Hawkins, using a computer, found an "astonishing" number of correlations between the alignments of recognized Stonehenge positions—stones, stone holes, mounds—and the solar and lunar positions as of 1500 B.C. when Stonehenge was built.[3] The alignments made possible an accurate calendar and the prediction of the rising and setting of the sun and moon.

Stonehenge is the best-preserved and perhaps best-known megalithic monument in Europe. The outer megaliths are arranged in a circle around a central stone altar.

Mesopotamia: The First Civilization

Authorities do not all agree about the definition of *civilization*. Most accept the view that "a civilization is a culture which has attained a degree of complexity usually characterized by urban life." In other words, a civilization is a culture capable of sustaining a substantial number of specialists to cope with the economic, social, political, and religious needs of a populous society. Other characteristics usually present in a civilization include a system of writing to keep records, monumental architecture in place of simple buildings, and an art that is no longer merely decorative, like that on Neolithic pottery, but representative of people and their activities. All these characteristics of civilization first appeared in Mesopotamia.

The Geography of Mesopotamia

Around 6000 B.C., after the agricultural revolution had begun to spread from its place of origin on the northern fringes of the Fertile Crescent, Neolithic farmers started filtering into the Fertile Crescent itself. Although this broad plain received insufficient rainfall to support agriculture, the eastern section was watered by the Tigris and Euphrates rivers. Known in ancient days as Mesopotamia (Greek for "between the rivers"), the lower reaches of this plain, beginning near the point where the two rivers nearly converge, was called Babylonia. Babylonia in turn encompassed two geographical areas—Akkad in the north and Sumer, the delta of this river system, in the south.

Broken by river channels teeming with fish and refertilized frequently by alluvial silt laid down by uncontrolled floods, Sumer had a splendid agricultural potential if the environmental problems could be solved. "Arable land had literally to be created out of a chaos of swamps and sand banks by a 'separation' of land from water; the swamps . . . drained; the floods controlled; and lifegiving waters led to the rainless desert by artificial canals."[4] In the course of the several successive cultural phases that followed the arrival of the first Neolithic farmers, these and other related problems were solved by cooperative effort. Between 3500 B.C. and 3100 B.C. the foundations were laid for a type of economy and social order markedly different from anything previously known. This far more complex culture, based on large urban centers rather than simple villages, is what we associate with civilization.

Prelude to Civilization

By discovering how to use metals to make tools and weapons, late Neolithic people effected a revolution nearly as far-reaching as that wrought in agriculture. Neolithic artisans discovered how to extract copper from oxide ores by heating them with charcoal. Then about 3100 B.C., metal workers discovered that copper was improved by the addition of tin. The resulting alloy, bronze, was harder than copper and provided a sharper cutting edge.

Thus the advent of civilization in Sumer is associated with the beginning of the Bronze Age in the West, which in time spread to Egypt, Europe, and Asia. The Bronze age lasted until about 1200 B.C., when iron weapons and tools began to replace those made of bronze.

The first plow was probably a stick pulled through the soil with a rope. In time, however, domesticated cattle were harnessed to drag the plow in place of the farmer. Yoked, harnessed animals pulled plows in the Mesopotamian alluvium by 3000 B.C. As a result, farming advanced from the cultivation of small plots to the tilling of extensive fields. "By harnessing the ox man began to control and use a motive power other than that furnished by his own muscular energy. The ox was the first step to the steam engine and gasoline motor."[5]

Since the Mesopotamian plain had no stone, no metals, and no timber except its soft palm trees, these materials had to be transported from Syria and Asia Minor. Water transport down the Tigris and Euphrates solved the problem. The oldest sailing boat known is represented by a model found in a Sumerian grave of about 3500 B.C. Soon after this date wheeled vehicles appear in the form of ass-drawn war chariots. For the transport of goods overland, however, people continued to rely on the pack ass.

Another important invention was the potter's wheel, first used in Sumer soon after 3500 B.C. Earlier, people had fashioned pots by molding or coiling clay by hand, but now a symmetrical product could be produced in a much shorter time. A pivoted clay disk heavy enough to revolve of its own momentum, the potter's wheel has been called "the first really mechanical device."

The Emergence of Civilization in Sumer, c. 3100–2800 B.C.

By 3100 B.C. the population of Sumer had increased to the point where people were living in cities and had developed a preponderance of those elements previously noted as constituting civilization. Since these included the first evidence of writing, this first phase of Sumerian civilization, to about 28 B.C., is called the Protoliterate period.

This painted drinking cup was made in Iran over 5000 years ago when the Sumerian civilization was just beginning to take form.

The original homeland of the Sumerians is unknown. It is believed that they came from the east, but whether by sea or from the highlands is unknown. Their language is not related to those major language families that later appear in the Near East—Semites and Indo-Europeans. (The original home of the Semitic-speaking peoples is thought to have been the Arabian peninsula, while the Indo-Europeans seem to be migrated from the region north of the Black and Caspian seas. A third, much smaller language family is the Hamitic, which included the Egyptians and other peoples of northeastern Africa.)

How would life in Protoliterate Sumer have appeared to visitors seeing it for the first time? As they approached Ur, one of about a dozen Sumerian cities, they would pass farmers working in their fields with ox-drawn plows. They might see some of the workers using bronze sickles. The river would be dotted by boats carrying produce to and from the city. Dominating the flat countryside would be a ziggurat, a platform (later a lofty terrace, built in the shape of a pyramid) crowned by a sanctuary, or "high place." This was the "holy of holies," sacred to the local god. Upon entering the city, visitors would see a large number of specialists pursuing their appointed tasks as agents of the community and not as private entrepreneurs—some craftsmen casting bronze tools and weapons, others fashioning their wares on the potter's wheel, and merchants arranging to trade grain and manufactures for the metals, stone, lumber, and other essentials not available in Sumer. Scribes would be at work incising clay tablets with picture signs. Some tablets might bear the impression of cylinder seals, small stone cylinders engraved with a design. Examining the clay tablets, the visitors would find that they were memoranda used in administering a temple, which was also a warehouse and workshop. Some of the scribes might be making an inventory of the goats and sheep received that day for sacrificial use; others might be drawing up wage lists. They would be using a system of counting based on the unit 60—the sexagismal system rather than the decimal system which is based on the unit 10. It is still used today in computing divisions of time and angles.

Certain technical inventions of Protoliterate Sumer eventually made their way to both the Nile and the Indus valleys. Chief among these were the wheeled vehicle and the potter's wheel. The discovery in Egypt of cylinder seals similar in shape to those used in Sumer attests to contact between the two areas toward the end of the fourth millennium B.C. Certain early Egyptian art motifs and architectural forms are also thought to be of Sumerian origin. And it is probable that the example of Sumerian writing stimulated the Egyptians to develop a script of their own.

Sumerian Writing

As we have noted, the symbols on the oldest Sumerian clay tablets, the world's first writing, were pictures of concrete things such as a person, a sheep, a star, or a measure of grain. Some of these pictographs also represented ideas; for example, the picture of a foot was used to represent the idea of walking, and a picture of a mouth joined to that for water meant "to drink." This early pictograph writing gave way to phonetic (or syllabic) writing when the scribes realized that a sign could represent a sound as well as an object or idea. Thus, the personal name "Kuraka" could be written by combining the pictographs for mountain (pronounced *kur*), water (pronounced *a*), and mouth (pronounced *ka*). By 2800 B.C., the use of syllabic writing had reduced the number of signs from nearly two thousand to six hundred.

In writing, a scribe used a reed stylus to make impressions in soft clay tablets. The impressions took on a wedge shape, hence the term *cuneiform* (Latin *cuneus*, "wedge"). The cuneiform system of writing was adopted by many other peoples of the Near East, including the Babylonians, Assyrians, Hittites, and Persians.

The Old Sumerian Period, c. 2800–2300 B.C.

By 2800 B.C. the Sumerian cities had emerged into the light of history. This first historical age, called the Old Sumerian (or Early Dynastic) period, was characterized by incessant warfare as each city sought to protect or enlarge its land and water rights. Each city-state was a theocracy, for the chief local god was believed to be the real sovereign. The god's earthly representative was the *ensi*, the high priest and city governor, who acted as the god's steward in both religious and secular functions. Though endowed with divine right by virtue of being the human agent of the god, the *ensi* was not considered divine.

Early Sumerian society was highly collectivized, with the temples of the city god and subordinate deities assuming a central role. "Each temple owned lands which formed the estate of its divine owners. Each citizen belonged to one of the temples, and the whole of a temple community—the officials and priests, herdsmen and fishermen, gardeners, craftsmen, stonecutters, merchants, and even slaves—was referred to as 'the people of the god *X.*'"[6] That part of the temple land called "common" was worked by all members of the community, while the remaining land was divided among the citizens for their support at a rental of from one third to one sixth of the crop. Priests and temple administrators, however, held rent-free lands.

In addition to the temple lands, a considerable part of a city's territory originally consisted of land collectively owned by clans, kinship groups comprising a number of extended families. By 2600 B.C., these clan lands were becoming the private property of great landowners called *lugals* (literally "great men"). Deeds of sale record the transfer of clan lands to private owners in return for substantial payments in copper to a few clan leaders and insignificant grants of food to the remaining clan members. These private estates were worked by "clients" whose status resembled that of the dependents of the temples.

In time, priests, administrators, and *ensis* became venal, usurping property and oppressing the common people. This frequently led to the rise of despots who came to power on a wave of popular discontent. Since these despots were usually *lugals, lugal* became a political title and is generally translated as "king."

The Sumerian *lugals* made the general welfare their major concern. Best known is Urukagina, who declared himself *lugal* of Lagash near the end of the Old Sumerian period and ended the rule of priests and "powerful men," each of whom, he claimed, was guilty of acting "for his own benefit." Urukagina's inscriptions describe his many reforms and conclude: "He freed the inhabitants of Lagash from usury, burdensome controls, hunger, theft, murder, and seizure (of their property and persons). He established freedom. The widow and the orphan were no longer at the mercy of the powerful man."[7]

The Akkadian Period, c. 2300–2150 B.C.

Immediately north of Sumer lay the narrow region of Akkad, inhabited by Semites who had absorbed Sumerian culture. Appearing late in the fourth millennium B.C., the Akkadians were the earliest of the Semitic peoples who filtered into Mesopotamia from Arabia. A generation after Urukagina, Sargon I (2370–2315 B.C.), an energetic Akkadian ruler, conquered Sumer and went on to establish an empire that extended from the Persian Gulf to the Mediterranean Sea.

Very proud of his lower-class origins, Sargon boasted that his humble, unwed mother had been forced to abandon him: "She set me in a basket of rushes . . . [and] cast me into the river." Rescued and brought up by a gardener, Sargon rose to power through the army. As *lugal*, Sargon looked after the welfare of the lower classes and

This bronze head, dating from 2350 B.C., was found at Nineveh and is sometimes identified as Sargon, founder of the Akkadian dynasty.

aided the rising class of private merchants. At the latter's request he once sent his army to far-off Asia Minor to protect a colony of merchants from interference by a local ruler. We are told that Sargon "did not sleep" in his efforts to promote prosperity and that in this new free enterprise economy trade moved as freely "as the Tigris where it flows into the sea, . . . all lands lie in peace, their inhabitants prosperous and contented."[8]

Sargon's successors, however, were unable either to withstand the attacks of semibarbaric highlanders or to overcome the desire for independence of the priest-dominated Sumerian cities. As a result, the house of Sargon collapsed about 2150 B.C.

The Neo-Sumerian Period, c. 2100–2000 B.C.

Order and prosperity were restored by the *lugals* of the Third Dynasty of Ur. By creating a highly centralized administration in Sumer and Akkad, these rulers solved the problem of internal rebellion that had plagued Sargon and his successors. The formerly temple-dominated cities became provinces administered by closely watched governors. The "church" became an arm of the state; the high priests were state appointees, and the temple economic organization was used as the state's agent in rigidly controlling the nascent free enterprise economy that Sargon had encouraged came to a temporary halt.

At the head of this bureaucratic state stood the now-deified ruler, celebrated in hymns as a heaven-sent messiah who "brings splendor to the land, . . . savior of orphans whose misery he relieves, . . . the vigilant shepherd who conducts the people unto cooling shade."[9] Much of what we now call social legislation was passed by these "vigilant shepherds." Such laws were called "rightings" (Sumerian *nig-si-sa*, usually translated "equity"), since their object was the righting of wrongs that were not covered by the old customary law *(nig-ge-na,* "truth"). The prologue to the law code of Ur-Nammu, founder of the dynasty, declared that it was the king's purpose to see that "the orphan did not fall a prey to the wealthy" and that "the man of one shekel did not fall a prey to the man of one mina (sixty shekels)."[10]

Disaster struck Ur about 2000 B.C., when Elamites from the highlands to the east destroyed the city. The Sumerians were never again a dominant element politically, but their culture persisted as the foundation for all subsequent civilizations in the Tigris-Euphrates valley.

For more than two centuries following the destruction of Ur, disunity and warfare again plagued Mesopotamia, along with depression, inflation, and acute hardship for the lower classes. Merchants, however, utilized the absence of state controls to become full-fledged capitalists who amassed fortunes that they invested in banking operations and land. (Thee merchants used a form of double-entry bookkeeping they called "balanced accounts." Their word for capital, *qaqqadum*, meaning "head," influenced later peoples; our word *capital* is derived from the Latin *caput* "head." The stronger local rulers of the period freed the poor from debt slavery and issued a variety of reform laws best illustrated by the legislation of Hammurabi.

The Old Babylonia Period, c. 2000–1600 B.C.

Semitic Amorites (from *Amurru,* the "West"), under the rule of their capable king, Hammurabi of Babylon (c. 1792–1750 B.C.), for a time brought most of Mesopotamia under one rule by 1760 B.C. (see Reference Map 1).

Hammurabi is best known for his code of nearly three hundred laws whose stated objective was "to cause justice to prevail in the land, to destroy the wicked and evil, to prevent the strong from oppressing the weak . . . and to further the welfare of the people."[11] Hammurabi's legislation reestablished a state-controlled economy in which merchants were required to obtain a "royal permit," interest was limited to 20 percent, and prices were set for basic commodities and for fees charged by physicians, veterinarians, and builders. Minimum wages were established, and debt slavery was limited to three years. Other laws protected wives and children, although a wife who had "set her face to go out and play the part of a fool, neglect her house, belittle her husband" could be divorced without alimony, or the husband could take another wife and compel the first to remain as a servant. Unless a son committed some grave offense, his

Hammurabi Legislates Women's Rights

Hammurabi's code is a compilation of new laws called *misharum,* literally meaning "rightings." Their purpose is to right the injustices for which the old tribal customary law had no specific remedy.

If a man takes a wife and does not arrange a contract for her, that woman is not a wife.

If the wife of a man is caught lying with another man, they shall bind them and throw them into the water. If the husband of the woman wishes to spare his wife, then the king shall spare his servant.

If a man force the (betrothed) wife of another who has not known a male and is still living in her father's house, and he lie in her bosom and they catch him, that man shall be put to death and that woman shall go free.

If a man has accused his wife but she has not been caught lying with another man, she shall take an oath in the name of god and return to her house.

If a man deserts his city and flees and afterwards his wife enters into another house, if that man returns and wishes to take back his wife, the wife of the fugitive shall not return to her husband because he hated his city and fled.

If a man wishes to divorce his wife who has not borne him children, he shall give her money to the amount of her marriage price and he shall make good to her the dowry which she brought from her father's house and then he may divorce her.

If a woman hates her husband and says, "You may not possess me," the city council shall inquire into her case; and if she has been careful and without reproach and her husband has been going about and greatly belittling her, that woman has no blame. She may take her dowry and go to her father's house.

If a man takes a wife and she does not present him with children and he sets his face to take a concubine, that man may take a concubine and bring her into his house. That concubine shall not rank with his wife.

If a man takes a wife and she gives a maidservant to her husband, and that maidservant bears children and afterwards claims equal rank with her mistress because she has borne children, her mistress may not sell her, but she may reduce her to bondage and count her among the slaves.

If a man gives to his wife a field, garden, house, or goods and delivers to her a sealed deed, after (the death of) her husband her children cannot enter a claim against her. The mother may will her estate to her son whom she loves, but to an outsider she may not.

If a man, who has brought a gift to the house of his father-in-law and has paid the marriage price, looks with longing upon another woman and says to his father-in-law, "I will not marry your daughter," the father of the daughter shall take to himself whatever was brought to him.

If a man takes a wife and she bears him children and that woman dies, her father may not lay claim to her dowry. Her dowry belongs to her children.

Based on the translation by Robert F. Harper, *The Code of Hammurabi* (Chicago: University of Chicago Press, 1904).

father could not disinherit him. (Only Louisiana among American states has a similar "forced heirship" law.) If the state failed to maintain law and order, the victim of that failure received compensation from the state: the value of the property stolen, or "one mina of silver" to the kin of a murder victim.

Punishments were graded in their severity; the higher the culprit in the social scale, the more severe the penalty.

In the epilogue to the code, Hammurabi eloquently summed up his efforts to provide social justice for his people.

Let any oppressed man, who has a cause, come before my image as king of righteousness! Let him read the inscription on my monument! Let him give heed to my weighty words! And may my monument enlighten him as to his cause and may he understand his case! May he set his heart at ease! (and he will exclaim): "Hammurabi indeed is a ruler who is like a real father to his people . . . ."[12]

This paternalistic concern for the general welfare helps explain why the people of Mesopotamia—as well as of Egypt and all other areas of the ancient Near East—never moved on to democracy, as the Greeks will be the first to do. The Greek explanation, in Aristotle's words, was that these people "were by nature slaves" and so incapable of democracy. It would seem, rather, that they were content to be ruled by enlightened despots like Hammurabi. Today in Mesopotamia (present-day Iraq), the situation is little different. Saddam Hussein, the despotic ruler of Iraq, was enormously popular—at least before his ill-fated invasion of Kuwait in 1991. "Since Hammurabi," one Iraqi has said, "we have lived without choosing our own head of state, so we have a different feeling about leadership. In this part of the world, we have an instinctive love for our leader, if he is a leader. . . . [Saddam Hussein is] the symbol of their aspirations, who really cares for them. . . . Saddam Hussein is in their hearts."[13]

Mathematics and Science

Building on the work of the Sumerians, the Babylonians made advances in arithmetic, geometry, and algebra. For ease of computation with both whole numbers and fractions, they compiled tables for multiplication and division and for square and cube roots. They knew how to solve linear and quadratic equations, and their knowledge of geometry included the theorem later formulated by the Greek philosopher Pythagoras: the square of the hypotenuse of a right-angled triangle is equal to the sum of squares of the other two sides. Perhaps their greatest achievement was the principle of place-value notation that gave numbers a value according to their position in a series. To represent zero, they employed the character for "not," which is the same as our "naught," still used in place of zero.

The Babylonians achieved little that today can accurately be called science. They did observe nature and collect data, which is the first requirement of science; but to explain natural phenomena, they did not go beyond the formulation of myths that explained things in terms of the unpredictable whims of the gods. The sun, moon, and five visible planets were thought to be gods who were able to influence human lives; accordingly, their movements were watched, recorded, and interpreted. Thus was born the pseudoscience of astrology.

Literature and Religion

The Babylonians took over from the Sumerians a body of literature ranging from heroic epics that compare favorably with the *Iliad* and the *Odyssey* to wisdom writings that have their counterparts in the Old Testament books of Job, Proverbs, and Ecclesiastes. The *Epic of Gilgamesh* recounts the exploits of a heroic ruler of Uruk who lived about 2700 B.C. The central theme of the epic is Gilgamesh's hope for everlasting life. He seeks out and questions Utnapishtim, who was granted eternal life because he saved all living creatures from the flood. Utnapishtim's story has many remarkable similarities with the Hebrew account of Noah and the flood. But Gilgamesh's quest is hopeless, and he is so informed on several occasions:

Gilgamesh, whither rovest thou?
The life thou pursuest thou shalt not find.
When the gods created mankind,
Death for mankind they set aside,
Life in their own hands retaining.

Thou, Gilgamesh, let full be thy belly.
Make thou merry by day and by night.
Of each day make thou a feast of rejoicing,
Day and night dance thou and play! . . .
Pay heed to the little one that holds on to thy
*   hand,*
Let thy spouse delight in thy bosom!
For this is the task of mankind![14]

The ancient Mesopotamians never progressed beyond this early view that immortality is reserved for the gods. Unlike the Egyptians, they did not go on to develop a belief in an attractive life after death as a reward for good behavior on earth. They did come to believe in divine rewards for moral conduct, but these were rewards to be enjoyed in this life—increased worldly goods, numerous offspring, and long life. Thus the sun-god Shamash was celebrated in hymns which proclaimed that "the honest merchant . . . is pleasing to Shamash, and he will prolong his life. He will enlarge his family, gain wealth . . . and his descendants will never fail." The dishonest merchant, on the other hand, "is disappointed in the matter of profit and loses his capital."[15]

The ethical content of Babylonian religion was largely lost when the numerous priesthoods—more than thirty different types of priests and priestesses are known—became preoccupied with an elaborate set of rituals, particularly those designed to ward off evil demons and divine the future. Good deeds, the priests insisted, could not protect a person from demons that have the power to make their part-human and part-animal bodies invisible:

Doors and bolts do not stop them;
High walls and thick walls they cross like
*   waves;*
They leap from house to house . . . ;
Under the doors they slip like serpents.[16]

While one large class of priests provided amulets inscribed with incantations and magic formulas to exorcise demons, another group dealt with divining the future. Almost anything could be viewed as an omen, but most popular were dreams, the movements of birds and animals, the internal organs of sacrificed animals, the shape taken by oil poured on the surface of water, the casting of lots, and astronomical phenomena. Some of these methods of divination have survived virtually unchanged through the ages.

The End of an Era

The pattern of disunity and warfare, all too familiar in Mesopotamia, reasserted itself following Hammurabi's death. In 1595 B.C. the Hittites, an Indo-European people who had established themselves in Asia Minor (see p. 23), mounted a daring raid down the Euphrates, sacking Babylon and destroying the weakened dynasty of Hammurabi. The next five centuries is a dark age about which little is known; yet the cultural heritage left by the Sumerians and Babylonians survived. Meanwhile, in a neighboring river valley, another civilization had emerged.

Egypt: Gift of the Nile

Egypt is literally "the gift of the Nile," as the ancient Greek historian Herodotus observed. The Nile valley, extending 750 miles from the first cataract to the Mediterranean, is a fertile oasis cut out of a limestone plateau. Its soil was renewed annually by the rich silt deposited by the flood water of the river that, unlike the unpredictable floods of Mesopotamia, rose and fell with unusual precision. The rise began early in July and continued until the banks were overrun, reaching its crest in September. By the end of October the river was once more contained within its banks.

Predynastic Egypt

By 4000 B.C. Neolithic villagers had begun to build dikes and a canal network to control the Nile for irrigation. As population grew, a central authority was required because this necessary work involved many communities. Two distinct kingdoms emerged: Lower Egypt comprised the broad Nile delta north of Memphis, while Upper Egypt extended southward along the narrow ten- to twenty-mile-wide valley as far as the first cataract at Syene (Aswan). Each kingdom contained about a score of tribal districts, or *nomes*, which had formerly been ruled by independent chieftains.

The Predynastic period ended soon after 3100 B.C. when Menes (also known as Narmer), ruler of Upper Egypt, united the two kingdoms and founded the First Dynasty with its capital at Memphis. As little is known of these first two dynasties, the period is called Egypt's archaic age.

The Old Kingdom, c. 2700–2200 B.C.

The kings of the Third through the Sixth Dynasties—the period called the Old Kingdom or Pyramid Age—firmly established order and stability and the essential elements of Egyptian civilization. The nobility lost its independence, and all power was centered in the king, or pharaoh (Per-ao, "Great House"). The pharaoh was considered a god rather than the human agent of a god, as was usual in Mesopotamia. As the god of Egypt, the pharaoh owned all the land (although frequent grants were made to temples and private persons), controlled the irrigation system, decided when the fields should be sown, and received the surplus from the crops produced on the huge royal estates. This surplus supported a large corps of specialists—administrators, priests, scribes, artists, artisans, and merchants—who labored in the service of the pharaoh. The people's welfare was thought to rest on absolute fidelity to the god-king. "If you want to know what to do in life," advised one Egyptian writer, "cling to the pharaoh and be loyal. . . ." As a consequence, Egyptians felt a sense of security that was rare in Mesopotamia.

The belief that the pharaoh was a god led to the practice of mummification and the construction of colossal tombs—the pyramids—to preserve the pharaoh's embalmed body for eternity. The ritual of mummification restored vigor and activity to the dead pharoah; it was his passport to eternity: "You live again, you live again forever, here you are young once more for ever." The pyramid tombs, in particular those of the Fourth Dynasty at Gizeh near Memphis, which are the most celebrated of all ancient monuments, reflect the great power and wealth of the Old Kingdom pharaohs. Although pyramid construction provided employment during the four months of the year when the land was flooded by the Nile, the Egyptian masses performed it primarily as an act of faith in their god-king, on whom the security and prosperity of Egypt depended.

Security and prosperity came to an end late in the Sixth Dynasty. The burden of building and maintaining pyramid tombs for each new king exhausted the state. The Nile floods failed and crops were diminished, yet taxes were increased. As the state and its god-king lost credibility, royal tombs were plundered and government files were thrown into the street. The nobles assumed the prerogatives of the pharaohs, including the claim to immortality, and the nomes again became independent.

For about a century and a half, known as the First Intermediate Period (c. 2200–2050 B.C.), civil war raged among contenders for the throne. Outsiders raided and infiltrated the land. The lot of the common people became unbearable as they faced famine, robbery, and oppression by petty tyrants. "All happiness has vanished," wrote a contemporary. "I show you the land in turmoil, . . . Each man's heart is for himself. . . . A man sits with his back turned, while one slays another."[17]

The Middle Kingdom, c. 2050–1800 B.C.

Egypt was rescued from anarchy by the pharaohs of the Eleventh and Twelfth Dynasties, who reunited the country and ruled from Thebes. Stressing their role as watchful shepherds of the people, the Middle Kingdom pharaohs promoted the welfare of the downtrodden. One of them claimed: "I gave to the destitute and brought up the orphan. I caused him who was nothing to reach [his goal], like him who was [somebody]."[18] No longer was the nation's wealth expended on huge pyramids, but on public works. The largest of these, a drainage and irrigation project in the marshy Fayum district south of Memphis, resulted in the reclamation of 27,000 acres of arable land. Moreover, a concession that has been called "the democratization of the hereafter" gave the lower classes the right to have their bodies mummified and thereby to enjoy immortality like the pharaohs and the nobility.

Following the Twelfth Dynasty, Egypt again was racked by civil war as provincial governors fought for the pharaoh's throne. During this Second Intermediate Period (c. 1800–1750 B.C.), the Hyksos, a mixed but preponderantly Semitic people, invaded Egypt from Palestine about 1720 B.C. They easily conquered the Delta and made the rest of Egypt tributary. It was probably at this time that the Hebrew Joseph, who had risen to a high position under a Hyksos king, invited his relatives to settle in the Delta ("the land of Goshen") during a famine (see p. 26).

The New Kingdom or Empire, c. 1570–1090 B.C.

The Egyptians viewed the Hyksos conquest as a great humiliation imposed on them by detestable barbarians. An aggressive nationalism emerged, promoted by the native prince of Thebes who proclaimed: "No man can settle down, when despoiled by the taxes of the Asiatics. I will grapple with him, that I may rip open his belly! My wish is to save Egypt and to smite the Asiatics!"[19] Adopting the new weapons introduced by their conquerors—the composite bow, constructed of wood and horn, and the horse-drawn chariot—the Egyptians expelled the Hyksos and pursued them into Palestine. The pharaohs of the Eighteenth Dynasty, who reunited Egypt and founded the New Kingdom, made Palestine the nucleus of an Egyptian empire in western Asia (see Reference Map 1).

The outstanding representative of the aggressive state that Egypt now became was Thutmose III (1490–1436 B.C.). After inheriting the throne as a child, Thutmose was shoved aside by his stepmother, Hatshepsut (1490–1469 B.C.), a former concubine who acted as regent during his minority. Supported by the powerful priests of the sun-god Amon, Hatshepsut proclaimed herself "king." In many of her statues and reliefs she was portrayed wearing the customary royal crown and helmets—sometimes even sporting the royal beard! She employed all the customary royal titles with the exception of "Mighty Bull," which clearly was not appropriate for a woman who described herself as "exceedingly good to look upon, . . . a beautiful maiden, fresh, serene of nature, . . . altogether divine."

When Hatshepsut died after twenty years of rule, Thutmose ordered her name and inscriptions erased, her reliefs effaced, and her statues broken and thrown into a quarry. Then this "Napoleon of Egypt," as Thutmose III has been called, led his army on seventeen campaigns as far as Syria, where he set up his boundary markers on the banks of the Euphrates, called by the Egyptians "the river that runs backward." Nubia and northern Sudan were also brought under his sway. The native princes of Palestine, Phoenicia, and Syria were left on their thrones, but their sons were taken to Egypt as hostages. Here they were brought up and, thoroughly Egyptianized, eventually sent home to rule as loyal vassals. Thutmose III erected obelisks—tall, pointed shafts of stone—to commemorate his reign and to record his wish that "his name might endure throughout the future forever and ever." Four of his obelisks now adorn the cities of Istanbul, Rome, London, and New York.

Under Amenhotep III (c. 1402–1363 B.C.) the Egyptian Empire reached its peak. Tribute flowed in from conquered lands; and Thebes, with its temples built for the sun-god Amon east of the Nile at Luxor and Karnak, became the most magnificent city in the world. The Hittites and the rulers of Babylonia and Crete, among others, sent gifts, including princesses for the pharaoh's harem. In return, they asked the pharaoh for gold, "for gold is as common as dust in your land."

During the reign of the succeeding pharaoh, Amenhotep IV (1363–1347 B.C.), however, the Empire went into sharp decline as the result of an internal struggle between the pharaoh and the powerful and wealthy priests of the sun-god Amon, the king of the gods. The pharaoh undertook to revolutionize Egypt's religion by proclaiming the worship of the sun's disk, Aton, in place of Amon and all the other deities. Often called the first monotheist (although, as Aton's son, the pharaoh was also a god), Amenhotep changed his name to Akhenaton ("Devoted to Aton"), left Amon's city to found a new capital (Akhetaton), and concentrated upon religious reform. Most of Egypt's vassal princes in Asia defected when their appeals for aid against invaders went unheeded. Prominent among these invaders were groups of people called the Habiru, whose possible identification with the Hebrews of the Old Testament has interested modern scholars. At home the Amon priesthood encouraged dissension. When Akhenaton died, his nine-year-old brother, Tutankhamen ("King Tut," c. 1347–1338 B.C.)—now remembered for his small but richly furnished tomb discovered in 1922—returned to the worship of Amon and to Thebes, where he became a puppet of the priests of Amon. At this point the generals of the army took control of Egypt.

A relief from the temple of Aton at Tel el Amarna depicts Akhenaton and Nefertete worshipping the sun god Aton in the form of the sun's disk.

One of the new army leaders founded the Nineteenth Dynasty (c. 1305–1200 B.C.), which sought to re-establish Egyptian control over Palestine and Syria. The result was a long struggle with the Hittites, who in the meantime had pushed south from Asia Minor into Syria. This struggle reached a climax in the reign of Ramses II (1290–1224 B.C.), the pharaoh of the Hebrew Exodus from Egypt under Moses. Ramses II regained Palestine, but when he failed to dislodge the Hittites from Syria, he agreed to a treaty. Its strikingly modern character is revealed in clauses providing for nonagression, mutual assistance, and extradition of fugitives.

The long reign of Ramses II as Egypt's last period of national grandeur. The number and size of Ramses' monuments rival those of the Pyramid Age. Outstanding among them are the great Hypostyle Hall, built for Amon at Karnak, and the temple at Abu Simbel, with its four colossal statues of Ramses, which has now been raised to save it from inundation by the waters of the High Dam at Aswan (Syene). After Ramses II, royal authority gradually decayed as the power of the priests of Amon rose.

Period of Decadence, 1090–332 B.C.

During the early part of the Period of Decadence the Amon priesthood at Thebes became so strong that the high priest was able to found his own dynasty and to rule over Upper Egypt. At the same time, merchant princes set up a dynasty of their own in the Delta. Libyans from the west moved into central Egypt, where in 940 B.C. they established a dynasty whose founder, Shishak, was a contemporary of King Solomon of Israel. Two centuries later Egypt was conquered by the black Kushites of Nubia, who established the Twenty-Fifth Dynasty and ruled from Napata, near the Fourth Cataract (see Reference Map 1). Kushite domination ended in 671 B.C., when the Assyrians of Mesopotamia made Egypt a province of their empire. The Egyptianized Kushite rulers transferred their capital southward to Meroë, just above the Sixth Cataract. Here they recorded their royal annals in a script based on Egyptian hieroglyphs, and when they died their bodies were mummified and laid to rest in small replicas of the pyramid tombs of the Old Kingdom.

Egypt enjoyed a brief Indian summer of revived glory during the Twenty-Sixth Dynasty (663–525 B.C.), which expelled the Assyrians with the aid of Greek mercenaries. The revival of ancient artistic and literary forms proved sterile, and after attempts to regain Palestine failed, "the king of Egypt came not again any more out of his land" (2 Kings 24:7). Only the commercial policies of these rulers were successful. In about 600 B.C., to facilitate trade, Pharaoh Necho ordered a canal dug between the Nile mouth and the Red Sea (it was later completed by the Persians), and he commissioned a Phoenician expedition, which circumnavigated Africa in three years—a feat not to be duplicated until A.D. 1497 by the Portuguese.

The thirty Egyptian dynasties which had existed for nearly three thousand years came to an end when Egypt passed under Persian rule in 525 B.C. Two hundred years later this ancient land came within the domain of Alexander the Great.

Egyptian Society and Economy

Although most Egyptians were virtual serfs and subject to forced labor, class stratification was not rigid, and people of merit could rise to a higher rank in the service of the pharaoh. The best avenue of advancement was education. The pharaoh's administration needed many scribes, and young men were urged to attend a scribal school: "Be a scribe, who is freed from forced labor, and protected from all work. . . . he directeth every work that is in this land." Yet then as now the education of a young man was beset with pitfalls: "I am told thou forsakest writing, that thou givest thyself up to pleasures; thou goest from street to street, where it smelleth of beer, to destruction. Beer, it scareth men from thee, it sendeth they soul to perdition."[20]

Compared with their Greek and Roman successors, Egyptian women enjoyed extraordinary freedom. Equality of the sexes in Egypt is reflected in statues and paintings. Wives of pharaohs and nobles are shown standing or sitting beside their husbands, and little daughters are depicted with the same tenderness as little sons. The right of succession to the throne was based on royal descent from the mother as well as the father. Marriages between brothers and sisters often took place within the ruling family to assure the most divine strain and reduce the number of rival claimants to the throne. Business and legal documents show that women in general had rights to own, buy and sell property without reliance on legal guardians, and to make wills and testify in court. A few became scribes and members of the administration.

The economy of Egypt has been called "theocratic socialism" because the state, in the person of the divine pharaoh, owned the land and monopolized commerce and industry. (Compare the role of temples in the collectivized economy of the Early Sumerian period, p. 11.) Because of the Nile and the proximity to the Mediterranean and Red seas, most of Egypt's trade was carried on by ships. Boats plied regularly up and down the Nile, which, unlike the Tigris and the Euphrates, is easily navigable in both directions up to the first cataract at Aswan (Syene). The current carries ships downstream, and the prevailing north wind enables them to sail upstream easily. Trade reached its height during the Empire, when commerce traveled along four main routes: the Nile River; the Red Sea, which was connected by caravan to the Nile bend near Thebes; a caravan route to Mesopotamia and

The largest of the colossal columns of the temple at Karnak rise more than 70 feet and are more than 20 feet in diameter.

A seated scribe holds on his lap a scroll of papyrus, a reed that provided the Egyptians with a cheap and plentiful material on which to write. Flattened and dried reeds could be rolled in scrolls and easily stored or transported.

southern Syria; and the Mediterranean Sea, connecting northern Syria, Cyprus, Crete, and Greece with the delta of the Nile. Egypt's indispensable imports were lumber, copper, tin, and olive oil, paid for with gold from its rich mines, linens, wheat, and papyrus rolls—the preferred writing material of the ancient world. (Our word *paper* is derived from the Greek *papyros*.)

Egyptian Religion

During the Old Kingdom Egyptian religion had no strong ethical character. Relations between humans and gods were based largely on material considerations, and the gods were thought to reward those who brought them gifts of sacrifice. But widespread suffering during the First Intermediate Period led to a revolution in religious thought. It was now believed that instead of sacrificial offerings the gods were interested in good character and love for one's fellows: "More acceptable [to the gods] is the character of one upright of heart than the ox of the evildoer. . . . Give the love of thyself to the whole world; a good character is a remembrance."[21]

Osiris, the mythical god of the Nile whose death and resurrection explained the annual rise and fall of the river, became the center of Egypt's most popular religious cult when the new emphasis on moral character was combined with the supreme reward of an attractive afterlife. "Do justice whilst thou endurest upon earth," people were told. "A man remains over after death, and his deeds are placed beside him in heaps. However, existence yonder is for eternity. . . . He who reaches it without wrongdoing shall exist yonder like a god."[22] The original premoral myth told how Osiris had been murdered by Seth, his evil brother, who cut the victim's body into many pieces. When Isis, the bereaved widow, collected all the pieces and wrapped them in linen, Osiris was resurrected. The moralized Osiris cult taught that Osiris was the first mummy and that every mummified Egyptian could become another Osiris, capable of resurrection from the dead and a blessed eternal life.

But only a soul free of sin would be permitted to live forever in what was described as the "Field of the Blessed, an ideal land where there is no wailing and nothing evil; where barley grows four cubits high, and emmer wheat seven ells high; where, even better, one has to do no work in the field oneself, but can let others take care of it."[23] In a ceremony called "counting up character," Osiris weighed the deceased's heart against the Feather of Truth. If the heart was heavy with sin and outweighed the Feather of Truth, a horrible creature devoured it. During the Empire the priesthood of Osiris became corrupt and claimed that it knew clever methods of surviving the soul testing, even if a person's heart were heavy with sin. Charms and magical prayers and formulas were sold to the living as insurance policies guaranteeing them a happy outcome in the judgment before Osiris. They constitute much of what is known as the Book of the Dead, which was placed in the tomb.

Akhenaton's religious reformation was directed against the venal priests of Osiris as well as those of the supreme god Amon. As we have seen, Akhenaton failed to uproot Amon and the multiplicity of lesser gods; his monotheism was too cold and intellectual to attract the masses who yearned for a blessed hereafter.

Mathematics and Science

The Egyptians were much less skilled in mathematics than were the Mesopotamians. Their arithmetic was limited to addition and subtraction, which also served them when they needed to multiply and divide. They could cope with only simple algebra, but they did have considerable knowledge of practical geometry. The obliteration of field boundaries by the annual flooding of the Nile made land measurement a necessity. A knowledge of geometry was also essential in computing the dimensions of ramps for raising stones during the construction of pyramids. In these and other engineering projects the Egyptians were superior to their Mesopotamian contemporaries. Like the Mesopotamians, the Egyptians acquired a "necessary" technology without developing a truly scientific method. Yet what has been called the oldest known scientific treatise, *The Edwin Smith Surgical Papyrus*, was composed during the Old Kingdom. Its author described forty-eight cases requiring surgery, drawing conclusions solely from observation and rejecting supernatural causes and treatments. In advising the physician to "measure for the heart" that "speaks" in various parts of the body, he recognized the importance of the pulse and approached the concept of the circulation of the blood. This text remained unique, however, for in Egypt as elsewhere in the ancient Near East, thought failed to free itself permanently from domination by priests and bondage to religion. The Greeks were to be the first to accomplish this task.

The Old Kingdom also produced the world's first known solar calendar, the direct ancestor of our own. In order to plan their farming operations in accordance with the annual flooding of the Nile, the Egyptians kept records and discovered that the average period between inundations was 365 days. They also noted that the Nile flood coincided with the annual appearance of

In this scene from a funerary papyrus, or "Book of the Dead," Princess Entiu-ny stands to the left of a set of scales on which Anubis, the jackal-headed god, weighs her heart against the Feather of Truth, while Osiris, Lord of the Dead, judges from his throne. His wife, Isis, stands behind the princess.

the Dog Star (Sirius) on the eastern horizon at dawn, and they soon associated the two phenomena. (Since the Egyptian year was six hours short of the true year, Julius Caesar in Roman times corrected the error by adding an extra day every four years.)

Monumentalism in Architecture

Because of their impressive, enduring tombs and temples, the Egyptians have been called the greatest builders in history. The earliest tomb was the mud-brick *mastaba*, so called because of its resemblance to a low bench. By the beginning of the Third Dynasty stone began to replace brick, and an architectural genius named Imhotep, now honored as "the father of architecture in stone," constructed the first pyramid by piling six huge stone mastabas one on top of the other. Adjoining this Step Pyramid was a temple complex whose stone columns were not freestanding but attached to a wall, as though the architect was still feeling his way in the use of the new medium.

The most celebrated of the true pyramids were built for the Fourth Dynasty pharaohs Khufu, Khafre, and Menkaure. Khufu's pyramid, the largest of the three, covers thirteen acres and originally rose 481 feet. It is composed of 2,300,000 limestone blocks, some weighing fifteen tons, and all pushed and pulled into place by human muscle. This stupendous monument was built without mortar, yet some of the stones were so perfectly fitted that a knife cannot be inserted in the joints. The Old Kingdom's eighty pyramids are a striking expression of Egyptian civilization. Their dignity and massiveness reflect the religious basis of Egyptian society—the dogma that the king was a god who owned the nation and that serving him was the most important task of the people.

As the glory and serenity of the Old Kingdom can be seen in its pyramids, constructed as an act of faith by its subjects, so the power and wealth of the Empire survives in the Amon temples at Thebes, made possible by the booty and tribute of conquest. Here on the east side of the Nile stand the ruins of the magnificient temples of Karnak and Luxor. The Hypostyle Hall of the temple of Karnak, built by Ramses II, is larger than the cathedral of Notre Dame. Its forest of 134 columns is arranged in sixteen rows, with the roof over the two broader central aisles (the nave) raised to allow the entry of light. This technique of providing a clerestory over a central nave was later used in Roman basilicas and Christian churches.

Sculpture and Painting

Egyptian art was essentially religious. Tomb paintings and relief sculpture depict the everyday activities that the deceased wished to continue enjoying in the afterlife, and statues glorify the god-kings in all their serenity and eternity. Since religious art is inherently conservative, Egyptian art seldom departed from the traditions established during the vigorous and self-assured Old Kingdom. Sculptors idealized and standardized their subjects, and the human figure is shown either looking directly ahead or in profile, with a rigidity very much in keeping with the austere architectural settings of the statues.

Yet on two occasions an unprecedented naturalism appeared in Egyptian sculpture. The faces of some of the Middle Kingdom rulers appear drawn and weary, seemingly reflecting the burden of reconstructing Egypt after the collapse of the Old Kingdom. An even greater naturalism is seen in the portraits of Akhenaton and his queen, Nefertete, which continued on into the following reign of Tutankhamen. The pharaoh's brooding countenance is realistically portrayed, as is his ungainly paunch and his happy but far from godlike family life as he holds one of his young daughters on his knee or munches on a bone. The "heretic" pharaoh, who insisted on what he called "truth" in religion, seems also to have insisted on truth in art.

Painting in Egypt shows the same precision and mastery of technique that are evident in sculpture. However, no attempt was made to show objects in perspective, and the scenes give an appearance of flatness. The effect of distance was conveyed by making objects in a series or by putting one object above another. Another convention employed was to depict everything from its most characteristic angle. Often the head, arms and legs were shown in side view and the eyes, shoulders, and chest were shown in front view.

Writing and Literature

In Egypt, as in Sumer, writing began with pictures. But unlike the Mesopotamian signs, Egyptian hieroglyphs ("sacred signs") remained primarily pictorial. At first the hieroglyphs represented only objects, but later they came to stand for ideas and syllables. Early in the Old Kingdom the Egyptians took the further step of using the alphabetic characters for twenty-four consonant sounds. Although they also continued to use the old pictographic and syllabic signs, this discovery had far-reaching consequences. It influenced their Semitic neighbors in Syria to produce an alphabet that, in its Phoenician form, became the forerunner of our own.

Egypt's oldest literature is the Pyramid Texts, a body of religious writing found inscribed on the walls of the burial chambers of Old Kingdom pharaohs. Their recurrent theme is a monotonous insistence that the dead pharaoh is really a god and that no obstacle can prevent him from joining his fellow gods in the heavens.

The troubled life that followed the collapse of the Old Kingdom produced the highly personal literature of the First Intermediate Period and Middle Kingdom. It contains protests against the ills of the day, demands for social justice, and praise for the romantic excitements of wine, women, and song as a means of forgetting misery. The universal appeal of this literature is illustrated by the following lines from a love poem, in which the beloved is called "sister":

> I behold how my sister cometh, and my heart
>   is in gladness.
> Mine arms open wide to embrace her; my
>   heart exulteth within me; for my lady has
>   come to me. . . .
> She kisseth me, she openeth her lips to me:
>   then am I joyful even without beer.[24]

A classic of Egyptian literature is Akhenaton's *Hymn to the Sun*, which is similar in spirit to Psalm 104 in the Old Testament ("O Lord, how manifold are thy works!"). A few lines indicate its lyric beauty and its conception of one omnipotent and beneficient Creator:

> Thy dawning is beautiful in the horizon of the
>   sky,
> O living Aton, beginning of life! . . .
> How manifold are thy works!

In addition to the religious reform that he sponsored, Akhenaton also fostered a new style in art, evident here in this low-relief portrait.

> They are hidden before men,
> O sole god, beside whom there is no other.
> Thou didst create the earth according to thy
>   heart
> While thou wast alone.[25]

The Hittites, c. 2000–1200 B.C.

Except for brief mention in the Old Testament (Uriah the Hittite, for example, whose wife Bathsheba had an affair with King David) very little was known about the Hittites until archaeologists began to unearth the remains of their civilization in Asia Minor in 1906. By 1920 Hittite writing had been deciphered, and it proved to be the earliest example of a written Indo-European language. The Hittites are thought to have entered Asia Minor from the north about 2000 B.C., and their superior military means—particularly the horse-drawn chariot—enabled them to conquer the native people of central Asia Minor.

The Rosetta Stone, discovered in 1799 by an officer in Napoleon's army, supplied the means by which Egyptian writing was deciphered. The stone contains a message inscribed in three languages: the bottom layer is Greek, the middle layer is Egyptian popular writing, and the top layer is the more formal system of Egyptian hieroglyphics.

The Hittite Empire

After 1450 B.C. a series of energetic Hittite kings created a more centralized government and an empire that included Syria, lost by the Egyptian pharaoh Akhenaton. Pharaoh Ramses II moved north from Palestine in a vain attempt to reconquer Syria. Ambushed and forced back to Palestine after a bloody battle, Ramses agreed to a treaty of "good peace and good brotherhood" in 1269 B.C. (see p. 18). The Hittites may have been eager for peace with Egypt because of the threat posed by a new movement of Indo-European peoples, notably the Dorian Greeks. Many survivors of the resulting upheavals, which possibly included the fall of Troy, fled by sea

seeking new lands to conquer and settle. Collectively known as the Sea Peoples, these uprooted people included Philistines, Sicilians, Sardinians, and Etruscans. They left their names in the areas where they eventually settled. The destruction of the Hittite empire, shortly after 1200 B.C., was a by-product of these migrations.

Hittite Civilization

The Hittite state under the empire was modeled after the older oriental monarchies of Mesopotamia and Egypt. The king claimed to represent the sun god and was deified after death. The nobles held large states from the king and in return provided warriors armed increasingly with iron weapons. The Hittites are credited with being the first people to work iron from local deposits, which afforded them a jealouly guarded monopoly. Not until after 1200 B.C. did iron metallurgy become widespread.

The Hittites adopted the Mesopotamian cuneiform script together with some works of Babylonian literature. While their law code showed some similarity to the code of Hammurabi, it differed in prescribing more humane punishments. Instead of retaliation ("an eye for an eye"), the Hittite code made greater use of restitution and compensation.

The chief importance of Hittite culture lies in the legacy it left to the Phrygians and Lydians and, through them, to the Greeks who settled along the Aegean coast of Asia Minor. The Hittite goddess Kubaba, for example, became the great Phrygian goddess Cybele, the "Great Mother" whose worship became widespread in Roman times.

The Era of Small States, 1200–700 B.C.

After 1200 B.C., with the Hittite empire destroyed and Egypt in decline, the Semitic peoples of Syria and Palestine ceased being pawns in a struggle between rival imperialisms. For nearly 500 years, until they were conquered by the Assyrians, these peoples played an independent and significant role in history.

The Phoenicians

Phoenician is a name the Greeks gave to those Canaanites who dwelt along the Mediterranean coast of Syria, an area that is today Lebanon. Hemmed in by the Lebanon Mountains to the east, the Phoenicians turned to the sea and by the eleventh century B.C. had become the greatest traders, shipbuilders, navigators, and colonizers before the Greeks (see map below). To obtain silver and copper from Spain and tin from Britain, Gades (Cadiz) was founded on the Atlantic coast of Spain. Carthage, one of a number of Phoenician trading posts around the shores of the Mediterranean, was destined to become Rome's chief rival in the third century B.C.

Although the Phoenicians were essentially traders, their home cities—notably Tyre, Sidon, and Byblos—also produced manufactured goods. Their most famous export was woolen cloth dyed with the purple dye obtained from shellfish found along their coast. They were also skilled makers of furniture (made from the famous cedars of Lebanon), metalware, glassware, and jewelry. The Greeks called Egyptian papyrus rolls *biblia* ("books"), because Byblos was the shipping point for this widely used writing material; and later the Hebrew and Christian Scriptures were called "the Book" (Bible).

Culturally, the Phoenicians were not creative. They left behind no literature and little art. Yet they made one of the greatest contributions to human progress, the perfection of the alphabet, which, along with the Babylonian sexagesimal system of notation, they carried westward. Between 1800 and 1600 B.C. various Canaanite peoples, influenced by Egypt's semialphabetical writing, started to evolve a simplified method of writing. The Phoenician alphabet of twenty-two consonant symbols (the Greeks later added the vowel signs) is related to the thirty-character alphabet of Ugarit, a Canaanite city (see map, p. 0), which was destroyed about 1200 B.C. by the raiding Sea Peoples.

The half-dozen Phoenician cities never united to form a strong state, and in the last half of the eighth century B.C. all but Tyre were conquered by the Assyrians. When Tyre finally fell to the

GREEK AND PHOENICIAN COLONIZATION

☐ Greeks   ☐ Phoenicians

Chaldeans in 571 B.C., the Hebrew prophet Ezekiel spoke what reads like an epitaph to the once great role played by the Phoenicians:

> When your wares came from the seas, you satisfied many peoples; with your abundant wealth and merchandise you enriched the kings of the earth. Now you are wrecked by the seas, in the depths of the waters; your merchandise and all your crew have sunk with you. (Ezek 27: 33–34)

The Arameans

Closely related to the Hebrews were the Arameans, who occupied Syria east of the Lebanon Mountains. The most important of their little kingdoms was centered on Damascus, one of the oldest continuously inhabited cities of the world. The Arameans dominated the camel caravan trade connecting Mesopotamia, Phoenicia, and Egypt and continued to do so even after Damascus fell to the Assyrians in 732 B.C. The Aramaic language, which used an alphabet similar to the Phoenician, became the international language of the Near East. In Judea it displaced Hebrew as the spoken language and was used by Jesus and his disciples.

The Hebrew Kingdoms

In war, diplomacy, inventions, and art, the Hebrews made little splash in the stream of history. In religion and ethics, however, their contribution to the world civilization was tremendous. Out of their experience grew three great religions: Judaism, Christianity, and Islam.

Much of Hebrew experience is recorded in the Holy Writ of Israel, the Old Testament of the Christian Bible, whose present content was approved about A.D. 90 by a council of rabbis. As a work of literature it is outstanding; but it is more than that. "It is Israel's life story—a story that cannot be told adequately apart from the conviction that God had called this people in his grace, separated them from the nations for a special responsibility, and commissioned them with the task of being his servant in the accomplishment of his purpose."[26]

The Biblical account of the history of the Hebrews (later called Israelites and then Jews) begins with the patriarchal clan leader Abraham, called in Genesis 14:15 "the Hebrew" (Habiru; see p. 17). About 1800 B.C. Abraham led his people out of Ur in Sumer, where they had settled for a time in their wanderings, and eventually they arrived in the land of Canaan, later called Palestine.

About 1700 B.C., driven by famine, some Hebrews followed Abraham's great-grandson Joseph, son of Israel (also called Jacob), into Egypt. Joseph's rise to power in Egypt, and the hospitable reception of his people there, is attributed to the presence of the largely Semitic Hyksos, who had conquered Egypt about 1720 B.C. (see p. 16). Following the expulsion of the Hyksos by the pharaohs of the Eighteenth Dynasty, the Hebrews were enslaved by the Egyptians. Shortly after 1300 B.C. Moses led them out of bondage and into the wilderness of Sinai, where they entered into a pact or covenant with their God, Yahweh. The Sinai Covenant bound the people as a whole—the nation of Israel, as they now called themselves—to worship Yahweh before all other gods and to obey his Law. In return, Yahweh made the Israelites his chosen people whom he would protect and to whom he granted Canaan, the Promised Land "flowing with milk and honey." The history of Israel from this time on is the story of the working out of this covenant.

The Israelites had to contend for Palestine against the Canaanites, whose Semitic ancestors had migrated from Arabia early in the third millennium B.C. Joined by other Hebrew tribes already in Palestine, the Israelites formed a confederacy of twelve tribes and, led by war leaders called *judges*, in time succeeded in subjugating the Canaanites.

The decisive battle in 1125 B.C. at Megiddo, called Armageddon ("Hill of Megiddo") in the New Testament, owed much to Deborah the prophetess who "judged Israel at that time" (Judges 4:4). God bade Deborah, already famed throughout Israel for her wisdom, to accompany the discouraged war leaders and stir them to victory. For this reason she has been called the Hebrew Joan of Arc.

The vigorous and decisive role played by Deborah and other Israelite women (Moses' sister Miriam, for example), reflects the absence of female inferiority in early Israel. Genesis describes the two sexes as being equal and necessary for human livelihood: "So God created mankind in his image, . . . male and female he created them. And God blessed them and said to them, 'Be fruitful and multiply and fill the earth and subdue it [together]'" (1:27–28). And in the Song of Songs the maiden and the youth share equally in the desire and expression of love; there is no sense of subordination of one to the other. But the continuing dangers that faced the nation led to the creation of a strong centralized monarchy, and with it came male domination and female subordination. Deborah was the last Israelite woman upon whom God's spirit and wisdom descended.

Soon after the Canaanites were defeated, a far more formidable foe appeared. The Philistines,

part of the Sea Peoples who had tried unsuccessfully to invade Egypt and from whom we get the word *Palestine*, settled along the coast about 1175 B.C. Aided by the use of iron weapons, which were new to Palestine, the Philistines captured the Ark of the Covenant, the sacred chest described as having mysterious powers, in which Moses had placed the Ten Commandments. By the middle of the eleventh century B.C., the Philistines were well on their way to dominating the entire land.

The loose twelve-tribe confederacy of Israel could not cope with the Philistine danger. "Give us a king to govern us," the people demanded, "that we also may be like all the nations, and that

The Old Testament (Exodus 19): "Moses Brought the People to Meet God"

On the third new moon after the people of Israel had gone forth out of the land of Egypt, on that day they came into the wilderness of Sinai. . . . and there Israel encamped before the mountain. And Moses went up to God, and the LORD called him out of the mountain, saying, "Thus you shall say to the house of Jacob, and tell the people of Israel: You have seen what I did to the Egyptians, and how I bore you on eagles' wings and brought you to myself. Now therefore, if you will obey my voice and keep my covenant, you shall be my own possession among all peoples; for all the earth is mine, and you shall be to me a kingdom of priests and a holy nation. These are the words which you shall speak to the children of Israel." . . . And the LORD said to Moses, "Go to the people and consecrate them today and tomorrow, and let them wash their garments and be ready by the third day; for on the third day the LORD will come down upon Mount Sinai in the sight of all the people. And you shall set bounds for the people round about, saying, 'Take heed that you do not go up into the mountain or touch the border of it; whoever touches the mountain shall be put to death; no hand shall touch him, but he shall be

stoned or shot; whether beast or man, he shall not live.' When the trumpet sounds a long blast, they shall come up to the mountain." So Moses went down from the mountain to the people, and consecrated the people; and they washed their garments. And he said to the people, "Be ready by the third day, do not go near a woman."

On the morning of the third day there were thunders and lightnings, and a thick cloud upon the mountain, and a very loud trumpet blast, so that all the people who were in the camp trembled. Then Moses brought the people out of the camp to meet God; and they took their stand at the foot of the mountain. And Mount Sinai was wrapped in smoke, because the LORD descended upon it in fire; and the smoke of it went up like the smoke of a kiln, and the whole mountain quaked greatly. And as the sound of the trumpet grew louder and louder, Moses spoke, and God answered him in thunder. And the LORD came down upon Mount Sinai, to the top of the mountain; and the LORD called Moses to the top of the mountain, and Moses went up.

Exodus 19: 1–6, 10–20. *The Holy Bible Revised Standard Version* (New York: Thomas Nelson and Sons, 1952.)

our king may govern us and go before us and fight our battles." This move was strongly opposed by the conservative upper class, led by the prophet-judge Samuel. He warned the assembled Israelites that if they set up a king they would reject the "rule of God" and incur divine disapproval. He predicted that a king would subject them to despotic tyranny. But the Israelite assembly rejected Samuel's advice and elected Saul as their first king. Thereupon "the Lord said to Samuel, 'Hearken to the voice of the people in all that they say to you; for they have not rejected you, but they have rejected me from being king over them' " (1 Samuel 8:7). This appears to have been a grudging concession on God's part—like that of a father who allows his wayward son to learn from experience the folly of his ways.

Saul's reign (1020–1000 B.C.) was not successful. Continuously undercut by the conservatives led by Samuel and overshadowed by the fame of the boy-hero David, who had slain the Philistine giant Goliath in single combat, Saul made no attempt to transform Israel into a centralized state. He collected no taxes, and his army was composed of volunteers. A victim also of his own tempestuous and moody nature, Saul finally committed suicide after an unsuccessful battle with the Philistines. "How are the mighty fallen," the Old Testament concludes the story of Saul—a story with all the pathos of a Greek tragedy.

Saul's successor, the popular David (1000–961 B.C.), not only restricted the Philistines to a narrow coastal strip but became the ruler of the largest state in the ancient history of the area, stretching from the Euphrates to the Gulf of Aqaba. David also conquered Jerusalem from the Canaanites and made it the private domain of his royal court, separate from the existing twelve tribes. His popularity was enhanced when he deposited the recovered Ark of the Covenant in his royal chapel, to which he attached a priesthood. The priests in turn proclaimed that God had made a special covenant with David as "the Lord's servant," and with the throne of David through all generations to come.

David's work was completed by his son Solomon (961–922 B.C.), under whom Israel reached a pinnacle of worldly power and splendor as an oriental-style monarchy. In the words of the Bible:

> *Solomon ruled over all the kingdoms from the Euphrates to the land of the Philistines and to the border of Egypt; they brought tribute and served Solomon all the days of his life. . . . And Judah and Israel dwelt in safety, from Dan even to Beersheba, every man under his vine and under his fig tree, all the days of Solomon. . . . And God gave Solomon wisdom and understanding beyond measure, and largeness of mind. . . . Now the weight of gold that came to Solomon in one year was six hundred and sixty-six talents of gold, besides that which came from the traders and from the traffic of the merchants, and from all the kings of Arabia and from the governors of the land. . . . The king also made a great ivory throne, and overlaid it with the finest gold. . . . (1 Kings 4:20 f.; 10:14 f.)*

But the price of Solomon's vast bureaucracy, building projects (especially the palace complex and the Temple at Jerusalem), standing army (1400 chariots and 12,000 horses), and harem (700 wives and 300 concubines) was great. High taxes, forced labor, and the loss of tribal independence led to dissension. The Old Testament attributed this dissension to Solomon's feeble old

ANCIENT ISRAEL
8TH CENTURY B. C.

Damascus

Tyre

Kadesh

PHOENICIA

MEDITERRANEAN
SEA

Sea of
Galilee

KINGDOM
OF
ARAM

Megiddo

KINGDOM
OF
ISRAEL

Samaria

Joppa

Shiloh

Bethel

Jordan R.

Jericho

Jerusalem

Bethlehem

PHILISTIA

KINGDOM

Gaza

OF   Hebron

DEAD
SEA

AMMON

JUDAH

Beersheba

MOAB

NEGEV
(DESERT)

EDOM

Uncertain   Boundary

age, "For when Solomon was old, his wives turned away his heart after other gods; and his heart was not wholly true to the Lord his God, as was the heart of David his father. . . . Therefore the Lord said to Solomon, 'Since . . . you have not kept my covenant and my statutes which I have commanded you, I will surely tear the kingdom from you'" (1 Kings 11: 4–11).

When Solomon died in 922 B.C., the realm split into two kingdoms—Israel in the north and Judah in the south (see map, p. 28). These two weak kingdoms were in no position to defend themselves when new, powerful empires rose again in Mesopotamia. In 721 B.C. the Assyrians captured Samaria, the capital of the northern kingdom, taking 27,290 Israelites into captivity (the "ten lost tribes") and settling foreign peoples in their place. The resulting mixed population, called Samaritans, made no further contribution to Hebrew history or religion.

The southern kingdom of Judah held out until 586 B.C. when Nebuchadnezzar, the Chaldean ruler of Babylonia, destroyed Jerusalem and carried away an estimated 15,000 captives; "none remained, except the poorest people of the land" (2 Kings 25:14). Thus began the famous Babylonian Exile of the Jews (Judeans), which lasted until 538 B.C. when Cyrus the Persian, having conquered Babylon, allowed them to return to Jerusalem where they rebuilt the Temple destroyed by Nebuchadnezzar.

Persian rule was followed by that of the Hellenistic Greeks and Romans. From A.D. 66 to 70, the Jews rebelled against Rome, and Jerusalem was largely destroyed in the savage fighting that ensued. The Jews were again driven into exile, and the Diaspora—the "scattering"—was at its height.

Hebrew Religion

From the time of Abraham the Hebrews worshiped one god, a stern, warlike tribal deity whose name Yahweh (Jehovah) was first revealed to Moses. Yahweh differed from the many Near Eastern nature gods in being completely separate from the physical universe which he had created. This view of Yahweh as the Creator of all things everywhere was inevitably to lead to the monotheistic belief that Yahweh was the sole God in the universe.

After their entrance into Palestine, many Hebrews adopted the fertility deities of the Canaanites as well as the luxurious Canaanite manner of living. As a result, prophets arose who "spoke for" (from the Greek word *prophetes*) Yahweh in insisting on strict adherence to the Sinai Covenant and in condemning the "whoring" after other gods, the selfish pursuit of wealth, and the growth of social injustice.

Between roughly 750 and 550 B.C. appeared a series of great prophets who wrote down their messages. They sought to purge the religion of Israel of all corrupting influences and to refine the concept of Yahweh. As summed up by Micah (c. 750 B.C.) in a statement often cited as the essence of all advanced religions, "He has shown you, O man, what is good; and what does the Lord require of you but to do justice, and to love kindness, and to walk humbly with your God" (Micah 6:8)? Micah's contemporary, the shepherd-prophet Amos, stressed the need for social justice: "Thus saith the Lord: . . . [the rich and powerful] sell the righteous for silver, and the needy for a pair of sandals. They trample the head of the poor into the dust of the earth, and turn aside the way of the afflicted . . . so that they have profaned my holy name" (Amos 2:6–7).

The prophets viewed the course of Hebrew history as being governed by the sovereign will of Yahweh, seeing the Assyrians and the Chaldeans as "the rod of Yahweh's anger" to chastise his stubborn, wayward people. They also developed the idea of a coming Messiah (the "anointed one" of God), a descendant of King David. As "a king in righteousness," the Messiah would inaugurate a reign of peace and justice. This ideal would stir the hopes of Jews for centuries.

Considered the greatest of the Hebrew prophets are Jeremiah and the anonymous Second Isaiah, so-called because his message was incorporated in the Book of Isaiah (chapters 40–55). Jeremiah witnessed the events that led to Nebuchadnezzar's destruction of Jerusalem and the Temple and to the Babylonian Captivity of the Jews. He prepared the people for these calamities by affirming that Yahweh would forgive their sins and restore "a remnant" of his people by proclaiming a "new covenant." The old Sinai Covenant had been between Yahweh and the nation, which no longer existed. It had become overlaid with ritual and ceremony and centered in the Temple, which had been destroyed. The new covenant was between Yahweh and each individual; religion was now a matter of one's own heart and conscience, and both the nation and the Temple were considered superfluous. Second Isaiah, who lived at the end of the Babylonian Captivity, capped the work of his predecessors by proclaiming Israel to be Yahweh's "righteous servant," purified and enlightened by suffering and ready to guide the world to the worship of the one, eternal, supreme God. Thus the Jews who returned from the Exile were provided with a renewed faith in their destiny and a new comprehension of their religion that would sustain them through the centuries.

Later Empires of Western Asia, c. 700–500 B.C.

By 700 B.C. the era of small states had ended with the emergence of the Assyrian empire. The great contribution of the Assyrians was the forcible unification of weak, unstable nations and the establishment of an efficient imperial organization.

The Assyrian Empire

For two centuries before 700 B.C. the Assyrians had been bidding to translate the growing economic unity of the Near East—evidenced by Solomon's trading operations and even more by the activities of Aramean merchants—into political unity. The Assyrian push toward the Mediterranean began in the ninth century B.C. and after a lapse was resumed in the eighth century, when Babylon was also subdued. By 671 B.C. the Assyrians had annexed Egypt and were the masters of the Fertile Crescent (see map, p. 5).

A Semitic people long established in the hilly region of the upper Tigris, the Assyrians had experienced a thousand years of constant warfare. But their matchless army was only one of several factors that explain the success of Assyrian imperialism: a policy of calculated terrorization, an efficient system of political administration, and the support of the commercial classes that wanted political stability and unrestricted trade over large areas.

The Assyrian army, with its chariots, mounted cavalry, and sophisticated siege engines, was the most powerful yet seen in the ancient world. Neither troops nor walls could long resist the Assyrians who, in Byron's well-known phrase, "came down like a wolf on the fold." Conquered peoples were held firmly in control by systematic terrorization. "From some I cut off their noses, their ears and their fingers, of many I put out the eyes. . . . I bound their heads to tree trunks round about the city"[27] is a characteristic statement from the Assyrian royal inscriptions. Mass deportations, like that of the Israelites discussed above, were employed as an effective means of destroying national feeling.

The well-coordinated Assyrian system of political administration was another factor in the success of the empire. Conquered lands became provinces ruled by governors who exercised extensive military, judicial, and financial powers. Their chief tasks were to ensure the regular collection of tribute and the raising of troops for the permanent army that eventually replaced the native militia of sturdy Assyrian peasants. An efficient system of communications carried the "king's word" to the governors as well as the latter's reports to the royal court—including one prophetic dispatch reading: "The king knows that all lands hate us." Nevertheless, the Assyrians must be credited with laying the foundations for the later more humane administrative systems of their successors, the Persians and Alexander the Great.

Assyrian Culture

The Assyrians borrowed from the cultures of other peoples and unified the elements into a new product. This is evident in Assyrian architecture and sculpture, the work of subject artisans and artists. Both arts glorified the power of the Assyrian king. The palace, serving both as residence and administrative center, replaced the temple as the characteristic architectural form. A feature of Assyrian palace architecture was the structural use of the arch and the column, both borrowed from Babylonia. Palaces were decorated with splendid relief sculptures that glorified the king as warrior and hunter. Assyrian sculptors were especially skilled in portraying realistically the ferocity and agony of charging and dying animals.

THE ASSYRIAN EMPIRE
ABOUT 670 B.C.

into Babylonia, revolted in 626 B.C. In 612 they joined the Medes in destroying Nineveh, the Assyrian capital. From one end of the Fertile Crescent to the other people rejoiced: "Nineveh is laid waste: who will bemoan her? . . . All who hear the news of you clap their hands over you. For upon whom has not come your unceasing evil?" (Nahum 3:7, 19).

The Lydians and the Medes

The fall of Assyria left four states to struggle over the crumbs of empire: Chaldea and Egypt vied over Syria-Palestine, while Media and Lydia clashed over eastern Asia Minor.

After the collapse of the Hittite empire about 1200 B.C., the Lydians had followed the Phrygians, whose last king was the semilegendary Midas (d. c. 680 B.C.), in establishing a kingdom in western Asia Minor. When Assyria fell, the Lydians expanded eastward until stopped by the Medes at the Halys River. Lydia profited from being astride the commercial land route between Mesopotamia and the Aegean and from the possession of valuable gold-bearing streams. About 675 B.C. the Lydians invented coinage, which replaced the silver bars hitherto in general use. Lydia's most famous king was Croesus, and the phrase "rich as Croesus" is a reminder of Lydian opulence. With his defeat by the Persians in 547 B.C. Lydia ceased to exist as an independent state.

The Medes were an Indo-European people who by 1000 B.C. had established themselves on the Iranian plateau east of Assyria. In the seventh century B.C. they had created a strong kingdom with Ecbatana as capital and with the Persians, their kin to the south, as vassals. Following the collapse of Assyria, the Medes expanded into Armenia and eastern Asia Minor, but their short-lived empire ended in 550 B.C. when they, too, were absorbed by the Persians.

The Chaldean (Neo-Babylonian) Empire

While the Median kingdom controlled the highland region, the Chaldeans, with their capital at Babylon, were masters of the Fertile Crescent. Nebuchadnezzar, becoming king of the Chaldeans in 604 B.C., raised Babylonia to another epoch of brilliance after more than a

Assyrian kings were interested in preserving written as well as pictorial records of their reigns. King Ashurbanipal (d. 631 B.C.) left a record of his great efforts in collecting the literary heritage of Sumer and Babylon, and the 22,000 clay tablets found in the ruins of his palace at Nineveh provided modern scholars with their first direct knowledge of this literature.

Downfall of the Assyrian Empire

Revolt against Assyrian terror and tribute was inevitable when Assyria's strength waned and effective opposition arose. By the middle of the seventh century B.C. the Assyrians had been decimated by wars, and the Assyrian kings had to rely on unreliable mercenary troops and conscripted subject peoples. Egypt regained its independence under the Twenty-Sixth Dynasty, and the Medes refused further tribute. The Chaldeans, a new group of Semites who had filtered thousand years of eclipse. By defeating the Egyptians in Syria, Nebuchadnezzar ended their hopes of re-creating their empire. As we have seen (p. 29), he destroyed Jerusalem in 586 B.C. and carried thousands of Jews captive to Babylonia.

Nebuchadnezzar reconstructed Babylon, making it the largest and most impressive city of its day. The tremendous city walls were wide enough at the top to have rows of small houses on either side. In the center of Babylon ran the famous Procession Street, which passed through the Ishtar Gate. This arch, which was adorned with brilliant tile animals, is the best remaining example of Babylonian architecture. The immense palace of Nebuchadnezzar towered terrace upon terrace, each resplendent with masses of ferns, flowers, and trees. These roof gardens,

the famous Hanging Gardens of Babylon, were so beautiful that they were regarded by the Greeks as one of the seven wonders of the ancient world.

Nebuchadnezzar also rebuilt the great temple-tower or ziggurat, the Biblical "Tower of Babel," which the Greek historian Herodotus viewed a century later and described as

a tower of solid masonry, a furlong [220 yards] in length and breadth, upon which was raised a second tower, and on that a third, and so on up to eight. The ascent to the top is on the outside, by a path which winds round all the towers.[28]

Nebuchadnezzar was the last great Mesopotamian ruler, and Chaldean power quickly crumbled after his death in 562 B.C. The Chaldean

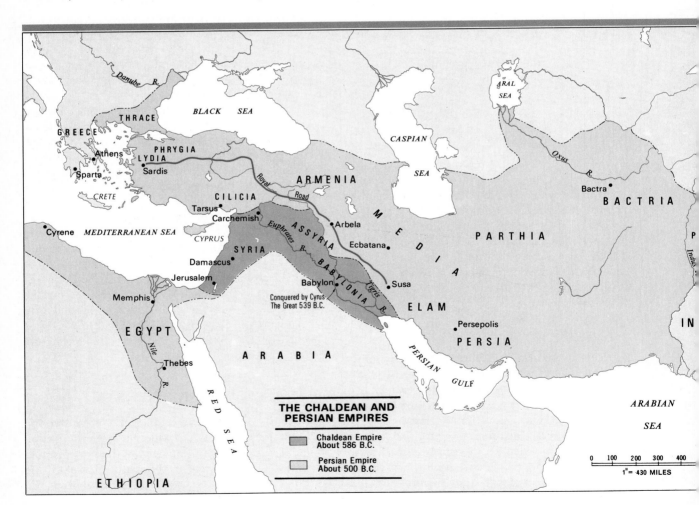

THE CHALDEAN AND PERSIAN EMPIRES

Chaldean Empire About 586 B.C.

Persian Empire About 500 B.C.

priests—whose interest in astrology so greatly added to the fund of Babylonian astronomical knowledge that the word "Chaldean" came to mean astronomer—continually undermined the monarchy. Finally, in 539 B.C., they opened the gates of Babylon to Cyrus the Persian, thus fulfilling Daniel's message of doom upon the notorious Belshazzar, the last Chaldean ruler: "You have been weighed in the balances and found wanting" (Dan. 5:27).

The Persian Empire

Cyrus the Persian was the greatest conqueror in the history of the ancient Near East. In 550 B.C. he ended Persian vassalage to the Medes by capturing Ecbatana and ousting the Median dynasty. The Medes readily accepted their vigorous new ruler, who soon demonstrated that he deserved to be called "the Great." When King Croesus of Lydia moved across the Hals River in 547 B.C. to pick up some of the pieces of the Median empire, Cyrus defeated him and annexed Lydia, including those Greek cities on the coast of Asia Minor that were under the nominal control of Lydia. Then he turned east, establishing his power as far as the frontier of India. Babylon and its empire was next on his list (see map, p. 32). Following the death of Cyrus, his son Cambyses conquered Egypt. The next ruler, Darius I (522–486 B.C.), added the Punjab region in India and Thrace in Europe. He also began a conflict with the Greeks that continued intermittently for more than 150 years until the Persians were conquered by Alexander the Great. Long before this event the Persian nobility had forgotten Cyrus the Great's answer to their suggestion that they "leave this small and barren country of ours" and move to fertile Babylonia:

Do so if you wish, but if you do, be ready to find yourselves no longer governors but governed; for soft lands breed soft men; it does not happen that the same land brings forth wonderful crops and good fighting men.[29]

Persian Government

Although built upon the Assyrian model, the Persian administrative system was far more efficient and humane. The empire was divided into twenty provinces, or satrapies, each ruled by a governor called a satrap. To check the satraps, a secretary and a military official representing the "Great King, King of Kings" were installed in every province. Also, special inspectors, "the Eyes and Ears of the King," traveled throughout the realm.

Imperial post roads connected the important cities. Along the Royal Road between Sardis and Susa there was a post station every fourteen miles, where the king's couriers could obtain fresh horses, enabling them to cover the 1600-mile route in a week. "Nothing mortal travels so fast as these Persian messengers," wrote Herodotus. "These men will not be hindered . . . , either by snow, or rain, or heat, or by the darkness of night."[30] These words were at one time used as the motto of the United States Postal Service.

The Persian empire was the first to attempt to govern many different racial groups on the principle of equal responsibilities and rights for all peoples. So long as subjects paid their taxes and kept the peace, the king did not interfere with local religion, customs, or trade. Indeed, Darius was called the "shopkeeper" because he stimulated trade by introducing a uniform system of gold and silver coinage on the Lydian model.

Persian Religion and Art

The humaneness of the Persian rulers may have stemmed from the ethical religion founded by the prophet Zoroaster, who lived in the early sixth century B.C. Zoroaster sought to replace what he called "the lie"—ritualistic, idol-worshiping cults and their Magi priests—with a religion centered on the sole god Ahura-Mazda ("Wise Lord"). This "father of Justice" demanded "good thoughts of the mind, good deeds of the hand, and good words of the tongue" from those who would attain paradise (a Persian word). The new religion made little progress until first Darius and then the Magi adopted it. The Magi revived many old gods as lesser deities, added much ritual, and replaced monotheism with dualism by transforming what Zoroaster had called the principle or spirit of evil into the powerful god Ahriman (the model for the Jewish Satan), rival of Ahura-Mazda, "between which each man must choose for himself." The complicated evolution of Zoroastrianism is revealed in its holy writ, the *Avesta* ("The Law"), assembled in its present form between the fourth and sixth centuries A.D. Zoroastrian eschatology—"the doctrine of final things" such as the resurrection of the dead and a last judgment—influenced later Judaism. Following the Muslim conquest of Persia in the seventh century A.D., Zoroastrianism died out in its homeland. It exists today among the Parsees in India.

In art the Persians borrowed largely from their predecessors in the Fertile Crescent, particularly the Assyrians. Their most important work was in palace architecture, the best remains of which are at Persepolis. Built on a high terrace, the royal residence was reached by a grand stairway faced with beautiful reliefs. Instead of the warfare and violence that characterized Assyrian sculpture, these reliefs depict hundreds of soldiers, courtiers, and representatives of twenty-three nations of the empire bringing gifts to the king for the festival of the new year.

Conclusion

Human history necessarily begins with the appearance of writing, which the historian uses to describe and explain human behavior through time. (Earlier human prehistory is the province of the anthropologist.) We say that "history begins at Sumer," because there writing first appeared about 3500 B.C.

In this chapter we have surveyed the history of the ancient Near East, beginning about 3100 B.C. with the Sumerians, and ending about 500 B.C. with the Persians—a period of nearly three thousand years. It is startling to reflect on the fact that this long span is half of all human history. Clearly, half of history deserves our attention. It has its own intrinsic interest—what did people think and do during this long period?—and it has left a heritage that in important ways affects us today.

In our daily living we are surrounded by our heritage from the ancient Near East. When we purchase a carton of twelve (rather than ten) eggs at a grocery store, divide the hour into sixty

minutes, or consult the horoscopes in our daily newspapers, we are indebted to the peoples of ancient Mesopotamia. Our calendar comes to us from ancient Egypt. The concept of Satan—and even the word *paradise*—is a heritage from Persia. Above all, the Hebrew religion with its sacred library of religious and literary masterpieces has entered into the moral and cultural structure of our Western civilization.

Indeed, studying the history of the ancient Near East should leave us with our own special understanding of Hammurabi's admonition at the end of his code of laws:

> *My words are weighty, my deeds are unrivaled; only to the fool are they vain, to the wise they are worthy of every praise.*

Suggestions for Reading

J. Gowlett, *Ascent to Civilization: The Archaeology of Early Man** (Knopf, 1984) is a copiously illustrated account of the origins of humanity and the science of archaeology. See also John Reader, *Missing Links: The Hunt for Earliest Man**, rev. ed. (Penguin, 1989) and A. Sheratt, ed., *The Cambridge Encyclopaedia of Archaeology* (Cambridge, 1980). Also recommended are D. C. Johanson and M. R. Edey, *Lucy: The Beginnings of Mankind* (Granada, 1981) and Richard E. Leakey, *The Making of Mankind* (Michael Joseph, 1981). See also F. Bordes, *The Old Stone Age* (McGraw-Hill, 1968); S. Cole, *The Neolithic Revolution*, 5th ed. (British Museum, 1970); A. Sieveking, *The Cave Artists* (Thames & Hudson, 1979); and J. Mellaart, *Çatal Hüyük* (Thames & Hudson, 1967).

C. Redman, *The Rise of Civilization: From Early Farmers to Urban Society in the Ancient Near East** (Freeman, 1978) is highly recommended. W. Hallo and W. Simpson, *The Ancient Near East: A History** (Harcourt Brace Jovanovich, 1971) is comprehensive. Short surveys are M. Covensky, *The Ancient Near Eastern Tradition** (Harper & Row, 1966); V. G. Childe, *What Happened in History** (Penguin, 1950); and S. Moscati, *The Face of the Ancient Orient** (Quadrangle, 1962). H. W. F. Saggs, *Civilization before Greece and Rome** (Yale, 1989) is a lively topical treatment.

G. Roux, *Ancient Iraq** (Penguin, 1976) is a detailed history of Ancient Mesopotamia. See also S. N. Kramer, *The Sumerians: Their History, Culture, and Character** (Univ. of Chicago, 1971) and the same author's popular *History Begins at Sumer** (Univ. of Pennsylvania, 1981) and *Cradle of Civilization* (Time-Life, 1967).

T. G. H. James, *An Introduction to Ancient Egypt** (Harper & Row, 1990) and L. Casson, *Ancient Egypt* (Time-Life, 1965) are brief surveys. A. Gardiner, *Egypt of the Pharaohs** (Galaxy, 1966) is a detailed political history. On the New Kingdom, see G. Steindorff and K. Steele, *When Egypt Ruled the East** (Phoenix, 1957) and C. Desroaches-

Noblecourt, *Tutankhamen** (New York Graphic Society, 1976). For the history of Kush, see W. Fairservis, Jr., *The Ancient Kingdoms of the Nile* (Crowell, 1962) and F. M. Snowden, *Blacks in Antiquity: Ethiopians in the Greco-Roman Experience* (Harvard, 1970).

H. Frankfort et al., *The Intellectual Adventure of Ancient Man** (Phoenix, 1977) is a notable interpretation of Mesopotamian, Egyptian, and Hebrew thought. Also highly recommended are John A. Wilson, *The Culture of Ancient Egypt** (Phoenix, 1956); H. Frankfort, *Ancient Egyptian Religion: An Interpretation** (Torchbooks); J. H. Breasted, *The Dawn of Conscience* (Scribner, 1933); and T. Jacobsen, *The Treasures of Darkness: A History of Mesopotamian Religion* (Yale, 1976).

O. P. Gurney, *The Hittites*, 2nd ed. (Penguin, 1972); G. Herm, *The Phoenicians: The Purple Empire of the Ancient World* (Morrow, 1975); and N. Sanders, *The Sea Peoples: Warriors of the Ancient Mediterranean, 1250–1150 B.C.* (Thames & Hudson, 1978).

D. F. Goldberg and J. D. Raynor, *The Jewish People: Their History and Their Religion** (Penguin, 1989) and H. Orlinsky, *Ancient Israel,** 2nd ed. (Cornell, 1960) are succinct overviews. Excellent longer surveys are Bernhard W. Anderson, *Understanding the Old Testament*, 4th ed. (Prentice-Hall, 1986); Michael Grant, *The History of Ancient Israel** (Macmillan, 1984); and John Bright, *A History of Israel*, 3rd ed. (Westminster, 1981).

A. Olmstead, *History of Assyria* (Univ. of Chicago, 1923) and *History of the Persian Empire** (Phoenix, 1948) are the standard accounts. See also R. Masani, *Zoroastrianism: The Religion of the Good Life* (Macmillan, 1968).

On ancient Near Eastern art and architecture, see Seton Lloyd, *The Art of the Ancient Near East* (Oxford, 1961), H. Frankfort, *The Art and Architecture of the Ancient Orient** (Penguin, 1978) and I. E. S. Edwards, *The Pyramids of Egypt** (Penguin, 1975).

For significant source readings, see J. B. Pritchard, ed. *The Ancient Near East: An Anthology of Texts and Pictures** Princeton, 1958) and N. Bailkey, *Readings in Ancient History: Thought and Experience from Gilgamesh to St. Augustine*, 4th ed. (Heath, 1992).

*Indicates a less expensive paperbound edition.

Notes

1. Richard E. Leakey, *The Making of Mankind* (London: Michael Joseph, 1981), p. 148.
2. Thorkild Jacobsen, "Primitive Democracy in Ancient Mesopotamia," *Journal of Near Eastern Studies* 2 (1943), pp. 159–72; Nels Bailkey, "Early Mesopotamian Constitutional Development," *American Historial Review* 72 (1967), pp. 1213–1217.
3. G. S. Hawkins and John B. White, *Stonehenge Decoded* (New York: Dell, 1966), pp. 117–118. Cited approvingly by J. Briard, *The Bronze Age in Barbarian Europe* (London: Routledge & Kegan Paul, 1979), p. 95; and refuted by J. Daniel, *Scientific American*, July 1980, p. 78.
4. V. Gordon Childe, *New Light on the Most Ancient East* (London: Routledge & Kegan Paul, 1954), p. 114.
5. V. Gordon Childe, *What Happened in History* (New York: Pelican Books, 1946), p. 74.
6. H. Frankfort, *The Birth of Civilization in the Near East* (London: Williams and Norgate, 1951), p. 60.
7. "The Reforms of Urukagina" in Nels M. Bailkey, ed., *Readings in Ancient History: Thought and Experience from Gilgamesh to St. Augustine*, 4th ed. (Lexington, MA: D. C. Heath, 1992), p. 21.
8. A. Falkenstein and W. von Soden, trans., *Sumerische and Akkadische Hymnen und Gebete* (Zurich: Artemis-Verlag, 1953), p. 188. For a partial translation and full discussion of this text, see S. N. Kramer, *History Begins at Sumer* (Garden City, NY: Doubleday Anchor Books, 1959), pp. 228–232.
9. H. de Genouillac, trans., in *Revue d'Assyriologe* 25 (Paris, 1928), p. 148.
10. Quoted in S. N. Kramer, *History Begins at Sumer*, p. 53.
11. R. F. Harper, *The Code of Hammurabi* (Chicago: University of Chicago Press, 1904), p. 3.
12. R. F. Harper, *The Code of Hammurabi*, p. 101.
13. *The New Yorker*, Oct. 12, 1987, p. 106, 108.
14. From *Epic of Gilgamesh*, trans. E. A. Speiser in *Ancient Near Eastern Texts Relating to the Old Testament*, 2nd ed. (Princeton University Press, 1953), p. 90.
15. Nels M. Bailkey, ed., *Readings in Ancient History*, p. 29.
16. Quoted in Sabatino Moscati, *The Face of the Ancient Orient* (Garden City, NY: Doubleday Anchor Books, 1962), p. 71.
17. Miriam Lichtheim, *Ancient Egyptian Literature: A Book of Readings*, Vol. 1: *The Old and Middle Kingdoms* (Berkeley: University of California Press, 1973), pp. 141–142.
18. John A. Wilson, trans., *The Burden of Egypt* (Chicago: University of Chicago Press, 1951), p. 117.
19. John A. Wilson, *The Burden of Egypt*, p. 164.
20. Adolf Erman, *The Literature of the Ancient Egyptians*, trans. Aylward M. Blackman (London: Methuen & Co., 1927), pp. 190, 196, 197.
21. From "The Instruction of Meri-ka-Re" in *The Burden of Egypt*, trans. John A. Wilson, p. 120.
22. From "The Instruction of Meri-ka-Re" in *The Burden of Egypt*, trans. John A. Wilson, p. 119.
23. Quoted in George Steindorff and George Hoyingen-Huene, *Egypt* (Locust Valley, NY: J. J. Augustin, 1943), p. 23.
24. George Steindorff and Keith E. Steel, trans., *When Egypt Ruled the East* (Chicago: University of Chicago Press, 1942), p. 125. Copyright 1942 by the University of Chicago Press.
25. Quoted in J. H. Breasted, *The Dawn of Conscience* (New York: Charles Scribner's Sons, 1939), p. 284.
26. B. W. Anderson, *Understanding the Old Testament*, 2nd ed. (Englewood Cliffs, NJ: Prentice-Hall, 1966), p. 559.
27. D. D. Luckenbill, *Ancient Records of Assyria and Babylonia* (Chicago: University of Chicago Press, 1926), vol. 1, p. 147.
28. Herodotus *History of the Persian Wars* 1.181, trans. G. Rawlinson.
29. Herodotus *History* 9.122, trans. A. R. Burn, *Persia and the West* (New York: St. Martin's Press, 1962), p. 61.
30. Herodotus *History* 8.88, trans. G. Rawlinson.

Chapter 2

The Glory That Was Greece

Aegean, Hellenic, and Hellenistic Civilizations

Scarred by time and weather, the ruins of the Athenian Acropolis stand against a vivid blue sky and overlook the trees and buildings of a modern city sprawled beneath. These ruins are striking symbols of a departed civilization, whose principal center was Athens.

In the fifth century B.C. the temples and statuary of the Acropolis were gleaming and new, fresh from the hands of builders and sculptors. Five hundred years later, when Greece was a province of the Roman Empire, they still appeared so to Plutarch:

> The works . . . are wonderful; they were quickly created and they have lasted for ages. In beauty each one appeared venerable as soon as it was finished, but in freshness and vigor it looks even now new and lately built. They bloom with an eternal freshness that seems untouched by time, as though they had been inspired by an unfading spirit of youth.[1]

Today the Acropolis no longer appears "untouched by time"; yet for us no less than for Plutarch, ancient Athens has retained an "eternal freshness." This quality, together with a refined sense of symmetry and proportion, are characteristic of the Greek spirit and the famed achievements of Greek civilization. The ancient Greeks repeatedly demonstrated an ability to regard the world about them from a fresh perspective and to inject a love of proportion not only into their architecture but into almost everything they attempted.

Yet in the crucial sphere of politics, their sense of proportion failed them. Instead of compromising their differences, the city-states quarreled continually. Their ardent city-state patriotism blinded them to the necessity of cooperation.

Thus the political life of the Greeks was marked by conflicts between the city-states until they were at last subjugated by King Philip of Macedonia.

Greece's accomplishments were to prove so enduring that its magnificent intellectual and artistic legacy would provide much of the cultural heritage of Western civilization.

The Background: Aegean Civilization, 2000–1200 B.C.

Greek civilization was unique in so many ways that a student of history might infer that it developed free from outside influences, springing full-blown from the mountains and plains of this small land. The Greek achievement, however, was preceded by an advanced civilization located on the lands surrounding the Aegean Sea. This Aegean civilization, which came into full flower about 2000 B.C. and collapsed suddenly following 1200 B.C., developed through two major periods.

Minoan and Mycenaean Phases

The first and longer phase of Aegean civilization, which ended about 1450 B.C., is called Minoan after the legendary Cretan King Minos. Crete was the center of Minoan civilization, which spread to the Aegean Islands, the coast of Asia Minor, and mainland Greece. The last period of Aegean civilization, the two and one-half centuries following 1450 B.C. when the center of Aegean political power and culture lay on the Greek

Two examples of Minoan art are the palace of Minos at Knossos on Crete and the figure of the Minoan snake goddess. Shown here is the queen's chamber of the palace, its walls richly decorated with frescoes of frolicking fish and dolphins. The writhing snakes in the snake goddess's hands exemplify the rhythmic motion that is characteristic of Minoan art.

mainland, is called Mycenaean after its most important site at Mycenae.

The Minoans

The narrow, 160-mile-long island of Crete was a stepping stone between Europe, Asia, and Africa. Stimulated by immigrants from Asia Minor and by contacts with Mesopotamia and Egypt, a brilliant civilization emerged here by 2000 B.C.

Minoan prosperity was based on large-scale trade that ranged from Sicily, Greece, and Asia Minor to Syria and Egypt. The Minoans employed the first ships capable of long voyages over the open sea. Chief exports were olive oil, wine, metalware, and magnificent pottery. This trade was the monopoly of an efficient bureaucratic government under a powerful ruler whose administrative records were written on clay tablets, first in a form of picture writing and later in a syllabic script known as Linear A. As neither script has been deciphered, our knowledge of Minoan civilization is scanty and imprecise; most of it is derived from the material remains uncovered by archaeologists.

It was the epoch-making discoveries of the English archaeologist Sir Arthur Evans that first brought to light this civilization, whose existence had previously only been hinted at in the epics of Homer and in Greek legends such as that of the minotaur, half bull and half man, who devoured youths and maidens sent as tribute from Greece. Between 1900 and 1905 Evans unearthed the ruins of a great palace at Knossos, the dominant city in Crete after 1700 B.C. Rising at least three stories high and sprawling over nearly six acres, this "Palace of Minos," built of brick and limestone and employing unusual downward-tapering columns of wood, was a maze of royal apartments, storerooms, corridors, open courtyards, and broad stairways. Furnished with running water, the palace had a sanitation system that surpassed anything constructed in Europe until Roman times. Walls were painted with elaborate frescoes in which the Minoans appear as a happy, peaceful people with a pronounced liking for dancing, festivals, and athletic contests. Women are shown enjoying a freedom and dignity unknown elsewhere in the ancient Near East or classical Greece. They are not secluded in the home but are seen sitting with men and taking an equal part in public festivities—even as toreadors in a form of bull fighting. Their dresses are very elaborate, with gay patterns and colors, pleats, puffed sleeves, and flounces. Bodices are open in front to the waist, and hair is elaborately fashioned with ringlets over the forehead and about the ears.

The glory of Minoan culture was its art, spontaneous and full of rhythmic motion. Art was an essential part of everyday life and not, as in the ancient Near East, an adjunct to religion and the state. What little is known of Minoan religion also contrasts sharply with conditions in the Near East: there were no great temples, powerful priesthoods, or large cult statues of the gods. The principal deity was the Mother Goddess; her importance reflected the important position held by women in Cretan society. A number of recovered statuettes show her dressed like a fashionable Cretan woman with flounced skirts, a tightly laced, lowcut bodice, and an elaborate coiffure. She was probably the prototype of such later Greek goddesses as Athena, Demeter, and Aphrodite.

The Mycenaeans

About 2000 B.C. or shortly thereafter, the first Indo-European Greek tribes, collectively called Achaeans, entered Greece, where they absorbed the earlier settlers and ruled from strongly fortified citadels at Mycenae, Pylos, Athens, and other sites. By 1600 B.C. the Achaeans—or Mycenaeans, as they are usually called—had

Mycenaean palaces were built as hilltop fortresses enclosed by walls of mammoth stone blocks. Above the gateway that leads into the ancient city of Mycenae stand two stone lionesses placed there to guard the inhabitants. Built about 1250 B.C., the Lion Gate is the most impressive remnant of such massive fortifications.

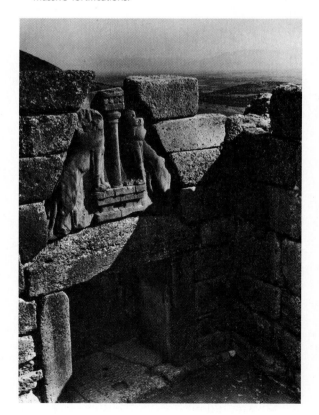

adopted much of the advances culture of the Minoans. They remained warlike, however, and plied the seas as raiders as well as traders. Mycenaean women adopted Cretan fashions and added a variety of sumptuous jewelry from bracelets to earrings.

Some of the wealth accumulated by the kings of Mycenae—the greatest single hoard of gold, silver, and ivory objects found anywhere before the discovery of Tutankhamen's tomb—was unearthed in 1876 by Heinrich Schliemann, fresh from his even more sensational discoveries at Troy (see this page). The royal palace on the acropolis, or citadel, of Mycenae had well-proportioned audience rooms and apartments, fresco-lined walls, floors of painted stucco, and large storerooms. Noteworthy also were the royal "beehive" tombs, constructed of cut stone and covered with earth.

The expansive force of Mycenaean civilization led to the planting of colonies in the eastern Mediterranean (Hittite sources refer to Achaeans in Asia Minor) and to the conquest of Knossos about 1450 B.C. The latter event was made possible by the destruction of the labyrinthian palace at Knossos by fire—the aftereffect, it is now conjectured, of a great tidal wave caused by the eruption of the small volcanic island of Thera (Santorini) eighty miles north of Crete. The palace at Knossos was rebuilt by the Mycenaeans (to be destroyed finally about 1380 B.C. by earthquake and fire), and the center of Aegean civilization shifted to the Greek mainland.

This story of Achaean-Cretan relations was unclear until after 1952 when a young English architect, Michael Ventris, startled the scholarly world by deciphering a type of Cretan script known as Linear B, many examples of which had been found by Evans at Knossos and by later archaeologists at Pylos, Mycenae, and Thebes. When Linear B turned out to be an early form of Greek written in syllabic characters, it followed that the rulers of Knossos after 1450 B.C. must have been Achaean Greeks who had adopted the Cretan script to write their own language.

The Linear B texts, which are administrative documents and inventories, greatly add to our knowledge of Mycenaean life. The Mycenaean centers were fortified palaces and administrative centers and not, as in Crete, true cities. The bulk of the population lived in scattered villages where they worked either communal land or land held by nobles or kings. The nobles were under the close control of the kings, whose administrative records were kept daily by a large number of scribes. Prominent in these records are details of the disbursement of grain and wine as wages and the collection of taxes in kind. The most important item of income was olive oil, the major article in the wide-ranging Mycenaean trade, which was operated as a royal monopoly. Perhaps it was their role as merchantmonopolists that led the Achaean kings about 1250 B.C. to launch the famous expedition against Troy in order to eliminate a powerful commercial rival.

Troy, Site of Homer's Iliad

The city of Troy occupied a strategic position on the Hellespont (the strait from the Aegean to the Black seas now known as the Dardanelles). Thus Troy could command both sea traffic through the straits and land caravans going between Asia and Europe. For many years scholars thought this city existed only in the epic poems of Homer. Henrich Schliemann (1822–1890), a German romantic dreamer and amateur archaeologist, believed otherwise. As a boy, he had read Homer's *Iliad*, and thereafter he remained firmly convinced that Troy had actually existed. At the age of forty-eight, having amassed a fortune in the California gold rush and in world-wide trade, Schliemann retired from business to put his persistent dream of ancient Troy to the test.

In 1870 Schliemann began excavations at the legendary site of Troy, where he unearthed nine buried cities, built one on top of another. He discovered a treasure of golden earrings, hairpins, and bracelets in the second city (Troy II), which led him to believe that this was the city of Homer's epics. Excavations in the 1930s, however, showed that Troy II had been destroyed about 2200 B.C., far too early to have been the scene of the Trojan War, and that Troy VIIa, clearly destroyed by human violence about 1250 B.C., was probably the one made famous by Homer.

Neither the view that Troy was the victim of commercial rivalry nor the other widely held theory that it was destroyed by Achaean pirates seeking booty corresponds to Homer's view that the Trojan War was caused by the abduction of Helen, queen of Sparta, by the Trojan prince Paris. Led by Agamemnon, king of Mycenae, the wrathful Achaeans besieged Troy for ten long years. Homer's *Iliad* deals only with a few weeks during the tenth year of the siege.

The Fall of Mycenaean Civilization

About 1200 B.C. a new wave of Indo-Europeans, the Dorian Greeks, materially aided by weapons made of iron instead of bronze, invaded Greece. First of the Mycenaean strongholds to fall was Pylos, whose Linear B archives contain numerous references to hastily undertaken preparations to repel the invaders. We find orders directing women and children to places of safety; instructions to armorers, "rowers," and food suppliers; and a report entitled "How the watchers are guarding the coastal regions."[2] The preparations were in vain, however. Pylos was sacked and burned, and the destruction of the other major Mycenaean citadels soon followed. Mycenaean refugees found a haven at Athens and in Ionia (see map, p. 41) on the western coast of Asia Minor.

In the painting on the interior of the Arkesilas Cup, dating from about 560 B.C., the king of Cyrene, a Greek colony in North Africa, is shown supervising the preparation of hemp or flax for export.

The Rise of Hellenic Civilization, 1150–500 B.C.

The four centuries from c.1150 to 750 B.C., the Greek Dark Ages, were marked by the disappearance of the major characteristics of Mycenaean civilization—centralized and bureaucratic administration, wide-ranging commerce, sophisticated art forms (including monumental architecture), and writing. Yet while the Dorian invasion was an undoubted catastrophe, it was also vital to the ultimate rise of a unique Hellenic (from *Hellas*, the Greek name for Greece) civilization that was not largely an offshoot of the Near East, as was Aegean civilization. A fresh start now had to be made.

The Influence of Geography

Geographical factors played an important part in shaping the events of Greek history. The numerous mountain ranges that crisscross the peninsula, which is about the size of Maine, severely hampered internal communication and led to the development of fiercely independent city-states and the failure of the Greeks to unite into a single state. The mountains cover two thirds of the surface, and along the west coast they come close to the sea, leaving few harbors and arable plains. Elsewhere the deeply indented coast provides many natural harbors that invite maritime adventure. The major cleft is the Gulf of Corinth, which made southern Greece almost an island—hence, it was called the Peloponnesus ("Pelop's island"). The indented coastline and the many islands offshore stimulated seagoing trade, and the rocky soil (less than a fifth of Greece is arable) and few natural resources encouraged the Greeks to establish colonies abroad.

The Homeric Age

Most of our information about the Greek Dark Ages, which followed the Dorian invasion, is derived from the epics put in final form during the last century of this period and attributed to the blind Ionian poet Homer. Controversy surrounds

THRACE

Byzantium

SEA OF
MARMARA

PHRYGIA

MYSIA

LYDIA

Pergamum

Sardis

Hermus

R.

Maeander R.

Ephesus

Miletus

Halicarnassus

RHODES

Hellespont

Ilium (Troy)

LESBOS

CHIOS

SAMOS

SPORADES
SEA

AEGEAN

SEA

CRETAN
SEA

SEA

SAMOTHRACE

LEMNOS

NAXOS

IOS

THERA

PAROS

CYCLADES

MELOS

Knossos

CRETE

MACEDONIA

MT. OLYMPUS

THESSALY

EPIRUS

AETOLIA

EUBOEA

ATTICA
Athens
Praeus

BOEOTIA
Delphi Thebes

Corinth
Mycenae
Argos

ARCADIA

PELOPONNESUS

Sparta
LACONIA

MESSENIA

ACHAIA

Olympia

Pylos

CYTHERA

MEDITERRANEAN

LEUCAS

CEPHALLENIA

ZACYNTHUS

CORCYRA

THE AEGEAN WORLD

0   25   50   75

the question of Homer's existence and whether he or several poets composed the *Iliad* and *Odyssey*. The Homeric epics retain something of the material side of the Mycenaean period. Yet in filling in the details of political, economic, and social life; the religious beliefs and practices; and the ideals that gave meaning to life; the poet could only describe what was familiar to him in his own age.

The values that gave meaning to life in the Homeric Age were predominantly heroic values—the strength, skill, and valor of the preeminent warrior. Such was the earliest meaning of *aret*, "excellence" or "virtue," a key term throughout the course of Greek culture. To obtain *aret*—defined by one Homeric hero as "to fight ever in the forefront and outvie my peers"—and the imperishable fame that was its reward, men welcomed hardship, struggle, and even death. Honor, like fame, was a measure of *aret*, and the greatest of human tragedies was the denial of honor due to a great warrior. Homer makes such a denial the theme of the *Iliad*: "The ruinous wrath of Achilles that brought countless ills upon the Achaeans" when Achilles, insulted by Agamemnon, withdraws from battle.

To the Homeric Greeks, the gods were plainly human. Zeus, the king of the gods, was often the undignified victim of the plots of his wife Hera and other deities, and he asserted his authority through threats of violence. Hades, the abode of the dead, was a subterranean land of dust and darkness, and Achilles, as Homer tells us in the *Odyssey*, would have preferred to be a slave on earth than a king in Hades.

Society was clearly aristocratic—only the *aristoi* ("aristocrats") possessed *aret*—and the common man was reviled and beaten when he dared to question his betters. Yet the common man had certain political rights as a member of the assembly that was summoned whenever a crisis, such as war, required his participation. Two other instruments of government described by Homer were the tribal king and his council. The king was hardly more than a chief among his peers, his fellow nobles, who sat in his council to advise him and to check any attempt he might make to exercise arbitrary power. The economy was that of a simple, self-sufficient agricultural system much like that of the early Middle Ages in western Europe.

The City-State: Origin and Political Evolution

The *polis*, or city-state, the famed Greek political unit, did not exist in the Greek Dark Ages. The nucleus of the *polis*, was the elevated, fortified site—the *acropolis*—where people could take refuge from attack. In time this defensive center took on added significance as the focus of political and religious life. When commerce revived in the eighth and seventh centuries B.C., a trading center developed below the acropolis. The two areas and the surrounding territory, usually smaller than a modern county, formed the *polis*, from which our word "politics" is derived.

The political development of the *polis* was so rich and varied that it is difficult to think of a form of government not experienced—and given a lasting name—by the Greeks. Four major types of government evolved: (1) monarchy, limited by an aristocratic council and a popular assembly, as described in the Homeric epics; (2) oligarchy ("rule of the few"), arising when the aristocratic council ousted the king and abolished or restricted the popular assembly; (3) tyranny, imposed by one man who rode to power on the discontent of the lower classes; (4) democracy ("rule of the people"), the outstanding political achievement of the Greeks, which emerged after the tyrant was deposed and the popular assembly revived and made the chief organ of government. After dissatisfaction with democratic government became widespread in the fourth century B.C., many of the city-states returned either to oligarchy or to one-man rule.

From Oligarchy to Tyranny

By the middle of the eighth century B.C., the nobles, who resented the power wielded by the tribal kings, had taken over the government, ushering in an age of oligarchy. Ruthlessly exercising their superior power, the nobles acquired a monopoly of the best land, reducing many commoners to virtual serfdom and forcing others to seek a living on rocky, barren soil.

The hard lot of common people under oligarchy produced the anguished protest of Hesiod's *Works and Days* (c. 700 B.C.). A commoner who had been cheated out of his parcel of land by his evil brother in league with "bribe-swallowing"

The ostrakon was used to cast a vote to decide whether a person would be banished from the city of Athens for a period of ten years. The name inscribed on the first line is Themistocles.

aristocratic judges, Hesiod was the prophet of a more exalted conception of the gods and a new age of social justice. To establish a just society, Hesiod argued, people must learn to pursue moderation *(sophrosyn)* in all things—apparently the first expression of this famous Greek ideal—and realize that "far-seeing" Zeus and the other gods punish evildoers and reward the righteous. In contrast to Homer with his aristocratic heroes, Hesiod defined human excellence, or *aret*, in a way to make it attainable for common people. Its essential ingredients were righteousness and work—honest work in competition with one's fellows being a form of strife in moderation. "Gods and men hate him who lives without work," Hesiod insisted. "His nature is like the drones who sit idle and eat the labor of the bees." Furthermore, "work is no shame, but idleness is a shame," and "esteem," "glory," and "riches" follow work.[3] All this sounds much like the Protestant ethic of disciplined restraint, sobriety, frugality, and industry taught by John Calvin and his followers.

Hesiod's new ideals of moderation and justice were slow to take root. The poor found relief only by emigrating to new lands overseas. As Plato later noted, the wealthy promoted colonization as a safety valve to ward off a threatened political and economic explosion:

> When men who have nothing, and are in want of food, show a disposition to follow their leaders in an attack on the property of the rich—these, who are the natural plague of the state, are sent away by the legislator in a friendly spirit as far as he is able; and this dismissal of them is euphemistically termed a colony.[4]

From 750 to 550 B.C. the Greeks planted colonies throughout much of the Mediterranean world (see map, p. 25), a development often compared with the expansion of Europe in modern times. Settlements sprang up along the northern coast of the Aegean and around the Black Sea. So many Greeks migrated to southern Italy and eastern Sicily that the region became known as *Magna Graecia*, or Great Greece. Colonies were also founded as far west as present-day France—at Massilia, modern Marseilles for example—and Spain and on parts of the African coast. Unique was Naucratis in Egypt, not a true colony but a trading post whose residents gained extraterritorial rights (their own magistrates and law courts) from the Egyptians.

In time colonization ameliorated Greece's economic and social problems. By 600 B.C. economic progress and the use of coined money, learned from the Lydians, had created the beginnings of a middle class. The Greek home states gradually became "industrialized" as a result of concentrating upon the production of specialized wares—vases, metal goods, textiles, olive oil, and wine—for export in exchange for foodstuffs and raw materials. But before this economic revolution was completed, the continuing land hunger of the peasants contributed to a political revolution.

Despite the poor quality of Greek soil, farming was important in ancient Greece. Olives were widely cultivated, and the production of olive oil was an important component of Greek commerce.

After 650 B.C. tyrants arose in many Greek states and, supported by the aggrieved peasantry and rising merchant class, seized the reins of government from the nobility. They were supported by a new heavy-armed infantry (the hoplite phalanx), composed of middle-class citizens wealthy enough to furnish their own equipment. These tyrants (the word meant simply "master" and did not at first have today's unfavorable meaning) not only distributed land to the peasants but, by promoting further colonization, trade, and industry, completed the Greek economic revolution.

Athens to 500 B.C.

Athens and Sparta, the city-states destined to dominate the history of Greece during the classical period (the fifth and most of the fourth centuries B.C.), underwent markedly different developments during the period prior to 500 B.C. While Athens' political, economic, and social evolution was typical of most other Greek states, Sparta's development produced a unique way of life that elicited the wonder and often the admiration of other Greeks.

During the seventh century B.C., the council of nobles became supreme in Athens. The popular assembly no longer met, and the king was replaced by nine aristocratic magistrates, called archons, chosen annually by the council to exercise the king's civil, military, and religious powers. While the nobles on their large estates prospered, the small farmers and sharecroppers suffered. Bad years forced them to borrow seed from their rich neighbors, and when they were unable to repay they were sold into slavery. To the small farmers' clamor for the cancellation of debts and the end to debt slavery was added the voice of the landless for the redistribution of land.

When the Athenian nobles finally realized that their failure to heed the cry for reform would result in the rise of a tyrant, they agreed to the policy of compromise advocated by the liberal aristocrat Solon. In 594 B.C. Solon was made sole archon with broad authority to reconcile the lower classes. Inspired by the ideals of moderation and justice promoted by Hesiod a century earlier, Solon instituted middle-of-the-road reforms that have made his name a byword for wise statesmanship.

Examples of Greek painting have totally disappeared except for those found on vases. This vase (c. 545 B.C.) depicts Achilles and Ajax, two of the heroes of Homer's *Iliad,* playing dice.

For the lower classes, Solon agreed to canceling all debts and forbidding future debt bondage, but he rejected as too radical the demand for the redivision of the land. His long-range solution to the economic problem was to seek full employment by stimulating trade and industry. To achieve this goal, Solon required fathers to teach their sons a trade, granted citizenship to foreign artisans who settled in Athens, and encouraged the intensive production of olive oil for export.

Moderation also characterized Solon's political reforms—the common people were granted important political rights, but not equality. While laws continued to originate in a new aristocratic Council of Four Hundred, they now had to be ratified by the popular assembly, which Solon revived. And since wealth, not birth, became the qualification for membership in the

Council and for the archonships, wealthy commoners acquired full political equality. Furthermore, the assembly could now act as a court to hear appeals from the decisions of the archons and to try them for misdeeds in office.

Unfortunately, Solon's moderate reforms satisfied neither party. The poor had received neither land nor full political equality, while the nobles thought Solon a radical who had betrayed his class. Deeply discouraged, Solon described what is too often the lot of moderate reformers: "Formerly their eyes sparkled when they saw me; now they coldly scorn me, no longer friends but enemies."[5]

Solon had warned the Athenians to accept his reforms lest "the people in its ignorance comes into the power of a tyrant." He lived to see his prediction fulfilled. In 560 B.C., after a period of civil strife, Pisistratus, a military hero and champion of the commoners, usurped power as tyrant. He solved the economic problem by banishing many nobles, whose lands he distributed among the poor, and by promoting commerce and industry. Together with extensive public works and the patronage of culture — thus starting Athens on the road to cultural leadership in Greece — these reforms gave rise to a popular saying that "Life under Pisistratus was paradise on earth."

Pisistratus was succeeded by his two sons, one of whom was assassinated and the other exiled after he became suspicious and cruel. When the nobles, aided by a Spartan army, took this opportunity to restore oligarchy, Cleisthenes temporarily seized power in 508 B.C. and put through constitutional reforms that destroyed the remaining power of the nobility. He disregarded the old noble-dominated tribes and created ten new ones, each embracing citizens of all classes from widely scattered districts. The popular assembly soon acquired the right to initiate legislation and became the sovereign power in the state; there could be no appeal from its decisions. A new and democratic Council of Five Hundred, selected by lot from the ten tribes, advised the assembly and supervised the administrative actions of the archons. Cleisthenes' final reform was the peculiar institution of *ostracism*, an annual referendum in which a quorum of citizens could vote to exile for ten years any individual thought to be a threat to the new Athenian democracy. (A quorum consisted of 6000 of the 50,000 male citizens over the age of eighteen. The average attendance at an Athenian assembly, whose ordinary meetings were held every ten days, was about 5000.) The 2500th anniversary of the establishment of the Athenian democracy will be celebrated in 1993.

Sparta to 500 B.C.

In sharp contrast to Athens was its rival Sparta. Sparta had not joined the other Greek cities in trade and colonization but had expanded instead by conquering and enslaving its neighbors. To guard against revolts by the state slaves (helots), who worked the land for their conquerors, Sparta deviated from the normal course of Greek political development and transformed itself into a militaristic totalitarian state. Aristotle called the government of Sparta a "mixed constitution";

Bronze statue of a Greek warrior from the sixth century B.C. The warrior is draped in a cloak and wears a helmet of the Corinthian type, covering the head and face.

for the small minority of ruling Spartans, it was a democracy, but for the great mass of subjected people it was an oligarchy. The government included two kings, an aristocratic council, and an assembly of all 9000 Spartan citizens. Great power resided in five magistrates called ephors ("overseers"), created originally as an aristocratic check on royal authority, but later elected annually by the assembly.

While the Athenian state required only two years of military training for young men, the Spartan system—traditionally attributed to a legendary lawgiver named Lycurgus—was designed to make every Spartan a professional soldier and to keep him in a constant state of readiness for war. To this end, the state enforced absolute subordination of the individual to its will.

State officials examined all newborn children, and any found sickly or deformed were abandoned to die. At the age of seven a boy was taken from his family and placed in the charge of state educators, who taught him to bear hardship, endure discipline, and devote his life to the state. At twenty the young Spartan enrolled in the army and lived in barracks, where he contributed food from his allotment of land granted by the state and worked by helots. At thirty he was allowed to marry, but he continued to live in barracks, visiting his wife only at night. Finally, at sixty, he was released from the army and could live at home with his family.

This lifelong discipline produced formidable soldiers and inspired them with the spirit of obedience and respect for law. Plutarch reports that Spartan training "accustomed the citizens to have neither the will nor the ability to lead a private life, but, like bees, to be organic parts of their community, clinging together around their leader, forgetting themselves in their enthusiastic patriotism, and belonging wholly to their country."

Although many Greeks admired the Spartan way of life, the typical Spartan was crude and aggressive, took few baths, and spoke few words. According to Plutarch:

> One may judge their character by their jokes; for they are taught never to talk at random, nor to utter a syllable that does not contain some thought. For example, when one of them was invited to hear a man imitate the nightingale, he answered, "I have heard the original."[6]

Spartan girls also received state training in order to become healthy mothers of warrior sons. Clad in short tunics, which other Greeks thought immodest, they engaged in running, wrestling, and throwing the discus and javelin. As their men marched off to war, Spartan women bade them a laconic farewell: "Come back with your shield or on it."

According to Plutarch, the Spartans

> did away with all seclusion and retirement for women, and ordained that girls, no less than boys, should go naked in processions, and dance and sing at festivals in the presence of the young men. . . . This nakedness of the maidens had in it nothing disgraceful. It was done modestly, not licentiously, and it produced habits of simplicity and taught them to desire good health and beauty of body, and to love honor and courage no less than the men. This it was that made them speak and think as Gorgo, the wife of Leonidas, is said to have done. Some foreign lady, it seems, said to her, "You Spartan women are the only ones who rule men." She answered, "Yes, for we are the only ones who give birth to men."

While Sparta developed the finest military machine in Greece, it remained backward culturally and economically. Trade and travel were prohibited because the city fathers feared that alien ideas might disturb the status quo. Sparta is a classic example of how intellectual stagnation accompanies rigid social conformity and military regimentation.

To provide additional assurance that its helots remained uncontaminated by democratic ideas, Sparta allied itself with oligarchic parties in other Peloponnesian states and aided them in suppressing their democratic opponents. The resulting Spartan League of oligarchic states, in operation by the end of the sixth century B.C., was shortly to be faced by an Athenian-led union of democratic states (see map, p. 47).

Unity and Strife in the Hellenic World, 500–336 B.C.

The leaders of the Greek economic and cultural revival after 750 B.C. were the Ionian Greeks, descendants of the Mycenaeans who had fled the

**GREEK POLITICAL ALLIANCES
ABOUT 431 B. C.**

- Athens and Allies
- Sparta and Allies
- Neutral Greek States

Dorian invaders and settled the Aegean coast of Asia Minor and its offshore islands. Influenced by contacts with Phoenician traders (from whom they borrowed the alphabet in the eighth century B.C.), neighboring Lydia, and Egypt, the Ionians "first kindled the torch of Hellenism." They were also the first Greeks to face the threat of the great powers of the Near East.

The Persian Wars

When the Persians conquered Lydia in 547 B.C., they also annexed Ionia, which had been under nominal Lydian rule. Chafing under Persian-appointed tyrants, the Ionian cities revolted in 449 B.C., established democratic regimes, and appealed to the Athenians, who were also Ionians,

for aid. Athens sent twenty ships, but to no avail. By 494 B.C. Darius I had crushed the revolt, burning Miletus in revenge.

Darius knew that Ionia was insecure as long as Athens remained free to incite its kin to revolt, and thus in 490 B.C. a Persian force about 20,000 strong sailed across the Aegean and debarked on the plain of Marathon near Athens. Darius' aim of forcing the Athenians to accept the exiled son of Pisistratus as a pro-Persian tyrant was frustrated when the Athenian army, half the size of the Persian, won an overwhelming victory, killing 6400 of the foe while losing only 192.

The battle of Marathon was one of the most decisive in history. It destroyed the belief in Persian invincibility and demonstrated, in the words of the Greek historian Herodotus, that "free men fight better than slaves." The victory also gave the Athenians the self-confidence that would soon make their city the leading Greek state.

Ten years later the Greeks were well prepared for a new Persian invasion under Xerxes, Darius' successor, whose objective was the subjection of all of Greece. Athens now had 200 ships, the largest fleet in Greece, and Sparta had agreed to head a defensive alliance of thirty-one states.

The Persian army—reckoned by Herodotus at 1,700,000 but more likely 150,000 or so—was too huge to be transported by ship. Crossing the swift-flowing, mile-wide Hellespont near Troy on two pontoon bridges—a notable feat of engineering—the army marched along the Aegean coast accompanied by a great fleet carrying provisions. The Spartans wanted to abandon all of Greece except the Peloponnesus to the invaders but finally agreed to a holding action at the narrow pass of Thermopylae. Here 300 Spartans and a few thousand other Greeks held back the Persians for three days, until a Greek traitor led them over a mountain path to the rear of the Greek position. The Spartans fought magnificently until all were slain, together with 700 other Greeks. The Spartan dead were immortalized on a monument erected at the pass: "Go tell the Spartans, you who pass us by, that here, obedient to their laws, we lie."

The Persians then burned Athens, whose inhabitants had fled, for they placed their faith in "wooden walls"—their fleet. Their faith was not misplaced; in the Bay of Salamis the Greek fleet, largely Athenian, turned the tide of victory with the shout: "On, sons of the Greeks! Set free your country, set free your children free, your wives, the temples of your country's gods, your fathers' tombs; now they are all at stake."[7] With 200 of his 350 ships destroyed and his lines of communication cut, Xerxes had no alternative but to retreat to Asia, although he left a strong force in Greece. The following summer (479 B.C.) the Greek army, with the Spartan contingent in the vanguard, routed the Persian force at Plataea, and Greece was for the time being safe from invasion.

Culmination of Athenian Democracy

The part they played in the Greek victory over the mighty Persian empire exhilarated the Athenians and gave them the confidence and energy

Pericles led Athens during its Golden Age, the era during which the city reached the height of its literary, artistic, and philosophical achievements.

that made them the leaders of the Greek world during the remainder of the fifth century B.C. During this period, known as the Golden Age of Greece, the Athenians "attempted more and achieved more in a wider variety of fields than any nation great or small has ever attempted or achieved in a similar space of time."[8]

For more than thirty years (461–429 B.C.) during this period, the great statesman Pericles guided Athenian policy. In Pericles' time the actual executive power no longer resided in the archons who were chosen by lot, but in a board of ten elected generals. This board operated much like a modern-day governmental cabinet. The generals urged the popular assembly to adopt specific measures, and the success or failure of their policies determined whether they would be reelected at the end of their annual term. Pericles failed of reelection only once, and so great was his influence on the Athenians that, in the words of the contemporary historian Thucydides, "what was in name a democracy was virtually a government by its greatest citizen."[9]

To enable even the poorest citizen to participate in government, Pericles extended payment to jurors (a panel of 6000 citizens chosen annually by lot) and to members of the council. While his conservative opponents called this political bribery, Pericles insisted that it was essential to the success of democracy:

> *Our constitution is named a democracy, because it is in the hands not of the few but of the many. But our laws secure equal justice for all in their private disputes, and our public opinion welcomes and honours talent in every branch of achievement, not as a matter of privilege but on grounds of excellence alone.... [Athenians] do not allow absorption in their own various affairs to interfere with their knowledge of the city's. We differ from other states in regarding the man who holds aloof from public life not as "quiet" but as useless; we decide or debate, carefully and in person, all matters of policy, holding, not that words and deeds go ill together, but that acts are foredoomed to failure when undertaken undiscussed."[10]*

Athenian Society

The majority of the inhabitants of Athens, however, were not recognized as citizens. Women, slaves, and resident aliens were denied citizenship and had no voice in the government. Legally, women were first the property of their fathers, then of their husbands. They could not possess property in their own name, or, as the law expressly stated, "make a contract about anything worth more than a bushel of barley."

Athens was distinctly a man's world. A wife's function was to bear children and manage the home, where she was restricted to the women's quarters when her husband entertained his friends. Men did not marry until they were about thirty, and they usually married girls half their age. Marriages were normally arranged by the families, and prospective brides and bridegrooms seldom met before their betrothal. Families were rather small, and infanticide, usually by exposure, of unwanted infants (especially girls)

was practiced as a primitive form of birth control. The average life expectancy was little more than thirty years.

Athenian society sanctioned a double moral standard, and the philandering of a husband was not the occasion for adverse public comment. A peculiar institution, catering to the needs and desires of upper-class Athenian males, was that of the "companions" *(hetaerae)*. These females were normally resident aliens and therefore not subject to the social restrictions imposed on Athenian women. A few of the *hetaerae,* such as Aspasia, the mistress of Pericles, were cultivated women who entertained at salons frequented by Athenian political and cultural leaders. Generally speaking, however, champions of the social emancipation of Athenian women were rare, and the women themselves accepted their status. Aside from a few cases in which wives murdered their husbands (usually by poison), married life seems to have been stable and peaceful. Attic gravestones in particular attest to the love spouses felt for one another. The tie to their children was strong, and the community set high store by the honor owed by sons and daughters to their parents.

Athenian women were responsible for running the household and directing the work of servants and slaves, but they were entirely excluded from public life.

Male homosexuality is frequently pictured on Athenian vases and mentioned in literature. Socially acceptable was "boy love," a homosexual relationship between a mature man and a young boy just before the youth attained puberty. This relationship was viewed as pedagogical—a rite of initiation into adult society. Like initiation rites in general, it contained a strong element of humiliation. Adult male homosexuality and homosexual prostitution, however, were not socially acceptable. Such relationships were looked upon as "contrary to nature," and the Athenian government issued stringent legal prohibitions against them.

No ancient society did without slaves, although their importance is often overstated; almost everyone, free as well as slave, had to work for a living. In fifth-century Athens it is estimated that one out of every four persons was a slave. Some were war captives, others were children of slaves, but most came from outside Greece through slave dealers. No large slave gangs were employed on plantations, as they were in Roman times and in the American South before the Civil War. Small landowners owned one or more slaves, who worked in the fields alongside their masters. Those who owned many slaves—one rich Athenian owned a thousand—hired them out to private individuals or to the state where they worked beside Athenian citizens and received the same wages.

Other slaves were taught a trade and set up in business. They were allowed to keep one sixth of their wages, and many of them were able to purchase their freedom. Although a few voices argued that slavery was contrary to nature and that all people were equal, the Greek world as a whole agreed with Aristotle that some people—non-Greeks in particular—were incapable of full human reason; thus they were by nature slaves who needed the guidance of a master.

Athenian Imperialism

The victory over Persia had been made possible by a partial unity of Hellenic arms; but that unity quickly dissolved when Sparta, fearful of helot rebellion at home, recalled its troops and resumed its policy of isolation. Because the Persians still ruled the Ionian cities and another invasion of Greece seemed probable, Athens in 478 B.C. invited the city-states bordering on the Aegean to form a defensive alliance called the Delian League. To maintain a 200 ship navy that would police the seas, each state was assessed ships or money in proportion to its wealth. From the beginning, Athens dominated the league. Since almost all of the 173 member states paid their assessments in money, which Athens was empowered to collect, the Athenians furnished the necessary ships.

By 468 B.C., after the Ionian cities had been liberated and the Persian fleet destroyed, various league members thought it unnecessary to continue the confederacy. In suppressing all attempts to secede, the Athenians were motivated by the fear that the Persian danger still existed and by the need to maintain and protect the large free-trade area so necessary for Greek—and especially Athenian—commerce and industry. The Athenians created an empire because they dared not unmake a confederation. By aiding in the suppression of local aristocratic factions within its subject states, Athens both eased the task of controlling its empire and emerged as the leader of a union of democratic states.

To many Greeks—above all to the members of the oligarchic Spartan League and the suppressed aristocratic factions within the Athenian empire—Athens was a "tyrant city" and an "enslaver of Greek liberties." Pericles, on the other hand, justified Athenian imperialism on the ground that it brought "freedom" from fear and want to the Greek world:

> We secure our friends not by accepting favours but by doing them.... We are alone among mankind in doing men benefits, not on calculations of self-interest, but in the fearless confidence of freedom. In a word I claim that our city as a whole is an education to Hellas.... [11]

The Peloponnesian War

In 431 B.C. the Peloponnesian War broke out between the Spartan League and the Athenian empire. While commercial rivalry between Athens and Sparta's major ally Corinth was an important factor, the conflict is a classic example of how fear can generate a war unwanted by either side. The contemporary historian Thucydides wrote:

> *The real but unavowed cause I consider to have been the growth of the power of Athens, and the alarm which it inspired in Lacedaemon [Sparta]; this made war inevitable.*[12]

Several incidents served to ignite the underlying tension, and Sparta declared war on the "aggressors."

Sparta's hope for victory lay in its army's ability to besiege Athens and lay waste its fields. Pericles, on the other hand, relied on Athens' unrivaled navy to import foodstuffs and to harass its enemies' coasts. Fate took a hand in this game, however. In the second year of the war a plague carried off a third of the Athenian population, including Pericles. His death was a great blow to Athens, for leadership of the government passed to demagogues. In the words of Thucydides:

> *Pericles, by his rank, ability, and known integrity, was able to exercise an independent control over the masses—to lead them instead of being led by them. . . . With his successors it was different. More on a level with one another, and each grasping at supremacy, they ended by committing even the conduct of state affairs to the whims of the multitude. This, as might have been expected in a great imperial state, produced a host of blunders. . . .*[13]

Eight more years of indecisive warfare ended in 421 B.C. with a compromise peace. During the succeeding period Athenian imperialism manifested itself in its worst form through the actions of Pericles' less able successors. In 416 B.C. an expedition embarked for Melos, a neutral Aegean island, to force it to join the Athenian empire. Thucydides reports the Athenian argument used to justify their naked imperialism; not until Machiavelli's *Prince* (1513 A.D.) would power politics again be so ruthlessly and candidly presented:

> *We believe that Heaven, and we know that men, by a natural law, always rule where they are stronger. We did not make that law nor were we the first to act on it; we found it existing, and it will exist forever, after we are gone; and we know that you and anyone else as strong as we are would do as we do.*[14]

The Athenians executed Melians of military age and sold the women and children into slavery.

The war was resumed in 415 B.C. with an Athenian expedition against Syracuse, the major Greek state in Sicily (see map, p. 25), that ended in disaster. Acting on the invitation of states that feared Syracusan expansion, the Athenians hoped to add Sicily to their empire and so become powerful enough "to rule the whole of the Greek world."[15] But ill luck and incompetent leadership resulted in two Athenian fleets and a large army being destroyed by the Syracusans, supported by Sparta. The war dragged on until 404 B.C., when Athens capitulated after its last fleet was destroyed by a Spartan fleet built with money received from Persia in exchange for possession of the Greek cities in Ionia. At home, Athens had been weakened by the plots of oligarchic elements to whom Sparta now turned over the government. The once great city-state was also stripped of its empire and demilitarized.

Aftermath of the War

Anarchy and depression were the political and economic legacies of the Peloponnesian War. Having ended the "tyranny" of Athens over Greece, the Spartans substituted their own form of rule which made the Athenian empire seem mild in comparison. Everywhere democracies were replaced by oligarchies supported by Spartan troops. The bloody excesses of these oligarchs soon led to democratic revolutions at Athens and elsewhere. As one of their generals admitted, the Spartans did not know how to govern free people. Incessant warfare between a bewildering series of shifting alliances filled the fourth century B.C. The alliances were usually financed by Persia, which wanted to keep Greece disunited and weak.

Political instability in turn contributed to the economic and social ills that plagued Greece during this period. Commerce and industry languished, and the unemployed who did not go abroad as soldiers of fortune supported demagogues and their radical schemes for the redivision of wealth. The wealthy, for their part, became increasingly reactionary and uncompromising. Even most intellectuals—including Plato and Aristotle—lost faith in democracy and joined with the wealthy in looking for "a champion powerful in action" who would bring order and security to Greece. They found him, finally, in the person of the king of Macedonia.

The Macedonian Unification of Greece

To the north of Greece lay Macedonia, inhabited by hardy peasants and nobles who were related to the Greeks but were culturally inferior to them. Macedonia became a centralized, powerful state under the able and crafty Philip II (359–336 B.C.), who created the most formidable army yet known by joining the crack Macedonian cavalry of nobles with the infantry phalanx used by the Greeks. In his youth, Philip had been a hostage at Thebes, where he acquired an appreciation of Greek culture, an understanding of Greek political weakness, and a desire to win for Macedonia a place in the Hellenic world.

After unifying Macedonia — including a string of Greek colonies that had been established along its coast during the earlier centuries of Macedonia's weakness—Philip turned to the Greek city-states, whose wars afforded him the opportunity first to intervene, then to dominate. Demosthenes, the great Athenian orator and democratic leader, warned in vain that "democracies and dictators cannot exist together" and urged the Athenians and other Greeks to stop Philip before it was too late. Belatedly, Athens and Thebes acted, but their combined forces were shattered at Chaeronea in 338 B.C. Philip then forced the Greeks into a league in which each state, while retaining self-government, swore to "make war upon him who violates the general peace" and to furnish Philip with men and supplies for a campaign against Persia. Two years later, before setting out for Asia Minor, Philip was assassinated by a noble with a personal grudge, leaving the war against Persia as a legacy for his gifted son Alexander.

Incapable of finding a solution to the anarchy that tore their world to shreds, the Greeks ended as political failures and at the mercy of a great outside power, first Macedonia and then Rome. They retained their cultural leadership, however, and the culture of the new Hellenistic Age and its successor, the world of Rome, was to be largely Greek.

The Greek Genius

The Greeks were the first to formulate many of the Western world's fundamental concepts in politics, philosophy, science, and art. How was it that a relative handful of people could bequeath such a legacy to civilization? The definitive answer may always elude the historian, but a good part of the explanation lies in environmental and social factors.

Unlike the Near Eastern monarchies, the *polis* was not governed by a "divine" ruler, nor were the thoughts and activities of its citizens limited by powerful priesthoods. Many Greeks, and most notably the Athenians, were fond of good talk and relished debate and argument. As late as the first century A.D., St. Paul was welcomed by the Athenians because they "liked to spend all their time telling and listening to the latest new thing." (Acts 17:21)

The Greek Character

The Greeks felt a need to discover order and meaning both in nature and in human life. This quest for order produced exceptional results in science, art, and philosophy. Beginning with Hesiod (see p. 43), the Greeks stressed the virtue of *sophrosyn* (moderation, self-control) as the key to happiness and right living. Its opposite was *hubris*, meaning pride, arrogance, and unbridled ambition. The result of human excesses and lying at the root of personal misfortune and social injustice, *hubris* invariably provoked *nemesis*, or retribution. According to the Greeks, an inexorable law would cause the downfall or disgrace of anyone guilty of *hubris*. The Athenian dramatists often employed this theme in their tragedies, and Herodotus attributed the Persian defeat by the Greeks to Xerxes' overweening pride, for "Zeus tolerates pride in none but himself."[16]

The Greeks exhibited human frailties and failings—at times they were irrational, vindictive, and cruel. But at their best they were guided by the ideals that permeate their intellectual and artistic legacy. The philosopher Protagoras is credited with the statement, "Man is the measure of all things"—a saying that sums up the outstanding feature of Greek thought and art.

The lyre player in this vase painting suggests that music was important to the Greeks. The invention of the lyre is attributed to the Greek god Hermes, who fashioned it from a tortoise shell.

Greek Religious Development

Early Greek religion abounded in gods and goddesses who personified the forces of nature. Thus Demeter (literally "Earth Mother"), was the earth and giver of grain; Apollo, the sun and giver of light; and Poseidon, who dwelled in the sea, was the ruler of the waters. Other deities had special functions, such as Aphrodite, the goddess of love; Dionysus, the god of fertility and wine; and Athena, the goddess of wisdom and guardian of Athens. The Greeks of Homeric times believed in humanlike deities, capable of malice, favoritism, and jealousy, and differing from ordinary people only in their immortality (the result of a special diet) and their possession of supernatural powers. Zeus, the king of sky, earth, and human beings, ruled the world from Mount Olympus with the aid of lesser deities.

By the time of Hesiod (see p. 43), a religious reformation had begun that changed the vengeful and capricious gods of Homer into austere arbiters of justice who rewarded the good and punished the wicked. From the famous oracle at Delphi the voice of Zeus' son Apollo urged all Greeks to follow the ideal of moderation: "Nothing in excess" and "Know thyself" (meaning "know your limitations").

A century after Hesiod, the Orphic and Eleusinian mystery cults emerged as a new type of Greek religion. Their initiates *(mystae)* were promised an afterlife of bliss in Elysium, formally the abode after death of a few heroes only. The basis of Orphic cult was an old myth about Dionysus as a son of Zeus who was slain and eaten by the evil Titans before Zeus arrived on the scene and burned them to ashes with his lightning bolts. Orpheus taught that Zeus then created man from the Titans' ashes. Human nature, therefore, is composed of two disparate elements: the evil titanic element (the body), and the divine Dionysian element (the soul). Death, which frees the divine soul from the evil body, is therefore to be welcomed. "Happy and blessed one!" reads a typical Orphic tomb inscription, "Thou shalt be god instead of mortal."

Early Greek Philosophy

What the Greeks were the first to call philosophy ("love of wisdom") arose from their curiosity about nature. The early Greek philosophers were called *physikoi* (physicists) because their main interest was in investigating the physical world. ("It is according to their wonder," wrote Aristotle, "that men begin to philosophize, pursuing science in order to know.") Only later, beginning with Socrates, would the chief concern of philosophy be not in natural science but in ethics—how people ought to act in the light of moral principles.

The Mesopotamians, as noted in chapter 1, were skilled observers of astronomical phenomena which, like the Greeks of Homer's time, they attributed to the action of gods. The early Greek philosophers, beginning with Thales of Miletus around 600 B.C., changed the course of human knowledge by insisting that the phenomena of the universe be explained by natural rather than supernatural causes. This rejection of mythological explanations and the use of reason to explain natural phenomena has been called the "Greek miracle."

Called "the father of philosophy," Thales speculated on the nature of the basic substance from which all else in the universe is composed. He concluded that it was water, which exists in different states and is indispensable to the maintenance and growth of organisms. Thales' successors in Ionia proposed elements other than water as the primal substance in the universe. One called it the "boundless," apparently a general concept for "matter"; another proposed "air," out of which all things come by a process of "rarefying and condensing"; a third asserted that fire was the "most mobile, most transformable, most active, most life-giving" element. This search for a material substance as the first principle or cause of all things culminated two centuries after Thales in the atomic theory of Democritus (c. 460–370 B.C.) To Democritus, reality was the mechanical motion of indivisible atoms, which differed in shape, size, position, and arrangement but not in quality. Moving about continuously, atoms combined to create objects.

While these and other early Greek philosophers were proposing some form of matter as the basic element in nature, Pythagoras of Samos (c. 582–500 B.C.) countered with the profoundly significant notion that the "nature of things" was something nonmaterial—numbers. By experimenting with a vibrating cord, Pythagoras discovered that musical harmony is based on arithmetical proportions, and he intuitively concluded that the universe was constructed of numbers and their relationships. His mystical, nonmaterial interpretation of nature, together with his belief that the human body was distinct from the soul, greatly influenced Plato.

An important consequence of early Greek philosophical speculation was the undermining of conventional beliefs and traditions. In religion, for example, Anaximander argued that thunder and lightning were caused by blasts of wind and not by Zeus' thunderbolts. Xenophanes went on to ridicule the traditional view of the gods: "If oxen and lions had hands, . . . they would make portraits and statues of their gods in their own image."

The eroding of traditional views caused Greek inquiry to turn away from the physical world to a consideration of human values and institutions. During the last half of the fifth century B.C., professional teachers, called Sophists ("intellectuals"), taught a variety of subjects—the nucleus of our present arts and sciences—which they claimed would lead to material success. The most popular subject was rhetoric, the art of persuasion, or how to take either side of an argument—"the sort of thing one learns today in law school." The Sophists submitted all conventional beliefs to the test of rational criticism. Concluding that truth was relative, they denied the existence of universal standards to guide human actions.

Socrates, a Martyr to Truth

The outstanding opponent of the Sophists was the Athenian Socrates (c. 470–399 B.C.). Like the Sophists, Socrates turned from cosmic to human affairs; in the words of the Roman statesman Cicero, Socrates was "the first to call philosophy down from the heavens and to set her in the cities of men, bringing her into their homes and compelling her to ask questions about life and morality and things good and evil."[17] But unlike the Sophists, Socrates believed that by asking salient questions and subjecting the answers to logical analysis, agreement could be reached about ethical standards and rules of conduct. And so he would question passers-by in his function of "midwife assisting in the birth of correct ideas" (to use his own figure of speech). Taking as his motto the famous inscription on the temple of Apollo at Delphi, "Know thyself," he insisted that "the unexamined life is not worth living." To Socrates, human excellence or virtue (aret) is knowledge, and evil and error are the result of ignorance.

In time Socrates' quest for truth led to his undoing, for the Athenians, unnerved by their defeat in the Peloponnesian War, arrested him on the charge of impiety and corrupting the youth. By a slim majority a jury of citizens condemned Socrates to die, a fate he accepted without rancor and with a last request:

When my sons are grown up, I would ask you, my friends, to punish them, and I would have you trouble them, as I have troubled you, if they seem to care about riches, or anything, more than about virtue; or if they pretend to be something when they are really nothing, then reprove them, as I have reproved you, for not caring about that for which they ought to care, and thinking that they are something when they are really nothing. And if you do this, both I and my sons will have received justice at your hands.[18]

Plato and His Theory of Ideas

After Socrates' death, philosophical leadership passed to his most famous disciple, Plato (427–347 B.C.). Like Socrates, Plato believed that truth exists, but only in the realm of thought, the spiritual world of Ideas or Forms. Such universals as Beauty, Good, and Justice exist apart from the material world, and the beauty, good, and justice encountered in the world of the senses are only imperfect reflections of eternal and changeless Ideas. The task for humans is to come to know the True Reality—the eternal Ideas—behind these imperfect reflections. Only the soul, and the "soul's pilot," reason, can accomplish this, for the human soul is spiritual and immortal, and in its prenatal state it existed "beyond the heavens" where "true Being dwells."[19]

Disillusioned with the democracy that had led Athens to ruin in the Peloponnesian War and had condemned Socrates to death, Plato expounded his concept of an ideal state in the *Republic*, the first systematic treatise on political science. The state's basic function, founded on the Idea of Justice, was the satisfaction of the common good. Plato described a kind of "spiritualized Sparta" in which the state regulated every aspect of life, including thought. Thus those poets and forms of music considered unworthy were banished from the state. Private property was abolished on the grounds that it bred selfishness. Plato believed there was no essential difference between men and women; therefore, women received the same education and held the same occupations as men, including "the art of war, which they must practice like men."[20] Individuals belonged to one of three classes and found happiness only through their contribution to the community: workers by producing the necessities of life, warriors by guarding the state, and philosophers by ruling in the best interests of all the people.

Plato founded the Academy in Athens, the famous school that existed from about 388 B.C. until A.D. 529, when it was closed by the Christian emperor Justinian. Here he taught and encouraged his students, whom he expected to become the intellectual elite who would go forth and reform society.

Aristotle, the Encyclopedic Philosopher

Plato's greatest pupil was Aristotle (384–322 B.C.), who set up his own school, the Lyceum, at Athens. Reacting against the other worldly tendencies of Plato's thought, Aristotle insisted that Ideas have no separate existence apart from the material world; knowledge of universal Ideas is the result of the painstaking collection and organization of particular facts. Aristotle's Lyceum, accordingly, became a center for the analysis of data from many branches of learning.

To us today, Aristotle's most significant treatises are the *Ethics* and the *Politics*. They deal with what he called the "philosophy of human affairs," whose object is the acquisition and maintenance of human happiness. Two kinds of virtue *(aretē)*, intellectual and moral, which produce two types of happiness, are described in the *Ethics*. Intellectual virtue is the product of reason, and only people like philosophers and scientists ever attain it. Much more important for the good of society is moral virtue—virtues of character, such as justice, bravery, and temperance—which is the product less of reason than of habit and thus can be acquired by all. In this connection Aristotle introduced his Doctrine of the Mean as a guide for good conduct. He considered all moral virtues to be means between extremes; courage, for example, is the mean between cowardice and rashness.

In the *Politics* Aristotle viewed the state as necessary "for the sake of the good life," because its laws and educational system provide the most effective training needed for the attainment of moral virtue and hence happiness. Thus to Aristotle the viewpoint popular today that the state stands in opposition to the individual would be unthinkable.

Aristotle's writings on formal logic, collectively known as the *Organon* ("Instrument"), describe two ways in which new truths can be acquired. The first, induction, moves from particular facts to general truths. Deductive logic, on the other hand, moves from the general to the particular. To facilitate deductive reasoning from general truths, Aristotle devised the syllogism, a logical

Aristotle Criticizes Communism

Aristotle foreshadows the failure of communist regimes in our world today.

Next let us consider what should be our arrangements about property: should the citizens of the perfect state have their possessions in common or not? . . .

There is always a difficulty in men living together and having things in common, but especially in their having common property. . . .

The present arrangement, if improved as it might be by good customs and laws, would be far better, and would have the advantages of both systems. Property should be in a certain sense common, but, as a general rule, private; for, when every one has a distinct interest, men will not complain of one another and they will make more progress, because every one will be attending to his own business. And yet among the good, and in respect of use, 'Friends,' as the proverb says, 'will have all things common' . . .

For, although every man has his own property, some things he will place at the disposal of his friends, while of others he shares the use with them. . . . Again, how immeasurably greater is the pleasure, when a man feels a thing to be his own; for the love of self is a feeling implanted by nature and not given in vain, although selfishness is rightly censured; this, however, is not the mere love of self, but the love of self in excess, like the miser's love of money; for all, or almost all, men love money, and other such objects in a measure. And further, there is the greatest pleasure in doing a kindness or service to friends or guests or companions, which can only be rendered when a man has private property. The advantage is lost by the excessive unification of the state. . . . No one, when men have all things in common, will any longer set an example of liberality or do any liberal action; for liberality consists in the use which is made of property.

Such [communistic] legislation may have a specious appearance of benevolence; men readily listen to it, and are easily induced to believe that in some wonderful manner everybody will become everybody's friend, especially when some one is heard denouncing the evils now existing in states, suits about contracts, convictions for perjury, flatteries of rich men and the like, which are said to arise out of the possession of private property. These evils, however, are due to a very different cause—the wickedness of human nature. Indeed, we see that there is much more quarrelling among those who have all things in common, though there are not many of them when compared with the vast numbers who have private property.

Again, we ought to reckon, not only the evils from which the citizens will be saved, but also the advantages which they will lose. The life which they are to lead appears to be quite impracticable. The error of Socrates [i.e., Plato] must be attributed to the false notion of unity from which he starts. Unity there should be, both of the family and of the state, but in some respects only. For there is a point at which a state may attain such a degree of unity as to be no longer a state, or at which, without actually ceasing to exist, it will become an inferior state, like harmony passing into unison, or rhythm which has been reduced to a single foot. The state, as I was saying, is a plurality, which should be united and made into a community by education. . . . Let us remember that we should not disregard the experience of ages.

From the translation by Benjamin Jowett, *Aristotle's Politics* (Oxford: Clarendon Press, 1908), pp. 60–64.

structure requiring a trio of propositions. The first two propositions (the major and minor premises) must be plainly valid and logically related so that the third proposition, the conclusion, inevitably follows. For example, (1) all Greeks are human; (2) Socrates is a Greek; (3) therefore Socrates is human.

There have probably been few geniuses whose interests were so widespread as Aristotle's. He investigated such diverse fields as biology, mathematics, astronomy, physics, literary criticism, rhetoric, logic, politics, ethics, and metaphysics. His knowledge was so encyclopedic that there is hardly a college course today that does not take note of what Aristotle had to say on the subject. Although his works on natural science are now little more than historical curiosities, they held a place of undisputed authority until the scientific revolution of the sixteenth and seventeenth centuries. But in no important sense are his humanistic studies, such as the *Ethics* and the *Politics*, out of date.

Medicine

Superstitions about the human body blocked the development of medical science until 420 B.C., when Hippocrates, the "father of medicine," founded a school in which he emphasized the value of observation and the careful interpretation of symptoms. Such modern medical terms as "crisis," "acute," and "chronic" were first used by Hippocrates. He was firmly convinced that disease resulted from natural, not supernatural, causes. Writing of epilepsy, considered at the time a "sacred" or supernaturally inspired malady, one Hippocratic writer observed:

> It seems to me that this disease is no more divine than any other. It has a natural cause just as other diseases have. Men think it supernatural because they do not understand it. But if they called everything supernatural which they do not understand, why, there would be no end of such thing![21]

The Hippocratic school also gave medicine a sense of service to humanity which it has never lost. All members took the famous Hippocratic Oath, still in use today. One section states: "I will adopt the regimen which in my best judgment is beneficial to my patients, and not for their injury or for any wrongful purpose. I will not give poison to anyone, though I be asked . . . nor will I procure abortion."[22]

Despite their empirical approach, the Hippocratic school adopted the theory that the body contained four liquids or humors—blood, phlegm, black bile, and yellow bile—whose proper balance was the basis of health. This doctrine was to impede medical progress until modern times.

The Writing of History

If history is defined as an "honest attempt first to find out what happened, then to explain why it happened," Herodotus of Halicarnassus (484?–425? B.C.) deserves to be called the "father of history." In his highly entertaining history of the Persian Wars he discerned the clash of two distinct civilizations, the Hellenic and the Near Eastern. His portrayal of both the Greeks and Persians was eminently impartial, but his fondness for a good story often led him to include tall tales in his work. As he stated more than once, "My duty is to report what has been said, but I do not have to believe it."

The first truly scientific historian was Thucydides (460–400? B.C.), who wrote a notably objective chronicle of the Peloponnesian War. Although he was a contemporary of the events and a loyal Athenian, a reader can scarcely detect whether he favored Athens or Sparta. Thucydides believed that his history would become "an everlasting possession" for those who desire a clear picture of what has happened and, human nature being as it is, what is likely to be repeated in the future. His belief was based on his remarkable ability to analyze and explain human behavior. (Two examples—his definition of statesmanship and his account of Athenians justifying their empire on grounds of power alone—have been quoted on page 51.) In describing the character and purpose of his work, Thucydides probably had Herodotus in mind:

> The absence of romance in my history will, I fear, detract somewhat from its interest; but I shall be content if it is judged useful by those inquirers who desire an exact knowledge of the past as an aid to the interpretation of the future, which will according to human nature recur in much the same way. My history has been composed to be an everlasting possession, not the show-piece of an hour.[23]

Hellenic Poetry and Drama

Greek literary periods can be classified according to dominant poetic forms that reflect particular stages of cultural evolution in Greece. First came the time of great epics, followed by periods in which lyric poetry and then drama flourished.

Sometime during the eighth century B.C. in Ionia, the *Iliad* and the *Odyssey*, the two great epics attributed to Homer, were set down in their present form. The *Iliad*, describing the clash of arms between the Greeks and Trojans "on the ringing plains of windy Troy," glorifies heroic valor and physical prowess against a background of divine intervention in human affairs. (See also p. 42.) The *Odyssey*, relating the adventure-filled wanderings of Odysseus on his return to Greece after Troy's fall, places less stress on divine intervention and more on the cool resourcefulness of the hero in escaping from danger and in regaining his kingdom. These stirring epics have provided inspiration and source material for generations of poets in the Western world.

As Greek society became more sophisticated, a new type of poetry, written to be sung to the accompaniment of the lyre, arose among the Ionian Greeks. Unlike Homer, authors of this lyric poetry sang not of legendary events but of present delights and sorrows. This new note, personal and passionate, can be seen in the following examples, in which the contrast between the new values of what is called the Greek Renaissance and those of Homer's heroic age is sharply clear. Unlike Homer's heroes, Archilochus of Paros (seventh century B.C.) unashamedly throws away his shield and runs from the battlefield:

My trusty shield adorns some Thracian foe; I left it in a bush — not as I would! But I have saved my life; so let it go. Soon I will get another just as good.[24]

And in contrast to Homer's view of an unromantic, purely physical attraction between Paris and the abducted Helen, Sappho of Lesbos (sixth century B.C.), the first and one of the greatest of all female poets, saw Helen as the helpless, unresisting victim of romantic love:

She, who the beauty of mankind Excelled, fair Helen, all for love The noblest husband left behind;

Afar, to Troy she sailed away, Her child, her parents, clean forgot; The Cyprian [Aphrodite] led her far astray Out of the way, resisting not.[25]

Drama (in verse) developed from the religious rites of the Dionysian mystery cult in which a large chorus and its leader sang and danced. Thespis, a contemporary of Solon, added an actor called the "answerer" *(hypocrites,* the origin of our word "hypocrite") to converse with the chorus and its leader. This made dramatic dialogue possible. By the fifth century B.C. in Athens, two distinct forms — tragedy and comedy — had evolved. Borrowing from the old familiar legends of gods and heroes for their plots, the tragedians reinterpreted them in the light of the values and problems of their own times.

In reworking the old legends of the heroic age, Aeschylus (525–456 B.C.) sought to spread the new values of the religious reformation, first expressed by Hesiod, by showing how the old premoral beliefs cause suffering. In his trilogy, the *Oresteia*, for example, he concerned himself with *hubris* (see p. 00) as applied to the murder of the hero Agamemnon by his queen following his return from the Trojan War, and then proceeded to work out its ramifications — murder piled on murder until people through suffering learn to substitute the moral law of Zeus for the primitive law of the blood feud. Like the prophets of Israel, Aeschylus taught that while "sin brings misery," misery in turn leads to wisdom:

Zeus the Guide, who made man turn Thought-ward, Zeus, who did ordain Man by Suffering shall Learn. *So the heart of him, again Aching with remembered pain, Bleeds and sleepeth not, until Wisdom comes against his will.*[26]

A generation later, Sophocles (c. 496–406 B.C.) largely abandoned Aeschylus' concern for the working out of divine justice and concentrated upon character. To Sophocles, a certain amount of suffering was inevitable in life. No one is perfect; even in the best people there is a tragic flaw that causes them to make mistakes. Sophocles dwelled mainly on the way in which human beings react to suffering. Like his contemporary, the sculptor Phidias, Sophocles viewed humans as ideal creatures — "Many are the wonders of the world, and none so wonderful as Man"—and he displayed human greatness by depicting people experiencing great tragedy without whimpering. It has been said that to Sophocles—and to Shakespeare—"tragedy is essentially an expression, not of despair, but of the triumph over despair and of confidence in the value of human life."[27]

Euripides (c. 480–406 B.C.), the last of the great Athenian tragedians, reflects the rationalism and critical spirit of the late fifth century B.C. Gone is Sophocles' idealized view of humanity. To Euripides, human life was pathetic, the ways of the gods ridiculous. His recurrent theme was "Since life began, hath there in God's eye stood one happy man?" For this he has been called "the poet of the world's grief." Euripides has also been called the first psychologist, for he looked deep into the human soul and described what he saw with intense realism. His *Medea*, for example is a startling and moving account of a woman's exploitation and her retaliatory rage. When Medea's overly ambitious husband discards her for a young heiress, she kills her children out of a bitter hatred that is the dark side of her once passionate love:

He, even he,
Whom to know well was all the world to me,
The man I loved, hath proved most evil. Oh,
Of all things upon earth that bleed and grow,
A herb most bruised is woman.
. . . but once spoil her of her right
In man's love, and there moves, I warn thee
    well,
No bloodier spirit between heaven and hell.[28]

Far more than Aeschylus or even Sophocles, Euripides strikes home to us today.

Comedies were bawdy and spirited. There were no libel laws in Athens, and Aristophanes (c. 445–385 B.C.), the famous comic-dramatist and a conservative in outlook, brilliantly satirized Athenian democracy as a mob led by demagogues, the Sophists (among whom he included

The Persian invasion reduced Athens to a heap of ruins, but the invaders' withdrawal left the Athenians free to reconstruct the Acropolis (below) into a treasury of temples and statues. The Parthenon (right), originally brightly painted, was designed to be a structurally and visually perfect building.

Aristophanes on the Shortcomings of Athenian Democracy

In *The Frogs*, Aristophanes exhorts the Athenians to elect better quality leaders.

[The LEADER *of the chorus comes forward and addresses the audience:*]

We chorus folk two privileges prize:
  To amuse you, citizens, and to advise.
  So, mid the fun that marks this sacred day,
We'll put on serious looks, and say our say. . . .

But if we choose to strut and put on airs
While Athens founders in a sea of cares,
In days to come, when history is penned,
They'll say we must have gone clean round the bend . . .

I'll tell you what I think about the way
This city treats her soundest men today:
By a coincidence more sad than funny,
It's very like the way we treat our money.
The noble silver drachma, that of old
We were so proud of, and the recent gold,
Coins that rang true, clean-stamped and worth their weight
Throughout the world, have ceased to circulate.

Instead, the purses of Athenian shoppers
Are full of shoddy silver-plated coppers.
Just so, when men are needed by the nation,
The best have been withdrawn from circulation.
Men of good birth and breeding, men of parts,
Well schooled in wrestling and in gentler arts,
These we abuse, and trust instead to knaves,
Newcomers, aliens, copper-pated slaves,
All rascals—honestly, what men to choose!
There was a time when you'd have scorned to use
Men so debased, so far beyond the pale,
Even as scapegoats to be dragged from jail
And flogged to death outside the city gate.
My foolish friends, change now, it's not too late!
Try the good ones again: if they succeed,
You will have proved that you have sense indeed. . . .

From the translation by David Barrett, *Aristophanes, The Frogs and Other Plays* (Baltimore, MD: Penguin Books, 1964), pp. 181–183.

Socrates) as subversive, and Euripides as an underminer of civic spirit and traditional faith. Another favorite object of Aristophanes' satire was the youth of Athens; in the following lines from *The Wasps*, they are lampooned by the chorus of old men:

> *Yes, we may be poor old crocks,*
> *But the whiteness of our locks*
> *Does the City better credit, I would say,*
> *Than the ringlets and the fashions*
> *And the pederastic passions*
> *Of the namby-pamby youngsters of today.*[29]

Hellenic Architecture

In the sixth century B.C. architecture flourished in Ionia, Greece, and the Greek colonies in Sicily and Italy with the construction of large temples of stone. Their form was a development from earlier wooden structures that had been influenced by the remains of Mycenaean palaces. Architecture reached its zenith in Athens during the fifth century B.C., the height of the city's power and wealth.

The Parthenon, the Erechtheum, and the other temples on the Athenian Acropolis exhibit the highly developed features that make Greek structure so pleasing to the eye. All relationships, such as column spacing and height and the curvature of floor and roof lines, were calculated and executed with remarkable precision to achieve a perfect balance, both structurally and visually. The three orders, or styles, usually identified by the characteristics of the columns, were the Doric, which was used in the Parthenon; the Ionic, seen in the Erechtheum; and the later and more ornate Corinthian.

Located where everyone could see and enjoy them, Greek temples afford an interesting comparison with those of Egypt. Whereas the Egyptian temple was enclosed and mysterious, the Greek temple was open, with a colonnade porch and an inside room containing a statue of the god. Sacrifice and ritual took place outside the temple, where the altar was placed.

Other types of buildings, notably the theaters, stadiums, and gymnasiums, also express the Greek spirit and way of life. In the open-air theaters the circular shape of the spectators' sections and the plan of the orchestra section set a style that has survived to the present day.

Hellenic Sculpture and Pottery

Greek sculpture of the archaic period (c. 700–480 B.C.), although crude in its representation of human anatomy, has the freshness and vigor of youth. Influenced partly by Egyptian models, the statues of nude youths and draped maidens usually stand stiffly with clenched fists and with one foot thrust awkwardly forward. The fixed smile and formalized treatment of hair and drapery also reveal the sculptors' struggle to master the technique of their art.

The mastery of technique by 480 B.C. ushered in the classical period of fifth-century Greek sculpture whose "classic" principles of harmony and proportion have shaped the course of Western art. Sculpture from this period displays both the end of technical immaturity and the beginning of idealization of the human form, which reached its culmination in the dignity and poise of Phidias' figures in the continuous frieze and pediments of the Parthenon. Carved with restraint and "calm exaltation," the frieze depicts the citizens of Athens participating in the Panathenaic procession in honor of their patron goddess Athena, which took place every four years.

The more relaxed character of fourth-century B.C. Hellenic sculpture, while still considered classical, lacks some of the grandeur and dignity of fifth-century art. Charm, grace, and individuality characterize the work of Praxiteles, the most famous sculptor of the century. These qualities can be seen in his supple statues of the god Hermes holding the young Dionysus and of Aphrodite stepping into her bath.

The making of pottery, the oldest Greek art, started at the beginning of the Greek Dark Ages with crude imitations of late Mycenaean forms. Soon the decayed Mycenaean motifs were replaced by abstract geometric designs. With the advent of the archaic period came paintings of scenes from mythology and daily life. From surviving Greek pottery and mosaics, we can get an idea of what Greek painting, now lost, was like.

The Hellenistic Age, 336–30 B.C.

The Hellenistic Age is a 300-year period from Alexander the Great to Augustus, the first Roman emperor. Alexander conquered the Near East up to the borders of India. Following his death, three large empires were carved from his conquests. The Hellenistic Age was a period of economic expansion, cosmopolitanism, striking intellectual and artistic achievements, and the wide diffusion of Greek culture.

Alexander the Great

When Philip of Macedonia was assassinated in 336 B.C., his crown fell to his twenty-year-old son Alexander who proved himself a resolute king at the very beginning of his reign by crushing rebellion in the Greek League, which had been founded by his father (see p. 52). As an object lesson, Alexander destroyed the city of Thebes and sold its inhabitants into slavery. The Greeks were horrified and cowed.

Alexander soon repented this atrocity for, having been tutored by Aristotle, he was alive to the glories of Hellenic culture. Reveling in the heroic deeds of the *Iliad*, which he always kept beside his bed, Alexander saw himself as a second Achilles waging war against barbarians when he planned to revenge the Persian attacks on Greece. In 334 B.C., he set out with an army of 35,000 soldiers recruited from Macedonia and the Greek League. In quick succession he subdued Asia Minor, Syria, Palestine, and Egypt. Then the young leader marched into Mesopotamia and there, in 331 B.C., defeated the last powerful army of Darius III, the Persian monarch. Alexander ventured as far east as the rich river valleys of India, where his weary

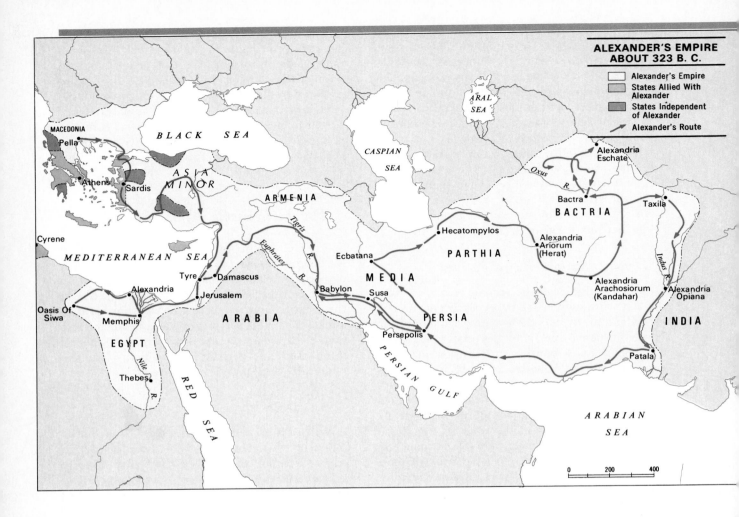

ALEXANDER'S EMPIRE ABOUT 323 B. C.

- ☐ Alexander's Empire
- ▨ States Allied With Alexander
- ▩ States Independent of Alexander
- → Alexander's Route

soldiers forced him to turn back (see map above). In 323 B.C., while he was planning the circumnavigation of Arabia, Alexander fell ill with a mysterious fever, following a long bout of heavy drinking, and died suddenly at the age of thirty-two. With the Greeks now masters of the ancient Near East, a new and distinctly cosmopolitan period in their history and culture began—the Hellenistic Age.

Alexander the Great is a puzzling figure to modern historians. Some view him as a ruthless conqueror who never lost a battle and a despot who ordered even his European subjects to prostrate themselves when in his presence. Others, however, influenced by Greek and Roman writers and by their own humanitarian outlook, picture him as an idealistic visionary seeking to unite East and West in one world.

Some of Alexander's military and administrative policies sought to unify the lands he conquered and to promote what he himself called "concord and partnership in the empire" between easterners and westerners. He blended Persians with Greeks and Macedonians in his army and administration; he founded numerous cities—seventy, according to tradition—in the East and settled many of his followers in them; and he married two oriental princesses and encouraged his officers and men to take foreign wives. Finally, for egotistical and political reasons, he ordered the Greek city-states to accord him "divine honors."

Alexander was a remarkable blend of the romantic idealist and practical realist, contrasting traits that he inherited from his parents. His fiery and emotional mother, Olympias, who practiced the orgiastic rites of primitive religions and claimed to be a descendant of the Greek hero Achilles, instilled in her son a consciousness of a divine mission that drove him onward, even to seeking the end of the earth beyond India. From his father he inherited his remarkable abilities as military commander, expert diplomat, and political administrator. Alexander was an egocentric idealist who was excited by challenges, but meeting those challenges forced him to take actions that were practical and pragmatic. For example, he could not merely conquer the king of Persia, he had to act as his successor as well. Alexander ruled for only thirteen years, but the world was never the same again.

The Division of Alexander's Empire

For several decades following Alexander's sudden death, his generals vied for the spoils of empire. Three major Hellenistic kingdoms emerged and maintained a precarious balance of power until the Roman conquests of the second and first centuries B.C.: Egypt, ruled by Ptolemy and his successors; Asia, comprising most of the remaining provinces of the Persian empire and

held together with great difficulty by the dynasty founded by Seleucus; and Macedonia and Greece, ruled by the descendants of Antigonus the One-Eyed (see map below).

While the Antigonids in Macedonia followed the model of Alexander's father Philip in posing as national kings chosen by the army, the Ptolemies ruled Egypt as divine pharaohs, and some of the Seleucids became deified "saviors" and "benefactors." Ptolemaic and Seleucid administrations were centralized in bureaucracies staffed by Greeks, an arrangement that created a vast gulf between rulers and ruled:

> *"What a mob!"* [the Greek poet Theocritus has a Greek woman residing in Alexandria say to her friend], *"They're like ants, no one can count them. Ptolemy, you've done many good things . . . . No more hoods creep up on you nowadays and do you in—an old Egyptian habit. The tricks those scoundrels used to play! They're all alike—dirty, lazy, good-for-nothings!"*[30]

Plagued by native revolts, dynastic troubles, and civil war, the Hellenistic kingdoms soon began to crumble. Macedonia lost effective control of Greece when Athens asserted its independence and most of the other Greek states resisted Macedonian domination by forming two federal leagues, the Achaean and the Aetolian. Their constitutions have long commanded the attention of students of federal unions—including the founders of the American constitution.

The eastern reaches of Alexander's empire—Indian, Bactria, and Parthia—gradually drifted out of the Seleucid sphere of influence. Pergamum, in northwestern Asia Minor, renounced its allegiance to the Seleucids and became an independent kingdom famous for its artists and scholars. In 200 B.C. the new power of Rome entered upon the scene, and by 30 B.C. Rome had annexed the last remaining Hellenistic state, Egypt.

Hellenistic Economy and Society

The Hellenistic Age was a time of economic expansion and social change. In the wake of Alexander's conquests, thousands of Greeks flocked eastward to begin a new era of Greek colonization, ending the long economic depression that followed the breakup of the Athenian empire. An

THE HELLENISTIC EMPIRES ABOUT 300 B.C.

Claimed by Macedonia
Claimed by Seleucids

economic union between East and West permitted the free flow of trade, and prosperity was stimulated further when Alexander put into circulation huge hoards of Persian gold and silver and introduced a uniform coinage. The result was a much larger and more affluent middle class than had hitherto existed.

By the third century B.C. the center of trade had shifted from Greece to the Near East. Largest of the Hellenistic cities, and much larger than any cities in Greece itself, were Antioch in northern Syria and Alexandria in Egypt. The riches of India, Persia, Arabia, and the Fertile Crescent were brought by sea and land to these Mediterranean ports.

Alexandria outdistanced all other Hellenistic cities as a commercial center. Its merchants supplied the ancient world with wheat, linen, papyrus, glass, and jewelry. Boasting a population of about a million, the city had a double harbor in which a great lighthouse, judged one of the wonders of the ancient world, rose to a height estimated at 370 feet. Its busy streets were filled with a mixture of peoples—Greeks, Macedonians, Jews, and Egyptians. As in all other Hellenistic cities in the Near East, the privileged Greeks and Macedonians were at the top of the social scale and the mass of natives at the bottom; the large Jewish population lived apart and was allowed a large degree of self-government. Free labor was so cheap that slavery hardly existed in Hellenistic Egypt. As a consequence, worker-organized strikes were frequent.

Hellenistic Philosophy

Developments in philosophy reflected the changed environment of the Hellenistic Age. With the growing loss of political freedom and the prevalence of internal disorder, philosophers concerned themselves less with the reform of society and more with the attainment of happiness for the individual. "There is no point in saving the Greeks," is the way one Hellenistic philosopher summed up the new outlook, quite in contrast to that of Socrates, Plato, and Aristotle. This emphasis on peace of mind for the individual living in an insecure world led to the rise of four principal schools of Hellenistic philosophy, all of which had their start at Athens.

The Skeptics and Cynics reflected most clearly the doubts and misgivings of the times. The Skeptics achieved freedom from anxiety by denying the possibility of finding truth. The wise, they argued, will suspend judgment and not dogmatize because they have learned that sensory experience, the only source of knowledge, is deceptive. The Skeptics were like modern pragmatists in substituting probability for certainty and insisting that even the probable must be tested by experience and exposed to the possibility of contradiction. To drive the point home they were famous for arguing both sides of the same question.

The Cynics carried negativism further; their ideal was nonattachment to the values and conventions of society. Cynic philosophers, like Diogenes, wandered from city to city, haranguing the public to pursue a nonconformist concept of virtue: "Look at me, I am without house or city, property or slave. I sleep on the ground. I have no wife, no children. What do I lack? Am I not without distress or fear? Am I not free?"[31]

More practical and popular were Epicureanism and Stoicism. The Athenian Epicurus (342–270 B.C.) taught that happiness could be achieved simply by freeing the body from pain and the mind from fear—particularly the fear of death. To reach this dual goal, people must avoid bodily excesses, including sensual pleasures, and accept the scientific teaching of Democritus that both body and soul are composed of atoms that fall apart at death. Thus beyond death there is no existence and nothing to fear. Epicurus maintained that the finest pleasures are intellectual, and that the gods, if they exist, do not concern themselves with humans but spend their time pursuing true pleasure like good Epicureans.

The Stoics, followers of Zeno (c. 336–c. 264 B.C.), a Semite who settled in Athens, argued in contrast to Epicureanism that the universe is controlled by some power—variously called Destiny, Reason, Natural Law, Providence, or God—which determines everything that happens. Fortified by this knowledge, wise Stoics conform their will to the World Will and "stoically" accept whatever part fortune allots them in the drama of life. While the Epicurean retreated from worldly responsibilities, the Stoic urged participation. Stoicism's stern sense of duty and belief in the equality of all people under a single ruling force made it particularly attractive to the Roman conquerors of the ancient world.

Science and Mathematics

The Greek concern for rational, disinterested inquiry reached a zenith in the Hellenistic period, particularly at Alexandria where the Ptolemies subsidized a great research institute, the Museum, and a library of more than half a million books. Emphasizing specialization and experimentation, and enriched by Near Eastern astronomy and mathematics, Greek science in the third century B.C. achieved results unmatched until early modern times.

The expansion of geographical knowledge resulting from Alexander's conquests incited scientists to make accurate maps and to estimate the size of the earth, which had been identified as a globe through observation of its shadow in a lunar eclipse. Eratosthenes, the outstanding geographer of the century, drew parallels of latitude and longitude on his map of the inhabited world and calculated the circumference of the globe with only 1 percent error (195 miles) by measuring the difference in the angles of the noonday sun's shadows at Aswan and Alexandria.

In astronomy, Aristarchus put forward the radical theory that the earth rotates on its axis and moves in an orbit around the sun. Most of his contemporaries adhered, however, to the prevailing geocentric theory, which stated that the earth was stationary and the sun revolved around it. This view was supported not only by the powerful authority of Aristotle, but it also seemed to explain all the known facts of celestial motion. This was particularly true after Hipparchus in the next century added the new idea of epicycles—each planet revolves in its own small orbit while moving around the earth. Aristarchus' heliocentric theory was forgotten until the sixteenth century A.D., when it was revived by Copernicus.

Mathematics also made great advances in the third century B.C. Euclid systematized the theorems of plane and solid geometry, and Archimedes of Syracuse, who had studied at Alexandria, calculated the value of π, invented a terminology for expressing numbers up to any magnitude, and laid the foundations of calculus. Archimedes also discovered specific gravity by noticing the water he displaced in his bath. And despite his disdain for making practical use of his knowledge, he invented the compound pulley, the windless, and the endless screw for raising water.

The Hellenistic Greeks extended the advances in medicine made earlier by Hippocrates and his school. By dissecting bodies of dead criminals, they were able to trace the outlines of the nervous system, to understand the principle of the circulation of the blood, and to ascertain that the brain, not the heart, was the true center of consciousness.

Hellenistic Art and Literature

The host of new cities that sprang up in Hellenistic times served as a tremendous impetus to architecture. The new cities benefited from town planning; the streets were laid out according to a rectangular plan. The great public edifices were elaborate and highly ornamented; this was an age that preferred the more ornate Corinthian to the simple Doric and Ionic orders.

Hellenistic sculptors continued and intensified the realistic, dramatic, and emotional approach that began to appear in late classical sculpture. Supported by rulers and other rich patrons in Alexandria, Antioch, Rhodes, and Pergamum, they displayed their technical virtuosity be depicting violent scenes, writhing forms, and dramatic poses—all with a realism that could make stone simulate flesh. Little evidence remained of the balance and restraint of classical Greek sculpture. The famous Laocoön group and the frieze from the altar of Zeus at Pergamum, with their twisted poses, contorted faces, and swollen muscles, remind one of the Baroque sculpture of seventeenth-century Europe, which replaced the classical art of the Italian Renaissance.

The quality of literature from the Hellenistic Age was generally inferior to that of the Hellenic Age. Scholarship flourished, and we are indebted for the preservation of much of Greek classical literature to the subsidized scholars at the Alexandrine library—"fatted fowls in a coup," as a Skeptic philosopher called them. They

This detail from the west pediment of the Parthenon frieze depicts two horsemen riding in the Panathenaia, the procession held every four years in honor of Athena, patron of the city.

composed epics in imitation of Homer (one new feature was romantic love, not found in Homer), long poems on dreary subjects like the weather, and short, witty epigrams—all in a highly polished style. These sophisticated scholars also invented a new type of romantic, escapist literature: pastoral poetry extolling the unspoiled life and loves of shepherds and their rustic maids. (Later, both Roman and modern poets and painters would adopt this Hellenistic tradition of celebrating the charms of unsophisticated country life.) The best of the new poetry was written by Theocritus at Alexandria in the third century B.C. The following short example, written by a contemporary, well illustrates its character and appeal:

> Would that my father had taught me the craft
>   of a keeper of sheep,
> For so in the shade of the elm tree, or under
>   the rocks on the steep,
> Piping on reeds I had sat, and had lulled my
>   sorrow to sleep.[32]

The Hellenistic Contribution: The East

The greatest contribution of the Hellenistic Age was the diffusion of Greek culture throughout the ancient East and the newly rising Roman West. In the East, the cities that Alexander and his successors built were the agents for spreading Hellenistic culture from the Aegean Sea to India. Literate Asians learned Greek to facilitate trade and to read Greek literature. In Judea, upper-class Jews built Greek theaters and gymnasia and adopted Greek speech, dress, and even names.

For a time the Seleucid empire provided the peace and economic stability necessary to ensure the partial Hellenization of a vast area. But with an insufficient number of Greeks to colonize so large an area as the Near East, the Greek city-states remained only islands in an Asian ocean. As time elapsed, this ocean encroached more and more upon the Hellenized areas.

The gradual weakening of the loosely knit Seleucid empire eventually resulted in the creation of independent kingdoms on the edge of the Hellenistic world. Bactria achieved independence in the middle of the third century B.C. Its Greek rulers, descendants of Alexander's veterans, controlled the caravan route to India and issued some of the most splendid Greek coins. In 183 B.C. the Bactrians crossed into India and conquered the province of Gandhara (see map, p. 108). One result was a strong Greek influence on Indian art (see chapter 4).

In the middle of the third century, a nomad chieftain founded the kingdom of Parthia, situated between the Seleucid and Bactrian kingdoms. Claiming to be the heirs of the Persians, the Parthians expanded until by 130 B.C. they had wrested Babylonia from the Seleucids. Although Parthia was essentially a native Iranian state, its inhabitants absorbed some Hellenistic culture.

The Hellenistic Contribution: The West

In the history of Western civilization there is little of greater significance than Rome's absorption of Greek civilization and its transference of that heritage to modern Europe. The stage on which this story began was the cosmopolitan Hellenistic Age, which "longed and strove for *Homonoia*, Concord between man and man . . . [and] proclaimed a conception of the world as One Great City."[33] The process by which the Roman West was Hellenized will be described in the next chapter.

Conclusion

What is it about the Greeks that leads us to speak so admiringly? The answer lies in the originality with which they met every situation. They examined each problem in a spirit of critical inquiry and sought natural rather than mythological explanations. Thus their view of life, something entirely new in the world's history, tended to be secular rather than religious, rational instead of credulous. This clear-cut, straightforward approach to life may have been the Greeks' most lasting contribution to Western civilization.

What more specific contributions have the Greeks made? A clue can be found in the large number of Greek words in the English language. For example, the terms *philosophy, logic, poetry, tragedy, aesthetics, politics, democracy, geometry, physics* reflect Greek contributions to Western civilization. Although exaggerated, there is much truth in the enthusiastic statement of the English Romantic poet Percy Bysshe Shelley, "We are all Greeks."

Suggestions for Reading

John Boardman et al., eds., *The Oxford History of the Classical World* (Oxford, 1986); Alan Samuel, *Promise of the West: The Greek World, Rome, and Judaism* (Routledge, 1988); and Peter Green, *Classical Bearings: Interpreting Ancient History and Culture* (Thames & Hudson, 1990) are valuable treatments.

P. MacKendrick, *The Greek Stones Speak** (Norton) is an account of the great archaeological discoveries in the Aegean area. See also R. Willetts, *The Civilization of Ancient Crete* (Univ. of California, 1978); E. Vermeule, *Greece in the Bronze Age** (Univ. of Chicago, 1972); and C. G. Starr, *The Origins of Greek Civilization, 1100–650 B.C.* (Knopf, 1961). R. Castledon, *The Knossos Labyrinth: A New View of the 'Palace of Minos' at Knossos* (Routledge, 1990); C. W. Blegen, *Troy and Trojans* (Praeger, 1963); and A. J. B. Wace, *Mycenae* (Princeton, 1949). M. Renault, *The King Must Die** (Bantam, 1974) is an absorbing novel set in Mycenaean times.

J. Fine, *The Ancient Greeks: A Critical History** (Harvard, 1985); A. R. Burn, *The Pelican History of Greece** (Penguin, 1966); M. I. Finley, *The Ancient Greeks** (Penguin, 1977); and Antony Andrewes, *The Greeks** (Norton, 1978) are valuable analyses. J. B. Bury and R. Meiggs, *A History of*

Greece to the Death of Alexander the Great, 4th ed. (St. Martin, 1975) is a standard detailed history. M. I. Finley, *The World of Odysseus**, 2nd ed. (Penguin, 1977) is excellent on the historical value of Homer. On the transition from oligarchy to democracy see Antony Andrewes, *The Greek Tyrants** (Humanities Press, 1956); and W. G. Forrest, *The Emergence of Greek Democracy, 800–400 B.C.** (McGraw-Hill, 1970).

Valuable special studies on politics, economics, and society include A. R. Burn, *Persia and the Greeks: The Defense of the West, 546–478 B.C.* (St. Martin, 1962); H. Mitchell, *Sparta** (Cambridge, 1952); A. H. M. Jones, *Athenian Democracy* (Johns Hopkins, 1988); M. M. Austin and P. Vidal-Naquet, *Economic and Social History of Ancient Greece** (Univ. of California, 1979); John Boardman, *The Greeks Overseas: Their Early Colonies and Trade*, 3rd ed. (Thames & Hudson, 1980); R. Meiggs, *The Athenian Empire* (Oxford, 1980); Cyril Robinson, *Everyday Life in Ancient Greece* (Greenwood, 1978); Frank Frost, *Greek Society,** 3rd ed. (Heath, 1987); M. I. Finley, *Ancient Slavery and Modern Ideology** (Penguin, 1983); H. A. Harris, *Sport in Greece and Rome* (Cornell, 1972); K. J. Dover, *Greek Homosexuality* (Harvard, 1978); and Chester Starr, *The Influence of Sea Power in Ancient History* (Oxford, 1989).

Sarah Pomeroy, *Goddesses, Whores, Wives, and Slaves: Women in Classical Antiquity** (Schocken, 1976) is a short popular account. Bonnie S. Anderson and Judith P. Zinsser, *A History of Their Own: Women in Europe from Prehistory to the Present*, Vol.1 (Harper & Row, 1988) and Mary Kinnear, *Daughters of Time: Women in the Western Tradition* (Univ. of Michigan, 1982) are outstanding recent studies. See also Eva Cantarella, *Pandora's Daughters: The Role and Status of Women in Greek and Roman Antiquity* (Johns Hopkins, 1988).

Edith Hamilton, *The Greek Way** (Norton) is a popular appreciation of the beauty and values of Hellenic literature. W. Jaeger, *Paideia: The Ideals of Greek Culture,** 2nd ed. (Galaxy, 1945) has been called "the most illuminating work on Greece." See also A. Lesky, *A History of Greek Literature** (Crowell, 1976).

W. Burkert, *Greek Religion* (Harvard, 1985) is called "the standard work for our time on the subject." See also W. F. Otto, *The Homeric Gods: The Spiritual Significance of Greek Religion** (Thames & Hudson, 1979); M. Grant, *Myths of the Greeks and Romans** (Mentor, 1964); W. K. Guthrie, *The Greeks and Their Gods** (Beacon, 1968); E. R. Dodds, *The Greeks and the Irrational** (Univ. of California); and J. Fontenrose, *The Delphic Oracle** (California, 1978).

Good introductions to Greek philosophy and science include W. K. Guthrie, *Greek Philosophers from Thales to Aristotle** (Torchbooks); F. M. Cornford, *Before and After Socrates** (Cambridge); G. E. Lloyd, *Early Greek Science: Thales to Aristotle** (Norton, 1974); *Greek Science After Aristotle** (Norton, 1974); and E. Ackernecht, *A Short History of Medicine,** rev. ed. (Johns Hopkins, 1982)

Recommended for fine arts students are J. Pollitt, *Art and Experience in Classical Greece** (Cambridge, 1972); B. R. Brown, *Anticlassicism in Greek Sculpture of the Fourth Century B.C.* (New York Univ., 1973); Martin Robertson, *A*

History of Greek Art, 2 vols. (Cambridge, 1976); A. W. Lawrence, *Greek Architecture*, rev. ed. (Viking, 1975); M. Bieber, *The Sculpture of the Hellenistic Age*, 2nd ed. (Hacker, 1980); and James H. Butler, *The Theatre and Drama of Greece and Rome* (Harper & Row, 1972).

W. W. Tarn, *Hellenistic Civilisation*,* 3rd ed. (Meridian, 1961) is a detailed survey. See also F. A. Walbank, *The Hellenistic World*,* (Harvard, 1982); J. Onians, *Art and Thought in the Hellenistic Age* (Thames & Hudson, 1979); and E. Gruen, *The Hellenistic World and the Coming of Rome*,* (California, 1986). On the career and motives of Alexander the Great, see the biographies by Peter Green (Praeger, 1970), U. Wilcken (Norton*), J. R. Hamilton (Univ. of Pittsburgh,* 1974), and W. W. Tarn (Beacon*).

*Indicates a less expensive paperbound edition.

Notes

1. Plutarch *Lives* "Pericles" 13.
2. See Leonard R. Palmer, *Mycenaeans and Minoans: Aegean Prehistory in the Light of the Linear B Tablets* (New York: Alfred A. Knopf, 1961), ch. 5, "The Last Days of Pylos."
3. Quoted in Werner Jaeger, *Paideia: The Ideals of Greek Culture* (New York: Oxford University Press, 1939), vol. 1, p. 70.
4. Plato *Laws* 5.735. In *The Dialogues of Plato*, trans. B. Jowett (New York: Random House, 1937), vol. 2, p. 503.
5. Plutarch *Lives* "Solon" 16.
6. Plutarch *Lives* "Lycurgus" 20.
7. A. R. Burn, trans., *The Pelican History of Greece* (Baltimore: Penguin Books, 1966), p. 186.
8. C. E. Robinson, *Hellas: A Short History of Ancient Greece* (Boston: Beacon Press, 1955), p. 68.
9. Thucydides *History of the Peloponnesian War* 2.65.
10. Thucydides *History of the Peloponnesian War* 2.37, 40.
11. Thucydides *History of the Peloponnesian War* 2.40, 41.
12. Thucydides *History of the Peloponnesian War* 1.23.
13. Thucydides *History of the Peloponnesian War* 2.65.
14. Thucydides *History of the Peloponnesian War* 5.105.
15. Thucydides *History of the Peloponnesian War* 6.90.
16. Herodotus *History of the Persian Wars* 7.10.
17. Quoted in M. Cary and T. J. Haarhoff, *Life and Thought in the Greek and Roman World*, 5th ed. (London: Methuen & Co., 1959), p. 200.
18. Plato *Apology* 41.
19. Plato *Phaedrus* 247.
20. Plato *Republic* 451.
21. Quoted in M. Cary and T. J. Haarhoff, *Life and Thought in the Greek and Roman World*, p.192.
22. Quoted in A. R. Burn, *The Pelican History of Greece*, p. 272.
23. Thucydides *History of the Peloponnesian War* 1.22.
24. Quoted in A. R. Burn, *The Lyric Age of Greece* (New York: St. Martin's Press, 1960), p. 166.
25. Quoted in A. R. Burn, *The Lyric Age of Greece*, p. 236.
26. Aeschylus *Agamemnon*. In *Ten Greek Plays*, trans. Gilbert Murray and ed. Lane Cooper (New York: Oxford University Press, 1929), p. 96.
27. Joseph Wood Krutch, *The Modern Temper* (New York: Harcourt Brace Jovanovich, 1956), p. 84.
28. Sophocles *Medea*, trans. Gilbert Murray, *Ten Greek Plays*, pp. 320, 321.
29. Aristophanes *The Wasps* 1065–1070 in *Aristophanes: The Frogs and Other Plays*, trans. David Barrett (Baltimore: Penguin Books, 1964), p.77.
30. Theocritus *Idyl* 15, trans. Nels Bailkey.
31. Quoted in *The Cambridge Ancient History* (Cambridge: The University Press, 1936), vol. 11, p. 696.
32. Moschus *Idyl* 9, trans. Andrew Lang.
33. G. Murray, *Hellenism and the Modern World* (Boston: Beacon Press, 1953), pp. 56–57.

Chapter 3

The Grandeur That Was Rome

The Roman World 509 B.C. to A.D. 180

A s the Athenians saw the symbol of their city-state's democracy and culture in the rock-jutting Acropolis, so the Romans viewed the Forum as the symbol of imperial grandeur. Temples were to be found there, but in contrast to the Acropolis, the Forum was dominated by secular buildings—basilicas used for judicial and other public business; the nearby Colosseum, used for gladiatorial shows; and the great palaces of the emperors rising on the neighboring Palatine Hill. While the Acropolis was crowned with statues to Athena, the Forum gloried in triumphal arches and columns commemorating military conquests. Rome was the capital of a world-state, extending from Britain to the Euphrates, and its citizens were proud of their imperial mission.

Although the buildings in the Forum appear fundamentally Greek in style, they are more monumental and sumptuous. Here, then, are two clues to an understanding of the Romans: they borrowed much from the Greeks and others, and they modified what they took.

Rome was the great intermediary—the bridge over which passed the rich contributions of the ancient Near East and especially Greece, to form the basis of modern Western civilization. The Romans replaced the anarchy of the Hellenistic Age with law and order and embraced the intellectual and artistic legacy of the conquered Greeks. As Rome's empire expanded, this legacy was spread westward throughout most of Europe.

Yet Rome was more than an intermediary, for it made many important and original contributions to our Western culture. Throughout a history that led from a simple farming community in the plain of Latium to a strong state that

became the master of the Mediterranean world as well as Gaul, Britain, and part of Germany, the Romans met one challenge after another with practicality and efficiency. In the shadows of its marching legions went engineers and architects, so that today, scattered throughout the lands that once were part of the Roman world, the remains of roads, walls, baths, basilicas, amphitheaters, and aqueducts offer convincing evidence of the Romans' practical skills. Most lasting and far-reaching of all were Roman law and administration—for example, the separation of powers (magistrates, Senate, and assembly) and checks and balances in Rome's republican constitution were models for the U.S. Constitution.

Rome to 509 B.C.

The history of Rome extends from 753 B.C., the traditional date for the founding of the city by Romulus, Rome's legendary first king, to A.D. 476 when another Romulus, Romulus Augustulus, the last Roman emperor in the West, was deposed. The first period in this span of more than a thousand years ended in 509 B.C. with the expulsion of the seventh and last of Rome's kings, Tarquin the Proud, and the establishment of a republic.

Geography and Early Settlers of Italy

Geography did much to shape the course of events in Italy. The Italian peninsula is 600 miles long and about four times the size of Greece and two-thirds that of California. A great mountainous backbone, the Apennines, runs down

ROMAN ITALY BEFORE AUGUSTUS

Rhine R.

Rhone

A L P S

Danube

Drava

Sava

R.

R.

VENETIA

TRANSPADANE GAUL

Po R.

LIGURIA

•Parma

CISPADANE GAUL

•Genoa

APENNINE

UMBRIAN MOUNTAINS

Pisa•

Arno R.

•Florentia

Rubicon R.

ETRURIA

•Spoletium

Tiber R.

CORSICA

ADRIATIC SEA

SAMNIUM

•Rome

Ostia•

LATIUM

APULIA

CAMPANIA

MT. VESUVIUS

•Pompeii

Brundisium•

Tarentum•

SARDINIA

LUCANIA

TYRRHENIAN SEA

BRUTTIUM

MEDITERRANEAN

•Messina

MT. ETNA

SICILY

SEA

•Syracuse

•Carthage

AFRICA

0   50   100

almost the entire peninsula. But the land is not so rugged as Greece, and the mountains do not constitute a barrier to political unification. Unlike in Greece, a network of roads could be built to link the regions. Furthermore, the plain of Latium and its city, Rome, occupied a strategic position. It was easy to defend, and once the Romans had begun a career of conquest, they occupied a central position which made it difficult for their enemies to unite successfully against them. The strategic position of Rome was repeated on a larger scale by Italy itself. Italy juts into the Mediterranean almost in the center of that great sea. Once Italy was unified, its commanding position invited it to unify the entire Mediterranean world (see map, p. 70).

Italy's best valleys and harbors are on the western slopes of the Apennines. The Italian peninsula faced west, not east. For a long time, therefore, culture in Italy lagged behind that of Greece because cultural contact was long delayed.

Both Greeks and Romans were offshoots of a common Indo-European stock, and settlement of the Greek and Italian peninsulas followed broadly parallel stages. Between 2000 and 1000 B.C., when Indo-European peoples invaded the Aegean world, a western wing of this nomadic migration filtered into the Italian peninsula, then inhabited by indigenous Neolithic tribes. The first invaders, skilled in the use of copper and bronze, settled in the Po valley. Another wave of Indo-Europeans, equipped with iron weapons and tools, followed; in time the newer and older settlers intermingled and spread throughout the peninsula. One group, the Latins, settled in the plain of Latium, in the lower valley of the Tiber River.

For ages history had bypassed the western Mediterranean, but it was soon to become an increasingly significant area. During the ninth century B.C. the Etruscans, a non-Indo-European people who probably came from Asia Minor, brought the first city-state civilization to Italy. Expanding from the west coast up to the Po valley and south to the Bay of Naples, the Etruscans organized the backward Italic peoples into a loose confederation of Etruscan-dominated city-states. After 750 B.C. Greek colonists migrated to southern Italy and Sicily, where they served as a protective buffer against powerful and prosperous Carthage, a Phoenician colony established in North Africa about 800 B.C. Yet the future was not to belong to these various invaders but to an insignificant village on the Tiber River, then in the shadow of Etruscan expansion. This was Rome, destined to be ruler of the ancient world.

Rome's Origins

According to ancient legend, Rome was founded in 753 B.C. by the twin brothers Romulus and Remus, who were saved from death in their infancy by a she-wolf who sheltered and suckled them. According to Virgil's *Aeneid* Romulus' ancestor was Aeneas, a Trojan who after the fall of Troy founded a settlement in Latium. The Aeneas story, invented by Greek mythmakers, pleased the Romans because it linked their history with that of the Greeks.

Turning from fable to fact, modern scholars believe that in the eighth century B.C. the inhabitants of some small Latin settlements on hills in the Tiber valley united and established a common meeting place, the Forum, around which the city of Rome grew. Situated at a convenient place for fording the river and protected from invaders by the hills and marshes, Rome was strategically located. Nevertheless, the expanding Etruscans conquered Rome about 625 B.C., and under their tutelage Rome first became an important city-state.

Some aspects of Etruscan culture were borrowed from the Greek colonies in southern Italy, and much of this, including the alphabet, was passed on to the conquered Romans. (Etruscan writing can be read phonetically but not understood.) From their Etruscan overlords, the Romans acquired some of their gods and the practice of prophesying by examining animal entrails and the flight of birds. From the conquerors, too, the conquered learned the art of building (especially the arch), the practice of making statues of their gods, and the staging of gladiatorial combats. Even the name *Roma* appears to be an Etruscan word.

The Roman Monarchy, 753–509 B.C.

Rome's political growth followed a line of development similar to that of the Greek city-states:

limited monarchy of the sort described by Homer, oligarchy, democracy, and, finally, the permanent dictatorship of the Roman emperors. We shall see that in moving from oligarchy to democracy, the Romans, unlike the Greeks, succeeded in avoiding the intermediate stage of tyranny.

According to tradition, early Rome was ruled by kings elected by the people. After the Etruscan conquest, this elective system continued, although the last three of Rome's seven kings were Etruscan. The king's executive power, both civil and military, was called the *imperium*, which was symbolized by an ax bound in a bundle of rods *(fasces)*. In the 1920s the *fasces* provided both the symbol and name for Mussolini's political creed of fascism.

Although the *imperium* was conferred by a popular assembly made up of all arms-bearing citizens, the king turned for advice to a council of nobles called the Senate. Senators had lifelong tenure, and they and their families belonged to the patrician class. The other class of Romans, the plebeians, or commoners, included small farmers, artisans, and many clients, or dependents, of patrician landowners. In return for a livelihood, the clients gave their patrician patrons political support in the assembly.

The Early Republic, 509–133 B.C.: Domestic Affairs

The history of the Roman Republic can be divided into two distinct periods. During the first, from 509 to 133 B.C., two themes are dominant: a constitutional change from oligarchy to democracy, the result of the gradual extension of political and social equality to the plebeian lower class; and the expansion of Rome, first in Italy and then in the Mediterranean area.

Establishment of the Republic

In 509 B.C., the patricians expelled the last Etruscan king, Tarquin the Proud, claiming that he had acted despotically. (According to the Roman historian Livy, Tarquin was called the Proud because he "was the first king of Rome to break the established tradition of consulting the Senate on all matters of public business, and to govern by the mere authority of himself and his household.") The patricians replaced the monarchy with an oligarchy that, apparently to gain the support of the plebeians, they called a republic *(res publica,* "commonwealth"). The *imperium* was transferred to two new magistrates, called *consuls.* Elected annually from the patrician class, the consuls invariably exercised power in its interest. In the event of war or serious domestic emergency, a *dictator* could be substituted for the two consuls, but he was given absolute power for six months only.

Struggle for Equal Rights

For more than two centuries following the establishment of the Republic, the plebeians struggled for political and social equality. Outright civil war was averted by the willingness, however reluctant and delayed, of the patricians to compromise. This largely explains why it was unnecessary for the plebeians to resort to tyrants to help them gain their goals, as had happened in the Greek city-states. Much of the plebeians' success in this struggle was due to their having been granted the right to organize themselves as a corporate body capable of collective action. (Rome's constant wars gave the plebeians, who were indispensable in filling the ranks of Rome's conscript army, great bargaining power.) This concession, granted by the Senate early in the fifth century B.C. after the plebeians threatened to leave Rome and found a city elsewhere, established a sort of state within a state known as the *Concilium Plebis* ("gathering of the plebeians"), which was presided over by plebeian leaders called *tribunes.* The tribunes also received the right to stop unjust or oppressive acts of the patrician consuls and Senate by uttering the word *veto* ("I forbid").

The next major concession was in the field of law. Because the consuls often interpreted Rome's unwritten customary law to suit patrician interests, the plebeians demanded that it be written down and made available for all to see. As a result, about 450 B.C. the law was inscribed on twelve tablets of bronze and set up publicly in the Forum. This Law of the Twelve Tables was the first landmark in the long history of Roman law, and Roman schoolchildren were required to memorize it.

Livy: Horatius at the Bridge

Livy relates how one man saved Rome from reconquest by the Etruscans, about 506 B.C.

On the approach of the Etruscan army, the Romans abandoned their farmsteads and moved into the city. Garrisons were posted. In some sections the city walls seemed sufficient protection, in others the barrier of the Tiber. The most vulnerable point was the wooden bridge, and the Etruscans would have crossed it and forced an entrance into the city, had it not been for the courage of one man, Horatius Cocles— that great soldier whom the fortune of Rome gave to be her shield on that day of peril. . . . Proudly he [Horatius] took his stand at the outer end of the bridge; conspicuous amongst the rout of fugitives, sword and shield ready for action, he prepared himself for close combat, one man against an army. The advancing enemy paused in sheer astonishment at such reckless courage. Two other men, Spurius Lartius and Titus Herminius, both aristocrats with a fine military record, were ashamed to leave Horatius alone, and with their support he won through the first few minutes of desperate danger. Soon, however, he forced them to save themselves and leave him; for little was now left of the bridge, and the demolition squads were calling them back before it was too late. Once more Horatius stood alone; with defiance in his eyes he confronted the Etruscan chivalry, challenging one after another to single combat, and mocking them all as tyrants' slaves who, careless of their own liberty, were coming to destroy the liberty of others. For a while they hung back, each waiting for his neighbour to make the first move, until shame at the unequal battle drove them to action, and with a fierce cry they hurled their spears at the solitary figure which barred their way. Horatius caught the missiles on his shield and, resolute as ever, straddled the bridge and held his ground. The Etruscans moved forward, and would have thrust him aside by the sheer weight of numbers, but their advance was suddenly checked by the crash of the falling bridge and the simultaneous shout of triumph from the Roman soldiers who had done their work in time. The Etruscans could only stare in bewilderment as Horatius, with a prayer to Father Tiber to bless him and his sword, plunged fully armed into the water and swam, through the missiles which fell thick about him, safely to the other side where his friends were waiting to receive him. It was a noble piece of work—legendary, maybe, but destined to be celebrated in story through the years to come.

From the translation by Aubrey De Sélincourt, *Livy, The Early History of Rome* (Harmondsworth, England: Penguin Books, 1960), Book II, Chapter 10.

In time the plebeians acquired other fundamental rights and safeguards: they secured the right to appeal a death sentence imposed by a consul and to be retried before the popular assembly; marriage between patricians and plebeians, prohibited by the Law of the Twelve Tables, was legalized; and the enslavement of citizens for debt was abolished.

Little by little the plebeian class acquired more power in the government. In 367 B.C. one consulship was reserved for the plebeians, and before the end of the century plebeians were eligible to hold other important magistracies that the patricians had created in the meantime. Among these new offices, whose powers originally had been held by the consuls, were the *praetor* (in charge of the administration of justice), *quaestor* (treasurer), and *censor* (supervisor of public morals and the letting-of-state contracts). The right to hold high political offices proved to be a stepping stone to the Senate, and some rich plebeians succeeded in gaining entry to that august body.

The long struggle for equality ended in 287 B.C. when the *Concilium Plebis* was recognized as a constitutional body, henceforth known as the Tribal Assembly, with the right to pass laws that were binding on all citizens, patricians as well as plebeians. The plebeians demanded this right because of the undemocratic organization and procedure of the older popular assemblies, which the patricians had been able to control. The Roman Republic was now technically a democracy, although in actual practice a senatorial oligarchy of patricians and rich plebeians continued to control the state. Having gained political and social equality, the plebeians were usually willing to allow the more experienced Senate to run the government from this time until 133 B.C., a period of almost constant warfare.

After 287 B.C. conflict in Roman society gradually assumed a new form. Heretofore, the issue had been primarily social and political inequality between the hereditary classes of patricians and plebeians. After equality was achieved, many rich plebeians were elected to the highest offices and became members of an expanded senatorial aristocracy. This new Roman "establishment" was prepared to guard its privileges even more tenaciously than the old patricians had done. This became evident in 133 B.C. when a popular leader arose to challenge the establishment (see p. 79). But by this time the Roman

The relief on this sarcophagus depicts a Roman youth reciting his lessons. From an early age, Roman children learned respect for Roman laws, customs, and virtues.

populace had lost many of the qualities that had characterized the citizens of the early Republic.

Society and Religion

The basic unit of early Roman society was the family. The father's power was absolute, and strict discipline was imposed to instill in children those virtues to which the Romans attached particular importance—loyalty, courage, self-control, and respect for laws and ancestral customs. The Romans of the early Republic were stern, hard-working, and practical. Cato the Elder (d. 149 B.C.), for example, took inspiration from frequent visits to view the small farm and humble cottage of a former consul, who

though he had become the greatest of Romans, had subdued the most warlike nations, and driven Pyrrhus out of Italy, nevertheless tilled this little patch of ground with his own hands and occupied this cottage, after three triumphs. Here it was that the ambassadors of the Samnites once found him seated at his hearth cooking turnips, and offered him much gold; but he dismissed them, saying that a man whom such a meal satisfied had no need of gold.[1]

In contrast to the frequency of divorce in the late Republic, marriage in the early Republic was viewed as a lifelong union based on mutual affection. An early epitaph (second century B.C.) reads:

Stranger, what I say is short, stay and read. Here is the unbeautiful grave of a beautiful woman. Her parents named her Claudia. She loved her husband with her whole heart. She bore two sons: one of whom she left alive on earth, the other she buried in the earth. Her speech was gay, but her bearing seemly. She kept the home. She made the wool. I have spoken. Go away.[2]

The religion of the early Romans had little connection with ethics, and views concerning life after death were very vague. Religious practices were confined to placating the spirits *(numina)* of the family and the state by the repetition of complicated formulas, or spells. Mispronunciation of even a single syllable was enough to cause the spell to lose its power. Under Etruscan influence the major spirits were personified. Thus the sky-spirit Jupiter became the patron god of Rome; Mars, spirit of vegetation, became god of war; and Janus, whose temple doors remained open when the army was away at war, was originally the spirit of the city gate.

While early Roman religion had little to do with morals, it had much to do with morale. It strengthened family solidarity and enhanced a patriotic devotion to the state and its gods. But the early Romans' respect for hard work, frugality, and family and state gods was to be undermined by Rome's expansion in Italy and over much of the Mediterranean area during the early Republic.

The Early Republic, 509–133 B.C.: Foreign Affairs

The growth of Rome from a small city-state to the dominant power in the Mediterranean world in less than 400 years (509–133 B.C.) is a remarkable success story. Roman expansion was not deliberately planned; rather, it was the result of dealing with unsettled conditions, first in Italy and then abroad, which were thought to threaten Rome's security. Rome always claimed that its wars were defensive.

By 270 B.C. the first phase of Roman expansion was over. Ringed by hostile peoples— Etruscans in the north, predatory hill tribes in central Italy, and Greeks in the south—Rome had subdued them all after long, agonizing effort and found itself master of all Italy south of the Po valley. (After Rome's fall in the fifth century A.D., Italy was not again unified until 1870.) In the process the Romans developed the administrative skills and traits of character—both fair-minded and ruthless—that would lead to the acquisition of an empire with possessions on three continents by 133 B.C.

Roman Conquest of Italy

Soon after ousting their Etruscan overlords in 509 B.C., Rome and the Latin League, composed of other Latin peoples in Latium, entered into a defensive alliance against the Etruscans. This new combination was so successful that by the beginning of the fourth century B.C. it had become the chief power in central Italy. But at this time (390 B.C.) a major disaster almost ended the history of Rome. A horde of marauding Celts, called Gauls by the Romans, invaded Italy from central Europe, wiped out the Roman army, and almost destroyed the city by fire. The elderly members of the Senate, according to the traditional account, sat awaiting their fate with quiet dignity before they were massacred. Only a garrison on the Capitoline Hill held out under siege. After seven months and the receipt of a huge ransom in gold, the Gauls retired. The stubborn Romans rebuilt their city and protected it with a stone wall, part of which still stands. They also remodeled their army by replacing the solid line of fixed spears of the phalanx formation, borrowed from the Etruscans and Greeks, with the much more maneuverable small units of 120 men, called *maniples*, armed with javelins instead of spears. It would be 800 years before another barbarian army would be able to conquer the city of Rome.

The Latin League grew alarmed at Rome's increasing strength, and war broke out between the former allies. With Rome's victory in 338 B.C., the League was dissolved, and the Latin cities were forced to sign individual treaties with Rome. Thus the same year that saw the rise of Macedonia over Greece also saw the rise of a new power in Italy.

Border clashes with aggressive highland Samnite tribes led to three fiercely fought Samnite wars and the extension of Rome's frontiers to the Greek colonies in southern Italy by 290 B.C. Fearing Roman conquest, the Greeks prepared for war and called in the Hellenistic Greek king, Pyrrhus of Epirus, who dreamed of becoming a second Alexander the Great. Pyrrhus' war elephants, unknown in Italy, twice routed the Romans, but at so heavy a cost that such a triumph is still called a "Pyrrhic victory." When a third battle failed to induce the Romans to make peace, Pyrrhus is reported to have remarked, "The discipline of these barbarians is not barbarous," and returned to his homeland. By 270 B.C. the Roman army had subdued the Greek city-states in southern Italy.

Treatment of Conquered Peoples

Instead of slaughtering or enslaving their defeated foes, the Romans treated them fairly, in time creating a strong loyalty to Rome throughout the peninsula. Roman citizenship was a prized possession that was not extended to all peoples on the peninsula until the first century B.C. Most defeated states were required to sign a treaty of alliance with Rome, which bound them to adhere to Rome's foreign policy and to supply troops for the Roman army. No tribute was required, and each allied state retained local self-government. Rome did, however, annex about one fifth of the conquered lands, on which nearly thirty colonies were established by 250 B.C.

The First Punic War

After 270 B.C. only Carthage remained as Rome's rival in the West. Much more wealthy and populous than Rome, with a magnificent navy that controlled the western Mediterranean and with a domain that included the northern coast of Africa, Sardinia, Corsica, western Sicily, and parts of Spain. Carthage seemed more than a match for Rome. But Carthage was governed by a commercial aristocracy which hired mercenaries to do the fighting. In the long run, the lack of a loyal body of free citizens and allies, such as Rome had, proved to be Carthage's fatal weakness.

The First Punic War (from *punicus*, Latin for "Phoenician") broke out in 264 B.C. when Rome sought to oust a Carthaginian force that had occupied Messina on the northeastern tip of Sicily just across from Roman Italy. According to Polybius, a Hellenistic Greek historian, the Romans "felt it was absolutely necessary not to let Messina fall, or allow the Carthaginians to secure what would be like a bridge to enable them to cross into Italy."[3] Rome and its Italian allies lost 200,000 men in disastrous naval engagements before Carthage sued for peace in 241 B.C. Sicily, Sardinia, and Corsica were annexed as the first provinces of Rome's overseas empire, governed and taxed—in contrast to Rome's allies in Italy—by Roman officials called *proconsuls*.

The Contest with Hannibal

Thwarted by this defeat, Carthage concentrated upon enlarging its empire in Spain. Rome's determination to prevent this led to the greatest and most difficult war in Roman history. While both powers jockeyed for position, a young Carthaginian general, Hannibal, precipitated the Second Punic War by attacking Saguntum, a Spanish town claimed by Rome as an ally. Rome declared war, and Hannibal, seizing the initiative, in 218 B.C. led an army of about 40,000 men, 9000 cavalry troops, and a detachment of African elephants across the Alps into Italy. Although the crossing had cost him nearly half of his men and almost all of his elephants, Hannibal defeated the Romans three times within three years.

Hannibal's forces never matched those of the Romans in numbers. At Cannae, for example, where Hannibal won his greatest victory, some 70,000 Romans were wiped out by barely 50,000 Carthaginians. On the whole, Rome's allies remained loyal—a testimony to Rome's generous and statesmanlike treatment of its Italian subjects. Because the Romans controlled the seas, Hannibal received little aid from Carthage. Thus Hannibal was unable to inflict a mortal blow against the Romans.

The Romans finally found a general, Scipio, who was Hannibal's match in military strategy and who was bold enough to invade Africa. Forced to return home after fifteen years spent on Italian soil, Hannibal clashed with Scipio's legions at Zama, where the Carthaginians suffered a complete defeat (see map, p. 77). The power of Carthage was broken forever by a harsh treaty imposed in 201 B.C. Carthage was forced to pay a huge indemnity, disarm its forces, and turn Spain over to the Romans. Hannibal sought asylum in the Seleucid empire where he stirred up anti-Roman sentiment.

Roman Intervention in the East

The defeat of Carthage left Rome free to turn eastward and settle a score with Philip V of Macedonia. Fearful of the new colossus that had risen in the west, Philip had allied himself with Hannibal during the darkest days of the war. Now, in 200 B.C., Rome was ready to act, following an appeal from Pergamum and Rhodes for aid in protecting the smaller Hellenistic states from Philip, who was advancing in the Aegean, and from the Seleucid emperor, who was moving into Asia Minor. The heavy Macedonian phalanxes were no match for the mobile Roman legions, and in 197 B.C. Philip was soundly defeated. His dreams of empire were ended when Rome deprived him of his warships and military bases in Greece. The Romans then proclaimed the independence of Greece and were eulogized by the grateful Greeks for playing a role similar to that assumed by Americans twenty centuries later:

> *There was one people in the world which would fight for others' liberties at its own cost, to its own peril, and with its own toil, not limiting its guaranties of freedom to its neighbors, to men of the immediate vicinity, or to countries that lay close at hand, but ready to cross the sea that there might be no unjust empire anywhere and that everywhere justice, right, and law might prevail.*[4]

A few years later Rome declared war on the Seleucid emperor who had moved into Greece, urged on by Hannibal and a few greedy Greek states that resented Rome's refusal to dismember Macedonia. The Romans forced the emperor to vacate Greece and Asia Minor, pay a huge indemnity, and give up his warships and war elephants. The Seleucids were checked again in 168 B.C. when a Roman ultimatum halted their invasion of Egypt, which became a Roman protectorate. A year later Rome supported the Jews in their successful revolt against the Seleucids by addressing this message to the Seleucid ruler:

> *Wherefore hast thou made thy yoke heavy upon our friends and confederates the Jews? If therefore they complain any more against*

THE ROMAN WORLD 133 B.C.

☐ Roman Territories

◼ Allies Of Rome By Treaty

thee, we will do them justice, and fight with thee by sea and by land.[5]

Most of the East was now a Roman protectorate, the result of a policy in which Roman self-interest was mingled with idealism. But Roman idealism turned sour when anti-Romanism became widespread in Greece, particularly among the radical masses who resented Rome's support of conservative governments and the status quo in general. (The Romans, for example, helped crush a socialist revolution in Sparta.) The new policy was revealed in 146 B.C. when, after many Greeks had supported an attempted Macedonian revival, Rome destroyed Corinth, a hotbed of anti-Romanism, as an object lesson. (It is not coincidental that the predominantly working-class population of Corinth was anti-Roman, and that later, after the city was resettled, they would welcome Paul "teaching Christ" for a lengthy eighteen months.) The Romans also supported oligarchic factions in all Greek states, and placed Greece under the watchful eye of the governor of Macedonia, which had been made a Roman province two years earlier.

Destruction of Carthage

In the West, meanwhile, Rome's hardening policy led to suspicion of Carthage's reviving prosperity and to a demand by extremists for war—*Carthago delenda est* ("Carthage must be obliterated"). Treacherously provoking the Third Punic War, the Romans besieged Carthage, which resisted heroically for three years. They destroyed the city in 146 B.C., the same year they destroyed Corinth, and annexed the territory as a province.

Rome, Supreme in the Ancient World

In 133 B.C. Rome acquired its first province in Asia when the king of Pergamum, dying without heir, bequeathed his kingdom to Rome. Apparently he feared that the discontented masses would revolt after his death unless Rome, with its reputation for maintaining law and order in the interest of the propertied classes, took over. Rome accepted the bequest and then spent the next three years suppressing a proletarian revolution in the new province called Asia. With provinces on three continents—Europe, Africa, and Asia-the once obscure Roman Republic was now supreme in the ancient world.

The Late Republic, 133–30 B.C.

The century following 133 B.C., during which Rome's frontiers reached the Euphrates and the Rhine, witnessed the failure of the Republic to solve the problems that were the by-products of the acquisition of an empire.

Effects of Roman Expansion

The political history of Rome thus far has consisted of two dominant themes: the gradual extension of equal rights for all citizens and the expansion of Roman dominion over the Mediterranean world. Largely as a result of this expansion, important social and economic problems faced Rome by roughly the midpoint of the second century B.C.

One of the most pressing problems was the decline in the number of small landowners, whose spirit had made Rome great. Burdened by frequent military service, their farm buildings destroyed by Hannibal, and unable to compete with the cheap grain imported from the new Roman province of Sicily, small farmers sold out and moved to Rome. Here they joined the unemployed, discontented proletariat, so-called because their only contribution was *proles*, "children." The proletariat comprised a majority of the citizens in the city.

On the other hand, improved farming methods learned from Greeks and Carthaginians encouraged rich aristocrats to buy more and more land. Abandoning the cultivation of grain, they introduced large-scale scientific production of olive oil and wine, or of sheep and cattle. This change was especially profitable because an abundance of cheap slaves from conquered areas was available to work on the estates. These large slave plantations, called *latifundia*, were now common in many parts of Italy.

The land problem was further complicated by the government's practice of leasing part of the territory acquired in the conquest of the Italian peninsula to anyone willing to pay a percentage of the crop or animals raised on it. Only the patricians or wealthy plebeians could afford to lease large tracts of this public land, and in time they treated it as if it were their own property. Plebeian protests led to an attempt to limit the holdings of a single individual to 320 acres of public land, but the law enacted for that purpose was never enforced.

Corruption in the government was another mark of the growing degeneracy of the Roman Republic. Provincial officials seized opportunities for lucrative graft, and a new class of Roman businessmen scrambled selfishly for the profitable state contracts to supply the armies, collect taxes and loan money in the provinces, and lease state-owned mines and forests. An early example of corrupt business practices occurred during the Second Punic War. According to the Roman historian Livy, "Two scoundrels, taking advantage of the assumption by the state of all risks from tempest in the case of goods carried by sea to armies in the field," fabricated false accounts of shipwrecks. "Their method was to load small and more or less worthless cargoes into old, rotten vessels, sink them at sea . . . , and then, in reporting the loss, enormously to exaggerate the value of the cargoes." When the swindle was reported to the Senate, it took no action because it "did not wish at a time of such national danger to make enemies of the capitalists."[6]

Although in theory the government was a democracy, in practice it remained a senatorial oligarchy. Wars tend to strengthen the executive power in a state, and in Rome the Senate had such power. Even the tribunes, guardians of the people's rights, became for the most part puppets of the Senate. Thus by the middle of the second century B.C., the government was in the hands of a wealthy, self-seeking Senate, which became increasingly incapable of coping with the problems of governing a world-state. Ordinary citizens were for the most part impoverished and landless; and Rome swarmed with fortune hunters, imported slaves, unemployed farmers, and discontented war veterans. The poverty of the many, coupled with the opulence of the few, hastened the decay of the old Roman traits of discipline, simplicity, and respect for authority.

The next century (133–30 B.C.) saw Rome convulsed by civil strife, which led to the establishment of a permanent dictatorship and the end of the Republic. The Senate was noticeably inefficient in carrying on foreign conflicts, but its most serious weakness was its inability to solve the economic and social problems following in the wake of Rome's conquests.

Reform Movement of the Gracchi

An awareness of Rome's profound social and economic problems led to the reform program of an idealistic young aristocrat named Tiberius Gracchus. His reforming zeal was the product of the newly imported liberal learning of Greece and an awareness that the old Roman character and way of life were fast slipping away. He sought to arrest Roman decline by restoring the backbone of the old Roman society—the small landowner. Supported by a few liberal Senators, Tiberius was elected tribune for the year 133 B.C. at the age of twenty-nine.

Tiberius proposed to the Tribal Assembly that the act limiting the holding of public land to 320 acres per person be reenacted. Much of the public land would in the future be held by the

To protect the poor during times of famine, Gaius Gracchus initiated a relief plan for the distribution of free food. This ticket entitled the bearer to a ration of grain.

present occupants and their descendants as private property, but the surplus was to be confiscated and allotted to landless Roman citizens. In his address to the assembly Tiberius noted that

> *it is with lying lips that their commanders exhort the soldiers in their battles to defend sepulchres and shrines from the enemy; . . . they fight and die to support others in wealth and luxury, and though they are styled masters of the world, they have not a single clod of earth that is their own.*[7]

When it became evident that the Tribal Assembly would adopt Tiberius' proposal, the Senate induced one of the other tribunes to veto the measure. On the ground that a tribune who opposed the will of the people thereby forfeited his office, Tiberius took a fateful—and, the Senate claimed, unconstitutional—step by having the assembly depose the tribune in question. The agrarian bill was then passed.

To ensure the implementation of his agrarian reform, Tiberius again violated custom by standing for reelection after completing his one-year term. Claiming that he sought to make himself king, partisans of the Senate murdered Tiberius and 300 of his followers. The Republic's failure at this point to solve its problems without bloodshed stands in striking contrast to its earlier history of peaceful reform.

Tiberius' work was taken up by his younger brother, Gaius Gracchus, who was elected tribune for 123 B.C. In addition to the reallocation of public land, Gaius proposed establishing Roman colonies in southern Italy and on the site of Carthage. To protect the poor against speculation in the grain market (especially in times of famine), Gaius committed the government to the purchase, storage, and subsequent distribution of wheat to the urban masses at about half the former market price. Unfortunately, what Gaius intended as a relief measure later became a dole, whereby free food was distributed—all too often for the advancement of astute politicians—to the entire proletariat.

Another of Gaius' proposals would have granted citizenship to Rome's Italian allies, who were now being mistreated by Roman officials. This proposal cost Gaius the support of the Roman proletariat, which did not wish to share the privileges of citizenship or endanger its control of the Tribal Assembly. Consequently, in 121 B.C.

Gaius failed to be reelected to a third term and the Senate again resorted to force. It decreed what is today called martial law by authorizing the consuls to take any action deemed necessary "to protect the state and suppress the tyrants." Three thousand of Gaius' followers were arrested and executed, a fate Gaius avoided by committing suicide.

The Senate had shown that it had no intention of initiating needed domestic reforms, or of allowing others to do so, and the Gracchi's deaths were ominous portents of the way the Republic would decide its internal disputes.

In foreign affairs, too, the Senate soon demonstrated its incapability. Rome was forced to grant citizenship to its Italian allies after the Senate's failure to deal with their grievances goaded them into revolt (90–88 B.C.). Other blunders led to the first of the civil wars that destroyed the Republic.

The First Civil War: Marius vs. Sulla

Between 111 and 105 B.C. Roman armies, dispatched by the Senate and commanded by senators, failed to protect Roman equestrians (capitalists) in North Africa. Nor were they able to prevent Germanic tribes from overrunning southern Gaul, now a Roman province, and threatening Italy itself. Accusing the Senate of lethargy and incompetence in directing Rome's foreign affairs, the capitalists and common people joined together to elect Gaius Marius consul in 107 B.C., and the Tribal Assembly commissioned him to raise an army and deal with the foreign danger. Marius first pacified North Africa and then crushed the first German threat to Rome. In the process he created a new-style Roman army that was destined to play a major role in the turbulent history of the late Republic.

Unlike the old Roman army, which was composed of conscripts who owned their own land and thought of themselves as loyal citizens of the Republic, the new army created by Marius was recruited from landless citizens for long terms of service. These professional soldiers identified their own interests with those of their commanders, to whom they swore loyalty and looked to for bonuses of land or money after the Senate had irresponsibly refused their requests. Thus the character of the army changed from a militia

In this relief from the Column of Marcus Aurelius, Germans loyal to Rome are shown executing rebel Germans under the watch of the Roman cavalry.

of draftees to a career service in which loyalty to the state was no longer paramount. Aspiring generals were in a position to use their military power to seize the government.

In 88 B.C. the ambitious king of Pontus in Asia Minor, encouraged by the growing anti-Roman sentiment in the province of Asia and in Greece caused by corrupt governors, tax collectors, and money lenders, declared war on Rome. The Senate ordered Cornelius Sulla, an able general and a staunch supporter of the Senate's prerogatives, to march east. As a countermove, the Tribal Assembly chose Marius for the eastern command. In effect both the Senate and the Tribal Assembly, whose power the Gracchi had revived, claimed to be the ultimate authority in the state. The result was the first of a series of civil wars between rival generals, each claiming to champion the cause of either the Senate or Tribal Assembly. The first civil war ended in a complete victory for Sulla, who in 82 B.C. was appointed by the Senate to serve for an unlimited term as "dictator for the revision of the constitution."

Sulla set out to restore the preeminence of the Senate. He drastically curtailed the powers of the tribunes and Tribal Assembly, giving the Senate the control of legislation it had enjoyed 200 years before. Having massacred several thousand of the opposition, Sulla, was convinced that his work would be permanent, and in 79 B.C. he voluntarily resigned his dictatorship. His reactionary changes, however, were not to last.

The Second Civil War: Pompey vs. Caesar

The first of the civil wars and its aftermath increased factionalism and discontent and nursed the ambitions of individuals eager for personal power. The first to come forward was Pompey, who had won fame as a military leader. In 70 B.C. he was elected consul. Although he was a former partisan of Sulla, he courted the populace by repealing Sulla's laws curtailing the power of the tribunes and Tribal Assembly. Pompey then put an end to anarchy in the East caused by piracy (the result of the Senate's neglect of the Roman navy), the continuing threat of the king of Pontus, and the death throes of the Seleucid Empire. New Roman provinces and client states set up by Pompey brought order eastward as far as the Euphrates (see map below). These included the province of Syria—the last remnant of the once vast Seleucid Empire—and the client state of Judea, supervised by the governor of Syria.

Still another strong man made his appearance in 59 B.C., when Julius Caesar allied himself politically with Pompey and was elected consul. Following his consulship, Caesar spent nine years conquering Gaul on the pretext of protecting the Gauls from the Germans across the Rhine, where he accumulated a fortune in plunder and trained a loyal army of veterans. During his absence from Rome, he cannily kept his name before the citizens by publishing a lucidly written account of his military feats, *Commentaries on the Gallic War*.

Caesar's conquest of Gaul was to have tremendous consequences for the course of Western civilization, for its inhabitants quickly assimilated Roman culture. Consequently, when the Roman Empire collapsed in the West in the fifth century A.D., Romanized Gaul—or France—emerged before long as the center of medieval civilization.

Jealous of Caesar's achievements in Gaul and fearful of his growing power, Pompey conspired with the Senate to ruin him. When the Senate demanded in 49 B.C. that Caesar disband his army, he crossed the Rubicon, the river in northern Italy that formed the boundary of Caesar's province. By crossing the Rubicon—a phrase

THE GROWTH OF THE ROMAN EMPIRE 44 B.C. TO 180 A.D.

Acquired before the Death of Caesar, 44 B.C.
Acquired before the Death of Augustus, 14 A.D.
Acquired before the Death of Marcus Aurelius, 180 A.D.

employed today for any step that commits a person to a given course of action—Caesar in effect declared war on Pompey and the Senate. He marched on Rome while Pompey and most of the Senate fled to Greece, where Caesar defeated them at Pharsala. "They would have it so" was Caesar's curt comment as he walked among the Roman dead after the battle. Pompey was killed in Egypt when he sought refuge there, but the last Pompeian army was not defeated until 45 B.C.

Caesar assumed the office of dictator for life, and during the six-month period before his death he initiated far-reaching reforms. He granted citizenship liberally to non-Italians and packed the Senate with many new provincial members, thus making it a more truly representative body as well as a rubber stamp for his policies. In the interest of the poorer citizens, he reduced debts, inaugurated a public works program, established colonies outside Italy, and decreed that one third of the laborers on the slave-worked estates in Italy be persons of free birth. As a result, he was able to reduce from 320,000 to 150,000 the number of people in the city of Rome receiving free grain. (The population of Rome is estimated to have been 500,000.) His most enduring act was the reform of the calendar in the light of Egyptian knowledge; with minor changes, this calendar of 365 1/4 days is still in use today.

Caesar realized that the Republic was, in fact, dead. In his own words, "The Republic is merely a name, without form or substance." He believed that benevolent despotism alone could save Rome from continued civil war and collapse. But Caesar incurred the enmity of many, particularly those who viewed him as a tyrant who had destroyed the Republic. On the Ides (the fifteenth) of March, 44 B.C., a group of conspirators, led by ex-Pompeians whom Caesar had pardoned, stabbed him to death in the Senate, and Rome was once more plunged into conflict.

Caesar's assassins had been offended by his trappings of monarchy—his purple robe, the statues erected in his honor, the coins bearing his portrait—and they assumed that with his death the Republic would be restored to its traditional status. But the people of Rome remained unmoved by the conspirators' cry of "Liberty! Freedom! Tyranny is dead!" The majority of them were prepared to accept a successor whose power and position stopped just short of a royal title. The real question was: Who was to be Caesar's successor?

The Third Civil War: Antony vs. Octavian

Following Caesar's death, his eighteen-year-old grandnephew and heir, Octavian, allied himself with Caesar's chief lieutenant, Mark Antony, against the conspirators and the Senate. Although he was not a conspirator, Cicero, the renowned orator and champion of the Senate, was put to death for his hostility to Antony, and the conspirators' armies were routed. Then for more than a decade Octavian and Antony exercised dictatorial power and divided the Roman world between them. But the ambitions of each man proved too great for the alliance to endure.

Antony, who took charge of the eastern half of the empire, became infatuated with Cleopatra, the last of the Egyptian Ptolemies. He even went so far as to transfer Roman territories to her dominions. Octavian took advantage of this high-handedness to arouse Rome and Italy against Antony and his queen. The ensuing struggle was depicted as a war between the West and the East. When Octavian's fleet met Antony's off Actium in Greece, first Cleopatra and then Antony

This silver coin was struck to commemorate the assassination of Julius Caesar. The legend reads "The Ides of March." On the other side is a profile of Brutus.

deserted the battle and fled to Egypt. There Antony committed suicide, as did Cleopatra soon afterwards when Alexandria was captured in 30 B.C.

The Early Empire, 30 B.C.– A.D. 180

At the end of a century of civil violence Rome was at last united under one ruler, and the Republic gave way to the permanent dictatorship of the Empire. Two centuries of imperial greatness, known as the *Pax Romana* (Roman Peace), followed.

Reconstruction under Augustus

Following his triumphal return to Rome, Octavian in 27 B.C. announced that he would "restore the Republic." But he did so only outwardly by blending republican institutions with strong personal leadership. He provided the Senate with considerable authority, consulted it on important issues, allowed it to retain control over Italy and half of the provinces, and gave it the legislative functions of the nearly defunct Tribal Assembly. The Senate in return bestowed upon Octavian the title *Augustus* ("The Revered," a title previously used for gods), by which he was known thereafter.

During the rest of his forty-five-year rule, Augustus never again held the office of dictator, and he seldom held the consulship. Where, then, did his strength lie? Throughout his career he kept the power of a tribune, which gave him the right to initiate legislation and to veto the legislative and administrative acts of others. He also kept the governorship of the frontier provinces, where the armies were stationed. Augustus' control of the army meant that his power could not be successfully challenged. From his military title, *imperator* ("victorious general"), is derived our modern term *emperor*.

Augustus thus effected a compromise "between the need for a monarchical head of the empire and the sentiment which enshrined Rome's republican constitution in the minds of his contemporaries."[8] He preferred the modest title of *princeps*, "first citizen" or "leader," which he felt best described his position, and his form of disguised dictatorship is therefore known as the Principate. At the beginning of the Empire, then, political power was ostensibly divided between the *princeps* and the senatorial aristocrats. This arrangement was continued by most of Augustus' successors during the next two centuries.

Because Augustus faced the problem of removing the scars resulting from a century of civil strife, he concentrated on internal reform. He did extend the Roman frontier to the Danube as a defense against barbarian invasions, but he failed in an attempt to conquer Germany up to the Elbe River (see map, p. 82). As a result of this failure, the Germans were never Romanized, like the Celts of Gaul and Spain, and the boundary between their language and the Roman-based Romance languages of France and Spain is still the Rhine.

Augustus also sought to cure a sick society–to end the mood of utter hopelessness felt by many concerned Romans, among them the poet Horace:

Time corrupts all. What has it not made worse?
Our grandfathers sired feebler children; theirs Were weaker still—ourselves; and now our curse
Must be to breed even more degenerate heirs.[9]

Through legislation and propaganda, Augustus sought with some success to check moral and social decline and revive the old Roman ideals and traditions. He rebuilt deteriorated temples, revived old priesthoods, and restored religious festivals. He sought to reestablish the integrity of the family by legislating against adultery, the chief grounds for divorce, which had become commonplace during the late Republic. A permanent court was set up to prosecute adulterous wives and their lovers. Among those found guilty and banished from Rome were Augustus' daughter and granddaughter. Finally, to disarm the gangs that had been terrorizing citizens, he outlawed the carrying of daggers.

Augustus greatly reduced the corruption and exploitation that had flourished in the late Republic by creating a salaried civil service, open to all classes. He also established a permanent standing army, stationed in the frontier provinces and kept out of politics. More than

This marble portrait statue of Augustus Caesar presents the emperor in an idealized, militaristic pose. The carvings on his breastplate commemorate a diplomatic incident during his reign.

pretense that they were only the first among all citizens: Caligula was a madman who demanded to be worshiped as a god and made his favorite horse a senator; Nero was infamous for his immorality, the murder of his wife and his mother, and his persecution of Christians in Rome.

In A.D. 64, a great fire raged for nine days, destroying more than half of the capital. The Roman historian Tacitus has left us a vivid account of how Nero made the unpopular Christians scapegoats for the fire:

> . . . large numbers . . . were condemned—not so much for incendiarism as for their anti-social tendencies. Their deaths were made farcical. Dressed in wild animals' skins, they were torn to pieces by dogs, or crucified, or made into torches to be ignited after dark. . . . Nero provided his Gardens for the spectacle, and exhibited displays in the Circus . . . Despite their guilt as Christians, and the ruthless punishment it deserved, the victims were pitied. For it was felt they were being sacrificed to one man's brutality rather than to the national interest.[10]

The Julio-Claudian line ended in A.D. 68 when Nero, declared a public enemy by the Senate and faced by army revolts, committed suicide. In the following year four emperors were proclaimed by rival armies, with Vespasian the final victor. For nearly thirty years (A.D. 69–96) the Flavian dynasty (Vespasian followed by his two sons, Titus and Domitian) provided the Empire with effective, if autocratic, rule. The fiction of republican institutions gave way to a scarcely veiled monarchy as the Flavians openly treated the office of emperor as theirs by right of conquest and inheritance.

forty colonies of retired soldiers were founded throughout the Empire; among them were Palermo in Sicily, Patras in Greece, and Baalbek in Syria.

Augustus' reforms engendered a new optimism and patriotism that were reflected in the art and literature of the Augustan Age (discussed later in this chapter).

The Julio-Claudian and Flavian Emperors

Augustus was followed by four descendants of his family, the line of the Julio-Claudians, who ruled from A.D. 14 to 68. Augustus' stepson Tiberius, whom the Senate accepted as his successor, and Claudius were fairly efficient and devoted rulers; in Claudius' reign the Roman occupation of Britain began in A.D. 43. The other two rulers of this imperial line disregarded the

The Antonines: "Five Good Emperors"

An end to autocracy and a return to the Augustan principle of an administration of equals—emperor and Senate—characterized the rule of the Antonine emperors (A.D. 96–180), under whom the Empire reached the height of its prosperity and power. Selected on the basis of proven ability, these "good emperors" succeeded, according to Tacitus, in "reconciling things long incompatible, supreme power and liberty." Two of these emperors are especially worthy of notice.

Hadrian reigned from A.D. 117 to 138. His first important act was to stabilize the boundaries of the Empire. He gave up as indefensible recently conquered Armenia and Mesopotamia and erected protective walls in Germany and Britain, the latter an imposing structure of stone twenty feet high. Hadrian traveled extensively, inspecting almost every province of the Empire. New towns were founded, old ones restored, and many public works were constructed, among them the famous Pantheon in Rome.

The last of the "five good emperors" was Marcus Aurelius, who ruled from A.D. 161 to 180. He approached Plato's ideal of the "philosopher king" and preferred the quiet contemplation of his books to the blood and brutality of the battlefield. Yet he was repeatedly troubled by the invasions of Parthians (see p. 66) from the east and Germans from across the Danube. While engaged in his Germanic campaigns, he wrote his *Meditations*, a collection of personal thoughts notable for its lofty Stoic idealism and love of humanity. (Ironically, the stoic manner in which

A passion for detailed artistic realism produced this equestrian statue of Marcus Aurelius. The portrait statue captures the ideal of the emperor as a philosopher-king who rules by wisdom rather than by force.

Christian martyrs accepted death did not impress him: "What an admirable soul that is which is ready, if at any moment it must be separated from the body. . . . This readiness must come from a man's own judgment, not from mere obstinacy, as with the Christians, but with reason and dignity if it is to persuade another, and without tragic show." (*Meditations* XI,3) Like a good Stoic, Marcus Aurelius died at his post at Vindobona (Vienna). At Rome his equestrian statue still stands on the Capitoline Hill, "returning the salute of legions which have been dead for two thousand years."

The "Immense Majesty of the Roman Peace"

In its finest period, the Empire was a vast area stretching from Britain to the Euphrates and containing upwards of 100 million people. It was welded together into what Pliny the Elder, in the first century A.D., termed the "immense majesty of the Roman peace" *(Pax Romana)*. Writing during the rule of Augustus, the Roman poet Virgil was the spokesman for what enlightened Romans felt to be the mission of Rome:

> *Others, doubtless, will mould lifelike bronze with greater delicacy, will win from marble the look of life, will plead cases better, chart the motions of the sky with the rod and foretell the risings of the stars. You, O Roman, remember to rule the nations with might. This will be your genius—to impose the way of peace, to spare the conquered and crush the proud.*"[11]

Non-Romans were equally conscious of the rich benefits derived from Roman rule. The mass of the inhabitants of the Empire welcomed the peace, prosperity, and administrative efficiency of the Principate.

The *Pax Romana* began with Augustus and reached its height under the Five Good Emperors. Cities increased in number and were largely self-governed by their own upper-class magistrates and senates. They formed nerve centers linked together by a network of roads and waterways. Secure behind natural frontiers guarded by well-trained armies, the *Pax Romana* created a cosmopolitan world-state where races and cultures intermingled freely.

The "True Democracy" of the Roman Empire

At the head of this huge world-state stood the emperor, its defender and symbol of unity as well as an object of veneration. "The whole world speaks in unison," proclaimed a Greek orator, "more distinctly than a chorus; and so well does it harmonize under this director-in-chief that it joins in praying this Empire may last for all time."[12] The major theme of the many encomiums written to celebrate the generally enlightened government of the Principate was that liberty had been exchanged for order and prosperity. The Empire was said to represent a new kind of democracy: "the true democracy and the freedom that does not fail"—"a democracy under the one man that can rule and govern best." The last century of the Republic, by contrast, exhibited "the evils found in every democracy. . . . The cause is the multitude of our population and the magnitude of the business of our government; for the population embraces men of every kind, . . . and the business of the state had become so vast that it can be administered only with the greatest difficulty."[13]

Economic Prosperity

Rome's unification of the ancient world had far-reaching economic consequences. The *Pax Romana* was responsible for the elimination of tolls and other artificial barriers, the suppression of piracy and brigandage, and the establishment of a reliable coinage. Such factors, in addition to the longest period of peace the West has ever enjoyed, explain in large measure the great expansion of commerce that occurred in the first and second centuries A.D. Industry was also stimulated, but its expansion was hindered since wealth remained concentrated and no mass market for industrial goods arose. Industry remained organized on a small-shop basis with producers widely scattered, resulting in self-sufficiency.

The economy of the Empire remained basically agrarian, and the huge estates, *latifundia*, prospered. On these tracts, usually belonging to absentee owners, large numbers of *coloni*, free tenants, tilled the soil as sharecroppers. The *coloni* were replacing slave labor, which was becoming increasingly hard to secure with the disappearance of the flow of war captives.

Early Evidence of Economic Stagnation

Late in the first century A.D. the first sign of economic stagnation appeared in Italy. Italian agriculture began to suffer from overproduction as a result of the loss of its markets for wine and olive oil in Roman Gaul, Spain, and North Africa, which were becoming self-sufficient in those products. To aid the Italian wine producers, the Flavian emperor Domitian created an artificial scarcity by forbidding new vineyards in Italy to be planted and by ordering half the existing vineyards in the provinces to be plowed under. A century later the Five Good Emperors sought to solve the continuing problem of overproduction by subsidizing the buying power of consumers. Loans at 5 percent interest were made to ailing landowners, with the interest to be paid into the treasuries of Italian municipalities and earmarked "for girls and boys of needy parents to be supported at public expense." This system of state subsidies was soon extended to the provinces.

Also contributing to Roman economic stagnation was the continuing drain of money to the East for the purchase of such luxury goods as silks and spices (see "The Meeting of East and West in Ancient Times," p. 124), and the failure of city governments within the Empire to keep their finances in order, thus making it necessary for the imperial government to intervene. As an official sent by one of the Five Good Emperors to investigate the fiscal troubles of some cities in Asia Minor reported:

> *Many sums of money are detained in private hands for a variety of reasons, and in addition some are disbursed for quite illegitimate expenditures. . . . The city of Nicomedia, my lord, has expended 3,329,000 sesterces on an aqueduct, which has been abandoned still unfinished and has even been torn down. Again they disbursed 200,000 sesterces for another aqueduct, but this, too, has been abandoned. So now, after throwing away all that money they must make a new expenditure in order to have water.[14]*

Such early evidence of declining prosperity foreshadowed the economic crisis of the third century A.D., when political anarchy and monetary inflation caused the economy of the Empire to collapse (see ch. 5).

Rome, Imperial Capital

At the hub of the sprawling Empire was Rome, with about a million inhabitants. Augustus boasted that he had found a city of brick and had left one of marble. Nonetheless, Rome presented a great contrast of magnificence and tawdriness, of splendid public buildings and squalid tenements, which often collapsed or caught fire. The crowded narrow streets, lined with apartment houses and swarming with all manner of people, are described by the satirist Juvenal early in the second century A.D.:

> ... Hurry as I may, I am blocked
> By a surging crowd in front, while a vast mass
> Of people crushes onto me from behind.
> One with his elbow punches me, another
> With a hard litter-pole; one bangs a beam

Against my head, a wine-cask someone else.
With mud my legs are plastered; from all sides
Huge feet trample upon me, and a soldier's
Hobnails are firmly planted on my toes.[15]

Social Life

At the top of the social order were the old senatorial families who lived as absentee owners of huge estates and left commerce and finance to a large and wealthy middle class. In contrast to the tenements of the poor, the homes of the rich were palatial, as revealed by excavations at Pompeii, which was buried by the eruption of Vesuvius in A.D. 79. These elaborate villas contained courts and gardens with fountains, rooms furnished with marble walls, mosaics on the floors, and numerous frescoes and other works of art. An interesting feature of Roman furniture was the abundance of couches and the scarcity of chairs. People usually reclined, even at meals—a custom which may have had its value during the sumptuous dinners served by the wealthy gourmands, who were not above administering emetics to permit disgorging and starting afresh on more food and wine.

The lower classes in the cities found a refuge from the dullness of their existence in social clubs, or guilds, called *collegia*, each comprising the workers of one trade. The activity of the *collegia* did not center on economic aims, like modern trade unions, but on the worship of a god and on feasts, celebrations, and decent burials for members.

The living conditions of slaves varied greatly. Those in domestic service were often treated humanely, and their years of efficient service frequently rewarded by emancipation. Nor was it uncommon for freed slaves to rise to places of eminence in business, letters, and the imperial service. On the other hand, conditions among slaves on the large estates could be indescribably harsh. Beginning with Augustus, however, numerous enactments protected slaves from mistreatment; Hadrian, for example, forbade private prisons and the killing of a slave without judicial approval.

Recreation played a key role in Roman social life. Both rich and poor were exceedingly

A typically furnished bedroom in a villa illustrates the Roman view of domestic comfort. Though sparsely furnished, the room retains its elegant atmosphere, created in part by the elaborate wall decorations and intricate mosaic floor pavement.

fond of their public baths, which in the capital alone numbered 800 during the early days of the Empire. The baths served the same purpose as our modern-day athletic clubs. The larger baths contained enclosed gardens, promenades, gymnasiums, libraries, and famous works of art as well as a sequence of rooms through which one moved—the sweat room, the warm room where sweat was scraped off by a slave (soap was unknown), the tepid room for cooling off, and the invigorating cold bath. Another popular room was the lavatory with its long row of marble toilets equipped with comfortable arm rests. Here Romans liked to sit and chat for an hour or more.

Foot races, boxing, and wrestling were minor sports; chariot racing and gladiatorial contests were the chief amusements. The cry for "bread and circuses" reached such proportions that by the first century A.D. the Roman calendar had as many as a hundred days set aside as holidays, the majority of which were given over to games furnished at public expense. The most spectacular sport was chariot racing. The largest of six race courses at Rome was the Circus Maximus, a huge marble-faced structure seating about 150,000 spectators. The games, which included as many as twenty-four races each day, were presided over by the emperor or his representative. The crowds bet furiously on their favorite charioteers, whose fame equaled that of the sports heroes of our own day.

Scarcely less popular, but infinitely less civilized, the gladiatorial contests were organized by both emperors and private promoters as a regular feature on the amusement calendar. These cruel spectacles, which have no exact counterpart in any other civilization, were held in arenas, the largest and most famous of which was the Colosseum. The contests took various forms. Ferocious animals were pitted against armed combatants or occasionally even against unarmed men and women who had been condemned to death. Another type of contest was the fight to the death between gladiators, generally equipped with different types of weapons but matched on equal terms. It was not uncommon for the life of a defeated gladiator who had fought courageously to be spared at the request of the spectators. Although many Romans decried these blood-letting contests, they

The Colosseum, largest of the Roman amphitheaters, was used for gladiatorial combats, animal fights, and even for naval exhibitions—water pipes for flooding the interior still exist in some arenas.

continued until the fifth century, when Christianity forbade them.

The Roman Contribution

Unlike the Greeks, the Romans were not gifted in abstract thought. They constructed no original system of philosophy, invented no major new literary forms, and made no outstanding scientific discoveries. Yet they excelled in the art of government. The Romans created a workable world-state and developed a skill in administration, law, and practical affairs. The *Pax Romana* was fashioned and maintained by a people who were, on the whole, conscious of their responsibilities to others.

The Roman Spirit

The Roman spirit was compounded of many factors. Never completely forgotten was the tradition of plain living that stemmed from Rome's early history as a nation of farmers. Geography was another factor; for centuries the Romans were faced with the need to conquer or be conquered, and they had to stress discipline and duty to the state. But the Roman spirit also had another side. It could be arrogant and cruel, and its sense of justice was often untempered with mercy. In A.D. 84, a Scottish chieftain is reported to have said of his Roman conquerors, "To robbery, slaughter, plunder, they give the lying name of empire; they create a desert and call it peace."[16]

Rome's answer to such criticism was delivered a few years earlier by a Roman general to some tribes in Gaul that had revolted after the infamous emperor Nero had arrested some of their leaders:

> Gaul always had its petty kingdoms and intestine wars, until you submitted to our authority. We, though so often provoked, have used the right of conquest to burden you only with the cost of maintaining peace.... You often command our legions. You rule these and other provinces. There is no privilege, no exclusion.... Endure the passions and rapacity of your masters, just as you bear barren seasons ... and other natural evils. There will be vices as long as there are men. But they are not perpetual....
>
> Should the Roman be driven out ... what can result but wars between all these nations? ... Let the lessons of fortune ... teach you not to prefer rebellion and ruin to submission and safety.[17]

Evolution of Roman Law

Of the contributions made by the Romans in government, Roman law is preeminent. Two great legal systems, Roman law and English common law, are the foundation of jurisprudence in most modern Western nations. Roman law is the basis for the law codes of Italy, France, Scotland, Louisiana, and the Latin American countries. Where English common law is used, as in the United States (except in Louisiana), there is also a basic heritage of great legal principles originated by ancient Roman jurists. In addition, Roman legal principles have strongly affected the development of the canon law of the Roman Catholic Church; and international law has borrowed principles inherent in the Roman system.

Roman law evolved slowly over a period of about a thousand years. At first, as in all early societies, the law was unwritten, mixed with religious custom, and harsh in its judgments. In the fifth century B.C., this law was put in writing in the Law of the Twelve Tables, as the result of plebeian demand. During the remainder of the Republic the body of Roman law (jus civile, "law of the citizen") was enlarged by legislation passed by the Senate and the assembly and by judicial interpretation of existing law to meet new conditions. By the second century A.D. the emperor had become the sole source of law, a responsibility he entrusted to scholars "skilled in the law" (jurisprudentes). These scholars stuck fast to the idea of equity ("Follow the beneficial interpretation"; "Letter of law is height of injustice") and to stoic philosophy with its concept of a "law of nature" common to all people and ascertainable by means of human reason. Finally, in the sixth century A.D., the enormous bulk of Roman law from all sources was codified (see p. 172) and thus easily preserved for posterity.

Roman Engineering and Architecture

The Empire's needs required a communication system of paved roads and bridges as well as huge public buildings and aqueducts. As road builders, the Romans surpassed all previous peoples. Constructed of layers of stone and gravel according to sound engineering principles, their roads were planned for the use of armies and messengers and were kept in constant repair. The earliest and best known main Roman highway was the Appian Way. Running from Rome to the Bay of Naples, it was built about 300 B.C. to facilitate Rome's expansion southward. It has been said that the speed of travel possible on Roman highways was not surpassed until the early nineteenth century.

In designing their bridges and aqueducts, the Romans placed a series of stone arches next to one another to provide mutual support. At times several tiers of arches were used, one above the other. Fourteen aqueducts, stretching a total of 265 miles, supplied some fifty gallons of water daily for each inhabitant of Rome. They were proudly described by Rome's superintendent of aqueducts as "a signal testimony to the greatness of the Roman Empire," to be contrasted with "the idle pyramids or all the useless, though famous, works of the Greeks."[18]

At first the Romans copied Etruscan architectural models, but later they combined basic Greek elements with distinctly Roman innovations. The structural simplicity of Hellenic buildings was too restrained for the Romans. By utilizing concrete—a Roman invention—faced with brick or stone, they developed new methods for enclosing space. The Greeks' static post and lintel system was replaced by the more dynamic techniques of vaulting derived from the arch, borrowed from the Etruscans.

Heavy concrete barrel vaults, cross (or groin) vaults and domes—all so solid that they exerted no sidewise thrust—made possible the vast interiors that distinguish Roman architecture. The barrel vault was essentially a series of connected arches resembling a tunnel, and the cross vault consisted of two barrel vaults intersecting at right angles. The largest Roman domed structure is the Pantheon, the oldest important roofed building in the world that is still intact. As its name indicates, it was dedicated to "all the gods" by the emperor Hadrian as a symbol of the union of Greeks and Romans on equal terms. The massive dome rests on thick round walls of poured concrete that could not be weakened by window openings. The only light enters through a great hole, thirty feet wide, at the top of the dome. The size of the dome remained unsurpassed until the twentieth century.

The typical Roman basilica, which served as a social and commercial center and as a law court, was not domed or vaulted. It was a rectangular structure with a light wooden ceiling held up by rows of columns that divided the interior into a central nave and side aisles. The roof over the nave was raised to admit light, creating a clerestory like that found in the temple of Karnak in Egypt. The Roman basilica was to have a remarkable future as a Christian church (see illustration, p. 300).

Roman buildings were built to last, and their size, grandeur, and decorative richness aptly symbolized the proud imperial spirit of Rome. Whereas the Greeks evolved the temple, theater, and stadium, the Romans contributed the triumphal arch, bath, basilica, amphitheater, and the multistoried apartment house. Perhaps the most famous Roman edifice is the Colosseum, a huge amphitheater about one quarter of a mile around on the outside and with a seating capacity of about 45,000. Its three stories of arches are decorated with Doric, Ionic, and Corinthian columns.

Sculpture and Painting

After the conquest of Greece thousands of statues and other art pieces were brought to Rome. Many Romans acquired a passion for art, and the homes of the wealthy were filled with all kinds of Greek art, either brought to Rome as booty or copied there in great number.

Although strongly influenced by Etruscan and Greek models, the Romans developed a distinctive sculpture of their own, which was remarkably realistic, secular, and individualistic. Lifelike portraiture flourished, probably originating in the early practice of making and preserving wax images of the heads of important families. During the Principate, portraiture and relief sculpture tended to idealize the likenesses of the

This portrait bust is typical of the lifelike portraiture that flourished in Rome. While likenesses of private citizens were intensely individualistic, depictions of emperors (see pp. 84, 85) tended to be more heroic and idealized.

emperors. Portraits on coins also served to glorify the Empire and particular emperors. Equestrian statues, sculptured coffins, or sarcophagi, and the reliefs found on imperial monuments were exceptionally fine works of art. The Romans developed a great fund of decorative motifs, such as cupids, garlands of flowers, and scrolls of various patterns, which are still used today.

What little Roman painting has been preserved clearly reflects the influence of Hellenistic Greek models. The Romans were particularly skilled in producing floor mosaics—often copies of some Hellenistic painting—and in painting frescoes. The frescoes still to be seen in Pompeii and elsewhere show that the artist drew the human figure accurately and showed objects in clear though imperfect perspective.

Literary Rome

In literature as in art, the Romans turned to the Greeks for their models. Roman epic, dramatic, and lyric poetry forms were usually written in conscious imitation of Greek masterpieces. Compared with Greek literature, however, Latin literature is for the most part inferior to its Greek models. But it remains one of the world's great literatures largely because of its influence upon medieval, Renaissance, and modern culture.

Formal Latin literature did not begin until the third century B.C. when a Greek slave named Livius Andronicus translated Homer's *Odyssey* and several Greek plays into Latin. By the end of the same century the first of a series of Latin epics dealing with Rome's past was composed. Only a few fragments have survived.

The oldest examples of Latin literature to survive intact are the twenty-one comedies of Plautus (c. 254–184 B.C.), which were adapted from Hellenistic Greek originals but with many Roman allusions, colloquialisms, and customs added. Plautus' comedies are bawdy and vigorously humorous, and their rollicking plots of illicit love and stock characters of the shrewish wife ("Look at you! Gadding about, reeking of scent; you ought to know better, at your time of life"), henpecked husband ("But dear, I was only helping a friend buy a bottle of perfume"), lovelorn youth, clever slave, and swashbuckling soldier reveal the level of culture and taste in early Rome. The works of Plautus suggest many of the types that modern comedy has assumed—the farce, burlesque, and the comedy of manners. From him Shakespeare got ideas for his *Comedy of Errors* and *The Merry Wives of Windsor;* the modern musical and movie, *A Funny Thing Happened on the Way to the Forum*, is an adaptation of three of Plautus' plots.

The Golden Age of Latin Literature

Latin literature entered its first great period of creative activity in the first century B.C., when an outpouring of intellectual effort coincided with the last years of the Republic. This period marks the first half of the Golden Age of Latin literature, known as the Ciceronian period because of the stature of Marcus Tullius Cicero (106–43 B.C.), the greatest master of Latin prose and the outstanding intellectual influence in Roman history.

Acclaimed as the greatest orator of his day, Cicero found time during his busy public life to write extensively on philosophy, political theory, and rhetoric. Some 900 of his letters still exist. Together with fifty-eight speeches, they give us insight into Cicero's personality as well as life in republican Rome. Cicero also made a rich contribution by passing on to the Romans and to later ages much of Greek thought—especially that of Plato and the Stoics—and at the same time interpreting it from the standpoint of a Roman intellectual and practical man of affairs. He did more than any other Roman to make Latin a great literary language.

Other works of the Ciceronian period include the personal lyrical poetry of Catullus (c. 87–54 B.C.), a young man about town who wrote intensely of his loves and hates:

I hate and love—the why I cannot tell,
But by my tortures know the fact too well.[19]

Catullus' contemporary, Lucretius (99–55 B.C.), found in the philosophy of Epicurus an antidote to his profound disillusionment with his fellow citizens who, he wrote, "in their greed of gain . . . amass a fortune out of civil bloodshed: piling wealth on wealth, they heap carnage on carnage. With heartless glee they welcome a brother's tragic death."[20] Lucretius' long philosophical poem, *On the Nature of Things,* is discussed on page 94.

Augustus provided the Roman world with a stability that was conducive to a further outpouring of literary creativity. The second phase of the Golden Age of Latin literature, the Augustan Age, was notable particularly for its excellent poetry. Virgil (70–19 B.C.) is considered the greatest of all Roman poets. His masterpiece, a great national epic called the *Aeneid,* glorifies the work of Augustus and eloquently asserts Rome's destiny to conquer and rule the world (see quotation, p. 86). Using Homer's *Odyssey* as his model, Virgil recounted the fortunes of Aeneas, the legendary founder of the Latin people, who came from burning Troy to Italy. The *Aeneid* breathes Virgil's deep and enthusiastic patriotism and is as much a piece of imperial symbolism as Rome's triumphal arches.

As Augustus' poet laureate after the death of Virgil, Horace (65–8 B.C.) often sincerely praised the emperor's achievements:

> *Now Parthia fears the fist of Rome, the fasces*
> *Potent on land and sea; now the once haughty*
> *Ambassadors from the Caspian and the Indus*
>   *Sue for a soft reply.*
> *Now Faith and Peace and Honor and*
>   *old-fashioned*
> *Conscience and unremembered Virtue venture*
> *To walk again, and with them blessed Plenty,*
>   *Pouring her brimming horn.[21]*

Most of Horace's poetry, however, is concerned with everyday human interests and moods, and succeeding generations up to the present have been attracted by his serene outlook on life:

> *Happy the man, and happy he alone,*
> *He, who can call today his own:*
> *He who secure within, can say,*
> *Tomorrow do thy worst, for I have lived*
>   *today.[22]*

Quite a different sort was Ovid (43 B.C.–A.D. 17). His partiality for themes of sensual love in his *Art of Love* and other poems ("There she stood, faultless beauty in front of me, naked") caused Augustus to exile him to the shores of the Black Sea, Rome's equivalent to Russia's Siberia. But Ovid was also a first-rate storyteller, and it is largely through his *Metamorphoses,* a witty verse collection of Greek stories about the life of the gods—not neglecting their lovelife—that classical mythology was transmitted to the modern world.

The Silver Age of Latin Literature

The literature of the Silver Age, the period between the deaths of Augustus and Hadrian (A.D. 14–138), substituted a more critical and negative spirit for the patriotism and optimism of the Augustan Age. Despite a great emphasis on artificial stylistic devices, the Silver Age was memorable for its moral emphasis, seen in Tacitus, Plutarch, Seneca, and especially in Juvenal (d. A.D. 130), who has been called "the greatest satiric poet who ever lived." With moral indignation and bitter irony he assailed the shortcomings of Roman society: the common people of the city, no longer having votes to sell, are interested only in free "bread and circuses;" a good woman is a "rare bird," as "uncommon as a black swan," but "worse still is the well-read menace" who "with antiquarian zeal quotes poets I've never heard of." (See also quotation p. 87.)

The Writing of History

Two Roman historians produced notable works during the Golden and Silver Ages. The first, Livy (59 B.C.–A.D. 17), was a contemporary of Virgil; Livy's immense *History of Rome,* like the latter's *Aeneid,* is of epic proportions and glorifies Rome's conquests and ancestral ways. By assembling the legends and traditions of early Roman history and welding them into a continuous narrative, Livy, like Virgil, sought to advance Augustus' program of moral and social regeneration. He praised the virtues of the ancient Romans—their heroism, patriotism, and piety—and sought to draw moral lessons from an idealized past:

> *What chiefly makes the study of history wholesome and profitable is this, that you behold the lessons of every kind of experience set forth as on a conspicuous monument; from these you may choose for yourself and for your own state what to imitate, from these mark for avoidance what is shameful in the conception and shameful in the result.[23]*

Tacitus (A.D. 55–117), like his contemporary Juvenal, was concerned with improving society, but he used history rather than satiric poetry to serve his ends. In his *Germania* Tacitus contrasted the life of the idealized, simple Germanic tribes with the corrupt and immoral existence of the Roman upper classes. In the *Annals* and *Histories* he used his vivid, epigrammatic prose to depict the shortcomings of the emperors and their courts from the death of Augustus to A.D. 96. For example: "Tyrants merely procure infamy for themselves and glory for their victims" and "The more corrupt the state, the more numerous the laws." Tacitus suffered from the bias of his own senatorial class; he looked upon the emperors as tyrants and thus could not do justice to the positive contributions of imperial government.

The most famous Greek author in the Empire was Plutarch (A.D. 46?–126?). He lectured on philosophy at Rome before retiring to his small hometown to pursue research on the outstanding figures in Roman and Greek history in order to discover what qualities make people great or ignoble. His *Parallel Lives*, containing forty-six biographies of famous Greeks and Romans arranged in pairs for the purpose of comparison, is one of the eminently readable classics of world literature. Because many of the sources Plutarch used have been lost, his *Lives* is a mine of invaluable information for the historian.

Stoicism and Epicureanism

The Romans contributed no original philosophical theories, preferring to adapt existing Greek systems of thought to suit their needs. As people of action with grave governmental responsibilities, the Romans paid scant attention to such abstract problems as the nature of the universe and of human knowledge. But the corrupting effects of life that began in the late Republic on the old Roman virtues and traditions caused thoughtful Romans to be concerned over problems of behavior. As a consequence, they were attracted to the two chief Hellenistic ethical philosophies, Epicureanism and Stoicism.

Epicureanism made its greatest impact during the last days of the Republic, since some people found its tenets comforting in a period of political upheaval when no one knew what the future would bring. As young men, Virgil and Horace embraced Epicureanism, but Lucretius was the most important Roman interpreter of this philosophy. In *On the Nature of Things*, Lucretius followed Epicurus in basing his explanation of the "nature of things" on materialism and atomism (see p. 64). He called on people to free themselves from the superstitious fear of death, which was drawing them to the emotional mystery religions of Greece and the East. Lucretius exhorted his readers to seek pleasure in philosophical serenity, rather than in sensuous gratification, and to have no fear of death since souls, like bodies, are composed of atoms that fall apart when death comes: "What has this bugbear Death to frighten man/If souls can die, as well as bodies can?"

More enduring, especially in the days of the Empire, was the appeal of Stoicism to the Roman ruling classes. The emphasis of Roman Stoicism was on a just life, constancy to duty, courage in adversity, and service to humanity. It had a humanizing effect on Roman law by introducing such concepts as the law of nature and the brotherhood of all—including slaves. The law of nature, as defined by Cicero, "is not a product of human thought, nor is it any enactment of peoples, but something eternal which rules the whole universe by its wisdom in command and prohibition." It is the source of "the rational principles on which our laws must be based."[24]

One of the outstanding Roman Stoics was Seneca (4 B.C.–A.D. 65), Nero's tutor and a writer of moral essays and tragedies. He was regarded with high favor by the leaders of the early Christian Church, for his Stoicism, like that of the ex-slave Epictetus (d. A.D. 135) and the emperor Marcus Aurelius (see p. 86), had the appearance of a religious creed. He stressed an all-wise Province, or God, and believed that each person possessed a spark of the divine:

> God is near you, he is with you, he is within you. This is what I mean, Lucilius: a holy spirit indwells within us, one who marks our good and bad deeds, and is our guardian. . . . No man can be good without the help of God.[25]

Christians assumed that Seneca must have been influenced by St. Paul during the latter's stay in Rome. By A.D. 400 a fictitious collection of letters between the two was being circulated.

Lucretius: "Avoid Enticement into the Snares of Love"

Epicurean philosophers regarded love as one of many vain pursuits that lead to unhappiness. "By clinging to it," Lucretius writes, "you assure yourself of heartsickness and pain."

To avoid enticement into the snares of love is not so difficult as, once entrapped, to escape out of the toils and snap the tenacious knots of Venus. And yet, be you never so tightly entangled and embrangled, you can still free yourself from the curse unless you stand in the way of your own freedom. First, you should concentrate on all the faults of mind or body of her whom you covet and sigh for. For men often behave as though blinded by love and credit the beloved with charms to which she has no valid title. How often do we see blemished and unsightly women basking in a lover's adoration! . . . A sallow wench is acclaimed as a nut-brown maid. A sluttish slattern is admired for her 'sweet disorder'. Her eyes are never green, but grey as Athene's. If she is stringy and woody, she is lithe as a gazelle. A stunted runt is a sprite, a sheer delight from top to toe. A clumsy giantess is 'a daughter of the gods divinely tall'. She has an impediment in her speech—a charming lisp, of course. She's as mute as a stockfish—what modesty! A waspish, fiery-tempered scold—she 'burns with a gem-like flame'. She becomes 'svelte' and 'willowy' when she is almost too skinny to live; 'delicate' when she is half-dead with coughing. Her breasts are swollen and protuberant: she is 'Ceres suckling Bacchus'. Her nose is snub—'a Faun', then, or 'a child of the Satyrs'. Her lips bulge: she is 'all kiss'. It would be a wearisome task to run through the whole catalogue. But suppose her face in fact is all that could be desired and the charm of Venus radiates from her whole body. Even so, there are still others. Even so, we lived without her before.

From the translation by Ronald Latham, *Lucretius, On the Nature of the Universe* (Harmondsworth, England: Penguin Books, 1951), Book IV, Lines 1146ff.

Science in the Roman Empire

The Romans had little scientific curiosity, but by putting the findings of Hellenistic science to practical use, they became masters in engineering, applied medicine, and public health.

The Romans pioneered in public health service and developed the extensive practice of hydrotherapy—the use of mineral baths for healing. Beginning in the early Empire, doctors were employed in infirmaries where soldiers, officials, and the poor could obtain free medical care. Great aqueducts and admirable drainage systems also indicate Roman concern for public health.

Characteristic of their utilitarian approach to science was the Romans' predilection for amassing immense encyclopedias. The most important of these was the *Natural History* compiled by Pliny the Elder (A.D. 23–79), an enthusiastic collector of all kinds of scientific odds and ends. In writing his massive work, Pliny is reputed to have read more than 2000 books. The result is an intriguing mixture of fact and fable thrown together with scarcely any method of classification. Nevertheless, it was the most widely read work on science during the Empire and the early Middle Ages.

Pliny was well aware of the lack of creative scientific activity in his day. "In these glad times of peace," he wrote, "no addition whatever is being made to knowledge by means of original research, and in fact even the discoveries of our predecessors are not being thoroughly studied." To Pliny, the cause of this state of affairs was "blind engrossment with avarice," and he cited this example: " . . . now that every sea has been opened up . . . , an immense multitude goes on voyages—but their object is profit not knowledge."[26] Pliny himself was suffocated by a rain of hot ashes while he was studiously observing the eruption of Mount Vesuvius near

Pompeii, an awesome event that killed two thousand people and was described by Pliny's nephew: "Many lifted up their hands to the gods, but a great number believed there were no gods, and that this night was to be the world's last, eternal one."[27]

The last great scientific minds of the ancient world were two Greeks, Claudius Ptolemy and Galen, both of whom lived in the second century A.D. Ptolemy resided at Alexandria, where he became celebrated as a geographer, astronomer, and mathematician. His maps show a comparatively accurate knowledge of a broad section of the Old World, and he used an excellent projection system. But he exaggerated the size of Asia, an error that influenced Columbus to underestimate the width of the Atlantic and to set sail from Spain in search of Asia. His work on astronomy, usually called the *Almagest* ("the great work") from the title of the Arabic translation, summed up the geocentric, or earth-centered, view of the universe that prevailed until the sixteenth century. In mathematics, Ptolemy's work in improving and developing trigonometry became the basis for modern knowledge of the subject.

Galen, born in Pergamum in Asia Minor, was a physician for a school of gladiators. His fame spread, and he was called to Rome where he became physician to Marcus Aurelius. Galen was responsible for notable advances in physiology and anatomy; for example, he was the first to explain the mechanism of respiration. Forbidden by the Roman government to dissect human bodies, Galen experimented with animals and demonstrated that an excised heart can continue to beat outside the body and that injuries to one side of the brain produce disorders in the opposite side of the body.

Galen's account of how he discovered the cause of a Roman matron's chronic insomnia shows that he was aware of the psychosomatic factor in illness: he noted that the lady's pulse "suddenly became extremely irregular" whenever the name of a famous actor was mentioned. "Now what was it that escaped the notice of previous physicians when examining the aforesaid woman?" Galen wrote. "They have no clear conception of how the body tends to be affected by mental conditions."[28] Galen's medical encyclopedia, in which he summarized the medical knowledge of

antiquity, remained the standard authority until the sixteenth century.

Conclusion

The story of Rome's rise from an insignificant muddy village along the banks of the Tiber to the mighty ruler of an empire that included most of western Europe, the Mediterranean area, and the Near East will always remain one of the most fascinating stories in world history. Rome's expansion was accompanied by much devastation and suffering, yet it was less disastrous than continued international anarchy would have been.

Rome's greatest achievement was the *Pax Romana*, peace and prosperity over a vast area for long periods under a stable and acceptable government. The Roman citizens who accomplished this task were characterized by Livy, Rome's great historian at the end of the Republican period, in words that anticipate what modern Americans have often said of themselves:

> *I hope that my passion for Rome's past has not impaired my judgment; for I do honestly believe that no country has ever been greater or purer than ours or richer in good citizens and noble deeds; none has been free for so many generations from the vices of avarice and luxury; nowhere have thrift and plain living been for so long held in such esteem.*[29]

Suggestions for Reading

K. Christ, *The Romans: An Introduction to Their History and Civilization** (California, 1984) and Michael Grant, *History of Rome** (Scribner, 1979) are highly recommended general accounts. Also excellent are D. R. Dudley, *The Civilization of Rome** (Mentor, 1960); R. Barrow, *The Romans** (Penguin, 1975); and P. Arnott, *The Romans and Their World** (St. Martin, 1970). M. Cary and H. Scullard, *A History of Rome Down to the Reign of Constantine*, 3rd ed. (St. Martin, 1975) is a standard detailed account.

M. Pallotino, *The Etruscans*,* rev. ed. (Penguin, 1975) and E. Richardson, *The Etruscans: Their Art and Civilization* (Univ. of Chicago, 1964) are detailed accounts. See also Michael Grant, *The Etruscans** (Scribner, 1981); and P. MacKendrick, *The Mute Stones Speak: The Story of Archaelogy in Italy** (Norton, 1976).

Recommended special studies: R. Errington, *The Dawn of Empire: Rome's Rise to World Power* (Cornell, 1972); D.

Dating from the late Paleolithic Age (c. 28,000–10,000 B.C.), this painting is one of those found on the walls of Lascaux cave in central France. Paleolithic artists used paints prepared from natural deposits found in the soil, ground to a fine powder, mixed with animal fat and water, and applied with the fingers or pointed tools. The paintings, in pigments of black, brown, red, and yellow, suggest that the cave may have been used for the performance of hunting and religious rites.

The *Standard of Ur,* above, (c. 2460 B.C.) is a flat, lectern-shaped box decorated on four sides with inlaid figures of shells and lapis lazuli. The two longer sides of the box, known respectively as *War* (shown here) and *Peace,* depict various aspects of Sumerian life. Sumerian jewelry, like the bracelet at left found in the royal tombs at Ur, was fashioned from precious stones and metals imported into Sumer in exchange for grain, wool, cloth, and other Sumerian goods and manufactures.

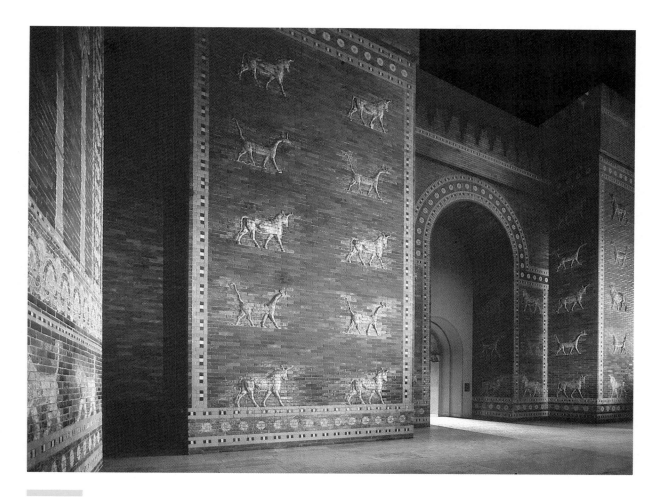

The brilliantly glazed bricks of the Ishtar Gate suggest the splendor of the Neo-Babylonian Empire under Nebuchadnezzar (604–562 B.C.). Adorning the brick is a stately procession of realistic-looking bulls and fantastic dragons, which feature a serpent's head and tail, a lion's body and forelegs, and a falcon's hind legs. Separately molded and glazed bricks were used to form the animals, which appear in raised relief on the gate.

The artistic traditions of the New Kingdom of Egypt include both the wall painting (left) of Ahmes-Nefertari and the funerary mask of King Tutankhamen (below). Ahmes-Nefertari was the wife of Ahmose the Liberator, who founded the Eighteenth Dynasty, the beginning of the New Kingdom. Tutankhamen's mask is made of solid, beaten gold and inlaid with semiprecious stones and colored glass. The heads of the vulture goddess and the serpent on the headdress represent the divine protectors of Upper and Lower Egypt.

Like the Egyptian pharaohs, the royal dead of Mycenae were mummified and their faces covered with funeral masks. The mask at left, known as the Mask of Agamemnon, dates from about 1500 B.C., nearly three centuries before the Trojan War, during which Agamemnon is said to have reigned. Most of what has survived of Greek painting is in the form of vase decoration, as shown by the kylix (drinking cup) below, which dates from about 540 B.C. The scene depicted is Dionysus, god of wine, reclining in a boat and surrounded by seven dolphins and seven bunches of grapes for good luck.

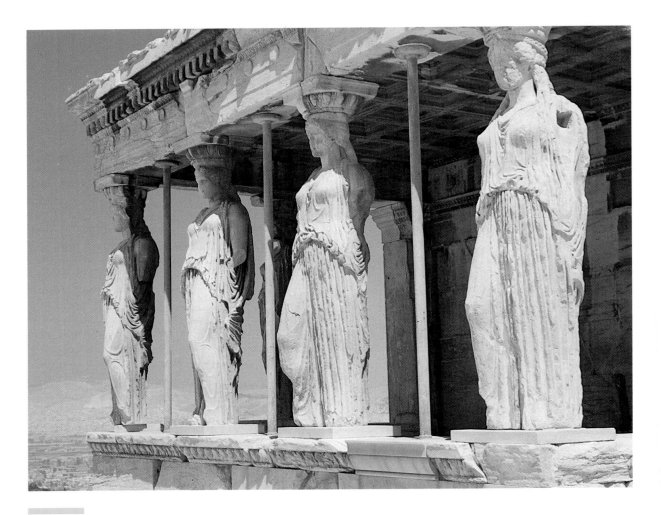

Facing the Parthenon on the Athenian Acropolis is the south porch of the Erechtheum, a temple in the Ionic style. The so-called Porch of the Maidens, built about 407 B.C., features six caryatids (draped female figures) supporting the roof in a graceful blend of beauty and strength. The folds of the draperies resemble the fluting of columns, while the bent knee of each maiden supplies a hint of motion. Grouped as in a procession, the caryatids seem to suggest a ceremony honoring the heroic dead.

The Etruscans equipped their dead with familiar objects of everyday life; thus excavations of Etruscan tombs provide an accurate reconstruction of Etruscan households. The square columns of the Tomb of the Reliefs (third century B.C.) are decorated with stucco reliefs of the common household articles of a prosperous Etruscan family—cooking utensils, tools, crockery, bedding, and weaponry. Above one couch is a relief of the ferryman Charon and his three-headed dog Cerberus, guardian of the entrance to Hades, the underground abode of the dead.

Brilliant decoration often adorned the interior walls of well-appointed Roman homes of the late Republican period. A stunning example is this wall painting from the summer dining room of the Villa of Livia, third wife of the emperor Augustus, at Prima Porta. The painting, which covered the walls of the room, creates the illusion of an exquisite garden of fruit trees, flowering shrubs, and songbirds just outside the viewer's reach beyond the low fence and wall.

Portfolio One

Stockton, *The Gracchi* (Oxford, 1979); E. Gruen, *The Last Generation of the Roman Republic* (California, 1973); M. Gelzer, *Caesar: Politician and Statesman** (Harvard, 1985); Lily R. Taylor, *Party Politics in the Age of Caesar** (California, 1961); R. Syme, *The Roman Revolution** (Oxford, 1939); P. Brunt, *Social Conflicts in the Roman Republic** (Norton, 1974); A. H. Jones, *Augustus** (Norton, 1972); F. Millar, *The Emperor in the Roman World* (Cornell, 1977); H. Rowell, *Rome in the Augustan Age** (Univ. of Oklahoma, 1971); Alan Watson, *The Law of the Ancient Romans* (Southern Methodist Univ., 1970).

Michael Grant, *Cities of Vesuvius: Pompeii and Herculaneum** (Penguin, 1978) re-creates the daily life of these buried cities. See also Mary Johnston, *Roman Life* (Scott, Foresman, 1957); J. Balsdon, *Life and Leisure in Ancient Rome* (McGraw-Hill, 1969); and *Roman Women: Their History and Habits* (Knopf, 1975); Mary Lefkowitz and Maureen Fant, eds, *Women's Life in Greece and Rome: A Source Book in Translation*, rev. ed. (Johns Hopkins, 1982); H. Boren, *Roman Society: A Social, Economic, and Cultural History** (Heath, 1977); B. Rawson, ed., *The Family in Ancient Rome: New Perspectives* (Cornell, 1986); H. Mattingly, *The Man in the Roman Street** (Norton, 1966); and Michael Grant, *The Jews in the Roman World* (Scribner, 1973).

Other books of interest are Martin L. Clarke, *The Roman Mind: Studies in the History of Thought from Cicero to Marcus Aurelius** (Norton, 1968); C. G. Starr, *Civilization and the Caesars: The Intellectual Revolution in the Roman Empire** (Cornell, 1954); M. Laistner, *The Greater Roman Historians* (California, 1963); S. Bonner, *Education in Ancient Rome** (California, 1978); J. Landels, *Engineering in the Ancient World* (Univ. of California, 1978); M. Henig, *A Handbook of Roman Art* (Oxford, 1983); M. Wheeler, *Roman Art and Architecture** (Oxford, 1964); and H. J. Rose, *Religion in Greece and Rome** (Torchbooks). Edith Hamilton, *The Roman Way** (Norton, 1932) is a popular treatment of Roman literature.

Recommended historical novels: W. Bryher, *The Coin of Carthage** (Harvest, 1965); T. Wilder, *The Ides of March** (Avon, 1975); John Williams, *Augustus** (Penguin, 1979); R. Graves, *I Claudius** (Vintage, 1977); and M. Yourcenar, *Memoirs of Hadrian** (Modern Library, 1984).

*Indicates a less expensive paperbound edition.

Notes

1. Plutarch *Lives* "Cato the Elder" 2, trans. Bernadotte Perrin, The Loeb Classical Library (Cambridge: Harvard University Press).
2. Donald R. Dudley, trans., *The Civilization of Rome* (New York: New American Library, 1962), p. 21.
3. Polybius *Histories* 1.10, trans. Evelyn S. Shuckburgh.
4. Livy *Roman History* 33, trans. E. T. Sage, The Loeb Classical Library (Cambridge: Harvard University Press), vol. 9, p. 367.
5. 1 Macc. 9:31—32 (King James Version of the Bible).
6. Livy *Roman History* 25.3, trans. Aubrey de Sélincourt, *Livy: The War with Hannibal* (Baltimore: Penguin Books, 1965), p. 296.
7. Plutarch *Lives* "Tiberius Gracchus" 9.5, trans. Bernadotte Perrin, The Loeb Classical Library (Cambridge: Harvard University Press), vol. 10, pp. 165, 167.
8. M. Hammond, *City-State and World State in Greek and Roman Political Theory Until Augustus* (Cambridge: Harvard University Press, 1951), p. 153.
9. Horace *Odes* 3.6, trans. James Michie, *The Odes of Horace* (Indianapolis: Bobbs-Merrill, 1965), p. 138.
10. Tacitus *Annals* 15:44, trans. Michael Grant (Baltimore: Penguin Books, 1959), p. 354.
11. Virgil *Aeneid* 6.847—853, in *Roman Civilization: Selected Readings*, ed. Naphtali Lewis and Meyer Reinhold (New York: Columbia University Press, 1955), vol. 2, p. 23.
12. Aelius Aristides *To Rome*. Oration 26, trans. S. Levin (Glencoe, IL: The Free Press, 1950), p. 126.
13. The advice of Maecenas, Rome's richest capitalist, to Augustus in Dio Cassius *Roman History* 52.14—15, trans. Earnest Cary, The Loeb Classical Library (Cambridge: Harvard University Press), vol. 6, pp. 109ff.
14. Pliny the Younger *Letters* 10.17a in *Roman Civilization: Selected Readings*, ed. Naphtali Lewis and Meyer Reinhold, vol. 2, p. 342.
15. R. C. Trevelyan, *Translations from Horace, Juvenal and Montaigne* (New York: Cambridge University Press, 1941), p. 129.
16. Tacitus *Agricola* 30.
17. Tacitus *Histories* 4.74.
18. Frontinus, quoted in Michael Grant, *The World of Rome* (New York: New American Library, 1960), p. 298.
19. *Carmen* 85, trans. Theodore Martin.
20. Lucretius *On the Nature of the Universe* 3.70, trans. Ronald Latham (Baltimore: Penguin Books, 1951), p. 98.
21. Horace "The Centennial Hymn," trans. James Michie, *The Odes of Horace*, p. 227.
22. Horace *Odes* 3.29, trans. John Dryden.
23. Livy *History of Rome* 1.10, trans. B. O. Foster, The Loeb Classical Library (Cambridge: Harvard University Press), vol. 1, p. 7.
24. Cicero *De Legibus* 1.4.14–6.20.
25. Seneca *Epistles* 41, quoted in Chester G. Starr, *Civilization and the Caesars: The Intellectual Revolution in the Roman Empire* (New York: Norton, 1965), p. 228.
26. Pliny *Natural History* 2.14.117—118, trans. H. Rackham, The Loeb Classical Library (Cambridge: Harvard University Press), vol. 1, pp. 259, 261.
27. Pliny the Younger *Letters* 6.16.20.
28. Galen "On Prognosis," in Thomas W. Africa, *Rome and the Caesars* (New York: John Wiley & Sons, 1965), p. 217.
29. Livy *Roman History* 1.1, trans. Aubrey de Sélincourt, *Livy: The Early History of Rome* (Baltimore: Penguin Books, 1960), p. 34.

Chapter 4

The Asian Way of Life

Ancient India and China to A.D. 220

This chapter will trace the genesis and development of the two oldest continuous civilizations—the Indian and the Chinese—in order to obtain an understanding of the Asian way of life and allow comparison with the West. In addition, this chapter will examine the early trade and diplomatic exchanges between East and West. These exchanges provide us with our first view of historical development on a global scale.

A modern Indian scholar has said: "All that India can offer to the world proceeds from her philosophy." Indian thinkers have consistently held a fundamental belief in the unity of all life, establishing no dividing line between the human and the divine. This pervasive belief in the unity of life has made possible the assimilation and synthesis of a variety of beliefs and customs from both native and foreign cultures. Thus, despite its almost continual political disunity, India has achieved and maintained a fundamental cultural unity.

While political disunity has characterized most of India's history, China has been united for more than 2000 years—the longest-lived political institution in world history. While religion had dominated the customs and attitudes of India's people, the Chinese have been much more humanistic and worldly. "We find in China neither that subordination of the human order to the divine order nor that vision of the world as a creation born of ritual and maintained by ritual which are part of the mental universe of India."[1] The Chinese attitude toward life had led to a concern for the art of government, the keeping of voluminous historical records, and the formulation of down-to-earth ethical standards.

This chapter traces the important threads of Indian and Chinese history to the beginning of the third century A.D., a time when the *Pax Romana* in the West was coming to an end. This was the formative age of both civilizations, the period in which the major elements of the Indian and Chinese way of life were established.

Early India

About 2500 B.C. a counterpart of the civilizations that had emerged earlier along the Tigris-Euphrates and the Nile rivers appeared along the Indus River in India. Coinciding with the collapse of this Indus civilization, Indo-European invaders—the Aryans—began a conquest that produced numerous contending states in northern India by 326 B.C. Long before that date, Aryan and native Indian beliefs and customs had undergone a process of assimilation and development that produced what is called classical Hinduism—an amalgam of religious and philosophical ideas (humankind's relation to the cosmic order) and socioeconomic institutions (the caste system in particular). Most of the elements that today are characteristic of Indian thought and action are the products of this period.

Geography of India

We can think of India* as a gigantic triangle, bounded on two sides by the warm waters of the

*Until the text deals with the creation of the separate states of India and Pakistan in 1947, the word *India* will refer to the *entire* subcontinent.

Indian Ocean and on the third by the mountain wall of the Himalayas. The highest mountains in the world, the Himalayas and their western extensions cut India off from the rest of Asia, making it an isolated subcontinent as large as Europe. Through the Khyber and other mountain passes in the northwest have come the armed conquerors, restless tribes, and merchants and travelers who did much to shape India's turbulent history (see map at right).

In addition to the northern mountain belt, which shields India from cold Arctic winds, the Indian subcontinent comprises two other major geographical regions, both characterized by India's most important ecological feature, an enervating subtropical climate.

In the north is the great plain known as Hindustan, which extends from the Arabian Sea to the Bay of Bengal. It forms the watersheds of two great river systems, the Indus and the Ganges, which have their sources in the Himalayas. South of this great plain rises a high plateau that covers most of the southern, or peninsular, part of India and is called the Deccan (the "South"). The mountains along the western edge of the Deccan plateau, called the Western Ghats ("Steps"), caused the monsoon winds that blow across the Arabian Sea to drop their rain on the Malabar coast. Since Roman times, the pepper and other spices that grow abundantly on this coast have attracted Western traders.

Our focus is presently on western Hindustan, now part of the state of Pakistan, where India's earliest civilization arose. This area is made up of an alluvial plain watered by the upper Indus and its tributaries (called the Punjab, "Land of the Five Rivers"), and the region of the lower Indus (called Sind, from *sindhu*, meaning "river," and the origin of the terms *Hindu* and *India*).

The Indus Civilization (c. 2500–1500 B.C.)

The rise of civilization in the Indus valley around 2500 B.C. duplicates what occurred in Mesopotamia nearly one thousand years earlier. In both areas, Neolithic farmers lived in food-producing villages situated on the hilly flanks of a large river valley. Under pressure from increased population and the need for more land and water, they moved to the more abundant and

ANCIENT INDIA

Indus Valley Civilization

fertile soil of the river valley. Here their successful adaptation to a new environment led to the more complex way of life called a civilization. In India's case, four or five of the farming villages had grown into large cities with as many as 40,000 inhabitants by 2300 B.C. Excavations of two of these cities, Mohenjo-Daro in Sind and Harappa in the Punjab, have provided most of our knowledge of this civilization.

Although Harappa and Mohenjo-Daro were 400 miles apart, the Indus River made possible the maintenance of a uniform administration and economy over the large area. The cities were carefully planned, with straight paved streets intersecting at right angles and an elaborate drainage system with underground channels. A standard system of weights was used throughout the area. The spacious two-storied houses of

Excavations at Mohenjo-Daro have unearthed mother goddess figurines and cylinder seals that may have had a religious significance. The seals bear Indus writing, essentially a pictographic script employing about 250 symbols and 400 characters, which are still undeciphered. The copper artifact from northern India, made in about 1000 B.C., was probably a weapon used to hunt animals.

the well-to-do contained bathrooms and were constructed with the same type of baked bricks used for roads. A uniform script employing some 400 pictographic signs has not yet been deciphered. The only known use of the script was on engraved stamp-seals, which were probably used to mark property with the name of the owner.

The economy of the Indus civilization, like that of Babylonia and Egypt, was based on irrigation farming. Wheat and barley were the chief crops, and the state collected these grains as taxes and stored them in huge granaries. The importance of agriculture explains the presence of numerous mother-goddess figurines; representing the principle of fertility, they exaggerate female anatomy. For the first known time in world history, chickens were domesticated as a food source, and cotton was grown and used in

making textiles. The spinning and weaving of cotton continues in modern times to be India's chief industry.

Copper and bronze were used for tools and weapons, but the rarity of weapons indicates that warfare was uncommon. Trade was sufficiently well organized to obtain needed raw materials—copper, tin, silver, gold, and timber—from the mountain regions to the west. There is also evidence of active trade contacts with Mesopotamia, some 1500 miles to the west, as early as 2300 B.C. (the time of Sargon of Akkad).

For centuries the people of the Indus valley pursued a relatively unchanging way of life. However, excavations of Mohenjo-Daro show clearly that decline had set in about 1700 B.C., when a series of great floods caused by earthquakes altered the course of the Indus. Harappa to the north appears to have suffered a similar disaster. The invaders who came through the northwest passes about 1500 B.C. found little remaining of a once-flourishing civilization.

The Aryan Invasion and the Early Vedic Age (c. 1500–1000 B.C.)

The invaders who brought an end to what was left of Indus civilization called themselves *Aryans*, meaning "nobles." They spoke Sanskrit, an Indo-European language, and were a part of the great Indo-European migrations of the second millennium B.C., whose profound effects on the ancient world we have noted in earlier chapters. The Aryans were pastoralists who counted their wealth in cattle and whose chief interests were war and cattle rustling. Like the Homeric heroes of Greece, no greater shame could befall these warriors than to take flight in the face of the enemy. Their horse-drawn chariots, which were new to India, made them invincible.

The native population, later called Dravidians, was either conquered by the Aryans as they expanded eastward into the Ganges plain, or driven south into the Deccan. The Aryans contemptuously referred to these darker-skinned but more civilized conquered people as *Dasas*, "slaves."

We know more about the Aryans than we know about their Indus civilization predecessors. Our knowledge comes largely from the four *Vedas* ("Knowledge"), great collections of hymns to the gods and ritual texts composed and handed down orally between 1500 and 500 B.C. by the Aryan priests, the Brahmins. Hence this thousand-year period is commonly called the Vedic Age.

The earliest and most important of the *Vedas*, the *Rig-Veda* ("Royal Veda"), the earliest surviving Indo-European work of literature, gives an insight into the institutions and ideas of the Early Vedic Age, which ended about 1000 B.C. Each tribe was headed by a war leader called *rajah*, a word closely related to the Latin word for king, *rex*. Like the early kings of Sumer, Greece, and Rome, the rajah was not considered divine; nor was he an absolute monarch. Two tribal assemblies, one a small council of the great men of the tribe and the other a larger gathering of the heads of families, approved his accession to office and advised him on important matters.

The earliest hymns in the *Rig-Veda* mention only two social classes, the Kshatriyas (nobility) and the Vaishyas (commoners). But by the end of the Early Vedic Age two additional classes were recognized: the Brahmins, or priests, who because of their specialized religious knowledge had begun to assume the highest social rank; and the Shudras, the non-Aryan conquered population of workers and serfs at the bottom of the social scale. From these four classes the famous caste system of India was to develop during the Later Vedic Age.

The early Aryans had an unsophisticated premoral religion. It involved making sacrifices to the deified forces of nature in return for such material gains as victory in war, long life, and many offspring. The gods were conceived in the image of humans—virile and warlike, fond of charioteering, dancing, and gambling (dice, like chess, is an Indian invention). They were addicted to an intoxicating drink called *soma*, which was believed to make them immortal. The most popular god of the *Rig-Veda* was Indra, storm-god and patron of warriors, who is described leading the Aryans in destroying the forts of the Dasas. Virile and boisterous, Indra personified the heroic virtues of the Aryan warrior aristocracy as he drove his chariot across the sky, wielded his thunderbolts, ate bulls by the score, and quaffed entire lakes of intoxicating *soma*. Another major Aryan god was Varuna, the sky-god. Viewed as the king of the gods, he lived in a great palace in the heavens where one of his associates was Mitra, known as Mithras to the Persians and widely worshiped in the Roman Empire. Varuna was the guardian of *rita*, which is the right order of things. *Rita* is both the cosmic law of nature (the regularity of the seasons, for example), and the customary tribal law of the Aryans.

The Later Vedic Age (c. 1000–500 B.C.)

Most of our knowledge about the five hundred years that comprise the Later Vedic Age is gleaned from two great epics, the *Mahabharata* and the *Ramayana*, and from the religious compositions of the Brahmin priests. The latter comprise three major groups: (1) the three later *Vedas*, containing many hymns along with spells and incantations designed to avoid harm or secure blessings to the worshiper, (2) the *Brahmanas*, which describe and explain the priestly ritual of sacrifice and reflect the dominant position achieved by the Brahmin class in society; and (3) the more philosophical speculations collectively known as the *Upanishads*.

The kernel of the two Indian epics, which glorify the Kshatriyan (noble or warrior) class, was originally secular rather than religious. The core of the *Mahabharata* is a great war between rivals for the throne of an Aryan state situated in the upper Ganges plain in the region of the modern Delhi. Many passages dwell on the warriors' joy of battle as they fight for glory and booty. As in the Greek *Iliad's* account of the Trojan War, all rulers of Aryan India participate in a decisive battle, which rages for eighteen days near the beginning of the Later Vedic Age. The epic came to be used in royal sacrificial ritual, and a long succession of priestly editors added many long passages on religious duties, morals, and statecraft.

One of the most famous additions is the *Bhagavad-Gita (The Lord's Song)*, a philosophical dialogue which stresses the performance of duty, or *dharma*, without passion or fear. It is still the most treasured piece in Hindu literature. *Dharma*, whose broad meaning is moral law and is often translated as "virtue," had by this time replaced the earlier Vedic term *rita* which, as noted above, originally meant premoral customary and cosmic law.

The other great epic, the *Ramayana*, has been likened to the Greek *Odyssey*. It recounts the wanderings of the banished prince Rama and his faithful wife Sita's long vigil before they are reunited and Rama gains his rightful throne. In the course of time priestly editors transformed this simple adventure story into a book of devotion. Rama became the ideal man and the incarnation of the great god Vishnu, while Sita emerged as the perfect woman, devoted and submissive to her husband. Her words were memorized by almost every Hindu bride:

> Car and steed and gilded palace,
>   vain are these to woman's life;
> Dearer is her husband's shadow
>   to the loved and loving wife.

The two epics, together with the last three *Vedas* and the *Brahmanas*, reflect the many changes that occurred in Indian life during the Later Vedic Age. By the beginning of this age, the Aryans had mastered iron metallurgy, which they may have learned from the Near East. The Aryans had also moved eastward from the Punjab, conquering the native population and forming larger and frequently warring states in the upper Ganges valley. These were territorial rather than tribal states. Although some were oligarchic republics, most were ruled by rajahs. Despite the presence of an advisory council of nobles and priests, the rajahs' powers were greater than those of the tribal leaders of the earlier period. The rajahs now lived in palaces and collected taxes—in the form of goods from the villages—in order to sustain their courts and armies. A few small cities arose, some as administrative centers connected with a palace, and some as commercial centers. Trade contacts with Mesopotamia were renewed, and merchants probably brought back from the West the use of coinage and the Aramaic alphabet, which was adapted to Sanskrit.

Village, Caste, and Family

In the Later Vedic Age, the three pillars of traditional Indian society—the autonomous village, caste, and the joint family—were established. India has always been primarily agricultural, and its countryside is still a patchwork of thousands of villages. The ancient village was made up of joint families governed by a headman and a council of elders. Villages enjoyed considerable autonomy; the rajah's government hardly interfered at all as long as it received its quota of taxes.

The four classes, or castes—Kshatriyas (nobles), Vaishyas (commoners), Brahmins (priests), and Shudras (workers or serfs)—have remained constant throughout India's history. But during the Later Vedic Age, the Brahmins assumed the highest social rank. The four castes also began to subdivide into numerous subcastes, each with a special social, occupational, or religious character. For example, such new occupational groups as merchants and artisans became subcastes of the Vaishyas. Furthermore, another main social division was formed, consisting of those whose occupations were the most menial and degrading—scavengers, sweepers, tanners (because they handled the carcasses of dead animals), and carriers of human and animal waste. These outcasts were called Untouchables because their touch was considered defiling to the upper castes.

Although the inequalities of the caste system clearly contributed to the wealth and influence of the upper castes, the lower caste groups came to accept the system. One reason for this was the manner in which a caste performed the functions of a guild in maintaining a monopoly for the caste in its occupation and in securing other favorable conditions for its members. By maintaining discipline in accordance with caste rules, the caste leaders in each village also gave Indian society a stability that partially compensated for the lack of political stability over a wide area through much of Indian history.

The third pillar of Indian society was the joint family, in which the wives of all the sons of the patriarch of the family came to live and raise the children. When the patriarch died, his authority was transferred to his eldest son, but his property was divided equally among all his sons. Women could not inherit property. Nor could they participate in sacrifices to the gods; their presence at the sacrifice was considered a source of pollution.

The emphasis placed on the interest and security of the group rather than on the individual is a common denominator of the three pillars of Indian society—the autonomous village, the caste system, and the joint family. Thus Indian society has always been concerned with stability rather than with progress in the Western sense, and the Indians have had a more passive outlook toward life than their Western counterparts.

The Brahmanas *and the* Upanishads

Radical changes in Indian religion and thought occurred during the Later Vedic Age, producing what became one of the world's most complex religious and philosophical systems. The first phase of this development is clearly seen in the *Brahmanas*. It began about 1000 B.C. and is often called Brahmanism because it was the product of the emergence of the Brahmin priests to a position of supreme power and privilege in society. During the Early Vedic Age, sacrifice had

been only a means of influencing the gods in favor of the offeror; now it became the means of compelling the gods to act, provided the correct ritual was employed. Since only the priests possessed the technical expertise to perform the complex and lengthy rites of sacrifice (some of which lasted for months), and since the slightest variation in ritual was thought to turn the gods against people, the Brahmins strengthened their position over the nobles and rulers of the Kshatriya class.

Equally important, the priests gave the caste system a religious sanction by extending the concept of *dharma*, moral duty, to include the performance of caste functions as social duty—behavior suitable to a person's hereditary caste.

The more than 250 *Upanishads* were composed between 800 and 600 B.C. by some members of the Brahmin and Kshatriya classes who rejected both the simple nature worship of the *Rig-Veda* and the complicated sacrificial system of the *Brahmanas*. The Upanishadic thinkers speculated on the nature of reality, the purpose of life, and immortality. (The Rig-Vedic Aryans, pursuing their heroic warrior values, had not been particularly interested in life after death.)

These first Indian gurus wandered in the forests as hermits, where they meditated and taught their disciples. One of them summed up their quest as follows:

From the unreal lead me to the real!
From darkness lead me to light!
From death lead me to immortality!

The following beliefs ultimately became an integral part of Indian religion and philosophy:

1. The fundamental reality, the essence of all things, is not something material, as most of the early Greek philosophers at about the same time concluded, but spiritual—the World Soul.

2. Each individual possesses a soul, which is a part of the World Soul.

3. The material world is an illusion *(maya)* and the cause of all suffering. As long as such earthly goals as fame, power, and wealth are sought, the result will be pain and sorrow.

4. Salvation, or deliverance from *maya*, can only come through the reabsorption of the individual soul into the World Soul.

5. This release from *maya* is part of a complicated process of reincarnation. The individual soul must go through a long series of earthly reincarnations from one body to another.

6. Intertwined with the doctrine of reincarnation is the immutable law called *karma* (meaning "deed"). This law holds that the consequences of one's deeds determine one's future after death. A person's status at any particular point is not the result of chance but depends on his or her soul's actions in previous existences. Together with the doctrine of *maya*, *karma* gives a satisfactory explanation to the question of why suffering exists, a question that has troubled thoughtful people all over the world. The Indian answer is that the wicked who prosper will pay later, while the righteous who suffer are being punished for acts committed in former existences.

Hindusism: A Religious Synthesis

Upanishadic thought became a part of Hinduism, the developing religion of India, when the Brahmin priests incorporated it into their teaching. In doing so they gave the caste system additional religious support by linking it to *karma* and the process of reincarnation. In effect, caste became the essential machinery for the educative process of the soul as it went through the long succession of rebirths from the lowest categories in caste to that of the Brahmin, who presumably is near the end of the cycle. The priests made individual salvation, now a conspicuous part of Indian religion, dependent on the uncomplaining acceptance of one's position at birth. Marriage outside one's caste was forbidden.

But because the Upanishadic doctrine of salvation by absorption of the individual soul into the World Soul was too intellectual and remote for the average person to grasp fully, devotion to personal redeemer gods emerged. This new devotion centered on gods who, as manifestations of *Brahman* (the World Soul), stood in close relationship to their worshippers.

The major Aryan gods gradually faded away, and Hinduism acquired a trinity consisting of Brahma the Creator, Vishnu the Preserver, and Shiva the Destroyer. Brahma, the personification of the World Soul whose name is the masculine form of *Brahman*, never acquired the popular following achieved by Visnu and Shiva, a position they continue to maintain. These two popular deities evolved from Vedic and Dravidian origins.

In the old Vedic pantheon of the Aryans, Vishnu was a god associated with the sun. He now evolved into the friend and comforter, the savior who works continuously for the welfare of humanity. "No devotee of mine is lost," is Vishnu's promise. His followers believe that he has appeared in ten major "descents" in human form to save the world from disaster. Two of Vishnu's incarnations are described in great Indian epics. As Krishna in the *Mahabharata*, he is the friend and adviser of princes and the author of *The Lord's Song* (*Bhagavad-Gita;* see p. 102). As Rama, the hero of the *Ramayana*, he saves the human race from the oppressions of a great demon before returning to the "City of the Gods" and resuming the form of Vishnu.

Shiva, the other great popular god of classical and modern Hinduism, evolved from a minor Aryan Vedic god who was the guardian of healing herbs but whose arrows also brought disease. Another prototype of Shiva was a pre-Aryan fertility god who was worshipped in the cities of the Indus civilization. For this reason, Shiva is often associated with phallic symbols. His spouse is the pre-Aryan mother goddess who under various forms, from grossly sexual to gentle and benevolent, often plays a more important role than her husband.

With such a background, Shiva is a very different character from Vishnu. Shiva personifies the cosmic force of change that destroys in order to build anew. He exemplifies another major characteristic of Hinduism, the reconciliation of extremes—violence and passivity, for example, and eroticism and asceticism. Some representations portray Shiva in terrifying guise, garlanded with skulls; others show him as the Lord of Dancers, whose activities are the source of all movement within the cosmos.

Most Hindus are devotees of either Vishnu or Shiva and their respective emanations, wives, and children. However, animals—especially the cow—vegetation, water, and even stones are also worshiped as divine. In time literally thousands of deities, demigods, and lesser spirits came to form the Hindu pantheon, the world's largest. Hindus, however, do not think of their religion as polytheistic, for all gods and spirits are viewed as manifestations of *Brahman,* the World Soul, which pervades everything.

Hinduism is probably the world's most tolerant religion. It possesses no canon, such as the Bible or the Koran; no single personal founder, such as Christ or Muhammad; and no precise body of authoritative doctrine. Hindus can believe what they like, and they remain Hindus as long as they observe the rules of their caste. Depending on one's intellectual and spiritual needs and capacities, Hinduism can be a transcendental philosophy, a devotional adherence to a savior god such as Vishnu, or simple idolatry. From its earliest origins, Hinduism has exhibited an unusual organic quality of growth and adaptation. The last major element in the Hindu synthesis was provided by Gautama Buddha.

The Middle Way of Gautama Buddha

By taking over Upanishadic thought, the Brahmins had laid the foundations of classical Hinduism, but they continued to place great emphasis upon the importance of sacrifice, priestly ritual, and magical spells. This led in the sixth century B.C. to the rise of more ascetics and reformers who sought to pursue the goals of Upanishadic thought by bypassing the priests and other mechanical ceremonialism. To achieve salvation from the cycle of birth and death, most of these dissenters lived as hermits, meditating on the true nature of human beings as part of the World Soul. They demonstrated by their indifference to worldly matters that they had realized their oneness with the underlying essence of all

things. The most important of these ascetics, who soon rejected extreme asceticism and found his own "Middle Way" to salvation, was Guatama, who called himself the Buddha ("The Enlightened One").

Gautama (c. 563–483 B.C.) was the son of a leading noble in a small oligarchic republic located at the foot of the Himalayas. In his twenty-ninth year, according to tradition, Gautama was deeply shocked by the misery, disease, and sorrow that he saw as he walked through the streets of his native city. He renounced his wealth and position and, forsaking his wife and child, determined to seek a meaningful answer to the question of human suffering. For six years he lived in a forest, practicing the self-mortification rites of the ascetics he found there. Gautama almost died from fasting and self-torture and at last concluded that these practices did not lead to wisdom.

One day, while sitting beneath a sacred fig tree meditating on the problem of human suffering, Gautama received "enlightenment." The meaning, the cause, and the conquest of suffering became clear to him. From this insight, he constructed a religious philosophy that has affected the lives of millions of people for 2500 years.

Dressed in a simple yellow robe, with begging bowl in hand, he wandered through the plain of the Ganges, speaking with everyone regardless of caste and attracting disciples. At last, when he was eighty years old and enfeebled, he was invited by a poor blacksmith to a meal. According to legend, the food was tainted, but Gautama ate it rather than offend his host. Later in the

Buddha on the Middle Way

There are two extremes, O disciples, which the man who has given up the world ought not to follow—the habitual practice, on the one hand, of those things whose attraction depends upon the passions, and especially of sensuality—a low and pagan way unworthy, unprofitable, and fit only for the worldly-minded—and the habitual practice, on the other hand, of asceticism, which

is painful, unworthy, and unprofitable.

There is a middle path, O disciples, avoiding these two extremes . . . a path which opens the eyes and bestows understanding, which leads to peace of mind, to the higher wisdom, to full enlightenment, to Nirvana!

Translated by T. W. Rhys David, *Sacred Books of the East,* XI (Oxford: Oxford University Press, 1881), pp. 146–147.

day the Buddha had severe pains, and he knew death was near. Calling his disciples together, he gave them this parting message: "Be ye lamps unto yourselves. Be a refuge to yourselves. Hold fast to the truth as to a lamp. Look not for refuge to anyone beside yourselves."

What is "the truth" that the Buddha believed could be discovered by individual effort, without the need for priestly assistance? The answer had been revealed to him during the Great Enlightenment in the form of the Four Noble Truths: (1) existence is suffering; (2) suffering springs from desire and craving; (3) the cure for suffering is the extinction of desire; and (4) to achieve the absence of desire, there is an Eightfold Path of right conduct, which is the Middle Way between worldly pursuits and extreme asceticism. The Buddha offered Five Moral Rules of right conduct: do not kill any living being; do not take what is not given to you; do not speak falsely; do not drink intoxicating drinks; do not be unchaste.

Like so many reform movements in the history of religion, the Buddha's teaching aimed at restoring the purity of an existing creed. The Buddha sought to strip the Upanishadic teachings of the corruptions that had enveloped them. Thus he restored the ethical basis of the doctrines of *karma* and reincarnation, which the priests had made dependent on the performance of ritual rather than on moral behavior. He also repudiated the belief that only members of the Brahmin caste could attain release from the wheel of birth and rebirth, insisting that release was possible for everyone regardless of caste. Nor was there any place in his system for the popular gods of Hinduism. Indeed, what the Buddha taught was more a philosophy than a religion. Thus, Buddhism became a movement separate from Hinduism.

The Buddhists came to form two groups—monks and laity. The Buddha's close disciples, who included women as well as men, renounced the world, donned yellow robes, and lived for part of the year in the world's first monastic communities (many in caves cut out of rock), with staves and begging bowls as their only possessions. By means of a strict discipline of mind and body, they aspired to achieve "the supreme peace of *nirvana*"—release from the wheel of birth and rebirth. The literal meaning of *nirvana* is "to extinguish," and it refers to the extinguishing of

desire, which feeds on sensual pleasures and is the cause of suffering. *Nirvana* is also a state of superconsciousness, attained by a type of yoga concentration in which the individual personality or ego dissolves and becomes united with the spirit of life, which the Buddha taught exists in all creatures.

To the ascetic monks, Buddhism's major purpose is the dissolution of the ego and the sense of release and spiritual joy that results. To the ordinary Buddhist laity, who continue to live in the world (although they often "retreat" to a monastery for short periods), the Buddha's ethical teachings serve as a guide to right living.

The Buddha was a reformer who censured the rites and dogmas of the Brahmins, broke with the rules of caste, taught that all people are equal, and proclaimed a code of ethics whose appeal is universally recognized. Buddhism reached its height in India in the third century B.C. Soon thereafter Buddhism began to decline, and ultimately it disappeared in its homeland.

One reason for this development was a successful counterreformation of Hinduism. For most people accustomed to elaborate ritual and the worship of benevolent personal gods, original Buddhism seemed stern and austere, and in time the Buddha's simpler followers began to worship him as a god and the savior of humanity. Temples were built and statues were erected honoring the savior, and *nirvana* was viewed as a sort of heaven. Then when the Brahmins proclaimed the Buddha to be the ninth incarnation of the Hindu god Vishnu, Buddhism began to fade as an independent religion in India. (Destroyed completely by persecution following the Muslim conquest of India in the eighth century A.D., Buddhism revived on a small scale in the mid-twentieth century.)

Buddhism's impact on Hinduism was nevertheless profound, for it served to rejuvenate and purify the older religion. More emphasis was henceforth placed on ethical conduct as a means of salvation and less on sacrifices, ritual prayers, and magic spells.

Another order of monks and lay followers who reject the authority of the Brahmin priests was Jainism. Its founder was Mahavira, a younger contemporary of the Buddha. Jainism has much in common with Buddhism, but it has never attained Buddhism's popularity. It places far more emphasis on asceticism and the doctrine of non-violence (*ahimsa*) toward any living creature. It is probably more through the influence of Jainism than of Buddhism that nonviolence became a significant aspect of Hinduism.

The First Indian Empire

By the end of the Later Vedic Age about 500 B.C., a thousand years after the collapse of the Indus civilization, the Aryan invaders of India had established sixteen major kingdoms and tribal oligarchies in northern India, stretching from modern Pakistan to Bengal. The shock of Alexander the Great's invasion of India provided the spark that led to the unification of India.

In 326 B.C. Alexander the Great, continuing his conquest of the Persian Empire (see ch. 2), brought his phalanxes into the easternmost Persian satrapy in the Indus valley, defeating local Punjab rulers. When his weary troops refused to advance further eastward into the Ganges plain, Alexander constructed a fleet and explored the Indus to its mouth. From there he returned overland to Babylon, while his fleet skirted the coast of the Arabian Sea and reached the Persian Gulf.

After Alexander's death in 323 B.C., the empire he had built so rapidly quickly disintegrated, and by 321 B.C. his domain in the Punjab had completely disappeared. But he had opened routes between India and the West that would remain open during the following Hellenistic and Roman periods, and by destroying the petty states in the Punjab he facilitated—and perhaps inspired—the conquests of India's own first emperor.

Chandragupta Maurya, India's First Emperor

In 322 B.C., shortly after Alexander's death, a new era began in India. In that year Chandragupta Maurya seized the state of Magadha in the Ganges valley. Over the next twenty-four years Chandragupta conquered northern India and founded the Maurya Dynasty, which endured until about 185 B.C. At its height the empire included all the subcontinent except the extreme south.

India's first empire reflected the imperial vision of its founder. He created an administrative system whose efficiency was not surpassed until the advent of British rule in the nineteenth century. Chandragupta was also a brilliant general and administrator. He was responsible for the first military victory of the East over the West; in 305 B.C. he defeated Seleucus, the general who had inherited the major part of Alexander's empire and had crossed the Indus in an attempt to regain Alexander's Indian conquests. Seleucus gave up his Indian claims in return for five hundred war elephants and established friendly diplomatic relations with the Indian emperor.

Life in the Mauryan Empire

Seleucus' ambassador to the court of Chandragupta, whose name was Megasthenes, wrote a detailed account of India, fragments of which have survived. They give a fascinating picture of life in the empire. Pataliputra, Chandragupta's capital known today as Patna, covered eighteen square miles and was probably the largest city in the world. Outside its massive wooden walls was a deep trench used for defense and the disposal of sewage.

The remarkably advanced Mauryan empire was divided and subdivided into provinces, districts, and villages whose headmen were appointed by the state. The old customary law, preserved and administered by the Brahmin priesthood, was superseded by an extensive legal code that provided for royal interference in all matters. A series of courts ranging from the village court presided over by the headman to the emperor's imperial court administered the law. So busy was Chandragupta with the details of his surprisingly modern administration that, according to Megasthenes, he had to hear court cases during his daily massage.

Two other agencies were very important in holding the empire together. One was the professional army, which Megasthenes reports was an incredibly large force of 700,000 men, 9000 elephants, and 10,000 chariots. The other was the secret police, whose numbers were so large that the Greek writer concluded that spies constituted a separate class in Indian society. So great was the danger of conspiracy that Chandragupta lived in strict seclusion, attended only by women who cooked his food and in the evening carried him to his apartment, where they lulled him to sleep with music.

Complementing this picture of an efficient but harsh bureaucracy is a remarkable book, *Treatise on Material Gain (Arthashastna)*, written by Chandragupta's chief minister, Kautilya, as a guide for the king and his ministers. Kautilya exalts royal power as the means of establishing and maintaining "material gain," meaning political and economic stability. The great evil is anarchy, such as had existed among the small warring states in northern India. To achieve the aims of statecraft, Kautilya argues, a single authority is needed that will employ force when necessary. Like Machiavelli, the Renaissance Italian author of a famous book on statecraft (*The Prince*), Kautilya advocates deception or unscrupulous means to attain desired ends.

The Mauryan state also controlled and encouraged economic life. Kautilya's treatise, which is thought to reflect much actual practice, advises the ruler to "facilitate mining operations," "encourage manufacturers," "exploit forest wealth," "provide amenities" for cattle breeding and commerce, and "construct highways both on land and on water." Price controls are advocated because "all goods should be sold to the people at favorable prices," and foreign trade should be subsidized: "Shippers and traders dealing in foreign goods should be given tax exemptions to aid them in making profits." Foreign trade did flourish, and in the bazaars of Pataliputra were displayed goods from southern India, China, Mesopotamia, and Asia Minor. Agriculture, however, remained the chief source of wealth. In theory, all land belonged to the state, which collected one fourth of the produce as taxes. Irrigation and crop rotation were practiced, and Megasthenes states that there were no famines.

ASHOKA'S EMPIRE

- Cities
△ Rock Edicts
▲ Pillar Edicts

Ashoka, India's Greatest King

Following Chandragupta's death in 297 B.C., his son and grandson expanded the empire southward into the Deccan Peninsula (see map, left). However, Chandragupta's grandson Ashoka (269–232 B.C.), the most renowned of all Indian rulers, was more committed to peace than to war. His first military campaign was also his last; the cruelty of the campaign horrified him, and he resolved never again to permit such acts of butchery. Soon thereafter he was converted to Buddhism, whose teachings increased his aversion to warfare.

Throughout his empire, Ashoka had his edicts carved on rocks and stone pillars. They remain today as the oldest surviving written documents of India and are invaluable for appreciating the spirit and purpose of Ashoka's rule. For example, they contain his conception of the duty of a ruler:

> He shall . . . personally attend the business . . . of earth, of sacred places, of minors, the aged, the afflicted, and the helpless, and of women. . . . In the happiness of his subjects lies his happiness.[2]

Although a devout Buddhist, Ashoka did not persecute the Brahmins and Hindus but proclaimed religious toleration as official policy:

The king ... honors every form of religious faith ...; whereof this is the root, to reverence one's own faith and never to revile that of others. Whoever acts differently injures his own religion while he wrongs another's.[3]

Ashoka was a successful propagator of his faith. He sent Buddhist missionaries to many lands—the Himalayan regions, Tamil Land (India's far south), Ceylon (Sri Lanka), Burma, and even as far away as Syria and Egypt—and transformed Buddhism from a small Indian sect to an aggressive missionary faith. Modern Indians revere his memory, and the famous lion on the capital of one of his pillars has been adopted as the national seal of the present Indian republic.

Fall of the Mauryan Empire

Almost immediately after Ashoka's death in 232 B.C., the Mauryan Empire began to disintegrate. The last emperor was assassinated about 185 B.C. in a palace revolution led by a Brahmin priest. Some five centuries of disintegration and disorder followed. Northern India was overrun by a series of invaders, and the south broke free from northern control.

The sudden collapse of the powerful Mauryan state, and the grave consequences that ensued have provoked much scholarly speculation. Some historians have felt that the fall of the Mauryas can be traced to a hostile Brahmin reaction against Ashoka's patronage of Buddhism. Others believe that Ashoka's doctrine of nonviolence curbed the military ardor of his people and left them vulnerable to invaders. More plausible explanations for the fall of the Mauryan state take into account the communications problems facing an empire than included most of the Indian subcontinent, the difficulty of financing a vast army and bureaucracy, and the intrigues of discontented regional groups within the empire.

New Invaders of India

The Mauryan Empire was the first of two successful attempts to unify India in ancient times. The second—the work of the Gupta dynasty (A.D. c. 320–350)—will be described in chapter 8. In the five centuries between these two eras of imperial splendor, a succession of foreign invaders entered from the northwest and added new racial and cultural elements to the Indian scene.

Bactrian Greeks and Kushans

The first of the new invaders of India were Greeks from Bactria (see map, p. 108). They were descendants of the soldiers settled there by Alexander to serve as the strong point of his empire in the east. After Alexander, Bactria continued as a province of the Seleucid Empire, a bastion against the attacks of wandering nomads from the north and a center for trade with India to the southeast. The decline of the Seleucid Empire allowed the Bactrian Greeks to establish an independent kingdom about 245 B.C.

In 183 B.C., two years after the death of the last Mauryan emperor of India, the fourth Bactrian king, Demetrius, crossed the Hindu Kush mountains as Alexander had done 150 years earlier and occupied the northern Punjab. From their base at Taxila, Demetrius and his successors ruled an area stretching from Bactria to the upper Ganges valley (modern Afghanistan and northern Pakistan), but soon after 150 B.C., Bactria itself was overrun by nomads. Thereafter Greek rule in India steadily declined until the last remnants disappeared late in the first century B.C.

The Greeks in India established the farthest outpost of Hellenism in the Hellenistic Age. Demetrius and his successors came closer than any Hellenistic ruler to realizing Alexander's supposed goal of a union of races. Their cities were not artificial Greek enclaves in a hostile land, like Alexandria in Egypt and Antioch in Syria. Indians were enrolled as citizens, a bilingual coinage was issued bearing Greek inscriptions on one side and Indian on the other, and at least one king, Menander, became a Buddhist.

Hordes of nomadic peoples, migrating out of central Asia, replaced the Greeks in Bactria and northwest India. First to arrive were the Indo-European Scythians, who had been pushed out of central Asia by other Indo-European nomads known in Chinese sources as the Yueh-chih. In their turn the Yueh-chih occupied Bactria, and about A.D. 40 they crossed the Hindu Kush and conquered the Punjab. The Kushans, as the

Yueh-chih were called in India, expanded eastward to the Middle Ganges valley and southward perhaps as far as the borders of the Deccan. In contrast to the highly centralized Mauryan Empire, the Kushan state was more feudal than bureaucratic—its kings were overlords rather than direct rulers—yet it gave northern India two centuries of peace and prosperity before collapsing soon after A.D. 200.

Hinayana and Mahayana Buddhism

Buddhism in the meantime had split into two major branches. The older branch was contemptuously called Hinayana or "Lesser Vehicle" (to salvation) by its opponents. It continued the early tradition of regarding the Buddha as a teacher who taught how the individual could achieve salvation by becoming an *arhant*, a saint who eliminated his ego and entered into *nirvana*. *Arhants* renounced the world to seek their own enlightenment and salvation through meditation. To the followers of the newer branch, the Mahayana or "Great Vehicle" (to salvation), the Hinayana goal was considered to be selfish and incomplete. They replaced the ideal of the *arhant* with that of the *bodhisattva* ("one whose essence is enlightenment"), a saint who postponed his own entry into *nirvana* in order to act as a compassionate and loving savior to others in reaching that goal.

Mahayana Buddhism, with its message of hope and salvation for the masses, spread rapidly along the overland trade route to Tibet and China, and from China to Korea, Japan, and Vietnam. (The spiritual leader of Tibetan Buddhism, the famous Dalai Lama, is a personification of the *bodhisattva* concept). The more austere Hinayana became the southern branch of Buddhism, spreading from India and Ceylon to Burma, Thailand, and Cambodia.

While Buddhism was becoming a world religion, Hinduism continued to maintain a strong hold on the Indian people. Unlike the Buddhists, who had disregarded caste and accepted both the Greeks and the Kushans, the Hindus rejected the foreign invaders as outcasts. Gradually the Indians came to consider Hinduism a more characteristically Indian movement than Buddhism, and Buddhism began to lose its popularity within India.

Buddhist Sculpture and Architecture

The most lasting Western influence on India in ancient times was on Buddhist sculpture. Before the Kushan period, Indian artists were influenced by the Buddha's prohibitions against idolatry and refrained from portraying the Buddha in human form. His presence was indicated by symbols only, such as his footprints, his umbrella, or the tree under which he attained enlightenment. Beginning in the first century A.D., however, the Buddha himself was portrayed in numerous statues and reliefs. Most of these early Buddha figures come from Gandhara, the center of the Kushan empire and the earlier Graeco-Bactrian kingdom.

The primary inspiration for this Gandharan art came from Greece. Apparently Hellenistic sculptors and craftsmen migrated to Grandhara via the central Asian trade routes. The result was a blending of Greek technique and Indian motifs.

A second inspiration for Gandharan art came from Mahayana Buddhism, which viewed the Buddha as a savior. This devotional form of Buddhism needed images for worship, and figures of the Buddha as a *bodhisattva* savior, as well as many *bodhisattva* saints, were produced in large numbers. Mahayana Buddhism and Graeco-Buddhist images of the Buddha, both of which developed in the Kushan empire, spread together through eastern Asia.

The magnificent buildings of the Mauryan emperors have disappeared. All that remain are Buddhist *stupas*, dome-shaped monuments that were used as funeral mounds to enshrine the relics of the Buddha and Buddhist saints, or to mark a holy spot. Originally made only of earth, the mounds were later fashioned out of earth faced with brick and surrounded by railings and four richly carved gateways of stone. (Those built by Ashoka at Sanchi include voluptuous mother-goddess figures that illustrate the Indian belief in the unity of life—human and divine, erotic and ascetic.) On top of the dome was a boxlike structure surmounted by a carved umbrella, the Indian emblem that symbolizes the Buddha's princely birth. As centuries passed, the low dome was heightened into a tall, tapered structure more like a tower. Later, when Buddhism spread to other countries, the *stupa* type of architecture went along. Its gateway was widely copied, and the *stupa* itself may have been the prototype of the Buddhist pagodas that are common in East Asia today.

South India

With the exception of a short period during the Mauryan Empire, the vast tableland of south India—the Deccan—and its fertile coastal plains remained outside the main forces of political change in the north. The Dravidian peoples of this area, with their dark skin and small stature, differed in appearance, language, and culture from the Aryan-speaking peoples of the north. Gradually, however, as Brahmin priests and Buddhist monks infiltrated the south, Hinduism and Buddhism were grafted onto the existing Dravidian culture.

Politically the south remained divided into numerous warring states, the most interesting being three Tamil-speaking (a Dravidian dialect) kingdoms in the far south. Tamil folk poetry, which describes the people at work and at play, is justly famous. By the first century B.C., Tamil Land had become an intermediary in the maritime trade extending eastward to the East Indies and westward to the Hellenistic kingdoms.

When Augustus became head of the Roman world, the Tamil and Kushan rulers sent him congratulatory embassies. At least nine other embassies from India visited the Roman emperors, and Roman-Indian trade greatly increased. Indian birds (particularly talking parrots, costing more than human slaves) became the pets of wealthy Roman ladies, and Indian animals (lions, tigers, and buffaloes) were used in the wild beast shows of Roman emperors. In view of these contacts, we can understand why Ptolemy's second-century A.D. map of the world shows considerable knowledge of the geography of India.

The peace and prosperity that the Kushans brought to much of northern India ended about A.D. 220. The collapse of the Kushan state was followed by a century of chaos and almost total obscurity before a new era of unified imperial rule, which rivaled that of the Mauryas, began in India under the Guptas (see chapter 8). In the meantime another great civilization had arisen in China.

The formative period of Chinese history—the era of the Shang and Chou dynasties, before China was unified politically—was, like the early

The Great Stupa at Sanchi was constructed during the reign of King Ashoka. This circular Buddhist shrine is surrounded by stone railings pierced at each cardinal point of the compass by a ceremonial stone gateway *(torana)*. Each gateway is decorated, like the west gate shown here, with intricate relief sculptures depicting *Jataka* tales (events in the life of the Buddha) and popular mythological figures.

history of India before its unification by the Mauryan Dynasty, a time during which most of China's cultural tradition arose. As in India, this tradition has lasted into the present century.

The Land

Chinese civilization arose and developed in a vast area, one-third larger than the United States if such dependencies as Manchuria, Inner Mongolia, and Tibet are included. For centuries China was almost completely isolated from the other centers of civilization by mountains, deserts, and seas. This isolation helps explain the great originality of China's culture.

China proper is a vast watershed drained by three river systems that rise close together on the high Tibetan plateau and flow eastward to the Pacific. Three mountain systems also rise in the west, diminishing in altitude as they slope eastward between the river systems. The Yellow River (Huang Ho), traditionally known as "China's Sorrow" because of the misery caused by its periodic flooding, traverses the North China plain. In this area, the original homeland of Chinese culture, the climate is like that of western Europe. The Yangtze River and its valley forms the second river system. South of this valley lie the subtropical lands of South China, the home of ancient cultures that were destroyed or transformed by Chinese expansion from the north. Here the shorter rivers and valleys converging on present-day Canton formed the third major river system.

This pattern of mountain ranges and river systems has, throughout China's history, created problems of political unity. At the same time, the great river valleys facilitated the spread of a homogeneous culture over a greater land area than any other civilization in the world.

China's Prehistory

The discovery of Peking man in 1927 made it evident that ancient humanlike creatures with an early Paleolithic culture had dwelled in China (see p. 3). Certain physical characteristics of Peking man are thought to be distinctive marks of the Mongoloid branch of the human race. Skulls of modern humans (*Homo sapiens*) have also been found.

Until recently, archaeologists believed that the earliest Neolithic farming villages (the Yang Shao culture) appeared in the Yellow River valley about 4500 B.C. Now a series of newly discovered sites has pushed back the Neolithic Age in China to 6500 B.C. The evidence indicates that China's Neolithic culture, which cultivated millet and domesticated the pig, originated independently from that in the Near East.

The people of China's last Neolithic culture, called Lung Shan, lived in walled towns and produced a wheel-made black pottery. Their culture spread widely in North China. Most scholars believe that this Neolithic culture immediately preceded the Shang period, when civilization emerged in China about 1700 B.C. Others now believe that the Hsia Dynasty, considered—like the Shang had been—to be purely legendary, actually existed and flourished for some three centuries before it was conquered by the Shang.

The Shang Dynasty: China Enters History

With the establishment of Shang rule over most of North China and the appearance of the first written texts, China completed the transition from Neolithic culture to civilization. Shang originally was the name of a nomadic tribe whose vigorous leaders succeeded in establishing themselves as the overlords of other tribal leaders in North China. The Shang capital, a walled city to which the tribal leaders came to pay tribute, changed frequently; the last capital was at modern Anyang (see map, p. 113).

The Shang people developed bronze metallurgy and carried it to heights hardly surpassed in world history. Bronze was used to cast elaborate ceremonial and drinking vessels (the Shang leaders were notorious for their drinking bouts) and weapons, all intricately decorated with both incised and high-relief designs.

The Shang people also developed a distinctive writing system employing nearly 5000 characters, some of which are still in use today. These characters represent individual words rather than sounds and consist of pictographs, recognizable as pictures of observable objects, and ideographs representing ideas.

Most Shang writing is found on thousands of "oracle bones," fragments of animal bones and

ANCIENT CHINA

Shang kings and nobles lived in imposing buildings, went to battle in horse-drawn chariots resembling those of Homer's Greece, and were buried in sumptuous tombs together with their chariots, still-living servants and war captives. Warfare was frequent, and the chariot, a new military weapon, facilitated the spread of Shang power through North China. The power of the kings and nobles rested on their ownership of the land, their monopoly of bronze metallurgy, their possession of expensive war chariots, and the kings' religious functions.

Unlike the common people, the kings and nobles had recorded ancestors and belonged to a clan. They were the descendants in the male line from a common ancestor to whom they rendered worship and who was usually a god or a hero, but sometimes a fish, an animal, or a bird. The chief deity, called God on High, was the ancestor of the king's own clan. There were regular animal sacrifices and libations of a beerlike liquor were poured on the ground. The object was to win the aid or avoid the displeasure of the spirits.

Magic was employed to maintain the balance of nature, which was thought to function through

Bronze vessels, such as this one from the early tenth century B.C., were designed to contain water, wine, meat, or grain used during the sacrificial rites in which the Shang and Chou prayed to the memory of their ancestors. Animals were a major motif of ritual bronzes.

tortoise shells on which were inscribed questions put to the gods and ancestral spirits, which were thought to continue a close relationship with their living descendants as members of the family group. The diviner would ask such questions as "Will the king's child be a son?" and "If we raise an army of 3000 men to drive X away from Y, will we succeed?" The shell or bone would then be heated and the resulting cracks would be interpreted as an answer to the question.

Shang China was ruled by hereditary kings who were also priests acting as intermediaries between the people and the spirit world. Their power was not absolute, being constantly limited by an aristocratic "Council of the Great and Small." The oracle bones reveal that the kings often appealed to the ancestral spirits in order to overcome the opposition of the council.

the interaction of two opposed but complementary forces called *yang* and *yin*. *Yang* was associated with the sun and all things male, strong, warm, and active. *Yin* was associated with the moon and all things female, dark, cold, weak, and passive. In later ages, Chinese philosophers—all male—would employ these concepts to work out the behavior pattern of obedience and passivity that was expected of women.

The common people were peasants who belonged to no clans and apparently worshiped no ancestors. Their gods were the elementary spirits of nature, such as rivers, mountains, earth, wind, rain, and heavenly bodies. Peasants were virtual serfs, owning no land but working plots periodically assigned to them by royal and noble landowners. They collectively cultivated the fields retained by their lords.

Farming methods were primitive, not having advanced beyond the Neolithic level. Bronze was used for weapons, not tools or implements, and the peasants continued to reap wheat and millet with stone sickles and till their allotted fields with wooden plows.

The Chou Dynasty: The Feudal Age

Around 1122 B.C., the leader of the Chou tribe overthrew the Shang ruler, who, it was claimed, had failed to rule fairly and benevolently. The Chou leader announced that Heaven (*T'ien*) had given him a mandate to replace the Shang. This was more than a rationalization of the seizure of power. It introduced a new aspect of Chinese thought: the cosmos is ruled by an impersonal and all-powerful Heaven, which sits in judgment over the human ruler, who is the intermediary between Heaven's commands and human fate.

The Chou was a western frontier tribe that had maintained its martial spirit and fighting ability. Its conquest of the Shang can be compared with Macedonia's unification of Greece. The other Chinese tribes switched their loyalty to the Chou leader, who went on to establish a dynasty that lasted for more than 800 years (1122–256 B.C.), the longest in Chinese history.

Comprising most of North China, the large Chou domain made the establishment of a unified state impossible. Consequently, the Chou kings set up a feudal system of government by delegating local authority to relatives and noble magnates. These vassal lords, whose power was hereditary, recognized the over-lordship of the Chou kings and supplied them with military aid.

The early Chou kings were vigorous leaders who were able to retain the allegiance of their vassals (when necessary, by their superior military power) and fend off attacks from barbarians on the frontiers. In time, however, weak kings succeeded to the throne, and the power and independence of their vassals increased. By the eighth century B.C., the vassals no longer went to the Chou capital for investiture by the Son of Heaven, as the Chou king called himself.

The remnants of Chou royal power disappeared completely in 771 B.C., when an alliance of dissident vassals and barbarians destroyed the capital and killed the king. Part of the royal family managed to escape eastward to Lo-yang, however, where the dynasty survived for another five centuries doing little more than performing state religious rituals as the Son of Heaven. Seven of the stronger feudal princes gradually conquered their weaker neighbors. In the process they assumed the title *wang* ("king"), formerly used only by the Chou ruler, and began to extinguish the feudal rights of their own vassals and establish centralized administrations. Warfare among these emerging centralized states was incessant, particularly during the two centuries known as the Period of Warring States (c. 450–221 B.C.). By 221 B.C., the ruler of the Ch'in, the most advanced of the seven warring states, had conquered all his rivals and established a unified empire with himself as absolute ruler.

Chou Economy and Society

Despite its political instability, the Chou period is unrivaled by any later period in Chinese history for its material and cultural progress. These developments led the Chinese to distinguish between their own high civilization and the nomadic ways of the "barbarian dogs" beyond their frontiers. A sense of the superiority of their own civilization became a lasting characteristic of the Chinese.

During the sixth century B.C., iron was introduced and mass producing cast iron objects from molds came into general use by the end of the Chou period. (The first successful attempts at casting iron were not made in Europe until the end of the Middle Ages.)

The ox-drawn iron-tipped plow, together with the use of manure and the growth of large-scale irrigation and water-control projects, led to great population growth based on increased agricultural yields. Canals were constructed to facilitate moving commodities over long distances. Commerce and wealth grew rapidly, and a merchant and artisan class emerged. Brightly colored shells, bolts of silk, and ingots of precious metals were the media of exchange; by the end of the Chou period small round copper coins with square holes were being minted. Chopsticks and finely lacquered objects, today universally considered as symbols of Chinese and East Asian culture, were also in use by the end of the period.

Class divisions and consciousness became highly developed under Chou feudalism and have remained until modern times. The king and the aristocracy were sharply separated from the mass of the people on the basis of land ownership and family descent.

The core units of aristocratic society were the elementary family, the extended family, and the clan (see p. 102), held together by patriarchal authority and ancestor worship. Marriages were formally arranged unions between families. Among the peasants, however, marriage took place after a woman became pregnant following the Spring Festival at which boys and girls, beginning at age fifteen, sang and danced naked.

The customs of the nobles can be compared in a general way to those of Europe's feudal nobility (see ch. 9). Underlying the society was a complex code of chivalry, called *li*, practiced in both war and peace. It symbolized the ideal of the noble warrior, and men devoted years to its mastery.

The art of horseback riding, developed among the nomads of central Asia, greatly influenced late Chou China. In response to the threat of mounted nomads, rulers of the Warring States period began constructing defensive walls, later joined together to become the Great Wall of China. Inside China itself, chariots were largely replaced by swifter and more mobile cavalry troops wearing tunics and trousers adopted from the nomads.

The peasant masses, still attached serflike to their villages, worked as tenants of noble landholders, paying one tenth of their crop as rent. Despite increased agricultural production, resulting from large-scale irrigation and the ox-drawn iron-tipped plow, the peasants had difficulty eking out an existence. Many were forced into debt slavery. A major problem in the Chinese economy, evident by late Chou times, has been that the majority of farmers have worked fields so small that they could not produce a crop surplus to tide them over periods of scarcity.

The Rise of Philosophical Schools

By the fifth century B.C., the increasing warfare among the feudal lords and Warring States had destroyed the stability that had characterized Chinese society under the Shang and early Chou dynasties. Educated Chinese had become aware of the great disparity between the traditions inherited from their ancestors and the conditions in which they themselves lived. The result was the birth of a social consciousness that focused on the study of humanity and the problems of society. Some scholars have noted the parallel between the flourishing intellectual life of China in the fifth century B.C. and Greek philosophy and Indian religious thought at the same time. It has been suggested that these three great centers of world civilization stimulated and influenced each other. However, little or no historical evidence exists to support such an assertion. The birth of social consciousness in China, isolated from the other centers of civilization, can best be understood in terms of internal developments rather than external influences.

Confucianism: Rational Humanism

The first, most famous, and certainly most influential Chinese philosopher and teacher was K'ung-fu-tzu ("Master K'ung, the Sage," 551–479 B.C.), known in the West as Confucius after Jesuit missionaries to China in the seventeenth century latinized his name.

Later Confucianists attributed to the master the role of composing or editing the Five Confucian Classics (two books of history and one book each on poetry, divination, and ceremonies), which were in large part a product of the early Chou period. But the only work that can be accurately attributed to Confucius is the *Analects* ("Selected Sayings"), a collection of his responses to his disciples' questions.

Confucius, who belonged to the lower aristocracy, was more or less a contemporary of the Buddha in India, Zoroaster in Persia, and the early philosophers of Greece. Like the Buddha and Zoroaster, Confucius lived in a troubled time—an age of political and social turmoil—and his prime concern, like theirs, was the improvement of society. To achieve this goal, Confucius did not look to the gods and spirits for assistance; he accepted the existence of Heaven (*T'ien*) and spirits, but he insisted it was more important "to know the essential duties of man living in a society of men." "We don't know yet how to serve men," he said, "how can we know about serving the spirits?" And, "We don't yet know about life, how can we know about death?" He advised a ruler to "respect the ghosts and spirits but keep them at a distance" and "devote yourself to the proper demands of the people."

Confucius believed that the improvement of society was the responsibility of the ruler and that the quality of government depended on the ruler's moral character: "The way (*Tao*) of learning to be great consists in shining with the illustrious power of moral personality, in making a new people, in abiding in the highest goodness." Confucius' definition of the Way as "moral personality" and the "the highest goodness" was in decided contrast to the old premoral Way in which gods and spirits, propitiated by offerings and ritual, regulated human life for good or ill. Above all, Confucius' new Way meant a concern for the rights of others, the adherence to a Golden Rule:

> *Tzu-king [a disciple] asked saying, "Is there any single saying that one can act upon all day and every day?" The Master said, "Perhaps the saying about consideration: 'Never do to others what you would not like them to do to you.'"*[4]

Although Confucius called himself "a transmitter and not a creator," his redefinition of *Tao* was a radical innovation. He was, in effect, putting new wine into old bottles. He did the same thing with two other key terms, *li* and *chün-tzu. Li*, meaning "honorable behavior," was the chivalric code of the constantly fighting *chün-tzu*, the hereditary feudal "noblemen" of the Chou period. As refined and reinterpreted by Confucius, *li* came to embody such ethical virtues as righteousness and love for one's fellow humans. The *chün-tzu*, under the influence of the new definition of *li*, became "noble men," or "gentlemen," whose social origins were not important. As Confucius said, "The noble man understands what is right; the inferior man understands what is profitable." Confucius' teachings have had a greater and longer-lasting influence on China, and much of East Asia, than those of any other philosopher.

Taoism: Intuitive Mysticism

A second philosophical reaction to the troubled life of the late Chou period was the teaching of Lao-tzu ("Old Master"), a semi-legendary figure who was believed to have been a contemporary of Confucius. As with Confucius, the key term in Lao-tzu's teaching is *Tao*, from which his philosophy derives its name. But while Confucius defined *Tao* as a rational standard of ethics in human affairs, Lao-tzu gave it a metaphysical meaning—the course of nature, the natural and inevitable order of the universe.

The goal of Taoism, like Confucianism, is a happy life. Lao-tzu believed that this goal could be achieved by living a life in conformity with nature, retiring from the chaos and evils of contemporary Warring States society and shunning human institutions and opinions as unnatural and artificial "outside things." Thus at the heart of Taoist thought is the concept of *wu-wei*, or "nonaction"—a manner of living which, like nature itself, is nonassertive and spontaneous. Lao-tzu pointed out that in nature all things work silently; they fulfill their function and, after they reach their bloom, they return to their origins. Unlike Confucius' ideal gentleman, who is constantly involved in society in order to better it, Lao-tzu's sage is a private person, an egocentric individualist.

Taoism is a revolt not only against society but also against the intellect's limitations. Intuition, not reason, is the source of true knowledge; and books, Taoists said, are "the dregs and refuse of the ancients." One of the most famous Taoist philosophers, Chuang-tzu (fourth century B.C.), who made fun of Confucians as tiresome busybodies, even questioned the reality of the world of the senses. He said that he once dreamed that he was a butterfly, "flying about enjoying itself." When he awakened he was confused: "I do not know whether I was Chuang-tzu dreaming that I was a butterfly, or whether now I am a butterfly dreaming that I am Chuang-tzu."

Similar anecdotes and allegories abound in Taoist literature, as in all mystical teachings that deal with subjects that are difficult to put into words. (As the Taoists put it, "The one who knows does not speak, and the one who speaks does not know.") But Taoist mysticism is more philosophical than religious. Unlike Upanishadic philosophy or Christian mysticism, it does not aim to extinguish the personality through the union with the Absolute or God. Rather, its aim is to teach how one can obtain happiness in this world by living a simple life in harmony with nature.

Confucianism and Taoism became the two major molds that shaped Chinese thought and civilization. Although these rival schools frequently sniped at one another, they never became mutually exclusive outlooks on life. Taoist intuition complemented Confucian rationalism; during the centuries to come, Chinese were often Confucianists in their social relations and Taoists in their private life.

Taoism, with its individual freedom and mystical union with nature, would in time have a deep impact on Chinese poetry and art.

Mencius' Contribution to Confucianism

The man whose work was largely responsible for the emergence of Confucianism as the most widely accepted philosophy in China was Mencius, or Meng-tzu (372–289 B.C.). Born a century after the death of Confucius, Mencius added important new dimensions to Confucian thought in two areas—human nature and government.

Although Confucius had only implied that human nature is good, Mencius emphatically insisted that all people are innately good and tend to seek the good just as water tends to run downhill. But unless people strive to preserve and develop their innate goodness, which is the source of righteous conduct, it can be corrupted by the bad practices and ideas existing in the environment. Mencius taught that the opposite of righteous conduct is selfishness, and he attacked the extreme individualism of the Taoists as a form of selfishness. He held that "all men are brothers," and he would have agreed with a later Confucian writer who summed up in one sentence the teaching of a famous Taoist: "He would not pluck so much as a hair out of his head for the benefit of his fellows."

The second area in which Mencius elaborated on Confucius' teaching was political theory. Mencius distinguished between good kings, who ruled benevolently, and the rulers of his day (the Period of Warring States), who governed by naked force and spread violence and disorder.

Mencius on Human Nature

Kao Tzu said: "The nature of man may be likened to a swift current of water: you lead it eastward and it will flow to the east; you lead it westward and it will flow to the west. Human nature is neither disposed to good nor to evil, just as water is neither disposed to east nor west." Mencius replied: "It is true that water is neither disposed to east nor west, but is it neither disposed to flowing upward nor downward? The tendency of human nature to do good is like that of water to flow downward. There is no man who does not tend to do good; there is no water that does not flow downward. Now you may strike water and make it splash over your forehead, or you may even force it up the hills. But is this in the nature of water? It is of course due to the force of circumstances. Similarly, man may be brought to do evil, and that is because the same is done to his nature."

Source: Theodore de Bary, ed., *Sources of Chinese Tradition* (New York: Columbia University Press, 1960), pp. 102–3.

Because good rulers are guided by ethical standards, he said, they will behave benevolently toward the people and provide for their well-being. Unlike Confucius, who did not question the right of hereditary kings to rule, Mencius said that the people have a right to rebel against bad rulers and even kill them if necessary, because they have lost the Mandate of Heaven.

As we have seen, this concept has been used by the Chou to justify their revolt against the Shang. On that occasion, the concept had had a religious meaning, being connected with the worship of Heaven, who supported the ruler as the Son of Heaven. Mencius, however, secularized and humanized the Mandate of Heaven by equating it with the people: "Heaven hears as the people hear; Heaven sees as the people see." By redefining the concept in this way, Mencius made the welfare of the people the ultimate standard for judging government. Indeed, he even told rulers to their faces that the people were more important than they were.

Modern commentators, both Chinese and Western, have viewed Mencius' definition of the Mandate of Heaven as an early form of democratic thought. Mencius did believe that all people were morally equal and that the ruler needed the consent of the people, but he was clearly the advocate of benevolent monarchy rather than popular democracy.

Legalism

Another body of thought emerged in the fourth and third centuries B.C. and came to be called the School of Law, or Legalism. It had no single founder, as did Confucianism and Taoism, nor was it ever a school in the sense of a teacher leading disciples. What it did have in common with Confucianism and Taoism was the desire to establish stability in an age of turmoil.

The Legalists emphasized the importance of harsh and inflexible law as the only means of achieving an orderly and prosperous society. They believed that human nature was basically bad and that people acted virtuously only when forced to do so. Therefore, they argued for an elaborate system of laws defining fixed penalties for each offense, with no exceptions for rank, class, or circumstances. Judges were not to use their own conscience in estimating the gravity

of the crime and arbitrarily deciding on the punishment. Their task was solely to define the crime correctly; the punishment was provided automatically by the code of law. This procedure is still a characteristic of Chinese law.

Since the enforcement of law required a strong state, the immediate goal of the Legalists was to enhance the power of the ruler at the expense of other elements, particularly the nobility. Their ultimate goal was the creation of a centralized state strong enough to unify all China and end the chaos of the Warring States period. The unification of China in 221 B.C. was largely the result of putting Legalist ideas of government into practice.

China: The First Empire

Some 1500 years after the founding of the Shang Dynasty around 1700 B.C., China was unified. The first centralized Chinese empire was the proud achievement of two dynasties, the Ch'in and the Han. The Ch'in Dynasty collapsed soon after the death of its founder, but the Han lasted or more than four centuries. Together the two dynasties transformed China, but the changes were the culmination of earlier developments.

Rise of Legalist Ch'in

Throughout the two centuries of the Warring States period (c. 450–221 B.C.) there was the hope that a king would emerge who would unite China and inaugurate a great new age of peace and stability. While the Confucians believed that such a king would accomplish the task by means of his outstanding moral virtue, the Legalists substituted overwhelming might as the essential element of effective government. The political philosophy of the Legalists, who liked to sum up and justify their doctrine in two words—"It works"—triumphed, and no state became more adept at practicing that pragmatic philosophy than the Ch'in.

The Ch'in's rise to preeminence began in 352 B.C., when its ruler selected Lord Shang, a man imbued with Legalist principles, to be chief minister. Recognizing that the growth of Ch'in's

Legalism: The Theories of Han Fei Tzu (d. 233 B.C.)

When the sage rules the state, he does not count on people doing good of themselves, but employs such measures as will keep them from doing any evil. If he counts on people doing good of themselves, there will not be enough such people to be numbered by the tens in the whole country. But if he employs such measures as will keep them from doing evil, then the entire state can be brought up to a uniform standard. Inasmuch as the administrator has to consider the many but disregard the few, he does not busy himself with morals but with laws.

. . . Therefore, the intelligent ruler upholds solid facts and discards useless frills. He does not speak about deeds of humanity and righteousness, and he does not listen to the words of learned men.

Those who are ignorant about government insistently say: "Win the hearts of the people." If order could be procured by winning the hearts of the people, then even the wise ministers Yi Yin and Kuan Chung would be of no use. For all that the ruler would need to do would be just to listen to the people. Actually, the intelligence of the people is not to be relied upon any more than the mind of a baby. If the baby does not have his head shaved, his sores will recur; if he does not have his boil cut open, his illness will go from bad to worse. However, in order to shave his head or open the boil someone has to hold the baby while the affectionate mother is performing the work, and yet he keeps crying and yelling incessantly. The baby does not understand that suffering a small pain is the way to obtain a great benefit.

. . . The sage considers the conditions of the times . . . and governs the people accordingly. Thus though penalties are light, it is not due to charity; though punishment is heavy, it is not due to cruelty. Whatever is done is done in accordance with the circumstances of the age. Therefore circumstances go according to their time, and the course of action is planned in accordance with the circumstances.

. . . Now take a young fellow who is a bad character. His parents may get angry at him, but he never makes any change. The villagers may reprove him, but he is not moved. His teachers and elders may admonish him, but he never reforms. The love of his parents, the efforts of the villagers, and the wisdom of his teachers and elders—all the three excellent disciplines are applied to him, and yet not even a hair on his shins is altered. It is only after the district magistrate sends out his soldiers and in the name of the law searches for wicked individuals that the young man becomes afraid and changes his ways and alters his deeds. So while the love of parents is not sufficient to discipline the children, the severe penalties of the district magistrate are. This is because men become naturally spoiled by love, but are submissive to authority. . . .

That being so, rewards should be rich and certain so that the people will be attracted by them; punishments should be severe and definite so that the people will fear them; and laws should be uniform and steadfast so that the people will be familiar with them. Consequently, the sovereign should show no wavering in bestowing rewards and grant no pardon in administering punishments, and he should add honor to rewards and disgrace to punishments—when this is done, then both the worthy and the unworthy will want to exert themselves.

Source: Theodore de Bary, ed., *Sources of the Chinese Tradition* (New York: Columbia University Press, 1960), pp. 141–47.

power depended on a more efficient and centralized bureaucratic structure than could exist under feudalism, Lord Shang undermined the old hereditary nobility by creating a new aristocracy based on military merit. He also introduced a universal draft beginning at approximately age fifteen. As a result, chariot and cavalry warfare, in which the nobility has played the leading role, was replaced in importance by masses of peasant infantry equipped with swords and crossbows.

Economically, Lord Shang further weakened the old landowning nobility by abolishing the peasants' attachment to the land and granting them ownership of the plots they tilled. Thereafter the liberated peasants paid taxes directly to the state, thereby increasing its wealth and power. These reforms made Ch'in the most powerful of the Warring States. It soon began to extend the area of its political and social innovations.

Ch'in Unites China

In the middle of the third century B.C., a hundred years after Lord Shang, another Legalist prime minister helped the king of Ch'in prepare and carry out the conquest of the other Warring States that ended the Chou Dynasty in 256 B.C. and united China by 221 B.C. The king then declared himself the "First August Supreme Ruler" (Shih Huang-ti) of China, or "First Emperor," as his new title is usually translated. He also enlarged China—a name derived from the word Ch'in—by conquests in the south as far as the South China Sea (see map below).

The First Emperor gathered the old nobility— some 120,000 families, according to tradition— near the capital, where they could be closely watched. To further forestall rebellion, he ordered the entire civilian population to surrender its weapons to the state. A single harsh legal code, which replaced all local laws, was so detailed in its provisions that it was said to have been like "a fishing net through which even the smallest fish cannot slip out." The entire realm, which extended into South China and Vietnam, was divided into forty-eight provinces, administrative units drawn to obliterate traditional feudal units and to facilitate direct rule by the

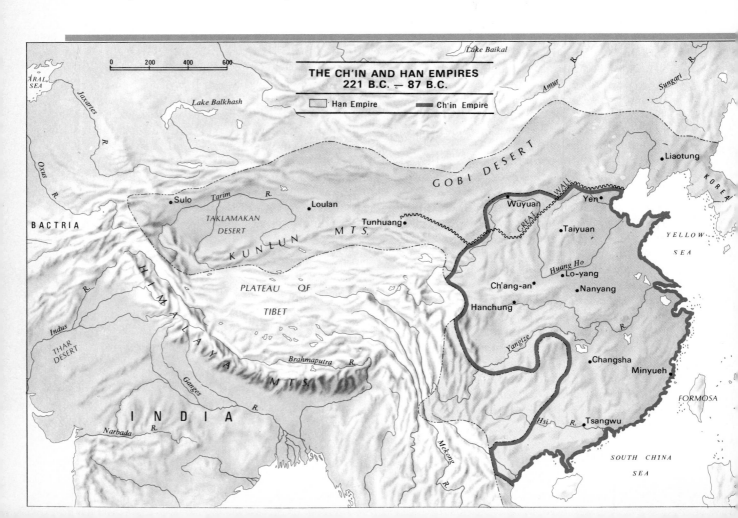

THE CH'IN AND HAN EMPIRES
221 B.C. – 87 B.C.

Han Empire   Ch'in Empire

emperor's centrally controlled civil and military appointees. To destroy the source of the aristocracy's power and to permit the emperor's agents to tax every farmer's harvest, private ownership of land by peasants, promoted a century earlier in the state of Ch'in by Lord Shang, was decreed for all of China. Thus the Ch'in empire reflected the emerging social forces at work in China—the peasants freed from serfdom, the merchants eager to increase their wealth within a larger political area, and the new military and administrative upper class.

The most spectacular of the First Emperor's many public works was repairing remnants of walls built earlier by the northern Warring States and joining them into the Great Wall, extending from the sea into Central Asia for a distance of over 1400 miles. Constructed by forced labor, it was said that "every stone cost a human life." The wall was both a line of defense against the barbarians who habitually raided into China and a symbol of the distinction between China's agricultural society and the nomadic tribes of Central Asia. It remains today one of the greatest monuments to engineering skill in the preindustrial age and one of the wonders of the world. It is said to be the only man-made structure on earth that can be seen from the moon.

The First Emperor tried to enforce intellectual conformity and make the Ch'in Legalist system appear to be the only natural political order. He suppressed all other schools of thought— especially the Confucians who idealized Chou feudalism by stressing the obedience of sons to their fathers, of nobles to the lord, and of lords to the king. To break the hold of the past, the emperor put into effect a Legalist proposal requiring all privately owned books reflecting past traditions to be burned and "all those who raise their voice against the present government in the name of antiquity [to] be beheaded together with their families."

The First Emperor constructed a huge mound tomb for himself and, nearby, three large pits filled with the life-sized terra cotta figures of his imperial guard. Over half a million laborers were employed at the site. The mausoleum has not been excavated, but the partial excavation of the pits revealed an estimated 7000 soldiers. Strangely, each head is a personal portrait—no two faces are alike.

When the First Emperor died in 210 B.C. while on one of his frequent tours of inspection, he was succeeded by an inept son who was unable to control the rivalry among his father's chief aides. Ch'in policies had alienated not only the intellectuals and the old nobility but also the peasants, who were subjected to ruinous taxation and forced labor. Rebel armies rose in every province of the empire, some led by peasants, others by aristocrats. Anarchy followed, and by 206 B.C. the Ch'in Dynasty, which the First Emperor had claimed would endure for "ten thousand generations," had completely disappeared. But the Chinese Empire itself, which Ch'in created, would last for more than 2000 years, the longest-lived political institution in world history.

At issue in the fighting that continued for another four years was not only the question of succession to the throne but also the form of government. The peasant and aristocratic leaders, first allied against Ch'in, became engaged in a furious and ruthless civil war. The aristocrats sought to restore the oligarchic feudalism of pre-Ch'in times. Their opponents, whose main leader was Liu Pang, a peasant who had become a Ch'in general, desired a centralized state. In this contest between the old order and the new, the new was the victor.

The Han Dynasty: The Empire Consolidated

In 202 B.C., the year that the Romans defeated the Carthaginians at the battle of Zama, the peasant Liu Pang defeated his aristocratic rival and established the Han Dynasty. Named after the Han River, a tributary of the Yangtze, the new dynasty had its capital at Ch'ang-an. It lasted for more than 400 years and is traditionally divided into two parts: the Earlier Han, from 202 B.C. to A.D. 8, and the Later Han, from A.D. 23 to A.D. 220, with its capital at Lo-yang. In time and importance, the Han corresponded to the late Roman Republic and early Roman Empire; ethnic Chinese still call themselves "Men of Han."

The empire and power sought by Liu Pang and his successors were those of the Ch'in, but they succeeded where the Ch'in had failed because they were tactful and gradual in their approach. Liu Pang reestablished for a time some of the vassal kingdoms and feudal states in regions distant from the capital. Peasant discontent was mollified by lessened demands for taxes and forced labor. But the master stroke of the Han emperors was to enlist the support of the Confucian intellectuals. They provided the empire with an ideology that would last until recent times. The Ch'ins' extreme Legalistic ideology of harsh punishment and terror had not worked.

The Han emperors recognized that an educated bureaucracy was necessary for governing so vast an empire. The ban on the Confucian classics and other Chou literature was lifted, and the way was open for a revival of the intellectual life that had been suppressed under the Ch'in.

In accord with Legalist principles, now tempered by Confucian insistence on the ethical basis of government, the Han emperors established administrative organs staffed by a salaried bureaucracy to rule their empire. Talented men were chosen for government service through an examination system based on the Confucian classics, and they were promoted by merit.

The examinations were theoretically open to all Chinese except merchants. (The Han inherited both the Confucian bias against trade as an unvirtuous striving for profit and the Legalist suspicion of merchants who put their own interests ahead of those of the state and society.) The bureaucrats were drawn from the landlord class because wealth was needed to obtain the education needed to pass the examinations. Consequently, the earlier division of Chinese society between aristocrats and peasants was transformed into a division between peasants and landowner-bureaucrats. The latter are also called scholar-gentry, a term first used in the eighteenth century by the British. They saw a parallel with the gentry who dominated the countryside and administration of their own country.

Wu Ti and the Pax Sinica

After sixty years of consolidation, the Han Empire reached its greatest extent and development during the long reign of Wu Ti ("Martial Emperor"), who ruled from 141 to 87 B.C. To accomplish his goal of territorial expansion, he raised the peasants' taxes but not those of the great landowners, who remained virtually exempt from taxation. In addition, he increased the amount of labor and military service the peasants were forced to contribute to the state.

The Martial Emperor justified his expansionist policies in terms of self-defense against Mongolian nomads, the Hsiung-nu, known to the West later as the Huns. Their attacks had caused the First Emperor to complete the Great Wall to obstruct their raiding cavalry. To outflank the nomads in the west, Wu Ti extended the Great Wall and annexed a large corridor extending through the Tarim River basin of Central Asia to the Pamir Mountains close to Bactria. This corridor has ever since remained a part of China (see Reference Map 3).

Wu Ti failed in an attempt to form an alliance with the Scythians in Bactria, but his envoy's report of the interest shown in Chinese silks by the peoples of the area was the beginning of a commercial exchange between China and the West. This trade brought great profits to wealthy merchant families.

Wu Ti also outflanked the Hsiung-nu in the east by the conquest of southern Manchuria and northern Korea. In addition, he completed the conquest of South China, begun by the Ch'in, and added North Vietnam to the Chinese Empire. All the conquered lands experienced considerable Chinese emigration. Thus at a time when the armies of the Roman Republic were laying the foundations of the *Pax Romana* in the West, the Martial Emperor was establishing a *Pax Sinica* ("Chinese Peace") in the East.

Han Decline

Wu Ti's conquests led to a fiscal crisis. As costs increased, taxes increased, and the peasants' burdens led to revolt. The end result was that the central government had to rely more and more on local military commanders and great landowners for control of the population, giving them great power and prestige at its own expense. This cycle of decline after an initial period of increasing prosperity and power has been the pattern of all Chinese dynasties. During the Han this "dynastic cycle," as Western historians of China call it, led to a succession of mediocre rulers after Wu Ti's death and a temporary usuration of the throne (A.D. 9–23), which divided the Earlier from the Later Han.

The usurper, Wang Mang, united Confucian humanitarianism with Legalist practice. Like his contemporary in the West, the Roman Emperor Augustus, his goal was the rejuvenation of society. By Wang Mang's day the number of large tax-free estates had greatly increased while the number of tax-paying peasant holdings had declined. This was a by product of the private landownership that, under the Ch'in, had replaced the old communal use of the land. Rich officials and merchants were able to acquire the lands of small peasant-owners, who became tenants paying exorbitant rents. The conflict of landlordship and tenancy, along with the concentration of power of great families, became a major problem in Chinese history.

More and more peasants fell behind in their rents and were forced to sell themselves or their children into debt slavery. To remedy this situation and increase the government's tax income, Wang Mang decreed that the land was the property of the nation and should be portioned out to peasant families, who would pay taxes on their allotments.

Wang Mang sought to solve the long-standing problem of inflation, which had greatly increased since Wu Ti first began debasing the coinage when he found himself in financial difficulties, by setting maximum prices on basic commodities. He also sought to stabilize prices by instituting "leveling"—the government bought surplus commodities when prices fell and sold them when scarcity caused prices to rise. (In 1938, a chance reading of Wang Mang's "leveling" proposal inspired the "ever-normal granary" program of President Roosevelt's New Deal.[5])

Wang Mang's remarkable reform program failed, however; officials bungled the difficult administrative task, and the powerful landowners rebelled against the ruler who proposed to confiscate their land. Although Wang Mang rescinded his reforms, he was killed by the rebels in A.D. 23.

The Later Han Dynasty never reached the heights of its predecessor. Warlords who were members of the rich landowner class seized more and more power, and widespread peasant rebellions (one band was led by "Mother Lu," a woman skilled in witchcraft) sapped the state's resources. Surviving in name only during its last thirty years, the Han Dynasty ended in A.D. 220, when the throne was usurped by the son of a famous warlord. Three and a half centuries of disunity and turbulence followed—the longest in China's long history and often called China's "Middle Ages"—as it did in Europe after the fall of the Roman Empire. But China eventually succeeded where Europe failed: in A.D. 589 China once again was united by the Sui Dynasty (see ch. 8). With minor exceptions, it has remained united to this day.

Han Scholarship, Art and Technology

Politically and culturally, the relation of the Han to the Chou paralleled that of ancient Rome to Greece. Politically, the disunity of Greece and the Chou was followed by the imperial unity and administrative genius of the Romans and the Han. Culturally, just as the Romans owed a great debt to the Greeks, so did the Han to the Chou. Furthermore, Greek and Chou intellectual creativity was not matched by the Romans and the Han.

Scholarship flourished under the Han, but it was mainly concerned with collecting and interpreting the classics of Chinese thought produced in the Chou period. As the basis of education for prospective bureaucrats, Wu Ti established an imperial university in 124 B.C.; a century later it had 3000 students. The Han scholars venerated Confucius as the ideal wise man, and Confucianism became the official philosophy of the state. Great respect for learning, together with the system of civil service examinations based on the Five Confucian Classics, became fundamental characteristics of Chinese civilization.

Han scholars started another scholarly tradition with their historical writings. Their antiquarian interest in researching the past produced a comprehensive history of China, the *Historical Records (Shih chi)*. This voluminous work of 130 chapters has been highly praised, in part for its inclusion of a vast amount of information, beginning with the legendary past, but even more for its freedom from superstition and careful weighing of evidence. In the Later Han, a scholar wrote the *History of the (Earlier) Han*, and thereafter it was customary for each dynasty to write the official history of its immediate predecessor. The Chinese believed that the successes and failures of the past provided guidance for one's own time and the future. As stated in the *Historical Records*, "Events of the past, if not forgotten, are teachings about the future."

Archaeological investigation was used as an aid to the writing of history. One scholar anticipated modern archaeologists by more than a thousand years in classifying human history by "ages": "stone" (Old Stone Age), "jade" (New Stone Age), "bronze," and "the present age" when "weapons are made of iron."[6]

Another monument to Han scholarship was the world's first dictionary, *Shuo Wen* (*Words Explained*), produced during Wu Ti's reign. It listed the meaning and pronunciation of more than 9000 Chinese characters.

In contrast to Han scholarship, Han art was clearly creative. The largely decorative art of the past, which served a religious purpose, was replaced by a realistic pictorial art portraying ordinary life. The result was the first great Chinese flowering of sculpture, both in relief and in the round.

Some of the finer examples of this realistic secular art are the sculptured models of the tall and spirited horses that Wu Ti imported from Bactria. The Han greatly admired these proud "celestial" and "blood-sweating" horses from the West, and their artists brilliantly captured their high spirit.

During the Han period, China surpassed the level of technological development in the rest of the world. Notable inventions included a primitive seismograph capable of indicating earthquakes several hundred miles away; the use of water power to grind grain and to operate a piston bellows for iron smelting; the horse collar, which greatly increased the pulling power of horses; paper made from cloth rags, which replaced cumbersome bamboo strips and expensive silk cloth as writing material; and the humble but extremely useful wheelbarrow. By the end of the first century B.C., the Han Chinese had recognized sunspots and accurately determined the length of the calendar year.

Popular Taoism and Buddhism

By the time the First Emperor united China at the end of the third century B.C., a decadent or popular form of Taoism had emerged. Popular Taoism was a religion of spirits and magic that provided the spiritual comfort not found in either philosophical Taoism or Confucianism. Its goals were long life and personal immortality. These goals were to be achieved not so much as a reward for ethical conduct but through magical charms and spells and imbibing an "elixir of immortality." The search for such an elixir, which was thought to contain the vital forces of nature, led to an emphasis on diet and ultimately to the culinary art for which the Chinese are famous.

Popular Taoism also became a vehicle for the expression of peasant discontent. In A.D. 184, the Yellow Turbans (one of the earliest of many such uprisings throughout China's history) led a widespread peasant revolt inspired by Taoist followers of a now-deified Lao-tzu. Over 300,000 rebels destroyed much of China and greatly contributed to the anarchy that fatally weakened the Later Han Dynasty.

Buddhism, which appeared in China during the first century A.D., provided another answer to the need for religious assurance. It was brought to China by missionaries and traders through Central Asia. About A.D. 184 a Buddhist missionary established a center for the translation of Buddhist writings into Chinese at the Later Han capital. However, relatively few Chinese were attracted to the religion during this period. Buddhism's great attraction of converts and influence on Chinese culture came after the fall of the Han Dynasty, when renewed social turmoil made its emphasis on otherworldly salvation appealing to the great majority of Chinese.

The Meeting of East and West in Ancient Times

In the centuries immediately preceding and following the birth of Christ, the great civilizations of the world—Roman, Indian, and Chinese—were connected by commercial and diplomatic exchanges. These contacts began to decline in the third century A.D. and were eventually cut off. But each civilization remembered that beyond the mountains and the deserts to the east or to the west lay other great civilizations.

Many centuries later this knowledge would incite adventurous spirits in the West to bring the "halves" of world civilizations together once again.

Beyond the Roman Frontiers

During the first and second centuries A.D., the prosperous years of the *Pax Romana*, the peoples of the Roman Empire maintained trade contacts extending far beyond the imperial boundaries. Chinese silk, which the Romans believed was produced from the leaves of trees, was sold in the market quarter of Rome, and Indian cotton was converted into cloth at Alexandria. Contacts between West and East had progressively increased after 334 B.C., when Alexander the Great invaded Asia, until a chain of intercommunicating states stretched across Eurasia from the Atlantic to the Pacific.

After Alexander's death, the Seleucid and Ptolemaic kingdoms of the Hellenistic Age maintained trade contacts with India over two routes, one by land and the other by sea (see map below). The most frequented route was the caravan road that began in Syria or Asia Minor, crossed Mesopotamia, then skirted the Iranian plateau to either Bactra (modern Balkh) or Kandahar before crossing the Hindu Kush to reach Taxila in India. The sea route began either at the Red Sea ports of Egypt or at the head of the Persian Gulf and moved along the coast to India.

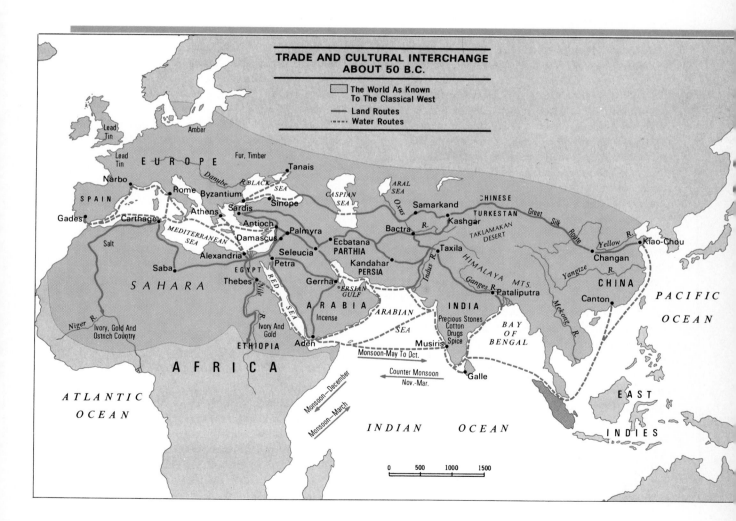

Sea Traffic to India

By the late first century B.C., after Egypt and Syria had succumbed to Rome, Roman capital and appetite for the luxury goods of India—ivory, pearls, spices, dyes, and cotton—greatly stimulated trade with the East. By this time, however, the existing trade routes had serious disadvantages. The Parthians, whose kingdom extended from the Euphrates to the borders of Bactria, were levying heavy tolls on the caravan trade, and the Sabaean Arabs of southwest Arabia had cut off the Red Sea route at Aden and were in control of much of the overseas trade with India. From Aden, the Sabaeans sent Indian goods north by caravan to Petra, which grew rich as a distribution point to Egypt via Gaza and to the north via Damascus.

Augustus broke the hold of the Parthian and Arab middlemen on the Eastern trade by establishing direct commercial connections by sea with India. By 1 B.C., he had reopened the Red Sea by forcing the Sabaeans out of Aden and converting it into a Roman naval base. Ships were soon sailing from Aden directly to India across the Arabian Sea, blown by the monsoon winds recently discovered by a Greek mariner named Hippalus. From May to October the monsoon blows from the southwest across the Arabian Sea, while the countermonsoon blows from the northeast between November and March. Thus, direct round-trip voyages, eliminating middlemen and the tedious journey along the coasts, could be made in eight months. Strabo, a Greek geographer during the time of Augustus, stated that 120 ships sailed to India every year from Egyptian ports. Augustus claimed that "to me were sent embassies of kings from India," probably to specify the towns within the Roman Empire and in India where foreign merchants might freely conduct their business and practice their own customs and religions.

During the first century A.D., Roman-financed ships reached the rich markets of southern India and Ceylon (Sri Lanka). Christianity may have reached India at this time. Indian Christians claim that their small group of about 2 million was founded by St. Thomas, one of Jesus' original twelve disciples, who may have sailed to India about A.D. 50. In A.D. 166, according to the Chinese *History of the Later Han Dynasty*, some merchants from Ta Ch'in ("Great Ch'in," the Chinese name for Rome), claiming to represent "King Antun" (the emperor Marcus Aurelius Antoninus), arrived in South China by sea across the Bay of Bengal and around the Malay Peninsula.

The Silk Trade with China

The Chinese made the first move to pierce the land barrier separating them from the West. In 138 B.C. the Han emperor Wu Ti dispatched an envoy to Bactra to seek allies against the Hsiung-nu (Mongolian nomads). Although the envoy failed to secure an alliance, the information he brought back amounted to the Chinese discovery of the West.

Intrigued above all by his envoy's report indicating great interest in Chinese silks and his description of the magnificent Western horses, Wu Ti resolved to open trade relations with the West. His armies pushed across the Pamir Mountains to a point close to Alexandria Eschate (Khojend), founded by Alexander the Great as the northern limit of his empire (see map, p. 62, and Reference Map 1). Shortly after 100 B.C. silk began arriving in the West, transmitted by the Parthians. Wealthy private merchants carried on this trade, organized into caravans that required large outlays of capital. When the Chinese soon moved back across the Pamirs, the Kushans of India became middlemen, selling the silk to the Parthians and later to Western merchants coming by sea to India.

It was not until about A.D. 120 that the Parthians allowed some Western merchants to cross their land. Ptolemy used the information they brought back on the Chinese in constructing his map of the world.

The Economic Consequences for the West

To satisfy the Roman world's insatiable appetite for luxury goods, Western trade with the East grew immensely in the first two centuries A.D. But because such Roman exports as wool, linen, glass, and metalware to the East did not match in value Rome's imports of silk, spices, perfumes, gems and other luxuries, the West suffered seriously from an adverse balance of trade. Gold and silver had to be continually exported to Asia. Late in the first century A.D.,

Pliny estimated that India, China, and Arabia drained away annually at least 100 million sesterces (perhaps 10 million 1991 dollars), declaring, "That is the sum which our luxuries and our women cost us." The discovery of large hoards of Roman coins in India supports Pliny's statement. This serious drain was one of the factors in the general economic decline of the Roman world in the third century A.D.

Severance of East-West Contacts

Beginning in the third century A.D., contacts between the East and the West gradually declined. With the overthrow of the Han Dynasty in A.D. 220, China's power and prestige dwindled in Central Asia. By coincidence, the Kushan empire in northeast India fell at the same time, and India entered a period of change and transition. But probably the most significant factor in the disruption of East-West relations was the political and economic decline of the Roman world in the third century A.D., a topic that will be described in the following chapter.

Conclusion

India and China today are the direct heirs of the two longest-living civilizations in the world. By the beginning of the third century A.D., the formative ages of these two civilizations had produced an Indian tradition and a Chinese tradition that have endured into modern times. These two traditional ways of life differ sharply.

During India's formative age, the youthful energy and optimistic self-assurance of the early Aryan warriors of India was replaced by Hinduism's ideology of ascetic withdrawal from life. Indian society became so strongly dominated by priests and religion that government usually played a minor role. Even Buddhism, which challenged the power of the priests, had as its primary goal not social change but, like Hinduism, the dissolution of the ego and renunciation of the world. The great bulk of Indian thought seeks not to challenge the existing social order but to explain and justify it. Duty (*dharma*) and not, as in the West, freedom, individual rights, and the idea of progress, dominates Indian thought. Individual rights in this world are overshadowed by the requirements of eternal salvation, and freedom means escape from the cycle of birth, death, and rebirth. Both are to be obtained through the faithful discharge of caste duties.

In India there has been little demand for a better life in this world. Social injustice is too often treated with indifference. In the words of a modern scholar, "The tragedy of India is that it became a land where tragedy had become irrelevant."[7]

The Chinese, on the other hand, did not lose their relish for life. They reacted to human suffering not, as in India, by pursuing a long and arduous religious quest that Indians often described as "leaving the world," but by aiding the afflicted and directing the power of the state toward the amelioration of social evils and the relief of distress. This was the product of two of the main ingredients in the Chinese tradition—Confucianism, with its humanistic concern for the individual within society, and Legalism, with its stress on the power of the state.

Today some scholars view the present Communist dictatorship in China as another imperial dynasty, the last in a long succession of imperial regimes. But communism is a foreign import at variance with Chinese tradition, which the Communist leaders have rejected—Confucianism in particular. Nevertheless, the humane values of the Chinese tradition have persisted. This was demonstrated in the spring of 1989, when hundreds of thousands of university students in forty-one cities, supported by many workers, massed and demanded "democracy" and an end to corruption. Their slogan, "People Power," echoed Mencius' view that the people's contentment is the indispensable criterion for Heaven's choice of the ruler "since Heaven sees with the eyes of the people." Perhaps, too, they remembered the opening line of the *Analects* of Confucius: "To study and in due season to practice what one has learned, is this not a pleasure?"

Suggestions for Reading

S. Wolpert, *A New History of India,** 3rd ed. (Oxford, 1989); A. Thapar, *A History of India,** Vol. I (Penguin); and A. L. Basham, *The Wonder That Was India,** rev. ed. (Merrimack, 1983) are comprehensive. See also C. Drekmeier,

Kingship and Community in Early India (Stanford, 1962); W. Tarn, *The Greeks in Bactria and India* (Ares, 1984); Mortimer Wheeler, *The Indus Civilization,* 3rd ed. (Cambridge Univ., 1968) and E. Lengyel, *Asoka the Great: India's Royal Missionary* (Watts, 1969).

K. Sen, *Hinduism* (Penguin, 1962) describes the nature and function of Hinduism. Also recommended are P. Bowes, *The Hindu Religious Tradition* (Routledge & Kegan Paul, 1978), a forceful statement of Hindu's dynamic creativity until the Middle Ages, and S. Radhakrishnan. *The Hindu View of Life* (Allen & Unwin, 1980). W. T. De Bary, et al. eds., *Sources of Indian Tradition,* 2 vols. (Columbia, 1958) contains significant selections with illuminating introductions. Modern translations of the *Rig Veda, Mahabarata, Ramayana, Bhagavad Gita,* and *Upanishads* are published by Penguin. See also N. Frith, *The Legend of Krishna* (Schocken, 1976).

E. Conze, *A Short History of Buddhism* (Allen & Unwin, 1980), is a good updated introduction. See also Edward J. Thomas, *The Life of Buddha as Legend and History* (Routledge & Kegan Paul, 1975); C. Humphreys, *Buddhism* (Penguin, 1951); and Richard Robinson and W. L. Johnson, *The Buddhist Religion: A Historical Introduction,* 2nd ed. (Dicenson, 1977).

W. Rodzinski, *The Walled Kingdom: A History of China from Antiquity to the Present* (Free Press, 1984); J. Gernet, *A History of Chinese Civilization* (Cambridge, 1982); and J. Fairbank and E. Reischauer, *China: Tradition and Transformation* (Houghton Mifflin, 1978) are highly acclaimed histories. Shorter are W. Eberhard, *A History of China,* 4th ed. (California); and R. Yang and E. Lazzerini, *The Chinese World* (Forum, 1978). See also K. C. Chang, *The Archaeology of Ancient China,* 4th ed. (Yale, 1986) and *Shang Civilization* (Yale, 1980); R. Grousset, *The Rise and Splendour of the Chinese Empire* (California); and M. Loewe, *Everyday Life in Early Imperial China* (Harper & Row, 1965). A. Cottrell, *The First Emperor of China* (Penguin) is a well-illustrated and popular account of the founder of the Ch'in dynasty and the archaeological discoveries at his tomb.

Benjamin Schwartz, *The World of Thought in Ancient China* (Harvard, 1985) is an authoritative fresh view. Fung Yulan, *A Short History of Chinese Philosophy* (Free Press, 1966) is an excellent introduction. See also A. Waley, *Three Ways of Thought in Ancient China* (Stanford); M. Granet, *The Religion of the Chinese People* (Torchbooks); and R. Van Over, ed., *Taoism Tales* (Mentor, 1973). W. T. DeBary, et al., eds., *Sources of Chinese Tradition* (Columbia, 1960) is an outstanding collection of translations with valuable commentaries.

On Indian and Chinese art see A. Coomaraswamy, *History of Indian and Indonesian Art* (Dover, 1985); Michael Sullivan, *The Arts of China* 3rd ed. (California, 1984); and T. Froncek, ed., *The Horizon Book of the Arts of China* (American Heritage, 1969).

Robert E. Wheeler, *Rome Beyond the Imperial Frontiers* (Greenwood, 1972) is a study of Rome's trade with the East. J. W. Sedlar, *India and the Greek World: A Study in the Transmission of Culture* (Rowman & Littlefield, 1980) seeks to answer the question: Can we speak of a true Indian influence on the Greek world?

*Indicates a less expensive paperbound edition.

Notes

1. Jacques Gernet, *A History of Chinese Civilization* (New York: Cambridge University Press, 1982), p. 28.
2. Quoted in Vincent Smith, *The Oxford History of India* (Oxford: Oxford University Press, 1958), p. 131.
3. Quoted in Charles Drekmeier, *Kingship and Community in Early India* (Stanford, CA: Stanford University Press, 1962), p. 175.
4. Quoted in Jack Finegan, *The Archeology of World Religions* (Princeton, NJ: Princeton University Press, 1952), p. 351.
5. Wm. Theodore de Bary, *East Asian Civilizations: A Dialogue in Five Stages* (Cambridge, MA: Harvard University Press, 1988), p. 19.
6. Kwang-chih Chang, *The Archaeology of Ancient China,* 4th ed. (New Haven, CT: Yale University Press, 1986), p. 5.
7. Charles Drekmeier, *Kingship and Community in Early India,* p. 300.

Chapter 5

The City of God

The Fall of Rome and the Rise of Christianity

To the inhabitants of the Graeco—Roman world, Rome was the "Eternal City," a proud title that conveyed the sense of confidence that Romans had in their capital. Thus when the Visigoths entered Italy and sacked the city in A.D. 410, anguish reverberated throughout the crumbling Empire. In distant Bethlehem, St. Jerome wrote, "The lamp of the world is extinguished, and it is the whole world which has perished in the ruins of this one city."

This chapter examines the decline and fall of the City of the Caesars and the emergence of the "City of God." It was St. Augustine, in the wake of the Visigoths' capture of Rome, who devised that phrase to describe the rise of a new Christian society on the ruins of paganism and a once invincible empire—and to assure Christians that the "community of the Most High" would endure, even though the greatest city on earth had fallen.

This period in history has several facets. One concerns the progressive decline of the Roman Empire, beginning in the third century A.D. In the gloomy words of a contemporary, "Our history now descends from a kingdom of gold to one of iron and rust." Another facet concerns the migration and settlement of the Germanic peoples in the western half of the Roman Empire. A third element is the national history of the Jews, the coming of Jesus in the midst of their turbulent relations with the Romans, and the eventual triumph of Jesus' teachings.

Decline and Division in the Roman World

In the third century A.D., internal anarchy and foreign invasion drastically transformed the Roman Empire. Augustus' constitutional monarchy, in which the emperor shared power with the Senate (see p. 84), changed to a despotic absolute monarchy in which the emperors made no attempt to hide the fact that they were backed by the military and would tolerate no senatorial interference. By the late third century, the emperor was no longer addressed as *princeps*, meaning first among equals, but as *dominus et deus*, "lord and god." The Principate had been replaced by the absolute rule known as the Dominate.

The Crisis of the Third Century

The transformation of the Roman Empire in the third century was foreshadowed by the reign of Commodus, who in A.D. 180 succeeded his

In this relief Roman tenants pay tribute to the owner of a farm by bringing their produce to him.

father, Marcus Aurelius. Unlike his stern father with his Stoic sense of duty (see p. 86), Commodus was an incompetent voluptuary whose dissipations, cruelties, and neglect of affairs of state motivated a group of conspirators to have him strangled in 192. Civil war followed as rival armies fought for the imperial throne—on one occasion troops holding Rome sold the throne to the highest bidder—until Septimus Severus emerged on top and established a dynasty that provided some measure of order.

The Severan dynasty (193–235) marks the approaching end of the Principate. The Senate, which under the Principate retained some governing power and functioned as an advisory body, was ignored and the army was pampered and enlarged. Septimus Severus' dying words to his sons, "Enrich the soldiers and scorn all others," reflect the trend of the times.

The dire effects of this toadying to the soldiery became apparent after 235, when the last member of the Severan dynasty was murdered by his own mutinous troops. During the next fifty years, the Empire suffered both from bloody civil wars and foreign invasions. Generals murdered emperors with no second thoughts, intimidated all opposition, and put themselves or their puppets on the throne. Of the twenty-six who claimed the title of emperor during this half-century of military anarchy, only one died a natural death.

Meanwhile, whole German tribes moved across the imperial frontiers: the Franks devastated Gaul, the Saxons invaded Britain, and the Goths occupied Dacia (modern Romania). For the first time since Hannibal's invasion five centuries earlier, it was felt necessary to protect Rome itself with a wall twenty feet high and twelve feet wide, which still stands. In Asia a powerful new menace appeared after 226—a reinvigorated Persia under the rule of the Sassanid dynasty, which proceeded to attack Roman Syria. In 260 the Persians defeated and captured a Roman emperor, who died in captivity—a severe blow to Roman prestige.

Economic Decline

As deadly to the well-being of the Empire as military anarchy and foreign invasions was prolonged economic decline. The Empire was no longer expanding; the economy had become static. In the past, military expansion had paid off in rich booty, and the tapping of new sources of wealth had justified a large army. Now, however, wars were defensive, and the army had become a financial liability rather than an asset. Gold and silver were also being drained away because of an unfavorable trade balance with India and China (see p. 126).

In the western half of the Empire the trend toward the concentration of land ownership in a few hands was greatly accelerated by the turbulent conditions of the third century. Small farmers abandoned their lands, which were then bought up cheaply by large landowners or confiscated by the emperors. The number of tenant farmers, or *coloni* (see p. 87), increased as small farming decreased. People fled the insecurity of city life to find jobs and protection on the large estates (*latifundia*) with their fortified villas. There they cultivated their patches of land, paying rent to the landowner and providing free labor at sowing and reaping time. The condition of the *coloni* deteriorated as they fell behind in their rents and taxes and finally were bound to their tenancies by imperial order until they had discharged their debts. This was a first step toward serfdom and the social and economic pattern of the early Middle Ages.

The frequent civil wars disturbed trade and thus undermined the prosperity of the cities, whose populations decreased correspondingly. To make matters worse, inflation spiraled because the government spent more than it took in. In order to meet their military and administrative expenses, the emperors repeatedly devalued the coinage by reducing its silver content. Ultimately the amount of alloy reached 98 percent, and prices soared as people lost confidence in the debased currency. The government soon refused to accept its own money for taxes and required payment in goods and services.

Diocletian and Constantine

A much-needed reconstruction of the Empire was accomplished by Diocletian (285–305), a rough-hewn soldier and shrewd administrator. Diocletian's work of stabilization is often compared to that of Augustus after a similar period of turmoil. But while Augustus had established a form of constitutional monarchy, Diocletian founded an undisguised oriental despotism.

To increase the strength of the government, Diocletian completed the trend toward autocracy. The Senate was relegated to the status of a city council, while the person of the emperor was exalted. Adorned in robes laden with jewels, Diocletian surrounded himself with all the splendor of an oriental despot. An imperial etiquette was established that transformed the emperor into a veritable god; rigid ceremony demanded that people bow low before him, kiss the hem of his robe, and address him as "the most sacred lord."

Diocletian realized that the Empire's problems had become too great for one man, so he divided the Empire, retaining the more prosperous eastern half for his own administration. In the West he created a co-emperor who, like himself, was designated an Augustus. Each Augustus in turn entrusted the direct rule of half his realm to an assistant, called a Caesar. Since each Caesar was to succeed his Augustus when the senior official died or retired, the problem of succession seemed to be resolved.

Diocletian greatly increased the number and variety of administrative units within the four divisions of the Empire. The provinces were reduced in size and more than doubled in number. (Italy lost its hitherto favored position and was divided into provinces.) The provinces were grouped into thirteen dioceses, each under a vicar. The dioceses in turn were grouped into four prefectures, each under a prefect who served directly under one of the four emperors. Paralleling this civil administration was a separate hierarchy of military officials. Command of armies was given to generals called *duces* (from which the title *duke* was later derived). Finally, a large secret service was created to keep close watch over this vast bureaucracy.

Diocletian also made strenuous efforts to arrest economic decay in the Empire. He gradually restored confidence in the debased currency by issuing new standard silver and gold coins. In the meantime, in an effort to stem the runaway inflation, he issued an edict fixing maximum prices for all essential goods and services, from peas and beer to haircuts and freight rates.

After Diocletian and his fellow Augustus retired in 305, his scheme for the succession collapsed, and civil war broke out once again. Within a few years Constantine (306–337) forged to the front. After sharing the Empire for a few years with an eastern rival, Constantine became sole emperor in 324.

Constantine carried on Diocletian's work of reconstructing and stabilizing the Empire. He was the first emperor to use the Christian religion as a means of strengthening his position. In 312 Constantine was in the midst of a desperate battle for the city of Rome with a rival when, as tradition has it, he saw emblazoned across the sky a cross with the words *In hoc signo vinces* ("By this sign you will conquer.") Constantine won the battle, and in 313 he issued the Edict of Milan, which legalized Christianity throughout the Empire and put it on an equal footing with the pagan cults. The emperor himself waited until

Diocletian and his co-Augustus, each with his appointed Caesar, are shown in an embrace symbolic of the unity that Diocletian hoped to maintain despite administrative division of the empire. This sculpture now adorns St. Mark's Cathedral in Venice.

This colossal head of Constantine captures the emperor's vision of himself as a man in close contact with God.

on his deathbed before receiving baptism, but during his reign he actively supported Christianity by granting many favors to the church, thereby gaining the loyalty of many Christians, the bishops in particular. His mother, a barmaid named Helena (St. Helena), converted to Christianity and made a famous pilgrimage to the Holy Land where she is reputed to have discovered the remains of the True Cross on the site of Christ's Crucifixion. She presented her son with two nails from the cross. One he set in his crown, the other in the bridle of his war horse.

To ensure the production of essential goods and services as well as the collection of taxes, Constantine, like Diocletian earlier, issued a series of decrees that froze people in their occupations and places of origins. Henceforth, no *colonus* could leave the soil, and the children of a *colonus* had to accept the same status as that of their father. A soldier's son, too, had to follow his father's profession. In the cities the same restrictions were applied to members of those guilds whose activities were essential to the state, such as baking and transportation. Thus, to serve the interests of the state and to arrest further economic decline, a kind of caste system was established.

Division of the Empire

The center of gravity in the Roman world shifted eastward during the age of Diocletian and Constantine. The administrative reforms swept away Italy's former primacy, and Rome ceased to be a seat of imperial authority. Diocletian's coemperor in the West ruled from Milan, while Diocletian himself chose to govern the eastern half of the Empire and set up his court at Nicomedia in northwestern Asia Minor. His was a logical choice; the East had declined less than the West, and the greatest dangers to the Empire came from beyond the Danube River and from Persia. But even more strategic than Nicomedia was the old Greek colony of Byzantium, just across the straits in Europe, which Constantine selected for a new capital. Reached only through a narrow, easily defended channel, Byzantium possessed a splendid harbor at the crossroads of Europe and Asia. Constantine dubbed his capital New Rome, but it soon became known as Constantinople ("City of Constantine").

The establishment of an eastern capital foreshadowed the impending division of the Empire into two completely separate states (see map, p. 133). For about fifty years following the death of Constantine in 337, the unity of the Empire was preserved, although there were often two joint emperors, one in the East and the other in the West. But after Theodosius I divided the Empire between his two sons in 395, the Roman world was never again governed as a single unit. Henceforth we can speak of a western Roman empire, which soon fell, and an eastern Roman—or Byzantine—empire, which endured for another thousand years during which it adhered to the paternalistic and authoritarian pattern laid down by Diocletian and Constantine.

Upheaval in the West

Weakened by economic, social, and political decline, Rome had turned to the most extreme

**THE ROMAN EMPIRE
ABOUT 400 A.D.**

forms of absolutism in an effort to survive. But the Empire's internal crisis was compounded by mounting external pressures that threatened its far-flung frontiers. The greatest danger was in the north, the home of restless tribes of barbarians—the Germans. When they defeated the Romans in the battle of Adrianople in 378, the gates of the Empire burst open.

The Germanic Tribes

While the westernmost German tribes (Franks, Angles, and Saxons) had achieved a settled agricultural life, the others (including Goths, Vandals, and Lombards) were largely nomadic. All were far less advanced than their Roman contemporaries. For example, they engaged in so little commerce that cattle, rather than money, sufficed as a measure of value.

According to the Roman historian Tacitus, the Germans were notorious as heavy drinkers and gamblers. On the other hand, Tacitus praised their courage, respect for women, and freedom from many Roman vices. A favorite amusement was listening to the tribal bards recite old tales of heroes and gods.

Each warrior leader had a retinue of followers, who were linked to him by personal loyalty. According to Tacitus:

> On the field of battle it is a disgrace to the chief to be surpassed in valour by his companions, to the companions not to come up to the valour of their chief. As for leaving a battle alive after your chief has fallen, that means lifelong infamy and shame. To defend and protect him, to put down one's own acts of heroism to his credit—that is what they really mean by "allegiance." The chiefs fight for victory, the companions for their chief.[1]

"The war band—*comitatus* in Latin—had an important bearing on the origin of medieval feudalism, which was based on a similar personal bond between knights (companions) and their feudal lords (chiefs). The heroic values associated with the *comitatus* also continued into the Middle Ages, where they formed the basis of the value system of the feudal nobility.

In an effort to eliminate blood feuds, the tribal law codes of the Germans encouraged the payment of compensation as an alternative for an aggrieved kin or family seeking vengeance. For the infliction of specific injuries, a stipulated payment, termed a *bot*, was listed. The amount of compensation varied according to the severity of the crime and the social position of the victim. For example, the compensation for killing a male of high rank was forty times greater than that for killing a commoner.

It was often necessary to hold a trial to determine guilt or innocence. A person standing trial could produce oath-helpers who would swear to his innocence. If unable to obtain oath-helpers, the accused was subjected to trial by ordeal, of which there were three kinds. In the first, the defendant had to lift a small stone out of a vessel of boiling water; unless his scalded arm healed within a prescribed number of days, he was judged guilty. In the second, he had to walk blindfolded and barefoot across a floor on which lay pieces of red-hot metal; success in avoiding the metal was a sign of innocence. In the third, the bound defendant was thrown into a stream; if he sank he was innocent, but if he floated he was guilty because water was considered a divine element that would not accept a guilty person. Trial by ordeal lasted until the thirteenth century, when it was outlawed by Pope Innocent III and various secular rulers.

During the many centuries that the Romans and Germans faced each other across the Rhine-Danube frontier, there was much contact—peaceful as well as warlike—between the two peoples. Roman trade reached into Germany, and Germans entered the Empire as slaves. During the troubled third century, many Germans were invited to settle on vacated lands within the Empire or to serve in the Roman legions. By the fourth century, the bulk of the Roman army and its generals in the West were German.

The Germans beyond the frontiers were kept in check by force of arms, by frontier walls, by diplomacy and gifts, and by employing the policy of playing off one tribe against another. In the last decades of the fourth century, however, these methods proved insufficient to prevent a series of great new invasions. A basic factor behind Germanic restlessness seems to have been land hunger. Their numbers were increasing, much of their land was forest and swamp, and their agricultural methods were inefficient.

Barbarian Invasions

The impetus behind the increasing German activity on the frontiers in the late fourth century was the approach of the Huns. These nomads, superb horsemen and fighters from Central Asia, had plundered and slain their Asian neighbors for centuries. In 372 they crossed the Volga and soon subjugated the easternmost Germanic tribe, the Ostrogoths. Terrified at the prospect of being conquered in turn by the advancing Huns, the Visigoths petitioned the Romans to allow them to settle as allies inside the Empire. Permission was granted, and in 376 the entire tribe crossed the Danube into Roman territory. But soon corrupt Roman officials cheated and mistreated the Visigoths, and the proud barbarians went on a rampage. Valens, the inept East Roman emperor, sought to quell them, but he lost both his army and his life in the battle of Adrianople in 378.

Adrianople has been described as one of history's decisive battles, since it destroyed the legend of the invincibility of the Roman legions and ushered in a century and a half of chaos. For a few years the capable emperor Theodosius I held back the Visigoths, but after his death in 395 they began to migrate and pillage under their leader, Alaric. He invaded Italy, and in 410 his followers sacked Rome. The weak West Roman emperor ceded southern Gaul to the Visigoths, who soon expanded into Spain. Their Spanish kingdom lasted until the Muslim conquest of the eighth century (see map p. 135).

To counter Alaric's threat to Italy, the Romans had withdrawn most of their troops from the Rhine frontier in 406 and from Britain the following year. The momentous consequence of this action was a flood of Germanic tribes across the unguarded frontiers. The Vandals pushed their way through Gaul to Spain and, after pressure from the Visigoths, moved on to Africa, the granary of the Empire. In 455 a Vandal raiding force sailed over from Africa, and Rome was sacked a second time. Meanwhile the Burgundians settled in the Rhone valley, the Franks gradually spread across northern Gaul, and the Angles, Saxons, and Jutes invaded Britain. Although each of these several tribes set up a German-ruled kingdom within the confines of the Empire, only the Franks in Gaul and the Angles and Saxons in Britain managed to perpetuate their kingdom longer than a few centuries.

Meanwhile, the Huns pushed farther into Europe. Led by Attila, the "scourge of God," the mounted nomads crossed the Rhine in 451. The remaining Roman forces in Gaul, joined by the Visigoths, defeated the Huns near Troyes. Attila then plundered northern Italy and planned to take Rome, but disease, lack of supplies, and the dramatic appeal of Pope Leo I—which was to give the papacy great prestige—caused him to return to the plains of eastern Europe. The Huns disintegrated after 453, when Attila died on the night of his marriage to a Germanic princess immortalized in legend as Krimhild of the *Nibelungenlied*. Modern Hungary derives its name from Attila's followers who remained in that location.

The End of the West Roman Empire

As previously noted, after the death of Theodosius I in 395 the Empire had been divided between his two sons. The decline of Roman rule in the West was hastened as a series of incompetent emperors abandoned Rome and sought safety behind the marshes at the northern Italian city of Ravenna. The leaders of the imperial army, whose ranks were now mainly German, wielded the real power.

In 475 Orestes, the German commander of the troops, forced the Senate to elect his young son Romulus Augustulus ("Little Augustus") as emperor in the West. In the following year another German commander, Odovacar, slew Orestes. Seeing no reason for continuing the sham of an imperial line in the west, he deposed Romulus Augustulus and proclaimed himself head of the government. The deposition of this boy, who by a strange irony bore the names of the legendary founder of Rome and the founder of the Empire, marks the traditional "fall" of the Roman Empire.

Actually, no single date is accurate, for the fall of Rome was a long and complicated process. Yet at least 476 symbolizes the end of the Roman Empire in the West, for in this year the long line of emperors inaugurated by Augustus ended and the undisguised rule of Italy by German leaders began.

Theodoric's Kingdom in Italy

The disintegration of the Hunnic empire following the death of Attila freed the Ostrogoths to migrate as other tribes were doing. Under

This gold coin bears a likeness of Theodoric and is inscribed "King Theodoric," but the absence of a robe and diadem shows that he was not considered the equal of the emperor.

their energetic king, Theodoric (c. 454–526), the Ostrogoths were galvanized into action.

Theodoric accepted a commission from the emperor in the East to reimpose imperial authority over Italy, now in Odovacar's hands. In 488 Theodoric led his people into the Italian peninsula, where, after hard fighting, Odovacar sued for peace and was treacherously murdered. Theodoric then established a strong Ostrogothic kingdom in Italy with its capital at Ravenna. Because he appreciated the culture he had seen at Constantinople, Theodoric maintained classical culture on a high level. Following his death without a male heir in 526, civil war broke out in Italy, paving the way for a twenty-year war of reconquest (535–555) by the armies of the East Roman emperor Justinian. Italy was ravaged from end to end by the fighting, and the classical civilization that Theodoric had carefully preserved was in large part destroyed.

The Lombards

In 568, three years after the death of Justinian, the last wave of Germanic invaders, the Lombards, reputed to have been the most brutal and fierce of all the Germans, poured into Italy. The emperor in the East held on to southern Italy, as well as Ravenna and Venice, and the pope became the virtual ruler of Rome. Not until the late nineteenth century would Italy again be united under one government. The Lombard kingdom in Italy, weakened by the independent actions of many strong dukes, did not last long. In 774 it was conquered by the Franks, who had in the meantime established the most powerful and longest lasting of all the Germanic kingdoms that arose on the territory of the West Roman Empire.

The Problem of the Fall of Rome

The shock and dismay felt by contemporaries throughout the Roman world on learning of Alaric's sack of the Eternal City in 410 were to echo down the centuries, leaving the impression that the fall of Rome was a major calamity, one of the greatest in history.

Pagan writers attributed the sack of Rome to the abandonment of their ancient gods. In *The City of God*, St. Augustine argued against this

This World or the Other World

Six years after Alaric's sacking of Rome in 410, Rutilius Namatianus, a man still faithful to his pagan past, retired as prefect of the city of Rome and returned by sea to his home in Romanized Gaul. Passing a Christian monastery on the shore, he recalls that a young man of great promise, because of some "madness," had left "the lands and company of men" to become a monk and was now "buried here alive."

And in the middle of the water rises
 The isle of Gorgon, with the Pisan coast
 On one side, that of Cyrnos on the other.
And opposite, a rock that held for me
A memory of lately suffered loss:
A man of my own city, buried here
Alive; a youth of noble ancestors
And matching them in marriage and estate.

At least, he was. A madness came upon him
To leave the lands and company of men
And go to exile and ignominy
Among the shades. Poor, superstitious fool,
To think uncleanliness is godliness
And bring more savage torments on himself
Than heaven in its anger could devise.

Source: Peter D. Arnott, *The Romans and Their World* (New York: St. Martin's Press, 1970), p. 310.

Paulinus of Nola (c. 355–431) provides an answer to Rutilius' anguished question, Why? The governor of a Roman province before he was thirty, Paulinus gave up his post and his vast estates in Gaul, Spain, and Italy to become a humble Christian priest at Nola in Italy.

Not that they beggared be in mind, or
 brutes,
That they have chosen their dwelling
 place afar
In lonely places: but their eyes are
 turned
To the high stars, the very deep of
 Truth.
Freedom they seek, an emptiness apart
From worthless hopes: din of the mar-
 ketplace,
And all the noisy crowding up of things,
And whatsoever wars on the divine,
At Christ's command and for His love,
 they hate;
By faith and hope they follow after God,
And know their quest shall not be
 desperate,

If but the Present conquer not their souls
With hollow things: that which they see
 they spurn
That they may come at what they do not see,
Their senses kindled like a torch, that may
Blaze through the secrets of eternity.
The transient's open, everlastingness
Denied our sight; yet still by hope we
 follow
The vision that our minds have seen,
 despising
The shows and forms of things, the love-
 liness
Soliciting for ill our mortal eyes.
The present's nothing: but eternity
Abides for those on whom all truth, all
 good,
Hath shone, in one entire and perfect light.

Source: Helen Waddell, *Medieval Latin Lyrics* (London: Constable, 1929), p. 35.

charge and put forth the view that history unfolds according to God's design. Thus Rome's fall was part of the divine plan—"the necessary and fortunate preparation for the triumph of the heavenly city where man's destiny was to be attained."

This view was challenged in the eighteenth century by Edward Gibbon, author of the famous *Decline and Fall of the Roman Empire*, who saw Rome's fall as the "triumph of barbarism and religion." Not only the Germans, but also the Christian's had played an important role in undermining the imperial structure: "The clergy successfully preached the doctrines of patience and pusillanimity; . . . the last remains of the military spirit were buried in the cloister."[2]

Modern historians advance a variety of theories to explain why Rome fell. Some explanations have been rooted in psychological theory. Thus the basic cause has been attributed to a weakening of morale in the face of difficulties, to a "loss of nerve." Or it has been argued that the ultimate failure of Rome came from its too complete success—the easy acquisition of power and wealth and the importing of ready-made cultures from conquered peoples led to indolence and self-gratification among the ruling classes. Corrupt high-ranking bureaucrats and military leaders seeking private gain have also been cited as a key factor. Some historians blame nonhuman causes such as an exhaustion of the soil, drought, malaria, plague, or the presence of toxic amounts of lead in Roman dining pottery and water pipes. Such single-cause explanations usually reflect a personal bias or axe to grind. Thus the popular television star Joan Collins, much concerned about the spread of such afflictions as herpes and AIDS, argues that Rome's fall is "a good reason for celibacy. It's like the Roman Empire. Wasn't everybody running around just covered in syphilis? And then it was destroyed by volcano."[3]

Most historians today attribute Rome's decline to a combination of interacting forces over a long period of time. On the political side, no effective system of imperial succession had ever been worked out, and this, plus the failure of the emperors to control the army, resulted in military anarchy, the disintegration of central authority, and the weakening of Rome's ability to withstand external pressures. Beginning in the third century, the emperors had to increase the military establishment despite a growing manpower shortage caused by a declining birthrate and by recurrent plagues from Asia (perhaps smallpox or measles). This decision led to Germanization of the army and to German colonization within the Empire. The West was becoming "barbarized" before the barbarian invasions took place.

The economy of the Empire had been declining for two centuries (see p. 136). Rome had grown rich on the spoils of conquest. This source of wealth ended when expansion ceased with the stabilization of the frontiers. Without manufactures and other sources of new wealth, Rome's capitalistic economy contracted. To pay their armies and other costs of government, the emperors continually debased the coinage. To escape the resulting inflation, the rich invested their wealth in land, which, unlike money, retained its value. Inflation and a crushing tax burden destroyed much of the middle class. Eventually, the rigid economic and social reforms of Diocletian and Constantine created a vast bureaucracy that merely aggravated the existing ills in the western half of the Empire, already far along the road to decline.

In addition to asking how it ended, one should ask how the Roman Empire lasted so long. Any discussion of the reasons for the collapse of Roman power in the West must also explain why the Roman Empire in the East, centered on Constantinople, survived for another thousand years. This subject will be explored in chapter 7.

The Rise and Triumph of Christianity

Through the long centuries that witnessed the decline of the Roman Empire and the invasions of the Germans, an increasingly powerful force became evident in the Mediterranean world. The Christian religion's long and arduous struggle for converts eventually led to victory over Roman and German alike. Some older historians have singled Christianity out as the most significant cause of Rome's fall. Most scholars today would not agree with that earlier judgment, but none would deny that Christianity played a vital role in the transformation of the classical world into the new civilization of medieval Europe.

Post-Exilic Jewish Nationalism

When the Principate of Augustus was laying the foundations of Rome's imperial greatness, events were taking place in the distant Roman province of Judea that would one day alter the course of Western history. Following the conquests of Alexander the Great in the Near East, Palestine was ruled first by the Ptolemies and then by the Seleucids. Since their return from exile in Babylonia in 538 B.C., the Jews in Palestine had created a theocratic community, based on the Torah, God's Law, originally revealed to

Moses and contained in the Pentateuch (the first five books of the Old Testament), and later supplemented by the teachings of the prophets and the writings of priests and scholars.

Religious life centered on the Temple at Jerusalem, which echoed with the cry "Hallelujah" ("Praise Yahweh") in thanksgiving for Yahweh's gracious dealing with his people. The most powerful figure was the high priest, who was assisted by the Sanhedrin, the high court for the enforcement of the Law. Since there was no distinction between civil and religious law, the jurisdiction of the Sanhedrin covered all aspects of Jewish life.

The Hebrews, the "People of God," were tightly knit; even Jewish groups outside Palestine were linked by spiritual bonds to the Temple and to a law they believed to be divinely inspired. But, unable to participate in the services of the Temple at Jerusalem, the Jews of the Diaspora (the "Scattering") met in local synagogues (from the Greek word for "assembly") for public worship and instruction in the Scriptures. In the long run, the synagogue, which probably first arose during the Babylonian Exile, outlived the Temple to become the heart of Judaism. Ultimately, it influenced the forms of worship in the Christian church and the Muslim mosques.

During the Hellenistic Age, Greek influences were constantly at work among the Jews. Most Jews outside Palestine spoke Greek, and a Greek translation of the Hebrew Scriptures became a necessity. Called the Septuagint (Latin for "seventy") from the tradition that it was the work of seventy scholars whose independent translations were miraculously identical, it was produced at Alexandria in the third century B.C.

Greek influences contributed to factionalism among the Jews in Judea. Eventually, one extremely pious group came to blows with the aristocratic pro-Greek Sadducees, as they came to be called, who were favored by the Seleucid rulers of Palestine. This internal conflict gave the Seleucid king an opportunity to intervene, and in 168 B.C., seeking to Hellenize the Jews, he ordered the Temple dedicated to the worship of Zeus. Viewing this decree as a blasphemous defilement, the Jews rebelled. Under their leader, Judas Maccabaeus, they rededicated the Temple to Yahweh and in 142 B.C. won their independence from the Seleucids.

Although Judas and his immediate successors contented themselves with the title of high priest, later members of the family were known as kings. In time these rulers became worldly and corrupt; factionalism flared up again, resulting in persecution and bloodshed. It was in the midst of a civil war that the Roman legions first made their appearance.

Roman Occupation of Palestine

Adopting the practice habitually followed by eastern Mediterranean states, one Jewish faction appealed to Rome for aid. Pompey, who was then completing his pacification of Asia Minor and Syria (see p. 82), ended the civil war in 63 B.C. by making Judea subject to the Roman governor of Syria.

Eventually, Herod the Great, a half-Jewish, half-Arab leader from Edom just south of Judea, rose to power as a tool of the Romans. Appointed by Mark Antony, Herod served as king of Judea from 37 to 4 B.C. He erected a magnificent palace, a theater, and a hippodrome and rebuilt the Temple on a lavish scale. To the Jews, however, Herod remained a detested usurper who professed Judaism as a matter of expediency. Soon after his death, Judea was made into a minor Roman province ruled by governors called procurators. The best known procurator is Pontius Pilate (A.D. 26–36), under whom Jesus was crucified.

The Jews themselves remained unhappy and divided under Roman domination. For centuries the prophets had taught that God would one day create a new Israel when righteousness prevailed under a God-anointed leader, the Messiah. In time, many Jews lost hope in a political Messiah and an earthly kingdom and instead conceived of a spiritual Messiah who would lead all the righteous, including the resurrected dead, to a spiritual kingdom. But a group of ardent Jewish nationalists, called Zealots, favoring the use of force to drive the hated foreigner out of "God's land," precipitated a fatal clash with the Romans. The atmosphere had long been poisoned by such incidents as the following, reported by the contemporary Jewish historian Josephus:

The people had assembled in Jerusalem for the Feast of Unleavened Bread [Passover], and the Roman cohort stood on guard over the

Temple colonnade, armed men always being on duty at the feasts to forestall any rioting by the vast crowds. One of the soldiers pulled up his garment and bent over indecently, turning his backside towards the Jews and making a noise as indecent as his attitude. This infuriated the whole crowd, who noisily appealed to Cumanus [the procurator] to punish the soldier, while the less restrained of the young men and the naturally tumultuous section of the people rushed into battle, and snatching up stones hurled them at the soldiers. Cumanus, fearing the whole population would rush at him, sent for more heavy infantry.[4]

Destruction of Jerusalem

In A.D. 66 violence erupted into war after the Zealots massacred the small Roman garrison at Jerusalem. After a five-month siege of Jerusalem in A.D. 70, Titus, son of the emperor Vespasian, laid waste to most of the city. What came to be called the "Wailing Wall," a small part of the Temple complex, remained standing. The story is that it was protected by angels whose tears cemented the stones in place forever. It was later prophesied that a third Temple would be erected on the site when the Messiah came. (The Dome of the Rock, a mosque built by the Muslims, has occupied the site since the eighth century A.D.) The wholesale destruction of Jerusalem in A.D. 70 spelled the end of the Hebrew state, although the fortress of Masada near the Dead Sea held out for two more years. The Jewish dream of an independent homeland was to remain unrealized for almost nineteen centuries, until the Republic of Israel was proclaimed in 1948.

Development of Jewish Religious Thought

The destruction of Jerusalem did not destroy the most important single aspect of Jewish culture—its religion. Through centuries of suffering, captivity, and subjugation, the Jews had been taught by a succession of prophets and priests to hold to their covenant with Yahweh and to safeguard their religious inheritance.

In the centuries just preceding and following the birth of Christ, Judaism exhibited much vigor. While the aristocratic Sadducees, who controlled the office of high priest, stood for strict adherence to the written Law, or Torah, the more numerous Pharisees believed that, with divine guidance, human beings could modify and amend the Law. The Pharisees accepted the belief in personal immortality and the kingdom of heaven. From their ranks came the rabbis, scholars who expounded the Law and applied it to existing conditions. The "oral law" propagated by the Pharisees became the core of the later Talmud, the great commentary on Jewish law that laid down in the most detailed way a code of daily living for Jews. Moreover, following the destruction of the Temple and the end of the high priesthood, the rabbinical schools of the Pharisees did much to ensure that Judaism would endure.

The Dead Sea Scrolls

The discovery of the Dead Sea Scrolls added greatly to our knowledge of another Jewish sect, the Essenes. While exploring caves around the desolate western shore of the Dead Sea in 1947,

The partially unrolled Thanksgiving Scroll, one of the Dead Sea Scrolls, preserved at the Hebrew University in Jerusalem, is composed of religious hymns that poetically develop the Essenes' theological doctrines.

two Bedouin boys came across several clay jars containing long manuscripts wrapped in linen. Later, many more scrolls were found in other caves. Nearby were the ruins of a monastery built by the Essenes "to separate themselves," as the scrolls state, "from the abode of perverse men." Occupied between the second century B.C. and A.D. 68, the monastery was destroyed by the Romans during the great Jewish revolt. Prior to its destruction the Essenes hid their manuscripts in the caves.

Some scrolls are portions of the Old Testament dating from the first century B.C. and thus are about a thousand years older than the earliest previously known text. Biblical scholars have been thrilled to read the Book of Isaiah in such an ancient manuscript and to discover that the version now in use is virtually unchanged.

Those scrolls that describe the Essene sect in the first century B.C.—that is, just prior to the appearance of Christianity—have been said to constitute "a whole missing chapter of the history of the growth of religious ideas between Judaism and Christianity."[5] Some scholars have attached much significance to common elements in the beliefs and practices of the Essenes and early Christians. (John the Baptist, who baptized Jesus and whom Jesus viewed as the chosen herald of a God-given message, may have been a member of the Essene sect.)

The Essenes' founder, a shadowy figure known as the Righteous Teacher, suffered persecution and perhaps martyrdom late in the second century B.C. The sect considered itself the true remnant of God's people, preached a "new covenant," and waited patiently for the time when God would destroy the powers of evil and inaugurate His Kingdom

Similar views concerning the transition from the "Old Age" to the "New Age" were held by many other Jews as well as by Christians. For the Christians, however, the gap had been bridged. The Messiah had come, and his resurrection was proof that the New Age had arrived. "The New Testament faith was not a new faith, but the fulfillment of an old faith. . . . Lines of continuity between Moses and Jesus, Isaiah and Jesus, the Righteous Teacher and Jesus, John the Baptist and Jesus should occasion no surprise. On the contrary, a biblical faith insists on such continuities."[6]

The Life and Teaching of Jesus

Whatever its parallels with the Essene sect—including baptism and a communal meal—Christianity bears the unmistakable imprint of the personality of its founder, Jesus of Nazareth. According to the Biblical account, he was born in Bethlehem during the reign of Herod; therefore he may have been born by the time of Herod's death (4 B.C.) rather than in the year that traditionally begins the Christian era. After spending the first years of his life as a carpenter in the village of Nazareth, Jesus began his brief mission, preaching a gospel of love for one's fellow human beings and urging people to "Turn away from your sins. The kingdom of heaven is near" (Matthew 4:17).

The fame of Jesus' teaching and his "mighty works"—miracles such as casting out demons, healing the sick, raising the dead, and walking on the water—spread among the Jews as he and his twelve Apostles traveled from village to village in Palestine. When he came to Jerusalem to observe the feast of the Passover, he was welcomed triumphantly by huge crowds as the promised Messiah. But Jesus was concerned with a spiritual, not an earthly, kingdom, and when people saw that he had no intention of leading a nationalistic movement against the Romans, they turned against him. His enemies then came forward—the moneylenders whom he had denounced, the Pharisees who resented his repudiation of their minute regulations of daily behavior, the people who considered him a disturber of the status quo, and those who saw him as a blasphemer of Yahweh. Betrayed by Judas, one of his disciples, Jesus was condemned by the Sanhedrin for blasphemy "because he claimed to be the Son of God" (John 19:7). Before the procurator Pontius Pilate, however, Jesus was charged with treason for claiming to be the king of Jews:

"Are you the king of Jews?" he [Pilate] asked him. Jesus answered, . . . "My kingdom does not belong to this world; if my kingdom belonged to this world, my followers would fight to keep me from being handed over to the Jews. No, my kingdom does not belong here. . . . You say that I am a king. I was born and came into the world for this one purpose, to speak about the truth. Whoever belongs to the truth listens to me." (John 18:33–38)

Jesus' Parable of the Weeds

The heart of Jesus' teaching was "The Kingdom of Heaven is near." This eschatological (from the Greek word for "end" or "final") message concerns such things as the coming "end of the age" of evil, the Devil ("the Evil One"), the Last Judgment, resurrection of the dead, angels, and the "Son of Man" who will usher in the Kingdom of Heaven. Jesus employed easy to understand parables to convey to his listeners the meaning of the Kingdon of Heaven—also called the Kingdom of God.

Jesus told them another parable: "The Kingdom of heaven is like a man who sowed good seed in his field. One night, when everyone was asleep, an enemy came and sowed weeds among the wheat, and went away. When the plants grew and the heads of grain began to form, then the weeds showed up. The man's servants came to him and said, 'Sir, it was good seed you sowed in your field; where did the weeds come from?' 'It was some enemy who did this,' he answered. 'Do you want us to go and pull up the weeds?' they asked him. 'No,' he answered, 'because as you gather the weeds you might pull up some of the wheat along with them. Let the wheat and weeds both grow together until harvest, and then I will tell the harvest workers: Pull up the weeds first and tie them in bundles to throw in the fire; then gather in the wheat and put it in my barn.'"

Then Jesus left the crowd and went indoors. His disciples came to him and said, "Tell us what the parable of the weeds in the field means." Jesus answered: "The man who sowed the good seed is the Son of Man; the field is the world; the good seed is the people who belong to the Kingdom; the weeds are the people who belong to the Evil One; and the enemy who sowed the weeds is the Devil himself. The harvest is the end of the age, and the harvest workers are angels. Just as the weeds are gathered up and burned in the fire, so it will be at the end of the age: the Son of Man will send out his angels and they will gather up out of his Kingdom all who cause people to sin, and all other evildoers, and throw them into the fiery furnace, where they will cry and gnash their teeth. Then God's people will shine like the sun in their Father's Kingdom. Listen, then, if you have ears!"

Matthew 13: 24–30, 36–43. *The Holy Bible: Revised Standard Version* (New York: Thomas Nelson and Sons, 1952).

Jesus was condemned to the death that Rome inflicted on enemies of the state—crucifixion.

With Jesus' death it seemed as though his cause had been exterminated. No written message had been left behind, and his few loyal followers were disheartened. Yet in the wake of his martyrdom, the Christian cause took on new impetus. Reports soon spread that Jesus had been seen after his crucifixion and had spoken to his disciples, giving them solace and inspiration. At first there were few converts within Palestine itself, but the Hellenized Jews living in foreign lands, in contact with new ideas and modes of living, were less firmly committed to traditional Jewish doctrines. The new faith first made real headway among the Jewish communities in such cities as Damascus, Antioch (where its followers were first called "Christians" by the Greeks), Corinth, and Rome (see map, p. 143).

The Work of Paul

The followers of Jesus, like their master, had no thought of breaking away from Judaism. They sought only to revivify their faith spiritually and ethically. Because they adhered to the requirements of the Jewish law, with its strict dietary requirements and practice of circumcision, the new message could not attract non-Jews. Largely through the more liberal and cosmopolitan preachings of Paul, this obstacle was removed. Because of his influence, Paul has been called the second founder of Christianity.

Born Saul, of Jewish ancestry but a Roman citizen by birth, and raised in the cosmopolitan city of Tarsus in Asia Minor, he possessed a wide knowledge of Greek culture. Saul was also a strict Pharisee who considered Christians to be traitors to the Sacred Law and took an active part in their persecution. One day, about A.D. 33, on the road to Damascus, determined to wipe out the Christian community there, Saul had an experience that changed his life. In Saul's own words:

As I was traveling and coming near Damascus, about midday a bright light suddenly flashed from the sky around me. I fell to the ground and heard a voice saying to me, "Saul, Saul! Why do you persecute me?" "Who are you, Lord?" I asked. "I am Jesus of Nazareth, whom you persecute," he said to me. The men with me saw the light but did not hear the voice of the one who was speaking to me. I asked, "What shall I do, Lord?" and the Lord said to me, "Get up and go into Damascus, and there you will be told everything that God has determined for you." (Acts 22:6–10)

Saul, henceforth known by the Roman name, Paul, turned from being a persecutor into the greatest of Christian missionaries.

Paul taught that Jesus was the Christ (from *Christos*, Greek for "Messiah"), the Son of God, and that he had died to atone for the sins of all people. Only faith in the saving power of Jesus Christ was necessary for the salvation to Jews

THE SPREAD OF CHRISTIANITY

- Christians: 50% or more of population, 300 A.D.
- Christians: 30-50% of population, 300 A.D.
- Paul's travels
- ■ Christian communities in the 1st Century

and Gentiles (non-Jews) alike. The Jewish Law was unnecessary:

A man is put right with God only through faith in Jesus Christ, never by doing what the Law requires. . . . So there is no difference between Jews and Gentiles, between slaves and free men, between men and women; you are all one in union with Christ Jesus. (Galatians 2:16, 3:28)

After covering 8000 miles teaching and preaching, Paul was beheaded at Rome about A.D. 65 (as was also Peter, founder of the church at Rome) during the reign of Nero. By this time Christian communities had been established in all important cities in the East and at Rome. Paul performed a very important service to these infant communities of believers by instructing them, either through visits or letters, in the fundamental beliefs of the new religion. He served as an authority by which standardization of belief could be achieved.

Persecution of the Christians

The Roman government tolerated any religion that did not threaten the safety or tranquility of the Empire. Christianity, however, was perceived as a subversive danger to society and the state. Christians were notorious in their refusal to offer sacrifice—even a few grains of incense cast upon an altar—to the state cults on behalf of the emperor. Although not required by law before the troubled third century, this was considered an essential patriotic rite uniting all Roman subjects in common loyalty to the imperial government. To Christians, however, there was only one God; they could sacrifice to no other. In the eyes of the Roman officials, this attitude branded them as traitors and "atheists." In addition, the Christians seemed to be a secret, unsociable group forming a state within a state—"walling themselves off from the rest of mankind," as a pagan writer observed. Many were pacifists who refused to serve in the army, and all were intolerant of other religious sects and refused to associate with pagans or take part in social functions that they considered sinful or degrading.

During the first two centuries A.D., persecution was only sporadic and local, like that at Rome under Nero (see p. 85). But during the late third and early fourth centuries, when the Empire was in danger of collapse, three organized empire-wide efforts were made to suppress Christianity. By far the longest and most systematic campaign against the Christians, who now comprised perhaps one tenth of the population, was instigated by the emperor Diocletian from 303 to 311. The death penalty was stringently enforced for those who refused to sacrifice to the Roman gods. But the inspired defiance of the Christian martyrs, who seemed to welcome death, could not be overcome. "The blood of the martyrs is the seed of the Church" became a Christian rallying cry.

Official Recognition and Acceptance

In 311 the emperor Galerius recognized that persecution had failed and issued an edict of toleration making Christianity a legal religion in the East. Two years later, Constantine's Edict of Milan granted Christians freedom of worship throughout the Empire.

Constantine accepted baptism when near death, and his successors were all Christians, with one exception. In his brief reign (361–363) the scholarly emperor Julian, Constantine's nephew, who had been raised a Christian, renounced his faith and sought to revive paganism; as a result, he was branded the Apostate. Julian did not persecute the Christians ("Those who are in the wrong in matters of supreme importance," he wrote, "are objects of pity rather than of hate,"[7]) and his efforts to revive paganism failed dismally. On his deathbed he is supposed to have said, "Thou hast conquered, O Galilean."

The emperor Theodosius I (379–395) made Christianity the official religion of the Empire. Henceforth paganism was persecuted, and even the Olympic games were suppressed.

A famous victim of this new persecution was the woman Hypatia, who in 415 was killed by a Christian mob in Alexandria. By the age of twenty-five she had become famous throughout the eastern half of the Empire as a lecturer on Greek philosophy. Her popularity aroused the resentment of the bishop of Alexandria, who had already led a mob in destroying the homes and businesses of the city's Jews. He now incited a mob to abduct Hypatia. She was dragged into a nearby church and hacked to death. This display of fanatical intolerance shocked Christian leaders throughout the Roman world.

Reasons for the Spread of Christianity

In its rise to preeminence, Christianity competed with the various philosophies and religions of the day. The philosophies were becoming more religious and other-worldly, however, which made it easy for their adherents to accept a Christianity whose doctrines, as we shall see, were becoming more philosophical. During the early Empire, most Roman intellectuals had embraced Stoicism, which, unlike Epicureanism with its unyielding materialism, had room for God (see p. 94). The dominant philosophy of the third century, Neoplatonism, rejected human reason and taught that the only reality is spiritual. The soul's principal objective is to escape from the material world and, by union with God, return to its spiritual home.

The popular mystery religions that the Romans had imported from Greece and the Near East during the troubled last century of the Republic, gave spiritual satisfaction not provided by Rome's early ritualistic forms of worship (see p. 74). These religions included the worship of the Phrygian Cybele, the Great Mother (Magna Mater); the Egyptian Isis, sister and wife of Osiris and also viewed as a Great Mother; the Greek Dionysus, called Bacchus by the Romans; and the Persian sun-god Mithras, the intermediary between the great Lord of Light, Ahura Mazda, and mere mortals, whose sacred day of worship was called Sunday, and from whose cult women were excluded. Common to all the mystery religions were the notions of a divine savior and the promise of everlasting life. Their followers found Christian beliefs and practices familiar enough to make conversion easy to achieve.

But Christianity had far more to offer than did the mystery religions. Its founder was not a creature of myth, like the gods and goddesses of the mystery cults, but a real historic personality whose lofty ethical teachings and whose death and resurrection as the divine incarnation of God were preserved in detail in a unique record, the New Testament. Shared only with the Jews was the Christian concept of God—the omnipotent, jealous, yet loving God of the Hebrew Scriptures as the God of all humanity. Moreover, Christianity was a dynamic, aggressive faith. It upheld the equality of all people—rich and poor, slave and freeborn, male and female. (Women were among Jesus' audiences, and Paul's letters give much evidence of women active in the early church. One of Jesus' helpers was Mary Magdalene. According to the so-called Gnostic Gospels, which were declared heretical in the early fourth century and ordered destroyed, "Christ loved her more than all the disciples."[8]) Christianity taught that a loving Father had sent his only Son to atone for human sins, and offered a vision of immortality and an opportunity to be "born again" cleansed of sin. Its converts were bound together by faith and hope, and they took seriously the obligation of caring for orphans, widows, and other unfortunates. The courage with which they faced death and persecution impressed even their bitterest enemies. In time, a church organization was created that was far more united and efficient than any of its competitors.

Church Organization

The years immediately following the death of Jesus passed with little organization in the Christian movement. Viewing the present world as something that would end quickly with the imminent Second Coming of their Lord and the Last Judgment of the living and the dead, the early Christian converts saw no necessity for organization. But after it became clear that the Second Coming had been delayed, a definite church organization began to emerge.

At first there was little or no distinction between laity and clergy. Traveling teachers visited Christian communities, preaching and giving advice where needed. But the steady growth in the number of Christians made necessary special church officials who could devote all their time to religious work, clarifying the body of Christian doctrine, conducting services, and collecting money for charitable purposes.

The earliest officials were called presbyters (elders) or bishops (overseers). By the second century, the offices of bishop and presbyter had become distinct. Churches in the villages adjacent to the main church, which was usually located in a city, were administered by priests (a corruption of *presbyter*), who were responsible to a bishop. Thus evolved the diocese, a territorial administrative division under the jurisdiction of a bishop. The bishops were recognized as the direct successors of the Apostles and, like them, the guardians of Christian teaching and tradition.

A number of dioceses made up a province. The bishop of the most important city in each province enjoyed more prestige than his fellows and was known as an archbishop or metropolitan. The provinces were grouped into larger administrative divisions called patriarchates. The title of patriarch was applied to the bishop of such great cities as Rome, Constantinople, and Alexandria.

Primacy of the Bishop of Rome

A development of outstanding importance was the rise of the bishop of Rome to a position of preeminence in the hierarchy of the church. At preeminence in the hierarchy of the church. At first only one of several patriarchs, the Roman bishop gradually became recognized as the leader of the church in the West with the title of pope—from the Greek word meaning "father."

Many factors explain the emergence of the papacy at Rome. As the largest city in the West and the capital of the Empire, Rome had an aura of prestige that was transferred to its bishop. When the Empire in the West collapsed in the fifth century, the bishop of Rome emerged as a stable and dominant figure looked up to by all. The primacy of Rome was fully evident during the pontificate of Leo I the Great (440–461), who provided both the leadership that saved Italy from invasion by the Huns and the major theoretical support for papal leadership of the church—the Petrine theory. This doctrine held that since Peter, whom Christ had made leader of the apostles, was the first bishop of Rome, his authority over all Christians was handed on to his successors at Rome. The church in the East, insisting on the equality of all the apostles, never accepted the Petrine theory.

Foundations of Christian Doctrine and Worship

While the administrative structure of the church was being erected, Christian beliefs were being defined and systematized. We have seen that this process of fixing Christian doctrine, or dogma, began with Paul, who stressed the divinity of Jesus and explained his death as an atonement for mankind's sins ("Christ died for us" Romans 5:8).

In time, differences of opinion over doctrinal matters caused many controversies. One of the most important was over a belief called Arianism. At issue was the relative position of the three persons of the Trinity—God the Father, God the Son, and God the Holy Spirit. The view that the Father and Son were equal was vigorously denied by Arius (256–336), a priest from Alexandria. He believed that Christ was not fully God because he was not of a substance identical with God and, as a created being, was not coeternal with his creator. The controversy became so serious that in 325 the emperor Constantine convened the first ecumenical church council, the Council of Nicaea, to resolve the problem. (This was the first of nine "world" councils in early church history. They decided matters democratically by a majority vote of the attending bishops, who were themselves elected. The modern world's democratic ideal may stem as much from Christianity as from democratic Athens or republican Rome.) With Constantine presiding, the council branded Arian belief a heresy—an opinion or doctrine contrary to the official teaching of the church—and Christ was declared to be of the same substance as God, uncreated, and coeternal with him. This mystical concept of the Trinity, without which the central Christian doctrine of the incarnation—God becoming man in Christ—would be undermined, received official formulation in the Nicene Creed.

The liturgy of the early churches was plain and simple, consisting of prayer, Scripture reading, hymns, and preaching. Early Christians worshiped God and sought salvation largely through individual efforts. Following the growth of church organization and dogma, however, the church was believed to be the indispensable intermediary between God and humans. Without the church, the individual could not hope for salvation.

The development of the church's dogma owed much to the church Fathers of the second through fifth centuries. Since most of them were intellectuals who came to Christianity by way of

Neoplatonism and Stoicism, they maintained that Greek philosophy and Christianity were compatible. Because reason (*logos* in Greek) and truth came from God, "philosophy was a preparation," wrote Clement of Alexandria (d. 215), "paving the way towards perfection in Christ," the latest and most perfect manifestation of God's reason. Thus Christianity was viewed as a superior philosophy that could supersede all pagan philosophies and religions.

In the West three church Fathers stand out. The scholarship of St. Jerome (340–420) made possible the famous Vulgate translation of the Bible into Latin. In a revised form, it is still the official translation of the Roman Catholic church. Jerome also justified Christian use of the literature and learning of the classical world. Why should not the Christian take what was good from the pagans, he argued, since the Hebrews had taken "spoil" from Egypt when they fled from Egyptian bondage. (Exodus 3:22)

St. Ambrose (340–397) resigned his government post to become bishop of Milan, where he employed his great administrative skills to establish a model bishopric. By reproving the actions of the strong emperor Theodosius I and forcing him to do public penance, St. Ambrose was the first to assert the church's superiority over the state in spiritual matters.

St. Augustine (354–430) was the most important of all the church Fathers. At the age of thirty-two, as he relates in his *Confessions*, one of the world's great autobiographies, he found in Christianity the answer to his long search for meaning in life. Before, he had shared the doubts of men "who rush hither and thither, to this side or that, according as they are driven by the impulse of erratic opinion." Now, "by the pity, mercy, and help of God" he had come to anchor in Christianity. "What man shall teach another to understand this?" Augustine asks. No one can teach him; he must come to it on his own after much travail: "This must be asked of you, sought in you, knocked for at you; thus only shall it be received, thus shall it be found, thus shall it be opened to us."[9] Here Augustine echoes the view expressed by many church Fathers, that "Christians are not born, they are made."

As bishop of Hippo in North Africa, St. Augustine wrote more than a hundred religious works, which blended classical logic and philosophy with Christian belief and became the foundation of much of the church's theology.

The Regular Clergy

So far we have discussed the secular clergy, who moved through the world (*saeculum*) administering the church's services and communicating its teachings to the laity. But another type of clergy also arose—the regular clergy, so called because they lived by a rule (*regula*) within monasteries. These monks sought seclusion from the distractions of this world in order to prepare themselves for the next.

The monastic way of life was older than Christianity, having existed in Judaism, for example, among the Essenes. Christian ascetics, who had abandoned the worldly life and become hermits, could be found in the East as early as the third century A.D. In pursuit of spiritual perfection by denying their physical feelings, they tortured themselves and fasted to excess. In Syria, for example, St. Simeon Stylites sat for thirty-three years on top of a pillar sixty feet high. His disciple then beat his record by three months.

As a more moderate expression of asceticism, Christians in Egypt developed the monastic life in which, seeking a common spiritual goal, they lived together under a common set of regulations. St. Basil (330–379), a Greek bishop in Asia Minor, drew up a rule based on work, charity, and a communal life that still allowed each monk to retain most of his independence. The Rule of St. Basil became the standard system in the Eastern church.

In Western monasticism the work of St. Benedict (c. 480–543) paralleled St. Basil's efforts in the East. About 529, Benedict led a band of followers to a high hill between Rome and Naples, named Monte Cassino, where they erected a monastery on the site of an ancient pagan temple. Here he composed a rule that gave order and discipline to Western monasticism. Benedictine monks took the three basic vows of poverty, chastity, and obedience to the abbot, the head of the monastery. Unlike Eastern monks, the daily activities of the Benedictine monks were closely regulated: they participated in eight divine services, labored in field or workshop for six or seven hours, and spent about two hours studying and preserving the writings of Latin antiquity at a time when western Europe suffered widespread illiteracy. Benedictine monasticism was to be the most dynamic civilizing force in medieval Europe between the sixth and the twelfth centuries.

Women played an important role in establishing the new monastic style of Christianity. In Egypt, an early fifth-century bishop declared that 20,000 women—twice as many as men—were living in desert communities as nuns. In the West, several fourth-century biographies of aristocratic women describe how they turned their villas and palaces into monasteries for women of all classes and remained firmly in control of their institutions. These communities became famous for their social and educational services, in addition to providing a different way of life for women who were unwilling to conform to the usual pattern of marriage, motherhood, and subordination to men.

Conclusion

By the sixth century in the West the Empire was no more than a dim memory. In its place were new states that foreshadowed the major political divisions of modern Europe: Visigothic Spain, Anglo-Saxon England, Frankish Gaul, and a divided Italy ruled by Lombard dukes, the Eastern emperor, and the pope.

Vast tracts of formerly cultivated land were left untilled. The failure of communications and transportation, coupled with the flight of the labor force from the cities to the country, had brought on a progressive decentralization of the economy. With much industry transferred from cities to large country estates, scores of once flourishing towns near the frontiers ceased to exist, while those closer to the Mediterranean shrunk in size and importance. "Roman civilization had been essentially urban; medieval civilization was to be essentially rural. With the decline of the towns the general level of civilization was lowered and western Europe began to assume its medieval aspect."[10]

The unified and systematic body of Roman law, one of the greatest achievements of the Empire, was one of the most significant losses to sixth-century Europe. Germanic law was personal and tribal, and the Germans carried it into the Empire. Classical culture was also largely disregarded by the Germans, who had neither the desire nor the sophistication to utilize Roman engineering techniques, architecture, art, and literary style.

Yet the Germanic invasions were not as catastrophic as was once thought. True, the invaders pillaged ruthlessly, and in certain sections of the Empire, especially in Britain, Roman civilization was entirely wiped out. The Germans also seized a great deal of land, but most of this was either vacant or belonged to the emperors. In most areas the invaders still represented a minority of the population (few Germanic tribes exceeded 100,000 people) and a gradual blending of the cultures and the blood of the two people began. Thus the barbarians in time lost their Germanic customs, religion, and speech; that is why hardly a trace of the Germanic languages remains in Italy, France, and Spain. The church, under the dual leadership of Benedictine monasticism and the papacy, assisted the fusion between German and Roman.

By the sixth century, the foundations for the papacy's spiritual and political power had been laid. We have seen how Pope Leo the Great acquired the moral leadership of the West by successfully protecting Italy from the Huns and how the Lombard conquests in Italy gave the papacy its opportunity to achieve independence. In addition, ready for future use was the doctrine of the supremacy of the church over the state in spiritual matters, a doctrine implied by St. Augustine in his *City of God* and clearly expressed by St. Ambrose during his clash with the emperor Theodosius I.

By the sixth century, then, the three elements that were to create the pattern of Western civilization in the Middle Ages were being interwoven: Graeco-Roman culture, the Christian church, and the Germanic peoples and their institutions and values.

Suggestions for Reading

S. Katz, *The Decline of Rome and the Rise of Medieval Europe* (Cornell, 1955) is a concise, clear account. Peter Brown, *The World of Late Antiquity, A.D. 150–750* (Harcourt Brace Jovanovich, 1971); C. G. Starr, *The Roman*

Empire, 27 B.C.–A.D. 476: A Study in Survival (Oxford, 1982); and A. H. M. Jones, *The Decline of the Ancient World** (Longman, 1975) are detailed surveys. See also F. Lot, *The End of the Ancient World and the Beginning of the Middle Ages* (Barnes and Noble, 1953); R. MacMullen, *Constantine* (Dial, 1969).

Edward Gibbon, *The Decline and Fall of the Roman Empire** (Penguin, 1983), ed. by D. A. Saunders, is a useful abridgment of this eighteenth-century classic. For modern scholarly opinion on Rome's decline see Lynn White, Jr., ed., *The Transformation of the Roman World: Gibbon's Problem After Two Centuries* (Univ. of California, 1966); Michael Grant, *The Fall of the Roman Empire: A Reappraisal* (Annenberg School Press, 1976); R. Mac-Mullen, *Corruption and the Decline of Rome** (Yale, 1988); R. M. Haywood, *The Myth of Rome's Fall** (Greenwood, 1958); and D. Kagan, ed., *The End of the Roman Empire: Decline or Transformation?** 2nd ed. (Heath, 1978).

J. B. Bury, *The Invasion of Europe by the Barbarians** (Norton, 1967) is a good general work on the nature and effect of the Germanic invasions. Malcolm Todd, *The Northern Barbarians, 100 B.C.–A.D. 300*, 2nd. ed.*(Blackwell, 1987) describes German life before the invasions. See also E. A. Thompson, *The Early Germans* (Oxford, 1965); and O. J. Maenchen—Helfen, *The World of the Huns* (Univ. of California, 1973).

J. A. Hexter, *The Judaeo-Christian Tradition** (Harper & Row, 1966) is a brief but valuable survey of the evolution of ancient Judaism and Christianity. On the late ancient history of the Jews see E. Bickerman, *From Ezra to the Last of the Maccabees: Foundations of the Post-Biblical Judaism** (Schocken, 1949); and D. S. Russell, *The Jews from Alexander to Herod* (Oxford, 1967). Edmund Wilson, *The Dead Sea Scrolls, 1949–1969* (Oxford, 1969) is the most readable introduction to a fascinating subject. See also John Allegro, *The Dead Sea Scrolls: A Reappraisal** (Penguin, 1956); and Frank M. Cross, *The Ancient Library of Qumran and Modern Biblical Studies* (Greenwood, 1961).

H. Kee and F. Young, *Understanding the New Testament*, 4th ed. (Prentice-Hall, 1983) is highly recommended. See also E. J. Goodspeed, *A Life of Jesus** (Greenwood, 1950); Michael Grant, *Saint Paul** (Scribner, 1976); and R. Bultman, *Primitive Christianity** (Fortress, 1956).

J. W. C. Ward, *A History of the Early Church to A.D. 500,** 4th ed. (Methuen, 1975) and Henry Chadwick, *The Early Church** (Penguin, 1969) are excellent surveys of the first five centuries of church history. See also Cyril Richard-son, *Early Christian Fathers* (Macmillan, 1970); the superb biography by Peter Brown, *Augustine of Hippo** (Univ. of California, 1969); H. Mattingly, *Christianity in the Roman Empire** (Norton, 1967); R. MacMullen, *Paganism in the Roman Empire* (Yale, 1981); and *Christianizing the Roman Empire** (Yale, 1984); E. R. Dodds, *Pagan and Christian in an Age of Anxiety** (Norton, 1970); Luther H. Martin, *Hellenistic Religions: An Introduction* (Oxford, 1987); and C. N. Cochrane, *Christianity and Classical Culture: A Study of Thought and Action from Augustus to Augustine** (Galaxy, 1960).

On early monasticism see H. Waddell, *The Desert Fathers** (Univ. of Michigan, 1957) and Peter Brown, *The Making of Late Antiquity* (Harvard, 1978).

*Indicates a less expensive paperbound editon.

Notes

1. Tacitus *Germania* 14, trans. H. Mattingly, *Tacitus on Britain and Germany* (Harmondsworth: Penguin Books, 1948), p. 112.
2. E. Gibbon, *The History of the Decline and Fall of the Roman Empire* (London: Methuen & Co., 1896), ch. 38, "General Observations on the Fall of the Roman Empire in the West."
3. *Playboy*, April 1984, p. 66. Quoted in Chester G. Starr, *Past and Future in Ancient History*, Publications of the Association of Ancient Historians, I (Lanham, MD: University Press of America, 1987), p. 57.
4. Josephus *The Jewish War* 2.223, trans. G. A. Williamson (Baltimore: Penguin Books, 1970), p. 136.
5. E. Wilson, *The Scrolls from the Dead Sea* (New York: Oxford University Press, 1955), p. 60.
6. Frank M. Cross, Jr., *The Ancient Library of Qumran and Modern Biblical Studies*, rev. ed. (Garden City, NY: Doubleday Anchor Books, 1961), p. 242.
7. Quoted in Henry Betterson, ed., *Documents of the Christian Church* (London: Oxford University Press, 1943), p. 28.
8. Mary Kinnear, *Daughters of Time: Women in the Western Tradition* (Ann Arbor: University of Michigan Press, 1982), p. 55.
9. St. Augustine *Confessions* 13.38, trans. E. B. Pusey.
10. S. Katz, *The Decline of Rome and the Rise of Medieval Europe* (Ithaca, NY: Cornell University Press, 1955), p. 98.

Islam from the Beginning to 1300

Arabia was the birthplace of the Islamic religion; the Arabic language was the "tongue of the angels," since God chose to reveal himself through that vehicle to Muhammad, the founder of the faith. Arabia would become the center of the Islamic world, and the source of renewal and inspiration for the faithful believers throughout an emerging Islamic empire.

Arabia Before the Prophet

Arabia before the birth of Muhammad had been a culturally isolated and economically underdeveloped region. The Arabian peninsula is one-third the size of the continental United States. Most of the land is arid and desert; rainfall is scarce, vegetation scant, and very little of the land is suitable for agriculture. In the north of the region, several Arabic kingdoms were able to establish contacts with the Byzantine and the Persian Sassanian empires as early as the fifth century A.D. To the south, small Arabic kingdoms, including Saba (Sheba), were ancient centers of Arabic civilization. But in the interior, dotted only with occasional oases, the nomadic life was the only successful existence (see map, p. 151).

The Bedouins

The nomads, or Bedouins, lived according to ancient tribal patterns; at the head of the tribe was the elder, or sheik, elected and advised by the heads of the related families comprising the tribe. Driven from place to place in their search for pastures to sustain their flocks, the Bedouins

led a precarious existence. Aside from maintaining their herds, some relied on plunder from raids on settlements, on passing caravans, and on one another. The Bedouins enjoyed a degree of personal freedom unknown in more agrarian and settled societies. Sheiks could not always limit the freedoms of their tribesmen, who often rode off and hired themselves out as herdsmen or warriors if the authority of the tribe became too restrictive. The Bedouins developed a code of ethics represented in the word *muru'ah* or manly virtue. Far from brutishness and bragging, *muru'ah* was proven through grace and restraint, loyalty to obligation and duty, a devotion to do that which must be done, and a respect for women. Bedouin women also enjoyed a great degree of independence. They were allowed to engage in business and commerce; they could choose their own lovers, and conduct their lives without great restriction by the control of their husbands. The freedom and independence of Bedouins sprang from the realities of life in the desert, as did the values and ethics of the Arabs. One rule of conduct was unqualified hospitality to strangers. A nomad never knew when the care of a stranger might be necessary to provide the necessary water and shade to save his or her own life.

The Bedouins of the seventh century lacked a unifying religious system. Most looked at life as a brief time within which to take full advantage of daily pleasure. Ideas of an afterlife were not well defined or described. The Bedouins worshiped a large number of gods and spirits, many of whom were believed to inhabit trees, wells, and stones. Each tribe had its own gods, generally symbolized by sacred stones, which served as altars where communal sacrifices were offered.

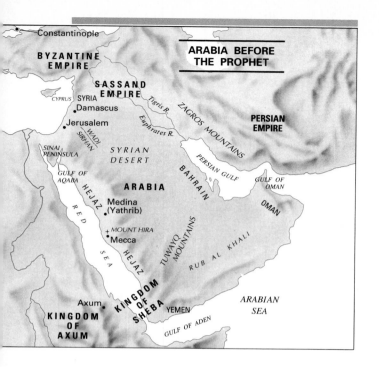

ARABIA BEFORE THE PROPHET

as a religious sanctuary. An ancient temple, an almost square structure built of granite blocks, stood near the well of Mecca. Known as the *Kaaba* (cube), this square temple contained the sacred Black Stone, which was said to have been brought to Abraham and his son Ishmael by the Angel Gabriel. According to tradition, the stone, probably a meteorite, was originally white but had become blackened by the sins of those touching it.

For centuries the *Kaaba* had been a holy place of annual pilgrimage for the Arabic tribes and a focal point of Arabic cultural and linguistic unity. The *Kaaba* itself was draped with the pelts of sarificial animals, and supposedly held the images and shrines of 360 gods and goddesses.

This miniature of the seventh heaven depicts the Bedouin conception of paradise as a lush garden of sensual delights.

Although the Bedouins of the interior led a primitive and largely isolated existence, some parts of Arabia were highly influenced by the neighboring and more highly sophisticated cultures of Byzantium, Persia, and Ethiopia. By the later half of the sixth century Christian and Jewish residents were found throughout the Arabian peninsula; their religious systems and philosophical positions probably had an influence on the Bedouin population.

Early Mecca

On the western side of the Arabian peninsula is a region known as the Hejaz, or "barrier." The Hejaz rises from the western coastal plain from Yemen in the south to the Sinai peninsula in the north. One of the oases in the Hejaz is Mecca, set among the barren hills fifty miles inland from the sea. This site had several advantages: Mecca possessed a well (the Zemzem) of great depth, and two ancient caravan routes met there. An east-to-west route ran from Africa through the peninsula to Iran and Central Asia, and a northwest-southeast route brought the spices of India to the Mediterranean world. Another significant advantage of Mecca was its importance

By the sixth century, Mecca was controlled by the Koraysh tribe, whose rulers organized themselves into syndicates of merchants and wealthy businessmen. The Koraysh held lucrative trading agreements with Byzantine and Persian contacts, as well as with the southern Arabian tribes and the Abyssinians (Ethiopians) across the Red Sea. In addition, a number of neighboring merchant fairs, such as one usually held at Ukaz, were taken over by the Koraysh to extend the economic influence of Mecca. The Koraysh were also concerned with protecting the religious shrine of the *Kaaba*, in addition to ensuring that the annual pilgrimage of tribes to the holy place would continue as a source of revenue for the merchants of the city.

Muhammad, Prophet of Islam

Into this environment at Mecca was born a man who would change completely the religious, political, and social organization of his people. Muhammad (c. 570–632) came from a family belonging to the Koraysh. His early years were difficult because of the deaths of both his parents and his grandfather who cared for him after his parents' loss. He was raised by his uncle, Abu Talib, a prominent merchant of Mecca. His early years were spent helping his uncle in the caravan trade. Even as a young man, Muhammad came to be admired by his fellow Meccans as a

sincere and honest person, and earned the nickname al-Amin, "the trustworthy." When he was about twenty years old, he accepted employment by a wealthy widow, Khadija, whose caravans traded with Syria. He later married Khadija and took his place as a leading influential citizen of the city. Muhammad's marriage to Khadija was a long and happy one, and produced two sons, who both died as infants, and two daughters, of whom the younger, Fatima, is best known.

A description of Muhammad, and probably a very accurate one, has been preserved in the *Sira*, the traditional biography of the Prophet. He is described as a handsome, large man with broad shoulders, black, shining eyes flecked with brown, and a fair complexion. His personality was reserved and gentle, but he was a man of impressive energy. He walked quickly, and always seemed to make it difficult for his friends to keep up with him. Although he was a popular companion, an energetic businessman, and a responsible husband and father, Muhammad was a very introspective man. Often he would escape from the society, which he considered too materialistic and irreligious, and spend long hours alone in a cave on nearby Mount Hira. In these hours of meditation Muhammad searched for answers to the metaphysical questions that many thoughtful Arabs were beginning to explore. Muhammad's meditations many times produced nearly total mental and physical exhaustion. During one such solitary meditation, Muhammad heard a call that was to alter the history of the world.

This Koran leaf from the eighth or ninth century illustrates the austere formality and elegance of the Kufic form of Arabic calligraphy. Vowel marks appear as dots of various colors, while the tenth verse marker (in the third line of this page) is a triangle of six dots. It is not unusual for as few as three lines of calligraphy to appear on a single page.

Muhammad's first communication from heaven came in the form of a command:

> Recite! In the name of your Lord, who created all things, who created man from a clot (of blood).
> Recite! And your Lord is Most Bounteous Who teaches by the Pen, teaches man that which he would not have otherwise known (Koran 96: 1–5)

The Arabic word for "recitation" or "reading" is *qur'an*, and the collected revelations given to Muhammad are known to us as the *Koran*. The revelations that continued to come over the next twenty years were sometimes terse and short, at other times elaborate and poetic. The early revelations did not immediately convince Muhammad that he was a messenger of God. In fact, his first reaction was fear and self-doubt. During his depressions brought on by fears over the source and nature of his revelations, he sought the comfort and advice of Khadija. As the revelations continued, Muhammad finally became convinced that the message he was receiving was the truth, and that he had been called to be a messenger of divine revelation. He came to think of himself and his mission as one similar to prophets and messengers who had preceded him in announcing the existence of the one God, Allah. Allah, "*the* God," was the same God worshiped by the Christians and Jews, but Allah had now chosen Muhammad to be his last and greatest prophet to perfect the religion revealed earlier to Abraham, Moses, the Hebrew prophets, and Jesus. The religion Muhammad preached is called *Islam*, which means surrender or submission to the will of God. The followers of Islam are called Muslims. The term *Muslim* refers to one who submits to God's law.

Muhammad's Message and Early Followers

At first Muhammad had little success in attracting followers in Mecca. The early message Muhammad brought to the Arabs was one of sternness and strength: that Allah was one and majestic, all-powerful and demanding of the faith of his followers. Furthermore, Allah demanded that his followers be compassionate, ethical, and just in all their dealings:

This manuscript illustration portrays a party of Muslim pilgrims making their way toward the holy city of Mecca. A pilgrimage to Mecca was one of the prerequisites for entering paradise.

> In the name of Allah, the most Beneficent, the Most Merciful
> by the night as it enshrouds
> by the day as it illuminates
> by Him Who created the male and female indeed your affairs lead to various ends.
> For who gives (of himself) and acts righteously, and conforms to goodness,
> We will give him ease.
> But as for him who is niggardly cleaning himself, self-sufficient and rejects goodness,
> We will indeed ease his path to adversity.
> Nor shall his wealth save him as he perishes for Guidance is from Us
> and to Us belongs the Last and First (92: 1–14)

Muhammad was able to win the early support of some of his relatives and close friends. His first converts were his wife, his cousin Ali, and Abu Bakr, a leading merchant of the Koraysh tribe who was highly respected for his integrity. Abu Bakr remained the constant companion of the Prophet during his persecution and exile and later became the first caliph (leader) of Islam. But opposition to Muhammad's message was very strong, especially from Mecca's leading citizens. Many thought Muhammad was a poor poet attempting to pass on his own literary creations as the word of God. Others believed him to be possessed by demons. Muhammad's strong monotheism worried those residents of Mecca who obtained their income from the pilgrims to the *Kaaba*. Most of Muhammad's early converts were among the poorest of the city's residents, and Mecca's leading citizens feared social revolution.

Since Muhammad was himself a member of the Koraysh tribe, its leaders first tried to convince Abu Talib to persuade his nephew to stop preaching. Next they tried to bribe Muhammad himself with the promise of a lucrative position in tribal affairs. When such offers were rejected, actual persecution of Muhammad's converts began, and a commercial and social boycott of the Prophet's family was attempted. During this time Abu Talib and Khadija both died, and Muhammad's faith and resolution was greatly tested. But inspired by the spirit and example of earlier prophets such as Abraham and Moses, who were also tested and persecuted, Muhammad persevered in his faith and continued his preaching.

The Hijrah

To the north of Mecca is the city of Medina, which was then called Yathrib. The residents of Medina were more familiar with monotheistic beliefs, perhaps because of the Jewish community in residence there. They also had no dependence on the revenues from a pagan site of pilgrimage, as the Meccans had. Some pilgrims from Medina saw in Muhammad a powerful and influential leader and invited him to come to Medina to settle differences among rival factions. Muhammad sent some of his followers from Mecca to take up residence in Medina in order to escape persecution. Muhammad and Abu Bakr were the last to leave when it became known that the Koraysh intended to kill the Prophet. They were followed, but escaped, the story goes, by hiding in a narrow cave whose entrance was quickly covered by a spider's web. The web convinced Koraysh that the cave had been abandoned for a long while.

The *Hijrah*, or "migration" from Mecca to Medina (often transliterated as *Hegira)*, took place in September 622. The event was such a turning point in the history of Islam that the year is counted as Year One of the Islamic calendar. In Medina, the Prophet met with entirely different circumstance than in his birthplace. His leadership turned Medina (*Madinat al Nali*, or the City of the Prophet) into the leading center of power in the Arabian peninsula.

The Community at Medina

Muhammad was received in Medina as a leader and a spiritual visionary. He and his followers set about the establishment of a genuine community, or *Ummah*, free of pressure and persecution. The community at Medina included a number of Jewish and Christian families, whom Muhammad tried to convert. His efforts were successful with some Jewish residents, but the Jews who did not choose to accept Muhammad's faith were allowed to continue their way of life, since they were also held to be "people of the Book" to whom Allah had made himself known through earlier prophets.

The care of the community at Medina was of grave concern to Muhammad. Many of those who followed the prophet to Medina were without work, and necessary food was sometimes obtained by plundering the caravans passing Medina on the way to Mecca. Also, Muhammad and his followers became steadily more agressive in their attempts to win converts to Islam. The word *jihad*, meaning struggle, was applied to the early efforts of the *Ummah* to win converts and strengthen its own recruiting. Military encounters with the pagan opponents of Islam began in 624, with the battle of Bedr. Muhammad defeated the stronger Koraysh army of Mecca, and the victory reinforced the resolve of the new religion's followers. Succeeding battles established the Muslims as the dominant force in Arabia, and finally a truce with Mecca was arranged, under which the Muslims could visit the holy shrines in the city.

Return to Mecca

In 629 Muhammad returned with his followers to take control of the city of Mecca and to cleanse the *Kaaba* of pagan idols. The temple itself, together with the Black Stone, was preserved as the supreme religious center of Islam, the "Mecca" to which all devout Muslims are to attempt to make a pilgrimage during their lifetimes. Muhammad urged his old enemies and unbelievers to accept Islam and become part of the *Ummah*. By 632, almost all of the Arabian peninsula had accepted Islam, and Muhammad had even sent ambassadors to the neighboring Byzantine and Persian empires to announce the new religion and encourage converts. Clearly Muhammad did not look upon Islam as only a religion of the Arabs, and certainly sought converts other than the residents of the Arabian peninsula.

The Death of Muhammad

Muhammad died on June 8, 632 in Medina. He succumbed to a fever, probably induced by the great strains brought on by constant campaigns for new converts and the unrelenting demands for his attention. Muslims at first refused to accept his death, but were reassured by Abu Bakr, who recited this verse from the *Koran:*

> *Muhammad is only a messenger: many are the messengers who have died before him; if he dies, or is slain, will you turn back on your heels? (3:144)*

On the day of Muhammad's death, the question of leadership of the faithful was solved by the democratic election of Abu Bakr, who became the Prophet's first successor or caliph (from the Arabic *khalifa*). Abu Bakr was not looked upon as a prophet; Muhammad was seen as the last and the greatest of Allah's messengers. The caliph was regarded as the head of the Islamic *Ummah.*

The significance of Muhammad to the birth and growth of Islam is impossible to overestimate. The Prophet and his message inspired his followers to create and work for the betterment of a society united by the Islamic faith. Tribal loyalties were replaced by faith in the One God, who chose to speak to his people in their own language through a messenger who was also one of their own.

Soon after Muhammad's death, his followers and companions, many of whom were scholars and teachers, began to collect and codify his teachings and actions. The result of their efforts was the *hadith,* or reports of the activities and sayings of Muhammad. The *hadith* has become an important source of values and ethical paths of behavior for the Islamic world. The *Sunnah,* the custom or practice of the Prophet, is grounded in the *hadith* and serves as a pattern for a model way of life to be imitated by the faithful. Sunni Islam is thus based on imitation of the Prophet's behavior as a proper goal for a meaningful life; 85 percent of the modern world's Muslims are Sunni.

The Islamic Faith and Law

Islam places great emphasis on the necessity of obedience to God's law in addition to faith. The *Koran* is the fundamental and ultimate source of knowledge about Allah and the proper actions of his followers. This holy book contains the theology of Islam, in addition to the patterns of ethical and proper conduct to which a Muslim must subscribe. Among the beliefs outlined in the *Koran,* there are some basic concepts which are held in common by the Islamic community as fundamental to the faith.

The Koran

Muslims believe that the *Koran* contains the actual word of God as it was revealed to Muhammad through divine inspiration. The revelations to the Prophet took place over a period of more than twenty years. Before Muhammad's death, many of these messages had been written down in order to be preserved. Muhammad himself began the work of preservation, and Abu Bakr, the first caliph, continued the process by compiling revelations which up to that time had been memorized by the followers and passed on by word of mouth. A complete written text of the *Koran* was produced shortly after Muhammad's death, with particular care taken to eliminate discrepancies and record only one standard version. This version was then transmitted to various parts of the new Islamic empire and used to assist in the conversion of unbelievers. The text of the *Koran* has existed virtually unchanged for fourteen centuries.

The *Koran* was intended to be recited aloud; much of the power of the *Koran* comes from the experience of reciting, listening, and feeling the

The Koran

The *Koran,* dictated to Muhammad by Allah, is one of the most significant of all religious works. It is also one of the world's most beautiful works of literature. The following is a selection from Surah XXIII, entitled "The Believers."

In the name of Allah, the Beneficent, the Merciful.
Successful indeed are the believers
Who are humble in their prayers,
And who shun vain conversation,
And who are payers of the poor-due;
And who guard their modesty—
Save from their wives or the (slaves) that their right hands possess, for then they are not blameworthy,
But whoso craveth beyond that, such are transgressors—
And who are shepherds of their pledge and their covenant,
And who pay heed to their prayers.
These are the heirs
Who will inherit Paradise. There they will abide.
Verily We created man from a product of wet earth;
Then placed him as a drop (of seed) in a safe lodging;
Then fashioned We the drop a clot, then fashioned We the clot a little lump, then fashioned We the little lump bones, then clothed the bones with flesh, and then produced it as another creation. So blessed be Allah, the Best of Creators!
Then lo! after that ye surely die.
Then lo! on the Day of Resurrection ye are raised (again).
And We have created above you seven paths, and We are never unmindful of creation.
And We send down from the sky water in measure, and We give it lodging in the earth, and lo! We are able to withdraw it.
Then We produce for you therewith gardens of date-palms and grapes, wherein is much fruit for you and whereof ye eat;
And a tree that springeth forth from Mount Sinai that groweth oil and relish for the eaters.
And lo! in the cattle there is verily a lesson for you. We give you to drink of that which is in their bellies, and many uses have ye in them, and of them do ye eat;
And on them and on the ship we are carried.
Then We sent Moses and his brother Aaron with Our tokens and a clear warrant
Unto Pharaoh and his chiefs, but they scorned (them) and they were despotic folk.
And they said: Shall we put faith in two mortals like ourselves, and whose folk are servile unto us?
So they denied them, and became of those who were destroyed.
And We verily gave Moses the Scripture, that haply they might go aright.
And We made the son of Mary and his mother a portent, and We gave them refuge on a height, a place of flocks and water-springs.
O ye messengers! Eat of the good things, and do right. Lo! I am Aware of what ye do.
And lo! this your religion is one religion and I am your Lord, so keep your duty unto Me.
Say: In Whose hand is the dominion over all things and He protecteth, while against Him there is no protection, if ye have knowledge?
They will say: Unto Allah (all that belongeth). Say: How then are ye bewitched?
Nay, but We have brought them the Truth, and lo! they are liars.
Allah hath not chosen any son, nor is there any God along with Him; else would each God have assuredly championed that which he created, and some of them would assuredly have overcome others. Glorified be Allah above all that they allege.
Knower of the invisible and the visible! and exalted be He over all that they ascribe as partners (unto Him)!

From *The Meaning of the Glorious Koran,* Mohammed Marmaduke Pickhall, trans. (New York: New American Library, 1980), pp. 248–252.

message. It was in this manner that Muhammad converted his followers. The *Koran* is never to be translated from the Arabic for worship. Because the followers of Islam had to learn the *Koran* in Arabic, the spread of Islam created a great amount of linguistic unity. Arabic replaced many local languages as the language of daily use, and the great majority of the Muslim world from Morocco to Iraq is still Arabic-speaking. In addition, the *Koran* remains the basic document for the study of Islamic theology, law, social institutions, and ethics. The study of the *Koran* remains at the heart of all Muslim scholarship, from linquistics and grammatical inquiry to scientific and technical investigation.

The Tenets of Islamic Faith

Monotheism is the central principle of Islam. *Tahwid* means the unity or oneness of God; there is no other God but Allah, and this belief is proclaimed five times daily as the believers are called to prayer with these words:

God is most great. I testify that there is no God but Allah. I testify that Muhammad is the

In this illustration from the book of Kalîlah and Dîmnali, a judge metes out punishment to the accused who stand before them.

Messenger of Allah. Come to prayer, come to revelation, God is most great! There is no God but Allah.

Allah is the one and only god, unapproached by other divinities and unlike all others in the strength of his creative power. All life, in fact all creation, is the responsibility of Allah alone. His nature is described in many ways and by many names, one of the most beautiful as "light."

Allah is the light of the heaven and the earth. . . . His light is as a niche wherein is a lamp. The lamp is in a glass. The glass is as it were a shining star. (The lamp is) kindled from a blessed tree, an olive neither of the East or the West, whose oil would almost glow forth (of itself) though no fire touched it. Light upon light, Allah guided unto His light whom He will. And Allah speaketh to mankind in allegories, for Allah is Knower of all things.

(This lamp is found) in houses which Allah hath allowed to be exalted and that His name shall be remembered therein. Therein do offer praise to Him at noon and evening. (24:35)

Islam also recognize the significance and contributions of prophets who preceded Muhammad. From the beginnings of human history, Allah has communicated with his people either by the way of the prophets, or by written scriptures:

Lo! We inspire thee as We inspired Noah and the Prophets after him, as We inspired Abraham and Ishmael and Isaac and Jacob and the tribes, and Jesus and Job and Jonah and Aaron and Solomon and as We imparted unto David the Psalms. (4:164)

Twenty-eight such prophets are mentioned in the *Koran* as the predecessors of Muhammad, who is believed to have been the last and greatest of all of Allah's messengers. Muhammad is given no divine status by Muslims, even though he was the one chosen to proclaim Allah's message of salvation in its perfected form and final revelation; in fact, Muhammad took great care to see that he was not worshiped as a god.

The creation of the universe and all living creatures within it is the work of Allah; harmony and balance in all of creation was ensured by God. In addition to humans and other creatures on the earth, angels exist to protect humans and to pray for forgiveness for the faithful. *Jinn* are spirits who may be good or bad, and forces known as "the unseen" exist on a level unknown to humans.

Men and women are given a special status in the pattern of the universe, since Allah has endowed them with the ability to know and react to him better than any living creatures. They can choose to obey, or to reject Allah's will and deny him. Allah's message includes the belief in a Day of Resurrection when people will be held responsible for their actions and rewarded or punished accordingly for eternity.

Geographic imagery played an important role in the Prophet's description of heaven and hell: both are depicted in a manner that calls forth an immediate reaction from people living in the desert. Those who have submitted to Allah's law—the charitable, humble, and forgiving—and those who have preserved his faith, shall dwell in a Garden of Paradise, resting in cool shades, eating delectable foods, attended by "fair ones with wide, lovely eyes like unto hidden pearls," and hearing no vain speech or recrimination but only "Peace! Peace!" This veritable oasis is far different from the agonies of the desert hell that awaits the unbelievers, the covetous, and the erring. Cast into a pit with its "scorching wind and shadow of black smoke," they will drink boiling water and suffer forever.

The Five Pillars

Islam is united in the observance of the Five Pillars, or five essential duties which all Muslims are required to perform as they are able. These obligations are accepted by Muslims everywhere and thus serve to further unite the Islamic world. The first obligation is a simple *profession of faith*, by which a believer becomes a Muslim. The simple proclamation *(shahada)* is repeated in daily prayers. Belief in the one God and emulation of the exemplary life led by his Prophet are combined in the profession of faith.

Prayer (salat) is said five times a day, when Muslims are called to worship by the *muezzin* (caller to prayer) who leads the recitation of the faithful from atop the minaret of the mosque *(masjid,* or place of prostration). During prayer, Muslims face Mecca, and in so doing give recognition to the birthplace of Islam and the unity

This illustration from a fourteenth-century manuscript depicts a congregation of Spanish Jews at worship in their synagogue.

of the Islamic community. Prayer can be given alone, at work, at home, or in the mosque.

A Muslim is required to give *alms (zakat)* to the poor, orphans, and widows, and to assist the spread of Islam. The payment of alms is not considered to be a charitable activity, but rather a social and religious obligation to provide for the welfare of the *Ummah.* Muslims are generally expected to contribute a percentage (usually 2.5 percent) of their total wealth and assets annually in alms.

Muslims are requested to *fast (siyam)* during the holy month of Ramadan, the ninth month of the Islamic calendar. From sunrise to sunset, adult Muslims in good health are to avoid food, drink, and sexual activity. Finally Muslims are called to make a *pilgrimage (hajj)* to Mecca at least once in his or her lifetime, in the twelfth month of the Islamic lunar calendar. The focus of the pilgrimage is the *Kaaba* in the Grand Mosque of Mecca. The *hajj* once again emphasizes the unity of the Islamic world community and the adherence to Islamic law no matter where a Muslim may reside.

Islamic Law

It is not possible to separate Islam from its law, because law in the Muslim community is religious by its nature. Islam is a way of life as well as a religion, and at its heart is the *Sharia*, or path, the law provided by Allah as a guide for a proper life. The *Sharia* gives the believers a perfect pattern of human conduct and regulates every aspect of a person's activities. Islamic law is considered to be established by God, and therefore unquestionably correct; God's decrees must be obeyed even if humans are incapable of understanding, since the *Sharia* is greater than human reason.

Islamic law, then, permeates all aspects of human conduct and all levels of activity—from private and personal concerns to those involving the welfare of the whole state. Family law is set forth in the *Koran* and is based on much earlier Arabic tribal patterns of development. Islamic law emphasizes the patriarchal nature of the family and society. Marriage is expected of every Muslim man and woman unless physical infirmity or financial inability prohibits it. Muslim men can marry non-Muslim women, preferably Christians or Jews, since they too are "People of the Book," but Muslim women are forbidden to marry non-Muslim men. The *Koran* had the effect of improving the status and opportunities of women in Islam, as opposed to the older and traditional Arabic patterns of conduct. Women can contract their own marriages, keep and maintain their own dowries, and manage and inherit property.

The *Koran* allows Muslim men to marry up to four wives, but polygamy is not required. Co-wives must be treated with equal support and affection. Many modern-day Muslims interpret the *Koran* as encouraging monogamy; the practice of polygamy may have arisen in order to provide protection and security in early Islamic society, when women outnumbered men because of the toll of constant warfare.

For Islamic society as a whole, the law is considered to be universal and equally applied. Islamic law is considered to be God's law for all humankind, not only for the followers of Islam. In addition to its theology, Islam offers to its believers a system of government, a legal foundation, and a pattern of social organization. The Islamic *Ummah* was and is an excellent example of a theocratic state, one in which all power resides in God, in whose behalf political, religious, and other forms of authority are exercised. In fact, there is not even the combination of church and state in Islam, because there is no "church" or religious organization. The role of the state is to serve as the guardian of religious law. Also a characteristic of Islam is the principle of religious equality. There is no priesthood—no intermediaries between people and God. There are leaders of worship in the mosques as well as the *ulema*, a class of learned experts in the interpretation of the *Koran*, but they are all members of the secular community.

The Spread of Islam

The Islamic state expanded very rapidly after the death of Muhammad through remarkable successes both at converting unbelievers to Islam and by military conquests of the Islamic community's opponents. Expansion of the Islamic state was an understandable development, since Muhammad himself had successfully established the new faith through conversion and conquest of those who stood against him. Immediately after the Prophet's death in 632, Abu Bakr, as the first Caliph, continued the effort to abolish paganism among the Arab tribes, and also to incorporate Arabia into a region controlled by the political power of Medina. United by their faith in God and a commitment to political consolidation, the merchant elite of Arabia succeeded in consolidating their power throughout the Arabian peninsula and began to launch some exploratory offensives north toward Syria.

Expansion Under the First Four Caliphs

During the reigns of the first four caliphs (632–661), Islam spread rapidly. The wars of expansion were also advanced by the devotion of the faithful to the concept of *jihad*. Muslims are obliged to extend the faith to unbelievers and to defend Islam from attack. The original concept of *jihad* did not include agressive warfare against non-Muslims, but "holy war" was sometimes waged by Muslims whose interpretation of the *Koran* allowed them such latitude. *Jihad* was directly responsible for some of the early conquests of Islam outside of the Arabian peninsula.

The Islamic cause was also aided by political upheavals occurring outside of Arabia. The Muslim triumphs in the Near East can be partly accounted for by the long series of wars between the Byzantine and Persian empires. Earlier Byzantine victories had left both sides exhausted and open to conquest. Moreover, the inhabitants of Syria and Egypt, alienated by religious dissent and resenting the attempts of the Byzantine Empire to impose Christianity on the population, were eager to be free of Byzantine rule. In 636, Arab armies conquered Syria. The Muslims then won Iraq from the Persians and, within ten years after Muhammad's death, subdued Persia itself. The greater part of Egypt fell with little resistance in 640 and the rest shortly afterward. By the end of the reigns of the first four caliphs, Islam had vastly increased its territory in the Near East and Africa.

The new conquests of Islam were governed with remarkable efficiency and flexibility. The centralization of authority typical of military organization aided in the incorporation of new peoples. Unbelievers in the conquered territories became increasingly interested in the new religion and accepted Islam in great numbers. In addition to the obvious power of the religious message of Islam, the imposition of a personal tax on all non-Muslims encouraged many to become converts. Contrary to exaggerated accounts in western Europe of the forceful imposition of Islam upon conquered peoples, Jews and Christians outside of Arabia enjoyed toleration because they worshiped the same God as the Muslims; many non-Muslims participated in the Islamic state and prospered financially and socially.

Islam was and remains one the most effective religions in removing barriers of race and nationality. Apart from a certain privileged position allowed Arabs, distinctions were mostly those of economic rank in the early days of conquest. The new religion converted and embraced peoples of many colors and cultures. This egalitarian feature of Islam undoubtedly aided its expansion.

Arab Domination Under the Umayyads

The first three caliphs of Islam were chosen in consultation with the elders and leaders of the Islamic community, and a pattern was established for selecting the caliph from the Karaysh tribe of Mecca. The fourth caliph, Ali, who was the son-in-law of Muhammad, was devoted to Islam and convinced that leadership of the Islamic community should remain in the family of the Prophet. The followers of Ali were later called Shii or Shi'ites (after *Shiat-u-Ali,* or "party of Ali"), and believed that the first three caliphs had been usurpers to legitimate power. Ali and his followers were opposed first by Muslims under the leadership of Muhammad's widow Aisha, daughter of Abu Bakr, and later by the forces of Muawiyah, the governor of Syria and a relative of the third caliph. In 661 Muawiyah proclaimed himself caliph, made Damascus his capital, and founded the Umayyad Dynasty, which lasted until 750. Thus the caliphate became in fact, although never in law, a hereditary office, not, as previously, a position filled by election.

Umayyad military campaigns of conquest for the most part were highly successful. The Umayyad navy held Cyprus, Rhodes, and number of Aegean islands, which served as bases for annual seaborne attacks on Constantinople from 674 to 678. With the aid of Greek fire (see p. 174) Constantinople was successfully defended, and the Arab advance was checked for the first time. Westward across North Africa, however, the Umayyad armies had much greater success. The Berbers, a warlike nomadic people inhabiting the land between the Mediterranean and the Sahara, resisted stubbornly but eventually converted to Islam. The next logical expansion for Islam was across the Strait of Gibraltar into the weak kingdom of the Visigoths in Spain. The governor of Muslim North Africa sent his general, Tarik, and an army across the Strait into Spain in 711. Seven years later the kingdom of the Visigoths completely crumbled. The Muslims advanced across the Pyrenees and gained a strong foothold in southwest France, where they carried out a major raid to explore the possibility of a further northward advance. However, they were defeated by Charles Martel near Tours in 732 (see p. 225), in a battle which, together with their defeat by the Byzantine emperor Leo III in 718, proved decisive in halting their northward expansion into Europe. Meanwhile the Muslims had been expanding eastward into Central Asia, and by the eighth

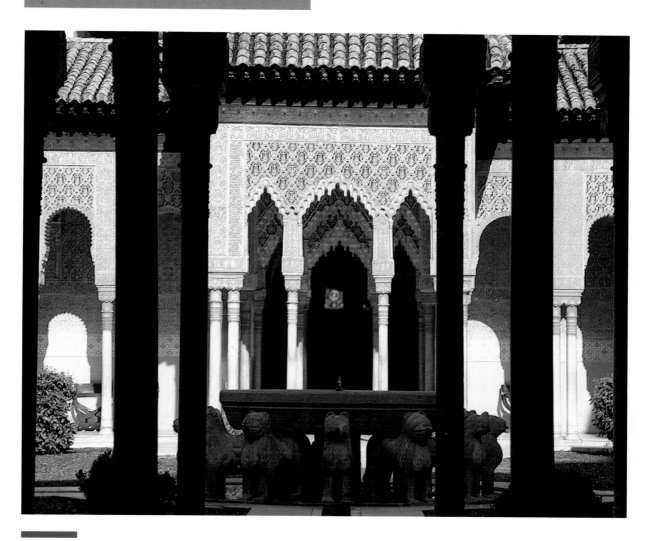

The ultimate stage of refinement of Moorish architecture, which combines Spanish and Islamic elements, is the Alhambra in Granada, the last Islamic stronghold in Spain during the late Middle Ages. Slender, rhythmically spaced columns and arches covered with an intricate design of molded stucco frame the Court of the Lions, the richest portion of the palace. Twelve carved beasts spurting water from their mouths form the Lion Fountain in the center of the Court.

The best and most typical examples of Gupta painting are the cave paintings at Ajanta, site of a Buddhist monastic community in the Deccan. The elegant and graceful figures, the rich costume, and the architectural detail all reflect the luxurious and aristocratic culture of Gupta India (A.D. 320–600). The painting here is of a court scene.

Combining the practical and the esthetic, the gilded bronze figure (right) is a functional oil lamp from the Han Dynasty of China (second century B.C.). The functional purpose of the figure in no way detracts from its artistic beauty. The small fan painting *Bare Willows and Distant Mountains* (below) by Ma Yüan eloquently expresses the Sung artist's mastery of landscape painting. The delicate tranquillity of the composition is upset only by the seals at right placed there by a Ming collector.

Portfolio Two

The artistic style of the Kamakura period in Japan emphasized strength and realism, as is evident in this battle scene. The scroll is from a series illustrating the Heiji Monogatari, an epic narrative describing the rise and fall of the Taira clan, rivals of the Minamoto, the eventual victors and founders of the Kamakura shogunate. The Heiji Monogatari chronicles the events of the winter of 1159—60 during which the Taira temporarily defeated the Minamoto.

century they could claim lands as far as Turkestan and the Indus valley (see map below).

The mainstay of Umayyad dynastic power was the ruling class consisting of an Arab military aristocracy, who formed a privileged class greatly outnumbered by non-Arabic converts to Islam—Egyptians, Syrians, Persians, Berbers, and others. Many of these converted peoples possessed cultures much more advanced than that of the Arabs, and the economic and cultural life of the Arab empire came to be controlled by these non-Arab Muslims *(mawali)*. Because they were not Arab by birth, they were treated as second-class citizens. High government positions were closed to them. They paid higher taxes than Arabs, and as soldiers they received less pay and loot than the Arabs. Resentment grew among the non-Arabic Muslims who objected to their lesser status as a violation of the Islamic laws of equality. Eventually the resentment of the *mawali* helped bring about the downfall of the Umayyads.

Shia Movement Against the Ruling Group

This resentment also found expression in the religious sphere, where large numbers of non-Arabic Muslims joined the sect known as the Shia, which had been forced from power on the accession of the Umayyads. The Shia continued to regard Ali and his descendants as the rightful rulers of the Islamic community, and believed that in every age a messiah-like leader would appear and that he must be obeyed. The Shia also

THE EXPANSION OF ISLAM TO 750 A.D.

Under Muhammad 622-632

Under The First Four Caliphs 632-661

Under the Umayyad Caliphs 661-750

0 200 400 600

rejected the Sunna, the body of later tradition concerning Muhammad that was not contained in the *Koran;* they insisted on the *Koran* as the sole and unquestioned authority on the life and teachings of the Prophet. Though originally an Arab party, the Shia in time became a general Islamic movement that stood in opposition to the ruling Arabic dynasty. The Shia evolved into one of the two major groups in Islam. The majority, called Sunni because they were the "orthodox" perpetrators of Muhammad's Sunna, or tradition, upheld the principle that the caliph owed his position to the consent of the Islamic community. The numerical superiority of the Sunni Muslims has continued to this day.

The Abbasids, Zenith of Islamic Civilization

In 750 the Umayyad Dynasty was removed from power by rebels, and a new dynasty, the Abbasid, ruled most of the Muslim world from 750 to 1258. The city of Baghdad was built in 762 as the capital of the new caliph, Abu-al-Abbas, a descendant of the Prophet's uncle. The Abbasids owed their initial success to the discontent of the non-Arabic Muslims, who were the primary leaders in the towns and in the Shia.

The fall of the Umayyad Dynasty marked the end of Arab domination within Islam; the Abbasid caliph made great effort to establish equalitarian treatment of all Muslims. The Arab aristocracy had led the forces of conquest during the great period of Islamic expansion, but with the advent of more stable political conditions, the important status previously held only by the Arab soldier was given to non-Arab administrators, merchants, and scholars. The traditional Arabic patterns of nomadism and warfare gave way before economic prosperity, the growth of town life, and the rise of a merchant class. Caliph Abu-al-Abbas forecast that Baghdad would become the "most flourishing city in the world"; and indeed it rivaled Constantinople for that honor, situated as it was on the trade routes linking West and East. Furthermore, Abbasid

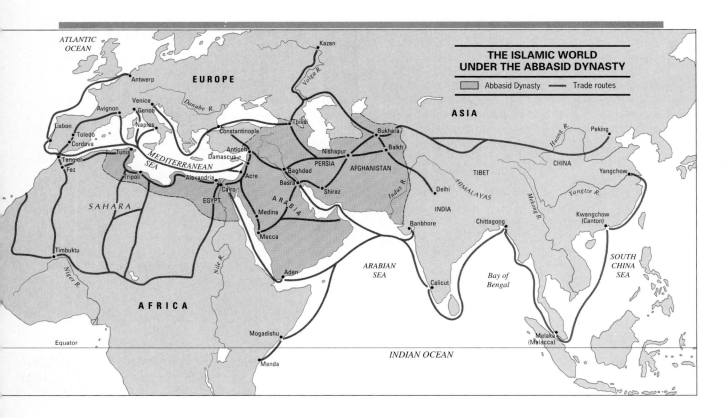

patronage of scholarship and the arts produced a rich and complex culture far surpassing that then existing in western Europe.

The location of a new capital at Baghdad shifted Islam's center of gravity to the province of Iraq, whose soil, watered by the Tigris and Euphrates, had nurtured the earliest human civilization. Here the Abbasid caliphs set themselves up as potentates in the traditional style of the ancient East (more particularly of Persia) so that they were surrounded by a lavish court that contrasted sharply with the simplicity of the lifestyle of the Prophet.

The Abbasid Dynasty marked the high point of Islamic power and civilization. The empire ruled by these caliphs was greater in size than the domain of the Roman Caesars; it was the product of an expansion during which the Muslims assimilated peoples, customs, cultures, and inventions on an unprecedented scale (see map, p. 162). This Islamic state, in fact, drew from the resources of the entire known world.

Trade, Industry, and Agriculture

From the eighth to the twelfth century the Muslim world enjoyed enormous prosperity. In close contact with three continents, the Muslims could shuttle goods back and forth from China to western Europe and from Russia to central Africa. The absence of tariff barriers within the empire and the tolerance of the caliphs, who allowed non-Muslim merchants and craftsmen to reside in their territories and carry on commerce with their home countries, further facilitated trade. The presence of such important urban centers as Baghdad, Cairo and Cordova stimulated trade and industry throughout the Muslim world.

The cosmopolitan nature of Baghdad was evident in its bazaars, which contained goods from all over the known world. There were spices, minerals, and dyes from India; gems and fabrics from Central Asia; honey and wax from Scandinavia and Russia; and ivory and gold dust from Africa. One bazaar in the city specialized in goods from China, including silks, musk, and porcelain. In the slave markets Muslim traders bought and sold Scandinavians, Mongolians from Central Asia, and Africans. Joint-stock companies flourished along with branch banking organizations,

and checks (an Arabic word) drawn on one bank could be cashed elsewhere in the empire.

Muslim textile industries turned out excellent cottons (muslins) and silks. The steel of Damascus and Toledo, the leather of Cordova, and the glass of Syria became internationally famous. Notable also was the art of papermaking, learned from the Chinese. Under the Abbasids, vast irrigation projects in Iraq increased cultivable land, which yielded large crops of fruits and grains. Wheat came from the Nile valley, cotton from North Africa, olives and wine from Spain, wool from eastern Asia Minor, and horses from Persia.

The Spectacular Reign of Harun al-Rashid

Just as the Abbasid Caliphate was the most impressive Islamic dynasty, so the rule of Harun al-Rashid (786–809) was the most spectacular of the Abbasid reigns. A contemporary of Charlemagne, who had revived the idea of a Roman Empire in the West (see ch. 9) there can be no doubt that Harun was the more powerful of the two and ruler of the more highly advanced culture. The two monarchs were on friendly terms, based on self-interest. Charlemagne wanted to exert pressure on the Byzantine emperor to recognize his new imperial title. Harun, on the other hand, saw Charlemagne as an ally against the Umayyad rulers of Spain, who had broken away from Abbasid domination. The two emperors exchanged embassies and presents. The Muslim sent the Christian rich fabrics, aromatics, and even an elephant named Abu-Lababah, meaning "the father of intelligence." An intricate water clock from Baghdad seems to have been looked upon as a miracle in the West.

Relations between the Abbasid caliphate and the Byzantine Empire were never very cordial, and conflicts often broke out along the constantly shifting border that separated Christian and Muslim territories. Harun al-Rashid once replied to a communique from the Byzantine emperor in the following terms:

In the name of God, the Merciful, the Compassionate. From Harun, Commander of the Faithful, to Nicephorus, the dog of the Greeks, I have read your letter, you son of a she-infidel, and you shall see the answer before you hear it.

Whereupon the irate caliph sent forth expeditions to ravage Asia Minor.

In the days of Harun al-Rashid, Baghdad's wealth and splendor equaled that of Constantinople, and its chief glory was the royal palace. With its annexes for eunuchs, officials, and a harem, the caliph's residence occupied a third of Baghdad. The caliph's audience chamber was the setting for an elaborate ceremonial, which imitated that of the Byzantines and Persians.

Disintegration of the Abbasid Empire

In some ways, the opulent reign of Harun al-Rashid marked the highpoint of Abbasid achievement. In others it exhibited the warning signs of weakness. Despite the unprecedented prosperity of the far-flung Abbasid Empire, the political unity of Islam began to crumble soon after the accession of the Abbasid caliphs. The first sign of political disintegration appeared in 756 when a member of the deposed Umayyad family founded his own dynasty at Cordova in Spain; in 929 his decendant assumed the title of caliph. Also in the tenth century the Fatimids—Shi'ites who claimed descent from Muhammad's daughter Fatima who had married Ali, the fourth caliph—proclaimed themselves the true caliphs of all Islam. From their capital at Cairo, which they founded, their rule eventually extended from Morocco to northern Mesopotamia.

Meanwhile, in the latter part of the tenth century Turkish nomads, called Seljuks, had migrated from Central Asia into the Abbasid lands, where they accepted Islam. After annexing most of Persia, the Seljuks gained control of Baghdad in 1055 and subjugated Iraq. Subsequently they conquered Syria and Palestine at the expense of the Fatimids and proceeded to annex most of Asia Minor from the Byzantines. It was the Seljuks' advance that prompted the First Crusade in 1095. The Seljuks permitted the Abbasids to retain nominal rule, but a new and powerful enemy now appeared and overran Abbasid lands.

Early in the thirteenth century Genghis Khan succeeded in uniting the nomads of Mongolia, and conquering much of China and Russia; he and his successors moved on to eastern and central Asia (see ch. 8) and swept into Persia and Iraq. In 1258 a grandson of Genghis Khan captured Baghdad and had the caliph put in a sack and trampled to death. Not only did the Abbasid Dynasty come to an end, but so did most of the vast irrigation system that had supported the land since the beginning of civilization; Iraq was not to recover until modern times. The dynasty established by the Mongols survived for only a short time, and the Mongol ruling class was eventually absorbed into the native populations of Persia and Iraq.

Muslim Egypt was saved from the Mongol advance by the Mamluks ("the owned ones"), captured Turkish slaves trained to become Muslims and soldiers. Serving as a elite guard for their Fatimid masters, the Mamluks rebelled, seized power in Egypt, and eventually took over Palestine and Syria, ejecting the last of the crusaders in 1291. Ultimately they fell before the onslaught of another Turkish force, the Ottomans, in 1517.

The Ottoman Turks

Having settled in northwestern Asia Minor in the thirteenth century as vassals of the Seljuks, the Ottoman Turks had organized their own aggressive state by the end of that century. The name Ottoman is derived from Osman I (d. 1324), founding chieftan of the dynasty, who organized Muslim volunteer fighters against the Byzantines on the western borders. These fighters committed themselves to *ghaza*, or Islamic holy war, in order to eliminate the unbelievers surrounding the Turkish homeland. The Ottomans pitted their considerable strength against the crumbling power of the Byzantines, pressed on into southeastern Europe, and finally captured Constantinople in 1453. Driving as far as Vienna, they were turned back with tremendous difficulty in 1529 and again in 1683. Meanwhile, in 1517, the Ottomans had conquered the Mamluk territories, and within a few years they added Iraq, much of Arabia, and all of the North African coastal belt to the borders of Morocco.

Islamic Culture

The attainments of the Muslims in the intellectual and artistic fields can be attributed not only to the genius of Arabs, but also to those peoples who embraced the Islamic faith in Persia, Mesopotamia, Turkey, Syria, Egypt, North Africa, and Spain. Muslim learning benefitted both from Islam's ability to absorb other cultures and from the native talents of the Islamic peoples. The cosmopolitan spirit permeating the Abbasid Dynasty supplied the tolerance necessary for a diversity of ideas, so that the science and philosophy of ancient Greece and India alike received a cordial reception in Baghdad. Under Harun al-Rashid and his successors, the writings of Aristotle, Euclid, Ptolemy, Archimedes, Galen, and other great Greek scientific writers were translated into Arabic. This knowledge, together with the teachings of the *Koran*, formed the basis of Muslim learning, which in turn was later transmitted to scholars in western Europe. In addition to being invaluable transmitters of learning, the Muslims made many original contributions to science and the arts.

Advances in Medicine

The years between 900 and 1100 can be called the golden age of Muslim learning. This period was particularly significant for medical advances. Muslim students of medicine were by all measures far superior to their European contemporaries. Muslim cities had excellent pharmacies and hospitals, and both pharmacists and physicians had to pass state examinations for licensure. Physicians received instruction in medical schools and hospitals.

Perhaps the greatest Muslim physician was the Persian al-Razi (d. 925), better known in the West as Rhazes. He wrote more than a hundred medical treatises in which he summarized Greek medical knowledge and added his own clinical observations. His most famous work, *On Smallpox and Measles*, is the first clear description of the symptoms and treatment of these diseases. The most influential Muslim medical treatise is the vast *Canon of Medicine* of the Persian scholar Avicenna (d. 1037), in which all Greek and Muslim medical learning is systematically organized. In the twelfth century the *Canon* was translated into Latin and was so much in demand in the West that it was issued sixteen times in the last half of the fifteenth century and more than twenty times in the sixteenth. It is still read and used in east Asia today.

Progress in Other Sciences

Muslim physicists were not just copyists, but highly creative scientists as well. Alhazen (d. 1039) of Cairo developed optics to a remarkable degree and challenged the theory of Ptolemy and Euclid that the eye sends visual rays to its object. The chief source of all medieval Western writers on optics, Alhazen interested himself in optic reflections and illusions and examined the refraction of light rays through air and water.

Although astronomy continued to be strongly influenced by astrology, Muslim astronomers built observatories, recorded their observations over long periods, and achieved greater accuracy than the Greeks in measuring the length of the solar year and in calculating eclipses. Interest in alchemy—the attempt to change base metals into precious ones and to find the magic elixir for the preservation of human life—produced the first chemical laboratories and caused an emphasis on the value of experimentation. Muslim alchemists prepared many chemical substances (sulfuric acid, for example) and developed methods for evaporation, filtration, sublimation, crystallization, and distillation. The process of distillation, invented around 800, produced what was called *alkuhl* (alcohol), a new liquor that had made Geber, its inventor, an honored name in some circles.

In mathematics the Muslims were indebted to the Hindus as well as to the Greeks. From the Greeks came the geometry of Euclid and the fundamentals of trigonometry, which Ptolemy had worked out. From the Hindus came arithmetic and algebra and the nine signs, known as Arabic numerals. The Muslims probably invented the all-important zero, although some scholars assign this honor to the Indians. Two Persian mathematicians made significant contributions: al-Khwarizmi (d. about 840), whose *Arithmetic* introduced Arabic numerals and whose *Algebra* first employed that mathematical term, and Omar Khayyám (d. c. 1123), whose work in algebra went beyond quadratics to cubic equations. Other scholars developed plane and spherical trigonometry.

In an empire that straddled continents, where trade and administration made an accurate knowledge of lands imperative, the science of geography flourished. The Muslims added to the

Hunayn ibn Ishaq's *Book of the Ten Treatises on the Eye* shows the Islamic scientist's outstandingly accurate under-standing of the anatomy of the eye. Written in the tenth century, the work was still standard in the thirteenth century, when the copy shown here was made.

geographical knowledge of the Greeks, whose treatises they translated, by producing detailed descriptions of the climate, manners, and cus-toms of many parts of the known world.

Islamic Literature and Scholarship

To Westerners, whose literary tastes have been largely modeled after the Graeco-Roman classics, Islamic literature may seem very alien. Whereas we are used to restraint and simplici-ty, Muslim writers have long enjoyed elegant ex-pression, subtle combinations of words, and fanciful and even extravagant imagery.

Westerners' knowledge of Islamic literature tends to be limited to the *Arabian Nights* and the poetry of Omar Khayyám. The former is a col-lection of often erotic tales told with a wealth of

local color; although it professedly covers differ-ent facets of life at the Abbasid capital, it is in fact often based on life in medieval Cairo. The fame of Omar Khayyám's *Rubáiyát* is partly due to the musical (though somewhat free) transla-tion of Edward FitzGerald. The following stan-zas indicate the poem's beautiful imagery and gentle resignation:

> *A Book of Verses underneath the Bough,*
> *A Jug of Wine, a Loaf of Bread—and Thou*
> *   Beside me singing in the Wilderness—*
> *Oh, Wilderness were Paradise enow!*
>
> *Some for the Glories of This World; and some*
> *Sigh for the Prophet's Paradise to come;*
> *   Ah, take the Cash, and let the Credit go,*
> *Nor heed the rumble of a distant Drum! . . .*

The Moving Finger writes; and, having writ,
Moves on: nor all your Piety nor Wit
    Shall lure it back to cancel half a Line,
Nor all your Tears wash out a Word of it.

And that inverted Bowl they call the Sky,
Whereunder crawling coop'd we live and die,
    Lift not your hands to It for help—for It
As impotently moves as you or I.[1]

The same rich imagery characterizes much Islamic prose. As the first important prose work in Arab literature, the *Koran* set the stylistic pattern for all Arabic writers. The holy book was designed particularly to be recited aloud; anyone who has listened to the chanting of the *Koran* can testify to its cadence, melody, and power.

Muslim philosophy, essentially Greek in origin, was developed by secular scholars and not, as in the West, by churchmen. Like the medieval Christian philosophers (see ch. 10), Muslim thinkers were largely concerned with reconciling Aristotelian rationalism and religion. The earlier Muslim thinkers, including Avicenna, the physician with many talents, sought to harmonize Platonism, Aristotelianism, and Islam. Avicenna's work was widely read in the West, where it was translated in the twelfth century. The last great Islamic philosopher, Averroës (d. 1198), lived in Cordova where he was the caliph's personal doctor. In his commentaries on Aristotle's works, which gave the Christian West its knowledge of Aristotle long before the original Greek texts were obtained from Constantinople,

Averroës rejected the belief in the ultimate harmony between faith and reason along with all earlier attempts to reconcile Aristotle and Plato. Faith and reason, he argued, operate on different levels; a proposition can be true philosophically but false theologically. On the other hand, Moses Maimonides, Averroës' contemporary who was also born in Muslim Spain, sought, in his still influential *Guide to the Perplexed*, to harmonize Judaism and Aristotelian philosophy. St. Thomas Aquinas, who in the next century undertook a similar project for Christianity, was influenced by these earlier attempts to reconcile faith and reason.

Islamic historiography found its finest expression in the work of ibn-Khaldun of Tunis (d. 1406), who has also been called a "father of sociology." Despite his busy life in public affairs, he found time to write a large general history dealing particularly with human social development, which he held to be the result of interaction of society and the physical environment. Ibn-Khaldun defined history thus:

It should be known that history, in matter of fact, is information about human social organization, which itself is identical with world civilization. It deals with such conditions affecting the nature of civilization as, for instance, savagery and sociability, group feelings, and the different ways by which one group of human beings achieves superiority over another. It deals with royal authority and . . . with the different kinds of gainful

Abd al-Rahman, "Date Tree"

Abd al-Rahman (d. 788), the first Omayyad ruler of Islamic Spain, is said to have written this poem as he observed a solitary Syrian date tree in his garden in Cordova, far from the ruler's native land.

O Palm, thou art a stranger in the
        West,
        Far from thy Orient home, like me
unblest.
Weep! But thou canst not. Dumb, dejected
    tree,
Thou art not made to sympathise with me.
Ah, thou wouldst weep, if thou hadst tears to
    pour,

For thy companions on Euphrates' shore;
But yonder tall groves thou rememberest not,
As I, in hating foes, have my old friends
    forgot.

From R. A. Nicholson, *The Literary History of the Arabs* (London: T. Fisher Unwin, 1907), p. 418.

occupations and ways of making a living, with the sciences and crafts that human beings pursue as part of their activities and efforts, and with all the other institutions that originate in civilization through its very nature.[2]

Ibn-Kaldun conceived of history as an evolutionary process, in which societies and institutions change continually.

Art and Architecture

Religious attitudes played an important part in Muslim art. Because the Prophet warned against idols and their worship, there was a prohibition against pictorial representation of human and animal figures. The effect of this injunction was to encourage the development of stylized and geometrical design. Muslim art, like Muslim learning, borrowed from many sources. Islamic artists and craftsmen followed chiefly Byzantine and Persian models and eventually integrated what they had learned into a distinctive and original style.

The Muslims excelled in the fields of architecture and the decorative arts. That Islamic architecture can boast of many large and imposing structures is not surprising, because it drew much of its inspiration from the Byzantines and Persians, who were monumental builders. In time an original style of building evolved; the great mosques embody such typical features as domes, arcades, and minarets, the slender towers from which the faithful are summoned to prayer. The horseshoe arch is another graceful and familiar feature of Muslim architecture.

On the walls and ceilings of their buildings, the Muslims gave full rein to their love of ornamentation and beauty of detail. The Spanish interpretation of the Muslim tradition is particularly delicate and elegant. Other outstanding examples of Islamic architecture are to be found in India; the Taj Mahal, for example, is based largely on Persian motifs.

Restricted in their subject matter, Muslim craftsmen conceived beautiful patterns from flowers and geometric figures. Even Arabic script, certainly one of the most beautiful ever devised, was used as a decorative motif. Muslim decorative skill also found expression in such fields as carpet and rug weaving, brass work, and the making of steel products inlaid with precious metals.

The Cordova Cathedral is a striking example of the Spanish interpretation of the Muslim tradition in architecture.

Conclusion

In this chapter, we have examined the origins and meteoric development of Islam—both the religion and the community. The great power of Muhammad's teachings enabled the creative but fragmented Arab tribes to unify and expand across three continents in an astoundingly brief period.

During the reigns of the first four caliphs and the century of the Umayyad Dynasty (661–750), great strides were made in annexing new territories and peoples. But the Umayyad Dynasty was based on a ruling hierarchy of Arabs, and the resentment that set the Abbasid Dynasty (750–1258) on a new throne in Baghdad.

During the early Abbasid period Islam reached the high point of its geographical expansion and cultural achievements, extending from Spain across three continents to east Asia. Unparalleled prosperity evolved from a combination of successful trade, industry, and agriculture. But the Muslims were not able to maintain an integrated empire; despite a religious unity—which still exists—politically the empire broke up into smaller Muslim states.

The Muslims were especially gifted in science, literature, and philosophy. Muslim intellectual life was in large part the product of a genius for synthesizing varying cultures, and the diffusion of this knowledge was a tremendous factor in the revival of classical learning and the coming of the Renaissance in Europe.

Ironically, while the arts and learning were beginning to thrive in the West, Islamic civilization itself declined. Various reasons have been advanced for this phenomenon, including the influx of semibarbarous peoples into Islamic lands, intellectual inflexibility resulting from rigid adherence to the Koran's sacred law, and the despotic and eventually corrupt rule of such Muslim dynasties as the Ottomans in Turkey, who destroyed most progressive political and economic movements.

Islam remains a powerful force in the world today. Its believers encompass the most highly educated scholars and unscholared peasants. The Islamic community likewise is made up of leading industrialized societies as well as nations just emerging from colonialism. The message of faith and the unity of communalism under Islam are powerful influences which will continue to play a part in world politics. Islam has begun its fifteenth century as one of the world's most influential religious and social forces. Present-day Islam still derives great meaning from the teachings of Muhammad and the community he and his disciples constructed. The power of the ancient message still plays a dominant role in the modern world.

Suggestions for Reading

P. K. Hitti, *The Arabs: A Short History** (Gateway) is an excellent abridgement of a scholarly general history. See also Richard C. Martin, *Islam** (Prentice-Hall, 1992) for an excellent brief summary of Islamic history. See also the outstanding work by John L. Esposito, *Islam: The Straight Path* (Oxford, 1988) and C. Brockelmann, *History of the Islamic Peoples** (Capricorn).

For the early development of Islam, see J. J. Saunders, *History of Medieval Islam** (Routledge & Kegan Paul, 1965) and Dominique Sourdel, translation by J. Montgomery Watt, *Medieval Islam* (Routledge & Kegan Paul, 1983). For an excellent evauation of the Umayyad period and its importance, see G. R. Hawting, *The First Dynasty of Islam* (Croom Helm, 1986).

W. M. Watt, *Muhammad: Prophet and Statesman** (Galaxy) is a brief but excellent account of the prophet's life and teachings. See also T. Andrae, *Mohammed: The Man and His Faith** (Torchbooks); M. Rodinson, *Mohammed* (Vintage, 1974); F. M. Denny, *An Introduction to Islam** (Macmillan, 1985); and Martin Lings, *Muhammad: His Life Based on the Earliest Sources* (Inner Traditions International, Ltd., 1983). For an interpretation and translation of the Koran, see M. Pickthall, *The Meaning of the Glorious Koran** (Mentor) and H. A. R. Gibb, *Mohammedism: An Historial Survey** (Galaxy), which is outstanding.

P. Coles, *The Ottoman Impact on Europe** (Harcourt Brace Jovanovich is a lucid survey. See also S. Runciman, *The Fall of Constantinople, 1453** (Cambridge) and N. Itkowitz, *The Ottoman Empire and Islamic Tradition** (Knopf, 1972).

R. A. Nicholson, *A Literary History of the Arabs** (Cambridge, 1969) traces the growth of Arab thought and culture through its literature, as does H. A. R. Gibb, *Arabic Literature*, 2nd ed. (Oxford, 1974). See also P. Hitti, *Makers of Arab History** (Torchbooks) and D. Talbot Rice, *Islamic Art** (Praeger).

*Indicates a less expensive paperbound edition.

Notes

1. *Rubaiyát of Omar Khayyám*, trans. by Edward Fitzgerald, Stanzas 12, 13, 71, 72.
2. Ibn Khaldun, *The Mugaddimah: An Introduction to History*, trans. by Franz Rosenthal, Vol. I (London: Routledge & Keegan Paul Ltd., 1958), p. 71.

The Byzantine Empire, Eastern Europe, and Russia to 1600

When we speak of the fall of the Roman Empire, we should not forget that in fact only the western portion of that empire succumbed to the Germanic invaders. In the east, the eastern Roman, or Byzantine, Empire stood for a thousand years as a citadel against the threats of expansion by the Muslims.

The Byzantine Empire made great contributions to civilization: Greek language and learning were preserved for posterity; the Roman imperial system was continued and Roman law codified; the Greek Orthodox church converted some Slavic peoples and fostered the development of a splendid new art dedicated to the glorification of the Christian religion. Situated at the crossroads of east and west, Constantinople acted as the disseminator of culture for all peoples who came in contact with the empire. Called with justification "The City," this rich and turbulent metropolis was to the early Middle Ages what Athens and Rome had been to classical times. By the time the empire collapsed in 1453, its religious mission and political concepts had borne fruit among the Slavic peoples of eastern Europe and especially among the Russians. The latter were to lay claim to the Byzantine tradition and to call Moscow the "Third Rome."

Byzantium: the Shining Fortress

At the southern extremity of the Bosphorus stands a promontory that juts out from Europe toward Asia, with the Sea of Marmora to the south and a long harbor known as the Golden Horn to the north. On this peninsula stood the ancient Greek city of Byzantium, which Constantine the Great enlarged considerably and formally christened "New Rome" in A.D. 330 (see chap. 5 and map, p. 133).

Constantine had chosen the site for his new capital with care. He placed Constantinople (now Istanbul) on the frontier of Europe and Asia, dominating the waterway connecting the Mediterranean and Black seas. Nature protected the site on three sides with cliffs; on the fourth side, emperors fortified the city with an impenetrable three—wall network. During the fourth and fifth centuries Visigoths, Huns, and Ostrogoths unsuccessfully threatened the city. In the seventh, eighth, and ninth centuries, first Persians, then Arab forces, and finally the Bulgarians besieged—but failed to take—Constantinople. Until 1453, with the exception of the Fourth Crusade's treachery (see p. 179), the city withstood all attacks.

The security and wealth provided by its setting helped Byzantium survive for more than a thousand years. Constantinople was a state-controlled, world trade center which enjoyed the continuous use of a money economy—in contrast to the localized systems found in the west. The city's wealth and taxes paid for a strong military force and financed an effective government. Excellent sewage and water systems supported an extremely high standard of living. Food was abundant, with grain from Egypt and Anatolia and fish from the Aegean. Constantinople could support a population of a million, at a time when it was difficult to find a city in Europe that could sustain more than 50,000.

Unlike Rome, Constantinople had several industries producing luxury goods, military

This oldest known view of Constantinople, drawn in 1420, shows both the city's wealth of monumental architecture and its outstanding fortifications.

supplies, hardware, and textiles. After silkworms were smuggled out of China about A.D. 550, silk production flourished and became a profitable state monopoly. The state paid close attention to business, controlling the economy: A system of guilds to which all tradesmen and members of the professions belonged set wages, profits, work hours, and prices and organized bankers and doctors into compulsory corporations.

Security and wealth encouraged an active political, cultural, and intellectual life. The widespread literacy and education among men and women of various segments of society would not be matched in Europe until, perhaps, eighteenth-century France. Until its fall in 1453, the Byzantine Empire remained a shining fortress, attracting both invaders and merchants.

The Latin Phase

Constantine and his successors struggled to renew the empire. Rome collapsed under the pressure of the Germanic invaders in 476 (see ch. 5). Thanks to its greater military and economic strength, Constantinople survived for a thousand years, despite revolutions, wars, and religious controversy.

Justinian (527–565) was the last emperor to attempt seriously to return the Roman Empire to its first-century grandeur. Aided by his forceful wife Theodora and a corps of competent assistants, he made lasting contributions to Western civilization and gained short-term successes in his foreign policy.

The damage caused by devastating earthquakes (a perennial problem in the area) in the 520s and 530s gave Justinian the opportunity he needed to carry out a massive project of empire-wide urban renewal. He strengthened the walls defending Constantinople and built the Church of the Holy Wisdom, which still stands in the city. The dome of the church is an architectural triumph with forty windows circling its base, producing a quality of light that creates the illusion that the ceiling is floating.

Justinian also reformed the government and ordered a review of Roman law. This undertaking led to the publication of the *Code of Justinian*, a digest of Roman and church law, texts, and other instructional materials that became the foundation of modern Western law. Justinian also participated actively in the religious arguments of his day.

In this 10th-century mosaic, which appears over the door of Hagia Sophia, Constantine offers his city and Justinian offers his church to the Virgin and Child.

The emperor's expensive and ambitious projects triggered outbreaks of violence among the political gangs of Constantinople, the circus crowds of the Greens and Blues.[1] Since ancient times city dwellers throughout the Mediterranean formed groups, each pursuing a set of economic, social, and religious goals. Much like contemporary urban gangs, members of the circus factions moved about in groups and congregated at public events.

In Constantinople the Circus took place in the Hippodrome, a structure that could hold 80,000 spectators. There contests of various types were held, including chariot races. The Blues and Greens backed opposing drivers and usually neutralized each other's efforts. In 532, however, the Blues and Greens united to try to force Justinian from the throne. The so-called Nike rebellion, named after the victory cry of the rioters, nearly succeeded. In his *Secret Histories*, Procopius relates that Justinian was on the verge of running away, until Theodora stopped him and told the frightened emperor:

> *I do not choose to flee. Those who have worn the crown should never survive its loss. Never shall I see the day when I am not saluted as empress. If you mean to flee, Caesar, well and good. You have the money, the ships are ready, the sea is open. As for me, I shall stay.*[2]

This mosaic from the Church of San Vitale at Ravenna features the Empress Theodora and her attendants.

Assisted by his generals, the emperor remained and put down the rebellion.

Justinian momentarily achieved his dream of re-establishing the Mediterranean rim of the Roman Empire. To carry out his plan for regaining the lost half of the empire from the Germanic invaders, he first had to buy the neutrality of the Persian kings who threatened not only Constantinople but also Syria and Asia Minor. After securing his eastern flank through diplomacy and bribery, he took North Africa in 533 and the islands of the western Mediterranean from the Vandals.

The next phase of the conquest was much more exhausting. Like warriors before and after him, Justinian had a difficult time taking the Italian peninsula. After twenty years, he gained his prize from the Ostrogoths, but at the cost of draining his treasury and ruining Rome and Ravenna. Justinian's generals also reclaimed the southern part of Spain from the Visigoths, but no serious attempt was ever made to recover Gaul, Britain, or southern Germany (see map, p. 173).

By a decade after Justinian's death, most of the reconquest had been lost. The Moors in Africa, Germanic peoples across Europe, and waves of Asiatic nomadic tribes threatened the imperial boundaries. Ancient enemies such as the Persians, who had been bribed into a peaceful relationship, returned to threaten Constantinople when the money ran out. In addition, the full weight of the Slavic migrations came to be felt. Peaceful though they may have been, the primitive Slavs severely strained and sometimes broke the administrative links of the empire. Finally, the empire was split by debates over Christian doctrine. Two of Justinian's successors succumbed to madness under the stress of trying to maintain order in the empire.

Heraclius: The Empire Redefined

Salvation appeared from the west when Heraclius (610–641), the Byzantine governor of North Africa, returned to Constantinople to overthrow the mad emperor Phocas. Conditions were so dismal and the future appeared so perilous when Heraclius arrived in the capital that he considered moving the government from Constantinople to Carthage in North Africa.

THE BYZANTINE EMPIRE
UNDER JUSTINIAN

Empire at his Accession 527
Empire at his Death 565

The situation did not improve soon. The Persians marched through Syria, took Jerusalem—capturing the "True Cross"—and entered Egypt. When Egypt fell to the Persians, the Byzantine Empire lost a large part of its grain supply. Two Asiatic invaders, the Avars and the Bulgars, pushed against the empire from the north. Pirates controlled the sea lanes and the Slavs cut land communication across the Balkans. At this moment of ultimate peril, the emperor decided to throw out the state structure that had been in place since the time of Diocletian and Constantine.

Heraclius created a new system that strengthened his army, tapped the support of the church and people, and erected a more efficient, streamlined administration. He determined that the foundation for the redefined empire would be Anatolia (present-day Turkey) and that the main supply of soldiers for his army would be the free peasants living there, rather than mercenaries. In place of the sprawling realm passed on by Justinian, Heraclius designed a compact state and an administration conceived to deal simultaneously with the needs of government and the challenges of defense.

Heraclius' system, known as the *theme* system, had been tested when the emperor had ruled North Africa. Acting on the lessons of the past four centuries, he assumed that defense was a constant need and that free peasant soldiers living in the *theme* (district) they were defending would be the most effective and efficient force. He installed the system first in Anatolia, and his successors spread it throughout the empire for the next two centuries. Heraclius'

This medallion commemorates Heraclius' victory over the Persians and his reclamation of the "True Cross." Here, the emperor rides in triumph into Constantinople.

The Byzantine Empire, Eastern Europe, and Russia to 1600 **173**

scheme provided sound administration and effective defense for half of the cost formerly required.[3] As long as the *theme* system with its self-supporting, land-owning, free peasantry endured, Byzantium remained strong. When the *theme* system and its free peasantry were abandoned in the eleventh century, the empire became weak and vulnerable.

Heraclius fought history's first holy war to reclaim Jerusalem from the Persians. By 626 he stood poised to strike the final blow and refused to be distracted by the Avar siege of Constantinople. He defeated the Persians at Nineva, marched on to Ctesiphon, and finally reclaimed the "True Cross" and returned it to Jerusalem in 630.

Heraclius was unable to savor his victory for long, because the Muslim advance (see p. 159) posed an even greater threat to Byzantium. The Muslims took Syria and Palestine at the battle of Yarmuk in 636. Persia fell the following year, and Egypt in 640. Constantinople's walls and the redefined Byzantine state withstood the challenge, enduring two sieges in 674–678 and in 717. When Byzantium faced a three-sided invasion from the Arabs, Avars, and Bulgarians in 717, the powerful leader Leo the Isaurian (717–741) came forward to save the empire. The Byzantines triumphed by using new techniques such as Greek fire, a sort of medieval equivalent of napalm. The substance, a powerful chemical mixture whose main ingredient was saltpeter, caught fire on contact with water and stuck to the hulls of the Arabs' wooden ships. Over the next ten years, Leo rebuilt those areas ruined by war and strengthened the *theme* system. He reformed the law, limiting capital punishment to crimes involving treason. He decreed the use of mutilation for a wide range of common crimes, a harsh but still less extreme punishment than execution.

The Iconoclastic Controversy

From the beginning, the Byzantine emperors played active roles in the calling of church councils and the formation of Christian doctrine. Leo the Isaurian took seriously his role as religious leader of the empire. He vigorously persecuted heretics and Jews, ordering that the latter must be baptized. In 726 he launched a theological crusade against the use of icons, images or

The Byzantine navy coupled its prowess in battle with the secret and powerful weapon, Greek fire, depicted here in a 14th-century manuscript illumination.

representations of Christ and other religious figures. The emperor was concerned that icons played too prominent a role in Byzantine life and that their common use as godparents, witnesses at weddings, and objects of adoration violated the Old Testament prohibition of the worship of graven images. Accordingly, the emperor ordered the army to destroy icons. This image-breaking, or iconoclastic, policy sparked a violent reaction in the western part of the empire, especially in the monasteries. The government responded by mercilessly persecuting those opposed to the policy. The eastern part of the empire, centered at Anatolia, supported the breaking of the images. By trying to remove what he considered an abuse, Leo split his empire in two.

In Byzantium's single-centered society, this religious conflict had far-reaching cultural, political, and social implications. In 731 Pope Gregory II condemned iconoclasm. Leo's decision to destroy icons stressed the fracture lines that had existed between east and west for the past four centuries, expressed in the linguistic differences between the Latin west and the Greek east.[4] Leo's successors continued his religious and political policies, and in 754 Pope Stephen II turned to the north and struck an alliance with the Frankish king Pepin. This was the first step in a process that half a century later would lead to the birth of the Holy Roman Empire and the formal political split of Europe into the east and west (see ch. 9).

There was a brief attempt under the regent, later empress, Irene (797–802), in 787, to restore

The Empress Irene, the only woman to rule the Byzantine Empire in her own right, attempted in 787 to restore icons. In 812 Irene was deposed and exiled to Lesbos.

win widespread support for her pro-icon policies, nor could she put together a marriage alliance with the newly proclaimed western emperor Charlemagne, a union which would have brought east and west together. As Irene spent the treasury into bankruptcy, her enemies increased. Finally in 802, they deposed her and exiled her to the island of Lesbos.[5]

The conflict over iconoclasm and Irene's ineptitude placed the empire in jeopardy once again. Her successor, Nicepherous (802–811), after struggling to restore the bases of Byzantine power, was captured in battle with the Bulgarians in 811. The Khan Krum beheaded him and had his skull made into a drinking mug. Soon the iconoclasts made a comeback, but this phase of image-breaking lacked the vigor of the first, and by 842 the policy had been abandoned.

The iconoclastic controversy marked a period when the split between east and west became final. Eastern emperors were strongly impressed by Islamic culture, with its prohibition of images. The emperor Theophilus (829–842), for example, was a student of Muslim art and culture, and Constantinople's painting, architecture, and universities benefited from the vigor of Islamic culture. This focus on the east may have led to the final split with the west, but it also produced

icons. In 797 she gained power after having her son—the rightful but incompetent heir—blinded in the very room in which she had given him birth. Irene then became the first woman to rule the empire in her own name. She could neither an eastern state with its theological house finally in order and its borders fairly secure by the middle of the ninth century (see map, p. 175).

The Golden Age: 842–1071

For two centuries, roughly coinciding with the reign of the Macedonian dynasty (867–1056), Byzantium enjoyed political and cultural superiority over its western and eastern foes. Western Europe staggered under the blows dealt by the Saracens, Vikings, and Magyars. The Arabs lost the momentum that had carried them forward for two centuries. Constantinople enjoyed the relative calm, wealth, and balance bequeathed by the *theme* system and promoted by a series of powerful rulers. The time was marked by the flowering of artists, scholars, and theologians as much as it was by the presence of great warriors. It was during this golden age that Constantinople made its major contributions to Eastern Europe and Russia.

Missionaries from Constantinople set out in the 860s to convert the Bulgarian and Slavic peoples and in the process organized their language, laws, esthetics, political patterns, and ethics, as well as their religion. But such transformation did not take place without struggle. Conflict marked the relationship between the Roman and Byzantine churches. The most significant indication of this competition was seen in the contest between the patriarch Photius and Pope Nicholas I in the middle of the ninth century.

Photius excelled both as a scholar and religious leader. He made impressive contributions to universities throughout the Byzantine empire and worked to increase the area of Orthodoxy's influence. Nicholas was his equal in ambition, ego, and intellect. They collided in their attempts to convert the pagan peoples such as the Bulgarians, who were caught between their spheres of influence.

The Bulgarian Khan Boris, as cunning and shrewd as either Photius or Nicholas, saw the trend toward conversion to Christianity that had been developing in Europe since the sixth century and realized the increased power he could gain by the heavenly approval of his rule. He wanted his own patriarch and church and dealt with the side that gave him the better bargain. Between 864 and 866 Boris changed his mind three times over the issue of which holy city to turn to. Finally, the Byzantines gave the Bulgarians the equivalent of an autonomous church, and in return the Bulgarians entered the Byzantine cultural orbit. The resulting schism between the churches set off a sputtering sequence of Christian warfare that went on for centuries.[6]

The work of the Byzantine missionaries Cyril and Methodius was more important than Bulgarian ambitions or churchly competition. The two, who were brothers, were natives of Thessalonica, a city at the mouth of the Vardar-Morava waterway that gave access to the Slavic lands. They learned the Slavic language and led a mission to Moravia, which was ruled by King Rastislav. The king no doubt wanted to convert to Orthodoxy and enter the Byzantine orbit in order to preserve as much independence for his land as he could in the face of pressure from his powerful German neighbors. Cyril and Methodius went north, teaching their faith in the vernacular Slavic language. Cyril devised an alphabet for the Slavs, adapting Greek letters. The two brothers translated the liturgy and many religious books into Slavic. Although Germanic missionaries eventually converted the Moravians by sheer force, the efforts of Cyril and Methodius profoundly affected all the Slavic peoples, whose languages are rooted in the work of the two brothers.

Byzantium continued its military as well as its theological intensity. Arab armies made continual thrusts, including one at Thessalonica in 904 that led to the Byzantine loss of 22,000 people through death or slavery. But during the tenth century the combination of the decline in Muslim combativeness and the solidarity of Byzantine defenses brought an end to that conflict. Basil II (963–1025), surnamed *Bulgaroctonus*, or Bulgar-slayer, stopped the Bulgarians at the battle of Balathista in 1014 (see p. 181). At the same time, the Macedonian emperors dealt from a position of strength with western European powers, especially in Italy, where their interests clashed. Western diplomats visiting the Byzantine court expressed outrage at the benign contempt with which the eastern emperors treated them, but this conduct merely reflected Constantinople's understanding of its role in the world.

By the eleventh century, succession to the Byzantine throne had degenerated into a power

This detail of a page from a 15th-century manuscript shows the Byzantine missionaries, the brothers Cyril and Methodius, composing the Cyrillic alphabet.

struggle between the civil and military aristocracies. On the other hand, the secular and theological universities flourished despite the political instability, and the emperors proved to be generous patrons of the arts. Basil I (867–886) and Leo VI (886–912) oversaw the collection and reform of the law codes. Leo, the most prolific lawgiver since Justinian, sponsored the greatest collection of laws of the medieval Byzantine empire, a work that would affect jurisprudence throughout Europe. Constantine VII Porphyrogenitus (912–959) excelled as a military leader, lover of books, promoter of an encyclopedia, and surveyor of the empire's provinces. At a time when scholarship in western Europe was almost nonexistent, Byzantine society featured a rich cultural life and widespread literacy among men and women of different classes.

The greatest contribution to Western civilization made during the golden age was the preservation of ancient learning, especially in the areas of law, Greek science, Platonic and Aristotelian philosophy, and Greek literature. Unlike in the West where the church maintained scholarship, the civil servants of Constantinople perpetuated the Greek tradition in philosophy, literature, and science. Byzantine monasteries produced many saints and mystics but showed little interest in learning and teaching.

Decline and Crusades

Empires more often succumb to internal ailments than to external takeovers and this was the case with the Byzantine empire. As long as Constantinople strengthened the foundations laid by Heraclius—the *theme* system and reliance on the free peasant-soldier—the empire withstood the military attacks of the strongest armies. When the Byzantine leaders abandoned the pillars of their success, the empire began to falter.

Inflation and narrow ambition ate away at the Heraclian structure. Too much money chased too few goods during the golden age. Land came to be the most profitable investment for the rich, and the landowning magnates needed labor. As prices went up, taxes followed. The peasant villages were collectively responsible for paying taxes, and the rising tax burden overwhelmed them. In many parts of the empire, villagers sought relief by placing themselves under the control of large landowners, thus taking themselves out of the tax pool and lowering the number of peasant-soldiers. Both the state treasury and the army suffered. Until the time of Basil II, the Macedonian emperors tried to protect the peasantry through legislation, but the problem was not corrected. Even though the free peasantry never entirely disappeared and each free person was still theoretically a citizen of the empire, economic and social pressures effectively destroyed the *theme* system. Exacerbating the problem was the growth of the church's holdings and the large percentage of the population entering church service, thus becoming exempt from taxation.

In the fifty years after the death of Basil II in 1025, the illusion that eternal peace had been achieved encouraged the opportunistic civil aristocracy, which controlled the state, to weaken the army and ignore the provinces. When danger next appeared, no strong leader emerged to save Byzantium. Perhaps this was because no enemies appeared dramatically before the walls of Constantinople.

Instead, a new foe arose, moving haphazardly across the empire. Around the sixth century, the first in a series of waves of Turkish bands appeared in southwest Asia. These nomads converted to Islam and fought with, then against, the Persians, Byzantines, and Arabs. When the Seljuk Turk leader Alp Arslan ("Victorious Lion")

made a tentative probe into the empire's eastern perimeter near Lake Van in 1071, the multilingual mercenary army from Constantinople fell apart even before fighting began at the battle of Manzikert. With the disintegration of the army, the only limit to the Turks' march for the next decade was the extent of their own ambition and energy.

Byzantium lost the heart of its empire (see map below), and with it the reserves of soldiers, leaders, taxes, and food that had enabled it to survive for the past four centuries. From its weakened position, the empire confronted Venice, a powerful commercial and later political rival. By the end of the eleventh century, the Venetians took undisputed trading supremacy in the Adriatic Sea and turned their attention to the eastern Mediterranean. The Byzantines also faced the challenges of the Normans, led by Robert Guiscard, who took the last Byzantine stronghold in Italy.

In 1081 the Comnenian family claimed the Byzantine throne. In an earlier time, with the empire in its strength this politically astute family might have accomplished great things. In the eleventh and twelfth centuries, though, the best they could do was play a balance-of-power game between east and west. Fifteen years later, in

Hagia Sophia (Church of the Holy Wisdom) in Constantinople is considered the architectural masterpiece of the Byzantine Empire. The crowning glory of the church, built during Justinian's reign, was its huge dome, abutted at both ends by a half-dome. The mosaics, painted over when the Ottomans captured the city in 1453, have now been partially restored.

for this crusade and persuaded the fighters to attack the Christian city of Zara in Dalmatia—a commercial rival of Venice—and Constantinople before going on to the Holy Land. Venice wanted a trade monopoly in the eastern Mediterranean more than a fight with the Muslims. Constantinople was paralyzed by factional strife, and for the first time, an invading force captured the city and devastated it far more than the Turks would 250 years later. A French noble described the scene:

> The fire... continued to rage for a whole
> week and no one could put it out.... What
> damage was done, or what riches and posses-
> sions were destroyed in the flames was be-
> yond the power of man to calculate.... The
> army... gained much booty; so much, indeed,
> that no one could estimate its amount or its
> value. It included gold and silver, table-
> services and precious stones, satin and silk,
> mantles of squirrel fur, ermine and miniver,
> and every choicest thing to be found on this
> earth... so much booty had never been
> gained in any city since the creation of the
> world.[8]

The Venetians made sure they got their share of the spoils, such as the bronze horses now found at St. Mark's Cathedral in Venice, and played a key role in placing a new emperor on the throne. The invaders ruled Constantinople until 1261. The Venetians put a stranglehold on commerce in the region and then turned their hostility toward the Genoese, who threatened their monopoly.

The Paleologus Dynasty (1261–1453), which ruled the empire during its final two centuries, saw the formerly glorious realm become a pawn in a new game. Greeks may have regained control of the church and the state, but there was little strength left to carry on the ancient traditions. The free peasant became ever rarer, as a form of feudalism (see ch. 8) developed in which nobles resisted the authority of the emperor and the imperial bureaucracy. The *solidus*, the Byzantine coin which had resisted debasement from the fourth through the eleventh century, now fell victim to inflation. The church, once a major support for the state, became embroiled in continual doctrinal disputes. Slavic peoples such as the Serbs, who had posed no danger to the empire in its former strength,

1096, the first crusaders appeared (see ch. 10), partially in response to the Council of Clermont, partially in response to the opportunity for gold and glory. Alexium Comnenus (1081–1118) had appealed to Pope Urban II for help against the Turks, but the emperor had not bargained on finding a host of crusaders, including the dreaded Normans, on his doorstep. Alexius sent them quickly across the Dardanelles where they won some battles and permitted the Byzantines to reclaim some of their losses in Asia Minor.[7]

Subsequent crusades, however, failed to bring good relations between east and west, whose churches had excommunicated each other in 1054. By the time of the Fourth Crusade, the combination of envy, hatred, and frustration that had been building up for some time led to an atrocity. The Venetians controlled the ships and money became threats. After the Mongol invasions of the thirteenth century destroyed the exhausted Seljuq Turks, a new, more formidable threat appeared—the Ottoman, or Osmanli, Turks.

Blessed after 1296 with a strong line of male successors and good fortune, the Ottomans rapidly expanded their power through the Balkans. They crossed the Straits into Europe in 1354 and moved up the Vardar-Morava valleys to take Serres (1383), Sofia (1385), Nish (1386), Thessalonica (1387), and finally Kossovo from the South Slavs in 1389. The Turks won their victories by virtue of their overwhelming superiority in both infantry and cavalry. But their administrative effectiveness, which combined strength and flexibility, solidified their rule in areas they conquered. In contrast to the Christians, both Roman and Byzantine, who were intolerant of religious differences, the Turks allowed monotheists, or any of the believers in a "religion of the book" (the Bible, Torah, or Koran), to retain their faith and be ruled by a religious superior through the *millet* system, a network of religious ghettoes.

In response to the Ottoman advance, the west mounted a poorly conceived and ill-fated crusade against the Turks at Nicopolis on the Danube in 1396 that led to the capture and slaughter of 10,000 knights and their attendants. Only the overwhelming force of Tamerlane (Timur the Lame), a Turko-Mongol ruler who devastated the Ottoman army in 1402, gave Constantinople and Europe some breathing space.

The end came finally in May 1453. The last emperor, Constantine XI, led his forces of 9,000, half of whom were Genoese, to hold off the 160,000 Turks for seven weeks. Finally, the Ottomans, with the help of Hungarian artillerymen, breached the walls of the beleaguered city. After 1123 years, the Christian capital fell.[9]

Eastern Europe

Following in the wake of the Germanic tribes' westward march, the Slavs spread from the Pripet marshes west to the Elbe, east to the Urals, north to Finland, and south to the Peloponnesus (see map above). As they settled throughout eastern and central Europe from the

EASTERN EUROPE ABOUT 900

Slavic homeland

sixth through the ninth centuries, they absorbed most of the original inhabitants of the region. This mixing of peoples produced the resulting blend of nations that make up present-day Central and Eastern Europe and the western portion of the Soviet Union.

The region's geography contributed to the diversity of the population. The climatic extremes range from Arctic cold to Mediterranean mildness. The soil varies from the rich topsoil of the Ukraine and the Danubian plain to the rocky dryness of the Dinaric Alps. Waterways include both the scenic though commercially useless rivulets of Greece and the broad and powerful Vistula and Danube rivers. Some of the nations were landlocked. Others, such as Greece, were blessed with fine harbors. The particular combinations of climate, soil, and water access dictated the economic possibilities of each nation.

The Slavs hunted, traded (usually forest products such as nuts, honey, and wax), or farmed. The usual farming practice was the "slash and burn" method of cutting down the forests, tilling the land until it was exhausted, and then moving on. With the exception of the Bulgarians, the Slavs formed themselves into male-dominated peasant tribal units, based on blood relations. The clan elders elected a leader from their ranks who would meet with other clan leaders to elect a person to coordinate activities throughout the district. From the ranks would come local officials and priests, as well as taxes and military payments.

Compared to the wealth and sophistication of the Byzantines, the Slavs' economic and social lives were primitive and their political and military structures were weak. Outsiders—Byzantines, Germans, Magyars, Mongols, or Turks—often ruled them. Each of the outsiders imposed a distinctive set of cultural, economic, political, and social traits. Religion was the key means through which these distinctive traits were imposed.

The Orthodox Orbit

The Orthodox church in the ninth and tenth centuries converted the Russians and Slavs south of a line formed by the Danube and Sava rivers and the South Carpathian Mountains. The Bulgarians, Serbs, Montenegrins, Romanians, and Russians—heard the liturgy in their native language, worshipped under a decentralized religious structure, and remained culturally isolated from western Europe. In addition, these Orthodox Christians, living on the eastern edge of Europe, endured the domination of the Mongols and the Turks, two despotic Asiatic powers that permitted the exercise of the Orthodox religion but controlled political authority. The combination of Byzantine autocracy and oriental despotism facilitated the growth of authoritar-

The Bulgarians. The Bulgarians, originally a Finno-Ugric group, came into the Balkans in the late seventh century. In the ninth and tenth centuries, they were ruled by inspired leaders such as Krum and Boris (see p. 175) and Tsar Symeon (893–927), who brought the first Bulgarian empire to its peak, claimed the mantle of Roman emperor, and challenged Constantinople. Not until Basil the Bulgar-Slayer conquered his ancient foe at the battle of Balathista in 1014 did the first Bulgarian empire come to an end. The Byzantine emperor captured 14,000 Bulgarians and divided them into groups of 100. He then blinded 99 of each group, sparing one eye of the hundredth man so that he could guide his sightless colleagues home. The shock of the ghastly sight of his blinded warriors killed Tsar Samuel and the first Bulgarian empire crumbled, though an independent Bulgarian orthodox church remained. After this drastic defeat, the Bulgarians did not pose a military threat for more than a century.

After the Fourth Crusade in 1204 put an end, temporarily, to the Byzantine state, John Asen II brought the second Bulgarian empire to its height, extending its power from Thrace through Macedonia and northern Albania into the area of present-day Yugoslavia. The Mongol invasion in the 1240s struck a decisive blow that removed the Bulgarians as a power in the Balkans, though the shell of the kingdom remained until the 1390s when the Ottoman Turks defeated them.

The Serbs. In the thirteenth century, the Serbs replaced the Bulgarians as the dominant Balkan power. Groups of Serbs converted to Orthodox Christianity in the ninth century and until the twelfth century remained under Bulgarian or Byzantine control. Stephen Nemanja (1168–1196) founded the Nemanjid dynasty and established the Serbian state. Although the Serbs fought the Byzantines, they remained their cultural and religious students, even after the fall of Constantinople. When the Serbs reached their peak during the reign of Stephen Dushan (1331–1355), they set up an imitation of the Byzantine court, revised their laws on the basis of the Code of Justinian, and rivaled the Byzantines with their intricate court ritual. They made significant contributions to Orthodox theology. From his capital at Skopje, Stephen fought off the Hungarians and Italians and proclaimed himself emperor of the Serbs, Greeks, Bulgars, and Albanians. The Serbian state declined rapidly after Stephen's death in 1355 and in 1389 the Ottomans defeated the Serbs at Kossovo. The Turks incorporated Serbia into their holdings, where it remained for the next five centuries.

Other Orthodox States. The other Orthodox Slavs—Bosnians and Montenegrins—each for a brief time stood strong and independent in the Balkans. The Bosnians enjoyed their greatest prosperity in the 1370s after the decline of the Serbs, Bulgarians, and Byzantines, before the arrival of the Turks. A century later the Turks made the area an Ottoman province. The entire Bosnian aristocracy converted to Islam—the only instance of conversion by an elite, as the Turks destroyed all the other Balkans' nobilities. Montenegro, ruled by a prince bishop, emerged in 1355 following Serbia's decline. From its mountainous fortress Montenegro tenaciously held on to its independence for five centuries, the only area in the Balkans to maintain its freedom from Ottoman control.

The Greeks had lost their political independence to outsiders beginning in the third century B.C., although they continued to exert powerful commercial and cultural influence, particularly in Constantinople. They emerged from two centuries of Slavic invasions with their civilization intact; they survived the period of Latin occupation after the crusades; and they endured Turkish control after the fifteenth century. They did not experience any substantial degree of self-government until the nineteenth century.

One area of the old Roman Empire retained its Latin legacy, the area of present-day Romania. The emperor Trajan extended Rome's control to the area of Dacia in 106, and by the time the Romans withdrew 165 years later, they left behind very little of the original civilization or language of the area. (In fact, Romanians refer to themselves as "an island of Latins in a sea of Slavs.") For the next thousand years Romania, and its provinces of Wallachia, Moldavia, Transylvania, Bessarabia, and Bukovina, served as the crossroads through which every invader came. Not until the end of that millennium could elements of a definably Romanian civilization and government be perceived. Thereafter, the efforts of fifteenth-century warriors such as Vlad Tepeš, the model for Dracula, held the Turks off, but the Romanians paid tribute to the Ottomans for the next three centuries.[10]

The Roman Catholic Orbit

The Eastern Europeans who found themselves in the Roman sphere—the Poles, Czechs, Slovaks, Hungarians, Slovenes, and Croats—joined religious framework knit together by the Latin language and papal authority. The Catholic community stretched from the Bug River to the Straits of Gibraltar to Iceland. Predominantly German monks and priests carried the Roman faith to this area, and they were followed and sustained by a Germanic population movement— the so-called *drang nach osten* (drive to the east). The region experienced a golden age of cultural and economic achievement in the fourteenth century. Universities were established in Prague (1348), Cracow (1364), and Pecs (1369), and scholars in those schools were active in the humanist movement of the fifteenth century (see ch. 12). This region experienced the great formative developments of Western civilization—the Renaissance, the Reformation, the Scientific Revolution, the rise of capitalism, the Enlightenment, and the French and Industrial Revolutions. The people of this area of Europe also participated directly in the development of the western European system of feudalism, the rise of the modern state system, and the growth of pluralistic society.

The Hungarians. The Hungarians, also known as the Magyars, arrived in eastern Europe from Asia. Unlike other nomadic peoples, however, the Hungarians remained and effectively split the Slavic peoples in two parts (see map, p. 180). They crossed the Carpathians in 896 and destroyed the remnants of the Great Moravian empire ten years later. Until their defeat by Otto the Great at Augsburg in 955, they terrorized Europe, ranging from the Baltic to the Pyrenees and into Italy.

By the time their advance was halted, they had established a more or less permanent state along the middle Danube, under the Arpad dynasty. Two outstanding kings, Geza (972–997) and Stephen (997–1038) laid the foundation of the country's county-based political system and stabilized the social and economic structure. Geza and his family accepted baptism from the Roman Catholic church, but it was Stephen who, by accepting his crown from Pope Sylvester II in 1000, brought Hungary into the western church's orbit. Stephen actively defended the faith against heretics and pagans, and the crown of St. Stephen, who was canonized (made a saint) by the Roman Church in 1083, remains the symbol of the Hungarian nation.

The Crown of St. Stephen. During his reign, Stephen, who is considered the patron saint of Hungary, endowed abbeys and suppressed paganism.

After Stephen's death Hungary experienced a century of crises brought on by internal competing factions and Polish and German intervention. The tenth-century structure erected by Geza and Stephen, modified somewhat to accommodate an elective monarchy, withstood these tests and by the reign of Bela III (1173–1196) Hungary stood as one of the most powerful countries in Europe, extending its influence deep into the Balkans. Domestically, the nobles gained enough strength to force the monarchy to agree to a limitation of its power in a Magna Carta-like document (see p. 250), the Golden Bull of 1222.

The Mongols ravaged the country so thoroughly in 1241 that two generations passed before the area recovered. However, the invaders did not remain to exploit their victory, and the Hungarians were able to rebuild their system by the 1280s. During the period of recovery, the more powerful nobles, the magnates, gained greatly in authority.

Charles Robert of Anjou (1308–1342) and his son Louis the Great (1342–1382) oversaw a period of rapid growth through the fourteenth century, as Hungary expanded its trade and political ties to the west. The two kings attempted to limit the powers of the provincial magnates by building support among the cities. Louis fought the Turks successfully in 1365 at Widin, while extending his power southward toward Serbia, Wallachia, and Moldavia and northward toward Poland. After Louis's death, the magnates soon regained any lost power, as his successors either through negligence or capitulation to noble demands weakened the central authority. Leadership of the country passed to those nobles living along the frontier. One of these nobles, John Hunyadi, in the fifteenth century ruled the country as regent for the infant king Ladislas V.

Matthias Corvinus, Hunyadi's son, brought Hungary to a high point from 1458 to 1490. Effectively running the state, Matthias excelled as a soldier, statesman, and scholar. He brought some of the great thinkers from Florence and Ferrara to his court at Buda, where he accumulated a library of over 10,000 manuscripts. He encouraged the development of Hungarian literature and brought a printing press to Hungary, two years before the first press was installed in France. He also founded the university at Buda. When Corvinus died in 1490, Hungary was the most powerful state in central Europe; its influence extended from the Turkish frontier to Austria to Poland.

The Czechs. After the Magyars put an end to the Great Moravian empire in 906, the Bohemian state centered at Prague became an important element in European history. For a thousand years before the Czechs—the common name for Bohemians and Moravians—had shown a deft balance in working with the Germans to maintain the maximum amount of leeway for their own policies and desires. They cooperated with Otto I (936–973) to drive back the Hungarians and thereafter established their church hierarchy under the archbishopric of Mainz. From the eleventh through the thirteenth centuries, Bohemia benefited from the influx of German settlers and money. There was considerable cultural and economic interchange. German and Czech families intermarried and both German and Czech merchants profited from trade. By the fourteenth century, Bohemia-Moravia had a strong Czech-dominated urban life, a balanced social structure with the only Slavic middle class that would develop in eastern Europe, and the beginnings of a broad-based spirit of nationalism.

The indigenous dynasty, the Premyslid, encouraged both the urban and the rural economy and gained a diversified and rich base of political and economic support. In contrast to Hungary and Poland where the nobles held the upper hand, in Bohemia the king maintained greater autonomy. In addition, the Premyslid monarchs followed the western European custom of primogeniture, by which the throne passed to the eldest son, instead of the system of seniority in which rule passed from one brother to the next in a given generation before the next generation was given its chance. The Czech ruler Otakar II (1253–1278) was the most powerful ruler in central Europe, until Rudolf of Habsburg defeated him in 1278.

After the Premyslid dynasty ended in the first decade of the fourteenth century, John of Luxembourg (1310–1347) came to the throne. He wasted much of the local Bohemian fortune to wage battles against all available heretics. When he was killed at the battle of Crécy—a conflict he entered even though he was blind—his peers praised him for his bravery and his subjects breathed a sigh of relief.

John's son Charles IV (1347–1378) proved to be almost the complete opposite of his father. Charles was a cosmopolitan statesman: He brought the best of Europe to Prague. He made the Bohemian city the capital of the Holy Roman Empire and turned it into an ecclesiastical center, separate from the dominance of the German city of Mainz. In 1348 he established the University of Prague, the first university north of the Alps and east of the Rhine, and brought to it the finest scholars in Europe. In addition, he built up other Bohemian and Moravian cities and showed his sensitivity to the area's population by first tolerating and then encouraging the use of the Czech language.

Charles set in motion developments that his successors could not control. While he was a student at the University of Prague in the 1390s, John Hus (1369?–1415) discovered the writings of the English theologian John Wycliffe (see p. 285), which called for a simplified, faith-based, Bible-oriented church that minimized the importance of the clerical bureaucracy and the role of the pope. Two years after receiving his M.A. in 1396, Hus became dean of philosophy and then rector of the university. His sermons, preached in Czech, repeated the desires for a simpler church, centered on the Bible, in which the believer was capable of judging right from wrong on the basis of reading the scriptures.

In this 16th-century manuscript illumination, John Hus, wearing the traditional heretic's cap adorned with devils, is burned at the stake.

The church in Mainz attempted to silence Hus, and in 1415 he was summoned to the reform Council of Clermont. The authorities promised his safe passage, but when he would not recant his views, they condemned him and burned him at the stake on July 6, 1415.[11]

A common disaster led to the demise of the rising nations of both Hungary and Bohemia. The king of Hungary, who was also the king of Bohemia, met his death while fighting the Turks in 1526. Terrified at the prospects of Muslim rule, both the Czechs and the Hungarians elected the same man to their vacant thrones—Ferdinand, the *Habsburg* archduke of neighboring Austria. The Turks, however, occupied most of Hungary (which they would hold until the end of the seventeenth century), leaving Ferdinand only a narrow strip along the western border. This intertwining of national fortunes explains how the *Habsburgs* at Vienna came to rule a vast empire of Bohemians, Hungarians, and German Austrians.

Poland. The Slavic tribes that came into the Vistula basin in the seventh century formed the Polish nation. They were united by faith with the Germans, and united by race with the Russians. Geography blessed and condemned the Poles: Poland is a land of rich plains, forested mountains, and broad navigable rivers; on the other hand, it lacks any natural features that might protect the area.

The Piast prince Mieszko led the Poles into the Roman Catholic community in 966 and, coincidentally, began an ecclesiastical relationship with Rome that culminated a millennium later in the election of a Polish pope. Polish Catholicism assumed the role of the advance guard of the faith against the infidel. This crusading tradition should have encouraged the growth of a strong, centralized, national military force. Instead the Poles developed a structure that featured close ties locally between the nobles and the church, usually at the expense of the king and always at the expense of the peasants. Catholicism, nonetheless, has been an essential element of the Polish character.

This is not to say that there were no strong kings in the early centuries. Boleslav I (992–1025) and Boleslav II (1058–1079) constructed the state and extended Polish authority far to the east. Vladislav IV (1305–1333) did much to restore Poland after the Mongol invasion. But the real power in Poland was the major noble families and the church. It was apparent that in the elective monarchy, kings could have power only by placating the nobles, especially after the Piast dynasty died out in the first decade of the fourteenth century. Under the Jagiellonian dynasty, which came to power in 1386 and ruled for nearly three centuries, the nobles' strength increased.

Poland's golden age occurred during the reign of Casimir the Great (1333–1370), who oversaw the progress of all parts of the nation's life. He encouraged the arts, sponsored the codification of the law, established the University of Cracow (1364), modeled after the University of Bologna, and centered his foreign policy on the Russians and the Lithuanians.

Poland's nobles dominated the nation's social, political, and economic structures. As the nobles' activities rested almost totally in agriculture, they did not invest in much urban development; so Jews and Germans dominated the cities, where an indigenous Polish urban class developed slowly. Such a development may have suited the nobles' interests, but it condemned Poland to fall behind western Europe after the 1400s. The nobles increased their dominance in the political realm with the accession of each new Jagiellonian monarch, who had to sign increasingly onerous contracts with the nobles to gain power.

The nobles made a major stride forward with the election of Princess Jadwiga, who gained power by granting them many concessions. When she married the pagan Lithuanian prince Jagiello, who ruled as Vladislav V from 1384 to 1434, she had to grant still more. The alliance of the Polish princess and the pagan Lithuanian prince produced one of the largest powers in Europe and brought the last European nation into the Christian fold, but it also allowed the nobles to solidify their position as one of the most privileged aristocracies on the continent.

As long as Poland was surrounded by relatively weak powers, the nobles' policies of expanding their position at the expense of the central government functioned well. They put down the Teutonic Knights at the battle of Tannenberg in 1410 as well as in the Second Peace of Torun in 1466, by the terms of which the Poles obtained control of the Vistula River and a corridor north to the Baltic Sea, including the important port of Danzig. In the history of modern Europe, the Polish corridor and Danzig have played important roles.

Other branches of the Jagiellonian family ruled Bohemia and Hungary, and for a brief time at the beginning of the sixteenth century, central Europe seemed ready to unite under them, until the Turks struck at the battle of Mohacs. The Polish nobles continued to extend their control over the monarchy to such a degree that the king was unable to muster a standing army or push through a program of reform. In addition, Poland faced the hostility of the ambitious tsars of Moscow, who sought to rule over all Russians, including those in the huge Polish-Lithuanian state.

Russia

Russia's history is largely a product of its geography. The combination of a large amount of land and comparatively small population have made the domination of the peasants by the landed interests—both individuals and the state—one of the continual themes of Russian history. Russia's difficulty in gaining access to sea lanes had important economic and cultural consequences, stunting the growth of a merchant class and encouraging the formation of an inward-looking population.

Russia's landscape is marked by rivers that flow either north or south. From the Dniester to the Volga, Russia's European rivers played a key role in the development of the country. They have served as thoroughfares for trade and cultural exchange as well as routes for invasion. Not tying into the western European region, the rivers dictated a line of communication that led early Russian traders to Constantinople rather than to the west. The Volkhov and Dnieper network tied together the Varangians (also known as the Vikings) and the Greeks, through Russia, while the Volkhov and Volga system reached toward the Near East and central Asia.

Russian historians stress that the interaction of the forests, and the steppes must be considered for a true understanding of their country. The forest provided protection, a means to make a living through fur trading and honey gathering, and a chance to escape the pressures of central authorities. The steppe featured extremely rich topsoil and provided agricultural wealth, more political control, and a grass-lined highway for nomadic invaders. Where the two zones come together is where much of early Russian history took place.

It is within this geographical framework that the Russian nation developed. Six centuries before the birth of Christ Asiatic tribes following the steppe belt crossed into Russian territory. The East Slavs began moving from the area near the Pripet marshes in the sixth century, and the various clans went as far north as the White Sea, as far east as the Urals, and to the region south of Kiev. To the north, around Lake Ilmen, the Slavs established a number of trading towns such as Novgorod, from which they founded other trading bases. By the ninth century, they had accumulated sufficient wealth to attract the attention of the Varangians, who came down from the Baltic to dominate the trading routes, especially those from the Dvina to the Dnieper to Constantinople.

Kiev

Russian history is usually held to begin with the entry of the Varangians into East Slavic affairs in the 860s. The Varangian Oleg (882?–913)

established his seat of government at Kiev, at the transition point between the forest and steppe zones (see map, p. 187). During the tenth century Oleg and Sviatoslav (964–972) created a state that was the equal of contemporary France. Oleg took control of both Kiev and Novgorod and with the strength gained, he launched an attack on Constantinople. Sviastoslav carried Kievan power to the Danube and the lower Volga. He fell victim to Asiatic invaders known as the Patzinaks, but he left a state strong enough to endure almost a decade of internal power struggle.

The most important ruler in the Kievan phase of Russian history was Vladimir, who overcame his brothers to rule the state from 980 to 1015. Vladimir learned his political lessons through dealing with the Byzantines and he consolidated his power in Kiev. At first he based his rule on the pagan party and erected statues to gods such as Perun the god of thunder, Volos the god of wealth, and others. He made peace with the Volga Bulgars to the east and worked with the Byzantines against the Bulgarians in pursuit of his diplomatic and political goals.

Vladimir noted that the nations surrounding him were converting to one organized religion or another: the Poles and Hungarians to Roman Catholicism, the Khazars to Judaism, the Volga Bulgars to Islam, and the Bulgarians to Orthodoxy. His grandmother, the shrewd and skillful Olga, had accepted Orthodoxy in 956, as had other members of his family. During the 980s he sent observers to judge the various religious alternatives. According to the *Chronicles*, they visited Santa Sophia cathedral in 988 and were impressed with the power and wealth of Constantinople. They recommended Vladimir choose the Orthodox faith.

Vladimir's decision to convert to Orthodoxy brought him many advantages. As part of the negotiation package, Vladimir agreed to help the Byzantine emperor Basil against his enemies. In return, Vladimir would receive the emperor's sister in marriage. After a successful campaign, Basil delayed carrying out his part of the bargain. Vladimir moved quickly to make his point and marched into the Crimea and took the Byzantine city of Cherson. The Kiev-Byzantine agreements were finally carried out in 990. Vladimir married into the Byzantine royal family and brought his country into the orthodox orbit.

Even before "becoming a saint," the *Chronicles* tell us he destroyed the pagan statues, converted his many concubines to nuns, and forced his people into the Orthodox faith.[12] After a period of Byzantine ecclesiastical stalling and confusion, the Russians gained their own church, received their own metropolitan, and adapted Byzantine ritual, theology, and monastic practices to their own use. They also took the Byzantine governmental theories and applied them to the Russian social hierarchy.

Other than Vladimir, few great monarchs ruled during the Kievan period. Instead, the process of political fragmentation intensified during the era. The Kievan state reached its high point under Yaroslav the Wise (1019–1054). Yaroslav undertook major building projects, revised the law code, and promoted the growth of the church. He built a dynastic alliance with Henry I of France. Unfortunately Kiev did not long maintain its prestigious position. Yaroslav introduced the seniority system of succession (see p. 184), and within two generations this practice led to the political breakup of Kiev, although the city retained it theoretical superiority within Russia.

Other factors working against Kiev were attacks from both east and west and the economic decline of Constantinople. Under Vladimir Monomakh (1113–1125), Kiev reemerged briefly as a center of power, but a half century of decline soon followed. Competing centers arose at Suzdal; Galicia, where the local aristocracy dominated; Vladimir, where the prince became all-powerful; and Novgorod, where the assembled citizens (the *veche*) were the major force.

RUSSIA ABOUT 1000

--- Varangian Trade Route

The Acceptance of Christianity

Russia's conversion to Orthodoxy was a fundamental step in the division of Europe between east and west. This excerpt from "The Russian Primary Chronicle" explains how the decision was made.

6494 (986). Vladimir was visited by Volga Bulgars of Mohammedan faith. . . . Then came the Germans, asserting that they came as emissaries of the Pope. . . . The Jewish Khazars heard of these missions, and came themselves. . . . Then the Greeks sent to Vladimir a scholar. . . .

6495 (987). Vladimir summoned together his vassals and the city elders, and said to them, "Behold, the Volga Bulgars came before me urging me to accept their religion. Then came the Germans and praised their own faith; and after them came the Jews. Finally the Greeks appeared, criticizing all other faiths but commending their own, and they spoke at length, telling the history of the whole world from its beginning. . . .

. . . The Prince and all the people, chose good and wise men to the number of ten, and directed them to go first among the Volga Bulgars and inspect their faith. The emissaries went their way, and when they arrived at their destination they beheld the disgraceful actions of the Volga Bulgars and their worship in the mosque; then they returned to their own country. Vladimir then instructed them to go likewise among the Germans, and examine their faith, and finally to visit the Greeks. They thus went into Germany, and after viewing the German ceremonial, they proceeded to Tsargrad (Constaninople), where they appeared before the Emperor. . . .

Thus they returned to their own country, and the Prince called together his vassals and the elders. Vladimir then announced the return of the envoys who had been sent out, and suggested that their report be heard. He thus commanded them to speak out before his vassals. The envoys reported, "When we journeyed among the Volga Bulgars, we beheld how they worship in their temple, called a mosque, while they stand ungirt. The Volga Bulgars bows, sits down, looks hither and thither like one possessed, and there is no happiness among them, but instead only sorrow and a dreadful stench. Their religion is not good. Then we went among the Germans, and saw them performing many ceremonies in their temples; but we beheld no glory there. Then we went on to Greece, and the Greeks led us to the edifices where they worship their God, and we knew not whether we were in heaven or on earth. For on earth there is no such splendor or such beauty, and we are at a loss how to describe it. We only know that God dwells there among men, and their service is fairer than the ceremonies of other nations. . . . Then the vassals spoke and said, "If the Greek faith were evil, it would not have been adopted by your grandmother Olga, who was wiser than all other men." Vladimir then inquired where they should all accept baptism, and they replied that the decision rested with him. . . .

By divine agency, Vladimir was suffering at that moment from a disease of the eyes, and could see nothing, being in great distress. The Princess declared to him that if he desired to be relieved of this disease, he should be baptized with all speed, otherwise it could not be cured. . . . The Bishop of Kherson, together with the Princess's priests, after announcing the tidings, baptized Vladimir, and as the Bishop laid his hand upon him, he straightway received his sight. Upon experiencing this miraculous cure, Vladimir glorified God, saying, "I have now perceived the one true God." When his followers beheld this miracle, many of them were also baptized.

From Samuel H. Cross, "The Russian Primary Chronicle," *Harvard Studies and Notes in Philology and Literature* (Cambridge, MA: Harvard University Press, 1930)

Even before the Mongols totally destroyed Kiev in 1240, the era of the city's dominance was effectively over.

The Mongol Conquest of Russia

Genghis Khan united the tribesmen of Mongolia and then launched them like a thunderbolt on a campaign of world conquest. By 1240 the Mongols had conquered Kiev and other Russian principalities, and in 1242 they penetrated to the outskirts of Vienna. Western Europe seemed theirs for the taking, but the death of the great warrior in far-off Mongolia caused the Tatar, or Mongol, armies to return to the lower Volga pending the election of a new khan.

Central Europe was not threatened again, but the Mongols continued to dominate Russia from their capital at Sarai on the Volga not far from the modern city of Volgograd. The various Russian principalities were allowed to govern themselves as long as they paid tribute to the Golden Horde, as the Tatars in Russia were called. The khanate of the Golden Horde was only one of the Mongol states, however; the successors of Genghis Khan ruled an empire that stretched from Korea on the east to Poland on the west. On the south their holdings included Persia and Afghanistan, as well as the area north of what is now India and Burma.

The Mongol domination of Russia lasted in name from 1240 to 1480, and during that time much of the land was cut off from contact with the rest of the world. This led to the development of a new center of power at Moscow, which for most of the period served as collector of tribute for the Mongol court. New internal markets developed and the Orthodox church, unhampered by the Mongols, grew in strength and influence. The city of Novgorod also managed to carry on despite the oriental overlord.

Novgorod and Alexander Nevsky

Novgorod had come under the control of the Varangians in the ninth century, but in 977 the citizens received a charter granting them self-government. For the next five centuries the *veche* elected its rulers. The city boasted an aggressive and prosperous merchant class which exploited the region from the Ural Mountains to the Baltic Sea and held its own against the German merchants. Throughout, Novgorod was the equal of most of the cities found along the Baltic and North seas. In the middle of the thirteenth century, Alexander Nevsky, the prince of Novgorod, led his fellow citizens in struggles to repel the Teutonic knights and the Swedes. A few years later he showed exceptional diplomatic skill in paying homage to the Mongols, even though they had stopped sixty miles short of the city and left Novgorod untouched. At a time when the rest of Russia suffered greatly under the first phase of Mongol domination, Novgorod's oligarchy continued to rule its own town.

The city's wealth and traditions permitted the *veche* to rule. The citizens elected their princes and forced them to sign a contract setting out what they could and could not do. In the words of a typical document between ruler and city, the citizens could show their prince "the way out" if he failed to live up to the terms of his agreement. The prince could function as leader of Novgorod only as long as he physically remained within the city's limits. The city's method of government permitted the rise of major class divisions that led to more than twenty major outbreaks of violence in the thirteenth and fourteenth centuries.

Novgorod was vulnerable to the changes in trade routes that took place in the fifteenth century. Baltic commerce declined, and Novgorod came to depend on Moscow for its grain supply. Those factors, plus the class conflict, weakened the city, and in 1478 Moscow absorbed the town, seized its *veche* bell, which was used to call the citizens to meet, and snuffed out its independence.

The Grand Duchy of Moscow

The obscure fortress town of Moscow, first mentioned in the records in 1147, came to be the core of the new Russia. Even before the Mongol invasion, a large number of Slavs migrated toward the north and east. This movement continued for centuries as that frontier offered opportunities for the oppressed. This constant flow to the northeast broke new ground for the Russian state. Moscow was well placed in a protective setting of marshy ground and forests and along an important north-south river route.

One of Alexander Nevsky's sons, Daniel, founded the Grand Duchy of Moscow, and he and his successors imitated Nevsky's ability to get along with the Mongols. As the Moscow princes skillfully acknowledged their inferior position to the Mongol khans, who wanted tribute and recruits, they worked to improve their political position in relation to the other Russian principalities by monopolizing tax collection duties for the Mongols. In addition, at the beginning of the fourteenth century, the Muscovite princes ensured that the seat of the Russian Orthodox church would be in Moscow, a reflection of the city's prestige.[13]

In the first century after the Mongol invasion, the Muscovite princes showed a great deal of ambition and ability, although sometimes in an unattractive way. Ivan I *Kalita* (surname means "moneybags"), who ruled from 1328 to 1341, greatly increased the wealth and power of the city through his aggressive tax collections.

On the surface, the fourteenth century appeared to be a time of decline, with the Mongol domination and western European encroachment along Russia's western boundary. In reality, however, Russia was laying foundations for its future, with Moscow becoming the religious and political center of the country. In 1380 Dmitri Donskoi (1359–1389) defeated the Mongols at the battle of Kulikovo. Although Mongol strength was far from broken, the Russian victory had great symbolic significance. The next century was a difficult one for the Russian, with civil war and invasions threatening the Moscow-based country. However, by the middle of the fifteenth century, Moscow's leadership in Russia was firmly based and its territory had expanded greatly through purchase, war, and marriage.

Ivan the Great

The Muscovite prince who laid the foundations for a Russian national state was Ivan III known as the Great (1462–1505). He conquered Novgorod in 1478 and two years later ceased to acknowledge Mongol domination. He then began the centuries-long advance toward the south and east against the Turks and Mongols (see map, p. 173). He married Sophia Palaeologus, the niece of the last Byzantine emperor, imitated the court ceremonies of the Byzantine emperors, and claimed to be their legitimate successor. He adopted the Byzantine two-headed eagle as the symbol of the Russian throne and sometimes called himself *tsar*, derived from "Caesar." He viewed Moscow as the Third Rome, the logical successor to Rome and Constantinople as the center of Christianity.

The doctrine that the Russian tsar was the successor of the Byzantine emperors was expressed by the monk Philotheos of Pskov in the fifteenth century. "Two Romes have fallen," he wrote, "and the third stands, and fourth one there shall not be." On the basis of the conviction that they were heirs of the Byzantine tradition, Russian rulers were later to press claims to the Dardanelles and parts of southeastern Europe. Moreover, as in the idea expressed by Philotheos when he said, "You are the only tsar for Christians in the whole world,"[14] the Russian tradition would henceforth encompass a great imperial mission.

Ivan brought to Russia Italian Renaissance architects and technicians such as Aristotle Fieravanti and Pietro Antonio Solari to design and build an enormous walled palace called the Kremlin. This use of Italian artists and craftsmen had no lasting cultural impact on the mass of Russians, but it nonetheless signified an opening up to and an awareness of the West. In recognition of the need to establish a standing army, Ivan began the difficult process of building up a modern state structure. He increased restrictions on the Russian peasants, an action foreshadowing serfdom. During the fifteenth century, Ivan was the peer of his west European colleagues Henry VII of England and Louis XI of France. After three centuries of isolation, the Russians were back in touch with Europe.[15]

Ivan the Terrible

The next great ruler of Moscow was Ivan III's grandson, Ivan IV (1547–1584), called "the Terrible." Russia became more despotic as Ivan ruthlessly subordinated the great nobles to his will, exiling or executing many on the slightest pretext. With little consideration for human life, Ivan ordered the destruction of Novgorod, Russia's second city, on suspicion of treason. Another time, in a rage, he struck and killed his gifted eldest son. But, Ivan was also a far-seeing statesman who established a new code of laws, reformed the morals of the clergy, and built the fabulous St. Basil's Cathedral that still stands in Moscow's Red Square.

During Ivan's reign eastern Russia was recovered from the Tatars, and Cossack pioneers then crossed the Ural Mountains in their push to the Pacific—a movement that can be compared with the simultaneous expansion of western Europe across the Atlantic. Ivan's efforts to reach the Baltic and establish trade relations with western Europe were forcibly stopped by Sweden and Poland. Later, however, he was able to inaugurate direct trade with the West by granting English merchants trading privileges at the White Sea port of Archangel (Arkhangelsk) in the far north.

Ivan's death in 1584 was followed by the Time of Troubles, a period of civil wars over the succession and resurgence of the power of the nobility. Both Poland and Sweden intervened in Russian affairs, and their invasions across an indistinct frontier that contains no major natural barriers demonstrated again the danger from the west and contributed to Russia's growing tendency to withdraw into its own distinctive heritage. Order was restored in 1613 when Michael Romanov, the grandnephew of Ivan the Terrible, was elected to the throne by a national assembly that included representatives from fifty cities. The Romanov dynasty ruled Russia until 1917.

Conclusion

In the thousand years after the fall of Rome, the nations of eastern Europe came into being. The first and most important state was the Byzantine Empire that preserved and enlarged the heritage of Western civilization, Christianized much of eastern Europe, and held off the Persian and Arab assaults. During its thousand-year existence, the Byzantine Empire enjoyed eight centuries of economic, intellectual, political, and military dominance. Perhaps its longest-lasting effect was on the Slavs.

As the Slavs moved to their new homelands from the fourth through the ninth centuries, they came under the influence of dominant outside

A contemporary woodcut of Ivan IV, The Terrible, the fierce despot of 16th-century Russia.

Ivan the Terrible

Ivan received the title "the terrible" for good reason. As was the case with many Renaissance despots, he was quick to use brutal methods to enforce his will. His treatment of Novgorod is one such example.

On Monday the second day of January, in the year 7079 [1570], after the creation of the world, the day of commemoration of the Holy Father and Roman Pope Silvester, the illustrious Tsar and Grand Prince Ivan Vasilevich, lord of All Russia, sent an advance guard of the army in forced march toward Great Novgorod. The army units consisted of *boyars*, army commanders, princes, nobles, courtiers, and an uncountable multitude of other troops.

. . . They erected sentinel towers near the posts and decreed that the inhabitants of the city be closely watched in order that not one human being could escape from the city.

On Saturday, the day after his arrival, the illustrious Tsar and Grand Prince Ivan Vasilevich, lord of All Russia, gave the order that the abbots, clergy, and monks who had previously been brought to the place of execution should be beaten to death with clubs. After they had all been killed, he ordered that each be buried at the monastery where he had resided. . . .

The Tsar commanded that the powerful *boyars*, the important merchants, the administrative officials, and the citizens of every rank be brought before him, together with their wives and children. The Tsar ordered that they be tortured in his presence in various spiteful, horrible, and inhuman ways. After many various unspeakable and bitter tortures, the Tsar ordered that their bodies be tormented and roasted with fire in refined ways. And the Tsar commanded his nobles to bind the hands and feet and heads of these tortured and roasted human beings with fine ropes in various ways. He ordered that each man be tied to a sled, be dragged to the Volkhov bridge behind the fast-moving sleds, and be thrown into the Volkhov River from the bridge. The Tsar ordered that their wives and children be brought to the Volkhov bridge, where a high platform had been erected. He commanded that they be chained on the arms and legs and that the children be tied to their mothers and then be thrown from the platform into the waters of the Volkhov River. Meanwhile, the Tsar's men, the nobles and soldiers, moved about in small boats on the Volkhov River, armed with spears, lances, hooks, and axes. When the people, men and women of all ages, surfaced, they were stabbed by the soldiers with hooks, lances, and spears, or they were struck with axes. In a horrible manner they were submerged without mercy in the depths of the river, and abandoned to a terrible and bitter death.

Because of our sins, this unspeakable shedding of Christian blood, caused by the excessive anger of the Tsar, continued uninterrupted each day for five weeks or more. . . .

Afterwards, the Orthodox Tsar and Grand Prince rode with all of his people and warriors through all of Novgorod and its suburbs, pitilessly robbing all the inhabitants, including the women, breaking windows and doors, and demolishing the houses and manors. (For several weeks similar treatment was given the region under control of Great Novgorod. The surviving citizens of Novgorod were pardoned, with the exception of those whom the Tsar had transported to Moscow and ordered beheaded.)

From *Polnoe Sobranie Russkikh Letopisei* (Complete Collection of Russian Chronicles) (St. Petersburg, 1885). Vol. 3, pp. 254–262. *Trans. Basil Dmytryshyn, in Medieval Russia: A source Book, 900–1700* (Holt, Rinehart, and Winston, Inc., New York, 1967.(pp. 203–207.

powers. In Russia and the Balkans, Byzantine patterns and traditions shaped the Slavs' lives. To the north, the Roman Catholic faith, as carried by the Germans, helped shape different national characteristics. The movement of peoples in eastern and southern Europe and the rise and fall of states culminated in the emergence of Poland, Bohemia, Hungary, and Russia. Russia was for years under the rule of the Mongols, but when the dukes of Moscow assumed leadership of the Russians, a long and eventually successful campaign was initiated against Mongol dominance.

By the fifteenth century, each of the peoples of eastern Europe had enjoyed a brief moment of triumph. Byzantium had disappeared from the scene and the Balkans were under Turkish control, but Russia, Poland, Bohemia, and Hungary remained as dominant powers, capable of playing important roles in the development of modern Europe.

Suggestions for Reading

An excellent short introduction to Byzantium is S. Runciman's classic *Byzantine Civilization* (Meridian, 1969). J. Hussey's *The Byzantine World** (Torchbooks, 1957) is clear and lively. For an exhaustive treatment, see the *Cambridge Medieval History*, IV, *The Byzantine Empire*, Pt. 1, "Byzantium and Its Neighbours"; Pt. 2, "Government, Church, and Civilization." George Ostrogorsky's *History of the Byzantine State* (Rutgers, 1957) provides the best institutional overview. John W. Barker, *Justinian and the Later Roman Empire* (University of Wisconsin, 1966); R. Browning, *Justinian and Theodora* (Praeger, 1971); and G. Downey, *Constantinople in the Age of Justinian* (Oklahoma, 1968) give complementary analyses of the sixth century. Romilly Jenkins, *Byzantium: The Imperial Centuries* (Vintage, 1969) is a beautifully written treatment of medieval Byzantium. Francis Dvornik's works on the Photian schism (see Note #6) and *The Slavs in Europen History and Civilization* (Rutgers, 1970) address the matters of conversion. C. M. Brand's *Byzantium Confronts the West, 1184–1204* (Harvard, 1968) and D. Queller, ed., *The Latin Conquest of Constantinople* (Wiley, 1971) describe the tragedy of the Crusades for Byzantium and complement Runciman's three-volume *History of the Crusades* (Penguin, 1965). Donald Nicol's *The Last Centuries of Byzantium* (St. Martin's, 1972) discusses the empire in its state of weakness. D. Talbot Rice, *Art of the Byzantine Era* (Oxford, 1962) gives a competent overall assessment of Byzantine aesthetics. Andre Grabar, *Byzantium* (Thames and Hudson, 1966) is a beautifully illustrated, thorough discussion of art and architecture before 600. H. Magoulias, *Byzantine Christianity: Emperor, Church, and the West* (Rand McNally, 1970) and T. Ware, *The Orthodox Church* (Penguin, 1963) are two good surveys.

G. Vernadsky, *Kievan Russia,** 2nd ed. (Yale, 1973) is detailed and authoritative. G. Fedotov's *The Russian Religious Mind: Kievan Christianity, The Tenth to the Thirteenth Centuries* (Torchbooks, 1975) notes the impact of orthodoxy on Russian civilization. See the Notes for useful primary readings of Villehardouin, Procopius, and the Russian Chronicles. John Fennell, *The Crisis of Medieval Russia 1200–1304* (Longman, 1983) and Robert Crummey, *The Formation of Muscovy* (Longman, 1983) are two concise surveys of Russian history. Oscar Halecki's *Borderlands of Western Civilization* (Ronald, 1952) gives the outlines of East European history, especially the northern region. See also N. Riasanovsky, *History of Russia*, 2nd ed. (Oxford, 1969); I. Grey *Ivan III and the Unification of Russia** (Collier, 1964); and S. Graham, *Ivan the Terrible* (ShoeString, 1968).

*Indicates a less expensive paperbound edition.

Notes

1. Alan Cameron, *Circus Factions: Blues and Greens at Rome and Byzantium* (Oxford: Clarendon Press, 1976), pp. 310–311.
2. Procopius of Caesarea, *History of the Wars*, I, XXIV, 36–38, trans. S. R. Rosenbaum in Charles Diehl, *Theodora: Empress of Byzantium* (New York: Frederick Ungar, 1972), pp. 87–88.
3. George Ostrogorsky, *History of the Byzantine State*, trans. Joan Hussey (New Brunswick, NJ: Rutgers University Press, 1957), pp. 86–90.
4. A.N. Stratos, *Byzantium in the Seventh Century*, I, trans. Marc Ogilvie Grant (Amsterdam: Adolf M. Hakkert, 1968), pp. 37–39.
5. Romilly Jenkins, *Byzantium: The Imperial Centuries, A.D. 610–1071* (New York: Vintage Books, 1969), pp. 90–104.
6. Francis Dvornik, *The Photian Schism: History and Legend* (New Brunswick, NJ: Rutgers University Press, 1970), passim.
7. For an eastern perspective, see Amin Maalouf, *The Crusades Through Arab Eyes* (New York: Schocken Books, 1985).
8. Geoffrey de Villehardouin, *The Conquest of Constantinople* in M. R. B. Shaw, *Chronicles of the Crusades* (Baltimore: Penguin Books, 1963), pp. 79, 92.
9. Steven Runciman, *The Fall of Constantinople* (Cambridge: Cambridge University Press, 1965), passim.
10. René Ristelhueber, *Histoire des Peuples Balkaniques* (Paris: Arthème Fayard, 1950), pp. 1–107.
11. S. Harrison Thomson, *Europe in Renaissance and Reformation* (New York: Harcourt, Brace & World, 1963), pp. 191–211.
12. *The Russian Primary Chronicle*, trans. S. H. Cross and O. P. Sherbowitz—Wetzor (Cambridge: The Mediaeval Academy of America, 1953), pp. 110–118.
13. John Fennell, *The Crisis of Medieval Russia, 1200–1304* (London: Longman, 1983), passim.
14. Quoted in M. Cherniavsky, " 'Holy Russia': A Study in the History of an Idea," *The American Historical Review* 63, no. 3 (April 1958), p. 625.
15. Donald Treadgold, *The West in Russia and China*, I (Cambridge: Cambridge University Press, 1973), pp. 2–4.

The Rising Flood of Asian Culture, 300–1300

After the fall of Rome, eight centuries passed before Europe began its transition to modernity. The civilizing process was more continuous in Asia, high cultures flourishing in both India and China between 300 and 1300. Their wealth and cultural achievements helped prepare the way for Western revival after the fourteenth century.

This was a time of preservation, consolidation, and innovation for the old Asian civilizations. Earlier values and institutions were reaffirmed so effectively that the characteristic Hindu and Chinese culture patterns have endured down to modern times, despite frequent invasions of both homelands. Moreover, each civilization produced significant contributions to the world's common culture. India made remarkable advances in mathematics, medicine, chemistry, textile production, and imaginative literature. China excelled in political organization, scholarship, and the arts, while producing such revolutionary technical inventions as printing, explosive powder, and the mariner's compass.

The preserving function of the Indo-Chinese heritage was reinforced by the roles of women. Although developing militarism and elitism emphasized masculine views and often contributed to the abuse of women as sex objects and playthings, older feminine values lingered on, particularly within families, where women continued to maintain traditional values and make important decisions. With the possible exception of Muslim women in India, they played more significant social roles than in Europe or the Middle East.

Cultural growth in the old Asian centers led naturally toward diffusion into other locations and the emergence of fringe civilizations. In Southeast Asia, new civilizations rose as contacts with India and China increased through trade, missionary efforts, colonization, and conquest. First Korea, and then Japan after the seventh century, imported cultural bases from China. Similarly, Central Asian nomads—Turks, Uighurs, Mongols, and numerous other steppe peoples—who were just beginning to create urban civilizations in this period, learned as merchants, subjects, or conquerors from the Chinese. During their briefly maintained states, climaxed by the great Mongol Empire in the thirteenth and fourteenth centuries, they passed on to Arabs and Europeans many items in the expanding Asian culture stream.

India: The Imperial Guptas

Through most of the fourth and fifth centuries the monarchs of the Gupta dynasty ruled in what has been termed India's classical age. For a century, the land had suffered political disintegration while Buddhism partially replaced the old Vedic religion of the brahmins. The Guptas brought unity and fostered a revival of traditional religion, Sanskrit literature, and native art. During this period, Hindu culture spread widely through Southeast Asia, as we shall see in chapter 14. After the fifth century, India became a mélange of warring states, some ruled by Muslim dynasties, but the Hindu tradition continued to exert its influence.

The Gupta State and Society

The Gupta state began its rise with the accession to power of Chandra Gupta I (not related to

Chandragupta Maurya) in 320. His son and grandson were successful conquerors, extending the boundaries of an original petty state in Maghada until it included most of northern India from the Himalayas to the Narbada River and east to west from sea to sea (see map, right). Within this domain, the Gupta monarchs developed a political structure along ancient Mauryan lines, with provincial governors, district officials, state-controlled industries, and an imperial secret service. This centralized system was effective only on royal lands, however, which were much less extensive than in Mauryan times. With a smaller bureaucracy, the Gupta rulers depended upon local authorities and communal institutions, raising revenues primarily through tribute and military forces by feudal levy.

Peace and stabilized government under the later Guptas increased agricultural productivity and foreign trade. Flourishing commerce with

INDIA 400–650 A. D.

☐ Gupta Empire, 413 A.D.

■ Area Under Gupta Influence

▬ Harsha's Dominions, 606 A.D.

Gupta sculpture reached a pinnacle of refinement at Sārnāth, where this high-relief statue of the Buddha preaching the First Sermon was discovered.

Rome in the last decades of the fourth century brought a great influx of gold and silver into the Empire. Hindu traders were also active in Southeast Asia, particularly in Burma and Cambodia, contributing to the emergence of civilizations there (see ch. 14). The resulting prosperity of India was reflected in the erection of great public buildings and in the luxuries of the elite, particularly at the Gupta court.

Although the Gupta rulers generally practiced religious toleration, they favored Hinduism, providing the brahmins with imperial patronage, both in wealth and prestige. As it crystallized into a final form, Hinduism thus became dominant over Buddhism. By recognizing the validity of all religious experience—and particularly by incorporating basic Buddhist doctrines, such as nonviolence and respect for life—the traditional religion developed tremendous tenacity, lasting into modern times. The Hindu revival of this period brought a great upsurge of devotion to old gods, such as Vishnu and Siva, in a popular quest for personal identity and serenity. This new religious fervor was reflected in a wave of popular religious books, the *Puranas*, which emphasized in simple tales, the compassion of the personal gods. By promoting such emotional Hinduism, the Gupta monarchs gained great favor among all classes of their subjects.

Much of our knowledge of Gupta society comes from the journal of a Buddhist monk, Fa-Hsien, who traveled in India for fifteen years at the opening of the fifth century. He reported the people to be happy, relatively free of government oppression, and inclined towards courtesy and charity. Other references in the journal, however, indicate that the caste system was rapidly assuming its basic features, including "untouchability," the social isolation of a lowest class that is doomed to menial labor. The caste system certainly provided security of status and occupation for many, but it also justified economic and social inequality. Gupta material prosperity was monopolized by the elite.

Class inequality was matched by a growing inequality of the sexes. Gupta women still received the respect of their husbands and children; some women, particularly those of the upper class, were also active in the arts, commerce, and professions. Sometimes, upon the death of rulers, their queens became capable regents for infant sons. But growing wealth and power during the Gupta period steadily eroded the traditional status of women. Girls were contracted to arranged marriages at early ages and forced to live with the families of future husbands. Subordination of women was most evident in developing customs that denied widows the right to remarry and even encouraged them to commit suicide, in the *suttee* ceremony, by burning themselves on the funeral pyres of their husbands.

Gupta Art and Literature

Indian art of the Gupta period depicts an age of classical brilliance, mingling stability and serenity with an erotic love of life. The Gupta artistic spirit is perhaps best expressed in the twenty-eight monasteries and temples at Ajanta, hewn out of a solid rock cliff and portraying in their wall frescoes not only the life of Buddha

Interior of the rock-cut temple at Ajanta, dating from the 2nd-century B.C. The Ajanta caves were Buddhist sanctuaries containing both assembly halls and monasteries.

but also life in general: lovers embracing, beds of colorful flowers, musicians, dancers, and a young lady preparing her toilette. Numerous lightly clad women reveal the beauty of the human form, attesting to the traditional belief of Gupta artists that the divine is not separate from the human nor the spirit from the body.

The Gupta era was also a golden age for literature, written in Sanskrit, the ancient language of the brahmins. Authors supported by royal patronage poured forth a wealth of sacred, philosophical, dramatic, poetic, and prose works. Among the latter were fables, fairy tales, and adventure stories featuring a wide range of characters—thieves, courtesans, hypocritical monks, and strange beasts. The *Panchatantra* is a collection of stories about animals facing human problems. A most renowned literary figure

The Farmer's Wife

This tale, from the fourth book of the *Panchatantra,* presents the typical moral twist but does not have animal characters. Like other stories in this book, it does not well fit a "framing story" and was probably added to the original work as an addendum.

There was once a farmer who lived with his wife in a certain place. And because the husband was old, the wife was forever thinking of lovers, and could not possibly be contented at home. Her one idea was strange men.

Now a rogue who lived by pilfering, noticed her and said: "You lovely creature, my wife is dead, and I am smitten with love at the sight of you. Pray enrich me with love's perfect treasure."

And she said: "You beautiful man, if you feel that way, my husband has a great deal of money, and he is so old that he cannot stir. I will bring it, so that I may go somewhere with you and enjoy the delights of love."

"That is satisfactory to me," he replied. "Suppose you hasten to this spot at dawn, so that we may go together to some fascinating city where life may bear for me its perfect fruit." "Very well," she agreed, and went home with laughing countenance.

Then at night, while her husband slept, she took all the money, and reached the rendezvous at dawn. The rogue, for his part, put her in front, started south, and traveled two leagues, gaily enjoying the delights of conversation with her. But when he saw a river ahead, he reflected: "What am I to do with this middle-aged female? Besides, someone might perhaps pursue her. I will just take her money and be off."

So he said to her: "My dear, this is a great river, hard to cross. I will just take the money and put it safe on the far bank, then return to carry you alone on my back, and so transport you in comfort." "Do so, my belovèd," said she.

So he took the money to the last penny, and then he said: "Dearest, hand me your dress and your wrap, too, so that you may travel through the water unembarrassed."

And when she did so, the rogue took the money and the two garments and went to the place he had in mind.

Then the farmer's wife sat down woebegone on the river-bank, digging her two hands into her throat. At that moment a she-jackal came to the spot, carrying a piece of meat. As she came up and peered about, a great fish leaped from the water and was stranded on the bank. On spying him, she dropped the meat and darted at the fish. Whereupon a vulture swooped from the sky and flew off with the meat. And the fish, perceiving the jackal, struggled into the river. So the she-jackal had her pains for nothing, and as she gazed after the vulture, the naked woman smiled and said:

"You poor she-jackal!

The vulture has your meat;
*   The water holds your fish:*
Of fish and flesh forlorn,
*   What further do you wish?"*

And the she-jackal, perceiving the woman was equally forlorn, having lost her husband's money and her lover, said with a sneer:
"You nakéd thing!

Your cleverness is twice
*   As great as mine, 'twould seem;*
Lover and husband lost,
*   You sit beside the stream"*

"The Farmer's Wife," from *The Panchatantra,* translated from the Sanskrit by Arthur W. Ryder, (Chicago: University of Chicago Press, 1956), pp. 412–14.

of this era was India's greatest poet and dramatist, Kalidasa (c. 400–455), who wrote at the court of Chandra Gupta II. His work best known in the West is *Shakuntala*, a drama of lovers separated by adversity for many years and then by chance reunited. The play is full of vivid imagery and a loving sympathy for nature.

Gupta Scholarship and Science

The Gupta era brought a great stimulus to learning. Old Vedic schools were revitalized, and Buddhist centers, which had spread after the Maurya period, were given new support. The foremost Indian university was at Nalanda, founded in the fifth century. Although Buddhist in its basic orientation, it tolerated all creeds and attracted students from all over Asia. The organization of Hindu philosophy into six orthodox systems, with a common concern for salvation, owed much to the Hindu-Buddhist dialogue in the Gupta universities.

Accomplishments in art, literature, scholarship, and philosophy were not more remarkable than those in science. The most famous Gupta scientist was the astronomer-mathematician, Aryabhatta, who lived in the fifth century. He discussed (in verse) quadratic equations, solstices, and equinoxes, along with the spherical shape of the earth and its rotation. Other Hindu mathematicians of this period popularized the use of a special sign for zero, later passing it on to the Arabs.

In addition to employing their skills in Yoga, Hindu physicians sterilized wounds and prepared for surgery by fumigation, performed Caesarean operations, set broken bones, and practiced plastic surgery. They used drugs then unknown in the West, such as chaulmoogra oil for treating leprosy, a practice still used today.

Achievements in pure science were matched by practical applications. Gupta craftsmen made soap, cement, superior dyes, and the finest tempered steel in the world.

India in Turmoil

For eight hundred years after the Gupta era ended, India languished in an abyss of political confusion, with only temporary periods of political unity. First Huns, then Turks, and finally Mongols invaded the land; their wars against Hindu kings and among themselves, as well as internal Hindu conflicts, contributed largely to the general decline. Religious extremism and corruption also played a part. Hindu sectarianism increased, the brahmins grew more arrogant and greedy, concern for personal salvation lessened personal initiatives, the poor became more oppressed, the economy faltered, and cities lost population. Some art and literature survived, but scientific investigation almost stopped. Not until the sixteenth century would Indian culture regain Gupta levels.

While their kindred ravaged Europe in the late 400s, Huns invaded northwestern India, shattering the Gupta Empire. They were stopped by a Hindu confederation, but this terrible disruption was followed by more incursions of Central Asians, who intermarried with local populations to produce a class of fighting aristocrats known as Rajputs. These fierce warriors carved out kingdoms among the Hindu states of northern India.

A bronze statue of the elephant-headed deity, Ganesha, the god of good luck. His fat body symbolizes prosperity, which he brings to those who worship him.

The resultant near-anarchy was alleviated for a while in the seventh century by Harsha, a strong Hindu leader. In six years he reconquered much of what had been the Gupta Empire, restoring order and partially reviving learning. Unfortunately, Harsha left no heir when he died in 647, and the country again dissolved in civil war and confusion. This paved the way, in 712, for an Arab conquest of Sind, the coastal gateway to northwest India.

Muslim Invasions of India

The Arab Caliphate, which annexed Sind, threw its shadow over the Middle East in the 700s; as it weakened during succeeding centuries, various Central Asian peoples, notably the Turks, entered the area. The Turkish flood into Persia and Mesopotamia spilled over into India during the late tenth century. Hindu-Muslim conflict was by then centuries old; but the Turkish invaders, only partially civilized and recently converted Muslims, were most zealous in pursuing a holy crusade against infidels. They were also fearsome marauders. One of their leaders, the ruler of a small Afghan state, annexed the Punjab in 1022. For another two centuries, fighting continued between Turks and Rajputs, until Muhammed Ghuri, another Muslim commander, conquered most of northern India.

After Muhammed Ghuri was assassinated in 1206, one of his generals seized power as sultan at Delhi, setting the stage for another unification of India. At the peak of its power in the thirteenth century, the Delhi Sultanate held not only the north but part of the Deccan in the south (see map, right). Its political unity and power, however, was often wasted or abused. While often patrons of the arts, builders of splendid monuments, and proponents of philosophy, the sultans regularly murdered their political rivals, tortured prisoners, and wasted resources. By the middle of the fourteenth century, they had lost control of the south and were hard-pressed by various Hindu and Muslim challengers. Although experiencing brief periods of revival, the regime continued to disintegrate internally before it was destroyed by the Turko-Mongol Tamerlane in 1388.

Muslim rule in India brought about some cultural integration, particularly among ordinary

DELHI SULTANATE

Delhi Sultanate, 1236

Empire of Muhammed ibn Tuglhuq, 1335

0   500
MILES

Hindus. Many of the people found emotional appeal in the Muslim faith, sought to lighten their taxes, hoped to raise their caste status, or tried to qualify for public service by converting to Islam. An example of the cultural integration is the creation of Urdu, a spoken language using Persian, Arabic, and Turkish words within Hindu grammatical constructions.

Assimilation of Islamic values led to a further degradation in the status of Hindu women. Girls were married younger, education of females was practically eliminated, widows were absolutely prohibited from remarrying, and *suttee* became an almost universal custom. Very few Hindu queens administered affairs of state after the eleventh century. Muslim discrimination in sexual morality also penetrated Hindu culture. Adultery and infidelity became criminal offenses for women (but not for men), and the veiling of upper-class women (*purdah*), which had earlier been only sporadic among Hindu women, became the norm. Perhaps the most dramatic illustration of women's lowered status came in the refusal of Hindu society to accept returning women who been captured and carried off to Muslim harems.

Cultural synthesis, however, could not eliminate the Hindu-Muslim contention over polytheism, religious images, and closed castes. Aristocratic Hindu leaders desperately resisted Islam, often suffering cruel persecution. After the Delhi Sultanate, life in India was largely divided into Hindu and Muslim streams, which mingled only superficially.

Hindu India During the Delhi Sultanate

Southern India during the period of the Delhi Sultanate was governed by a number of struggling Hindu monarchies, each organized on a semi-feudal basis and heavily dependent upon peasant agriculture. Some of these fell to the sultan's armies, but a few survived. One such kingdom was Chola, on the southeast coast. By the eleventh century it had become a great maritime power, prominent in the trade and politics of Southeast Asia. As India grew weaker prior to the Mongol invasions of the thirteenth century, Chola and the other petty Hindu states of the south continued to maintain a semblance of their ancient culture in Sanskrit texts and massive temple architecture, with its characteristic symbolic statues.

Chinese Continuity: T'ang and Sung

In contrast with India or medieval Europe, China achieved both political and cultural continuity between the sixth and thirteenth centuries. Political unity was attained briefly under the Sui dynasty (589–618), consolidated under the T'ang (618–906), and maintained percariously in the south under the Sung (960–1279). Despite periods of internal disruption, this political structure, recreated from Han precedents, survived repeated invasions and civil wars. Its stability resulted from a common written language; an ancient family structure, guided by mature and conservative-minded matriarchs; an enduring Confucian tradition; and a Chinese elite of hereditary nobles and scholar-bureaucrats, who

shared power while subtly contending for dominance. Their efforts promoted a flowering of Chinese culture during the expansionary T'ang period, when China was the largest state in the world, and during the ensuing economic prosperity of the Sung.

Before the T'ang Dynasty

Following the fall of the Han Empire in 220, China suffered three centuries of disorder and division. Various nomadic peoples, mainly Huns (Hsiung-nu) and Turks (Yueh-chih), pillaged northern China, setting up petty states. Because these were administered mostly by Chinese, they gradually absorbed Chinese culture. Central and southern China, escaped these intrusions and experienced relative prosperity and an expanding population, resulting from an influx of northern emigrés and an increasingly productive rice cultivation. The growing economy supported a series of political regimes at Nanking, all maintaining classical traditions and the notion of a united state under a "Son of Heaven."

During turbulent times in the fourth century, as the old Confucian ideal of a balanced social order appeared less realistic, Buddhism had spread rapidly in China. Its promise of salvation, particularly to common people, its special compassionate appeal to women, its offer to meek men of monastic security in troubled times, and its long incubation within Chinese culture, all ensured its popularity. Although challenged by native Taoism (which adopted many of its ideas), scorned by some Confucian intellectuals, and periodically persecuted by rulers jealous of its strength, Buddhism ultimately won adherents among all of its critics, especially among the barbarian monarchs of the north, including the Sui emperors. Most of them patronized Buddhism by building splendid temples and generously endowing monasteries.

The two Sui monarchs, tempered in the rough frontier wars of the north, reconquered all of China, thus ending nearly four centuries of localized confusion. They established an imperial military force and a land-based militia, centralized the administration, and revived a civil service recruited through an examination system. They also started building a canal, a forerunner of the later famous Grand Canal (see map, p. 201), to link the rice-growing Yangtse basin with northern China. Their unpredictable cruelty, oppression and conscription of labor for the canal, led to a rebellion that ended the dynasty; nevertheless, the Sui emperors deserve much credit for later T'ang successes.

Political Developments Under the Rising T'ang Dynasty, 618–756

During the early T'ang period to 756, China attained a new pinnacle of glory. The first three emperors subjugated Turkish Central Asia, made Tibet a dependency, and conquered Annam (North Vietnam). This era of growth and grandeur was marked by the extraordinary reign of the able Empress Wu, a concubine of the second and third emperors, who controlled the government for twenty years after the latter's death, torturing and executing her political opponents but also consolidating the T'ang Dynasty (see map below). In the process, she greatly weakened the old aristocracy by favoring Buddhism and strengthening the examination system for civil servants. Moreover, she decisively defeated the northern Koreans, making Korea a loyal vassal

The Empress Wu, the only woman to rule China in name as well as in fact. She usurped the imperial throne and assumed the special title of "Holy Mother Divine Imperial One."

state. Largely because she was a woman and a usurper, she found little favor with some Chinese historians and politicians, who emphasized her vices, particularly her many favorites and lovers. Her overthrow in 712 ended an era of contention

THE T'ANG DYNASTY

and ushered in a new age of cultural development in the long reign of Emperor Hsuan-tsung (713–756).

T'ang rulers perfected a highly centralized government, utilizing a complex bureaucracy organized in specialized councils, boards, and ministries, all responsible directly to the emperor. Local government functioned under fifteen provincial governors, aided by subordinates down to the district level. Military commanders supervised tribute collections in semi-autonomous conquered territories. Office-holders throughout the Empire were, by the eighth century, usually degree-holders from government schools and universities, who had qualified by passing the regularly scheduled examinations. These scholar-bureaucrats were steeped in Confucian conservatism but were more efficient than the remaining minority of aristocratic hereditary officials. One notable T'ang institution was a nationalized land register, designed to check the growth of large estates, guarantee land to peasants, and relate their land tenure to both their taxes and their militia service. Until well into the eighth century, when abuses began to show, the system worked to merge the interests of state and people.

T'ang Economy and Society

The T'ang economy was carefully regulated. The government maintained monopolies on salt, liquor, and tea and used licensing in an attempt to discourage undesirable enterprises. In operating its monopolies, it issued receipts that circulated among merchants. These receipts were antecedents of the paper money that came into use under the Sung. The state also built roads and canals to facilitate commerce. Perhaps the most functional of these projects was the magnificent Grand Canal, stretching some 650 miles between Hangchow and Tientsin. Other typical government enterprises included post houses and restaurants for official travelers, as well as public granaries for insurance against famine.

Economic productivity, both agricultural and industrial, rose steadily during the early T'ang period. The introduction of tea and wet rice from Annam turned the Yangtse area into a vast irrigated food bank and the economic base for T'ang power. More food and rising population

brought increasing manufactures. Chinese techniques in the newly discovered craft of paper-making, along with iron-casting, porcelain production, and silk processing, improved tremendously and spread west through the Middle East.

Foreign trade and influence increased significantly under the T'ang emperors in a development that would continue through the Sung era. Chinese control in Central Asia reopened the old overland silk route; but as porcelains became the most profitable exports and could not be easily transported by caravan, they swelled the volume of sea trade through southeast Asia. Most of this trade left from southern ports, particularly from Canton, where more than 100,000 aliens—Hindus, Persians, Arabs, and Malays—handled the goods. Foreign merchants were equally visible at Ch'ang-an, the T'ang capital and eastern terminus of the silk route.

Although largely state-controlled and aristocratic, T'ang society was more dynamic and flexible than those of the past. It was particularly responsive to new foreign stimuli, which it eagerly absorbed. A strongly pervasive Buddhism, a rising population, and steady urbanization fostered this open-mindedness. Many city

In the T'ang Dynasty, earthenware models of people and objects, like this one of traders with a bullock and cart, were buried with the dead. Such objects were believed to be useful in the afterlife.

populations exceeded 100,000; four cities had more than a million people; and one of these—the capital of Ch'ang-an—was the largest city in the world. Commercial prosperity naturally benefitted the merchants, but they were still considered socially inferior; merchants often used their wealth to educate their sons for the civil service examination, thus promoting the rising class of scholar-bureaucrats. The latter, as they acquired land, gained status and power at the expense of the old aristocratic families. Conditions among artisans and the expanding mass of peasants improved somewhat, but life remained hard and sometimes unpredictably disastrous.

In the early T'ang era, women had been considered equal enough socially to play polo with the men. By the eighth century, however, T'ang legal codes had imposed severe punishments for wifely disobedience or infidelity to husbands. New laws also limited womens' rights to divorce, inheritance of property, and remarriage as widows. Women were still active in the arts and literature but were excluded from civil examinations for public service. Although some wielded influence and power at royal courts, many were confined to harems, a practice without precedent in Chinese traditions and probably borrowed from Islam in the late T'ang era. These obvious regressions were only partially balanced by the continued high status and authority of older women within the families.

T'ang Literature and Scholarship

A fresh flowering of literature occurred during the early T'ang period. It followed naturally from a dynamic society, but it was also greatly furthered by the development of paper-making and the invention in about 600 of block printing in China, whence the technique soon spread to Korea and Japan. Movable type, which would later revolutionize Europe, was little used in East Asia during this period, because all writing was done in word characters. Still, printing helped meet a growing demand for the religious and educational materials generated by Buddhism and the examination system.

T'ang scholarship is best remembered for historical writing. Chinese of this period firmly believed that lessons from the past could be guides to the future. As an early T'ang emperor remarked, "by using a mirror of brass, you may . . . adjust your cap; by using antiquity as a mirror you may . . . foresee the rise and fall of empires."[1] History itself came under investigation during this era, for example in *The Understanding of History*, a work which stressed the need for analysis and evaluation in the narration of events.

Writers produced works of all types, but poetry was the accepted medium, composed and repeated by emperors, scholars, singing courtesans, and common people in the marketplaces. T'ang poetry was marked by ironic humor, deep sensitivity to human feeling, concern for social justice, and a near-worshipful love of nature. Three of the most famous among some 3000 recognized poets of the era were Po Chu, Tu Fu, and Li Po. The last, perhaps the greatest of them all, was an admitted lover of pleasure, but he could pinpoint life's mysteries, as in the following poetic expression of Taoist philosophy (see p. 117):

Chuang Tzu in a dream
 became a butterfly,
And the butterfly became
 Chuang Tzu at waking.
Which was the real—the
 butterfly or the man?[2]

A painting from the Sung Dynasty showing the poet Li Po in repose. Li Po's poetry is renowned for its exquisite imagery, rich allusions, and beautiful cadence.

This glazed earthenware figurine of a Bactrian camel dates from the T'ang Dynasty of the early 8th century.

T'ang Sculpture and Painting

The T'ang literary revival was paralleled by movements in painting and sculpture. The plastic arts, dealing with both religious and secular subjects, became a major medium for the first time in China. Small tomb statues depicted both Chinese and foreign life with human realism, verve, and diversity. Religious statuary, even in Buddhist shrines, showed a strong humanistic emphasis, often juxtaposed with the naive sublimity of Buddhas carved in the Gandara (Greek Hellenistic) style of northwest India. Similar themes were developed in T'ang painting, but the traditional preoccupation with nature prevailed in both northern and southern landscape schools. The most famous T'ang painter was Wu Tao-tzu, whose landscapes and religious scenes were produced at the court of the Emperor Ming Huang in the early eighth century.

T'ang Decline

After the middle of the eighth century, T'ang China began to decline. A warning came in 751, when Arabs reconquered the Tarim basin. Meanwhile, as the fiscal system weakened under attack from various vested interests, military governors took over control of outlying provinces. One of them, a former favorite named An Lu-shan, marched on Ch'ang-an in 755. The aged Emperor Hsuan-tsung, while fleeing the capital, was forced by his troops to approve the execution of his favorite concubine, who had dominated his court and weakened his dynasty. According to legend, he died of sorrow less than a month later.

The rebellion was put down after seven years, but the disruption was so extensive that the late T'ang emperors never recovered their former power. Following a breakdown of the old land registration system, revenues declined and peasants rebelled against rising taxes. The government alienated more people by seizing Buddhist property and persecuting all foreign religions. At the capital, weak emperors lost their authority to eunuchs who had originally been only harem servants. Finally, in 907, a military commander killed all the eunuchs and deposed the last T'ang emperor.

Even as the T'ang dynasty was ending, it prepared the way for the Sung. South China, under T'ang rule, had developed a strong economy that could not be contained within the rigid T'ang system. The T'ang collapse permitted a commercial expansion that in turn generated much of the Sung's remarkable cultural achievement.

Political Developments During the Sung Era, 960–1279

For nearly a half century after the fall of the T'ang dynasty, China experienced political division, at times approaching anarchy. During the period of the Five Dynasties in the north and the Ten Kingdoms in the south, barbarian attacks continued to alternate with internal conflicts among contending warlords. A military leader of the northern Chou staged a palace coup and founded the Sung line in 960. He and his successor reunited the country, although certain frontier provinces and the tributary areas held by T'ang rulers were never regained (see map, p. 205).

Although they were northerners, early Sung emperors abandoned their military traditions in deference to the powerful landed magnates of the south, upon whom the state depended for economic support. Instead of using officials personally committed to the emperor, the Sung rulers relied upon the civil service, recruited through an examination system that largely favored the scholarly elite. Without an effective military, and plagued with internal bureaucratic dissension, Sung ministers tried first to defend the steppe frontiers by diplomacy. When that failed, they temporarily avoided invasion of the empire by paying tribute in silver and silk to neighboring barbarian kingdoms, such as the Khitan.

In addition to external threats, Sung rulers faced serious internal problems. A booming economy encouraged an individualism that affected all classes. The cost of foreign tribute, in addition to losses resulting from tax evasion by the wealthy, brought rising deficits as well as peasant unrest. To meet this crisis, the emperor called upon an eminent statesman, Wang An-shih (1081–1086). Wang sponsored a program which enforced state-controlled interest rates on agricultural loans, fixed commodity prices, provided unemployment benefits, established old age pensions, and reformed the examination

system by stressing practical rather than literary knowledge. These measures brought some improvements but evoked fanatic opposition from scholars, bureaucrats, and moneylenders. In the next generation, most of the reforms were rescinded.

Sung efforts to govern a united China came to an inglorious end early in the twelfth century. A nomadic people from Manchuria, the Jurchen, having established the Chin dynasty in north China, soon destroyed the Khitan regime and took the northern Sung capital in K'ai-feng. The Sung court fled in panic to Nanking and later established a capital at Hangchow. After a decade of indecisive war, a treaty in 1141 concluded a humiliating and uneasy peace with the Chin. For more than another century the southern Sung state survived, almost completely cut off by land from the north and west, but still capable of great commercial and cultural advances.

Economic and Social Conditions During the Sung Period

Although militarily weak, the Sung state was the economic nucleus for most of east Asia. Its water control projects and intensive agriculture doubled rice production within a century after 1050, while industry increased rapidly, pouring out the finest silk, lacquer wares, and porcelains for home and foreign markets. Sung economic advances were furthered by such technical innovations as water clocks, paddle-boats, explosive projectile weapons, seagoing junks, the sternpost rudder, and the mariner's compass. The resulting rise in productivity forced commerce out of government control, at the same time encouraging banks to depend upon paper currency. Foreign trade, formerly dominated by aliens, was taken up by Chinese, who established commercial colonies throughout East Asia.

Such profound and rapid change brought tensions to Sung society. Along with rising material affluence came urban expansion. The Chinese population swelled from 60 to 115 million, an increase of more than twice the world average. For all classes, life presented a unique contrast between confidence and anxiety. Relatively safe from nomad attack behind southern water barriers, most people were more concerned than in

THE SUNG DYNASTY

MANCHURIA

GREAT WALL

Peking

HAN
NORTHERN CHINA
CHOU

Kaifeng

YELLOW SEA

KOREA

Huang Ho R.

Nanking

NAN-PING

SHU
Yangtze R.

SOUTHERN CHINA

Hangchow

EAST CHINA SEA

CHU

NAN-TANG

WU YÜEH

NAN CHAO

HAN-HAN

Canton

FORMOSA

ANNAM

Mekong R.

HAINAN

SOUTH CHINA SEA

PHILIPPINES

Memorial on the Crop Lands Measure

Wang-An shih wrote this proposal in 1069. It was presented by a government commission to the Emperor Shen-tsung, who applied it first in a few provinces. Later it was extended to other areas.

The cash and grain stored in the Ever-Normal and the Liberal-Charity granaries of the various circuits, counting roughly in strings of cash and bushels of grain, amount to more than 15,000,000. Their collection and distribution are not handled properly, however, and therefore we do not derive full benefit from them. Now we propose that the present amount of grain in storage should be sold at a price lower than the market price when the latter is high; and that when the market price is low, the grain in the market should be purchased at a rate higher than the market price. We also propose that our reserves be made interchangeable with the proceeds of the land tax and the cash and grain held by the Fiscal Intendants, so that conversion of cash and grain may be permitted whenever convenient.

With the cash at hand, we propose to follow the example set by the crop loan system in Shensi province. Farmers desirous of borrowing money before the harvest should be granted loans, to be repaid at the same time as they pay their tax, half with the summer payment and half with the autumn payment. They are free to repay either in kind or in cash, should they prefer to do so if the price of grain is high at the time of repayment. In the event disaster strikes, they should be allowed to defer payment until the date when the next harvest payment would be due. In this way not only would we be prepared to meet the distress of famine, but, since the people would receive loans from the government, it would be impossible for the monopolistic houses to exploit the gap between harvests by charging interest at twice the normal rate.

Under the system of Ever-Normal and Liberal-Charity granaries, it has been the practice to keep grain in storage and sell it only when the harvest is poor and the price of grain is high. Those who benefit from this are only the idle people in the cities.

Now we propose to survey the situation in regard to surpluses and shortages in each circuit as a whole, to sell when grain is dear and buy when it is cheap, in order to increase the accumulation in government storage and to stabilize the prices of commodities. This will make it possible for the farmers to go ahead with their work at the proper season, while the monopolists will no longer be able to take advantage of their temporary stringency. All this is proposed in the interests of the people, and the government derives no advantage therefrom. Moreover, it accords with the idea of the ancient kings who bestowed blessings upon all impartially and promoted whatever was of benefit by way of encouraging the cultivation and accumulation of grain.

From *Sources of Chinese Tradition*, compiled by William T. de Bary, Wing-tsit Chan, and Burton Watson. (New York: Columbia University Press, 1963), pp. 475–76.

the past with their personal freedom, amusement, and advancement. The new affluence also brought cruel competition and undermined the old family values and moral obligations to the state. Such influences, however, did little to affect the class structure. Merchants, no matter how wealthy, could not replace the dominant scholar-bureaucrats, who continued to prosper as landowners. Admittedly, many of these were from middle-class families, financially able to educate their sons for the civil service examinations.

Social changes in the Sung era were especially difficult for women. Rising economic growth and competition helped erode Buddhist compassion and encouraged a revival of the Confucian doctrine of male dominance, particularly among the elite. For some lower-class women, commercial development brought new freedoms and opportunities to work, even conduct business, outside the home. In contrast, upper-class Sung women were now more restricted than in the past. Usually betrothed by their fathers, they lived in near servile status within their husbands' families, producing children and providing social decoration. The binding of little girls' feet, as preparation for this sterile adult life, became common practice under the Sung, as did female infanticide, restrictions on the remarriage of widows, and harsh legal penalties including death for violating the accepted code of prescribed wifely conduct.

Sung Philosophy, Literature, and Art

A rapidly changing social scene and the political debate over Wang An-shih's reforms led to philosophical dissension during the Sung era. Most reformers claimed that their proposals were based upon Confucian principles, but they were nevertheless strongly opposed by the majority of Confucian scholars, who were part of the established bureaucracy. Although Buddhist and Taoist spokesmen supported few standard arguments in the debate, their general opposition to government gave them many opportunities to increase the confusion. Thus the fragile compromise between Buddhism and Confucianism, achieved during the T'ang period, was placed under severe strain. Ultimately, these problems were resolved by a new compromise known as Neo-Confucianism, which was to become the intellectual foundation for Chinese thought until the twentieth century.

Chu Hsi (1129–1200), founder of the new philosophic school, was a brilliant scholar and respected commentator on the Confucian classics. His teaching sought to reconcile the mystical popular faiths of Buddhism and Taoism with Confucian practicality. Like his near contemporary in Europe, St. Thomas Aquinas (see p. 276), Chu Hsi synthesized faith and reason; but unlike Aquinas, Chu's highest priority was disciplined reason. He believed that people are neither naturally good nor bad, but are inclined either way by experience and education. The universe, according to Chu, is a self-generating and self-regulating order, to which humans may adjust rationally. Faith and custom, however, are necessary supports for reason and proper training.

A scroll painting by the Sung Dynasty emperor-artist Hui Tsung portrays women beating and preparing silk. An ineffectual ruler, Hui Tsung is best remembered as a painter, calligrapher, and patron of the arts.

Chu Hsi contended that self-cultivation required the extension of knowledge, best achieved by the "investigation of things." As a consequence, Neo-Confucianism was accompanied by significant advances in experimental and applied sciences. Chinese doctors, during the period, introduced innoculation against smallpox. Their education and hospital facilities far surpassed anything in the West. In addition, there were notable achievements in astronomy, chemistry, zoology, botany, and cartography. Sung algebra was also the most advanced in the world.

Sung aesthetic expression was more secular and less introspective than during the earlier era of Buddhist influence. This encouraged versatility; as during the later European Renaissance, the universal man—public servant, scholar, poet, or painter—was the ideal. Ironically, the most famous Chinese poetess, Li Ch'ing-chao (b. 1181), whose work was enthusiastically promoted by her scholar-husband, wrote her uniquely personal verse during the southern Sung period. Generally, however, Sung poetry did not match the growing quality of novels and drama. Historical and philosophical works reflected the main literary interests of the time, but the traditional love of nature was still displayed in landscape painting, which reached a peak under the Sung. Artists gave more attention to detail and were therefore more precisely naturalistic than T'ang painters, although the latter were often more imaginative.

Spreading Chinese Influence Abroad

Although not overly impressed by foreign culture, the Sung Chinese exerted much more influence upon the outside world than did their T'ang predecessors. Sung maritime trade affected all of East Asia, particularly the coastal regions to the south, where Chinese merchants were emigrant culture carriers. Sung technology exerted a long-range impact upon India, the Middle East, and even Europe. From China, Europe acquired metal horseshoes, the padded horse collar, and the wheelbarrow. Chinese cartographic knowledge, along with the compass and the stern-post rudder, helped prepare Europe's age of expansion. Later, gunpowder and movable type arrived in Europe via Asian intermediaries.

The Emergence of Japan

The rise of Japan after the sixth century was part of a much larger process in which a number of new fringe cultures developed rapidly in the shadows of the old major civilizations. In Europe, Africa, southeast and central Asia, Korea, and Japan, these later "third round" civilizations were able to appropriate the cultural experience of centuries without developing through the much slower process of trial, error, and conditioning. The results, however, were compromises. In its early evolution, for example, Japan borrowed much from China; but this cultural raw material was mingled and reworked into a new Japanese pattern.

Geographic, Ethnic, and Historical Backgrounds

Much that is distinctive in Japanese culture has resulted from geographic factors, which provided harsh challenges but maximum national security (see map, p. 209). The inland sea marked by the islands of Kyushu, Shikoku, and Honshu, with their lush and beautiful sheltered plains, was the center of Japanese civilization until the twelfth century. Yet even this area, along with the other 3000 islands of the archipelago, has frequently experienced earthquakes and typhoons. Location was the most important early factor; approximately 200 miles of water separate the highly populated islands from the mainland. Isolated as they were during their early history, the Japanese were secure enough to experiment with new ways while retaining a deep attachment to their land and its traditional culture.

Ethnically, the Japanese are of mixed origins, a result of many prehistoric migrations from the mainland, by way of Korea and Southeast Asia, through the island chain to the south. The resulting common ethnic community was predominantly Mongoloid, though darker and hairier than Asian mainland types. The language was derived from the basic Altaic family of northern Asia, which also produced Mongol and Korean variations. As the Japanese population expanded and moved north, after the second century

A.D., it began exterminating and absorbing the Ainu, a people of less developed culture, who had first occupied the area. This process continued into the modern era.

In ancient times, the mountainous Japanese islands facilitated the growth of numerous small tribal states, each ruled by a hereditary chieftain who claimed descent from a tribal deity. According to Japanese folklore, one of these chieftains named Jimmu ("Divine Warrior"), a descendent of the sun goddess, began the current line of Japanese emperors in 660 B.C. Historians generally believe that the present imperial family originated with the most powerful ruling group—the Yamato clan—which emerged in Kyushu and whose chieftains, beginning in the first century A.D., led the conquest eastward against the Ainu in Honshu.

The religion of the Japanese, known as Shinto, or "Way of the Gods," was a simple worship of natural forces and ancestral spirits, with no organized priesthood or ethical system. The chieftains served as priests as well as war leaders. With the growth of Yamato power, Shinto centered primarily on the sun goddess as the divine ancestress of the Yamato and, eventually, of all the Japanese people.

Agriculture was the basis of the economy. The nobles controlled the land, which was worked by peasants and slaves. Clans engaged in constant struggle for land and against the Ainu. Warfare was the order of the day, and the dominant role in society was played by noble families, whose fighting men were equipped with bows and iron swords and rode horses. Unlike China, where scholar-bureaucrats eventually rose to positions

The Rising Flood of Asian Culture, 300–1300 **209**

of dominance, the warrior class maintained its social prestige and political power through most of Japanese history. But despite this military emphasis, early Japanese society was largely matriarchal, as was evidenced by the prevalence of female deities. Women enjoyed a social status comparable to that of men; children were raised within the wife's family household; and women rulers were common until the eighth century.

During the first few centuries A.D., the Yamato clan settled on a plain north of modern Osaka and extended its power in central Japan. Its chieftain began to regard himself as a kind of emperor, while the other clan chieftains, some of whom had better lineage than their Yamato overlord, were attached to his court. Thus the Japanese state emerged as a loose association of clans under the suzerainty of the Yamato.

Influences from China and the Taika Reforms

After the third century, when the Han dynasty extended its sway over Korea, Chinese culture began to reach Japan. At first the process was very gradual, but in the sixth century, when the Japanese began consciously borrowing Chinese ways, a new age in Japanese history began.

The Great Buddha at Nara, Japan. This 1200-year-old bronze image is Japan's largest Buddha. Its face is said to be 16 feet long.

Buddhism was the main vehicle for transporting Chinese culture to sixth century Japan. In 522, a Korean king presented to the Japanese court an image of the Buddha, some Buddhist texts, and a recommendation of the new faith as "hard to comprehend" but "excellent" and widely adhered to in Korea. Whether or not they were moved by this particular plea, Yamato rulers embraced the new faith, with its accompanying Chinese values, even more fervently than contemporary Germanic tribes in Europe accepted Christianity. Before 600, Buddhism and respect for Chinese culture had spread throughout Japan.

In the seventh century the Yamato regime deliberately attempted to establish a centralized absolutism modeled on T'ang China. A group of young Japanese, including students recently returned from China, seized power in 645 and proclaimed the new order, with the Yamato ruler named as *Tenno*, or "Heavenly Emperor." The resulting Taika (Great Change) reforms asserted the absolute authority of the monarch at the expense of the former clan chieftains. The reformers also established a centralized bureaucracy, a legal code, a tightly controlled provincial system, a standing army, and a land tax similar to that of the T'ang.

From the beginning, differences between Japanese and Chinese societies required drastic adjustments. Most positions in the Japanese bureaucracy, held by members of the old clan nobility, quickly became hereditary. Recruitment through an examination system, after the Chinese model, never developed in Japan. The newly asserted power of direct taxation could not be effective at any distance from the court, so the emperors were forced to grant tax-exempt estates to some nobles in return for their services or support. Such estates also tended to become hereditary.

The reforms nevertheless exerted a great impact upon Japanese society, not the least being the construction of Japan's first city, Nara, as a capital where the new ways could flourish. Built in the early eighth century, Nara was carefully planned as a miniature version of Ch'ang-an, with broad streets, imposing new palaces, and many Buddhist edifices. Some of these temples and monasteries still survive as among the best remaining examples of T'ang architectural style.

Two Taika Reform Edicts

The reforms came in a series of decrees in 645 and 646. This section covers local administration.

2nd year [646], Spring, 1st month, 1st day. As soon as the ceremonies of the new year's congratulations were over, the Emperor promulgated an edict of reform, as follows:

"I. Let the people establish by the ancient Emperors, etc., as representatives of children be abolished, also the Miyake of various places and the people owned as serfs by the Wake, the Imperial Chieftains, the Deity Chieftains, Court Chieftains, Local Chieftains and the Village Headmen. Let the farmsteads in various places be abolished." Consequently fiefs were granted for their sustenance to those of the rank of Daibu and upwards on a descending scale. Presents of cloth and silk stuffs were given to the officials and people, varying in value.

"Further We say. It is the business of the Daibu to govern the people. If they discharge this duty thoroughly, the people have trust in them, and an increase of their revenue is therefore for the good of the people.

"II. The capital is for the first time to be regulated, and Governors appointed for the Home provinces and districts. Let barriers, outposts, guards, and post-horses, both special and ordinary, be provided, bell-tokens made, and mountains and rivers regulated.

"For each ward in the capital let there be appointed one alderman, and for four wards one chief alderman, who shall be charged with the superintendence of the population, and the examination of criminal matters. For appointment as chief alderman of wards let men be taken belonging to the wards, of unblemished character, firm and upright, so that they may fitly sustain the duties of the time. For appointment as aldermen, whether of rural townships or of city wards, let ordinary subjects be taken belonging to the township or ward, of good character and solid capacity. If such men are not to be found in the township or ward in question, it is permitted to select and employ men of the adjoining township or ward.

"The Home provinces shall include the region from the River Yokogawa at Nabari on the east, from Mount Senoyama in Kii on the south, from Kushibuchi in Akashi on the west, and from Mount Afusakayama in Sasanami in Afumi on the north. Districts of forty townships are constituted Greater Districts, of from thirty to four townships are constituted Middle Districts, and of three or fewer townships are constituted Lesser Districts. For the district authorities, of whatever class, let there be taken Local Chieftains of unblemished character, such as may fitly sustain the duties of the time, and made Tairei and Shōrei. Let men of solid capacity and intelligence who are skilled in writing and arithmetic be appointed assistants and clerks. . . .

"III. Let there now be provided for the first time registers of population, books of account and a system of the receipt and regranting of distribution-land.

"Let every fifty houses be reckoned a township, and in every township let there be one alderman who shall be charged with the superintendence of the population, the direction of the sowing of crops and the cultivation of mulberry trees, the prevention and examination of offenses, and the enforcement of the payment of taxes and of forced labor.

"For rice-land, thirty paces in length by twelve paces in breadth shall be reckoned a *tan*. Ten *tan* make one *chō*. For each *tan* the tax is two sheaves and two bundles [such as can be grasped in the hand] of rice; for each *chō* the tax is twenty-two sheaves of rice. On mountains or in valleys where the land is precipitous, or in remote places where the population is scanty, such arrangements are to be made as may be convenient.

From *Sources of the Japanese Tradition*, compiled by Ryusaku Tsunoda, William T. de Bary, and Donald Keene, 2 vols. (New York: Columbia University Press, 1964), Vol. 1, pp. 70–72.

Scholars, priests, and artisans from the mainland were welcomed at Nara, and later at Kyoto, the second capital, also copied from Ch'ang-an. Chinese culture-carriers found ready apprentices among the Japanese, including the first Japanese historians, who recorded, in Confucian contexts, myths and legends of the past which supported the emperor's right to his throne as a descendent of the Sun Goddess.

A New Japanese Order: The Heian Period, 794–1185

A recreated Japanese cultural and political system, part traditional, part Chinese, part imperial, and primarily feudal, came into being during the Heian period. In 794, a Confucian trained emperor built a new capital at Heian-kyo (now called Kyoto) to free himself from the growing political power of the Buddhist clergy; here the imperial court remained for nearly a thousand years, until 1868. During the next three and a half centuries, "peace and tranquility" (a literal translation of "Heian-kyo") generally characterized Japanese life. The era of Chinese—inspired reforms was over. Imperial authority weakened, and a court aristocracy flourished without much political power. What was left of central government came under domination of the Fujiwara family, while local lords became practially independent in the provinces.

By the tenth century, the Fujiwara family was accepted as the source of hereditary regents, who ruled the country for figurehead emperors, a system continued, in varied forms, to the present. Fujiwara Michinaga (966–1027), who held dominion over the court for thirty years, was the brother of two empresses and the father of four, the uncle of two emperors, the grandfather of two more, and the great-grandfather of another. Controlled by such a web of family intrigue and influence, the Heian court functioned in accord with its own stately rhythms. The sacred emperor performed his ceremonial duties, some Shinto and some Buddhist. Fujiwara women, as imperial consorts, produced future emperors. Monarchs were pressured to retire to Buddhist monasteries when their male heirs, usually little boys, were old enough to perform the prescribed rituals. As maternal uncles or grandfathers of the child-sovereigns, Fujiwara regents managed affairs until the emperors matured and abdicated in their turns.

While the Fujiwara, the puppet emperors, and the effete court nobles played their formal roles at Heian-kyo, political power was shifting toward the provinces, where many local lords were becoming independent governors and military commanders. Some of the strongest and most adventurous lords organized campaigns against the Ainu, seizing and colonizing territories with their followers. A network of feudal relationships, linking land grants with pledges of personal loyalty and service, developed among these provincial nobles and their subordinates, often completely outside imperial authority. The *bushi* (warrior) lords and their mounted *samurai* retainers, generated a primitive value system, the code of *Bushido*, which stressed courage, endurance, discipline, and loyalty unto death. The long-range effect of the *Bushido* tradition among Japanese men was recognized by many American soldiers in World War II.

Culture of the Heian Period

The court at Heian-kyo produced an artificial culture, largely imported from China; but behind this facade of Chinese traditions and aristocratic pretensions, the Japanese by the tenth century had developed a cultural perspective quite distinct from China's. Although also nature lovers, the Japanese were much less scholarly than the Chinese and more moved by intuitional preferences for balance, restraint, delicate precision, and economy. Indeed, "cultivation of the little" has been identified as a characteristic Japanese culture trait, which may have resulted from people living closely together on small secluded islands.

Perhaps the most obvious signs of Chinese influence were the temples. Generally, they followed the characteristic T'ang style and were lavishly adorned with both imported and Japanese statues of the Buddha, executed in bronze or wood and showing the typical benign expression of the Gandaran schools. Surviving temples include the Horyuji at Nara and the Phoenix Hall of the Byodoin at Uji, not far from Kyoto. The latter features perfect symmetry,

A fine example of architecture during the Heian period in Japan is Phoenix Hall, near the modern city of Kyoto. The building shows the influence of Chinese style.

commonly seen in picture-scroll illustrations for literary works.

Heian literature, while reflecting clearly the aristocratic life of its setting, was even more independent of Chinese influence than the other arts. Most Japanese intellectuals were men, trained to write in Chinese characters that could not easily represent Japanese syllables or thought; upper-class Japanese women, on the other hand, were not as well educated in Chinese and therefore wrote in a phonetic script, expressing Japanese sensitivities in charming poems, diaries, and novels. These works contained analyses of personal feeling that had no precedents in Chinese literature. The finest example is undoubtedly *The Tale of Genji*, a long novel by Lady Murasaki, who depicted her narrow court life with great psychological profundity and aesthetic appreciation for human emotion. As Lady Murasaki explained in the words of her hero, Genji, an author does not only write to tell a story but to express an "emotion so passionate that he can no longer keep it shut up in his heart" or "let it pass into oblivion."[3]

Well before Lady Murasaki, in the early eighth century, the countryside beyond Heian-kyo had begun producing its own literature. The *Manyoshu*, a collection of some 4000 poems, reflects a fresh outpouring of the native Japanese spirit in treating the old religion, the brevity of life, love of nature, and appreciation of friends. These short poems have never been surpassed in equating natural phenomena and human emotion, clinching each point in typical Japanese fashion with a twist of thought at the end of a set syllabic sentence.

extravagant decoration, and striking contrasts of white and bright red colors. Although symbolizing the Buddhist paradise, it also expresses the Japanese appreciation of the harmony between a subject and its natural setting. The hall stands beside a pond, its reflection creating an inverse picture of the building in the water.

Painting developed from Chinese models but, like architecture, soon showed a distinctive Japanese flavor. Buddhist themes predominated at first, but later artists chose more secular subjects drawn from everyday life. The new Japanese style, known as *Yamato-e*, was noted for its use of bright colors and for filling in finely sketched outlines. It was often used in decorating sliding doors and screens, but it was most

A portrait of Lady Murasaki, courtier and writer, and author of the *Tale of Genji,* which is considered the great classic of Japanese literature.

The Kamakura Shogunate

Cultural development continued past the thirteenth century in directions set during the Heian era, but the Fujiwara regency broke down much sooner as the result of warfare among the noble clans. In 1185, after a long struggle still celebrated in Japanese literature, movies, and television, a clique dominated by the Minamoto clan emerged victorious. Its leader, an outstanding soldier-statesman named Yoritomo, forced the emperor to grant him the title of *shogun* (generalissimo) and established a capital at Kamakura. Subsequent *shoguns* paid utmost respect to the emperors and governed at a discreet distance from the imperial court at Heian-kyo; but the *shoguns*, not the emperors, were the real rulers of Japan.

The resulting Kamakura Shogunate was a superfeudal order, designed to control an earlier one created by the Fujiwara court. It employed constables and stewards in every province but still relied on a complex web of personal obligations among local aristocrats and their common adherence to the code of Bushido. The prevailing values were extended to women, who were now expected to bear hardships with Spartan endurance; to fight, and if necessary, to die beside their husbands. Their lives were much harder, but they could hold the rights of a vassal and inherit property under the code. Kamakura noblewomen were often successful administrators. One of the ablest was Masako, Yorimoto's widow, also known as the "nun-*shogun*", who was the power behind the *shogun*, after her husband died.

A 13th-century wooden statue of Minamoto Yoritomo, Japan's first *shogun*.

interrupting the course of its development. Yet despite such serious disruptions, the Mongol era dramatically illustrated the importance of newly emerging civilizations in bringing peoples closer together.

The Role of the Central Asian Nomads

The Mongols were part of an old and developing tradition. Just prior to their conquests, they had been steppe nomads, ranging widely and pitching their black felt tents wherever they could find pasturage for their animals, like similar peoples who had terrorized settled Eurasian populations since the fourth century B.C.

Mongol society on the steppe fostered a strange mixture of values, combining the fierce ruthlessness and brutality of fighting men with a crude democratic equality. Males, particularly the ruling Khans, held almost unlimited authority. Polygamy was common among the warriors, although marital fidelity was equally enforced among men and women. Wives sometimes rode and fought beside their men, but usually confined their activities to domestic affairs. In addition to caring for children, women milked the mares and made all clothing. They were also responsible for many tasks required by their nomad life, such as breaking camp, loading the ox-wagons, and driving animals on the march. This division of labor was obviously uneven, but

The Mongol Impact

In the latter half of the thirteenth century, a rapidly rising Mongol Empire significantly altered the course of history. East Asia, India, the Middle East, and even Europe felt either the direct impact or indirect shockwaves from Mongol invasions. To the Middle East, the Mongols brought long-range disaster; India suffered but survived to produce another imperial age a century later. China, as in the past, ultimately assimilated its invaders without seriously within its context, women were honored and afforded a rough approximation of social equality.

As was true of their predecessors, the Mongols held military advantages in their superior cavalry tactics and mobility. Their disadvantages were their relatively few numbers, plus their dependence upon the administrative skills of their subjects. This situation, however, changed steadily as civilization spread on the Central Asian steppes after the sixth century. Even the Mongols were by then quite familiar with new urban influences.

The Turks, who had figured in Eurasian history for a thousand years before the emergence of the Mongols, were even more aware that times were changing. Originating in the Altai mountains, near the Orkhon River north of Tibet, the Turks began attacking northwest China in the third century and continued to be mentioned in Chinese annals as the Yueh-chih, a special branch of the Hsiung-nu frontier barbarians. As some Turks began living in cities in 500, they were noted for their skills as iron workers. According to the Chinese, Turks produced the first written language among Central Asian peoples in the sixth century, although the earliest known Turkish records date from two hundred years later. By that time, the Turks had produced their first steppe empire.

Between the sixth and eighth centuries, Turkish and Chinese regimes competed for control of the steppes. With Chinese support, the first Turkish empire (552–583) extended its dominion over most of Central Asia. Internal dissension caused it to split briefly into eastern and western Khanates, followed by Chinese conquest under the early T'ang emperors. Later, as the T'ang regime weakened, a second Turkish empire dominated the steppes (684–734), only likewise to succomb to internal weaknesses. Although maintaining many old tribal institutions, these states had central bureaucracies and appointed provincial officials, as did many petty Turkish monarchies in border areas.

During and after their imperial experiments, the Turks absorbed and disseminated much of the culture of the more advanced neighboring areas. Trade, religion, and warfare facilitated the process. Eastern Turks borrowed early from China, adopting Buddhism and converting their western kinsmen in distant Ferghana. After the eighth century, when the rising Caliphate brought Islam to the steppes, the combined pressures of population increases and Muslim fanaticism led the Turks on to complete conquests in the Middle East and India. Such incursions, which were still occurring in the fifteenth century, usually brought short-range disaster to

Two views of Mongols as seen by their contemporaries. Left is Persian miniature showing Mongols preparing food at their tents. Right is a Chinese painting of a mounted Mongol archer.

occupied regions; but they spread civilization in Central Asia.

For more than five centuries before the Mongol conquests, this process had been growing in intensity. Westward and to the north of the Chinese frontiers, a series of large states, partially urbanized but still containing large nomad populations, rose and fell. The two best known were the Uighur Empire of the ninth century and the Tangut state which succeeded it. Both of these regimes prospered on the overland trade with China, which continued to grow. For all Central Asians—Turks, Uighurs, Tanguts, Tibetans, Mongols, and a host of others—trade was one of many stimuli that turned their attention toward the outside world in the thirteenth century.

Formation of the Mongol Empire

At the opening of the thirteenth century, slightly more than a million Mongols began their whirlwind conquests and empire-building. Within less than a century, they had subdued most populations from the Pacific to the Danube, terrorized the rest, and established the *Pax Tatarica*, which permitted more trade and travel across Eurasia than the world would see until the seventeenth century. This was the largest empire ever known, comparable in geographic area only with the current Soviet Union (see map below). Like all steppe empires, however, it was extended so far beyond its native human resources that it began to weaken even as it was being formed and extended.

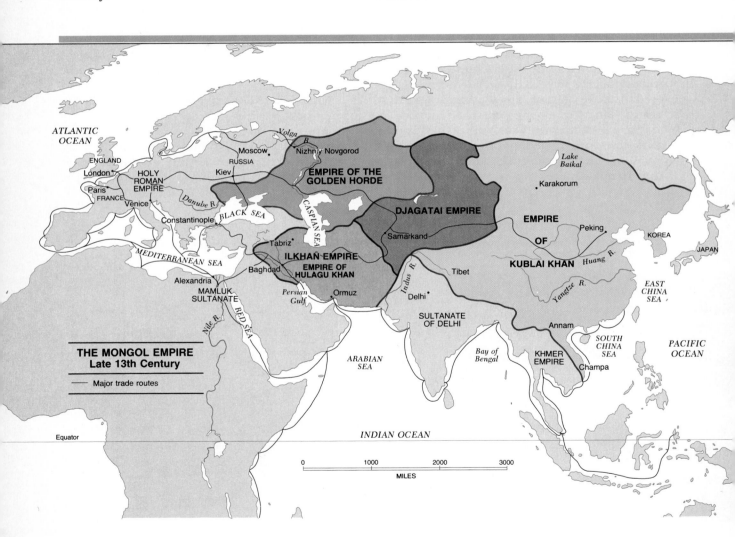

Mongol successes against such great odds resulted largely from the leadership of a guiding genius who launched his people into history. The son of a minor Mongol chief, he was born in 1162 and named Temujin, or "man of iron." When Temujin's father was killed by enemies, the young warrior was forced into a lonely exile on the steppe, where he nursed his desire for vengeance though barely managing to survive. Using cunning, courage, brutality, and patience, he gathered followers, persevering through tribal wars and confederacies. Ultimately, a convocation of all the tribes in 1206 recognized him as "Genghis Khan," unquestioned leader of the Mongols.

During the first stage of empire building, to 1241, the Mongols concentrated on the steppe and its less developed border areas. Genghis Khan subdued the barbarian kingdoms north of the Chinese wall, destroyed the western Muslim states on the steppes, and occupied eastern Russia. After his assassination in 1227, his son conquered the semibarbarian Chin state in northern China and extended Mongol control in Russia beyond Kiev.

In their second phase of conquest the Mongols extended their domain to include old civilized areas. They gained dominance over eastern Tibet (1252), Korea (1258), and Sung China (1274–1279). Kublai Khan, grandson of Genghis and conqueror of the southern Sung, also seized major areas in Burma, Annam, and Cambodia. Meanwhile, Mongol armies in the Middle East, led by Hulagu Khan, were toppling nearly every Muslim state in Persia, Mesopotamia, and Syria. The Mongol tide was finally arrested by an Egyptian army in Palestine (1260), by the failure of Kublai's naval attacks against Japan (1281) and Java (1293), and by contention among Mongol rulers of the far-flung territories.

Because they were so few in number, the Mongols relied upon terror to control conquered peoples. They routinely resorted to mass torture, killing, destruction, and resettlement of whole populations. In Baghdad, for example, Hulagu Khan executed 800,000 men, women, and children, sparing only a few skilled craftsmen. By destroying the irrigation system, the Mongols almost permanently ruined Mesopotamian agriculture. Even under more benign Mongol rule, China's population dropped from 100 million to less than 70 million during the period.

The Mongol Political Structure

The ultimate base of authority in the sprawling Mongol territories was a cavalry force of 130,000. Small contingents of this superbly armed and disciplined body were usually sufficient in areas already demoralized by terrorism. Communications were maintained by the famous Mongol couriers and thousands of post stations, which radiated in all directions from the imperial capital at Karakorum. Under watchful Mongol military commanders, local rulers or officials collected tribute, maintained routine services, and enforced native law, unless it violated Mongol custom or the Khan's decrees.

By the mid-thirteenth century, this military foundation was supporting a central bureaucracy of Turkish, Tibetan, and Chinese officials, in various ministries, such as justice, treasury, and military affairs. An examination system provided recruits for the expanding civil service, and young Mongols trained for the examinations at an imperial academy. Under this central government, the empire was divided into four parts: the Grand Khanate (Central Asia and North China), and three sub-Khanates of Asia, Persia, and Russia.

China Under the Mongols

During the reign of Kublai Khan (1260–1294), China briefly gained new significance in the Mongol system. Although Kublai successfully maintained his titular authority over the sub-Khanates, he moved his capital from Karakorum to Peking; proclaimed himself the founder of the Yuan dynasty, ruled a unified China; and turned attention primarily to his Chinese territories. This strain on Mongol unity led directly to imperial decline after Kublai's time.

For most of our knowledge about China in this era, we are indebted to the Venetian traveler Marco Polo. As a youth, he had accompanied his father and uncle, Venetian merchants, eastward to Kublai's court, arriving there about 1275. Polo served the Khan seventeen years as a trusted administrator, before returning home. His fabulous story, dictated to a fellow prisoner of war in

Marco Polo on Mongol Military Prowess

You see, when a Tartar prince goes forth to war, he takes with him, say, one hundred thousand horse. Well, he appoints an officer to every ten men, one to every hundred, one to every thousand, and one to every ten thousand, so that his own orders have to be given to ten persons only, and each of these ten persons has to pass the orders only to other ten, and so on; no one having to give orders to more than ten. And every one in turn is responsible only to the officer immediately over him; and the discipline and order that comes of this method is marvelous, for they are a people very obedient to their chiefs. Further, they call the corps of one hundred thousand men a *Tuc;* that of ten thousand they call a *Toman;* the thousand they call *Miny;* the hundred *Guz;* the ten *On.* And when the army is on the march they have always two hundred horsemen, very well mounted, who are sent a distance of two marches in advance to reconnoitre, and these always keep ahead. They have a similar party detached in the rear, and on either flank, so that there is a good lookout on all sides against a surprise. When they are going on a distant expedition they take no gear with them except two leather bottles for milk; a little earthenware pot to cook their meat in, and a little tent to shelter them from rain. And in case of great urgency they will ride ten days on end without lighting a fire or taking a meal. On such an occasion they will sustain themselves on the blood of their horses, opening a vein and letting the blood jet into their mouths, drinking till they have had enough, and then staunching it.

They also have milk dried into a kind of paste to carry with them; and when they need food they put this in water, and beat it up till it dissolves, and then drink it. It is prepared in this way: they boil the milk, and when the rich part floats on the top they skim it into another vessel, and of that they make butter; for the milk will not become solid till this is removed. Then they put the milk in the sun to dry. And when they go on an expedition, every man takes some ten pounds of this dried milk with him. And of a morning he will take a half pound of it and put it in his leather bottle, with as much water as he pleases. So, as he rides along, the milk paste and the water in the bottle get well churned together into a kind of pap, and that makes his dinner.

When they come to an engagement with the enemy, they will gain the victory in this fashion. They never let themselves get into a regular medley, but keep perpetually riding round and shooting into the enemy. And as they do not count it any shame to run away in battle, they will sometimes pretend to do so, and in running away they turn in the saddle and shoot hard and strong at the foe, and in this way make great havoc. Their horses are trained so perfectly that they will double hither and thither, just like a dog, in a way that is quite astonishing. Thus they fight to as good purpose in running away as if they stood and faced the enemy, because of the vast volleys of arrows that they shoot in this way, turning round upon their pursuers, who are fancying that they have won the battle. But when the Tartars see that they have killed and wounded a good many horses and men, they wheel round bodily, and return to the charge in perfect order and with loud cries: and in a very short time the enemy are routed. In truth they are stout and valiant soldiers, and inured to war. And you perceive that it is just when the enemy sees them run, and imagines that he has gained the battle, that he has in reality lost it; for the Tartars wheel round in a moment when they judge the right time has come. And after this fashion they have won many a fight.

From *The Travels of Marco Polo* (New York: Grosset & Dunlap, 1931), pp. 79–81.

A manuscript illumination from Marco Polo's journal depicts the Great Khan riding in a palanquin (an enclosed litter) borne by elephants.

Genoa, reported the wondrous world of Cathay (China)—its canals, granaries, social services, technology, and such strange customs as regular bathing. Polo's contemporaries considered him to be a braggart and a colossal liar.

Yuan China strongly resembled the picture presented under earlier dynasties, with some exceptions. The country was governed mainly by foreigners: Mongols at the top, other Central Asians on the next rung, northern Chinese in lower positions, and southern Chinese almost completely excluded from office. Kublai retained the traditional ministries and local governmental structure. Generally, Mongol law prevailed, but the conquerors were often influenced by Chinese legal precedents, as in the acceptance of brutal punishments for loose women or those unfaithful to their husbands. Most religions were tolerated unless they violated Mongol laws; for example, Muslim rules for slaughtering animals and circumcising infants led to persecutions under Kublai. According to Polo, the state insured

against famine, kept order, and provided care for the sick, the aged, and the orphaned. To the awed Venetian, the Yuan state appeared fabulously wealthy, as indicated by the Khan's 12,000 personal retainers, bedecked in silks, furs, fine feathers and sparkling jewels.[4]

In its cultural preferences, the Yuan court reverted to Chinese traditions. Taoism and Confucianism were subordinated at first to Buddhism but both revived during Kublai's reign. Chinese drama remained popular although influenced somewhat by Central Asian dance. Interest in drama encouraged the development of classical Chinese opera, a combination of singing, dancing, and acting, which reached maturity in the Yuan period. Some of the most influential Chinese painters were also producing at this time, and the novel emerged as a reflection of Chinese concerns. An example was the *Romance of the Three Kingdoms*, a long and rambling tale, set in late Han times but written in the fourteenth century.

Pax Tatarica: *Relinking of East and West*

During the century of the Mongol Peace, when much of Eurasia was unified and pacified by Mongol armies, East and West were in closer communication than ever before, even in Han and Roman times. Hosts of missionaries, traders, and adventurers journeyed to and from Asia, Africa, and Europe, thus partially preparing for the coming age of exploration.

Even before the Polos, Christian missionaries had led the way eastward, encouraged by hopes for Mongol conversion and alliance against the Muslims. John of Piani Carpini, dispatched by the Council of Lyons with the pope's blessing, visited Karakorum in 1245 but failed to convert the khan or enlist him as a papal vassal. A few years later, a Flemish Franciscan, William of Rubruck, met with similar results; but another Franciscan, John of Monte Corvino, converted thousands between his arrival in Peking in 1289 and his death in 1322. Meanwhile, Mongol religious toleration drew Near Eastern Christians into Central Asia and Buddhists into the Middle East.

In addition to the missionaries, swarms of other people, responding to the Mongol interest in foreign knowledge and skills, moved continuously on the travel routes. Between 1325 and 1354, Ibn Batuta, the famous Muslim globetrotter from the Sudan, visited Constantinople, every Middle Eastern Islamic state, India, Ceylon, Indonesia, and China. In Hangchow, he encountered a man from Morocco whom he had met before in Delhi. Some travelers went the opposite way. Rabban Sauma, a Nestorian monk from Central Asia, traveled to Paris; and a Chinese Christian monk from Peking, while in Europe as an envoy from the Persian khan to the pope, talked with the English and French kings.

Eurasian traders—Persians, Arabs, Greeks, and western Europeans—were the most numerous and worldly wise of all travelers. They were enticed by Mongol policies that lowered tolls in the commercial cities and provided special protection for merchants' goods. A Florentine document published about 1340 described favorable conditions on the silk route as "perfectly safe whether by day or night . . . Whatever silver the merchants carry . . . the lord of Cathay takes from them . . . and gives . . . paper money . . . in exchange . . . and with this money you can readily buy silk and whatever you desire to buy and all the people of the country are bound to receive it."[5]

Land trade between Europe and China, particularly in silk and spices, increased rapidly in the fourteenth century. The main western terminals were Nizhni Novgorod, east of Moscow, where the China caravans made contact with merchants of the Hanseatic League; Tabriz, in northeast Persia, which served as the eastern terminal for Constantinople; and the Syrian coastal cities, where the caravans met Mediterranean ships, mostly from Venice.

Expanding land trade along the old silk route did not diminish the growing volume of sea commerce. Indeed the Mongol devastation of Middle Eastern cities provided a quick stimulus, particularly to the spice trade, which was redirected through the Red Sea and Egypt to Europe. Within a few decades, however, the Egyptian monopoly drove prices up sharply, and the European demand for cheaper spices helped revive overland trade. By now, however, the southern sea route was thriving for other reasons. The Mongol conquest of China had immediately opened opportunities to Japanese and Malayan sea merchants, causing a modest commercial revolution. Later, after China stabilized and became involved in the exchange, the volume of ocean trade between northeast Asia and the Middle East surpassed that of Sung times.

The Mongol Legacy

Although their conquests brought immediate—and in some cases, long-term—havoc, Mongol control ultimately promoted stability. Their inexperience forced the Mongols to encourage trade and borrow freely from civilized peoples, while their commercial contacts spread knowledge of explosives, printing, navigation, shipbuilding, and medicine to the West. In the Middle East they furthered art, architecture, and historical writing, and to China they brought Persian astronomy and ceramics, plus sorghum, a new food from India. The Mongol era also saw great commercial and population growth in Japan and Southeast Asia. Not least important was a new awareness of the wider world, which the Mongols gave to a Europe poised for global exploration.

This European gain, however was far outweighed by negative effects upon Asia, best indicated by declining populations. Iraq, Iran, and Afghanistan lost about three million people before 1350, a drop of 30 percent. Significant declines also occurred in Burma (10 percent), Korea (19 percent), and China (30 percent). In territories formerly controlled by the Sung, the loss was approximately 29 million,[6] and this was accompanied by discrimination which seriously depressed the native population. Chinese insecurities under Mongol rule led directly to the narrow provincialism of the later Ming dynasty. For the Middle East and most of Asia, the Mongol era produced formidable handicaps in the upcoming period of European expansion.

While decisively affecting Eurasian history, the Mongols were incapable of creating a lasting state. Indeed, their empire dissolved almost as fast as it was formed, because the Mongols were divided by the diverse cultures they absorbed. Thus Kublai's Mongols turned Buddhist, while those in the Middle East and Russia became Muslims. In time, even the Mongol Muslims fought among themselves. The Yuan regime declined rapidly after Kublai's death, as the economy became more oppressive and the Mongol aristocracy weakened. A nationalist rebellion, beginning in southern China, ultimately ended the foreign dynasty. After the Chinese reconquered most of Mongolia and Manchuria, many northern Mongols reverted to nomadism. Others, on the western steppes, were absorbed into Turkish states.

Conclusion

The centuries following the collapse of Rome in the West saw significant cultural revivals in Asia. First India, then China, experienced golden ages, when old political structures were restored and social systems revitalized, in accordance with traditional values. The Gupta era brought a lasting synthesis of Hindu thought, along with notable advances in painting, architecture, literature, drama, medicine, and the physical sciences. China perfected its administrative structure while further developing its characteristic Confucian philosophy, poetry, landscape painting, and practical technology. Each civilization served as a culture bank, preserving and extending knowledge when much was being lost in the West.

As time passed, cultural diffusion gained increasing momentum throughout Eurasia. From both India and China, culture spread through migrations, invasions, missionary activities, and trade to Southeast Asia, Japan, the Asian steppes, and Europe. The result was a third wave in the civilizing process. The first wave had washed over the Near East before 500 B.C.; the second brought great empires in China, India, and the Mediterranean basin; the third generated new fringe civilizations in Southeast Asia and Japan while contributing largely to another in western Europe.

Steppe nomads played an increasingly important role in this period of Eurasian history. Many remained nomad warriors, attacking and pillaging the high civilizations on their frontiers. Others adopted civilized ways—shifting from herding to farming, living in cities as craftsmen or traders, or becoming state administrators. This development was climaxed by the Mongols, who greatly furthered contacts between East and West. Unfortunately for Asia, they also fostered a turning inward, away from the outside world, particularly in China. In doing this, the Mongol's inadvertently prepared for a modern world dominated by the West.

Suggestions for Reading

Two standard treatments of the Gupta era are Sir Percival Spear, *India, a Modern History*, rev. ed. (Univ. of Michigan, 1972) and R. C. Majumdar and A. D. Pulsaker, eds., *The Classic Age*, vol. III of *The History and Culture of the Indian Peoples* (Bharatiya Vidya, 1954). Reliable and informative recent surveys include B. G. Gokhale, *A Political and Cultural History of India* (Sterling, 1982); Hermann A. Kulke, *A History of India* (Barnes and Noble, 1986); and Stanley Wolpert, *A New History of India*, 3rd ed. (Oxford, 1989). Steven Warshaw, *India Emerges* (Diablo, 1987), is a concise and readable paperback for the student and general reader. A view from the Soviet perspective is provided in K. Antonova, G. Bongard-Levin, and G.

Kotovsky, *A History of India* (Moscow: Progress Publishers, 1979). B. H. Gokhale, *Samudra Gupta* (Asia, 1962), is an interesting biography. The best special treatment of women is A. S. Altekar, *The Position of Women in Hindu Civilization,* 3rd ed. (Sundar Lal Jam and Motilal Banarsidass, 1962). For a well illustrated account of Indian influence upon the art of neighboring countries, see B. Rowland, *The Art and Architecture of India* (Penguin, 1971).

Among the best general histories of China for the Tang and Sung periods are William Scott Morton, *China, Its History and Culture* (Lippincott and Crowell, 1980); Witold Rodzinzki, *A History of China,* 2 vols., (Pergamon, 1979); and Charles O. Hucker, *China's Imperial Past* (Stanford Univ., 1975). Others deserving mention are Wolfram Eberhard, *A History of China* (Univ. of Calif., 1977); John Meskill, *An Introduction to Chinese Civilization* (Heath, 1973); Raymond Dawson, *Imperial China* (Hutchinson, 1972); and Hilda Hookham, *A Short History of China* (St. Martin's Press, 1970). A recent readable paperback is Steven Warshaw, *China Emerges* (Diablo, 1987). For complete coverage of Chinese technology and engineering, see Joseph Needham, *Clerks and Craftsmen in China and the West* (Cambridge Univ., 1970). Esther Yao, *Chinese Women Past and Present* (Idle House, 1987) provides complete coverage of social conditions and important personalities.

The T'ang historical background is ably presented in Arthur F. Wright, *The Sui Dynasty* (Knopf, 1978) and in Woodbridge Bingham, *The Founding of the T'ang Dynasty* (Octagon Books, 1975). Arthur F. Wright and Dennis Twitchett provide special insights in *Perspectives on the T'ang* (Yale, 1973). A classic study of T'ang decline is E. G. Pulleyblank, *The Background of the Rebellion of An Lushan* (Oxford, 1955). C. Hartman, *Han Yu and the T'ang Search for Unity* (Princeton, 1986) depicts the famous philosopher's efforts to synthesize meaning from traditional values during the late T'ang troubles. Interesting and revealing special studies of the Sung period include Jingshen Tao, *Two Sons of Heaven* (University of Arizona, 1988); W. W. Lo, *An Introduction to the Civil Service System of Sung China* (Univ. of Hawaii, 1987; and H. C. Lee, *Government, Education, and the Examinations in Sung China* (St. Martin's Press, 1985).

G. B. Sansom, *A History of Japan,* 3 vols., (Stanford, 1958–1963) is still the best exhaustive work in English. Also valuable are J. K. Fairbank, *East Asia, Tradition and Transformation* (Houghton Mifflin, 1973); Eric Tomlin, *Japan* (Walker, 1973); Mikiso Hane, *Japan, A Historical Survey* (Scribner, 1972); and Edwin Reischauer, *Japan: the Story of a Nation* (Knopf, 1970). Noteworthy recent surveys include R. H. P. Mason, *A History of Japan* (Charles C. Tuttle, 1987) and Steven Warshaw, *Japan Emerges* (Diablo, 1987). Two penetrating special studies of early Japanese society are Jonathan E. Kidder, *Early Buddhist Japan* (Praeger, 1972) and Peter Judd Arensen, *The Medieval Japanese Daimyo* (Yale, 1979). Rose Hempel, *The Golden Age of Japan* (Rizzoli, 1983) is the only recent study of Japanese art and architecture in the Heian period.

Luc Kwanten, *Imperial Nomads: A History of Central Asia, 500–1500* (Univ. of Pa., 1979) is a superb and long overdue study of the nomadic steppe peoples, including Turks, Uighurs, and Uzbegs, as well as the Mongols. It has been ably augmented by two later works on Mongol life and conquests: David Morgan, *The Mongols* (London: Basil Blackwell, 1986) and Thomas T. Allsen, *Mongol Imperialism* (Univ. of Calif., 1987). Other standard and adequate treatments of the Mongol impact are: Rene Grousset, *The Empire of the Steppes* (Rutgers, 1970); Eustace D. Phillips, *The Mongols* (Praeger, 1969); John J. Saunders, *History of the Mongol Conquests* (Barnes and Noble, 1971); and Bertold Spuler, *The Mongols in History* (Praeger, 1971). A very sound treatment of the *Pax Tatarica* is presented in G. F. Hudson's *Europe and China* (Gordon, 1976). For early relations between the Chinese and the Mongols, see H. D. Martin, *The Rise of Ghenghis Khan and the Conquest of North China* (Octagon, 1971). L. Olschki, *Marco Polo's Precursors* (Johns Hopkins, 1943) and *Marco Polo's Asia* (Berkeley, 1960) provide complete accounts of the long-range trade leading to Polo's mission. A readable Polo biography is Henry Hart *Marco Polo, Venetian Adventurer* (Univ. of Oklahoma, 1967). The best recent accounts of the Yuan regime of China are Elizabeth E. West, *Mongolian Rule in China* (Harvard, 1989); Morris Rossabi, *Kublai Khan: His Life and Times* (Univ. of Calif., 1987); and John D. Langlois, *China Under Mongol Rule* (Princeton, 1981).

Notes

1. Quoted in H. H. Gowen and H. W. Hall, *An Outline History of China* (New York, D. Appleton and Co., 1926), p. 117.
2. *The Works of Li Po,* trans. by Shigeyoshi Obata (New York: E. P. Dutton, 1950), no. 71.
3. Quoted in Ryusaku Tsunoda *et al.,* eds., *Sources of Japanese Tradition* (New York: Columbia University Press, 1958), pp. 181–182.
4. Marco Polo, *Travels,* (New York: Grosset and Dunlap, 1931), pp. 133–149, p. 30.
5. Quoted in G. F. Hudson, *Europe and China* (Boston: Beacon Press, 1931), p. 156.
6. Population estimates in this chapter were taken from Colin McEvedy and Richard Jones, *Atlas of World Population History* (New York: Penguin Books), p. 171.

Europe's Search for Stability

The Early Middle Ages, 500–1000

We last examined developments in Europe at a crucial turning point in Western civilization—the fifth century (see ch. 5). The Roman Empire in the West was breaking apart under a variety of pressures, and unity and stability gave way to fragmentation and localism.

The first dominant kingdom to emerge from the decentralization of the early Middle Ages was that of the Germanic tribe of the Franks. From 714 to 814, the Carolingian House of the Franks brought stability and progress to northern Europe. A large portion of the West enjoyed military and political security as well as religious unity.

This accomplishment was not to last, however. The Frankish empire did not endure, partly because it lacked the strong economic bases that has supported the Romans. By the ninth century, Muslim conquests and commercial activity successfully competed with the Franks; inland trade declined sharply and urban life almost disappeared in the north. In addition, the empire had no strong administrative machinery to compensate for the weak rulers who followed the dominating leadership of the emperor Charlemagne; the empire disintegrated amid civil wars and invasions.

The impressive achievements of the Carolingians towards building a unifying governmental system were not able to counteract the decentralization of political, military, and economic activity in most of western Europe. A system of government sometimes referred to as feudalism attempted to provide stability and to serve as an effective political substitute for a powerful, effective central government. Economic life centered on a concern for subsistence and security, which could only be provided by the acceptance of local and rural customs and practices designed to ensure the necessities of life through resisting change and fostering self-sufficiency. The church continued its efforts to convert and standardize the belief of its members, and in so doing attempted to provide spiritual security in a troubled and insecure world.

A New Empire in the West

In the merging of Roman and Germanic cultures and institutions, the Franks played an especially significant role. The kingdom of the Franks was not only the most enduring of the Germanic states established in the West, but it became, with the active support of the church, the center of the new Europe that attempted to assume the place of the western Roman Empire.

The Kingdom of the Franks Under Clovis

Before the Germanic invasions of the fourth century, the Franks lived along the east bank of the Rhine, close to the North Sea. Late in the fourth century the Franks began a slow movement south and west across the Rhine into Gaul. By 481 they occupied the northern part of Gaul as far as the old Roman city of Paris; in that year Clovis I of the Merovingian House became ruler of one of the small Frankish kingdoms. By the time of his death in 511, Clovis had united the Franks into a single kingdom that stretched south to the Pyrenees.

Germanic tribes were either pagan or Arian Christians (see p. 146).

The conversion of the Franks to Christianity is considered a decisive event in European history. Ultimately it led to an alliance of the Franks and the papacy, and immediately it assured Clovis the loyalty of the Gallo-Roman bishops, the leaders of the native Christian population of Gaul. This was a political advantage not open to the Arian Visigothic and Burgundian kings. With the help of the native population of Gaul, Clovis was able to expand his control in the name of Christian orthodoxy.

In 507 Clovis attacked the Visigoths, who ruled Gaul south of the Loire River and all of Spain (see map, p. 135). The Visigothic king was killed, and his people abandoned most of their Gallic territory. Clovis died four years later at

The baptism of Clovis, king of the Franks. As bishops and nobles look on, a dove representing the Holy Spirit and symbolizing God's approval, descends bringing oil to be used in the ceremony.

Clovis achieved his aims by the crafty manipulation of marriage alliances, treachery, assassination, and the use of religion. Clovis first allied himself with other kings of the small Frankish states to dispose of Syagrius, the last Roman general in Gaul. He then turned against his own allies and subdued them.

According to the sixth century Gallo-Roman bishop and historian Gregory of Tours, whose *History of the Franks* is the most detailed account of any of the early Germanic peoples, Clovis was converted to Christianity in 496 as a result of a battle against the Alemanni, a pagan Germanic tribe whose name became the French word for Germany, *Allemagne*. On the verge of being defeated, Clovis called on the Christian god for help:

> *O Christ . . . if you accord me the victory . . . I will believe in you and be baptized in your name. I have called on my gods, but I have found from experience that they are far from my aid . . . it is you whom I believe to be able to defeat my enemies.[1]*

Clovis won the battle and was baptized together with his whole army. He became the only mainstream Christian ruler in the West, for the other

KINGDOM OF CLOVIS I

NORTH SEA

Elbe R.

Cologne
Tournai
Rhine R.
Seine R.
Paris
Strasbourg
Danu
Loire R.
Tours
Bordeaux
Garonne R.
Rhône R.
Po R.
Toulouse
PYRENEES
ALPS
MEDITERRANEAN SEA

the age of forty-five; his conquests formed the core of what would eventually become the French nation (see map, p. 224).

Decline of the Merovingians

Clovis' sons and grandsons conquered the Burgundian kingdom and extended Frankish control to the Mediterranean and further into Germany. After a century, however, the Merovingian House began to decay from inner weaknesses. The Germanic practice of treating the kingdom as personal property and dividing it among all the king's sons resulted in constant and bitter civil wars. Potential heirs plotted murders, intrigue, and treachery. Merovingian kings proved themselves incompetent and ineffectual as rulers. Soon the Frankish state broke up into three separate kingdoms; in each, power was concentrated in the hands of the chief official of the royal household, the mayor of the palace, a powerful noble in whose interest it was to keep the king weak and ineffectual. The Merovingian rulers were mere puppets, the *rois fainéants* ("do-nothing kings").

A Dark Age

By the middle of the seventh century the Frankish state had lost many of the essential characteristics of its Roman predecessor. The Roman system of administration and taxation had completely collapsed. The dukes and counts who represented the Merovingian king received no salary and usually acted on their own initiative in commanding fighting men and presiding over the courts in their districts. International commerce had ceased except for a small trade in luxury items carried on by adventurous Greek, Syrian, and Jewish traders. The old Roman cities served mainly to house the local bishop and his staff. The absence of a vibrant middle class meant that society was composed of the nobility, a fusion through intermarriage of aristocratic Gallo-Roman and German families who owned and exercised authority over large estates, and the lower class *coloni*, who were bound to the land. These serfs included large numbers of formerly free German farmers. Only about 10 percent of the peasant population of Gaul maintained a free status.

Coinciding with the Merovingian decay, new waves of invaders threatened every part of Europe. A great movement of Slavic people from the area that is now Russia had begun in about A.D. 500 (see p. 185). The Slavs fanned out from this point, filling the areas left by the Germanic tribes when they pushed south into the Roman Empire. By 650 the western Slavs had reached the Elbe River, across which they raided German territory. More danger threatened western Europe from the south; in the late seventh century the Muslims prepared to invade Spain from North Africa.

Charles Martel and the Rise of the Carolingians

The Frankish kingdom revived when Charles Martel became mayor of the palace in 714. His father, one of the greatest Frankish landowners, had eliminated all rival mayors. Although Charles ruled a united Frankish kingdom in all but name, the Merovingian kings were kept as figureheads at the court.

Charles is best remembered for his victory over a Muslim invasion of Frankish territory, which earned him the surname Martel, "The Hammer." In 711 an army of Muslims from North Africa had invaded Spain, and by 718 the weak kingdom of the Visigoths had collapsed. With most of the peninsula under their control, the Muslims began making raids across the Pyrenees. In 732 Charles Martel met them near Tours, deep within the Frankish kingdom. Muslim losses were heavy, and during the night they retreated to Spain.

A major military reform coincided with the Battle of Tours. For some time before this conflict, the effectiveness of mounted soldiers had been growing, aided by the introduction of the stirrup, which allowed mounted warriors to keep a firm seat while wielding their weapons. To counteract the effectiveness of the quick-striking Muslim cavalry, Charles recruited a force of professional mounted soldiers whom he rewarded with sufficient land to enable each of them to maintain a family, equipment, and war horses.

Pepin the Short

Charles Martel's son, Pepin the Short, who ruled from 741 to 768, was a worthy successor to his father. To legalize the power already being exercised by the mayors of the palace, Pepin requested and received from the pope a decision that whoever exercised the actual power in the kingdom should be the legal ruler. In 751 Pepin was elected king by the Franks; the last Merovingian was quietly sent to a secluded monastery. In 754 the pope reaffirmed the election of Pepin by crossing the Alps and personally anointing the new king in the Old Testament manner, as the Chosen of the Lord.

Behind the pope's action lay his need for a powerful protector. In 751 the Lombards had conquered the Exarchate of Ravenna, the center of Byzantine government in Italy, were demanding tribute from the pope, and threatened to besiege Rome. Following Pepin's coronation, the pope secured the new ruler's promise of armed intervention in Italy and his pledge to give the papacy the Exarchate of Ravenna, once it was conquered. In 756 a Frankish army forced the Lombard king to relinquish his conquests, and Pepin officially gave Ravenna to the pope. Known as the "Donation of Pepin," the gift made

the pope a temporal ruler over the Papal States, a strip of territory that extended diagonally across northern Italy.

The alliance between the Franks and the papacy affected the course of politics and religion for centuries. It accelerated the separation of the Roman from the Greek Christian church by providing the papacy with a dependable western ally in place of the Byzantines, previously its only protector against the Lombards; it created the Papal States, which played a major role in Italian politics until the late nineteenth century; and, by the use of the ritual of anointment, it carried on a tradition that kingship in the West was to be affirmed by approval of church officials.

Charlemagne's Accomplishments

Under Pepin's son, Charlemagne (Charles the Great), who ruled from 768 to 814, the Frankish state and the Carolingian House reached the summit of their power. Charlemagne's biographer, Einhard, described the king as a natural leader—tall, physically strong, and a great

Left, a gold bust of Charlemagne made in the 14th century and presently kept in the treasury of the Palace Chapel of Charlemagne at Aachen, Germany. The accompanying relief, below, shows the emperor weeping over the death of his soldiers.

Einhard, Life of Charlemagne

Einhard was the Emperor Charlemagne's secretary and biographer. The following is an excerpt from Einhard's *Life of Charlemagne*.

Charles was large and strong, and of lofty stature, though not disproportionately tall (his height is well known to have been seven times the length of his foot); the upper part of his head was round, his eyes very large and animated, nose a little long, hair fair, and face laughing and merry. Thus his appearance was always stately and dignified, whether he was standing or sitting; although his neck was thick and somewhat short, and his belly rather prominent; but the symmetry of the rest of his body concealed these defects. His gait was firm, his whole carriage manly, and his voice clear, but not so strong as his size led one to expect. His health was excellent, except during the four years preceding his death, when he was subject to frequent fevers; at the last he even limped a little with one foot. Even in those years he consulted rather his own inclinations than the advice of physicians, who were almost hateful to him, because they wanted him to give up roasts, to which he was accustomed, and to eat boiled meat instead. In accordance with the national custom, he took frequent exercise on horseback and in the chase, accomplishments in which scarcely any people in the world can equal the Franks. He enjoyed the exhalations from natural warm springs, and often practiced swimming, in which he was such an adept that none could surpass him; and hence it was that he built his palace at Aix-la-Chapelle, and lived there constantly during his latter years until his death. He used not only to invite his sons to his bath, but his nobles and friends, and now and then a troop of his retinue or bodyguard, so that a hundred or more persons sometimes bathed with him.

Charles was temperate in eating, and particularly so in drinking, for he abominated drunkenness in anybody, much more in himself and those of his household; but he could not easily abstain from food, and often complained that fasts injured his health. He very rarely gave entertainment, only on great feastdays, and then to large numbers of people. His meals ordinarily consisted of four courses, not counting the roast, which his huntsmen used to bring in on the spit; he was more fond of this than of any other dish. While at table, he listened to reading or music.

Charles had the gift of ready and fluent speech, and could express whatever he had to say with the utmost clearness. He was not satisfied with command of his native language merely, but gave attention to the study of foreign ones, and in particular was such a master of Latin that he could speak it as well as his native tongue; but he could understand Greek better than he could speak it. He was so eloquent, indeed, that he might have passed for a teacher of eloquence. He most zealously cultivated the liberal arts, held those who taught them in great esteem, and conferred great honors upon them. He took lessons in grammar of the deacon Peter of Pisa, at that time an aged man. Another deacon, Albin of Britain, surnamed Alcuin, a man of Saxon extraction, who was the greatest scholar of the day, was his teacher in other branches of learning. The King spent much time and labor with him studying rhetoric, dialectics, and especially astronomy; he learned to reckon, and used to investigate the motions of the heavenly bodies most curiously, with an intelligent scrutiny. He also tried to write, and used to keep tablets and blanks in bed under his pillow, that at leisure hours he might accustom his hand to form the letters; however, as he did not begin his efforts in due season, but late in life, they met with ill success.

From Samuel Epes Turner, trans., *Life of Charlemagne by Einhard* (Ann Arbor: University of Michigan Press, 1960), pp. 50–57.

horseman who always led the charge at the hunt. Although he was primarily a successful warrior-king, leading his armies on yearly campaigns, Charlemagne also tried to provide an effective administration for his kingdom. In addition, he had great appreciation for learning and attempted to further the arts in his court.

Taking advantage of feuds among the Muslims in Spain, Charlemagne sought to extend his kingdom southward. In 778 he crossed the Pyrenees and met with some success. As the Frankish army headed back north, it was met by the Christian Basques, who attacked the Franks from the rear. In this skirmish the Frankish leader, a count named Roland, was killed. The memory of his heroism was later recorded in the great medieval epic, the *Chanson de Roland* (*Song of Roland*). On later expeditions the Franks drove the Muslims back to the Ebro River and establshed a frontier area known as the Spanish March, or Mark, centered near Barcelona. French immigrants moved into the area, later called Catalonia, giving it a character culturally distinguishable from the rest of Spain.

Charlemagne conquered the Bavarians and the Saxons, the last of the independent Germanic tribes. It took thirty-two campaigns to subdue the Saxons, who lived between the Rhine and Elbe rivers. Charlemagne divided Saxony into bishoprics, built monasteries, and instituted severe laws against paganism. Eating meat during the penitential period of Lent, cremating the dead (an old pagan practice), and pretending to be baptized were offenses punishable by death.

Like his father before him, Charlemagne was concerned with Italian politics. The Lombards resented the attempts of the papacy to expand civil control in northern Italy. At the request of the pope, Charlemagne attacked the Lombards in 774, defeated them and proclaimed himself their king. While in Italy, he reaffirmed his father's alliance with the church through the Donation of Pepin.

The empire's eastern frontier was continually threatened by the Avars, Asiatic nomads related to the Huns, and the Slavs. In six campaigns Charlemagne almost eliminated the Avars and then set up his own military province in the valley of the Danube to guard against any future plundering by eastern nomads. Called the East Mark, this territory later was named Austria.

Charlemagne's Coronation in Rome

One of the most important events in Charlemagne's reign took place on Christmas Day, 800. In the previous year the Roman nobility had ousted the pope, charging him with corruption. Charlemagne came to Rome and restored the pope to his office. Then, at the Christmas service while Charlemagne knelt before the altar at St. Peter's, the pope placed a crown on his head amid the cries of the assembled congregation: "To Charles Augustus crowned of God, great and pacific Emperor of the Romans, long life and victory!"

This ceremony demonstrated that the memory of the Roman Empire still survived as a meaningful tradition in Europe and that there was a strong desire to reestablish a political unity. In fact, Charlemagne had named his capital at Aix-la-Chapelle (Aachen) "New Rome" and was about to take the title of emperor in an attempt to revive the idea of the Roman Empire in the West. By seizing the initiative and crowning Charlemagne, the pope attempted to assume a position of superiority as a maker of emperors.

Charlemagne's Administration

The extent of Charlemagne's empire was impressive. His territories included all of the western area of the old Roman Empire except Africa, Britain, southern Italy, and southern Spain (see map, p. 229). Seven defensive provinces, or marks, protected the empire against hostile neighbors.

The Carolingian territories were divided into some three hundred administrative divisions, each under a count (*graf*) or, in the marks along the border, a margrave (*markgraf*). In addition, there were local military officials, the dukes. In an effort to solve the problem of supervising the local officials, a problem that plagued all Germanic rulers, Charlemagne issued an ordinance creating the *missi dominici*, the king's envoys. Pairs of these itinerant officials, usually a bishop and a lay noble, traveled throughout the realm to check on the local administration. To make the *missi* immune to bribes, they were chosen from men of high rank, were frequently transferred from one region to another, and no two of them were teamed for more than one year.

The Carolingian Renaissance

Charlemagne also promoted a revival of learning and the arts. His efforts in this area were destined to be far more lasting than his attempt to revive the Roman Empire in the West, and they have prompted historians to speak of this period as one of cultural rebirth.

In 789 Charlemagne decreed that every monastery must have a school for the education of boys in "singing, arithmetic, and grammar." As he stated in a letter to the abbot of Fulda, Charlemagne was greatly concerned over the illiteracy of the clergy:

> *Since in these years there were often sent to us from divers monasteries letters in which . . . owing to neglect of learning, the untutored tongue could not express [itself] without faultiness. Whence it came that we began to fear lest, as skill in writing was less, wisdom to understand the Sacred Scriptures might be far less than it ought rightly to be.*[2]

At his capital of Aix-la-Chapelle, the emperor also sponsored a palace school for the education of the royal household and the stimulation of learning throughout the realm. Alcuin, the Anglo-Saxon scholar in charge of the school, began the difficult task of reviving learning by writing textbooks on grammar, spelling, rhetoric, and logic. "Ye lads," Alcuin exhorted his students, "whose age is fitted for reading, learn! The years go by like running water. Waste not the teachable days in idleness!"[3]

The reform of handwriting and the preservation of classical manuscripts were significant achievements of the Carolingian revival. Copyists labored in monasteries to preserve the classics of pagan and Christian thought with the result that the oldest manuscripts of most of the Latin

Alcuin, Epitaph

Alcuin of York, reportedly one of the most brilliant scholars of his day, was a friend and advisor to the Emperor Charlemagne. The following is Alcuin's epitaph.

Here halt, I pray you, make a little
    stay
  O wayfarer, to read what I have writ,
And know by my fate what thy fate shall be,
What thou art now, wayfarer, world-renowned,
I was; what I am now, so shall thou be.
The world's delight I followed with a heart
Unsatisfied: ashes am I, and dust.

Wherefore bethink thee rather of thy soul
Than of thy flesh;—this dieth, that abides.
Dost thou make wide thy fields? In this small
    house
Peace holds me now; no greater house for
    thee.
Wouldst have thy body clothed in royal red?
The worm is hungry for that body's meat.

Even as the flowers die in a cruel wind,
Even so, of flesh, shall perish all thy pride.

Now in thy turn, wayfarer, for this song
That I have made for thee, I pray you, say:
"Lord Christ, have mercy on thy servant
    here,"
And may no hand disturb this sepulchre,
Until the trumpet rings from heaven's height,
"O thou that liest in the dust, arise,
The Judge of the unnumbered hosts is here!"

Alcuin was my name; learning I loved.
O thou that readest this, pray for my soul.

From Ruth Brantl, ed., *Medieval Culture: The Image and the City* (New York: George Braziller, 1966), pp. 66–67.

---

classics that have come down to us date from the age of Charlemagne. The almost illegible script of the Merovingian period was replaced by a more readable style of writing, known as Carolingian minuscule—"little letters," in contrast to the capitals used by the Romans. Carolingian miniscule became the foundation for the typefaces still used in present-day printing, including that used in this textbook.

At Aix-la-Chapelle Charlemagne also strove to recapture something of the magnificence of ancient Rome by building a stone palace church modeled after a sixth-century church in Ravenna. Its mosaics were probably the work of Byzantine artisans, and its marble columns were taken from ancient buildings in Rome and Ravenna.

Charlemagne's Legacy

Charlemagne must be considered one of the most significant figures of European history. He extended Christian civilization in Europe, set up barriers to prevent invasions of the Slavs and Avars, and created a new Europe whose center was in the north rather than on the Mediterranean and a state in which law and order was again enforced after three centuries of disintegration. His patronage of learning began a cultural revival that later generations would build upon, producing a European civilization distinct from the Byzantine to the east and the Muslim to the south.

Charlemagne's empire was not long-lived, however, for its territories were too vast and its nobility too divisive to be held together after the dominating personality of its creator had passed from the scene. Charlemagne had no standing army; his foot soldiers were essentially the old Germanic war band summoned to fight by its war leader, and his mounted warriors served him, as they had Charles Martel, in return for grants of land. Charlemagne did not have a bureaucratic administrative machine comparable to that of Roman times. The Frankish economy was agricultural and localized, and there was no system of taxation adequate to maintain an effective and permanent administration. Under Charlemagne's weak successors the empire collapsed in the confusion of civil wars and devastating new invasions. Progress toward a centralized and effective monarchy in Europe ended with Charlemagne's death.

The Division of the Empire

Before his death in 814, Charlemagne himself, ignoring the pope, placed the imperial crown on the head of his only surviving son, Louis the Pious, a well-meaning man who was loved by the clergy, ignored by the nobility, and resented by his own family. Louis, in accord with Frankish custom, divided the kingdom among his sons, and bitter rivalry and warfare broke out among the brothers and their father.

Louis the Pious died in 840, and strife continued among his three surviving sons. Lothair, the oldest, was opposed by his two younger brothers—Louis the German and Charles the Bald. In 842 the two younger brothers joined

forces by swearing the Strasbourg Oaths. The text of these oaths is significant in that one part was in an early form of French, the other in German. The first could be understood by Charles' followers, who lived mainly west of the Rhine; the other by Louis' followers, who lived east of the Rhine. These oaths are evidence that the Carolingian empire was splitting into two linguistic and cultural sections—East Frankland, the forerunner of modern Germany, and West Frankland, or France.

In 843 the three brothers met at Verdun, where they agreed to split the Carolingian lands three ways. Charles the Bald obtained the western part of the empire and Louis the German the eastern; Lothair, who retained the title of emperor, obtained an elongated middle kingdom, which stretched a thousand miles from the North Sea to central Italy (see map at left).

The Treaty of Verdun is important because it began the shaping of modern France and Germany by giving politcal recognition to the cultural and linguistic division shown in the Strasbourg Oaths. Lothair's middle kingdom soon collapsed into three major parts, Lorraine in the north, Burgundy, and Italy in the south. Lorraine included Latin and German cultures, and although it was divided in 870 between Charles and Louis, the area was disputed for centuries. Lorraine became one of the battlegrounds of Europe.

The rival Carolingian houses produced no strong leaders worthy of being called "Hammer" (Martel) or "Great"; instead, we find kings with such revealing names as Charles the Fat, Charles the Simple, Louis the Child, and Louis the Sluggard. The last of the East Frankish Carolingians died in 911. In West Frankland the nobles, ignoring the eighteen-year-old Carolingian prince, chose Odo, the count of Paris, as king in 888.

The New Invasions

During the ninth and tenth centuries the remnants of Charlemagne's empire were also battered by new waves of invaders. Scandinavians attacked from the north, Muslims from the south, and a new wave of Asiatic nomads, the Magyars, conducted a series of destructive raids on central Europe and northern Italy. Christian Europe had to fight for its life against these aggressive and warlike newcomers, who did far

PARTITION OF CHARLEMAGNE'S EMPIRE 843

more damage to life and property than the Germanic invaders of the fifth century.

From bases in North Africa, Muslim adventurers in full command of the sea plundered the coasts of Italy and France. In 827 they began the conquest of Byzantine Sicily and southern Italy. From forts erected in southern France they penetrated far inland to attack the caravans of merchants in the Alpine passes. What trade still existed between Byzantium and western Europe, except for that undertaken by Venice and one or two other Italian towns, was now almost totally cut off, and the Mediterranean Sea became a virtual Muslim lake.

The most widespread and destructive raids came from Scandinavia. During the ninth and tenth centuries Swedes, Danes, and Norwegians—collectively known as Vikings—began to move south from their remote forests and fiords. The reason for this expansion is not clear, but some historians cite overpopulation and a surplus of young men as causes. Other scholars view these raiders as defeated war bands expelled from their homeland by the gradual emergence of strong royal power. Still others see a clue in the fact that the Vikings had developed

seaworthy ships capable of carrying a hundred men and powered by long oars or by sail when the wind was favorable. Viking sailors also had developed expert sailing techniques; without benefit of the compass, they were able to navigate by means of the stars at night and the sun during the day.

The range of Viking expansion was impressive. The Vikings explored as far as North America to the west, the Caspian Sea to the east, and the Mediterranean to the south. Few areas seemed immune from their raids, which filled civilized Europeans with a fear that was reflected in a new prayer in the litany of the church: "From the fury of the Northmen, O Lord deliver us."

Three main routes of Viking expansion can be identified. The outer path, which was followed principally by the Norwegians, swung westward to Ireland and the coast of Scotland. Between 800 and 850 Ireland was ravaged severely. Many monasteries, the centers of the flourishing Irish Celtic culture, were destroyed. By 875 the Norwegians were beginning to occupy remote Iceland, and it was here rather than in their homeland that the magnificent Norse sagas were

Wooden carvings like that below on Viking ships were meant to instill terror. The Viking head shown here is from the Oseberge ship, right, from the early Viking period.

preserved, little affected by either classical or Christian influences. During the tenth century the Icelandic Norsemen ventured on to Greenland and, later, to North America.

Another route, the eastern line, was followed chiefly by the Swedes, who went down the rivers of Russia as merchants and soldiers of fortune and, as was described in chapter 7, founded the nucleus of a Russian state.

The Danes took the middle passage, raiding Britain and the shores of Germany, France, and Spain. By the 870s they had occupied most of Britain north of the Thames. Also in the middle of the ninth century their raids increased upon the Continent, where their long boats sailed up the Rhine, Scheldt, Seine, and Loire rivers. In particular the Danes devastated northwest France, destroying dozens of abbeys and towns. Unable to fight off the Viking attacks, the weak Carolingian king Charles the Simple arranged a treaty with Rollo, a Norse chieftain, in 911. This agreement created a Viking buffer state, later called Normandy, and recognized Rollo as duke and vassal of the French king. Like Viking settlers elsewhere, these Northmen, or Normans, soon adopted Christian civilization. By the eleventh century, Normandy was a powerful duchy, and the Viking spirit of the Normans contributed in producing the most vigorous crusaders, conquerors, and administrators in Europe.

Europe in 900

Europe's response to the invasions of the ninth and tenth centuries was not uniform. By 900, the Viking occupation of England initiated a strong national reaction, which soon led to the creation of a united British kingdom. Similarly, Germany in 919 reacted to the Magyar threat by installing the first of a new and able line of kings who went on to become the most powerful European monarchs since Charlemagne.

The Viking attacks on France accelerated the trend toward political fragmentation that began under the Merovingians but was temporarily halted by the strong personal leadership provided by the Carolingians. When Charlemange's weak successors were unable to cope with constant Viking assaults, and the government could not hold together its vast territory without either a bureaucracy or a dominating king, the result

was that small independent landowners surrendered both their lands and their personal freedoms to the many counts, dukes, and other local lords in return for protection and security. The decline of trade further strengthened the position of the landed nobility, whose large estates, or manors, tended to become economically self-sufficient. In addition, the nobility became increasingly dependent on military service rendered by a professional force of heavily armed mounted knights, many of whom still lived in the house of their noble retainers in return for their military service.

In response to all these elements—the disintegration of central power, the need for protection, the decrease in the number of freemen, the rise of a largely independent landed aristocracy, and the increased reliance on the mounted knight—patterns of society took shape.

Political Organization in the Early Middle Ages

The centralization of the Carolingian state was not long a source of political stability in western Europe in the early Middle Ages. In those areas where the Carolingian Empire had little impact, and even in the regions which were at some time controlled by Carolingian rulers, personal safety and security were the primary concerns for most individuals. In circumstances that make strong central government impossible, individual security must be guaranteed by other means—usually through local custom and practice. Historians have used the term *feudalism* to apply generally to these individual patterns of decentralized government. The diversity of political structure in the early Middle Ages was great, and varied from region to region. We must be aware that in using the term to describe medieval political structures, we are attempting a simplification of an extremely diversified and complex set of local practices.

Feudalism

Feudalism can be described as a type of government in which political power is exercised locally by private individuals rather than through the bureaucracy of a centralized state. It is seen as a transitional stage which may follow the collapse of a unified political system. The term has been used to describe political practices in various areas and times in world history—in ancient Egypt and in twelfth-century Japan, for example—but the most famous of all feudal patterns emerged in France following the collapse of Charlemagne's empire.

In general, medieval political institutions involved three basic elements: (1) a personal element, called lordship or vassalage, by which one nobleman, the vassal, became the loyal follower of a stronger nobleman, the lord or suzerain; (2) a property element, called the fief (usually land), which the vassal received from his lord in order to enable him to fulfill the obligations of vassalage; and (3) a governmental element, meaning the private exercise of governmental functions over vassals and fiefs. The roots of these three elements run back to late Roman and early Germanic times.

By the fifth century the Roman emperor was no longer able to protect his subjects, and citizens had to depend on the patronage system, by which a Roman noble organized a group of less powerful men as a personal bodyguard and in return looked after their wants and interests. A similar arrangement existed among the Germans—the war band or *comitatus*, described by Tacitus (see p. 133). Vassalage, the personal element in feudalism, arose from the combination of the use of patronage and the *comitatus*.

The origin of the property element, the fief, also derives from Roman practices. In the late Roman Empire the owners of great estates (*latifundia*) added steadily to their already extensive holdings. Unable to manage their large tracts directly, the nobles granted the temporary use of portions to other people in exchange for dues and services. Such land was called a *beneficium*, or benefice (literally, a "benefit"). As an example, in late Merovingian times, when mounted warriors rather than old-style foot soldiers were needed to deal effectively with Muslim raiders from Spain, Charles Martel granted numerous benefices to compensate his followers for the added expense of maintaining horses. During the civil wars and foreign invasions of late Carolingian times, the competition among Charlemagne's successors for the available supply of mounted knights led not only to the wholesale granting of benefices but also to making the benefice hereditary. On the death of the vassal, the benefice passed to an heir instead of reverting to the king. Hereditary benefices were commonly called fiefs.

The third basic element, the exercise of governmental power by private individuals, also had antecedents in late Roman times. As the imperial government weakened, the powerful Roman landowners organized their own private armies to police their estates and fend off governmental agents, particularly tax collectors. The emperors also favored certain estates with grants of immunity from imperial authority, a practice the Germanic kings often followed and that became the rule with Charlemagne's successors in their competitive efforts to fill their armies with mounted fief-holding vassals. And where immunity from the king's authority was not freely granted, it was often usurped.

With the combining of these three elements, a definable, although highly complex and variable, governmental pattern emerged in the West by the end of the ninth century.

The Theoretical Feudal Hierarchy

In theory, feudalism was a vast hierarchy. At the top stood the king, and all the land in his kingdom belonged to him. He kept large areas for his personal use (royal or crown lands) and, in return for the military service of a specified number of mounted knights, invested the highest nobles—such as dukes and counts (in Britain, earls)—with the remainder. Those nobles holding lands directly from the king were called tenants-in-chief. They, in turn, in order to obtain the services of the required number of mounted warriors (including themselves) owed to the king, parceled out large portions of their fiefs to lesser nobles. This process, called *subinfeudation*, was continued until the lowest in the scale of vassals was reached—the single knight whose fief was just sufficient to support one mounted warrior.

Subinfeudation became a problem when a conflict of loyalties arose. Since the Count of Champagne, for example, was vassal to nine different lords, on whose side would he fight should two of his lords go to war against one

Impressive symbolism surrounded the knighting ceremony. Here the knight is being armed. Two attendants behind him held his helmet and shield; two others fasten his sword and spurs.

another? This dilemma was partially solved by the custom of liege homage. When a vassal received his first fief, he pledged liege or prior homage to that lord. This obligation was to have top priority over services that he might later pledge to other lords.

Except for the knight with a single fief, a nobleman was usually both a vassal and a lord. Even a king might be a vassal; John of Britain was vassal to King Philip of France for certain French lands, yet he in no way thought himself inferior to Philip.

By maintaining a king at the head of the theoretical feudal hierarchy, custom kept the traces of monarchy intact. Although many feudal kings were little more than figureheads who might be less powerful than their own vassals, the institution of the monarchy was retained out of tradition.

Relation of Lord and Vassal: The Contract

Basic to politcal order was the personal bond between lord and vassal. In the ceremony known as the act of *homage,* the vassal knelt before his lord, or suzerain, and promised to be his "man." In the *oath of fealty* that followed, the vassal swore on the Bible or some other sacred object that he would remain true to his lord. Next, in the ritual of *investiture,* a lance, glove, or even a clump of dirt was handed the vassal to signify his jurisdiction (not ownership) over the fief.

The contract entered into by lord and vassal was usually considered sacred and binding upon both parties. Breaking this tie of mutual obligations was considered a serious offense, because the agreement was the basis of feudalism and hence of early medieval society. The lord on his part was usually obliged to give his vassal protection and justice. The vassal's primary duty was military service. In some instances, he was expected to devote forty days' service each year to the lord without payment. In addition, a vassal could be obliged to assist the lord in rendering justice in the lord's court. At certain times, such as when he was captured and had to be ransomed, the lord also had the right to demand money payments, called *aids.* Unusual aids, such as defraying the expense of going on a crusade, might not be levied without the vassal's consent.

The lord also had certain rights, called *incidents,* regarding the administration of the fief. These included *wardship* (the right to administer the fief during the minority of a vassal's heir) and *forfeiture* of the fief if a vassal failed to honor his obligations.

The final authority in this era was force, and the general atmosphere of the time was one of violence. Defiant vassals frequently made war upon their lords. But warfare was also considered the normal occupation of the nobility, for success offered glory and rich rewards. If successful, warfare enlarged a noble's territory; and, if they produced nothing else, forays and raids kept one active. To die in battle was the only honorable end for a spirited gentleman; to die in bed was a "cow's death."

The Church and Feudalism

The inclusion of the church in the sytem became a political reality. The unsettled conditions caused by the Viking and Magyar invasions forced church officials to enter into close relations with the only power able to offer them protection—the barons in France and the kings in Germany. Bishops and abbots thus became vassals, receiving fiefs for which they were obligated to provide the usual feudal services. The papacy fared even worse; during much of the tenth and early eleventh centuries the papacy became a political prize sought after by local Roman nobles.

In time, the church sought to improve the behavior of the warrior nobility. In addition to attempting to add Christian virtues to chivalry, the code of knightly conduct, (see ch. 10), the church sought to impose limitations on warfare. In the eleventh century bishops called the attention of the knights to the Peace of God and Truce of God. The Peace of God banned from the sacraments all persons who pillaged sacred places or refused to spare noncombatants. The Truce of God established "closed seasons" on fighting: from sunset on Wednesday to sunrise on Monday and certain longer periods, such as Lent. These regulations were generally ignored.

Class Structure

Medieval society essentially consisted of three classes: nobles, peasants, and clergy. Each of these groups had its own role. The nobles were primarily fighters, belonging to an honored society distinct from the freemen and serfs who made up the peasantry. In an age of physical violence, society obviously would accord first place to the man with the sword rather than to the man with the hoe. Members of the clergy came from both the noble and peasant classes. Although most higher churchmen were sons of nobles and held land as vassals under local custom, the clergy formed a class that was considered separate from the nobility and peasantry.

The Early Medieval Economy

The terms *manorial system* and *manorialism* refer to the economic and social system based on the manors, the great estates whose origins go back to the Roman *latifundia* (see p. 87). In Gaul in particular, these estates survived the Germanic invasions. During the early Middle Ages they were held either by the descendants of their Roman owners, by Germanic kings, nobles, or the church. The medieval serf was the direct heir of the Roman *colonus* who worked the land, paid rent in kind, and could not leave the estate without the owner's permission.

The Manor

The manor usually varied in size from one locality to another. A small one might contain only about a dozen households. Since the allotment to each family averaged about 30 acres, the small manors probably included about 350 acres of tillable land, not counting meadows, woods, wasteland, and the lord's *demesne*—the land reserved for the lord's use alone. A large manor might contain fifty families and a total area of 5000 acres.

The center of the manor was the village, with the thatched cottages of the peasants grouped together along one street. Around each cottage was a space large enough for a vegetable patch, chicken yard, haystack, and stable. An important feature of the landscape was the village church, together with the priest's house and the burial ground. The lord's dwelling might be a castle or a more modest manor house.

Distribution of the Land

Every manor contained two types of land, arable and nonarable. Part of the arable land, called the *demesne*, was reserved for the lord and was cultivated for him by his serfs. The remainder of the arable land was held by the villagers. The nonarable land, consisting of meadow, wood, and wasteland, was used in common by the villagers and the lord.

From one sixth to one third of the arable land was given over to the lord's demesne. The demesne might be either sharply set off from the tenures of the villagers or distributed among the lands of the tenants. The land not held in demesne was allotted among the villagers under the open-field system, whereby the fields were subdivided into strips. The strips, each containing about an acre, were separated by narrow paths of uncultivated turf. The serf's holding was not all in one plot, for all soil throughout the manor was not equally fertile, and a serious attempt was made to give each of the villagers land of the same quality. Each tenant was really a shareholder in the village community, not only in the open fields but also in the meadow, pasture, wood, and wastelands. Tenants' rights in these common lands were determined by the number of acres they held in the open fields.

Wooded land was valuable as a place to graze pigs, the most common animal on the manor. Again, tenants were limited in the number of pigs that they might turn loose there. Tenants could also gather dead wood in the forest, but cutting down green wood was prohibited unless authorized by the lord.

Medieval Farming Methods

It is dangerous to generalize about agricultural methods, because differences in locality, fertility of soil, crop production, and other factors resulted in a variety of farming methods. But if we study farming as practiced in northwestern Europe, we can discover some common factors. The implements the peasants used were extremely crude; the plow was a cumbersome instrument with heavy wheels, often requiring as many as eight oxen to pull it. (By the twelfth century plow horses were common.) There were also crude harrows, sickles, beetles for breaking up clods, and flails for threshing. Inadequate methods of farming soon exhausted the soil. It has been estimated that the average yield per acre was only six to eight bushels of wheat, a fourth of the modern yield. In classical times farmers had learned that soil planted continually with one crop rapidly deteriorated. To counteract this, they employed a two-field system, whereby half of the arable land was planted while the other half lay fallow to recover its fertility. Medieval farmers learned that wheat or rye could be planted in the autumn as well as in the spring. As a result, by the ninth century they were dividing the land into three fields, with one planted in the fall, another in the spring, and the third left

A medieval print capturing the whole life of a medieval village. In the foreground is a hunting party, tthe ladies riding behind the knights. On the most elevated level in the countryside stands the castle with its moat and draw-bridge. The village church at the center is surrounded by the houses of the villagers. At the left is the mill and millrace; to the right of the mill is what appears to be a wine or cider press. In the upper right, a serf plows the ground using the heavy plow common to northwestern Europe.

lying fallow. This system not only kept more land in production but also required less plowing in any given year.

Administration of the Manor

Although the lord might live on one of his manors, each manor was usually administered by such officials as the steward, the bailiff, and the reeve. The steward was the general overseer who supervised the business of all his lord's manors and presided over the manorial court. It was the bailiff's duty to supervise the cultivation of the lord's demesne, collect rents, dues, and fines, and inspect the work done by the peasants. The reeve was the "foreman" of the villagers, chosen by them and representing their interests.

In status and function, the various social classes that made up the manor community differed not only from locality to locality but from period to period. Nonetheless, they can be roughly divided into three major categories: the lord and his officials, the free peasants, and the nonfree peasants (serfs).

There often were freemen on the manor, although they may have constituted only a small portion of its population. Freemen were not subject to the same demands as the serfs. The freeman did not have to work in the lord's fields himself but could send substitutes. He paid rent for his holding and, if he wanted to leave, could locate a new tenant for the land, provided the transfer took place in open court and the new man was acceptable to the lord. Aside from these privileges, however, the freeman was little different from a serf. His strips in the open field adjoined those of the serf and he lived in a cottage in the same village.

Serfs were bound to the manor and could not leave without the lord's consent. Serfdom was a hereditary status; the children of a serf were attached to the soil as their parents were. The lord of the manor was bound by the force of custom to respect certain rights of his serfs. So long as they paid their dues and services, serfs could not be evicted from their hereditary holdings. Although a serf could not appear in court against his lord or a freeman, he could appeal to the manor court against any of his fellows.

The peasants based their economic, political, legal, and social life in the manor, but to the lord the manor was essentially a source of income from three obligations imposed on the peasantry: (1) services in the form of labor, (2) dues levied on the peasant, and (3) manorial monopolies. The most important service was *week-work*. The peasant had to donate two or three days' work each week to the lord. The week-work included such jobs as repairing roads or bridges or carting manure to the fields. Because the lord's demesne "had always to be plowed first, sowed first, and reaped first," the peasant also had to perform extra *boon-work* at these times.

Various dues or payments, in money where available, but usually in produce, were made to the lord. The *taille* (or tallage), a tax on whatever

Both peasant men and women toiled in the fields. Here women reap with sickles, while behind them a man binds the sheaves.

property a peasant managed to accumulate, was the most common. It was levied on all peasants at least once a year. Another burdensome tax was imposed when a peasant died; before a son could inherit his father's cottage and strips, the lord claimed the best beast or moveable possession as inheritance tax.

In addition to service and dues, the lord profited from certain monopolies. He operated the only grain mill, oven for baking bread, and wine and cider press on the manor, and he collected a toll each time these services were needed.

The Life of the Peasants

On the manors of the Middle Ages the margin between starvation and survival was narrow, and the life of the peasant was not easy. Famines were common; warfare was a consant threat; grasshoppers, locusts, caterpillars, and rats repeatedly destroyed the crops. Men and women alike had to toil long hours in the fields. A medieval poem vividly describes the life of a peasant family:

> I saw a poor man o'er the plough bending . . .
> All befouled with mud, as he the plough
>   followed. . . .
> His wife walked by him with a long goad, . . .
> Barefoot on the bare ice, so that the blood
>   followed.
> And at the field's end lay a little bowl,
> And therein lay a little child wrapped in rags,
> And twain of two years old upon anothe side;
> And all of them sang a song that sorrow was
>   to hear,
> They cried all a cry, a sorrowful note,
> And the poor man sighed sore, and said
> "Children, be still."[4]

The difficulties of peasant life were reflected in the home, a cottage with mud walls, clay floor, and thatched roof. The fire burned on a flat heartstone in the middle of the floor; and unless the peasant was rich enough to afford a chimney, the smoke escaped through a hole in the roof. The windows had no glass and were stuffed with straw in the winter. Furnishings were meager, consisting usually of a table, a kneading trough for dough, a cupboard, and a bed, often either a heap of straw or a box filled with straw, which

An illumination from the Flemish *Hours of the Virgin* (c. 1515) illustrates several pastoral activities: milking the cow, herding livestock, and churning butter.

served the entire family. Pigs and chickens wandered about the cottage continually, while the stable was frequently under the same roof, next to the family quarters.

The peasants, despite their hard, monotonous life, enjoyed a few pleasures. Wrestling was exceedingly popular, as were cockfighting, a crude type of football, and fighting with quarter-staves, in which the contestants stood an excellent chance of getting their heads bashed in. Around the porch of the parish church the peasants often congregated to dance and sing on the numerous holy days. The church preached in vain against "ballads and dancings and evil and wanton songs and such-like lures of the Devil." The peasants refused to give up these amusements, a small enough compensation for the constant exploitation they suffered.

The Church in the Early Middle Ages

As Europe gradually emerged from the destruction of the Roman Empire, the church became one of the mainstays of civilization. During the pontificate of Gregory I the Great (590–604), the medieval papacy began to assert its authority. Gregory's achievement was to go beyond the claim of papal primacy in the church (see p. 146) by beginning to establish the temporal power of the papacy.

Gregory the Great and the Early Medieval Papacy, 600–1000

A Roman aristocrat by birth, Gregory witnessed and commented on the devastation of Rome as the city changed hands three times during Justinian's long struggle to retake Italy from the Ostrogoths:

Ruins on ruins.... Where is the senate? Where the people? All the pomp of secular dignities has been destroyed.... And we, the few that we are who remain, every day we are menaced by scourges and innumerable trials.[5]

Concluding that the world was coming to an end, Gregory withdrew from it to become a Benedictine monk. In 579 the pope convinced him to undertake a fruitless mission seeking Byzantine aid against the Lombards, who had invaded Italy a few years before. After Gregory was elected pope in 590, he assumed the task of protecting Rome and its surrounding territory from the Lombard threat. Thus Gregory was the first pope to act as temporal ruler of a part of what later became the Papal States.

Gregory the Great also laid the foundation for the elaborate papal machinery of church government. He took the first step toward papal control of the church outside of Italy by sending a mission of Benedictine monks to convert the pagan Anglo-Saxons. The pattern of church government Gregory established in England—bishops supervised by archbishops, and archbishops by the pope—became standard in the church.

The task of establishing papal control of the church and extending the pope's temporal

An ivory panel of Pope Gregory the Great. A dove perched on his shoulder is said to have inspired Gregory as he wrote his *Commentaries.*

authority was continued by Gregory's successors. In the eighth century, English missionaries transferred to Germany and France the pattern of papal government they had known in England; and the Donation of Pepin (see p. 226), by creating the Papal States, greatly increased the pope's temporal power. The papacy's spiritual and temporal power was restrained, however, with the onset of feudalism. Beginning in the late ninth century, the church, including the papacy, fell more and more under the control of secular lords and kings.

Benedict of Nursia, Rule of St. Benedict

The *Rule of St. Benedict* was adopted as a creed of life by monks from the fifth century throughout the Middle Ages. The following is a selection from the Rule.

Idleness is an enemy of the soul. Because this is so the brethren ought to be occupied at specified times in manual labour and at other fixed hours in holy reading. We therefore think that both these may be arranged for as follows: from Easter to the first of October, on coming out from Prime, let the brethern labour till about the fourth hour. From the fourth till close upon the sixth hour let them employ themselves in reading. On rising from table after the sixth hour let them rest on their beds in strict silence; but if anyone shall wish to read, let him do so in such a way as not to disturb any one else.

Let *None* be said somewhat before the time, about the middle of the eighth hour, and after this all shall work at what they have to do till evening. If, however, the nature of the place or poverty require them to labour at gathering in the harvest, let them not grieve at that, for then are they truly monks when they live by the labour of their hands, as our Fathers and the Apostles did. Let everything, however, be done with moderation for the sake of the faint-hearted.

From the first of October till the beginning of Lent let the brethren be occupied in reading till the end of the second hour. At that time *Tierce* shall be said, after which they shall labour at the work enjoined them till *None*. At the first signal for the hour of *None* all shall cease to work, so as to be ready when the second signal is given. After their meal they shall be employed in reading or on the psalms.

On the days of Lent, from the morning till end of the third hour, the brethren are to have time for reading, after which let them work at what is set them to do till the close of the tenth hour. . . .

It is of much import that one or two seniors be appointed to go about the monastery at such times as the brethren are free to read, in order to see that no one is slothful, given to idleness or foolish talking instead of reading, and so not only makes no profit himself but also distracts others. If any such be found (which God forbid) let him be corrected once or twice, and if he amend not let him be subjected to regular discipline of such a character that the rest may take warning. Moreover one brother shall not associate with another at unsuitable hours.

On Sunday also, all, save those who are assigned to various offices, shall have time for reading. If, however, any one be so negligent and slothful as to be unwilling or unable to read or meditate, he must have some work given him, so as not to be idle. For weak brethren or those of delicate constitutions, some work or craft shall be found to keep them from idleness, and yet not such as to crush them by the heavy labour or to drive them away. The weakness of such brethren must be taken into consideration by the abbott. . . .

Let him (the abbot) make no distinction of persons in the monastery. Let not one be loved more than another, save such as be found to excel in obedience or good works. Let not the free-born be put before the serf-born in religion, unless there be other reasonable cause for it. If upon due consideration the abbot shall see such cause he may place him where he pleases; otherwise let all keep their own places, because *whether bond or free we are all one in Christ*, and bear an equal burden of service under one Lord; for *with God there is no accepting of persons*. For one thing only are we preferred by Him, if we are found better than others in good works and more humble. Let the abbot therefore have equal love for all and let all, according to their deserts, be under the same discipline. . . .

From *The Rule of St. Benedict*, trans. Cardinal Gasquet (London: Chatto and Windus Ltd., 1936).

Missionary Activities of the Church

The early Middle Ages was a period of widespread missionary activity. By spreading Christianity, missionaries aided in the fusion of Germanic and classical cultures. Monasteries served as havens for those seeking a contemplative life, as repositories of learning for scholars, and often as progressive farming centers. The zeal with which the monks approached their faith often extended beyond the monastic walls.

One of the earliest Christian missionaries to the Germans was Ulfilas (c. 311–383), who spent forty years among the Visigoths and translated most of the Bible into Gothic. Ulfilas and other early missionaries were followers of Arius, and so the Arian form of Christianity (see p. 146) was adopted by all the Germanic tribes in the empire except the Franks and Anglo-Saxons. As we saw earlier, the Franks' adoption of Roman Catholicism produced an important alliance between Frankish rulers and the papacy.

Another great missionary, Patrick, was born in England about 389 and later fled to Ireland to escape the Anglo-Saxon invaders. As a result of his missionary activities in Ireland, monasteries were founded and Christianity became the dominant religion. In the late sixth and seventh centuries a large number of monks from the Irish monasteries went to Scotland, northern England, the kingdom of the Franks, and even to Italy. The Irish monks eagerly pursued scholarship, and their monasteries became storehouses for priceless manuscripts.

When Gregory the Great became pope, the papacy joined forces with monasticism to take an active role in the missionary movement. Gregory sent a Benedictine mission to England in 596. Starting in Kent, where an archbishopric was founded at Canterbury ("Kent town"), Roman Christianity spread through England, and finally even the Irish church founded by St. Patrick acknowledged the primacy of Rome.

The English church, in turn, played an important part in the expansion of Roman-controlled Christianity on the Continent. Boniface, the greatest missionary from England in the eighth century, spent thirty-five years among the Germanic tribes. Known as the "Apostle to the Germans," he established several important monasteries, bishoprics, and an archbishopric at Mainz before he turned to the task of reforming the church in France. There he revitalized the monasteries, organized a system of local parishes to bring Christianity to the countryside, and probably was instrumental in forming the alliance beween the papacy and the Carolingian house. Roman Catholic missionaries also worked among the Scandinavians and the western Slavs.

The Preservation of Knowledge

One of the great contributions of the monasteries was the preservation of the learning of the classical world and that of the church. Learning did not entirely die out in western Europe, of course. Seeing that the ability to read Greek was quickly disappearing, the sixth-century Roman scholar Boethius, an administrator under the Ostrogothic king Theodoric, determined to preserve Greek learning by translating all of Plato and Aristotle into Latin. Only Aristotle's treatises on logic were translated, and these remained the sole works of that philosopher

Detail of a manuscript illumination from Fulda Abbey depicting Saint Boniface, Apostle to the Germans, baptizing a convert.

available in the West until the twelfth century. Unjustly accused of treachery by Theodoric, Boethius was thrown into prison, where he wrote *The Consolation of Philosophy* while awaiting execution. This little work later became a medieval textbook on philosophy.

Cassiodorus, a contemporary of Boethius who had also served Theodoric, devoted most of his life to the collection and preservation of classical knowledge. By encouraging the monks to copy valuable manuscripts, he was instrumental in making the monasteries centers of learning. Following his example, many monasteries established scriptoria, departments concerned exclusively with copying manuscripts.

During the early Middle Ages most education took place in the monasteries. In the late sixth and seventh centuries, when the effects of the barbarian invasions were still being felt on the Continent, Irish monasteries provided a safe haven for learning. There men studied Greek and Latin, copied and preserved manuscripts, and in illuminating them produced masterpieces of art. *The Book of Kells* is a surviving example of their skill.

An outstanding scholar of the early Middle Ages, the Venerable Bede (d. 735), followed the Irish tradition of learning in a northern English monastery. Bede described himself as "ever taking delight in learning, teaching, and writing." His many writings, which included textbooks and commentaries on the Scriptures, summed up most knowledge available in his age. Through Alcuin later in the century, Bede's learning influenced the Carolingian Renaissance (see p. 229). Bede's best work, the *Ecclesiastical History of the English People*, with its many original documents and vivid character sketches, is our chief source for early British history.

The Chi-Rho page from the Book of Kells. The Irish monks applied Celtic and Germanic motifs to their illuminations of Holy Writ, thereby creating a dynamically restless abstract style, largely removed from physical reality.

Conclusion

During the period known as the early Middle Ages (500–1000), the focus of European civilization shifted from the Mediterranean to France. The conversion of Clovis to Christianity and the subsequent Frankish alliance with the papacy united the most energetic of the Germanic tribes with the greatest existing force for civilization in western Europe—the Christian church. The foundation of the new Europe was completed by Charlemagne, but his empire depended too heavily on the forceful personality of its founder and did not survive his less dynamic successors. After the Carolingian collapse, new political and economic patterns evolved to meet the turbulent conditions of the time.

The decentralized political systems and customs of government during the early Middle Ages are sometimes generally referred to as feudalism. This term is helpful in describing a theoretical pattern of government, although in reality local diversity and custom were more the rule. Blending of Germanic and Roman practices to suit regional needs resulted in a great variety of political patterns.

Manorialism is the term sometimes employed to generalize the condition of life for the vast majority of commoners in the early Middle Ages.

On the manors, serfs grew the food for all segments of medieval society and performed the exhausting labor required. They were politically restricted, bound to their estates, and very rarely in a position to control their own destinies.

Throughout the period, the church attempted to serve the spiritual needs of the populace, in addition to strengthening its position as an institution of power and influence. The church also spread its influence through missionary activity across the Continent and into England and Ireland. Monasteries served not only as centers from which missionary activity spread, but also as repositories for the preservation of the learning of the classical world and the church itself.

Suggestions for Reading

M. Keen, *The Pelican History of Medieval Europe** (Penguin); D. Hay, *The Medieval Centuries*• (Torchbooks); and H. Trevor-Roper, *The Rise of Christian Europe** (Harcourt Brace Jovanovich) are valuable surveys of the Middle Ages. See also N. Zacour, *An Introduction to Medieval Institutions*, 2nd ed. (St. Martin's, 1976) and C. Erickson, *The Medieval Vision: Essays in History and Perception** (Oxford, 1976).

R. E. Sullivan, *Heirs of the Roman Empire** (Cornell), and A. R. Lewis, *Emerging Medieval Europe, A.D. 400–1000** (Knopf) are excellent brief surveys of the early Middle Ages. See John Morris, *The Age of Arthur* (Scribner's, 1973) for a history of the British Isles to A.D. 650. For greater detail see H. Moss, *The Birth of the Middle Ages, 395–814** (Oxford); C. Dawson, *The Making of Europe** (Meridian); M. Deanesley, *History of Early Medieval Europe, 476–911** (Varnes and Noble); C. H. Lawrence, *Medieval Monasticism** (Longmans, 1984); and G. Barraclough, *The Crucible of Europe: The Ninth and Tenth Centuries* (Univ. of California, Berkeley, 1976).

H. Fichtenau, *The Carolingian Empire: The Age of Charlemagne* (Torchbooks) is the best work on the subject. See also R. Winston, *Charlemagne: From the Hammer to the Cross** (Peter Smith); S. F. Wemple, *Women in Frankish Society** (Pennsylvania, 1981); and P. Munz, *Life in the Age of Charlemagne** (Capricorn). On the Carolingian Renaissance see F. Heer, *The World of Charlemagne* (Macmillan, 1975), which is scholarly and readable; E. Duckett, *Alcuin, Friend of Charlemagne: His World and His Work* (Shoe String); and M. Laistner, *Thought and Letters in Western Europe, A.D. 500 to 900** (Cornell).

J. Brondsted, *The Vikings** (Penguin) and Gwyn Jones, *A History of the Vikings* (Galaxy, 1973) are outstanding on Viking activities. G. Turvill-Petre, *The Heroic Age of Scandinavia* (Greenwood, 1976) describes the Norse way of life as reflected in their heroic legends.

Carol Stephenson, *Mediaeval Feudalism** (Cornell) is a clear introduction. See also F. Ganshof, *Feudalism** (Torchbokks); and M. Bloch, *The Feudal Society,** 2 vols., (Phoenix). S. Painter, *French Chivalry** (Cornell) is a delightful essay on the many aspects of chivalry. See also R. Barber, *The Knight and Chivalry** (Harper and Row, 1982).

On rural life and the manorial system see *The Agrarian life of the Middle Ages*, Vol. 1, in *The Cambridge Economic History of Europe*, 2nd ed. (Cambridge, 1967); and G. Duby, *Rural Economy and Country Life in the Medieval West* (South Carolina, 1968). G. G. Coulton, *Medieval Village, Manor, and Monastery* (Peter Smith); H. S. Bennett, *Life on the Medieval Manor** (Cambridge); and E. Power, *Medieval People** (Barnes and Noble) are worthwhile accounts. See also D. Herliky, *Opera Muliebria: Women and Work in Medieval Europe** (McGraw-Hill, 1990).

*Indicates a less expensive paperbound edition.

Notes

1. Gregory of Tours, *History of the Franks II*, 30; quoted in Eleanor Duckett, *The Gateway to the Middle Ages* (New York: The Macmillan Company, 1938), p. 231.
2. Quoted in M. L. W. Laistner, *Thought and Letters in Western Europe, A.D. 500 to 900* (Ithaca, NY: Cornell University Press, 1931), pp. 196–197.
3. M. L. W. Laistner, *Thought and Letters in Western Europe*, p. 390.
4. Quoted in E. M. Hulme, *History of the British People* (New York: Century Co., 1929), pp. 121–122.
5. Quoted in R. H. C. Davis, *A History of Medieval Europe: From Constantine to Saint Louis* (London: Longmans, Green & Co., Ltd., 1957), p. 80.

Chapter 10

The High Middle Ages, 1000–1300

Medieval Politics, Economics, Religion, and Learning

Between 1000 and 1300, drastic political, economic, and social change occurred in Europe. Not only did trade revive, cities grow, and a new bourgeois social class emerge, but in several regions kings enforced their power at the expense of the nobility, and strong centralized government was realized in several regions of Europe.

The growth of trade and commerce to national and international scale is one of the impressive achievements of the High Middle Ages. The revitalization of trade and commerce, coupled with a revival of urban life, helped foster the growth of the bourgeoisie, or middle class.

Political and economic change, of course, had a direct impact on the culture of the High Middle Ages. In these years, the Church reached the apex of its power, and religion played a crucial role in the development and definition of medieval intellectual life.

The Making of Modern Britain

After the Romans withdrew from England in the fifth century, Germanic tribes known as Anglo-Saxons invaded the island and divided it among more than a dozen hostile tribal kingdoms. Gradually, rivalries among the kingdoms diminished, and the overlordship of the island was held in turn by the different rulers. In the ninth century the kingdom of Wessex (see map, p. 229) held the dominant position. Its king, Alfred the Great (871–899), was confronted with the task of turning back a new wave of invaders, the Danes, who overran all the other English king-

doms. Alfred defeated the Danes and forced them into a treaty whereby they settled in what came to be called the Danelaw (see map, p. 231) and accepted Christianity.

In addition to being a successful warrior, Alfred the Great made notable contributions to the creation of a stronger nation. He reorganized the militia of freemen (*fyrd*) so that some were always ready for battle while the rest tilled the

A successful warrior and a patron of intellectual activity, Alfred the Great also made notable contributions to government in order that, as he wrote, he "might worthily and fittingly steer and rule the dominion that was entrusted to me."

soil, and the ships he built to repel future Viking attacks won for him the title of founder of the English navy.

Following the example of Charlemagne, Alfred also advanced the intellectual life of his country, inviting scholars from the Continent to the palace school he founded. He also encouraged monks to keep an account of current affairs, the *Anglo-Saxon Chronicle*, which continued to be written for hundreds of years after his reign.

Alfred's successors were able rulers who conquered the Danelaw, the northern portion of the island previously conquered by the Danes, and created a unified English monarchy. Danes and Saxons intermarried, and soon most differences between two peoples disappeared. After 975, however, the power of the central government lagged, and with it the ability to keep order at home and repel outside attacks. The weakness of the kingdom is well illustrated in the reign of Ethelred the Unready (978–1016), who constantly struggled to keep a firm hand on the great nobles and who was forced to cope with a new attack by the Danes.

Following Ethelred's reign, the Anglo-Saxons were again overrun by the Danes, and King Canute of Denmark ruled England as well as Norway. Canute proved to be a wise and civilized king and was well liked by his Anglo-Saxon subjects because he respected their rights and customs. Canute's empire fell apart after his death in 1035, and in 1042 the English crown was secured by Ethelred's son, Edward the Confessor. Although famous for his devotion to religion, Edward was a weak ruler who had little control over the powerful earls who had usurped most of the king's authority in their regions. This decline in government was reversed after the Normans conquered the island in 1066.

William the Conqueror and the Norman Conquest

Norman influence in England really began in the reign of Edward the Confessor. Edward had spent most of his early life in Normandy, and as king of England he showed a strong pro-Norman bias. When Edward died without heir in 1066, the *Witan*—the council of the kingdom—selected Harold Godwinson, a powerful English earl, as the new ruler. Immediately William, duke of Normandy, claimed the English throne, basing his demand on a flimsy hereditary right and on the assertion that Edward had promised him the crown.

An outstanding statesman and soldier, William as duke of Normandy had subdued the rebellious nobles and established an effective centralized feudal state. William effectively controlled his vassals, and his feudal army of a thousand knights made him the most powerful ruler west of Germany. His centralized authority in Normandy contrasted sharply with the situation in England, where the powerful earls were continually challenging the king.

William and his army of five thousand men crossed the English Channel to enforce the Norman claim to the English throne. On October 14, 1066, William's mounted knights broke through the English infantry at Hastings. Resistance ceased when Harold was slain. The defeat ended Anglo-Saxon rule and brought a new pattern of government that would make England the strongest state in Europe.

William introduced the Norman system of feudalism into England. As owner of all England by right of conquest, William retained some land as his royal domain and granted the remainder as fiefs to royal vassals called tenants-in-chief, among whom were bishops and abbots. In return for their fiefs, the tenants-in-chief provided William with a number of knights to serve in the royal army. To furnish the required service, the great vassals—most of whom were French-speaking Normans—granted parts of the fiefs among their own vassals. But from all the landholders in England, regardless of whether they were his immediate vassals, William exacted homage and an oath that they would "be faithful to him against all other men." Both the tenants-in-chief holding fiefs directly from the king and the lesser tenants holding fiefs as vassals of the tenants-in-chief swore this loyalty, which meant that a disgruntled noble could not call out his own vassals against the king, because every person owed his first allegiance to William.

The Domesday Survey, which was originally a survey for payments of money to buy off the Danes from Anglo-Saxon territory, was retained by William and turned into an efficient source of royal revenue. Because William, as all medieval kings, constantly needed money, he

Beowulf

Beowulf is the oldest epic poem of the English people. Its origins go back to an oral tradition well before the 10th century, at which time it was written in final form.

The monstrous dragon inflamed with
the feud,
Rushed on the king when the
opening offered,
Fierce and flaming; fastened its fangs
In Beowulf's throat; he was bloodied with
gore;
His life-blood streamed from the welling
wound,
As they tell the tale, in the king's sore need
His shoulder-companion showed forth his
valor,
His craft and courage, and native strength.
To the head of the dragon he paid no heed,
Though his hand was burned as he helped his
king.
A little lower the stalwart struck
At the evil beast, and his blade drove home
Plated and gleaming. The fire began
To lessen and wane. The king of the Weders
Summoned his wits; he drew the dagger
He wore on his corselet, cutting and keen,
And slit asunder the worm with the blow.
So they felled the foe and wrought their
revenge;
The kinsmen together had killed the dragon.
So a man should be when the need is bitter!
That was the last fight Beowulf fought;
That was the end of his work in the world.
The wound which the dragon had dealth
him began
To swell and burn; and soon he could feel
The baneful venom inflaming his breast.
The wise, old warrior sank down by the wall

And stared at the work of the giants of old,
The arches of stone and the standing columns
Upholding the ancient earth-hall within.
His loyal thane, the kindest of comrades,
Saw Beowulf bloody and broken in war;
In his hands bore water and bathed his
leader,
And loosened the helm from his dear lord's
head.
Beowulf spoke, though his hurt was sore,
The wounds of battle grevious and grim.
Full well he weened that his life was ended,
And all the joy of his years on earth;

That his days were done, and Death most
near;
'My armor and sword I would leave to my
son
Had Fate but granted, born of my body,
An heir to follow me after I'm gone.
For fifty winters I've ruled this realm,
And never a lord of a neighboring land
Dared strike with terror or seek with sword.
In my life I abode by the lot assigned,
Kept well what was mine, courted no
quarrels,
Swore no false oaths. And now for all this
Though my hurt is grevous, my heart is glad.
When life leaves body, the Lord of mankind
Cannot lay to my charge the killing of
kinsmen!

From *Beowulf: The Oldest English Epic*, trans. Charles W. Kennedy (New York: Oxford University Press, 1940), pp. 86–91.

ordered an accurate census of the property and property holders in his realm as a basis for collecting all the feudal aids and incidents (see p. 235) owed to him.

In line with his policy of controlling all aspects of the government, William revamped the old Anglo-Saxon *Witan*, which had elected and advised the kings. The new Norman ruler changed its title to the Great Council—also called *curia regis*, the king's council or court—and converted it into a body composed of his tenants-in-chief. The Great Council met at least three times a year as a court of justice for the great barons and as an advisory body in important matters. At other times a small permanent council of barons advised the king.

The Bayeux tapestry, a woolen embroidery on linen, dates from the 11th century. Over 230 feet long, it depicts events in the Norman Conquest of England in 1066 accompanied by a commentary in Latin and surrounded by a decorative border portraying scenes from fables and everyday life. In the section here a woman and child, symbolizing the widow and orphan, the eternal victims of warfare, rush from a burning building.

William also dominated the English church. He appointed bishops and abbots and required them to provide military service for their lands. Although he permitted the church to retain its courts he denied them the right to appeal cases to the pope without his consent. Nor could the decrees of popes and church councils circulate in England without royal approval.

William II, who succeeded his father in 1087, was an ineffective king who inspired several baronial revolts before being shot in the back—accidently, it was said—while hunting. Succeeding him was his brother, Henry I (1110–1135), a more able monarch who easily put down the only baronial revolt that challenged him.

While the Great Council, made up of the chief nobles, occasionally met to advise the king, the small permanent council of barons grew in importance. From it appeared specialized organs of government. The exchequer, or court of accounts, supervised the collection of royal revenue, greatly increased with the revival of a money economy. Notable was *scutage* or "shield money," a fee the king encouraged his vassals to pay in lieu of personal military service. The well-

trained "barons of the exchequer" also sat as a special court to try cases involving revenue.

Henry I's achievements in strengthening the monarchy were obviated by the nineteen years of chaos that followed his death. Ignoring their promise to recognize Henry's only surviving child, Matilda, wife of Geoffrey Plantagenet, count of Anjou in France, many barons supported Henry's weak nephew Stephen. During the resulting civil war the nobility became practically independent of the crown and, secure in their strong castles, freely pillaged the land.

Henry II

Anarchy ceased with the accession of Matilda's son, Henry II (1154–1189), the founder of the Plantagenet, or Angevin, House in England. As a result of his inheritance (Normandy and Anjou) and his marriage to Eleanor of Aquitaine, the richest heiress in France, Henry's possessions stretched from Scotland to the Pyrenees (see map, p. 249). Henry's great military skill and restless energy were important assets to his reign. He quickly recaptured the rights and lands of his grandfather Henry I and began rebuilding the power of the monarchy in England.

Henry's chief contribution to the development of the English monarchy was to increase the jurisdiction of the royal courts at the expense of the feudal courts. This produced three major results: a permanent system of circuit courts presided over by itinerant justices, the jury system, and a body of law common to all England.

Itinerant justices on regular circuits were sent out once each year to enforce the "King's Peace." To make this system of royal criminal justice more effective, Henry employed the method of inquest used by William the Conqueror in the Domesday Survey. In each shire a body of important men were sworn (*juré*) to report to the sheriff all crimes committed since the last session of the circuit court. Thus originated the modern grand jury that presents information for an indictment.

Henry's courts also used the jury system to settle private lawsuits. Instead of deciding such civil cases by means of oath-helpers or lengthy trial by ordeal (see p. 134), the circuit judges handed down quick decisions based upon evidence sworn to by a jury of men selected because they were acquainted with the facts of the case. This more efficient system caused litigants to flock to the royal courts, a procedure facilitated by the sale of "writs," which ordered a sheriff to bring the case to a royal court.

Henry's judicial reforms promoted the growth of the common law—one of the most important factors in welding the English people into a nation. The decisions of the royal justices became the basis for future decisions made in the king's courts, superseded the many diverse systems of local justice in the shires, and became the law common to all English people.

Thomas à Becket, Victim of Church-State Rivalry

Although Henry strengthened the royal courts at the expense of the baronial courts, he was not so successful against another rival—the church courts. When he appointed Thomas à Becket archbishop of Canterbury, the king assumed that his close friend and former chancellor could easily be persuaded to cooperate, but Becket proved to be stubbornly independent and upheld the authority of the church courts over Henry's.

In 1164 Henry stipulated that clergyman found guilty by a church court of committing crimes, such as murder and grand larceny, were to be unfrocked and tried by a royal court, where punishments were more severe. Henry's idea was to prevent the abuses resulting from "benefit of clergy," the principle that the church alone had legal jurisdiction over its clergy. Becket refused to yield, claiming that clergymen would suffer unjust "double punishment" for a crime by being both unfrocked by the church and punished by the state.

When Becket received no support from the English clergy, he fled to France and appealed to the pope for aid. After a few years the pope resolved the quarrel, and the archbishop returned to England. Becket's first act, however,

THE DOMINIONS OF HENRY II

- Inheritance
- Suzerainty
- Acquisitions by Marriage to Eleanor of Aquitaine
- French Royal Domain

SCOTLAND
Bannockburn
NORTH SEA
IRELAND
ATLANTIC OCEAN
Dublin
York
WALES
ENGLAND
London
Canterbury
Calais
×Sluys
Rhine R.
Crecy×
×Agincourt
English Channel
Rouen
NORMANDY
Paris
BRITTANY
MAINE
Orléans
Nantes
ANJOU
Tours
BAY OF BISCAY
×Poitiers
AQUITAINE
Bordeaux
Garonne R.
GASCONY
TOULOUSE
Rhône R.

A detail from the Carrow Psalter depicts the murder of Thomas à Becket by the knights of Henry II in Canterbury Cathedral. One knight has broken his sword over the archbishops's head.

was to excommunicate the bishops who, in his absence, had supported the designation of Henry's oldest son as heir to the throne. When this news reached Henry, in a fit of passion he roared: "What a pack of fools and cowards I have nourished in my house, that not one of them will avenge me of this turbulent priest."[1] Responding to this tirade, four knights went to Canterbury and murdered Becket before the high altar of the cathedral.

Popular outrage over this murder destroyed Henry's chances of reducing the power of the church courts. Becket became a national hero and, after miracles were reported to have occurred at his tomb, was canonized a saint.

The Successors of Henry II

Henry's promising beginning was marred by the mistakes of his successors. Having no taste for routine tasks of government, Richard the Lion-Hearted (1189–1199) spent only five months of his ten-year reign in Britain, which he regarded as a source of money for his overseas adventures. Richard wasted his country's wealth in winning a great reputation as a crusader (see p. 263) and in fighting the king of France. The royal bureaucracy worked so well, however, that Richard's absence made little difference.

Richard's successor, his brother John (1199–1216), was an inept ruler who lacked both his brother's chivalrous qualities and his father's genius. John's cruelty and unscrupulousness cost him the support of his barons at the time he needed them most in his struggles with the two ablest men of the age, Philip II of France and Pope Innocent III. As feudal overlord for John's possessions in France, Philip found an occasion to declare John an unfaithful vassal and therefore his fiefs forfeit. John put up only feeble resistance, and after losing more than half his possessions in France he became involved in a struggle with Innocent III in which he was forced to make complete surrender (see p. 269). In the meantime, John had completely alienated the British barons, who rebelled and in 1215 forced John to affix his seal to Magna Carta, which bound the king to observe all feudal rights and privileges. Although in later centuries, people looked back on Magna Carta as one of the most important documents in the story of political

The Great Seal of King John of England. This seal was affixed to Magna Carta. The Great Charter limited the power of the king and protected the feudal rights of the nobles.

freedom, to the English of the time, Magna Carta did not appear to introduce any new constitutional principles. It was an agreement between barons and the king, the aristocracy and the monarchy.

The importance of Magna Carta does not lie in its original purpose but rather in the subsequent use made of it. Two great principles were potential in the charter: The law is above the king; and the king can be compelled by force to obey the law of the land. This concept of the rule of law and the limited power of the crown was to play an important role in the development of English history.

The Origins of Parliament

The French-speaking Normans commonly used the word *Parlement* (from *parler*, "to speak") for the Great Council. Anglicized as *Parliament*, the term was used interchangeably with Great Council and *curia regis*. Modern historians, however, generally apply the term to the Great Council only after 1265, when its membership was radically enlarged.

The first meeting of Parliament, the enlarged Great Council, took place in the midst of a baronial rebellion against Henry III (1216–1272), the son of King John. In an effort to gain the widest possible popular support, Simon de Montfort, the leader of the rebellion, summoned not only the barons but also two knights from every shire and two burghers from every borough to the Great Council in 1265.

Parliament first became truly influential during the reign of Henry III's son, Edward I (1272–1307), one of England's most outstanding monarchs. Beginning with the "Model Parliament" of 1295, Edward followed the pattern set by Simon de Montfort in summoning representatives of shires and towns to meetings of the Great Council. In calling parliaments, Edward had no idea of making any concession to popular government.

Early in the fourteenth century the representatives of the knights and the burghers, called the "Commons," adopted the practice of meeting separately from the lords spiritual and temporal. Thus arose the division of Parliament into what came to be called the House of Commons and the House of Lords.

Edward I at a session of Parliament. Edward was the first monarch to give real standing to the institution of Parliament and to expand it to include representatives of the shires and boroughs.

Parliament, particularly the Commons, soon discovered its power as the major source of revenue for the king. It gradually became the custom for Parliament to exercise this "power of the purse" by withholding its financial grants until the king had redressed grievances, made known by petitions. Parliament also presented petitions to the king with the request that they be recognized as statutes, as the laws drawn up by the king and his council and confirmed in Parliament were called. Gradually the right to initiate legislation through petition was obtained. Again, Parliament's "power of the purse" carried the day.

Widening the Boundaries of the Realm

Edward I was the first English king who was determined to be master of the whole island of Britain—Wales, Scotland, and England. In 1284, after a five-year struggle, English law and administration were imposed on Wales. As a concession to the Welsh, Edward gave his oldest son the title of Prince of Wales.

A dispute over the succession to the Scottish throne in the 1290s gave Edward his opportunity to intervene in the land to the north. After calling upon Edward to settle the dispute, the Scots accepted him as their overlord. Then Edward unwisely demanded that the Scots furnish him with troops to fight in England's wars. Under the courageous William Wallace, rebellion quickly flared up. After winning several victories against the English, Wallace was defeated and hanged as a traitor. But Scottish nationalism was not defeated. In 1307 Edward once again invaded Scotland, but he fell ill and died before his dreams of conquest could be realized. Edward II (1307–1327) attempted to humble the Scots, but at the battle of Bannockburn (1314) the Scots, led by Robert Bruce, won their independence. The two peoples remained bitter enemies, with the Scots often joining the French in their wars against the English. Not until 1603 were the two kingdoms united under a common monarch.

The Beginnings of the French Nation

As we saw in chapter 9, the later Carolingian rulers were generally weak and unable to defend the realm from Viking incursions. This task fell

FEUDAL FRANCE ABOUT 1000
Ile de France

to the local counts and dukes, who built castles to protect the countryside and exercised the powers of the king in their territories. In France by the beginning of the tenth century there were more than thirty great feudal princes who were nominally vassals of the king but who gave him little or no support. When the last Carolingian, Louis the Sluggard, died in 987, the nobles elected as his successor Hugh Capet, count of Paris.

The "kingdom" that Hugh Capet (987–996) theoretically ruled was roughly comparable to, but smaller than, modern France. The territory Hugh actually controlled was a small feudal county extending from Paris to Orléans. It was almost encircled by rivers. The royal domain was surrounded by many independent duchies and counties, such as Flanders, Normandy, Anjou, and Champagne, which were fiercely independent (see map at left).

The Early Capetians

Starting with little power and limited territory under their direct rule, the Capetian monarchs gradually extended their control over the great nobles who resisted centralization. France was literally made by its kings, for ultimately the royal domain, in which the king's word was law, came to coincide with the boundaries of the entire realm.

In the late tenth and eleventh centuries, however, there was little evidence that the Capetian kings would accomplish much of anything. They were weaker than many of their own vassals; compared to them, they had little historical impact. One of their vassals, the duke of Normandy, seized the throne of England; another, the count of Flanders, became a leader of the First Crusade and ruler of the kingdom of Jerusalem; another vassal became the founder of the kingdom of Portugal.

The major accomplishment of the first four Capetian kings was their success in keeping the French crown within their own family. The nobles who elected Hugh Capet had no thought of giving the Capetian family a monopoly on the royal office. But the Capetian kings, with the support of the church, which nurtured the tradition of monarchy as a sacred office, cleverly arranged for the election and coronation of their heirs. Before the king died, the young prince was crowned by the church and became "associated" with his father in his rule. For 300 years the House of Capet never lacked a male heir, and by the end of the twelfth century the hereditary principle had become so ingrained that French kings no longer took the precaution of crowning their sons during their own lifetime.

The advent of the fifth Capetian king, Louis VI (1108–1137), also known as Louis the Fat, marked the end of Capetian weakness. Louis' pacification of the royal domain, the Ile de France, paralleled on a smaller scale the work of William the Conqueror in England. With the support of the church (which supplied him with able advisers), Louis determined to crush the lawless barons who were defying royal authority in the Ile de France. Castles of the defiant vassals were captured and in many cases torn down. Louis made his word law in the Ile de France, established a solid base from which royal power could be extended, and increased the prestige of the monarchy so much that the great duke of Aquitaine deigned to marry his daughter Eleanor to Louis' son. Unfortunately, Eleanor's behavior so scandalized Louis' pious son ("I thought I married a king," Eleanor once exclaimed, "but instead I am the wife of a monk") that he had the marriage annulled, and Aquitaine passed to Eleanor's second husband, Henry II of England.

The Growth of the French Monarchy

The first great expansion of the royal domain was the work of the next Capetian, Philip II Augustus (1180–1223), during whose reign the French king for the first time became more powerful than any of his vassals and France replaced Germany as the strongest monarchy in continental Europe. Philip's great ambition was to take from the English Plantagenets the vast territory they held in France. Philip made little headway against Henry II, except to make Henry's life miserable by encouraging his faithless sons, Richard the Lion-Hearted and John, to revolt. Philip took Normandy, Maine, Anjou, and Touraine from John, thereby tripling the size of the French royal domain (see map below).

Philip also greatly strengthened the royal administrative system by devising new agencies for centralized government and tapping new sources of revenue, including a money payment from his vassals in lieu of military service. Salaried officials, called bailiffs, performed duties similar to those carried out in England by itinerant justices and sheriffs. A corps of loyal officials, like the bailiffs recruited not from the feudal nobility but from the ranks of the bourgeoisie, was collected around the king. As in England, special administrative departments were created: the *parlement*, a supreme court of justice (not to be confused with the British Parliament, which became primarily a legislative body); the chamber of accounts, or royal treasury; and the royal or privy council, a group of advisers who assisted the king in the conduct of the daily business of the state.

In this phase of consolidation of royal power, the papacy, which was struggling with the German emperors, usually allied itself with the French monarchy. As in England and Germany, however, the kings sometimes collided with the popes. Philip II defied Innocent III by having French bishops annul his marriage; but when the pope imposed an interdict (see p. 271) on France, Philip backed down, and his wife again became his queen.

On the other hand, the church inadvertently helped expand the royal domain. In southern France, particularly in Toulouse, the Albigensian sect flourished. Determined to stamp out this heresy, Innocent III in 1208 called the Albigensian Crusade (see p. 272). Philip, faced with the hatred of King John and the German emperor, did not take part, but he allowed his vassals to do so. After Philip's death, his son Louis VIII (1223–1226) led a new crusade to exterminate the remnants of Albigensian resistance. Later in the century Toulouse reverted to the French crown when its count died without heir. The royal domain now stretched from the coast of the English Channel to the shores of the Mediterranean Sea.

After the brief reign of Louis VIII, France came under the rule of Louis IX (1226–1270), better known today as St. Louis. In contrast to the cunning opportunism of his grandfather, Louis' ideal was to rule justly, and he made some sacrifices to that end. For example, special officials were created to check on the bailiffs, who were forbidden to encroach on the feudal rights of the nobility. On the other hand, Louis believed himself responsible only to God, who had put him on the throne to lead his people out of a life of sin. Accordingly, he was the first French king to issue edicts for the whole kingdom without the prior consent of his council of great vassals. He also ordered an end to trial by battle and the time-honored feudal right of private warfare. Certain matters, such as treason and crimes on the highways, were declared to be the exclusive jurisdiction of the royal courts. Furthermore, Louis insisted on the right of appeal from the feudal courts of his vassals to the high royal court of *parlement* at Paris. Just, sympathetic, and peace-loving, Louis IX convinced his subjects that the monarchy was the most important agency for assuring their happiness and well-being.

Apex of Capetian Rule Under Philip IV

The reign of Philip IV, the Fair (1285–1314), climaxed three centuries of Capetian rule. The opposite of his saintly grandfather, Philip was a man of craft, violence, and deceit. He took advantage of the growing anti-Semitism that had appeared in Europe with the Crusades to expel the Jews from France and confiscate their possessions. (Philip's English contemporary, Edward I, had done the same.) Heavily in debt to the Knights Templars, who had turned to banking after the Crusades (see p. 264), Philip had the order suppressed on trumped-up charges of heresy.

Philip's need for money also brought him into conflict with the last great medieval pope. Pope Boniface VIII refused to allow Philip to tax the French clergy and made sweeping claims to supremacy over secular powers. But such leaders as Philip IV would not tolerate interference with their authority, no matter what the source. The result of this controversy was the humiliation of Boniface, a blow from which the influence of the medieval papacy never recovered.

In domestic affairs the real importance of Philip's reign lay in the king's ability to increase the power and improve the organization of the royal government. Philip's astute civil servants, recruited mainly from the middle class, concentrated their efforts on exalting the power of the monarch. Trained in Roman law and inspired by its maxim that "whatever pleases the prince has the force of law," they sought to make the power of the monarch absolute.

As did Edward I in England, Philip enlarged his feudal council to include representatives of the third "estate" or class—the townspeople. This Estates-General of nobles, clergy, and burghers was used as a means of obtaining popular support for Philip's policies, including the announcement of new taxes. Significantly, Philip did not seek to ask the Estates-General's consent for his tax measures, and thus it did not acquire the "power of the purse" that characterized the English Parliament.

The Christian Reconquista in Spain

The unification of Spain was by a different route than that of either France or England. The customary rivalry between the feudal aristocracy and the royal authority was complicated by another significant element—a religious crusade. National unification required the ejection of the Muslims, with their foreign religion and culture.

Unity also called for the consolidation of several distinct Christian states.

During the long struggle to drive the Muslims from Spain, a mounting patriotism blended with a fanatical religious spirit. As early as the ninth century northern Spain became caught up in a religious zeal centering around Santiago de Compostela, reputed to be the burial site of the apostle St. James. His bones were enshrined in a great cathedral visited by thousands of pilgrims. Banners were consecrated there, and the battle cry of the Christian soldiers became "Santiago" (a contraction of *Sante Iago*, St. James' name in Spanish).

Another symbol of national awakening was an eleventh-century soldier of fortune, El Cid (Arabic for "lord"). His exploits against the Muslims thrilled Europe, and he became the hero of the great Spanish epic, *Poema de Mio Cid*. In the epic El Cid appears as a perfect Christian knight, although in reality he was an adventurer seemingly more interested in booty and power than in religion.

In 1212, at Las Navas de Tolosa, the Christians achieved a decisive victory over the Muslims. A few years later they captured first Cordova, whose great mosque was reconsecrated as a cathedral, and then Seville. The conquest of Seville effectively doubled the territory of the Spanish kingdom. By the end of the thirteenth century, when the reconquest halted, until the latter part of the fifteenth century, Moorish political control was confined to Granada (see map, p. 255). The Christian victors allowed their new Muslim subjects to enjoy their own religion and traditions. Muslim traders and artisans were protected because of their economic value, and Muslim culture—art in particular—was often adapted by the Christians.

Government in Germany and Italy

When the Carolingian kingdom of the East Franks proved incapable of coping with the attacks of Magyar horsemen in the late ninth and early tenth centuries, the task was taken over by the tribal leaders (or dukes) of the Saxons, Bavarians, Swabians, and Franconians. These dukes—along with the duke of Lorraine—usurped the

The jeweled crown of Otto I, probably made for his coronation. The eight gold panels of the crown are hinged; thus, the crown can be flattened for transport.

royal power and crown lands in their duchies and also took control over the church.

When the last Carolingian, Louis the Child, died in 911, the dukes elected the weakest among them, Conrad of Franconia, to be their king. The new monarch ruled just eight years and was incapable of meeting the menace of the Magyar raids. On his deathbed he recommended that the most powerful of the dukes, Henry the Fowler, duke of Saxony, be chosen as his successor. Henry, who ruled as Henry I (919–936), was the first of the illustrious Saxon Dynasty, which ruled until 1024 and under which Germany became the most powerful state in western Europe. Henry exercised little authority outside of his own duchy, and his kingdom was hardly more than a confederation of independent duchies. Against Germany's border enemies, he was more successful. He pushed back the Danes and established the Dane Mark as a protective buffer. He also made inroads against the Slavs to the east, and further to the southeast, in Bohemia, forced the Slavic Czech to recognize his overlordship.

Otto the Great and the German Empire

Realizing that the great hindrance to German unity was the opposition of the dukes, Henry's son and heir, Otto I, the Great (936–973), initiated a policy of gaining control of the unruly duchies by setting up his own relatives and favorites as their rulers. As an extra precaution he appointed as supervising officials counts who were directly responsible to the king.

Through an alliance with the church, Otto constructed a German monarchy. The king protected the bishops and abbots and granted them a free hand over their vast estates; in return the church leaders furnished the king with the officials, income, and troops that he lacked. Otto appointed bishops and abbots, and since their offices were not hereditary, he could be sure that their first obedience was to the king. This alliance of crown and church was a natural one at the time. At his coronation at Aaachen, Otto had insisted on being anointed *rex et sacerdos* ("king and priest").

Otto also put an end to the Magyar invasions, thereby enhancing his claim that the king, and

Irish monks of the seventh and eighth centuries applied traditional Germanic and Celtic styles and motifs to their Gospel illuminations to produce magnificent, intricately patterned works of art. The animal interlace pattern on the decorative page from the Book of Durrow (left), an Irish manuscript of the seventh century, is remarkably similar to that of the solid gold buckle (below) from Sutton Hoo, the apparent burial site of an East Anglian king of the seventh century.

The artworks on these pages trace successive artistic styles of the Middle Ages. The gold and jeweled front cover of the Lindau Gospels (left), made in the ninth century, is an example of the Carolingian style. Some of the most beautiful examples of Romanesque painting are the illuminated manuscripts produced in the abbeys of northern France and southern England in the eleventh and twelfth centuries. One such work is the *Life, Miracles, and Passion of St. Edmund* (right), the earliest example of an illustrated life of an English saint. Below, the *Annunciation* (1333) of Simone Martini (1284–1344) represents a blend of the French Gothic style with the Sienese artistic tradition, which emphasized brilliant color, lavish costume, and elegant shapes.

The Death, or Dormition, of the Virgin from the Kariye Camii (formerly the Church of the Savior of Chora) in Istanbul typifies Byzantine mosaic production of the fourteenth century. The Virgin is surrounded by the Apostles, while Christ, at the center, holds a small child, who represents the soul of the Virgin.

Map labels:
NORTH SEA · FRIESLAND · Brandenburg · SAXONY · Magdeburg · Elbe R. · Vistula R. · POLAND · Oder R. · Aix-la-Chapelle (Aachen) · LORRAINE · Rhine R. · Frankfurt · Prague · Mainz · FRANCONIA · BOHEMIA · Saale R. · Strasbourg · Lechfeld · Danube R. · Vienna · HUNGARY · KINGDOM OF FRANCE · SWABIA · Salzburg · BAVARIA · GERMANY ABOUT 1000 · Holy Roman Empire · CARINTHIA · KINGDOM OF BURGUNDY · Rhine R. · Milan · LOMBARDY · Po R. · Venice · CROATIA · Danube R. · Genoa · PAPAL · SERBIA · TUSCANY · STATES · SPOLETO · ADRIATIC SEA · CORSICA · Rome · SARDINIA · Naples · TYRRHENIAN SEA · IONIAN SEA

not the dukes, was the true defender of the German people. In 955 Otto crushed the Magyars at Lechfeld, near Augsburg. The surviving Magyars settled in Hungary, and by the year 1000 they had accepted Christianity.

Otto the Great wanted to establish a German Empire, modeled after the Roman and Carolingian examples. The conquest and incorporation of Italy into that empire was one of Otto's primary objectives. In 951 he crossed the Alps and proclaimed himself king of Italy.

On his second expedition to Italy in 962, Otto was crowned emperor by the pope, whose Papal States were threatened by an Italian duke. No doubt Otto thought of himself as the successor of the imperial Caesars and Charlemagne; and, in fact, his empire later became known as the

Holy Roman Empire (see map above). But Otto also needed the imperial title to legitimize his claim to Lombardy, Burgundy, and Lorraine, which had belonged to the middle kingdom of Lothair, the last man to hold the imperial title. Otto's coronation brought Italy and Germany, pope and emperor, into a forced and unnatural union.

The adverse effects of the German pursuit of empire in Italy are apparent in the reign of Otto III (983–1002), who promoted his grandiose scheme for "the renewal of the Roman Empire." Ignoring Germany, the real source of his power, he made Rome his capital, built a palace there, and styled himself "emperor of the Romans." As the "servant of Jesus Christ," another of his titles, Otto installed non-Italian popes in Rome and conceived of the papacy as a partner in ruling an empire of Germans, Italians, and Slavs. But notwithstanding Otto's love for Italy, the fickle Roman populace revolted and forced him to flee the city. He died a year later while preparing to beseige Rome.

Despite the distractions in Italy, the Saxon rulers were the most powerful in Europe. They had permanently halted Magyar pillaging and, by utilizing the German church as an ally, had limited tendencies toward feudalism in their homeland. They had also fostered economic progress. German eastward expansion had begun, and the Alpine passes had been freed of Muslim raiders and made safe for the Italian merchants.

The Salian Emperors

The Saxon kings were succeeded by a new royal line, the Salian House, which ruled from 1024 to 1125 and whose members tried to establish a centralized monarchy. To the dismay of many nobles, a body of lowborn royal officials was recruited; and the power of the dukes was

weakened further when the crown won the allegiance of the lesser nobles.

The reign of Henry IV (1056–1106) was a watershed in German history. The monarchy reached the height of its power, but it also experienced a major reverse. For a century the Ottonian system, by which the king had governed his kingdom through the clergy, whom he appointed, had functioned smoothly. Under Henry IV, however, the revival of a powerful papacy led to a bitter conflict, centering on the king's right to appoint church officials who were also his most loyal supporters. This disagreement between state and church culminated in Henry himself suffering the humiliation of begging the pope's forgiveness by dressing as a penitent and standing in the snow at Canossa, the papal winter residence. This conflict, known as the Investiture Controversy (see p. 267), resulted in the loss of the monarchy's major sources of strength: the loyalty of the German church, now transferred to the papacy; the support of the great nobles, now openly rebellious and insistent on their "inborn rights"; and the chief material base of royal power, the king's lands, which were

Scenes from the Investiture Controversy. In the top panel Henry IV is seated with Bishop Guibert of Ravenna, Henry's choice to replace Pope Gregory VII, who is being expelled from his throne. In the bottom panel, Gregory, mourned by his faithful followers, dies in exile.

Bronze bust of Frederick Barbarossa. Claiming that his empire was descended from Rome, he gave the title "Holy Roman Empire" to his realm.

diminished by grants to nobles who would stay loyal only if such concessions were made.

The real victors in the Investiture Controversy were the German nobles, many of whom allied themselves with the papacy and continued to defy the monarchy long after the reign of Henry IV. From the time of Henry's death in 1106 until the accession of Frederick Barbarossa in 1152, the Welfs of Bavaria and the Hohenstaufens of Swabia, along with the other noble factions, fought over the throne, which they made elective rather than hereditary.

Italy, the Hohenstaufen Emperors, and the Papacy

Italy was even less unified than Germany. Jealous of one another and of their independence, the properous city-states in northern Italy joined the struggle between the German emperors and the papacy. A brilliant civilization also flourished on the island of Sicily. The kingdom of Naples and Sicily, under the able rule of

Roger II (1130–1154), was one of the strongest and wealthiest states in Europe. Intellectuals from all over the East and Europe traveled to Roger's court, which ranked next to Spain's in Arabic scholarship. Life and culture in the Sicilian kingdom, which included Norman, Byzantine, Italian, and Arabic elements, was diverse and colorful.

The second Hohenstaufen emperor, Frederick I Barbarossa ("Red-beard"), who reigned from 1152 to 1190, realistically accepted the fact that during the preceding half century Germany had become thoroughly decentralized; his goal was to give himself the supreme power by forcing the great nobles to acknowledge his overlordship. Using force when necessary, he was largely successful, and Germany became a centralized feudal monarchy.

To maintain his hold over Germany Frederick needed the resources of Italy—particularly the income from taxes levied on wealthy north Italian cities, which, encouraged by the papacy, joined together in the Lombard League to resist him. Frederick spent about twenty-five years fighting intermittently in Italy, but the final result was failure; the opposition from the popes and the Lombard League was too strong. Frederick did score a diplomatic triumph, however, by marrying his son to the heiress of the throne of Naples and Sicily.

Frederick Barbarossa's grandson, Frederick II (1194–1250), was able to meet the pope's challenge to the threat of Hohenstaufen encirclement. Orphaned at an early age, Frederick was brought up as the ward of Innocent III, the most powerful medieval pope. With the pope's support, Frederick was elected emperor in 1215, one year before Innocent's death.

The papacy and the north Italian cities successfully defied Frederick II throughout his reign, and in the end he experienced the same failure as had Frederick Barbarossa. Frederick also clashed with the papacy in another sphere. Embarking on a crusade at the pope's insistence, he fell ill and turned back. For this, he was promptly excommunicated. When Frederick resumed the crusade a few months later, he was again excommunicated, this time for crusading while excommunicated. When Frederick acquired Jerusalem by negotiation (see p. 261) and agreed to allow Muslims to worship freely in the city, the pope excommunicated him a third time, describing the emperor as "this scorpion spewing poison from the sting of its tail."

Frederick sacrificed Germany in his efforts to unite all Italy under his rule. He transferred crown lands and royal rights to the German princes in order to keep them quiet and to win their support for his Italian wars. Born in Sicily, he remained devoted to the southern part of his empire. He shaped his kingdom in Sicily into a vibrant state. Administered by paid officials who were trained at the University of Naples, which he founded for that purpose, his kingdom was the most centralized and bureaucratic in Europe. Economically, too, it was far in advance of other states; Frederick minted a uniform currency and abolished interior tolls and tariffs, and his powerful fleet promoted and protected commerce.

As long as he lived, this brilliant monarch held his empire together, but it quickly collapsed after his death in 1250. In Germany his son ruled ineffectively for four years before dying, and soon afterward Frederick's descendants in Sicily were killed when the count of Anjou, brother of St. Louis of France, was invited by the pope to annihilate what remained of what he called the "viper breed of the Hohenstaufen."

The victory of the papacy over the Hohenstaufen was more apparent than real, for its struggle against the emperors lost it much of its prestige. Popes had used spiritual means to achieve earthly ambitions—by preaching a crusade against Frederick II and his descendants, for example. More and more, popes acted as though they were Italian princes, playing the game of diplomacy amid shifting rivalries.

The Holy Roman Empire never again achieved the brilliance it had enjoyed during the reign of Frederick Barbarossa. Later emperors usually did not try to interfere in Italian affairs, and they ceased going to Rome to receive the imperial crown from the pope. In German affairs the emperors no longer even attempted to assert their authority over the increasingly powerful nobles. After the fall of the Hohenstaufens, Germany lapsed more and more into the political disunity and ineffectual elective monarchy that remained characteristic of its history until the late nineteenth century.

A pilgrim's guide to Jerusalem, dating from about 1150. The journey to Jerusalem was one of the most popular Christian pilgrimages. The drawing here is a fairly accurate rendering of the city's important religious shrines.

The Crusades

The most dramatic expression of Europe on the offensive in the High Middle Ages was the Crusades. For hundreds of years peaceful pilgrims had been traveling from Europe to worship at the birthplace of Christ. By the tenth century bishops were organizing mass pilgrimages to the Holy Land; the largest of these, which set out from Germany in 1065, included about seven thousand pilgrims.

During the eleventh century, however, Christian pilgrims to the Holy Land became especially concerned and aggravated when the Seljuk

Turks, who were new and fanatical converts to Islam, took over Jerusalem from the more tolerant Abbasid Muslims. Byzantine forces desperately tried to bar the Seljuks, but at the battle of Manzikert (1071) the eastern emperor was captured and his army scattered. Within a few years Asia Minor, the chief source of Byzantine revenue and troops, was lost, and the emperor was writing to western princes and to the pope seeking mercenaries with which to regain lost territories. In addition, tales of alleged Turkish mistreatement of Christian pilgrims circulated throughout Europe, and though there is evidence that these stories were propaganda, they inflamed Christian public opinion.

In 1095 Pope Urban II proclaimed the First Crusade to regain the Holy Land. Preaching at the Council of Clermont in that year, he exhorted Christians to take up the cross and strive for a cause that promised not merely spiritual rewards but material gain as well. At the end of his impassioned oration the crowd shouted "God wills it"—the expression the crusaders later used in battle.

Although the pope saw in the crusade an outlet for the restlesss energy of quarreling nobels—their warring fervor would be channeled for the glory of God—the primary impetus behind the crusade was probably religious. It was viewed as a holy war, and following Pope Urban's appeal, there was a real and spontaneous outpouring of religious enthusiasm. The word *crusade* itself is derived from "taking the cross," after the example of Christ.

The Results of the Crusades

From the end of the eleventh century to the end of the thirteenth, there were seven major crusades, as well as various small expeditions that from time to time, warred against the Muslims in the Near East, whom the crusaders called Saracens. The First Crusade, composed of feudal nobles from France, parts of Germany, and Norman Italy, proceeded overland to Constantiople. Having expected the help of European mercenaries agains the Seljuks, the emperor Alexius Comnenus was taken aback when confronted by an unruly horde of what Pope Urban himself had called "aforetime robbers." He hastily directed the crusaders out of Constantinople to fight the Turks. The First Crusade was the most successful of the seven; with not more than 5000 knights and infantry, it overcame the resistance of the Turks, who were no longer united. Above all, it captured Jerusalem, the Holy City. The First Crusade conquered a narrow strip of land stretching from Antioch to Jerusalem (see map, p. 173) and created the Latin kingdom of Jerusalem (distinct from the city itself), over which Crusaders and Muslims continued to battle until the region finally was retaken by the Muslims in 1291.

When the kingdom of Jerusalem became endangered, St. Bernard of Clairvaux induced the kings of France and Germany to lead the Second Crusade in 1147. It never reached Jerusalem, having turned aside to attack Damascus where its forces were routed.

The fall of Jerusalem in 1187 to the Muslims, reinvigorated under the leadership of Saladin, the Kurdish sultan of Egypt and Syria, provoked the Third Crusade in 1189. Its leaders were three of the most famous medieval kings—Frederick

The Battle of Jerusalem, from a 12th-century manuscript. Events in the life of Christ are depicted in the upper windows. Crusaders are storming the walls, while the artillery (below at right) uses the counterweighted trebuchet to hurl rocks at the enemy.

The First Crusade, The Fall of Jerusalem

This selection describes the fall of Jerusalem during the First Crusades in 1099, as witnessed by the author, a Frankish knight.

During this siege, we suffered so badly from thirst that we sewed up the skins of oxen and buffaloes, and we used to carry water in them for the distance of nearly six miles. We drank the water from these vessels, although it stank, and what with foul water and barley bread we suffered great distress and affliction every day, for the Saracens used to lie in wait for our men by every spring and pool, where they killed them and cut them to pieces; moreover they used to carry off the beasts into their caves and secret places in the rocks.

Our leaders then decided to attack the city with engines, so that we might enter it and worship at our Saviour's Sepulchre. They made two wooden siege-towers and various other mechanical devices. Duke Godfrey filled his siege-tower with machines, and so did Count Raymond, but they had to get the timber from far afield. When the Saracens saw our men making these machines, they built up the city wall and its towers by night, so that they were exceedingly strong. When, however, our leaders saw which was the weakest spot in the city's defences, they had a machine and a siege-tower transported round to the eastern side one Saturday night.

On Friday at dawn we attacked the city from all sides but could achieve nothing, so that we were all astounded and very much afraid, yet, when that hour came when our Lord Jesus Christ deigned to suffer for us upon the cross, our knights were fighting bravely on the siege tower . . . all the defenders fled along the walls and through the city, and our men went after them, killing them and cutting them down as far as Solomon's Temple, where there was such a massacre that our men were wading up to their ankles in enemy blood.

Then the amir who held David's Tower surrendered to the count, and opened for him the gate where pilgrims used to pay their taxes, so our men entered the city, chasing the Saracens and killing them up to Solomon's Temple, where they took refuge and fought hard against our men for the whole day, so that all the temple was streaming with their blood. At last, when the pagans were defeated, our men took many prisoners, both men and women, in the temple. They killed whom they chose, and whom they chose they saved alive. On the roof of the Temple of Solomon were crowded great numbers of pagans of both sexes, to whom Tancred and Gastin of Bearn gave their banners.

After this our men rushed round the whole city, seizing the gold and silver, horses and mules, and houses full of all sorts of goods, and they all came rejoicing and weeping from excess of gladness to worship at the Sepulchre of our Savior Jesus, and there they fulfilled their vows to him. Next morning they went cautiously up on to the Temple roof and attacked the Saracens, both men and women, cutting off their heads with drawn swords. Some of the Saracens threw themselves down headlong from the Temple. Tancred was extremely angry when he saw this.

Our leaders then took counsel and ordered that every man should give alms and pray that God would choose for himself whomsoever he wished, to rule over the others and to govern the city. They also commanded that all the Saracen corpses should be thrown outside the city because of the fearful stench, for almost the whole city was full of their dead bodies. So the surviving Saracens dragged the dead ones out in front of the gates, and piled them up in mounds as big as houses. No-one has ever seen or heard of such a slaughter of pagans, for they were burned on pyres like pyramids, and no-one save God alone knows how many there were.

From Rosalind Hill, ed., *Gesta Francorum* (London: Thomas Nelson, 1962), pp. 89–92.

Barbarossa of Germany, Richard the Lion-Hearted of England, and Philip Augustus of France. Frederick was drowned in Asia Minor; and, after many quarrels with Richard, Philip returned home. Saladin and Richard remained the protagonists, but finally agreed to a three year truce and free access to Jerusalem for Christian pilgrims.

The Fourth Crusade (1202–1204) was a disaster from a religious perspective. No kings answered Pope Innocent II call, and the knights who did were unable to pay the Venetians the agreed-upon transport charges. The Venetians persuaded the crusaders to pay off the sum by capturing the Christian town of Zara on the Adriatic coast, which had long proved troublesome to Venetian trading interests. Then, in order to absorb all Byzantine commerce, the Venetians pressured the crusaders into attacking Constantinople. After conquering and sacking the greatest city in Europe, the crusaders set up the Latin empire of Constantinople (see map below) and forgot about recovering the Holy Land.

The thirteenth century saw other crusades. The youngsters of the ill-fated Children's Crusade in 1212 fully expected the waters of the Mediterranean to part and make a path to the Holy Land, which they would take without fighting, but thousands of them were sold into slavery by Marseilles merchants. The Fifth Crusade in 1219 failed in its attack on Egypt, the center of Muslim power in the Near East. The unique Sixth Crusade in 1228 was organized and led by the excommunicated enemy of the pope, the emperor Frederick II, who by skillfull diplomacy succeeded in acquiring Jerusalem, Bethlehem, and Nazareth from the sultan of Egypt without striking a blow. This arrangement ended in 1244 with the Muslim reconquest of the Holy City. The loss inspired the saintly Louis IX of France to organize the Seventh Crusade in 1248, but despite his zeal it ended in a fiasco when Louis was captured in Egypt and forced to pay an enormous ransom. This was the last major attempt to regain Jerusalem, and the era of the crusades ended in 1291 when Acre, the last stronghold of the Christians in the Holy Land, fell to the Muslims.

The Crusader States

Altogether four crusader principalities, with the kingdom of Jerusalem dominant, had been established along the eastern Mediterranean coast. By the time Jerusalem fell to Saladin in 1187, however, only isolated pockets of Christians remained surrounded by hostile Muslims.

The crusader states were able to survive only by reason of frequent transfusions of strength from Europe in the form of supplies and manpower.

The crusader states were defended by three semi-monastic military orders: the Templars, or Knights of the Temple, so called because their first headquarters was on the site of the old Temple of Jerusalem; the Hospitalers, or Knights of St. John of Jerusalem, who were founded originally to care for the sick and wounded; and the Teutonic Knights, exclusively a German order. Combining monasticism and militarism, these orders had as their aims the protection of all pilgrims and perpetual war against the Muslims.

The Crusades Evaluated

Even though the crusades failed to achieve their specific objective permanently, they cannot be written off as mere adventures. On the contrary, their influence extended over a much wider geographical field than just the Holy Land. Much of the crusading fervor carried over to the fight against the Muslims in Spain and the Slavs in eastern Europe. Politically the crusades weakened the Byzantine Empire and accelerated its fall (see ch. 7). Although the early crusades strengthened the moral leadership of the papacy in Europe, the bad luck of the later crusades, together with the preaching of crusades against Christian heretics and political opponents, weakened both the crusading ideal and respect for the papacy.

Contact with the East widened the scope of the Europeans, ended their isolation, and exposed them to an admirable civilization. Although it is easy to exaggerate the economic effects of the crusades, they did influence the reopening of the eastern Mediterranean to Western commerce, which itself had an effect on the rise of cities and the emergence of a money economy in the West.

The Rise of Trade and Towns

Although scholars have long debated the extent of trade and urban life during the early Middle Ages, there is general agreement that increased trade activity was evident before the crusades. With the ending of Viking and Magyar attacks in the tenth century, a northern trading area developed, which extended from the British Isles to the Baltic Sea.

The center of this northern trade system was the county of Flanders. By 1050 Flemish artisans were producing a surplus of woolen cloth of such fine quality that it was in great demand. Baltic furs, honey and forest products, and British tin and raw wool were exchanged for Flemish cloth. From the south by way of Italy came oriental luxury goods—silks, sugar, and spices.

Trade Routes and Trade Fairs

A catalyst of the medieval commercial revolution was the opening of the Mediterranean trading area. In the eleventh century, Normans and Italians broke the Muslim hold on the eastern Mediterranean, and the First Crusade revived trade with the Near East. Arab vessels brought luxury goods from the East to ports on the Persian Gulf and Red Sea. From there they were shipped by caravan to Alexandria, Acre, and Joppa, and from those ports the merchants of Venice, Genoa, and Pisa transported the goods to Italy on their way to the markets of Europe. Other trade routes from Asia came overland, passing through Baghdad and Damascus and on to ports, such as Tyre and Sidon, in the crusader states. The easiest route north from the Mediterranean was by Marseilles and up the Rhône valley.

Early in the fourteenth century two more major trade lanes developed within Europe. An all-sea route connected the Mediterranean with northern Europe via the Strait of Gibraltar. The old overland route from northern Italy through the Alpine passes to central Europe was also developed. From Venice and other northern Italian cities, trade flowed through such passes as the Brenner, sharply reducing the business of the Rhône valley route and the famous fairs of Champagne.

Along the main European trade routes, astute lords set up fairs, where merchants and goods from Italy and northern Europe met. During the twelfth and thirteenth centuries the fairs of Champagne in France functioned as the major clearing house for this international trade.

A 15th-century illustration of the fair of Lendit, held every June in a field outside Paris. Here the bishop of Paris gives his blessing to the fair.

Fairs were important and elaborate events held either seasonally or annually in specified areas of each European country. The feudal law of the region was set aside during a fair, and in its place was substituted a new commerical code called the "law merchant." Special courts, with merchants acting as judges, settled all disputes. In England such courts were called "pie-powder courts," from the French *pied poudré*, meaning "dusty foot." Fairs also greatly stimulated the revival of a money economy and early forms of banking and credit.

Factors in the Rise of Towns

The resurgence of trade in Europe was a prime cause of the revival of towns; the towns arose because of trade, but they also stimulated trade by providing greater markets and by producing goods for the merchants to sell..

In this revival, geography played a significant role. Rivers, important to the evolution of ancient civilizations, were also important in the development of medieval towns. They were natural highways on which articles of commerce could be easily transported.

Another factor contributing to the rise of towns was population growth. In Britian, for example, the population more than tripled between

1066 and 1350. The reasons for this rapid increase in population are varied. The ending of bloody foreign invasions and, in some areas, the stabilization of feudal society were contributing factors. More important was an increase in food production brought about by the cultivation of wastelands, clearing of forests, and draining of marshes.

Merchant and Craft Guilds

In each town the merchants and artisans organized themselves into guilds, which were useful not only for business but also for social and political purposes. There were two kinds of guilds: merchant and craft.

The merchant guild ensured a monopoly of trade within a given locality. All alien merchants were supervised closely and made to pay tolls. Disputes among merchants were settled at the guild court according to its own legal code. The guilds also tried to make sure that the customers were not cheated: they checked weights and measures and insisted upon a standard quality for goods. To allow only a legitimate profit, the guild fixed a "just price," which was fair to both producer and customer.

The guild's functions stretched beyond business and politics into charitable and social activities. A guildsman who fell into poverty received aid from the guild. The guild also provided financial assistance for the burial expense of its members and looked after their dependents. Members attended social meetings in the guildhall and periodically held processions in honor of their patron saints.

With the increase of commerce in the towns, artisans began to organize as early as the eleventh century. Craftsmen in each of the medieval trades—weaving, cobbling, tanning, and so on—joined forces. The result was the craft guild, which differed from the merchant guild in that membership was limited to artisans in one particular craft.

The general aims of the craft guilds were the same as those of the merchant guilds—the creation of a monopoly and the enforcement of a set of trade rules. Each guild had a monopoly of a certain article in a particular town, and every effort was made to prevent competition between

In this illustration of the Draper's Market at Bologna, a tailor (center) measures a prospective client. Cloth making contributed greatly to European economic growth during the Middle Ages.

members of the same guild. The guild restricted the number of its members, regulated the quantity and quality of the goods produced, and set prices. It also enforced regulations to protect the consumer from bad workmanship and inferior materials.

The craft guild also differed from the merchant guild in its recognition of three distinct classes of workers—apprentices, journeymen, and master craftsmen. The apprentice was a youth who lived at the master's house and was taught the trade thoroughly. Although the apprentice received no wages, all his physical needs were supplied. Apprenticeship commonly lasted seven years. When the apprentice's schooling was finished, the youth became a journeyman. He was then eligible to receive wages and to be hired by a master. At about age twenty-three, the journeyman sought admission into the guild as a master. To be accepted he had to prove his ability. Some crafts demanded the making of a "master piece'"—for example, a pair of shoes that the master shoemakers would find acceptable in every way.

Acquiring Urban Freedom

The guilds played an important role in local government. Both artisans and merchants, even though freemen, were subject to the feudal lord or bishop on whose domain the city stood. The citizens of the towns resented the fact that their overlord collected tolls and dues as though they were serfs. The townsmen demanded the privileges of governing themselves—of making their own laws, administering their own justice, levying their own taxes, and issuing their own coinage. Naturally the overlord resented the impertinent upstarts who demanded self-government. But the towns won their independence in various ways.

One way was to become a commune, a self-governing town. The merchant guilds took the lead in acquiring charters of self-government for the towns. Often a charter had to be won by revolt; in other circumstances it could be purchased, for a feudal lord was always in need of money. By 1200 the Lombard towns of northern Italy, as well as many French and Flemish towns, had become self-governing communes.

Where royal authority was strong, a town could be favored as "privileged." In a charter granted to the town by the monarch, the inhabitants won extensive financial and legal powers. The town was given management of its own finances and paid its taxes in a lump sum to the king. It was also generally given the right to elect its own officials. The king was usually glad to grant such a charter, for it weakened the power of the nobles and won for the monarch the support of the townspeople.

Founding new towns was still another way in which feudal restrictions were broken down. Shrewd lords and kings, who recognized the economic value of having towns in their territories, founded carefully planned centers with well-designed streets and open squares. As a means of obtaining inhabitants, they offered many inducements in the form of personal privileges and tax limitations.

Interacting with the growth of towns was the decline of serfdom. Many serfs escaped from the manors and made their way to the towns. After living a year and a day in the town, a serf was considered a freeman.

The Bourgeoisie

The triumph of the townspeople in their struggle for greater self-government meant that a new

A guild master judges the work of two craftsmen, a mason and a carpenter.

class evolved in Europe—a powerful, independent, and self-assured group, whose interest in trade was to revolutionize social, economic, and political history. The members of this class were called burghers and came to be called *bourgeoisie*. Kings came to rely more and more on them in combating the power of the feudal lords, and their economic interest gave rise to an early capitalism. Also associated with the rise of towns and the bourgeoisie were the decline of serfdom and the manorial system and the advent of modern society.

A medieval townsman's rank was based on money and goods rather than birth and land. At the top of the social scale were the princes of trade, the great merchants and banking families, bearing such names as Medici, Fugger, and Coeur. Then came the moderately wealthy merchants and below them the artisans and small shopkeepers. On the lowest level were the unskilled laborers, whose miserable lot and discontent were destined to continue through the rest of the Middle Ages.

The Church in the High Middle Ages

When the German king Otto the Great revived the Roman Empire in the West in 962 (see p. 257), his act reemphasized the concept of the dual leadership of pope and emperor. Otto claimed to be the successor of Augustus, Constantine, and Charlemagne, although his actual power was confined to Germany and Italy. At first the papacy looked to the German king for protection against the unruly Italian nobles who for a century had been making a political prize of the papacy. From the church's viewpoint, however, this arrangement had its drawbacks, for the German kings continued to interfere in ecclesiastical affairs and even in the election of popes.

During the eleventh century controversy arose between church and state over the problem of lay investiture. Theoretically, on assuming office a bishop or abbot was subject to two investitures; his spiritual authority was bestowed by a church official, and his feudal or civil authority by a layman—a feudal lord or a king. In actual fact, however, feudal lords and kings came to control both the appointment and the installation of church officials. As noted earlier (see p. 256), this practice was most pronounced in Germany, where control of the church was the foundation of the king's power. The German church was in essence a state church.

Gregory VII and the Investiture Struggle

The most ambitious advocate of church reform was Pope Gregory VII (1073–1085), who claimed unprecedented power for the papacy. Gregory held as his ideal the creation of a Christian commonwealth under papal control. In the *Dictatus Papae* ("Dictate of the Pope") Gregory claimed:

> *That the Roman pontiff alone is rightly called universal.*
> *That he alone has the power to depose and reinstate bishops.*
> *That he alone may use the imperial insignia.*
> *That all princes shall kiss the foot of the pope alone.*
> *That he has the power to depose emperors.*
> *That he can be judged by no one.*
> *That no one can be regarded as catholic who does not agree with the Roman church.*
> *That he has the power to absolve subjects from their oath of fealty to wicked rulers.*[2]

In 1075 Gregory VII formally prohibited lay investiture and threatened to excommunicate any layman who performed it and any ecclesiastic who submitted to it. This drastic act virtually declared war against Europe's rulers, since lay investiture had been employed since the emperor Constantine's time. The climax to the struggle occurred in Gregory's clash with the German emperor Henry IV. Henry was accused of simony and lay investiture in appointing his own choice to the archbishopric of Milan and was summoned to Rome to explain his conduct. Henry's answer was to convene in 1076 a synod of German bishops, which declared Gregory a "false monk" and unfit to occupy the office of pope. In retaliation, Gregory excommunicated Henry and deposed him, absolving his subjects from their oaths of allegiance.

At last, driven by a revolt among the German nobles to make peace with the pope, Henry appeared before Gregory in January 1077 at Canossa, a castle in the Apennines. Dressed as a penitent, the emperor is said to have stood barefoot in the snow for three days and begged forgiveness until, in Gregory's words: "We loosed the chain of the anathema and at length received him into the favor of communion and into the lap of the Holy Mother Church."[3]

This dramatic humiliation of the emperor did not resolve the quarrel, nor do contemporary accounts attach much significance to the incident—public penance was not uncommon in those days, even for kings. After the episode at Canossa, Henry returned to Germany and crushed his opponents; in the short term the whole incident cost Gregory the support of the German nobility. Yet the pope had made progress toward freeing the church from lay interference and increasing the power and prestige of the papacy.

The problem of lay investiture was settled in 1122 by the compromise known as the Concordat of Worms. By the terms of this agreement, the church maintained the right to elect the holder of an ecclesiastical office, but only in the presence of the king or his representative. The

At Canossa, the penitent Henry IV pleads with Abbot Hugh of Cluny and Countess Matilda of Tuscany to intercede with Pope Gregory VII to rescind Henry's excommunication.

candidate, such as a bishop, was invested by the king with the scepter, the symbol of his administrative jurisdiction, after which he performed the act of homage and swore allegiance as the king's vassal. Only after this ceremony had taken place was the candidate consecrated by the archbishop, who invested him with his spiritual functions, as symbolized by the ring and pastoral staff. Since the kings of England and France had earlier accepted this compromise, the problem of lay investiture ended.

The Papacy's Zenith: Innocent III

Under Innocent III (1198–1216), a new type of administrator-pope, papal power reached its zenith. Unlike Gregory VII and other earlier reform popes, who were monks, Innocent and other great popes of the late twelfth and thirteenth centuries were lawyers, trained in the newly revived and enlarged church, or canon law. Innocent was like Gregory VII, however, in holding an exalted view of his office:

> *The Lord Jesus Christ has set up one ruler over all things as His universal vicar, and as all things in heaven, earth and hell bow the knee to Christ, so should all obey Christ's vicar, that there be one flock and one shepherd.*[4]

So successful was Innocent III in asserting his temporal and spiritual supremacy that many states formally acknowledged vassalage to the pope. In the case of King John of England, a struggle developed over the election of the archbishop of Canterbury, and Innocent placed England under interdict for five years and excommunicated John. Under attack from his barons, John capitulated to Innocent by becoming his vassal, receiving England back as a fief, and paying him an annual monetary tribute. Innocent forced Philip Augustus of France to comply with the church's moral code by taking back as his queen the woman he had divorced with the consent of the French bishops. As for the Holy Roman Empire, Innocent intervened in a civil war between rival candidates for the throne, supporting first one, then the other. In the end Innocent secured the election of his ward, the young Hohenstaufen heir Frederick II, who promised to respect papal rights and to go on a crusade.

The medieval papacy reached the height of its power under Innocent III, who firmly believed in the papal right to exercise authority over temporal monarchs. Innocent called the Fourth Lateran Council, which legislated many reforms in Church administation.

Church Administration

The universality and power of the church rested not only upon a systematized, uniform creed but also upon the most highly organized administrative system in the West. At the head was the pope, or bishop of Rome (see ch. 5). He was assisted by the Curia, the papal council or court, which in the twelfth and thirteenth centuries developed an intricate adminstrative system. Judicial and secretarial problems were handled by the papal Chancery, financial matters by the Camera, and disciplinary questions by the Penitentiary. Special emissaries called legates, whose powers were superior to those of the local churchmen, carried the pope's orders throughout Europe.

The church was ahead of secular states in developing a system of courts and a body of law.

Innocent III, Letter to King John, 1214

The spiritual and political authority of Pope Innocent III is reported to have been the greatest of any medieval clergyman. Innocent sent this letter to King John of England after John had agreed to give the pope both England and Ireland in return for release from the papal interdiction imposed on John's lands. The surrender of England and Ireland to the pope was little more than a symbolic gesture, but that very symbolism left a clear impression of Innocent's authority on all observers.

Innocent, bishop, servant of the servants of God, to his well-beloved son in Christ, John illustrious king of the English, and to his legitimate free-born heirs for ever.

The King of kings and Lord of lords, Jesus Christ, a priest for ever after the order of Melchisedech, has so established in the Church His kingdom and His priesthood that the one is a kingdom of priests and the other a royal priesthood, as is testified by Moses in the law and by Peter in his Epistle; and over all He has set one whom He has appointed as His Vicar on earth, so that, as every knee is bowed to Jesus, of things in heaven, and things in earth, and things under the earth, so all men should obey His Vicar and strive that there may be one fold and one shepherd. All secular kings for the sake of God so venerate this Vicar, that unless they seek to serve him devotedly they doubt if they are reigning properly. To this, dearly beloved son, you have paid wise attention; and by the merciful inspiration of Him in whose hand are the hearts of kings which he turns whithersoever He wills, you have decided to submit in a temporal sense yourself and your kingdom to him to whom you knew them to be spiritually subject, so that kingdom and priesthood, like body and soul, for the great good and profit of each, might be united in the single person of Christ's Vicar. He has deigned to work this wonder, who being alpha and omega has caused the end to fulfil the beginning and the beginning to anticipate the end, so that those provinces which from of old have had the Holy Roman Church as their proper teacher in spiritual matters should now in temporal things also have her as their peculiar sovereign. You, whom God has chosen as a suitable minister to effect this, by a devout and spontaneous act of will and on the general advice of your barons have offered and yielded, in the form of an annual payment of a thousand marks, yourself and your kingdoms of England and Ireland, with all their rights and appurtenances, to God and to SS Peter and Paul His apostles and to the Holy Roman Church and to us and our successors, to be our right and our property.

From C. R. Cheney and W. H. Semple, eds., *Selected Letters of Pope Innocent III Concerning England* (London: Thomas Nelson, 1955), pp. 177–178.

Church or canon law was based on the Scriptures, the writings of the church Fathers, and the decrees of church councils and popes. In the twelfth century the church issued its official body of canon law, which guided the church courts in judging perjury, blasphemy, sorcery, usury (the medieval church denounced the taking of interest), and heresy. Heresey was the most horrible of all crimes in medieval eyes. A murder was a crime against society, but the heretic's disbelief in the teaching of Christ or His church was considered a crime against God.

The papacy's chief weapons in support of its authority were spiritual penalties. The most powerful of these was excommunication, by which people became anathema, "set apart" from the church and all the faithful. A person who was excommunicant could not act as judge, juror, notary, witness, or attorney. That person could not be a guardian, an executor, or a party to any contracts. When one died as an excommunicant, one received no Christian burial; and if by chance he or she was buried in consecrated ground, the body was dug up and thrown away.

An excommunicant who entered a church during Mass was to be expelled, or the Mass discontinued. After the reading of a sentence of excommunication, a bell was rung as for a funeral, a book closed, and a candle extinguished, to symbolize the spiritual death of the guilty person.

Interdict, which has been termed "an ecclesiastical lockout," was also a powerful instrument. Whereas excommunication was directed against individuals, interdict suspended all public worship and withheld all sacraments other than Baptism and Extreme Unction in the realm of a disobedient ruler. Pope Innocent III successfully applied or threatened the interdict eighty-five times against disobedient kings and princes.

From the reign of Innocent III until the end of the thirteenth century, the church radiated power and splendor. It possessed perhaps a third of the land in Europe, and all secular rulers and church prelates acknowledged the power of Christ's vicar, the pope. Innocent III and his successors could and did "judge all and be judged by no one."

Yet while the church's wealth enabled it to perform educational and charitable functions that the states were too poor and weak to provide, this wealth also encouraged abuses and worldliness among the clergy. Cracks were appearing in the foundation even while the medieval religious structure received its final embellishments. Weaknesses were evident in the lessening of religious zeal in the later crusades, in the need for renewed internal reform, and in the growth of heresy.

Monastic Reform

A religious revival, often called the medieval reformation, began in the tenth century and reached full force in the twelfth and thirteenth. The first far-reaching manifestation of the revival was the reformed Benedictine order of monks at Cluny, founded in 910. From the original monastery in Burgundy radiated a powerful impulse for the reform of the feudalized church. The Cluniac program began as a movement for monastic reform, but in time it influenced the enforcement of clerical celibacy and the abolition of simony, the purchase and sale of church offices. The ultimate goal of the Cluniac reformers was to free the entire church from secular

control and subject it to papal authority. Some three hundred Cluniac houses were freed from lay control, and in 1059 an attempt was made to rid the papacy itself of secular interference by the creation of the College of Cardinals, which henceforth elected the pope.

The medieval reformation gained momentum late in the eleventh century with a second wave of monastic reform brought on by the failure of the Cluniac reform to end all the abuses associated with the monastic life. Among the new orders were the severely ascetic Carthusians and the very popular Cistercians.

The Cistercian movement received its greatest impetus from the zealous efforts of St. Bernard of Clairvaux (1091–1153). The order's abbeys were situated in solitary places, and their strict discipline emphasized fasts and vigils, manual labor, and a vegetarian diet. Their churches contained neither stained glass nor statues, and the puritanical Bernard denounced the beautification of churches in general.

The Cistercian order had founded 343 abbeys in western Europe by the time of Bernard's death in 1153 and more than double that number by the end of the century. Yet in one important sense these austere new monastic orders were failures. Being exclusively agricultural and dwelling apart from society, these orders were

This illumination from a 12th-century manuscript portrays a Cistercian monk harvesting grain.

unsuited to cope with religious discontent in the towns and the consequent increase of heresy.

Heresy

Heresy, the deliberate belief in doctrines officially condemned by the church, flourished particularly in the towns, where an increasing consciousness of sin and a demand for greater piety went largely unheeded by old-style churchmen. This fertile ground produced many heresies, among which the Albigensian and Waldensian were major ones.

Harking back to an early Christian heresy, the Cathari ("Pure") or Albigensians—so called because Albi in southern France was an important center—went to extremes in regarding the world as the battleground for the opposing forces of good and evil. The Albigensians denounced many activities of the state and the individual, even condemning marriage for perpetuating the human species in this sinful world. The Albigensi-

ans went on to denounce even the church as an institution, since it too was a part of the earth and thereby inherently evil.

The Waldensians derived their name from Peter Waldo, a merchant of Lyons who gave his wealth to charity and founded a lay order, the Poor Men of Lyons, to serve the needs of the people. He had parts of the New Testament translated into French, held that laymen could preach the Gospel, and denied the effectiveness of the sacraments unless administered by worthy priests.

For ten years, Innocent III tried to reconvert these heretical groups. Failing, in 1208 he instigated a crusade against the prosperous and cultured French region of Toulouse, where the Albigensian heresy was widespread. The crusade began with horrible slaughter to the cry of "Kill them all, God will know his own." Soon the original religious motive was lost in a selfish rush to seize the wealth of the accused. In time the Albigensian heresy was destroyed, along with the

In this 15th-century Flemish manuscript illumination, the Church is depicted as a citadel besieged by the Seven Capital Sins (all women) and heretics blindfolded against the True Faith. Efforts to suppress heresy could lead to savage torture and persecution of heretics, as in the Inquisition.

An altarpiece depicting Saint Francis of Assisi surrounded by six scenes of his life, painted just nine years after the saint's death. The marks on his hands and feet are stigmata—symbolic wounds representing his identification with Christ—which he is said to have received at the end of his life.

flourishing culture of southern France, and the Waldensians were scattered. Until the rise of Protestantism, the church was generally successful in its efforts to crush heresy.

The Inquisition

In 1233 a special papal court called the Inquisition was established to cope with the rising tide of heresy and to bring about religious conformity. Those accused were tried in secret without the aid of legal counsel. Those who confessed and renounced heresy were "reconciled" with the church on performance of penance. Those who did not voluntarily confess could be tortured. If this failed, the prisoners could be declared heretics and turned over to the secular authorities, usually to be burned at the stake.

A rationalization for torture was that the soul was considered incomparably more important than the body, so therefore it was believed that torturing a suspected heretic was justifiable if

confession could save the soul from the greater torments of hell. The use of torture, secret testimony, and the denial of legal counsel prevailed in all courts that followed Roman legal procedure. But some of the church's courts of inquisition, and in particular the Spanish courts, abused their authority and became almost fanatical in their prosecution of suspected heretics.

The Franciscans and Dominicans

As a more positive response to the spread of heresy and the conditions that caused it, Innocent III approved the founding of the Franciscan and Dominican orders of friars ("brothers"). Instead of living an isolated existence in a remote monastery, the friars moved among the people, ministering to their needs, preaching the Gospel, and teaching in the schools.

The Franciscans were founded by St. Francis of Assisi (1182?–1226), who rejected riches and spread the gospel of poverty and Christian simplicity. Love of one's fellow human beings and all God's creatures, even "brother worm," were basic in the Rule of St. Francis, which was inspired by Jesus' example.

The second order of friars was founded by St. Dominic (1170–1221), a well-educated Spaniard who had fought the Albigensians in southern France. There he decided that to combat the strength and zeal of it opponents, the church should have champions who could preach the Gospel with the dedication of the Apostles. Dominic's order of friar-preachers dedicated themselves to preaching as a means of maintaining the doctrines of the church and of converting heretics.

The enthusiasm and sincerity of the friars in their early years made a profound impact on an age that had grown increasingly critical of the worldliness of the church. But after they took charge of the Inquisition, became professors in the universities, and served the papacy in other ways, the friars lost much of their original simplicity and freshness. Yet their message and zeal had done much to provide the church with moral and intellectual leadership at a time when such leadership was badly needed.

The Intellectual Synthesis of the High Middle Ages

In addition to the general level of education, interest in intellectual matters declined rapidly in the period following the fall of the Roman Empire and the establishment of the early Germanic kingdoms. And even among the intellectual community that did survive, a controversy raged over the value of studying subjects not directly pertinent to the saving of souls for the church. So dim had the light of learning become by the end of the eighth century that Charlemagne found it necessary to order the monasteries to revive their schools and resume instruction in the rudiments of "singing, arithmetic, and grammar."

Despite the fate of his political achievements, Charlemagne's modest educational revival survived his death. At least partly as a result of this stimulus, western Europe by the late eleventh century was on the threshold of one of the most productive and energetic periods of the history of Western thought.

Scholasticism

Living "religiously in a studious manner" characterizes the scholars of the High Middle Ages. With few exceptions, medieval people did not think of truth as something to be discovered by themselves; rather, they saw it as already existing in the authoritative Christian and pagan writings of antiquity. Spurred by a new zest for employing reason (through the use of logic or dialectic), medieval scholars of the twelfth and thirteenth centuries succeeded in understanding and reexpressing those elements in the Christian and pagan heritage that seemed significant to them. Since this task was carried out largely in the schools, these scholars are known as schoolmen, or *scholastics*, and the intellectual synthesis they produced is called scholasticism.

Each scholar formed his own judgments and earnestly sought to convince others. This led to much debate, often uncritical but always exuberant, on a wide range of subjects. Most famous was the argument over universals known as the nominalist-realist controversy. This philosophical controversy centered on the question of whether universal ideas—beauty, truth, and justice for example—had a reality other than existing in people's minds as abstract notions. The realists held that these universal ideas did have a reality, but the nominalists believed that the universal ideas were nothing more than names (nomina) used to identify abstract concepts. The debates and arguments between nominalists and realists found receptive audiences in medieval universities and in the writings of philosophers and theologians.

The Contribution of Abélard

The extreme views of nominalists and realists, along with other examples of the sterile use of logic ("whether the pig is led to the market by the rope or by the driver"), outraged the brilliant young student Peter Abélard (1079–1142), later a popular teacher at the cathedral school of Notre Dame in Paris.

Abélard's great contribution to medieval thought was an approach called conceptualism, his common-sense solution to the nominalist-realist controversy. Abélard held that universals, while existing only in the mind as thoughts or concepts, are nevertheless valid (real) since they are the product of observing the similar qualities that exist in a particular class of things. Thus, by observing many chairs and sitting in them, we arrive at the universal concept "chair."

In addition to redefining the purpose of scholastic thought, Abélard perfected the scholastic method. Like others before him, Abélard emphasized the importance of understanding. However, Abélard's predecessors had begun with faith; Abélard started with doubt. We must learn to doubt, he insisted, for doubting leads us to inquire, and inquiry leads us to the truth.

In a very influential work, *Sic et Non* (*Yes and No*), Abélard demonstrated his method. Listing 158 propositions on theology and ethics, he appended to each a number of statements pro and con taken from the authoritative writings of the church. Abélard did not reconcile these apparent contradictions, but he urged his students to do so by rational interpretation. Abélard's successors used his methods to absorb and interpret the pagan as well as the Christian heritage of the past. The resulting scholarly compilations, which bear such apt titles as *concordantia* (concordance), *speculum* (mirror), and *summa* (total), constitute a crowning achievement of the medieval intellectual synthesis.

Abélard is remembered as a great lover as well as a great scholar—a rather uncommon combination. His ill-starred romance with his pupil, the learned and beautiful Héloïse, niece of the canon of Notre Dame, cut short his promising career as a teacher. The two lovers were married in secret but Héloïse's uncle, falsely believing that Abélard planned to abandon Héloïse, hired thugs who attacked and castrated the scholar. Both Abélard and Héloïse then sought refuge in the church—he as a monk and she as the abbess of a convent.

The New Material and the Task of Reconciliation

In the twelfth century Western scholars flocked to Spain and Sicily and there translated Muslim editions of ancient writings. As a result of these translations a host of new ideas, particularly in science and philosophy, were introduced to Western scholars. Western knowledge was expanded to include not only Arabic learning but also such important classical works as Euclid's *Geometry*, Ptolemy's *Almagest*, Hippocrates' and Galen's treatises in medicine, and all of Aristotle's extant writing except the *Poetics* and the *Rhetoric*.

Because of the emphasis on authority and the all-pervasive influence of the church, the medieval atmosphere was not conductive to free scientific investigation. Those who studied science were churchmen, and their findings were supposed to illuminate rather than contradict the dogmas of the theologians.

When Greek and Arabic works were translated in the twelfth century, the West inherited a magnificent legacy of mathematical and scientific knowledge. Algebra, trigonometry, and Euclid's *Geometry* became available, and Arabic numerals and the symbol for zero made possible the decimal system of computation. Physics was based on Aristotle's theory of four elements (water, earth, air, and fire) and on his theories of dynamics—doctrines that took centuries to disprove. Some fourteenth-century nominalists were the first to challenge Aristotle's theory, later conclusively disproven by Galileo, that a heavy object falls faster than a light one. Chemistry was based on Aristotelian concepts, mixed with magic and alchemy. Like the Muslim alchemist, the European counterpart tried in vain to transmute base metals into gold and silver and to obtain a magic elixir that would prolong life; in both cases the attempts did much to advance true findings in the field of chemistry.

Two notable exceptions to the medieval rule of subservience to authority were the emperor Frederick II (see p. 259) and the English Franciscan Roger Bacon. Frederick had a genuine scientific interest in animals and was famed for his large traveling menagerie, which included elephants, camels, panthers, lions, leopards, and a giraffe. He also wrote a remarkable treatise, *The Art of Falconry*, which is still considered largely accurate in it observations of the life and habits of various kinds of hunting birds. At his Sicilian court Frederick gathered about him many distinguished Greek, Muslim, and Latin scholars, and he wrote to others in distant lands seeking their views on such problems as why objects appear bent when partly covered by water. He indulged in many experiments; one was a test to determine what language children would speak if raised in absolute silence. The experiment was a failure, because all the children died.

Roger Bacon (1214–1292) also employed the inductive scientific method, he coined the term "experimental science" and boldly criticized the deductive syllogistic reasoning used by scholastic thinkers. Bacon never doubted the authority of the Bible or the church—his interest lay only in natural science—yet his superiors considered him dangerous because of his criticism of scholastic thought.

By the thirteenth century learned Muslim commentaries on the medical works of Galen and Hippocrates and on Aristotle's biology were available in the West. This knowledge, coupled with new discoveries and improved techniques, made medieval doctors more than just barbers who engaged in bloodletting. Yet the overall state of medical knowledge and practice was, by our standards at least, still primitive.

As his works became known, Aristotle became "the philosopher" to medical students, and his authority was generally accepted as second only to that of the Scriptures. But because the church's teachings were considered infallible, Aristotle's ideas, as well as those of other great thinkers of antiquity, had to be reconciled with religious dogma. Using logical approaches, the scholastic thinkers of the thirteenth century succeeded in this task of reconciliation.

Scholasticism reached its zenith with Thomas Aquinas (1225?–1274). In his *Summa Theologica*, this brilliant Italian Dominican dealt exhaustively with the great problems of theology, philosophy, politics, and economics. Thomas'

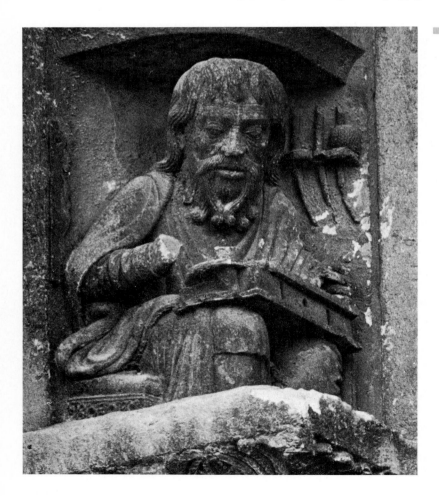

A relief from Chartres Cathedral of the Greek philosopher Aristotle with the tools of a scribe. Scholars of the 13th century relied on Latin translations of Aristotle's texts, which they reinterpreted to reconcile his theories with Church teachings.

In this work by the Siennese painter Giovanni di Paolo, Saint Thomas Aquinas confounds the Arab philosopher Averroës. The tableau symbolizes the triumph of Aquinas' scholasticism over Averroës' doctrines.

major concern was to reconcile Aristotle and church dogma—in other words, the truths of natural reason and the truths of faith. There can be no real contradiction, he argued, since all truth comes from God. In case of an unresolved contradiction, however, faith won out, because of the possibility of human error in reasoning.

The Decline of Scholasticism

Having reached its zenith, scholasticism declined rapidly. The assumption that faith and reason were compatible was vigorously denied by two Franciscan thinkers, Duns Scotus (d. 1308) and William of Occam (d. c.1349), who elaborated on Aquinas' belief that certain religious doctrines are beyond discovery by the use of reason. They argued that if the human intellect could not understand divinely revealed truth, it could hope to comprehend only the natural world and should not intrude upon the sphere of divine truth.

After the thirteenth century, scholasticism increasingly became criticized, for its adherents were obsessed with theological subtleties, discouraged independent thought, and in general lost touch with reality. But it should be remembered that the scholastics sought to compile and then to interpret the vast body of Christian and pagan knowledge left to them by an earlier civilization. In terms of their needs and objectives—an intelligible and complete synthesis of faith, logic, and science—the scholastics were extremely successful.

Origin of Universities

The rebirth of learning in the twelfth century, with especially its revival of classical learning, its unprecedented number of students flocking to the schools, and its development of professional studies in law, medicine, and theology, led to the rise of organized centers of learning—the universities, which soon eclipsed monastic and cathedral schools. Originally the word *university* meant a group of persons possessing a common purpose. In this case it referred to a guild of learners, both teachers and students, similar to the craft guilds with their masters and apprentices. In the thirteenth century the universities had no campuses and little property or money, and the masters taught in hired rooms or religious houses. If the university was dissatisfied with its treatment by the townspeople, it could migrate elsewhere. The earliest universities—Bologna, Paris, and Oxford—were not officially founded or created, but in time the popes and kings granted them and other universities charters of self-government. The charters gave legal status to the universities and rights to the students, such as freedom from the jurisdiction of town officials.

Two of the most famous medieval universities were at Bologna in northern Italy and at Paris. The former owed its growth to the fame of Irnerius (d. 1130), who taught civil law. Because of his influence, Bologna acquired a reputation as the leading center for the study of law. The students soon organized a guild for protection against the townspeople, who were demanding exorbitant sums for food and lodging. Because the guild went on to control the professors, Bologna became a student paradise. In the earliest statutes we read that a professor requiring leave of absence even for one day first had to obtain permission from his students. He had to begin his lecture with the bell and end within one minute of the next bell. The material in the text had to be covered systematically, with all difficult passages fully explained. The powerful position of the students at Bologna developed as a result of the predominance of older students studying for the doctorate in law.

At the university in Paris conditions developed differently. This university, which had grown out of the cathedral school of Notre Dame, specialized in liberal arts and theology and became the most influential intellectual center in medieval Europe. Its administration was far different from Bologna's. The chancellor of Notre Dame, the bishop's officer who exercised authority over the cathedral school, refused to allow the students or the masters to obtain control of the burgeoning university. Charters issued by the French king in 1200 and by the pope in 1231 freed the university from the bishop's authority by making it an autonomous body controlled by the masters. Oxford, the oldest university in England, was founded in the early twelfth century by scholars who were attracted to the town by the favorable reception from the nearby court, and the large number of religious houses established there. After numerous conflicts local residents and students, the university became the beneficiary of the king's support, and Oxford's security was assured.

Letter from a Student at Oxford University

The following is a letter from a student at Oxford ca. 1220 written in an effort to receive more money from his parents. The continuity of some aspects of university life clearly have not changed in 900 years.

B. to his venerable master A., greeting. This is to inform you that I am studying at Oxford with the greatest diligence, but the matter of money stands greatly in the way of my promotion, as it is now two months since I spent the last of what you sent me. The city is expensive and makes many demands; I have to rent lodgings, buy necessaries, and provide for many other things which I cannot now specify.

Wherefore I respectfully beg your paternity that by the promptings of divine pity you may assist me, so that I may be able to complete what I have well begun. For you must know that without Ceres and Bacchus Apollo grows cold. . . . . . .

From Charles Homer Haskins, *The Renaissance of the Twelfth Century* (Cambridge, MA: Harvard University Press, 1927), p. 395.

In a classroom at the University of Paris the French theologian and mystic Amaury de Bène lectures to four student clerics. The doctrines that Amaury taught were condemned by Pope Innocent III and by the Fourth Lateran Council.

Conclusion

The period from 1000 to 1300, called the High Middle Ages, witnessed significant changes and high levels of advancement from a wide variety of perspectives. In England, William the Conqueror secured a unified kingdom in 1066, and successive English kings managed to keep their competitors under control and build up the machinery of royal administration. In France, the movement toward the consolidation of royal power emanated from the minuscule Ile de France. Each of the many counties and duchies that constituted feudal France had to be subordinated and brought within the framework of royal authority. It took the French kings three centuries to accomplish what William the Conqueror had done in one generation. The German kings dissipated their energies by seeking the prize of empire over the Alps in Italy and Sicily. Nation-making in Spain was unique, since it acquired the religious fervor of a crusade. In the mid-eleventh century the Christian Spanish states began the *Reconquista* in earnest, but not until the end of the fifteenth century would the task be completed.

Economically, Europe was transformed by new forces: increased food production and population, revitalized trade, new towns, expansion of industry, and a money economy. A new society began to take shape—the bourgeoisie emerged, and serfdom declined.

During the High Middle Ages, the church developed the first unified system of law and administration in medieval Europe and intimately affected the life of every person. It gave people a sense of security against the dangers on earth and those beyond. Within the church, thinkers wrestled with philosophical issues, such as the realist-nominalist controversy. In the thirteenth century, such famous scholars as St. Thomas Aquinas made impressive attempts to reconcile faith and reason, church authority and classical thought; and universities were established.

Suggestions for Reading

J.H. Mundy, *Europe in the High Middle Ages* (Basic Books, 1973); F. Heer, *The Medieval World: Europe, 1100–1350** (Mentor, 1964); and J. R. Strayer, *Western Europe in the Middle Ages** (Scott, Foresman, 1982), are excellent syntheses. See also C. Brooke, *Europe in the Central Middle*

Ages, 962–*1154*,* 2nd ed. (Longman, 1975). H. Cam, *England Before Elizabeth** (Torchbooks, 1960); G. Sayles, *The Medieval Foundations of England** (A. S. Barnes, 1968); and C. Brooke, *From Alfred to Henry III, 871–1272** (Norton, 1961) are valuable surveys of English history during the period covered in this chapter. See also F. Stenton, *Anglo-Saxon England*, 3rd ed. (Oxford, 1971), the standard account; D. Kirby, *The Making of Early England* (Schocken, 1968); and E. King, *Medieval England, 1066–1485* (Salem House, 1989).

R. Allen Brown, *The Normans and the Norman Conquest* (Crowell, 1970); J. A. Matthew, *The Norman Conquest* (Schocken); and H. A. Cronne, *The Reign of Stephen* (Trinity Press, 1970) are all outstanding treatments. H. Muntz, *The Golden Warrior* (Popular Library, 1978) is a first-rate novel dealing with the Norman conquest.

Works on English monarchs of the period include E. Duckett, *Alfred the Great: The King and His England** (Phoenix, 1958); Amy Kelly, *Eleanor of Aquitaine and the Four Kings** (Howland, 1971); W. L. Warren, *King John* (Univ. of Calif. Press, 1978); S. Painter, *The Reign of King John** (Johns Hopkins, 1949); James A. Brundage, *Richard Lion Heart* (Scribner's, 1974); and W. L. Warren, *Henry II* (Univ. of Calif., 1973). See also R. Winston, *Thomas Becket* (Knopf, 1967) and T. M. Jones, ed., *The Becket Controversy** (Wiley, 1970).

On English constitutional history see J. C. Holt, *Magna Carta: The Idea of Liberty** (Wiley, 1973); G. L. Haskins, *The Growth of English Representative Government** (A. S. Barnes, 1948); B. Lyon, *A Constitutional and Legal History of Medieval England* (Harper & Row, 1960); and A. Pollard, *The Evolution of Parliament* (Russell, 1926).

For French history see R. Fawtier, *The Capetian Kings of France, 987–1328** (St. Martin's, 1969), the best account. See also J. B. Henneman, ed., *Medieval French Monarchy** (Krieger, 1973) and M. W. Labarge, *Saint Louis* (Macmillan, 1968).

R. Morriman, *The Rise of the Spanish in the Old World and in the New*, vol. I, (Cooper Square, 1918) and J. F. O'Callaghan, *A History of Medieval Spain** (Cornell, 1983) are standard works on medieval Spain. See also Gabriel Jackson, *The Making of Medieval Spain** (Harcourt Brace Jovanovich, 1972), and R. Menedez Pidal, *The Cid and His Spain* (Frank Cass, 1971).

For Germany in the Middle Ages see G. Barraclough, *The Origins of Modern Germany** (Capricorn, 1963). See also the diverse scholarly opinions presented in R. Herzstein, ed., *The Holy Roman Empire in the Middle Ages: Universal State or German Catastrophe?** (Heath, 1966). P. Munz, *Frederick Barbarossa: A Study in Medieval Politics* (Cornell, 1969); E. Kantorowicz, *Frederick the Second, 1194–1250* (Ungar, 1931); and T. van Cleve, *The Emperor Frederick II of Hohenstaufen* (Oxford, 1972) are instructive biographies. See also F. Baume, *Medieval Civilization in Germany* (Praeger, 1969).

William F. Butler, *The Lombard Communes: A History of the Republics of North Italy* (Haskell, 1969) is a reprint of a standard work. L. Salvatore, *A Concise History of Italy* (AMS, 1976) is a good general survey, as is J. K. Hyde, *Society and Politics in Medieval Italy** (Macmillan, 1973).

M. Keen, *The Pelican History of Medieval Europe** (Penguin); D. Hay, *The Medieval Centuries** (Torchbooks); and H. Trevor-Roper, *The Rise of Christian Europe** (Harcourt Brace Jovanovich) are valuable surveys of the Middle Ages. See also N. Zacour, *An Introduction to Medieval Institutions*, 2nd ed. (St. Martin's, 1976) and C. Erickson, *The Medieval Vision: Essays in History and Perception** (Oxford, 1976).

*Indicates a less expensive paperbound edition.

Notes

1. Quoted in W. S. Churchill, *The Birth of Britain*, vol. 1 of *A History of English-Speaking Peoples* (New York: Dodd, Mead & Co., 1965), p. 210.
2. Pope Gregory VII *Dictatus papae*, quoted in M. W. Baldwin, *Christianity Through the Thirteenth Century* (New York: Harper & Row, 1970), pp. 182–183.
3. Quoted in J. H. Robinson, *Readings in European History*, vol. 1 (Boston: Ginn and Co., 1904), p. 283
4. Quoted in Margaret Deanesly, *A History of the Medieval Church, 590–1000* (London: Metheun Co. Ltd., reprinted with corrections, 1972), p. 141.

Europe in Transition

Religion, Politics, and Culture, 1300–1500

In Europe, the fourteenth and fifteenth centuries were marked by the gradual passing of the culture that is thought of as typically "medieval." In the years of the High Middle Ages, European civilization had reached a pinnacle of development. But after 1300, the nature of civilization during the High Middle Ages began to change. In thought and art, a rigid formalism replaced the creative forces that had given the Middle Ages such unique methods of expression as scholasticism and the Gothic style. Economic and social progress yielded to depression and social strife, with peasant revolts a characteristic symptom of instability.

Church government in Rome experienced a loss of prestige, and a series of challenges weakened its effectiveness after 1300. The church was gravely weakened from within by would-be reformers and dissidents as well as by external factors, chiefly political and economic. By the sixteenth century these forces would be strong enough to bring about the Protestant and Catholic reformations.

Despite the desolation and death brought about by the Hundred Years' War between France and England, the process of nation-making continued during the fourteenth and fifteenth centuries. In western Europe the contrasting political trends clearly evident at the end of the thirteenth century—unification in England, France, and Spain, and fragmentation in Germany and Italy—reached their culmination. In much of Europe by the end of the fifteenth century, the conflicting aims of what are sometimes called the "new monarchies" were superseding the quarrels of feudal barons.

The Decline of the Medieval Church

The history of the medieval church divides roughly into three periods—dissemination, domination, and disintegration. In the initial period, which lasted from about the fifth through the eleventh centuries, Roman Catholic Christianity spread throughout the West. The advent of feudalism in the tenth century hindered the development of the church's administrative structure dominated by the papacy; but late in the eleventh century, the curch, directed by strong popes, became the most powerful institution in the West. The period of the papacy's greatest power—the twelfth and thirteenth centuries—reached its height with the pontificate of Innocent III, who exerted his influence over kings and princes without challenge. The church then seemed unassailable in its prestige, dignity, and power. Yet that strength soon came under new attack, and during the next two centuries the processes of disintegration were to gain in influence.

Papal power was threatened by the growth of nation-states, which challenged the church's temporal power and authority. Joined by some of the local clergy, rulers opposed papal interference in state matters and favored the establishment of general church councils to limit papal power. In addition, the papacy was criticized by reformers, who had seen earlier reform movements and the crusades transformed from their original high-minded purposes to suit the ambitions of the popes, and by the bourgeoisie, whose realistic outlook was fostering growing

Pope Gregory XI returning to Rome from Avignon, site of the papacy during the so-called Babylonian Captivity, 1305–1377.

skepticism, national patriotism, and religious self-reliance. During the fourteenth and fifteenth centuries these challenges to papal authority were effective, and papal influence rapidly declined.

Boniface VIII

A century after the papacy's apex under Innocent III, Pope Boniface VIII (1294–1303) was forced to withdraw his fierce opposition to taxes levied on the great wealth of the church by Edward I in Britain and Philip IV in France. Modeling his actions after Innocent, Boniface threatened to depose the "impious king," as he termed Philip, but he gave way when Philip with the support of the Estates-General prohibited the export of money to Rome.

A final and more humiliating clash with the French king had long-term implications for the papacy. When Boniface boldly declared, in the papal bull, *Unam Sanctam* (1302), that "subjection to the Roman pontiff is absolutely necessary to salvation for every human creature," Philip demanded that the pope be tried for his "sins" by a general church council. In 1303 Philip's henchmen broke into Boniface's summer home at Anagni to arrest him and take him to France to stand trial. Their kidnapping plot was foiled when the pope was rescued by his friends. Humiliated, Boniface died a month later, perhaps from the shock and physical abuse he suffered during the attack.

The Avignon Papacy

The success of the French monarchy was as complete as if Boniface actually had been dragged before Philip to stand trial. Two years after Boniface's death, a French archbishop was chosen pope. Taking the title of Clement V, he not only excused Philip but praised his Christian zeal in bringing charges against Boniface. Clement never went to Rome, where feuding noble families created turmoil in the city, but moved the papal headquarters to Avignon in southern France, where the papacy remained under French influence from 1305 to 1377. During this period, the so-called Babylonian Captivity of the church, papal prestige suffered enormously. All Christendom believed that Rome was the only suitable capital for the church. Moreover, the English, Germans, and Italians accused the popes and the cardinals, who were also French, of being instruments of the French king.

The Avignon papacy added fuel to the fires of those critics who were attacking church corruption, papal temporal claims, and the apparent lack of spiritual dedication. Increasing their demands for income from England, Germany, and Italy, and living in splendor in a newly built fortress-palace, the Avignon popes expanded the papal bureaucracy, added new church taxes, and collected the old taxes more efficiently. Such actions produced denouncements of the wealth of the church and a demand for its reform.

The Great Schism

When the papacy paid attention to popular opinion and returned to Rome in 1377, it seemed for a time that the fortunes of the Roman church

Pope Boniface VIII, Unam Sanctam

Unam Sanctam (1302), written to Philip IV of France by Pope Boniface VIII, is one of the most extreme statements of papal superiority and one of the final assertions of the temporal power of the church in an age growing more distant from effective political power exercised by the pope.

We are compelled, our faith urging us, to believe and to hold—and we do firmly believe and simply confess—that there is one holy catholic and apostolic church, outside of which there is neither salvation nor remission of sins; her Spouse proclaiming it in the canticles: "My dove, my undefiled is but one, she is the choice one of her that bare her;" which represents one mystic body, of which body the head is Christ; but of Christ, God. In this church there is one Lord, one faith and one baptism. There was one ark of Noah, indeed, at the time of the flood, symbolizing one church; and this being finished in one cubit had, namely, one Noah as helmsman and commander. And, with the exception of this ark, all things existing upon the earth were, as we read, destroyed. This church, moreover, we venerate as the only one, the Lord saying through His prophet: "Deliver my soul from the sword, my darling from the power of the dog." He prayed at the same time for His soul—that is, for Himself the Head—and for His body—which body, namely, he called the one and only church on account of the unity of the faith promised, of the sacraments, and of the love of the church. She is that seamless garment of the Lord which was not cut but which fell by lot. Therefore of this one and only church there is one body and one head—not two heads as if it were a monster:—Christ, namely, and the vicar of Christ, St. Peter, and the successor of Peter. For the Lord Himself said to Peter, Feed my sheep. My sheep, He said, using a general term, and not designating these or those particular sheep; from which it is plain that He committed to Him *all* His sheep. If, then, the Greeks or others say that they were not committed to the care of Peter and his successors, they necessarily confess that they are not of the sheep of Christ; for the Lord says, in John, that there is one fold, one shepherd and one only. We are told by the word of the gospel that in this His fold there are two swords,—a spiritual, namely, and a temporal. For when the apostles said "Behold here are two swords"—when, namely, the apostles were speaking in the church—the Lord did not reply that this was too much, but enough. Surely he who denies that the temporal sword is in the power of Peter wrongly interprets the word of the Lord when He says: "Put up thy sword in its scabbard." Both swords, the spiritual and the material, therefore, are in the power of the church; the one, indeed, to be wielded for the church, the other by the church; the one by the hand of the priest, the other by the hand of kings and knights, but at the will and sufferance of the priest. One sword, moreover, ought to be under the other, and the temporal authority to be subjected to the spiritual. For when the apostle says "there is no power but God, and the powers that are of God are ordained," they would not be ordained unless sword were under sword and the lesser one, as it were, were led by the other to great deeds. Whoever, therefore, resists this power thus ordained by God, resists the ordination of God, unless he makes believe, like the Manichean, that there are two beginnings. This we consider false and heretical, since by the testimony of Moses, not "in the beginnings," but "in the beginning" God created the Heavens and the earth. *Indeed we declare, announce and define, that it is altogther necessary to salvation for every human creature to be subject to the Roman pontiff.* The Lateran, Nov. 14, in our 8th year. As a perpetual memorial of this matter.

From Ernest F. Henderson, ed., and trans., *Select Historial Documents of the Middle Ages* (London: G. Bell & Sons, 1912), pp. 435–37.

would improve. But the reverse proved true. In the papal election held the following year, the College of Cardinals, perhaps influenced by a shouting mob milling around the Vatican, elected an Italian pope. A few months later the French cardinals declared the election invalid and elected a French pope, who returned to Avignon. The church was now in an even worse state than it had been during the Babylonian Captivity. During the Great Schism, as the split of the church into two allegiances was called, there were two popes, each with his college of cardinals and capital city, each claiming universal sovereignty, each sending forth papal administrators and taxing Christians, and each excommunicating the other. The nations of Europe gave allegiance as their individual political interests prompted them. In order to keep that allegiance, the rival popes had to make numerous concessions to their political supporters and largely abandoned the practice of interfering in national politics.

The Great Schism continued after the original rival popes died and each camp elected a replacement instead of working to heal the breach in the church. Religious life suffered, for "Christendom looked upon the scandal helpless and depressed, and yet impotent to remove it. With two sections of Christendom each declaring the other lost, each cursing and denouncing the other, men soberly asked who was saved."[1] Doubt and confusion caused many to question the legitimacy and true holiness of the church as an institution.

The Conciliar Movement

Positive action came in the form of the Conciliar Movement, a return to the early Christian practice of solving church problems by means of a general council of churches. In 1395 the professors at the University of Paris proposed that a general council, representing the universal church, should meet to heal the schism. A majority of the cardinals of both factions accepted this solution, and in 1409 they met at the council of Pisa, deposed both pontiffs, and elected a new pope. But neither of the two deposed popes would give up his office, and the papal throne now had three claimants.

Such an intolerable situation necessitated another church council. In 1414 the Holy Roman emperor assembled at Constance the most impressive church gathering of the period. For the first time voting took place on a purely national basis. Instead of the traditional assembly of bishops, the council included lay representatives and was organized as a convention of "nations" (German, Italian, French, and English, the Spanish entering later). Each nation had one vote. The nationalistic structure of the council was significant as an indication that the tendency toward such alignments was being recognized by the church's hierarchy. Finally, through the deposition of the various papal claimants and the election of Martin V as pope in 1417, the Great Schism was ended, and a single papacy was restored at Rome.

Failure of Internal Reform

The Conciliar Movement represented a reforming and democratizing influence in the church, aimed at transforming the papacy into an institution similar to a limited monarchy. But the movement was not to endure, even though the Council of Constance had solemnly decreed that general councils were superior to popes and that they should meet at regular intervals in the future. Taking steps to preserve his position, the pope announced that to appeal to a church council without having first obtained papal consent was heretical. The restoration of a single head of the church, together with the inability of later councils to bring about much-needed reform and with lack of support for such councils by secular rulers, enabled the popes to discredit the Conciliar Movement by 1450. Not until almost a century later, when the Council of Trent convened in 1545, did a great council meet to reform the church. By that time the church had already irreparably lost many countries to Protestantism.

Unfortunately, as the popes hesitated to call councils to effect reform, they failed to bring about reform themselves. The popes busied themselves not with internal problems but with Italian politics and patronage of the arts. Thus "the papacy emerged as something between an Italian city-state and a European power, without forgetting at the same time the claim to be the vice-regent of Christ. The pope often could not make up his own mind whether he was the successor of Peter or of Caesar. Such vacillation had much to do with the rise and success . . . of the Reformation."[2]

Wycliffe and Hus

Throughout the fourteenth century the cries against church corruption became louder at the same time that heretical thoughts were being publicly voiced. In England *Piers Plowman* mercilessly ridiculed the corruption, ignorance, and worldliness of the clergy, and a professor at Oxford named John Wycliffe (1320?–1384) attacked not only church abuses but especially church doctrines. Because of his beliefs that the church should be subordinate to the state, that salvation was primarily an individual matter between human beings and God, that transubstantiation as taught by the church was false, and that outward rituals and veneration of relics were idolatrous, Wycliffe has been called the forerunner of the Protestant revolt. He formed bands of "poor priests," called Lollards, who spread his views, and he provided the people with an English translation of the Bible, which he considered the final authority in matters of religion. Although Wycliffe's demands for reform did not succeed, the Lollards, including the famous John Ball, spread a more radical version of Wycliffe's ideas until the movement was driven underground early in the next century.

In Bohemia, where a strong reform movement linked with the resentment of the Czechs toward their German overlords was under way, Wycliffe's doctrines were popularized by Czech students who had heard him at Oxford. In particular, his beliefs influenced John Hus (1369?–1415), an impassioned preacher in Prague and later rector of the university there (see ch. 7). Hus' attacks on the abuses of clerical power led him, like Wycliffe, to conclude that the true church was composed of a universal priesthood of believers and that Christ alone was its head. But Hus, who was more preacher and reformer than theologian, did not accept Wycliffe's denial of the validity of transubstantiation.

Alarmed by Hus' growing influence, the church excommunicated him. Summoned to the Council of Constance to stand trial for heresy, Hus was promised safe conduct. But Hus refused

Two influential Church reformers of the 14th century were the Oxford theologian John Wycliffe (top) and John Hus (bottom), the leading proponent of Wycliffe's teachings in Prague.

to change his views, and the council ordered him burned at the stake. This action made Hus a martyr to the Czechs, who rebelled against both the German emperor and the Catholic church. In the sixteenth century the remaining Hussites merged with the Lutheran movement in frustration with a church deaf to their protests.

Reasons for Church Decline

The reasons for the church's decline during the fourteenth and fifteenth centuries can be divided into internal and external ones. By the early sixteenth century, these forces were strong enough to bring about the Reformation. Valid criticisms of the clergy had come from a variety of sources, and the Conciliar Movement had challenged the supreme power of the papacy itself. While criticisms increased, the church continued to decline in spiritual leadership. The worldly concerns of the fourteenth- and fifteenth-century popes—including their deep involvement in Italian politics—pushed the church further and further away from religious concerns.

Among the outside pressures that led to the church's decline, the growing spirit of inquiry resulted in a new critical attitude toward the institutionalization of the church. Further, the newly invented printing press provided the means for the rapid dissemination of ideas. From a socioeconomic view, the medieval church was slow in adapting itself to the new environment of the towns. The problems arising from town life too often went unanswered by the church, which failed to provide enough parish priests to keep pace with the growth of urban population. It is no accident that the towns became centers of heresy. Finally, the development of nationalism and the growing reluctance of kings to obey any opposing institution, including the church, were evident in the encounters between Boniface VIII and the French ruler Philip IV.

Crisis in England and France

Nation-making in both France and England was greatly affected by the long conflict that colored much of their history during the fourteenth and fifteenth centuries. In both lands the crisis of war led to a temporary resurgence of the feudal nobility at the expense of the king. Another modification in the rise of royal power was the increase in the power of the representative assemblies, Parliament and the Estates-General. Nevertheless, in the long run the increasing anarchy and misery of the times stimulated nationalistic feelings and a demand for strong rulers who could guarantee law and order. Thus by the late fifteenth century the French

and English kings were able to resume the task of establishing the institutions of the modern nation-state.

The Hundred Years' War

The Hundred Years' War had its origins in a fundamental conflict between the aims of the English and the French monarchies. The English kings wanted to regain the large holdings in France that had been theirs in the days of Henry II. The French kings, on the other hand, were determined not only to keep what had been taken from John of England but to expand further (see map below). Their ultimate goal was a centralized France under the direct rule of the monarchy at Paris.

Another cause was the clash of French and English economic interests in Flanders. This

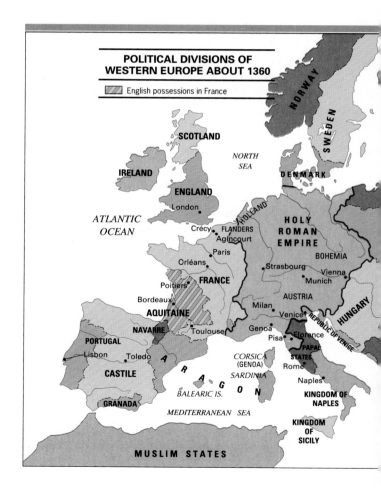

POLITICAL DIVISIONS OF WESTERN EUROPE ABOUT 1360

English possessions in France

An English view of the Battle of Agincourt. The English victory at Agincourt, as well as those at Crécy and Poitiers, were attributed in part to the well-disciplined English longbowmen.

region was coming more and more under French control, to the frustration of the English wool growers who supplied the great Flemish woolen industry, and of the English king whose income came in great part from duties on wool.

The immediate excuse for the Anglo-French conflict was a dispute over the succession to the French throne. In 1328, after the direct line of the Capetians became extinct, Philip VI of the House of Valois assumed the throne. The English king, Edward III, maintained that he was the legitimate heir to the French throne because his mother was a sister of the late French king. The French nobility disputed this claim, which became a pretext for war. Interrupted by several peace treaties and a number of truces, this devastating conflict stretched from 1337 to 1453. At the naval battle of Sluys (1340) the English gained command of the Channel and thus were able to send their armies to France at will. Thereafter England won a series of great victories— at Crécy (1346), Poitiers (1356), and Agincourt (1415), where the French lost some 7000 knights, including many great nobles, and the English only 500. In the aftermath of Agincourt large portions of France fell to the English.

The English armies were much more effective than those of the French. With no thought of strategy, the French knights charged the enemy at a mad gallop and then engaged in hand-to-hand conflict. The English had learned more effective methods. Their secret weapon was the longbow, apparently taken over from the Welsh. Six feet long and made of special wood, the longbow shot steel-tipped arrows that were dangerous at 400 yards and deadly at 100. The usual English plan of battle called for the knights to fight dismounted. Protecting them was a forward wall of bowmen just behind a barricade of iron stakes planted in the ground to slow down the enemy's cavalry charge. By the time the enemy cavalry reached the dismounted knights, only a few remained to be taken care of; the "feathered death" had done its work.

English military triumphs stirred English pride and what we now think of as nationalism—love of country, identification with it, and a sense of difference from, and usually superiority to, other peoples. However, patriotism was stirring in France also. The revival of French spirits is associated with Joan of Arc, who initiated a series of French victories.

Inspired by inward voices which she believed divine, Joan persuaded the timid French ruler to allow her to lead an army to relieve the besieged city of Orléans. Clad in white armor and riding a white horse, she inspired confidence and a feeling of invincibility in her followers, and in 1429 Orléans was rescued from what had seemed certain conquest. But Joan met a tragic end. Captured by the enemy, she was found guilty of bewitching the English soldiers and was burned at the stake, while the French king remained indifferent to her fate.

The martyrdom of the Maid of Orléans was a turning point in the long struggle. The nucleus of a permanent standing army was developed and the use of gunpowder to propel missiles began to transform the art of war. English resistance crumbled as military superiority now turned full circle; the English longbow was outmatched by French artillery. Of the vast

A 15th-century portrait of Joan of Arc in battle dress. After leading the French to victory at Orléans in 1429, she was captured by the English, who tried and convicted her of witchcraft and heresy and burned her at the stake in 1431. The French king Charles VII, whose kingdom she helped save, did nothing to save her.

territories they had once controlled in France, the English retained only Calais when the war ended in 1453.

Aftermath of the War in England

The Hundred Years' War exhausted England, and discontent was rife in Parliament and among the peasants. Richard II (1377–1399), the last Plantagenet king, was unstable, cruel, power-hungry, and firm in his belief that the king should control the lives and property of his subjects. His seizure of the properties of Henry, the duke of Lancaster, led to a revolt in which Henry was victorious.

Henry IV established the House of Lancaster, which ruled England from 1399 to 1461. He was given the support of Parliament, which had deeply resented Richard's autocratic reign and was determined that its authority should not again be slighted. Hard pressed for money to suppress revolts at home and carry on the war in France, the Lancastrian kings became more and more financially dependent upon Parliament. In return for money grants, Parliament acquired such gains as the guarantee of freedom of debate, the right to approve the appointment of the king's chief officials and members of his council, the stipulation that money bills must originate in the House of Commons, and the rule that the king's statutes should exactly duplicate petitions presented by the Commons. Not until 1689, when England became a constitutional monarchy, would Parliament again exercise such powers.

Baronial rivalry to control both Parliament and the crown flared up during the reign of the third Lancastrian king, and when he went completely insane in 1453, the duke of York, the strongest man in the kingdom, became regent. Two years later full-scale civil war broke out between the House of York and the partisans of the Lancaster family. The struggle became known as the Wars of the Roses; the white rose was the badge of the House of York, and the red rose that of the House of Lancaster. In 1461 the Yorkists managed to have their leader, Edward IV, crowned king. Ten years later, Edward had succeeded in controlling the nobles and in winning the support of the English middle classes, who saw a strong monarchy as the only alternative to anarchy. Edward's power became practically

Henry Tudor, who ruled England as Henry VII, was the first of the Tudor line. His victory over Richard III in Bosworth Field in 1485 ended the rule of the House of York.

absolute, foreshadowing the strong rule of the Tudors that was to follow.

The promise of the House of York ended in 1483 when Edward IV died, leaving two young sons as his heirs. Their uncle bribed and intimidated Parliament to declare his nephews illegitimate and took the throne as Richard III. The two boys were imprisoned in the Tower of London, where they were secretly murdered. The double murder was too scandalous for the nation to bear, and support was thrown to the cause of Henry Tudor, who in his lineage and later marriage to Edward IV's daughter, united the Houses of Lancaster and York. At Bosworth Field in 1485 Richard III died fighting as his army deserted him. According to tradition, his crown was found in a bush on the battlefield and placed on the head of Henry VII, the first of the Tudors, who ruled England from 1485 to 1603.

Beginning of Tudor Rule

Under Tudor rule England achieved full development into a nation. During the reigns of the shrewd Henry VII (1485–1509) and his successor, Henry VIII (1509–1547), strong, almost absolute government was reintroduced into England, with the people supporting the monarchy because it held the nobility in check. The Court of Star Chamber, established by Edward IV, was the most effective royal instrument in suppressing the unruly barons; it bypassed the established common law courts, whose judges and juries were too often intimidated and bribed by powerful nobles, and operated secretly and swiftly without benefit of juries. Because the Tudor rulers restored order, promoted trade at home and abroad, and restored security, they won the support of the people of middle rank, the burghers and landed gentry, and upon this support their power was primarily built. Though often highhanded, Tudor kings always worked through Parliament, where their wishes were generally honored.

France After the Hundred Years' War

The Hundred Years' War left France with a new national consciousness and royal power that was stronger than ever before. In 1438 the king had become very influential over the church in France by decreeing that it should be controlled by a council of French bishops whose appointment was to be regulated by the monarch. Furthermore, the *taille*, a land tax voted during the war to support a standing army, became permanent, making the king financially independent of the Estates-General. Thus the purse strings, which the English Parliament used to gain concessions from the king, were kept firmly under royal control in France.

After the war, Louis XI (1461–1483), son of the king aided by Joan of Arc, continued the process of consolidating royal power. Physically unattractive and completely lacking in scruples, Louis XI earned himself the epithet the "universal spider." In his pursuit of power he used any weapon—violence, bribery, or treachery—to obtain his ends. When the French nobles rose in revolt, dignifying themselves as the League for the Public Welfare, Louis outfoxed them by

Louis XI of France. The wily and ruthless French king used violence, bribery, and treachery to secure his rule and lay the foundation for absolute monarchy in France.

agreeing to their Magna Carta-like demands and then ignoring his pledged word. The "spider-king" devoted his reign to restoring prosperity to his nation and to reducing the powers of the noble families still active and ambitious after the long war.

Louis XI's most powerful antagonist was the duke of Burgundy, Charles the Bold, whose possession of Flanders and the other Low Countries or Netherlands (modern Holland, Belgium, and Luxembourg) made him one of Europe's richest rulers. After Charles' death in 1477, Louis seized most of Burgundy, while the remainder of the duke's possessions passed to his daughter Mary. When she married the German emperor Maximilian I, the Netherlands came into the hands of the House of Habsburg (see map, p. 450). Like Henry VII of England, Louis XI was one of the "new monarchs" who created the absolute states that were to dominate Europe in the early modern period.

The Political Unification of Spain and Portugal

Another "new monarchy" emerged in 1479 when Isabella of Castile and Ferdinand of Aragon, who had married ten years earlier, began a joint rule that united the Iberian peninsula except for Granada, Navarre, and Portugal. The "Catholic Majesties," the title the pope conferred on Ferdinand and Isabella, set out to establish an effective royal despotism in Spain. The Holy Brotherhood, a league of cities that had long existed for mutual protection against unruly nobles, was taken over by the crown, and its militia was used as a standing army and police force.

In this romantic Flemish tapestry Ferdinand and Isabella reign in splendor, attended by richly costumed courtiers and ladies-in-waiting.

The powerful and virtually independent military orders of knights, which had emerged during the *Reconquista*, were also brought under royal control.

Ferdinand and Isabella: "One King, One Law, One Faith"

Ferdinand and Isabella believed that the church should be subordinate to royal government—a belief they shared with the other "new monarchs" of Europe. By tactful negotiations, the Spanish sovereigns induced the pope to give them the right to make church appointments in Spain and to establish a Spanish Court of Inquisition, largely free of papal control. The Inquisition confiscated the property of most Jews and Muslims and terrified the Christian clergy and laity into accepting royal absolutism as well as religious orthodoxy. Although the Inquisition greatly enhanced the power of the Spanish crown, it also caused many talented people to flee the land of persecution. About 150,000 Spanish Jews, mainly merchants and professional people, fled to Holland, England, North Africa, and the Ottoman Empire. Calling themselves Sephardim, these exiles retained their Spanish language and customs into the twentieth century.

A final manifestation of Spanish absolutism, defined by Isabella herself as "one king, one law, one faith," was the virtual ignoring of the *Cortes* of Castile and Aragon. These representative assemblies, having emerged in the twelfth century, were thus older than the English Parliament, but had not been effective for some time.

The most dramatic act of the Catholic Majesties was the conquest of Granada in 1492, the same year that Columbus claimed the New World for Spain. Before Ferdinand died in 1516, twelve years after Isabella, he seized that part of Navarre that lay south of the Pyrenees Mountains. This acquisition, together with the conquest of Granada, completed the national unification of Spain.

Results of Spanish Unification

Royal absolutism and unification, coupled with the acquisition of territory in the New and Old Worlds, made Spain the strongest power in sixteenth-century Europe. But the process of unifying Spain had some unfortunate results. Centuries of fighting against the Muslims left a legacy of warlike spirit and excessive national pride. Religious fervor was generated as a means to an end, and the sequel was a heritage of religious bigotry and the death of that tolerance, intellectual curiosity, and sense of balance that had been characteristic of Muslim culture in Spain. Spanish contempt for the Muslims created a scorn for those activities in which the "unbelievers" had engaged—commercial involvement and agriculture. This attitude hampered Spanish economic development in subsequent centuries.

Portugal

The nucleus of the area that eventually became Portugal was a part of Castile until 1095. In that year the king of Castile gave his daughter in marriage to Count Henry of Burgundy, one of many French knights who had helped take Toledo. Her dowry was the country of Portugal, named after its chief town Oporto ("The Port") at the mouth of the Duero River. The son of this marriage organized a revolt against his overlord, the king of Castile, and in 1139 proclaimed himself king of Portugal.

Attempts by Castile to regain Portugal ended in 1385 when John I, aided by English archers, decisively defeated the Spanish invaders. The following year John signed an alliance with England which has been reaffirmed down the centuries and remains the oldest alliance in existence. In 1415 John took Ceuta in North Africa, thus initiating Portuguese overseas expansion; carried on by his son, Henry the Navigator, this policy eventually led to the creation of a great overseas empire (see ch. 16).

Disunity in Germany and Italy

Between 1254 and 1273 the German monarchy was made virtually nonexistent by the election of two rival foreign princes, neither of whom received great recognition. Then in 1273 the imperial crown was bestowed upon the obscure Count Rudolf (1273–1291) of the House of Habsburg—from Habichtsburg (Castle of the Hawk), the family's home in northern Switzerland. During the remainder of the Middle Ages and in modern times, the Habsburgs had amazing success in adding to their ancestral lands. Rudolf himself acquired Austria through marriage, and thereafter the Habsburgs ruled their holdings from Vienna. In the sixteenth century they obtained Bohemia and part of Hungary.

The effective end of German imperial influence after 1250 left the three major divisions of Italy—the city-states of northern Italy, the Papal States, and the Kingdom of Naples (see map, p. 286)—free to follow their own desires. Such city-states as Venice, Florence, Milan, Genoa, and Pisa had grown wealthy from their thriving industries, lucrative trade, and banking houses that handled papal revenues and made loans to European monarchs.

The Early Habsburgs and the Golden Bull

In the thirteenth century, the Habsburg hold on the imperial crown proved to be brief. After Rudolf's reign it was passed from one family to another. Then in 1356 the nobility won another significant victory. The Golden Bull, a document that served as the political constitution of Germany until early in the nineteenth century, established the procedure for election of the emperor by seven German dignitaries—three archbishops and four lay princes. The electors and other important princes were given rights that made them virtually independent rulers, and the emperor could take no important action without the consent of the imperial feudal assembly, the Diet, which met infrequently.

It has been said that the Golden Bull "legalized anarchy and called it a constitution"; in reality it stabilized the political situation in Germany by recognizing the independence of the princes, thereby encouraging them to create stable governments in their principalities. It also ended disputed elections and civil wars over the succession. But with the emperor virtually powerless, people thereafter commonly referred to the welter of duchies, counties, bishoprics, and free cities as the Germanies, not Germany.

The imperial crown of Germany was returned to the Habsburg family in 1438. From this time until 1806, when the Holy Roman Empire disintegrated, the Habsburgs held the crown almost without interruption. Maximilian I (1493–1519) helped make the Habsburgs the most important royal family in sixteenth-century Europe by taking as his wife Mary of Burgundy (see p. 290), heiress of the rich Low Countries, and by marrying his son to the heiress of Spain.

Inspired by the accomplishments of other contemporary European monarchs, Maximilian attempted to strengthen his power. His program for a national court system, army, and taxation was frustrated by the German princes who insisted on guarding what they called "German freedom." The emperor continued to be limited in power; nor did the empire have an imperial treasury, an efficient central administration, or a standing army. And so the phantom Holy Roman Empire lived on as Voltaire later characterized it: "Neither Holy, nor Roman, nor an Empire."

Italy: Wealthy but Divided

Within each of the northern Italian city-states there were intense rivalries and feuds. Unlike the situation in northern Europe, where bourgeoisie inhabited the towns but the nobles lived on country manors, the Italian nobility had city houses as well as country villas. In some Italian cities arcaded streets enabled the townspeople to go about their business safe from the arrows that from time to time flew between the towered houses of feuding nobles.

In both the intracity rivalries and the struggles between city-states, mercenary soldiers under the command of leaders called *condottieri* were employed. Coming from all over Europe, these adventurers sold their swords to the highest bidder, but, in order to live and fight another day, they carried on their fighting with a minimum of bloodshed. Far different from the twentieth-century wars of annihilation, these petty conflicts did not interfere with the spectacular progress in art and learning called the Italian Renaissance (see ch. 12).

Civic patriotism advanced rapidly under the influence of the prosperous townspeople, who finally succeeded in removing the restless feudal aristocrats from positions of power. Ingenious city charters and civic constitutions were drafted, and there was much trial and error in the art of government. Until the end of the thirteenth century the prevailing political trend in the cities was toward republicanism and representative government.

Venice and Florence

Two city-state republics are of special interest. Venice, the "Pearl of the Adriatic," was one of the richest cities of its time, controlling an empire of ports and islands in the eastern Mediterranean and carrying much of Europe's maritime

A portrait of Maximilian I by Albrecht Dürer, appointed painter to the emperor in 1512. The portrait was done in 1519, the year of the emperor's death. In the 11th and 12th centuries, Germany seemed on the way to becoming the strongest state in Europe, but by 1500 the emperor's authority had declined in favor of the power of princes and nobles.

The two great Italian city-states, Venice (right) and Florence (below). The large building at the right in the portrait of Venice is the Palace of the Doge. Behind it are the domes of St. Mark's Cathedral. In this 15th-century view of Florence, an artist (lower right) is sketching the busy and crowded urban center, which has spread beyond the city walls to the hills of the Apennines.

trade in its great fleets. The government of this rich republic had been in the hands of a doge (duke), together with a popular assembly, but beginning in the thirteenth century the rich merchants gradually took over the reins of power. They alone sat in the Great Council, which replaced the popular assembly. This oligarchic council appointed the doge and the members of smaller councils that administered the government. Most famous among the smaller councils was the secret Council of Ten, which dealt swiftly with suspected enemies of the government. The merchant oligarchy of Venice provided good government and, unlike other Italian city-states, resolutely squashed internal strife.

Florence—the center of flourishing wool, leather, and silk industries—boasted merchants and bankers who were among the most prosperous in Europe, and its gold florin circulated in many lands as a standard coin. With its many checks and counterchecks of power, the Florentine constitution was bewilderingly complex. For example, the head of the state held office for two months only, and all measures needed a two-thirds majority in five different committees or assemblies to become laws. In theory Florence was a democracy but, as in Venice, real political power was wielded by wealthy business owners.

During the fourteenth century, republicanism declined and most Italian city-states came under the rule of despots. Conspiracy, confusion, and incompetence caused many citizens to welcome a strong leader as political despot. Although Venice maintained the benevolent oligarchy of its merchants with the doge as a figurehead, Florence fell under the influence of the Medici family, and its republican institutions because largely empty forms. The Medici had no aristocratic ancestors; their status was based on the family's great success in commerce and finance. The significance of the family emblem—six red balls on a field of gold—is unknown, but we are all familiar with the later modification of this insignia—the three balls of the pawnbroker.

The Papal States and the Kingdom of Naples

The Papal States, extending from fifty miles south of the mouth of the Tiber to the northeast across Italy as far as the mouth of the Po River, were poorly organized. The popes found it difficult to force their will upon various local rulers who defied their political authority. Although they headed the great international church, in Italy the popes acted little differently from the rulers of the other states in the matter of hiring troops, waging wars, and making treaties.

The Kingdom of Naples covered the southern half of the Italian peninsula as well as Sicily. After 1250 the houses of Aragon and Anjou disputed each other over the kingdom until Aragon won out early in the fifteenth century. But southern Italy and Sicily were both impoverished by the warfare of foreign armies and damaged by the rebelliousness of their own nobles. With anarchy prevailing, southern Italy and Sicily sank into a decline that was to continue into the twentieth century.

Cultural Expression During the Middle Ages

During the entire Middle Ages Latin served as an international means of communication. This common tongue provided much of the cohesion of the Middle Ages, for virtually all the crucial communications of the church, governments, and schools were in Latin. But any misconception that the Middle Ages were simply "otherworldly" is shattered by glancing at the Latin poetry written during the twelfth and thirteenth centuries by students. Known as Goliardic verse because its authors claimed to be disciples of Goliath, their euphemism for the devil, it unhesitatingly proclaimed the pleasures of the good life.

> Let us live like gods above!
> Worthy is this sentiment,
> See, the hunting nets of love
> Wait for those on loving bent
> To our vows let us attend!
> That is what the custom says.
> Let us to the streets descend,
> To the maidens' choruses.
> Time we're wasting speedily
> While to books confined,
> Tender youth suggests that we
> Be to fun inclined.[3]

Vernacular Literature

A rising tide of literature in the vernacular, or common, tongues began to appear by the twelfth century, with the epic as the earliest form. The greatest of the French epics, or *chansons de geste* ("songs of great deeds"), is the late eleventh century *Song of Roland,* which recounts the heroic deeds and death of Count Roland in the Pyrenees while defending the rear of Charlemagne's army. The great Spanish epic, the *Poema del Mio Cid* is a product of the twelfth century. These stirring epic poems, with their accounts of prowess in battle, mirror the warrior virtues of early chivalry.

Dante Alighieri

The vernacular was also used by two of the greatest writers of the period—Dante and Chaucer. Combining a profound religious sense with a knowledge of scholastic thought and the Latin classics, the Italian Dante Alighieri (1265–1321) produced one of the world's greatest and most skillfully written narrative poems. The *Divine Comedy,* which Dante said described his "full experience," is an allegory of medieval man (Dante)

The Ménagier's Wife

The following selection was written in the fifteenth century by a French upper middle class businessman who wished to give his wife a book of instructions on how she should work to make her husband happy.

Fair sister, if you have another husband after me, know that you should think much of his comfort, for after a woman has lost her first husband she commonly finds it difficult to find another according to her estate, and she remains lonely and disconsolate for a long time; and more so still, if she lose the second. Wherefore cherish the person of your husband carefully, and, I pray you, keep him in clean linen, for 'tis your business. And because the care of outside affairs lieth with men, so must a husband take heed, and go and come and journey hither and thither, in rain and wind, in snow and hail, now drenched, now dry, now sweating, now shivering, ill-fed, ill-lodged, ill-warmed and ill-bedded; and nothing harms him, because he is upheld by the hope that he has of his wife's care of him on his return, and of the ease, the joys and pleasures which she will do to him, or cause to be done to him in her presence; to have his shoes removed before a good fire, his feet washed and to have fresh shoes and stockings, to be given good food and drink, to be well served and well looked after, well bedded in white sheets and night-caps, well covered with good furs, and assuaged with other joys and amusements, privities, loves, and secrets, concerning which I am silent; and on the next day fresh shirts and garments. Certes, fair sister, such service maketh a man love and desire to return to his home and to see his goodwife and to be distant with other women.

And therefore I counsel you to make such cheer to your husband at all his comings and goings and to persevere therein; and also to be peaceable with him and remember the rustic proverb, which saith that there be three things which drive the goodman from home, to wit, a dripping roof, a smoking chimney and a scolding woman. Wherefore, fair sister, I pray you that in order to keep yourself in love and good favour with your husband you be unto him gentle, amiable and debonair. Do unto him what the good simple women of our country say has been done unto their sons, when the lads have set their love elsewhere and their mothers cannot wean them from it. It is certain that when fathers and mothers be dead, and stepfathers and stepmothers argue with their stepsons, and scold them and repulse them, and take not thought for their sleeping, nor for their food and drink, their hose and their shirts and all their other needs and affairs, and the same children find elsewhere a good home and good counsel from some other woman, who receives them and takes thought to warm them with some poor gruel with her and to give them a bed and keep them tidy, mending their hosen, breeches, shirts, and other garments, then those lads cleave to her and desire to be with her, and to sleep warm between her breasts. . . . Wherefore, dear sister, I pray you thus to bewitch and bewitch again your husband, and beware of dripping roof and smoking fire, and scold him not, but be unto him gentle and amiable and peaceable. Be careful that in winter he has good fire without smoke, and let him rest well and be well covered between your breasts and thus bewitch him. . . . And so on the road, husbands will think of their wives, and no trouble will be a burden to them for the hope and love they will have of their wives, whom they will long to see, even as poor hermits, penitents and fasting monks long to see the face of Christ Jesus; and husbands served thus will never desire to abide elsewhere or in other company but will withhold, withdraw and abstain themselves there-from; all the rest will seem to them but a bed of stones compared with their home.

From Eileen Power, *Medieval People* (London: Methuen & Co., 1924), pp. 104–07.

A fresco by Domenico di Francesco, called Michelino, of Dante and his poem also includes the Cathedral of Florence (right), where the fresco is located, and scenes from the *Divine Comedy*, Dante's medieval allegory of the journey from hell (left) through purgatory to heaven and union with God (center).

moving from bestial earthiness (hell) through conversion (purgatory) to the sublime spirituality of union with God (paradise). Dante describes how

> Midway this way of life we're bound upon,
> I woke to find myself in a dark wood,
> Where the right road was wholly lost and
>   gone.[4]

Dante then accepts the offer of Virgil, symbol of pagan learning to be his "master, leader, and lord" to guide him through hell and purgatory. But Beatrice, the lady whom he had once loved from afar and who is now the symbol of divine love, guides him through paradise. At last Dante stands before God, and words fail him as he finds peace in the presence of the highest form of love:

> Here my powers rest from their high fantasy,
> but already I could feel my being turned—
> instinct and intellect balanced equally ... [5]

The Wit of Chaucer

In the *Canterbury Tales*, Geoffrey Chaucer (1340?–1400), one of the greatest figures in medieval literature, reveals a cross section of contemporary English life, customs, and thought. The twenty-nine pilgrims who assembled in April 1387 at an inn before journeying to the shrine of St. Thomas à Becket at Canterbury were a motley group. The "truly perfect, gentle knight," just returned from warring against the "heathen in Turkey," was accompanied by his son, a young squire who loved so much by night that "he slept no more than does a nightingale." The clergy was represented by the coy prioress who "would weep if she but saw a mouse caught in a trap,"[6] the rotund monk who loved to eat fat swan and ride good horses, the friar who knew the best taverns and all the barmaids in town, and the poor parish priest who was a credit to his faith.

François Villon, "On Death" and "The Ballad of Dead Ladies"

François Villon (d. 1463) was perhaps the greatest French poet of his time. His poetry reflects the realism and pessimism which seem to permeate French society in the fifteenth century.

"On Death"

I know this well, that rich and poor,
Fools, sages, laymen, friars in cowl,
Large-hearted lords and each mean boor,
Little and great and fair and foul,
Ladies in lace, who smile or scowl,
From whatsoever stock they stem,
Hatted or hooded, prone to prowl,
Death seizes every one of them.

And Paris dying, or Helen, still
Who dies, dies wretchedly and apart.
Whoever loses breath and will,
The black gall breaks upon his heart;
He sweats—God knows how sweat will start!—
Nor gains aid as his eyes grow dim:
Child, brother, none will play the part
Of hostage in death's hands for him.

Death makes him shudder and turn pale.
Pinches his nose, distends his veins,
Swells out his throat, his members fail,
Tendons and nerves grow hard with strains.
O female flesh, like silken skeins,
Smooth, tender, precious, in such wise
Must you endure so awful pains?
Aye, or go living to the skies.

From J. V. Nicholson, *The Complete Works of François Villon* (New York: Covici, Friede, 1931), pp. 191–92.

"The Ballad of Dead Ladies"

Tell where, in what country,
Is Flora the beautiful Roman,
Archipiada or Thaïs
Who was first cousin to her once,
Echo who speaks when there's a sound
On a pond or a river
Whose beauty was more than human?
But where are the snows of yesteryear?

Where is the learned Heloise
For whom they castrated Pierre Abelard
And made him a monk at Saint-Denis,
For his love he took this pain,
Likewise where is the queen
Who commanded that Buridan
Be thrown in a sack into the Seine?
But where are the snows of yesteryear?

The queen white as a lily
Who sang with a siren's voice,
Big-footed Bertha, Beatrice, Alice,
Haremburgis who held Maine
And Jeanne the good maid of Lorraine
Whom the English burnt at Rouen, where,
Where are they, sovereign Virgin?
But where are the snows of yesteryear?

From Sylvia Wright, ed., *Age of Chivalry* (New York: Watts, 1988) p. 288.

Chaucer's fame rests securely upon his keen interest in human nature and his skill as a storyteller. The Midland dialect he used was the linguistic base for the language of future English literature, just as Dante's use of the Tuscan dialect fixed the Italian tongue.

Artistic Correlation

The *Summa Theologica* of St. Thomas Aquinas and the *Divine Comedy* of Dante represent the best intellectual expressions of the medieval spirit. Similarly, the Gothic cathedral is the ultimate artistic expression of the age. Each of these masterpieces represents a different aspect of the attempt to organize everything into an overall pattern that would glorify God.

The order and form of scholastic thought find their counterparts in the structure and style of the Gothic edifices. A scholastic treatise was systematically arranged in logical parts; the cathedral was similarly articulated in space. The

At the bottom of this detail of the *Last Judgment* from Autun Cathedral, the dead rise from their graves in fear. At the top, their souls are weighed in the scales. The saved cling to angels, while grotesque devils seize the damned and throw them into hell.

main sections, the nave, transept, and apse, were individually distinctive yet integrated into a coherent structure.

Cathedral Architecture

In the eleventh century a tremendous architectural revival occurred, marked by the recovery of the art of building in stone rather than in wood, as was common during the early Middle Ages. At a much later date the name *Romanesque* came to be applied to this new style, because, like early Christian architecture, it was based largely on Roman models. Although details of structure and ornamentation differed with locality, the round arch was a standard Romanesque feature. Both barrel and cross vaults (see p. 91) were used, particularly in northern Europe, where the need to build fireproof churches made it impractical to follow the common Italian practice of using flat wooden roofs. While there was often one long barrel vault over the nave (the part of a church between the aisles, where the congregation assembles), the aisles were divided into square areas or bays with a cross vault over each bay. Thick outside walls and huge interior piers were necessary to support the heavy stone barrel and cross vaults. Because the walls would be weakened by large window apertures, the clerestory (the uppermost portion of the nave walls) windows were small or nonexistent. Thus the northern Romanesque interior was dark and gloomy, the exterior massive and monumental.

No clear distinction exists between Romanesque and Gothic architecture. There was a gradual evolutionary process, which reached its culmination in the thirteenth and fourteenth centuries. The architects of the Gothic cathedral developed ribbed-groin vaults with pointed rather than round arches. This invention enabled them to solve the technical problem of cross-vaulting the nave, which, being wider than the aisles, could not easily be divided into square bays covered by Romanesque cross vaults. The light ribbed-groin vaults, whose sides were of different length to fit the rectangular bays of the nave, replaced the heavy barrel vault, and the roof of the nave could be raised to permit the use of large clerestory windows. The thrust of the vaults over both the nave and the aisles was concentrated on a few strong structural supports. Part of the weight was carried down to the ground by columns within the building, and part by flying buttresses at points along the walls. With such vaulting and flying buttresses, the weight of the roof was largely shifted off the walls. Large stained-glass windows were set into the walls between the buttresses. The dark, somber interior of the Romanesque churches gave way to the jeweled light of the Gothic interiors.

Interior and exterior views of the Cathedral of St. Pierre at Angoulême, a typical example of Romanesque architecture. The cathedral's ribbed groin vaults are derived from the Roman intersecting vaults. As shown in the drawing, the ribbed vault is made up of arches that span the sides of a square bay, with groin vaults crossing diagonally from corner to corner.

Sculpture and Painting

Most Romanesque and Gothic sculpture served an architectural function by being carved into the total composition of a church. To use sculpture to the best architectural advantage, the artist often distorted the subject to achieve a particular effect. Like sculpture, medieval painting in the form of stained-glass windows was integral part of architecture. Composed of small pieces of colored glass held together in a pattern by metal strips, which both braced the glass and emphasized the design, stained glass was an art whose excellence has not been

The effect of the fully developed Gothic sytle, as shown here in the interior and exterior views of Amiens Cathedral, is one of awesome but ordered intricacy. The drawings below are a cross section and floor plan of the cathedral. Vaults, arches, buttresses, and weighted pinnacles were important structural elements in the Gothic style of architecture.

duplicated in modern times. By adding various minerals to Molten glass, thirteenth-century craftsmen achieved brilliant hues. Details such as hair were painted on the glass. The object, however, was not realism but the evoking of a mood—to shine with the radiance of heaven itself.

Secular Architecture

What the cathedral was to religious life, the castle was to everyday living. Both were havens and both were built to endure. The new weapons and techniques of siege warfare, which the

Medieval cathedrals, like that at Amiens in France, were rich in sculptures of saints, episodes from the Old and New Testaments, and allegorical representations. The Vierge Dorée, which appears over the south portal, conveys the deeply felt emotion and ability to communicate by glance and gesture which are characteristic of the Gothic style.

Crusaders brought back with them, necessitated more massive castles. By the thirteenth century castle building in Europe reached a high point of development. The towers were rounded, and bastions stood at strategic points along the walls. The castle as a whole was planned in such a skillful manner that if one section was taken by attackers, it could be sealed off from the remaining fortifications. Whole towns were fortified in the same way, with walls, watchtowers, moats, and drawbridges.

Toward the end of the Middle Ages there was less of a need for fortified towns and castles. At the same time the wealth accruing from the revived trade and increased industry encouraged the development of secular Gothic architecture. Town and guild halls, the residences of the rich, and the chateaux of the nobility all borrowed the delicate Gothic style from the cathedrals.

Conclusion

Medieval idealism hoped for a Europe united as a Christian commonwealth and ruled by dual powers, the universal church and an all-embracing Holy Roman Empire. In theory, the emperor would rule in the temporal or earthly realm, and the pope in the spiritual. Because papal authority was not restricted by national boundaries, the church was nearly all-encompassing. By contrast, the emperor's authority was limited for the most part to Germany and Italy, and even there imperial power was intermittent.

During the fourteenth and fifteenth centuries, a number of forces threatened and eventually undermined the medieval ideal. The church was badly weakened from within as a result of the "Babylonian Captivity", the Great Schism, and the demands of reformers; and despite continuous opposition from both the church and the feudal nobles, the national state had become a reality in Europe by the end of the sixteenth century.

Influencing nation-making in both England and France was the Hundred Years' War, which stimulated nationalism in the hearts of the English and French alike. Other significant changes resulted from that conflict: in England, the power of Parliament was increased, and the upsurge in the power of the nobility led to the War of the

Roses, which ended finally with the accession of the Tudors; in France, royal power was consolidated under Louis XI, and further progress in national unification was made because of his abilities in government. Ferdinand and Isabella completed the creation of a national state in Spain and laid the foundations for its future greatness. On the other hand, Germany and Italy continued divided and weak; there national unification would not be achieved until the nineteenth century.

The beauty and harmony of the medieval cathedral is in many ways paralleled by the effort of the medieval theologians to construct "cathedrals of thought and learning." The achievements in learning and in art were similarly dedicated to the glory of God, the source of all knowledge and order. Even the political might of the organized church could be viewed as a similar attempt for perfection and order.

Suggestions for Reading

W.K. Ferguson, *Europe in Transition, 1300 to 1500* (Houghton Mifflin, 1963) is a comprehensive work. See also D. Hay, *Europe in the Fourteenth and Fifteenth Centuries* (Harcourt Brace Jovanovich, 1966); E. Cheyney, *The Dawn of a New Era, 1250–1453** (Torchbooks); R. E. Lerner, *The Age of Adversity: The Fourteenth Century** (Cornell); Jerah Johnson and W. Percy, *The Age of Recovery: The Fifteenth Century** (Cornell); and D. Waley, *Later Medieval Europe** (Longman, 1985).

A. R. Myers, *England in the Late Middle Ages** (Penguin) and George Holmes, *The Later Middle Ages, 1272–1485**

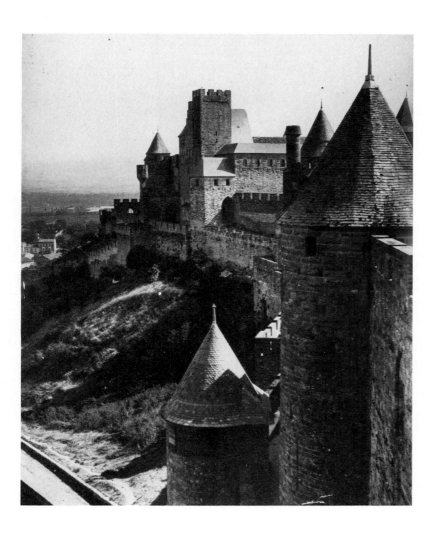

A fine example of medieval secular architecture is the castle at Carcasonne, France, which dates from the 13th century. The earliest castles, which appeared in about the 9th century, were built entirely of wood. By the late 11th century, stone was used for the construction of the castle tower. Massive stuctures built entirely of stone appeared in the 12th and 13th centuries.

(Norton) are excellent surveys of English history during the period. See also Faith Thompson, *A Short History of Parliament, 1295–1642* (Minnesota). P.S. Lewis, *Later Medieval France* (St. Martin's, 1968) covers government and society in the later Middle Ages. Also recommended are two biographies: J. Michelet, *Joan of Arc** (Michigan) and John H. Smith, *Joan of Arc* (Scribner's, 1973).

Gabriel Jackson, *The Making of Medieval Spain* (Harcourt Brace Jovanovich) is brief and highly readable with many illustrations. Other excellent surveys are F. Fernandez-Arnesto, *Ferdinand and Isabella* (Taplinger, 1975); J. H. Elliot, *Imperial Spain, 1469–1716** (Penguin); and C. Roth, *The Spanish Inquisition** (Norton).

G. Barraclough, *The Origins of Modern Germany** (Capricorn) is the best account of this period of German history. J. A. Symonds, *The Renaissance in Italy*, Vol. I, *The Age of the Despots* (Peter Smith) is a celebrated account of Italian politics in the fourteenth and fifteenth centuries. D. Hay, *The Church in Italy in the Fifteenth Century* (Cambridge, 1977) and D. S. Chambers, *The Imperial Age of Venice, 1380–1580** (Harcourt Brace Jovanovich) are brief and well done. See J. Burrow, *The Ages of Man: A Study in Medieval Writing and Thought** (Oxford, 1989) for an outstanding review of medieval literature. An excellent social history is J. Bennett, *Women in the Medieval English Countryside** (Oxford, 1989).

A good account of church history during this period is L. Elliot-Binns, *History of the Decline and Fall of the Medieval Papacy* (ShoeString, 1967). See also G. Leff, *Heresy in the Later Middle Ages*, 2 vols. (Barnes and Noble, 1967); K. McFarlane, *John Wycliffe and the Beginnings of English Nonconformity* (Verry); and M. Spinka, *John Hus: A Biography* (Princeton, 1968).

* Indicates a less expensive paperbound edition.

Notes

1. A. C. Flick, *Decline of the Medieval Church*, vol. I (London: Kegan Paul, Trench, Trubner and Co., 1930), p. 293.
2. R. H. Bainton, *The Reformation of the Sixteenth Century* (Boston: Beacon Press, 1952), p. 15.
3. "Adieu to Studies" in *Vagabond Verse*, trans. Edwin H. Zeydel (Detroit: Wayne State University Press, 1966), p. 157.
4. *L'Inferno*, Canto I, lines 1–3, trans. Dorothy L. Sayers, *Dante, The Divine Comedy, I: Hell* (Harmondsworth: Penguin Books, 1949), p. 71.
5. Dante Alighieri, *The Paradiso*, Canto XXXIII, lines 142–144, trans. John Ciardi (New York: Mentor Books, 1961), p. 365.
6. Geoffrey Chaucer, *Canterbury Tales*, trans. J. U. Nicolson (New York: Crown Publishers, 1936), pp. 3–5.

"Man Is the Measure"

Renaissance Thought and Art, 1300–1600

In Italy during the fourteenth and fifteenth centuries thinkers and artists began to view the thousand years that had elapsed since the fall of Rome as the "Dark Ages" — a time of stagnation and ignorance — in contrast to their own age which appeared to them wise and beautiful. They exuberantly proclaimed that they were participating in an intellectual and aesthetic revolution sparked by the "rebirth" (renaissance) of the values and forms of classical antiquity. Modern historians have accepted the term Renaissance as a convenient label for this exciting age of intellectual and artistic revival, which continued through the sixteenth century. But since the Renaissance had deep roots in the Middle Ages, which also made rich contributions to civilization, in what ways can the Renaissance be said to signify a "rebirth"?

First of all, there was an intensification of interest in the literature of classical Greece and Rome. This Classical Revival, as it is called, was the product of a more wordly focus of interest — a focus on human beings and on this life as an end in itself rather than a temporary halting place on the way to eternity. Renaissance scholars searched the monasteries for old Latin manuscripts that had been unappreciated and largely ignored by medieval scholars, and they translated hitherto unknown works from Greek into Latin, the common language of scholarly discourse. Thus the humanists, as these scholars were called, greatly added to the quantity of classical literature that had been entering the mainstream of Western thought since the Middle Ages. Second, while Renaissance scholars found a new significance in classical literature, artists in Italy were stimulated and inspired by their study and imitation of classical sculpture and architecture.

But the spirit of the Renaissance was not characterized by a mere cult of antiquity, a looking backward into the past. The humanists of the Renaissance were — except for a lack of interest in science — the harbingers of the modern world, enthusiastically engaged in widening the horizon of human interests. Renaissance culture strikingly exhibits belief in the worth of the individual and the desire to think and act as a free agent. The Renaissance spirit was admirably summed up by the Florentine humanist Leon Battista Alberti, when he declared, "Men can do all things if they will."

In some respects every age is an age of transition, but it may be fair to state that the Renaissance marks one of the major turning points in Western civilization. The dominant institutions and thought systems of the Middle Ages were in decline; scholasticism, church authority, and conformity were on the wane. A more modern culture that depended on individualism, skepticism, and ultimately on science was taking its place.

The Renaissance originated in the cities of central and northern Italy. We shall begin with a description of the new secular interests and values that rose in these urban centers, then note the relationship between these urban interests and the Classical Revival and flowering of art, and conclude with a discussion of the spread of the Renaissance as it crossed the Alps to France, Germany, and England. It was in England that the underlying optimism and dynamism of the entire Renaissance period was epitomized by Shakespeare:

O, wonder!
How many goodly creatures are there here!
How beauteous mankind is! O brave new
  world,
That has such people in't![1]

The Italian Renaissance: The Background

The culture of the Italian Renaissance did not arise in a vacuum. Historians today find a clue to the intellectual and esthetic changes of the age in economic, social, and political change.

The "Brave New World" of the Italian City-States

We have seen in chapter 10 that during the twelfth and thirteenth centuries of the High Middle Ages a new economy and a new society emerged in western Europe. Commerce and a money economy revived, towns arose and became self-governing communes, and townspeople constituted a new middle class, the bourgeoisie. While Italy had been one of the leaders in these twelfth- and thirteenth-century developments, during the next two centuries it moved dramatically ahead of the rest of Europe.

During the fourteenth and fifteenth centuries the city-states of northern and central Italy experienced a tremendous growth of population and expanded to become small teritorial states. These included the Papal States, where the restored authority of the popes extinguished the independence of many little city-states in central Italy. Feudalism had died out in Italy during the twelfth and thirteenth centuries.

Unlike the French nobility, who spent their time participating in the vigorous court life of their fellow nobles, the Italian nobles moved to the cities and joined with the rich merchants to form a patrician ruling class. Together they successfully fought off the German emperors Frederick Barbarossa and Frederick II (see p. 259). By 1300 nearly all the land of northern and central Italy was owned by profit-seeking urban capitalists who produced for city markets. In the large export industries, such as woolen cloth, a capitalistic system of production was emerging—the "putting out" system in which the merchant-capitalist retained ownership of the raw material and paid others to work it into the finished product. Additional great wealth was gained from commerce, particularly the import-export trade in luxury goods from the East. So much wealth was accumulated by these merchant-capitalists that they turned to money-lending and banking. From the thirteenth to the fifteenth centuries, Italians monopolized European banking. It is no wonder that in this prosperous, worldly Italian society, money transformed values and became a new virtue, celebrated in poetry:

Money makes the man,
Money makes the stupid pass for bright, . . .
Money buys the pleasure-giving women,
Money keeps the soul in bliss, . . .
The world and fortune being ruled by it,
Which even opens, if you want, the doors of
  paradise.
So wise he seems to me who piles up
What more than any other virtue
Conquers gloom and leavens the whole spirit.[2]

These economic and political successes made the Italian upper-class groups strongly assertive, self-confident, and passionately attached to their city-states. Literature and art reflected their self-confidence. Poets described them riding "self-assuredly through the streets"; every major sculptor and painter produced their portraits, sometimes tucked away in corners of religious paintings; and architects affirmed their importance by constructing their imposing palaces— the *palazzi* of the Medici, Rucellai, Pitti, and Pazzi families, for example, still standing in Florence.

Furthermore, the humanists provided them with an ideology. The humanists' focus on individuals and society, and their insistent theme of "the dignity of man," were entirely in keeping with the outlook, manners, and accomplishments of the dominant urban groups. These groups patronized the new more secular art and the new secular values, both largely alien to the church-dominated culture of the Middle Ages.

Renaissance Patrons

The despots and the wealthy merchants, bankers, and maufacturers conspicuously displayed their wealth and bolstered their own importance and that of their cities by patronizing artists and humanists. Most of the latter were provided with governmental, academic, and tutorial posts.

Renaissance artists had the benefit of the security and protection offered by their patrons and enjoyed the definite advantage of working exclusively on commission. Artists knew where their finished work would repose, in cathedral, villa, or city square. This situation contrasts with some later periods, when artists painted as they wished and then attempted to sell the work to anyone who would buy it.

Among the most famous patrons were members of the Medici family who, by acting as champions of the lower classes, ruled Florence for sixty years (1434–1494) behind a facade of republican forms. Lorenzo de' Medici, who was first citizen of Florence from 1469 until his death in 1492, carried on his family's proud traditions and added so much luster to Florence that he became known as Lorenzo the Magnificent. When he added up the principal expenditures made by his family between 1434 and 1471 for commissions to artists and architects, as well as for charities

A prime example of the Renaissance nobleman, statesman, and patron of the arts was the Florentine Lorenzo de' Medici, known as Lorenzo the Magnificent. Under his patronage and guidance, Florence became the leading city of the Italian Renaissance, renowned for the splendor of its buildings and lavish support for the arts.

and taxes, and it came to the astounding total of 663,755 gold florins, he remarked: "I think it casts a brilliant light on our estate and it seems to me that the monies were well spent and I am very well pleased with this."[3]

The Renaissance popes, with few expections as worldly as their fellow citizens, were lavish patrons who made Rome the foremost center of art and learning by 1500. What Pope Nicholas V (1447–1455) said of himself applies to most of the Renaissance popes through the pontificate of Clement VII (1523–1534), who was a member of the Medici family: "In all things I have been liberal: in building, in the purchase of books [the Vatican Library is still one of the world's greatest], in the constant transcription of Greek and Latin manuscripts, and in the rewarding of learned men."

The Classical Revival

During the Middle Ages, the writers of antiquity had been interpreted within the framework of the Christian religion and often cited as authorities to bolster church dogma. Although many aspects of antiquity were avoided because of their disturbingly pagan quality, churchmen did make use of pagan literature for a variety of

Under Pope Leo X, the son of Lorenzo the Magnificent, Rome became a great center of art and learning. This portrait by Raphael shows Leo, flanked by two cardinals—also members of the Medici family—perusing an illuminated manuscript.

narratives that could be interpreted allegorically and given a Christian meaning. Consequently, the true nature of the classical legacy was generally distorted or obscured.

Humanism and the Classical Revival

In fourteenth-century Italy a new perspective on life was attained and a fresh appreciation of classical literature emerged. Successors to a small group of medieval teachers of grammar and rhetoric, the representatives of this new movement called themselves humanists, a name derived from the *studia humanitatis*, or "humanistic studies," a term Roman authors had used in the sense of a liberal or literary education. Writing in praise of the *studia humanitatis*, an early Italian humanist identified them as "those studies which perfect and adorn man."

Medieval scholastic education had emphasized logic, science, and professional training in law, medicine, and theology at the expense of the "arts," or literary side of the curriculum. Hence the scholastics had centered their attention on Aristotle's *Logic, Metaphysics,* and his scientific writings and on other ancient works on astronomy, medicine, and mathematics. Reflecting the urban society's interest in the problems and values of human living, the humanists reversed this medieval emphasis and called attention to the importance of an education in the humanities —history, grammar, rhetoric, poetry, and moral philosophy. The humanists disdained the sciences because, as Petrarch—the first of the Italian humanists—wrote:

> ... *they help in no way toward a happy life, for what does it advantage us to be familiar with the nature of animals, birds, fishes, and reptiles, while we are ignorant of the nature of the race of man to which we belong, and do not know or care whence we come or whither we go?*[4]

Thus, despite the fact that both the humanist and the scholastic looked to the past and venerated its heritage, they differed widely in their choice of the ancient material to be revered.

Humanists and scholastics also differed in the manner in which they saw themselves in relation to the writers of ancient times. While the scholastic always felt inferior to the ancients and looked

In *The Prince,* Niccolò Macchiavelli expounds his theory of government and provides a handbook on practical statecraft for the ruler who would establish a lasting state.

up to them as child to parent or pupil to teacher, humanists saw themselves equal to the ancients and boldly hailed them as individual to individual and friend to friend. At the beginning of his *Divine Comedy* Dante describes medieval reliance on the authority of the ancients in allegorical terms. Dante (symbolizing medieval man) is lost in the "dark wood" that is this life until he is rescued by Virgil (a favorite medieval symbol of ancient wisdom), who thereafter guides him along the right path. "Losing me," Virgil is made to say to Dante, "ye would remain astray."

The noticeably different attitude of the humanists was well expressed by Machiavelli, in his strictly secular and realistic treatise on politics, *The Prince* (1513): "I enter the ancient courts of the men of antiquity. Received with affection by them, . . . I do not hesitate to hold conversation with them and to inquire the reason for their actions. They, in their humanity, reply to me."[5] It was in this spirit that Petrarch wrote his *Letters to Ancient Authors*, addressing Homer, Plato, Cicero, and others in familiar terms and sharing with them his own thoughts and experiences. This feeling of equality with ancient authors was also behind the humanists' practice of stuffing their own writings with apt quotations from the classics. The humanists' purpose, however, differed from that of the scholastics, who also quoted extensively from the ancients. As the French humanist Montaigne explained in his essays, he quoted the ancients not because he agreed with them but because they agreed with him.

Petrarch and Boccaccio

The "father of humanism" is a title that was given to Francesco Petrarca, better known to us as Petrarch (1304–1374), by later Italian humanists because he was the first to play a major role in making people conscious of the attractions of classical literature. Distressed by the condition of society in fourteenth-century Italy —political and social unrest, the decline of the church, the shortcomings of scholasticism—and resentful of being forced by his father to study law at Bologna, Petrarch found consolation and escape in the literature of ancient Rome. As he explained later in his *Letter to Posterity*, "In order to forget my own time I have constantly striven to place myself in spirit in other ages." And, in the same vein, "Nothing that we suffer but has happened to others before us."

In 1327 he met Laura and fell in love with her. Little is known of Laura other than that she was married. Inspired by his love for her, Petrarch wrote sonnets that made him one of the greatest lyric poets of all time. His portrayal of Laura represents a fresh approach. Earlier poets had woven about their heroines an air of courtly love and religious idealization, which made the characters quite unreal. Petrarch's Laura was a flesh-and-blood creature whom all readers could recognize as human. Petrarch praised her chastity, which had withstood his entreaties. And even though he wrote that she had "mocked, despised, scorned" him "with an air of haughty disdain," he forever after viewed her as an ennobling influence on his life.

A miniature portrait of Petrarch within the illuminated letter A from his manuscript of *Remedies Against Fortune.* Drawing upon a classical tradition, Petrarch composed many letters—which he edited for publication—that were in effect literary essays expressing his own attitudes and humanistic concerns.

Zeal for the Study of Greek Literature

Petrarch had tried without success to learn Greek. Not until Greek scholars arrived in Italy from Constantinople were competent instructors available. Manuel Chrysoloras, the first of these scholars, came to Venice in 1393, sent by the Byzantine emperor to secure help against the Turks. Three years later he was invited to come to Florence, where he remained for three years as a teacher of Greek language and literature. Leonardo Bruni (1370–1444) tells how he took this opportunity to throw himself enthusiastically into the study of Greek.

Chrysoloras the Byzantine, a man of noble birth and well versed in Greek letters, brought Greek learning to us. When his country was invaded by the Turks, he came by sea, first to Venice. The report of him soon spread, and he was cordially invited and besought and promised a public stipend, to come to Florence and open his store of riches to the youth. I was then studying Civil Law, but . . . I burned with love of academic studies, and had spent no little pains on dialectic and rhetoric. At the coming of Chrysoloras I was torn in mind, deeming it shameful to desert the law, and yet a crime to lose such a chance of studying Greek literature; and often with youthful impulse I would say to myself: "Thou, when it is permitted thee to gaze on Homer, Plato and Demosthenes, and the other poets, philosophers, orators, of whom such glorious things are spread abroad, and speak with them and be instructed in their admirable teaching, wilt thou desert and rob thyself? Wilt thou neglect this opportunity so divinely offered? For seven hundred years, no one in Italy has possessed Greek letters; and yet we confess that all knowledge is derived from them. How great advantage to your knowledge, enhancement of your fame, increase of your pleasure, will come from an understanding of this tongue? There are doctors of civil law everywhere; and the chance of learning will not fail thee. But if this one and only doctor of Greek letters disappears, no one can be found to teach thee." Overcome at length by these reasons, I gave myself to Chrysoloras, with such zeal to learn, that what through the wakeful day I gathered, I followed after in the night, even when asleep.

Source: Henry Osborn Taylor, *Thought and Expression in the Sixteenth Century* (New York: Macmillan, 1920), pp. 36–37.

The ancient writers' attitude toward life struck a sympathetic chord in Petrarch. In *On the Secret Conflict of My Cares,* Petrarch has an imaginary conversation with St. Augustine that forcibly brings out the conflict between his new worldly interests and those of traditional Christianity. St. Augustine accuses Petrarch of pursuing false goals: "What are you doing, poor little man? What are you dreaming?" Petrarch concludes that, although St. Augustine's arguments cannot be refuted, he will not renounce his chosen path: "The care of mortal things must come first in mortal minds."

This inner conflict between his concern for "mortal things" and his loyalty to the traditional Christian ideal of self-denial and other-worldliness exemplifies the transitional position Petrarch occupied in Western culture. He could not accept a depreciation of an individual's importance or a constriction of one's mental horizons. Thus he condemned the rigidity and arid logic of scholasticism and the narrow limits of medieval education. He took as his motto a line from the Roman dramatist Terence: "I am a man, and nothing human do I consider alien to myself." Petrarch was not a careful scholar and never learned Greek, yet he gave humanism its first great impetus.

Another celebrated early humanist was Giovanni Boccaccio (1313–1375), who began his career as a writer of poetry and romances. In 1348 the calamitous Black Death struck—a disaster that wiped out nearly two thirds of Florence's population. Boccaccio used this event to establish the setting of his masterpiece, the *Decameron*. To escape the pestilence, his characters—three young men and seven young women—seek seclusion in a country villa, where they while away the time by telling stories. Boccaccio suffused the hundred tales of the *Decameron*, based on the old fabliaux and on chivalric accounts, with a new and different spirit. Recounted by sophisticated city dwellers, the tales satirize the follies of knights and other medieval types and express clearly the contempt that had developed for the old, and by then threadbare, ideals of feudalism. Many tales are bawdy and even scandalous—a charge Boccaccio undertook to refute:

> Some of you may say that in writing these tales I have taken too much license, by making ladies sometimes say and often listen to matters which are not proper to be said or heard by virtuous ladies. This I deny, for there is nothing so unchaste but may be said chastely if modest words are used; and this I think I have done.[6]

The *Decameron* offers a wealth of anecdotes, portraits of flesh-and-blood characters, and a vivid (although one-sided) picture of Renaissance life.

The *Decameron* closed Boccaccio's career as a creative artist. Largely through the influence of Petrarch, whom he met in 1350, Boccaccio gave up writing in the Italian vernacular and turned to the study of antiquity. He attempted to learn Greek, wrote an encyclopedia of classical mythology, and went off to monasteries in search of manuscripts. By the time Petrarch and Boccaccio died, the study of the literature and learning of antiquity was growing throughout Italy.

The search for manuscripts became a mania, and before the middle of the fifteenth century works by most of the important Latin authors had been found. The degree of difference between humanist and scholastic is indicated by the ease with which the early humanists recovered the "lost" Latin literary masterpieces: they were found close at hand in monastic libraries,

covered by the undisturbed dust of many centuries. The books had always been there; what had been largely lacking was a mature and appreciative audience of readers. In addition to these Latin works, precious Greek manuscripts were brought to Italy from Constantinople after it fell to the Turks in 1453.

Civic Humanism

For the humanists of the fifteenth century—the "civic humanists," as they are called—humanism became the foundation of a course of study designed not for pure contemplation, as it was for Petrarch, but as an educational program delineating what was relevant and useful in the classics for the leaders of the Italian city-states. One of them warned against letting literature "absorb all the interests of life. . . . For the man who surrenders himself entirely to the attractions of letters or speculative thought perhaps follows a self-regarding end and is useless as a citizen or prince." While Petrarch wrote of the "much sweetness and charm" he found in the writings of his "dear friend" Cicero "when the difficulties of life are pressing on me so sharply and inexorably," the civic humanists honored Cicero more for his stress on moral philosophy, rhetoric (the art of persuasion), and his commitment to public affairs. They found the ancient historians, notably Livy and Plutarch, especially valuable. "The careful study of the past," one of them wrote, "enlarges our foresight in contemporary affairs."

Revival of Platonism

During the late fifteenth century, many humanists gravitated to Platonic and Neoplatonic philosophy as a result both of their lack of interest in the Aristotelian emphasis on natural science and of their search for a classical philosophy that stressed moral purpose and religious and even mystical values. A factor in this revival was the study of Plato in the original Greek, particularly at Florence were Cosimo de' Medici, one of the great patrons of the Renaissance, founded the informal club that came to be known as the Platonic Academy. Its leader, Marsilio Ficino (1433–1499), who always kept a candle burning before a bust of Plato, made the first complete Latin translation of Plato's works.

Ficino sought to synthesize Christianity and Plato, much as St. Thomas Aquinas had done with Aristotle. In his principal work, appropriately titled *The Platonic Theology,* Ficino viewed Plato as essentially Christian and Plato's "religious philosophy" as a God-sent means of converting intellectuals. He coined the expression "Platonic love" to describe an ideal, pure love, and this concept found its way into Renaissance literature and art.

Ficino's disciple, Pico della Mirandola (1463–1494), was driven by an enormous appetite for knowledge. In addition to Latin and Greek, he learned Hebrew and Arabic in order to read everything available. At the age of twenty-three he announced to the world that he knew everything, and he invited all interested scholars to join him in Rome for a public debate on 900 theological and philosophical propositions. (The pope considered some propositions heretical and forbade the debate.) As an introduction to his list of propositions, Pico composed *Oration on the Dignity of Man,* an essay that remains one of the most glowing tributes to the human race in all Renaissance writing. With youthful exuberance he expounded on the theme that "There is nothing to be seen more wonderful than man. . . . To him it is granted to have whatever he chooses, to be whatever he wills."

Aristotelianism

Despite its great attraction for many humanists, Platonism still had a formidable rival in Aristotelianism. Concerned chiefly with natural science, logic, and metaphysics, Aristotelian commentators still dominated teaching in the Italian universities.

The most influential Aristotelians were the Latin Averroists, followers of the Muslim philosopher Averroës (see p. 167). The Averroists followed Aristotle in teaching that matter is eternal and in denying the immortality of the soul. Since such views were contrary to the Biblical story of creation and the belief in personal immortality, the Averroists advocated the doctrine of "double truth"—a truth in philosophy need not be valid in religion.

By the fifteenth century the University of Padua had become the center of Aristotelianism, which reached its peak in the next century. By championing a secular rationalism that kept philosophy separate from theology, its adherents maintained an environment necessary for the triumph of scientific thought in the seventeenth century. Some of the pioneers of that "scientific revolution" (see ch. 20) were connected with Padua. Copernicus studied there before publishing his *Revolutions of the Heavenly Spheres* in 1543; the anatomist Vesalius, whose revolutionary *Fabric of the Human Body* appeared in the same year, was a professor there; and the astronomer and physicist Galileo lectured there early in the next century. Ironically, the experimentalism that Aristotelianism encouraged was destined to overthrow Aristotle's own theories in physics and other fields of science.

Evaluation of Humanism

In the meantime the humanists continued to downgrade science as sterile, and they did not teach it in the schools they established. Their educational goal, which is still the goal of a liberal education, was the cultivation of the mind both for individual happiness and for equipping a person to play a worthy role in society.

To the humanists we owe the modern ideal of the all-around person, the versatile, accomplished, socially-at-ease citizen of the world. Called by the humanists the "complete man," such a person was the subject of eagerly read books on correct social behavior that were produced during the Renaissance.

The most famous book on Renaissance manners, published in 1528, was *The Courtier* by Baldassare Castiglione (1478–1529), which was soon translated into French, German, English, and Spanish and which established a model for the Renaissance gentleman. To Castiglione, good manners and deportment were essential to the ideal courtier because women now played a freer and more active role in polite society, to which they added such feminine refinements as music and dancing. It is, however, the verdict of a modern feminist historian that "There was no renaissance for women . . . during the Renaissance."[7]

In *The Courtier,* Baldassare Castiglione, shown here in a portrait by Raphael, preserved the tenor of Italian courtly life. The dialogue of the book illustrated the value placed on speech and behavior. The courtier was above all a gentleman: a man of good breeding, physically attractive, and accomplished in all things—a Renaissance man.

The courtier must please the ladies as well as the prince; he must master the social graces. But Castiglione's central idea was that a courtier's true worth was more commensurate with his strength of character and excellence of intellect than with his hereditary social position. Well-read in the classics but no pedant, the courtier should be a well-rounded individual, capable in the arts both of war and of peace.

Reviving the ancient ideal of a healthy mind in a sound body, Renaissance educators and writers stressed the importance of exercise and sports. But not any sport: in 1531 an English author of a book on manners wrote that football ought to be shunned by all gentlemen because there is in it "nothing but beastly furie and exstreme violence; whereof precedeth hurte, and consequently rancour and malice do remaine. . . . "[8]

On the other hand, while we owe the humanists a debt of gratitude for reintroducing the whole of Latin and Greek literature into the mainstream of Western thought, theirs was otherwise a closed culture whose boundaries had been set by ancient Greece and Rome. Their course was to retravel old ground, not to explore uncharted territory. The humanists resented the centuries separating them from the golden days of antiquity. Unfortunately, this viewpoint resulted in their disparagement of the best works (Dante excepted) produced in the Middle Ages.

The cult of classical letters gave rise to another defect. By the late fifteenth century the humanists' passion for writing Latin prose in imitation of Cicero's graceful, eloquent, and polished style had become a pernicious vogue. One eminent humanist, who was also a cardinal of the church, even hesitated to read St. Paul's epistles for fear they might corrupt his Latin style. A reaction in favor of the native language ensued; Castiglione and Machiavelli, for example, chose to write in the vernacular.

The humanist men of letters contributed nothing new to philosophy or to science and did little or no original thinking. Nevertheless, they did contribute indirectly to the coming scientific revolution. Their search for Roman and Greek manuscripts resulted in the recovery of more ancient scientific writings than were available to medieval scholars. These were at hand later when the interests of scholars turned decisively toward science. (Copernicus' heliocentric theory of planetary motion, for example, came from his reading of ancient authors.) Furthermore, modern critical scholarship began with the humanists' emphasis upon verified facts. They compared manuscripts in order to eliminate errors and establish authentic texts. In their writings they exposed historical myths and eliminated supernatural causes. This critical and objective outlook would be of great value in later scientific research.

Italian Renaissance Art

North of the Alps during the fourteenth and fifteenth centuries there was a continuation of "Gothic" art—in painting and sculpture, the same emphasis on realistic detail; in architecture, an elaboration of the Gothic style.

Fourteenth- and fifteenth-century Italy, however, saw innovations that culminated in the classic High Renaissance art of the early sixteenth century. All this was the product of a new society centered in rich cities, the humanist spirit in thought and religion, and a revived interest in Classical art.

Transitional Period in Painting

The greatest figure in the transitional painting of the fourteenth century was the Florentine painter Giotto (1266–1336), who, it was said, "achieved little less than the resurrection of painting from the dead." While earlier Italian painters had copied the unreal, flat, and rigidly formalized images of Byzantine paintings and mosaics, Giotto observed from life and painted a three-dimensional world peopled with believable human beings dramatically moved by deep emotion. He humanized painting much as Petrarch humanized thought and St. Francis, whose life was one of his favorite subjects, humanized religion. Giotto initiated a new epoch in the history of painting, one that expressed the religious piety of his lay patrons and their delight in images of everyday life.

Quattrocento Painting, Sculpture, and Architecture

The lull in painting that followed Giotto's death in 1338, during which his technical innovations were retained but the spirit and compassion that make him one of the world's great painters were lost, lasted until the beginning of the quattrocento (Italian for "four hundred," an abbreviation for the 1400s). In his brief lifetime the Florentine Massaccio (1401–1428) completed the revolution in technique begun by Giotto. As can be seen in his few surviving paintings, Masaccio largely mastered the problems of perspective, anatomical naturalism of flesh and bone, and the modeling of figures in light and shade (chiaroscuro) rather than by sharp line. Masaccio was also the first to paint nude figures (Eve, in his Expulsion from Eden), thus reversing the trend of Christian art, which, since its inception in late Roman times, had turned its back on the beauty of the human form. Masaccio died in debt and poor in Rome, having received few commissions in Florence. Apparently his work was too austere and lacking in elegance to attract many patrons.

Inspired by Masaccio's achievement, most quattrocento painters constantly sought to improve technique. This search for greater realism culminated in such painters as Andrea Mantegna

(1431–1506) and Piero della Francesca (c. 1420–1492). Mantegna's painting of the dead body of Christ lying feet first on a marble slab well shows the results of his lifelong study of perspective. His group portrait of the family of his chief patron, the Gonzaga duke of Mantua, is "done in the grand manner" and reflects the self-assurance of the Renaissance elite.

Piero della Francesca's approach to painting was scientific and intellectual. His zeal to reduce perspective to a mathematical science—he wrote a book on the subject—led him to neglect motion. The figures in his *Discovery and Proving of the True Cross*, showing Constantine's mother Helena discovering the cross used for Christ's crucifixion (see p. 132), are as still as if hewn out of marble. Piero's restrained, undramatic, unemotional, and mathematically precise paintings prefigure the abstract painting of our own time. For such reasons, fashionable taste today has transferred its allegiance from Botticelli's lyrical exquisiteness to Piero's hushed serenity.

While Masaccio's successors in the last half of the fifteenth century were intent upon giving their figures a new solidity and resolving the problem of three-dimensional presentation, the

Masaccio, *Expulsion from Eden*. Masaccio's mastery of perspective creates the illusion of movement as the angel drives Adam and Eve from Paradise.

Piero della Francesca, *Discovery and Proving of the True Cross.* The solemn heroic figures in the fresco cycle from the Church of San Francesca at Arezzo are reminiscent of classical Greek sculpture.

After winning the commission to design the bronze doors for the Baptistery in Florence, Ghiberti spent most of his life making the 28 panels for the doors. This panel illustrates the biblical story of Joseph.

Florentine Sandro Botticelli (1447–1510) proceeded in a different direction, abandoning the techniques of straightforward representation of people and objects. Botticelli used a highly sensitive, even quivering, line to stir the viewer's imagination and emotion and to create a mood in keeping with his more subtle and sophisticated poetic vision. This unconventional artist was associated with the Platonic Academy at Florence, where the Christian faith was fused with pagan mythology. Thus, although his *Birth of Venus* depicts the pagan myth of the goddess of love rising from the sea, there is little that is human or material about her ethereal figure. Like the Virgin Mary, she has become the symbol of a higher kind of love—divine love. The allegory is reinforced by making the winds that blow Venus onto the shore look like Christian angels.

In the meantime progress was being made also in sculpture, and it, like painting, reached stylistic maturity at the beginning of the quattrocento. Like the humanists, the sculptors found in ancient Rome the models they were eager to imitate; they, too, saw what seemed related to their own experience and aspirations.

In his second pair of bronze doors for the baptistery in Florence, Lorenzo Ghiberti (1378–1455) achieved the goal he had set for himself: "I strove to imitate nature as closely as I could, and with all the perspective I could produce." These marvels of relief sculpture, which resurrect the form and spirit of Roman sculpture and architecture and drew from Michelangelo the declaration that they were worthy to be the gates of paradise, depict skillfully modeled human figures—including some classically inspired nudes—which stand out spatially against architectural and landscape backgrounds.

Although Ghiberti was a superb craftsman, he was less of an innovator than his younger contemporary in Florence, Donatello (1386–1466), who visited Rome to study the remains of antique sculpture. Divorcing sculpture from the architectural background it had in the Middle Ages, Donatello produced truly freestanding statues based on the realization of the human body as

Donatello, *David*. Donatello learned the technique of bronze sculpture in the workshop of Lorenzo Ghiberti.

supreme self-confidence and even arrogance of Renaissance public figures.

Renaissance architecture, which even more than sculpture reflects the influence of ancient Roman models, glorifies the worldly success of its patrons. It began with the work of Filippo Brunelleschi (1377–1446). As a youth Brunelleschi accompanied Donatello to Rome where he employed measuring stick and sketchbook to master the principles of classical architecture. Returning to Florence, Brunelleschi constructed there the uncompleted dome of the cathedral, the first dome to be built since Roman times. Although strongly influenced by classical architecture, Brunelleschi's buildings in Florence, which include churches and palaces, were not just copies of Roman models. Employing arcades of Roman arches, Roman pediments above the windows, and Roman columns and other decorative motifs, Brunelleschi recreated the Roman style in a fresh and original manner. So began

Verrocchio, Monument to Colleoni. Verrocchio's equestrian statue captures well the spirit and individuality of the condottiere (professional soldier) Bartolomeo Colleoni.

a functional, coordinated mechanism of bones, muscles, and sinews, maintaining itself against the pull of gravity. His *David* is the first bronze nude made since antiquity, and his equestrian statue of the army commander Gattamelata, clad in Roman armor, is the first of its type done in the Renaissance. The latter clearly reveals the influence of classical models and was probably inspired by the equestrian statue of the emperor Marcus Aurelius in Rome (see p. 86).

More dramatic than either of these equestrian statues is that of the Venetian general Bartolomeo Colleoni, the creation of Andrea del Verrocchio (1435–1488). A versatile Florentine artist noteworthy as a sculptor, painter, and the teacher of Leonardo da Vinci, Verrocchio designed the statue of Colleoni to permit one of the horse's forelegs to be unsupported—a considerable achievement. The posture and features of the famous general convey dramatically the

the Renaissance style of architecture that, with many modifications, has lasted to the present time.

The High Renaissance, 1500–1530

By the time of the High Renaissance in Italy, when painting, sculpture, and architecture reached a peak of perfection, the center of artistic activity had shifted from Florence to Rome. The popes were lavish patrons, and the greatest artists of the period worked in the Vatican at one time or another. It did not seem inconsistent to popes and artists to include representations of pagan mythological figures in the decorations of the papal palace, and thus the Vatican was filled with secular as well as religious art.

The great architect of the High Renaissance was Donato Bramante (1444–1514) from Milan. Bramante's most important commission came in 1506 when Pope Julius II requested him to replace the old basilica of St. Peter, built by the emperor Constantine, with a monumental Renaissance structure. Bramante's plan called for a centralized church in the form of a Greek cross surmounted by an immense dome. His design for St. Peter's exemplifies the spirit of High Renaissance architecture—to approach nearer to the monumentality and grandeur of Roman architecture. In Bramante's own words, he would place "the Pantheon on top of the Basilica of Maxentius." Bramante died when the cathedral was barely begun, and it was left to Michelangelo and others to complete the work. Michalangelo's dome has influenced the design of most major domes down to the beginning of the present century.

The painters of the High Renaissance inherited the solutions to such technical problems as perspective space from the quattrocento artists. But whereas the artists of the earlier period had been concerned with movement, color, and narrative detail, painters in the High Renaissance strove to eliminate nonessentials and concentrated on the central theme of a picture and its basic human implications. By this process of

St. Peter's Basilica, Rome. After Michelangelo took charge of the construction of the basilica, he modified Bramante's original plan. For the dome, Bramante had planned a stepped hemisphere similar to the dome of the Pantheon. Michelangelo redesigned the dome to add a high drum and strongly projecting buttresses accented by double columns. Later a long nave was added to the front of the church, giving it the form of a Latin, rather than a Greek, cross.

elimination, many High Renaissance painters achieved a "classic" effect of seriousness and serenity and endowed their work with idealistic values.

Leonardo da Vinci, Raphael, and Michelangelo

The great triad of High Renaissance painters consists of Leonardo da Vinci, Raphael, and Michelangelo. An extraordinary man, Leonardo da Vinci (1452–1519) was proficient in a variety of fields: engineering, mathematics, architecture, geology, botany, physiology, anatomy, sculpture, painting, music, and poetry. He was always experimenting, with the result that few of the projects he started were ever finished.

A superb draftsman, Leonardo was a master of soft modeling in light and shade and of creating groups of figures perfectly balanced in a given space. But in addition to an advanced knowledge of technique, what makes Leonardo one of the great masters is his deep psychological insight into human nature. As he himself expressed it, "A good painter has two chief objects to paint, man and the intention of his soul."

One of Leonardo's most famous paintings is the *Mona Lisa,* a portrait of a woman whose enigmatic smile captures an air of tenderness and humility, which, Freud suggests, the memory of his mother called to his mind. Another is *The Last Supper,* a study of the dramatic impact of Christ's announcement to his disciples, "One of you will betray me." When he painted this picture on the walls of the refectory of Santa Maria delle Grazie in Milan, Leonardo was experimenting with the use of an oil medium combined with plaster, and, unfortunately, the experiment was unsuccessful. The painting quickly began to disintegrate and has had to be repainted several times.

The second of the great triad of High Renaissance painters was Raphael (1483–1520). By the time he was summoned to Rome in 1508 by Pope Julius II to aid in the decoration of the Vatican,

Leonardo da Vinci, *The Last Supper.* In early Renaissance art, architecture sometimes overpowered the figures, but here the architectural details are subordinate to the figures. The main opening in the rear wall, for example, acts a halo for Christ's head.

Michelangelo, *The Creation of Adam,* one of the hundreds of figures from the ceiling of the Sistine Chapel. Michelangelo is widely regarded as the most influential artist who ever lived. "Until you have seen the Sistine Chapel," wrote the German poet Goethe, "you have no adequate conception of what man is capable of accomplishing."

Raphael had absorbed the styles of Leonardo and Michelangelo. His Stanze frescoes in the Vatican display a magnificent blending of classical and Christian subject matter and are the fruit of careful planning and immense artistic knowledge. Raphael possessed neither Leonardo's intellectuality nor Michelangelo's power, but an appealing serenity, particularly evident in his lovely Madonnas, characterizes his work. Most critics consider him the master of perfect design and balanced composition.

The individualism and idealism of the High Renaissance have no greater representative than Michelangelo Buonarroti (1475–1564). Stories of this stormy and temperamental personality have helped shape our ideas of what a genius is like. Indeed, there is something almost superhuman about both Michelangelo and his art. His great energy enabled him to complete in four years the entire work of painting the ceiling of the Vatican's Sistine Chapel for Julius II, an area of several thousand square yards, and his art embodies a superhuman ideal. With his unrivaled genius for rendering the human form, he devised a wealth of expressive positions and attitudes

for his figures in scenes from Genesis. Their physical splendor is pagan, but their spirit is Christian. The *Creation of Adam* depicts God, with the unborn Eve under his left arm, instilling the divine spark of the soul into the body of Adam.

Michelangelo considered himself first and foremost a sculptor, and this *uomo universale* ("complete man"), who also excelled as poet, engineer, and architect, was undoubtedly the greatest sculptor of the Renaissance. The glorification of the human body, particularly the male nude, was Michelangelo's great achievement. Fired by the grandeur of such newly discovered pieces of Hellenistic sculpture as the Laocoön group and strongly influenced by Platonism with its dualism of body and soul, he expressed in such works as his *David*, commissioned in 1501 when he was twenty-six, his idealized view of human dignity and majesty. Succeeding Bramante as chief architect of St. Peter's in 1546, Michelangelo designed the great dome and was still actively creative as a sculptor when he died, almost in his ninetieth year, in 1564. He had long outlived the High Renaissance.

The Venetian School

Following the sack of Rome in 1527 during the Italian Wars (see next column), the rich trading city of Venice became the center of art. This wealthy, sophisticated milieu produced a secular rather than a devotional school of painting. Most Venetian artists were satisfied with the here and now; while they sometimes painted Madonnas, they more often painted wealthy merchants and proud doges, attired in rich brocades, jewels, and precious metals. There is a sensuousness in the Venetian painting of this period, which is evident in the artists' love of decoration, rich costumes, striking nude figures, and radiant light and color. It has been said that while earlier painting consisted of drawing plus coloring, at Venice color and light became paramount ingredients of painting.

The first master of the Venetian High Renaissance was Giorgione (1477–1510), who, like Botticelli, rejected the quattrocento concern to be scientific and realistic and substituted a delicate and dreamily poetic lyricism. Common to all of his paintings is a mood of languor and relaxation that is called Giorgionesque. The lyrical grace of his *Sleeping Venus*, for example, has no erotic overtones. His paintings are fanciful idylls that have no narrative content—they tell no story. Viewers are left free to extract their own meaning from them.

Giorgione, *Sleeping Venus*. Although his use of classical themes and idyllic landscapes demonstrate Giorgione's indebtedness to antiquity, his Venuses are no unearthly mythological figures but rather quite real Venetian models.

The paintings of Titian (1477?–1576), who was probably born in the same year as his friend Giorgione but outlived him by sixty-five years, are less subtle and poetic. His Venuses, for example, are buxom Venetian models—mature, opulent, and sex-conscious. During his long working life he proved himself the master of every kind of subject ranging from religion to pagan mythology and including portraits of the self-satisfied upper class, for which he was most famed among his contemporaries. With his robust sensuousness and view of all things in terms of light and color, Titian is the type-figure of the Venetian painter, and his work has influenced many generations of modern painters.

Mannerism: The "Anti-Renaissance" Style

In 1494, the French king Charles VIII crossed into Italy with an army of 40,000 men and inaugurated the Italian Wars that lasted until 1559 and turned Italy into a battleground for the powerful new monarchies of France and Spain. While Italians were losing control of their destiny, Machiavelli in *The Prince* (1513) lamented his native land as being

> more a slave than the Hebrews, more a servant than the Persians, more scattered than the Athenians; without head, without government; defeated, plundered, torn asunder, overrun; subject to every sort of disaster.[9]

In 1527 the unruly army of Charles V, Spanish king and German emperor, sacked Rome, the major center of High Renaissance patronage and culture, and its many artists, writers, and scholars fled the city.

Such unsettling developments, including the Protestant and Catholic Reformations, produced a radical change of outlook on life. The earlier optimistic emphasis on "the dignity of man" was replaced by a pessimistic belief in man's evil nature—one of the basic assumptions in Machiavelli's *Prince*. Michelangelo, who as we noted had long outlived the High Renaissance, expressed a similar pessimism in the tortured figures of his late sculptures and in his painting of the *Last Judgment*, filled with huddled figures pleading for mercy before a wrathful God, painted on a wall of the Sistine Chapel in the 1530s

Parmigianino, *Madonna with the Long Neck.* Parmigianino's smooth, elongated, languid figures embody an ideal of unearthly beauty and perfection that bears little resemblance to real human beings. Characteristic of Mannerist painting is huge discrepancy in scale, here shown by the tiny figure of the prophet beside the gigantic column.

after the sack of Rome and more than forty years after his glorious *Creation of Adam* on the ceiling. "Led by long years to my last hours," Michelangelo wrote, "too late, O world, I know your joys for what they are. You promise a peace which is not yours to give."

From about 1530 to the end of the sixteenth century, Italian artists responded to the stresses of the age in a new style called Mannerism. Consciously revolting against the classical serenity and poise of High Renaissance art, Mannerist artists sought to express their own inner vision—often, like Michelangelo in his later years, their doubts and indecisions—in a manner that evoked shock in the viewer.

Typical are the paintings of Parmigianino, who returned to his native Parma from Rome after it was sacked, and the Venetian Tintoretto. Parmigianino's *Madonna with the Long Neck* (1535) shows no logic of structure. One cannot tell whether the distorted figure of the Madonna is seated or standing. Her cloak billows out in defiance of gravity, and her Child seems to be slipping off her lap. The prophet in the background, standing beside a gigantic and purposeless column, is absurdly tiny.

Tintoretto, *Abduction of the Body of St. Mark*. The leading proponent of the Mannerist style in Venice, Tintoretto combined strong use of light and shade with a gift for dramatic storytelling.

The contemporaries of Tintoretto (1518–1594) had good reason to call him "the thunderbolt of painting." His *Abduction of the Body of St. Mark*, depicting the legend that three Venetians stole the body of their patron saint from Alexandria during a storm, replaces the harmony, proportion, balance, and idealized reality of the High Renaissance with dramatic force and movement, violent contrast in light and color, imbalanced composition, and crowded figures in uneasy and agitated poses. The upholders of the pure classical tradition who opposed the innovations of the Mannerists considered Tintoretto's work to be marred by careless execution and eccentric

taste. One of them wrote that "had he not abandoned the beaten track but rather followed the beautiful style of his predecessors, he would have become one of the greatest painters seen in Venice."

The outstanding Mannerist sculptor was the unconscionable braggart, Benvenuto Cellini (1500–1571). Both his sculpture and his famous *Autobiography* reflect his violent and corrupt age's rejection of artistic and moral standards. (He boasts of the number of personal enemies he has killed and quotes a pope as excusing him on the ground that "men like Benvenuto, unique in their profession, stand above the law.") His work,

Cellini: Mannerist "Gewgaws" vs. High Renaissance "Elegance"

In his *Autobiography,* the Mannerist sculptor Benvenuto Cellini describes an incident that reveals the popularity of the new anti-Renaissance style. While still a journeyman, Cellini produced for a Roman matron an ornate jeweled ornament "in the form of a fleur-de-lys, . . . ornamenting it with little masks, children, and animals, exquisitely enamelled, whereby the diamonds which formed the lily were more than doubled in effect." At the same time, his master executed for the pope a typical High Renaissance "silver piece," technically called "large plate" and described by Cellini as a vase "adorned with . . . masses of lovely foliage, in as exquisite a style of elegance as could be imagined." In the following passage, Cellini gleefully describes his master's discomfiture when it became known that the latter's compensation was only half of what Cellini received.

He cursed his art and those who taught it him, vowing that thenceforth he would never work at large plate, but give his whole attention to those whoreson gewgaws, since they were so well paid. Equally enraged on my side, I answered that every bird sang its own note; that he talked after the fashion of the hovels he came from; but that I dared to swear that I should succeed with ease in making his lubberly lumber, while he would never be successful in my whoreson gewgaws. Thus I flung off in a passion, telling him that I spoke truth. The bystanders openly declared against him, holding him to be a lout, as indeed he was, and me for a man, as I had proved myself.

The Autobiography of Benvenuto Cellini, Bk. I, chs. 20, 21; trans. by John Addington Symonds.

Cellini, *Saltcellar of Francis I.* The utilitarian purpose of the condiment dish is subordinate to its lavish decoration. Neptune, god of the sea, guards the boat-shaped salt container, while a personification of Earth watches over the pepper. Figures around the base represent the four seasons and the four parts of the day. The intricacy of the design is a showcase of the sculptor's virtuosity.

like the gold cup decorated with enamel and precious stones now in the Metropolitan Museum of Art in New York, consists largely of similar elegant, showy trifles, which Michelangelo described as "snuff-box ornaments."

Mannerist architects developed the Jesuit style, named for the new Jesuit Order that first sponsored it in its *Gesù* (Jesus) church in Rome (c. 1575). The classical components of Renaissance architecture were manipulated to achieve anticlassical effects. Columns and pilasters were paired for greater richness, curved lines ending in volutes replaced straight lines, and statues were often fixed to upper stories and roofs. The parts were arranged to form a climax in the center and fused into one complex pattern.

Tintoretto's *Abduction of the Body of St. Mark* pictures both the old architecture and the new. In the left background is a typical Renaissance building with its repetition of the same pattern;

the whole is no greater than the sum of its parts. To the rear is a Jesuit-style structure whose effect is much more than the sum of its parts—to leave out any part would destroy its essential unity.

The Mannerist Jesuit style prefigures the fully developed Baroque architecture of the seventeenth century, just as the Mannerist style of Tintoretto—and El Greco (d. 1614) in Spain a generation later—prefigures Baroque painting (see ch. 17). There is no clear dividing line between the Mannerism of the sixteenth century and the Baroque of the seventeenth.

Renaissance Music

In contrast to the simple single-voiced or monophonic music—called plain song or Gregorian chant—of the early Middle Ages, the late medieval composers of church music wrote

Gesù Church, Rome. The Mannerist style in architecture is characterized by a deliberate contradiction of classical rules and a conscious effort to produce an effect of discord and strain rather than harmony and repose, the ideals of Renaissance style.

many-voiced or polyphonic music. Polyphony often involved a shuttling back and forth from one melody to another—musical counterpoint. By the fifteenth century as many as twenty-four voice parts were combined into one intricately woven musical pattern. The composers of the High Renaissance continued to produce complicated polyphonic music, but in a calmer and grander manner. Compared with the style of his predecessors, that of the Flemish composer Josquin des Prés (c. 1440–1521), the founder of High Renaissance music, "is both grander and more simple . . . and the rhythms and forms used are based on strict symmetry and mathematically regular proportions. Josquin handled all technical problems of complicated constructions with the same ease and sureness one finds in the drawings of Leonardo and Raphael."[10] During the sixteenth century, also, instruments such as the violin, spinet, and harpsichord developed from more rudimentary types.

The Renaissance in Italy stimulated many new forms of secular music, especially the madrigal, a love lyric set to music. Castiglione in *The Courtier* insists that the ability to sing, read music, and play an instrument was essential for gentlemen and ladies. In addition to the Italian madrigal, French *chansons* and German *Lieder* added to the growing volume of secular music.

The Northern Renaissance

The Italian Renaissance had placed human beings once more in the center of life's stage and infused thought and art with humanistic values. In time the stimulating ideas current in Italy spread to other areas and combined with indigenous developments to produce a French Renaissance, an English Renaissance, and so on.

Throughout the fifteenth century the matriculation records of Italian universities listed hundreds of northern European students. While their chief interest was the study of law and medicine, many were influenced by the intellectual climate of Italy with its new enthusiasm for the classics. When these students returned home, they often carried manuscripts—and later printed editions—of classical and humanist writers. By this time, scholasticism had declined into

Facsimile copy of a page from the Gutenberg Bible, the Book of Genesis. With the development of printing, learning was no longer the private domain of the Church and those few persons wealthy enough to own hand-copied volumes.

sterile repetition and logical subleties, and literate laymen and pious clerics in the North were ready to welcome the new outlook of humanism.

The Influence of Printing

Very important in the diffusion of the Renaissance and later in the success of the Reformation was the invention of printing in Europe. The essential elements—paper and block printing—had been known in China since the eighth century. During the twelfth century the Spanish Muslims introduced papermaking to Europe; in the thirteenth century Europeans were in close contact with China (see ch. 8) and block printing became known in the West. The crucial step was taken in the 1440s at Mainz, Germany, where Johann Gutenberg and other printers invented movable type by cutting up old printing blocks to form individual letters. Gutenberg used movable type to print papal documents and the first printed version of the Bible (1454).

Soon all the major countries of Europe possessed the means for printing books. In 1465 two Germans brought printing to Italy, and within four years the works of eight classical authors (including Cicero, Livy, Virgil, Pliny, and Caesar) had been printed there. In all of Europe during the remainder of the century an estimated 40,000 titles were published. It is said that the prices of books sank to one eighth of their former cost thus placing books within the reach of many people who formerly had been unable to buy them. In addition, pamphlets and controversial tracts soon were widely circulated, and new ideas reached a thousand times more people in a relatively short span of time. In the quickening of Europe's intellectual life, it is difficult to overestimate the effects of the printing press. Without printing it is doubtful that a German writer at the end of the fifteenth century could have made the exaggerated boast that "once upon a time Germany was poor in wisdom, power, and wealth; now it is not only equal to others in glorious work, but surpasses loquacious Greece, [and] proud Italy."

Erasmus and Northern Humanism

The intellectual life of the first half of the sixteenth century was dominated by the Dutch humanist, Desiderius Erasmus (1466?–1536).

Portrait of Erasmus by Hans Holbein the Younger (see p. 334). Erasmus' principal scholarly achievements include a Greek edition of the New Testament and editions of the writings of St. Jerome and other early Church Fathers. Erasmus is best known, however, for his popular works, especially *In Praise of Folly*.

Although born in Rotterdam, he passed most of his long life elsewhere—in Germany, France, England, Italy, and especially Switzerland. The most influential and cosmopolitan of the northern humanists, he corresponded with nearly every prominent writer and thinker in Europe and knew personally popes, emperors, and kings. He was *the* scholar of Europe, and his writings were read eagerly everywhere.

Perhaps the most famous and influential work by Erasmus was *The Praise of Folly*, a satire written in 1511 at the house of the English humanist Sir Thomas More. Folly, the term used in the Middle Ages as a synonym for human nature, is described by Erasmus as the source not only of much harmless enjoyment in life but also of many things that are wrong and need correcting. A historian has described the work in these words:

> *At first the book makes kindly and approving fun of the ways of action and the foibles and weaknesses of mankind. It is not mordant, only amused. But gradually from fools innocent and natural and undebased, it passes to those whose illusions are vicious in their setting and results.[11]*

Among such are merchants ("they lie, swear, cheat, and practice all the intrigues of dishonesty"), lawyers ("they of all men have the greatest conceit of their own abilities"), scholastic philosophers ("that talk as much by rote as a parrot"), and scientists ("who esteem themselves the only favorites of wisdom, and look upon the rest of mankind as the dirt and rubbish of the creation"). Most roughly handled are churchmen, in particular monks, who are "impudent pretenders to the profession of piety," and popes, cardinals, and bishops, "who in pomp and splendor have almost equalled if not outdone secular princes." While his satire is indeed harsh, Erasmus was himself balanced, moderate, and intolerant only of bigotry, ignorance, greed, and violence.

The Praise of Folly points up a significant difference between the northern humanists and their Italian predecessors. Most Italian humanists—the civic humanists—spoke to and for the upper-class elements in their city-states. They urged political leaders to become more statesmanlike, businessmen to become more generous with their wealth, and all to become more moral. They did not dissent or speak out in opposition; in urging the elite groups to assume their responsibilities, they were actually trying to defend, not condemn, them. Italian humanism "centered on the liberality or parsimony of princes, on the moral worth of riches, and on the question of how to define true 'nobility.' "[12] The northern humanists, on the other hand, like Erasmus in *The Praise of Folly*, spoke out against a broad range of political, social, economic, and religious evils. They faced reality and became ardent reformers of society's ills.

The northern humanists also went further than the Italians in broadening their interest in ancient literature to include early Christian writings—the Scriptures and the works of the church Fathers. This led them to prepare new and more accurate editions of the Scriptures (Erasmus' Greek edition of the New Testament became famous and was used by Luther) and to compare unfavorably the complexities of the church in their own day with the simplicity of early Christianity. Since they held that the essence of religion was morality and rational piety—what Erasmus called the "philosophy of Christ"—rather than ceremony and dogma, it is not surprising that the church became a major target of their reforming zeal.

Sir Thomas More's Utopia

The most significant figure in English humanism was Sir Thomas More (1478–1535), the friend of Erasmus. More is best known for his *Utopia*, the first important description of an ideal state since Plato's *Republic*. In this extraordinarily realistic work, More criticized his age by using as his spokesman a fictitious sailor who contrasts the ideal life he has seen in Utopia (The Land of Nowhere) with the harsh conditions of life in England. More's denunciations centered on the new acquisitive capitalism, which he blamed for the widespread insecurity and misery of the lower classes. More felt that governments

> *are a conspiracy of the rich, who, in pretence of managing the public, only pursue their private ends, . . . first, that they may, without danger, preserve all that they have so ill acquired, and then, that they may engage the*

A map of Utopia from the 1518 edition of More's social satire. More's creation was so convincing that travelers tried to learn the location of the ideal state and a priest sought to become its bishop. To fellow humanists, however, More's satire was plain: Utopia means "nowhere" and Hythloday, the name of the fictitious sailor who narrates the tale, means "peddler of nonsense."

poor to toil and labor for them at as low rates as possible, and oppress them as much as they please.[13]

In Utopia, by contrast, no one is in want because the economy is planned and cooperative and because property is held in common. Utopia is the only true commonwealth, concludes More's imaginary sailor:

In all other places, it is visible that while people talk of a commonwealth, every man only seeks his own wealth: but there, where no man has any property, all men zealously pursue the good of the public. . . . [I]n Utopia, where every man has a right to every thing, they all know that if care is taken to keep the public stores full, no private man can want any thing; for among them there is no unequal distribution, so that no man is poor, none in necessity; and though no man has anything, yet they are all rich; for what can make a man so rich as to lead a serene and cheerful life, free from anxieties; neither apprehending want himself, nor vexed with the endless complaints of his wife?[14]

More was the first of the modern English socialists, but his philosophy should not be considered a forerunner of the socialism of our day. His economic outlook was a legacy from the Middle Ages, and his preference for medieval collectivism over modern economic individualism was of a piece with his preference for a church headed—medieval style—by popes rather than by kings, a view that prompted Henry VIII, who had appropriated the pope's position as head of the church in England, to execute him for treason.

Rabelais' Gargantua and Pantagruel

One of the best known of the French humanists was François Rabelais (1494–1553). A brilliant, if coarse, lover of all life from the sewers to the heavens, Rabelais is best remembered for his *Gargantua and Pantagruel*. Centering on figures from French folklore this work relates the adventures of Gargantua and his son Pantagruel, genial giants of tremendous stature and appetite, to whom were ascribed many marvelous feats.

Michel de Montaigne. Montaigne's *Essays* influenced both English and French literature in form, style, and thought.

With much burlesque humor—hence the term "Rabelaisian"—Rabelais satirized his society while putting forth his humanist views on educational reform and inherent human goodness. He made vitriolic attacks on the abuses of the church and the shortcomings of scholastics and monks, but he had no patience with overzealous Protestants either. What Rabelais could not stomach was hypocrisy and repression and for those guilty of these tendencies he reserved his choicest invective. He bid his readers to flee from that

> *rabble of squint-minded fellows, dissembling and counterfeit saints, demure lookers, hypocrites, pretended zealots, tough friars, buskinmonks, and other such sects of men, who disguise themselves like masquers to deceive the world. . . . Fly from these men, abhor and hate them as much as I do, and upon my faith you will find yourself the better for it. And if you desire . . .* to live in peace, joy, health, making yourselves always merry, *never trust those men that always peep out through a little hole.*[15]

Von Hutten: German Humanist and Patriot

One of the outstanding German humanists was Ulrich von Hutten (1488–1523). In him was blended a zeal for religious reform and German nationalist feelings. This member of an aristocratic family, who wanted to unite Germany under the emperor, led a tumultuous life as a wandering Greek scholar and satirist. He supported Luther as a rallying point for German unity against the papacy, to which he attributed most of his country's ills. Von Hutten reflected the tensions and aspirations of the German people in the early years of the Protestant revolt against the papacy (see ch. 13).

Montaigne's Essays

The last notable northern humanist was the French skeptic Michel de Montaigne (1533–1592). At the age of thirty-eight he gave up the practice of law and retired to his country estate and well-stocked library, where he studied and wrote. Montaigne developed a new literary form and gave it its name—the essay. In ninety-four essays he set forth his personal views on many subjects: leisure, friendship, education, philosophy, religion, old age, death, and so forth. He did not pretend to have the final answer to the subjects he discussed. Instead, he advocated open-mindedness and toleration—rare qualities in the sixteenth century, when France was racked by religious and civil strife.

Montaigne condemned the pedantry and formalism into which humanism and humanistic education had largely degenerated by the end of the sixteenth century. "To know by heart is not to know; it is to retain what we have given our memory to keep," he wrote, and added that

Our tutors never stop bawling into our ears, as though they were pouring water into a

funnel; and our task is only to repeat what has been told us. I should like the tutor to correct this practice. . . . I want him to listen to his pupil speaking in his turn.[16]

Montaigne's final essay, entitled "Of Experience," which developed the thought that "when reason fails us we resort to experience," is an acknowledgment of the bankruptcy of humanism and a foreshadowing of the coming triumph of science.

Cervantes' Don Quixote

In the national literatures that matured during the Northern Renaissance, the transition from feudal knight to Renaissance courtier finds its greatest literary expression in a masterpiece

Title page from an early English translation of *Don Quixote* by Cervantes. Part one of the novel first appeared in 1605 and was reprinted in Madrid in 1608. It was printed in Brussels in 1607 and 1611, in Milan in 1610. It appeared in English in 1612 and in French two years later. In its burlesque of chivalric romances, *Don Quixote* represents a great ideological change from the outworn concepts of the Middle Ages to the ideology of a newer age, one infinitely more complex and practical.

Spanish satire, *Don Quixote de la Mancha,* the work of Miguel de Cervantes (1547–1616). By Cervantes' day knighthood had become an anachronism, though its accompanying code of chivalry still retained its appeal. It remained for a rationalist like Cervantes to show up the inadequacies of chivalric idealism in a world that had acquired new, and intensely practical, aims. He did so by creating a pathetic but infinitely appealing character to serve as the personification of an outmoded way of life.

Don Quixote, the "knight of the woeful countenance," mounted on his "lean, lank, meagre, drooping, sharp-backed, and raw-boned" steed Rozinante, sets out in the Spanish countryside to right wrongs and uphold his lady's and his own honor. In his misadventures he is accompanied by his squire, the much less gallant but infinitely more realistic Sancho Panza, whose peasant adages and hard-grained common sense serve as a contrast to the unpractical nature of his master's chivalric code. Tilting at windmills, mistaking serving wenches for highborn ladies and inns for castles, and lamenting the invention of gunpowder as depriving ardent knights of a chance to win immortality, Don Quixote is, on the surface at least, a ridiculous old man whose nostalgia for the "good old days" is a constant source of grief to him. Thus the story represents a superb satire directed against the outworn ideology of the Middle Ages; in particular, it laughed the ideal of chivalric romance into the world of make-believe.

And yet *Don Quixote* is still more. Cervantes instilled in his main character a pathos born in large measure of the author's own career of frustrated hopes and ambitions. As a result, Don Quixote becomes more than a romantic lunatic; he serves to embody that set of ideals each of us would like to see realized but that we must compromise in a world that has other interests to serve.

Secular Drama Appears

Like Greek drama, medieval drama developed out of religious ceremonies. A complete divorce of the church and stage did not occur until the middle of the fifteenth century when the Renaissance era of drama began in Italian cities with the performance of ancient Roman comedies. In the following century appeared the *commedia dell' arte,* reflections of everyday life in vulgar and slapstick fashion, usually improvised by the players from a plot outline.

As secular dramas grew in popularity, theaters were built as permanent settings for their presentations. Great ingenuity was shown in the design of elaborate, realistic stage scenery as well as in lighting and sound effects. Theaters embodying these innovations only gradually appeared outside Italy. Not until 1576 was the first public theater erected in London; three years later, a similar theater was constructed in Madrid.

Imitating the ancient models they admired, French and Italian writers followed what they believed were the rigid conventions of the classical drama and, to a large extent, catered to the tastes of the aristocracy. By contrast, Spanish and English playwrights created a theatrical environment that was at once more socially democratic, more hospitable to national themes, and less concerned with classical models.

William Shakespeare

The reign of Queen Elizabeth I (1558–1603) climaxed the English Renaissance and produced such a galaxy of talented writers that one would have to go back as far as Athens in the fifth century B.C. to find an age as rich with literary genius. Strongly influenced by the royal court, which served as the busy center of intellectual and artistic life, these writers produced works that were highly colored, richly romantic, and often wildly extravagant in spite of all their poetic allusions to classical times.

The supreme figure in Elizabethan literature and perhaps in all literature is William Shakespeare (1564–1616). His rich vocabulary and poetic imagery were matched by his turbulent imagination. He was a superb lyric poet, and numerous critics have judged him the foremost sonnet writer in the English language.

Shakespeare wrote thirty-seven plays—comedies, histories, tragedies, and romances. His historical plays reflected the patriotic upsurge experienced by the English after the defeat of the Spanish Armada in 1588. For his comedies, tragedies, and romances, Shakespeare was content in a great majority of cases to borrow plots from earlier works. His forte lay in his creation of character—perhaps the richest and most diversified collection conceived by the mind of one man—and in his ability to translate his knowledge of human nature into dramatic speech and action. Today his comedies are played to enthusiastic audiences: *The Taming of the Shrew*, *As You Like It*, *A Midsummer Night's Dream*, *The Merchant of Venice*, are but a few. But it is in his tragedies that the poet-dramatist runs the gamut of human emotion and experience. Shakespeare possessed in abundance the Renaissance concern for human beings and the world around them. Hence his plays deal first and foremost with the human personality, passions, and problems. In such works as *Romeo and Juliet*, *Measure for Measure*, and *Troilus and Cressida*, the problems of love and sex are studied from many angles. Jealousy is analyzed in *Othello*, ambition in *Macbeth* and *Julius Caesar*, family relationships in *King Lear*, and a man's struggle with his own soul in *Hamlet*. Shakespeare's extraordinary ability to build every concrete fact and action upon a universal truth makes his observations as applicable today as they were when first presented in the Globe Theater. Small wonder that next to the Bible, Shakespeare is the most quoted of all literary sources in the English language.

Northern Painting

Before the Italian Renaissance permeated the artistic circles of northern Europe, the painters of the Low Countries had been making significant advances on their own. Outstanding was the Flemish Jan van Eyck (1385?–1440), whose work has been called "the full flowering of the spirit of the late Middle Ages," for he continued to paint in the realistic manner developed by medieval miniaturists. Van Eyck also perfected the technique of oil painting, which enabled him to paint with greater realism and attention to detail. In his painting of the merchant Arnolfini and his wife, for example, he painstakingly gives extraordinary reality to every detail, from his own image reflected in the mirror in the background to individual hairs on the little dog in the foreground.

Jan Van Eyck, *Wedding Portrait*. The double portrait painting is one of great psychological insight, meticulously rendered realistic detail, and rich symbolism. The dog, for instance, stands for marital fidelity.

The first talented German painter to be influenced deeply by Italian art was Albrecht Dürer (1471–1528) of Nüremberg. Dürer made more than one journey to Italy, where he was impressed both with the painting of the Renaissance Italians and with the artists' high social status—a contrast with northern Europe where artists were still treated as craftsmen. His own work is a blend of the old and the new; thus his engraving *Knight, Death, and the Devil*, fuses the realism and symbolism of the Gothic with the nobility of Verrocchio's equestrian statue of Colleoni. In the long run Dürer became better known for his numerous engravings and woodcuts than for his paintings.

Another famous German painter, Hans Holbein the Younger (1497–1543), chiefly painted portraits and worked abroad, especially in England. His memorable portraits blend the realism and concern for detail characteristic of all northern painting with Italian dignity.

Two northern painters who remained completely isolated from Italian influences were Hieronymus Bosch (1480–1516) and Pieter Brueghel the Elder (1525?–1569). Brueghel retained a strong Flemish flavor in his portrayal of the faces and scenes of his native land. He painted village squares, landscapes, skating scenes, peasants at work and at leisure just as he saw them, with a reporter's eye for detail.

Very little is known about the Dutch master Bosch other than that he belonged to one of the many puritanical religious sects that were becoming popular. This accounts for his most famous painting, *The Garden of Delights,* a triptych whose main panel is filled with innumerable naked men and women reveling in the sins of the flesh. The smaller left panel, by contrast, depicts an idyllic Garden of Eden, while the right panel portrays a nightmarish Hell filled with frenzied sinners undergoing punishment. Bosch was a stern moralist whose obsession with sin and Hell reflects the fears of his contemporaries, which contributed to the religious movement to be described in the next chapter—the Reformation.

Conclusion

In the Middle Ages people had thought and acted primarily as members of a community—a manor, a guild, or, above all, the universal community represented by the Roman church. But gradually, individuals began to attach importance to themselves and to develop an interest in worldly things for their own sake. This new individualistic and secular spirit, the period in which it became prominent, and the ways in which it manifested itself in art, literature, and learning we call the Renaissance.

The change took place earliest in the cities of fourteenth- and fifteenth-century Italy, and its intellectual and artistic aspects were linked to the practical activities of Renaissance civic life. Its intellectual manifestation, known as humanism, was a revival of classical literature and learning; it led citizens to what was relevant and useful in the classics. Scholars eagerly searched for ancient manuscripts and introduced the literature of Greece and Rome into contemporary life.

Italian humanists also laid the foundation for modern scholarship. Thus they helped prepare the way for modern science, even though they themselves generally disdained the subject.

Artists, too, reflected the new human-centered view of the world. The extent to which the Italian Renaissance sculptor, architect, and painter succeeded remains one of the glories of Western civilization. But the "anti-Renaissance" art called Mannerism, which arose during the last two thirds of the sixteenth century after the peak of perfection had been reached in the High Renaissance, has also of late received much favorable attention. Long dismissed as "the grotesque Renaissance" and described as "variations on ugliness," in the twentieth century the appearance of such styles as Surrealism and Expressionism has led to a new understanding and appreciation of Mannerism. The Mannerist period is also seen as one of invention and exploration out of which arose the Baroque style of the seventeenth century.

In the sixteenth century the stimulating ideas current in Italy spread beyond the Alps and combined with local developments to produce renaissances in France, England, and elsewhere. While influenced by Italian antecedents, thought and art beyond the Alps developed in distinctive ways. These developments included the invention of printing from movable type, the impact of the reforming zeal of the northern humanists on society, some of the great classics of European national literature, and achievements in painting that blended late medieval Gothic realism with Italian Renaissance dignity.

Suggestions for Reading

Margaret Aston, *The Fifteenth Century: The Prospect of Europe** (Norton, 1979) is a short, first-rate introduction to the Renaissance period. J. Huizinga, *The Waning of the Middle Ages** (Anchor, 1924) is a notable study of "fading and decay" in the culture of northern Europe during the fourteenth and fifteenth centuries.

Jacob Burckhardt, *The Civilization of the Renaissance in Italy,** 2 vols. (Torchbooks, 1958), first published in 1860, inaugurated the view that the Italian Renaissance of the fourteenth and fifteenth centuries was a momentous turning point in the history of Western civilization. The editors of this edition insist that Burckhardt's major insights "remain essentially unimpaired." On the many interpretations of the Renaissance, see Walter K. Ferguson. *The Renaissance in Historical Thought: Five Centuries of Interpretation* (Houghton Mifflin, 1948).

L. Martines, *Power and Imagination: City-States in Renaissance Italy** (Knopf, 1979) is an outstanding synthesis stressing the relationship between social change and culture. See also G. Brucker, *Renaissance Florence,* rev. ed. (California, 1983); C. Hibbert, *The House of Medici: Its Rise and Fall* (Morrow, 1975); Denys Hay, *The Italian Renaissance in Its Historical Background,** 2nd ed. (Cambridge, 1977); and G. F. Lytle, and S. Orgel, eds., *Patronage in the Renaissance* (Princeton, 1952).

Philip L. Ralph, *The Renaissance in Perspective** (St. Martin, 1973); J. H. Plumb, *The Italian Renaissance: A Concise Survey of Its History and Culture** (Torchbooks) are good introductions. P.O. Kristeller, *Renaissance Thought: The Classic, Scholastic, and Humanist Strains** (Torchbooks, 1961) is excellent on Italian humanism. See also Herschel Baker, *The Image of Man: A Study of the Idea of Human Dignity in Classical Antiquity, the Middle Ages, and the Renaissance* (Harper & Row, 1961); R. Weiss, *The Renaissance Discovery fo Classical Antiquity** (Blackwell, 1988); and John H. Whitfield, *Petrarch and the Renascence* (Haskell, 1969).

Margaret M. Phillips, *Erasmus and the Northern Renaissance*, rev. ed. (Rowman, 1981) is a valuable introduction. See also J. Huizinga, *Erasmus of Rotterdam* (Phaidon, 1952); Raymond W. Chambers, *Thomas More** (Univ. of Michigan, 1958); J. H. Hexter, *More's Utopia: The Biography of an Idea* (Princeton 1952); M. Chute, *Shakespeare of London** (Dutton, 1957); and S. J. Greenblatt, *Sir Walter Raleigh: The Renaissance Man and His Roles* (Yale, 1973).

On printing and its effect on culture see P. Butler, *The Origin of Printing in Europe* (Univ. of Chicago, 1940) and Marshall McLuhan, *The Gutenberg Galaxy** (Univ. of Toronto, 1969).

F. B. Artz, *From the Renaissance to Romanticism: Trends in Style in Art, Literature, and Music, 1300–1830** (Phoenix, 1962) is an overall view of the arts. Also recommended are Peter and Linda Murray, *The Art of the Renaissance** (Thames and Hudson, 1985); Michael Levey, *Early Renaissance** (Penguin, 1978) and *High Renaissance** (Penguin, 1975), which contain many illustrations of paintings; and A. Hauser, *A Social History of Art*, Vol. II, *Renaissance to Baroque** (Vintage, 1957). B. Berenson, *Italian Painters of the Renaissance* (Cornell, 1980); and R. Wittkower, *Architectural Principles in the Age of Humanism** (Norton, 1971) are two classics of art history. See also B. Lowry, *Renaissance Architecture** (Braziller, 1962). On northern painting see O. Benesch, *The Art of the Renaissance in Northern Europe*, rev. ed. (Phaidon, 1965) and W. Stechow, *Northern Renaissance Art: 1400–1600* (Prentice Hall, 1966).

Two excellent biographies of Renaissance artists are D. Merejkowski, *The Romance of Leonardo da Vinci* (Modern Library) and H. Hibbard, *Michelango** (Torchbooks, 1975).

On the slow emergence of science see J. Bronowski, "Leonardo da Vinci," in J. H. Plumb, ed., *Renaissance Profiles** (Torchbooks, 1965) and J. H. Randall, Jr., "The Development of Scientific Method in the School of Padua," in P. Kristeller and Wiener, *Renaissance Essays* (Harper & Row, 1968).

On music see Alfred Einstein, *A Short History of Music** (Vintage, 1954) and G. Reese, *Music in the Renaissance*, rev. ed. (Norton, 1959).

*Indicates a less expensive paperbound edition.

Notes

1. *The Tempest*, act 5, sc. 1, lines 182–185.
2. Quoted in Lauro Martines, *Power and Imagination: City States in Renaissance Italy* (New York: Alfred A. Knopf, 1979), p. 83.
3. Lauro Martines, *Power and Imagination*, p. 243.
4. Quoted in J. H. Randall, Jr., *The Making of the Modern Mind* (Boston: Houghton Mifflin, 1976), p. 213.
5. Letter to Francesco Vettori; see Allan Gilbert, *The Letters of Machiavelli* (New York: Capricorn Books), p. 142.
6. *The Decameron of Giovanni Boccaccio*, trans. Richard Addington (New York: Garden City Publishing Co., 1949), p. 559.
7. Joan Kelly, quoted in Bonnie S. Anderson and Judith P. Zinsser, *A History of Their Own: Women in Europe from Prehistory to the Present*, Vol. I (New York: Harper & Row, 1988), p. xvii.
8. Sir Thomas Elyot, *The Book of the Governor*, quoted in Eugene F. Rice, *The Foundations of Early Modern Europe, 1460–1559* (New York: Norton, 1970), p. 88.
9. Trans. A. H. Gilbert, *Machiavelli: The Prince and Other Works* (Chicago: Packard & Co., 1941), p. 177 (Ch. 26).
10. F. B. Artz, *From the Renaissance to Romanticism: Trends in Style in Art, Literature, and Music, 1300–1830* (Chicago: University of Chicago Press, 1962), p. 102.
11. H. O. Taylor, *Thought and Expression in the Sixteenth Century* (New York: Macmillan, 1920), vol. 1, p. 175.
12. Lauro Martines, *Power and Imagination*, p. 208.
13. From the 1684 translation by Gilbert Burnet, in *Introduction to Contemporary Civilization in the West: A Source Book* (New York: Columbia University Press, 1946), vol. 1, p. 461.
14. *Introduction to Contemporary Civilization*, p. 460.
15. Quoted in H. O. Taylor, *Thought and Expression in the Sixteenth Century*, pp. 328–329.
16. Montaigne, "Of the Education of Children," in *The Complete Works of Montaigne*, trans. D. M. Frame (Stanford, CA: Stanford University Press, 1957), p. 112.

"Here I Take My Stand"

The Protestant and Catholic Reformations

On April 18, 1521 in the German city of Worms, an Augustinian monk named Martin Luther publicly refused to renounce his heresies, thus defying Charles V, the Holy Roman Emperor, and the assembled Imperial Diet. On that day, Luther launched the Protestant Reformation and a new age of religious zeal that contrasted with the practical indifference of the late medieval Catholic Church. Protestantism denied accepted doctrines about salvation and the role of the clergy, but it also challenged the social and political theories of the medieval church on such issues as the significance of marriage and the proper balance between secular and religious political authorities. In addition, the movement generated a determined Catholic reaction and stimulated Catholic reforms. Ultimately, the ensuing controversy caused frightful persecution and bloody civil war; but it also engendered new vitality to millions, for whom religion was a dominant concern in daily life.

Although the Protestant Reformation brought revolutionary change, its spirit reflected medieval values. Like the Renaissance, it fostered individualism and lamented church abuses, but its authorities were early church fathers, like St. Paul and St. Augustine, not Greek and Roman writers. Generally, for Protestants, man was not "the measure"; they saw humanity as corrupt, trusted faith over reason, and disdained worldly pleasures in favor of seeking salvation. Northern humanists who became Protestants usually held views quite different from the earlier Italian humanists.

To Luther and his critics, Catholic as well as Protestant, the Reformation was significant as a great theological controversy; modern historians see it also as reflecting a total European transformation, involving the shift from an agrarian to a commercial urban economy, the rise of a middle class, the emergence of new nation-states, overseas expansion, and a reaction of northern Europe against Italian domination. The Reformation promoted all of these changes, from which emerged the modern world.

From a political point of view, there were two successive Reformations. The first exerted its greatest influence before the 1550s in supporting secular rulers against the papacy. It was represented by the Lutheran state churches in Germany and Scandinavia and by the Anglican establishment in England. The second Reformation began in the 1520s but only came to fruition in the century of violence efore the Peace of Westphalia in 1648. It was well illustrated by later Calvinism and by more extreme sects like the Anabaptists (see map, p. 338).

Background of the Protestant Reformation

The Reformation was a response to both religious and social needs. It promised subjective comfort and security in a tension-ridden age. The Catholic Church, itself facing confusing upheaval, was often accused of violating Christian principles, wasting resources, abusing power, and failing its mission. These charges from Protestant reformers were not without truth. There were, however, other pertinent sources of religious revolt in social and political conditions, external to the Church.

**THE REFORMATION AND
THE COUNTER–REFORMATION**

- Lutheran
- Calvinist
- Church of England
- Catholic
- Huguenot Centers

Adverse Economic and Social Conditions

A major factor in the reformers' success was the avalanche of materials printed by the new movable type process. By 1500, they had already spewed out six million publications in more than 200 European towns; Luther himself between 1517 and 1520 produced thirty works totaling 300,000 copies. The multiplicity of printers can be largely explained by growing literacy and by terrible roads, which made reprinting books more economical than transporting them. Profit was surely a major stimulus to printers, who were eager to exploit an exploding market. For reformers, the printed word offered seemingly unlimited opportunities for spreading their ideas.

This rising demand for print reflected a dynamic urban expansion. Although 90 percent of the population remained rural, cities grew considerably in size and number, swelled by the general population increase and by expanding

trade. The rapid urban growth brought social distress. In most instances, the urban dweller was estranged from family and village ties while recoiling from strange ideas and galling frustrations. Fees and tolls exacted by the Church or feudal lords, as well as trade restrictions imposed by guild monopolies, were sources of discontent among craftsmen and petty merchants. Their ambitions, insecurities, and resentments provided a most fertile seed bed for Protestantism, which was largely an urban movement.

Much has been written about the alliance between Protestantism and capitalism, but this union did not become readily apparent until later, when developing Calvinism provided a capitalistic ethic. But even in the early sixteenth century, many people felt adverse effects from the new money economy. Inflation brought serious economic dislocations and suffering among the poor. Capitalistic agriculture tended to erode peasants' traditional rights, subject them to rents beyond their resources, and drive them from the land into the towns, where they added to the chorus of discontent. Much of this protest was directed against the church because it was a most visible source of authority.

Conditions Affecting Women

These prevailing social dislocations affected everyone but were most disturbing to women. They had attained some social status during the medieval period, but their social privileges were still less than those of men. Now, in the sixteenth century, the new economy, their declining marriage prospects, and the changing nature of the Church itself, combined to increase their miseries and insecurities. When Protestant preachers proclaimed a new Jerusalem, women were inclined to listen.

Even during the late medieval period, the social position of European women was markedly ambiguous. They were excluded from the universities, from most professions except midwifery and prostitution, from most guilds, from elective municipal offices, and from the deliberative councils of states, unless they were queens. Yet many women made important social contributions. As nuns, they symbolized the Catholic ideal of feminine purity, associated with the Virgin. Outside the cloister, they provided necessary

Among the household tasks that fell to women was laundry. Here, women in an English village wash their laundry in a stream.

labor. In addition to their many household tasks, which included gardening, tending animals, cooking, cleaning, child-rearing, and family nursing, they were active in almost every light craft. They also operated market stalls and established shops, managed estates, and were sometimes engaged in foreign trade. On the continent, some held appointed municipal offices, such as heading public health agencies.

The tumultuous transition from medievalism drastically altered this relatively favorable situation for women. As capitalism developed, it drew industry from the home and emphasized specialization. Because of their household duties, women were not free to seek outside jobs, and what work they could get on a part-time basis, such as field labor, paid very little. They were further disadvantaged by tightening competition and male resentment, which led to the completion of their exclusion from craft guilds. Women outnumbered men in most cities, a situation which helped flood the job market while it increased women's difficulties in finding husbands. The number of single women increased, not only because their marriage prospects were few, but also because the religious wars of the era had widowed many.

The declining status of women was reflected in the witchcraft mania which spread over Europe after 1450, reaching a climax in the latter sixteenth century. The idea of witches as agents of the devil originated in pre-Christian times but waned in the late medieval era. Its revival after

In this woodcut from a 1555 publication, the devil carries off a witch to hell. Misfortunes that fell upon a particular family or group were often attributed to the activity or power of witches.

1450 was sudden and fanatical. Accused witches were usually tried in religious courts, both Catholic and Protestant, where many were tortured until they confessed. Over 100,000 of these unfortunates were executed by strangling, drowning, burning, and beheading. The victims were sometimes men, but more than 70 percent were women. Some 40 percent of the latter were widows, and most were old and eccentric. Punishment of accused witches was justified by their alleged association with the devil and opposition to the true faith. Supposedly, they had succumbed to Satan because women were weak and innately evil, as indicated by the biblical account of Eve's role in corrupting Adam.

Adverse Political Conditions

An aspect of the transition from medievalism much more directly threatening to the Church than economic and social change was the consolidation of nonfeudal governments, with their attendant nationalism. Rulers of such states found themselves competing with the popes and their major political allies, the Habsburg Holy Roman Emperors. The surface issues were political, involving control of courts, law, public support, and military power; but significant economic interests were also at stake. The Church owned vast properties and collected fortunes in tithes, fees, and religious gifts, all of which were coveted by secular rulers, who hoped to achieve national independence by taking over church functions.

The political position of the church was perhaps strongest in eastern Germany, Poland, Bohemia, and that part of Hungary not lost to the Turks in the 1520s. In these agrarian hinterlands, dependent upon trade with the Hanse Baltic ports, local nobles ruled their serfs on manorial estates and fought against each other, regularly defying their monarchs. Common fear of the Turks, amid this general anarchy, brought a very tenuous unity. The church sought stability in alliance with eastern royal families. It held many lands, exercising considerable influence at royal courts, within feudal councils, and in local affairs. But even here, where medieval traditions lingered longest, frequent disputes among royal families and ambitious nobles wanting to become kings threatened Church interests.

After Titian painted this portrait of Charles V, the emperor conferred noble status on the artist, giving him the title Count Palatine.

For its part, the Church relied upon the Habsburg family, which in the early sixteenth century was personified by Charles V, king of Spain, Bohemia, and Hungary; sovereign over the Netherlands, Burgundy, Austria, Styria, Milan, Naples, and Sicily; and titular head of the Holy Roman Empire. His far-flung holdings and wars with the Turks left him little potential for protecting the church. The Empire, including 2000 independent lesser nobles, 66 autonomous cities, over 100 imperial counts, and 30 secular princes, was loosely governed by a quarrelsome Imperial Diet, which functioned primarily to protect the independence of the princes and cities. With its 70 quasi-independent bishoprics and its close ties with the Emperor, the Church was naturally an object of resentment within the Diet.

The Church faced even more serious political difficulties with the new independent monarchies of western Europe. During the fifteenth century, English, French, and Spanish rulers began freeing themselves from feudal restrictions and gaining independence from the papacy. In Spain, Charles V's maternal grandparents, Ferdinand and Isabella, made taxation of the church a major revenue source and the Inquisition a political tool for removing enemies of the monarchy. French kings, by the mid-fifteenth century, had won the right of clerical appointment and used it to control the Church. In England, the Tudor dynasty after 1485 crushed the nobility and raised new revenues; the break with Rome under Henry VIII climaxed a long and bitter struggle between English kings and the papacy over appointments and church incomes.

No longer able to prevail over secular rulers by its religious authority alone, the papacy fared poorly in an era of power politics in foreign relations. Free Italian cities, such as Venice and Florence, had helped generate the new diplomacy, but the peninsula soon became embroiled in a desperate struggle between the Habsburgs and France, lasting from the 1490s to 1559. In this maelstrom of deceit, intrigue, and violence, the Papal States were simply another pawn in the game of power politics. Both the papacy's moral and physical weaknesses were demonstrated by Catholic armies plundering papal territories, as when troops of Charles V sacked Rome in 1527.

Internal Decay of the Church

To many western Europeans in this period, the politicizing of the Church was only one sign of its internal decay. The charge was based upon considerable evidence that the clerical hierarchy, particularly at the upper levels, had been seriously infected by the prevailing viruses of power, profit, and sensual pleasures, at the expense of spiritual concerns.

The Church was already notorious for many specific abuses. Some priests were illiterate; they could neither read scripture nor conduct the Mass. Others, even some popes, took mistresses, fathered children, and paid fees for absolution. High clergymen lived as well as they could, seeking pleasure in scholarship, art collecting,

fine wines, and rich foods. Church offices were regularly sold, while church revenues were swollen by innumerable fees levied upon superstitious parishioners. One rich source of income was the sale of sacred relics, including reputed bones of the saints, vials of blood from Christian martyrs, and other equally grotesque items. A most objectionable practice was the sale of indulgences. These were theoretically shares of surplus grace, earned by Christ and Christian saints and available for exceptional papal dispensation to worthy souls in purgatory. Originally, indulgences were not sold or described as tickets to heaven. By the sixteenth century, however, papal hucksters regularly peddled them as guarantees of salvation.

One subject of Protestant criticism, the Catholic monasteries, involved abuses directly affecting women. Although the sheltered life was extolled as offering an option to women, who could not participate in many church-sponsored activities for men, convent life had its oppressive side. Many girls were put in convents while they were children and admitted as nuns while still very young. They were often subjected to rigid disciplines, punished for minor infractions, and held in virtual captivity. Many became housemaids or concubines for priests. Reports of such conditions were confirmed by escaping nuns, who were increasing in number during the sixteenth century.

Theological Controversy

Such practices provided telling arguments for Protestant reformers' but of greater concern to them were the errors incorporated into church theology during the late medieval period. In the reformers' view, these changes had seriously violated scriptural principles and had to be corrected.

Reformers reacted particularly against scholastic philosophers who had seen reason as God's greatest gift, permitting humans to understand the nature of good and evil. In his *Summa Theologica*, St. Thomas Aquinas, perhaps the best-known schoolman, labored to reconcile Aristotle's logic with church teaching. Unfortunately for the sixteenth-century Church, scholastic logic, later carried to extremes, was employed to rationalize many ritualistic and mechanical paths to salvation: good works earned credits against sins; popes could dispense grace through indulgences; the clergy were direct representatives of God and therefore only they could minister the sacraments. These and similar propositions all emphasized the idea that salvation required services from the Church and its clergy more than piety or faith.

Northern humanists, many reforming clergy, and Protestants held to earlier Christian principles. Humanist scholars such as Erasmus ridiculed scholasticism as pedantic and outmoded. Augustinian monks, following the ideas of their founder, St. Augustine, believed humans were depraved sinners who could only be saved through personal repentance and faith in God's mercy. Augustinians accepted only the scriptures as religious truth. They denied emphatically that the clergy held the keys to heaven, and they condemned all deviations from the early primitive church, including veneration of relics, celibacy of the clergy, priests as intermediaries, the necessity of most sacraments, and the infallibility of the pope. They denounced scholastic superstitions but valued faith over reason. Some believed in witches; others, like Luther, often saw the devil in human or animal form.

Differences between accepted church theology and the reformers was especially marked on marriage, celibacy, and the position of women. Official church doctrine viewed wives as subordinate to their husbands because women were less capable of sound moral judgment, being emotional and sex-oriented creatures. The celibate life, as exemplified by the clergy, was held to be the surest way to salvation. By rejecting celibacy as unnatural, extolling marriage as Christian duty, and stressing salvation through faith and redemption, Protestantism offered hope to many priests and nuns who had suffered torments of conscience for their sins of the flesh. Protestantism, unlike the church, also offered some prospects for divorce in unfortunate marriages.

Differences within the church had surfaced long before Luther. John Huss, the Bohemian reformer, had voiced dissent before the Council of Constance in 1415; he was burned at the stake as a heretic. Huss and his English mentor, John Wycliffe (1320–1384), preached against clerical abuses and the necessity of priests for guaranteeing salvation (see p. 285). A third of Wycliffe's followers and many of his preachers were women. Other late medieval dissenters included the German and Dutch mystics, who sought direct spiritual communion with God. Each of these movements, although not protected by secular authorities, lived on into the sixteenth century.

Luther and Charles V

On October 31, 1517, Martin Luther issued a call for debate on his celebrated ninety-five theses concerning indulgences and other theological questions.[1] The ensuing controversy, which soon raged far beyond Wittenberg, not only split Christendom; it also brought significant political changes, affecting the German princes, the Holy Roman Emperor, and most western European states.

Development of the Lutheran Movement

German social, political, and cultural conditions had prepared the way for Luther. Changes in the traditional manorial economy had disturbed both nobles and peasants; prosperity and its accompanying sophistication were also turning some of the urban middle classes against medieval commercial values. Moreover, Germany had long been politically divided and dominated by the papacy. The Empire had been weakening since the thirteenth century; by the 1400s, a number of German princes were seeking independence from both the Empire and Rome.

Conditions in Germany help explain the acceptance of Luther's ideas, but his unique personality must also be credited. Although sometimes fanatic and bigoted, he was a charismatic religious leader and an accomplished scholar, who counted humanists among his friends and yet was capable of rough rural humor in the peasants' vernacular. He possessed great self-confidence and strength of character, arising from personal religious experience. Born in 1483, the son of a Thuringian peasant turned miner and petty capitalist, the boy was subjected to strict discipline and lectured on the penalties

Martin Luther at the Diet of Worms

In April 1521, Emperor Charles V called the Imperial Diet into session to hear Luther's defense of statements against Church teachings and the papal authority. Luther's refusal to recant resulted in his being put under an imperial ban aimed at enforcing the pope's Bull of Excommunication.

Most Serene Lord Emperor, Most Illustrious Princes, Most Gracious Lords . . . I have thought and written in simplicity of heart, solely with a view to the glory of God and the pure instruction of Christ's faithful people . . .

. . . Your Imperial Majesty and Your Lordships; I ask you to observe that my books are not all of the same kind.

There are some in which I have dealt with piety in faith and morals with such simplicity and so agreeably with the Gospels that my adversaries themselves are compelled to admit them useful, harmless, and clearly worth reading by a Christian. . . . If I should begin to recant here, what, I beseech you, should I be doing but condemning, alone among mortals, that truth which is admitted by friends and foes alike, in an unaided struggle against universal consent?

The second kind consists in those writings levelled against the papacy. . . . If then I recant these, the only effect will be to add strength to such tyranny, to open not the windows but the main doors to such blasphemy, which will thereupon stalk farther and more widely than it has hitherto dared. . . .

The third kind consists of those books which I have written against private individuals. . . . But it is not in my power to recant them, because that recantation would give that tyranny and blasphemy an occasion to lord over those whom I defend and to rage against God's people more violently than ever. . . .

And so, through the mercy of God, I ask Your Imperial Majesty, and Your Illustrious Lordships, or anyone of any degree, to bear witness, to overthrow my errors, to defeat them by the writings of the Prophets or by the Gospels; for I shall be most ready, if I be better instructed, to recant any error, and I shall be the first in casting my writings into the fire. . . .

Thereupon the Orator of the Empire, in a tone of upbraiding, said that his answer was not to the point, and that there should be no calling into question of matters on which condemnations and decisions had before been passed by Councils. He was being asked for a plain reply, without subtlety or sophistry, to this question: Was he prepared to recant, or no?

Luther then replied: Your Imperial Majesty and Your Lordships demand a simple answer. Here it is, plain and unvarnished. Unless I am convicted of error by the testimony of Scripture or (since I put no trust in the unsupported authority of Pope or of councils, since it is plain that they have often erred and often contradicted themselves) by manifest reasoning I stand convicted by the Scriptures to which I have appealed, and my conscience is taken captive by God's word, I cannot and will not recant anything, for to act against our conscience is neither safe for us, nor open to us.

On this I take my stand. I can do no other. God help me. Amen.

From *Documents of the Christian Church*, edited by Henry Bettenson. (New York: Oxford University Press, 1963), pp. 280–83.

MARTHIN LVTHER.　　　CATHARINA.

In this cartoon Luther is shown carting a host of former priests away from their vows of chastity. Following Luther is his wife, Katherine von Bora, who had been a nun.

incurred by worldly sins. After four years of law study at Erfurt University, young Martin disappointed his father by entering an Augustinian monastery at the age of twenty-two. His decision followed a miraculous (to him) survival in a violent thunderstorm. Yet even as a monk, he was tormented by awareness of his sins and unworthiness for salvation. Then, in his mid-thirties, he found liberation from despair in reading St. Paul's Epistle to the Romans:

> Then I grasped that the justice of God is that righteousness by which through grace and sheer mercy God justifies us through faith. Thereupon, I felt myself to be reborn and have gone through open doors into paradise.[2]

Luther's immediate adversary in 1517 was a Dominican monk named Johann Tetzel, commissioned by the pope to sell indulgences. This was part of a large undertaking, by which Leo X hoped to finance completion of St. Peter's Cathedral in Rome. Although indulgences were supposed to gain only partial forgiveness for repentant sinners, Tetzel used every appeal in convincing thousands of the country people around Wittenberg that they were buying salvation for themselves and their loved ones. Luther and many other Germans resented Tetzel's methods and his Roman connections. Luther also rejected Tetzel's Dominican theology, which differed from Augustinian beliefs.

The resulting Lutheran movement succeeded because it combined a passionate loyalty to religious traditions and a pragmatic acceptance of social change. It satisfied those who wanted a return to simple faith; it also appealed to those, like the humanists, who were aroused by church abuses and irrationality; it provided an outlet for German resentment against Rome; and it promised advantages to those princes seeking

Johann Tetzel, commissioner of indulgences, was said to have convinced concerned Christians that "as soon as coin in coffer rings, the soul to heaven springs."

political independence. They were impressed by the practical flexibility of Lutheran reformers, who easily accepted political commitments in order to achieve their religious goals.

Luther's theses were printed and reprinted, plunging Germany into religious controversy. The theses denied the pope's ability to effect salvation and declared that indulgences were not necessary for a contrite and repentant Christian. The pope was not immediately alarmed, but the Dominicans leveled charges of heresy. Luther might have faced the fate of Huss had he not won the support of his secular lord, Frederick, Elector of Saxony. Even so, the Dominicans pushed Luther to defend publicly his theological principles.

Luther had already begun his defense in a series of pamphlets. In 1519, he debated the eminent theologian, John Eck at Leipzig. Denying that the pope or church councils were infallible, Luther declared that the Scriptures constituted the only doctrinal authority and that salvation could only be gained by faith. When the pope issued a decree requiring that he renounce these heresies, Luther burned the document. In 1521, Pope Leo ordered Luther excommunicated.

That same year, a last effort at reconciliation failed completely. Charles V, only recently crowned emperor and aware of Luther's growing following among the princes, heeded advice to give the rebellious monk an audience before the Imperial Diet. Luther came to Worms but publicly refused to recant any of his stated principles. Subsequently, in private sessions, he would not concede the slightest point which could allow his opponents to save face and retain him in the Church. Ultimately, the Diet declared him a heretic and an outcast. The decree, however, was not enforceable. Immediately after he left Worms, Luther was kidnapped and secretly detained for his own protection in Wartburg Castle by Elector Frederick.

At Wartburg, Luther set his course for life, as he began organizing an evangelical church, distinct from Rome. He also translated the Bible into German and composed the sermons which would be repeated in hundreds of Lutheran pulpits all over Germany and Scandinavia. Soon he was able to leave Wartburg. He put off his clerical habit in 1523 and two years later married a former nun, Katherine von Bora, who bore him

The title page from Leo X's papal bull ordering Luther to recant his teachings. When Luther refused, the pope excommunicated him.

six children, raised his nieces and nephews, managed his household, secured his income, entertained his colleagues, and served as his supportive companion. As his church grew and sustained its independence, Luther became more confident and strident, pouring forth verbal abuse upon his enemies in 156 published works between 1530 and 1535. His verbal diatribes against Jews, Catholics, and even other Protestants, became increasingly violent and vulgar in his old age. He died in 1546, pleased to see his church firmly established but disappointed by its meager spiritual accomplishments.

The Lutheran Church

The common contention that Lutheranism was a religion of rulers is only partially true. Former Catholic congregations organized themselves into Lutheran churches and, in many places, influenced secular authorities to go along. Luther was protected by the Elector of

Title page from the last edition of the *New Testament* reviewed by Martin Luther, printed in 1546 at Wittenberg.

Saxony largely because Frederick the Wise was a practical politician.

The fundamental principle of the Lutheran creed was salvation by the faith that Christ's sacrifice alone could wash away sin. This was opposed to the Catholic doctrine of salvation by faith and good works, including conformance to prescribed dogma and participation in rituals. Along with the Lutheran emphasis upon faith went belief in an all-powerful and all-knowing God, beyond human rational understanding. A Christian, in Lutheran doctrine, could experience God only through personal faith and the revealed word of scripture.

Following these basic tenets, Lutheranism abandoned much of the Catholic ritual. Sacraments not mentioned in the New Testament were eliminated. The Catholic Mass became the Lutheran "Communion," involving all those attending services and requiring no priestly blessing to transform the bread and wine into Christ's body and blood, which, in Lutheran theory, automatically "coexisted" with the wafer and the wine. Other changes included church services in German instead of Latin, an emphasis on preaching, and the curtailment of formal ceremonies foreign to the personal experiences of ordinary people.

The Lutheran Church claimed to be a "priesthood of all believers," in which each person could approach God directly, with no absolute need for clerical mediation. Ordained clergymen and lay members were equally responsible for keeping the faith, helping others, and saving their own souls. Luther saw a clerical hierarchy as, at best, a necessary evil. Having denied papal infallibility and denounced Catholic clerical privileges, he followed the same principles in dealing with his own hard-working and often impoverished preachers.

Luthr's ideas on marriage and Christian equality promised women new opportunities, which were only partially realized. He stressed the importance of wives as marriage partners and, contrary to Catholic doctrine, even condoned divorce in cases of adultery and desertion. During the 1520s, his views drew numerous women, including his own wife, to Wittenberg, where they found refuge from monasteries or Catholic husbands. Some Lutheran women became wandering preachers, but they evoked protests from the male clergy and legal prohibitions from many German municipal councils, including those of Nuremburg and Augsburg. Although teaching that women were equal to men in opportunities for salvation and necessary in their family roles, Luther's later writings described women as subordinates to their husbands and not meant for the pulpit.

Despite his prejudices against hierarchies, Luther established a church organization as well as a doctrine. At first, each congregation conducted its own affairs, but by the late 1520s, Luther saw a need for discipline to maintain unity of faith and combat ignorance of the scriptures. This led to a central committee in Saxony, whose members visited and instructed the congregations. Ultimately, each of the four Saxon districts was put under a superintendent. This Saxon system became the model for subsequent Lutheran state churches in Germany and Scandinavia.

The Political Orientation of Lutheranism

Although the Lutheran Church gained sincere popular support, it probably could not have survived without the protection of German princes and Scandinavian kings. Luther understood this early and developed a political philosophy which, unlike Catholic theory, separated religious and worldly spheres, leaving the latter to secular authority. At first, he interpreted this to mean accepting demands of the state, except for false religious requirements, a position which avoided his being regarded as a revolutionary. Under pressure later from rebellious German Protestant princes, he wrote and spoke for armed resistance to Rome.

Protection of Lutheranism by the princes was often the result of feminine influence. Even Charles v's sister Mary (1505–1558), Queen of Hungary in the late 1520s, had Lutheran ministers at her court, for which she was scolded by her brother. Later, as regent of the Nether- lands, she kept the inquisition out of her realm and sought to mitigate the punishment of Luthe- rans tried for heresy. Elizabeth, Duchess of Braunschweig (1510–1558), despite the indiffer- ence of the duke, battled most of her life to main- tain Lutheranism in their territories. In various other places, throughout northern Germany and also in Denmark, high-born women achieved comparable results.

Lutheranism's political orientation was more clearly revealed in 1522–1523, during a rebellion of German knights. Seeing themselves ruined by decaying manorialism, these petty lords sought an alliance with the Emperor against their com- mon enemies; Rome, the princes, and the free ci- ties. Led by ultranationalists such as Ulrich von Hutten and Franz von Sickingen, they attacked the Archbishop of Trier, while proclaiming their Lutheranism. When Lutheran support was not forthcoming, the rebellion was quickly crushed. Luther took no part in the struggle but was em- barrassed by opponents who claimed his religion threatened law and order.

A better example of Luther's political conser- vatism was provided by the peasant revolt of 1524–1525. Encouraged by Lutheran appeals for Christian freedom, the rebels drew up a petition,

The scandalous behavior of the Bor- gia Pope Alexander VI (1492–1503) prompted this bit of critical propa- ganda. A flap lifts to transform Alex- ander into a satanic monster who proclaims, ''I am the pope.''

asking for religious autonomy but also for the abolitions of serfdom, tithes, enclosure of common lands, excessive rents, and harsh punishments. Luther publicly showed sympathy for the demands, particularly the peasants' request to select their own pastors; still, he advised them to obey the law, which was God's will, and desist from using force. Later, when the movement became violently rebellious, Luther penned a virulent pamphlet entitled *Against the Thievish and Murderous Hordes of Peasants*. In it, he called on the princes to "knock down, strangle, . . . stab . . . and think nothing so venomous, pernicious, or Satanic as an insurgent."[3]

Martin Luther and His Friends by Lucas Cranach the Elder. Luther (left) and other Protestant reformers surround their protector, Elector Frederick of Saxony.

After the revolt was stamped out in 1525 at a cost of 100,000 lives, many German peasants returned to Catholicism or joined other Protestant sects. Alienating the peasants and some poor townspeople helped Luther confirm his position with the nobles and princes. From this time on, Lutheranism was a religion associated with the secular status quo, as indicated by the formality and dignity of the Lutheran services.

The Political Effects of Lutheranism

As a political movement, Lutheranism encouraged submission of subjects while bolstering the security, independence, and solvency of emergent monarchies. Its repudiation of Catholicism was also a renunciation of foreign political control, and it provided secular rulers with justification for swelling their treasuries by seizing Catholic properties.

In Germany, the movement soon precipitated a struggle between the emperor and the Lutheran princes. The preliminary verbal skirmishes occurred in Imperial Diets during the late 1520s, when the Catholics sought to maintain religious uniformity. Lutheran leaders drew up a formal protest, from which the word *Protestant*, was derived. When their statement of principles, the Augsburg Confession (1530), was rejected, the Lutheran princes banded together for defense in the Schmalkaldic League. Because Charles V was preoccupied with the French and the Turks, open hostilities were minimized, but a sporadic civil war dragged on until after Luther's death in 1546. It was ended, for the next fifty-eight years, by the Peace of Augsburg in 1555.

This settlement ended the Reformation's first phase in Germany. By authorizing the princes to choose between Lutheranism and Catholicism in their state churches, it increased their independence of the Emperor. In addition, Catholic properties, confiscated before 1552, were to be retained by Lutheran principalities, thus confirming a means for financing their policies. Although no concessions were made to other Protestant groups, such as the Calvinists, the treaty brought a new political balance which was much less favorable to the empire and the church.

Outside of Germany, Lutheranism furnished the religious medium for national monarchies in Scandinavia. Here, as in Germany, rulers not

Pen sketches of peasants executing an indulgence salesman. Both Catholics and Protestants were guilty of incredible atrocities in their respective attempts to achieve religious uniformity.

only welcomed Lutheran religious ideas but also the chance to acquire confiscated Catholic properties. They were especially glad to have ministers preaching obedience to constituted secular authority. In Sweden, Gustavus Vasa (1523–1560) used Lutheranism in leading a successful struggle for Swedish independence from Denmark. In turn, the Danish king, who also ruled Norway, issued an ordinance in 1537, establishing a national Lutheran Church, with its bishops as salaried officials of the state.

Henry VIII and Anglicanism

The early English Reformation created an Anglican Church even more politically oriented than Lutheranism. The leader of the Reformation in England was not a dissenting priest but rather the reigning monarch, Henry VIII (1504–1547). His primary motive was securing his Tudor dynasty, although access to the wealth of the English Catholic Church was also a major consideration. Protestant ideas concerning theology and ritual did not much interest him, as was demonstrated by his persecution of dissident Protestants as well as Catholics. While Henry lived, the English Church reflected his will, but after his death, the country was nearly torn apart by corrupt politics and religious fanaticism.

The Annulment Issue

Henry's immediate problem in the 1520s was the lack of a male heir. After eighteen years of marriage, he had only a sickly daughter and an illegitimate son. His queen, Catherine of Aragon (1485–1536), after four earlier pregnancies, gave birth to a stillborn son in 1518, and by 1527, when she was 42, Henry had concluded that she would have no more children. His only hope for the future of his dynasty seemed to be a new marriage with another queen. This, of course, would require an annulment of his marriage to Catherine. In 1527, he appealed to the pope, asking for the annulment.

Normally, the request would probably have been granted; the situation, however, was not normal. Catherine had first been the wife of Henry's deceased brother Arthur. Her marriage to Henry had required a papal dispensation, based on her oath that the first marriage had never been consummated. Now Henry professed concern for his soul, tainted by living in sin with Catherine for eighteen years. He also claimed that he was being punished, citing a passage in the Book of Leviticus, which predicted childlessness for the man who married his dead brother's wife. The pope was sympathetic and certainly aware of an obligation to Henry, who for his verbal attacks against Luther had been named "Defender of the Faith" by a grateful earlier pontiff; but granting the annulment would have been admission of papal error, perhaps even corruption, in issuing the dispensation. Added to the Lutheran problem, this would have been doubly damaging to the papacy.

A more formidable problem for Henry was Catherine. She was a cultured Spanish woman, a respected consort, and a devoted wife, who had had successfully conducted a war against Scotland while Henry was campaigning in France. Henry recognized her strong character in their daughter, Mary, whom he appointed Princess of Wales and heir apparent, in the absence of a prince. As late as the mid-1520s, he sought Catherine's counsel and her companionship. Henry soon learned that Catherine would never accept an annulment, and he was afraid she might lead rebellion against him. As the aunt of Charles v, whose armies occupied Rome in 1527, she also exerted considerable pressure on the pope.

Despite these difficulties, Henry could hope for success in his appeal to the pope. Any conflict with Rome was in accord with national pride, often expressed in traditional resentment against Roman domination. Late medieval English kings had challenged the popes over Church appointments and revenues. More than a century and a half before Luther, an Oxford professor named John Wycliffe had denounced the false claims of popes and bishops. In more recent times, English Christian humanists, such as Sir Thomas More, had criticized the artificialities of Catholic worship. Thus when the pope delayed making a decision, Henry was relatively secure in his support at home.

The English Reformation and Reaction

During the three years after 1531, when Catherine saw him for the last time, Henry took control of affairs. Lodging his daughter and his banished wife in separate castles, he forbade them from seeing each other. He also intimidated the clergy into proclaiming him head of the English Church "as far as the law of Christ allows," extracted from Parliament the authority to appoint bishops, and designated his willing tool, Thomas Cranmer (1489–1556), as Archbishop of Canterbury. In 1533, Cranmer pronounced Henry's marriage to Catherine invalid, at the same time legalizing the king's union with Ann Boleyn, a lady of the court who was already carrying his unborn child. Parliament also ended all payments of revenues to Rome. Now, having little choice, the pope excommunicated Henry, making the breach official on both sides.

Amid a marked anti-Catholic campaign in the 1530s, Henry secured the Anglican establishment, which became an engine for furthering royal policies, with the king's henchmen controlling every function, from the building of chapels to the wording of the liturgy. Former church revenues, including more than £40,000 a year from religious fees alone, poured into the royal treasury. In 1539, Parliament completed its seizure of monastery lands, selling some for revenue and dispensing others to secure the loyalties of crown supporters. Meanwhile, Catholics suffered. Dispossessed nuns, unlike monks and priests, could find no place in the new church and were often reduced to despair. One, the famous "holy maid of Kent," who dared to rebuke the king publicly, was executed, as were other Catholic dissidents, including the king's former chancellor, Sir Thomas More, and the saintly Bishop Fisher of Rochester. Henry even forced his daughter, Mary, to accept him as head of the church and admit the illegality of her parents' marriage.

The new English Church, however, brought little change in doctrine or ritual. The "Six Articles," Parliament's declaration of the new creed

Detail from the title page illustration of the first Bible issued by the Church of England. Henry VIII presents copies to the Lord Chamberlain, Thomas Cromwell, and to Thomas Cranmer, Archbishop of Canterbury.

Henry VIII confers the royal succession on Edward VI, Henry's son by Jane Seymour, his third wife. The birth of a male heir was cited as Henry's triumph over the pope, who lies defeated at Edward's feet.

and ceremonies in 1539, reaffirmed most Catholic theology, except papal supremacy. Henry, in his later years after the execution of Anne in 1536, grew increasingly suspicious of popular Protestantism, which was spreading into England and Scotland from the Continent. He refused to legalize clerical marriage, which caused great hardships among many Anglican clergymen, including some bishops, and their wives. Henry's sixth wife, the former Catherine Parr, who was sympathetic to the reformers, narrowly escaped the king's displeasure by humbly appealing to his vanity. Others were not so lucky. Perhaps the most notable among many Protestant martyrs was Anne Askew, a woman of Lincolnshire, who was tried before a church court for heresy and so confounded her judges that she became a legend. She was nevertheless burned in 1546, a year before Henry died.

The Turmoil of Extremes

The decade after Henry's death brought social and political upheaval, as religious fanaticism shook the country. For six years, amid growing political corruption, Protestants ruled the country and the frail young King, Edward VI (1547–1553), who was the son of Henry's third wife, Jane Seymour. When he died in 1553, Mary Tudor came to the throne and strove to restore Catholicism until her death in 1558. The succeeding reign of Elizabeth (1558–1603), Henry's

daughter by Anne Boleyn, triggered a national awareness that diminished religious strife.

In Edward's reign, the government was controlled by a Regency Council, dominated first by the Duke of Somerset and then, after 1549, by his rival, the Duke of Northumberland. While the Council members furthered their own ambitions, many parishes were engulfed by a wave of Protestantism, which overturned religious traditions. Foreign refugees contributed to the unrest, although many were aided by English sympathizers like Catherine Willoughby, Duchess of Suffolk, and other Protestant court ladies. Starting slowly under Somerset and moving faster under Northumberland, the government sought political support by courting Protestants. It repealed the Six Articles, permitted priests to marry, replaced the Latin service with Cranmer's English version, and adopted the Forty-Two Articles, an embodiment of extreme Protestantism. Such policies frightened Catholics, but there were only two religious burnings, and one of these victims was an Anabaptist woman.

Frightful persecutions of Protestants marked the reign of Mary Tudor. Although known in history as "Bloody Mary," the new queen possessed many admirable qualities, including intelligence, dignity, compassion, and a strong moral sense; but she was handicapped by a religious obsession and by a hopeless love for her husband, Philip II of Spain, who married her in 1554, courteously abandoned her soon after, and

Both Catholics (left) and Protestants (right) suffered persecution during the English Reformation. Which group was being persecuted depended upon the religion of the reigning monarch.

returned only once, briefly, to ask her aid. At first successful in putting down rebellion, Mary squandered her early popularity by imposing her will on a divided people. This involved restoring the Catholic church service, proclaiming papal authority, forging a Spanish alliance, and burning 300 Protestants, including Cranmer and two other bishops. Most victims, however, were of the middle and lower classes; 55 of these were women; and two were blind girls. At the end, Mary died pitifully, rejected by her husband and people, but unmoved from her determined hope to save English Catholicism.

The Second Reformation

While Anglicanism and Lutheranism were developing as state churches, other forms of Protestantism were emerging in western Europe. Calvinism was the most popular and most conservative of these, but there were many others, including multiple forms of Anabaptism (see p. 357). All of them went farther than Lutheranism and Anglicanism in rejecting Catholic dogma and ritual. The were also marked by their intensity in pursuing objectives. Generally, they were opposed to monarchy, but this did not become very apparent until they became deeply involved in the religious wars after 1560.

The Early Reformation in Switzerland

Popular Protestantism developed early in Switzerland, where conditions favored its growth. During the late medieval period, the country prospered in the growing trade between Italy and northern Europe. Busy Swiss craftsmen and merchants in such cities as Zurich, Berne, Basel, and Geneva, became alienated by their Habsburg overlords and by papal policies, particularly the sale of indulgences. In 1499, the Confederation of Swiss cantons won independence from the Holy Roman Empire and the Habsburgs. To many Swiss, this was a first step in repudiating the authority of the pope.

The Swiss Reformation began in Zurich, shortly after Luther published his theses at Wittenberg. It was led by Ulrich Zwingli (1484–1531), a humanist scholar, priest, and former military chaplain, whose regime of clergymen and magistrates at Zurich supervised government, religion, and individual morality. Zwingli agreed with Luther in repudiating papal in favor of scriptural authority. He simplified services, preached justification by faith, attacked monasticism and opposed clerical celibacy. More rational than Luther, he was also more interested in practical reforms, going beyond Luther in advocating more ground for divorce and in denying any mystical conveyance of grace by baptism or communion; both, to Zwingli, were only symbols. These differences proved irreconcilable when Luther and Zwingli met to consider merging their movements in 1529.

As Zwingli's influence spread rapidly among the northern cantons, religious controversy separated north from south, rural from urban areas, and feudal overlords, both lay and ecclesiastical, from towns within their dominions. When, in the 1520s, Geneva repudiated its feudal obligations and declared its independence from its local bishop and the Count of Savoy, the city became a hotbed of Protestantism, with preachers swarming in from Zurich. Zwingli was killed in the resulting religious war of 1531; fortunately, the fighting ended quickly in a peace which permitted each Swiss canton to choose its own religion.

Origin and Early Development of Calvinism

Hoping to secure Protestantism in Geneva after the religious wars, enthusiastic reformers invited John Calvin (1509–1564) to Geneva. Calvin

John Calvin formulated his doctrine of predestination to explain the relationship between God and humans. The view that human souls are predestined for salvation or damnation contrasted sharply with the Catholics' selling of indulgences to "buy a place in heaven."

Woodcut portrait of Swiss religious reformer Ulrich Zwingli, who was also a leader in political affairs in Switzerland.

arrived from Basel in 1536. His preaching ultimately won enough followers to make his church the official religion. From Geneva, the faith spread widely in all directions after the early 1540s.

Calvin was a dour and dogmatic Frenchman of the middle class. Like Luther, he had an unsympathetic father, who let a friend of the family send his son to the University of Paris. At first, Calvin studied theology but later transferred to Orleans, where, at his father's urging, he took up law. He read some humanist writings, talked to Lutherans, experienced a personal conversion, was suspected of heresy by the authorities, and ultimately fled to Basel. There, in 1536, he published the first edition of his *Institutes of the Christian Religion*, a most influential theological work because it transformed the general Lutheran doctrines into a profoundly rational legal system. It also earned Calvin an invitation to Geneva.

There, Calvin's original plan for a city government dominated by the clergy aroused a storm of opposition, forcing him into exile at Strasbourg, where he was associated with other reformers who urged him to take a wife. In 1539, he married Idellette de Bures, a sickly widow with two children. She came back to Geneva with him in 1541, when his party regained power. Henceforth, as Protestant refugees packed the city, Idellette managed Calvin's household, took in friends and refugees, nursed him through frequent headaches, tried unsuccessfully to bear his children, and left him bereft when she died in 1549.

Calvin personally ruled Geneva, exercising his power through influence and republican forms. The town council approved all legislation, including laws governing morality and religion, but it recognized the Bible as supreme law and the *Institutes* as a manual for behavior. Legislative interpretations of these sources were prepared by the "Congregation of the Clergy," reviewed by the Consistory, a committee of the clergy plus twelve lay members, and sent to the town council for final action. The Consistory also apprehended violators of the law, sending its members into households to check every detail of private life. Offenders were reported to secular magistrates for punishment.

Punishments at Geneva were severe, in keeping with the religious fanaticism of the time. Punishable offenses included missing church, laughing during services, wearing bright colors, dancing, playing cards, and swearing. Religious dissent brought much heavier penalties. The consistory frequently banished offenders for blasphemy, mild heresies, adultery, or suspected witchcraft. Magistrates sometimes used torture to obtain confessions and often executed heretics, averaging more than a dozen annually in the 1540s. Michael Servetus (1511–1553), the Spanish theologian-philosopher and refugee from the Catholic Inquisition, was burned for heresy because he had denied the doctrine of the Trinity. The Consistory in this period showed little sexual discrimination, punishing men and women with equal severity.

Calvin's Theology

Although he accepted most of Luther's theological principles, Calvin placed heavier emphasis upon God's unlimited power. For Luther, God's majesty "served to point up the miracle of forgiveness," but "for Calvin it gave rather the assurance of the impregnability of God's purpose."[4] In pursuing this mysterious purpose, God had created the world and human beings in his image. The same divine will had caused Adam and Eve to fall from a state of sinlessness, leaving humans utterly depraved and lost, without God's grace.

Unlike the Catholic Theologians, Calvin did not emphasize Eve's guilt in Adam's fall. Both, in his mind, were guilty and so were men and women equally full of sin. Both were also equal in God's eyes and in the hope of salvation. Thus, in the 1540s, as he sought recruits, Calvin stressed the rights of women to read the Bible and participate in church services, a promise of sexual equality which attracted women to his movement. Very soon, however, he expressed a conviction that, in practical affairs, even in the conduct of church business, women were naturally subordinate to their husbands. Without female patron saints or priestly confessors, they were now expected to seek protection and moral discipline from their spouses.

Calvin's idea of God's omnipotence, carried to its logical conclusion, produced his famous docrine of predestination. Since God is all-powerful, He must also know who are to be saved and who are to be damned eternally. The human purpose, then, is not to win salvation—for this has already been determined—but to honor God. Calvin did not profess to know absolutely who were God's chosen, although he believed that some tests might be partially successful in identifying the elect: a moral life, a public profession of faith, and participation in the two sacraments of Baptism and the Lord's Supper.

Impact of Calvinism Before the Peace of Augsburg

Before 1555, Calvinism was growing but had not yet gained official status except in Geneva and the tiny Kingdom of Navarre, on the French side of the Pyrenees. It was not even recognized as an option by the German princes in the Peace of Augsburg. Among European governing elites, it was generally regarded with suspicion if not contempt.

John Calvin on God's Omniscience and Predestination

This selection from Calvin's most famous work summarizes one of the two most significant points in his theology. The other was justification by faith.

Of the Eternal Election, by Which God Has Predestined Some to Salvation, and Others to Destruction.

The predestination by which God adopts some of the hope of life, and adjudges others to eternal death, no man who would be thought pious ventures simply to deny; but it is greatly cavilled at, especially by those who make prescience its cause. We, indeed, ascribe both prescience and predestination to God; but we say that it is absurd to make the latter subordinate to the former (see chap. xxii. sec. 1). When we attribute prescience to God, we mean that all things always were, and ever continue, under his eye; that to his knowledge there is no past or future, but all things are present, and indeed so present, that it is not merely the idea of them that is before him (as those objects are which we retain in our memory), but that he truly sees and contemplates them as actually under his immediate inspection. This prescience extends to the whole circuit of the world, and to all creatures. By predestination we mean the eternal decree of God, by which he determined with himself whatever he wished to happen with regard to every man. All are not created on equal terms, but some are preordained to eternal life, others to eternal damnation; and, accordingly, as each has been created for one or other of these ends, we say that he has been predestined to life or to death. This God has testified, not only in the case of single individuals; he has also given a specimen of it in the whole posterity of Abraham, to make it plain that the future condition of each nation was entirely at his disposal. . . .

. . . We say, then, that Scripture clearly proves this much, that God by his eternal and immutable counsel determined once for all those whom it was his pleasure one day to admit to salvation, and those whom, on the other hand, it was his pleasure to doom to destruction. We maintain that this counsel, as regards the elect, is founded on his free mercy, without any respect to human worth, while those whom he dooms to destruction are excluded from access to life by a just and blameless, but at the same time incomprehensible judgment. In regard to the elect, we regard calling as the evidence of election, and justification as another symbol of its manifestation, until it is fully accomplished by the attainment of glory. But as the Lord seals his elect by calling and justification, so by excluding the reprobate either from the knowledge of his name or the sanctification of his Spirit, he by these marks in a manner discloses the judgment which awaits them. I will here omit many of the fictions which foolish men have devised to overthrow predestination. There is no need of refuting objections which the moment they are produced abundantly betray their hollowness. I will dwell only on those points which either form the subject of dispute among the learned, or may occasion any difficulty to the simple, or may be employed by impiety as specious pretexts for assailing the justice of God.

From *Institutes of the Christian Religion* in Harry J. Carroll, et al., eds., *The Development of Civilization* (Glenview, IL: Scott, Foresman, 1970), pp. 91–93.

The most promising area for growth was France, Calvin's own homeland. His message attracted many members of the urban middle classes, who had begun to feel alienated from both church and state. Missionaries from Geneva carried Calvin's message to France where the church was organized in a national system of congregations and synods. French Calvinists, or Huguenots as they were called, made up an aggressive minority of discontented nobles and middle-class urban citizens. The new movement also enlisted a large proportion of women, drawn by opportunities for direct participation in the services. Many joined reading groups, where they discussed the Bible and theological issues. Early Calvinist women worked diligently for the cause, not only converting their husbands and families but also founding religious schools, nursing the sick, and aiding the poor.

French aristocratic women also promoted the growth of Calvinism. As the Renaissance moved north, many young French women were educated in the new humanism and began to question the traditional Catholic dogma. Margaret of Angouleme, Queen of Navarre (1492–1549) and sister of the French king, often petitioned her brother on behalf of Protestants accused of heresy and kept reformers at her court, where Calvin was sheltered at one time. Her daughter, Jeanne d'Albret (1528–1572), who became queen in 1549, established Calvinism in Navarre, having converted her second husband, the French aristocrat, Antone de Bourbon. Because Calvinism had enlisted many French dissident nobles who were intent upon resisting royal power, the Bourbon leader hoped to gain their support and use it later to further his family's claim to the French throne. Jeanne, however, was dedicated to Calvinist principles, raising money and enlisting recruits among her contempories. She was a powerful member of the aristocratic Huguenot clique, headed by Admiral de Coligny and the Bourbon Prince, Louis of Condé.

Calvinism made gains elsewhere but did not win political power. In Italy, the Duchess of Ferrara copied the Navarre church service for her private chapel and harbored Calvinist refugees; and Zofia Olesnicka, wife of a Polish noble, endowed a local Calvinist church. Strasbourg, in the 1530s, was a free center for Protestant reformers such as Matthew Zell and his wife,

Marguerite of Navarre, a supporter of Protestantism, was the author of the *Heptameron,* a collection of tales modeled on Boccaccio's *Decameron.*

Katherine, who befriended many Calvinist preachers, including Martin Bucer, the missionary to England during the reign of Edward VI. In the same period, John Knox spread the Calvinist message in Scotland. Such efforts, however, were most significant in preparing for later aggressive action.

Although Calvin himself was inclined to respect secular authority and to oppose revolt from below, his political support naturally oriented him against established governments. Calvin's solution to this problem, like Luther's, was a compromise. He advised obedience to magistrates but argued that lower officials were justified in resisting tyrants who commanded violation of God's laws. He also insisted that the church, under its elected ministers and elders, was superior to bishops or kings in religious matters. Although this declaration defined "tyranny" almost exclusively in religious terms, Calvin's theoretical system strongly implied the necessity for representative government, an idea which would later challenge absolute monarchy.

Anabaptism and the Protestant Sects

Even more extreme than Calvinism were many divergent Protestant splinter groups, each pursuing its own "inner lights." Some saw visions of the world's end; some advocated a Christian brotherhood of shared wealth; some opposed social distinctions and economic inequalities; some, like the Anabaptists, repudiated infant baptism as a violation of Christian responsibility; and some denied the need for any clergy. Most of the sects emphasized biblical literalism and direct emotional communion between the individual and God. The majority of them were indifferent or antagonistic to secular government; many favored pacifism and substitution of the church for the state.

Women were prominent among the sects. They helped found religious communities, wrote hymns and religious tracts, debated theology, and publicly challenged the authorities. Some preached and delivered prophecies, although such activities were soon suppressed by male ministers. More women that men endured torture and suffered martyrdom. Their leadership opportunities and relative freedoms in marriage, compared to women of other religions, were bought at a high price in hardship and danger.

Persecution of the sects arose largely from their radical ideas, but Catholics and other Protestants usually cited two revolutionary actions. Some radical preachers took part in the German Peasants' Revolt of the 1520's and shared in the savage punishments that followed. In 1534, a Catholic army beseiged Munster, a German city near the northern Netherlands, where thousands of recently arrived Anabaptist extremists had seized control and expelled dissenters. Facing desperate circumstances, the new regime confiscated property, institutionalized polygamy, and laid plans to convert the world. John of Leyden, a former Dutch tailor who claimed divine authority, headed a terroristic regime during the final weeks before the city fell. Many of its defenders suffered horrible torture and execution.

The army that recaptured the city of Münster executed the Anabaptist leaders and displayed their bodies as a warning to others. The siege of Münster touched off a widespread persecution of Anabaptists.

Two Edicts Issued by the Twelve Elders of Münster

In mid-1534 the Anabaptist regime in the German city of Münster reached its nadir of extremism. This is partially indicated by these decrees relating to private life and public behavior.

Although all of us in this holy church of Muenster, in whose hearts the law and the will of God are inscribed by the finger of God . . . should readily fulfill them, we, twelve elders of the nation, shall nevertheless summarize them briefly in a list in order that the new state may be protected so that each one may see what to do and what not to do. . . .

The Scripture directs that those who are disobedient and unrepentant regarding several sins shall be punished with the sword:

1. Whoever curses God and his holy Name or his Word shall be killed (Lev. 24).

2. No one shall curse governmental authority (Ex. 22, Deut. 17), on pain of death.

3. Whoever does not honor or obey his parents (Ex. 20, 21) shall die.

4. Servants must obey their masters, and masters must be fair to their servants (Eph. 6).

5. Both parties who commit adultery shall die (Ex. 20, Lev. 20, Matt. 5).

6. Those who commit rape, incest, and other unclean sexual sins should die (Ex. 22, Lev. 20). . . .

7. Avarice is the root of all evil (I Tim. 6).

8. Concerning robbery, you shall not steal (Ex. 20, Deut. 27): Cursed be he who narrows his neighbor's boundary.

9. Concerning fraud and overcharging (I Thess. 4): The Lord will judge this.

10. Concerning lying and defamation (Wisd. [of Sol.] 1): A lying mouth destroys a soul.

11. Concerning disgraceful speech and idle words (Matt. 12): Men must account for every idle word they speak, on the Day of Judgment.

12. Concerning strife, disputes, anger, and envy (Gal. 5, I John 4): Whoever hates his brother is a murderer.

13. Concerning slanderer, murmuring, and insurrection among God's people (Lev. 19): There shall be no slanderer or flatterer among the people.

. . . Whoever disobeys these commandments and does not truly repent, shall be rooted out of the people of God, with ban and sword, through the divinely ordained governmental authority.

The elders of the congregation of Christ in the holy city of Muenster, called and ordained by the grace of the most high and almighty God, desire that the following duties and articles be faithfully and firmly observed by every Israelite and member of the house of God.

1. What the Holy Scriptures command or prohibit is to be kept by every Israelite at the pain of punishment.

2. Everybody is to be industrious in his vocation and fear God and his ordained government. Government authority does not carry the sword in vain, but it is the avenger of evildoers.

6. Every day from seven to nine o'clock in the morning and from two to four o'clock in the afternoon, six elders are to sit in the market at the appointed place and settle all differences with their decisions.

9. In order to keep the proper order concerning the administration of good, the food-masters are every day to prepare dishes of the kind as was hitherto customary for the brothers and sisters. These are to sit modestly and moderately at separate tables. They must not demand anything apart from what is served to them. . . .

30. A baptized Christian is not to converse with any arriving person or pagan stranger and is not to eat with him, lest there arise the suspicion of treacherous consultation. . . .

Source: Lowell H. Zuck, ed., *Christian and Revolution* (Philadelphia: Temple University Press, 1975), pp. 95–97.

Among the most damaging charges against the Munster rebels were their reputed sexual excesses and the dominant role played by women in this immorality. Such charges were mostly distortions. The initiation of polygamy in the city, while justified by references to the Old Testament, was a response to problems arising from a shortage of men, many of whom had fled the city. Many other men were killed or injured in the fighting. The leaders of the city required women to marry, so that they could be protected and controlled by husbands. Most Anabaptist women accepted the requirement as a religious duty. Although some women paraded through the streets, shouting religious slogans, the majority prepared meals, did manual labor on the defenses, fought beside the men as the city fell, and died by the hundreds, in the fighting or at the stake. Many of the original Munster women, however, fiercely resisted forced marriage, choosing instead imprisonment or execution.

For more than a century, memories of Munster plagued the radical Protestant sects. They were almost immediately driven underground throughout Europe. Their persecution continued, long after they had abandoned violence. In time, they dispersed over the continent and to the New World, as Mennonites, Quakers, and Baptists, to name only a few denominations. For obvious reasons, the voices of the radicals were among the first raised for religious liberty. Their experiences with established governments made them even more suspicious of authority than were Calvinists. In both the Netherlands and in England, they participated in political revolutions and helped frame the earliest written demands for constitutional government, representative institutions, and civil liberties.

The Catholic Reformation

The era of the Protestant Reformation was also a time of rejuvenation for the Roman Catholic Church. This revival was largely caused by the same conditions which evoked Protestantism. Many sincere and devout Catholics had recognized a need for reform and had begun purifying their church before Luther acted at Wittenberg. There can be no doubt, however, that the success of Protestant reformers, plus the political weakness of Catholicism in the early sixteenth century, promoted a Catholic Counter-Reformation, demonstrated in stubborn resistance to and militant attacks on Protestantism. Both internal reform and external militancy gave Catholicism new life, securing its place as a major religion in the modern world.

Catholic Reform and Rededication

Even before the 1520s, almost every variety of reform opinion had been raised within the Catholic Church. Erasmus, Sir Thomas More, and other Christian humanists provided an impetus for Luther but refused to follow him out of the Church. In a category of his own was Savonarola (1452–1498), a Dominican friar, ardent puritan, and mystic, who ruled Florence during the last four years before his death. This "Catholic Calvin" consistently invoked the wrath of God upon worldly living and sinful luxuries, criticizing the pope and the clergy in terms more caustic than Luther's. At the other extreme, on the side of the establishment, was Cardinal Ximenes (1437–1517) in Spain, who disciplined the clergy, encouraged biblical studies, and instilled a new spirit of dedication into the monastic orders.

After the Protestant revolt began, the primary Catholic reformer was Pope Paul III (1534–1549). Coming into office at a time when the Church appeared ready to collapse, Paul struggled to overcome the legacy of his Renaissance predecessors and restore integrity to the papacy. Realizing that issues raised by the Protestants would have to be resolved and errors corrected, he attacked the indifference, the corruption, and the vested interests of the clerical organization. In pursuing these reforms, he appointed a commission which reported the need for correcting such abuses as the worldliness of bishops, the traffic in benefices (church appointments with guaranteed incomes), and the transgressions of some cardinals. This beginning led Paul to advocate calling a church council, an idea which he continued to press against stubborn opposition for more than ten years.

When Paul died in 1549, he had already set the Church a new direction, although his proposed church council had only begun its deliberations. Perhaps his greatest contribution was his appointment of worthy members to the College of Cardinals, filling that body, among whose duties was the election of the pope, with eminent scholars and devout stewards of the Church. His labors in this area resulted in the cardinals' electing a succession of later popes who were prepared intellectually and spiritually to continue the process of regeneration.

Paul's reform initiatives received support from the great church council, held in three sessions between 1545 and 1563 in the north Italian city of Trent. While devoting much attention to the external struggle against Protestantism, the council also sought to eliminate internal church abuses by ordering changes in church discipline and administration. It strictly forbade absenteeism, false indulgences, selling church offices, and secular pursuits by the clergy. Bishops were ordered to supervise their clergies—both priests and monks—and to appoint competent men to church positions. Seminaries were to be established for the education of priests. The clergy, in turn, were enjoined to set examples and preach frequently to their flocks.

The spirit of reform was reflected in a number of new Catholic clerical orders, which sprang up in the early sixteenth century. The Theatines were a body of devoted priests who worked to regenerate faith among the clergy. The Capuchins, a revived Franciscan brotherhood, became known for preaching and ministering to the poor and the sick. The most significant of the new orders was the Society of Jesus, commonly known as the Jesuits. It was founded by Ignatius Loyola (1491–1556), a Spanish nobleman and former soldier. While recovering from battle wounds in 1521, he experienced a religious vision similar to the one that transformed Luther. Loyola then became a wandering pilgrim, a self-styled religious teacher, and the author of *Spiritual Exercises*, a work of great psychological insight and Christian inspiration. In 1524, he launched his Society at the University of Paris; six years later, Pope Paul gave it official authorization.

Societies of women also furthered the work of reform. Some of these, such as the Sisters of the Common Life and the Beguines, continued their work of charity and nursing among the poor from the medieval period into the sixteenth century. The Ursuline order of teaching nuns, founded by St. Angela Merci (1473–1540), educated

St. Teresa of Avila, mystic and visionary. Her devotional works and her personal example inspired the spiritual rebirth of Spanish Catholicism.

girls in morality and the faith. Even more renowned were the Carmelites, founded by St. Teresa of Avila (1515–1582), whose determination and selfless devotion were legendary in her own time. She inspired mystical faith and reforming zeal in written works, such as *Interior Castle* and *The Ladder of Perfection*. Her nuns were models of Christian charity and compassion who helped restore the pride and integrity of the Church.

The War Against Protestantism

Along with the Catholic reform movement came a determined Catholic campaign against Protestantism. While strengthening itself with a new discipline, the Church launched a many-faceted crusade in Protestant areas, using political influence, allied secular military forces, and hundreds of committed missionaries. In Catholic countries, where the war was defensive, the main weapon was the Inquisition, a medieval church court, given new significance in Spain after 1478, under Cardinal Ximenes. It was used then primarily to eliminate heretic Moors and Jews, and in the sixteenth century it was turned against Protestants.

A second and most effective weapon was the Jesuit order. Organized along military lines, with Loyola as general and the pope as the commander-in-chief, its members were an army of soldiers, sworn to follow orders and defend the faith. As preachers, teachers, confessors, organizers, diplomats, and spies, they took the field everywhere, founding schools and colleges, serving as missionaries on every continent, and working their way into government wherever possible. Their efforts were probably most responsible for the decided check which Protestantism received after the 1560s. They zealously defended Catholicism in France and may be accurately credited with saving Poland and south Germany for the church. Jesuit missions overseas also helped Spain and Portugal develop their empires.

Jesuits played prominent roles at the Council of Trent in imposing uniformity and discipline upon the church as it faced the Protestant challenge. Rejecting all compromise, the council retained the basic tenets of Catholic doctrine, including the necessity of good works as well as faith for salvation, the authority of church law and traditions, the sanctity of all seven sacraments, the use of only Latin in the mass, and the spiritual value of indulgences, pilgrimages, veneration of saints, and the cult of the Virgin. The council also strengthened the power of the papacy. Led by Jesuit theologians, the pope's party defeated all attempts to place supreme church authority in any general council. When the final session voted that none of its decrees were valid without papal approval, the church became more than ever an absolute monarchy.

The full significance of Trent became evident after the 1560s, when the Catholic reaction to Protestantism acquired new vigor and militancy. Having steeled itself within, the church and its shock troops, the Jesuits, went to war against Protestants and other heretics. The new crusade was both open and secret. In Spain, Italy, and the Netherlands, the Inquisition, more than ever before, became the dreaded scourge of Protestants. Jesuit universities trained scholars and missionaries, who served as both priests and organizers in Protestant countries, such as England. Many died as martyrs, condemned by Protestant tribunals; others suffered similar fates, meted out by pagan authorities in America or Asia.

Whatever the price of security, the church paid in blood and treasure. Consequently, Protestantism made no more significant gains in Catholic lands after Trent. Indeed the geographic scope of Catholicism expanded, particularly overseas.

In this uncompromising and bloody conflict of faiths, women were both unappreciated heroines and victims. Out of 41 heretics executed in Spain during 1559, 26 were women. A typical earlier example, in 1534, was Maria Cazalla, accused of laughing at Aristotle, scoffing at scholasticism, reading Erasmus, and being familiar with Luther's ideas. Other Catholic women who defended the faith faced frustrating problems. In Protestant lands, some dispossessed nuns, with no place to go, were the most stubborn holdouts against secularizing the convents. Many of them wrote and preached against Luther, and others tried to organize against the Protestants. An order of Jesuit nuns beccame quite active, though it never received papal approval. Such efforts, moreover, alarmed church leaders. The Council of Trent reaffirmed the prohibition against women preachers; and after Trent, the church forced the Ursulines into convents. The Catholic prejudice against the female orders is illustrated best by the ordeal of St. Teresa of Avila, who struggled for years and was even brought before the Inquisition before her Carmelites were approved.

Conclusion

By the 1570s the Catholic Church had checked the spread of Protestantism. The first phase of the Reformation was over; it had not eliminated Catholicism, but it had nearly destroyed the medieval world. The second phase, coinciding with the religious wars of the seventeenth century, confirmed the religious division of Christendom and the diversity of Protestantism. It also exerted a major force in completing the transition to modern times.

No sixteenth-century religious reformers, either Catholic or Protestant, had envisioned this result. Protestant reformers, particularly, were disturbed by the worldliness, pleasure-seeking, commercialism, and sophisticated complexity which they saw increasing around them. They sought salvation, not happiness or progress in this world, and expected to approach heaven through early simplicity and mystical faith. Although rejecting the authority of priests, bishops, and popes as restrictions on Christian liberty, they still believed in Christian brotherhood. The individualism of the early Reformation was therefore narrowly restricted within the religious boundaries of dogmatic systems.

Another early promise of the Reformation remained unfulfilled in this era and for a long time to come. Encouraged by a few humanists like Erasmus, many European women had seen in the reformers' message of Christian equality a hope for new recognition and status. Many were moved by religious fervor, suffering hardships and even martyrdom for the Protestant cause. They were to be disappointed. Having lost the protection of the cloister and having been released from the discipline of the confessional, they were reconsigned by male reformers, including both Luther and Calvin, to the overlordship of their husbands, who would reign as patriarchs and interpreters of the Bible in the new Protestant family. Women's hopes for a new freedom had to wait for the Reformation's effects upon government and education.

These effects were recognized early in education: The emphasis begun by the humanists was taken up by both Protestants and Catholics, who wanted their youth of both sexes trained to read the Bible and follow its teachings. As part of their crusade to reconvert Protestants, the Jesuits, in particular, developed a school system so superior and so attractive that many Protestants attended. Both Luther and Calvin worked to establish schools, and the former championed an early version of compulsory public education.

In many other ways, the Reformation helped create the modern world. By breaking the religious monopoly of European Catholicism, it encouraged the growth of national monarchies. Lutheranism and Anglicanism, as state churches, contributed quite positively to this end. Later, the puritan values and "work ethic" of Calvinism helped justify the activities of the middle classes, at the same time promoting capitalism. Calvinism and the more radical Protestant sects later provided a strong impetus to the decline of absolutism, in Europe's second stage of political transition to modernity. The ideal of religious liberty in separation of church and state, theories concerning natural rights, and the actual institutions of representative government all had some origins in the radical sects.

Suggestions For Reading

Steven B. Ozment, *The Age of Reform* (Yale Univ., 1980) is excellent for social and political, as well as religious, topics. More recent but less comprehensive works include J. H. d'Aubigne, *History of the Reformation of the Sixteenth Century* (Baker Books, 1986); E. W. Spitz, *The Protestant Reformation* (Harper and Row, 1985); E. H. Harbison, *The Age of the Reformation* (Greenwood Press, 1982); and Peter James Klassen, *Europe in the Reformation* (Prentice-Hall, 1979). Among older but still sound general treatments are Hans J. Hillerbrand, *The World of the Reformation* (Scribner's, 1973); J. Russell Major, *The Age of the Renaissance and Reformation* (Lippincott, 1970); Harold Grimm, *The Reformation Era* (Macmillan, 1968); George L. Mosse, *The Reformation* (Holt, Rinehart, and Winston, 1966); and the classic, Roland H. Bainton, *The Reformation of the Sixteenth Century*, rev. ed. (Boston, Beacon Press, 1985).

Criticism of the church by northern humanists is ably described in J. Huizinga, *Erasmus and the Age of the Reformation* (Princeton Univ., 1984) and in Arthur G. Dickens, *The Age of Humanism and the Reformation* (Prentice-Hall, 1972). For social conditions in the Reformation era, see R. Po-chin Hsia, *The German People and the Reformation* (Cornell Univ., 1988) and R. W. Scribner, *Popular Culture and Popular Movements in Reformation Germany* (Hambledon Press, 1987). A penetrating study of the urban environment is provided in Steven Ozment, *The Reformation in the Cities* (Yale Univ., 1975). *When Fathers Ruled* (Harvard Univ., 1983), by the same author, reveals the patriarchial nature of the Reformation family. The sad plight of women in the era is treated in Susan Cahn, *The Industry of Devotion* (Colgate Univ., 1987); Mary E. Wiesner, *Working Women in Renaissance Germany* (Rutgers Univ., 1986); and Retha M. Warnicke, *Women of the English Renaissance and Reformation* (Greenwood Press, 1983). For the most inclusive treatment of this subject, see Roland Bainton's three volumes, *Women of the Reformation* (Augsburg Press, 1971–1977).

The old standard biography by Roland H. Bainton, *Here I Stand: A Life of Martin Luther* (Abingdon-Cokesbury Press, 1950) is still moving and interesting. A sound recent biography of Luther, based on newly-discovered documents and promising to be definitive, is M. Brecht, *Martin Luther* (Fortress, 1985). Subsequent years have brought a spate of new biographies, including Bernard Lohse, *Martin Luther* (Clark T. and T., 1987); J. M. Kittelson, *Luther, the Reformer* (Augsburg Press, 1986); and W. von Loewnich, *Martin Luther* (Augsburg Press, 1986). For an interesting contrast, compare E. Erikson, *Young Man Luther* (Norton, 1962) and Mark U. Edwards, *Luther's Last Battles* (Cornell Univ., 1983), which presents a portrait of an aging, prejudiced, and politically motivated reformer. Other noteworthy special works are Hubert Kirchner, ed., *Luther and the Peasants' War* (Fortress Press, 1972); and

J. C. Thompson, *The Political Thought of Martin Luther* (Barnes and Noble, 1984).

William J. Bouwsma, *John Calvin* (Oxford Univ., 1988) is a fresh and scholarly portrayal of Calvin's human side, emphasizing his inner conflict against the humanistic trend of his time. Another competent study, based upon primary materials, is George R. Potter and M. Greengrass, *John Calvin* (St. Martins, 1983). See also T. H. L. Parker, *John Calvin* (Lion, 1987); A. Ganoczy, *The Young Calvin* (Westminster Press, 1987); and F. Wendel, *Calvin* (Labrynth Press, 1987). Rewarding special studies of Calvinism include M. Greengrass, *The French Reformation* (Blackwell, 1987); D. Martin, *John Knox, the Scottish Reformer* (Moody Press, 1982); J. D. Douglas, *Women, Freedom, and Calvin* (Westminster Press, 1985); and Willem Balke, *Calvin and the Anabaptist Radicals* (Eerdmans, 1981). U. Gabler, *Huldriych Zwingli* (Augsburg Fortress, 1986) is a recent biography of the Swiss reformer.

Two solid and informative accounts of English society and the Anglican Reformation, are J. J. Scarisbrick, *The Reformation and the English People* (Blackwell, 1984) and Robert S. Feuerlicht, *The Life and World of Henry VIII* (Crowell-Collier, 1970). See also Peter Lake and Maria Dowling, *Protestantism and the National Church in the Sixteenth Century* (Croom Helm, 1987). G. J. R. Parry, *A Protestant Vision* (Cambridge Univ., 1987) is a thoughtful interpretation of William Harrison's Puritan theology. The Henrican economic and social revolution is described effectively in S. M. Harrison, *Henry VIII and the Dissolution of the Monasteries* (Macmillan, 1985). For the roles played by Tudor women, see Margaret P. Hannay, *Silent but for the Word* (Kent State Univ., 1985) and Carolly Erickson, *Bloody Mary* (Doubleday, 1978). Paul Hogrife has also produced two volumes on the subject: *Tudor Women* (Iowa State Univ., 1975) and *Women of Action in Tudor England* (Iowa State Univ., 1977).

For the "left wing" of Protestantism see Peter C. Clasen, *Anabaptism, a Social History* (Cornell Univ., 1972); George H. Williams, *The Radical Revolution* (Westminster Press, 1962); and E. Belfort Bax, *The Rise and Fall of Anabaptism* (A. Kelley, 1970). A good more recent treatment of Anabaptism is in a collection of essays edited by James M. Stayer: *The Anabaptists and Thomas Munzer* (Kendall Hunt, 1980).

Nicholas S. Davidson, *The Counter-Reformation* (Blackwell, 1987) and M. A. Mullet, *The Counter-Reformation* (Methuen, 1984) are among the latest adequate works on the Catholic revival. G. Dickens, *The Counter-Reformation* (Harcourt Brace Jovanovich, 1969) is brief but richly illustrated. A sympathetic Catholic account is in P. Janelle, *The Catholic Reformation* (Bruce Pub. Co., 1963). Also worth noting is J. Brodrick, *The Origin of the Jesuits* (Greenwood, 1976).

Notes

1. Luther probably never actually posted his theses on the church door at Wittenberg. See H. G. Halle, *Luther* (New York: Doubleday, 1980), pp. 177–178.
2. Quoted in R. Bainton, *Here I Stand: A Life of Martin Luther* (New York: Abingdon-Cokesbury Press, 1950), p. 54.
3. Quoted in Harold Grimm, *The Reformation Era* (New York: Macmillan, 1968), p. 175.
4. Quoted in Roland H. Bainton, *The Reformation of the Sixteenth Century* (Boston: Beacon Press, 1952), p. 114.

Chapter 14

The Transition to Modern Times in Asia, 1300–1650

During the three-and-a-half centuries after 1300, when western Europe was turning toward overseas expansion and empire building, Asian centers of power and wealth were shifting inland toward the steppes and the Muslim lands of the south. Ming China, after a brief experiment with a maritime policy, turned in upon itself and was already in decline by the sixteenth century. Japan and Southeast Asia, meanwhile, were weakened by internal conflicts. On the other hand, Central Asia spawned an Islamic revival which spread from the Middle East to Malaysia. By the sixteenth century, it had produced the great Ottoman and Mughul empires in the Middle East and India.

Europeans were active in Asia during this period but exerted relatively little influence. Awed by the wealth and power of Asian empires, they were generally held in disdain by most Asians, who felt themselves and their cultures superior. Akbar, the great Mughul emperor, referred to the "savage Portuguese"[1] at his court; Cambodian and Burmese kings used Portuguese slaves in their armies; Ottoman sultans regarded European envoys as supplicants; and Ming emperors considered European diplomats as tribute-bearers, subjecting them to humiliating delays or even imprisonment.

Asian superiority over Europe, so obvious in the fourteenth century, was definitely waning three hundred years later, amid a global economic revolution. While rising Muslim states disrupted intercontinental land trade, advancing European technology encouraged maritime commerce. This reorientation of trade routes, a significant portent for the future, was largely ignored by Asians, who were concerned with building their own empires. As the Dutch and Portuguese steadily exploited their growing technical and commercial advantages, most of Asia experienced serious difficulties: Japan cut itself off from the outside world; the weakening Ming dynasty fell before the Manchu invasion; Southeast Asia continued its petty conflicts in the shadow of Dutch imperialism; and the great Muslim empires languished in their excesses of riches and power.

New Muslim Powers in Middle Eurasia

The fall of Constantinople to the Ottoman Turks in 1453 confronted Europe with a dangerous new threat in the Middle East, but the Ottomans also symbolized a new Muslim world, emerging between the eastern Mediterranean and Indonesia. Culturally, this world was centered in Persia, under the Shi'ite Safavid dynasty. Safavid Persia, however, was overshadowed by the dazzling wealth of the Mughul empire in India and by the military might of the Ottoman empire, which was far more formidable than any country in Europe at the time.

Within the expansive Muslim world were a multitude of other struggling states, held together by the Islamic faith, common steppe traditions, and a set of evolving values, among them a pervading emphasis upon the special importance, if not the literal superiority, of males. To be sure, Muhammad's original teaching emphasized humane treatment of women. The idea found expression in later Islamic law, which granted to women certain rights, such as owning property and legally divorcing cruel husbands. But as time passed, these principles were largely ignored. Muslim women were subjected to an obsessive concern for their chastity and were restricted behind veils and harem walls. They became victims of the steady transition from tribal solidarity to the ruthless conflicts of a warrior society.

Background: The Steppe Frontier

After the fourteenth century, the disintegrating Mongol empire left the steppe in chaos but supporting many states, which dissolved and reformed in new combinations of nomad peoples. The old Khanates survived for a while in Russia and Central Asia. War was almost continuous along the steppe frontier, from the Crimea to China. Such were the tumultuous conditions which generated rising Muslim empires.

The continuing steppe influence was well illustrated by the quick rise and collapse of the Timurid empire at the close of the fourteenth century. Timur the Lame, sometimes called Tamerlane, a Turk claiming descent from Genghis Kahn, rose to power during the 1370s as emir under the Mongol khan of Central Asia. In his quest to restore the original Mongol Empire, Timur led whirlwind campaigns through the western steppe, the Crimea, Persia, and parts of the Levant. He crushed Ottoman resistance, ravaged northern India beyond anything yet experienced there, and was planning to invade Ming China when he died in 1405. But Timur's realm, like earlier Mongol regimes ruled from horseback, soon divided into contending states.

For more than a century after Timur resurrected the spirit of Ghengis Khan, a dream of universal empire lingered in the minds of his descendants, real or imagined, among the many Turko-Mongol rulers in northern Persia and Transoxania (present-day Russian Turkestan). The Ottoman sultans, who had established their hegemony in Asia Minor before Timur's time and only barely survived his onslaught, were not direct heirs of his timur traditions but they had been involved in the wars on their frontiers in the Crimea and eastern Asia Minor. Another danger spot was northern India, where multiplying Muslim regimes sprouted after Timur's horde had plundered Delhi in 1398 and destroyed the last semblance of political unity.

The steppe frontier changed drastically after the latter fifteenth century. As populations settled around cities, firearms took away the advantages of nomad cavalry. The Uzbegs, who seized most of Transoxania in this era were among the last nomad steppe-conquerors. But long after the Uzbeg conquest, old nomadic family ambitions continued to shape policies in the Muslim Middle-East.

Rise of the Ottoman Empire

Beginning as petty vassals of the Seljuk sultans in the thirteenth century, early Ottoman rulers won independence in the chaos of the Mongol wars. They had united Muslim Asia Minor and started to move into southeastern Europe when Timur's army stopped their expansion and forced a half-century of internal restoration. Then, after 1451, two able sultans resumed the Ottoman conquests. The first, Mehmet II (1451–1481), took Constantinople, Roumania, and the Crimea. The second, Selim I (1512–1520) annexed Kurdistan, northern Mesopotamia, Syria, and Egypt. After winning Egypt, Selim moved the moribund Caliphate to Constantinople. By the end of his reign, the Ottoman domain touched three continents, controlling coasts of the Black Sea, the eastern Mediterranean, and the southern Red Sea area beyond the sacred Arab cities.

Ottoman power peaked during the reign of Selim's only son, Suleiman (1520–1566). Upon his accession at the age of twenty-six, Suleiman was described as tall and thin, with a sparse beard and a neck "too long."[2] Despite this unimposing appearance, he soon became the most feared ruler among a generation of European monarchs that included Henry VIII of England, Francis I of France, and Charles V of Spain.

Suleiman waged successful wars on all his borders. He was most triumphant in Europe at the expense of the Habsburgs. After taking Belgrade (1521) and Rhodes from the Knights of St. John (1523), he invaded Hungary in 1526 with 100,000 men and 300 artillery pieces. At Mohacs, the Turks won an overwhelming victory, slaughtering thousands of Hungarian nobles and the Hungarian king. Hungary was then integrated

This 16th-century European equestrian portrait by the Flemish artist Hans Eworth captures the majesty and severity of the Ottoman rulers.

for weeks. Foreign ambassadors, such as those from Francis I after 1536, were required to recognize the sultan's exalted position. Even in his own time, he was known as "Suleiman the Magnificent."

The Empire Under Suleiman

In Suleiman's time, the empire was a peculiar blend of tribalism, feudalism, and Oriental absolutism. Like steppe tribes earlier, it was still supported primarily by plunder. Conquered lands were given as fiefs to the governing class of warriors. Above this feudal base was the sultan's central administration, copied from the Byzantine Empire after 1453. Its main ministries and special military force, filled with Suleiman's favorites and slaves, were completely at his command.

Political competition in this system consisted largely of struggles to gain the sultan's ear and shape his policies. Ministers and religious leaders were constantly conspiring and maneuvering

into the Ottoman Empire. Allied with France after 1536, Suleiman continued to threaten Habsburg interests in Europe and in the Mediterranean. Meanwhile, his forces took lower Mesopotamia from Persia, thus acquiring access to the Persian Gulf. From there and from the lower Red Sea, the Ottomans whittled away at Portuguese positions along the south Arabian coast and in the Indian Ocean (see map at right).

Suleiman's life was luxurious and his rule was absolute. A son and grandson who rebelled against him were executed. He moved amid pomp and splendor exceeding that of Louis XIV's France. An army of servants awakened, bathed, dressed, and entertained him. At meals, each course was served on dishes of silver, gold, and fine porcelain, while a physician stood by, ready to minister instantly against poisoning. In the hours between waking and sleeping, Suleiman met with advisors and petitioners, read, or listened to music, when he was not in the field. For amusement, he watched wrestling matches, listened to court jesters, and attended banquets, which sometimes were part of festivities lasting

OTTOMAN EMPIRE
1566

- Ottoman Empire, 1359
- Ottoman Empire, 1566

0   500
MILES

for power, but some women of the harem also competed for influence. At first the sultan's mother dominated the government, and after her death, Suleiman's favorite wife, Roxelana, occupied this position of power. Often listening from behind a curtain while he discussed state matters, Roxelana advised the sultan on all state matters. Her primary goal was succession to the throne for her son. To this end, she influenced Suleiman to execute his chief minister, a life-long friend, and then the heir-apparent, another of Suleiman's sons.

Suleiman governed the mightiest state of his day. Stretching from Poland to the Yemen and from Persia to Tripoli, it comprised twenty-one provinces and even more nationalities. Economically it was nearly self-sufficient, with expanding production and flourishing trade. The empire produced annual revenues of 10,000 ducats (approximately $80,000,000), an amount larger than that available to any contemporary European monarch. With such incomes, Suleiman maintained a standing army of 70,000 and a navy of 300 ships. He could muster more than 200,000 additional troops for a campaign.

This sprawling realm was largely governed locally by Turkish fief-holders, who were expected to bring cavalry contingents for the sultan's annual campaigns. At other times they lived on their lands (*timars*) and administered local affairs, collecting taxes and keeping order. Unlike earlier European feudal lords, they were not closely attached to their localities because they were often away in distant wars. Governors (*beys*) of provinces (*sanjaks*) comprised a high nobility but came from the same military aristocracy. The whole governing class was heavily dependent upon the sultan.

The Ottoman religious establishment, as in the other Muslim lands, was an integral part of government. A corps of learned religious scholars, the *ulema*, represented the sultan as provincial judges (*kadis*), dispensers of charities, and ministers of education. The Grand Mufti was chief religious and legal advisor to the sultan, but as Caliph, the sultan claimed religious authority over all Muslims. Non-Muslims were regarded as inferior but granted religious toleration in agreements with their religious leaders, who were responsible for the civil obedience of their groups.

By Suleiman's reign, the sultan's central bureaucracy had usurped the political power of the nobles over their *timars*. The bureaucracy functioned under a *vizier*, or chief minister, with separate agencies, each headed by an official. These met regularly as the sultan's council (*divan*) to advise the ruler. Most of the bureaucrats were slaves, recruited from subject nationalities and trained to serve in the harem, household, and military. The famed Turkish infantry (*janissaries*), which was the nucleus of the standing army, was an elite slave force and served as the main support of Ottoman absolutism against the nobles.

Society in this despotic system was rigidly stratified but afforded some freedom within its specified legal guidelines. The ruling class of Ottoman soldiers and administrators enjoyed wealth and privilege in varying degrees, but members of this elite were subject to strict observance of law. Aristocratic Muslim women, for example, while guaranteed legal rights, were accorded dignity and status only in their prescribed roles as secluded mothers and home managers. In some respects, members of the subject classes, considered primarily as economic producers and traders, were freer than the Ottomans. They lived under their own laws and religions, pursuing their private interests inside limits imposed by Islamic law and Ottoman economic needs. Some subjects lived better than others. Non-Muslim women were generally less restricted than those of the ruling class, if they could escape slave markets and harems, which often claimed new war captives.

Rising Ottoman power brought a vigorous cultural awakening, most evident in architecture. Mehmet II rebuilt his decaying capital, from sewers to palaces. His monumental Faith Mosque and great Seraglio Palace, with its fortress-walls, fountains, and courtyards, were models of the new Byzantine-Ottoman style. Suleiman surpassed the Seraglio's splendor with *Suleimanye*, his own mosque and mausoleum. These were but three architectural wonders among thousands scattered throughout the Empire. In addition, the period saw a great outpouring of Turkish learning and poetry, mostly following Persian traditions, but reflecting a new productive spirit.

Despite its apparent strength, the Ottoman system demonstrated obvious flaws. Continued

Front view of Suleimanye, the magnificent mosque and mausoleum of Suleiman the Magnificent.

conquests produced serious communication problems; but when conquests lagged, both the nobles and the *janissaries* became rebellious. Religious contention, intensified by Shi'ite Persia, which challenged the Sunni orthodoxy of the sultans, further split the empire. Finally, as they were corrupted by power, the sultans became increasingly cruel, not only torturing and slaughtering their enemies but also their own servants and relatives. Indeed, Selim's terrible punishments generated a contemporary curse: "may you become the vizier of Sultan Selim."[3]

Ottoman Decline

After Suleiman's reign, slow but steady decay permeated the empire. Cheap silver from the New World and reckless extravagance led to rising inflation, rebellions, and military mutinies which often paralyzed the government. Favored concubines, wives, and mothers manipulated irresponsible rulers, who sought the sensory pleasures of the harem at the expense of public affairs. Among the nine who followed Suleiman before 1648, only Murad III (1623–1640) was competent, and he was a cruel tyrant. One was known as "the sot"; another was an opium addict; a third killed nineteen of his brothers at his inaugural reception; and still another was a profligate who wore diamonds in his beard and

had 280 concubines drowned in the Bosporus. Such antics of the sutlans help explain Ottoman losses to the Russians and Habsburgs in Europe, stalemated wars with Persia, and the fall of Ottoman supremacy in the Red Sea.

With Suleiman's death, the Ottoman Empire passed its zenith, but it had made a significant impression on history. By dominating overland trade with Asia, it contributed to European maritime expansion. The sultans prevented Portuguese domination of the Indian Ocean, thus inadvertently aiding the Dutch and English in the East while humbling their Habsburg rivals in Europe. In fact, trade with England in the late sixteenth century led to a diplomatic partnership, which later protected the Ottoman Empire, characterized as the "sick man of Europe," into the present century.

The Iranian Revival

The Ottoman Empire's most formidable enemy was Persia, where a fanatic Shi'ite nationalist movement took over the country in 1500, replacing a descendant of Timur with fourteen-year-old Shah Ismail (1499–1524), founder of the Safavid dynasty. Under the Safavids, Persia exerted contrasting influences. Its literature and art evoked feelings of cultural unity among Muslims from Africa to Southeast Asia, but its fanatical rejection of Sunni Orthodoxy defied Ottoman sultans and divided the Islamic world.

During most of the sixteenth century, Safavid shahs struggled with only moderate success against the Ottomans and against their own religious supporters. What started as a militant religious state gradually evolved toward a secular bureaucracy. Meanwhile, both Ismail and his son, Tahmasp (1524–1576), suffered humiliating defeats by Ottoman invaders. Tahmasp endured only by abandoning the cities and taking refuge in the mountains. Still, the regime retained respect at home and within other Muslim states, particularly among Shi'ites in Anatolia, where Selim had executed 40,000 at the opening of Ismail's reign. Tahmasp even effected half-hearted diplomatic communications with Charles V in seeking leverage against the Turks.

After Tahmasp died in 1576, contention among Turkish, Persian, and Caucasian tribes led to near-anarchy. Ismail II, fourth son of the late shah, having been imprisoned by his father for twenty-five years, ultimately gained the throne. He had eight rivals blinded or murdered but died within a year of poisoning or an opium overdose. His older brother, Mohamed, succeeded Ismail. Nearly blind and notoriously weak, Mohamed was incapable of dealing with a Turkish-Uzbeg invasion and a rebellion favoring his son, Abbas. Shah Mohamed was assassinated in 1587.

The Reign of Abbas the Great

Shah Abbas (1588–1629) the Persian version of Suleiman, was eight years old at his succession. Although conditioned from childhood to ruthless cruelty in holding power, he ultimately became a pragmatic politician, a wise statesman, a brilliant strategist, and a sensitive patron of the arts. During his reign, Persia acquired security, economic prosperity, and a reputation for cultural creativity, exemplified by the Shah's lovely capital at Isfahan.

Shah Abbas the Great of Persia created Persia's first standing army. He fought a long war with the Ottomans from whom he regained lost Persian Territory.

At first Abbas directed most of his attention to the foreign threat posed by the Ottoman-Uzbeg alliance, which had almost destroyed his country. He reorganized his government and his army, creating a "third force" of Caucasian imperial slaves to man his elite military contingents and fill government offices, thus accenting his independence from competing ethnic and religious factions. Within the army, Abbas increased his artillery and musketeer forces, relying less on the traditional cavalry charge. During the 1590s he slowly recovered lost territory in northern Persia. In 1612, he gained a stunning victory over the Ottomans at Lake Urmia, forcing them to abandon most of their gains in the south. Wars continued intermittently to the end of Abbas' reign, but subsequent Turkish campaigns brought no significant territorial changes.

Despite continuing wars, Persia prospered under Abbas. Hundreds of new roads, bridges, and hostels encouraged trade and swelled urban populations. Government monopolies, particularly in silk, furthered various crafts; and skilled immigrants, enticed by the government, stimulated agriculture and industry. A commercial agreement with the English East India Company led subsequently to the forceful ejection of the Portuguese from Ormuz in 1622. This development permitted direct export of Persian silk to Europe by sea, thus avoiding Turkish tolls on the overland routes.

Persia was less wealthy than the other great Muslim empires of this era, but it was the unchallenged cultural center of Islam. Its fine arts—ceramics, tapestries, and carpets—were eagerly sought from Alexandria to Calcutta. Persian literary forms, particularly in poetry, were imitated at both the Ottoman and Mughul courts, even by the rulers themselves. Persian painters were recruited abroad. Two Persian emigres, Khwaja Abdus Samad and Mir Sayyid Ali, founded the famous Mughul school of miniature painting (see p. 373). Persian architecture, with its bright colors, intricate designs, luxurious gardens, and artificial streams exerted the most pervasive influence in Muslim countries.

Despite his innovative genius and unique accomplishments, Abbas was in many ways a typical Muslim ruler. He held his holy men in political check but labored to project an image of his Shi'ite piety. Like most monarchs of his day, he was cruel, ordering the murder of real or suspected enemies, including members of his own family. When distraught, he found relaxation and amusement in his harem, an object of pride he was determined to protect. On one campaign against the Turks, when the enemy threatened to overrun his mobile harem, Abbas ordered that his women be decapitated, if necessary to prevent their capture. Luckily for them, the Turks did not attack.

Shah Abbas was a remarkable statesman, whose accomplishments far surpassed his resources. He inherited a war-torn country, isolated from western markets, and steeped in paralyzing traditions. Even at the end of his reign, it depended largely upon English naval power. Yet Abbas gave his country security, pride, and a degree of prosperity. No other shah has been so loved or respected by his people.

The Origins of the Mughul Empire

The Safavid and Ottoman states were contemporaries of the mighty Mughul Empire in India. It originated in the same tumultuous areas of Central Asia which had generated the other two, and it shared with them certain characteristics, blending the ruthless militarism of the steppes with Muslim law, feudal bureaucracy, and luxuries accompanying unlimited power.

In 1520, India was still suffering from Timur's terrible visitation more than a century before. The Delhi Sultanate, having been practically destroyed and having spawned a number of independent contending Turkish states, had been finally partially resurrected under an Afghan dynasty. The Rajput Confederacy in the northwest and the great Hindu state of Vijayanger in the south still existed, although both were weak politically. Despite some promising efforts to synthesize Muslim and Hindu cultures, the subcontinent remained fragmented, politically and socially. The moribund Delhi Sultanate was a vacuum, attracting outside forces.

One of these forces was led by the adventurous Turko-Mongol ruler of Kabul, Babur (the "Tiger"), a descendent of both Timur and Ghengis Khan. He had inherited the Afghan principality of Ferghana and twice conquered Timur's capital at Samarkand, before losing everything to the Uzbegs. After years of wandering and

Babur the Tiger. His memoirs, written in Turkish, provide an invaluable and quite rare record of the man and his times.

fighting, he managed to seize the throne of Kabul in 1504. But according to his memoirs, he was not content and thought constantly of conquering Hindustan. He prepared for this venture by acquiring a Turkish specialist, who trained his troops in the use of artillery and muskets. In 1525, Babur invaded India, winning three decisive battles against the Delhi Sultanate and the Rajput Confederacy. When he died, this most colorful representative of his dynasty had laid firm foundations for the later Mughul (Mongol) Empire.

Babur was succeeded by his conscientious but erratic and drug-addicted son, Humayun. Driven from the country by an eastern uprising, Humayun fled to Persia, where he gained support by accepting Shi'ite principles. Ultimately he reconquered northern India but died soon after when he fell down a flight of stairs.

The Reign of Akbar

Hymayun's son, Akbar (1556–1605), was thirteen years old when he succeeded his father.

Babur, Account of the Battle of Panipat

The Battle of Panipat was the decisive battle in Babur's last invasion of India, when he won the Mughul throne.

When the enemy first came in sight, they seemed to bend their force most against the right division. I therefore detached Abdal-aziz, who was stationed with the reserve, to reinforce the right. Sultan Ibrahim's army, from the time it first appeared in sight, never made a halt, but advanced right upon us, at a quick pace. When they came closer, on getting a view of my troops, and finding them drawn up in the order and with the defences that have been mentioned, they were brought up and stood for a while, as if considering, 'Shall we halt or not? Shall we advance or not?' They could not halt, and they were unable to advance with the same speed as before. I sent orders to the troops stationed as flankers on the extremes of the right and left divisions, to wheel round the enemy's flank with all possible speed, and instantly to attack them in the rear; the right and left divisions were also ordered to charge the enemy. The flankers accordingly wheeled on the rear of the enemy, and began to make discharges of arrows on them. Mahdi Khwajeh came up before the rest of the left wing. A body of men with one elephant advanced to meet him. My troops gave them some sharp discharges of arrows, and the enemy's division was at last driven back. I dispatched from the main body Ahmedi Perwanchi, Terdi Beg, Kuch Beg, and Muhibb Ali Khalifeh, to the assistance of the left division. The battle was likewise obstinate on the right. I ordered Muhammedi Gokultash, Shah Mansur Birlas, Yunis Ali, and Abdallah, to advance in front of the centre and engage. Ustad Ali Kuli also discharged his guns many times in front of the line to good purpose. Mustafa, the cannoneer, on the left of the centre, managed his artillery with great effect. The right and left divisions, the centre and flankers having surrounded the enemy and taken them in rear, were now engaged in hot conflict, and busy pouring in discharges of arrows on them. They made one or two very poor charges on our right and left divisions. My troops, making use of their bows, plied them with arrows, and drove them in upon their centre. The troops on the right and left of their centre, being huddled together in one place, such confusion ensued, that the enemy, while totally unable to advance, found also no road by which they could flee. The sun had mounted spear-high when the onset of battle began, and the combat lasted till mid-day, when the enemy were completely broken and routed, and my friends victorious and exulting. By the grace and mercy of Almighty God, this arduous undertaking was rendered easy for me, and this mighty army, in the space of half a day, laid in the dust. Five or six thousand men were discovered lying slain, in one spot, near Ibrahim. We reckoned that the number lying slain, in different parts of this field of battle, amounted to fifteen or sixteen thousand men. On reaching Agra, we found, from the accounts of the natives of Hindustan, that forty or fifty thousand men had fallen in this field. After routing the enemy, we continued the pursuit, slaughtering, and making them prisoners. Those who were ahead, began to bring in the Amirs and Afghans as prisoners. They brought in a very great number of elephants with their drivers, and offered them to me as *peshkesh*. . . .

From *Memories of Zehir-Ed-Din Muhammed Babur,* translated by John Leyden and William Erskine and edited by Sir Lucas King, 2 vols. (London: Oxford University Press, 1921, (Vol. 2, pp. 186–88; 193–95.

Although fond of the military arts, he could not read and was initially dominated by his regent; he did not take personal charge until the age of twenty. When Afghanistan later threatened rebellion, he quelled it with 50,000 horsemen and 500 elephants. His foreign campaigns subdued the five northern Muslim states, plus the Rajput Confederacy and four Deccan sultanates. At his death in 1605, he had united India north of the Vindhya mountains and extended loose Mughul control over much of the Deccan.

Akbar's character was a mixture of contrasts. He certainly demonstrated traits of a typical Turko-Mongol ruler: At thirteen he led troops in battle; in his thirties he challenged an enemy commander to personal combat; in late middle age he still hunted wild animals with sword and lance. He regularly wallowed in luxury, surrounded by thousands of courtiers and servants, plus a harem of 5000 women, including 300 wives and innumerable concubines. Yet beneath these surface indications of egomania were depths of thought quite uncommon among Muslim monarchs. Akbar avidly sought knowledge in frequent discussion with scholars, whose advice he welcomed but did not always take. His concern for morality and social justice was indicated by his advice to a son: "avoid religious persecution; be strong but magnanimous; accept apologies, sincerely given."[4]

Akbar's most statesmanlike achievement came in his policies favoring Hindus. He married a number of Rajput princesses, making alliances with their families and taking the men into his service. He issued decrees outlawing Hindu child marriages and *suttee* (already established in Chap. 8), two reforms which violated Hindu traditions but promised better lives for Hindu women. He also abolished taxes on non-Muslims, stopped taxing Hindu pilgrims, permitted the construction of Hindu temples, and paid Muslim officials salaries rather than feudal taxing rights. These measures alienated the diverse Muslim elite of Turks, Afghans, Mongols, and Persians, but won new support among millions of Hindus.

Frustration with the *ulema* (see p. 159), who objected strenuously to his religious toleration of non-Muslims, drove Akbar steadily away from Sunni orthodoxy. In pondering this problem, he began regular discussions in his famous "Hall of

This illustration from "Akbarnama" shows the Mughul Emperor Akbar on an expedition to hunt and train elephants.

Worship," built in 1575. He first met with Muslim holy men and was thoroughly disillusioned. Then he talked with Hindus, Jains, Zoroastrians, and Christians. Still neither satisfied nor converted, he declared himself supreme over the *ulema* in interpreting the Koran and, in 1582, proclaimed a new religion, the *Din Ilahi*, or "Divine Faith." This embraced basic tenets of all the great religions, with the emperor as its ordained voice. The new creed gained few adherents, and the government was forced to suppress numerous Muslim uprisings.

The Mughul State and Its Culture

Having inherited an imperial system deeply permeated with feudal weaknesses, Akbar labored successfully to introduce a uniform centralized administration. His officials, 70 percent of whom were foreign-born Muslims, were organized in military ranks and paid salaries, according to the number of soldiers they commanded. This policy decreased the number of *jagadirs,* or officials who held estates in return for their services. They were now made more dependent upon the emperor. Akbar further weakened the *jagadirs* and tributary rulers by requiring them to attend his court, where he could watch them. The new central bureaucracy, organized in imperial agencies under the *vakil* (vizier), had its counterparts in fifteen provinces, each divided into districts and subdistricts. In every province, responsibilities were divided between a governor (*subahdar*) and a financial officer (provincial *diwan*), who both reported directly to the central government and therefore balanced each other.

In the early seventeenth century, the Mughul Empire was the wealthiest state in the world, with revenues ten times greater than France. The population of 100,000,000 was growing rapidly, partially swelled by immigration. Cities were numerous and large by European standards. Akbar's capital at Agra, for example, housed 200,000 people—twice the population of contemporary London. In the towns and villages, many industries flourished, particularly cotton textiles, which were exported to most of Asia and Africa. The majority of subjects were Hindu peasants. One third of their produce, paid in land taxes, supported the mostly Muslim elite in unbelievable luxury. What was left kept the country self-sufficient and barely maintained the peasants, although they lived better under Akbar than in later times.

The early Mughul period saw a new Hindu-Muslim cultural synthesis, well illustrated in literature. Beginning with Babur, each emperor considered himself a poet, scholar, and collector of books. Akbar founded a great library and brought scholars to his court. The resulting cosmopolitan literature reflected a fresh originality, expressed in a variety of languages, including Turkish, Persian, Hindi, Arabic, and Urdu, a combination of all the others. While Persian, the official language, was favored as a literary medium, Akbar encouraged a Hindu literary revival by sponsoring the translation of Hindu classics into Persian or Urdu and by maintaining a Hindu poet laureate at his court.

Despite the Muslim prohibition of represented figures, human or animal, painting developed rapidly as an art in the early Mughul period. Akbar had studied drawing as a child under Abdus Samad, the Persian whom Humayan had brought to Kabul and later took to India. Samad was the leading artist in Akbar's "painting department," which included more than a hundred others, mostly Hindus. Their works, brought before the emperor every week, combined Persian color and elegance with Hindu symbolism and Arabic precision. They mainly produced miniatures of court life, but they also created large murals for Akbar's palaces. The Mughul school of painters was given even more support by Janangir, Akbar's son, who appreciated European painting and had it expertly copied by his artists.

The most imposing symbols of Mughul glory are to be seen in its architecture. Fusing Persian and Indic styles, it featured the lavish use of mosaics, bulbous domes, cupolas, slender spires, lofty vaulted gateways, and formal gardens, all carefully harmonized. Akbar's major building project was his capital city at Fathpur-Sikri. Within its seven-mile circuit were elaborate palaces, a superb mosque, and numerous statues and paintings. Akbar's two immediate successors, his son Jahangir (1605–1627), and his grandson, Shah Jahan (1627–1658), continued this tradition. The latter replaced Akbar's sandstone buildings at Delhi with new ones of marble. At Agra, he erected the Taj Mahal, a mausoleum for his favorite wife. Visitors still marvel at its luminous white marble and beautiful tracery of semiprecious stones.

Beginning of Decline After Akbar

Architectural improvements after Akbar's reign contrasted decisively with political administration, which began deteriorating, eventually collapsing in the next century. Difficulties arose from the increasing extravagances of the court, the growing complexities in governing large territories (see map, p. 374), and the impossibility of raising revenues through continuing conquests.

Neither Jahangir nor Shah Jahan had the ability to continue Akbar's policies. Jahangir was

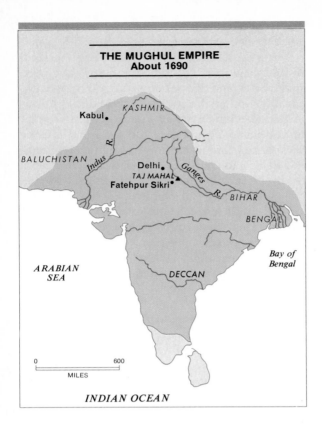

THE MUGHUL EMPIRE
About 1690

KASHMIR
Kabul
BALUCHISTAN
Indus R.
Delhi
TAJ MAHAL
Fatehpur Sikri
Ganges R.
BIHAR
BENGAL
ARABIAN SEA
DECCAN
Bay of Bengal
0   600
MILES
INDIAN OCEAN

craftsmen and merchants, the sources of revenue, were subjected to burdensome taxes. Peasants suffered the most—Shah Jahan, for example, raised land taxes above 50 percent but refused government relief in time of famine.

Unfortunately, Akbar's reform efforts brought few long-term gains for women, Hindu or Muslim. Even in Akbar's time, *suttee* and child marriage continued to be practiced; one observer in Bengal noted that the average marital age for girls was seven. Female education was practically nonexistent, except in a few very affluent families. Sexual exploitation of Hindu peasant women by their Muslim overlords was also common practice.

Despite the Mughul weakening, relations with Europeans before 1650 were relatively insignificant. Akbar recognized the value of trade with the Portuguese and respected their strength enough to admit their missionaries but would not convert to Christianity. Later, after the English had crippled Portuguese sea power, Jahangir and Shah Jahan drove the Portuguese from the empire. English imports, however, remained negligible, consisting largely of arms and curios for the leisure classes.

East Asia on the Defensive

While Middle Eurasia was generating great Muslim empires in the sixteenth century, the old East Asian cultures were experiencing internal problems which hampered their progress and turned them away from the outside world. Although the Japanese economy was expanding and society was in ferment, political disunity was a major concern. Korea, with a culture and political structure older than Japan's, remained restricted by its location between Japan and China. Under the early Ming emperors, China showed a definite interest in maritime expansion; but continued barbarian pressures soon led to stabilization within encrusted traditions, plus another cycle of political degeneration.

The Early Ming Era

In the mid-fourteenth century, the Mongol regime in China, facing rising inflation and

learned and artistically sensitive, but he was also a wastrel, addicted to drink and drugs and lacking the strength to make decisions or conduct policy. He lost Kandahar to the Persians. His rebellious son, Shah Jahan, fancying himself a holy crusader for Islam, vigorously persecuted Hindus and destroyed their temples. He also launched three unsuccessful campaigns to retake Kandahar, a disastrous jaunt into Central Asia, four costly invasions of the Deccan, and an extravagant fiasco involving 150,000 men to dispossess 1000 Portuguese and their Indian auxiliaries and Hugli.

These deficiencies of Mughul rulers were similar to those weakening Persia and the Ottoman Empire. Traditional methods of conquest and exploitation were continued long after they were outmoded. Although collecting bountiful revenues, the later emperors did not build a navy nor improve their armies. They depended heavily upon foreign advisors and imported weapons. Idle nobles and inefficient bureaucrats were permitted, even encouraged, to copy the wasteful extravagance of the imperial court. Independent bureaucratic breakdown, was overthrown by a popular uprising. One of the leaders was a young Buddhist monk who founded the Ming dynasty, adopting the reign title, Hung-wu (1368–1398). Aided by his consort, the legendary Empress Ma, the Hung-wu emperor restored stability to the Chinese government. He and his son, called the Yung-lo emperor (1403–1424), labored to strengthen imperial authority and revive a spirit of national pride. They restored the examination system and the traditional law, harshly punishing violators but respecting individual rights of those, even Mongols, who accepted Ming rule. The early Ming emperors also restored a degree of local autonomy and fostered traditional education, while keeping firm control of national government and the military.

Policy in the first two reigns reflected a definite interest in the wider world. Both emperors fought successful campaigns against the Mongols, and Yung-lo forcibly reannexed Annam. The Ming government encouraged foreign trade with Japan, Southeast Asia, and India, officially promoting cotton production, introduced earlier from the West, as a new staple export. Yung-lo regularly sent diplomatic and commercial missions to neighboring states. Between 1405 and 1431, he launched seven spectacular naval expeditions to the south and west. With some ships exceeding 500 tons and carrying crews of 700, the Chinese flotillas visited Sumatra, India, the Persian Gulf, Aden, and East Africa. There they exchanged porcelains and pottery for ivory, ostrich feathers, and exotic animals, such as zebras and giraffes. China had already penetrated the Indian Ocean while Portuguese captains were still cautiously exploring the Atlantic coast of Morocco.

Even in this period, however, the Ming emperors were more concerned about recovering the past than pioneering the future. They won support by playing upon popular prejudices against the Mongols and the Chinese elite who had served the foreign oppressors. In the process, they tried to build a welfare state, funded by "soaking the rich" and managed by former peasants and tradesmen instead of the old scholar-bureaucrats. But despite their zeal for some change, the emperors perpetuated many old bureaucratic sources of corruption and weakness, such as the excesses of court eunuchs.

Continuing destructive Mongol raids, compounded by pirate attacks along the coasts, brought further problems. Consequently, economic revival remained only moderate, population stayed low, and revenues declined while expenditures rose. Such conditions soon forced China to abandon maritime expansion and ultimately open Asia to Europeans.

The Ming inclination to perpetuate misfortune by clinging to tradition is well illustrated by the declining status of women in this era. This trend had been steady under the Sung and Yuan dynasties, but it reached a new low under the Ming. Footbinding, for example, was most common in the Ming period, when it was copied by rising middle-class families hoping to be accepted into the governing elite. The recognition of concubinage under Ming law encouraged a traffic in young virgins from poor families. They were bought by concubine brokers, who supplied wealthy merchants and officials. Increases, under the Ming, in the number of suicides or self-mutilations among widows seeking to show grief and prove their loyalty to dead husbands is a further indication of the new social atmosphere. Before 1644, 8600 Ming widows killed themselves, compared with 359 under the Yuan and 150 under the Sung.

Ming China and Its Culture in the Sixteenth Century

As time passed, Chinese rulers lost the drive and enthusiasm of the first two reigns, becoming more immune to innovation. Yet this inflexibility, so common among a long line of "do-nothing" emperors, generated an aura of stabiliy through most of the 1500s, when Chinese culture remained a model for East Asia.

Sixteenth-century European visitors were impressed by Chinese courtesy, respect for law, confidence, and stately ceremonies. They saw material prosperity in the bustling markets, stone-paved roads, and beautiful homes of Ming officials. The elaborate Ming examination system, with its proclaimed principle of advancement on merit, often evoked favorable surprise. But European commentators were perhaps most lavish in praising Chinese justice; one concluded that China was "one of the best governed" countries "in all the world."[5] Such recognized

Polygamy in a Ming Household

This selection reveals the kind of competition and petty jealousy that could develop within a middle-class family with multiple wives.

Now that she was the favorite, Lotus became more and more intent on having her own way. She was never at peace. . . . One day, in a bad mood over nothing, she upbraided her maid Plum. . . . That morning she had risen earlier than usual to help Moon, the principal wife, get ready for a funeral. She had been so tired she took a nap, and was just going back to her own suite. On her way there she ran into Jade, the third wife.

"Why are you looking so worn out?" Jade asked.

"Don't ask me! I had to get up early," Lotus replied, then added, "Sister, where are you coming from?"

"I stopped at the kitchen."

Did the one there tell you anything?"

"No, not that I can think of."

. . . She and Jade sat down and passed some time doing needlework. After finishing the tea and cakes Plum and Chrysanthemum set out, they decided to play a game of chess. But no sooner had their game become exciting than Hsi-men was announced and entered the room. . . .

When Jade asked about Moon, Hsi-men said she would be coming later in the sedan chair and that he had sent two servant boys to meet her. He sat down next to them and asked, "What were your stakes in this game?"

"Oh, we were just playing for the fun of it," Lotus answered.

"Then let me challenge you each to a game. Whoever loses forfeits a tael of silver to pay for a party."

"But we don't have any money with us." Lotus objected.

"Never mind. You can give me a hairpin as security."

First he played with Lotus and she lost. He began to reset the pieces for a game with Jade, but Lotus suddenly tipped over the board, causing the chessmen to fall in a jumble. Then she ran out of the room and into the garden.

Hsi-men chased her and found her picking flowers. "What a spoilsport! You run away because you lost, my lovable little oily-mouth," he called to her, panting. . . .

Their diversions were soon interrupted by Jade who called, "Moon has just returned. We'd better go."

Lotus broke loose from Hsi-men and said she would talk to him more later. Then she hurried after Jade to pay her respects to Moon.

Moon asked them, "What makes you two so merry?"

"Lotus lost a tael of silver playing chess with the master, so she will have to host a party tomorrow," Jade answered. "You must come."

Moon smiled and Lotus soon took her leave. She rejoined Hsi-men in the front suite and had Plum light some incense and draw a hot bath so that later they could amuse themselves like a couple of fish.

Although Moon was Hsi-men's principal wife, her ill-health usually kept her from fulfilling all the duties of the mistress of the house. Grace, the second wife, performed most of the social duties such as paying visits and receiving guests, and handled the household budget. Snow, the fourth wife, took charge of the servants and was the chief cook. Wherever Hsi-men was in the house, if he wanted something to eat or drink, he would send his request to Snow via one of the maids of the lady he was visiting.

From the novel *Chin P'ing Mei* (1610) in Patricia B. Ebrey, ed., *Chinese Civilization and Society: A Sourcebook* (New York: Macmillan, 1981), pp. 167–68.

superiority, along with the resulting Chinese satisfaction, was a major obstacle to progress in the later Ming period.

Ming respect for learning was most evident in the production of vast multi-volumed collections, including 1500 local histories and a dry but famous medical work, *The Outline of Herb Medicine*, which took thirty years to complete. There were, however, more dynamic intellectual developments, encouraged by the increased printing of books and by the growth of education in private academies preparing students for public examinations. A pragmatic counterinfluence against orthodox Neo-Confucianism was provided by the soldier, poet, and philosopher Wang Yang-ming (1472–1528), who taught that knowledge is intuitive and thought is inseparable from action.

Some Ming literature deviated from classical poetic styles. Written in colloquial language, it describes ordinary life, often including explicit pornography. Three of the best-known novels

The Temple of Good Harvest, the main part of the Temple of Heaven at Peking, built during the Ming dynasty. The original was destroyed in a fire in 1889; this is an exact copy.

Woodcut of Wang Yang-ming wearing the court dress of high rank and holding a tablet emblematic of his office.

date from the sixteenth century. *Monkey* is a rollicking semisatiric tale about a Buddhist monk, traveling to India with his pig and a monkey, which had led an earlier human life. Another example is the partially pornographic *Chin P'ing Mei*, which describes a pharmacist's romantic adventures. Perhaps the best-read work is *All Men Are Brothers*, the story of an outlaw band, like Robin Hood's merry men, who robbed the rich and helped the poor.

Ming artists and architects produced great quantities of high-quality works but generally lacked originality. The horizontal lines of the Forbidden City, the imperial family's area of temples and palaces, dating from 1403–1424, well illustrates the period's values of acceptance, balance, and formalism. In painting, slight exceptions from the norm are found in the naturalistic landscapes of Shen Chou (1427–1509) and his most talented pupil, Wen Cheng-Ming (1470–1559). The greatest later Ming painter, Tung Ch'i-ch'ang (1555–1636), was noted for the formal discipline of his brush strokes. By far the period's major artistic achievement was its porcelains, painted under the glaze and copied unsuccessfully from Japan to Europe.

Ming Decline

Despite many signs of early vigor, the Ming regime steadily weakened after the middle of the fifteenth century. This decline resulted largely from dynamic change, which the emperors and their bureaucrats tried to ignore, until the government was beset with serious difficulties on every side.

Economic and social signs of the process were particularly evident in the late 1500s. Population had expanded rapidly from less than 75 million in 1400 to over 150 million.[6] This rising human flood swelled the number and size of market towns, particularly in the heavily populated south. The overflow of determined emigrants poured into Indonesia and the Philippines. Trade expanded voluminously within the country, and smuggling increased along the coasts, despite the government's desperate attempts to prevent it. Portuguese traders, banned in 1517, were permitted restricted operations from Macao after 1557. Soon foreign foods, goods, and money, especially Spanish silver, disrupted the economy and contributed to inflation. These changes drew the gentry and peasants into the towns, away from rising land taxes. They became prosperous but discontented members of a middle class that was increasing even faster than the burgeoning general population.

Urban unrest and inflation were only two of the converging problems facing later Ming emperors. Technical progress lagged and production failed to supply the rising population. Corruption, waste, conservatism, and bureaucratic inertia permeated every level of government. The armed forces, badly equipped and generally poorly led, suffered a serious drop in morale; disorder increased throughout the country; hordes of pirates ravaged the coasts; Mongol attacks brought near-anarchy along the wall; and war with Japan in the 1590s almost caused a complete breakdown.

Success in addressing these misfortunes depended on the efficiency of local governors and commanders. One such leader, in the southwest, was the famous female general, Ch'in Liang-yu, whose troops put down local rebellion and restored order. Known for her bravery and strength of character, she was also a refined woman who wrote elegant poetry. The central government, meanwhile, nearly ceased to function. Most emperors were prisoners of the highly formalized system and puppets of their eunuch-ministers, who generally pursued their own interests in directing policies increasingly frivolous and unrealistic.

Until about 1650, China seemed to influence Europe more than Europe influenced China, but the Western impact, viewed in historical

A 16th-century engraving of Macao shows Portuguese ships anchored at the port.

perspective, was perhaps greater than it appeared at the time. Its most visible signs were the Portuguese ships and traders at Macao, the few Portuguese artillerymen employed against the Manchus, and the Jesuit advisors in Peking, who followed Father Ricci to the Ming court after 1601. As missionaries, they were not very successful, converting only some 100,000 Chinese—a tiny fraction of the population. But Jesuit treatises on the practical sciences, such as medicine, shipbuilding, and metal casting, were widely read and highly valued. Even more lasting effects came with European trade and western food crops, which helped expand an increasingly contentious population.

In the summer of 1644, after trying to kill his oldest daughter and succeeding only in cutting off her arm, the last Ming emperor, Ch'ung-cheng (1627–1644), hanged himself in his imperial garden, leaving a pitiful note which indicated

MING AND MANCHU CHINA

- Ming China, 1368 - 1644
- Areas added by Manchus, 1644 - 1912
- Provinces of Manchu China

The Jesuit missionary, Father Matteo Ricci, shown here with Ly Paulus, a Chinese convert priest, introduced Christianity to China. Ricci made a great impression on the Ming court with his knowledge of mathematics, astronomy, and practical engineering.

his shame in meeting his ancestors. An insurgent government had already formed to the west in Szechwan; another rebel army was approaching Peking; only a few Portuguese mercenaries and some imperial guard contingents remained nominally loyal. But neither of the Chinese counter-movements would succeed. As the Ming regime collapsed, Manchu forces crossed the northern borders. By 1683, a Manchu emperor controlled the whole country.

Korea: Cultural Intermediary

The Ming defensive orientation was habitual for Korea, China's northern satellite (see map above). An ancient kingdom, clinging resolutely to its own identity, it had survived for centuries by accepting tributary status under Chinese emperors and adapting imported Chinese culture, much of which it passed on to Japan.

Originally a steppe people like the Mongols and Manchus, the Koreans settled early on the north Asian peninsula opposite Japan. Some were subjugated by China in the Han period, but the independent tribes slowly formed three separate kingdoms, which retained their independence during the interval between the Chinese Han and T'ang dynasties. Even then, however, Korea borrowed agricultural techniques, written characters, and Buddhism from China. In the late seventh century, the three states were united, with the aid of T'ang China, under the ruling dynasty of Silla, one of the original kingdoms. The next three centuries brought prosperity and growth, followed by near breakdown, before the country was united again in the late 900s, by the founder of the Koryo dynasty, which gave Korea its name. Koryo monarchs paid tribute to Sung China, encouraging Neo-Confucianism and adopting the Chinese imperial structure, including the examination system. Although relatively independent under the Sung, the Koryo rulers became virtual puppets of Yuan emperors. Koreans blamed them for the heavy Yuan taxes and manpower levies.

When the Yuan regime was overthrown in China, Korean military leaders seized power, dispossessing the old landed aristocrats of the Koryo establishment and redistributing their lands among scholar-bureaucrats supporting the rebellion. In 1392, one of the military leaders, Yi Song-Gye, was recognized as the first king of the new Yi dynasty, which lasted unto 1910.

The early Yi monarchs, even more than their Ming overlords, effected positive changes. They created a new land register, abolished feudal relations in the armed forces, eliminated many Buddhist privileges, and made Confucianism the state religion. In foreign affairs, the Yi rulers expanded into Manchuria and conducted successful operations against Japanese coastal pirates. Improved agricultural techniques, better communications, and innovations in the crafts increased economic productivity. The manufacture of cotton cloth, learned from China, also stimulated trade. Such economic growth increased the number of craftsmen and merchants, although most were employed in government monopolies.

Like Ming China, which it imitated, Korea under the early Yi dynasty promised more than it delivered. In less than a century, Neo-Confucianism and the new centralized administration had spawned another class of privileged bureaucrats who were as corrupt, inefficient, and overbearing as those in Ming China. With

their growing power came higher taxes and service requirements for common people, most of whom were peasant tenants or slaves. As in China, the Neo-Confucian revival brought more difficulties for women. Through the tenth century, women had enjoyed near legal equality with men in property, inheritance, and marriage rights. Many Silla rulers were women, either as queens, exercising royal authority directly, or as powers "behind the screen," acting through royal consorts or sons. This all changed drastically with the Koryo dynasty. New laws restricted women's legal rights, and women were prohibited from participating in games, attending feasts, appearing in public unveiled, or even walking alone outside the home.

The period of the early Yi dynasty produced a mild upsurge of cultural expression, particularly in literature. The treatises produced by the scholarly ruling class were often dull, but some reflected a genuine respect for rational knowledge and the promotion of learning. Their message helped promote a Korean alphabet, the use of newly invented movable type, and practical curricula in the academies. By the fifteenth century government printing presses were publishing many works in various literary forms. Some of these were prose compositions on serious subjects, such as moral responsibility. Poetry, stressing love of nature, personal grief, and romantic love, also became quite popular. Many of the lyric poets were women. The other arts, however, were less promising. Painting, sculpture, and architecture generally followed Chinese models, producing many creditable works but generally lacking originality.

The end of the Ming era brought troubled times to Korea. Factionalism, as too many bureaucrats competed for positions of power, plagued the government. When Ming protective power waned, the Japanese invaded, hoping to use Korea for a base against China. Disaster was temporarily averted by Korean armored "tortoise boats," which cut supply lines of the invading forces, but deliverance was not assured until 1598 when Hideyoshi, the Japanese *shogun*, died. In the seven years of Japanese partial occupation and military deliverance by Ming armies, Korea's wealth was plundered. The determined efforts of King Kwang-haegun (1608–1623) to rebuild the country came too late. After aiding Ming China in war against the Manchus, Korea was invaded, defeated, and forced to accept Manchu overlordship in 1637. Thousands of Koreans, held hostage by the Manchus, suffered great cruelty and privation before they could be ransomed. Many Korean women were never accepted again by their families, because they had been sexually violated and therefore dishonored.

Upheaval in Japan

The defensive orientation and subsequent decline of Ming China were not paralleled in Japan as they were in Korea. During the fifteenth century, the imperial government lost almost all of its power to great feudal lords, the *daimyo*, who fought among themselves for control of the country. Their wars actually stimulated the economy and temporarily opened Japan to foreign influences. Later, Japan isolated itself, not from a sense of superiority or a desire to ignore the outside world but in order to achieve political stability.

The rising *daimyo*, strangely enough, prepared a way for their own decline. Greatly weakened by the Mongol wars, the Kamakura government (see p. 214) ultimately faced a feudal uprising against the *shogun*, in favor of the emperor. For some sixty years, two emperors claimed authority, each supported by contending forces. In 1336, the dominant one of these forces proclaimed the Ashikaga shogunate as successor to the Kamakura, but the new regime soon lost control of its vassals. The *daimyo*, in time, assumed complete authority over their fiefs, not only in raising armies but also in taxing had lawmaking. By the late fifteenth century, their sporadic fighting had become protracted and full-scale conflicts. When civil war broke out between rival Ashikaga houses in 1467, more than 250,000 men fought around Kyoto. Intensified by the use of firearms, the conflagration spread throughout the country and lasted, with brief lapses, for over a century; it reduced the number of *daimyo* from roughly 260 in 1467 to 45 in 1580.

Despite political instability, the period brought economic growth and dynamic social change. The *daimyo* were so occupied with their wars that they were forced to be more lenient with peasants and the commercial classes, who paid taxes and served in mercenary armies. The *daimyo*, needing weapons, supplies, and money, sought to foster trade, build towns, and encourage industry. Agricultural production continued to rise, as it had done since the thirteenth century. The resulting economic boom brought an exploding population, rapid city growth, and more social mobility. Prosperity and change, however, also generated insecurities, well illustrated by the growing popularity of mystical religions in which people sought relief. These included Zen Buddhism and other evangelical cults, like the "Pure Land" movement, which stressed individual salvation, congregational worship, and street preaching.

The same interests which impelled the *daimyo* toward trade led them toward Europeans. Because Portuguese captains could supply efficient firearms and help foster profitable enterprises, the *daimyo* competed for the foreigners' favor. After 1544, various *daimyo* concluded commercial agreements with the Portuguese, who took over most trade with the mainland, exchanging Japanese silver and copper for Chinese silks. Portuguese operations after 1580 expanded Nagasaki from a tiny fishing village to one of the largest ports in Asia.

Behind the traders came the missionaries, who were generally welcomed by *daimyo* eager to establish commercial contacts. Francis Xavier began preaching near Kyoto in 1549; by 1600, there may have been 300,000 Japanese Christians, including some *daimyo* of Kyushu. The Jesuits worked closely with Portuguese merchants, sometimes acting as commercial agents among the *daimyo*.

Between 1560 and 1598, two powerful warlords, Oda Nobunaga, and his able commander, Toyotomi Hideyoshi, gained control over the *daimyo*. Nobunaga, in 1573, set aside the last of the Ashikaga *shoguns*, put down the Buddhist military orders, and drove the powerful Mori family from central Japan. Hideyoshi, who succeeded to the regency in 1584, completed the conquest of the *daimyo*. He disarmed the populace, ended all feudal grants of political authority, and separated the *samurai* from the land by nationalizing their service. In the decade after 1590, Hideyoshi made war against Korea and China, hoping to gain Christian support for a religious crusade. When these hopes were not realized, he began sporadic persecution of Christians.

内宮次三拾五道海東
府中

As a defense measure, the Tokugawa banned the building of bridges across major rivers. Thus, rivers were crossed by palanquin, an enclosed litter which men bore on their shoulders by means of poles. Or one might cross the river on the back of a coolie.

The Tokugawa Shogunate

Hideyoshi died in 1598 and the country lapsed again into civil war. Within a few years, however, Hideyoshi's former deputy in eastern Japan, Tokugawa Ieyasu, became the strongest warlord. He won the decisive battle of Seikigahara in 1600, was appointed *shogun* in 1603, and forced Hideyoshi's son to commit suicide after the siege of Osako in 1615. Thus began the Tokugawa shogunate, which molded Japanese culture for the next two and half centuries.

Ieyasu was among the shrewdest, most patient, most ruthless, and most successful rulers in Japanese history. Reared amid the cruel uncertainties of the civil wars, he became equally appreciative of wisdom and lack of principle. To obtain favor with Nobunaga, he murdered his own wife and compelled a son to commit suicide. He won many battles by treachery. Yet his personal philosophy extolled self-criticism, quiet patience, and humble bearing. Above all, he was characterized by an iron will and by a desire for political security for himself and his family.

Ieyasu's politcal structure was a model of efficient organization and stability, exploiting both feudal and imperial traditions. As in the past, the emperor symbolized national unity, while the *shogun* held the real power over the fiscal and military bureaucracies. Local government remained under the *daimyo*, who paid tribute to the capital. Their privileges varied, but all were required to attend court, leaving close relatives as hostages when they returned home. This system, similar to that of the Muslim empires, was more successful; however, a major weakness was its conservatism amid the burgeoning economic productivity and unheralded urban expansion which its stability encouraged.

Along with the strengthening of central authority, the Tokugawa period brought a new social order, headed by a rising merchant class, which partially superseded the *daimyo* and their fighting retainers, the *samurai*. Members of the latter class were still honored as they rode the social momentum of recent civil wars, but they had been reduced to an ornamental petty aristocracy of state mercenaries. Lacking real purpose or practical judgment and addicted to their own amusement, many became indebted to moneylenders and merchants, who profited from *samurai* misfortunes. Merchants also benefited from the new roads and better communications, from a stabilized currency, and from the rising trade, spreading outward from former castle towns.

These changes in the class structure were reflected in difficulties faced by Japanese women. During the civil wars, *samurai* women often fought beside their men, expecting to die in battle with their husbands or commit suicide if they survived alone. Thus late in the Ashikaga period, *samurai* women were still honored and respected. But other emphases of the time definitely lowered their status. Marriages, negotiated by fathers and brothers, became the common means for promoting family military alliances. Similar family interests were involved in the turn toward inheritance by primogeniture. In the early Tokugawa era, women were granted the legal right to divorce but otherwise relegated, under the prevailing Neo-Confucian philosophy, to a subordinate position. These conditions were most common among the aristocracy, where male dominance compensated for the humbling of the *daimyo* and the *samurai*. Within the middle classes, however, the situation was quite different; marriage partners often demonstrated real affection, based upon equal sharing and individual decision making.

The early Tokugawa period brought a dramatic end to most European influence. At first, Ieyasu tolerated Christianity in his hope for maintaining foreign trade. Despite the arrogance of Spanish Franciscan missionaries, he tried to negotiate a commercial agreement with the Spanish, but the latter refused admission of Japanese ships into Phillippine or Mexican ports. Ieyasu was also alienated by the desperate intrigues of recently arrived Dutch and English merchants. His feelings were undoubtedly influenced by the possibility of uniting Japanese against foreigners. Consequently, in 1612, 1613, and 1614, Ieyasu issued edicts prohibiting Christianity. Thousands of Japanese Christians suffered martyrdom during succeeding years. A climax came in 1637, when a popular revolt, led by some Christian *daimyo*, was put down. Japan expelled all Europeans, except for one regulated Dutch station at Nagasaki. At the same time, all Japanese were prohibited from leaving the country or even building ships for overseas voyages.

Japanese Cultural Expression

Like the European Renaissance, which was a unique variation on its classical heritage, Japanese culture in this period continued to accent its peculiar identity within Chinese forms. It also expressed the curious duality of Japanese society: a striving for calm serenity and a contrasting lusty vitality, as shown in explicit literature, massive architecture, and brilliant color. Although often obscured by tradition, these latter characteristics beame inceasingly evident in the Tokugawa era.

During the late Ashikaga period, Zen Buddhism spread from the great monasteries to impress thought and art with respect for things elegantly simple. Its best-known expressions were flower arranging, landscape gardening, and the famous tea ceremony, with its accented restraint and quiet contemplation. Zen also influenced painting, as artists strove, through the discipline of their brush strokes and the austerity of their subject matter, to demonstrate economy in artistic creativity. The most enduring literary vehicle of the period was the *Noh*, a traditional form of lyric drama which combined stately mimetic dancing, music, and song. All such pursuits continued to be popular, particularly among the elite, into the Tokugawa era.

The era of political unification brought new styles. Known as the Momoyama period in

An engraving illustrating the persecution of Christians in Japan in 1623. Shogunate officers strike down both Jesuit priests and Japanese converts to Christianity.

Father Xavier's Difficulties as a Missionary in Sixteenth-Century Japan

This is from one of Father Xavier's letters, written in 1549 to friends in India. Note references to recent wars of the *daimyo*.

I went on with Joam Fernandez to Amanguchi. . . . The city contains more than ten thousand household. . . . We found many here, both of the common people and of the nobility, very desirous to become acquainted with the Christian law. We thought it best to preach twice a day in the streets and cross roads, reading out parts of our book, and then speaking to the people about the Christian religion. Some of the noblemen also invited us to their houses, that they might hear about our religion with more convenience. They promised of their own accord, that if they came to think it better than their own, they would unhesitatingly embrace it. Many of them heard what we had to say about the law of God very willingly; some, on the other hand, were angry at it, and even went so far as to laugh at what we said. So, wherever we went through the streets of the city, we were followed by a small crowd of boys of the lowest dregs of the populace, laughing at us and mocking us with some such words as these: "There go the men who tell us that we must embrace the law of God in order to be saved, because we cannot be rescued from destruction except by the Maker of all things and by His Son! There go the men who declare that it is wicked to have more than one wife!"

. . . We had spent some days in this office of preaching, when the king, who was then in the city, sent for us and we went to him. He asked us wherever did we come from? why had we come to Japan? And we answered that we were Europeans sent thither for the sake of preaching the law of God, since no one could be safe and secure unless he purely and piously worship God and His Son Jesus Christ, the Redeemer and Saviour of all nations. Then the king commanded us to explain to him the law of God. So we read to him a good part of our volume; and although we went on reading for an hour or more, he listened to use diligently and attentively as long as we were reading, and then he sent us away. We remained many days in the city, and preached to the people in the streets and at the cross roads. Many of them listened to the wonderful deeds of Christ with avidity, and when we came to His most bitter death, they were unable to restrain their tears. Nevertheless, very few actually became Christians.

Finding, therefore, that the fruit of our labours was small, we went on to Meaco, the most famous city in all Japan. We spent two months on the road, and passed through many dangers, because we had to go through countries in which war was raging. I say nothing of the cold of those parts, nor of the roads so infested by frequent robberies. When we arrived at Meaco, we waited for some days that we might obtain leave to approach the king, and ask of him to give us permission to publish the divine law in his kingdom. But we found all ways of access to him altogether closed. And as we discovered that the edicts of the king were generally thought little of among the princes and rulers, we laid aside our design of obtaining from him any such licence, and I determined to sound and try the minds and dispositions of the people themselves, so as to find out how disposed that city was to receive the worship of Christ. But as the people were under arms, and under the pressure of a severe war, I judged that the time was most inopportune for the preaching of the Gospel. . . .

Source: William H. McNeill and Mitsuko Iriye, eds., *Modern Asia and Africa* (New York: Oxford University Press, 1971), pp. 15–17.

Japanese art, the age from Nobunaga to Ieyasu was often marked by ostentation and flamboyance, incompatible with cultural traditions, and similar, in its own contexts, to European baroque. It was most obvious in architecture, particularly in massive stone castles. Hideyoshi's famous fortress at Osaka, for example, had 48 towers; the base of the central tower was 75 feet high and the main structure rose another 102 feet. Within the castles, other arts were displayed in wild profusion, featuring woodcarving, sliding doors, folding screens, and brilliantly colored walls. Doors and screens contrasted their colors against gold leaf. Paintings were often grandiose, in keeping with the pretensions of the castle lords. To this melange of traditional simplicity and showy elegance, Ieyasu added a revival of Confucian philosophy at his court, in his effort to pacify the *samurai*, while promoting their respect for authority.

Contending Cultures in Southeast Asia

Situated adjacent to India and China, on the main sea route between East Asia and the Indian Ocean, and divided geographically into diverse subregions, Southeast Asia had long been an area of contending cultures and states. Although containing varied cultural mixes from elsewhere in Asia, each country was fiercely committed to its own national interests and to defending its independence or conquering neighboring states, which were usually held in contempt. During the three and a half centuries after 1300, this competition intensified hampering development and turning attention away from the shrinking outside world.

Background Before 1350

The most obvious geographical difference separated the mainland, with its agrarian peasant traditions, from the archipelago, which was naturally oriented toward the sea (see map above right). Both subregions were further divided. Malaya and the many islands were scattered over a thousand miles of open ocean. On the mainland, great rivers—the Irrawaddy, Salween,

EARLY EMPIRES IN SOUTHEAST ASIA
- Srivijaya Empire, 8th C.
- Khmer Empire c. 1200
- Kertanagara Empire, c. 1292

and Mekong—flowed in valleys through forested mountains. For hundreds of years, successive migrations of Malays, Vietnamese, Chams, Mon-Khmer, and Thai peoples came south through the valleys, driving their predecessors into the highlands and the archipelago.

The early foreign influences upon the region came from India. These were mainly commercial but some resulted from colonizing and missionary efforts, even before the fourth century. The Gupta period witnessed an explosion eastward of Hindu culture and Buddhist evangelical zeal. For a thousand years, this Hindu-Buddhist cultural combination, featuring Sanskrit literature, Indian architecture, and traditional Gupta court ceremonies, was common in both mainland and island states. Native values, however, always tempered such trends; the Hindu caste system, for example, found little acceptance in Southeast Asia.

Nearly constant struggle marked the political history of the mainland. Funan, a great Indianized Malay power between 200 and 500, dominated emerging northern states and extended control into Java and Sumatra. After its decline, beginning in the later sixth century, a series of new states fought for leadership: Chenla in Cambodia, a Mons confederacy in lower Burma, a new Thai monarchy, and a unified kingdom in Burma.

The most impressive early mainland state was the Khmer Empire. At its peak, around 1200, it controlled territories in Burma and the Malay Peninsula, plus everything in between. It was noted for its Hindu and Buddhist learning centers, its great prosperity and its building projects, particularly the great temple city of Angkor Wat, with its sunken pyramid base, its lotus-bud spires, its wide balustrades, and its hundreds of relief carvings. The empire's demise was probably hastened by such costly religious obsessions, which maintained 300,000 priests and 21,000 temples.

While mainland states competed for territory, Indianized socio-political systems in the archipelago sought control of the sea and its commerce. The most successful was Srivijaya, on the island of Sumatra. At the apex of its power in the eleventh and twelfth centuries, Srivijaya dominated sea lanes through the Malacca and Sudra straits. Ultimately the Srivijayan monarchs held sway over most of Java and Indonesia, as well as Sumatra, and much of the Malay peninsula. They were proponents of Mahayana Buddhism, but other rulers in the area followed orthodox Hindu beliefs. The ancient Indian cultural traditions were illustrated by the great carved mountain of Borobudor, in central Java, with its nine successive terraces and its numerous sculptured illustrations from Buddhist texts.

Indian cultural influence was less potent than Chinese only in Vietnam (Annam). Chinese cultural conditioning began with colonists in Han times; it continued through centuries of subjection during the Han, T'ang, and Sung periods; and it remained after the Vietnamese won their independence in the late 900s. Under the Ly and Tran dynasties, through the thirteenth century, Vietnam struggled against Chinese political and cultural pressures, although its language, main religion (*Mahayana Buddhism*), imperial structure, Confucian examination system, literature, art, and architecture were largely imported from China. Yet for all its preoccupation with this problem, Vietnam waged frequent exhaustive wars against its Hindu neighbors, particularly Champa and Cambodia.

The Transition to Modern Times in Southeast Asia

As Southeast Asia approached the modern era after 1350, difficulties intensified. The Mongols, who temporarily controlled the mainland and parts of Java, seriously disrupted all existing governments, facilitated the rise of a strong Thai state, and indirectly contributed to ruinous petty wars. Later, Muslim regimes replaced many traditional Hindu states in Indonesia, which also felt the effects of European empire-building, first by the Portuguese and then by the Dutch. Before 1650, however, the European impact on the mainland was negligible.

There, during the fifteenth century, Vietnam completely overshadowed its neighbors. Rulers of the early dynasty after 1428 drove out the Chinese and absorbed Champa, while threatening Laos, Cambodia, and Burma. The latter were all in decline; indeed, Burma broke into a number of feudal domains. A slight exception to the general trend was the little Thai polity, under King Trailock (1448–1488), who was partially successful in creating an efficient army and establishing a civil administration.

First Burma and then Thailand, held dominance in the sixteenth and early seventeenth centuries. Under King Bayinnaung, Burma absorbed Laos and conquered Thailand with an army estimated at 500,000, the largest ever assembled in Southeast Asia. Bayinnaung's capital at Pegu was a center of Buddhist culture, a thriving commercial center, and the site of his wondrous palace, roofed in solid gold. But his successor wasted resources in unsuccessful invasions of Thailand. Ultimately, the Thai state gained supremacy, humbling Cambodia and profiting from a commercial alliance with the Dutch. This favorable situation changed,

Angkor Wat in Cambodia is considered by many to be the finest example of Indian architecture. One of the courtyards of the gigantic complex contains a half-mile of sculptured reliefs.

however, during the reign of Prasat T'ong, an era characterized by "petticoat intrigue, savage cruelty, and court debauchery."[7]

Generally, mainland governments successfully maintained their independence against Europeans. Portuguese missionaries, at first active in Vietnam, were expelled by the end of the period. Portuguese traders and mercenary soldiers served everywhere, but they were usually controlled. Some were enslaved in Burma; only in weakened Cambodia and Laos did they acquire significant political influence. By the seventeenth century, the Portuguese were giving way to the Dutch, who courted the Vietnamese in only partially successful efforts to monopolize trade with Thailand and Burma.

Maritime interests and religious revolution transformed Indonesian states after 1400. *Sufi* Muslim missionaries were drawn to the area by expanding India-China trade, particularly when Chinese interests waned in the decade after 1424. Many local rulers embraced Islam to gain independence from the great Hindu state of Madjapahet on Java; others sought a share of Indian commerce. This motive was reflected by the rising Muslim commercial center of Malacca, on the Malay coast opposite Sumatra. Founded in 1400

under protection of China, its rulers became Muslims, won independence from Thailand, and built a Muslim empire of commercial vassal states in the region. Before 1511, when it fell to the Portuguese, Malacca was the busiest port in Asia, linking China and the Spice Islands with India and Africa. Its growing success paralleled Muslim expansion through western Indonesia to the Philippines in the sixteenth century.

Well before 1650, Europeans were becoming very active in Indonesia. The Portuguese tried to use Malacca as a base for dominating trade in the region; but Muslim confederacies forcefully ejected them from Java and Sumatra, while limiting their operations in the Moluccas. In the late 1500s, Portugal was allied with Spain when the latter acquired a foothold in the Philippines. The Spanish established a colonial capital at Manila and successfully converted the country to Christianity. But such activities did not protect the Portuguese from Dutch competition. The newcomers quickly took control of the Moluccas and expelled the Portuguese in 1641. Soon after, the Dutch concluded a long war in Java by forcing a treaty upon the sultans which guaranteed a Dutch commercial monopoly in return for political autonomy. Dutch plantation agriculture soon began undermining Indonesian economies.

Nearly 1500 bas-relief carvings and over 400 life-size images of Buddha adorn the great Buddhist temple at Borobudur in central Java.

Conclusion

Numerous significant changes occurred in Asia between 1350 and 1650. Steppe nomads, represented by the Uzbegs and the Manchus, made their last significant conquests of civilized areas. The balance of power shifted noticeably from the Orient toward Middle Eurasia, and Islam expanded rapidly in Southeast Asia. But at a time when the world was ready for oceanic expansion, the old Asian civilizations remained preoccupied with their traditional territorial imperialism.

In the three-and-a-half centuries before 1650, Europe still lagged behind Asia in many respects. No European state, not even the polyglot empire of Charles V, could compare in manpower and resources with the realms of Suleiman, Akbar, or even the later Ming emperors. In the engineering of its roads and canals, as well as the objectivity of its justice, China evoked awe from Europeans, who were equally impressed by the recognition of merit within the Turkish governing system. Opportunities for minorities and toleration for dissenting religions were greater in the Muslim countries and in East Asia than in Europe. Asian cities were usually better planned, more tastefully adorned with works of art, and even better supplied with water and sewage disposal. Moreover, Asian art, literature, and philosophy inspired general European admiration.

Europe's advantages, which began to be most evident after the beginning of the seventeenth century, were confined primarily to technology, specifically to the production of projectile weapons and ocean-going ships. These technical assets suggest other, more fundamental, differences. The Asian states were all land-based imperial systems, attempting to use massive armies and elaborate bureaucracies to control and administer vast territories. Europe, on the other hand, was ushering in a new age, when powerful states would depend upon strategic control of sea lanes and world markets. The gap between these two systems, which would become so wide in succeeding centuries, was already beginning to open in the early part of the seventeenth century.

Suggestions for Reading

Colin E. Tweddell, *Introduction to the Peoples and Cultures of Asia* (Prentice-Hall, 1985) is good for general background. Two older works are recommended as readable, comprehensive, and integrated: John A. Garraty and Peter Gay, *A History of the World*, 3 vols., (Harper & Row, 1972), vol. II, *Toward Maturity;* and Chester G. Starr, et al., *A History of the World*, 2 vols., (Rand McNally, 1960), vol. I, *to 1500.* Edwin O. Reischauer, *East Asia* (Houghton Mifflin, 1973) also provides a good sweep of the whole area. For a very recent general survey, see C. A. Schirokaier, *A Brief History of the Chinese and Japanese Civilizations* (Harcourt Brace Jovanovich, 1989). Frank C. Darling, *The Westernization of Asia* (Schenkman, 1980) is a rare attempt to synthesize a complex subject. It is a valuable study but full of technical detail and abstract jargon. Rhoads Murphy, *The Outsiders: The Western Experience in India and China* (Univ. of Michigan, 1977) is interesting but gives only slight attention to the era before 1800.

Luc Kwanten, *A History of Central Asia: Imperial Nomads, 500–1500* (Univ. of Pennsylvania, 1979) is an illuminating study of a subject long neglected in standard texts. See also David Morgan, *The Mongols* (Basil Blackwell, 1986) and Berthold Spuler, *The Mongols in History* (Praeger, 1971). More on the steppe background for other civilizations in this period can be found in Wilfrid Blunt, *The Golden Road to Samarkand* (Viking, 1973); Gavin Hambly, ed., *Central Asia* (Delecorte, 1969); William H. McNeil, *Europe's Steppe Frontier* (Univ. of Chicago, 1964); and John Joseph Saunders, *The Muslim World on the Eve of Europe's Expansion* (Prentice-Hall, 1966). The latter work also presents excellent coverage of high Muslim civilizations in southern Asia.

The Ottoman Golden Age is ably depicted in Norman Itkowitz, *The Ottoman Empire and the Islamic Tradition* (Univ. of Oklahoma, 1980); Lord Kinross, *The Ottoman Centuries (Morrow, 1977);* Stanford Shaw, *A History of the Ottoman Empire*, 2 vols. (Cambridge Univ., 1976); and Halil Inalcik, *The Ottoman Empire* (Praeger, 1973). For effects of the Ottomans upon Europe, see Paul Coles, *The Ottoman Impact upon Europe* (Harcourt Brace and World, 1968); C. Max Kortepeter, *Ottoman Imperialism During the Reformation* (New York Univ., 1972); and C. A. Fazee, *Catholics and Sultans* (Cambridge Univ., 1983). D. Nicolle, *Armies of the Ottoman Turks, 1300–1774* (London: Osprey, 1985) provides a good appraisal of the janissaries. Noel Barber, *The Sultans* (Simon and Schuster, 1973) reveals the intimate and often lurid personal lives of Ottoman rulers. The classic biography of Suleiman is Roger Bigelow Merriman, *Suleiman the Magnificent* (Harvard Univ., 1978). For Suleiman's military campaigns and the art of his times, see A. Bridge, *Suleiman the Magnificent, Scourge of Heaven* (Franklin Watts, 1983) and E. Etil, *The Age of Sultan Suleyman, the Magnificent* (Abrams, 1987). Another captivating and revealing biography is Franz Babinger, *Mehmed the Conqueror and His Time* (Princeton Univ., 1978).

David Morgan, *Medieval Persia 1040–1797* (Longman, 1988), a brief but very lucid book in a new series on the history of the Near East, has been called "the best short treatment in the English language." See also Roger Savory, *Iran Under the Safavids* (Cambridge Univ., 1980) and Clive Irving, *Crossroads of Civilization: 3000 Years of Persian History* (Barnes and Noble, 1979). Until recently, coverage in English of the Safavid period was limited for practical purposes to the thorough but ancient standard study: Percy M. Sykes, *A History of Persia* (Gordon, 1976) [reprint of 1938 ed.].

An excellent and very complete survey of Indian culture with good brief coverage of the Mughul period is Stanley A. Wolpert, *A New History of India*, 3rd. ed. (Oxford, 1989). See also G. Kupperman, *India Through the Ages* (Delhi: Sundeep Parakashan, 1988); Sir W. W. Hunter, *History of the Indian Peoples* (Cosmo, 1984); and Sheikh Mohammed, *Muslim Civilization in India* (Columbia Univ., 1964). The Mughul imperial system is ably described in Stephen M. Edwards and H. L. Garrett, *Mughul Rule in India* (Delhi: S. Chand, 1962) and A. L. Srivastva, *The Mughul Empire* (Agra: S. L. Agarwala, 1966). For excellent studies of individual emperors, see Michael Charol, *Builders of the Mogul Empire* (Barnes and Noble, 1965) and Bamber Gascoigne, *The Great Moghuls* (Harper & Row, 1971. The best-known biography of Akbar is J. M. Shelat, *Akbar* (India: Bharatiya Bidya Bhavan, 1964).

William Scott Morton, *China: Its History and Culture* (McGraw-Hill, 1982) is a well-researched and well-written survey, with excellent broad coverage of the Ming era. See also a recent special study by Albert Chan, *The Glory and Fall of Ming China* (Univ. of Oklahoma, 1982). Ray Huang, *1587, A Year of No Significance* (Yale Univ., 1981) is noteworthy for its penetrating case study of late Ming weaknesses. A commendable special study of the early Ming period is Bruce Swanson, *The Eighth Voyage of the Dragon; a History of China's Quest for Sea Power* (Naval Institute, 1982). Other scholarly but readable treatments of the Ming era are available in Charles O. Hucker, *China's Imperial Past* (Stanford Univ., 1975); Raymond S. Dawson, *Imperial China* (Hutchinson, 1972); and Hilda Hookham, *A Short History of China* (St. Martin's, 1970). Esther S. Yao, *Chinese Women: Past and Present* (Idle House, 1983) provides a complete treatment of the Ming period. Older but still valuable studies include G. Francis Hudson, *Europe and China* (Beacon, 1961); Donald Lach, *China in the Eyes of Europe: The Sixteenth Century* (Univ. of Chicago, 1968; and Arnold Silcock, *Introduction to Chinese Art and History*) Greenwood, 1972).

For the Yi period in Korea, the best work in English is Ki-baik Lee, *A New History of Korea* (Harvard Univ., 1984). See also Jon Carter Covell, *Korea's Cultural Roots* (Moth House, 1981) and Andrew C. Nahm, *Tradition and Transformation: A History of the Korean People* (Hollym International, 1983). Yung-Chung Kim, *Women of Korea* (Ewha Women's Univ., 1979) provides a readable and informative treatment of the period.

George B. Sansom, *A History of Japan*, 3 vols. (Stanford Univ., 1958–1963) and Edwin O. Reischauer, *Japan* (Alfred A. Knopf, 1970) are the standard detailed scholarly works. Peter Duus, *Feudalism in Japan* (Alfred A. Knopf, 1969) remains a useful institutional study. A number of other well-known books are recommended for the period between 1300 and 1650: Mikiso Hane, *Modern Japan* (Westview, 1986); Noel E. Busch, *Japan* (American Heritage,

1972); Eric Tomlin, *Japan* (Walker, 1973); Peter Duus, *Japan: A Short Cultural History* (Knopf, 1974); John W. Hall, et al., *Japan Before Tokuqawa* (Yale Univ., 1981); and William S. Martin, *Japan, Its History and Culture* (McGraw-Hill, 1984 [1970]). Conrad Totman, *Japan Before Perry* (California Univ., 1981), which devotes much attention to the early modern period, is well organized despite an awkward periodization framework. Recent informative works include R. H. Mason, *A History of Japan* (Charles C. Tuttle, 1987); and S. Fewster, *Japan From Shogun to Super-State* (St. Martin's, 1988). Two excellent biographies, which also mirror the time, are Mary Elizabeth Berry, *Hideyoshi* (Harvard Univ., 1982) and Conrad Totman, *Tokuqawa Ieyasu* (Heian Int., 1983). Mary R. Beard, *The Force of Women in Japanese History* (Public Affairs Press, 1953) is still a reliable source. Steven Warshaw, *Japan Emerges* (Diablo, 1987) will appeal to the nonspecialist.

A. Reid, *Southeast Asia in the Age of Commerce, 1400–1680* (Yale Univ., 1988) supplies brilliant coverage of separate cultures and attempts a synthesis of the whole in terms of affecting Western commercialism. Two recent revisions of older general works are well worth examining: G. Coedes, *The Making of Southeast Asia*, 2nd. ed. (Allen and Unwin, 1983) and Steven Warshaw, *Southeast Asia Emerges*, rev. ed. (Diablo, 1987). In addition, the following standard surveys are still useful: John F. Cady, *Southeast Asia* (McGraw-Hill, 1964); G. Coedes, *The Indianized States of Southeast Asia* (East-West Center, 1968); D. G. H. Hall. *A History of Southeast Asia* (St. Martin's, 1964); and B. R. Pearn, *An Introduction to the History of Southeast Asia* (Longmans of Malaysia, 1963. See also Robert C. Lester *Theravada Buddhism in Southeast Asia* (Univ. of Michigan, 1973). The best regional treatments may be found in Michael Aung-Thwin, *Pagan: The Origins of Modern Burma* (Univ. of Hawaii, 1985); D. K. Wyatt, *Thailand* (Yale Univ., 1983); David P. Chandler, *A History of Cambodia* (Westview Press, 1983; Joseph Buttinger, *A Oragon Defiant* (Praeger, 1972); Barbara W. Andaya, *A History of Malaysia* (Macmillan, 1985); and John David Legge, *Indonesia* (Prentice-Hall, 1965).

Notes

1. Vincent A. Smith, *Akbar, the Great Mogul*, 2nd ed. (Mystic, CT: Verry, 1966), p. 522.
2. Quoted in Roger Bigelow Merriman, *Suleiman the Magnificent* (Cambridge, MA.: Harvard Univ. Press, 1944), p. 33.
3. Quoted in Sir Edward S. Creasy, *A. History of the Ottoman* Turks (Beirut: Khayats, 1961), p. 127.
4. Quoted in Bamber Gascoigne, *The Great Moghuls* (New York: Harper and Row, 1971), p. 128.
5. Quoted in G. F. Hudson, *Europe and China* (Boston: Beacon Press, 1931), p. 244.
6. Colin McEvedy and Richard Jones, *Atlas of World Population History* (New York: Penguin Books, 1978), p. 171.
7. Quoted in John F. Cady, *Southeast Asia* (New York: McGraw Hill, 1965), p. 263.

Emerging Civilizations in Sub-Sahara Africa and the New World

B y A.D. 1200, the process of civilization was approaching global dimensions. At the same time that Europe, Asia, and the Middle East were experiencing dynamic cultural growth during the late medieval period, sub-Sahara Africa and the New World were undergoing similar changes. Indeed, both regions had developed high civilizations before the European impact of the fifteenth and sixteenth centuries.

African and American civilizations were each distinctive, although generally similar to those in Eurasia. In all three areas, flourishing agriculture supported expanding populations, large cities, highly skilled crafts, expanding trade, complex social orders, and developing states. The basic culture of sub-Sahara Africa evolved mainly from its own traditions, while imported Eurasian culture, such as Islam, was relatively superficial. American civilizations were even more original, having developed in complete isolation from the Old World.

The most noteworthy native American civilizations were those of the Mayas in Yucatan and Guatemala, the Aztecs in central Mexico, and the Incas in Peru. The Mayas are especially famous for their mathematics, their solar calendar, and their writing system, still largely undeciphered. The Aztecs and Incas conquered large populations and governed large states. Each civilization produced distinctive art, religion, values, and customs, some of which have become part of the Latin American heritage. Even today, Latin American artists often take their themes from these traditions.

African civilizations before the sixteenth century compared favorably with those in Europe. Ethiopia, in East Africa, was already flourishing while the Roman Empire was disintegrating. In the tenth century, and possibly two centuries earlier, East African cities were trading by sea with Persia and India. Shortly after, the Kingdom of Ghana rose in the western Sudan. After about A.D. 1200, when European states were becoming centralized monarchies, comparable kingdoms were rising in sub-Sahara Africa, particularly in regions drained by the Niger, Congo, and Zambesi rivers. Europeans arriving after the 1400s found well-organized governments and societies bound by strong traditions.

Native Cultures in Sub-Sahara Africa

As late as the fifteenth century, cultures in sub-Sahara Africa were still somewhat distinct from the states, which were relatively new and often shaped by foreign influences among the ruling minorities. Most sub-Saharan Africans, even those living in powerful states, still held firmly to old loyalties associated with lineage, village, and religion. Because this respect for tradition was so typical of all these societies, we can understand them better if we first take note of their ancient cultural foundations.

Geographic, Ethnic, and Historical Backgrounds

Geographic factors help explain sub-Sahara Africa's relatively late state-building. Climatic changes between 5000 and 1500 B.C., which produced the Sahara Desert, limited cultural contacts with the Middle East and the Mediterranean basin. When such contacts became more frequent in the Christian era, local African traditions were deeply rooted and resistant to change. In addition, the vast space open to migration south of the Sahara decreased conflict over land, thereby lessening what had been a significant stimulus in the formation of many early Eurasian states. This factor, too, helps account for delayed political development.

Although most Americans have traditionally thought of sub-Sahara Africa as an immense jungle, more than half of the area comprises grassy plains, known as savanna. The northern savanna, sometimes called the Sudan, stretches across the continent, just south of the Sahara. Other patches of savanna are interspersed among the mountains of East Africa, and another belt of grassland runs east and west across the southern continent, north of the Kalahari Desert. Between the northern and southern savannas, in the region of the equator, is jungle. Heavy rainfall here permitted the cultivation of some nutritious crops, but soils were not very fertile, and the rain forests produced many dangers, including sleeping sickness, to which both humans and animals are susceptible. Generally, the most habitable regions have been the savannas, which have favored transportation and agriculture.

After the Sahara became arid, the most prominent sub-Saharan peoples were Negroid speakers of diverse but related Bantu languages. Originating in west central Africa, between the savanna and the forests, the Bantu began migrating after about 1000 B.C. For centuries, they moved south and east, ultimately spreading along the east coast. By A.D. 1000, they had reached central Natal, in what is now the Republic of South Africa. During their migrations, the Bantu absorbed or displaced other Negroid peoples of eastern and southern Africa, driving pygmies, Bushmen, and Khoisan-speaking pastoralists into the southern jungle, the Kalahari Desert, or the extreme southwestern savanna. Thus Bantu migrants provided most of sub-Sahara Africa with a common cultural identity (see map above right).

The Bantu migrations were closely related to agriculture and iron-working in a continuous reciprocal process. Developing agriculture expanded Bantu populations; iron tools and weap-

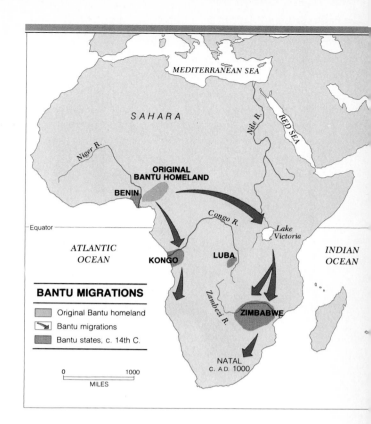

ons provided the means to acquire new lands; and the resulting migrations spread both technologies through the whole sub-Sahara region.

Until recently, most scholars believed that early Bantu peoples acquired agriculture from the upper Nile, via the northern savanna. More recent linguistic and archeological investigations suggest that plant domestication began independently in Ethiopia, the central Sudan, and the upper Niger, centuries before the Sahara became a desert. Regardless of which theory is correct, it is clear that a number of native crops, most notably bulrush millet and sorghum, were cultivated in the western savannah by 2000 B.C. These were diffused south to the original Bantu homelands, where they were augmented by African yams.

The vitality of early Bantu agrarian society is well illustrated by the Nok culture, which flourished in central Nigeria after 1000 B.C. Its skilled gardeners provided economic support for great artists, who produced beautiful terracotta (baked clay) sculpture. Later, as the Bantu

This stylized terra cotta head, dating from about 500 B.C., is an outstanding example of Nok sculpture. The head, which represents a human face, was probably used for religious purposes.

moved east and south, leaving the forest, they improved their gardening techniques and their food stocks by adopting Near Eastern grains and plantains. They also began herding cattle, sheep, and goats.

With the Bantu migrations, iron-working diffused rapidly through sub-Sahara Africa. This revolution, which had recently stirred all Eurasian civilizations, was brought from Egypt to Nubia in the seventh century B.C. It appeared in the western Sudan at about the same time, apparently brought south across the Sahara by Berbers, in contact with Phoenician or Carthaginian traders. Iron was produced in the Nok culture by 500 B.C., and iron-working was known to the earliest Bantu migrants, who ultimately brought it down the east coast beyond the Zambezi by the fifth century A.D. African ironmasters became very proficient and were highly respected. In some areas of West-Central Africa, their craft assumed such ritualistic significance that their furnaces were located in secluded places. After about A.D. 900, during the second iron age,

African furnaces were capable of generating higher temperatures than those in Europe before the 1700s. By then, Bantu craftsmen were producing high quality implements, as well as beautiful jewelry in copper and gold.

This later era brought a climax in social evolution. Between 1300 and 1500, for example, the Bantu population increased from 21 to 30 million people.[1] Trade also expanded significantly, not only within sub-Sahara Africa but also with the Mediterranean basin and other Eurasian areas. Rising commerce encouraged the growth of cities and the organization of large states. Such changes were most typical of the western Sudan and East Africa, which combined native African and non-African cultures. But even in the Bantu hinterlands, where foreign influences were nonexistent or only indirect, cities appeared and strong kingdoms emerged. In their institutions and values, these proto-civilizations were predominantly African.

The General Culture Pattern

Although Bantu-speaking societies were remarkably diverse, their institutions, values, and aesthetic styles reflected a common pattern. Usually, authority was strongest in the village, where it was exercised by elders of extended families (lineages), who claimed descent from a great ancestor. Both custom and religion supported this system. Traditional rules governed an individual's social functions and activities, which were often performed within his or her age group. Respect for the community was paramount, speculative innovation was suspect, and selfish behavior was discouraged or punished. Political authority beyond the village was most effective where it depended upon these local loyalties. Kings based their right to rule on descent from divine ancestors but exercised such rights within the limits of customary law.

Sub-Saharan economies, outside of the Sudan, Ethiopia, and the east coast, were based largely upon simple agriculture without plows and draft animals, although a primitive irrigation was in evidence. Pastoralism was common throughout the savannas, particularly among seminomadic peoples, including some Bantu-speakers. Most of the basic handicraft industries were well developed, including spinning, weaving, pottery-making, carpentry, and metal-working. Using relatively crude methods, African miners procured iron, copper, and gold ores. Highly skilled craftsmen sought to protect their secrets by organizing their families into tightly knit groups. Trade was usually a function of the crafts, although specialized merchants and trading societies were often present in the cities. Generally, these economies depended upon individual skills, employed within community and family traditions.

The kinship principle was fundamental to social organization throughout sub-Sahara Africa. Loyalties to the clans, each comprising all members of an extended family, living and dead, were more compelling than class interests, even in the cities. Sometimes, clans were combined in more artificial tribal systems. Tribal chiefs were often hereditary, but most were also confirmed by clan elders, who were all presumed to be at least distantly blood-related. Because tribes and lineages were older than the villages, the latter were often divided into separate kinship groups. Grouping individuals of different lineages into age-sets, such as children, apprentice warriors, and elders, helped alleviate divisiveness. Secret societies, including members drawn from mature age groups, also united lineages and encouraged loyalty to village or tribal communities.

Kinship societies were typical; but many changed as they experienced productive economies, property relationships, and increasingly prevalent warfare. In the process, ancient matrilineal clans, with descent traced through women, gave way gradually to patrilineal groups, with men in control. The change was reflected in marriage customs, where the traditional dowry, supplied by the wife's family, was replaced by "bride-price," paid by the prospective husband. This enforced the idea that wives are valuable property, to be protected and used for economic gain. Within patrilineal societies, a minority of male elders governed, while women did most of the work, including agricultural labor. Such practices, however, do not prove the complete demise of matriarchal values, many of which lingered on. There were instances where wives still dominated their husbands, demanding gifts when they produced children and going back to their families when at odds with their spouses.

The confusion of male and female roles is perhaps best illustrated in Bantu political institutions. Most states were headed by kings, but matrilineal descent was quite common in royal lines. This could involve complex relationships, resulting from the effort to reconcile male royal authority with the traditional practice of matrilineal succession. To solve this problem, the heir apparent was sometimes a nephew of the queen and a son of her oldest brother. In another scenario, where kings followed the common practice of marrying their sisters, the relationship may not have been sexual but merely symbolic, permitting women to share royal power in nominal patrilineal systems. There were also numerous examples of queens who held supreme authority, with or without a consort. This was not typical, but even in states where male supremacy was most pronounced, women were often powers behind the thrones. The king's mother, the queen, or both usually advised the monarch, particularly on matters pertaining to women and economic organization. On occasion, women also served as councilors or officials; they were often priests; and in a few instances, they fought as soldiers.

The newer patrilineal political systems developed slowly but directly from older kinship structures. Although many Bantu-speaking societies remained "stateless," some developed kingdoms from tribal bases. Monarchs were at first tribal chiefs, some of whom managed to conquer or otherwise unite other tribes. Kings generally carried on the traditions of the lineages, claiming descent from divine ancestors who lived in a half-mythical "dreamtime" of the distant past, when they had brought a message from the gods, led their blood brothers on a great migration, or found land to settle. Kings were considered semi-divine, but their actual powers were limited by traditional ceremony and law. Their rule depended upon support from lineage chiefs, village headmen, and secret societies. Some later kings appointed their own officials, but these were usually selected from local leaders.

The most abiding part of the sub-Saharan African heritage was its value system, rather than its social or political institutions. Supporting such institutions were customary beliefs which shaped all aspects of life. Most common to these beliefs was a profound awareness of human interdependence. Appreciation for community and law, mingled in primitive superstitions and intuitive insights, found expression in hundreds of oral myths and stories, known to Africans from the Niger to the Limpopo. The rich Bantu heritage in art and music reflected the same communal perspectives. Such values have been common to tribal societies everywhere, but nowhere else have they endured so tenaciously into advanced stages of civilization.

Religion touched every phase of human experience in sub-Sahara Africa. Specific beliefs varied from tribe to tribe, but some general tenets were common. Most Bantu-speaking peoples believed that the dead continued to influence the lives of their survivors; indeed, the ancestors were considered to remain in spirit, eliciting respect and concern from the living, who might welcome ancestors at meals or appease them when they were angry. Sub-Saharan Africans also recognized many spirits identified with natural forces, both benign and dangerous. Most of these societies also believed in a supreme being as the highest power, the source of all excellence and virtue but far removed from human understanding.

Sub-Saharan Africans were remarkably skilled and sensitive artists, particularly in sculpture. Ancient sculptors carved wood, ivory, or soapstone and cast in bronze, as well as working with baked clay. The famous bronze statuary of Benin, climaxing a long development in Nigeria, has been compared in craftsmanship and aesthetic sensitivity with the best work of the European Renaissance. Statuary and sculptured architectural decorations were often used to record historical events. Despite its characteristic realism, black African sculpture also symbolized religious themes.

Symbolism, religious and otherwise, was also typical of African music, especially of drum rhythms and dance. Like law and religion, music was a part of everyday life. Bantu songs recounted real life experiences such as hunting, planting, cattle trading, courtship, and the adventures of famous heroes. Unlike musical events in Europe or contemporary America, where the performing artist plays to an audience, all individuals present tended to participate. Exceptions were mostly to be found in such states as Mali and Axum, where professional musicians

Bronze relief fashioned by artisans of Benin. The king (center) is flanked by pages and guards. Plaques like these adorned the walls and square pillars of the Royal Palace of Benin.

were kept at royal courts, according to customs prevalent in North Africa or the Middle East. African audiences in the traditional Bantu societies usually became involved by clapping or dancing. Nothing could better illustrate the prevailing adherence to communal values.

Representative Bantu States

The ancient common culture pattern was well illustrated by a number of emerging Bantu states in the late medieval period. They include Zimbabwe and Mutapa in contemporary Zimbabwe; Kongo, which straddled the great river in the southwest; and Benin, near the mouth of the Niger. The Mossi and Yoruba states, which arose in the Niger backcountry, were typical of numerous less powerful Bantu polities.

Upon arriving in East Africa at the opening of the sixteenth century, the Portuguese found the Kingdom of Mutapa controlling 700 miles of the upper Zambezi. They learned from Mutapan oral tradition about two recent kings who had conquered an empire between the Zambezi and the Limpopo. The last conqueror had moved his capital north to the Zambezi, but his successors still revered the ancient stone ruins of the original capital at Zimbabwe in the southern highlands. Great Zimbabwe, which reached its peak of development between 1250 and 1450, is the most impressive among hundreds of stone ruins, dating from the same era in that region. Its great buildings, extending over sixty acres, included a palace capable of housing a thousand servants and a temple with walls ten feet thick and twenty feet high. Labor for such projects was supported by a flourishing gold trade with the coastal cities, continued later by Mutapa. Without written records, scholars cannot precisely describe the Zimbabwe polity, but Portuguese accounts of Mutapa provide some indication of what the parent civilization was like.

The royal capital of Mutapa contained a palace complex within a wooden palisade. Here, in addition to the king's quarters, were those for

The massive stone wall dominates the ruins of the valley of Zimbabwe, which means "the sacred graves of the chiefs."

the queens and the royal pages, who were young hostages from subject peoples, sent to serve at the Mutapan court. The royal household also included the king's personal aides, such as the captain of the guard, the king's pharmacist, the head musician, and the doorkeeper. The most powerful officials, however, were the nine "wives of the king." Of these, the top ranking "wife" was the king's sister, who was in charge of foreign affairs. Only one queen, who ranked third in the hierarchy, was a true wife. The others were chief ministers and regional governors, with their own estates, vassals, and revenues. Some were not even women, but all were related to the dynasty by symbolic marriage ties, a practice evidently carried over from a past when all the ministers were women. Another sign of an earlier female emphasis was a military contingent of women, who played a decisive part in the election of kings. This tradition-bound bureaucracy and its related lineages imposed practical limits upon the king, despite his recognized divinity.

Another notable kingdom was Kongo, located near the mouth of the Congo River. It was formed in the fourteenth century when a petty northern prince named Wene led a migration into the south, married into the local ruling family, and began acquiring vassals through conquest and voluntary submission of local rulers. A typical Bantu hero, Wene took the title of *ManiKongo* (lord of the Kongo). His successors governed a realm which united six former states between the coast and Stanley Pool.

By the time the Portuguese arrived in the 1400s, Kongo had already developed a bureaucratic monarchy. The king had a paid bodyguard and a central government, collecting taxes in copper and cloth, which served as currency in regular trade between the coast and the interior. Appointed governors and district officials enforced authority in the six provinces. In the late fifteenth century, the whole system was based upon innumerable agricultural villages, which were still organized in the old matrilineal lineages but governed by brothers and nephews. Wives and daughters did most of the work in the fields.

North of Kongo, on the forested coast of southern Nigeria, was Benin, a prosperous and powerful kingdom two centuries before the Portuguese arrived. Unlike Kongo, it had grown wealthy from its merchants' overland trade with the Sudan, although it did not become Muslim or import Sudanese culture. Among Benin's greatest rulers was Ewuare, who killed his rival and took the throne in 1440. He was remembered as a powerful magician and healer but was more famous as a conqueror of 200 towns, extending Benin's boundaries to the Niger and into the Yoruba hinterlands.

The kings of Benin, known as Obas, lived in a huge palace, protected by a surrounding maze of courtyards. They maintained large, well-trained armies. Aiding the king was a council, comprised of hereditary officials who were royal family members. Government outside of the capital, Benin City, was largely in the hands of town and village chiefs, also related to the ruling dynasty.

In addition to Benin, other states in the Niger region profited from contacts with the Sudan but continued developing their Bantu culture. Commerce, traditionally monopolized by women at the local level, had become thriving long-distance trade by the fifteenth century, when tribal towns north and west of Benin were heavily involved in military struggles for commercial dominance. The kings (Alafins) of Oyo, one Yoruba state, began building a tributary empire. It functioned, before 1500, as a complex mix of palace councils, subkings, secret societies, and lineage organizations at the village level. Later, in the sixteenth century, Oyo would become a strong rival of Benin.

The Bantu heritage was equally striking among the Mossi states of the upper Volta, on the borders of Mali and Songhai in the western Sudan. By the fifteenth century, the five original Mossi kingdoms were united in a federation of subkings, each recognizing one ruler as overlord. This potentate headed a government of sixteen ministries, his palace housed hundreds of servants, and his army included efficient cavalry units. The Mossi polity resembled its greater Muslim neighbors, except for its religion and its orientation toward the outside world. In these respects, its rulers were loyal to the spirit of their ancestral religion and their customary law.

All of the states described here were closer to their native traditions than were the older and more complex polities in the Sudan, in Ethiopia, and along the East Coast. Most of these latter states espoused Islam, while Ethiopia had been Christian since the fourth century. In addition, they imported non-African languages, writing systems, art, and cultural traditions. Because they developed earlier, they have often been regarded as sources of civilization spreading into the African interior. Such a process did take place, as is most evident on the borders of the northern savanna. Yet all innovations were integrated into older African cultures. This was true of all sub-Saharan states, but especially true of emerging southern Bantu monarchies after A.D. 1000.

Hybrid Civilizations of Sub-Sahara Africa

While Bantu states in the forests and the southern highlands were evolving toward centralized monarchies, other sub-Saharan cultures were maturing into complex but varied civilizations. The western Sudan produced great empires, comparing in reputation with Eurasian imperial states. Ethiopia, a compact Christian monarchy, developed a unique identity while relatively isolated in the Abyssinian highlands. The Swahili sultanates on the east coast were independent cities, prospering in sea trade with Asia. But despite their differences, these societies were more economically advanced, more complex in political organization, more literate, and more aware of the larger world than those of the southern Bantu. Indeed, they were hybrid civilizations, with a layer of non-African values and institutions superimposed upon their native cultural foundations.

Early Contacts with Non-African Civilizations

Outside influences reached sub-Sahara Africa from ancient times, despite its relative isolation. Egypt expanded southward into the eastern Sudan before 2000 B.C.; Phoenicians, in their day, circumnavigated the continent, trading along the way. Later, Carthaginian galleys sailed the northwest coast, and still later, Romans reached the east coast through the Red Sea. They also traded across the Sahara, particularly after the second century A.D., when they brought Asian camels to North Africa. Following the Roman era, Eurasian influences reached Africa via the upper Nile, the ports of western Asia, and the rapidly developing caravan trade of the western Sahara.

The major source of Egyptian influence upon sub-Sahara Africa was the black Nubian Kingdom of Kush (see map at right). Once an Egyptian province, Kush became independent in the eighth century B.C. Its kings governed Egypt briefly before the 600s; after being driven from the north, they continued to rule the upper Nile, perpetuating an Africanized version of Egyptian culture, complete with pyramids. During the early Christian era, their capital city at Meroë became a famous iron-smelting center. Kush conducted a lively trade with Egypt, the central Sudan, Ethiopia, and Arabia. An Axumite invasion destroyed the kingdom in the fourth century, but two surviving Nubian states maintained Christianity and the traditional civilization until they were overrun by Arabs in the fourteenth and fifteenth centuries.

A second foreign influence upon sub-Sahara Africa came from pre-Islamic Arabs, who crossed the Red Sea and colonized the Eritrean coast around 1000 B.C. They interbred with native Africans to form a state called Axum, which rose on the Somali coast of Ethiopia. After destroying Kush in 350 B.C., Axum extended its control into the highlands. It brought many Semitic influences to northeast Africa, including some aspects of Judaism and a distinctive language. It also accepted Coptic Christianity from Egypt, maintaining close contacts with Near Eastern centers until it was isolated by the rise of Islam in the seventh century.

Of all the early foreign influences in sub-Sahara Africa, the Islamic religion was undoubtedly the most significant. Originating in western Arabia, it spread rapidly through the Near East and North Africa in the seventh century. From Morocco, Tunisia, and Egypt, it was carried into the northern savanna by traders, missionaries, and conquerors. It also followed Arab and Persian sea trade from the Red Sea and the Persian Gulf to East Africa. With Islam came monotheism, Arabic language and writing, Arabic and Persian literature, coined money, and

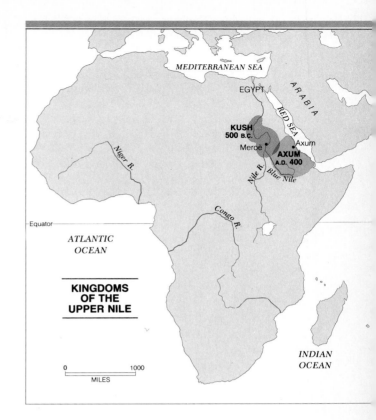

KINGDOMS
OF THE
UPPER NILE

bureaucratic government. Islam was considerably modified by African customs, but it became a potent force, particularly in the western Sudan.

Ethiopia

Among the later sub-Saharan states, Ethiopia was the oldest. Historians usually record its beginnings with Axum's conquest of Kush, but Ethiopian monarchs traced their lineage back to the Hebrew King Solomon and the Queen of Sheba, or Sabea, an ancient state in southwestern Arabia. Whether this is true, Axum's strong roots in Near Eastern culture were strengthened after its conversion to Christianity. Although predominantly black, its people were ethnically, culturally, and linguistically different from the Bantu.

In the sixth century, the country was wealthy and powerful. Cities boasted stone houses and beautiful churches; the king wore luxurious robes and rode in chariots pulled by elephants. Axum also produced its own distinctive gold

Beit Giorgis, one of the rock-hewn churches of Ethiopia. The churches, eleven in all, were hewn out of solid rock, entirely below ground level, then carved both internally and externally.

coins and conducted trade throughout the Near East, transacting business in Greek or in its own official language, known as Ge'ez.

This picture changed drastically after Muslims conquered North Africa in the seventh century. They soon drove the Axumites from the Red Sea coast and into the highlands of the interior, where they fought to preserve their independence, their Christianity, and their culture. This struggle became particularly intense after the tenth century, when the country was weakened by a revolt, led by a reputedly Jewish queen in the southwest who played off Muslims against Christians, killed the Ethiopian king in battle, seized the throne, and reigned for forty years, persecuting Ethiopian Christians throughout the land. In the twelfth century, another rebellious local queen helped further Muslim influence. By the fifteenth century, however, Ethiopian monarchs had united local tribes, Christian and Muslim, into a tributary empire, whose monarch termed himself "King of Kings."

The outstanding emperor of the era was Zara Yakob (1434–1468), who achieved internal unity for Ethiopia and security among its warlike Muslim neighbors, most of whom he defeated and reduced to vassalage. He is best remembered as a stern reformer who stamped out heresy, strengthened the Ethiopian Church, and reorganized the bureaucracy. He also established tentative relations with the pope, seeking European aid against his Muslim enemies. Unpopular at the time, this policy later led to alliance with the Portuguese.

Zara Yakob held sway over a loosely controlled tributary state, but within his immediate environs he ruled as an absolute autocrat, surrounded by hundreds of courtiers and servants. He was aided by two chief ministers, two chief justices, a secretary, and a chaplain. The "Negus" (Emperor), as head of the Church, appointed the bishops and took an active part in church administration. Although he traveled constantly about the country, accompanied by his enormous retinue, the Negus allowed the public to see him only on rare occasions, when he appeared on a high platform, specially built for the purpose.

Like the Middle Eastern states, to which it was closely related in history and culture, Ethiopia developed a male-centered society. According to Ethiopian legend, the first king, a son of the Queen of Sheba, swore at his coronation that Ethiopia would never be ruled by a woman. The king, though a Christian, usually had three wives and numerous concubines, who were kept secluded in their own quarters of the household. They had few political duties. Although the queen mothers were honored, and one might occasionally serve as regent for a young son, their political influence, like that of the royal wives, usually had to be exerted through some sympathic male of status. As among Arabs and Jews, this influence was often beneficial and decisive, despite its unofficial nature. On the other hand, it could be quite disruptive when it resulted in palace intrigues and conspiracies among royal mothers, maneuvering to gain the throne for their sons.

The economy of medieval Ethiopia was based primarily upon local agriculture. Axum's extensive commerce declined after the eighth century, as it shifted gradually from the sea to land trade with the interior. Nevertheless, the country enjoyed moderate prosperity, as evidenced by bountiful public revenues and lavish expenditures in church-building. The Emperor received tribute and taxes, mostly in goods, which were stored in warehouses. In addition, the monarch's daily needs were largely supplied by local rulers or officials, who entertained his entourage as it moved from place to place.

Ethiopia acquired a rich cultural heritage, drawn mainly from the Middle East. Its traditions, even before the Christian era, were generated from the religious lore of Palestine and Arabia. Consequently, its most enduring cultural expressions were its churches, the most famous of which are the beautiful and awe-inspiring rock-hewn cathedrals of Roha, built after the eleventh century in the reign of the legendary Emperor Lalibela, who was declared a saint by the Ethiopian Church. These huge architectural projects compare favorably with similar temples in India for their ingenious engineering. This religious accent was typical of all scholarly and aesthetic pursuits, particularly in the fourteenth and fifteenth centuries, when Ethiopians produced innumerable biblical translations, theological treatises, biographies of saints, historical chronicles, illuminated manuscripts, and mural paintings.

Swahili Cities in East Africa

From ancient times the East African coast was involved in long-range maritime trade. Phoenician, Greek, Roman, and Arab traders regularly operated as far south as Zanzibar before Bantu migrants arrived in early Christian times. The rise of Islam furthered commercial expansion in the Indian Ocean, but East Africa was not much affected until the twelfth century, when a wave of Arab and Persian commercial colonists began transforming primitive trading settlements into flourishing Muslim commercial cities.

During the peak period of Swahili civilization, between 1200 and 1500, the east coast was studded with thirty-seven city-states along the 1500 miles between Mogadishu in the north and Sofala in the south. Among the best known were Malindi, Mombasa, and Kilwa. Most Swahili cities were on islands, protected by sea from the foreign Bantu world of the mainland. Common people in the cities were from that world, either as descendants or migrants. Free intermarriage between a Middle Eastern elite and native inhabitants had produced a diverse racial mixture, described later by the Portuguese as varying from black through tawny to light, according to locality and social class. Swahili, the language of these cities, was mainly Bantu, but included some Arabic, Persian, and Hindu. Islam was usually the official religion, although shaped by local beliefs and customs. Generally, the culture was a synthesis of African and Middle Eastern, with the latter more pronounced among the upper classes.

The Swahili cities were independent, with some temporary exceptions. At times, one city might exact tribute from its neighbors, or a number of states might federate in time of war. But commercial competition made such cooperation difficult to maintain and curtailed political expansion toward the Bantu interior, where kingdoms like Mutapa played one coastal city against another. Within the cities, governments were usually headed by monarchs (sultans), assisted by merchant councils, holy men, or royal relatives. Although the sultans were typical Muslim rulers in most respects, the common order of succession was drawn from the Bantu matrilineal tradition. When a sultan died at Kilwa, Pate, or numerous other cities, the throne passed to one of the head queen's brothers.

As the Muslim Middle East became the commercial center of Eurasia, maritime trade of the Swahili cities figured largely in the commercial development of three continents. Kilwa became the major port for gold sent through Egypt to Europe. Iron ore, exported from Malindi and Mombasa, supplied the furnaces of India. A number of Chinese expeditions visited the coast in the early 1400s (see ch. 8), exchanging porcelain for typical African products, including exotic animals such as ostriches, zebras, and giraffes.

Emperor Zara Yakob's Coronation and His Concern for the Church

This fifteenth-century ruler pulled the central administration together after a long period of feudal decentralization. His several daughters assisted in the task by taking over provincial governments.

When our King Zara Yaqob went into the district of Aksum to fulfil the law and to effect the coronation ceremony according to the rites followed by his ancestors, all the inhabitants, including the priests, came to meet him and welcomed him with great rejoicing; the chiefs and all the soldiers of Tigre were on horseback carrying shield and lance, and the women, in great numbers, gave themselves up, according to the ancient custom, to endless dancing. When he entered the gates of the town the King had on his right and left the governors of Tigre and Aksum who, according to custom, both waved olive branches. . . . After arriving within the walls of Aksum the King had gold brought to him which he scattered as far as the city gate on the carpets spread along his route. This amount of gold was more than a hundred ounces. . . .

On the twenty-first of the month of Ter *(January 16)* the day of the death of our Holy Virgin Mary, the coronation rite was carried out, the King being seated on a stone throne. This stone, together with its supports, is only used for the coronation. There is another stone on which the King is seated when he receives the blessing, and several others to the right and left on which are seated the twelve chief judges. There is also the throne of the metropolitan bishop.

While at Aksum the Emperor made a number of regulations for the church.

During his stay at Aksum our King regulated all the institutions of the church and ordered that prayers which had up to that time been neglected should be recited each day at canonical hours. For this purpose he convened a large number of monks and founded a convent, the headship of which he entrusted to an abbot with the title of Pontiff of Aksum, who received an extensive grant of land called Nader. The King accomplished this work through devotion to the Virgin Mary and to perpetuate his own memory and that of his children and his children's children. He summoned some catechists and presented to the church a great number of ornaments and a golden ewer, revived all the old traditions, spread joy in these places, and returned thence satisfied.

Zara Yaqob also founded churches and regulated religious affairs in other provinces.

Arriving in the land of Tsahay in Amhara, he went up a high and beautiful mountain, the site of which he found pleasing; at the top of this mountain and facing east he found a wall which had been raised by his father, King Dawit, with the intention of erecting a shrine. His father, however, had not had the time to complete the work, in the same way that the ancient King David, who planned to build a temple to the Lord, could not accomplish his task which was completed by his son Solomon. Our king Zara Yaqob fulfilled his father's intention by building a shrine to God on the west of the mountain. Everyone, rich and poor alike and even the chiefs, were ordered to carry the stones with the result that this edifice was speedily erected. They embellished this locality, which underwent a great transformation; two churches were built there, one called Makana Gol and the other Dabra Negwadgwad. The King attached to them a certain number of priests and canons to whom he gave grants of land. He also founded a convent and placed in it monks from Dabra Libanos, whom he endowed in a similar manner.

From *The Ethiopian Royal Chronicles*, edited by Richard K. Pankhurst. (London: Oxford University Press, 1967), pp. 34–36.

Giotto, *Adoration of the Magi.* Renowned as the true founder of Florentine painting, Giotto imbued his art with the illusion of texture, weight, expression, and depth to give his figures their convincing lifelike quality. Body and drapery create a single unit in Giotto's paintings, and his expression of human emotions is both simple and subtle. Although he was nominated in 1334 to be the architect of the Florence cathedral and the city fortifications, he continued to maintain that painting was superior to other arts.

Botticelli, *The Birth of Venus* (above). The last great Florentine painter of the Early Renaissance, Botticelli did most of his best-known work, including *The Birth of Venus,* for Lorenzo de' Medici and his circle. In *The Birth of Venus,* the artist blends ancient mythology with Christian faith. The figures, while voluptuous, are also serene and ethereal and seem to float rather than touch the ground. Leonardo da Vinci, *Mona Lisa* (right). The earliest of the masters of the High Renaissance, Leonardo was a painter, sculptor, architect, inventor, scientist, writer, and musician. *Mona Lisa,* arguably the most famous portrait ever painted, with her enigmatic smile expresses the artist's feeling for the mystery of human existence. In later life, Leonardo devoted himself to his scientific interests, filling notebooks (written backwards) with his observations on proportion, perspective, optics, anatomy, and geology. He created the art of scientific illustration, rendering with absolute clarity his vivid observations.

Michelangelo, *David* (right). To Michelangelo, the Florentine painter, sculptor, poet, and architect, sculpture was the noblest of the arts. The large marble *David,* the earliest monumental statue of the High Renaissance, was commissioned in 1501 to stand to the left of the entrance to the Palazzo Vecchio as a civic and patriotic symbol of the Republic of Florence. Even his contemporaries recognized Michelangelo's genius, referring to him as "the Divine M." Raphael, *Madonna of the Chair* (below). Along with Michelangelo and Leonardo da Vinci, Raphael is recognized as one of the three masters of the High Renaissance. Raphael combined qualities of Michelangelo and da Vinci to create a style that is both lyrical and dramatic. In 1508 Pope Julius II summoned Raphael to Rome and commissioned him to decorate the papal apartments at the Vatican, at the same time that Michelangelo was painting his frescoes on the ceiling of the Sistine Chapel.

Hieronymus Bosch, *The Garden of Delights* (above). From the Netherlands, Bosch was a religious painter who combined religious iconography with mood-setting landscape to express his satiric, pessimistic, medieval world view. Pieter Brueghel the Elder, *Peasant Wedding* (left). The last and one of the greatest of the artists of the Northern Renaissance, Brueghel was strongly influenced by Bosch, but the most outstanding quality of Brueghel's art is its independence from the Italian style or models. In *Peasant Wedding,* the artist provides a sympathetic but unsentimental close-up look at one of the few happy events in the lives of the peasant laborers.

In this era of their greatest prosperity, the Swahili cities built stone mosques and palaces, adorning their buildings with gold, ivory, and other wealth from nearly every major port in southern Asia. Kilwa impressed the famous Muslim scholar-traveler Ibn Batuta as the most beautiful and well-constructed city he had seen anywhere. Archeological excavations revealing the ruins of enormous palaces, great mansions, elaborate mosques, arched walkways, town squares, and public fountains have confirmed this evaluation. The main palace at Kilwa, built on the edge of an ocean cliff, contained over 100 rooms, as well as an eight-sided bathing pool in one of its many courtyards.

The Swahili cities produced their own characteristic culture. Their beautiful architecture, borrowed from Arabia and Persia, was matched by a Swahili literature, written in an Arabic script. Poems, ballads, and letters in Swahili reflected the perspectives of a Muslim urban elite. Most common people, however, were only indifferent converts to Islam, which they accepted while holding to their own orally expressed traditional beliefs. A few miles inland from the cities, the lives of Bantu villagers were relatively untouched by the ways of the coastal cities.

Empires of the Western Sudan

More than the Swahili cities and Ethiopia, the great states of the western Sudan were based upon native African traditions. The old Bantu ways remained very strong, particularly among women, who outwardly accepted the imported Muslim religion but retained their attachment to old customs and freedoms. Yet despite this pull of the past, the area was much affected by outside contacts, particularly those arising from trans-Saharan trade with the Mediterranean lands to the north.

Following the third century, when camels were first employed in this trade, large caravans, sometimes including 10,000 pack animals, made regular trips across the dangerous desert, carrying North African salt in exchange for West African gold. To these great expeditions, the Niger River offered a secure watering and resting place. Here were people who knew the savanna and could easily find the still distant gold-producing areas. Thus Africans living near the great bend of the river came into control of the lucrative gold and salt trade. Many traders were women, particularly those operating in local markets, where rising prosperity and accumulating wealth increased the traffic in foods and luxury goods.

Ghana   The earliest of the kingdoms of the western Sudan was Ghana (not to be confused with the modern state of the same name). It arose on the upper Niger during the fourth century as a loose federation of village states, inhabited by Soninke farmers (see map below). According to unconfirmed legends, it was first ruled by a Berber dynasty, which was overthrown about A.D. 700, when Kaya Maghau led his kinsmen in an uprising, killed the last white ruler, and established a Soninke dynasty. Kaya was remembered as a great warrior, who expanded Ghana's boundaries while furthering trade across the desert.

Ghana reached its peak in the eleventh century. The Arab chronicler al-Bakri noted in 1067 that the army was 200,000 strong, with many contingents wearing chain mail. The king, who

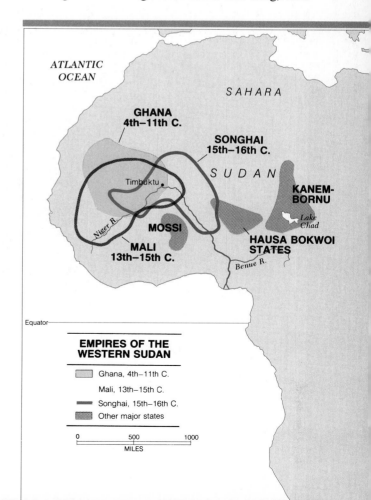

ATLANTIC OCEAN

SAHARA

GHANA
4th–11th C.

SONGHAI
15th–16th C.

S U D A N

Timbuktu

KANEM-BORNU

Lake Chad

MOSSI

MALI
13th–15th C.

HAUSA BOKWOI STATES

Niger R.

Benue R.

Equator

EMPIRES OF THE WESTERN SUDAN

Ghana, 4th–11th C.

Mali, 13th–15th C.

Songhai, 15th–16th C.

Other major states

0   500   1000

MILES

had not converted to Islam, was considered divine and able to intercede with the gods. He appointed all officials and served as supreme judge. When he appeared in public, he was surrounded by advisors and princes of the empire, along with personal retainers holding gold swords, horses adorned with gold-cloth blankets, and dogs wearing gold collars.

Ghana's wealth derived partially from its efficient irrigation agriculture, but the gold trade was an even more significant factor. The king claimed every gold nugget coming into the country, leaving ordinary citizens the right to buy and sell only gold dust. Taxes were levied on the many goods crossing Ghana's borders. The commercial emphasis is evident in al-Bakri's description of the capital, Kumbi-Saleh. This was really two towns, some six miles apart, one occupied by the king and his retinue and the other by foreign merchants. Even the merchants' town had twelve mosques, two-storied stone houses, and public squares. This, along with the Muslim legalists and theologians who lived in Kumbi-Saleh, suggests a prevailing Islamic influence, although the king publicly consulted priests of the traditional cults.

Ghana's decline and eclipse in the early thirteenth century remains something of a mystery.

One Muslim account of an Almoravid invasion from Morocco, around 1080, has been seriously questioned by recent scholarship, without completely resolving the question. Later kings apparently accepted Islam, but this may have been voluntary. At any rate, Ghana remained intact but weakening for another hundred years. In 1203, its rule was ended by the uprising of a petty vassal, who was later overthrown by Sundiata, founder of Mali.

Mali After defeating and killing the tyrant who had subjugated his kinsmen and murdered his brothers, Sundiata took over Ghana and gained control of the desert gold trade. Thus began a new ruling dynasty in the western Sudan. Sundiata's immediate descendants converted to Islam, which aided their further conquests, until by the fourteenth century, Malian kings ruled over more than forty million people and 400 towns in the entire Sudan-Sahel region of West Africa, which stretched from beyond the upper Niger to the Atlantic.

The kingdom was at the height of its power and prosperity during the reign of Mansa (King) Musa (1312–1337). Musa was perhaps the first African ruler to be known throughout the civilized world of western Asia and Europe. He was

In this 1375 map from the Catalan Atlas, Mansa Musa of Mali is holding a nugget of gold as he awaits the arrival of a Muslim trader. The inscription beside him reads: "This Negro lord is called Musa Mali, lord of all the Negroes of Guinea. So abundant is the gold which is found in his country that he is the richest and most noble king in all the land."

a great soldier, consolidating his control over a vast domain. He also encouraged the growth of Islam in his lands, importing Muslim scholars and architects to promote learning, build mosques, and implement his political authority. His fame abroad resulted mainly from his pilgrimage to Mecca in 1324, when his thousands of retainers and generous gifts completely amazed his hosts along the way. Gold expended then in Cairo caused ruinous Egyptian inflation for a generation.

Mansa Musa ruled over a state more efficiently organized than the relatively crude European kingdoms of the time. On the north and northeast were loosely held tributary kingdoms of diverse populations, including some Berbers. To the south were more closely controlled tributary states, under resident viceroys, appointed by the Mansa. Elsewhere, particularly in the cities, such as Timbuktu, provincial administrators governed directly in the king's name and at his pleasure. The central government included ministries for finance, justice, agriculture, and foreign relations.

Ibn Batuta visited Mali in 1352 and left a detailed description of the country. He was most impressed by its law and justice, which guaranteed that no man "need fear brigands, thieves, or ravishers" anywhere in the Mansa's vast domain. Batuta praised the king's devotion to Islam but was disappointed that so many Malians were not Muslim. He noted also that the unveiled women were most attractive but lacking in humility. He was astounded that they might take lovers without arousing their husbands' jealousy and might have male friends, with whom they regularly discoursed on learned subjects. Batuta was describing the city of Walata, where he found women better educated and enjoying more freedom that in other countries he had visited.[2] He might have said the same about a number of Sudanese trading cities, including Adoghast, Kumi Saleh, Gao, and Timbuktu.

After Mansa Musa's death, his successors found the large empire increasingly difficult to govern. They were plagued by poor communications, the diversity of cultures, and the competition of rising states, whose rulers were also converting to Islam. One of the rebellious states was Songhai, farther down the Niger. Before the end of the fourteenth century it had won its independence. Within another century it had conquered Mali.

Other Sudanese States Songhai reached its zenith during the reigns of Sonni Ali (1464–1492) and Askia Muhammed (1493–1528). Sonni Ali captured Timbuktu in 1468, while conquering most of Mali, When he died, after thirty years of ruthless military dictatorship, Askia Muhammed set about reorganizing the whole empire. He created central ministries, an appointed provincial administration, a professional army, and an enlarged fleet of canoes, which constantly patroled the Niger. He also reformed taxation, instituted a systems of weights and measures, and regularized judicial procedures. During his reign, the Sankore mosque in Timbuktu became so renowned as a center of learning that a contemporary traveler noted more profit being made from bookselling than from any other trade. When Askia Muhammed died, Songhai was respected throughout the western Islamic world.

Another rising Savanna state after the fourteenth century was Kanem-Bornu, located near Lake Chad in the central Sudan. By the eleventh century, the parent kingdom of Kanem was a prosperous contemporary of Ghana. After being overrun by invaders and then reconquered by earlier migrants to Bornu in the west, it emerged a second time after 1400. As did those of Mali, the women of Kanem-Bornu enjoyed a high social status. From the tenth century, they had held important government positions; the king's mother was an official advisor along with his chief wife and eldest sister. The kings commanded a large army, which they used to extend their territories. Like the Mansas of Mali, they attempted, with some success, to impose their Islamic religion upon their people. In the fifteenth century, they developed close relations with pro-Turkish regimes in North Africa and the Middle East, thus increasing their trade and their military support.

Farther west, between Lake Chad and the Niger, were the seven independent Hausa kingdoms, each organized as a city-state. Before the eleventh century, Hausa kings were hampered by a lingering matrilineal system, in which each

Mali, as Described by Ibn Batuta

Ibn Batuta (1304–1368) was a most famous Muslim traveler in the Near and Far East, as well as in Africa. He was the only medieval commentator who visited every land under Muslim rule.

The sultan of Mali is Mansa Sulayman, *mansa* meaning sultan, and Sulayman being his proper name. He is a miserly king, not a man from whom one might hope for a rich present. He held a banquet in commemoration of our master [the sultan of Morocco] to which the commanders, doctors, judge and preacher were invited, and I went along with them. Reading desks were brought in and the Koran was read through, then they prayed for our master and also for Mansa Sulayman. When the ceremony was over, I went forward and saluted Mansa Sulayman. The judge, the preacher, and Ibn al-Faquih told him who I was and he answered them in their tongue. They said to me "The sultan says to you 'Give thanks to God,'" so I said, "Praise be to God and thanks under all circumstances."

When I withdrew the sultan's hospitality gift was sent to me. Ibn al-Faquih came hurrying out of his house barefooted, and entered my room saying "Stand up; here comes the sultan's gift to you." So I stood up thinking that it consisted of robes of honour and money, and lo! it was three cakes of bread, and a piece of beef fried in native oil, and a calabash of sour curds. When I saw this I burst out laughing and thought it a most amazing thing that they could be so foolish. . . .

On certain days the sultan holds audiences in the palace yard, where there is a platform; this they call the *pempi*. It is carpeted with silk and has cushions placed on it. Over it is raised the umbrella, which is a sort of pavilion made of silk, surmounted by a bird in gold, about the size of a falcon. The sultan comes out of a door in a corner of the palace, carrying a bow in his hand and a quiver on his back. On his head he has a golden skull-cap bound with a golden band. His usual dress is a velvety red tunic, made of the European fabrics called *mutanfas*. The sultan is preceded by his musicians who carry gold and silver guimbris [two-stringed guitars],

and behind him come three hundred armed slaves. He walks in a leisurely fashion . . . and even stops from time to time. On reaching the *pempi*, he stops and looks around the assembly, then ascends it in the sedate manner of a preacher ascending a mosque-pulpit. As he takes his seat the drums, trumpets, and bugles are sounded. Three slaves go out at a run to summon the sovereign's deputy and the military commanders, who enter and sit down. Two saddled and bridled horses are brought, along with two goats, which they hold to serve as a protection against the evil eye.

The negroes are of all people the most submissive to their king and most abject in their behavior before him. They swear by his name, saying *Mansa Sulayman ki* [the Emperor Sulayman has commanded]. If he summons any of them while he is holding an audience in his pavilion, the person summoned takes off his clothes and puts on worn garments, removes his turban and dons a dirty skull-cap, and enters with his garments and trousers raised knee-high. He goes forward in an attitude of humility and dejection, and knocks the ground hard with his elbows, and stands with bowed head and bent back listening to what he says. If anyone addresses the king and receives a reply from him, he uncovers his back and throws dust over his head and back, for all the world like a bather splashing himself with water. . . . Sometimes one of them stands up before him and recalls his deeds in the sultan's service, saying, "I did so-and-so on such a day" or "I killed so-and-so." Those who have knowledge of this confirm his words, which they do by plucking the cord of the bow and releasing it with a twang.

Source: Rhoda Hoff, ed. and comp., *Africa: Adventures in Eyewitness History* (New York: Henry A. Walck, 1963), pp. 11–12.

monarch shared power with a queen mother and other female councilors. Later, as the cities began prospering in trans-Saharan trade, and as commercial rivalry increased, their weaknesses became more evident. This situation changed some after the fourteenth century, when most of the kings accepted Islam, using it to free them from old matriarchal restraints and prepare literate officials for governing the villages. The new Muslim age of despotism, competition, and warfare decisively weakened the traditional status of Hausa women. One king of Kano, in the late 1400s, even had his wives and thousand concubines secluded, as was the custom in the Muslim Middle East.

All the Sudanese states, despite their significance in the trans-Saharan trade, were relatively weak and insecure. Their Islamic culture, which generated literary and architectural achievements, was a thin veneer over a traditional African way of life. Royal administrators were hard pressed to control lineage chiefs and self-sustaining villages. Ultimately, Sudanese polities depended upon able kings; inefficient monarchs invariably brought collapse.

New World Civilizations

The rich traditions and vitality of African civilizations were also typical of those in America, long before Europeans saw them at the turn of the sixteenth century. Many prejudiced Spaniards considered these societies to be primitive; but others, who bothered to learn, soon discovered the Indians' technical efficiency, institutional complexity, and artistic creativity, as well as their superstitions and cruelty.

Historical Backgrounds

All American cultures originated with nomadic migrations from Asia to Alaska, across the Bering land bridge, which ceased to exist some 10,000 years ago. Scholars have placed the migrations from Asia between 13,000 and 28,000 years earlier. During countless generations, these early peoples moved south through North America, occupying most habitable areas. They reached Mexico by 20,000 years ago, Peru some

7000 years later, and ultimately the tip of South America by about 9000 B.C. In this long process, they split into hundreds of ethnic and linguistic groups and adapted to many different geographical environments.

The most significant modification of Amerindian culture came with agriculture. By 7000 B.C., some food crops were known in parts of the New World, but the major agricultural impact came with cultivated maize, shortly before 5000 B.C., in the Tehuacan Valley of Mexico. From this center, maize culture spread rapidly, particularly between 2000 and 1500 B.C. Within a few hundred years, village communities began developing as religious centers; by 500 B.C., large temple-communities were emerging; and during the last 500 years before the Spaniards arrived, city-states united to form large empires in Mexico and Peru.

Cultural levels varied widely at the end of the fifteenth century. Most of the indigenous tribes, including fur-clad Eskimos, mesolithic nomads of the North American plains, jungle headhunters of the Amazon, and naked savages of Tierra del Fuego, were hunters and gatherers. Advanced peasant cultures, however, flourished in a number of places. North of the Rio Grande, these ranged from the Pueblo culture of the southwest to the large confederacies of the eastern woodlands. In South America, proto-civilizations were emerging along the north coasts, near the mouth of the Amazon, and on the southeastern pampas. Finally, mature civilizations had been established among the Mayas of Central America, the Aztecs of Mexico, and the Incas of Peru (see map, p. 407).

In comparison with others, these civilizations shared certain general characteristics. They depended upon maize cultivation, which imposed special social requirements, and they were severely limited by their lack of iron, horses, and most common domesticated animals. They also shared unique customs such as the wearing of ear or lip plugs. On the other hand, they were remarkably similar to other civilizations in their theocratic organizations, sun cults, pyramids, and human sacrifices. Like the African cultures, they were still in transition from matriarchal to patriarchal institutions, although further advanced in this process. Finally, a common belief in divine monarchy among Aztecs and Incas was also typical of many other peoples, including Africans, Hindus, and Cambodians.

Emerging Civilizations in Mesoamerica

The term *Mesoamerican* identifies related Mexican and Central American cultures, after about 1200 B.C. They developed in a bewildering diversity of climates and terrains but were unified by their economic interdependence, since no one region was self-sufficient. Despite many differences, they shared a complex calendar, hieroglyphic writing, bark paper and deerskin books, team games played with solid rubber balls, large markets, chocolate bean money, and common legends, notably one about a culture hero identified with a feathered serpent. To facilitate our study of developing Mesoamerican culture, we may conveniently divide its history into three main periods: formative (to A.D. 150), classical (150–900), and postclassical (900–1492).

The emergence of Mesoamerican civilization began along a lowland strip of the Mexican Caribbean coast, some 125 miles long and 50 miles wide, near present-day Vera Cruz. Here, by 1200 B.C., food production became efficient enough to support an appreciable number of nonagricultural workers. The resulting Olmec civilization, renowned for its large building projects and colossal sculptured stone heads, was centered first at San Lorenzo. After about 900 B.C., when San Lorenzo was destroyed by invaders, the center of the civilization moved to La Venta in Tabasco, until it collapsed at the end of the fourth century B.C.

Scattered throughout the Olmec heartland were numerous sparsely populated religious centers, supported by outlying peasant villages. Labor and stone for the massive construction projects, jade for carving, luxury goods, raw materials for the crafts, and food were brought to the centers, often from distant places. These goods were probably not the spoils of conquest; Olmec society left little evidences of war or violence, excepting those produced by foreign invaders. Its priestly ruling class evidently governed by exploiting fear and respect, even in Olmec colonies as distant as the Pacific coast. This theocratic orientation is reflected most obviously in the great temple mounds, in the huge stone conical pyramid at La Venta, rising over

A magnificent monumental stone head from the Olmec center at San Lorenzo. Some scholars have suggested that these massive heads are portraits of rulers.

ninety feet above the island, and in the characteristic jaguar motif of the carving and statuary, which undoubtedly represented a prevailing Olmec cult.

Olmec influence permeated most of Mesoamerica. A few independent Olmec centers may have been established in central Mexico, but it was probably more common for a number of Olmec priests and traders to live among a native population, conducting religious rituals and arranging for the transport of goods to the homeland. Such enclaves were typical of regions as distant as the Pacific coast of Central America. In other places, such as the Oaxaca Valley to the West or the southwestern Mexican highlands, the Olmec influence was more indirect, possibly resulting from Olmec intermarriage with local elites or cultural diffusion through simple trade. By such varied means, Olmec foundations were laid for the religion, art, and architecture—possibly for the calendars, mathematics, and writing systems—of later Mesoamerican civilizations, including the Mayan and Aztec.

The Early Classical Period in Mesoamerica

After the fall of La Venta, Olmec prestige waned, but civilizations continued to flourish, particularly in the Valley of Mexico, in the Oaxaca Valley, and in the Yucatan lowlands. By the second century A.D., these developments had progressed to a point of florescence known as the classical period, which lasted until the tenth century. This was a golden age, when literacy, complex time reckoning, a bewildering pantheon of gods, interregional trade, and a population increase of fortyfold over the Olmec period affected most of Mesoamerica. Hundreds of communities raised great buildings, "decorated them with beautiful frescoes, produced pottery and figurines in unbelieveable quantity, and covered everything with sculptures."[3]

Teotihuacan, in the northeastern Valley of Mexico, generated the most notable early classical culture. It was at its peak about A.D. 500, when it was the sixth largest city in the world, with a population between 125,000 and 200,000. As a great religious center, it featured the largest man-made structure in the New World, a great stone pyramid 180 feet high honoring the god Quetzalcoatl. Along with such imposing temples were wide avenues and bustling markets, drawing wares from throughout Mesoamerica. The city's governing elite enjoyed every luxury, while exploiting poor urban craftsmen and peasants in nearby areas. Over other states, including some among the lowland Mayas, Teotihuacan exerted a powerful influence, arising mainly from its cultural reputation, social connections, and commercial advantages.

Another impressive classical center in Mexico was located on the site of contemporary Monte Alban in the Oaxaca Valley. Between A.D. 300 and 700, this concentration of temples, pyramids, and shrines was a theocratic state, dominating adjacent residential hill settlements and a valley population of over 45,000 people. Although developed on a smaller scale than Teotihuacan, Monte Alban produced a similar pattern of external trade, class differentiation, elaborate religious architecture, artistic creativity, writing, and time reckoning. It derived most of its art styles from Teotihuacan and some from the Mayas but synthesized both in its own traditions. Politically, it remained independent through the classical era, although its elite sought the luxury goods and favor of Teotihuacan.

Classical Mayan Civilization

While Teohihuacan and Monte Alban flourished, Mayan peoples farther south in Yucatan and Guatemala produced the most splendid cultural achievements of the classical era and perhaps of native American societies in any time. Artistic and intellectual activity rose to new heights in numerous Mayan centers, each boasting its temples, palaces, observatories, and ball courts. Although it borrowed from Teotihuacan before the latter's fall in the seventh century A.D., Mayan civilization subsequently cast a brilliant shadow over the whole of Mesoamerica.

The earliest Mayas are thought to have migrated from the northwest coast of California to the Guatemalan highlands during the third millennium B.C. From that homeland, Yucatec and Cholian speakers settled the northern and central lowlands between 1500 B.C. and A.D. 100,

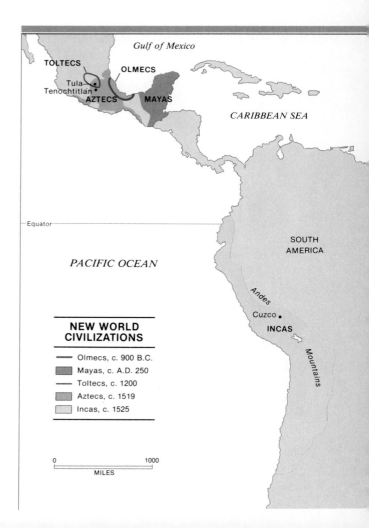

NEW WORLD CIVILIZATIONS

—— Olmecs, c. 900 B.C.
■ Mayas, c. A.D. 250
— Toltecs, c. 1200
▨ Aztecs, c. 1519
▢ Incas, c. 1525

0   1000
MILES

respectively. Mayan villages developed steadily, many becoming ceremonial centers by the Christian era. In the highlands, Kaminaljuyu had by then developed architecture and primitive writing under the influence of Oaxaca and Teotihuacan. In the early classical period before A.D. 550, Tikal in the central lowlands assumed the Mayan leadership, as it traded with Teotihuacan and allied with Kaminaljuyu. The fall of Teotihuacan brought temporary confusion, soon followed by the glorious renaissance of the late classical era at Tikal, Palenque, Yaxchilan, Uxmal, and many other Mayan centers.

Mayan communities were supported by productive economies, based upon agriculture but heavily involved in handicrafts and long distance trade. In the rich soil, improved by clearing, irrigating, and terracing, the Mayas raised squash, chile peppers, and many other crops, including maize, which supplied 80 percent of their food. Slaves did the hard labor in the fields and in construction. On the next social rung were common peasants, craftsmen, and merchants.

The governing class of priests and nobles, drawn from elite lineages, performed overlapping functions because religion and government were so closely allied. This social structure was rigidly differentiated, with each class distinct in rights and responsibilities.

Mayan women were respected and sometimes honored, but they exercised their limited freedoms within the bounds permitted by a culture characterized by male domination. As keepers of households and experts in handicrafts, they did all of the weaving and alone produced the highly artistic pre-wheel pottery, for which the Mayans are famous. In performing such important roles, Mayan women earned a modicum of respect and status. When a maiden married, her husband came to live in her family's house until he proved himself. She could divorce him and marry again, if she waited a year. She was also permitted to hold property. In many other ways, however, Mayan women were subordinated. They were prohibited from looking directly at men; they waited on men at meals, eating

A high caste Mayan woman working at the loom. One end of the loom is attached to the woman's waist, the other is fastened to a tree trunk. Weaving was considered a noble occupation.

El Castillo of Chicén Itzá is the largest and probably one of the oldest of seven such pyramid temples in the large group of buildings that was once the most holy city of the Mayan Empire. The temple is about 185 feet square at the base and 90 feet high. The four sets of 91 steps and the base make a total of 365 steps—the same number as the number of days in the Mayan calendar.

later with other women; and they could not hold public office or enter a temple. Those in elite or royal families were regularly exported for marriage into foreign families, serving as political trade goods for cementing alliances or clinching trade agreements.

Each Mayan center was governed by a hereditary priest-king, although some very few states may have had ruling queens in earlier times, before the sixth century. The typical ruler in the late classical period was considered to be a descendant of the sun god. He was assisted by a council of priests and nobles. His government levied taxes, supervised justice, conducted foreign relations, and made war—indeed, as time passed in this era, warfare became increasingly common. Headmen, selected after passing examinations, were appointed to administer affairs in outlying villages. They commanded local militias, subject to strict control by the top military officers of the states. Some centers remained independent, but most were members of loosely organized leagues, based on common religions, royal marriages, or diplomatic alignments.

Religion permeated all phases of Mayan life. Law and taxation, for example, were interpreted as religious principles and religious offerings. Education was conducted mainly as training for priests, who made reading, writing, and learning caste specialties. They conducted the numerous public rituals, including some human sacrifice by decapitation. Mayan thought was more ritualistic than scientific; mathematics and astronomy were considered necessary to schedule ceremonies honoring the divine heavenly bodies. These were but some among a vast hierarchy of deities, ruling the universe under a supreme god and his consort.

The two most enduring achievements of the Mayas were their calendar and their writing system. Neither of these was original, but both were more efficient than those of earlier Mesoamerican peoples. The Mayas perfected a solar calendar with eighteen months of 20 days each and a five-day period for religious festivals. Using an ingenious cyclical system of notation known as the "long count," they were able to date events of the distant past for accurate record-keeping and astronomical observations. Their notational mathematics, based on 20 rather than 10 in the current decimal system, employed combinations of dots and bars, in vertical sequences, to indicate numbers above 20. For nonnumerical records, they combined pictographic and glyphic symbols, which have only recently been partially deciphered.

Their remarkable accomplishments in mathematics, astronomy, and writing were more than matched by their truly magnificent art and architecture. The plaza of each Mayan community was marked by at least one pyramid, topped by a temple. With their terraced sides and horizontal lines, these buildings demonstrated a prevailing sense of proportion. The highly stylized sculpture which decorated their terraces is regarded by some authorities as the world's finest, even though Mayan sculptors accomplished their intricate carving with only stone tools. The Mayas also developed mural painting to a high art. Even their lesser arts, such as weaving, ceramics, and jewelry making, reveal aesthetic sense, sublety of design, and manipulative skills superior to artistic creations in many other high civilizations.

The Postclassical Era in Mesoamerica

Widespread disturbances brought a collapse of classical Mesoamerican civilization during the ninth century A.D. The causes are not yet fully understood but are presumed to have been a combination of overpopulation, resulting internal upheavals, and invading waves of fierce Chichimec barbarians from the far north. When civilized life revived on a more primitive level, it was in a new mode, which emphasized war, domination of society by military classes, human sacrifice, and gods thirsting for human blood. These characteristics had not been completely absent in the past, but they were much more typical of the postclassical era after 900.

Following the time of troubles that ended the classical period, a semicivilized group of Chichimeca known as Toltecs, created a new power in the Valley of Mexico. One of their legendary kings, Topiltzin, established his capital at Tula, which became a great urban center of 120,000 people, a hub of trade, and the center of an evolving Toltec confederacy, which assumed the leading role formerly played by Teotihuacan. In adopting the Teotihuacan god Quetzalcoatl, who opposed human sacrifice, Topiltzin alienated followers of the traditional Toltec war god, Tezcatlipoca. In the struggle for power which ensued, the war cult prevailed. Topiltzin was ultimately exiled, and the Toltecs expanded their empire by conquest and trade to include everything between the Gulf and the Pacific, including some Mayan cities to the south.

The tumultuous political conditions of the early postclassical period soon brought disaster to the Toltecs. Failing crops and internal dissension caused great outward migrations from Tula and abandonment of the capital at the end of twelfth century. Shortly after, the city was destroyed by the Chichimeca. For the next two centuries, Mesoamerica was a land of warring states, constantly forming and dissolving federations. Some cultural continuity, however, was maintained by peoples in the Oaxaca Valley, notably the Zapotecs, whose culture was as old as the Olmec. Although struggling constantly for supremacy over neighboring peoples, the Zapotec towns, temples, ball courts, and art helped preserve Mesoamerican traditions for later times.

As Toltec barbarism spread from central to southern Mexico, it left the less developed Mayan highlands relatively undisturbed but brought definite decline and reorientation to the old lowland centers. At Chichen Itza, in the tenth century, a Toltec elite established tributary hegemony over northern Yucatan and maintained a trading network, by land and sea, within the whole southern region. From the early thirteenth into the fifteenth century, Mayapan became a fortified center, defended by Mexican mercenaries and maintaining leverage over subkingdoms by keeping hostages from dependent royal families. Trade and population continued to grow among the postclassical Mayas, but art and cultural pursuits—including architecture—deteriorated. The Spaniards later described a Mayan people who were fiercely independent, blood-thirsty, and, like the Aztecs, inclined to sacrifice the hearts of war prisoners on the gods' altars.

The Aztecs

The Spaniards who later arrived with Hernando Cortés were completely dazzled by the Aztec capital at Tenochtitlan. They did not realize that Aztec culture, despite its material prosperity, was a relatively recent and somewhat crude version of ancient civilizations. The Aztecs, like the Toltecs earlier, retained much of their old barbarism and depended largely upon culture borrowed from those who went before. There was, however, one very significant Aztec innovation. Their hydraulic agriculture increased population in the environs of Tenochtitlan to more than 400,000. In 1500, the Valley of Mexico supported over a million people and some fifty city-states.

Before the opening of the fourteenth century, the Aztecs' history is obscure. They evidently migrated from the north into central Mexico some time before A.D. 1200. For a while they were dominated by other peoples, including the Toltecs. In time, they won their independence and about 1325 founded their capital, Tenochtitlan, on the present site of Mexico City. Constructed entirely on an island and connected to the mainland by causeways, Tenochtitlan was an architectural wonder. The Aztecs built a dam to control the lake level, provided a fresh water supply for the city, and created artificial islands, where irrigated fields supplied food for the capital. Within the city, beautiful avenues, temples, and religious monuments symbolized the Aztec power, which remained supreme in Mexico until Cortés destroyed Tenochtitlan in 1521.

The Aztec empire began assuming a recognizable form during the reign of Montezuma I (1440–1468). This strong-willed conqueror and governor, dubbed "the angry one" by his contemporaries, waged relentless war for more than twenty years, extending Aztec rule beyond the Valley of Mexico and acquiring the rich maize-producing areas on the Gulf coast. He suffered with his people through the great famine between 1450 and 1454 but lived to see them proud and prosperous, supported from tribute collected as far south as Guatemala.

Government-regulated horticulture was basic to the Aztec economy and social structure, but craftsmanship and trade also flourished, the latter furthered through military conquest. Class lines became more distinct as wealth increased during the fifteenth century. Slaves were numerous and generally well treated, apart from their use as ceremonial sacrifice victims. Peasants worked assigned plots of land, elected their own petty officials, and served the the army, where they rose according to their abilities. Craftsmen and merchants, organized in powerful guilds, paid taxes but were exempt from labor or military service; some merchants served the government as diplomats or spies in foreign states. At the top of the social structure were the privileged nobles and priests, who acquired great wealth and were exempt from taxes and labor services. The Aztec social order, like the Roman, was highly disciplined yet permitted individual advancement.

War and conquest not only shaped the emerging Aztec class structure but also the still surviving kinship system. The ancient clans (calpulli) were also territorial units, which held communal lands and governed the daily lives of all Aztecs. The calpulli were gradually changing from matrilineal to patrilineal after the fourteenth

The huge double pyramid sacred to Uitzilopochtli, the god of the sun and war, and Tlaloc, the god of rain, dominated the Great Temple precinct of the Aztec capital city of Tenochtitlán. A serpent wall and a moat separated the temple precinct from the rest of the city.

century, as males acquired more status and political power. When the Spaniards arrived, men were recognized heads of families, even those tracing descent through the female line. Women retained some rights. They could own and inherit personal property, go to court, enter business contracts, and divorce their husbands. When widowed, they could marry again, but only within the former husband's clan. They served as merchants, healers, or midwives, and even priestesses in some temples. Like the Mayan women, they were master weavers. But their most important social role was the care of their homes and children, for which they were trained from childhood, at home and in school; indeed pregnancy earned an Aztec woman her greatest respect. Some women also became prostitutes, public or private. Those who volunteered to service young warriors were honored; those who worked the streets were scorned; those captured in conquered territories were assigned to the barracks of Aztec soldiers.

The Aztec polity was a complex of provinces, independent states, and tribes, some governed directly and some as tributaries. The emperor was a hereditary despot, regarded as an incarnation of the sun god. His court was more lavish than many in Europe; his household swarmed with servants; and his secluded harem of concubines was managed by a head wife, who scheduled their assignments. Assisting the emperor were ministers of war, justice, treasury, storehouses, personnel, and religion. His capital and 38 provinces were administered directly by governors, most of whom were descended from former kings. They collected taxes, held court, arranged religious ceremonies, regulated economic affairs, and directed police activities. In addition, urban guilds, villages, and tribes had their own local officials. Beyond the villages were vassal states, governed under their own laws but paying homage and tribute to the emperor. This whole system, which maintained some control over three million people, was protected by a large military organization, comprising allied forces, local militias, and an imperial guard of elite troops.

Aztec religion developed from the worship of animistic spirits symbolizing natural forces in constant conflict while seeking balance. The cycle of life and death encouraged acceptance of

Xolotl, the Aztec god of death, depicted as a skeleton. In Aztec religion, the benevolence of the gods was assured through human sacrifice.

the Toltec belief that the gods required human sacrifice to sustain nature and continuing life. The Aztecs conceptualized their sun deity Uitzilopochtli as a blood-thirsty war god with an appetite for brave warriors captured in battle. In every Aztec city, they built pyramids, topped with temples to the sun. Here they honored Uitzilopochtli in great public ceremonies, when priests at the high altars tore out the living hearts of victims and held up the quivering organs to the sun. Ultimately the need for sacrificial victims became an obsession which justified continuing conquests.

While such theoretical exercises should not be taken too literally, a fair analogy may be drawn in comparing the Mayas and the Aztecs with the ancient Greeks and Romans. Generally speaking, the Mayas were more artistic and intellectual than the Aztecs and in these respects remind us somewhat of the Greeks. The Aztec calendar, mathematics, writing, art, and architecture were derived largely from Mayan-Toltec sources, just as Roman culture was taken largely from Greek models. Similarly, both Roman and Aztec cultures were characterized by respect for discipline, practicality, directness, and force. Aztec art, for example, was more suggestive of austerity, strength, violence, and brutality than was the Mayan.

The Inca Empire

Both the Mayan and Aztec political systems were surpassed in complexity by the great Inca empire which arose in the Andean highlands of western South America. At its height when the Spaniards arrived in the early 1500s, it extended some 2700 miles from what is now Ecuador to contemporary Chile. In area, this state was six times the size of France; yet it was governed in a more centralized system than any in Europe of its time. The Incas produced fine art and architecture, but their major achievement was imperial organization. In this respect, they compared favorably with the Romans or Chinese.

Although it rose very rapidly, immediately before the Spanish conquest, Inca civilization developed from very old cultural foundations. Ceremonial and commercial centers existed on the Peruvian coastal plain well before the Christian era. About A.D. 600, cities began rising in the highlands of the interior. During the next two centuries, tributary kingdoms drew together formerly isolated ceremonial centers of the Peruvian highlands. Some of the resulting states exercised control over the plain, along with territories in modern Bolivia and Chile. Two kingdoms had capitals at Huari and Tiahuanaco, in south-central Peru. When these states collapsed in the ninth century, they were succeeded by independent agrarian towns, organized along tribal lines and nearly consumed by continuous warfare.

Amid this ruthless struggle for survival, the Incas created their state. According to their own legends, these "children of the sun" settled the Valley of Cuzco, in the heartland of the Andes, about the eleventh century, having migrated from the south, possibly from the region of Tiahuanaco. During the 1100s, they extended their domain over the mountain tribes. Having conquered Tiahuanaco by 1250, they used it as a base for their steady conquest of the coastal cities and federations.

Their most rapid advances came during the reign of Pachacutic (1438–1471), a brilliant field commander but also a planner, organizer, builder and religious leader, who has been called "the greatest man ever produced by the American race."[4] Pachacutic completely pacified the Cuzco area, and with his successor, Topa Yupanqui, extended Inca rule from the Amazon forest to the coast and from Ecuador to Chile. Although he could be ruthless, as evidenced by his massacres of rebels, Pachacutic avoided violence whenever diplomacy could accomplish results. His reign produced a universal empire which emphasized mutual cooperation among its three million subjects. He also added worship of a supreme creator to the prevailing sun cult.

Exploiting their reputation as a chosen people and the unity derived from a common official language, the Incas developed a culture marked by integration. Every part of the pattern—economy, social structure, government, religion, and art—fitted together in a highly disciplined whole. Such internal cohesion had been common in smaller, simpler kinship societies. Before the Incas, however, few other territorial states had succeeded so quickly and so effectively in regimenting millions of people over such great distances. The accomplishment appears even more remarkable in view of the environmental difficulties, which hampered rather than encouraged unity. Throughout their history, the Incas struggled against the steep slopes and cruel weather of the towering Andes in achieving their organizational miracles.

Like all civilized peoples, the Incas faced the problem of population expansion against a limited food supply. They solved the problem well enough to support large military, bureaucratic, and priestly establishments by developing what economists call a "command economy." They used no money, no credit, and very little trade beyond the barter conducted locally by government agents. The state planned all economic operations and kept all accounts, assigning the land to be worked, supervising the worker who produced the crops, and collecting the harvests

Father Bernard Cobo, "The Greatest Inca"

This selection is from chapter 12 of Cobo's *History of the Inca Empire*. Cobo relied upon Indian legends and contemporary Indian testimony, as well as earlier Spanish writings.

Viracocha Inca left four sons by his principal wife; they were called Pachacutic Inca Yupanqui, Inca Roca, Tupa Yupanqui, and Capac Yupanqui. The first one succeeded him in the kingdom, and concerning the rest, although they were lords and grandees, nothing is said. Pachacutic married a lady named Mama Anahuarque, native to the town of Choco, near Cuzco, and he founded a family that they call Iñaca Panaca. This king was the most valiant and warlike, wise and statesmanlike of all the Incas, because he organized the republic with the harmony, laws, and statutes that it maintained from that time until the arrival of the Spaniards. He injected order and reason into everything; eliminated and added rites and ceremonies; made the religious cult more extensive; established the sacrifices and the solemnity with which the gods were to be venerated, enlarged and embellished the temples with magnificent structures, income, and a great number of priests and ministers; reformed the calendar; divided the year into twelve months, giving each one its name; and designated the solemn fiestas and sacrifices to be held each month. He composed many elegant prayers with which the gods were to be invoked, and he ordered that these prayers be recited at the same time that the sacrifices were offered. He was no less careful and diligent in matters pertaining to the temporal welfare of the republic; he gave his vassals a method of working the fields and taking advantage of the lands that were so rough and uneven as to be useless and unfruitful; he ordered that rough hillsides be terraced and that ditches be made from the rivers to irrigate them. In short, nothing was overlooked by him in which he did not impose all good order and harmony; for this reason he was given the name of Pachacutic, which means "change of time or of the world"; this is because as a result of his excellent government things improved to such an extent that times seemed to have changed and the world seemed to have turned around; thus, his memory was very celebrated among the Indians, and he was given more honor in their songs and poems than any of the other kings that either preceded him or came after him.

After having shown himself to be so devoted to the sun and having taken the care just mentioned that all worship him in the same way that his ancestors had done, one day Pachacutic began to wonder how it was possible that a thing could be god if it was so subject to movement as the Sun, that it never stops or rests for a moment since it turns around the world every day; and he inferred from this meditation that the Sun must not be more than a messenger sent by the Creator to visit the universe; besides, if he were God, it would not be possible for a few clouds to get in front of him and obscure his splendor and rays so that he could not shine; and if he were the universal Creator and lord of all things, sometimes he would rest and from his place of rest he would illuminate all the world and command whatever he wished; and thus, there had to be another more powerful lord who ruled and governed the Sun; and no doubt this was Pachayachachic. He communicated this thought to the members of his council, and in agreement with them, he decided that Pachayachachic was to be preferred to the Sun, and within the city of Cuzco, he built the Creator his own temple which he called Quishuarcancha, and in it he put the image of the Creator of the world, Viracocha Pachayachachic.

Source: Roland Hamilton, trans. and ed., *History of the Inca Empire* (Austin: University of Texas Press, 1979), pp. 133–135.

in warehouses. A similar approach was used in manufacturing. From its storehouses, the government distributed goods to individuals, to the military, and to government projects. In the process, it built roads, operated hospitals, and maintained schools. Private property was limited to the simplest personal possessions, including the luxuries of the privileged classes.

This economy functioned through four levels of precisely defined social gradations. At the top were the Incas, all related directly or indirectly to the reigning emperor. They held the highest positions in government, the army, and the priesthood. A notch lower were lesser aristocrats and nobles among conquered peoples, who held local offices, up to subgovernors in the provinces. The two upper classes made up a privileged elite. Trained in special schools, their members were identified by luxuries in food, dress, and housing. They were also exempted from taxes and cruel punishments. At the third level were common workers. They were generally confined to their villages, their work was prescribed, their dress and food were restricted, and the government even checked the cleanliness of their houses. Commoners were thus little better off than the lowest class of slaves, who were taken as war captives and assigned as servants to the upper classes.

Women occupied an inferior position in Inca society. Indeed, a fifteenth-century royal decree prohibited them from testifying in court, because they were by nature "deceitful, mendacious, and faint-hearted."[5] They were respected and honored, however, in pursuits considered appropriate. Those of the upper classes ate at banquets with their husbands, supervised household affairs, and cared for their children. Legal wives ruled over concubines, the number of which varied according to the husband's status and special permission from the emperor, who was permitted an unlimited number. Women of all classes could inherit personal property from a dead husband. As widows they were supported by the state, but a widow could not remarry, except to her former husband's brother. Concubines, with no legal status at all, were subject to banishment by their masters at any time. Women of the commoner class, which supplied most concubines, generally lived miserable lives, amid dirt, disease, and hard work. Those who were especially beautiful or

In this drawing from an Inca calendar, a woman irrigates the field with water drawn from a small reservoir.

highly intelligent might be drafted as young girls and specially trained. Some of these "chosen women," would become "virgins of the sun," serving as nuns and perhaps weaving cloth for the emperor in the temple workshops. Others would become concubines of nobles or the emperor. A few would be sacrificed. All of these were considered to be honored servants of the state.

All authority in this state originated with the hereditary divine emperor, who exercised the power of life and death over three million people. He was usually aloof and withdrawn, even among members of his own household, although he might, if he chose, delegate authority to the queen or take advice from his mother. With thousands of servants and concubines, his court was a magnificent display of wealth and power. It was also the locus of a central government which included ministries of rituals (religion), war, treasury, accounts, and public works. The chief

Machu Picchu, a natural fortress on a narrow ridge between two mountains, was built by the Incas probably after 1440. When the last Incan ruler died, the fortress was abandoned and lost until its rediscovery in 1911.

ministers were advisors to the Imperial Council, consisting of the emperor and four viceroys, who governed the four provinces. Each province, about the size of New York state, was divided into approximately 40 districts, under subgovernors and their helpers. Authority in the districts was further subdivided, ultimately into units of ten families. Officials at each level reported regularly to superiors and were subject to frequent inspections. This system regulated every aspect of life, including labor, justice, marriage, and even morals.

The power of the ruler depended largely on an excellent military system, which featured compulsory service. Instructors in the villages trained peasant boys for the army; the most promising were marked for advancement when they were called to active duty in their twenties. They served for two years before retiring to the labor reserve and militia. The army was organized in units of 10, 50, 100, 1000 and 10,000, under officers who held complete authority over subordinates. A combat force of 200,000 with support units, was always under arms. It was supplied from military storehouses throughout the country and garrisoned in mighty stone fortresses, each with independent water sources. Troops from these centers ruthlessly suppressed any resistance to the regime.

A second base for Inca authority was religion. As the empire grew, its priests appropriated the local and ancestral gods of conquered peoples. For example, the "virgins of the sun," their ceremonies, and their temples were copied from the earlier worship of a moon goddess among matrilineal societies. Thus the former local deities were formed into a vast pantheon, under the Inca sun god. Unfortunately, Pachacutic's nascent monotheism and humanitarianism did not prevail; his son and later emperors occasionally sacrificed war victims to the sun. As with the Aztecs, each conquest was rationalized as the god's will. The continuity of the state was considered proof of divine approval, and the emperor was regarded as the god's living embodiment. In emphasizing this rationale, dead emperors were mummified and seated on thrones in their sacred palaces, to be attended by servants, wives, and priests. On public occasions, these grotesque figures were paraded before the people, who bowed before them in reverence. Such ceremonies were conducted by a clerical establishment of 4000 in the capital and hundreds of thousands more throughout the country.

The characteristic values of order and security were reflected in Inca cultural expression, which gave little place to aesthetic concerns or philosophic speculation. Even religious theory was conditioned by practical necessities and the morality of power. Treason and cowardice were considered the worst offenses. The Incas had no common written literature and no complex writing system. They used a system of knotted cords to communicate quantitative information. Similarly, the Inca lunar calendar was inaccurate and had no starting point for historical identification of events. Although efficient craftsmen and producers of fine pottery and metal work in copper and gold, the Incas' main cultural accomplishments were in engineering and massive architecture. Without using mortar, they fitted immense slabs of stone into temple and fortress walls. This efficiency is still evident in existing road, bridges, terraced fields, and stone fortresses.

Conclusion

Sub-Sahara Africa and America before the coming of Europeans in the fifteenth century provide interesting case studies of the "civilizing process." They show examples of what has happened among all human societies when food production replaced hunting as a means of survival. Agriculture supplied the material sustenance for expanding populations. This, in turn, led to the formation of cities, and ultimately some urban communities developed into large territorial states. More food and more wealth also produced leisure classes, which had the time to think originally about religion, literature, art, and architecture. In both Africa and the New World native culture bases generated true civilizations.

All civilizations have sprung from similar economic conditions, but they have developed more rapidly when they have borrowed from each other to combine varied traits in unique ways. African civilizations tell us a good bit about such diffusion. Ethiopia, the East African city-states, and the Sudanese empires all mingled African and non-African traditions to enrich their cultures without succumbing to alien influences. Yet the African civilizations, because of their early isolation, were somewhat slower in their development when compared with Eurasia, where cultural interaction between the two continents had long prevailed, particularly in the Middle Eastern cradle of civilization. On the other hand, African estrangement from the great Eurasian culture bank was less than America's, which helps explain the quick collapse of American civilizations after the European impact.

Aside from these insights, native traditions in Africa and the New World are significant in themselves for contemporary students, because both traditions are still very much alive. The ancient African heritage lives today in the many new African states and in the minds of black people all over the world, particularly in the United States. Similar conclusions may be drawn concerning native American traditions, which remain in the culture of all contemporary Latin American peoples.

Suggestions for Reading

The best detailed coverage of African history can be found in two multi-volume series, each containing chapters by expert scholars: *The Cambridge History of Africa* and *The UNESCO General History of Africa*. For this chapter, the appropriate volumes in the Cambridge series are Volume I, edited by J. Desmond Clark, *From Earliest Times to 500 B.C.* (Cambridge Univ., 1982) and Volume III, edited by Roland Oliver and J. D. Fage, *From 1050 to 1600 A.D.* (Cambridge Univ., 1977). Appropriate volumes in the UNESCO series are Volume II, edited by G. Mokhtor, *Ancient Civilizations of Africa* (Univ. of California, 1981) and Volume IV, edited by D. T. Niane, *Africa from the Twelfth to the Sixteenth Century* (Univ. of California, 1984). An excellent one-volume survey is Robert July, *A History of the African People* (Scribner's, 1980).

In addition, the following general histories provide useful information: Roland Oliver and J. D. Fage, *A Short History of Africa* (Facts on File, 1989; Harry A. Gailey, *A History of Africa from Earliest Times to 1800* (Holt, Rinehart and Winston, 1981); Basil Davidson, *Africa: History of a Continent* (Macmillan, 1972); J. Maquet, *Civilizations of Black Africa* (Oxford, 1972); E. Jefferson Murphy, *A History of African Civilization* (Crowell, 1972); and Robin Hallett, *Africa to 1875* (Univ. of Michigan, 1970).

Cultural backgrounds and early influences on Africa are ably treated in John Addison, *Traditional Africa* (Greenhaven, 1980); J. Desmond Clark and Steven Brandt, eds., *From Hunters to Farmers* (Univ. of California, 1984); P. L. Shinnie, *The African Iron Age* (Oxford, 1971); Basil Davidson, *The Lost Cities of Africa*, rev. ed. (Little, Brown, 1988); and Margaret Shinnie, *Ancient African Kingdoms* (St. Martin's, 1965). P. L. Shinnie's *Meroe* (Thames and Hudson, 1967) is the classic study of that early Nubian state. An illuminating depiction of early Muslim diffusion into sub-Sahara Africa is presented in John Spencer Trimmingham's *The Influence of Islam Upon Africa* (Longman, 1980).

On the controversial issues relating to the origins of food production and iron working in Africa, see Christopher Ehret, "On the Antiquity of Agriculture in Ethiopia" in *The Journal of African History*, 20 (1979), pp. 168–197; Candice Goucher, "Iron is Iron Until It Rusts," in *The Journal of African History*, 22 (1981), pp. 179–189; and Krzyaniak Lech, "New Light on Food Production in the Central Sudan," in *The Journal of African History*, 19 (1978), pp. 159–172.

African philosophy and art are interpreted effectively in Basil Davidson, *The African Genius* (Little, Brown, 1970); Victor C. Ferkiss, *Africa's Search for Identity* (Braziller, 1966); and F. Willett, *African Art* (Thames Hudson, 1985).

Among the many regional and special works on Africa, the following are particularly noteworthy for West Africa: J. F. Ajayi and Michael Crowder, *The History of West Africa*, 2 vols. (Longman, 1987); George Brooks, *Western Africa to 1860 A.D.* (Indiana Africa, 1985); and G. T. Stride, *The Peoples and Empires of West Africa* (Africana, 1971). For more specialized works, see Michael Crowder, *The Story of Nigeria* (Faber and Faber, 1966) and Robert Smith, *Kingdoms of the Yoruba* (Methuen, 1969). The fall of Ghana is given a new interpretation by Humphrey Fisher in "The Conquest that Never Was," *History in Africa*, 9 (1982), pp. 21–59. Barbara Calloway, *Muslim Hausa Women in Nigeria* (Syracuse Univ., 1987) is a comprehensive study.

For other African regions, see David Birmingham and Phyllis M. Martin, *A History of Central Africa*, 2 vols. (Longman, 1983); Derek A. Wilson, *A History of South and Central Africa* (Cambridge Univ., 1975); and Gideon S. Were and Derek A. Wilson, *East Africa Through a Thousand Years* (Africana, 1970). On Ethiopia, the best works are Sir E. A. Wallis Budge, *A History of Ethiopia*, 2 vols. (Methuen, 1966); Arnold H. Jones and Elizabeth Monroe, *A History of Ethiopia* (Oxford, 1966); Taddene Tamrat, *Church and State in Ethiopia* (Oxford, 1972); and Mordechai Abir, *Ethiopia and the Red Sea* (F. Cass Co., 1980).

Two interesting special studies of the African experience are Rhoda Hoff, *Africa, Adventures in Eye-Witness History* (Henry Z. Walck, 1963) and David Killengray, *A Plague of Europeans* (Penquin, 1973). The latter deals with the impact of slave-trading.

A good general introduction to indigenous cultures in the southern regions of the New World is Robert Wauchope's *Indian Background of Latin American History* (Knopf, 1970). Note also the following three comparative studies: George Collier, ed., *The Inca and Aztec States, 1400–1800* (Academic Press, 1982); Geoffrey W. Conrad and Arthur A. Demarest, *Religion and Empire: the Dynamics of Aztec and Inca Expansionism* (Cambridge Univ., 1984); and Alfred Sundell, *A History of the Aztecs and the Maya and Their Conquest* (Collier Books, 1967).

Among the most informative works on pre-Columbian Mexico and Central America (Mesoamerica) are Michael D. Coe, *Mexico*, 3rd ed. (Thames and Hudson, 1986) and Robert R. Miller, *Mexico* (Univ. of Oklahoma, 1989). See also Shirley Gorenstein, *Not Forever on Earth: The Prehistory of Mexico* (Scribner's, 1975); Kenneth Pearce, *The View From the Top of the Temple* (Univ. of New Mexico, 1984); Jacques Soustelle, *The Olmecs: The Oldest Civilization in Mexico* (Univ. of Oklahoma, 1985); and Joseph W. Whitecotton, *The Zapotecs: Princes, Priests, and Peasants* (Univ. of Oklahoma, 1984).

For informative special studies on the Maya, see Michael D. Coe, *The Maya* (Thames and Hudson, 1987); Norman Hammond, *Ancient Maya Civilization* (Rutgers Univ., 1982); John S. Henderson, *The World of the Ancient Maya* (Cornell Univ., 1981); and Sylvania G. Morley, George W. Brainerd, and Robert J. Sharer, *The Ancient Maya* (Stanford Univ., 1983). For special insights into the Maya experience, see Victor Perara and Robert D. Bruce, *The Last Lords of Palenque* (Univ. of California, 1985) and Ralph Witlock, *Every Day Life of the Maya* (Dorset, 1987).

Three reliable standard studies on the Aztecs have been recently revised: Francis F. Berdan, *The Aztecs* (Chelsea House, 1989); Alfonso Caso, *The Aztecs, People of the Sun* (Univ. of Oklahoma, 1988); and Nigel Davies, *The Aztecs* (Univ. of Oklahoma, 1989). Older acclaimed works include Brian M. Fagan, *The Aztecs* (W. H. Freeman, 1984) and Burr Cartwright Brundage, *A Rain of Darts* (Univ. of Texas, 1972). Recent special studies on Aztec political institutions and development provide fresh interpretations: Susan Gillespie, *The Aztec Kings* (Univ. of Arizona, 1989) and Ross Hassig, *Aztec Warfare: Imparial Expansion and Political Control* (Univ. of Oklahoma, 1988). For an interesting description of social conditions, see Jacques Soustelle, *Daily Life of the Aztecs on the Eve of Spanish Conquest* (Stanford Univ., 1961); Rudolf van Zantwijk, *The Aztec Arrangement: The Social History of Pre-Spanish Mexico* (Univ. of Oklahoma, 1985); and June Nash, "The Aztecs and the Ideology of Male Dominance," *Signs* 4 (1978), pp. 349–362.

Bernabe Cobo, *A History of the Inca Empire* (Univ. of Texas, 1979) is still considered sound and complete. Another long respected anthropological approach to pre-Columbian Andean culture is J. Alden Mason's *Ancient Civilizations of Peru* (Penguin, 1988). Older standard works include Edward Hyams and George Ordish, *The Last of the Incas* (Simon and Schuster, 1963); Loren McIntyre, *The Incredible Inca and Their Timeless Land* (Nat. Geog., 1978); and Alfred Métraux, *The History of the Incas* (Schocken, 1970). Excellent depictions of the Inca command econo-

my can be found in two classic works: Louis Baudin, *Socialist Empire* (Van Nostrand, 1961) and Rafael Karsten, *A Totalitarian State of the Past* (Kennikat, 1969). For studies based on more recent scholarship, see Jonathon Haas, et al., *The Origin and Development of the Andean State* (Cambridge Univ., 1987); Frank Solomon, *The Native Lords of Quito in the Age of the Incas: The Political Economy of the North-Andean Chieftans* (Cambridge Univ., 1986); and John V. Murra, *The Economic Organization of the Inca State* (Jai Pr., 1980).

Notes

1. Colin McEvedy and Richard Jones, *Atlas of World Population History* (New York: Penguin, 1978), pp. 238–259.
2. Rhoda Hoff, *Africa: Adventures in Eyewitness History* (New York: A. Walck, 1963), pp. 10–13.
3. Quoted in Michael D. Coe, *Mexico*, (London: Thames and Hudson, 1984), p. 87.
4. Quoted from Clements Markham in Edward Hyams and George Ordish, *The Last of the Incas* (New York: Simon and Schuster, 1963), p. 99.
5. *Ibid.*, p. 88.

European Expansion: Exploration and Colonization, 1400–1650

During the fifteenth century, Europe began a process of unprecedented expansion that by 1650 had affected all areas of the world. This was actually part of a global tendency towards complexity among many human societies. Matching the empires of the Aztecs, the Inca, and the West Africans were rising states on the Eurasian fringes such as Japan or the European monarchies in England, France, Spain, and Portugal. In Eurasia, developing navigational technology, along with expanding trade, encouraged long sea voyages by Arabs, Japanese, Chinese, and Europeans. But only the Europeans linked up all the continents in a new global age, when sea power, rather than land-based armies, was the main force in empire-building.

Overseas expansion was obviously related—both as cause and effect—to the European transition from medievalism. The Crusades and the Renaissance stimulated European curiosity; the Reformation produced thousands of zealous religious missionaries seeking foreign converts and refugees seeking religious freedom; and the monarchs of emerging sovereign states sought revenues, first from trade with the Orient and later by exploiting a new world. Perhaps the most permeating influence was the rise of European capitalism, with its monetary values, profit-seeking motivations, investment institutions, and constant impulse toward economic expansion. Some historians have labeled this whole economic transformation "the Commercial Revolution." Others have used the phrase in a narrower sense, referring to the shift in trade routes from the Mediterranean to the Atlantic. Interpreted either way, the Commercial Revolution and its accompanying European expansion helped usher in the modern era.

The Iberian Golden Age

By the middle of the seventeenth century, the full impact of the Commercial Revolution had not yet been experienced in Europe. Neither the Portuguese nor the Spanish, who were dominant overseas until the late 1500s, could maintain their initial advantages over the long term. Portugal lacked manpower and resources required by an empire spread over three continents. Spain wasted the wealth of the New World in continuous wars, while neglecting to develop its own economy (see p. 453). Yet the fabulous "Iberian Age" brought a momentous transition, as Lisbon and Seville received the world's wealth in gold, silver, slaves, and spices. In 1503 Portuguese pepper cost 80 percent less than that which came through Venice and the eastern Mediterranean.[1] During the sixteenth century, Spanish bullion, flowing into northern banks and markets, provided a major stimulus to European capitalism and prepared the way for empire-building by the Dutch, English, and French after 1600. Iberian expansion also inspired other Europeans with hope and confidence while effecting a mixing of peoples, a diffusion of cultures, and an intercontinental exchange of plants and animals such as the world had never seen before.

Conditions Favoring Iberian Expansion

A number of conditions invited Iberian maritime expansion in the fifteenth century. Muslim

Using ships like these broad-beamed carracks, the Portuguese controlled much of the carrying trade with the East in the 15th and 16th centuries.

control over the eastern caravan routes, particularly after the Turks took Constantinople in 1453, brought rising prices while emphasizing European weaknesses against Turkish land forces. But the sprawling Islamic world lacked both unity and intimidating sea power. China after 1440 abandoned its extensive naval forays into the Indan Ocean. Portugal and Spain, still involved in their centuries-old struggle with Muslims in the Mediterranean, were thus encouraged to seek new sea routes to the east, where they might find the Turks vulnerable or drain the rich ports of sub-Sahara Africa and southern Asia.

By the 1400s, the Iberian states were already proficient in new naval technology and tactics. Like other Europeans, the Portuguese and Spanish and long since adopted the compass and astrolabe, thus partially freeing themselves from land-hugging on long voyages. They were skilled cartographers and chartmakers, especially the Portuguese. But their main advantages lay with their ships and naval guns. The stormy Atlantic required broad bows, deep keels and complex square rigging for driving and maneuvering fighting ships. Armed with brass cannons, such

A map from the Portolan Atlas, c. 1600, showing the West Indies from Florida to the Amazon. Portolani were sophisticated navigational charts, often prepared by sailors' firsthand observations.

ships could sink enemy vessels, without ramming or boarding at close quarters. They could also batter down coastal defenses. Even the great Chinese junks, although often much larger than European ships, could not equal European maneuverability and firepower.

In addition to their superior ships, the Iberians were aided by an unique psychological orientation. Long and bitter wars with the Moors had left the Portuguese and Spanish with fanatical religious obsessions, which encouraged them to covert heathen and destroy infidels in the name of Christ. Sailors with Columbus recited vespers every night, and Portuguese seamen were equally devout. Maritime missions were regarded as holy crusades.

For two centuries hopes that Ethiopia might become a powerful ally against the Muslims had encouraged Iberian religious prejudice against Islam. European crusaders had met Ethiopian pilgrims in the Holy Land since the twelfth century; other Ethiopians had later visited Rhodes and Cyprus, where they boasted of their emperor's power and his prowess against the infidels. Such tales helped generate the myth of "Prester John," a mighty Ethiopian king, somewhere on the other side of Africa, who might help launch another crusade. After 1400, a few Europeans reached Ethiopia. The results of their efforts are unrecorded, but in 1450, Zara Yakob, the reigning Negus, sent a delegation to Naples and Rome. His envoys conferred with the pope and enlisted European artisans, who returned with the delegation to Ethiopia.

This dream of war for the cross was sincere, but it also helped rationalize more worldly economic concerns. Both Spain and Portugal experienced dramatic population growth between 1400 and 1600. The Spanish population increased from five to eight and a half million; the population of Portugal more than doubled, rising from nine hundred thousand to two million, despite a manpower loss of 125,000 in the sixteenth century.[2] Hard times in rural areas prompted migration to cities, where dreams of wealth in foreign lands encouraged fortune-seeking overseas. Despite the obvious religious zeal of many Iberians, particularly among those in holy orders, a burning desire for gain was the driving motivation for most.

The structures of the Iberian states provided further support for overseas expansion. In both, the powers of the monarchs had been recently expanded and were oriented toward maritime adventure as the means for raising revenues, diverting the Turkish menace, spreading Catholic Christianity, and increasing national unity. The Avis dynasty in Portugal, after usurping the throne and alienating the great nobles in 1385, made common cause with the gentry and middle classes, who prospered in commercial partnership with the government. In contrast, Spanish nobles, particularly the Castilians, were very much like Turkish aristocrats, who looked upon conquest and plunder as their normal functions and sources of income. Thus the Portuguese and Spanish political systems worked in different ways toward similar imperial ends.

Perhaps the most significant factor furthering Iberian expansion in America was disease. Having lived for centuries in contact with diverse Eurasian and North African populations, the Spanish and Portuguese has acquired immunities against infectious diseases such as small pox and measles, which they carried to the Caribbean, Mexico, Peru, and Brazil. In these areas, native Americans died by the thousands, greatly facilitating their conquest and domination.

Staking Claims

During the fifteenth century, Portugal gained a long lead over Spain, staking claims along the entire coast of West Africa. But in 1492 the Spanish monarchs conquered Granada, the last Moorish state in the peninsula, and completed the unification of their country. They now turned attention to the west. The resulting historic voyage of Columbus provided a basis for Spanish claims to most of the western hemisphere.

The man most responsible for the brilliant Portuguese exploits was Prince Henry (1394–1460), known as "the Navigator" for his famous observatory at Sagres, where skilled mariners planned voyages and recorded their results. As a young man in 1411, Henry directed the Portuguese conquest of Ceuta, a Muslim port on the Moroccan coast, near the Mediterranean's western entrance. This experience imbued him with a life-long desire to divert the West African gold trade from Muslim caravans to Portuguese ships. He also shared the common dream of finding in Ethiopia Christian allies against the Turks on the other side of Africa. Such ideas motivated Henry for forty years as he sent expeditions down the West African coast, steadily charting and learning from unknown waters.

Before other European states began extended explorations, the Portuguese had navigated the West African coast to its southern tip (see map below). Henry's captains claimed the Madeira Islands in 1418 and the Azores in 1421. They had explored the Senegal River by 1450 and then traced the Guinea coast during the next decade. After Henry's death in 1460, they pushed south, reaching Benin in the decade after 1470 and Kongo, on the southwest coast, in 1482. Six years later, Bartholomew Diaz rounded the southern tip of Africa, but his disgruntled crew forced him to turn back. Nevertheless, King John II of Portugal (1481–1495) was so excited by the prospect of a direct route to India that he named Diaz's discovery "the Cape of Good Hope."

Spain soon challenged Portuguese supremacy. The specific controversy was over the Canary Islands, some of which were occupied by Castilians in 1344 and others by Portuguese after the 1440s. The issue, which produced repeated incidents, was ultimately settled in 1479 by the Treaty of Alcacovas, which recognized exclusive Spanish rights in the Canaries but banned Spain from the Madeiras, the Azores, the Cape Verdes, and West Africa. Spanish ambitions were thus temporarily frustrated until Columbus provided new hope.

Christopher Columbus (1451–1506, a Genoese sailor with an impossible dream, had been influenced by Marco Polo to believe that Japan could be reached by a short sail directly westward. Although he underestimated the distance by some 7000 miles and was totally ignorant of the intervening continents, Columbus persistently

VOYAGES OF DISCOVERY

Treaty of Tordesillas – 1494 → | ← Pope's Line of Demarcation – 1493 | Treaty of Saragossa – 1529 →

An engraving showing Columbus landing at Hispaniola. Columbus made four voyages to the New World but died believing that the islands he explored were off the coast of China.

urged his proposals upon King John of Portugal and the Spanish monarchs. He was most successful with Queen Isabella of Spain, who was captivated by Columbus' dream and became his most steadfast supporter until her death in 1504. Having obtained her sponsorship, Columbus sailed from Palos on August 3, 1492, in three small ships. He landed on San Salvadore in the West Indies on October 12, thinking he had reached his goal. In three more attempts, he continued his search for an Asian passage. His voyages touched the major Caribbean islands, Honduras, the isthmus, and Venezuela. Although he never knew it, he had claimed a new world for Spain.

Columbus' first voyage posed threats to Portugal's monopoly in the Atlantic and called for compromise if destructive war was to be averted. At Spain's invitation, the pope issued a "Bull of Demarcation," establishing a north-south line, about 300 miles west of the Azores. Beyond this line, all heathen lands were open to Spanish claims. The Portuguese protested, forcing direct negotiations, which produced the Treaty of Tordesillas (1494). It moved the line some 500 miles farther west. Later explorations showed that the new line gave Spain most of the New World but left eastern Brazil to Portugal.

The Developing Portuguese Empire

The Portuguese developed a world maritime empire while maintaining commercial supremacy through the first half of the sixteenth century. They established posts around both African coasts, in Brazil, and across southern Asia, driving Muslims from the Indian Ocean and dominating the spice trade of Southeast Asia.

Two voyages at the turn of the sixteenth century laid the foundations for the Portuguese empire in America and in the Orient. In 1497, Vasca da Gama (1469–1524) left Lisbon in four ships, rounding the Cape of Good Hope after ninety-three days on the open sea. While visiting and raiding among East African ports, da Gama picked up an Arab pilot, who brought the fleet across the Indian Ocean to Calicut, on the western coast of India. By the time he returned to Lisbon in 1499, da Gama had lost two ships and a third of his men, but his cargo of pepper and cinnamon brought sixty times the cost of the expedition. Shortly afterward, Pedro Cabral (1468–1520), commanding a large fleet on a second voyage to India, bore too far west and sighted the east coast of Brazil. The new western territory was considered so unpromising that it was left unoccupied until 1532, when a small settlement was established at Sao Vincente. In the 1540s it had attracted only some 2000 settlers, mostly men, although a few Portuguese women came after the arrival of the Lord Protector's wife and her retinue in 1535. The colony served mostly as a place to send convicts in the sixteenth century. By 1600, it had a population of only 25,000 Europeans; fifty years later this number had increased to 50,000.

Brazil was neglected in favor of extensive operations in the Indian Ocean and Southeast Asia. The most striking successes there were achieved under Alfonso de Albuquerque, eastern viceroy between 1509 and 1515. He completed subjugation of the East African sultanates and established fortified trading posts in Mozambique and Zanzibar. After a decisive naval victory over an Arab fleet, Albuquerque captured Ormuz, thus hampering Arab passage from the Persian Gulf. In 1510, the Portuguese acquired Goa on the west coast of India; it became a base for aiding Hindus against Indian Muslims and conducting trade with the interior. The next year a Portuguese force took Malacca, a Muslim stronghold in Malaysia, which controlled trade with China and the Spice Islands, through the narrow straits opposite Sumatra.

Although dominant in Indonesia, the Portuguese were mostly supplicants on the Asian mainland. Portuguese adventurers acquired temporary influence in Laos and Cambodia, but they were expelled from Vietnam and enslaved in Burma. Their arrogance and violence caused them to be banished from Chinese ports in 1522 and 1544. The Chinese gave them trading rights at Macao in 1557, but only under strict regulations. From then until they were expelled at the end of the Ming dynasty, the Portuguese in China conformed to law, serving as traders, advisors, and missionaries. In Japan, after the 1540s, they prospered, furnishing guns to the warring *daimyo*. Jesuit missionaries were also successful in converting thousands of Japanese. But as the country approached political unity, these conditions steadily worsened until all Europeans were forced out in the 1630s (see p. 381).

Long before this, the Portuguese empire had begun to decline. It did not have the special knowledge or skills required to maintain a global empire. This deficiency originated in Albuquerque's time, when he failed to recruit females from home to provide social stability and breed a Portuguese elite. The problem was magnified in the early seventeenth century by a sharp decline in Portuguese population. Portuguese men mated with native women in Africa, Brazil, India, Indonesia, and China. Sometimes they achieved meaningful and lasting relationships, but more often the women were exploited as prostitutes, slaves, or harem concubines and treated little better than household pets or work animals. After the turn of the seventeenth century, the Portuguese were on the defensive against the Turks in East Africa, the Spanish in the Philippines, and the Dutch everywhere. In the 1630s, the Dutch forced them from most of Indonesia, West Africa, and Brazil. Despite a later mild revival, the Portuguese empire never regained its former glory.

The Growth of New Spain

While Portugal concentrated on Asian trade, Spain was winning a vast empire in America. Shortly after 1492, Spanish settlements sprouted in the West Indias, most notably on Haiti (Hispaniola) and Cuba. In time, as the passage to Asia remained undiscovered, a host of Spanish adventurers—the famous *conquistadores*—set out for conquest in the New World. From the West Indies, they crossed the Caribbean to eastern Mexico, fanning out from there in all directions, toward Central America, the Pacific, and the vast hinterland of North America.

Unstable conditions within the Aztec Empire, a federation of recently conquered tribes who were forced to pay tribute and furnish victims to satisfy the Aztec obsession with human sacrifice (see p. 406) worked to the Spaniards' advantage in Mexico. A recently revived legend about the white-skinned and bearded Teotihuacan god Quetzalcoatl, who had been exiled by the Toltecs because he forbade human sacrifice and would return from across the sea to enforce his law, also facilitated the Spanish conquest. The Aztec emperor Montezuma II faced impending revolts by his resentful subjects and eroding morale among superstitious Aztecs, including himself.

In 1519, Hernando Cortés (1485–1574) arrived in Mexico from Cuba with 11 ships, 600 fighting

Cortés Meets Montezuma

After arriving in Tenochtitlan, Cortés wrote this famous report in a long letter to Charles V, the Spanish monarch. Such descriptions of fabulous wealth in the New World were major causes for Spanish adventuring overseas.

The next day after I had arrived in this city, I left, and having gone half a league, I reached another causeway, leading out into the lake a distance of two leagues to the great city of Temixtitan, which stands in the midst of the said lake. This causeway is two lances broad, and so well built that eight horsemen can ride abreast; and, within these two leagues, there are three cities, on one and the other side of the said highway, one called Mesicalsingo, founded for the greater part within the said lake, and the other two, called Niciaca, and Huchilohuchico, on the other shore of it, with many of their houses on the water.

The first of these cities may have three thousand families, the second more than six thousand, and the third four or five thousand. In all of them, there are very good edifices, of houses and towers, especially the residences of the lords and chief persons, and the mosques or oratories, where they keep their idols. These cities have a great trade in salt, which they make from the water of the lake, and from the crust of the land which is bathed by the lake, and which they boil in a certain manner, making loaves of salt, which they sell to the inhabitants in the neighbourhood.

I followed the said causeway for about half a league before I came to the city proper of Temixtitan. I found at the junction of another causeway, which joins this one from the mainland, another strong fortification, with two towers, surrounded by walls, twelve feet high with castellated tops. This commands the two roads, and has only two gates, by one of which they enter, and from the other they come out. About one thousand of the principal citizens came out to meet me, and speak to me, all richly dressed alike according to their fashion; and when they had come, each one in approaching me, and before speaking, would use a ceremony which is very common amongst them, putting his hand on the ground, and afterwards kissing it. . . . There is a wooden bridge, ten paces broad, in the very outskirts of the city, across an opening in the causeway, where the water may flow in and out as it rises and falls. This bridge is also for defence, for they remove and replace the long broad wooden beams, of which the bridge is made, whenever they wish; and there are many of these bridges in the city, as Your Highness will see in the account which I shall make of its affairs.

Having passed this bridge, we were received by that lord, Montezuma, with about two hundred chiefs, all barefooted, and dressed in a kind of livery, very rich, according to their custom, and some more so than others. They approached in two processions near the walls of the street, which is very broad, and straight, and beautiful, and very uniform from one end to the other, being about two thirds of a league long, and having, on both sides, very large houses, both dwelling places, and mosques. Montezuma came in the middle of the street, with two lords, one on the right side, and the other on the left, one of whom was the same great lord, who, as I said, came in that litter to speak with me, and the other was the brother of Montezuma, lord of that city Iztapalapan, whence I had come that day. All were dressed in the same manner, except that Montezuma was shod, and the other lords were barefooted. Each supported him below his arms, and as we approached each other, I descended from my horse, and was about to embrace him, but the two lords in attendance prevented me, with their hands, that I might not touch him. . . .

From *Hernando Cortés, His Five Letters of Relation to the Emperor Charles V* in Harry J. Carroll et al., eds., *The Development of Civilizations*, 2 vols. (Glenview, IL: Scott, Foresman, 1970), Vol. 1, pp. 56–57.

In battle, Aztec warriors carried spears while the Spanish conquistadores were armed with crossbows and guns. Although the Aztecs fought with valor, superior technology gave the Spaniards an obvious advantage.

Hernando Cortés. Lured to the New World by tales of adventure and treasure, Cortés captured the Aztec capital at Tenochtitlán, in the process destroying its buildings, looting its gold, and killing most of its inhabitants.

men, 200 native servants, 16 horses, 32 crossbows, 13 muskets, and 14 mobile cannon. Before marching against the Aztec capital at Tenochtitlan, he destroyed his ships to prevent his men from turning back. In a few battles, the Spanish horses, firearms, steel armor, and tactics produced decisive victories. Cortés was also able to exploit the Quetzalcoatl legend, which caused the Spaniards to be regarded as gods and helped gain allies among the Aztec tributaries. As the little army marched inland, they were welcomed, feasted, and given Indian women, including daughters of chiefs, whom Cortés distributed among his men. One woman named Malinche, later christened Dona Marina, became an invaluable interpreter, as well as Cortés' mistress, who later bore him a son. The thousands of Indian warriors who fought and died for Cortés contributed significantly to the Spanish victory. Without his Indians, Cortés would have been doomed.

When he reached Tenochtitlan, a city of more than 100,000 people, Cortés became a guest of Montezuma. Surrounded by thousands of armed Aztecs and fearing treachery, Cortés decided to seize the Indian ruler. Malinche then informed Montezuma, as if in confidence, that he must cooperate or die. The bold scheme worked temporarily, but soon the Aztecs rebelled, renouncing their emperor as a traitor, stoning and killing him when he tried to pacify them, and driving a battered band of Spaniards from the city in a

Antonio Pigafetta, "Magellan's Last Fight"

This firsthand account, recorded by an Italian crew member, describes the skirmish with natives on the Philippine island of Mactan, where Magellan was killed in April 1521.

On Friday the 26th of April, Zula, the chief of this island of Mattan, sent one of his sons to present two goats to the Captain, and to tell him that [he would send him everything that he had promised but that he could not send it] because of the other chief, Cilapulapu, [who] did not want to obey the king of Spain, [and asked] that on the following night he send him but one boat-load of men to help him and fight him. The Captain General decided to go there with three boats. And for a long time the others begged him not to go there, but like a good captain, he did not want to abandon his allies. At midnight sixty men armored with cuirasses and sallers left with the Christian king, the prince and some of the chieftains in twenty or thirty boats. And three hours before daylight they reached Mattan. . . . When day came, our men leaped into the water up to their thighs, forty-nine of them, and thus they waded more than two bowshots before they came to dry land. . . . When they arrived on land, these people had made three sections of more than one thousand and fifty persons. And as soon as they realized that they (Magellan's men) were coming, two sections attacked their flanks, and the other their front. When the Captain saw this, he divided his men into two groups and thus they began to fight. The musketeers and the bowmen shot from a distance for almost a half hour in vain, able only to penetrate the shields made of thin planks that they carried on their arms. The Captain shouted to cease firing, but they did not cease firing. [When the natives saw that we were firing muskets without any result] they cried out determined to stand firm. And when the muskets were fired, they shouted all the louder and would not keep still, but jumped hither and yon, covered with their shields shooting so many arrows and hurling bamboo lances, charred pointed stakes, stones and mud at the Captain that he could scarce defend himself. When the Captain saw this he sent some men to burn their houses to frighten them. And when they saw their houses burning they were all the more fierce, and they killed two of our men near the houses, and twenty or thirty burned. And so great a number came upon us that they pierced the right leg of the Captain with a poisoned arrow, wherefore he ordered that they gradually retreat, and they would follow them, and six or eight remained with the Captain. These people aimed only at their legs because they were not covered with armor. And they had so many spears, darts and stones that they (Magellan's soldiers) could not withstand them, and the artillery of the fleet was so far away that it could not help them. And our men withdrew to the shore, fighting all the while, even up to their knees in water, and they recovered their own spears four or five times in order to throw them at us. They recognized the Captain and so many assailed him that twice they knocked his sallet from his head. And he, like a good knight, continued to stand firm with a few others, and they fought thus for more than an hour and refused to retreat. An Indian threw his bamboo spear into his face and he immediately killed him with his own spear and it remained in [the Indian's] body. And the Captain tried to draw his sword and was able to draw it only half way, because he had been wounded in the arm with a spear. When our men saw this they turned their backs and made their way to the ships, still pursued with lances and darts until they were out of sight, and they killed their (the Europeans') guide.

Source: *The Journal of Antonion Pigafetta* in Paula S. Paige, trans., *The Voyage of Magellan* (Englewood Cliffs, NJ: Prentice-Hall, 1969), pp. 75–79.

bare escape. Later, having regrouped and gained new Indian allies, Cortés wore down the Aztecs in a long and bloody siege, which saw some of the Spaniards sacrificed at a distance but in full view of their comrades. Toward the end of this ordeal, the Spaniards fought their way, street by street, against Aztec warriors, both women and men. Finally, after fearful slaughter, some 60,000 exhausted half-starved defenders surrendered. Most tribes in central Mexico then accepted Spanish rule; many who resisted were ultimately enslaved.

Tenochtitlan, rebuilt as Mexico City, became the capital of an expanding Spanish empire. *Conquistadores* steadily penetrated the interior, but the fierce Mayas of Yucatan and Guatemala were not subdued until the 1540s. By then, settlements had been established thoughout Central America. The first colony in North America was founded at St. Augustine, on Florida's east coast, in 1565. Meanwhile, numerous expeditions, including those of Hernando de Soto (1500–1542) and Francisco de Coronado (1510–1554), explored what is now California, Arizona, New Mexico, Colorado, Texas, Missouri, Louisiana, and Alabama. Spanish friars began a mission at Santa Fe in 1610, providing a base for later missions. All of these territories, known as "New Spain," were administered from Mexico City after 1542.

The vice-royalty of Mexico later sponsored colonization of the Philippines, a project justified by the historic voyage of Ferdinand Magellan (1480–1521). Encouraged by the exploits of Vasca de Balboa (1479–1519) who crossed Panama and discovered the Pacific Ocean in 1513, Magellan sailed from Spain in 1520, steered past the ice-encrusted straits at the tip of South America, and sailed ninety-nine days to the Philippines, where he was killed by natives. Only one ship completed this first circumnavigation of the world, but it established a Spanish claim to the Philippines. It also prepared the way for the first tiny settlement at Cebu, in 1571, of four hundred Mexicans. By 1580, the capital at Manila had been secured against attacking Portuguese, Chinese, and Moro fleets, and the friars were beginning conversions which would reach half a million by 1622. The colony became moderately prosperous in trade with Asia but remained economically dependent upon annual galleons from Mexico. Here, as in Mexico, Spanish males, as a tiny elite, spawned an inter-racial population in liaisons with Filipino and Chinese women.

Development of Spanish South America

Like the conquest of Mexico, Spanish operations in Peru began another continuing process of empire-building. In both instances, a handful of daring adventurers destroyed a complex civilization. Each conquest initiated extensive explorations which won most of a continent for Spain.

This all began with a surprisingly easy victory over an Inca state of three million people scattered through Peru and Ecuador in hundreds of mountain towns and coastal cities. But like the Aztec Empire, the Inca state had only been recently unified and was torn by civil war between two princely contenders for the throne when the Spaniards arrived. This bitter "war of the brothers" had almost destroyed the last semblances of imperial unity.

Francisco Pizarro (1470–1541), the son of an illiterate peasant, conquered Peru in 1531, after two failures, with an army of two hundred men and sixty horses. Pizarro started inland soon after Altahualpa, one of the contending princes, defeated his brother. As Pizarro marched he appealed to both sides. At Cajamarco, he met and captured Altahualpa, forcing the Inca ruler to fill a room with gold as tribute. Then, having collected the ransom, Pizarro executed his royal prisoner and marched to the capital at Cuzco, where the Spaniards were welcomed as deliverers. Pizarro next secured tentative control of the country by proclaiming as his puppet-emperor the young son of Altahualpa's dead brother.

For two more decades, political anarchy reigned in Peru, while *conquistadores* fought, explored, and plundered. Indian rebellions and wars raged within the country and on distant borders, but fights among the Spaniards were equally violent and destructive. Meanwhile, expeditions moved south into Chile and north through Ecuador into Colombia. Expeditions from Chile and Peru settled in Argentina, founding the city of Buenos Aires. *Conquistadores* and Indian women produced a new *mestizo* (Spanish-Indian) population in Paraguay. But despite this dynamic activity, there was no effective government at Lima, the capital, until the middle of the sixteenth century.

Amid the terrible hardships of this male-dominated era, women played significant roles. As in Mexico, Indian women were bearers and camp-following concubines; they prepared food and bore children; when necessary, they fought beside the men. Generally, Spaniards did not take Indian wives, preferring Spanish women, who began arriving after 1534. Among their number were society matrons, estate managers, nuns, and shopkeepers. Some were present on all the pioneering ventures and others were direct participants in the intrigues, protests, and fearful sacrifices of the civil wars. In the first tumultuous decades after Pizarro's conquest, they found opportunities to defy convention and act independently.

By 1600, the two vice-royalties of Mexico and Peru were well established, governing over two hundred towns with a Spanish and *mestizo* population of 200,000. Nevertheless, the empire was already in decline. Peruvian silver, the main source of Spanish wealth, was either running out or requiring very expensive mining operations; the Indian labor force was depleted, while African slaves were both expensive and scarce. Even more serious problems were Spain's deteriorating home economy and waning sea power.

The Impact of Iberian Culture in the New World

European expansion overseas after the fifteenth century brought revolutionary change to all the world's peoples, but the Iberian period before 1600 was unique in its violence and ruthless exploitation. Not only were highly organized states destroyed in the New World, but whole populations were wiped out by European diseases, shock, and inhumane treatment. This carnage is one of the most tragic catastrophes in human history. It contributed to a decided change in the racial composition of Iberian America, as an influx of black slaves, with continued Spanish and Portuguese immigration, led to a variegated racial mixture, ranging through all shades of color between white and black. Fortunately, the Indian populations began recovering in the later 1500s, and their cultures,

combining with Iberian and African, formed a new configuration, to be known later as Latin American.

The Nature of Iberian Regimes

Iberian regimes in America faced serious problems. Their vast territories, far greater than the homelands, contained nearly impassable deserts, mountains, and jungles. Supplies had to be moved thousands of miles, often across open seas. Communications were difficult, native wars frequent, and disease often rampant. Such conditions help explain, if not justify, the brutality of Iberian imperialism.

Despite their unique natures, Iberian overseas empires were similar to Roman or Turkish provinces; they were meant to produce revenues. In theory, all Spanish lands were the king's personal property. The Council of the Indies, which directed the viceroys in Mecico City and Lima, advised him on colonial affairs. The high-born Spanish viceroys were aided (and limited) by councils (*audiencias*), made up of aristocratic lawyers from Spain. Local governors, responsible to the viceroys, functioned with their advisory councils (*cabildos*) of officials. Only the rich normally sat in such bodies; poor Spaniards and *mestizos* had little voice, even in their own taxation. Most taxes, however, were collected by Indian chiefs (*caciques*), still acting as rulers of Indian peasant villages.

Portuguese Brazil was less directly controlled than the Spanish colonies. It languished for years under almost unrestricted dominatin of fifteen aristocratic "captains," who held hereditary rights of taxing, disposing lands, making laws, and administering justice. In return, they sponsored settlement and paid stipulated sums to the king. This quasi-feudal administration was abandoned in 1548. When Philip II became King of Portugal in 1580, he established municipal councils, although these were still dominated by the hereditary captains.

Iberian Economies in America

Both the philosophies and social structures of the Iberian states limited colonial trade and industry. Most Spanish and Portuguese immigrants were disinclined toward productive labor. With few exceptions, commercial contacts were limited to the homelands; Mexican merchants fought a steadily losing battle to maintain independent trade with Peru and the Philippines. Local trade grew modestly in supplying the rising towns, but some crafts developed large-scale industrial establishments. A national transportation system, using mule teams, became a major Mexican industry. So did smuggling, as demand rose higher and higher for foreign goods.

Agriculture, herding, and mining silver, however, were the main economic pursuits. The early gold sources soon ran out, but silver strikes in Mexico and in Peru poured a stream of wealth back to Spain in the annual treasure fleets, convoyed by warships from Havana to Seville. Without gold to mine, many Spanish aristocrats acquired abandoned Indian land, raising wheat, rice, indigo, cotton, coffee, and sugar cane. Cattle, horses, and sheep were imported and bred on ranches in the West Indies, Mexico, and Argentina. Brazil developed similar industries, particularly those related to sugar, livestock, and coffee. Iberian economic pursuits in America

were potentially productive, revealing numerous instances of initiative and originality, but they were largely repressed by bureaucratic state systems.

Before 1650, plantations were not typical of agriculture in Iberian America, although they were developing in certain areas. Portugal had earlier established sugar plantations in its Atlantic islands (Madeiras, Cape Verde, and Saõ Tomé) before the system was introduced into Brazil around 1550. The Spanish experimented with plantations in the Canaries, later establishing them in the West Indies, the Mexican lowlands, Central America, and along the northern coasts of South America. Even in such areas, which were environmentally suited for intensive single-crop cultivation, it was not easy to raise the capital, find the skilled technicians, and pay for the labor required by the system.

Scarce labor, a perpetual problem in Iberian America, was solved primarily by the use of Indians, but African slaves were imported early and were coming in greater numbers by the latter sixteenth century (see map below). Some

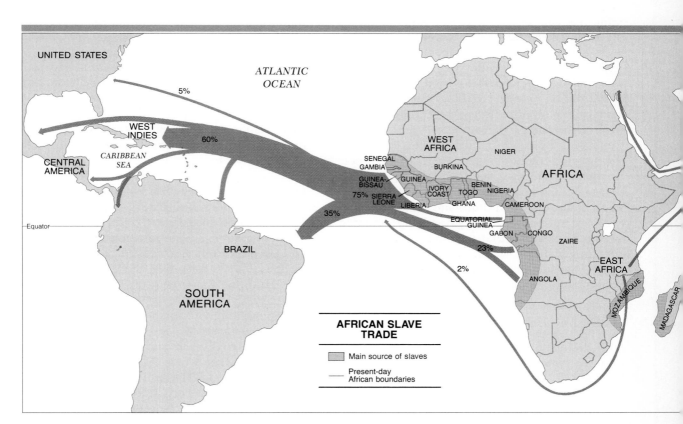

AFRICAN SLAVE TRADE

▇ Main source of slaves

— Present-day African boundaries

Indian slaves work a Spanish sugar plantation on the island of Hispaniola. Spanish treatment of the Native Americans was often brutal.

75,000 were in the Spanish colonies by 1600; over another 100,000 arrived within the next four decades. In Brazil, slave importing boomed after 1560, reaching annual figures of over 30,000 in the early 1600s. Some slaves were brutally oppressed as laborers in the mines. Others sweated on Spanish or Brazilian plantations, but they were the exceptions in this period. The great age of plantation slavery would come later and be most evident in other European colonies. Slaves were also teamsters, overseers, personal servants, and skilled craft workers. Particularly in the Spanish colonies, a good many earned their freedom, attaining a social status higher than that of Indian peasants. Free blacks, both men and women, operated shops and small businesses. Prostitution was understandably common among black and mulatto women, a profession encouraged by the sexual exploitation of female slaves, as concubines and slave-breeders, by Spanish and Portuguese owners.

The Iberian Impact upon Indian Life

The Spanish and Portuguese brought terrible disaster to most Indians. Having seen their gods discredited and their temples destroyed, the majority accepted Christianity as the only hope for survival, as well as salvation. Their Iberian

masters also introduced them to hard and sustained labor. Some died from overwork, some were killed, and others simply languished as their cultures disintegrated. The most effective killer was disease—European or African—to which the Indians had no immunities.

Epidemics arrived with Columbus and continued through the sixteenth century. Smallpox on Haiti in 1518 left only 1000 Indians alive there. Cortés carried the plague to Mexico, where it raged while he fought his way out of Tenochtitlan. From Mexico, the epidemic spread through Central America, reaching Peru in 1526. It killed the reigning emperor and helped start the civil war which facilitated Pizarro's conquest. Following these smallpox disasters in the 1540s and 1570s a wave of measles and other successive epidemics continued depleting the population. Precise accounting is not possible, but a reliable estimate shows a drop in the native American population by 25 percent during the sixteenth century.[3]

Depopulation of Indians was partially caused by their enslavement, despite disapproval from the Catholic Church and the Spanish home government. The worst excesses came soon after the conquests. The gentle Arawaks of Haiti, for example, were herded to work like animals by the first settlers; they soon became extinct.

The whole native population of the Bahamas—some 40,000 people—were carried away as slaves to Haiti, Cuba, and Puerto Rico. Cortés took slaves before he took Tenochtitlan; other Indians, captured in Panama, were regularly sent to Peru. The Portuguese organized jungle "Indian hunts" to acquire slaves before Africans arrived in appreciable numbers.

Another, more common, labor system in the Spanish colonies, was the *encomienda*. This was similar to earlier European serfdom, involving a grant which permitted the holder to take income or labor from specified lands and the people living on them. Abuses were so widespread and Indian complaints so insistent that the system was generally abandoned after the 1550s.

The Spanish government made some ineffective efforts to protect the Indians. The Dominican friar Bartolomé de Las Casas (1474–1566), protested the cruel treatment of the Indians and persuaded King Charles V that indigenous peoples held the same rights as other subjects. This led to the "New Law" of 1542, which ended existing *encomiendas*, on the death of their holders, prohibited native American slavery, and gave Indians full protection under Spanish law. Most of these provisions, however, were rescinded when the law evoked universal protest and open rebellion in Peru. Although later governors gradually eliminated *encomiendas*, many Indians were then put on reservations and hired out as contract laborers, under the direction of their *caciques* and local officials (*corriqodores*). Although this eliminated some of the worst excesses of the *encomiendas*, corrupt officials often exploited their wards, particularly those in Peru.

Most Indians were demoralized by their misfortunes, but some resisted. In Yucatan and Guatemala, where the Mayans did not believe the Spaniards were gods, bloody fighting lasted until the 1540s. About that time a revolt among Indians on the Mexican Pacific coast was put down with great difficulty by the Spaniards. As the silver mines opened in northern Mexico, the Chichimecas, relatives of the Apache, conducted border war into the 1590s, using horses and captured muskets. In Peru, an Inca rebellion led by a new emperor was only subdued in 1572. The most stubborn resistance came from the Araucanians of southern Chile, who fought the Spaniards successfully until the close of the sixteenth century.

Mission towns, established by the Dominican and Jesuit religious orders, afforded Indians the most effective protection. Las Casas led the way in founding such settlements, where the Indians were shielded from white exploitation, instructed in Christianity, and educated or trained in special skills. The prevailing philosophy in the missions stressed patient persuasion, "as rain and snow falls from heaven, not . . . violently . . . like a sudden shower, but gradually, with suavity and gentleness."[4] Large mission organizations developed in Brazil, Paraguay, Venezuela, and upper California. But even those protected by the missions died rapidly in this alien way of life.

Iberian Society and Culture

Iberian society was stratified but somewhat flexible. A small elite of Spanish officials and colonial aristocrats contended over native

Moved by the simplicity and gentle nature of the Native Americans, Bartolomé de Las Casas launched a vigorous campaign to ensure their protection. His *Apologetic History of the Indies* (1566) is an indictment of the Spaniards' harsh treatment of the Indians.

policy and foreign trade. Merchants and petty officials were on a lower social level but above *mestizos,* mulattos, and *zambos* (mixed Indo-Africans). Indians were considered incompetent wards of the king and black slaves were legally designated as beneath the law, but there were numerous individual exceptions. Many Indians went from the reservations to the towns, mines, or *haciendas;* some *caciques* enjoyed wealth and privilege; and a few old Indian families retained their nobility as early Spanish allies. Similarly, some black slaves were craftsmen, overseers, or privileged personal servants; others acquired freedom and became prosperous merchants; still others escaped slavery, organized free communities, and sucessfully defended their independence.

Iberian women in America played ambiguous roles. They were excluded through childhood from male contacts, educated in cloistered schools to become wives and mothers, married in their teens to achieve family interests, and legally subordinated to their husbands. Those who could not marry usually entered convents. There was, however, another side to the story. Spanish law guaranteed the wife's dowry rights, a legal protection against a squandering of her wealth and leverage to limit her husband's activities. The courts recognized separations and at times even granted annulments. Women, particularly widows acting for former husbands, operated businesses and held public offices. Some were wealthy, powerful, and even cruel *encomenderos,* supervising thousands of laborers. Whatever their special roles, Iberian women maintained stability, furthered continuity, defended religion, sponsored charities, dictated manners, and imbued children with family values.

Both the environment and the mix of peoples shaped Iberian-American culture toward a new distinctive unity. From southwestern Europe came the approach to government, disdain for manual labor, preference for dramatic over-precise expression, and ceremonial Catholic Christianity. From Indian traditions came characteristic foods, art forms, architecture, legends, practical garments like the poncho and serape, and hundreds of words. From Africa came agricultural knowledge, crafts, and animal husbandry, along with the rhythm and dance illustrated by Brazilian drums. By 1650, this characteristic Iberian culture was being preserved in its own universities, such as those at Lima and Mexica, both founded more than a century earlier.

This map of western Africa from the 16th century shows the Portuguese forts along the coast. Rulers in the West African states permitted the Portuguese to operate coastal stations but generally excluded them from the interior of the continent.

The Portuguese Impact upon Africa

Unlike the Spaniards in America, the Portuguese came to West Africa as traders rather than settlers. Their activities were largely dictated by circumstances. When they arrived in the fifteenth century, the West Africans had already built strong centralized states, with complex bureaucracies and effective fighting forces. Africans were also quite involved in the slave trade, which the Portuguese exploited by furnishing quicker sea transportation between African depots and also providing a way around Muslim middlemen, who had previously dominated the caravan trade of northwest Africa.

The Portuguese in West Africa

Portuguese coastal trade did not decisively divert traffic on the trans-Sahara routes until the seventeenth century, although it did somewhat intensify commercial and political competition among the Sudanese states. One of these was Songhai, which replaced Mali after 1468 as the dominant power on the upper Niger, maintaining an extensive empire, until it fell to Moroccan invaders in 1590. The next great Muslim kingdom in the area was Kanem-Bornu, during the reign of Mai Idris Alooma (1580–1617). Muslim elites in these and other Sudanese states often alienated their non-Muslim masses and were constantly involved in conflicts, within and beyond their borders. Regional disunity and contention contributed more to the destruction of Songhai than Moroccan conquest or the shift of trade routes to the Atlantic. Yet the continuing Sudanese monopoly of the caravan trade in gold and slaves caused the Portuguese to value highly their direct water route to Guinea in the fifteenth and sixteenth centuries.

Portuguese slaving on the West African coast developed gradually in accordance with negotiated agreements and local laws. Most coastal rulers carefully controlled commercial traffic with the interior, using this monopoly to bargain forcefully with the Portuguese, who were permitted only a very few fortified posts on the mainland. In these enclaves, Portuguese men and slave women produced a tawny population, which ultimately conducted most local trade with the host countries. The most independent Portuguese operations, however, were confined to offshore islands, such as Arguin, the Cape Verdes, and São Tomé.

One of the original coastal kingdoms was Benin, located in the forests of southern Nigeria. The land had been ruled by kings, called Obas,

This salt cellar from Benin depicts a Portuguese sailor sighting land from the crow's nest of his ship.

since the eleventh century. When the Portuguese arrived, Oba Eware the Great (1440–1473) ruled a large empire, which possessed a formidable army. Benin City, the capital, was a bustling metropolis, with wide streets, markets, and an efficient municipal government. The huge royal palace awed Europeans who chanced to see it, although the Portuguese—and later the Dutch—were generally prohibited from living in the city. The few visitors who gained entrance were amazed by the native metal work, such as copper birds on towers, copper snakes coiled around doorways, and beautifully cast bronze statues.

Portuguese relations with the Obas and other rulers along the Guinea coast were relatively calm during the sixteenth century, after Benin

Alfonso Appeals to the King of Portugal

This is an excerpt from a long letter, written by a Congolese schoolboy, who was a scribe for Dom Alfonso, the converted and disillusioned king of Kongo. The letter, dated October 5, 1514, contains many more complaints against Portuguese treachery and villainy.

We ask your Highness to demand of Fernão de Melo why he imprisoned our Dom Francisco, and why he did not allow him to proceed on your Highness' ships to the place we sent him, out of love—for your Highness had sent word that we should despatch 20 or 30 youths of our kin. And we sent our son to your Highness, so that he could present all the slaves and goods we were remitting—and Fernão de Melo did not wish to let him go, but kept him there on his island, with a stick in his hand, making him beg for the love of God—and likewise our nephews—for which reason we are keenly sorrowful. And as to the flesh, we feel much pain, because he is the fruit of our loins; but as to the soul, it grieves us not, for we sent our son to search for the things of God and learn them, and thus all the travails of the world that visit him, while he searches for the faith of our Lord Jesus Christ and learns it, we take to be blessings, and suffer them for the love of our Lord God, for He will ever remember us.

And now we beg of your Highness that, for the love of our Lord Jesus Christ, that you will not forsake us, nor allow the loss of the fruits of Christianity growing in our kingdom—for we can do no more, and have but one mouth to preach and instruct. We have already married, and all the nobles near us have been married—but those who are afar off do not want to be married, because of the evil examples they see every day, and they do not wish to obey us. So we ask your Highness to help us, so that we can make them get married. And if your Highness does not wish to help us in the spiritual realm, we will kiss your royal hands and ask that you send us five or six ships to take us and our sons and relatives, so that we will not witness so great a perdition. . . .

We shall not write more to your Highness because we would have need of a whole ream of paper to relate all the imbroglios that occur here, but Dom Pedro will give your Highness a detailed account of everything. And if anything in this letter be badly written, we ask pardon, because we do not know the styles of Portugal. And we write this with one of our schoolboys, for we do not dare to use any of the [Portuguese] men who are here, for those who best know how to write are guilty of one misdeed or another.

We would kiss the royal hands of your Highness if you would write a letter, on your own behalf, to the *Moynebata* Dom Jorge, and another to the *Moinepanguo*, who are the principal lords in our kingdom, in which your Highness would thank them for being good Christians, and also send them two priests, in addition to those sent to us, so that in their own churches they can say mass, hear confessions, and teach all the things pertaining to God's service. Your Highness should realize that these two lords live a good 80 or 90 leagues distant from us, and each of them has his own church wherein to see God. In both places we have put two schoolboys to teach them [the lords], and their sons and relatives. In this way we have begun the work there and may reap a great harvest. So now let your Highness see if you can complete it, for our powers are thinly spread out and that is all that we can do—but if they can have priests, to say mass to them and confess them, it will be of great merit and they will be strengthened.

Source: William H. McNeill and Mitsuko Iriye, eds., *Modern Asia and Africa* (New York: Oxford University Press, 1971), pp. 68–71.

began participating in the slave trade. The government completely controlled all transactions, while Portuguese traders paid taxes, followed official procedures, and conducted business only with the Oba's representatives. Portuguese visitors were regularly if not frequently invited to attend court, and the Obas at times sent emissaries to Lisbon. Oba Orghuba (1550–1578) actually became a Christian and admitted missionaries to the country.

By the end of the sixteenth century, slaving had become the major Portuguese commercial activity in West Africa. Although effectively limited in Benin, Portuguese traders operated on a larger scale among other coastal states, where they gained some political influence. They were particularly successful in the small kingdom of Warri, a Niger delta vassal state of Benin. Shortly after 1600, the Warri crown prince was educated in Portugal and brought home a Portuguese woman to be his queen. Warri supplied large numbers of slaves, as did other nearby states, which were now competing fiercely with one another. Before long, even Benin would accept dependence upon the trade to control its tributaries and hold its own against Europeans.

The Portuguese and the Kongo Kingdom

Farther south, near the mouth of the Congo River, the Portuguese attained their greatest success in Africa. The early navigators found a recently united Kongo Kingdom, still steeped in African traditions and maintaining a matriarchial system, in which the king was heavily influenced by the queen mother and other women on his council. Portuguese ships, goods, and their Catholic religion so impressed the monarch that in 1483, he invited the visitors to Christianize and modernize his country. Later he received Portuguese advisors and missionaries, reorganized his government, founded churches and schools, and even sent his chiefs, as well as his own son, to study in Portugal. He made Portuguese the official language, encouraging everyone to adopt European dress and manners, while changing his own name from Nzinga Myemba to Dom Alfonso. Many friendly letters subsequently passed between the two monarchs, Dom Alfonso of Kongo and Manuel of Portugal.

This happy state of affairs did not last long. As Alfonso became more dependent upon the Portuguese and more alienated from his own people, Portuguese slave traders from São Tomé ranged over the country. No longer satisfied with treaty terms which gave them prisoners of war and criminals, they ignored the laws and bought everyone they could get, thus creating dissension and weakening the country. Driven to despair, Alfonso wrote to his friend and ally, Manuel:

There are many traders in all corners of the country. They bring ruin . . . Every day, people are enslaved and kidnapped, even nobles, even members of the King's own family.[5]

Such pleas brought no satisfactory responses. For a while, Alfonso curbed the worst abuses, until he was shot by disgruntled Portuguese slavers while he was attending mass. Although the Kongo kingdom lasted for more than another century, retaining its Christian churches and many Portuguese ways, it faced serious internal difficulties, until civil war brought its collapse in 1641.

Upon losing their privileges in Kongo, the Portuguese concentrated their influence to the south in Angola, at the court of a Kongo vassal. Soon, they provoked a war in which Ndonga, the former tributary state, won its independence. By 1575, the Portuguese were following a more direct policy. Using black mercenaries, equipped with firearms, and sometimes allied with the feared Jaga cannibals, they began a long war of conquest. In the last stages of this war, they met the stubborn resistance of Queen Nzinga of Angola, a former ally, who finally broke with the Portuguese and rallied her country against them. These campaigns, even this early, were slave hunts as well as military operations. By 1650, after Angola had been completely conquered, the black cultures and states in this area, once so flourishing in the 1400s, were almost completely destroyed.

Portuguese Angola was never a very successful colony. It functioned primarily as a haven for slavers, amid the violence and vice which such a purpose entailed. The government sought to create a colony of settlement, sending female orphans and prostitutes as prospective wives for the colonists, but such efforts failed miserably. Angola, and its capital of Luanda, remained a sleepy outpost, containing a minority of Portuguese men, fewer white women, an increasing population of mulattoes and an indigenous population of Africans.

The Portuguese in East Africa

Portuguese exploits in East Africa were similar to those in Kongo and Angola. Here the native states were militarily weaker than most in the west. Moreover, the rich Swahili coastal cities, north of the Zambezi, were divided, militarily weak, Muslim, and strategically well located for trade with Asia, a combination that guaranteed Portuguese aggression.

The Swahili people scorned the Portuguese for their poor manners, unclean habits, and tawdry trade goods; but the cities had been prosperous and peaceful for so long that they could not effectively defend themselves. They were therefore plundered from Kilwa to Mombassa. At Mombassa, Portuguese sailors broke into houses with axes, looted, and killed before setting the town afire. The sultan of Mombassa wrote to the sultan of Malinde:

> He raged in our town with such might and terror that no one, neither man nor woman, neither the old or the young, nor even the children, however small, was spared to live . . . [6]

To control commerce, the Portuguese built fortified stations, from which they attempted to collect tribute and maintain trade with the interior. An early one, at Mozambique, became the main Portuguese port of call for vessels on the Asia route. In the 1590s the Portuguese built a fort at Mombassa, hoping to intimidate other cities and facilitate naval operations against Turks and Arabs in the Red Sea. Such efforts diminished the coastal trade but failed to achieve any military objectives.

In the 1520s, the Portuguese established regular diplomatic relations with Ethiopia, through the efforts of Queen Helene, the emperor's mother and the real power behind the throne. Helene sought Portuguese aid against Muslim invaders, but she died in 1525 and the projected alliance was not completed until the 1540s. Subsequently, a Portuguese contingent helped defeat a Muslim army which had almost taken over the country. For the rest of the sixteenth century, relations between Portugal and Ethiopia continued to improve. Ultimately, a Jesuit delegation was successful in popularizing Catholicism and converting Emperor Susenyos (1604–1632). But the arrogant zeal of Alphonso Mendez, who became head of the mission in 1626, led to bloody rebellion. The next emperor expelled the foreigners, and Ethiopia once again isolated itself from the rest of the world.

On the southeast coast, along the Zambezi River, Portuguese missionaries and traders penetrated the interior after 1561. Their arrival precipitated a bloody war which raged for fifteen years between the Portuguese and Vakaranga, a vast tributary empire, controlling seven hundred miles of the upper Zambezi. Finally, the Vakarangan monarch, known to the Portuguese as the Monomotapa, signed a treaty, granting trade rights and permitting missionaries into his country. Along with them came Portuguese adventurers, who established plantations (*prazos*) along the Zambezi, took black concubines, and fathered mulatto families. These women and their offspring often managed the estates, overseeing other black slave workers. Such conditions ultimately brought Vakarangia a fate similar to that of Kongo. The Monomotapa lost credibility among his subjects and was forced to seek Portuguese protection. This led to more discontent over Portuguese plantations and slave trading. Ultimately, warriors from Changamire, a central African state, drove both the Portuguese and the Vakarangas from the internal plateau.

The Portuguese impact upon Africa was not as immediately disastrous as Spanish effects upon the New World, although great damage was inflicted in Kongo, Angola, Vakaranga, and among the Swahili city states. Here were precedents for much greater African disasters in the seventeenth and eighteenth centuries. By their emphasis upon slavery, the Portuguese helped wed emerging black African states to war, militarism, rigid autocracy, and superstition. African economies were depressed because they did not develop their own productivity. The trade also promoted guilt and shame among Africans who enslaved each other. Even in this era, before the trade reached its peak, it created an enduring synthesis of African and European evils.

This detail from an Indian textile shows three women wearing the brightly colored Indian cottons known as calicoes. The new calicoes, lightweight and soft and smooth to the touch, became so popular so quickly that both England and France attempted to ban their import in order to protect their domestic clothing industries.

Beginnings of North European Expansion

European overseas expansion after 1600 entered a second phase, comparable to developments at home. As Spain declined, so did the Spanish empire and that of Portugal, which was tied to Spain by a Habsburg king after 1580 and plagued with its own developing imperial problems. These new conditions afforded opportunities for northern European states. The Dutch, between 1630 and 1650, almost cleared the Atlantic of Spanish warships and took over most of the Portuguese posts in Brazil, Africa, and Asia. The French and English also became involved on a smaller scale, setting up their global duel for empire in the eighteenth century (see Reference Map 7).

The Shifting Commercial Revolution

Behind this change was a decisive shift in Europe's early commercial revolution. Expanding foreign trade, new products, an increasing supply of bullion, and rising commercial risks created new problems, calling for energetic initiatives. During the sixteenth century the Spanish and Portuguese had depended upon quick profits, and because of weak home industries and poor management, wealth flowed through their hands to northern Europe, where it was invested in productive enterprises. Later, this wealth generated a new imperial age.

European markets after the sixteenth century were swamped with a bewildering array of hitherto rare or unknown goods. New American foods included potatoes, maize (Indian corn), peanuts, tomatoes, and fish from Newfoundland's Grand Banks. In an era without refrigeration imported spices, such as pepper, cloves, and cinnamon, made spoiled foods palatable. Sugar became a common substitute for honey, and cocoa, the Aztec sacred beverage, spread throughout Europe. Coffee and tea, from the New World and Asia, soon produced new social habits throughout Europe. North American furs, Chinese silks, and cottons from India and Mexico revolutionized clothing fashion. Luxury furnishings, using rare woods, ivory, and Oriental carpets appeared more frequently in homes of the wealthy. The use of American tobacco became almost a mania among all classes and contributed further to the booming European market.

Imported gold and, more significantly, silver probably affected the European economy more than all other foreign goods. After the Spaniards looted Aztec and Inca treasure rooms, the gold flowing from America and Africa subsided to a trickle, but seven million tons of silver poured into Europe before 1660. Spanish prices quadrupled and, because most of the silver went to pay for imports, prices in northern Europe more than tripled. The influx of bullion and the resulting inflation hurt landlords depending on fixed rents and creditors who were paid in cheap money, but the bullion bonanza ended a centuries-long gold drain to the East, with its attendant money shortage. It also increased the profits of merchants selling on a rising market, thus greatly stimulating north European capitalism.

At the opening of the sixteenth century, Italian merchants and money-lenders, mainly Florentines, Venetians, and Genoese, dominated the rising Atlantic economy. The German Fugger Banking house at Augsburg also provided substantial financing. All south European bankers,

Marketplace at Antwerp. In the 16th century, Antwerp was the leading city in international commerce. As many as 500 ships a day docked in its bustling harbor, and as many as 1000 wagons arrived each week carrying the overland trade.

particularly the Fuggers and the Genoese, suffered heavily from the Spanish economic debacles under Charles V and Philip II. As the century passed, Antwerp in the southern Netherlands became the economic hub of Europe. It was the center for the English wool trade as well as the entrepôt (way station) for southbound trade from the Baltic and Portuguese goods from Asia. It was also a great financial center, dealing in commercial and investment instruments. The Spanish sack of Antwerp (see p. 454) in 1576 ended Antwerp's supremacy, which passed to Amsterdam, where it furthered Dutch imperial ventures.

Meanwhile, north European capitalism flourished in nearly every category. Portuguese trade was rivaled by that of north European merchants in the Baltic and the North Atlantic. Northern joint stock companies pooled capital for privateering, exploring, and commercial venturing. The Dutch and English East India companies, founded early in the seventeenth century, were but two of the better known stock companies. In England, common fields were enclosed for capitalistic sheep runs. Throughout western Europe, domestic manufacturing, in homes or workshops, competed with the guilds. Large industrial enterprises, notably in mining, shipbuilding, and cannon-casting were becoming common. Indeed, the superiority of English and Swedish cannon contributed to the defeat of the Spanish Armada and the Catholic armies in the Thirty Years' War.

The Dutch Empire

By 1650, the Dutch were supreme in both southern Asia and the South Atlantic. Their empire, like the Portuguese earlier, was primarily commercial; even their North American settlements specialized in fur trading with the Indians. They acquired territory where necessary to further their commerce but tried to advance their interests by pragmatic policies, in accord with native cultures, rather than by conquest. Unlike the Spanish and Portuguese, they made little attempt to spread Christianity.

Systematic Dutch naval operations ended Iberian imperial supremacy, beginning in 1595 when the first Dutch fleet entered the East

Indies. Dutch captains soon drove the Portuguese from the Spice Islands. Malacca, the Portuguese bastion, fell after a long siege in 1641. The Dutch also occupied Ceylon and blockaded Goa, thus limiting Portuguese operations in the Indian Ocean. Although largely neglecting East Africa, they seized all Portuguese posts on the west coast north of Angola. Across the Atlantic, they conquered Brazil, drove Spain from the Caribbean, and captured a Spanish treasure fleet. Decisive battles near the English Channel coast of Kent (1639) and off Brazil (1640) delivered the final blows to the Spanish navy. What the English had begun in 1588, the Dutch completed fifty years later.

Trade with Asia, the mainstay of the Dutch empire, was directed by the Dutch East India Company. Chartered in 1602 and given a monopoly of all operations between South Africa and the Straits of Magellan, it served to concentrate resources and eliminate costly competition. In addition to its trade and diplomacy, it sponsored numerous explorations of Australia, Tasmania, New Guinea, and the South Pacific. With its great concentration of capital, larger than the wealth of most states, the company could easily outdistance its European rivals.

The Dutch empire in the East was established primarily by Jan Pieterszoon Coen (1587–1629), governor-general of the Indies between 1618 and 1629 and founder of the company capital at Batavia in northwest Java. At first he cooperated with native rulers in return for a monopoly of the spice trade. When this involved him in costly wars against local sultans as well as their Portuguese and English customers, Coen determined to control the trade at its sources. In the resulting many conflicts and negotiations, which lasted longer than Coen's time, the Dutch acquired all of Java, most of Sumatra, the spice-growing Moluccas, and part of Ceylon. They began operating their own plantations, supplying pepper, cinnamon, sugar, tea, tobacco, and coffee for a fluctuating world market.

Although commercially successful in Asia, the Dutch were not able to found flourishing settlement colonies. Many Dutchmen who went to the East wanted to make their fortunes and return home; those willing to stay were usually mavericks, uninterested in establishing families or permanent relationships. After 1620, the Dutch East India Company experimented with a policy of bringing European women to the Indies, but such efforts were abandoned when they failed to enlist much interest at home or in the foreign stations. Consequently, the Dutch colonies in Asia, as well as those in Africa, the Caribbean, and Brazil, remained primarily business ventures, with little racial mixing, compared with the Iberian areas.

After resuming war with Spain in 1621, the Dutch formed their West India Company, charged with overtaking Spanish and Portuguese holdings in Africa and America. The company wasted no time. It soon supplanted the Portuguese in West Africa and by 1630 dominated the slave trade with America. After driving the Spanish from the Caribbean, the Dutch invited other European planters to the West Indies as customers, keeping only a few bases for themselves. The company then launched a successful naval conquest of Brazil, from the mouth of the Amazon south to the San Francisco River. In Brazil the Dutch learned sugar planting, passing on their knowledge to the Caribbean and applying it directly in the East Indies.

Dutch settlements in North America never amounted to much because of the company's commercial orientation. In 1609 Henry Hudson (d. 1611), an Englishman sailing for Holland, explored the river named for him and established Dutch claims while looking for a northwest passage. Fifteen years later, the Dutch West India Company founded New Amsterdam on Manhattan Island; over the next few years, it built a number of frontier trading posts in the Hudson Valley and on the nearby Connecticut and Delaware rivers. Some attempts were made to encourage planting by selling large tracts to wealthy proprietors (patroons). Agriculture, however, remained secondary to the fur trade, which the company developed in alliance with the Iroquois tribes. This arrangement hindered settlement; in 1660 only 5000 Europeans were in the colony.

The French Empire

French exploration began early and was followed by attempted settlements in the New World, but no permanent colonies were established until the opening of the seventeenth

Batavia (present-day Djakarta) on the island of Java became the headquarters of the Dutch East India Company when the Dutch ousted the Portuguese and took command of the East Indies trade in the 17th century.

An early drawing shows the arrival of the first French colonists in North America, brought by Cartier on his third voyage in 1541, against a map of the Saint Lawrence estuary. The colony soon failed. (The map is drawn so that north is at the bottom of the drawing rather than at the top.)

century. France was so weakened by religious wars that most of its efforts, beyond fishing and privateering, had to be directed toward internal stability. While the Dutch were winning their empire, France was involved in the land campaigns of the Thirty Years' War. Thus serious French empire building was delayed until the reign of Louis XIV.

Early French colonization in North America was based on claims made by Giovanni da Verrazzano (1485–1528) and Jacques Cartier (1491–1557). The first, a Florentine mariner commissioned by Francis I in 1523, traced the Atlantic coast from North Carolina to Newfoundland. Eleven years later, Cartier made the first of two voyages, exploring the Saint Lawrence River. These French expeditions duplicated England's claim to eastern North America.

A wilderness stretching hundreds of miles separated the early French Canadian colonies from their English counterparts. A first French settlement was made at Port Royal (Nova Scotia) in 1605. Three years later, Samuel de Champlain (1567–1635), acting for a French-chartered company, founded Quebec on the Saint Lawrence. The company brought in colonists, but only a few came before Champlain's death in 1635 and only 2500 had arrived by 1663. The

company's emphasis on fur trading, the bitter cold of the winters, and the nearly continuous skirmishes with the Indians retarded growth. Montreal was established in 1642, after which French trapper-explorers began penetrating the region around the headwaters of the Mississippi. New France soon expanded over a wide area, but population remained sparse.

Elsewhere, the French seized opportunities afforded by the decline of Iberian sea power. They acquired the Isle of Bourbon in the Indian Ocean (1642) for use as a commercial base. In West Africa, they created a sphere of commercial interest at the mouth of the Senegal, where they became involved in the slave trade, with only slight opposition from the Dutch. Even more significant was the French presence in the West Indies. They occupied part of Saint Kitt's in 1625 and acquired Martinique and Guadeloupe ten years later. The burgeoning sugar trade helped make the French islands profitable, but fierce attacks by the Caribs limited colonization and economic development.

The English Empire

In terms of power and profit, English foreign expansion before 1650 was not impressive. Like

French colonialism, it was somewhat hampered by internal political conditions, particularly by the poor management and restrictive policies of the early Stuart kings, which led to civil war in the 1640s. A number of circumstances, however, promoted foreign ventures. The population increased from three to four million between 1530 and 1600, providing a large reservoir of potential indentured labor. Religious persecution encouraged migration of nonconformists, and surplus capital was seeking opportunities for investment. Such conditions ultimately produced a unique explosion of English settlement overseas.

During the sixteenth century, English maritime operations were confined primarily to exploring, fishing, smuggling, and plundering. English claims to North America were registered in 1497–1498 by two voyages of John Cabot, who explored the coast of North America from Newfoundland to Virginia but found no passage to Asia. For the next century, English expeditions sought such a northern passage, both in the East and in the West. All of them failed, but they resulted in explorations of Hudson Bay and the opening of a northern trade route to Russia. From the 1540s, English captains, including the famous John Hawkins of Plymouth, indulged in sporadic slave trading in Africa and the West Indies, despite Spanish restrictions. Their encounters on the Spanish main generated the exploits of English "sea dogs," like Sir Francis Drake, whose raids on Spanish shipping helped prepare the defeat of the Armada.

After failures in Newfoundland and on the Carolina coast, the first English colony in America was founded in 1607 at Jamestown in Virginia. For a number of years the colonists suffered from lack of food and other privations, but they were saved by their dauntless leader, Captain John Smith (1580–1631), whose romantic rescue by the Indian princess Pocahontas (a. 1595–1617), is an American legend. Jamestown set a precedent for all English colonies in North America. By the terms of its original charter, the London Company, which founded the settlement, was authorized to act as a miniature government for the colonists, who were to enjoy all the rights of native Englishmen. Consequently, in 1619, the governor called an assembly to assist in govern-

ing. This body later became the Virginia House of Burgesses, one of the oldest continuously operating representative legislatures.

Shortly after the founding of Jamestown, large-scale colonization began farther north. In 1620, a group of English Protestants who called themselves Pilgrims landed at Plymouth. Despite severe hardships, they survived, and their experiences inspired other religious dissenters against the policies of Charles I and Archbishop Laud (see p. 466). In 1629, the Massachusetts Bay Company settled a number of English Calvinists near the present-day site of Boston, where they were given the rights to virtual self-government. From this first enclave, emigrants moved out to other areas in present-day Maine, Rhode Island, and Connecticut. Before 1642 more than 25,000 people had migrated to New England, laying the foundations for a number of future colonies. This exodus firmly planted English culture and political institutions in North America.

Life in the North American English settlements was hard during those first decades, but a pioneering spirit and native colonial pride was already evident. In all areas, food was scarce, disease was ever present, and Indians were often dangerous. Yet from the beginning, and more than in other European colonies, settlers here looked to their futures in the new land because they had left less behind in Europe. Most were expecting to stay, establish homes, and raise families, as well as make their fortunes. The first Puritans included both women and men. A shipload of "purchase brides" arrived in 1619 at Jamestown to lend stability to the colony. This was but the first of many such contingents, all eagerly welcomed by prospective husbands. In addition, many women came on their own as indentured servants.

American colonial women were legally dependent upon their husbands, who controlled the property and the children. A widow achieved these rights, but it was not easy to outlive a husband. Hard work and frequent pregnancies—mothers with a dozen children were not uncommon—reduced female life expectancies. Nevertheless, women developed a rough endurance and gained confidence and practical independence. This independent spirit was revealed by Anne Hutchinson (1591–1643), who was banished from Massachusetts for preaching her own religious beliefs and then founded a settlement in Rhode Island. Another example is Anne Bradstreet (c. 1612–1672). Although made painfully aware that men considered her presumptuous, she continued to write thoughtful and beautiful poetry.

The English government considered the rough coasts and wild forests of North America less important in this period than footholds in the West Indies and Africa, where profit were expected from planting and slave-trading. A wave of English migrants descended upon the West Indies, after the Dutch opened the Caribbean. In 1613, English settlers established themselves on Bermuda, and by the 1620s others had planted colonies on Saint Kitt's, Barbados, Nevis, Montserrat, Antigua, and in the Bahamas. Tobacco planting was at first the major enterprise, bringing some prosperity and the promise of more. The white population expanded dramatically, especially on Barbados, which was not subject to Carib attack. There the English settlers increased from 7000 to 37,000 in seven years. As yet, however, there were few blacks on the English islands, although some were already being imported for the sugar plantations.

Meanwhile, English slaving posts in West Africa were beginning to flourish and English adventurers were starting operations in Asia. Captain John Lancaster, with four ships, visited Sumatra and Java in 1601, returning with a profitable cargo of spices. His voyage led to the founding of the English East India Company, which was chartered in 1609. But expansion outside of the Caribbean was difficult, because the Dutch were uncooperative. In the Moluccas, for example, they drove out the English in the 1620s, after repeated clashes. The English fared better in India. By 1622, the English East India Company had put the Portuguese out of business in the Persian Gulf. Subsequently, the English established trading posts on the west coast of India at Agra, Masulipatam, Balasore, and Surat. The station at Madras, destined to become the English bastion on the east coast, was founded in 1639.

Conclusion

Between 1450 and 1650, the era of the early commercial revolution, Europeans faced west

View of Jamestown in 1607 drawn by John Hull. Surrounded by water on three sides, the marshy peninsula on the James River seemed an easy-to-defend and thus ideal location for the Jamestown fort. By 1614 there were "two faire rowes of howses" protected by a palisade.

toward a new world and initiated a new age of oceanic expansion. In the process, they stimulated capitalistic development, found a sea route to Asia, became more familiar with Africa, began colonizing America, and proved the earth to have a spherical surface. For most of the period, Spain and Portugal monopolized the new ocean trade and profited most from exploiting American wealth, following precedents set by earlier Eurasian empires. Only at the end of the era, when leadership shifted toward the Dutch, French, and English, did European colonialism show signs of developing in new directions.

Overseas expansion exerted a tremendous effect upon European culture and institutions. Spain's political predominance in the sixteenth century was largely bought with American treasure; and Spain's quick decline was also caused primarily by the influx of American bullion, which inflated Spanish money and discouraged Spanish economic development. Northern European capitalism, developing in financial organization, shipbuilding, metal working, manufacturing, and agriculture, brought a new vitality to northern economies, in response to Spanish and Portuguese purchasing power. Economic advantages also contributed to Protestant victories in the Thirty Years' War. This first age of the commercial revolution increased north European confidence, enthusiasm, and initiative, in preparation for later world dominance.

In the New World the European impact was both dramatic and tragic. To win an empire, the Spanish *conquistadores* and the Portuguese captains nearly destroyed native peoples and subjected most of the survivors to terrible hardships, indignities, cultural deprivations, and psychological injuries. The plight of Latin American peasants today began with Iberian imperial policies of the sixteenth century. Yet the balance sheet is not all negative. The Spanish and Portuguese in America generated a new cultural synthesis, blending European, Indian, and African elements to produce a richness and variety not present in any one of the parent cultures. This integration was largely accomplished by a literal racial mixing, which created a new Latin American stock in the western hemisphere.

The European impact upon Africa was less apparent at the time but perhaps more damaging in the long run than what happened to the Indians of Latin America. When the Portuguese arrived, Africa was midway through a significant political revolution from tribalism to territorial states. In the Sudan and Ethiopia, this revolution was almost complete; south of the Sahara, it was already far advanced in a number of places. The state of political development prevented the Portuguese from effecting outright conquests, except in Angola and along the Zambezi. Instead, African states were domoralized by their increasing involvement in slave-trading. The trade maintained the political power of African states but slowed their economic development and weakened Africans' pride in themselves and their cultural heritage. This process, well begun before 1650, would reach its tragic climax in the next two centuries.

In Asia, the European impact before 1650 was mixed. Ceylon and the Spice Islands of the Malay archipelago, which were vulnerable to sea power, came under domination, direct or indirect, and were exploited by the Portuguese and Dutch. Elsewhere in Asia the European influence was present but less obvious. The Portuguese were run out of China twice before they learned respect for Chinese law. Other Europeans fared worse. All were ultimately excluded from Japan. Southern India was not entirely open, as the Portuguese found by the end of the period. In the main, Turks, Arabs, Chinese, Japanese, Thais, and Vietnamese felt superior to Europeans and were usually able to back their pride with effective action.

Suggestions for Reading

An excellent recent work which covers the whole subject is Geoffrey Scammell, *The First Imperial Age: European Overseas Expansion, 1400–1700* (Unwin Hyman, 1989). See also the two classic studies: Charles E. Nowell, *The Great Discoveries and the First Colonial Empires*, rev. ed. (Greenwood, 1982) and Samuel Eliot Morison's monumental *The European Discovery of America* in two volumes: *The Northern Voyages* (Oxford, 1971) and *The Southern Voyages* (Oxford, 1974). A briefer but still reliable and interesting volume along the same lines is Samuel Eliot Morison, *The Great Explorers* (Oxford, 1978). A number of other surveys are well worth consulting: Louis B. Wright, *Gold, Glory, and Gospel* (Atheneum, 1970); Daniel Devine, *The*

Opening of the World: The Great Age of Maritime Exploration (Putnam, 1973); and Daniel J. Boorstin, *The Discoverers* (Random House, 1985).

For more pointed analyses of early European imperialism, see Carlo M. Cipolla, *Guns Sails and Empires*, rev. ed. (Sunflower Univ. Press, 1985); William H. McNeil, *Plagues and People* (Doubleday, 1977); Eric R. Wolf, *Europe and the People Without History* (Univ. of California, 1982); and Nicholas Canny and Anthony Pagden, *Colonial Identity in the Atlantic World (Princeton Univ., 1989).*

Two time-tested secondary sources for the Iberian New World are H. Hering, *A History of Latin America* (Knopf, 1968) and Stanley J. and Barbara H. Stein, *The Colonial Heritage of Latin America* (Oxford, 1970). To these may be added a number of excellent later studies: Tzvetan Todorov, *The Conquest of America* (Harper and Row, 1984); Lyle N. McAlister, *Spain and Portugal in the New World 1492–1700* (Univ. of Minn., 1984); and Mark A. Burkholder, *Colonial Latin America* (Oxford Univ., 1989). For penetrating studies of Latin American social conditions, see Louisa Hoberman and Susan M. Socolow, eds., *Cities and Society in Colonial Latin America* (Univ. of New Mexico, 1986). The complex issues relating to slavery and plantations are ably indentified and evaluated in W. R. Aykroyd, *Sweet Malefactor* (Heinmann, 1967); Eric Williams, *From Columbus to Castro*, rev. ed. (Random House, 1984); and Herbert S. Klein, *African Slavery in Latin America and the Caribbean* (Oxford Univ., 1988). For the ambiguous status of women, see Ann M. Pescatello, *Power and Pawn: The Female in Iberian Families* (Greenwood, 1976) and Asuncion Lavin, ed., *Latin American Women* (Greenwood, 1978).

A general overview of Spanish empire-building in America is provided in Colin M. MacLachlan, *Spain's Empire in the New World* (Univ. of California, 1988). Three earlier works are also worth attention: Oskar H. K. Spate, *The Spanish Lake* (Univ. of Minnesota, 1979); J. H. Parry, *The Spanish Seaborne Empire* (Knopf, 1971); and Charles Gibson, *Spain in America* (Harper Torchbooks, 1968). Gianni Granzotto, *Christopher Columbus* (Univ. of Oklahoma, 1988) reveals the world of Columbus and a personalized account of his exploits.

On the whole subject of Spanish campaigns in the New World, William H. Prescott, *The Conquest of Mexico* (Bantam Books, 1964) and *The Conquest of Peru* (Mentor, 1961) are readable abridgements of memorable and dramatic historical classics. See also Frederick A. Kirkpatrick, *The Spanish Conquistadores* (Meridian, 1962). Luis Martin's *Daughters of the Conquistadores* (Southern Methodist Univ., 1989) documents the significant role of women in the grueling process and Nathan Wachtel's *Vision of the Vanquished* (Barnes and Noble, 1977) shows the Indians' views of their new masters. For the Spanish conquest of Mesoamerica, see Inga Clendinnon, *Ambivalent Conquest: Maya and Spaniard in Yucatan, 1517–1570* (Cambridge Univ., 1989); Kenneth Pearce, *The View from the Top of the Temple* (Univ. of New Mexico, 1984); R. Fehrenbach, *Fire and Blood* (Macmillan, 1973); and Jon M. White, *Cortés and the Downfall of the Aztec Empire* (Carroll and Graf, 1989). Good coverage of the Spanish campaigns in Peru is provided in Bernabe Cobo, *History of the Inca Empire* (Univ. of Texas, 1979) and John Hemming, *The Conquest of the Incas* (Harcourt Brace Jovanovich, 1973).

For more focused treatments on the colonial development of New Spain, see Peggy K. Liss, *Mexico Under Spain* (Univ. of Chicago, 1984) and James M. Lockhart, *Spanish Peru 1532–1600* (Univ. of Wisconsin, 1968). For political, economic, and social conditions, see Jonathan Irvine Israel, *Race, Class, and Politics in Colonial Mexico* (Oxford Univ., 1975); Leslie B. Simpson, *The Encomienda in New Spain*, 3rd. ed. (Univ. of California, 1982); Ross Hassig, *Trade, Tribute, and Transportation in the Sixteenth-Century Political Economy of the Valley of Mexico* (Univ. of Oklahoma, 1985); and William L. Sherman, *Forced Native Labor in Sixteenth Century Central America* (Univ. of Nebraska, 1979). The following works effectively depict the racial and cultural synthesis in colonial Mexico: Colin MacLachlan and James E. Rodriquez, *The Forging of the Cosmic Race* (Univ. of California, 1980); S. L. Cline, *Colonial Culhacan, 1580–1600: A Social History of an Aztec Town* (Univ. of New Mexico, 1986); Jacques Lafaye, *Quetzalcoatl and Guadalupe: The Formation of Mexican National Consciousness* (Univ. of Chicago, 1987); and Edward Murguca, *Assimilation, Colonialism, and the Mexican American People* (Univ. Press of Amer., 1989).

Two respected works on Portuguese exploration and colonization are Samuel Eliot Morison, *Portuguese Voyagers to America in the Fifteenth Century* (Octagon Books, 1965) and Charles R. Boxer, *Four Centuries of Portuguese Expansion* (Univ. of California, 1969). For the Portuguese in Asia, see Gerald R. Crone, *The Discovery of the East* (St. Martin's 1972); K. M. Matthew, *History of Portuguese Navigation in India* (South Asia Books, 1987); and Charles R. Boxer, *The Christian Century of Japan* (Univ. of California, 1974). For Portugal's policies in America, see E. Bradford Burns, *A History of Brazil* (Columbia, 1970) and Dagmar Schaeffer, *Portuguese Exploration in the West and the Formation of Brazil, 1450–1800* (J. C. Brown, 1988). An interesting and informative biography is Elaine Sanceau, *Henry the Navigator* (Archon Books, 1969).

For the best treatment of developing African culture during the era of European expansion see works cited in the preceding chapter, particularly Robert W. July, *A History of the African People* (Scribner, 1980). The calamities accompanying Portuguese policies in southwest Africa are graphically described in John Thornton, *Kingdom of the Kongo* (Univ. of Wisconsin, 1983) and Anne Hilton, *The Kingdom of Kongo* (Oxford Univ., 1985). On early slavery and the slave trade, see Charles Boxer, *Race Relations in the Portuguese Colonial Empire*, rev. ed. (Greenwood, 1985); Paul Lovejoy, *Transformations in Slavery* (Cambridge Univ., 1983); and James Walvin, *Slavery and the Slave Trade* (Univ. of Minnesota, 1983).

A good survey of Dutch imperial development is Charles R. Boxer, *The Dutch Seaborne Empire*, rev. ed. (Knopf, 1989). See also Charles E. Boxer, *The Dutch in Brazil* (Archon Books, 1973); Pieter Geyl, *The Netherlands in the Seventeenth Century* (Barnes and Noble, 1961); and Charles Wilson, *The Dutch Republic* (McGraw-Hill, 1968).

Yves F. Zoltvany, *The French Tradition in America* (South Carolina Univ., 1969) presents a definitive treatment of early French exploration and colonialism. See also John Hopkins Kennedy, *Jesuit and Savage in New France* (Archon Books, 1971); and George W. Wrong, *Rise and Fall of New France* (Octagon Books, 1970).

Angus Calder, *Revolutionary Empire* (E. P. Dutton, 1981) is a sweeping study of expanding English culture from the fifteenth to the eighteenth century. Barry Coward, *The Stuart Age* (Longman, 1984) deals effectively with expansion but also provides significant English economic, social, and political backgrounds. See also John Bowle, *The Imperial Achievement* (Little, Brown, 1974) and William Abbot, *The Colonial Origins of the United States* (Wiley, 1975). Carl Bridenbaugh, *Vexed and Troubled Englishmen* (Oxford, 1968) provides a penetrating analysis of perspectives among English colonists. For excellent special studies, see Alden T. Vaughn, *Captain John Smith and the Founding of Virginia* (Little, Brown, 1975); Grace Woodward, *Pocahontas* (Univ. of Oklahoma, 1980); and Cyril Hamshere, *The British in the Caribbean* (Harvard Univ., 1972).

Notes

1. Daniel J. B. Boorstin, *The Discoverers*, (New York: Random House, 1985), p. 178.

2. Colin McEvedy and Richard Jones, *Atlas of World Population History* (New York: Penguin, 1978), pp. 100–103.
3. *Ibid.*, pp. 272–73.
4. Quoted in H. Hering, *A History of Latin America* (New York: Alfred A. Knopf, 1968), p. 173.
5. Quoted in David Lillingray, *A Plague of Europeans* (New York: Penguin, 1973), p. 20.
6. Quoted in Robert Rotberg, *A Political History of Tropical Africa* (New York: Harcourt Brace Jovanovich, 1965), pp. 85–86.

The Strife of States and Kings

European Religion, Politics, and Art in a Century of Strife, 1560–1660

On a dark misty day in November 1632, two great armies, one Protestant and one Catholic, met in the German Saxon countryside near Lutzen. The Protestants won a decisive victory that day but lost their general, King Gustavus Adolphus (1594–1632) of Sweden, known as the "Lion of the North." According to a familiar story, the dying king was discovered on the battlefield and asked his name by enemy soldiers. "I am the King of Sweden," he replied, "who so seal the religion and liberty of the German nation with my blood."[1]

The fate of Sweden's warrior-king reflected the tragedy and the ambiguity of the age. This second phase of the Reformation was marked by bloody religious wars, economic depression, and rampant disease. It was also a time when religious fanaticism interacted with pragmatic politics, contributing, in the process, to the development of modern states. Sometimes religious conflict caused the reshaping of feudal values to justify movements against royal authority; more often, it promoted centralized monarchies, whose rulers promised to restore order by wielding absolute power. Despite pious declarations, kings and generals often conducted war with little regard for moral principles; indeed, as time passed, they steadily subordinated religious concerns to dynastic ambitions or assumed national interests. This change, however, came slowly and was completed only after Europe had been ravaged by the human suffering and material destruction of religious conflict.

A specific political result of the long religious conflict was a shift in the European balance of power. At the opening of the period, the Habsburg dynasty sought to maintain its dominant position in alliance with the Catholic Church. It failed in its struggle against opposing coalitions, which were often allied with Protestantism. The long-term beneficiary of this political struggle was France, a leading Catholic state.

Baroque art and literature somewhat ambiguously expressed the values of its period. The baroque style emphasized the heroic, the bizarre, and the powerful, in keeping with strong rulers and warring states. Despite its masculine values, the Baroque glorified women in the abstract at a time when ordinary women were losing social status. This apparent contradiction might be explained by the dominant contemporary roles of famous queens, powerful female regents, and the aristocratic women who acted as hostesses of the salons.

Internal Religious and Political Developments

Although it ended a short war in Germany, the Peace of Augsburg (1555) failed to end religious contention. Even before John Calvin died in 1564, his movement was spreading rapidly in France, Germany, Poland, Bohemia, and Hungary. The Council of Trent launched a formidable counteroffensive, led by the Jesuits and supported by Spain, against all Protestants. England narrowly avoided the religious civil wars that ended the Valois line in France; the Spanish Netherlands exploded in religious rebellion; and the militant counter-Reformation suppressed Protestantism in eastern Europe. For decades, problems of religion dominated politics within every European state.

**POLITICAL DIVISIONS OF
EUROPE ABOUT 1560**

- Spanish Habsburgs
- Austrian Habsburgs
- Boundary of the
  Holy Roman Empire

Spain as the Model for Catholic Absolutism

Under Philip II (1556–1598), Spain was recognized as the strongest military power in Europe and the major defender of the Catholic faith. This reputation arose from the rigidly disciplined Spanish infantry, silver that seemed to flow in unlimited quantities from America, and the record of the famed Spanish Inquisition, which had dealt effectively earlier with the Jews and Moors and was now being used to snuff out Spanish Protestantism. Philip accepted this interpretation, deliberately projecting an image of himself as the iron-willed champion of Catholic orthodoxy.

This responsibility was part of Philip's inheritance from his father, Charles V, whose long reign ended in 1556 when he abdicated his imperial throne and entered a monastery. As Charles stepped down from the throne, he split his holdings between his brother, Ferdinand, who received Austria, Bohemia, and Hungary; and his son, Philip, who received Naples, Sicily, Milan, the Netherlands, and Spain. Philip also gained control of a vast overseas empire, which was much more lucrative than had been his father's imperial crown in the Germanies.

indeed, the division of Habsburg lands appeared to be a blessing for Philip, allowing him to shed his father's worrisome "German problem" and concentrate more effectively upon his Spanish realm (see map, p. 450). There were, however, less favorable aspects of the legacy—Charles left his son the Turkish menace in the Mediterranean as well as the expensive task of leading the Catholic crusade against Protestantism.

Philip was an obedient son and took very seriously his father's admonitions. A slight, somber, and unemotional man, he was almost completely absorbed by his awesome official obligations. Charles had warned him about becoming too intimate with subordinates and, particularly, against trusting or depending upon women. Philip heeded this advice. Although he was involved briefly with mistresses, none of them influenced his judgment or policies. The same could be said about his four wives, Maria of Portugal, Mary of England, Elizabeth of France, and his niece, Anne of Austria, all of whom he married for political reasons. They bore his children, but did not eat at his table, except at official banquets. Elizabeth was his favorite and Philip doted on her daughters, to whom he wrote notes of tender and loving concern; but such revelations of his inner feelings were very rare.

The standard historical portrait of Philip, depicting him as a single-minded idealogue and lackey of the pope, is largely false. By using the Inquisition to destroy Islamic and Protestant heresies, Philip sought to enforce Spanish traditions, arouse patriotism, increase his popularity, and strengthen the state. But he was no tool of the papacy; indeed, like his father, he defied more than one pope, carefully weighing the costs of papal military proposals against the benefits and using the church for his own political purposes. He denied the pope jurisdiction over Spanish church courts, ignored objectionable papal decrees, defied the Council of Trent on church appointments in Spanish territories, and fought the Jesuits when they challenged his authority. Although a dedicated Catholic, Philip saw the church as an arm of his government, expecting its cooperation in return for his support.

Throughout his long reign, Philip tried with only moderate success to be an absolute monarch. His councilors, appointed as advisors more than as administrators, submitted most decisions for his resolution. In the *Escorial*, the cold and somber palace which he had built north of Madrid, he labored endlessly, reading and annotating their documents. His concerns were directed mainly towards Castile, where Philip furthered the process of developing absolutism, issuing royal edicts as law and using the *Cortes*, the traditional assembly of estates, as a device for measuring public opinion rather than as a legislative body. But such pretensions of centralized government were without much meaning in other parts of Spain. There, as well as in the Netherlands and Italy, proud noble families dominated the assemblies, jealously guarding their privileges and often opposing royal viceroys. They were aided by the weight of tradition, by poor communications, and—in the eastern

The lives of Europe's monarchs were interwoven through ties of marriage and kinship; these bonds were utilized to further the monarchs' nationalistic aims. While Philip II of Spain was married to Mary Tudor of England, it seemed that England might come under Spanish domination.

The Venetian Ambassador's Portrait of Philip II

This sketch of Philip II was written in a dispatch by Ambassador Paolo Tiepolo in 1563. Notice the king's characteristic physical weakness, hypochondria, languidness, religiosity, and penchant for privacy, even from his queen.

The king was born of the Empress Isabella, daughter of the king of Portugal, on May 21, 1527. He is slight of stature and round-faced, with very pale blue eyes, somewhat prominent lips, and pink skin, but his overall appearance is very attractive. His temperament is very phlegmatic and his condition weak and delicate; he often takes to his bed, sometimes with chest pains and shortness of breath and sometimes, others say, with more serious illnesses. I have heard doctors say that it is unlikely he will live for long. Like other Spaniards he sleeps a great deal; not only does he take a long siesta after dinner, but he does not get out of bed in the morning in any season of the year until two and a half hours before noon. As soon as he rises he hears mass, and then he has little time for anything else before dinner. Sometimes he dines with his court and sometimes privately—in fact, usually alone, since he rarely eats with his wife, child, and sister, and others are not considered worthy to be at his table. . . .

He appears to be extremely religious, since he goes to church very often and takes communion four times a year. When he assigns bishoprics and benefices what concerns him most about the candidates is their Christian learning and morality. He accepted the Council against the wishes and advice of the Spanish bishops, who enjoyed a very comfortable position and had no desire to endanger it. He maintains nearly perpetual hostilities with the infidels, persecutes heretics more than any other ruler, and claims to be the readiest and loyalest defender of the pope and the apostolic see. In everything he does he seeks to appear as a true Catholic king, guided by his conscience. But what religious zeal inspires always seems to coincide with his own purposes. . . .

From this anyone can see that his natural inclination is to avoid difficulties; he showed this trait during the fighting in the Netherlands when he got angry and frustrated over the way things were going. Anyone who ponders this king's way of life—how he enjoys staying in Spain and how unwillingly he wrestles with problems—is sure to conclude that when he can the king will stay at peace with everyone and keep far from the noise of battle. If he does start a fight with anyone, it will be with the infidels [Turks], because he could attack them without having to go in person; his soldiers would run all the dangers. . . .

The queen is little more than seventeen years old, and she has a lively personality but is not very pretty. So far she has shown no symptoms of pregnancy, but the truth is that she is still very young. The indications of maturity as a woman only appeared about ten months ago, as her own doctor told me. In public the king treats her as if he loves and respects her very much, but actually he does little to make her happy. He frequently stays away from her for long periods, and when he is at court he purposely visits her late at night; if he finds her sleeping he goes away, as if he does not want to awaken her, satisfied with having made this gesture. So the queen, in order not to miss having his company, many times has stayed up most of the night. She knows that the king has many affairs with other ladies, but she has learned from her mother to put up with this, and she patiently endures it without a murmur of complaint.

Source: James C. Davis, ed., *Pursuit of Power: Venetian Ambassadors' Reports on Spain, Turkey, and France in the Age of Philip II, 1560–1600* (New York: Harper & Row, 1970), pp. 81–84.

Spanish kingdoms of Aragon and Catalonia—by revenue potentials below the cost of subjecting them.

The backward Spanish sociopolitical system caused Philip many economic problems. Tax-exempt nobilities, comprising under 2 percent of the people, owned 95 percent of the land; the middle classes, overtaxed and depleted by purges of Jews and *Moriscos* (Spanish Muslims), were almost eliminated; and the peasants were so exploited that agricultural production, particularly grains, was insufficient to feed the population. The use of arable lands for the nobles' sheep runs worsened the situation. State regulation of industry and trade further limited revenues and forced primary reliance on specie from America, which ultimately brought ruinous inflation. When his income failed to meet expenses, Philip borrowed at rising interest rates. In 1557 and 1575, he had to suspend payments, effectively declaring national bankruptcy.

The Revolt of the Netherlands

Philip's Catholic absolutism encouraged some unity in Spain; in the Netherlands, which he also controlled, his policies promoted disaster. The seventeen provinces, each with its own feudal tradition, were originally suspicious of their Spanish king. When Philip confirmed their fears by attempting to enforce Catholic conformity, he generated resistance which soon grew into open rebellion.

This outcome could have been expected. The Netherlands then included much of modern Holland, Belgium, Luxembourg, and a few petty fiefs, located along 200 miles of marshy coast between France and Germany, an area not open to easy conquest. The geography promoted stron⌐ local nobilities but also relatively independent peasants and townsfolk. Even in medieval times, cities were centers of rapidly expanding commerce; of the 300 walled towns in 1560, nineteen had populations over 10,000 (England had only three or four); and Antwerp was the leading commercial and banking center of northern Europe. This combination of localism, feudalism, and commerce found a truly appropriate religious expression in the Reformation, first with Anabaptism and then with Calvinism after the 1550s.

Philip first appointed his illegitimate half-sister, Margaret of Parma, as regent of the Netherlands. An able administrator and like her father, a native of the region, this thick-set, hard-riding matron was at first popular because she understood her subjects. Philip wasted this asset by ordering her to combat heresy with the Inquisition, a policy which drove the leading nobles from her council and brought increasingly threatening popular protests. For years, Philip ignored Margaret's frantic appeals for leniency before permitting her to dismiss the hated Cardinal Granville from her government. Margaret also authorized Protestant preaching. Despite these belated concessions, Calvinist mobs began desecrating churches and terrorizing Catholics.

To meet this challenge, Philip dispatched the Duke of Alva, with 10,000 Spanish troops, a great baggage train, and 2000 prostitutes, to the Netherlands. Alva relieved Margaret of her regency and clamped a brutal military dictatorship on the country. By decree, he centralized church administration, imposed new taxes, and established a special tribunal—soon dubbed "The Council of Blood"—to stamp out treason and heresy. During Alva's regime, between 1567 and 1573, at least 8,000 people were killed, including the powerful Counts of Egmont and Horne. Women and children were often victims. In 1568, one woman was executed because she had refused to eat pork; an eighty-four-old woman whose son-in-law had given hospitality to a heretic, was condemned at Utrecht. In addition to such atrocities, the Catholic terror deprived 30,000 people of their property and forced 100,000 to flee the country.

By 1568, Alva's excesses had provoked open rebellion, led by William of Orange (1533–1584), nicknamed the silent. Born of Lutheran parents, William had been raised a Catholic at the court of Charles V, where he became a favorite, known for his practical statecraft. Alienated by Spanish violation of traditional rights, he reluctantly became a rebel. His gradual ideological transformation is illustrated by his four marriages. The first two, before 1561, were for status and convenience; the last two, after 1577, were to Charlotte de Bourbon and Louise de Coligny, both sincere French Huguenots, who served him as committed partners in a religious cause.

Until 1579, William persevered. Constant early defeats left him impoverished and nearly disgraced, but in 1572, the port of Brill fell to his notorious privateers, "the sea beggars," an event which triggered revolts throughout the north. Soon after, William cut the dikes, mired down a weary Spanish army, and forced Alva's recall to Spain. The continuing war was marked by savage ferocity, such as the sack of Antwerp by mutinous Spanish soldiers (1576). At the Spanish siege of Maestricht (1579), women fought beside their men on the walls, and soldiers massacred the population, raping the women before tearing some limb from limb in the streets. That same year, in the Pacification of Ghent, Catholics and Protestants from the seventeen provinces united to defy Philip, demand the recall of his army, and proclaim the authority of their traditional assembly, the States General.

Unfortunately for the rebel cause, this unity was soon destroyed by religious differences between militant northern Calvinists and Catholic southerners, particularly the many powerful nobles. The Spanish commander, Alexander Farnese, exploited these differences by restoring lands and privileges to the southern nobles. He was then able to win victories which induced the ten southern provinces to make peace with Spain in 1579. The Dutch, now alone, proclaimed their continued resistance to Spanish persecution and in 1581 declared their independence of Spain. They persisted after William was assissinated in 1584, while the Spanish continued their war on heresy, hanging, butchering, burning, and burying alive Protestants who would not renounce their faith. This cruelty lasted until a truce was negotiated in 1609.

Religious Wars in France

Although frustrated in the Netherlands, Philip did not face his father's French problem. By the Treaty of Cateau-Cambrésis in 1559, France gave up claims in Italy and the Netherlands. This humiliating surrender to the Habsburgs marked a definite hiatus in French history. Over the next four decades, France gradually lost its leverage in foreign affairs as the country was torn by internal dissension.

By the 1560s Calvinism had become a major source of that contention. Although outlawed and persecuted earlier, the movement appealed to the urban middle classes, particularly to women, who were among its most active promoters. It also attracted nobles through the influential friends of Jeanne d'Albret, the Calvinist Queen of Navarre and wife of Antoine de Bourbon, a Prince of the blood. In 1559, the Huguenots held a secret synod in Paris which drew representatives from seventy-two congregations and a million members. Although still a minority, the Calvinists were well organized, with articulate leaders and the promise of military support from an increasing number of converts from among the nobility.

The growing interest among nobles was largely political. When Henry II died in 1559, the throne passed to his sickly fifteen-year-old son, Francis II. Francis' queen was Mary Stuart (later Mary, Queen of Scots), whose uncles, the brothers Guise, assumed control of the government. The Guises championed the Catholic cause and were opposed, although not always openly, by the Bourbons, who were turning Protestant, and by the Montmorency family, some of whose members were Protestants.

Francis died in 1560 and was succeeded by his nine-year-old brother, Charles IX. The real power behind the throne, however, was his mother, Catherine de Médicis, the neglected wife of Henry II. She was a most able woman, single-minded, crafty, ready to take any advantage but also open to compromise, and determined to save the throne for one of her three sons, none of whom had produced a male heir. Exploiting the split between the Guises and their enemies, she assumed the regency for Charles. She then attempted, through reforms of the church, to reconcile the differences between Catholics and Protestants. In this endeavor she was unsuccessful, but she retained a tenuous control by using every political strategy, including a squadron of highborn ladies who solicited information by seducing powerful nobles.

Religious wars erupted in 1561, lasting through eight uneasy truces until 1593. Religious fanaticism evoked the most violent and inhumane acts on both sides. Assassinations, raids, and atrocities became commonplace. Catherine maneuvered through war and uneasy peace, first favoring the Guises and then the Bourbons. In 1572, when she feared the Huguenots were gaining supremacy over Charles, she joined a Guise plot which resulted in the murder of some 10,000 Huguenots in Paris. This "massacre of Saint Bartholomew's Eve" was a turning point in decisively dividing the country. The final "war of the three Henries" in the 1580s involved Catherine's third son, Henry III, who became king on the death of Charles IX in 1574, Henry of Guise, and the Protestant Henry of Navarre. When the first two were assassinated, Henry of Navarre proclaimed himself king of France in 1589.

Elizabethan England

England, like France in the late sixteenth century, was threatened with civil war and governed by a woman who sought stability in compromise. But unlike Catherine de Médicis, Elizabeth I of England had learned earlier to separate personal attachments from Tudor politics, where she almost lost her head as well as her chance for the crown. England became her family and her primary interest. She was skilled at judging people, projected charisma in public speeches, and dealt with foreign diplomats in their own languages. These talents were especially valuable at her succession in 1558, when the country's religious divisions invited foreign invasion.

The immediate danger was Scotland, where Mary of Guise, a stalwart proponent of Catholicism, was regent for her daughter, Mary Stuart, queen of both France and Scotland. French troops in Scotland supported this Catholic regime. Because Mary Stuart was also a direct descendent of Henry VII of England, she was a leading claimant for the English throne and a potential rallying symbol for Catholic interests, who hoped to reestablish their religion in England. These expectations were diminished in 1559 when a zealous Calvinist named John Knox (1505–1572), fresh from Geneva, led a revolt of Scottish nobles. Aided by English naval forces, they broke religious ties with Rome, established a Presbyterian (Calvinist) state church, and drove the French soldiers out of Scotland. Temporarily, Elizabeth had averted disaster.

She furthered her escape from the sectarian strife which was destroying France by a compromise policy more effective than that of Catherine de Médicis. Moving firmly but slowly, Elizabeth recreated an Anglican Church similar to her father's. It confirmed the monarch as its head, recognized only baptism and communion as sacraments, rejected the veneration of relics, conducted services in English, and avoided other controversial Protestant tenets. It also retained the old organization, under bishops and archbishops, along with much of the Catholic ritual.

This policy avoided open rebellion but failed to end the opposition of both Protestants and Catholics to the state church. Nonconformists attacked the establishment in sermons and pamphlets; some, like the Presbyterian minister Thomas Cartwright, were jailed by church courts. Catholics faced more severe persecution and were therefore even more determined and daring. A network of Jesuit priests operated throughout the country, particularly in the north and west, secretly performing masses and working with a Catholic political underground. Women played prominent roles on both sides. The Duchess of Suffolk and Lady Russell were two of the Protestant women who steadily pressured the queen; others organized meetings and distributed literature. Catholic women were most effective allies of the Jesuits; one of them, Margaret Clitherow, died under torture in 1586 rather than deny her faith.

While dealing with this internal dissension, Elizabeth faced a serious danger from abroad. In 1568, Mary Stuart was forced into exile by her Protestant subjects and received in England by her royal cousin. Although kept a virtual prisoner, Mary became involved in a series of Catholic plots, which appeared even more dangerous after the pope excommunicated Elizabeth in 1570. Philip of Spain aided the plotters but still hoped to enlist Elizabeth's cooperation in helping him create a Catholic hegemony in Europe.

Religious Conflict in the International Arena, 1571–1609

By 1580, the European religious conflict had burst beyond national boundaries and entered the international arena. Philip of Spain was the prime mover in this process. In his efforts to maintain leadership in the Counter-Reformation and achieve a Spanish hegemony in Europe, he shifted from a policy of diplomacy to one of direct military action. In the process, he succeeded only in weakening his country and strengthening its enemies, the Dutch, the English, and the French.

The Futile Spanish Bid for Supremacy

A number of factors combined to encourage Philip in his bid for supremacy. His diplomatic efforts, particularly his marriage to Mary Tudor in 1558, his next marriage to Elizabeth of Valois in 1560, and his clumsy efforts to court Elizabeth I of England had brought no lasting influence over English or French policies. Indeed, English captains were preying on Spanish shipping in the Atlantic and Dutch privateers, with English and Huguenot support, were interrupting the flow of vital supplies from northern Europe. Finally, after 1571, Spain was more free of the Turkish menace in the Mediterranean and therefore more able to move against Protestant enemies in northern Europe.

Philip's policies toward Turkey promoted his reputation as the champion of Catholicism, boosted Spanish morale, and revived the traditional national pride in defending the faith. When Cyprus, the last Christian stronghold in the eastern Mediterranean, fell to the Turks in 1570, Philp responded to the pope's pleas and formed a Holy League to destroy Turkish naval power. Spanish and Venetian warships, together with smaller squadrons from Genoa and the Papal States, made up a fleet of over two hundred vessels, which drew recruits from all over Europe. In 1571, the League's fleet and the Turkish navy clashed at Lepanto, off the western coast of Greece. The outcome was a decisive victory for Christian Europe; Ottoman sea power was never again to be a major threat to Christendom.

In 1580, after nine years of frustration in the Netherlands, Philip launched the first phase of his new offensive policy, enforcing his claim to the Portuguese throne by military force. As king of Portugal, he gained control of the Portuguese navy and Atlantic ports, where he began collecting an ocean-going fleet capable of operations against the Dutch and English in their home waters. International tensions increased in 1585, when Philip openly signed an alliance with the Guise faction and sent troops into France. Elizabeth, who had been engaging Philip in a game of duplicity, allowing him to think that she might turn Catholic and perhaps even marry him, was especially fearful of invasion from the Netherlands. To thwart such an invasion, she sent token military forces, in addition to the financial aid she was already providing, to the Dutch and French Protestants. By 1586, Philip's policies were about to precipitate a major war.

Philip's last hope for an easy solution to his problem was dashed in 1587. Pressed by the pope and the English Catholic exiles, he had tried for years to use Mary Stuart to overthrow Elizabeth, thereby regaining England for Catholicism and taking control of the country; but Mary's complicity in a plot against Elizabeth's life was discovered; and Elizabeth, reluctantly convinced that Mary alive was more dangerous than Philip frustrated, ordered Mary's execution. Mary's death confirmed Philip's earlier decision that England could only be conquered with powder and steel.

In pursuing this end, Philip planned a "great enterprise," an invasion of England, blessed by the pope. The Spanish strategy depended upon a massive fleet, known as the "Invincible Armada." It was ordered to meet a large Spanish army in the southern Netherlands and land this force on the English coast. But in 1588, when the Armada sailed for Flanders, Dutch ships blocked the main ports, preventing the convoying of troops to the Spanish galleons, which could not come into shallow waters. Philip's project was completely ruined when the smaller and more maneuverable English ships, commanded by Sir Francis Drake, defeated the Armada in the English Channel. A severe storm, the famed "Protestant wind," completed the debacle. After a long voyage around Scotland, the Armada limped back to Spain, having lost a third of its ships.

The Post-Armada Stalemate

Contrary to English expectations, defeat of the Armada brought no immediate shift of international power. While Spain built new ships and successfully defended its sea lanes, neither side gained dramatic victories. All the major combatants were exhausted, a factor which largely

An English view of the Spanish Armada shows the pope and the devil plotting the Spanish invasion of England. The engraving is dated 1620.

(1598–1621), who was also lazy, extravagant, and frivolous and whose henchmen increased an already prevalent graft and inefficiency.

Elizabeth experienced similar difficulties. Sea raids on Spanish shipping continued and returned some profits; yet all the grand projects failed, including a fiasco in 1596, when the English, commanded by the Earl of Essex, plundered Cadiz but missed the Spanish treasure fleet. Land campaigns in France and the Netherlands, plus a continuing rebellion in Ireland, depleted Elizabeth's carefully husbanded resources. When asked for grants, Parliament insisted on debating constitutional questions and hearing Puritan demands for reform of the Church. While the old queen grew crotchety, muttering about cutting off heads, the country needed peace. It didn't come until the year after her death in 1603.

The Dutch, meanwhile, were stumbling toward independence, fearing the advancing Spanish tide in the South and pleading for English or French Protestant aid, but stubbornly persevering. Their declaration of 1581, while displaying what could be interpreted later as democratic rhetoric, reflected more concern for aristocratic privilege and national survival. After failing to find a suitable French or English monarch, the Dutch created a republic in 1587 and held on to sign a truce with Spain in 1609. As time passed, their growing maritime trade and naval power guaranteed their security.

The post-Armada stalemate was most beneficial to war-torn France. With the death of the last Valois claimant in 1589, the Bourbon Protestant Henry of Navarre was proclaimed Henry IV, king of France. This provoked the Catholic Holy League to fanatic anti-royalist frenzy and caused Philip's military intervention in France to support his daughter's claim to the throne. But English aid and Henry's willingness to turn Catholic led to Philip's withdrawal and the Peace of Vervins in 1598. To pacify the Huguenot minority, Henry then issued the Edict of Nantes, which guaranteed the Huguenots some civil and religious rights while permitting them to continue holding more than a hundred fortified towns. Henry thus achieved peace, but the French economy was prostrated, and powerful Protestant armed forces within the country challenged royal authority.

explains the Bourbons' acquisition of the French crown and continued Dutch independence through the 1590s. Lingering war brought new opportunities for France and the Netherlands but only a strength-draining stalemate for England and Spain.

During the last decade of Philip's life, his developing failure foreshadowed the decline of his country. He encountered rebellion in Aragon, quarreled with Pope Clement VIII over recognizing the Bourbons, and sent two more naval expeditions against England, both of which were scattered by storms. In 1598, he handed over the southern Netherlands to his favorite daughter Isabel and her husband, Archduke Albert, an Austrian Habsburg. Then, before he died in 1598, Philip had to make peace with France. He left Spain bankrupt for the third time during his reign, having wasted the country's considerable resources and sacrificed its future to his dynastic pride. The same poor judgment was even more pronounced in his successor, Philip III

The Thirty Years' War

Spain's golden age had ended, but the religious and political strife of dynasties continued with even greater intensity. Despite the weakening of Spain, other nations still feared a Habsburg resurgence and other dynasties sought to win more territories and power. Moreover, the increasing number of Calvinists and proponents of the counter-Reformation were still hoping for complete victory in the struggle over "true religion." These issues ultimately produced the Thirty Years' War, which began in 1618. At enormous cost in lives and wealth, this war finally completed the political transition from medievalism by burning out old religious obsessions and clearly revealing the secular rivalries of European states.

Background and Setting of the Conflict

During the sixteenth century, Europeans had looked out upon the world with pride in their vitality and superiority. Now in the early 1600s, they faced severe economic depression, along with intensified conflict in every sphere of human relations. It was a time of disruption and frustration, quite in contrast with earlier optimism. A deepening sense of crisis gripped the continent.

The first few decades of the seventeenth century brought a marked decline to the European economy, even before the advent of open warfare. Prices fell until about 1660, reversing the inflation of the 1500s. International trade declined, as did Spanish bullion imports from America. Heavy risks on a falling market caused failures among many foreign trading companies; only the larger houses, organized as joint stock companies, were able to survive. European industry and agriculture also fell on hard times; urban craftsmen saw their wages drop, and peasants faced increasing exploitation.

Tensions accompanying economic depression added to those arising from religious differences. Calvinism was becoming a more formidable force, having become official in Scotland and Holland and achieving an uneasy toleration in France. It was also spreading in eastern Europe and Germany. In England, soon after James of Scotland succeeded Elizabeth, both the Anglicans and the more radical sects feared the southward march of Scottish Presbyterianism. A similar tension prevailed in the Dutch Republic, where a militant movement for Calvinist uniformity strove to wipe out all other churches. But the most dangerous area was Germany, which had directly experienced an increasingly militant Counter-Reformation since the Peace of Augsburg.

Although absolute monarchy was already a recognized ideal and a dominant trend in the early seventeenth century, every royal house from England to Russia was somewhat insecure. The usual threat was posed by nobles defending their traditional privileges. In England and Holland, however, where commercial development was most advanced, nobles tended to support central authority against the urban commercial classes. Theoretical opposition to absolutism, based on a monarch's contractural responsibilities to his subjects, had gained some popularity everywhere during the early religious wars. It was particularly common among radical Protestants; but the same theme had even been expressed among extreme royalists, such as the French Guises who opposed Henry IV.

France best illustrates developing absolutism during the period. Henry IV and his hard-headed chief minister, the Duke of Sully (1560–1641), produced a balanced budget and a treasury surplus in little more than a decade. At the same time, Henry ended the nobility's control of hereditary offices and council seats. This royalist centralization was temporarily disrupted in 1610, when Henry was assassinated; but his queen Marie de Médicis (1573–1642), served as regent for her son Louis XIII until 1617. Like her distant relative Catherine, Marie had survived a tragic marriage to play a dominant role in French affairs. Her peace policy toward Spain and her successful defenses, both military and diplomatic, kept the Huguenots and the great nobles in check, thus securing the succession. Meanwhile, she negotiated a marriage between her son and the Habsburg princess Anne of Austria.

When he was fifteen, the new king seized power from his mother. For the next thirteen years, mother and son vied for power. Marie favored a pro-Spanish and Catholic policy; Louis, following the advice of his famous minister, Cardinal Richelieu (1585–1642) saw the Habsburgs and the papacy as the main threats to French interests. Richelieu finally prevailed, and Marie was banished in 1631, after which she continued to conspire with Spain and the French Catholic party. Inside France, Richelieu relentlessly worked to increase the king's power. He organized a royal civil service, restricted the traditional courts, brought local government under royal agents (*intendants*), outlawed dueling, prohibited fortified castles, stripped the Huguenots of their military defenses, and developed strong military and naval forces.

Absolutism elsewhere in Europe was moving in the same general direction but with less success. The Vasa dynasty of Sweden, supported by a strong national church and an efficient army, was building an empire involving Finland, the Baltic states, parts of Poland, and Denmark. In Germany, many of the princes, particularly the Hohenzollerns of Brandenberg, hoped to become independent absolute monarchs. As was true of earlier Habsburgs, the Holy Roman Emperor, Ferdinand II (1619–1637), struggled to concentrate his control over Austria, Hungary, and Bohemia, while extending his limited authority in Germany at the expense of the princes. Other rulers, including those in England, Spain, Russia, and Poland, faced determined local opposition as they sought to centralize power.

This political contention within states was accompanied by rising internationl apprehensions. Although the European power balance in 1618 resembled that of the 1500s, it was much less fixed. The Habsburgs still evoked counteralliances, but their vulnerability was now greater, not only because Spain was weakening but also because other states—France, the Netherlands, and Sweden—were growing more powerful. Under these circumstances, European revolt against Habsburg dominance was almost inevitable. A general awareness of the coming conflagration was perhaps the most important source of European insecurity.

The Thirty Years' War, fought between 1618 and 1648, was a culmination of all these related religious and political dissensions. Almost all of western Europe, except England, was involved and suffered accordingly. Wasted resources and

manpower, along with disease, further checked economic development and curtailed population expansion. Germany was particularly hard hit, suffering great population loss in many areas. Despite the terrible devastation, neither Protestantism nor Catholicism won decisive victory. What began as a religious war in the German principalities turned into a complex political struggle, involving the ambitions of north German rulers, the expansionist ambitions of Sweden, and the efforts of Catholic France to break the "Habsburg ring."

Reviving Habsburg Prospects, 1618–1630

Despite the general decline of Habsburg supremacy, the early years of the war before 1629, usually cited as the Bohemian and Danish phases, brought a last brief revival of Habsburg prospects. The new Habsburg emperor, Ferdinand II, who had been raised by his mother as a fanatic Catholic, was determined to intensify the Counter-Reformation, set aside the Peace of

Cardinal Richelieu. The power behind the throne of Louis XIII, Richelieu was chiefly responsible for the direction of the government, including France's involvement in the Thirty Years' War.

Augsburg, and wipe out Protestantism in central Europe. For a time, he almost succeeded.

Ferdinand's succession came amid severe political tension. Spreading Calvinism, plus the aggressive crusading of the Jesuits, had led to the formation of a Protestant league of German princes in 1608 and a Catholic counter-league the next year. The two had almost clashed in 1610 over a territorial dispute in northwest Germany. Meanwhile, the Bohemian Protestants had extracted a promise of toleration from their Catholic king, the Holy Roman Emperor, Rudolf II (1576–1612). In 1618, the Bohemian leader, fearing that Ferdinand would not honor the promise, threw two of his officials out of a window—an incident which became known as the "defenestration of Prague." When Ferdinand mobilized troops, the Bohemians deposed him and offered their throne to Frederick, the Protestant Elector of the Palatinate, in western Germany.

In the short Bohemian war which followed, Frederick was quickly overwhelmed. At the urging of his wife, Elizabeth, the daughter of James I of England, Frederick reluctantly accepted the Bohemian crown. But while he and Elizabeth held court in Prague, no practical military support came from England, the Netherlands, or the Protestant German princes. Ferdinand, in contrast, deployed two superb armies, one from Spain and the other from Catholic Bavaria. In 1620 Frederick's meager forces were scattered at the Battle of the White Mountain, near Prague. Afterward, the hapless Bohemian monarch and his queen fled the country, ultimately settling at the Hague, in the Netherlands, where they continued to pursue their lost cause. Ferdinand gave their lands to Maximillian of Bavaria, distributed the holdings of Bohemian Protestant nobles among Catholic aristocrats, and proceeded to stamp out Protestantism in Bohemia.

War began again in 1625 when Christian IV (1588–1648), the Lutheran king of Denmark, invaded Germany. As Duke of Holstein and thus a prince of the Empire, he hoped to revive Protestantism and win a kingdom in Germany for his youngest son. Christian was luckier than Frederick had been in attracting support. The Dutch reopened their naval war with Spain; England provided subsidies; and the remaining independent German Protestant princes, now thoroughly alarmed, rose up against the Catholics and the

Emperor. All of these renewed efforts were in vain. Ferdinand's new general, Albert von Wallenstein, defeated the Protestants in a series of brilliant campaigns. By 1629, Christian had to admit defeat and withdraw his forces, thus ending the Danish conflict with another Protestant debacle.

Their successful campaigns of the 1620s gave the Habsburgs almost complete domination in Germany. Using the army Wallenstein raised in Bohemia, Ferdinand reconquered the north. In 1629, he issued the Edict of Restitution, restoring to the Catholics all properties lost since 1552. This seemed to be only a first step toward eliminating Protestantism completely and creating a centralized Habsburg empire in Germany.

The End of Habsburg Supremacy, 1630–1648

Fearing the Counter-Reformation and the growing Habsburg power behind it, the threatened European states resumed the war again in 1630. As the conflict rapidly spread and intensified, religious issues were steadily subordinated to power politics. This was evidenced by the phases of the conflict, usually designated as the Swedish (1630–1635) and the French (1635–1648), because these two countries led successive anti-Habsburg coalitions. Utlimately, their efforts were successful. By 1648, the Dutch Republic had replaced Spain as the leading maritime state and Bourbon France had become the dominant European land power.

Protestant Swedes and French Catholics challenged Ferdinand's imperial ambitions for similar political reasons. Gustavus Adolphus, the Swedish king, wanted to save German Lutheranism, but he was also determined to prevent a strong Habsburg state on the Baltic from restricting his own expansion and interfering with Swedish trade. A similar desire to liberate France from Habsburg encirclement motivated Cardinal Richelieu. He offered Gustavus French subsidies, for which the Swedish monarch promised to invade Germany and permit Catholic worship in any lands he might conquer. Thus the Catholic cardinal and the Protestant king compromised their religious differences in the hope of achieving mutual political benefits.

Gustavus invaded Germany in 1630 while the Dutch attacked the Spanish Netherlands. With

Hardships in a German Town During the Thirty Years' War

This account of disaster and suffering by a refugee from Calw, who returned to find his "beloved town" in "ashes and rubble," illustrates the terrible havoc experienced by ordinary German people during the conflict.

During the pillage of Calw by Croat Imperial troops in September 1634] I never totally forsook my flock and only sought to escape from falling into the hands of the enemy. I joined a band of women and children soon amounting to more than 200 people. Like ants we scurried over hills and rocks. The beneficial influence of Heaven helped up continuously throughout this time. If we had bad weather we would have fared even worse than we did.

After it became known that the town [Calw in Württemberg] had been burnt down, we escaped to Aichelberg, a rough place. We had agreed among ourselves where each of us should hide but since our presence had been betrayed to the enemy, we were barely able to escape a quarter of an hour before we would have been totally ruined. At this the enemy became angry and vented his wrath upon the richest peasant in the place, who after hideous torture was burnt along with his house. . . .

Since the enemy was also active in these parts, . . . we decided to make an attempt to ask the victor for mercy. But to our further consternation we had to flee once again into the hills where no one could readily follow us. From there we wandered around, divided into smaller bands, and on the 15 September alone with my nephew John Joshua and son Gottlieb I hid in the deep Lauterback valley near the stream in a barn on the fields. We spent the night calmly and also the next one.

Since our lodging was moved to another barn where a certain Peter Schill, whom I must praise for his great honesty among the wood-folk, provided us with food and drink, our lack of caution led us back to Gernsbach where we scarcely avoided falling into the net of the enemy. As we lived scattered about all the secret places on Obertsrot, Hilpertsau, Reichtal, Weissenbach, Langenbrand and elsewhere, the hue and cry was raised after us and huntsmen were hired who knew the forests to track us down with their dogs. We saw them in the distance and became heartily dispirited, but also took a serious warning from the event.

I finally arrived at a peasant's place where the wife was nearing her childbirth, and I had a sleepless night since three hours before dawn I had climbed over the peaks of the hills, gone through hill and dale and eventually arrived back at my own vineyard where I had placed my little son Ehrenreich [aged ten], and in which farm we now spent our exile [*exilierte*]. I found my little son much weakened and unable to stand cold and hunger. The Lord took him and released his spirit into the freedom of Heaven on the 20 September. But shortly before this I had already left. We were called back in a letter from our friends, since everything, as far as the times allowed, was back in order, which accorded with the enemy's own best interest.

When I saw my beloved town of Calw in ashes and rubble—it was however not the first time that I had seen a town in ruins—I felt a cold shudder and I brooded repeatedly on that which I neither can nor wish to repeat now. What struck me most deeply was that long ago I had already prophesied the calamity, and that my prophecy had now come true in as much as it had also included me.

Source: Gerhard Benecke, ed., *Germany in the Thirty Years' War* (London: Edward Arnold, 1978), pp. 85–87.

his mobile cannon and his hymn-singing Swedish veterans, Gustavus and his German allies won a series of smashing victories, climaxed in November 1632 at Lutzen, near Leipzig, where Wallenstein was decisively defeated. Unfortunately for the Protestant cause, Gustavus died in battle. Meanwhile, a Dutch army in Flanders advanced toward Brussels, where Philip II's aging daughter, Isabella, was still governing. Aware of her subjects' desperate need for peace, Isabella began negotiations, but the news from Lutzen raised Habsburg hopes in Vienna and Madrid. Subsequently, Isabella was removed, a Spanish army was dispatched to Germany, and Wallenstein was mysteriously murdered. This Habsburg flurry brought no significant victories but led to the compromise Peace of Prague in 1635 between the emperor and the German Protestant states.

The situation now demanded that France act directly to further its dynastic interests. The final, French phase of the war began in 1635 when Richelieu and Louis XIII declared war on the Habsburgs, sending French troops into Germany and toward the Spanish borders. They also subsidized the Dutch and Swedes, while recruiting an army of German Protestant mercenaries. France continued limiting Protestantism within its borders but gladly allied with Protestant states against Catholic Spain, Austria, Bavaria, and their Catholic allies. The war which had begun in religious controversy had now become pure power politics, completing the long political transition from medieval to modern times.

For thirteen more years the conflict wore on. France's allies, the Swedes and north Germans, kept Habsburg armies engaged in Germany, while French armies and the Dutch navy concentrated on Spain. In 1643, the French won a decisive battle at Rocroi in the southern Netherlands. Next, they moved into Germany, defeating the imperial forces and, with the aid of the Swedes, ravaging Bavaria. When Richelieu died in 1642, he had already unleased forces which would make the Bourbon dynasty supreme in Europe.

For all practical purposes the war was over, but years of indecisive campaigning and tortuous negotiations delayed the peace. The French held to rigid demands, despite the deaths of both Richelieu and Louis XIII in 1642 and 1643.

Richelieu's protege, Cardinal Mazarin, directed diplomacy, although he was technically responsible to Queen Anne, ruling as regent for her son, the future Louis XIV. Anne consistently supported her minister through budget crises and popular unrest. The Swedes took a more conciliatory approach after Queen Christiana, the daughter of Gustavus Adolphus, succeeded to the throne in 1644. A horde of emissaries from nearly every capital in Europe met that year at Westphalia to negotiate the peace. Although Spain and France could reach no agreement, a settlement for the Empire was finally completed in 1648.

The Peace of Westphalia

The Peace of Westphalia is among the most significant pacts in modern European history. It ended Europe's emergence from medievalism and prepared a way for the modern state system. Even so, it did not establish universal peace; the war between France and Spain lasted another eleven years, ending finally with the Peace of the Pyrenees in 1659.

The peace agreement at Westphalia signaled a victory for Protestantism and the German princes while dooming Habsburg imperial ambitions. France moved closer to the Rhine by acquiring Alsatian territory, Sweden and Brandenburg acquired lands on the Baltic, and Holland and Switzerland gained recognition of their independence (see map, p. 463). The German states won undisputed rights to self-government and the conduct of their foreign relations. The emperor was required to receive approval from the Imperial diet for any laws, taxes, military levies, or foreign agreements—provisions which practically nullified imperial power. The religious autonomy of the German states, as decreed at Augsburg, was reconfirmed, with Calvinism now permitted along with Lutheranism. In addition, Protestant states were conceded all Catholic properties taken before 1624.

In its religious implications, the Peace of Westphalia ended the dream of reuniting Christendom. Catholics and Protestants now realized that major faiths could not be destroyed; moreover, Europeans had finally tired of religious controversy, tending to think it dangerous. From such intuitions a spirit of toleration gradually

EUROPE AFTER THE PEACE OF WESTPHALIA, 1648

Spanish Habsburgs
Austrian Habsburgs
—— Boundary of the Holy Roman Empire

emerged. Although religious uniformity would be imposed within states for another century, it would not again be a serious issue in European foreign affairs.

The Peace confirmed the new European state system. Henceforth, states would customarily shape their policies in accord with the power of their neighbors, seeking to expand at the expense of the weaker and to protect themselves—not by religion, law, or morality—but by alliances against their stronger adversaries. The treaty also instituted the internationl conference as a means for negotiating power relationships among contending states.

Aside from its general implications, the peace left specific political legacies for Europe. Both Spain and Austria were weakened, and the Austrian Habsburgs shifted their primary attention from Germany to southeastern Europe. German disunity was perpetuated by the autonomy of many petty states. France, in contrast, emerged as the potential master of the continent and the model of successful absolute monarchy. The war also helped both Holland and England, although

This commemorative painting, *Signing of the Peace of Münster, May 15, 1648,* by the Dutch artist Gerard Ter Borch shows the scene in the Rathaus of Münster when the delegates swore the oath of ratification to the treaty, one of the agreements of the Peace of Westphalia ending the Thirty Years' War.

this was not evident for England in 1648 at the climax of its revolution (see pp. 466–467).

Perhaps the most significant legacy of Westphalia was a universal yearning for order and stability. The war disrupted trade, destroyed industries, undermined monetary systems, and caused the deaths of more than five million people. It perpetuated an economic depresssion in central Europe so severe that killing famines became commonplace. Armies on both sides lived from the land. Brutalized and half-starved mercenary soldiers looted, burned, tortured, and raped. Even in unoccupied areas, general disorder and crime prevailed among rural and urban populations, both of which declined drastically. In some places, law enforcement was virtually abandoned. For all who experienced these conditions directly, and for thousands of others who only heard the terrible rumors, restoration of order seemed a goal surpassing all others.

Emergence of Constitutional Governments

A notable development during the war was the emergence of constitutional governments in the Netherlands and England. The prolonged conflict affected the two countries in different ways. Holland prospered from developing trade and colonies, made possible by the weakening of Spain. Because other states were tied down in continental wars, England was free to experiment with its political structure. In both countries, rapidly developing commerce and rising middle classes encouraged a direct transition from feudalism to constitutional government, without a prolonged intermediate stage of absolute monarchy.

The Dutch Republic

The Thirty Years' War brought official independence to the Dutch Republic but its actual independence had long since been an established fact. Defeat of the Spanish Armada had bought the Dutch time in which to accumulate resources, create an efficient army, and drive out the Spaniards. After Spanish troops had sacked and then effectively blockaded Antwerp, most industry and banking moved north to Amsterdam, which became the leading port and financial center for northern Europe. The Dutch meanwhile developed a peculiar federal government, combining urban and feudal councils to limit executive power. The system was identified, in the Dutch independence declaration of 1581, with

The arts of Mughul India reflect the splendor and luxury of the great seventeenth-century empire. In the miniature painting *Jahangir's Dream* (c. 1618), left, the mighty emperor Jahangir embraces the frail Shah Abbas of Persia. In 1632 Jahangir's son, Shah Jahan, commissioned the building of the resplendent Taj Mahal, below, as a memorial to his late wife.

The outstanding artwork of Ming China is its porcelains, such as the mei p'ing vase, left. The vase is of the fa-hua type in which ridges of clay outline the design, then are filled with pale yellow and blue, in imitation of cloisonné enamel. The elegant simplicity of the late Ashikaga period in Japan is seen in the *Excursion to Takao*, below, of Kano Hideyori (d. 1557), which dates from the mid-sixteenth century.

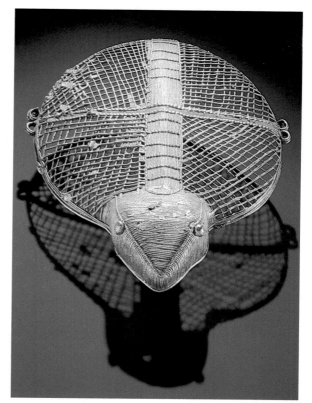

Government officials of the Ashanti kingdom of Africa wore gold badges like the turtle, right, or the double lizard, below, to identify their rank and role in the state system. The Ashanti state, a powerful kingdom of the eighteenth and nineteenth centuries, extended into the Gold Coast and present-day Ghana, Togo, and the Ivory Coast.

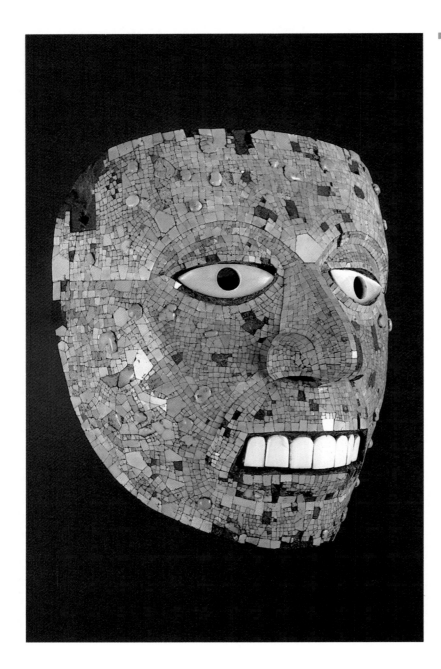

To the Aztecs, turquoise symbolized the preciousness of life, and turquoise mosaic was used to make ritual objects, such as masks, for statues of the gods. The turquoise mosaic on the mask, left, is placed on a backing of cedar wood, and the teeth and eyes are inlaid of white shell.

the abstract ideal of popular sovereignty, but this aristocratic polity of burghers and nobles only baguely resembled modern democracy. The Dutch system was, however, the first successful major challenge to absolute monarchy in western Europe, and it did provide a traditional base for many later democratic institutions.

Perhaps the most striking feature of the Dutch system was its internal pluralism. The Republic was literally a union of sovereign states, each empowered to veto any act of the States General (federal assembly). Theoretically, the *stadtholder*, as official chief of state, was merely a military commander, dependent upon the assembly for men and supplies. The provinces made public decisions in their own assemblies, which represented the nobles and the cities in varying proportions. Within the cities, policies were made by councils, whose members sat by inherited rights and usually represented the wealthy merchant-bankers. Local government, however, was a practical partnership between rich burghers and less affluent craftsmen. The latter held minor administrative posts and maintained peace through their service in the militias.

Concentration of power in any one office or individual was limited by this interaction of classes. Their differences were accented by their separate interests and by their indirect exercise of power, outside of government and often outside of the law itself. Wealthy urban merchants dominated the town councils, but their power was balanced against that of the nobles in the provincial assemblies. The merchants were also checked by differences within their own class and by dependence upon the urban militias. All three classes needed each other to maintain industry and commerce, upon which their prosperity depended. Because no one of the three major blocs could achieve absolute control, all regulations were lax, and individuals enjoyed more freedom than citizens anywhere else in Europe.

The internal Dutch power balance shifted during the early seventeenth century. Republicans, representing the great urban merchants, favored religious toleration, limited central authority, and peace. The monarchists, representing a majority of the urban lower classes, the nobles, and the House of Orange, wanted a Calvinist state church, a strong stadtholder, a large army, and an aggressive foreign policy against the Habsburgs. Until 1619, the republicans held power, but their leader, John Oldenbarnveldt (1547–1619), was ultimately overthrown and executed after a royalist uprising. Between 1619 and the Peace of Westphalia, the country was ruled by domineering stadtholders, who conducted the war against Spain and acquired a status similar to that of European kings.

At the end of the war the Dutch Republic enjoyed prosperity and power far beyond its natural potential. During the interval between the collapse of Spain and the maturation of England and France the Dutch Republic enjoyed naval, commerical, and colonial supremacy. The Dutch predominance, of course, could only be transitory. The country was so small and so divided that it could not afford open competition with France in Europe or with England overseas. But even as a secondary power, which it was destined to become after 1650, it remained economically progressive, culturally advanced, and a pioneer in developing constitutional government.

The English Constitutional Crisis

While the Dutch prospered and mainland Europe experienced near-anarchy in the Thirty Years' War, England faced its most dangerous internal crisis. Peace with Spain in 1604 left a debt of £100,000 and the end of privateering, which had netted handsome profits for many London financiers. The English, like the Dutch earlier, also resented a foreign king, his "popish" religion, and his taxes. Despite these similarities, the English struggle against absolutism brought different results. Because it came later and was better protected, it was more extreme, more secular, and more precise than the Dutch had been. Consequently, the English experience became the main historical precedent for western constitutional government.

Contention began shortly after James I (1603–1625) succeeded to the English throne. He was the son of Mary Stuart, a cousin of Elizabeth, and king of Scotland, where he had reigned as James VI since 1567. Understandably, he was a committed proponent of absolute monarchy, having written a book expounding his views on the subject.

James faced an English Parliament that had recently become aggressive in its demands for church reform, lower taxes, and security for its members. Most elected members were from the landed gentry, who also controlled local government. They naturally opposed a foreign king and the courtiers who served him. Therefore, a wide gap soon opened between the "country party" and those inside the royal circle.

The resulting political struggle was fought mainly in Parliament. James dismissed his first Parliament in 1611. The second sat for only two months in 1614. James then ruled by decree, without Parliament, until 1621, when he quickly ended another session by personally attending the House of Commons and angrily rejecting its proposals against his policies.

James' son, Charles I (1625–1649), fared even worse. After enduring many stormy debates with Parliament, he accepted the famous "Petition of Right" in 1628. Theoretically, this document affirmed ancient English rights by securing parliamentary approval of taxes, abolishing arbitrary imprisonment, ending the quartering of soldiers on citizens, and prohibiting martial law in peacetime. But Charles' cooperation was only temporary. From 1629 to 1640, he ruled without Parliament, alienating much of English society, particularly the Puritan church reformers and the gentry. When the Scots rebelled against his religious policies and invaded England in 1640, he was forced to conclude a humiliating peace and pay the invaders to withdraw.

In this age of religious strife, the early Stuart kings consistently provoked resentment from Protestant subjects. Although he was not a Catholic, James made peace with Spain, abandoned his Protestant son-in-law during the Thirty Years' War, and married Charles to a French princess, Henrietta Marie, who brought her Catholic confessor to England. Both James and Charles regarded Calvinism, with its independent clergy and elected synods, as threatening to monarchy. James resolutely fought reform of the Anglican Church, threatening to expel Calvinists from the country. Charles went further. Archbishop Laud, his Anglican advisor, forced absolute conformity; he whipped, mutilated, and jailed Protestant dissidents. As a result, thousands of religious refugees left the country. The Scottish invasion, which led directly to civil war, was a Calvinist reaction to Charles' religious policies.

The English crisis was nevertheless as much political as religious. The nation's governing class was divided; the economy was depressed; government expenses were rising; and the common people were suffering hard times. The struggle pitted the King's supporters, who advocated the king's divine right to rule, levy taxes, and control the economy, against the opposition who represented property owners and who wanted to govern in partnership with the king, control expenditures, and be free from government regulation of business affairs, particularly from royal monopolies. But the freedom that they advocated usually meant protection of a minority's profits. These aspirations reflected the country's commercial potential and the increasing self-awareness of the urban middle classes.

The English Civil War and Interregnum

After Charles agreed to buy off the Scots in 1640, he called Parliament to raise the money and secure his future finances. Known later as the "Long Parliament," because it sat through twenty years of constitutional debate and civil war, this Parliament immediately began limiting the king's powers. Led by the dauntless Puritan, John Pym, Parliament imprisoned Laud, executed Charles' hated chief minister, the Earl of Strafford, provided for its own regular meetings, abolished the royal courts of Star Chamber and High Commission, and eliminated taxes levied without parliamentary consent. The struggle with Charles would last another nine years; the monarchy would be replaced by a republic for a decade; and then the monarch would be restored, but absolutism was gone forever.

Increasingly intense contention between Charles and Parliament polarized public opinion and led to civil war, beginning in 1642. Charles left London in January of that year, raising his standard at Nottingham in August. London expected attack, but fighting began at South Molton, in Devonshire, where a mob of men and women, armed with rocks, clubs, and muskets, resisted royalist troops in the town square. During the ensuing civil war the royalists, or "cavaliers," were largely countrymen, led by noblemen, such as the dashing Prince Rupert, Charles' nephew and son of Elizabeth, the dethroned queen of Bohemia. The parliamentary forces included many townsmen, although some commanders, like the incompetent Earl of Essex, were aristocrats. English women were active on both sides, petitioning Parliament, handling business affairs while their men were fighting, and sometimes, as in the cases of the royalist Countess of Derby or the Parliamentarian Lady Harley, supervising defense of their homes against enemy soldiers.

At first, the royalist forces were successful, until the rebels turned to extreme measures. They made alliance with the Scots, reorganized their armies, enlisted popular support, and raised their morale by appeals to radical Protestantism. In 1646, they defeated Charles and took him prisoner. He escaped and renewed the war as dissension arose between the conservative Parliament and its more radical army. When Charles was defeated a second time, the army officers defied parliament and their own soldiers who wanted a democratic government. Led by the Puritan general, Oliver Cromwell (1599–1658), they executed the king in 1649 and proclaimed a republic.

Although their efforts were largely premature, some English rebels in this period first conceived of democracy. Their most striking pronouncements came from a group led by "honest John Lilburne" and known as "Levellers," because they advocated reforms to favor the common people. Many were active among the soldiers in Cromwell's army. Between 1646 and 1649, Levellers and the near-mutinous troops produced a series of documents, each known as an "Agreement of the People." These first written democratic constitutions proposed that the English government be organized as a republic, with a one-house legislature elected by universal manhood suffrage. They did not propose that women vote, but women were active in the movement, writing, speaking, and organizing. The program did, however, list civil and religious liberties, to be held as rights by all citizens. Thus the Levellers and their "Agreements" anticipated modern democratic theory.

The Leveller movement was suppressed when the officers regained control of the army and established a military regime. Their government, known as "the Commonwealth," was a republic dominated by property holders. It was never popular enough to be maintained without military force. After Cromwell's death in 1658, the system gave way almost immediately to a restored Stuart monarchy.

Despite these failures, the period of the civil war and the interregnum brought significant changes to England. Constitutionally, it confirmed Parliament's necessary role in the English system, thereby decisively checking the trend toward absolutism. At the same time, the royalist defeat opened opportunities for capitalisic development and imperial expansion under Cromwell. England effectively challenged the naval and maritime supremacy of the Dutch in the 1650s, while beginning to develop into the world's leading empire.

Cultural Expressions of the Age

European cultural expression during the century before 1650 reflected a strange ambiguity, combining reflections of the insecurity, violence, and general pessimism of the era with a great creative energy. For a time, artists and writers abandoned the confidence and enthusiasm of the Renaissance, seeking new forms of escape or becoming preoccupied with bizarre distortions of reality. Later, in the early seventeenth century, artistic works lacked balance and discipline but displayed a fresh vitality in symbolizing the power of religious upheaval and developing national states.

The Post-Renaissance Transition

Cultural ambiguity was most evident in the latter part of the sixteenth century. By then the Renaissance spirit was beginning to be transformed in Italy but was reaching a climax elsewhere in Europe (see pp. 327–328). The Counter-Reformation, stimulated by the Council of Trent, was also polarizing European thought and producing unique cultural developments. Sometimes, reviving religious sensitivities were accompanied by perplexing uncertainties. In other instances, lingering Renaissance values coexisted with Protestant Puritanism. Such incongruities were indications of a cultural transition, like those in political and social affairs, between medieval and early modern times.

John Lilburne, "The Agreement of the People"

John Lilburne, the nearly forgotten hero of the Puritan revolution, wrote this demand for popular sovereignty in 1647, when the common soldiers were near mutiny in the parliamentary army and before Cromwell and the army officers crushed the movement. This was the first among a number of such documents, which have been called the earliest appeals for democracy in the Western world.

Having by our late labors and hazards made it appear to the world at how high a rate we value our just freedom, . . . we do now hold ourselves bound in mutual duty to each other to take the best care we can for the future . . . so may we safely promise to ourselves that, when our common rights and liberties shall be cleared, their endeavors will be disappointed that seek to make themselves our masters. Since, therefore, our former oppressions and scarce-yet ended troubles have been occasioned, either by want of frequent national meetings in Council, or by rendering those meetings ineffectual, we are fully agreed and resolved to provide that hereafter our representatives be neither left to an uncertainty for the time nor made useless to the ends for which they are intended. In order whereunto we declare:

I. That, the people of England, being at this day very unequally distributed by Counties, Cities, and Boroughs for the election of their deputies in Parliament, ought to be more indifferently proportioned according to the number of the inhabitants. . . .

II. That, to prevent the many incoveniences apparently arising from the long continuance of the same persons in authority, this present Parliament be dissolved upon the last day of September which shall be in the year of our Lord 1648.

III. That the people do, of course, choose themselves a Parliament once in two years. . . .

IV. That the power of this, and all future Representatives of this Nation, is infereior only to theirs who choose them, and does extend, without the consent or concurrence of any other person or persons, to the enacting, altering, and repealing of laws, to the erecting abolishing of offices and courts, to the appointing, removing, and calling to account magistrates and officers of all degrees, to the making of war and peace, to the treating with foreign states, and, generally, to whatsoever is not expressly or impliedly reserved by the represented to the themselves:

Which are as follows:

1. That matters of religion and the ways of God's worship are not at all entrusted by us to any human power, because therein we cannot remit or exceed a tittle of what our consciences dictate to be the mind of God without wilful sin: nevertheless the public way of instructing the nation (so it be not compulsive) is referred to their discretion.
2. That the matter of impressing and constraining any of us to serve in the wars is against our freedom; and therefore we do not allow it in our Representatives. . . .
3. That after the dissolution of the present Parliament, no person be at any time questioned for anything said or done in reference to the late public differences. . . .
4. That in all laws made or to be made every person may be bound alike, and that no tenure, estate, charter, degree, birth, or place do confer any exemption from the ordinary course of legal proceedings whereunto others are subjected.
5. That as the laws ought to be equal, so they must be good, and not evidently destructive to the safety and well-being of the people.

These things we declare to be our native rights, and therefore are agreed and resolved to maintain them with our utmost possibilities against all opposition whatsoever.

Source: Lowell H. Zuck, ed., *Christianity and Revolution* (Philadelphia: Temple University Press, 1975), pp. 236–37.

In art and architecture, the post-Renaissance transition was reflected in a new style called mannerism (see p. 322). Perhaps the greatest of the "mannerists" was El Greco (1547–1614), who was born in Crete, studied in Italy, and settled in Spain. He is known for his imaginative but morbidly ascetic treatment of religious themes, using *chiaroscuro* (strong contrasts of light and shade). Andrea Palladio (1518–1580) exemplified the style in architecture with his Villa Rotunda, near Venice, which displays an exaggerated magnificence in its grouping of four identical temple facades on the sides of a square-domed building.

Like art and architecture, trends in music reflected the transition of the era, but in different ways. Both in Italy and in the northern Renaissance, music developed new complexities in keeping with a spirit of gaiety and respect for aesthetic beauty. This was evident in the increase of chordal writing, in great expansion of tonal ranges, and in the emergence of new secular forms, such as the chanson and the madrigal, which often had poetic lyrics. At the other extreme, church music also became very popular. Protestant hymn-writing and singing were given priorities by the reformers. Luther's "A Mighty Fortress is Our God" is only one example; many hymns were composed by women, who turned to this form of expression when they were prohibited from preaching. Catholic church music was also revolutionized after the Council of Trent ruled that it be simpler and more appealing. The new spirit, simple but emotionally powerful, was well expressed in the masses of Giovanni Palestrina (1525–1594), who has been called the "first Catholic Church musician."

The Baroque Era in the Arts

After 1600, European culture generated a new artisitic style, known as the Baroque. Taken literally, the term means "irregular" and is applied generally to the dynamic and undisciplined artistic creativity of the seventeenth century. At first, the Baroque style grew out of the Catholic pomp and confidence accompanying the Counter-Reformation. Later, as the style spread north, it became popular at royal courts, where it symbolized the emerging power of the new monarchies. Wherever it showed itself, the Baroque approach was likely to exhibit some combination of power, massiveness, or dramatic intensity, embellished with pageantry, color, and theatrical adventure. Without the restraints of the High Renaissance or the subjectiveness of Manneristic painting, the Baroque sought to overawe by its grandeur.

Baroque painting originated in Italy and spread north. One of its Italian creators was Michelangelo da Caravaggio (1565–1609), whose bold and light-bathed naturalism impressed many northern artists. The Italian influence was evident in the works of Peter Paul Rubens (1557–1640), a well-known Flemish artist who chose themes from pagan and Christian literature, illustrating them with human figures involved in dramatic physical action. Ruben also did portraits of Marie de Médicis and Queen Anne, at the French court of Louis XIII. Another famous Baroque court painter was Diego Velasquez (1599–1660), whose canvases depict the haughty formality and opulence of the Spanish royal household. A number of Italian women were successful Baroque painters, including Livonia Fontana (1552–1614), who produced pictures of monumental buildings, and Artemesia Gentileschi (1593–1652), a follower of Caravaggio.

While the Baroque style profoundly affected the rest of Europe, the Dutch perfected their own characteristic style, which grew directly from their pride in political and commerical accomplishments and emphasized the beauty of local nature and the solidity of middle class life. Dutch painting was sober, detailed, and warmly soft in the use of colors, particularly yellows and browns. Almost every town in Holland supported its own school of painters who helped perpetuate local traditions. Consequently a horde of competent artists arose to meet the demand for this republican art.

Only a few among hundreds can be cited here. The robust Frans Hals (1580–1666) employed a vigorous style that enabled him to catch the spontaneous and fleeting expression of his portrait subjects. He left posterity a gallery of types—from cavaliers to fishwives and tavern loungers. His most successful follower, whose works have often been confused with those of Hals, was Judith Leyster (1609–1660), a member of the Haarlem painter's guild with pupils of her own. Somewhat in contrast, Jan Vermeer (1632–1675) exhibited a subtle delicacy. His way of treating the fall of subdued sunlight upon interior scenes has never been equaled.

Towering above all the Dutch artists—and ranking with the outstanding painters of all time—was Rembrandt van Rijn (1606–1669). While reflecting the common characteristics of his school, he produced works so universally human that they not only expressed Dutch cultural values but also transcended them. His canvasses show tremendous sensitivity, depicting almost every human emotion except pure joy. This omission arose partially from his own troubled consciousness and partially from his republican, Calvinist environment. Nevertheless, his work furnished profound insights into the human enigma. He has been called the "Dutch Baroque version of da Vinci."

Baroque architecture, like painting, was centered in Italy, from whence it permeated western Europe. The most renowned architect of the school in the seventeenth century was Giovanni Bernini (1598–1660). He designed the colonnades outside St. Peter's Basilica, where his plan illustrates the Baroque style in the use of vast spaces and curving lines. Hundreds of churches and public buildings all over Europe displayed the elaborate Baroque decorativeness in colored marble, intricate designs, twisted columns, scattered cupolas, imposing facades, and unbalanced extensions or bulges. Stone and mortar were often blended with statuary and painting; indeed it was difficult to see where one art left off and the other began.

The seventeenth century also brought Baroque innovations in music. New forms of expression moved away from the exalted calmness of Palestrina and emphasized melody supported by harmony. Instrumental music—particularly for organ and violin—gained equal popularity, for the first time, with song. Outstanding among Baroque innovations was opera, which originated in Italy at the beginning of the century and quickly conquered Europe. The new form utilized many arts, integrating literature, drama, music and painting of the elaborate stage settings.

The literature of the Baroque age before 1650 showed a marked decline from the exalted heights of the northern Renaissance (see p. 327).

Even before 1600, however, Puritanism and the Counter-Reformation inclined many writers toward religious subjects. In England, this trend continued in the next century and was augmented by a flood of political tracts during the civil war. Religious concerns were typical of the two most prominent English poets, John Donne (1573–1631) and John Milton (1608–1674). Milton's magnificent poetic epic, *Paradise Lost* was planned in his youth but not completed until 1667. French literature during the early 1600s was much less memorable. The major advance came in heroic adventure novels, pioneered by Madeleine Scudery (1608–1701). Most other French writers, influenced by the newly formed French Academy, were increasingly active in salon discussions but more concerned with form than with substance.

Conclusion

The century after the Peace of Augsburg was an era of wrenching transition for Europe. At the opening of the period, most people were still imbued with the medieval concern for salvation, which gave meaning to the religious issues of both Reformations, Protestant and Catholic. Long and exhaustive religious wars burned out this obsession. As the wars continued, secular political concerns became increasingly evident, and at the end of the Thirty Years' War, in 1648, the Peace of Westphalia registered the existence of secular nation-states.

A major question raised by such states involved internal organization and sources of power. One answer, as provided by the Dutch and the English, called for representative political institutions, with power divided and balanced among a number of social groups or governmental offices. The idea of popular sovereignty, justified and maintained under law, developed from both feudal and religious precedents in this period. It caught on in Holland and England where developing commerce had already produced strong middle classes. These maritime states laid foundations for later constitutional governments.

Such precedents, however, exerted little influence in this era or in the half century that followed. A revolution in military tactics, the rise of professional militarism, and the disorders accompanying a century of warfare all contributed to the growth of centralized authority, as demonstrated in the emerging system of absolute monarchy. The trend was illustrated most obviously by the Bourbon dynasty in France. By the time of the Peace of Westphalia, the Bourbon monarchy had become a model for European absolutism, and the way was prepared for Louis XIV (1673–1715), who would soon be hailed as "the Grand Monarch."

A second innovation accompanying the emergence of secular sovereign states was the turn toward power politics in international relations. Although not entirely new, the practice had been obscured in Europe during the Middle Ages by the moral and religious claims of the Church. As the religious wars continued and religious diversities were intensified, rulers sought to realize national interests by looking to their own power, buttressed by alliances. Because each state tended to expand until checked by another, weaker states were forced to form alliances among themselves, no matter what their traditions or religions. The dominant state would thus be curtailed by a "balance of power." Wars to secure this balance ultimately elevated France above Habsburg Spain to dominance on the Continent. At the same time, Holland temporarily replaced Spain as the major maritime state.

The principle of unlimited sovereignty in conducting national affairs was questioned, even before 1648. In the 1620s, as the Thirty Years' War was beginning its terrible devastation, a few European thinkers called for European union to keep the peace. They included Emeric Cruce, an obscure French monk, the Duke of Sully, Louis XIII's chief minister and Hugo Grotius, the famous Dutch political authority. Their proposals were set aside but not forgotten. Since Westphalia, unlimited state sovereignty has generally prevailed, but much study has been devoted to averting international conflicts by subordinating international disputes to the rule of law.

Suggestions For Reading

Two excellent recent overall surveys of this period are Robert Bireley, *Religion and Politics in the Age of the Counter-Reformation* (Univ. of North Carolina, 1981) and

H. G. Koenigsberger, *Early Modern Europe, 1500–1789* (Longman, 1987). The classic treatment of the early seventeenth century, still worth reading, is Carl J. Friedrich, *The Age of the Baroque* (Torchbooks, 1961). For interesting special interpretations, see Trevor Henry Aston, ed., *Crisis in Europe, 1560–1660* (Torchbooks, 1974) and Perez Zagoren, *Rebels and Rulers, 1500–1660* (Cambridge Univ., 1982). Roland Bainton has produced two solid general works on the roles of women: *Women of the Reformation in France and England* (Augsburg Pub. House, 1973) and *Women of the Reformation: From Spain to Scandinavia* (Augsburg Pub. House, 1977). Helga Mobiusm *Women of the Baroque Age* (Abner Schram, 1984) provides good detail, particularly for women painters, but is less scholarly and more superficial in its generalizations.

Four sound studies of Spain during the period are John Lynch, *Spain Under the Habsburgs*, Vol. I, *Empire and Absolutism, 1516–1598* (New York Univ., 1984); Reginald Trevor-Davis, *The Golden Century of Spain, 1501–1621* (Greenwood Press, 1984); R. J. W. Evans, *The Making of the Habsburg Monarchy, 1550–1700* (Oxford Univ., 1984); and H. A. F. Kamen, *The Golden Age of Spain* (Humanities Press, Int., 1988). John H. Elliott, *Spain and Its World* (Yale Univ., 1989) is a collection of excellent previously published essays. A. W. Lovett, *Early Habsburg Spain* (Oxford Univ., 1986) is a readable teachers' manual but is weak on relevant developments in non-Spanish areas. The classic treatment of the Armada, appearing in a recent edition, is Garrett Mattingly, *The Armada* (Houghton Mifflin, 1988). Among a spate of books celebrating the four hundredth anniversary of the legendary battle, Peter Kemp, *The Campaign of the Spanish Armada* (Facts on File, 1988) is perhaps the most readable but, like the others, breaks no new ground. Felipe Fernóudez-Armesto, *The Spanish Armada* (Oxford Univ., 1988) presents the Spanish contention that defeat was caused by the elements rather than English naval guns. Peter Pierson, *Commander of the Armada* (Yale Univ., 1989) is a biography of the ill-fated Spanish admiral Median Sidonia. For a good analysis of Spanish decline after 1588, see Edward Grierson, *The Fatal Inheritance* (Doubleday, 1969).

The best-known account of the Dutch rebellion is Peter Geyl, *The Revolt of the Netherlands* (Barnes and Noble, 1958). Noel G. Parker, *The Dutch Revolt* (Cornell Univ., 1977) and John C. Cadoux, *Philip of Spain and the Netherlands* (Archon Books, 1969) are two excellent later studies, J. I. Israel, *The Dutch Republic and the Hispanic World, 1606–1661* (Oxford Univ., 1986) S. Schama, *The Embarrassment of Riches*, (Knopf, 1987); and C. R. Boxer, *The Dutch Sea-Borne Empire* (Penguin Books, 1989) depict the Republic's problems at the apex of its struggle for power and wealth. The social backgrounds are treated in S. Marshall, *The Dutch Gentry, 1500–1650* (Greenwood Press, 1987). See also K. H. Halley, *The Dutch in the Seventeenth Century* (Harcourt Brace Jovanovich, 1972); J. L. Price, *Culture and Society in the Dutch Republic During the Seventeenth Century* (Columbia Univ., 1974); and Charles H. Wilson, *The Dutch Republic* (McGraw-Hill, 1968). Cicely V. Wedgewood, *William the Silent* (Norton, 1968) is a superb biography.

French society and politics during the whole era are ably surveyed in Robert Briggs, *Early Modern France, 1560–1715* (Oxford Univ., 1977) and Natalie Davis, *Society and Culture in Early Modern France* (Stanford Univ., 1975). George D. Balsama, *The Politics of National Despair*

(Washington, 1978) describes the catastrophic religious wars. See also John E. Neale, *The Age of Catherine de Medici* (Harper Torchbooks, 1962). This tragic time is also reflected in Frederick J. Baumgartner's recent readable biography, *Henry II, King of France* (Duke Univ., 1988). Robert M. Kingdon, presents a Catholic view in *Myths About the Saint Bartholomew's Day Massacres 1572–1576* (Harvard Univ., 1988). For the early seventeenth century, see V. L. Tapie, *France in the Age of Louis XIII and Richelieu* (Cambridge Univ., 1984). The best biographies for this later period are A. Lloyd Moote, *Louis XIII* (Univ. of California, 1989); J. Bergin, *Richelieu* (Yale Univ., 1985); and Ruth Kleinman, *Ann of Austria* (Ohio State Univ., 1985). Elizabeth Warwick has produced two controversial but interesting studies in *Louis XIII, the Making of a King* (Yale Univ., 1986) and *The Young Richelieu* (Univ. of Chicago, 1983). The role of French Protestantism in both eras is clearly depicted in George A. Rothrock, *The Huguenots: a Biography of a Minority* (Nelson Hall, 1979).

A soundly researched coverage of economic, social, and political trends during the period in England by two New Zealanders is Michael A. R. Graves and Robin Silcock, *Revolution, Reaction, and the Triumph of Conservatism, 1558–1700* (Auckland, N. Z.: Longman Paul, 1984). Another outstanding survey of English social history is J. A. Sharpe, *Early Modern England: A Social History, 1550–1760* (E. Arnold, 1987). For the growing social and political awareness of English women in both the sixteenth and seventeenth centuries, see Katherine A. Henderson and Barbara McManus, *Half Humankind: Contexts and Texts of the Controversy About Women in England, 1540–1640* (Univ. of Illinois, 1985) and Mary Prior, ed., *Women in English Society, 1500–1800* (Methuen, 1985).

Excellent general interpretations of Elizabethan England are presented in Arthur Bryant, *The Elizabethan Deliverance* (St. Martin's, 1982) and David B. Quinn and A. N. Ryan, *England's Sea Empire, 1550–1642* (Allen and Unwin, 1983). A creditable but less creative work which supplies broad coverage of Elizabethan experience is S. White-Thomson, *Elizabeth I and Tudor England* (Bookwright Press, 1985). John E. Neale, *Queen Elizabeth I* (Cape, 1967) is still respected as an authoritative study, but a number of more recent biographies are worth consulting: Jasper G. Ridley, *Elizabeth: the Shrewdness of Virtue* (Viking, 1988); Allison Plowden, *Elizabeth Tudor and Mary Stuart* (Barnes and Noble, 1984); J. Mary Wormald, *Mary, Queen of Scots* (George Philip & Son, 1988); and Carolly Erickson, *The First Elizabeth* (Summit Books, 1983). For studies of Elizabethan politics and diplomacy, see Joel Hurstfield, *Elizabeth I and the Unity of England* (Torchbooks, 1967); Charles Wilson, *Queen Elizabeth and the Revolt of the Netherlands* (Univ. of Calif., 1970); and a pair of companion volumes by Richard B. Wernham. These are *Before the Armada: The Emergence of the English Nation, 1485–1588* (Norton, 1972) and *After the Armada: Elizabethan England and the Struggle for Western Europe*, revised ed. (Oxford Univ., 1984). Noteworthy special works on Elizabethan women include Pearl Hogrefe, *Women of Action in Tudor England* (Iowa State Univ., 1977); Retha M. Warnick, *Women of the English Renaissance and Reformation* (Greenwood Press, 1983); and Susan Cahn, *The Transformation of Women's Work in England, 1500–1600* (Col. Univ., 1987)

For the reigns of the first two Stuart monarchs and the civil war, see J. P. Kenyon, *Stuart England* (Penguin Books, 2nd. ed., 1986); Derek Hirst, *Authority and Conflict in England, 1603–1658* (Harvard Univ., 1986); David Underdown, *Revel, Riot, and Rebellion: Politics and Culture in England 1603–1660* (Oxford Univ., 1985); and Christopher Hill, *The Century of Revolution* (Norton, 1980). For political backgrounds of the civil war, see Perez Zagoren, *The Court and the Country* (Atheneum, 1970); Graham Perry, *The Golden Age Restored: the Culture of the Stuart Court* (St. Martin's, 1981); R. Malcolm Smuts, *Court Culture and the Origin of a Royalist Tradition in Early Stuart England* (Univ. of Pennsylvania, 1987); and Thomas Cogswell, *The Blessed Revolution: English Politics and the Coming of the War* (Cambridge Univ., 1989). Two recent relatively light biographies of Charles I are C. Carlton, *Charles I, the Personal Monarch* (Routledge & Kegan Paul, 1983) and Pauline Gregg, *King Charles I* (Univ. of California, 1984). For special studies on the civil war, see Christopher Hill, *The World Turned Upside Down* (Viking, 1972); G. E. Aylmer, *Rebellion or Revolution: England, 1640–1660* (Oxford Univ., 1986); and John P. Kenyon, *The Civil Wars of England* (Knopf, 1988). Among interesting studies of radicalism are Jerome Friedman, *Blasphemy, Immortality, and Anarchy: The Ranters and the English Revolution* (Ohio Univ., 1987); F. D. Dow, *Radicalism in the English Revolution* (Blackwell, 1985); Henry Noel Brailsford, *The Levellers and the English Revolution* (Stanford Univ., 1961); and Joseph Frank, *The Levellers* (Harvard Univ., 1955). For conditions facing women in Stuart England, see Alice Clark, *The Working Life of Women in the Seventeenth Century* (Routledge, Chapman, and Hall, 1982) and Margaret George, *Women in the First Capitalistic Society* (Univ. of Illinois, 1988).

Cicely V. Wedgewood, *The Thirty Years' War* (Anchor Books, 1961) is still reliable. Two other excellent treatments are Georges Pages, *The Thirty Years' War* (Torchbooks, 1970) and Josef V. Polisensky, *War and Society in Europe, 1618–1648* (Cambridge Univ., 1978). Michael Roberts, *Sweden's Age of Greatness* (St. Martin's, 1973) gives good coverage of both political background and military events of the conflict.

For the baroque artistic style in its historical setting, see Michael Kitson, *The Age of Baroque* (London: Paul Haslyn, 1966) and Victor L. Tapie, *The Age of Grandeur: Baroque Art and Architecture* (Praeger, 1961). Three excellent relevant biographies are Henry Bonnier, *Rembrandt* (G. Braziller, 1968); Christopher White, *Rembrandt and His World* (Viking, 1964); and Andrew M. Jaffe, *Rubens and Italy* (Cornell Univ., 1977).

Notes

1. Quoted in C. R. L. Fletcher, *Gustavus Adolphus and the Struggle of Protestantism in Europe* (New York: G. P. Putnam's Sons, 1923) p. 284.

L'Etat, C'Est Moi

European Absolutism and Power Politics

Louis XIV (1643–1715) of France is remembered best as a strong-willed monarch who reportedly once exclaimed to his fawning courtiers, "L'état, c'est moi" (I am the state). Whether or not he really said these words, Louis has been regarded by historians as the typical absolute monarch—a symbol of his era. Similarly, historians have often referred to this period, when kings dominated their states and waged frequent dynastic wars against one another as an age of absolutism.

Absolute monarchy, admittedly, was not exactly new in Europe. Since the late medieval period, rulers had been attempting to centralize their authority at the expense of feudal nobles and the church. In the sixteenth and early seventeenth centuries, however, religious strife blurred political issues and somewhat restricted developing monarchies. After the Peace of Westphalia, which ended the era of disastrous religious wars, absolutism rapidly gained popularity because it promised to restore order and security.

Parallel economic developments encouraged the maturing of absolutism. As the Spanish and Portuguese overseas empires declined, the Dutch, English, and French assumed commercial and colonial leadership, bringing the European economy to a second stage of expansion. The commercial revolution, centered in northern Europe, generated great wealth and brought increasingly complex capitalistic institutions, both of which furthered the process of state-building.

When the Peace of Westphalia ended the Thirty Years' War in 1648, it marked a significant turning point in European history. Peace, after such prolonged religious conflict and political chaos, renewed possibilities for centralizing royal authority within European states.

The Shift in Fundamental European Values

The era after Westphalia also saw a fundamental shift in European values. Although many Europeans—both Protestant and Catholic—were still concerned about personal salvation, they were now also apprehensive about prospects in this world. Like their Renaissance predecessors, they enjoyed sensual as well as aesthetic pleasures; but they put more emphasis on profits, power, and the need for security. With the memory of war and social upheaval still fresh, they were inclined toward a belief in order, which shaped their other values.

Secularism and Classicism

Although often subtle, the new secular outlook after 1650 was revealed in many ways. Despite their many expressed religious concerns, kings now routinely used religion for secular political ends. The prevailing secularism was also evident in the elegance, frivolity, intrigue, and sexual license that characterized royal courts and the private lives of the nobility. In educated circles, secularism was demonstrated in the growing popularity of science, with its avowed materialism and its implied refutation of scripture. But even unlearned common people shared a universal boredom with religious contention, along with the prevailing desire for stable social conditions.

This yearning for stability and order was clearly demonstrated in the arts. Earlier, during Europe's era of transitional turbulence, the baroque style had symbolized flamboyant power and restless frustration. Although the forms of baroque art and architecture remained popular, they were overshadowed in this era by a return to traditional classicism. Retaining the baroque deference to power, the revived classical mode emphasized order in its discipline, formality, and balance. Classicism owed much to the aristocratic world where it flourished. It reflected the growing scientific faith in an ordered universe, and it also expressed the political values of absolute monarchs, such as Louis XIV, who sponsored many artistic endeavors. Indeed, the French court led Europe's classical revival.

Classical literature was perhaps best exemplified in the polished and elegant French dramas of Pierre Corneille (1606–1684), Jean Racine (1639–1699), and Jean-Baptiste Molière (1622–1673). The first two were the great tragedians of the seventeenth century. They followed Aristotle's traditional rules of dramatic unity but produced works noted for psychological insights and beauty of language. Usually borrowing their plots from Greek and Roman antiquity, they often depicted heroes and hereoines as idealized portraits of contemporary courtiers. Molière, an author of witty comedies, contrasted the artificiality of his society with the dictates of moderation and good sense. All three writers were sometimes mildly critical of established institutions, although their criticism was not direct enough to offend patrons.

A similar deference for patronage and authority was revealed in classical architecture and painting. In these areas, France also led the way. A state-sponsored culture, begun by Richelieu and Louis XIII in the French Academy, was continued by Louis XIV in academies of architecture, painting, dance, and music. The latter's palace at Versailles, with its horizontal lines, ninety-degree angles, and formal gardens, was copied all over Europe. So was the work of French court painters, such as Charles Le Brun (1619–1690), who glorified the Grand Monarch and his society in colorful portraits and panoramic scenes, emphasizing the common values of elegance and order.

The Capitalistic Ethic

The worlds of art and business, apparently so far removed from each other, shared common perspectives in this era. Traders and bankers, like most Europeans after Westphalia, felt a sense of relief and some hope for more tranquil times in the future. They could now more freely follow their own capitalistic ethic, which usually placed acquisition of profit over humane or religious concerns. This commercial secularism was also oriented toward securing order. Social upheavals obviously hurt business, and a strong state could promote prosperity in an increasingly interdependent world economy.

By the seventeenth century, particularly after mid-century, this economy depended upon the exchange of bulk commodities, rather than imported gold and silver. Eastern Europe and the Baltic supplied grains, timber, fish, and naval stores. Western Europe supplied manufactures for its outlying regions and for overseas trade. Dutch, English, and French merchant-bankers controlled shipping and credit. Plantation agriculture in the tropics, particularly the cultivation of Caribbean sugar, produced the greatest profits from overseas commerce. The African slave trade, along with its many supporting industries, also became an integral part of the intercontinental system.

The New World economy widened European horizons while contributing to European wealth. New foods, such as potatoes, yams, lima beans, tapioca, and peanuts became part of the European diet. Tropical plantation crops, such as rice, coffee, tea, cocoa, and sugar ceased to be luxuries. Production from European industries, particularly metals, coal, and textiles, also increased noticeably. Although the European economy slowed considerably in the seventeenth century, some profits remained enormous, particularly in eastern Europe and on tropical plantations, where production depended on serfs and slave labor. Lagging wages in western Europe produced similar advantages for capitalists, who remained in a most favorable economic position.

Such conditions contributed directly to the development of capitalistic institutions. As the volume of business rose, great public banks, chartered by governments, replaced earlier family banks like the Fuggers of Augsburg. The Bank of Amsterdam (1609) and the Bank of England (1694) are typical examples. Such banks, holding public revenues and creating credit by issuing notes, made large amounts of capital available for favored enterprises. Another method of concentrating capital came with joint-stock companies, such as the Dutch and English East India Companies, which could pool the resources of many investors. In the late seventeenth century, exchanges for buying and selling stock were becoming common, as were maritime insurance companies. Lloyd's of London, the most famous of these, began operations about 1688 and is still in business. Such capitalistic institutions regularized business and helped justify materialistic values in the popular mind.

They also fitted into the emerging state systems. The new capitalism depended upon overseas trade, which, in turn, required government protection or subsidy. Government policies affected money, credit, and capital accumulation. If capitalists needed government, governments also needed them. Powerful states were increasingly expensive, and overseas trade was a vital source of revenue. Capitalists could often help monarchs acquire foreign credit. Military force and bureaucratic organization, so important to rising states, often depended on capitalistic support. This tacit partnership between kings and capitalists produced a system known as mercantilism (see p. 476). It was most typical of France, but all absolute regimes were conditioned by the integrated European economy. Consequently, both profit and power were compatible subordinates to order in the European value system.

Philosophical Justifications for Absolutism

The prevailing respect for power was most clearly revealed in theoretical justifications for absolute monarchy. In the past, defenders of royal authority had employed the idea of "divine right" in claiming that kings were agents of God's will. This religious argument for absolutism was still quite common during the period, but it was supplemented by new secular appeals to scientific principles.

Bishop Jacques Bossuet (1627–1704), a prominent French churchman and the tutor of Louis XIV's son, produced a classic statement of divine right theory. In *Politics Drawn from Scriptures*, Bossuet declared:

> the person of the king is sacred, and to attack him in any way is sacrilege . . . the royal throne is not the throne of a man, but the throne of God himself. . . . Kings should be guarded as holy things, and whosoever neglects to protect them is worthy of death. . . . the royal power is absolute . . . the prince need render accounts of his acts to no one . . . Where the word of a king is, there is power . . . Without this absolute authority the king could neither do good or repress evil[1]

The most penetrating and influential secular justification for absolutism came from the English philosopher, Thomas Hobbes (1588–1679), whose famous political treatise, *Leviathan*, appeared in 1651. The French religious wars, the Thirty Years' War, and the English civil war of the 1640s inclined Hobbes to view order as the primary social good and anarchy as the greatest social disaster. Unlike Bossuet, he did not see God as the source of political authority. According to Hobbes, people created governments as protection against themselves, because they were naturally "brutish," "nasty," "selfish," and as cruel as wolves. Having been forced by human nature to surrender their freedoms to the state, people had no rights under government except obedience. The resulting sovereign state could take any form, but according to Hobbes, monarchy was the most effective in maintaining order and security. Any ruler, no matter how bad, was preferable to anarchy. Monarchs were therefore legitimately entitled to absolute authority, limited only by their own deficiencies and by the power of other states.[2]

Absolutism as a System

Unlimited royal authority, as advocated by Bossuet and Hobbes, was the main characteristic of absolutism. It was demonstrated most obviously in political organization but also served to integrate into government most economic, religious, and social institutions. In this section, we will preview this general pattern of absolutism before assessing its development within specific European states.

Government and Religion Under Absolutism

Theoretically, the ruler made all major decisions in a typical absolute state. Although this was not actually possible, chief ministers were responsible directly to the monarch, and all of their actions were taken in the sovereign's name. The monarch was officially the supreme lawgiver, the chief judge, the commander of all military forces, and the head of all administration. Central councils and committees discussed policy, but these bodies were strictly advisory and concerned primarily with administrative matter. All authority originated in orders coming down from the top and going out to the provinces from the royal capital.

In conducting foreign policy, monarchs identified their personal dynastic interests with those of their countries. They usually considered the acquisition of foreign territory to be legitimate and pursued their objectives in a competitive game of power politics with other monarchs. This competition required a large military establishment, sometimes involving naval forces. Rulers sought to form alliances against the most dominant foreign state, giving little consideration to moral or religious principles. A concern for the "balance of power" exemplified the new secular spirit in foreign relations.

Local government was a concern to all aspiring absolute monarchs. Wherever possible, they replaced traditional local authorities, usually feudal nobles, with royal governors from other places. Where that could not be done, local nobles were rewarded so they would support the crown. Sometimes, new nobles were created and old land grants reassigned. Town governments were often brought under royal authority through contacts between urban guildsmen and the king's middle-class servants. Using such means as monopoly grants, political favors, or bribery, monarchs extended their control over local law and revenues.

Organized religion remained important under absolutism but lost its independence of government. Instead of dominating politics, as they had done earlier, churches—Protestant and Catholic alike—now tended to become government agencies. Even in Catholic countries, such as France, the king exerted more political control over the church than did the pope. Although this had been true of earlier secular rulers, they had faced much more religious opposition. After Westphalia, monarchs could deliberately use their clergies as government servants, to enlist and hold popular support. Such controlled churches exerted tremendous influence in support of absolute monarchies, not only in the formal services but also in their social and educational functions.

Mercantilism in the Structure of Absolutism

In typical absolute monarchies, the regulation of state churches was accompanied by a system of national economic regulations known as *mercantilism*. Although it had originated earlier, with the emergence of modern states, mercantilism was not adopted generally by European governments until the late seventeenth century. The expansion of overseas trade, expenses incurred in religious and dynastic wars, and the depression of the middle 1600s accentuated the trend toward mercantilism as states hoped to promote prosperity and increase their revenues.

The system attempted to apply the capitalistic principle of profit-seeking in the management of national economies. "Bullionism" was the fundamental maxim of mercantilist theory. Proponents of bullionism sought to increase precious metals within a country by achieving a "favorable balance of trade," in which the monetary value of exports exceeded the value of imports. The result, in a sense, was a national profit. This became purchasing power in the world market, an advantage shared most directly by the government and favored merchants.

Mercantilists believed state regulation of the economy to be absolutely necessary for effecting a favorable balance. Absolute monarchies used subsidies, chartered monopolies, taxes, tarriffs, harbor tolls, and direct legal prohibitions in order to encourage exports and limit imports. For the same purpose, state enterprises were given advantages over private competitors. Governments standardized industrial production, regulated wages, set prices, and otherwise encouraged or restricted consumer purchases.

Governments also built roads, canals, and docks to facilitate commerce.

Because mercantilists viewed the world market in terms of competing states, they emphasized the importance of colonial expansion. They regarded colonies as favored markets for home products and as sources of cheap raw materials. Colonial foreign trade and industries were controlled to prevent competition with the parent countries. In pursuing such policies, absolute states needed strong military and naval forces to acquire colonies, police them, and protect them from foreign rivals. Thus mercantilist policies often extended beyond commercial competition to international conflict.

Class Structure Under Absolutism

The class structures of absolute monarchies were marked by clear distinctions, precisely defined by law. Hereditary feudal aristocrats lost status unless they acquired an official appointment from the monarch. Such state nobles owed their privileges to their political service rather than birth. They often came from merchant families; indeed, the state often sold titles to wealthy commoners to provide income for the monarch. State nobles served in public administration, in the army, the church, or as attendants at court, where they accented the royal magnificence. They usually received tax exemptions, pensions, titles, and honors. Their legal rights, dress, and way of life differed markedly from even wealthy non-nobles.

In contrast, commoners, including middle-class townspeople, paid most of the taxes required by frequent wars and extravagant royal courts. Peasant landholders usually owed fees and labor dues to local aristocrats. The poorest peasants in western Europe were hired laborers or vagabonds; in eastern Europe, they were serfs. Slavery was rare in western Europe, but provided a major labor force on overseas plantations.

While tightening legal class distinctions, absolute monarchies also further downgraded the status of women. The Reformation had offered some opportunities for self-expression among women, and before 1650 many women had assumed temporary positions of leadership. The situation changed after Westphalia. Although a number of queens and regents were able to rule

The oppression of the peasantry is the subject of this engraving, which compares the noble and the peasant to the spider and the fly. The poor peasant brings all he has to the rich noble, who sits ready to receive all the produce.

as absolute monarchs, most aristocratic women could find recognition only as Catholic nuns, writers, artists, salon hostesses, court gossips, or royal mistresses, the latter gaining official status in this era. The status of commoner women did not fall as much or as quickly, but the advent of early capitalism and the decline of domestic economies was already excluding them from many industries and enterprises in the latter seventeenth century.

French Absolutism as the Model Under Louis XIV

Although absolutism was not a French invention, it appeared in a typically French form in the later seventeenth century. French armies had recently humbled the Habsburgs, bringing the Bourbon dynasty to predominance, and Louis XIV continued these military successes, at least for a while. Wealth poured into France from abroad, particularly from sugar islands in the

Louis XIV to His Son

This memoir, designed to instruct a young prince who never became king, nevertheless provides revealing insights into Louis' personal rationalizations for his one-dimensional view of government.

I laid a rule on myself to work regularly twice every day, and for two or three hours each time with different persons, without counting the hours which I passed privately and alone, nor the time which I was able to give on particular occasions to any special affairs that might arise. There was no moment when I did not permit people to talk to me about them, provided that they were urgent; with the exception of foreign ministers who sometimes find too favourable moments in the familiarity allowed to them, either to obtain or to discover something, and whom one should not hear without being previously prepared.

I cannot tell you what fruit I gathered immediately I had taken this resolution. I felt myself, as it were, uplifted in thought and courage; I found myself quite another man, and with joy reproached myself for having been too long unaware of it. This first timidity, which a little self-judgment always produces and which at the beginning gave me pain, especially on occasions when I had to speak in public, disappeared in less than no time. The only thing I felt then was that I was King, and born to be one. I experienced next a delicious feeling, hard to express, and which you will not know yourself except by tasting it as I have done. . . .

All that is most necessary to this work is at the same time agreeable: for, in a word, my son, it is to have one's eyes open to the whole earth; to learn each hour the news concerning every province and every nation, the secrets of every court, the mood and the weaknesses of each Prince and of every foreign minister; to be well-informed on an infinite number of matters about which we are supposed to know nothing; to elicit from our subjects what they hide from us with the greatest care; to discover the most remote opinions of our own courtiers and the most hidden interests of those who come to us with quite contrary professions. I do not know of any other pleasure we would not renounce for that, even if curiosity alone gave us the opportunity. . . .

I gave orders to the four Secretaries of State no longer to sign anything whatsoever without speaking to me; likewise to the Controller, and that he should authorise nothing as regards finance without its being registered in a book which must remain with me, and being noted down in a very abridged abstract form in which at any moment, and at a glance, I could see the state of the funds, and past and future expenditure.

The Chancellor received a like order, that is to say, to sign nothing with the seal except by my command, with the exception only of letters of justice, so called because it would be an injustice to refuse them, a procedure required more as a matter of form than of principle. . . . I let it be understood that whatever the nature of the matter might be, direct application must be made to me when it was not a question that depended only on my favour; and to all my subjects without distinction I gave liberty to present their case to me at all hours, either verbally or by petitions. . . .

Regarding the persons whose duty it was to second my labours, I resolved at all costs to have no prime minister; and if you will believe me, my son, and all your successors after you, the name shall be banished for ever from France, for there is nothing more undignified than to see all the administration on one side, and on the other, the mere title of King. . . .

From *A King's Lesson in Statecraft: Louis XIV: Letters to His Heirs* in Harry J. Carroll et al., eds., *The Development of Civilization*, 2 vols. (Glenview, IL: Scott, Foresman, 1970), Vol. 2, pp. 120–121.

Caribbean. The magnificent royal palace at Versailles, the luxury of the French court, and the brilliance of French cultural expression dazzled the rest of Europe. It is no wonder that Louis was considered the ultimate in political wisdom or that his arbitrary methods were widely copied. Like the solar system, then being emphasized in Newtonian physics, France appeared in the European state system as a central star, surrounded by its orbiting satellites.

The Grand Monarch

The strong absolutism of Louis XIV followed a long monarchical tradition. Francis I in the early sixteenth century had subordinated the feudal nobility, created a centralized administration, and waged continuous warfare against his Habsburg enemy, Charles V. Religious conflicts of the late 1500s ended the Valois dynasty but only temporarily disrupted the development of French absolutism. Henry IV, the first Bourbon, restored peace and royal authority. Cardinal

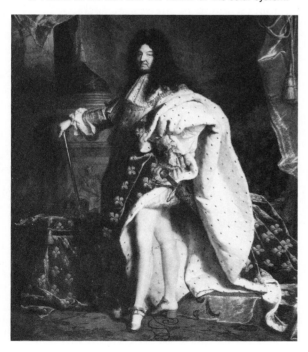

Louis XIV in Robes of State by court painter Hyacinthe Rigaud. The portrait captures the splendor of the Grand Monarch, known as the Sun King, who believed himself to be the center of France as the sun was the center of the solar system.

Richelieu, as minister in the next reign, broke the power of the nobility and the independent Protestant cities.

Yet for a while in the 1650s, the country appeared to be entering another time of troubles. It was nearly bankrupted by the Thirty Years' War, further drained of blood and treasure by continued conflict with Spain until 1659, and racked by the civil war of the Fronde between 1649 and 1653. More than once, Louis, as a boy, narrowly escaped capture by rebel forces. As a result he was deeply suspicious of the nobility, because many Fronde leaders had come from that class. He was particularly alienated by court ladies, such as Madame de Longueville, who organized rebel forces, and his cousin, Mademoiselle de Montpensier, who turned the guns of the Bastille on royalist troops. Louis' other nemesis was Cardinal Mazarin (1602–1661), his frantic mother's Italian lover and chief minister, who neglected Louis and ran the government. When Mazarin died in 1661, the twenty-three-year-old Louis took personal control of the state; he never appointed another chief minister.

During the remainder of his long reign, Louis worked at projecting an image of the "Grand Monarch." His personal political convictions were clearly revealed in a characteristic statement:

> All power, all authority resides in the hands of the king, and there can be no other in his kingdom than that which he establishes. The nation does not form a body in France. It resides entire in the person of the king.[3]

To symbolize his life-giving presence in the council chamber, Louis had a rising sun painted on his official chair. Today such overbearing egotism might appear as ridiculous as Louis' red-heeled shoes and enormous wig, but it was all taken seriously in his time. Louis, particularly, took his responsibilities very seriously. His lingering childhood insecurities produced in him an enormous capacity for work and an absolute dedication to the art of ruling, which he accomplished with remarkable shrewdness.

Louis constantly strove to inspire awe of the monarchy, as was evidenced by his great palace at Versailles, a short distance from Paris. It was set in 17,000 beautifully landscaped acres. The parks and buildings, surrounded by a 40-mile wall, contained 1400 fountains, 2000 standing statues, and innumerable rooms, decorated with marble columns, painted ceilings, costly draperies, mirrored walls, and hand-crafted furniture.

In this fairyland at Versailles, Louis lived amid studied elegance, formal manners, extravagant expressions of courtesy, and witty but shallow conversation. It was an artificial and carefully-ordered society, exemplified by the graceful minuet, with manners more important than either morals or religion. By requiring the nobles to attend his glittering court, Louis retained them in an elegant prison where they could be more easily controlled. Unfortunately, Louis was also imprisoned. Preoccupied with etiquette and protocol, he sacrificed his private life to hundreds of noble courtiers, who followed him about, observing the elaborate ceremonies associated with his every move, from the time he arose and was dressed in the morning, until he was disrobed and assisted into bed at night.

A marked characteristic of the court was its loose sexual morality. Here, again, Louis set the example. Before and after his marriage in 1659 to the Spanish Infanta, whom he formally honored but consistently neglected, Louis shared his bed with numerous women, each of whom was designated, in her time, as "head mistress." The best known among the early ones were the child-like Louise de la Vallière and the sensuous Madame de Montespan. Louis shared none of his problems with them and was extremely wary of their efforts to extract political favors. After his experience with the ladies of the Fronde, he made a conscious effort to limit female participation in government. He may have changed later in life; after his wife died, Louis secretly married Madame de Maintenon, the governess of his illegitimate children. This level-headed matron offered the companionship he had never known, but even she could provoke his ire. The grand monarch left his stamp upon an era when women's limited influence was mainly confined to the boudoir.

This point is well illustrated by seventeenth-century French cultural expression. During the early decades many aristocratic women became involved in amateur efforts as writers, artists, and critics. Their main milieu was the salons of Paris, where aristocratic women hosted regular meetings devoted to discussion of high culture, mostly literature. Ladies of the Fronde had frequented the salons, as did the well-known novelists Madame de Scudéry and Madame de Lafayette. But the collapse of the Fronde and Louis' accession depressed the salons until the eighteenth century. Competition from the carefully regimented art and literature sponsored by the French royal academies diminished their influence. Louis XIV's age of classicism was largely a reflection of state patronage.

The French Social and Political Structure

Court attendance was vitally important to the nobility, because honor and income depended on royal favor. Louis virtually eliminated independent feudal aristocrats from public service outside the church and the military. He gave or sold titles to his working middle-class officials known as "nobles of the robe," in contrast to the old landed "nobles of the sword." Those of the latter who remained away from court were suspect and subject to investigation. The nobility, thus divided, was a privileged class under law, along with the clergy. A third class, or estate, of taxpaying commoners, included merchants, craftsmen, and peasants. Most peasants owed manorial dues and services to their landlords, although they were no longer bound to the soil as serfs.

This aristocratic social structure was integrated with the administrative system developed earlier by Richelieu. Without a chief minister, Louis worked closely with his appointed council and the secretaries who headed major agencies. Subordinate councils supervised ministries and their large supporting corps of officials. One such body, the Council of Dispatches, received reports from the intendants, who were responsible for finance, police, and justice in the provinces. Louis professionalized this body of royal agents, increasing their powers, standardizing their salaries, and assigning them outside of their home areas. They supervised some 40,000 lesser officials. Within this vast organization, the king's government issued laws, censored litereature and art, conducted widespread spying, imprisoned its enemies, and dominated the courts. Within the limits imposed by space and technology, royal agents regulated everything.

Louis also claimed authority over the French church and the religious lives of his subjects, enforcing that authority against both Protestants and the papacy. The king was involved in a long struggle with the pope over revenues. Ultimately, after Bishop Bossuet and a convocation of the French clergy had upheld him, Louis won Rome's approval to collect the income from vacant bishoprics, although he abandoned the idea of heading an independent French church. In 1685, he revoked the Edict of Nantes, by which Henry IV had granted freedom of worship to the Protestant Huguenots almost a century before. The new law subjected practicing Protestants to torture or imprisonment. Luckily for them but not for France, some 200,000 of the most industrious French Huguenots escaped to other lands, taking with them valuable skills and knowledge.

This disastrous policy has been attributed to the influence of Madam de Maintenon. The charge has not been proved, although it is known that Louis was becoming increasingly concerned about his soul and that de Maintenon was an ardent Catholic with a missionary obsession. If she did not cause him to revoke the edict, there can be no doubt that she thoroughly agreed with the action.

French Mercantilism, Militarism, and Colonialism

State control of religion in France was paralleled by an all-embracing mercantilist system, deployed by Louis' comptroller of finance, Jean Baptiste Colbert (1619–1683). Colbert sought French economic self-sufficiency at the expense of Dutch overseas commerce. He created a comprehensive system of tariffs and trade prohibitions levied against foreign imports. French luxury industries—silks, laces, fine woolens, and glass—were subsidized or produced in government shops. The state imported skilled workers and prescribed the most minute regulations for each industry. Colbert also improved internal transportation by building some roads and canals. He chartered overseas trading companies, granting them monopolies on commerce with North America, the West Indies, India, Southeast Asia, and the Middle East. The system, called Colbertism, came to be identified with thoroughness.

French foreign and imperial policy under Louis XIV required a highly efficient war machine. To achieve it, the king's brutal but able minister of war, the Marquis de Louvois (1641–1691), revolutionized the French army. In addition to infantry and cavalry, he organized special units of supply, ordnance, artillery, engineers, and inspectors. Command ranks, combat units, drills, uniforms, and weapons were standarized for the first time in Europe. Louvois also improved weaponry by such innovations as the bayonet, which permitted a musket to be fired while the blade was attached. By raising military pay, providing benefits, and improving conditions of service, the war minister increased the size of the army from 72,000 to 400,000, a force larger than all belligerents put together at any one time during the Thirty Years' War. Louvois also improved and expanded the navy. In addition to a Mediterranean galley fleet based at Toulon, the overseas forces by 1683 consisted of 217 men-of-war, operating from Atlantic ports and served by numerous shipyards.

Jean Baptiste Colbert. His financial reforms were so successful that within six years a debt of 22 million French pounds had been transformed into a surplus of 29 million pounds.

The new navy was part of Colbert's grand strategy for building an enormous overseas dominion. In the last decades of the seventeenth century, the French Empire took shape on three continents. In North America, fur trappers and missionaries pushed south down the Mississippi. In 1683, when the Marquis de La Salle reached the Gulf of Mexico, he claimed the continental interior for his king, naming it Louisiana. A second important area was the West Indies, where a number of French sugar islands, particularly Martinique and Guadeloupe, experienced a booming prosperity. Across the Atlantic, French West African trading posts on the Senegal River supplied slaves for the West Indian plantations.

The other areas of interest were in East Africa and southern Asia, where the French had acquired footholds in Madagascar, the Isle of Bourbon in the Indian Ocean, and trading centers at Pondicherry and Chandernagore on the east coast of India.

The Gravitational Pull of French Absolutism

The popular image of Louis XIV as the Sun King symbolized his position in France but also implied that French absolutism exerted a magnetic influence upon other European states. Like all such symbolism, the idea was only partially true. As much as it was a response to French example, absolutism was accepted because it promised efficiency and security, the greatest political needs of the time. Yet French wealth and power certainly generated European admiration and imitation of the French example.

Typical Satellites of France

Among the most obvious satellites of the French sun were numerous German principalities of the Holy Roman Empire. By the Treaty of Westphalia, more than 300 were recognized as sovereign states. Without serious responsibilities to the emperor and with treasuries filled by confiscated church properties, their petty rulers struggled to increase their personal powers and play the exciting game of international diplomacy.

Many sought French alliances against the Habsburg emperor; those who could traveled in France and attended Louis' court. Subsequently, many a German palace became a miniature Versailles. Even the tiniest states were likely to have standing armies, state churches, court officials, and economic regulations. The ultimate deference to the French model was shown by the Elector of Brandenburg; although sincerely loyal to his wife, he copied Louis XIV by taking an official mistress, displaying her at court functions without requiring her to perform other duties usually associated with the position.

The era of the Sun King also witnessed an upsurge of absolutism in Scandinavia. After an earlier aristocratic reaction against both monarchies, Frederick III (1648–1670) in Denmark and Charles XI (1660–1697) in Sweden broke the power of the nobles and created structures similar to the French model. In 1661 Frederick forced the assembled high nobility to accept him as their hereditary king. Four years later, he proclaimed his exclusive right to issue laws. A similar upheaval in Sweden in 1680 allowed Charles to achieve financial independence by seizing the nobles' lands. These beginnings were followed by the development of thoroughly centralized administrations in both kingdoms. Sweden, particularly, resembled France with its standing army, navy, national church, and mercantilist economy. Although Swedish royal absolutism was overthrown by the nobles in 1718, the Danish system remained into the nineteenth century.

States in Irregular Orbits

Unlike the Sandinavian and German states, most European governments resembled Louis' system more in the way they developed rather than in their specific institutions. As agricultural economies became commercialized, restricting the developing interests of monarchs and commoners, rulers sought to ignore their feudal councils and exercise unlimited authority. Some states in this period had not yet developed as far in this direction as had France; others were already finding absolutism at least partially outmoded. All felt the magnetic pull of French absolutism, but their responses varied according to their traditions and local conditions.

The process is well illustrated by a time lag in the Spanish and Portuguese monarchies. United by Spanish force in 1580 and divided again by a Portuguese revolt in 1640, the two kingdoms were first weakened by economic decay and then nearly destroyed by the Thirty Years' War and their own mutual conflicts, which lasted until Spain accepted Portuguese independence in 1668. Conditions deteriorated further under the half-mad Alfonso VI (1656–1668) in Portugal and the feeble-minded Charles II (1665–1700) in Spain.

The nobilities, having exploited these misfortunes to regain their dominant position in both countries, could not be easily dislodged. Not until the 1680s in Portugal did Pedro II (1683–1706) successfully eliminate the Cortes (assembly of feudal estates) and restore royal authority. With new wealth from Brazilian gold and diamond strikes, John V (1706–1750) centralized the administration, perfected mercantilism, and extended control over the church. In Spain, similar developments accompanied the War of the Spanish Succession and the grant to Louis XIV's Bourbon grandson, Philip V (1700–1746), of the Spanish crown. Philip brought to Spain a corps of French advisors, including the Princess des Ursins, a friend of de Maintenon's and a spy for Louis XIV. Philip then followed French precedents by imposing centralized ministries, local intendants, and economic regulations upon the country.

Aristocratic limits on absolutism, so evident in the declining kingdoms of Portugal and Spain, were even more typical of the Habsburg monarchy in eastern Europe. The Thirty Years' War had diverted Habsburg attention from the Holy Roman Empire to lands under the family's direct control. By 1700, they held the Archduchy of Austria, a few adjacent German areas, the Kingdom of Bohemia, and the Kingdom of Hungary, recently conquered from the Turks. This was a very large domain, stretching from Saxony in the north to the Ottoman Empire in the southeast. It was strong enough to play a leading role in the continental wars against Louis XIV after the 1670s.

Leopold I (1657–1705) was primarily responsible for strengthening the Austrian imperial monarchy during this period. In long wars with the French and the Turks, Leopold modernized the army, not only increasing its numbers but also instilling professionalism and loyalty in its officers. He created central administrative councils, giving each responsibility for an arm of the imperial government or a local area. He staffed these high administrative positions with court nobles, rewarded and honored like those in France. Other new nobles, given lands in the home provinces, became political tools for subordinating the local estates. Leopold suppressed Protestantism in Bohemia and Austria and kept his own Catholic church under firm control. In 1687, the Habsburgs were accepted as hereditary monarchs in Hungary, a status they had already achieved in Austria and Bohemia.

In the eighteenth century, Maria Theresia (1740–1780) faced Leopold's problems all over again. When she inherited her throne at the age of twenty-two, her realm was threatened by Prussia and lacking both money and military forces. In the years after Leopold's time, the nobles had regained much of their former power and were again building their own dominions at the expense of the monarchy. Maria was a religious and compassionate woman, known as "Her Motherly Majesty," but she put aside this gentle image to hasten much needed internal reforms. Count Haugwitz, her reforming minister, rigidly enforced new laws which brought provincial areas under more effective royal control.

Despite its glitter and outward trappings, the Austrian Habsburg monarchy was not a truly absolute monarchy. The economy was almost entirely agricultural and therefore dependent upon serf labor. This perpetuated the power of the nobles and diminished revenues available to the state. In addition, subjects of the monarchy comprised a mixture of nationalities and languages — German, Czech, Magyar, Croatian, and Italian, to name only a few. Without real unity, the various Habsburg areas stubbornly persisted in their localism. Even the reforms of Leopold and Maria Theresia left royal authority existing more in name than in fact. Imposed on still functioning medieval institutions, it resulted in a strange combination of absolutism and feudalism.

While Habsburg absolutism wavered in an irregular orbit, Poland was in no orbit at all. Local trade and industry were even more insignificant in its economy; the peasants were more depressed; and land-controlling lesser nobles —

some 8 percent of the population—grew wealthy in supplying grain for western merchants. Nobles avoided military service and most taxes; they were lords and masters of their serfs. More than fifty local assemblies dominated their areas, admitting no outside jurisdiction. The national Diet (council), which was elected by the local bodies, chose a king without real authority. In effect, Poland was fifty small, independent feudal estates.

Western Maritime States

Although impressed by French absolutism, the agricultural states of eastern Europe were not yet capable of applying it. At the other extreme, England and Holland rejected the system, partially beause they had outgrown it. Yet both states felt the pull toward absolutism in their internal politics.

The Dutch Republic, in the seventeenth century, was a confusing mixture of medievalism and modernity. Its central government was a federation of seven nearly independent states. The stadtholder, as chief executive, led the military forces but had no control of budget or revenues. Neither did the States General, the legislative body, which could act only as a council of ambassadors from the provinces. These were governed by local estates, which limited the authority of their own executives. The main difference between this system and Poland's was the political weakness of the aristocracy. Although rural nobles were strong in some provincial assemblies, the cities, particularly those in the province of Holland, provided revenues that maintained the government. Thus wealthy bankers and merchants, who dominated the major town councils, held the real power.

Even in this political environment, absolutism was a political force. As successful military leaders, the Dutch stadtholders appealed to popular loyalties. The House of Orange supplied so many successive stadtholders that the office became virtually hereditary in the family. By the 1640s, stadtholders were addressed as "your highness" and intermarried with European royalty, including the English Stuarts. They created a political machine that controlled some provincial systems. Arguing for efficiency, they gained the right to name their councilors as working ministers. From 1618 to 1647 and again from 1672 to 1703, monarchists controlled the state. In the latter period, William III built a highly efficient army and centralized administration.

The Dutch state outdistanced contemporary monarchies in creating the first northern European empire overseas. Between 1609 and 1630, while at war with Spain and Portugal, the Dutch navy broke Spanish sea power, drove the Portuguese from the Spice Islands of Southeast Asia, and dominated the carrying trade of Europe. In this same period, the republic acquired Java, western Sumatra, the spice-producing Moluccas of Indonesia, and part of Ceylon. The Dutch East India Company took over most European commerce with ports between the Cape of Good Hope and Japan. Elsewhere, the Dutch acquired the Portuguese West African slaving stations, conquered most of Brazil, and established New Amsterdam (present-day New York City and the Hudson River valley) in North America. Dutch commercial and colonial predominance ended after 1650, but the Dutch Asian empire lasted into the twentieth century.

As Dutch commercial and imperial fortunes declined, England became the main rival of France for colonial supremacy. The two nations were already traditional enemies and different in many respects. While France was perfecting a model absolute monarchy, England was subordinating

A 1665 painting of the Dutch East India Company's trading station on the Hooghly River in Bengal. The station was a key link in the network of bases that made up the eastern trading empire of the Dutch Republic.

its kings to Parliament. Before 1688, however, England also felt the strong attraction of French absolutism.

The period from 1660 to 1688 was marked by increasingly severe struggles between English kings and Parliament. England had earlier been torn by fanatic religious controversy, political revolution, bloody civil war, the beheading of a king, and rigid military dictatorship (see ch. 17). Almost everyone welcomed the new ruler, Charles II (1660–1685), called back from exile in France and restored to the throne, with his lavish court and his mistresses. But Charles, the cleverest politician of the Stuart line, exploited this common desire for normality to violate the terms of his restoration, which bound him to rule in cooperation with Parliament.

Charles almost succeeded in becoming an absolute monarch. With the help of his favorite sister, Henrietta Anne, who had married Louis XIV's brother, Charles negotiated the secret Treaty of Dover, which bound him to further English Catholicism and aid France in war against Holland. In return, Charles received subsidies from France that made him independent of Parliament. He then used all of his deceit and cunning to create a political machine. This precipitated a political crisis, forcing him to back down. Ultimately, he dismissed four Parliaments. After 1681, Charles governed without Parliament, taking advantage of a strong desire among the propertied classes to avoid another civil war.

Charles' brother James II (1685–1688) proved to be a more determined absolutist. Like Charles, he was an admirer of Louis XIV and a known Catholic. His wife, Mary of Modena, had been persuaded by the pope to marry James as a holy commitment to save England for Rome. Having been repeatedly insulted by Protestants at Charles' court, she was now determined to accomplish her mission. James was quite willing to cooperate. Early in his reign, he suppressed an anti-Catholic rebellion in southwest England. With his confidence thus buttressed, he attempted to dominate the courts, maintain a standing army, take over local government, and turn the English church back to Catholicism. Most of this was done in defiance of the law while Parliament was not in session.

In 1688, after James had unsuccessfully tried to control parliamentary elections, the country was roused to near revolt by the birth of a royal prince, who might perpetuate a Catholic dynasty. A group of aristocrats met and offered the crown to the former heir, Mary Stuart, the Protestant daughter of James by an earlier marriage. Mary accepted the offer with the provision that her husband, William of Orange, be co-ruler. William landed with an efficient Dutch army, defeated James, and forced him into exile. This "Glorious Revolution" pushed England in the direction of limited monarchy (see p. 547).

After 1688, England turned away from French-styled absolutism but continued to follow mercantilist principles in building a worldwide empire. By enforcing the Navigation Act of 1651 and other similar laws passed under Charles, England sought to regulate foreign trade and exploit colonial economies.

Rising Absolute Monarchies in Eastern Europe

Following the Age of Louis XIV, strong absolute monarchies rose in eastern Europe. The area had formerly been an agricultural dependency of western European capitalism, retarded by its isolation and reliance upon serf labor. In time, the ideas and economic prosperity of western Europe spread slowly eastward, furthered by great wars and colonial contentions, which diverted western states from suspicion of eastern rulers and opened opportunities for two new despotisms. One was Prussia, under its Hohenzollern dynasty, and the other was Slavic Russia, under the Romanovs.

Prussia: The Typical Military State

The rise of the Hohenzollerns was among the most striking political development of the era. Once relatively unimportant nobles occupying a castle on Mount Zollern in southern Germany, they pursued their ambitious policies through marriage, intrigue, religious factionalism, and war. By the early seventeenth century, they held lands scattered across north Germany (see map. p. 486). The Thirty Years' War was almost disastrous for the Hohenzollerns but conditioned them to austerity, perseverence, and iron discipline.

Two reigns laid permanent foundations for the later monarchy. Frederick William (1640–1688), called "the Great Elector," used his small but well-trained army to win eastern Pomerania at the end of the Thirty Years' War. In the near anarchy which prevailed in Germany immediately after Westphalia, he reformed the administration in Brandenburg, crushed the nobles in Prussia and Cleves, created a tough army of 30,000 soldiers, and brought all three areas under his direct control. His son, Frederick I (1688–1713), exploited Russia's victory over Sweden to annex western Pomerania. As a reward for fighting France in the War of the Spanish Succession (see p. 492), Frederick was recognized as "King in Prussia" by the states which signed the Peace of Utrecht in 1713.

After Utrecht, Prussia was generally regarded as a drill yard, with the king as drillmaster. This reputation was largely created by Frederick William I (1713–1740), a crusty soldier-king, whose maxims were order, discipline, work, and loyalty. Demanding absolute obedience, he once told a group of subjects: "No reasoning! Obey orders." His conception of royal authority was simple. "Salvation belongs to the Lord," he once exclaimed and added, "Everything else is my business." With such unabashed absolutism, he reorganized the government under a General Directory, established a civil service for local administration, created a royal supreme court, taxed the nobles, required them to train for professional military careers, and built an army of 80,000, considered to be the best trained and equipped in Europe. At the end of his reign, the Hohenzollern monarchy was ready for military expansion.

Frederick William I held high hopes for his son, Frederick II (1740–1786). The young prince,

RISE OF PRUSSIA 1440-1795

- Brandenburg in 1440
- Acquisitions 1440-1624
- Acquisitions 1640-1740
- Acquisitions 1740-1786
- Acquisitions 1786-1795

Frederick the Great, Political Testament

In 1752 Frederick published his thoughts on government in *A Political Testament*. This excerpt is taken from that essay.

Politics is the science of always using the most convenient means in accord with one's own interests. In order to act in conformity with one's interests one must know what these interests are, and in order to gain this knowledge one must study their history and application. . . . One must attempt, above all, to know the special genius of the people which one wants to govern in order to know if one must treat them leniently or severely, if they are inclined to revolt . . . to intrigue. . . .

A well conducted government must have an underlying concept so well integrated that it could be likened to a system of philosophy. All actions taken must be well reasoned, and all financial, political and military matters must flow towards one goal: which is the strengthening of the state and the furthering of its power. However, such a system can flow but from a single brain, and this must be that of the sovereign. Laziness, hedonism and imbecility, these are the causes which restrain princes in working at the noble task of bringing happiness to their subjects . . . a sovereign is not elevated to his high position, supreme power has not been confined to him in order that he may live in lazy luxury, enriching himself by the labor of the people, being happy while everyone else suffers. The sovereign is the first servant of the state. He is well paid in order that he may sustain the dignity of his office, but one demands that he work efficiently for the good of the state, and that he, at the very least, pay personal attention to the most important problems. . . .

You can see, without doubt, how important it is that the King of Prussia govern personally. Just as it would have been impossible for Newton to arrive at his system of attractions if he had worked in harness with Leibniz and Descartes, so a system of politics cannot be arrived at and continued if it has not sprung from a single brain. . . . All parts of the government are inexorably linked with each other. Finance, politics and military affairs are inseparable; it does not suffice that one be well administered; the must all be . . . a Prince who governs personally, who has formed his [own] political system, will not be handicapped when occasions arise where he has to act swiftly; for he can guide all matters towards the end which he has set for himself. . . .

Catholics, Lutherans, Reformed, Jews and other Christian sects live in this state, and live together in peace; if the sovereign, actuated by a mistaken zeal, declares himself for one religion or another, parties will spring up, heated disputes ensue, little by little persecutions will commence and, in the end, the religion persecuted will leave the fatherland and millions of subjects will enrich our neighbors by their skill and industry.

It is of no concern in politics whether the ruler has a religion or whether he has none. All religions, if one examines them, are founded on superstitious systems, more or less absurd. It is impossible for a man of good sense, who dissects their contents, not to see their error; but these prejudices, these errors and mysteries were made for men, and one must know enough to respect the public and not to outrage its faith, whatever religion be involved.

From *A Political Testament* in George L. Mosse et al., comp. and eds., *Europe in Review* (Chicago: Rand McNally, 1962), pp. 110–112.

however, reacted against his Spartan training, secretly seeking escape in music, art, and philosophy. When caught after attempting flight to France, he was forced to witness the beheading of his accomplice and best friend. More years of severe training and discipline brought him into line with his father's wishes but robbed the future king of capacity for feeling. In later years, while retaining his cultural interests and mingling freely with writers and artists, he developed no lasting relationships, particularly not with women. He married early to escape his father's household, then ignored his wife, Elizabeth, subjecting her to a courteous but cold formality. Neither she nor any of his frequent but temporary mistresses could influence his judgment. This was also true of his family, after the old king died. Wilhelmina, the sister who had shared his youthful emnity against their father, lost his confidence as they both matured. Such was the price he paid to become a superb administrator, a master of Machiavellian diplomacy, and the greatest soldier of his day.

In 1780, the Prussia of Frederick II, called "the Great," was regarded as a perfectly functioning absolute monarchy. Stretching some 500 miles across northern Germany between the Elbe and Niemen rivers, its flourishing population had grown from three quarters of a million in 1648 to five million. For twenty-three years from 1740 to 1763, it had waged nearly continuous war. See pp. 492–494 in this chapter. The government ran as precisely as an efficient army. Like any good commander, Frederick claimed all ultimate authority. He required rigid discipline and deference to superiors from civilian officials as well as from military officers. Prussian nobles were honored over merchants or non-noble officials and were permitted complete mastery over their serfs. Frederick's mercantilism stressed tariff protection for agriculture, encouraged industry with government subsidies, imported artisans, and sought economic self-sufficiency as a means of achieving military superiority.

The Rise of Russia

Russia, the other eastern monarchy that rose to prominence in the eighteenth century, was even farther from the European economic hub than Poland and therefore even more backward

(see map, p. 489). The country had experienced a "time of troubles" in the latter sixteenth century, when the nobles engaged in civil war against the monarchy. Later, between 1613 and 1676, the first two Romanov tsars, Michael and Alexis, integrated most aristocrats into the state nobility and achieved some degree of stability. As in Prussia, the nobles and the government were united in their common exploitation of the serfs, and the primitive agricultural economy encouraged aristocratic independence. Russian ignorance and technical deficiencies, along with a conservative-minded nobility, made the country stagnant and retarded in comparison with western states.

A new era in Russian history began with Peter I (1682–1725). When he was ten years old, in 1682, Peter's half-sister, Sophia, effected a palace coup, in which her troops looted the palace, killing many of Peter's maternal uncles. For seven years, while Sophia ruled as regent for Peter and his demented half-brother, Ivan, the young co-tsar lived in fear and insecurity, without discipline or much formal education. He recruited and drilled his own guard regiments and roamed Moscow's foreign quarter, learning about boats and western ways. When he was sixteen, his mother arranged his marriage to a young noblewoman, Evdokia Lopukhina. From the first, this was a mismatch; after impregnating his wife, Peter abandoned her within three months. He was by now a young giant, weighing 230 pounds and standing six feet eight inches tall, with a temper to match his size. Fortunately, he also possessed a sharp mind and boundless energy.

After 1689, Peter took control of the country and his own life. When Sophia failed in an attempt to become sole ruler, he forced her into a convent, although Ivan remained co-tsar to his death in 1696. Peter amused himself with a mistress and wild drinking parties but continued his pursuit of western ways. His difficulties in wars with the Turks convinced him that he must modernize his army and build a navy. In 1697, he went incognito as a member of a great embassy to Poland, Germany, Holland, and England. He worked as a common ship's carpenter in Holland, learning Dutch methods at first hand. Back in Moscow, Peter crushed a rebellion of his palace guards with savage cruelty. This was followed by extensive reforms and wars against the

GROWTH OF RUSSIA: 1462;1676

1725

1796

Turks and Swedes, as Peter sought "a window on the sea." He achieved this goal in 1703, when he founded St. Petersburg, as his future capital on the Baltic. That same year, Peter met Marfa Skavronska, a Lithuanian peasant girl, who became his mistress, friend, campaign companion, and after Evdokia's death in a convent, his wife.

Peter's reforms made Russian absolutism functional, in fact as well as in theory. He completely centralized government, replacing all representative bodies with an appointed council and appointed ministries. Royal military governors assumed local authority. A Chancery of Police maintained order and collected information from an elaborate spy network. By forcing his nobles to shave their beards and don European clothes, he conditioned them to accept change and become living symbols of his power over them. They were now required to serve in the army, the government, or industry. Peter also officially abolished the office of Patriarch, as head of the state church, substituting a Holy Synod of bishops, dominated by a secular official, the procurator, who represented the Tsar. In copying European mercantilism, Peter established factories, mines, and shipyards, importing technical experts, along with thousands of laborers. He levied tariffs to protect native

industries and taxed almost everything, including births, marriages, and caskets. As revenues increased, he improved the army and navy, both of which were expanded, professionalized, and equipped with efficient western weapons.

Before and after Peter's time Russian absolutism also created its own empire in the forested wastes of Siberia. Russian cossacks and fur traders explored this enormous territory between 1580 and 1651. During the seventeenth century, it remained a vast game preserve, exploited by the Russian government for its fur. Agents responsible to the Siberian Bureau in Moscow or St. Petersburg governed the relatively peaceful native people, collecting tribute from them in furs and a percentage from the profits of chartered companies. With the tightly regulated fur trade so lucrative, the government discouraged settlement in Siberia. In the eighteenth century, however, restrictions were eased and western Siberia, between the Ob and Yenesei rivers, began attracting colonists, as well as convicts and political prisoners. Some 400,000 had come by 1763, but Siberia was largely undeveloped until the late nineteenth century.

Even after his death in 1725, Peter's policies continued to drive Russian politics through the eighteenth century. The main struggle was between "old believers," most prominent among the nobles and the clergy, who reacted strongly against the new ways and foreign influences Peter had sponsored. Another striking characteristic of the period was the prevalence of female rulers. Of the eight Russian monarchs in the eighteenth century, only three were tsars, who ruled a total of only three and a half disastrous years. The five tsarinas of the period were Catherine I (1725–1727), Peter's camp-following second wife and the first Russian empress; Anna Ivanovna (1730–1740), daughter of Peter's half-brother, Ivan; Elizabeth (1741–1762), daughter of Peter and Catherine I; and Catherine II (1762–1796), known as "the Great." All tried to continue Peter's policies, but Catherine I and Anna Ivanovna allowed foreigners too much power, thus alienating their Russian subjects. Elizabeth avoided this mistake. She was particularly successful in consolidating the central government and again winning respect in western Europe for Russian military power. She laid the foundations for the long and successful reign of Catherine the Great, whose role as an "enlightened despot" will be discussed in the next chapter.

Diplomacy and War in the Age of Absolutism

Because of dynastic and colonial rivalries, Europeans were constantly involved in conflicts in the Age of Absolutism. Fighting took place in America, Africa, and Asia—not only against non-Europeans but also in global wars among European colonial powers. At the same time, major wars battered Europe as dynastic states competed for dominance. While Spain, Sweden, and Poland were declining, Prussia, Russia, and even Austria were becoming first-class powers. Along with England's weight overseas, the last three exerted major influences on the European balance of power.

From Westphalia to Utrecht: The Dominance of France

France was the strongest and most threatening military power in Europe from the Peace of Westphalia (1648) to the Treaty of Utrecht (1713). Louis XIV first dreamed of expanding French frontiers to the Rhine; later he coveted the Spanish crown. Colbert also helped him plan the conquest of a large overseas empire in America, Africa, and Asia. The diplomacy of other European states in the era can largely be explained by their common efforts to unite against this French expansion.

One important exception to this general trend was the Russian policy. In early wars with the Turks Peter the Great took Azov on the Black Sea, but his main target in the Great Northern War (1709–1721) was Sweden. Peter's allies, Denmark and Poland, quickly fell to the Swedish warrior-king Charles XII (1697–1718). When the Swedes invaded Russia, they were first met with a "scorched earth" withdrawal, then annihilated at Poltavia (1709). The war ended in 1721 with Sweden exhausted and Peter gaining a section of the Baltic coast, where he had already begun building his new capital at St. Petersburg.

The three Anglo-Dutch naval wars between 1652 and 1674 provide an example of the intricate balance of power principle in action. Conflicting commercial and colonial interests of the two maritime states were the immediate issues. At the same time, both belligerents were increasingly aware of danger from a powerful and aggressive France. The Dutch were most directly affected because French expansion toward the northern Rhine threatened the survival of Holland as a nation. In order to deal with this problem, the Dutch came to terms, tacitly accepting English maritime supremacy while preparing the way for Anglo-Dutch alignment against Louis XIV. Ultimately the French menace was more decisive than naval actions in bringing an end to the Anglo-Dutch hostilities.

After 1670, Louis was the prime mover in European diplomacy. He fought four major wars, each with overseas campaigns. In the first, Louis claimed the Spanish Netherlands (Belgium). Thwarted by the Dutch and their allies, he next bought off Charles II of England and attacked the Dutch directly. Frustrated again by a combination of enemies, he tried in the 1690s to annex certain Rhineland districts. This time, almost all of Europe allied against him and forced him to back down. The climax to these repeated French efforts came between 1701 and 1713, in the War

Catherine the Great Assumes Power in Russia

Catherine became empress in 1762 in a coup which overthrew her estranged husband, Peter III. This selection is from her own written account of the episode.

The Hetman [Razumovsky,] Volkonsky and Panin were in the secret. I was sleeping calmly at Peterhof at 6 o'clock in the morning of the 28th [July Old Style] The day had been a very disturbing one for me as I knew all that was going on. [Suddenly] Alexius Orlov enters my room and says quite gently: "It is time to get up; all is ready for your proclamation. . . . " I dressed myself quickly without making my toilet and got into the carriage which he had brought with him. . . .

Five versts from the town I met the elder Orlov with the younger Prince Bariatinsky. Orlov gave up his carriage to me, for my horses were done up, and we got out at the barracks of the Ismailovsky Regiment. [At the gates] were only twelve men, and a drummer, who began sounding an alarm, when the soldiers came running out, kissing me, embracing my hands and feet and clothes, and calling me their deliverer. Then they began swearing allegiance to me. When this had been done, they begged me to get into the carriage, and the priest, cross in hand, walked on in front. We went [first] to the [barracks of the] Semenovsky Regiment, but the regiment came marching out to meet us, crying, Vivat! Then we went to the church of Kazan, where I got out. Then the Preobrazhensky Regiment arrived, crying, Vivat! "We beg your pardon," they said to me, for being the last. Our officers stopped us, but here are four of them whom we have arrested to shew you our zeal. We want what our brothers want." Then the horse-guards arrived frantic with joy, I never saw anything like it, weeping and crying at the deliverance of their country. . . . I went to the new Winter Palace where the Synod and the Senate were assembled. A manifesto and a form of oath were hastily drawn up. Then I went down and received the troops on foot. There were more than 14,000 men, guards and country regiments. As soon as they saw me they uttered cries of joy which were taken up by an innumerable crowd. I went on to the old Winter Palace to take [my] measures and finish [the business,] there we took counsel together, and it was resolved to go to Peterhof, where Peter III was to have dined with me, at their head. All the great roads had been occupied and rumours came in every moment. . . .

Peter III abdicated, at Oranienbaum, in full liberty, surrounded by 5000 Holsteiners, and came with Elizabeth Vorontsov, Gudovich and Ismailov to Perterhof, where, to protect his person, I gave him five officers and some soldiers. . . . Thereupon I sent the deposed Emperor to a remote and very agreeable place called Ropsha, 25 versts from Peterhof, under the command of Alexius Orlov, with four officers and a detachment of picked, good-natured men, whilst decent and convenient rooms were being prepared for him at Schlusselburg. But God disposed otherwise. Fear had given him a diarrhoea which lasted three days and passed away on the fourth; in this [fourth] day he drank excessively, for he had all he wanted except liberty. Nevertheless, the only things he asked me for were his mistress, his dog, his Negro and his violin; but for fear of scandal [sic] and increasing the agitation of the persons who guarded him, I only sent him the last three things. . . .

Source: Warren B. Walsh, comp. and ed., *Readings in Russian History* (Syracuse, NY: Syracuse University Press, 1948), pp. 185–187.

of the Spanish Succession, when Louis sought, upon the advice of Madame de Maintenon and with the later help of his spy, the Princess des Ursins, to secure the Spanish throne for his grandson, Philip. Although he finally succeeded in this project, the victory was a hollow one, bought at tremendous cost in lives and resources.

In this most destructive of Louis' wars, women played a major part behind the scenes. In England, during the early years, Sarah Churchill, wife of the English supreme commander, the Duke of Marlborough, consistently pressured the Queen and members of Parliament for vigorous prosecution of the war. On the other side, at the Spanish court and elsewhere on the continent, Mary of Modena, in exile with her husband, the deposed James I of England, exerted all of her influence to bolster support for France. Other women were most instrumental in bringing peace. Among them were Madame Maintenon and the Princess des Ursins, who helped persuade Louis to drop the idea of uniting the French and Spanish Bourbon monarchies. In England, after about 1709, Queen Anne, a patient and plodding monarch but at least one with some common sense, freed herself from Sarah Churchill's influence and guided her ministers toward the Peace of Utrecht.

Louis could not overcome all the power balanced against him. As France became stronger it invariably provoked more formidable counteralliances. At first, Louis faced Spain, Holland, Sweden and some German states. In the last two wars, England led a combination that included almost all of western Europe. In this anti-French alignment, the old Anglo-Dutch commercial rivalry and other traditional prejudices, such as Anglo-Dutch hatred of Spain, were subordinated to the balance of power principle.

The Treaty of Utrecht (1713) ushered in a period of general peace, lasting some thirty years. Philip V, Louis' grandson, was confirmed as king of Spain, with the provision that the two thrones would never be united. Since Spain had been declining for a century and France was drained financially, the Bourbon succession promised little for French ambitions in Europe. This was particularly true because Spain surrendered the southern Netherlands (Belgium) and its Italian holdings (Naples, Milan, and Sardinia) to the Austrian Habsburgs. In addition, Savoy was ceded to Sicily, which was subsequently traded (1720) to Austria for Sardinia. The Duke of Savoy was also recognized as a king, as was Frederick I of Prussia. In the nineteenth century, the House of Savoy would unify Italy and the Hohenzollerns would accomplish the same for Germany.

Almost all the participants except England lost more in the wars than they gained by the treaty. Holland had borne the cost of most land fighting against the French; France had been demoralized by a three-front war and a Huguenot uprising, for which it received no tangible compensation except the retention of Alsace; and Spain lost heavily to the Austrian Habsburgs. England, on the other hand, received both Newfoundland and Nova Scotia from France, plus French acceptance of English claims to the Hudson Bay area. England also retained the Mediterranean naval bases at Gilbraltar and Minorca, taken from Spain. Even more important commercially were the concessions permitting England to supply Spanish America with slaves and land one shipload of goods each year at Porto Bello in Panama. These stipulations helped England become the leading colonial power.

From Utrecht to Paris: The Duel for Empire and the Wavering Balance

The balance of European power wavered dangerously in the eighteenth century. Prussia and Russia—and even Habsburg Austria—attained great military potential, and each was tempted by power vacuums in Poland and Turkey. The situation was complicated by the difficulty in determining which of the eastern states was the most serious threat and therefore the logical object of counteralliances. To confuse matters more, both England and France were absorbed in their growing colonial rivalry, in which England was the obvious front runner. Major conflicts were on the way, although Europe was able to avoid them for some thirty years after Utrecht.

By 1730, it was apparent that France and England must soon clash over their conflicting colonial ambitions. Both empires were rapidly increasing their wealth and populations. In the Caribbean, French sugar production had surpassed the British, while French slavers were not only supplying their own islands but challenging

British trading privileges in Spanish America, as defined at Utrecht. On the other side of the world, the English and French were also scrambling to obtain influence among the petty rulers of southern India. The two powers, with their American Indian allies, were also fighting sporadic little wars in North America. In the preliminary diplomatic testing, French size and military force in Europe were balanced against British financial resources, naval power, and a larger American colonial population.

Conflict began in 1739 over British trade in Spanish America. An English captain testified before Parliament that Spanish authorities had boarded his vessel and cut off his ear, which he displayed, wrapped in cotton. The "War of Jenkins' Ear" soon spread, as France immediately supported Spain. Frederick II of Prussia, meanwhile, seized Silesia, part of the family holdings

of the Habsburg heiress, Maria Theresia, who had just succeeded to the Austrian throne. France and Spain now threw in with Frederick, along with the German states of Saxony and Bavaria. Fearful of France, England and Holland, allied with Hanover, joined Austria in 1742. By 1745, Prussia had almost knocked Austria out of the war, but fighting dragged on overseas in North America and India until 1748. The resulting Peace of Aix-la-Chapelle left Frederick with Silesia and the colonial positions of England and France about the same as they had been in 1739.

The agreements at Aix-la-Chapelle brought no peace but only a short truce of eight years. During the cessation of hostilities, France and England prepared to renew their global conflict. At the same time, Maria Theresia, having learned some lessons in international politics and effected some necessary internal reforms, joined with

THE PARTITION OF POLAND
1772–1795

☐ To Prussia
▨ To Russia
▨ To Austria
Boundary of Poland after the first partition 1772
Boundary of Poland after the second partition 1793

Tsarina Elizabeth of Russia to negotiate an alliance against Frederick, which also included Sweden and some German states. Her greatest coup, however, was recruiting France, the old Habsburg enemy, possibly with help from Madame Pompadour, Louis XV's mistress, who despised Frederick. Prussia was now effectively isolated but so was England, which was more concerned about colonial issues than agression on the continent. England therefore formed a new alliance with Prussia against France, Russia, and Austria. This shift in alliances is known as the diplomatic revolution of the 1750s.

Beginning in 1756, war was waged relentlessly on three continents—Europe, North America, and Asia (India). It is known in American history as the French and Indian War and in Europe as the Seven Years' War. Attacked on all sides by three major powers, Frederick marched and wheeled his limited forces, winning battles but seeing little prospect for ultimate victory. He even tried, with no success, to buy Madame Pompadour's influence for peace. Later he described the nearly hopeless predicament, comparing himself to a man assaulted by flies:

When one flies off my cheek, another comes and sits on my nose, and scarcely has it been brushed off than another flies up and sits on my forehead, on my eyes, and everywhere else.[4]

Frederick was saved and the war won by the narrowest of margins when a new pro-French tsar, Peter III, recalled the Russian armies from the gates of Berlin and withdrew from the war. Austria then sued for peace, leaving Frederick with Silesia.

The Seven Years' War confirmed the emergence of Prussia and Russia as great powers and prepared the way for a new diplomatic order in eastern Europe. Despite its tremendous losses, Prussia gained enormously in prestige; its internal damage would not be revealed until the nineteenth century. Russia regained the military reputation it had achieved under Peter without winning any striking victories. Austria lost prestige and was further weakened militarily but managed to retain its respectability. Turkey and Poland were the real losers in the postwar decades. In 1772, Poland lost most of its territory to the eastern powers in a three-way partition, despite Maria Theresia's protestations of remorse (see map, p. 493). In the 1790s, Poland was eliminated entirely in two partitions carried out by Prussia and Russia. Turkey, meanwhile, lost the Crimea and most of the Ukraine to the aggressive expansionist policies of Catherine the Great of Russia.

Much more significant than the war's effects on eastern Europe was its impact on Anglo-French colonial rivalry. Britain gained even more than it had at Utrecht while French colonial hopes were all but destroyed. By the Peace of Paris (1763), France lost to England the St. Lawrence Valley and the trans-Appalachian area east of the Mississippi. Spain also ceded Florida to England, receiving Louisiana west of the Mississippi from France as compensation. In the West Indies, France gave up Granada, Dominica, and St. Lucia. The French kept their main trading stations in India but were not permitted to fortify them or continue their political ties with local rulers. On the other hand, the British East India Company not only extended its political influence but acquired Bengal outright. The Peace of Paris made England the largest, wealthiest, and most powerful empire in the world.

Conclusion

The Peace of Westphalia marked a very significant turning point in European history. Following a century of destructive religious wars, it brought a new age, when Europeans longed for stability and order. This main concern was modified by the general attachment to worldly values associated with power, profit, and pleasure. Life became more frivolous as it became more secular, particularly among the wealthy. Acquiring money and credit became major objectives of businessmen looking for capital. Kings also sought money, not only for their personal enjoyment, but as the means to power. Even in the arts, there was much flamboyant display and luxurious elegance, along with a classical emphasis on order and formality.

Absolutism as a political system reached its European zenith in this era. With its control of the economy and the church, its large military establishments, and its rigid class distinctions, it met the psychological needs of its time and also supplied the force to effect necessary reforms. France under Louis XIV was a nearly perfect example of the system. Yet virtually all European states in this era were affected somewhat by absolutism in theory or fact.

The age produced its own approach to international relations. Absolute monarchy was a system for conducting war according to secular principles. Rulers felt compelled to follow their national interests, without reference to higher morality or religious maxims. Under these circumstances, it seemed that peace and international order could be achieved only by a balance of power, in which aggressive states would be checked by the counteralliances formed against them. The nearly continuous wars in this process between 1650 and 1763 brought varying fortunes to European states. Sweden, Turkey, Spain, and Poland slipped into decline or extinction. France and Austria achieved stability without establishing mastery. Prussia and Russia became major military powers, and England established its supremacy as a world empire.

Suggestions for Reading

Among the best general surveys of Europe in the period are H. O. Koenigsberger, *Early Modern Europe* (Longman, 1987); G. R. R. Treasure, *The Making of Modern Europe* (Methuen, 1985); Robert Zeller, *Europe in Transition, 1660–1815* (Univ. Press of America, 1988); and Maurice Ashley, *A History of Europe, 1648–1815* (Prentice Hall, 1973).

Special emphases on absolutism and its milieu may be found in Maurice Ashley, *The Age of Absolutism* (Merriam, 1974); William Doyle, *The Old European Order* (Oxford Univ., 1978), and Ragnhild Hatton, *Europe in the Age of Louis XIV*. The political side of absolutism is treated in J. Miller, *Bourbon and Stuart Kings and Kingship in France and England* (Duke Univ., 1988); and J. H. Shennan, *Liberty and Order in Early Modern Europe* (Longman, 1986). For economic aspects of the era and the system, see Michael Beaud, *A History of Capitalism* (Monthly Rev. Press, 1983); Philip W. Buck, *The Politics of Mercantilism* (Octagon, 1964); and Andre G. Frank, *World Accumulation, 1492–1789* (Monthly Rev. Press, 1978). Mary Fulbrook deals with religion and absolutism in *Piety and Politics: Religion and the Rise of Absolutism in England, Wurtemberg, and Prussia* (Cambridge Univ., 1984). For the burdens and accomplishments of women during the late seventeenth century, see Helga Mobius, *Women of the Baroque Age* (Abner Schram, 1984).

Excellent general overviews of the era in France are provided in Robin Briggs, *Early Modern France, 1560–1775* (Oxford Univ., 1977); V. Mallia-Milanes, *Louis XIV and France* (Macmillan, 1986); and Paul Sonnino, ed., *The Reign of Louis XIV* (Humanities Press, 1990).

Joseph Barry, *Passions and Politics: A Biography of Versailles* (Doubleday, 1972) is a highly personalized account of Louis XIV's glittering world at Versailles. See also Dianna De Marly, *Louis XIV and Versailles* (Holmes and Meier, 1987); Ragnhild Hatton, *Louis XIV and His World* (Putnam, 1972); and G. Walton, *Louis XIV's Versailles* (Univ. of Chicago, 1985). French political and social affairs are effectively depicted in Roger Mettam, *Power and Faction in Louis XIV's France* (Blackwell, 1987); W. Beik, *Absolutism and Society in Seventeenth-Century France* (Cambridge Univ., 1989); and Raymond F. Kersted, ed. *State and Society in Seventeenth-Century France* (Watts, 1975).

Three sound biographies of Louis XIV are John B. Wolf, *Louis XIV* (Hill and Wang, 1972); O. Bernier, *Louis XIV* Doubleday, 1987); and L. Marin, *Portrait of the King* (Univ. of Minnesota, 1988). For French women of the court, the salons, the markets, and the streets, see Louis Auchincloss, *False Dawn: Women in the Age of the Sun King* (Doubleday, 1984); Carolyn C. Lougee, *Le Paradis de Femmes* (Princeton Univ., 1976); Elborg Forster, ed., *A Woman's Life in the Court of the Sun King* (Johns Hopkins Univ., 1984); and the memoir of Madame de Maintenon, *The King's Way* (Penguin, 1985). See also Charlotte Haldane, *Madame de Maintenon* (Bobbs-Merrill, 1970).

For French-style absolutism in other countries, see Hajo Holburn, *A History of Modern Germany*, 3 vols., vol. I, (Knopf, 1964); T. K. Derry, *A History of Scandinavia* (Univ. of Minnesota, 1979); Eric Elstob, *Sweden, A Political and Cultural History* (Rowman and Littlefield, 1979); Michael Roberts, *Sweden's Age of Greatness* (St. Martin's, 1973); Samuel S. Franklin, *Sweden, the Nation's History* (Univ. of Minnesota, 1977); Stuart Oakley, *A Short History of Denmark* (Praeger, 1972); W. G. Jones, *Denmark* (Croom Helm, 1986); Henry A. Kamen, *Spain in the Latter Seventeenth Century* (Longman, 1980) and *Spain, 1469–1714: A Society in Conflict* (Longman, 1983); John Lynch, *Spain Under the Habsburgs*, vol. I: *Spain and America, 1598–1700* (New York Univ., 1984); R. A. Stradling, *Philip IV and the Government of Spain, 1621–1665* (Cambridge Univ., 1988); John Lynch, *Bourbon Spain* (Blackwell, 1989); and Harold V. Livermore, *A New History of Portugal* (Cambridge Univ., 1976).

For less developed absolutism in eastern Europe, see R. J. W. Evans, *The Making of the Habsburg Monarchy* (Oxford, 1984); the first volume of Norman Davies, *A History of Poland*, 2 vols. (Columbia Univ., 1981) and, by the same author, *Heart of Europe: A Short History of Poland* (Oxford, 1986). See also Robert N. Bain, *Slavonic Europe* (Arno Press, 1971).

An informative study of the Dutch maritime state is J. L. Price, *Culture and Society in the Dutch Republic During the Seventeenth Century* (Scribners, 1974). See also Pieter Geyl, *The Netherlands in the Seventeenth Century* (Barnes and Noble, 1961); Kenneth Haley, *The Dutch in the Seventeenth Century* (Harcourt Brace Jovanovich, 1972); and Charles Wilson, *The Dutch Republic and the*

Civilization of the Seventeenth Century (McGraw-Hill, 1968). Bernard H. Viekke, *The Evolution of the Dutch Nation* (Roy, 1945) is still useful.

Among the best general treatments of the whole Stuart period in England are Barry Coward, *The Stuart Age* (Longman, 1984); J. P. Kenyon, *Stuart England*, 2nd ed. (Penguin, 1986); and Blair Worden, *Stuart England* (Salem House, 1987). See also Antonia Fraser's study of English "women's lot" in the seventeenth century: *The Weaker Vessel* (Knopf, 1984) and James R. Jones, *Country and Court* (Harvard Univ., 1978).

D. Ogg, *England in the Reign of Charles II*, 2nd ed. (Oxford Univ., 1984) still provides solid coverage. For the Restoration, see R. Hutton, *The Restoration* (Oxford Univ., 1987); James R. Jones, *The Restored Monarchy* (Rowman and Littlefield, 1979); J. Miller, *Restoration England* (Longman, 1985); and H. Weber, *The Restoration Rake-Hero* (Univ. of Wisconsin, 1986). Political and social aspects of the reign are ably described in Kenneth H. Haley, *Politics in the Reign of Charles II* (Blackwell, 1985); James R. Jones, *Country and Court, 1658–1714* (Harvard Univ., 1978); and Tim Harris, *London Crowds in the Reign of Charles II* (Cambridge Univ., 1987). Among the best relevant biographies are Antonia Fraser, *Royal Charles* (Knopf, 1979); James R. Jones, *Charles II* (Allen and Unwin, 1987); and Bryan Bevan *Nell Gwyn* (Roy, 1970).

For the Glorious Revolution, see James R. Jones, *The Revolution of 1688 in England* (Weidenfield and Nicholson, 1984); K. M. Chacksfield, *The Glorious Revolution* (Winecanton Press, 1988); W. A. Speck, *Reluctant Revolutionaries: Englishmen and the Revolution of 1688* (Oxford Univ., 1989); and Stuart E. Prall, *The Bloodless Revolution* (Univ. of Wisconsin, 1985). D. Ogg, *England in the Reigns of James II and William III* (Oxford, 1984) and J. R. Weston, *Monarchy and Revolution* (Macmillian, 1985) are new editions of standard incisive works on the English political scene after the late 1680s. Among the best biographies of later English monarchs are Maurice Ashley, *James II* (Univ. of Minnesota, 1977) and Edward Gregg, *Queen Anne* (Routledge, Kegan Paul, 1980).

Two excellent short surveys of Prussian history in this period are H. W. Koch, *A History of Prussia* (Longman, 1978) and Otis Mitchell, *A Concise History of Brandenburg-Prussia to 1786* (Univ. Press of America, 1980). For revealing special studies of the Prussian political structure, see Hans Rosenberg, *Bureaucracy, Aristocracy, and Authority: The Prussian Experiment, 1660–1815* (Beacon, 1966) and Hubert C. Johnson, *Frederick the Great and His Officials* (Yale Univ., 1975). Robert R. Ergang, *The Potsdam Führer* (Octagon, 1972) is a colorful and stimulating portrait of Frederick William I, the founder of Prussian absolutism and militarism. Among the many biographies of Frederick the Great are three excellent recent ones: C. Duffy, *Frederick the Great* (Routledge, Kegan Paul, 1985); Robert

B. Asprey, *Frederick the Great* (Ticknor and Fields, 1986); and Mary Kittridge, *Frederick the Great* (Chelsea House, 1987).

The rise of the Romanov state is ably described in Otto Hoetzsch, *The Evolution of Russia* (Harcourt Brace and World, 1966) and W. Bruce Lincoln, *The Romanovs* (Dial, 1981). Sound historical studies of Peter the Great and his impact are Peter B. Putnam, *Peter, the Revolutionary Tsar* (Harper and Row, 1973); V. O. Kliuchevski, *Peter the Great* (Beacon, 1984); A. Tolstoy, *Peter the Great*, 2 vols, (Raduga, 1985); Robert K. Massie, *Peter the Great: His Life and World* (Ballantine, 1986); and H. Troyat, *Peter the Great* (Dutton, 1987).

For interesting studies of the great eighteenth-century Russian empresses who followed Peter, see Talbot T. Rice, *Elizabeth, Empress of Russia* (Praeger, 1970) and Robert Coughlan, *Elizabeth and Catherine* (New Amer. Lib., 1975). Among excellent biographies of Catherine are Vincent Cronin, *Catherine, Empress of All the Russias* (Morrow, 1978); Leslie Max-Mcguire, *Catherine the Great* (Chelsea House, 1986); and John T. Alexander, *Catherine the Great* (Oxford Univ., 1989). Perspectives on Catherine's impact are provided in Isabel De Madarlaga, *Russia in the Age of Catherine the Great* (Yale Univ., 1981) and G. S. Thomson, *Catherine the Great and the Expansion of Russia* (Greenwood, 1985).

For good general analyses of international relations in this age of developing power politics, see John B. Wolf, *Toward a European Balance of Power, 1620–1715* (Rand McNally, 1970); Geoffrey Symcox, *War, Diplomacy, and Imperialism, 1618–1763* (Walker, 1974); Theodore K. Rabb, *The Struggle for Stability in Early Modern Europe* (Oxford Univ., 1975); and Derek McKay and H. M. Scott, *The Rise of the Great Powers and the European State System* (Longman, 1983). For more specialized studies, see Carl J. Ekberg, *The Failure of Louis XIV's Dutch War* (Univ. of North Carolina Press, 1979); Michael Roberts, *The Swedish Imperial Experience, 1560–1718* (Cambridge Univ., 1984); and Paul Sonnino, *Louis XIV and the Origins of the Dutch War* (Cambridge Univ., 1989).

Notes

1. Quoted in James Harvey Robinson, *Readings in European History*, 2 vols. (Boston: Ginn and Co., 1906), vol. 1, pp. 273–275.
2. Thomas Hobbes, *Leviathan* (New York: Liberal Arts Press, 1958), pp. 106–170.
3. Quoted in F. Tyler, *The Modern World* (Farrar and Rinehart, 1939), p. 186.
4. Quoted in P. Gaxotte, *Frederick the Great* (London: G. Bell and Sons, 1941), p 357.

The Crisis of the Old Regime, 1714–1774

When Louis XIV died in 1715, he was succeeded by his five-year-old great-grandson, who later became Louis XV. This new Louis, however, was never capable of ruling as a "sun king." Although he retained all of his royal prerogatives, by the time he reached middle age he was so openly pessimistic about the future that he hoped only that the monarchy would last through his reign. He easily might have delivered the famous prophecy so often attributed to him: "Après moi, le déluge" (After me, the deluge).

Like his great-grandfather, Louis XV (1715–1774) was a symbol of European monarchy, but the monarchical system had changed significantly by the middle of the eighteenth century. It had lost prestige and was now often associated with the waste arising from costly wars and royal extravagances. An aristocratic revival, common all over Europe in the eighteenth century, also contributed to its decline. In a time which demanded reform, most European monarchies were mired down in tradition and vested interests.

While established regimes became more static, European society in the eighteenth century was increasingly dynamic. Foreign expansion entered a new phase after the seventeenth century, unleashing social and ecomomic forces that weakened monarchies and their social orders. The rising volume of colonial trade and the flood of information from the non-European world stimulated warfare and commercial rivalry among European powers. At the same time, increasing wealth further propelled the rising middle class, encouraged freedom in capitalistic endeavor, and escalated revolutionary changes almost beyond human control.

Inadequacies of the Old Regime

Absolute monarchy during the eighteenth century had developed a characteristic social structure and aristocratic way of life known as the Old Regime. By midcentury, it had acquired the sanctity of tradition, the confidence of long experience, the gentleness of maturity, and the infirmities of old age. Although no longer purposefully violent or vulgar, the Old Regime was marked by privileges, injustices, and political deficiencies.

A Social Order Based on Privilege

Perhaps the most striking feature of the Old Regime was its legalized privilege, conferring exclusive political power and fabulous wealth on a small elite, while dooming the masses to grinding poverty. The system cut across class lines. Most of the clergy and nobles were as poor as some peasants, and the great majority of the urban middle classes were denied the leisured comfort of the great bankers and merchants.

The aristocratic nature of the Old Regime derived partly from a successful counteroffensive by European nobilities after the Peace of Westphalia. Temporarily checked by such strong monarchs as Louis XIV and Peter the Great, the nobles retained or regained political power in the Habsburg domain, in Germany, and in Poland. Early in the eighteenth century, they recovered their supremacy in Sweden, in Spain, in Russia after Peter' death, and particularly in France under Louis XV.

A comparable development came in eighteenth-century England. After James II was

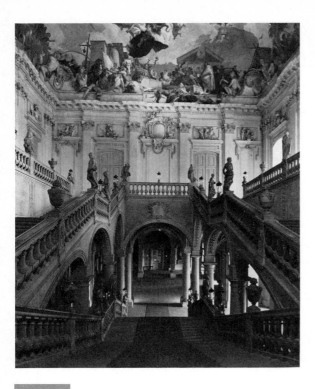

The ornate staircase and lavishly decorated ceiling of the Bishop's Palace in Würzburg, Germany, suggests the splendor and luxury enjoyed by the high clergy.

dethroned in 1688, the landed gentry—functionally a lower landed aristocracy—gained almost complete control of the House of Commons. From this base, they greatly influenced state policy through a prime minister and a cabinet that became responsible to Parliament. The gentry made government a closed system, putting members of their class into most public offices, most of the lucrative positions in the Anglican church, and most commissioned ranks in the army and navy. These privileges were shared only with a few remaining nobles, who sat in the House of Lords.

Europe's Old Regimes were topped by official ruling classes of high clergy and nobles. Combined, these two privileged orders accounted for less than 2 percent of the total European population; but the great magnates, who enjoyed real wealth and power, were concentrated in only 5000 families, among some four million titled aristocrats. Most of the true elite lived in city mansions and palaces, far away from their broad acres in the country. For their high incomes, tax

immunities, and numerous honors, they contributed almost nothing beyond decoration to church or state.

France provides a good illustration of the system. There, the church owned 20 percent of the land and collected returns equal to half those of the royal estates. The clergy included 130,000 churchmen and nuns. Although it supported some education, social work, and charities, most of its income went to 11,000 members of the higher clergy, particularly to 123 bishops and 28 archbishops. Some of their annual incomes exceeded the equivalent of $1 million, but many of the overworked lower clergy existed on $100 a year. Among the 400,000 nobles, only a thousand families were represented among the court nobility. Each aristocrat at Versailles held many honorific appointments in court service, inactive military commissions, honorary wardships of royal palaces, or obsolete provincial offices, requiring no work. Titled nobles held 20 percent of the land, most by feudal tenures, which permitted them to collect numerous customary fees from their peasants. From all such sources, high French nobles probably averaged the equivalent of well over $100,000 in annual income.

Throughout Europe, conspicuous consumption was typical of the high nobility, such as the Fitzwilliams in Ireland, the Newcastles in England, the Schönborns in Bohemia, the Radziwills in Poland, and the Esterhazys in Hungary. Prince Esterhazy owned about 10,000 acres in 29 estates. His lands included 160 market towns and 414 villages, while his revenues exceeded 700,000 florins annually, or the equivalent of $400,000. With such wealth, the magnates built elaborate town dwellings and sumptuous country retreats, filling them with priceless handcrafted furniture, rich tapestries, and fine works of art. While most people scratched for food, the high nobles enjoyed delicacies, meats, and rare fruits, which were almost unknown among common people. The nobles lived lavishly in a fantasy world, marred only by the dull ceremonies accompanying their brilliant but busy social activities.

Viewed from the top, the Old Regime appeared aristocratic, but it presented quite a different picture when viewed from the side. Most people in Europe were peasants, who constituted more than 80 percent of the total population; of these, 75 percent were landless, and many were serfs, bound to their villages, not only in Russia, Poland, and Prussia, but also in Denmark. Among city dwellers, only a tiny minority were wealthy bankers and overseas merchants. A larger number, some 10 percent of the population, were shopkeepers, artisans, and professional people. This proportion was higher in Holland, England, and northern Italy, but generally lower elsewhere, particularly in eastern Europe, where it dropped sharply. At the bottom of urban society was the mass of indigent poor, barely able to survive. Commoners of all economic levels paid most taxes. They were subject to legal discrimination in favor of the nobility, from whom they were also separated by differences in education, speech, manners, dress, and social customs.

This general pattern was evident in the French third estate. Consisting of some 26 million people, it was more varied in its extremes than the first two estates of clergy and nobles. At the top were about 75,000 wealthy bankers and merchants who had not bothered to buy titles. Another 3 million urban dwellers consisted largely of lesser merchants, shopkeepers, lawyers,

In *The Oyster Luncheon* (1731), the self-indulgent French nobles are more concerned with their own sensual pleasures than with the plight of the peasants or the well-being of the country as a whole.

doctors, craftsmen, and people of the streets, the latter being especially prevalent in Paris and the ports. The great mass of commoners in France, as in Europe generally, were the 23 million peasants who tilled the soil. Most held some property rights to their lands, but many were tenants or sharecroppers. As late as 1789 about a million were still serfs. Almost all peasants, serf or free, paid fees to their local nobles. Government taxes were irregular but heavy everywhere; the *taille*, or main land tax, fell heaviest on the class least able to pay. French peasants lived better than serfs in eastern Europe or the starving farm laborers of England, but life in a French village was a constant struggle for survival.

Malfunctioning Government

While the Old Regime favored the nobility and clergy at the expense of other citizens, its governmental system displayed major defects. Absolute monarchies had promised to bring order out of feudal chaos, correct the abuses of organized religion, and provide national economic security. By the eighteenth century, however, absolutism was failing. Nobilities were back in power, taxes were rising, economic enterprise was restricted, and most European monarchies were extravagant, corrupt, and inefficient.

Political inefficiency took many forms. Laws were a perlexing mix of variable local customs, feudal presumptions, and royal decrees. Provincial tolls were imposed on trade within states. Coinages, as well as weights and measures, were sometimes different in adjoining provinces. Because of overlapping authorities, courts and officials were not sure of their jurisdictions. Public servants avoided responsibilities, fearing they would be blamed for error, a situation which produced bureaucratic delay and elaborate red tape. Every form of bribery, fraud, and distortion characterized governments at every level. Such evils were difficult to combat, because legalized privilege was so common.

Again, France exemplifies the general situation. Despite all efforts at centalization, Louis XIV had left a chaotic jumble of councils and committees, each with its expanding network of officials and clerks, whose conflicting claims to authority were barely less perplexing than their fussy procedures. The French had no body comparable to the English Parliament for registering public opinion; the Estates General had not convened since 1614. Government was most deficient in handling revenues, which it attempted to do without budgets, regularized accounting, or uniform assessments. If possible, French local government was even more chaotic. Late medieval districts, with their bailiffs and seneschals, coexisted with ornamental provincial governors and royal intendants, who assumed most control of local affairs after the seventeenth century. Some 360 different legal codes and 200 customs schedules applied in different parts of the country. Attempts to achieve uniformity invariably provoked vested local interests, who sponsored exceptions and compromises, further complicating the situation.

French government, like some others, was severely damaged by the indolence of its monarch, Louis XV, who hated the tedium of governing. Until the 1740s, he turned his government over to an able minister, Cardinal Fleury, who maintained peace and reasonable stability. Even then, however, policy and appointments were affected by court intrigues. These endeavors often involved noblewomen, who traded their favors for political influence. Such indirect but effective "mistress power," not only flourished among the court nobility but also with the king himself. His Polish wife, Maria Leczinska, endured a series of Louis' chief mistresses, who were installed in the palace near the king's bedchamber, granted titles, showered with costly gifts, and paraded by Louis in public. They earned France a reputation for petticoat governance, but their influence was negligible during Fleury's tenure.

Mistress government came into full flower in France after 1745, the era of Madame Pompadour (1721–1764). Born Jeanne-Antoinette Poisson to middle-class parents and married later to a royal tax collector, as Madame d'Etioles, she contrived to meet and bewitch Louis at a public ball in 1745. For the next few years, as the newly titled Marquise de Pompadour and the king's favorite, she dominated court life at Versailles. She was also the recipient of 17 estates, had a personal staff of more than 50 attendants, and enjoyed unlimited access to the royal treasury. After 1749, she left Louis' bed but remained a trusted advisor, monitoring all of his appointments and sharing many of his conferences with officials and diplomats. She used her influence against the Jesuits and was an ardent advocate of the Austrian alliance, which led to French defeat in the Seven Years' War. She was a strong and determined woman, truly devoted to the king and to France, but the methods which she rose to power reflect the weakness of the system.

Four years after Pompadour's death, Louis took another mistress. Jeanne Bécu (1743–1793), the illegitimate daughter of a seamstress, was trained for her life's mission while living with Jean Du Barry, a notorious rake and minor noble on the fringe of the French court. He arranged for her to meet the king, who was immediately stricken by her beauty and took her into the palace. A contrived marriage with the brother of her former lover made her a countess. As Madame Du Barry, she was now qualified to enter the ruthless competition of the court arena. Lacking Pompadour's drive and political instincts, she nevertheless became a tool for the conservative nobles, who helped her overcome her rivals in a series of backbiting struggles for royal favor. Until Louis died in 1774, she revelled in her power, her jewels, and her luxurious houses. As if in expiation for these years of glory, she died nineteen years later on a Paris guillotine crying, "please do not hurt me."[1]

Like Louis, many European kings squandered fortunes on mistresses, palaces, courts, and idle aristocrats, thus contributing to the common problem of rising public debt. This was also partially encouraged by developing capitalism, which made borrowing possible. Another significant cause was the maintenance of military and naval forces strong enough to protect colonial possessions and play power politics in Europe. By the late eighteenth century, each of the major continental powers, France, Russia, and Austria, kept standing armies of 250,000 men.

European rulers might have borne these expenses if they had been able to govern by brute force, as former emperors had done. They were prevented from doing so by their dependence on an international market, which supplied their needs only in exchange for goods, bullion, or credit. Ultimately, they were forced to borrow, putting their states at the mercy of bankers and their own credit ratings. Such financial accountability, almost unknown in the ancient world, placed a serious restriction on European monarchies.

Public finance was even a serious problem for England, the most commercially advanced state in Europe. In 1700, after war with France, the state debt reached £13 million sterling and was secured by the bank of England. The public debt continued to rise, despite the government's efforts in the 1720s to eliminate it with profits from the South Sea Company, an overseas trading monopoly. This venture failed following a wild stock speculation (the "South Sea" bubble). Colonial wars with France drove the debt still higher. Between 1763 and 1783, it rose from £140 million to £238 million. England was very wealthy and could carry this tremendous burden relatively easily, but the debt nevertheless contributed to internal political unrest.

For France, where the economy was less expansive and commanded less foreign credit, the problem was more serious. Badly weakened by Louis XIV's wars, France averted financial disaster in the 1720s and 1730s only by Fleury's peaceful foreign policy and reduced military spending. After 1742, however, deficits mounted steadily while France fought three major wars. In 1780 the French debt amounted to an equivalent of $600 million; interest payments absorbed half the annual income of approximately $33,750,000; and total government expenditures were $40 million. Admittedly, the French debt was not excessive, in comparison with England's. What the French lacked, however, was the Dutch capital that poured into England. Without adequate foreign credit, France was thrown back on its own resources, which caused a tripling of taxes between 1715 and 1785. The ensuing tax burden, plus the growing anxiety of wealthy government creditors, created the most serious threat to the Old Regime in France.

Dynamic Forces in European Society

Economic and social forces challenged European absolutism as it was becoming more static and inefficient. Society had been changing steadily since the late medieval period, but the rate of change was so rapid in this era that the process itself seemed unique. Every part of Europe, from Holland past the Russian borders, and every social class, from peasants to the most tradition-bound nobles, felt the insecurity and restlessness inherent in a general social transformation.

Expanding Commercial Capitalism

The primary cause for change was a vibrant capitalistic economy, developing so rapidly that it could hardly be controlled or even predicted. Absolutism had risen on a steady wave of economic expansion, but the wave was now so strong that it tossed the political vessel about and determined the craft's direction, no matter how the tiller might be set. Capitalism generated new economic pursuits, developing almost spontaneously outside of established institutions. It also brought unprecedented increases in the volume of trade.

Four new conditions produced the commercial boom of the eighteenth century. First, government demand for goods reached astronomical heights, as huge standing armies required mountains of food, clothing, arms, and ammunition. The French army, varying between 140,000 and 250,000, was still the largest, but even Britain had a military establishment of some 80,000, including a strong navy. Rising European population created another expanding market, demanding bulk commodities. Developing plantation agriculture in the tropical colonies provided another decided stimulus to foreign trade. Finally, Brazilian gold and diamond strikes raised prices and encouraged all European business after the 1730s.

Inflation brought mixed economic results. Wages, for example, increased far less than food prices, thus depressing the condition of workers. French nobles, who received fixed money fees from their peasants, or English landlords who had let their fields on long-term leases, were also hurt badly. On the other hand, those landowners who rented to casual tenants or received payment in kind gained appreciably. The former were likely to be capitalistic investors of the same class who profited from the general increase in the cost of goods. At times their profits soared in a wildly speculative market.

The rapidly expanding volume of foreign commerce was a clear indicator of eighteenth-century business property. Although the Dutch imperial decline brought a decrease, English and French foreign trade increased 500 percent during the period. In 1789, imports from the French West Indies, an index of profits in sugar and slaves, were ten times higher than in 1716. At Liverpool, the major English port for sugar and slaves, annual imports jumped from 27,000 to 140,000 tons between 1700 and 1770.

The Growth of Free Enterprise

Such prosperity created serious problems for mercantilist systems. As opportunities for profit increased, capitalists sought gains outside traditional enterprises and even the legal limits set by governments. Some of these endeavors were deliberate efforts to evade the law; others — perhaps most — were responses to new, unanticipated economic conditions. This rising free-enterprise capitalism, as distinct from mercantilist state capitalism, was evident in every phase of the eighteenth-century economy.

A rising demand for food encouraged the trend in agriculture. As food prices soared, investors poured their surplus capital into land. This was most typical of England, but the agricultural boom, on somewhat smaller scales, touched France, Holland, the Austrian Netherlands, and even the vine cultures of Italy and Spanish Catalonia. Wherever it developed, capitalistic agriculture emphasized efficiency and profits, which usually required procedures that were inconsistent with the traditional cooperative methods of rural villages.

Three English commercial landowners pioneered in concentrating capital investments to improve agricultural techniques. Jethro Tull (1674–1741) carefully plowed the land, planted in neat rows, using a drill he invented, and kept the plants well cultivated as they grew to maturity. Viscount Charles Townshend (1674–1738), nicknamed "turnip Townshend," specialized in restoring soil fertility by such methods as applying clay-lime mixtures and planting turnips in crop rotation. Robert Bakewell (1725–1795) attacked the problem of scrawny cattle. Through his select breeding of choice animals, he was able to increase the size of meat animals and also the milk yields from dairy cows.

Another Englishman, Arthur Young (1741–1820), an ardent publicist for the new agriculture, lectured throughout Europe and edited a farm journal. Translated into many foreign languages his writings popularized the advantages of well-equipped farm and economical agricultural techniques. He did much to free European agriculture from the unproductive methods of the past.

New agricultural techniques required heavy capital investment and complete control of the land. The new methods could not be used on common fields, where villagers shared customary rights. Selective stockbreeding could not be practiced with animals in a community herd. Capitalistic landlords thus sought to fence, or enclose, their acres. By outright purchase, foreclosure, suit, fraud, or even legislation, they tried to free their lands from lingering manorial restrictions, particularly from traditional rights to community use of the commons.

The enclosure movement, which began in the sixteenth century, reached its peak after 1750. Most prevalent in England, it was also typical of the continent. Because French peasants were so important as taxpayers, the government could not allow many to be driven from the land. Consequently, French capitalistic landlords were still complaining about manorial restrictions in the late 1780s. In England, where the lower aristocracy (gentry) had already become capitalists and were also powerful in government, they were able to push 2000 enclosure laws through Parliament between 1760 and 1800 (see map, p. 503).

In industry, the movement toward free enterprise produced the "domestic system," which involved contractual arrangements between capitalists and handworkers. Capitalists supplied materials to the workers in their homes and later collected the products, to be sent through another stage of finishing or sold directly on the market. The system became common in industries where demand was high, returns attractive, and capital available. Domestic manufacturing moved early to the country, away from the regulations imposed by city guilds. The advantages and disadvantages were those associated with

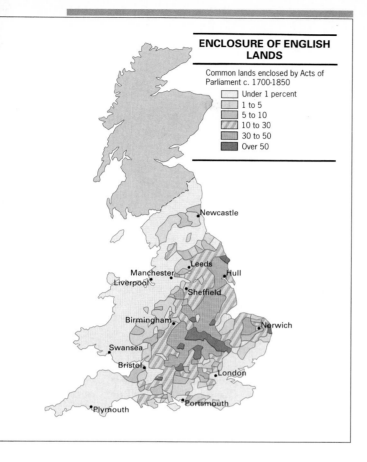

ENCLOSURE OF ENGLISH LANDS

Common lands enclosed by Acts of Parliament c. 1700–1850

- Under 1 percent
- 1 to 5
- 5 to 10
- 10 to 30
- 30 to 50
- Over 50

Newcastle

Leeds
Manchester
Liverpool
Hull
Sheffield

Birmingham

Norwich

Swansea

Bristol

London

Plymouth
Portsmouth

unregulated industry. Contracts were freely negotiated and prices were usually low, but capitalists, workers, and consumers faced considerable risks.

Domestic industry was common all over western Europe after 1500, but it developed most in the eighteenth century, particularly in England. It was typical of all essential processes in the woolen industries, notably spinning, weaving, fulling, and dyeing. The system also spread among other textile industries, such as linens and cottons, which provided a decided stimulus to the trend in the 1700s. Other industries affected were lace, leather, silk, paper, glass, pottery, and the metal trades. A high proportion of those employed in all these industries were woman, because they were readily available for part-time work at home and because they could be paid less than men. Children were also often employed. By 1750, English domestic manufacturing involved more than four million workers.

The career of Ambrose Crowley illustrates the domestic system in the infant English iron industry. Crowley started as a blacksmith who worked as a guildsman in Greenwich, where he accumulated a little capital. Around 1680, he moved to a small Durham village and built a domestic organization for the large-scale production of hardware. By 1700, the village had become a thriving town of 1500 workers. Most of them were employed by Crowley, who rented them their houses and supplied some of their tools as well as ore and fuel. The village produced nails, locks, bolts, hammers, spades, and other tools, which Crowley marketed elsewhere. As a wealthy and respected citizen, he was knighted in 1706.

In chapter 18 we described the rise of banks, stock exchanges, and insurance companies as part of the developing cooperation between capitalists and governments. Such cooperation does not fully explain the rise of these institutions. Although the great public banks usually operated under government charters and the new financial institutions affected government policies, all functioned within the opportunities and limitations of the free market. To this extent, they demonstrated the characteristics of free-enterprise capitalism.

Joint stock companies were drastically reoriented during the late 1600s. Originally they were exclusive monopolies, both in their areas of operation and in their limited number of stockholders. Prospective investors were denied stock or charged excessive fees. The companies were generally criticized and their trading rights were regularly violated by competitors and smugglers. Under pressure, the English East India Company and similar firms steadily liberalized their policies until eventually most stocks were sold on the open market. Free sale of stock greatly increased opportunities for investment and multiplied the number of joint stock companies. By 1715, more than 140 existed in England. This situation also encouraged a mushroom growth of stock exchanges, which sprang up in taverns and coffeehouses all over western Europe. In the early eighteenth century they had become necessary institutions in the private sector of Europe's economy.

Banking performed a similar necessary role. In a sense, the banks of Sweden, Amsterdam, and London were examples of state operation; their

Daniel Defoe, The Cloth Market at Leeds

The author of *Robinson Crusoe* also wrote on other subjects. This is a revealing picture of preindustrial capitalism in England.

Early in the Morning, Tressels are placed in two Rows in the Street, sometimes two Rows on a Side, cross which Boards are laid, which make a kind of temporary Counter on either Side, from one End of the Street to the other.

The Clothiers come early in the Morning with their Cloth; and, as few bring more than one Piece, the Market-days being so frequent, they go into the Inns and Public-houses with it, and there set it down.

At about Six o'Clock in the Summer, and about Seven in the Winter, the Clothiers being all come by that Time, the Market Bell at the Old Chapel by the Bridge rings; upon which it would surprise a Stranger, to see in how few Minutes, without Hurry, Noise, or the least Disorder, the whole Market is filled. . . .

As soon as the Bell has ceased ringing, the Factors and Buyers of all Sorts enter the Market, and walk up and down between the Rows, as their Occasions direct. Some of them have their foreign Letters of Orders, with Patterns sealed on them, in their Hands; the Colours of which they match, by holding them to the Cloths they think they agree to. When they have pitched upon their Cloth, they lean over to the Clothier, and, by a Whisper, in the fewest Words imaginable, the Price is stated; one asks, the other bids; and they agree or disagree in a Moment. . . .

If a Merchant has bidden a Clothier a Price, and he will not take it, he may go after him to his House, and tell him he has considered of it, and is willing to let him have it; but they are not to make any new Agreement for it, so as to remove the Market from the Street to the Merchant's House.

The Buyers generally walk up and down twice on each Side of the Rows, and in little more than an Hour all the Business is done. In less than half an Hour you will perceive the Cloth begin to move off, the Clothier taking it up upon his Shoulder to carry it to the Merchant's House. At about half an Hour after Eight the Market Bell rings again, upon which the Buyers immediately disappear, the Cloth is all sold; or if any remains, it is carried back into the Inn. . . .

Thus you see £10,000 or 20,000 worth of Cloth, and sometimes much more, bought and sold in little more than an Hour, the Laws of the Market being the most strictly observed that I ever saw in any Market in *England*.

If it be asked, How all these Goods at this Place, at *Wakefield*, and at *Halifax*, are vended and disposed of? I would observe,

First, That there is an Home-consumption; to supply which, several considerable Traders in *Leeds* go with Droves of Pack-horses, loaden with those Goods, to all the Fairs and Market-towns almost over the whole Island, not to sell by Retail, but to the Shops by Wholesale. . . .

There are others, who have Commissions from *London* to buy, or who give Commissions to Factors and Warehousekeepers in *London* to sell for them, who not only supply all the Shop-keepers and Wholesale Men in London, but sell also very great Quantities to the Merchants, as well for Exportation to the *English* Colonies in *America*, which take off great Quantities of the coarse Goods, especially *New England, New York, Virginia*, &c. as also to the *Russia Merchants*. . . .

The third Sorts are such as receive Commissions from abroad, to buy Cloth for the Merchants chiefly in *Hamburg*, and in *Holland, &c.* These are not only many in Number, but some of them very considerable in their Dealings, and correspond with the farthest Provinces in *Germany*.

From Daniel Defoe, *Tour Through Great Britain, 1724–1725* in Elizabeth K. Kendell, ed., *Source-Book of English History* (New York: Macmillan, 1912), pp. 321–24.

directors were often government advisors, authorized to perform semiofficial functions, such as issuing notes and financing public debts. In another sense, however, these institutions became integral parts of the free market economy, providing the necessary credit for business enterprise while creating their own nonofficial commercial methods and institutions. Moreover, smaller banks developed within the private monetary and credit systems. The first English country bank was founded as a private enterprise in 1716 at Bristol; by 1780, there were 300 in the country.

Major insurance companies, banks, and stock exchanges formed an integrated institutional system, functioning within a free international market. Their standardized procedures became so complicated that they could not be understood by ordinary people. That strange new world of business enterprise, unlike the political world, was not controlled directly by anyone, not even by the power of concentrated capital. Goods and credit, commodity prices and wages, monetary values and stock quotations, all interacted according to their own laws, which could be studied but only partially predicted.

A Turbulent European Society

This second stage of capitalist revolution was both cause and result of powerful social turbulence, marked by urbanism, migration, and an unprecedented population explosion. The number of people in Europe increased 68 percent, from about 110 million in 1700 to 185 million in 1800; some 50 million of the increase came after 1750. European population growth during the era was much higher than in Asia or Africa and also above that of any earlier comparable period; it has not been exceeded since, not even in the post-World War II era of the twentieth century.

This tremendous expansion was common to most of Europe between 1650 and 1800. The English population rose from 5 to over 9 million; that of Russia went up from 17 to 36 million; and the French population rose more moderately, from 21 to 28 million. The gain from 275,000 to 4 million in the English American colonies was by far the most striking. Other areas, which had earlier seen declines, posted gains.

Spanish population rose from 7.5 million to 11 million people, while that of Italy expanded from 11 to 19 million.[2]

Such statistics go far toward explaining the eighteenth-century social world. The incredible population increase may have been partially caused, for example, by the insecurity of impoverished rural families, who regarded children as sources of support or excuses for state aid. It is equally obvious that it was a product and a reflection of such varying social conditions as rising agricultural production; cleaner underclothes and dishes, made possible by the new textile and pottery industries; cheaper transportation of food supplies; better water and sewage facilities, resulting from wider use or iron piping; and improved medical techniques, which both combatted infant mortality and increased life expectancy. There can be little doubt that surging population contributed to the growth of cities, an increasing surplus of labor, vagabondage, and rising economic demand. It was thus an integral part of the universal social change.

As the population increased, people moved in all directions. Some, like the Swiss and Irish, became foreign mercenaries. Others, like the French Huguenots, were victims of religious persecution; of the original 300,000 refugees, 40,000 settled in England and some 20,000 of the most skilled went to Prussia. Both the Prussians and Russian governments regularly imported specialized craftsmen. German peasants by the thousands also went east to acquire land in the Hungarian or Russian Ukraines. In the eighteenth century, more than 750,000 English and 100,000 Irish settlers arrived in America. These were the largest national contigents of a European migration which numbered some 2 million people.

Life in the New World varied widely among the Spanish, Portuguese, French, and English colonists, but in all the colonies, the frontier atmosphere encouraged self-reliance and optimism. Upward mobility was everywhere much more possible overseas than in Europe at that time. This was particularly true in the English American colonies, where Benjamin Franklin could become rich after begininng life penniless or Thomas Jefferson, the son of a poor backcountry farmer, could marry into a wealthy family.

The adventurous spirit that had developed overseas returned to Europe in the eighteenth century. Europeans were fascinated by the cultures of foreigners, whether Chinese, Africans, or Native Americans. Everything American excited great curiosity, particularly after mid-century, when regular mail service brought Europe into closer contact with the colonies. Americans and British merchants developed strong ties based on common profits. Americans frequented certain London coffeehouses, and some former Americans won election to Parliament. Tremendous interest was aroused by retiring employees of the East India Company, many of whom had risked everything on making their fortunes in India and had succeeded beyond their wildest dreams. Their country estates excited widespread wonder and envy.

Migration overseas was accompanied by rising urban populations. This occured to some extent in eastern Europe, notably in Prussia and Austria, but the trend was especially pronounced in the west, where commerce and finance were centered. England was most affected. The populations of English towns and cities generally grew faster than those of rural areas, although migration from the country was a relatively insignificant factor. In England, as on the continent, population increased most decisively in those commercial centers which were involved in foreign trade.

The scope and significance of the trend may be quickly illustrated by a few figures. London's population rose from 400,000 to 900,000 between the Peace of Utrecht (1713) and the French Revolution (1789). Other English cities, such as Bristol, Norwich, Liverpool, Leeds, Halifax, and Birmingham, which had been country towns in the 1600s, became medium-sized cities, ranging in size between 20,000 and 50,000 inhabitants (see map below). On the continent, the population of Paris reached 800,00 by 1789, and the number of residents in Bordeaux, Nantes, Le Havre, and Marseilles all increased appreciably. Amsterdam, the nucleus of the Dutch urban cluster, increased from 200,000 residents in 1670 to 250,000 in 1800. Farther east were other expanding cities such as Hamburg, Frankfurt, Geneva, Vienna, and Berlin; populations of the latter two exceeded 100,000 in the eighteenth century.[3]

Cities, of course, were the breeding grounds of ideas and contention. There were the books and newspapers, coffeehouses, sailors from

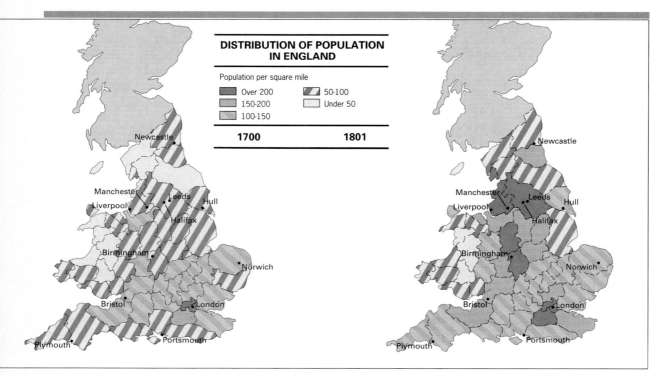

DISTRIBUTION OF POPULATION IN ENGLAND

Population per square mile

Over 200
150-200
100-150
50-100
Under 50

1700   1801

English artist William Hogarth used his engravings as "morality plays" to preach virtue and campaign against vice. *Gin Lane* depicts the London poor in alcoholic delirium, their escape from the misery of their lives.

The conspicuous display of wealth, more than birth, came to be associated with social status. Bewigged merchants as well as nobles were resplendent in white silk coats, knee breeches, silk stockings, and gold-braided hats. Young English fops, on their way up, might spend the equivalent of $2000 for a single outfit and lose that much more of borrowed money at the gaming tables. Well-to-do women decked themselves out in imported brocades, ostrich feathers, fans, furs, parasols, and silver lace. Home decor featured Persian rugs and imported draperies of chintzes and chiffons. There was also a passion for objects from China and Japan—china, screens, lacquered trays, and gilded tables. With their appetite for ostentation and uncultivated tastes, the newly rich, particularly low-born East India Company men, scandalized old English aristocrats.

Although sanitation and the quality of life among the poor remained terrible, there were some improvements for those above poverty level. In a few of the most progressive urban areas, some streets were paved and sewers constructed. Water was piped to some private mansions, and public baths were increasing. At the same time, social graces were becoming more refined. Manners, for example, improved somewhat, as middle-class Europeans set their tables with beautiful china and silver, provided napkins, and lifted food with forks rather than fingers. No longer did they throw bones on the floor or use pocket knives to pick their teeth. Eating, therefore, became more of an art than a simple necessity or a purely sensual satisfaction.

Such refinements suggested that the comforts of the nobility were being shared by the upwardly mobile middle classes. Some 250,000 European families had acquired this status by the middle of the eighteenth century. In France the middle class constituted about 8 percent of the population and had acquired about 25 percent of the land. Like their counterparts among the English landed gentry, they enjoyed privileges formerly confined largely to the aristocracy. Meanwhile, an increasingly large number of individuals entered the middle class from below. Shopkeepers, lawyers, and professionals improved their conditions and raised

foreign lands, and varied populations, exchanging views and challenging prejudices. Urban life was not only exciting, it was also more impersonal, dangerous, and frustrating. Using every kind of trick and deceit, a large criminal element flourished in the streets. Mobs were easily formed and more easily aroused, particularly in London and Paris, which regularly faced riots in the eighteenth century. Unlike the relatively placid inhabitants of rural villages, city dwellers thrived on such change and diversity.

Rising Expectations

New wealth and new ideas brought higher living standards to the middle classes, opening opportunities for social display and hopes for advancement. Even ordinary people could acquire the muslins and calicoes that permitted them to dress better and thus imitate their social superiors. More products stimulated appetites for even more goods, accenting the

Fantastic hair styles, like that shown in this engraving, were one of the ways in which the French upper classes displayed their extravagance.

their expectations. For the first time, they became truly conscious of individual interests, apart from those of a caste or a dynasty.

The rising middle class enjoyed luxuries but valued respectablility, rejecting the flamboyant display so typical of nobilities. Most accented the importance of private family life and religion. Indeed many shopkeepers and merchants had reinterpreted Calvinism as it spread among them, identifying usury and profit seeking with diligent stewardship in God's service and translating Calvin's original idea of a "calling" to mean profession or business. This integration of Calvinism and capitalism was also reflected in the similarity between elected church deacons and the representative boards of joint stock companies. Whether they were Calvinists or not—and many were not—members of the middle class were ambitious, aggressive, cunning, and, above all, competitive. They prided themselves on being "self-made." A perfect example was William Miles of Bristol, who started with almost nothing, amassed a fortune in the sugar trade, and ended by controlling the largest refining operation in his city.

Although largely denied government posts at the higher levels, many members of the new middle class possessed great potential for leadership. They were determined, confident, and often well educated. Many were members of the medical and legal professions, which were striving to earn respect. Physicians and lawyers often became very concerned about public issues. Lawyers, particularly, were familiar with parliamentary procedures and were trained to express themselves clearly. Middle-class leaders were also closer than the nobles to urban workers, with whom they could still share some common experiences and values.

Improving conditions among the middle classes brought some moderate gains for women. The refinement of manners, the growing concern for fads and fashions, along with the emphases upon family ties and religious morality, were all reflections of growing feminine influence. The same family emphasis and the middle class penchant for individualism encouraged women to demand more voice in choosing their husbands; fewer middle-class marriages were negotiated by parents without consulting their offspring. More wealth and leisure afforded increased opportunities for women's education, as indicated in the large number of new schools for girls, particularly in France and England. As a result, women became more prominent in literary and artistic fields. Educated and fashionable middle-class women often attended or hosted salons, which were centers for intellectual discussion, open to anyone with recognized talents. The salons originated in France but were copied all over Europe, a most notable example was the "bluestocking" gathering at the homes of wealthy English ladies.

Problems Facing Old Regimes

Despite its great promise, Europe's dynamic society generated countless ambitions, frustrations, and resentments associated with the rising middle classes, crowded cities, dispossessed peasants, rising populations, contrasting cultures, and an expanding world economy. Standing directly in the way of these forces were most absolute monarchies and their Old Regimes. Because of their vested interests and their rigidity, they were peculiarly incapable of dealing with social problems threatening from every side.

The Prevalence of Human Misery

Terrible human misery among the poor was typical of Europe in the eighteenth century. Like the conflicts that preceded it, the Seven Years' War had destroyed crops, ruined cities, created hordes of starving refugees, and depopulated whole provinces. Armies contributed to prevailing diseases, such as smallpox, typhus, and malaria. Flies swarmed about the sanitary waste and horse manure that filled roads and streets, encouraging the spread of typhoid and infantile diarrhea, which killed thousands of children.

Beggar Feeding a Child by Giacomo Ceruti. When they could not work, the poor turned to begging. When they could no longer beg, they died.

While epidemics of plague spread through central Europe, rickets and tuberculosis reflected the malnutrition preventing half the workers from achieving marginal proficiency. The mortality was appalling: half of the children died before they were six; 20 percent of fertile women died in childbirth; and life expectancy was only about 28 years. For a large proportion of Europeans, unemployment, homelessness, grinding poverty, and hunger was inevitable. Indeed, horrible reality could only be escaped, on rare affordable occasions, in alcohol.

Life in the cities may have been exciting, but it was also miserable for many. The urban poor made up some 20 to 25 percent of city populations; most had come in from the country seeking survival. Without homes, friends, or steady work, they lived, as best they could, working at transitory menial jobs, begging, stealing or selling themselves as prostitutes. Only a social notch higher were the apprentices and journeymen of the decaying craft guilds, who also faced real hardships. The discipline, particularly for apprentices, was hard, hours were long, and wages were barely enough to buy their food. Crowded into filthy quarters, without adequate light, air, or bathing facilities, they lived dull lives fraught with ignorance, disease, crime, and squalor. Bad as these conditions were, they might always get worse, for as the guilds faced competition, many shops were forced to close, forcing their journeymen to become wandering artisans among the vagabonds on the roads.

Most of these pitiful derelicts were products of the century's most serious social challenge: the problem of rural poverty. Despite a general prosperity, lasting until about 1770, European peasants suffered severely from rising food prices amid increasing agricultural specialization. The resulting seller's market turned aristocrats into aspiring capitalists, willing to gouge their peasants in order to realize greater profits. Some nobles, particularly on the continent, revived and enforced their old manorial rights to fees and services. Others moved in an opposite direction by eliminating the peasants' medieval rights and using hired labor to work their lands. Either way, the peasants lost a substantial amount of their livelihood and were likely to become criminals, vagrants, or part of an alienated subculture. They ceased to be assets

Arthur Young, Conditions Among Eighteenth-Century French Peasants

Young made these observations just before the French Revolution. He saw better conditions elsewhere but was appalled at the backward state of French agriculture and the great gap in living standards between the nobility and the lower classes in the country.

SEPTEMBER 1ST. To Combourg. The country has a savage aspect; husbandry not much further advanced, at least in skill, than among the Hurons, which appears incredible amidst enclosures; the people almost as wild as their country, and their town of Combourg one of the most brutal filthy places that can be seen; mud houses, no windows, and a pavement so broken, as to impede all passengers, but ease none; yet here is a château, and inhabited. Who is this Mons. de Chateaubriand, the owner, that has nerves strung for a residence amidst such filth and poverty? Below this hideous heap of wretchedness is a fine lake, surrounded by well-wooded enclosures. Coming out of Hédé, there is a beautiful lake belonging to Mons. de Blossac, Intendant of Poitiers, with a fine accompaniment of wood. A very little cleaning would make here a delicious scenery. There is a château [Château de Blossac], with four rows of trees, and nothing else to be seen from the windows in the true French style. Forbid it, taste, that this should be the house of the owner of that beautiful water; and yet this Mons. de Blossac has made at Poitiers the finest promenade in France! . . .

SEPT. 5TH. To Montauban. The poor people seem poor indeed; the children terribly ragged, if possible worse clad than if with no clothes at all; as to shoes and stockings they are luxuries. A beautiful girl of six or seven years playing with a stick, and smiling under such a bundle of rags as made my heart ache to see her. They did not beg, and when I gave them anything seemed more surprised than obliged. One-third of what I have seen of this province seems uncultivated, and nearly all of it in misery. . . .

JULY 11TH. Pass [Les] Islettes, a town (or rather collection of dirt and dung) of new features, that seem to mark, with the faces of the people, a country not French.

JULY 12TH. Walking up a long hill, to ease my mare, I was joined by a poor woman, who complained of the times, and that it was a sad country. Demanding her reasons, she said her husband had but a morsel of land, one cow, and a poor little horse, yet they had a *franchar* (42 lb.) of wheat, and three chickens, to pay as a quit-rent to one seigneur; and four *franchar* of oats, one chicken and 1 *sou* to pay to another, besides very heavy tailles and other taxes. She had seven children, and the cow's milk helped to make the soup. But why, instead of a horse, do not you keep another cow? Oh, her husband could not carry his produce so well without a horse; and asses are little used in the country. It was said, at present, that *something was to be done by some great folks for such poor ones, but she did not know who nor how,* but God send us better, *car les tailles et les droits nous écrasent.* This woman, at no great distance, might have been taken for sixty or seventy, her figure was so bent, and her face so furrowed and hardened by labour; but she said she was only twenty-eight. An Englishman who had not travelled cannot imagine the figure made by infinitely the greater part of the countrywomen in France; it speaks, at the first sight, hard and severe labour. I am inclined to think, that they work harder than the men, and this, united with the more miserable labour of bringing a new race of slaves into the world, destroys absolutely all symmetry of person and every feminine appearance. . . .

From Arthur Young, *Travels in France,* edited by Constantia Maxwell. (Cambridge: Cambridge University Press, 1929), pp. 107ff.

to the state—as either taxpayer or soldiers—and instead became potentially dangerous and expensive liabilities.

Although faring better than the serfs of eastern Europe, western peasants faced serious difficulties. Some in France were reduced from tenants to laborers when merchants bought up land to profit from rising food prices. Under Louis XV, some 30,000 rural vagrants thronged French roads. Some 35 percent of the peasants who had managed to acquire land were still paying manorial fees and services to local lords, in accordance with feudal law. Earlier these exactions had hurt the peasants' pride more than their chances for survival, but when the practice was stepped up during the depression of the 1780s, many lost their land.

In England, the situation was quite different. Although English manorial fees and services were abolished in the seventeenth century, many villages had retained their medieval rights to pasturage and fuel-gathering on the commons. These rights were lost to enclosures. From 1750 until the end of the century, 40,000 to 50,000 small farms disappeared into large capitalistic estates. Some of those forced from the land went to the cities, some because agricultural laborers at pitifully poor wages, and some went into parish poor houses, which were soon filled to overflowing.

Relief for the poor was one of the most persistent and perplexing problems facing England in the eighteenth century. Rural unemployment became a way of life, encouraged by the large landowners, who wanted cheap labor. More than a million unemployed people were languishing in 4000 parish work houses at the end of the century. Local taxpayers used every means to prevent vagrants from settling in their parishes, thus prohibiting the unemployed from finding work. Even a pregnant woman, or one with a sick child, might be given a few pennies and turned away. Ultimately the government built larger workhouses for fewer parishes, attempting to spread the cost of poor relief. Such policies destroyed the initiative of the poor, who turned to public welfare as their source for relief.

Oppressive Conditions for Women

Such conditions were especially oppressive to women, whose general prospects grew worse in the eighteenth century, despite some slight gains among those in the upper classes. Rising capitalism diminished work opportunities for all women, but poor widows were hit hardest, as suggested by the number starving in English workhouses. Women's life expectancy was five years less than men's. This fact is explained partially by the large proportion of mothers who

In some mining regions, women miners were common. In this engraving from an 18th-century French work, women work at the pit head of a primitive coal mine.

died in childbirth; a significant factor here was malnutrition. Poor women lacked calcium in their diets and were therefore subject to hemorrhaging. For women among the rural and urban poor, life was a nightmare of deprivation, suffering, and struggling to survive.

This was particularly true of poor country women, as noted by Arthur Young, who described a French peasant woman of 28 years but appearing to be 60 or 70. Capitalistic agriculture and the accompanying aristocratic encroachments depressed farm wages, forcing farm laborers to leave the villages in search of work. Women had to stay with the children and eke out support for the family in domestic spinning or weaving. Some worked in the fields for lower wages than men. As work opportunities declined, thousands of women took to the roads, carrying their babies and begging for food. Many died with their children by the roadsides. Others joined gangs of robbers or smugglers. The hardiest and the most determined reached the cities, where the best hope for a displaced peasant woman was employment as a cook or maid with a well-to-do family.

Among the urban poor, a woman's life was not much better than in the villages. The lucky few who were hired as household servants were paid much less than men, housed in cramped quarters, fed scraps, and frequently exploited sexually by their masters. Employment outside domestic service was extremely limited, because women were denied membership in most craft guilds. A few could find work in nonguild industries, spinning, weaving, sewing, or working leather for long hours at starvation wages in sweatshops. They were often employed at dirtier and heavier jobs in the metal trades and in the coal fields, both above and below ground. Another option, and one chosen by many women who could not easily find other work, was prostitution, which was growing rapidly in every large city, with 50,000 known prostitutes plying their trade in London and more than 40,000 in Paris at about the same time. Their lives were marked by social degradation, venereal disease, and continuous harassment by civil authorities, who allowed them to operate but subjected them to periodic imprisonment.

A vast social chasm separated poor women from those of the wealthy classes; yet at the top social levels another broad gulf divided the sexes. Royal and noble women, as we have seen, exercised considerable political power in this era, but except for the numerous ruling monarchs, women operated as satellites of the men they manipulated. Among both aristocratic women and those of the wealthy middle class, many were withdrawn from meaningful work as mothers and managers to become social drones, advertising, in an ornamental way, the positions of their husbands. Legally, upper-class wives remained subordinated to their husbands in the disposition of property and rights to divorce; the double standard concerning marital fidelity was still supreme, both socially and legally. Indeed, despite their improving education and their activities in literature and the arts, eminent eighteenth-century men, including Rousseau, Frederick the Great, and Lord Chesterfield, characterized women as childlike, irresponsible, and ruled by passion. In the council chambers and the counting houses, it was still a man's world.

Social Discontent

Even a quick survey of privileges, exploitation, and living conditions under the Old Regime reveals obvious sources of social discontent, which arose not only because of human misery and injustice—both conditions had been equally prevalent in earlier times. But now the spirit of change and improvement, coupled with the hopeless confusion and inefficiency of most monarchies, aroused general feelings of dissatisfaction. Peasants and city workers were certainly not pleased with their lot, although they lacked the confidence, education, and opportunities to register direct protest. The middle class, particularly the lawyers, were much better equipped to voice their grievances, which they did often. For monarchs, however, the most frightening development should have been the critical attitude of many nobles. The nobles' casual indifference proved that privilege no longer worked among the ruling class to ensure loyalty and leadership.

Because essential records are not available, no one can say for sure what were the attitudes of peasants on the continent. They surely varied from place to place, as did the conditions. Generally, peasants lacked long-range political objectives but were easily aroused by immediate threats to their well-being. Seventy-three peasant rebellions occurred in eighteenth-century Europe, including ones in Poland (1730s), Bohemia (1775), and Russia (1773–1775). The suffering English farm laborers rioted six times between 1710 and 1772. French peasants were generally docile, but nevertheless precipitated violent upheavals in 1709, 1725, 1740, 1749, and 1772. Arthur Young recognized the surly attitudes and contempt for authority among French peasants. In 1789, when they could express grievances to delegates headed for the Estates-General, they were universally bitter against feudal exactions and government taxes.

Workers, in general, were more aggressive and perhaps better informed than peasants but more confused by the complexities of their problems. While their numbers were increasing with the size of cities, they were becoming alienated from the upper classes by periodic unemployment and inflation. Rioting among workers and the idle poor of the cities was thus quite common, particularly in London and Paris. Such outbreaks, however, were usually more violent than politically significant. Workers did recognize two potential enemies. One was the capitalist who contracted for labor and used political influence to eliminate government welfare. The other enemy was the guild, which exploited the journeyman in favor of the master. To combat these enemies, workers formed some weak organizations in England and France. Their efforts, however, usually failed for want of leadership.

That leadership was available in the middle class, whose members were most conscious of defects in the Old Regime and most aggressive in their attitudes. Although they lent money or paid the taxes that supported governments, they were everywhere excluded from political participation. In England, the House of Commons was dominated by the gentry and the House of Lords by the nobles. Local government in England and France was monopolized by self-perpetuating cliques. In both France and England the middle class had wealth without responsibility, intelligence without authority, and ability without recognition. Small merchants and shopkeepers, in particular, were suspicious of government favors, lucrative offices, and monopolies. They

wanted, as one merchant told Colbert, to be left alone so they could mind their businesses. Their wants were in direct opposition to the absolutist political ideal.

Middle-class discontent, like some discontent of the peasants, arose more from thwarted expectations than from terrible suffering. Upward mobility, from middle class to aristocracy, was a by-product of economic prosperity all over Europe, particularly in England and France. Such upward movement took many forms—purchase of land and titles, marriage, even reward for personal services of lawyers, doctors, tutors, or governesses. This middle-class struggle for respectability was individualistic and competitive so long as opportunities were open. Unfortunately, room at the top was limited; as the middle class increased, more of its members sought to ascend the social ladder. They met with repeated frustrations as the Old Regime became stable. At this point, ambitious middle-class outsiders became dangerously hostile to the system.

Most dissenting action, whether physically violent or merely vocal, came from men, but women were also represented among the malcontents. They were regularly involved in local uprising against the high cost of bread, the introduction of machines to depress labor, and rising taxes. A striking case of female activism occurred in 1770, when a mob of Parisian women left their work places and protested the deporting of their vagrant children to the colonies; their endeavor succeeded temporarily but did not end the practice. Such actions were not yet directed against the Old Regime itself. Nor were the writings and agitations of middle-class women among the English humanitarians. One of these was Hannah More, who supported the English Evangelical movement against slavery. Other English women, led by the Countess of Huntingdon, helped popularize Methodism among the English working classes. Later in the century, as we shall see in chapter 21, other French and English women would go further, championing women's rights, along with "the rights of man."

The main voices of opposition from outside the Old Regime in this era came from middle-class men, but aristocratic insiders were also discontented. Gains achieved by the nobles in Sweden, Spain, Austria, and even France increased their confidence and whetted their appetites for more power. Nobles at the top were frantically determined to maintain their positions; indeed, they professed to believe that they were more legitimate rulers than were the kings. This was partially an effort to combat middle-class influence, for nobles were often heavily in debt and feared legal reforms that might require them to pay. Only a few lesser nobles, resenting the court cliques, dreamed of making common cause with the middle classes to change the system. Aristocratic criticism was indeed varied, but none of it promised cooperation with the kings in curtailing special privileges. On this point nearly all aristocrats were in rebellious agreement.

Difficulties in Enforcing Mercantilism

Perhaps the most serious problems facing monarchs were those related to enforcing mercantilism. In the sixteenth century, merchant-bankers had accepted the system because they shared common interests with kings in combatting the Catholic Church and the feudal nobilities. As time passed, however, monarchical states became increasingly paternalistic and ordered while capitalism developed spontaneously in the direction of more freedom.

In eighteenth-century Europe, the success of mercantilism varied widely between East and West. In Prussia and Russia, reforms were effected through state control and worked well, compared with what had gone before; state-imported craftsmen and tools from western Europe continued to improve the economies of both monarchies. Habsburg efforts met with less success, because the Empire was unable to impose regulations effectively on the aristocracy. Meanwhile, most states in western Europe could not easily keep their controlled maufactures competitive in the world market.

This was particularly true of France. Government regulations favored luxury goods over bulk commodities, which limited French participation in world trade. Reliance on urban guilds created another limitation. These medieval monopolies were given the responsibility for enforcing thousands of minute regulations in every aspect of industry. Government inspectors then sought to monitor the regulatory actions of the guilds. The system, which suffered from vested interests, local politics, corruption, and bureaucratic confusion, provoked periodic confrontations, particularly when it was extended into the countryside. In 1770, the guilds and the French government attempted to stop the domestic production of printed calicoes. More than 16,000 people died in the violent conflicts and subsequent executions. On one day in Valence, 631 offenders were sentenced to the galleys, 58 were put to torture on the wheel, and 77 were hanged. Yet despite all such efforts, printed calicoes continued to be printed and sold illegally in France.

England experienced another kind of industrial problem. Because most guild monopolies had passed with the seventeenth century, domestic industry faced few legal obstacles; but it did experience frequent functional crises. Despite widespread business prosperity, wages failed to keep up with the steady inflation. Between 1756 and 1786 wages rose by 35 percent, while food prices increased by more than 60 percent. Workers also had to accept periodic unemployment even in good times. They were thus inclined to resist the wage system and agitate for state intervention against low wages and high prices. Their bitter discontent was expressed in violent riots, most notably in 1765 and 1780.

Difficulties in industry were mild compared with those in foreign trade. All mercantilist economies attempted the careful control of external commerce, but the increased volume and consequent promise of rich profits from such enterprise encouraged widespread smuggling. No government of a coastal state was sufficiently wealthy to police a long and irregular coastline. Moreover, the coast guards, port authorities, and customs officials charged with enforcing trade restrictions were usually so corrupt that they were ineffective. Thus, despite feeble efforts to stop it, illegal trade flowed with growing pressure through rotten and fragile mercantilists sieves, violating increasingly complicated commercial laws. To meet this problem, governments resorted to private contractors, often granting immunity from the laws as payment for enforcing the regulations. The resulting monopolies assumed and usually abused government authority.

English controls were probably more successful than the French or the Spanish, but they were extremely costly in the long run. A great body of officials—more than 1250 in London alone—cost the government more than the amounts they were supposed to save in revenues. In the second half of the century, government imposed stricter controls over the trade of the American colonies. As the result of this mercantilist revival, smugglers almost took over the English coasts and the colonies were pushed toward armed rebellion.

Smuggling was big business in the New World, where it exceeded legal trade in the 1700s. West Indian planters of all nationalities conducted illicit commerce with English colonial merchants. New England timber and manufactures were regularly exchanged for French molasses, which was then made into rum and smuggled into Europe. Half the trade of Boston in 1750 violated English laws; Rhode Island and Pennsylvania merchants grew rich supplying the French during the Seven Years' War; and 80 percent of all teas used in the English colonies before 1770 came in free of duties. In addition, large quantities of tobacco were landed illegally in England with the connivance of Virginia and Carolina planters.

Smuggling was just as common in Europe, where every seacoast teemed with illegal traders. Families grew wealthy in the business, and fathers trained their sons to continue their enterprises. Contraband runners and government agents engaged in continual civil war, using intelligence operations, pitched battles, and prepared sieges. Systematic enforcement was almost impossible, because officials were bribed or personally involved, witnesses refused to testify, and juries often acquitted offenders caught in the act. During their classic era, after the Seven Years' War, English smugglers operated openly in almost all west country ports, including Bristol and Liverpool. On the other side of the country, desperate smuggling cliques roamed Kent, Sussex, and East Anglia. One of these, the notorious Hawkhurst gang of 500 armed men, forced farmers to store smuggled goods. The goods were then moved, under armed convoys, from depot to depot and ultimately to waiting London merchants. During the American Revolution, when the government attempted to stop this traffic, civil war nearly resulted, and smuggling was not appreciably curtailed.

Ordinary people accepted smuggling but tried to avoid entanglement in its dangerous web. One night in 1752, Horace Walpole found one inn filled with smugglers and moved on to the next, which was occupied by excise men. Walpole expressed relief in his diary for having passed safely as a "neutral" through "both armies." Another illuminating commentary was provided in 1765 by a Norfolk parson, who made the following entry in his journal:

> Andrews, the smuggler brought me this night about 11 o'clock a bag of Hyson tea of 6 lb. weight. He frightened us a little by whistling under the parlor window just as we were going to bed. I . . . paid him for the tea at 10s., 6d. per pound.[4]

Another illegal enterprise, closely related to smuggling, was piracy. It too was encouraged by the mercantilist policies of European states and by the fortunes to be made in foreign goods. In the seventeenth century, groups of freebooting adventurers operated out of the West Indies. By 1700 they were working with smugglers in western England, who refitted their ships and marketed their goods. They also did a thriving business with the colonies, where pirate ships were built to order in New England shipyards. Merchants in Carolina, Virginia, Rhode Island, Pennsylvania, and New York regularly took pirate cargoes after the English Navigation Acts prohibited foreign ships from entering colonial ports. Piracy, like smuggling, was considered a trade, and pirate crews were dedicated profit-seekers, organized to share their booty according to written contracts. Until the English navy cleared the Caribbean in the early eighteenth century, piracy ranked with slaving and smuggling as among the most profitable maritime enterprises.

The Failure of Monarchical Reform

At any time after the middle of the eighteenth century, an urgent need for reform challenged every major European state. Neither the nobles nor the clergy could provide the necessary leadership. Although they had acquired social status and power everywhere, they were committed to exercise that power, according to the code of their class, in protecting their privileges. Yet those privileges, particularly immunity from taxation, had to be limited if the states were to avoid collapse. Action by the monarchs, who symbolized their nations' well-being and supposedly wielded absolute power, seemed the best hope for solution of the problem.

The French Debacle: Enlightenment and Despotism

The necessity for monarchical leadership was well understood in France, where philosophers expressed it in the theory of "benevolent" or "enlightened" despotism. The proponents were mostly French middle-class intellectuals, such as Voltaire and Diderot (see ch. 20). Their writings were widely read in many European courts, a continued deference to French ideas, which were considered to be the latest in intellectual fashion. Their appeal, however, was more than a literary fad. European kings were easily influenced, because the need for forceful royal action was so pressing that it could hardly be ignored.

The last Bourbon kings in France were affected by these reforming ideas of the Enlightenment. Tax and budgetary reform, if not "enlightened despotism," was attempted half-heartedly in France under Louis XV and his grandson, Louis XVI (1774–1792). Although he was almost indifferent to affairs of state and dozed through his council meetings, Louis XV tried twice to tax the nobles and once to curtail the special privileges of the traditional courts, particularly the most prestigious, privileged, and aristocratic *Parlement* (court) of Paris. Each attempt led to years of controversy between the government and the nobles; in each instance, Louis ultimately gave up the fight.

Louis XVI was well meaning put poorly educated, indolent, and shy. Shirking government business, he spent his happiest hours in a workshop, tinkering with locks. His child-bride, the frivolous Habsburg princess, Marie Antoinette, furnished him with no wisdom or practical support. Although dimly aware of problems, Louis was no more successful than his grandfather. The clamor of the nobles forced him to abandon proposals for eliminating the more undeserved pensions and levying a very modest tax on all landed property.

Enlightened Despotism Outside France

Unlike the later Bourbons, some eighteenth-century kings were known as "enlightened despots." Perhaps the major figure in this "monarch's age of repentance" was Frederick II, the Great, of Prussia, who won a reputation as a model ruler during the last half of his reign. As an avowed admirer of Voltaire, his writings popularized the ideal monarch as "the first servant of the state," "the father of his people", and "the last refuge of the unfortunate."[5] "Old Fritz," as his subjects called him, was slavishly committed to his principles. He left his bed at five each morning and worked until dark, reading reports, supervising, traveling, listening to complaints, and watching over every aspect of government.

Under Frederick, Prussia was known as the best-governed state in Europe. Within only a few years, it had recovered economically from the terrible ravages of war, largely through the state's aid in distributing seed, livestock, and tools. Frederick imported new crops, attracted skilled immigrants, opened new lands, and tried to promote new industries, such as silk and other textiles. He codified the law and reorganized the courts, along with the civil service. Following the ideas of the French Enlightenment, he established civil equality for Catholics, abolished torture in obtaining confessions from criminals, decreed national compulsory education, and took control of the schools away from the church. Until he died in 1786, Frederick worked diligently at improving Prussia.

His achievements, nevertheless, were more despotic than enlightened, and his successes were matched by failures. Although Frederick played the flute, wrote French poetry, and corresponded with Voltaire, his reforms were continuations of his father's mercantilism rather than adjustments to changes in his time. His monetary policy caused inflation, and this, along with his penchant for state monopolies, seriously hurt many Prussian merchants. Frederick's agricultural program did not touch serfdom. His use of French tax collectors precipitated civil disorders, and his consistent appointment of aristocrats as officials helped exclude the middle class from government. Even his religious and educational reforms were marred by official discrimination against Jews and failure to provide necessary funds for schools. Frederick's approach succeeded so well because it came at a time when mercantilism still worked in Prussia. It left much to be done later, when social change would require quite different policies.

Frederick's contemporary, Catherine II of Russia was also known in her time as an enlightened despot. Having learned the politics of survival at the Russian court, she and her lover had conspired with palace guards to put aside her erratic husband, Peter, and have herself declared Czarina in 1762. Although a ruthless Machiavellian in foreign affairs and a libertine, Catherine was a sensitive woman who appreciated the arts, literature, and the advantages of being considered enlightened. She corresponded with Voltaire and gave Diderot a pension. The latter even stayed at her court for a year, meeting with her daily for private discussions on intellectual subjects, including improvements for her empire.

Catherine's reign brought considerable enlightenment and social progress. She subsidized artists and writers, permitted publication of controversial works, established libraries, patronized galleries, and transformed St. Petersburg with beautiful architecture. Catherine also founded hospitals and orphanages, notably those providing foundling children with improved education, one of her main interests. After many years of study, she launched a national system of elementary and secondary schools during the decade after 1775. In that same year, she began a reorganization of local government, including the cities, one of many administrative reforms which literally demilitarized the empire. She secularized church land, secured some rights for serfs, and restricted the use of torture; but her early, much publicized efforts to modernize and codify Russian laws were sabotaged by the aristocracy.

Catherine's program, however, like that of Frederick, was limited in scope and significance. Almost every reform had been attempted or suggested earlier and enhanced royal authority. For example, rigid state control and political indoctrination of the curriculum was fixed in the new educational system. Local government, after 1775, was controlled by aristocratic landowners. Such deference to the aristocracy was typical of Catherine's later internal policies after Pugachev's revolt, when the nobles' alarm forced

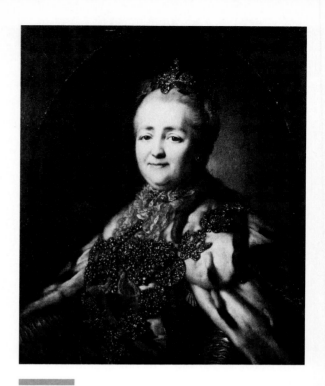

Catherine the Great of Russia. Although she is usually regarded as an enlightened despot, her liberalism was more eloquent theory than actual practice.

her to issue a charter giving them freedom from taxes, release from compulsory government service, and guaranteed ownership of their serfs. The reaction thus begun was continued during the French Revolution, when Catherine reversed most of her earlier stated libral opinions and imposed severe censorship. Her political legacy was a rigid autocracy, based on support from an aristocratic elite.

The most sincere of the would-be benevolent despots was Joseph II (1780–1790), the son of Maria Theresia and her successor as Habsburg ruler of Austria. He was a true product of the Enlightenment, intelligent and well educated; Catherine the Great called him "the most solid, profound, and best-informed mind I have ever met."[6] He was also completely converted to the principles of the philosophers. "I have made philosophy the legislator of my empire," he wrote to a friend in 1781, shortly after his succession.[7] During his whole reign, he fancied himself a royal voice of reason, fighting for human progress against ignorance, superstition, and vice.

Joseph II, Two Letters

Joseph's brand of "enlightened despotism," as well as his inflexibility and his jealousy of more renowned monarchs, are revealed in these private letters, written in the 1780s.

To Count Kollowrat, Grand Chancellor of Bohemia, and First Chancellor of Austria [October 1784].

Sir,—For the encouragement of home productions, and in order to check the progress of luxury and fashion, my commands respecting a general prohibition of foreign merchandise have been made known.

The Austrian commerce has become more passive in consequence of the increasing consumption of foreign productions, and the funds of the state, which has thereby lost more than twenty-four millions annually, would be this time have been nearly exhausted, but for the produce of our excellent mines.

It has been hitherto, one would almost think, the particular object of the Austrian government to benefit the manufacturers and merchants of the French, English, and Chinese, and to deprive itself of all the advantages the state must necessarily enjoy, when it provides for the national wants by national industry.

I know what sensations the prohibition caused among the merchants . . . and I have conversed with Prince Kaunitz on this subject, but I granted them nothing, except that I prolonged the term for their disposing of the foreign merchandise; and more they do not deserve; they are merely the commissioners of the other European merchants.

As to the rest, Prince Kaunitz will give the necessary instructions to the officers of the Custom-houses, that inventories may be made of the stock; that depots may be established; and in general, that such dispositions may be made as will ensure the execution of my orders.

To Tobias Philip, Baron von Gebler, Bohemian and Austrian Vice-Chancellor [March 1785].

Mr. Vice-Chancellor,—The present system of taxation in my dominions, and the inequality of the taxes which are imposed on the nation, form a subject too important to escape my attention. I have discovered that the principles on which it is founded are unsound, and have become injurious to the industry of the peasant; that there is neither equality, nor equity, between the hereditary provinces with each other, nor between individual proprietors, and therefore it can no longer continue.

With this view I give you the necessary orders to introduce a new system of taxation, by which the contribution, requisite for the wants of the state, may be effected without augmenting the present taxes, and the industry of the peasant, at the same time, be freed from all impediments.

Make these arrangements the principal object of your care, and let them be made conformably to the plan which I have proposed, particularly as I have nominated you President of the Aulic Commission, appointed for that purpose.

Adieu, Gebler! Hasten every thing that brings me nearer to the accomplishment of my plans for the happiness of my people, and, by your zeal, justify the respect which they have always had for your services.

Source: Harry J. Carroll et al., eds., *The Development of Civilization*, 2 vols. (Glenview, IL: Scott, Foresman, 1970), vol. 2, pp. 142–43.

Joseph's reign was an explosion of reform effort which threatened to topple much of the old aristocratic Habsburg structure. He proposed to simplify Catholic services, abolish the monasteries, take over church lands, remove religion from education, and grant civil equality to Protestants and Jews. Attacking the ancient landed establishment head-on, he planned to tax the nobles and free the serfs. With increasing revenues, he hoped to pay for a national education system, balance the budget, and improve opportunities for industry and trade. The whole undertaking would be consolidated and regulated under a comprehensive code of laws.

Despite their theoretical benefits, Joseph's endeavors aroused a storm of protest, which lasted throughout the reign and brought him practical failure. For all of his interest in progress, Joseph was a hard-headed and narrow-minded autocrat, incapable of flexibility, who was determined to build a centralized state on the Prussian model. His administrative reforms were aimed not only at higher efficiency but also at centralized government over all the many-cultured Habsburg territories. His attempted unification of administration alienated the Hungarians and caused revolts in Belgium, Bohemia, and the Tyrol. Peasants were angry because he subjected them to compulsory military service; the clergy harangued against him; and the nobles conspired to hinder the conduct of government at every level. He died in 1790, painfully aware of his failed policies and unfulfilled ideals.

Other less well known rulers of the period were probably more successful. One was Joseph's brother, Leopold of Tuscany, who was not only enlightened but also flexible and practical. Without throwing his little country into turmoil, he abolished the Inquisition and reformed the penal code, according to the principles of the well-known Italian humanist philosopher, Cesare Bonesana Beccaria (1735–1794). Another successful enlightened despot was Charles Frederick of Baden, who freed the serfs, promoted agrarian development, and achieved the fiscal regularity to make his little country a most prosperous German state. Gustavus III of Sweden seized power from the nobles by force. He then reorganized the justice system, abolished torture, reformed agriculture, made taxes more equitable, improved education, decreed religious toleration, and established freedom of the press. Unfortunately, he was assassinated. Charles III of Spain crushed the Jesuits, simplified the legal system, improved education, and balanced the budget, but his regime was a cruel dictatorship.

Even with all their good intentions and achievements, benevolent despots proved incapable of rooting out the deep-seated evils of the Old

Lithograph of Austrian emperor Joseph II working in the field. His abolition of serfdom was the most revolutionary decree of this enlightened despot, but his most lasting reform was his reorganization of the legal system.

Regime. Most of them underestimated the need for change and overestimated the durability of absolutist systems. All were dependent upon, and therefore prisoners of, outmoded aristocratic orders. Finally, they were often limited by chaotic administrative systems and mounting public debts. They were caught between a static past and a dynamic future.

Conclusion

Western European society in the eighteenth century was struggling hard against itself. The established regimes were becoming more fixed, while at the same time forces of change were growing with such intensity that they could not be permanently resisted.

These forces generated countless frustrations in conflicts arising from new middle-class interests, urbanism, expanding population, and tremendously widening opportunities for profit. Overseas expansion contributed, in one way or another, to the whole process. Free-enterprise capitalism was also common to all the forces of change. It substituted social incentives—mainly profit incentives—for the force and fear that drove the engines of absolutism. This new fuel could not fire safely in the old cylinders.

The situation called for radical adjustment, a complete retooling rather than a little tinkering. European monarchies were heavily in debt; their revenues could not meet expenses; they wasted vast sums on an upper class that gave little service; they openly perpetuated injustices; and their administrations were not only hopelessly inefficient but flagrantly corrupt. Even more dangerous was the growing alienation among nobles, as well as among the middle and lower classes.

Attempted reforms by kings produced too little and came too late. The policies of benevolent despots, for the most part, touched only the surface of the problems. Other monarchs, particularly the later Bourbons in France, were so lazy, bored, or naïve that they could not face realities. The nobles were in position to act decisively, but their efforts were naturally directed toward resisting necessary reforms.

Suggestions for Reading

Excellent general European surveys include Maurice Ashley, *A History of Europe, 1648–1815 (Prentice-Hall, 1973) and Matthew Smith Anderson, Europe in the Eighteenth Century*, 3rd ed. (Longman, 1987). For more interpretive coverage, see Vincent J. Knapp, *Europe in the Era of Social Transformation, 1700–Present* (Prentice-Hall, 1976); and Robert Zeller, *Europe in Transition, 1660–1815* (Univ. Press of America, 1988). Narrower national concentrations are provided in Louis R. Gottschalk, *Toward the French Revolution* (Scribner's, 1973); Dorothy Marshall, *Eighteenth-Century England* (Longman, 1974); and D. Jarrett, *England in the Age of Hogarth* (Yale Univ., 1986). *Britain in the Age of Walpole* (St. Martin's, 1985), edited by Jeremy Black, is a collection of interesting special studies.

William Doyle, *The Old European Order 1660–1800* (Oxford, Univ. 1978) is a superb study, covering all aspects of the Old Regime. In addition, see E. Neville Williams, *The Ancien Régime in Europe* (Harper and Row, 1970) and Catherine B. Behrens, *The Ancien Régime* (Norton, 1989). For France, see G. Chaussinand-Nogoret, *The French Nobility in the Eighteenth Century* (Cambridge Univ., 1985); Catherine B. Behrens, *Society, Government, and the Enlightenment* (Harper and Row, 1985); and J. C. Riley, *The Seven Years War and the Old Regime in France* (Princeton Univ., 1986). Intimate biographical insights into the French royal court are presented in O. Bernier, *Louis the Beloved* (Doubleday, 1984); Nancy Mitford, *Madame Pompadour* (Harper and Row, 1968); and Stanley Loomis, *Du Barry* (Lippincott, 1959). For similar analyses of the English system, see W. B. Willcox, *The Age of Aristocracy*, 4th ed. (Heath, 1983); John V. Beckett, *The Aristocracy in England*, (Blackwell, 1986); and T. H. White, *The Age of Scandal* (Oxford. Univ., 1986).

Michel Beaud, *A History of Capitalism* (Monthly Review, 1983) gives a brief but sound account of the major trend. The last two volumes of Immanuel Wallenstein's *The Modern World System* (3 vols.): vol. 2, *Mercantilism and the Consolidation of the World Economy* (Academic, 1980) and vol. 3, *The Second Era of Great Expansion of the Capitalist World Economy* (Academic, 1988) are excellent for fine details but hard going for beginners. See also Carlo M. Cipolla, *Before the Industrial Revolution* (Norton, 1980).

Dynamic European economic growth is strongly emphasized in Fernand Braudel, *Civilization and Capitalism* (2 vols.): vol. 2, *The Wheels of Commerce* (Harper and Row, 1986); N. Rosenberg, *How the West Grew Rich* (Basic Books, 1986); and Andre G. Frank, *World Accumulation, 1492–1789* (Monthly Review, 1978). See also Ralph Davis, *The Rise of the Atlantic Economies* (Cornell Univ., 1973); Herman Kellenberg, *The Rise of the European Economy* (Gerharde Benecke, 1976); and Gunnar Persson, *Economic Growth in Pre-industrial Europe* (Blackwell, 1988). For capitalistic development in England, see Ralph Davis, *The Rise of English Shipping in the Seventeenth and Eighteenth Centuries* (David and Charles, 1972); James A. Yelling, *Common Field and Enclosure in England, 1450–1750* (Archon, 1977); J. J. McCusker, *The Economy of British America, 1607–1789* (Univ. of North Carolina, 1986); and I. K. Steele, *The English Atlantic* (Oxford Univ., 1986).

For economic problems facing the old regimes, see, in addition to the above, Jan de Vries. *The Economy of Europe in an Age of Crisis, 1600–1750* (Cambridge Univ., 1976). Difficulties in regulating the import trade are ably treated in Frederick F. Nicholls, *Honest Thieves; the Violent Heyday of English Smuggling* (Heinemann, 1973); and R. Guttridge, *Smugglers* (Dorset, 1987). The following works depict the adventurous business of piracy: Philip Grosse, *The History of Piracy* (Rio Grande, 1988); Frank Sherry, *Raiders and Rebels: The Golden Age of Piracy* (Morrow, 1987); John F. Jameson, *Privateering and Piracy in the Colonial Period* (Kelley, 1970); John Esquemiling, *Buccaneers of America* (Dorset, 1988); and Robert R. Ritchie, *Captain Kidd and the War Against the Pirates* (Harvard Univ., 1989).

Numerous informative works treat the dynamic social trends of the period. Colin McEvedy and Richard Jones, *Atlas of World Population History* (Penguin, 1978) is a handy reference for monitoring population growth; and Herbert Moller, *Population Movements in Modern European History* (Macmillan, 1964) is still useful. For urban growth, see Jan de Vries, *European Urbanization, 1500–1800* (Harvard Univ., 1984) and Paul M. Hohenberg, *The Making of Urban Europe, 1000–1950* (Harvard Univ., 1987). Changes in the European class structure are treated in George Rude, *Europe in the Eighteenth Century: Aristocracy and the Bourgeois Challenge* (Harvard Univ., 1985) and Jerome Blum, *The End of the Old Order in Rural Europe* (Princeton Univ., 1978). Some obvious social threats to European monarchies are described in Jerome Blum, *The European Peasantry From the Fifteenth to the Nineteenth Century* (Prentice-Hall, 1978; M. S. Anderson, *War and Society in Europe of the Old Regime* (St. Martin's, 1988); and Frederick Krantz, *History from Below: French and English Popular Protest, 1600–1800* (Blackwell, 1988). For negative conditions affecting European women, see Helga Mobius, *Women of the Baroque Age* (Abner Schram, 1984).

For the French class structure and its discontents, see Isser Woloch, *The Peasantry in the Old Regime* (R. E. Kreiger, 1977); and Elinor G. Barber, *The Bourgeoisie in Eighteenth-century France* (Princeton Univ., 1975). Government bad judgment and oppression is convincingly established by Warren C. Scoville's *The Persecution of the French Huguenots and French Economic Development* (Univ. of California, 1960). See also R. D. Gwynn, *The Huguenot Heritage* (Routledge, Kegan Paul, 1985). For the role of eighteenth-century French women, see Sania Spencer, ed., *French Women of the Age of the Enlightenment* (Indiana Univ., 1984) and Joan Landes, *Women and Public Sphere in the Age of the French Revolution* (Cornell Univ., 1988).

Roy Porter, *English Society in the Eighteenth Century* (Penguin, 1983) and J. C. D. Clark, *English Society, 1688–1832*

(Cambridge Univ., 1985) provide excellent accounts of the social scene in England. Robert W. Malcolmson focuses on life among the working classes in his *Life and Labor in England, 1700–1780* (St. Martin's, 1981). For conditions in the country, see L. M. Cantor, *The Changing English Country-side, 1400–1700* (Routledge, Kegan Paul, 1987) and P. Horn, *Life and Labor in Rural England, 1760–1850* (Macmillan, 1987). Some indication of English social problems may be gained from Leslie A. Clarksin, *Death, Disease, and Famine in Pre-industrial England* (St. Martin's, 1975); and J. C. Clark, *Revolution and Rebellion: State and Society in England in the Seventeenth and Eighteenth Centuries* (Cambridge Univ., 1986). Problems facing English women are defined in Barbara Kanner, *Women of England* (Archon, 1979); Alice Clark, *Working Life of Women in the Seventeenth Century* (Routledge, Chapman, and Hall, 1982); and Bridget Hill, *Eighteenth-Century Women* (Unwin Hyman, 1987).

For the pros and cons of monarchical reform, see Geoffrey Bruun, *The Enlightened Despots* (Holt, Rinehart and Winston, 1967); John G. Gagliardo, *Enlightened Despotism* (Crowell, 1967); and J. F. Brennen, *Enlightened Despotism in Russia,* (P. Lang, 1987). Excellent biographies of Frederick the Great and Catherine the Great are included in Suggested Readings at the end of chapter 18.

Notes

1. Stanley Loomis, *Du Barry* (New York: J. B. Lippincott, 1959), p. 303.
2. Colin McEvedy and Richard Jones, *Atlas of World Population History* (New York: Penguin, 1978), pp. 18. 43, 57, 79, 101, 107, and 286.
3. For rising urbanization, see Jan de Vries, *The Economy of Europe in an Age of Crisis, 1600–1700* (New York: Cambridge University Press, 1976), pp. 87–88; William Doyle, *The Old European Order* (Oxford: Oxford University Press, 1978), pp. 28–33; and J. D. Chambers, *Population, Economy, and Society in Pre-industrial England* (New York: Oxford University Press, 1972), pp. 115–121.
4. Quoted in Neville Williams, *Contraband Cargoes* (Hampden, CT: Shoe String Press, 1961), p. 98. See also p. 128 for Walpole's entry.
5. Quoted in James Harvey Robinson and Charles A. Beard, *Readings in European History,* 2 vols. (Boston: Ginn and Co., 1908), vol. I, pp. 202–205.
6. E. Neville William, *The Ancien Régime in Europe* (New York: Harper and Row, 1970), p. 424.
7. Ibid.

The European Dream of Progress and Enlightenment

Science, Art, and Philosophy in the Eighteenth Century

In the eighteenth century, while royal absolutism faced serious problems, many learned and thoughtful Europeans held a shining vision of the future. They saw civilization advancing toward a future of diminished ignorance, brutality, and exploitation. Most believed that human reason, having finally reached its true potential, would bring the downfall of Old Regimes, which were being recognized as violating recently discovered laws of nature. Unlike Saint Augustine, who had described a City of God in the next world, many eighteenth-century thinkers confidently anticipated a happy earthly community. In the words of American historian Carl Becker they dreamed of a beautiful but terrestrial "heavenly city."[1]

Such ideas arose partially from social experience. European wealth was expanding rapidly, in comparison with all other societies. In fashionable European salons, philosophers and artists rubbed elbows with bored nobles and sons of enterprising bankers, who indulged in clever criticism of the Old Regime as a form of recreation. But a new popular philosophy appealed directly to the vested interests of the middle classes. By emphasizing the systematic regularity of nature, it automatically denied justification for most royal authority. The laws of nature promised to replace the laws of monarchs, along with their state churches, idle nobles, arbitrary courts, high taxes, and mercantilist control of business.

The concern for special interests was one source of the new vision, but it also rose from an intellectual stimulus. In the late seventeenth century, Europeans yearned for order, which scientists were finding throughout the universe. New discoveries in astronomy, physics, chemistry, and even biology strongly suggested that nature, from the smallest particle to the most distant stars, was an interlocking mechanism of harmoniously working parts. Here, apparently, was the simple answer to an everlasting search for certainty and the immediate origin of optimistic hopes for humanity.

Impact of the Scientific Revolution

By the later seventeenth century, science had won general acceptance and was beginning to dominate the European mind. The victory had been hard won. When during the late Renaissance the Italian universities and a few northern Europeans made advances in anatomy, medicine, and astronomy, their work was considered inconsequential or irreligious. Later scientists who persisted in taking their own conclusions seriously were either ignored or persecuted. Even the work of Copernicus was regarded more as mathematical exercise than a description of reality. This situation changed drastically after Sir Isaac Newton (1641–1727) expressed his universal law in mathematical terms and supported its validity by empirical results.

The Early Pioneering Era of Modern Science

The most notable of the scientific pioneers were astronomers, whose field of study was peculiarly suited to the new scientific method. As it was developed in the sixteenth century, this methodology involved a combination of two approaches, each depending upon human reason, with differing applications. The deductive approach started with self-evident truths and moved toward complex propositions, which might be applied to practical problems. It emphasized logic and mathematical relationships. The inductive approach started with objective facts, that is, knowledge of the material world. From facts, proponents of induction sought to draw valid general conclusions. In the past, the two procedures had often been considered contradictory. Early European astronomers were uniquely dependent on both kinds of reasoning.

The French scholar-mathematician René Descartes (1596–1650) initiated a new and critical mode of deduction. In his famous *Discourse on Method* (1627), Descartes rejected every accepted idea that could be doubted. He concluded that he could be certain of nothing except the facts that he was thinking and that he must therefore exist. From the basic proposition, "I think, therefore I am," Descartes proceeded in logical steps to deduce the existence of God and the reality of both the spiritual and material worlds.[2] He ultimately conceived a unified and mathematically ordered universe, which operated as a perfect mechanism. In the Cartesian physical universe, supernatural processes were impossible; everything could be explained rationally, and preferably in mathematical terms.

Descartes' method was furthered by discoveries in mathematics, and the method, in turn, popularized the study of the subject. Descartes' work coincided with the first use of decimals and the compilation of logarithmic tables. The latter advance, by halving the time required to solve intricate problems, may have doubled the effective influence of mathematics in the early 1600s. Descartes himself was successful in developing analytical geometry, which permitted relationships in space to be expressed in algebraic equations. Using such equations, astronomers could represent the movements of celestial bodies in

mathematical symbols. Astronomers received further aid later in the century when Sir Isaac Newton in England and Gottfried von Leibniz (1646–1716) in Germany independently perfected differential calculus, or the mathematics of infinity, variables, and probabilities.

The other great contributor to the theory of scientific methodology in this era was the Englishman Sir Francis Bacon (1561–1626). At a time when traditional systems of thought were crumbling, Bacon set forth a program extolling human reason, as applied to human sensory experiences. He advocated an inductive approach, using systematically recorded facts derived from experiments. These facts, he believed, would lead toward tentative hypotheses, which could then be tested by fresh experiments under new conditions. Ultimately, the method would reveal fundamental laws of nature. Bacon's ideas, outlined in his *Novum Organum* (1626), were the first definitive European statement of inductive principles.[3]

The inductive approach became even more practical with the remarkable improvement of scientific instruments. Both the telescope and the microscope came into use at the opening of the seventeenth century. Other important inventions included the thermometer (1597), the barometer (1644), the air pump (1650), and the pendulum clock (1657). With such devices, scientists were better able to study the physical universe.

Using both mathematics and observation, early astronomers before 1600 prepared the way for a scientific revolution. This was certainly true after 1543, the year of Copernicus' death and the publication of his famous book, *On the Revolutions of the Heavenly Spheres*. In the book, Copernicus posited a theory directly opposed to the traditional Ptolemaic explanation for passing days and the apparent movement of heavenly bodies. The old geocentric theory had assumed that the sun, the planets, and the stars all circled the earth. The new heliocentric theory postulated the sun as the center, around which the sun and planets moved.

Copernicus offered his idea as merely mathematical theory. By the end of the century, However, Tycho Brahe (1546–1601), a Danish astronomer, aided by his accomplished sister, Sophia (1556–1643), had recorded hundreds of observations that pointed to difficulties in the Ptolemaic explanation. Brahe even attempted, without much success, to find a compromise between the Ptolemaic and Copernican systems by postulating that the planets moved about the sun while the latter orbited the earth. This proposition raised even more problems and therefore met with little acceptance.

Brahe's data were used by his former assistant, the brilliant German mathematician, Johannes Kepler (1571–1630), to support the Copernican theory. While working mathematically with Brahe's records on the movements of Mars, Kepler was ultimately able to prove that the planet did not move in a circular orbit but in an ellipse. He also discovered that the paces of the planets accelerated when they approached the sun. From this he concluded that the sun might emit a magnetic force that directed the planets in their courses. The idea was not yet confirmed by a mathematical formula, but that would soon be achieved by Newton, using Kepler's hypothesis. Even in their own time, however, Kepler's laws of planetary motion almost completely undermined the Ptolemaic theory.

In 1596 Kepler created a model of the solar system with reference to five regular polyhedrons that fit between the spheres of the six known planets—Mercury, Venus, Earth, Mars, Jupiter, and Saturn.

During the early seventeenth century, growing acceptance of the heliocentric theory precipitated an intellectual crisis affecting organized religion, particularly the Catholic church. Medieval Catholicism had accepted Aristotle on physics and Ptolemy on astronomy. The church now felt its authority and reputation challenged by the new ideas. Copernicus and Brahe had both evaded the issue by purporting to deal only in mathematical speculations. Kepler and others of his time became increasingly impatient with this subterfuge. The most persistent of these scientific rebels was the Italian mathematician-physicist, Galileo Galilei (1564–1642).

Galileo discovered more facts to verify the Copernican theory, but as he wrote to Kepler,

> . . . up to now I have preferred not to publish, intimidated by the fortune of our teacher Copernicus, who though he will be of immortal fame to some, is yet by an infinite number (for such is the multitude of fools) laughed at and rejected.[4]

In 1609, Galileo made a telescope, and with it he discovered mountains on the moon, sunspots, the satellites of Jupiter, and the rings of Saturn. Having published his findings and beliefs, he was constrained by the Church in 1616 to promise that he would "not hold, teach, or defend" the heretical Copernican doctrines. After another publication, he was again hauled before a church court in 1633. This time, he was forced to make a public denial of his doctrines. Galileo was defeated, but by the end of the century the heliocentric theory had won common acceptance.

Newton and the Law of Gravitation

Great as were the contributions of Galileo and Kepler, their individual discoveries had not been synthesized into one all-embracing principle that would describe the universe as a unity. When Sir Isaac Newton achieved this goal, the opponents of science, such as Galileo's persecutors, were effectively silenced.

The notion of gravitation occurred to Newton in 1666, when he was only twenty-four. According to his own later account, he hit on the idea while sitting in thought under an apple tree. A falling apple roused him to wonder why it, and

Newton, Rule III of Reasoning

This selection, from Book III of the *Principia*, illustrates Newton's conception of universal gravity.

RULE III

The qualities of bodies, which admit neither intensification nor remission of degrees, and which are found to belong to all bodies within the reach of our experiments, are to be esteemed the universal qualities of all bodies whatsoever.

For since the qualities of bodies are only known to us by experiments, we are to hold for univeral all such as universally agree with experiments, and such as are not liable to diminution can never be quite taken away. We are certainly not to relinquish the evidence of experiments for the sake of dreams and vain fictions of our own devising; nor are we to recede from the analogy of Nature, which is wont to be simple and always consonant to itself. We in no other way know the extension of bodies than by our senses, nor do these reach it in all bodies; but because we perceive extension in all that are sensible, therefore we ascribe it universally to all others also. That abundance of bodies are hard we learn by experience; and because the hardness of the whole arises from the hardness of the parts, we therefore justly infer the hardness of the undivided particles, not only of the boides we feel, but of all others. That all bodies are impenetrable, we gather not from reason, but from sensation. The bodies which we handle we find impenetrable, and thence conclude impenetrability to be a universal property of all bodies whatsoever. That all bodies are movable and endowed with certain powers (which we call the inertia) of persevering in their motion, or in their rest, we only infer from the like properties observed in the bodies which we have seen. The extension, hardness, impenetrability, mobility, and inertia of the whole result from the extension, hardness, impenetrability, mobility and inertia of the parts; and hence we conclude the least particles of all bodies to be also all extended, and hard and impenetrable, and movable, and endowed with their proper inertia. And this is the foundation of all philosophy. Moreover, that the divided but contiguous particles of bodies may be separated from one another is a matter of observation; and, in the particles that remain undivided, our minds are able to distinguish yet lesser parts, as is mathematically demonstrated. But whether the parts so distinguished and not yet divided may, by the powers of Nature, be actually divided and separated from one another we cannot certainly determine. Yet had we the proof of but one experiment that any undivided particle, in breaking a hard and solid body, suffered a division, we might by virtue of this rule conclude that the undivided as well as the divided particles may be divided and actually separated to infinity.

Lastly, if it universally appears, by experiments and astronomical observations, that all bodies about the earth gravitate toward the earth, and that in proportion to the quantity of matter which they severally contain; that the moon likewise, according to the quantity of its matter, gravitates toward the earth; that, on the other hand, our sea gravitates toward the moon; and all the planets one toward another; and the comets in like manner toward the sun: we must, in consequence of this rule, universally allow that all bodies whatsoever are endowed with a principle of mutual gravitation. For the argument from the appearances concludes with more force for the universal gravitation of all bodies than for their impenetrability, of which, among those in the celestial regions, we have no experiments nor any manner of observation. Not that I affirm gravity to be essential to bodies; by their *vis insita* I mean nothing but their inertia. This is immutable. Their gravity is diminished as they recede from the earth.

Source: H. S. Thayer and John H. Randall, eds., *Newton's Philosophy of Nature* (New York: Hafner Publishing Co., 1953), pp. 3–5.

other objects, fell toward the center of the earth and not sideways or upward. There must be, he thought in a flash of insight, some drawing power associated with matter. If this were true, he reasoned, the drawing power was proportionate to quantity, which would explain why the smaller apple, despite its own attracting force, was pulled to earth. In his *Principia* (1687), Newton expressed this idea precisely in a mathematical formula. The resulting law of gravitation states that all material objects attract other bodies inversely according to the square of their distances and directly in proportion to the products of their masses. Hundreds of observations soon verified this principle, firmly establishing the validity of scientific methods.

Not only had Newton solved astronomical problems defined by Kepler and Galileo he had also confirmed the necessity of combining methods advocated by Descartes and Bacon. In the *Principia*, Newton stressed the importance of supplementing mathematical analysis with observation. Final conclusions, he insisted, must rest on solid facts; on the other hand, any hypothesis, no matter how mathematically plausible, must be abandoned if not borne out by obseavtion or experimentation.

Newton had also confirmed the basic premise of modern science that all nature is governed by laws. Indeed, his own major law was applicable to the whole universe, from a speck of dust on earth to the largest star in outer space. The magnitude of this idea—that is, the concept of universal laws—was almost infinitely exciting and contagious. Within decades it had spread throughout the Western world and had been applied in every area, including human relations.

The Widening Scope of Scientific Study

The impressive achievements of astronomers, climaxed by Newton's amazing revelations, encouraged scientific interest and endeavors in all related fields. As science widened its scope, the first advances outside of astronomy came in physics and physiology. Both fields owed much to earlier influences from Italian universities; both also reflected the new mechanistic ideas so prevalent in astronomy. Chemistry, long affected by medieval alchemy, did not reach maturity until the eighteenth century. By that time, in

general biology, apart from human anatomy and physiology, cellular studies and classification systems had begun to develop, although there was as yet no comprehensive evolutionary theory. Late in the century, however, geologists were suggesting such a scheme.

In astronomy the period after Newton was a time of elaboration and "filling in" the main outline, rather than one of new beginnings. A possible exception was the brilliant French astronomer-mathematician, Pierre Laplace (1749–1827), who has been called the Newton of France. Although a leading disciple of Newton, Laplace went beyond his master. Newton believed that God tended the universal machine to compensate for irregularities, but Laplace demonstrated that apparent inconsistencies, such as comets, were also governed by mathematical laws. Laplace is best known for his nebular hypothesis, which maintained that our sun, once a gaseous mass, threw off the planets as it solidified and contracted. Until recently, this hypothesis was widely accepted.

Despite their lack of opportunities for scientific education, a number of women became involved in astronomical studies during the eighteenth century. In France, Emilie du Châtelet (1706–1749), the sometime mistress and lifelong friend of Voltaire, translated the *Principia*, helping introduce Newton among the French *philosophes*. Maria Kirch (1670–1720), while assisting her husband, Gottfried, the royal astronomer in Berlin, discovered the comet of 1702. After her husband's death, she published their observations, which were widely read. Caroline Herschel (1750–1848), a native of Hanover working with her brother William in England, helped build huge telescopes, shared the discovery of 2500 new nebulae, and by herself found a number of new comets. The Herschels' work demonstrated that Newtonian principles applied to distant stars, outside the solar system.

In physics, the field most closely related to astronomy, Galileo was the pioneer. He defined the law of falling bodies, demonstrating that their acceleration is constant, no matter what their weight or size. His experiments also revealed the law of inertia: a body at rest or in motion will remain at rest or continue moving (in a straight line at constant speed) unless affected by an external force. In addition, he showed that the path of a fired projectile follows a parabolic curve to earth, an inclination explained later by the law of gravitation. Galileo made additional notable discoveries through his studies of the pendulum, hydrostatics, and optics. His work was clarified by two famous professors at the University of Bologna, Maria Agnesi (1718–1799), in mathematics, and Laura Bassi (1700–1778), in physics.

Other physicists made significant contributions. For example, Newton and the Dutch scientist, Christian Huygens (1629–1695) developed a wave theory to explain light. A more prosaic discovery, and one that promised more immediate practical results, demonstrated the material composition of air. The German physicist, Otto von Guericke (1602–1668), pumped air from two joined steel hemispheres, creating a vaccum so complete that the two sections could not be pulled apart by teams of horses. Ultimately, Guericke and other scientists proved that air could be weighed and that it could exert pressure, both properties in accord with Newton's law.

Although electricity remained a challenging mystery to physicists during this era, magnetic properties were recognized early. In 1600, the Englishman William Gilbert (1540–1603) published a book that described magnetic force and the possibilities of generating it by friction. Gilbert's suggestion of a similarity between magnetism and gravity exerted some influence on Newton. Electricity, generated by friction, was conducted short distances to produce sound and light in various experiments during the seventeenth century. The first crude storage battery—the Leyden Jar—was invented in 1745 at the Dutch University of Leyden. A last important achievement during the period came in 1752, when Benjamin Franklin (1706–1790), with his famous kite-and-key experiment, proved that lightning is natural electricity.

While physics and astronomy flourished, chemistry advanced more slowly. Robert Boyle (1627–1691), the son of an Irish nobleman and the father of modern chemistry, was the first to emphasize the difference between compounds (unified by chemical action) and mixtures. From his many experiments, he conceived a crude atomic theory, superseding the "four elements" and "four humors" of medieval alchemists and physicians. Boyle also investigated fire, respiration, fermentation, evaporation, and the rusting of metals. Joseph Priestley (1733–1804), an English dissenting minister and a famous eighteenth-century chemist, isolated ammonia, discovered oxygen, and generated carbon monoxide. Another Englishman, Henry Cavendish (1731–1810), discovered hydrogen (1766). His experiments, along with Priestley's, furnished an explanation for combustion.

More definitive studies of combustion were completed by the French scientist Antoine Lavoisier (1743–1794), who is generally considered the leading chemist of the eighteenth century. Lavoisier proved that burning is a chemical process involving the uniting of oxygen with the substances consumed. He also showed that respiration is another form of oxidation. Such discoveries led him to define the law of conservation: "matter cannot be created or destroyed." With this law, he laid a foundation for the discipline of quantitative analysis, which makes possible the precise measurement of substances in any compound. Much of the credit for Lavoisier's scientific success should go to his wife, Marie-Anne (1758–1836), whom he married when she was fourteen and educated in his laboratory. She assisted with all his major experiments, took notes, kept records, illustrated his books, and published her own papers. After he died on the guillotine during the French Revolution, she edited and published a compilation of his works.

Robert Boyle's seventeenth-century counterpart in the life-sciences was William Harvey (1578–1657). Born in England and educated at the University of Padua in Italy, Harvey continued in the tradition that had earlier produced Vesalius (see p. 313). Harvey's major contribution was a description of the human circulatory system: He traced the flow of blood from the heart, through the arteries, capillaries, and veins, and back to the heart. He also studied embryology in animals and put forth the theory of "epigenesis," which maintains that embryos develop progressively, through definite stages, prior to birth. Harvey provided medical science with many practical keys to understanding the human body. He also applied to biology the mechanistic interpretation developed by Galileo, Newton, and other modern scientists.

Biologists in the seventeenth century also achieved notable results. Jan Swammerdam (1637–1680) in Holland and Marcello Malpighi (1628–1694) in Italy studied circulation and added details to Harvey's general description. Anton van Leeuwenhoek (1627–1723), a Dutch biologist, discovered protozoa, bacteria, and human spermatozoa; Swammerdam studied the anatomies and life cycles of frogs and insects; and Robert Hooke (1635–1703), an Englishman, first described the cellular structure of plants. These studies, as did those of William Harvey, also furthered the idea of bodies as machines.

Biology in the eighteenth century was characterized by classification rather than the formulation of theory. An early example was Maria Sibylla Merian (1647–1717), a German entomologist who settled in Holland. She was a specialist on insects, and in 1705 published a well-known treatise dealing with those of Surinam, where she had studied for two years. Her work was just one approach to thousands of new species, discovered as a result of overseas expansion and collected in Europe, where they were classified and described. The most successful classifiers were John Ray (1627–1705) in England, Karl von Linné (1707–1778)—perhaps better known by his Latin name as Linnaeus—in Sweden, and Georges Buffon (1707–1788) in France. They established the basic terminology and categories still used in the twentieth century.

Three women deserve mention for their contributions to eighteenth-century anatomy and medicine. A recognized expert in anatomy was Anna Manzolini (1716–1774), professor at the University of Bologna, a lecturer at the Court of Catherine the Great, and a member of the Russian Royal Scientific Society. The French anatomist Genevieve d'Arionville (1720–1805), wrote treatises on chemistry, medicine, anatomy, and physiology. In addition to her self-illustrated textbooks on anatomy, she published a study on putrefaction and introduced bichloride of mercury as an antiseptic. Mary Motley Montague (1689–1762) was not a research scientist or a medical doctor, but she advocated innoculation against smallpox in England, a treatment she had observed in Turkey as the wife of the English ambassador there. Her efforts aided the English physician Edward Jenner (1749–1823), who published his famous defense of vaccination in 1798.

The most revolutionary thesis in modern biology, the evolutionary theory that all life has evolved from simpler organisms, was not yet widely accepted in the eighteenth century, although some classifiers, such as Buffon, were already speculating along these lines. A stronger case was argued by the Scottish gentleman farmer, James Hutton (1726–1797). In his *Theory of the Earth* (1795), Hutton described the earth as constantly wearing away and rebuilding itself through natural results of wind, water, and chemical reactions. This thesis contradicted traditional religious theories of creation and supported the concept of natural law.

Science as Popular Culture

The achievements of science, particularly its practical applications in such fields as medicine and navigation, completely transformed its social role. After long being suspect among the leaders of society, it now became respectable. By the beginning of the eighteenth century, scientists frequented the best salons, and scientific academies gained public support as they sprang up all over Europe. The most famous were the Royal Society of London, chartered in 1662, and the French Academy of Science, founded in 1664. Most academies published journals that circulated widely. Scientists and would-be scientists carried on voluminous correspondence, developing a cosmopolitan community with its own language, values, and common beliefs.

Rising enthusiasm on the public fringes of the scientific community was matched by a popular mania. Frederick the Great dabbled in scientific experiments, as did hundreds of other ordinary craftsmen, wealthy merchants, and bored nobles. Support for academies was merely one form of public endorsement. Kings endowed observatories; cities founded museums; and well-to-do women helped establish botanical gardens. Scientists became popular heroes. Giordano Bruno, an Italian philosopher-scientist, had been burned for heresy by the Holy Inquisition in 1600; Galileo was hounded by persecutors through his most productive years; but Newton received a well-paying government position. He was lionized and knighted during his lifetime, and after he died in 1727, he was buried in a state funeral at Westminster Abbey.

In sharp contrast to the robust exuberance and emotionalism of the Baroque style was the dainty elegance and delicate decoration of the Rococo, the characteristic style of the eighteenth century. The Rococo at its best is seen in the works of Antoine Watteau (1683–1721), who often painted scenes of aristocratic society in parklike settings. With the graceful gallantry and gay frivolity of its figures, *Les Plaisirs du Bal* (1719), above, is a typical example of the Rococo.

A popular English portraitist of the eighteenth century was Sir Joshua Reynolds (1723–92), first president of England's Royal Academy of Arts. In his portraits, such as *Lady Elizabeth Delmé and Her Children* (1777–80), right, Reynolds sought to show his subjects as models of nobility, grace, and elegance.

The leader of the Neoclassic style, a reaction against Baroque and Rococo excesses, was Jacques Louis David (1748–1825), who became the semiofficial artist of the French Revolution. *The Death of Socrates* (1787), below, was regarded as a political allegory and protest against the injustices of the Old Regime.

Thomas Jefferson (1743–1826), third president of the United States as well as a talented amateur architect, built his own home, Monticello, in Charlottesville, Virginia, in the Neoclassic style. The building, constructed of brick with wood trim, features a central dome on an octagonal base, a pedimented porch, and severely simple ornament to achieve the single-story effect of a Roman temple.

By 1700, science had surpassed the Reformation in affecting Western thought. Unlike the Reformation, science revolutionized people's view of their own purposes. No longer could they consider the universe as stage equipment, created by God expressly for the human drama of sin and salvation. People now looked up toward an unknown number of stars, each moving silently but regularly through infinite space. On one planet, orbiting one of the smaller stars, were human creatures, among other forms of life. Their obvious similarity was material composition, which also obeyed Newtonian principles. Matter and motion, the fundamental realities of this strange new universe, everywhere acted impersonally, without discernible human purpose. In all of this, the individual was apparently rendered insignificant, but some thinkers sensed more human potential than had been promised formerly by Christian free will. For if God were not directly determining human affairs, human reason might learn the natural laws and effect unlimited human progress.

Reflections of the Age in Cultural Expression

The eighteenth century, when Newtonian science exerted its greatest impact, was exceptionally noteworthy for European cultural expression. This was most evident in philosophy, which sought to find in human affairs natural laws similar to those science had discovered in the physical universe. This approach, with its optimistic utopianism, found some expression in literature, but it was much more obscured in the visual arts and barely noticeable in music. Because they were largely affected by tradition, individual feeling, and patronage, the arts were less responsive to scientific influence. They were, nevertheless, quite rich and varied, reflecting the increasing wealth, widening perspectives, and rising technical proficiency of European life.

Developments in the Arts

The quantity and diversity of artistic works during the period do not fit easily into categories for interpretation, but some loose generalizations may be drawn. At the opening of the century, baroque forms were still popular, as they would be at the end. They were partially supplanted, however, by a general lightening in the rococo motifs of the early 1700s. This was followed, after the middle of the century, by the formalism and balance of neoclassicism, with its resurrection of Greek and Roman models. Although the end of the century saw a slight romantic turn, the era's characteristic accent on reason found its best expression in neoclassicism.

In painting, rococo emphasized the airy grace and refined pleasures of the salon and the boudoir, of delicate jewelry and porcelains, of wooded scenes, artful dances, and women, particularly women in the nude. Rococo painters also specialized in portraiture, showing

Fragonard, *The Lover Crowned.* Fragonard's paintings contain the sensual subject matter, soft colors, and delicate curves typical of the Rococo style, which was a reaction against the heavy formal style characteristic of Louis XIV's court.

aristocratic subjects in their finery, idealized and beautified on canvas. The rococo painting of Antoine Watteau (1684-1721) blended fantasy with acute observations of nature, conveying the ease and luxury of French court life. Watteau's successors in France included François Boucher (1703–1770) and Jean Fragonard (1732–1806). Italian painters, such a Giovanni Tiepolo (1696–1730), also displayed rococo influences. English painting lacked the characteristic rococo frivolity, but the style affected works by Sir Joshua Reynolds (1723–1792) and Thomas Gainsborough (1727–1788), whose portraits tended to flatter their aristocratic subjects.

Eighteenth-century neoclassicism in painting is difficult to separate from some works in the era of Louis XIV. Both Charles Le Brun (1619–1690) and Nicolas Poussin (1594–1665) had earlier projected order and balance, often in grandiose scenes from antiquity or mythology. Jean Chardin (1699–1779) carried some of this over into the 1700s. The neoclassic approach, however, often expressed powerful dissatisfaction and criticism of the existing order, sometimes in stark realism and sometimes in colossal allegory. The most typical representative of this approach was Jacques Louis David (1748–1825), whose most famous work, *Death of Socrates* illustrates his respect for Greco-Roman tradition. His sketch of Marie Antoinette enroute to the guillotine clearly represents his revolutionary sympathies. The best examples of pure realism and social criticism are the London street scenes by the English painter William Hogarth (1697–1764) and the Spanish court portraits of Francisco Goya (1746–1828).

The number of women painters increased during the eighteenth century, but they were so limited by traditions and so dependent upon public favor that they could hardly maintain consistent styles. Very few were admitted to academies, where their work might be shown; in France, they were not permitted to work with nude models. The result was their practical restriction to still-life and portraiture. Among rococo painters, the two best-known were Rachel Ruysch (1664–1750), a court painter of flowers in Düsseldorf, and Rosalba Carriera (1675–1757), a follower of Watteau, who was admitted to the French Academy in 1720. Two very famous French portrait painters and members of the Academy, were Vigee Le Brun (1755–1842) and Adelaide Labille-Guiard (1749–1803). If possible, they were overshadowed by Angelica Kaufmann (1741–1807), a Swiss-born artist who painted in England and Italy. All three were celebrated in their time. Each produced grand scenes in the neoclassical style, but their market limited them to flattering portraits, at which they excelled.

Neoclassicism also found expression in architecture and sculpture. Architecture was marked by a return to the intrinsic dignity of what a contemporary called "the noble simplicity and tranquil loftiness of the ancients." The Madeleine of Paris is a faithful copy of a still-standing Roman temple, and the Brandenburg Gate in Berlin was modeled after the monumental entrance to the Acropolis in Athens. In England, where the classical style had resisted baroque influences, the great country houses of the nobility now exhibited a purity of design, which often included a portico with Corinthian columns. Mount Vernon is an outstanding example of neoclassicism in colonial America. The trend in sculpture often revived classical themes from Greek and Roman mythology; statues of Venus became increasingly popular. Claude Michel (1738–1814) and Jean Houdon (1741–1828) were

Francisco Goya, *Ni Por Esas*. In his series of engravings, *The Disasters of War*, Goya vividly depicted the brutality of war and the horrors of human suffering.

two French neoclassical sculptors who also achieved notable success with contemporary portraits. Houdon's *Portrait of Voltaire* is a well-known example.

At the opening of the eighteenth century, music demonstrated typical baroque characteristics. These were evident in instrumental music, especially that of the organ and the strings. The most typical baroque medium was opera, with its opulence and highly emotional content. The era culminated in the sumptuous religious music of Johann Sebastian Bach (1685–1750), a prolific German organ master and choir director. Bach's equally great contemporary, the German-born naturalized Englishman, George Frideric Handel (1685–1759), is known for his grand and dramatic operas, oratorios, and cantatas; he is best known today for his religious oratorio, *Messiah* (1742).

Composers of the late eighteenth century turned from the heavy and complex baroque styles to classical music of greater clarity, simpler structures, and more formal models. Plain, often folklike melodies also became common. With the appearance of symphonies, sonatas, concertos, and chamber music, less interest was shown in mere accompaniment for religious services or operatic performances. The general emphasis on technical perfection, melody, and orchestration is summed up in the work of the Austrian composers Franz Joseph Haydn (1732–1809) and Wolfgang Amadeus Mozart (1756–1791). Haydn wrote over 100 symphonies, along with numerous other works. Mozart wrote more than 600 works, including 41 symphonies, 22 operas, and 23 string quartets, climaxing his career with his three most famous operas: *The Marriage of Figaro* (1786) *Don Giovanni* (1787), and *The Magic Flute* (1791).

Musical expression at the turn of the century was touched by the genius of the immortal German composer Ludwig van Beethoven (1770–1827). The passion of his sonatas and symphonies expressed a revolutionary romanticism, which challenged the sedate classicism of his time.

Reflections of the Age in Literature

More than in art, neoclassicism in literature came closer to voicing the eighteenth century's fascination with reason and scientific law. Indeed, the verbal media of poetry, drama, prose, and exposition were commonly used to convey the new philosophic principles.

A typical poetic voice of the Age of Reason in England was Alexander Pope (1688–1744). In his most famous work, *An Essay on Man* (1733), Pope expressed the optimism and respect for reason that marked the era. He described a Newtonian universe in the following often quoted lines:

> *All are but parts of one stupendous whole,*
> *Whose body nature is, and God the soul . . .*
> *All nature is but art, unknown to thee;*
> *All chance, direction, which thou cannot see.*
> *All discord, harmony not understood;*
> *All partial evil, universal good*
> *And, spite of pride, in erring reason's spite,*
> *One truth is clear: Whatever is, is right.*[5]

Two other poetic voices deserve mention here. One belonged to the English Countess of Winchelsea (1661–1720), who extolled reason and feminine equality in her verse. The other was that of a Massachusetts slave girl, Phyllis Wheatley (1753–1784), whose rhyming couplets, in the style of Pope, pleaded the cause of freedom for the American colonies and for her race.

Reflecting the common disdain for irrational customs and outworn institutions were such masterpieces of satire as *Candide* (1759), by the French man of letters, François-Marie Arouet, better known as Voltaire (1694–1778). Another famous satirist, England's Jonathan Swift (1667–1745), ridiculed the pettiness of human concerns in *Gulliver's Travels* (1726), wherein Captain Gulliver, in visiting the fictitious land of Lilliput, found two opposing factions: the Big-endians, who passionately advocated opening eggs at the big end, and the Little-endians, who vehemently proposed an opposite procedure.

The novel became a major literary vehicle in this period. It caught on first in France during the preceding century and was then popularized in England. *Robinson Crusoe* (1719), by Daniel Defoe (1659–1731), is often called the first modern English novel. The straight prose of the novel satisfied a prevailing demand for clarity and simplicity; but the tendency in this period to focus on middle-class values, heroic struggle, and sentimental love foreshadowed the coming romantic movement. Writing along these lines,

Samuel Richardson (1689–1761) produced *Pamela* (1740–1741), the story of a virtuous servant-girl, and Henry Fielding (1707–1754) wrote the equally famous *Tom Jones* (1749), the rollicking tale of a young man's deep pleasures and superficial regrets. Each novel, in its own way, defined a natural human morality.

In both France and England women found a uniquely promising outlet for their long-ignored talents in the romantic novel, with its accent on personal feminine concerns and domestic problems. Two among the multitude of able French women novelists were Madame de Graffigny (1695–1758), whose *Lettres D'Une Peruvienne* (1730) became a best-seller, and Madame de Tencin (1682–1749), who wrote *The Siege of Calais*, a historical novel of love and danger. In England, Fanny Burney (1753–1840) was universally acclaimed after publication of her first novel, *Eveline* (1778), about "a young lady's entrance into the world." Aphra Behn (1640–1689) was an early playwright whose novel, *Oroonoko* (1688), was a plea for the natural person, long before the works of Defoe and Rousseau.

The Enlightenment and the Age of Reason in Philosophy

Western Europe's worship of reason, reflected only vaguely in art and literature, was precisely expressed in a set of philosophic ideas known collectively as the Enlightenment. It was not originally a popular movement. Catching on first among scientists, philosophers, and some theologians, it was then taken up by literary figures, who spread its message among the middle classes. Ultimately, it reached the common people in simplified terms associated with popular grievances.

The most fundamental concept of the Enlightenment were faith in nature and belief in human progress. Nature was seen as a complex of interacting laws governing the universe. The individual human being, as part of that system, was designed to act rationally. If free to exercise their reason, people were naturally good and would act to further the happiness of others. Accordingly, both human righteousness and happiness required freedom from needless restraints, such as many of those imposed by the state or the church. The Enlightenment's uncompromising hostility towards organized religion and established monarchy reflected a disdain for the past and an inclination to favor utopian reform schemes. Most of its thinkers believed passionately in human progress through education. They thought society would become perfect if people were free to use their reason.

Before the eighteenth century, the Enlightenment was confined to Holland and England. Its earlier Dutch spokesmen were religious refugees, like the French Huguenot Pierre Bayle (1674–1706), whose skepticism and pleas for religious toleration were widely known in France. Baruch Spinoza (1632–1687), a Jewish intellectual and Holland's greatest philosopher, was a spokesman for pantheism, the belief that God exists in all of nature. Spinoza's influence, along with Newton's, profoundly affected English thinkers. Mary Astell (1666–1731), perhaps the earliest influential English feminist, lauded rational thinking and cited Newton as proof of an ordered universe. Such ideas were given more credibility by John Locke (1632–1704), the famous English philosopher. Back home from exile in Holland after the Glorious Revolution of the 1680s, Locke applied Newton's recently published principles to psychology, economics, and political theory. With Locke, the Enlightenment came to maturity and began to spread abroad.

After the Peace of Utrecht (1713), the Enlightenment was largely a French Phenomenon. Its leading proponents were known as the *philosophes*, although the term cannot in this instance be translated literally as "philosophers." The *philosophes* were mostly writers and intellectuals who analyzed the evils of society and sought reforms in accord with the principles of reason. Their most supportive allies were the *salonnières*, that is, the socially conscious and sometimes learned women who regularly entertained them, at the same time sponsoring their discussion of literary works, artistic creations, and new political ideas. By 1750, the *salonnières*, their salons, and the *philosophes* had made France once again the intellectual center of Europe.

A leading light among the *philosophes* was the Marquis de Montesquieu (1688–1755), a judicial official as well as a titled nobleman. He was among the earliest critics of absolute monarchy. From his extensive foreign travel and wide reading he developed a great respect for English liberty and a sense of objectivity in viewing European institutions, particularly those of France. Montesquieu's *Persian Letters* (1721), which purported to contain reports of an Oriental traveler in Europe, describing the irrational behavior and ridiculous customs of Europeans, delighted a large reading audience. His other great work, *The Spirit of Laws* (1748), expressed his main political principles. It is noted for its practical common sense, its objective recognition of geographic influences on political systems, its advocacy of checks and balances in government, and its uncompromising defense of liberty against tyranny.

More than any of the *philosophes*, Voltaire personified the skepticism of his century toward traditional religion and the injustices of the Old Regimes. His caustic pen brought him two imprisonments in the Bastille and even banishment to England for three years. On returning to France, Voltaire continued to champion toleration. He popularized Newtonian science, fought for freedom of the press, and actively crusaded against the church. In such endeavors, he turned out hundreds of histories, plays, pamphlets, essays, and novels. His estimated correspondence of 10,000 letters, including many to Frederick the Great and Catherine the Great, employed his wry wit in spreading the gospel of rationalism and reform of abuses. Even in his own time, his reputation became a legend, among kings as well as literate commoners.

Voltaire had many disciples and imitators, but his only rival in spreading the Enlightenment was a set of books—the famous French *Encyclopédie*, edited by Denis Diderot (1713–1784). The *Encyclopédie*, the chief monument of the *philosophes*, declared the supremacy of the new science, denounced superstition, and expounded the merits of human freedom. Its pages contained critical articles, by tradesmen as well as scientists, on unfair taxes, the evils of the slave trade, and the cruelty of criminal laws.

More than has been widely understood, the *Encyclopédie*, and many other achievements of the *philosophes* were joint efforts with their female colleagues among the *salonnières*. Madame de Geoffrin (1699–1777) contributed 200,000 livres (roughly $280,000 equivalent) to the *Encyclopédie* and made her salon the headquarters for planning and managing it. Mademoiselle de Lespinasse (1732–1776), the friend and confidential advisor of Jean d'Alembert (1717–1783), who assisted Diderot in editing the work, turned her salon into a forum for criticizing prospective articles. Most of the *philosophes* relied upon such assistance. Voltaire was coached in science by Madame du Châtelet; and the Marquis de Condorcet (1742–1794), the prophet of progress and women's rights among the *philosophes*, was intellectually partnered by his wife, Sophie (1764–1812), who popularized their ideas in her own salon. Even Madame de Pompadour aided the *philosophes* in 1759, when she presuaded Louis XV to allow sale of the *Encyclopédie*.

Perhaps the best-known of all the *philosophes* was that eccentric Swiss-born proponent of romantic rationalism, Jean-Jacques Rousseau (1712–1778). Although believing in the general objectives of the Enlightenment, Rousseau distrusted reason and science. He gloried in human impulse and intuition, trusting emotions rather than thought, the heart rather than the mind. His early rebuffs from polite society encouraged his hatred for the Old Regime. He also professed admiration for "noble savages," who lived completely free of law, courts, priests, and officials. In his numerous writings, he spoke as a rebel against all established institutions. The most famous of these works, *The Social Contract* (1762), was Rousseau's indictment of absolute monarchy. It began with the stirring manifesto: "Man is born free, but today he is everywhere in chains."[6]

The French Enlightenment exerted a powerful influence on English thought. Many young upper-class Englishmen visited France to complete their education. Among them were three leading English thinkers: Adam Smith (1723–1790), the Scottish father of modern economics; David Hume (1711–1766), the best-known English skeptic; and Jeremy Bentham (1748–1832), the founder of utilitarian philosophy. Another famous English rationalist was the historian, Edward Gibbon (1737–1794), whose *Decline and Fall of the Roman Empire* markedly criticized early Christianity. Among English political radicals after 1770, Joseph Priestley, Richard Price (1723–1791) and Thomas Paine (1737–1809) were also very much affected by French thought. Paine, who figured prominently in the American and French revolutions, was also a leader in English radical politics.

The Enlightenment also affected English women. Hannah Moore and a coterie of lady intellectuals, known as "bluestockings," maintained a conservative imitation of the French salons after the 1770s. One atypical "bluestocking" was Catherine Macaulay (1731–1791), a leading historian who published eight widely acclaimed volumes on the Stuart period. A republican defender of the American and French Revolutions, Macaulay exerted a decided influence on Mary Wollstonecraft (1759–1797), whose life symbolized the Enlightenment and the emerging English feminist movement. Born in poverty and burdened by a dependent family, Wollstonecraft became a teacher and a successful professional writer. She was personally acquainted with leading English radicals, including Richard Price, Thomas Paine, and William Godwin (1756–1836), whom she later married. Her *Vindication of the Rights of Man* (1790) was the first serious answer to Edmund Burke's diatribe against the French Revolution, which Wollstonecraft personally observed and ardently supported.

The reforming rationalism of the Enlightenment spread over Europe and also reached the New World. A leading spokesman in Germany was Moses Mendelssohn (1729–1786), who wrote against dogmatism and in favor of natural religion. In Italy, the Marquis of Beccaria (1738–1794) pleaded for humanitarian legal reforms. The Enlightenment was popular among the upper classes in such absolutist strongholds as Prussia, Russia, Austria, Portugal, and Spain. French ideas were read widely in Spanish America and Portuguese Brazil. In the English colonies, Locke and the *philosophes* influenced such leading thinkers as Benjamin Franklin, Thomas Jefferson (1743–1826), Mercy Otis Warren (1728–1814), and Abigail Adams (1744–1818).

The Case Against Absolutism

The Enlightenment's highest achievement was the development of a tightly organized philosophy, purportedly based on scientific principles and contradicting every argument for absolute monarchy as it generally existed in the eighteenth century. The case against absolutism, as presented by the *philosophes* and their foreign sympathizers, condemned divine-right monarchy, aristocracy by birth, state churches, and mercantilism. Each was found to be irrational, unnatural, and therefore basically evil.

Basic Arguments in the Case

One fundamental indictment against absolutism was its lack of human concern. Critics argued that maintaining order by forcing or frightening people into conformity, destroyed the innate human potential for moral judgment. The social environment was responsible for corrupting people, who were naturally good. Human beings could be perfected by removing the corrupting influences. For example, Beccaria insisted that unjust and irrational laws should be changed, so that they would teach morality and not just punish those who were caught. Prisons, argued the English reformer John Howard (1726–1790) should rehabilitate criminals, not brutalize them. These and other eighteenth-century rationalists believed that humanitarian reforms, in conformity with nature's laws, would lead toward unlimited human progress. Their message was voiced effectively by Condorcet, the most idealistic of the *philosophes*, in his *Progress of the Human Mind* (1794).

Behind Condorcet's humanitarianism was a passionate faith in human freedom. Enlightenment thinkers saw the arbitrary policies of absolute monarchs as violations of innate rights, required by human nature. The most fundamental part of this nature was human reason, the means by which people learned and realized their potential. Learning, as described by Locke in his *Essay Concerning Human Understanding* (1690), consisted entirely of knowledge gained through the senses, interpreted by reason, and stored in memory. There were no internal sources of knowledge; indeed, the mind at birth was like blank pieces of paper, upon which experience would write. The individual, in short, was primarily a thinking and judging mechanism, which required maximum freedom to operate effectively. The best government, therefore, was the government that ruled least. This argument for human freedom was the heart of the anti-absolutist case.

Religious Arguments in the Case

By the late eighteenth century, organized religion in Europe faced serious problems. The preceding century of religious wars had produced many contending sects and shaken the unquestioning faith of medieval times. Overseas expansion and the resulting contacts with non-Christian religions contributed to the same result. State churches, often used by kings to support corrupt regimes, also undermined respect for traditional Christianity. Added to all of this was the impact of the Newtonian revolution as well as earlier religious persecution of scientists. Between the orderly universe described by scientists and the relative chaos of human society, the contrast was indeed shocking. It led to serious reconsideration of religious ideas and institutions.

For such early thinkers as Descartes, the major theoretical problem was reconciling the mechanistic, self-regulating universe with the traditional belief in an all-powerful God. Descartes solved this problem, for himself, by dividing all realities between the realms of mind and matter. According to Descartes, both realms were governed by a divine will, but they appeared disconnected to human beings. Through science, human reason could accurately comprehend the material world; through faith and theology, the mind might know, directly from God, those truths beyond the material world of science. Thus, Descartes, a loyal Catholic, sought to reconcile the old and the new. In contrast, his Dutch pupil, Baruch Spinoza, saw mind and matter as dual parts of nature, which was one with God. This pantheistic theory identified God with every natural process, leaving few mysteries to be revealed by theology or supernatural revelation.

John Locke's religious ideas were similar to Spinoza's, but a little more orthodox. In his *Reasonableness of Christianity* (1695), Locke confirmed the existence of God by the regularities and apparent purposes of nature. He then attempted to prove that Christianity was consistent with natural law. This effort was somewhat self-defeating because it required natural explanations of religious miracles, thus nullifying their traditional religious significance. Nevertheless, arguments for such rational Christianity

were quite common, particularly among "enlightened" clergymen in the eighteenth century.

The most popular religious belief of the later Enlightenment was deism. It was held by such well-known figures as Thomas Paine in England, Thomas Jefferson and Benjamin Franklin in the English American colonies, and Voltaire in France. To deists, God was an impersonal force—the master "clockwinder" of the universe. Generally, they rejected religious miracles and Christ's divinity. People, according to their view, were totally responsible for their actions. This "natural religion" required that individuals act morally without churches, clergy, ritual, or prayers. Although accepting the idea of an afterlife, deists attached no significance to emotional faith as a means to salvation. They placed all reliance on the individual reason and conscience.

Deism was popular but somewhat logically inconsistent. If the universe operated automatically, how could people possess free will and assume moral responsibility? What material evidence indicated an afterlife? Such questions led some thinkers to religious skepticism and even to atheism. Joseph Priestley, who was trained as an English minister and considered himself a Christian theologian, insisted that the soul did not exist independent of the body. David Hume (1711–1776), the famous English skeptic, questioned the existence both of God and of heaven. The most extreme views were professed in France, particularly in the circle of Paul Henri, Baron d'Holbach (1723–1789). In *The System of Nature* (1770), d'Holbach denied the existence of God or any human purpose in the universe. Such ideas, however, were held only by a minority of Enlightenment thinkers.

Despite some differences on the details of their beliefs, eighteenth-century rationalists were in almost perfect agreement on one point. They championed religious freedom of conscience. In addition, most were participants in a continuing struggle against the alleged fallacies of organized religion. Hundreds of their writings, especially those of Voltaire and the *philosophes*, depicted churches and priests as part of a vast conspiracy aimed at perpetuating injustice and tyranny. State churches were special targets for their attacks. Their crusade for religious liberty was particularly threatening to absolutism.

The Economic Argument

Natural law, a basic concept of the Enlightenment, was applied most consistently and effectively in economic arguments against absolutism. Contradictions that natural law raised in religious theory were not nearly so typical in economics. In addition, by the eighteenth century, developing capitalism clearly indicated the stimulus of profit to individual incentive. This realization, coming with the scientific revolution, strongly suggested that capitalism had outgrown mercantilism, with its state assistance and accompanying controls. The new economic philosophy contended that the free play of economic forces would ensure the greatest prosperity.

Such ideas were promoted by the physiocrats, a group of economic thinkers in eighteenth-century France. Their leading spokesman was François Quesnay (1694–1774), the personal physician to Louis XV but also a contributor to the *Encyclopédie*. Originally, Quesnay and his followers opposed Colbert's policy of subordinating agriculture to government-controlled industry. This narrow emphasis later developed into a comprehensive theory based on natural law. Quesnay, for example, compared the circulation of money to the circulation of blood. He likened mercantilist controls to tourniquets, which shut off a life-giving flow. Quesnay also denounced the mercantilist theory of bullionism, arguing that prosperity depended on production, not gold and silver in the royal treasury. According to another physiocrat, Robert Turgot (1720–1781), selfish profit-seeking in a free market would necessarily result in the best service and the most goods for society.

The most influential advocate of the new economic theory was Adam Smith, a Scottish professor of moral philosophy at Glasgow University, who had visited France and exchanged ideas with the physiocrats. In 1776, Smith published *An Inquiry into the Nature and Causes of the Wealth of Nations*, in which he set forth his systematic formulation of ideas. The work has since become the bible of classical economic liberalism, the doctrine of free enterprise, or *laissez-faire* economics.

Smith was indebted to the physiocrats for his views on personal liberty, natural law, and the role of the state as a mere "passive policeman." He argued that increased production depended largely on division of labor and specialization. Because trade increased specialization, it also increased production. The volume of trade, in turn, depended on every person being free to persue individual self-interest. In seeking private gain, each individual was also guided by an "invisible hand" (the law of supply and demand) in meeting society's needs:

> It is not from the benevolence of the butcher, the brewer, or the baker, that we expect our dinner, but from their reward to their own interests. We address ourselves, not to their humanity, but to their self-love ... [7]

Smith regarded all economic controls, whether by the state or by guilds and trade unions, as injurious to trade. He scoffed at the mercantilist idea that the wealth of a nation depended on achieving a surplus of exports, amassing bullion, and crippling the economies of other countries. In Smith's view, trade should work to the benefit of all nations, which would follow if the trade were free. In such a natural and free economic world, the prosperity of each nation would depend on the prosperity of all.

A number of other thinkers in the late eighteenth century combined or elaborated the ideas of Smith and the physiocrats. In France, d'Holbach repudiated mercantilism, arguing that free trade would permit one nation to supply the deficiencies of another. Jeremy Bentham, in England, followed Smith in developing his idea of utilitarianism "as the greatest good for the greatest number" but denied that economic equality would promote happiness, because it would destroy incentive and limit production. Other commentators, such as Richard Price and Benjamin Franklin, suggested that rising wealth naturally increased the population, except in new lands, where resources were almost unlimited. In one way or another, such propositions supported the basic idea that economic controls were futile or damaging the society.

A few radical thinkers of the Enlightenment, such as Richard Price and Mary Wollstonecraft, toyed with the idea of redistributing property, but the dominant creed was the laissez-faire philosophy, which sanctified capitalism and the

Adam Smith, On the Division of Labor Self-interest

The last section of this excerpt is perhaps the most often quoted. It is based on Mandeville's *Fable of the Bees (1729).*

This division of labor, from which so many advantages are derived, is not originally the effect of any human wisdom which foresees and intends that general opulence to which it gives occasion. It is the necessary, though very slow and gradual, consequence of a certain propensity in human nature which has in view no such extensive utility: the propensity to truck, barter, and exchange one thing for another.

Whether this propensity be one of those original principles in human nature, of which no further account can be given; or whether, as seems more probable, it be the necessary consequence of the faculties of reason and speech, it belongs not to our present subject to inquire. It is common to all men, and to be found in no other race of animals, which seem to know neither this nor any other species of contracts. Two greyhounds, in running down the same hare, have sometimes the appearance of acting in some sort of concert. Each turns her toward his companion, or endeavors to intercept her when his companion turns her toward himself. This, however, is not the effect of any contract, but of the accidental concurrence of their passions in the same object at that particular time. . . . When an animal wants to obtain something either of a man or of another animal, it has no other means of persuasion but to gain the favor of those whose service it requires. A puppy fawns upon its dam, and a spaniel endeavors by a thousand attractions to engage the attention of its master who is at dinner, when it wants to be fed by him. Man sometimes uses the same arts with his brethren, and when he has no other means of engaging them to act according to his inclinations, endeavors by every servile and fawning attention to obtain their good will. He has not time, however, to do this upon every occasion. In civilized society he stands at all times in need of the co-operation and assistance of great multitudes, while his whole life is scarcely sufficient to gain the friendship of a few persons. In almost every other race of animals each individual, when it is grown up to maturity, is entirely independent, and in its natural state has occasion for the assistance of no other living creature. But man has almost constant occasion for the help of his brethren, and it is in vain for him to expect it from their benevolence only. He will be more likely to prevail if he can interest their self-love in his favor, and show them that it is for their own advantage to do for him what he requires of them. Whoever offers to another a bargain of any kind proposes to do this. Give me that which I want, and you shall have this which you want, is the meaning of every such offer; and it is in this manner that we obtain from one another the far greater part of those good offices which we stand in need of. It is not from the benevolence of the butcher, the brewer, or the baker that we expect our dinner, but from their regard to their own interest. We address ourselves not to their humanity, but to their self-love, and never talk to them of our own necessities, but of their advantages. Nobody but a beggar chooses to depend chiefly upon the benevolence of his fellow citizens. Even a beggar does not depend upon it entirely. The charity of well-disposed people, indeed, supplies him with the whole fund of his subsistence. But though this principle ultimately provides him with all the necessities of life for which he has occasion, it neither does nor can provide him with them as he has occasion for them. . . .

From Adam Smith, *An Inquiry into the Nature and Causes of the Wealth of Nations,* edited by Bruce Mazlish. (New York: Bobbs-Merrill, 1961), pp. 13–15.

freely operating profit motive. The so-called economic laws seemed to parallel mathematically proven laws of science. Indeed, the middle classes came to consider free enterprise as practically equivalent in validity to the law of gravitation. In an age of high taxes, contradictory commercial regulations, and expanding opportunities for profit, the new principles seemed to provide practical solutions for all economic problems. They certainly went a long way toward discrediting mercantilism and the Old Regimes built upon it.

The Political Argument

Economic freedom, like religious freedom, depended ultimately on government, the source of most restrictions or coercion. For this reason, political principles in the case against absolutism were fundamental to all others. They were developed in two main categories: ideas concerning individual rights, and ideas concerning the organization of government. Both categories of thought were directed toward securing individual freedom against unnatural abuses of authority.

According to Locke and most political theorists of the Enlightenment, government existed to maintain the rights of its people. This idea ran directly counter to the divine-right theory, which was held by most reigning monarchs in the seventeenth and eighteenth centuries.

Locke at the opening of the period and Rousseau at its end answered the divine-right doctrine with the opposing theory of a "social contract." Thomas Hobbes had used the contract idea to justify royal authority; Locke turned Hobbes' argument around. In his famous *Second Treatise on Government* (1690), Locke contended that political systems were originally formed by individuals for defense of their natural rights to life, freedom, and property, against local or foreign enemies. They voluntarily ceded to government their individual right of protecting their liberties. In this transaction, government's authority was derived from the governed. It was not absolute but limited to maintaining the people's rights, for which it was constituted. When its authority was used for other purposes, the contract was broken and the people were justified in forming another government.

As insurance against abuses of political authority, political theorists of the Enlightenment generally advocated the separation of powers. Locke, for example, proposed that kings, magistrates, legislatures, and judges should share authority and check on one another. Spinoza also stressed the need for local autonomy and a locally based militia to guard against power concentrated in a central government. Montesquieu, although somewhat skeptical about natural laws or Locke's version of the social contract, developed a theory of separation of powers in his *Spirit of Laws;* most of the *philosophes* subscribed to this idea.[8]

Political freedom and guarantees for human rights were common goals, but ideas concerning the ideal form of government varied considerably. The majority of the *philosophes* were not opposed to monarchy, despite their rejection of the divine-right principle. Voltaire believed that the most likely way to attain desirable reforms was through the rule of an "enlightened despot." In a sense, this theory of government was akin to the Platonic ideal of the philosopher-king. A few monarchs professed to accept this role, although their policies did not always match their principles (see ch. 19).

Perhaps the most popular form of government among natural law theorists was constitutional monarchy on the English model. Locke, of course, was the recognized spokesman for the Glorious Revolution and the limited English monarchy established by Parliament. Both Voltaire and Montesquieu were very much impressed with the English system as they understood it. For Montesquieu, it appeared to be a practical balance of traditional forces, which secured liberty without sacrificing order.

Concern for internal order was typical of most political thought in the Enlightenment. Both Locke and Voltaire, to name only two well-known examples, advocated that political power be confined to property owners. This, they believed, would secure sound government against the ignorant masses, at the same time holding open opportunities to intelligent and industrious citizens. Presumably, those with most to lose from anarchy could best be trusted with political rights. Such ideas also squared with the English parliamentary system, dominated as it was by the propertied classes.

John Locke, On the Origin of Government

In this passage, Locke presents his well-known assumptions about human adversities in "a state of nature," which led to the cooperative forming of states and which made all governments logically responsible to their citizens.

Men being, as has been said, by nature all free, equal, and independent, no one can be put out of this estate, and subjected to the political power of another, without his own consent. The only way by which any one divests himself of his natural liberty and puts on the bonds of civil society is by agreeing with other men to join and unite into a community for their comfortable, safe, and peaceable living one amongst another, in a secure enjoyment of their properties, and a greater security against any that are not of it. This any number of men may do, because it injures not the freedom of the rest; they are left as they were in the liberty of the state of nature. When any number of men have so consented to make one community or government, they are thereby presently incorporated, and make one body politic, wherein the majority have a right to act and conclude the rest.

For when any number of men have, by the consent of every individual, made a community, they have thereby made that community one body, with a power to act as one body, which is only by the will and determination of the majority. For that which acts any community being only the consent of the individuals of it, and it being necessary to that which is one body to move one way, it is necessary the body should move that way whither the greater force carries it, which is the consent of the majority. . . . And therefore we see that in assemblies empowered to act by positive laws, where no number is set by that positive law which empowers them, the act of the majority passes for the act of the whole, and of course determines, as having by the law of nature and reason the power of the whole.

And thus every man, by consenting with others to make one body politic under one government, puts himself under an obligation to every one of that society, to submit to the determination of the majority, and to be concluded by it; or else this original compact, whereby he with others incorporates into one society, would signify nothing, and be no compact, if he be left free and under no other ties than he was in before in the state of nature. For what appearance would there be of any compact? What new engagement if he were no farther tied by any decrees of the society, than he himself thought fit, and did actually consent to? This would be still as great a liberty as he himself had before his compact, or any one else in the state of nature hath, who may submit himself and consent to any acts of it if he thinks fit. . . .

Whosoever therefore out of a state of nature unite into a community must be understood to give up all the power necessary to the ends for which they unite into society, to the majority of the community, unless they expressly agreed in any number greater than the majority. And this is done by barely agreeing to unite into one political society, which is all the compact that is, or needs be, between the individuals that enter into make up a commonwealth. And thus that which begins and actually constitutes any political society is nothing but the consent of any number of freemen capable of a majority to unite and incorporate into such a society. And this is that, and that only, which did or could give beginning to any lawful government in the world. . . .

From John Locke, *Second Treatise on Government* in *Sources of British Political Thought*, edited by Wilfrid Harrison. (New York: Macmillan, 1965), pp. 55–57.

Only a few eighteenth-century rationalists believed in democracy as a form of government. Like their more conservative colleagues, they were afraid of mob action but even more so of monarchs, aristocrats, and large centralized polities. They saw the ballot box as another check on arbitrary government and regarded political rights, particularly the franchise, as the ultimate security for personal liberty.

Because democratic ideas were so uncommon, they were often qualified in their expression. Thomas Jefferson suggested that common men should be represented in government, but he also accepted the property-based franchise. He harmonized the apparent contradiction by advocating that most land should be owned by small farmers. Other vague democratic references, sometimes contradictory, appeared in the political writings of Jeremy Bentham, Joseph Priestley, Richard Price, Thomas Paine, Mary Wollstonecraft, and William Godwin.

Since the late eighteenth century, Rousseau has been somewhat mistakenly considered the greatest democrat among the French *philosophes*. Admittedly, he respected the republican institutions of his native Geneva, but he did not think them appropriate for a large state such as France. He also exalted the "General Will" as representing the interests of the community or nation over the selfish interests of individuals. By "General Will," however, Rousseau meant the social contract as expressed in generally accepted law. This law secured each individual's freedom, up to the point where it threatened the freedom of others. Rousseau did not clearly oppose democracy, but he was more interested in the abstract ideas of popular sovereignty and equal rights under law. His so-called democracy was most evident in his general opposition to monarchy, aristocracy, and polite society.[9]

Such minor differences over forms of government were inconsequential, compared with the points of political agreement among Enlightenment thinkers. All of them rejected the idea of divine-right monarchy, considering kings as the public servants of their peoples and obligated to maintain natural rights for all. These rights to life, liberty, and property, as construed by the *philosophes* and their rationalist friends abroad, ran directly counter to absolutism.

The Argument for Women's Rights

The Enlightenment's case against absolutism brought the first clearly stated arguments for women's rights. Although such ideas were not implemented when they were most evident—during the French Revolution—and had largely been ignored when they were expressed earlier, this era saw them entered into the public consciousness.

Although a monarchist and a follower of Descartes rather than Locke, Mary Astell claimed legal equality for women on the basis of their natural rationality in her *Serious Proposal to the Ladies* (1694). This call for women's rights was not repeated for decades, but it was echoed in the writings of English women, such as Mary Montague, during the eighteenth century. In France, a number of *salonnières*, including Madame de Puisseux (1720–1798) and Madame Gacon-Dufour (1753–1835), authored books defending their sex. Outside the salons, between 1759 and 1758, the *Journal des Dames*, a magazine edited by women, preached freedom, progress, and women's rights. At about the same time, in the new United States, Abigail Adams chided her husband because the new American constitution ignored women.

Before the French Revolution, the "woman subject" did not concern many leading philosophers. Rousseau represented most of them when he described the ideal woman's proper role as housekeeper, mother, and quiet comforter of her husband, who was responsible for her protection and moral instruction. A few thinkers disagreed. Both Hobbes and Locke mildly questioned the idea that women were naturally subordinate to men. D'Alembert thought female limitations resulted from women's degradation by society, and Montesquieu saw absolute monarchy as the cause for women's lack of status. But Condorcet was the only *philosophe* who made a special plea for female equality. In his *Letters from a Bourgeois of New Haven* (1787), he claimed that women's rationality entitled them to full citizenship, including the right to vote and hold public office. Later, during the Revolution, he advocated full equality for women in public education. For the most part, however, his voice went unheard.

The fall of the Bastille and the subsequent *Declaration of the Rights of Man and Citizen* by the French National Constituent Assembly generated a wave of female intellectual agitation. Catherine Macaulay led the way in England, denouncing the prevailing "harem mentality" and advocating a liberal education for women in her *Letters on Education* (1790). In France, the first challenge came from a butcher's daughter and self-educated playwright, Olympe de Gouges (1748–1793). Her *Declaration of the Rights of Women* (1791) called for a social contract, which would give women equal rights in divorce, as well as free speech and assembly. The climax came with Mary Wollstonecraft's *Vindication of the Rights of Women* (1792). Like Condorcet, Macaulay, and de Gouges, Wollstonecraft used natural law arguments in justifying full civil rights and equal education for women, but she more effectively emphasized her demands with a withering attack upon the prejudice of Rousseau and his supporters. Her passionate appeal would become a future feminist tradition.

For a while during the 1790s, the flurry of concern continued. In England, Wollstonecraft's friend, Mary Hayes (1760–1843) took up the crusade, as did Mary Anne Radcliff (1764–1823), who stressed the lack of economic opportunities for women in *An Attempt to Recover the Rights of Women from Male Usurpation* (1799). Patricia Wakefield (1751–1832) also used an economic approach. Her book, *Reflections on the Present Condition of the Female Sex* (1798), followed Adam Smith in arguing that the exploitation of women would limit prosperity. Other voices were raised in Germany and America. In 1792, Theodore Hippel (1742–1796) rebuked the French for ignoring women in their new constitution. The American reaction came in the writings of Judith Sargent Murray (1751–1820) and Charles Brockden Brown (1771–1810), both of whom were influenced by Wollstonecraft.

The Reaction Against Reason

The eighteenth century was primarily an "Age of Reason," but in the latter decades there was a general reaction against rationalism. One form of the reaction came in philosophy with a new idealism, in opposition to the materialism of the early Enlightenment. Another form was an emotional religious revival, which won back many wavering Protestants and Catholics. A third form of reaction replaced reason with religion as the justification for humanitarian reforms. These movements stressed emotion over reason but continued the Enlightenment's accent upon individual liberty.

Idealistic Philosophy

Immanuel Kant (1724–1804), a kindly and contemplative professor of philosophy at the German University of Königsberg, was thoroughly aroused by the skeptical and materialistic extremes of the Enlightenment. While appreciating science and dedicated to reason, he determined to shift philosophy back to a more sensible position without giving up much of its newly discovered "rational" basis. His ideas, contained primarily in the *Critique of Pure Reason* (1781), ushered in a new age of philosophic idealism.

Kant agreed with Locke on the role of the senses in acquiring knowledge but insisted that sensory experience had to be interpreted by the mind's internal patterns. This meant that certain ideas—the mind's categories for sorting and recording experience—were *a priori*, that is, they existed before the sensory experience occurred. Typical innate ideas of this sort were width, depth, beauty, cause, and God; all were understood yet none were learned directly through the senses. Kant concluded, as had Descartes, that some truths were not derived from material objects through scientific study. Beyond the material world was a realm unapproachable by science. Moral and religious truths, such as God's existence, could not be proved by science yet were known to human beings as rational creatures. Reason, according to Kant, went beyond the mere interpretation of physical realities.

In Kant's philosophic system, pure reason, the highest form of human endeavor, was as close to intuition as it was to sensory experience. It proceeded from certain subjective senses, built into human nature. The idea of God was derived logically from the mind's penchant for harmony. The human conscience, according to Kant, might be developed or be crippled by experience, but it originated in the person's thinking nature. Abstract reason, apart from science and its laws, was a valid source of moral judgment and religious interpretation. Thus Kant used reason to give a philosophic base back to mystical religion.[10]

The Religious Reaction

Religious rationalism, despite its appeal to intellectuals, provoked considerable religious reaction. Part of this came from theologians such as Bishop Joseph Butler (1692–1752) and William Paley (1743–1805) in England, both of whom defended Christianity and challenged deism on its own rational grounds. Even more significant was a widespread emotional revival, stressing religion of the heart rather than the mind.

The new movement, known as pietism, began in England after 1738, when the brothers John (1703–1791) and Charles (1708–1788) Wesley began a crusade of popular preaching in the Church of England. The Anglican pietists discarded traditional formalism and stilted sermons in favor of a glowing religious fervor, producing a vast upsurge of emotional faith among the English lower classes. "Methodist," at first a term of derision, came to be the respected and official name for the new movement. After John Wesley's death in 1791, the Methodists officially left the Anglican church to become a most important independent religious force in England.

On the continent, Lutheran pietism, led by Philipp J. Spener (1635–1705) and Emanuel Swedenborg (1688–1772), followed a pattern similar to Methodism. Swedenborg's movement in Sweden began as an effort to reconcile science and revelation; after Swedenborg's death it became increasingly emotional and mystical. Spener, in Germany, stressed Bible study, hymn singing, and powerful preaching. The Moravian movement sprang from his background. Under the sponsorship of Count Nicholaus von Zinzendorf (1700–1760), it spread to the frontiers of Europe and to the English colonies in America.

The "Great Awakening," a tremendous emotional revival sustained by Moravians, Methodsts, Baptists, and Quakers, swept the colonial frontier areas from Georgia to New England in the late eighteenth century. Women played prominent roles in this activity, organizing meetings and providing auxiliary services, such as charities and religious instruction. Among the Quakers, women were often ministers and itinerant preachers. One was Jemima Wilkinson (1752–1819), leader of the Universal Friends; another was Ann Lee (1736–1784), who founded Shaker colonies in New York and New England.

By the 1780s, religious rationalism and pietism stood in opposition to each other. Proponents of each disagreed passionately on religious principles though they agreed on the issue of religious freedom. Both rationalists and pietists were outside the state churches, both feared persecution, and both recognized the flagrant abuses of religious establishments. The two movements were therefore almost equally threatening to state churches and the old regimes.

The New Humanitarianism

One dominant characteristic of the early Enlightenment — the concern for individual human worth — received new impetus from religion in the reaction against reason. The demand for reform and the belief in human progress were now equated with traditional Christian principles, such as human communality and God's concern for all people. Religious humanitarianism shunned radical politics and ignored the issue of women's rights, despite the movement's strong support among women. It did, however, seek actively to relieve human suffering and ignorance among children, the urban poor, prisoners, and slaves. This combination of humanitarian objectives and Christian faith was similar in some ways to the Enlightenment but markedly different in its emotional tone and religious justifications.

Notable among manifestations of the new humanitarianism was the antislavery movement in England. A court case in 1774 ended slavery within the country. From then until 1807, a determined movement sought abolition of the slave trade. It was led by William Wilberforce (1759–1833), aided by Hannah Moore and other Anglican Evangelicals, along with many Methodists and Quakers. Wilberforce repeatedly introduced bills into the House of Commons that would have eliminated the traffic in humans. His efforts were rewarded in 1807 when the trade was ended, although he and his allies had to continue to struggle for twenty-six more years, before they could achieve abolition in the British colonies.

Religious humanitarians enforced other movements that originated in the Enlightenment. For example, the movements for legal reform and prison reform were both supported by religious groups before 1800. Education, extolled by rationalist thinkers, also aroused interest among the denominations. The Sunday School movement, particularly in England, was a forerunner of many private and quasi-public church schools. Finally, concern for the plight of slaves, coupled with rising missionary zeal, brought popular efforts to improve conditions for native peoples in European possessions overseas.

While it was not as openly political as other aspects of the Enlightenment, the new humanitarianism played a significant part in weakening absolutism. In general, it contributed to a spirit of restlessness and discontent and encouraged independent thought, particularly as it improved education. Its successful campaign against the slave trade also struck a direct blow at the old mercantilist economies, which depended heavily on plantation agriculture overseas. In time, the missionaries would also prove to be the most consistent enemies of colonialism.

Conclusion

The Enlightenment brought a new vision of the future, which forecast the end of absolute monarchy. Philosophers of the Enlightenment thought they had discovered a simple formula for perpetual human happiness. They sought to deliver individuals from restraints so that they could act freely in accordance with their natures. On the one hand, the formula promised that pursuit of self-interest would benefit society; on the other, it promised that a free human reason would produce sound moral judgments. In other words, individual freedom permitted the operation of natural laws. Believing they had learned these laws, eighteenth-century rationalists thought they had found the secret of never-ending progress.

Rational philosophy undermined absolutism in all of its phases. Deism questioned the necessity of state churches and clergies. The physiocrats, Adam Smith, and other early economic liberals demonstrated the futility of mercantilism. Political theory in the Enlightenment substituted the social contract for divine right and emphasized natural human rights of political freedom and justice. Each of these ideas denied the absolute authority of monarchs.

Respect for rational philosophy was largely derived from the successes and popularity of science. The surprising discoveries of astronomers produced a new view of the individual's place in the universe; in his law of gravitation, Newton supplied mathematical evidence for their perspective. His laws, along with the other laws of science, suggested that human reason operated effectively only when it was interpreting sensory experience. Material reality was accepted as the only reality. Therefore, the natural laws affecting human society were also considered as basically materialistic.

Toward the end of the eighteenth century, a reaction against reason countered this materialism without affecting the fundamental objectives of the Enlightenment. Idealistic philosophy and pietism both challenged the scientific view of the individual, emphasizing that intuition and faith are human qualities as essential as reason. These new movements merged with the humane concerns of rational philosophy to produce a new humanitarianism, which accented both reason and sentimentality but also continued the eighteenth-century concern for human freedom. Together with the rationalism of the Enlightenment, the reaction against reason before 1800 also challenged absolutism's domination of the human body, mind, and spirit.

Suggestions for Reading

Good general surveys of intellectual developments during the early modern period in Europe may be found in two standard works that are still worth consulting: Jacob Bronowski and Bruce Mazlish, *The Western Intellectual Tradition from Leonardo to Hegel* (Torchbooks, 1962) and Crane Brinton, *The Shaping of Modern Thought* (P. Smith, 1968). Excellent coverage of general background is provided in William Doyle, *The Old Order in Europe* (Oxford, 1978).

Colin A. Ronan, *Science: Its History and Development Among the World's Cultures* (Facts on File, 1982) treats comprehensively the revolutionary developments of the seventeenth and eighteenth centuries. Two other useful general surveys of scientific achievements during the period are I. Bernard Cohen, *From Leonardo to Lavoisier* (Scribner, 1980) and Robert B. Downs, *Landmarks in Science* (Libraries Unlimited, 1982). For the changing place of science in society, Leonard M. Marsak, ed., *The Rise of Science in Reference to Society* (Macmillan, 1964) is still reliable. See also J. Weinberger, *Science, Faith and Society* (Cornell Univ., 1985). Mary Ornstein, *The Role of Scientific Societies in the Seventeenth Century* (Arno, 1975) is the classic study of this important subject. Overdue recognition of early women scientists is provdied in Margaret Alic, *Hypatia's Heritage: A History of Women in Science* (Beacon, 1986) and Marilyn B. Ogilive, *Women in Science* (M.I.T., 1986).

For the origins of scientific theory, see N. Jardine, *The Birth of the History and the Philosophy of Science* (Cambridge Univ., 1988). A flood of recent books deals with the special contributions of Descartes and Bacon. For Descartes, see T. Sorrel, *Descartes* (Oxford Univ., 1987); J. F. Scott, *The Scientific Work of René Descartes* (Garland, 1987); L. J. Beck, *The Method of Descartes* (Garland, 1987); and Desmond Clarke, *Descartes' Philosophy of Science* (Pennsylvania Sate Univ., 1982). For Bacon, see C. Whitney, *Francis Bacon and Modernity* (Yale Univ., 1986); P. Urbach, *Francis Bacon's Philosophy of Science* (Open Court, 1987); and Antonio Perez-Ramos, *Francis Bacon's Idea of Science and the Maker's Knowledge of Tradition* (Oxford Univ., 1989).

Alexander Koyre, *The Astronomical Revolution* (Cornell Univ., 1973) is a concise synthesis. Among the best interpretive biographies of the great astronomers are John Louis Emil Dreyer, *Tycho Brahe* (Dover, 1963); Arthur Koestler's study of Kepler, *The Watershed* (Univ. Press of America, 1984); Stillman Drake, *Galileo* (Hill and Wang, 1980); Ernan McMullin, *Galileo, Man of Science* (Scholar's Bookshelf, 1988). For Newton, see Gale E. Christianson, *In the Presence of the Creator* (Free Press, 1984) and Richard S. Westfall, *Never at Rest* (Cambridge Univ., 1983).

Achievements in biology and chemistry are covered in the following biographical works: Robert G. Frank, *Harvey and the Oxford Physiologists* (Univ. of California, 1980); Peter Alexander, *Qualities and Corpuscles: Locke and Boyle on the External World* (Cambridge Univ., 1985). For Lavoisier, see W. C. Anderson, *Between the Library and the Laboratory* (Johns Hopkins Univ., 1984); Vivian Grey, *The Chemist Who Lost His Head* (Coward Putnam, 1982); and Kenneth Sydney Davis' dual study of Lavoisier and Priestly, *The Cautionary Scientists* (Putnam's, 1966).

Hugh Honeur, *Neo-Classicism* (Penguin, 1987) is a well-balanced brief summary of the major artistic trend. Other sound treatments of art in this era are Halldor Soehner, *The Rococo Age: Art and Civilization in the Eighteenth Century* (McGraw-Hill, 1960); S. Jones, *The Eighteenth Century* (Cambridge Univ., 1985); Jean Starobinsky, *1789: The Emblems of Reason* (M.I.T., 1988); A. Boime, *Art in an Age of Revolution, 1750–1800* (Univ. of Chicago, 1987); and R. Paulson, *Representations of Revolution* (Yale Univ., 1987). For architecture, see Allan Braham, *The Architecture of the French Enlightenment* (Univ. of California, 1980);

Joseph Rykwert, *The First Moderns* (Harvard Univ., 1980); and J. L. Varriano, *Italian Baroque and Rococo Architecture* (Oxford Univ., 1986). Contributions of women artists are described in Helga Mobius, *Women of the Baroque Age* (Abner Schram, 1984); Karen Peterson, *Women Artists* (New York Univ., 1976); and Elsa H. Fine, *Women and Art* (Allenheld, Schram, and Prior, 1978).

Frederick Keener, *The Chain of Becoming* (Columbia Univ., 1983) is a thoughtful study of Enlightenment literature. It complements such other scholarly literary studies as J. Sambrook, *The Eighteenth Century—the Intellectual and Cultural Context of English Literature* (Longman, 1986) and P. Rogers, *Literature and Popular Culture in Eighteenth-Century England* (Barnes and Noble, 1985), for the intellectual and aesthetic atmosphere of early Georgian England, see Clive T. Probyn, *Jonathan Swift, the Contemporary Background* (Barnes and Noble, 1979). See also David Nokes, *Jonathan Swift* (Oxford Univ., 1985) and A. Ingram, *Intricate Laughter in the Satire of Swift and Pope* (Macmillan, 1986). Pope and his influence are covered in R. A. Brower, *Alexander Pope and the Arts of Georgian England*, 2nd ed. (Oxford, 1986); G. F. Plowden, *Pope on Classic Ground* (Ohio Univ., 1983); and M. Mack, *Alexander Pope* (Yale Univ., 1986). For a look at the French literary world at the end of the century, see Renée Winegarten, *Mme. de Staël* (St. Martin's, 1987) and C. Hogsett, *The Literary Existence of Germaine de Staël*.

Inclusive and coherent surveys of the Enlightenment are presented in Louis B. Snyder, *The Age of Reason* (Krieger, 1979) and Robert Anchor, *The Enlightenment Tradition* (Univ. of Pennsylvania, 1987). For intellectual origins of the movement, see Alan Kors and Paul J. Korshin, eds., *Anticipation of the Enlightenment in England, France, and Germany* (Univ. of Pennsylvania, 1987). Some common themes are treated in Henry Vyerberg, *Human Nature, Cultural Diversity, and the French Enlightenment* (Oxford Univ., 1989); Thomas J. Schlereth, *The Cosmopolitan Ideal in the Enlightenment* (Univ. of Notre Dame, 1977); and Donald C. Mell, et al, eds., *Man, God, and Nature in the Enlightenment* (Colleagues Press, 1989). For nationalistic variations, see Frederick Artz, *The Enlightenment in France* (Kent State Univ., 1968); John Redwood, *Reason, Ridicule, and Religion: The Age of the Enlightenment in England* (Harvard Univ., 1976); Henri Brunschwig, *Enlightenment and Romanticism in Eighteenth-Century Prussia* (Univ. of Chicago, 1974); Henry S. Commager, *The Empire of Reason: How Europe Imagined and America Realized the Enlightenment* (Peter Smith, 1984); and Ernest Cassirer, *The Enlightenment in America* (Univ. Press of Amer., 1988).

French and American colonial women who played roles in the Enlightenment are ably credited in Joan B. Lander, *Women and the Public Sphere in the Age of the French Revolution* (Cornell Univ., 1988); Samia I. Spender, *French Women and the Age of Enlightenment* (Indiana Univ., 1984); Margaret Hunt and Margaret Jacob, *Women and the Enlightenment* (Haworth Press, 1984); Linda K. Kerber, *Women of the Republic* (Univ. of North Carolina, 1980); and Mary Beth Norton, *Liberty's Daughters* (Little, Brown, 1980).

The following biographical studies are recommended for major participants in the Enlightenment: L. S. Feuer, *Spinoza and the Rise of Liberalism* (Transaction Books,

1987); Thomas L. Hankin, *Jean d'Alembert* (Oxford, 1970); Keith M. Baker, *Condorcet* (Univ. of Chicago, 1982); Otis E. Fellows, *Diderot* (Twayne, 1977); Alan C. Kors, *D'Holbach's Coterie* (Princetown Univ., 1976); Anthony Flew, *David Hume: Philosophy of Moral Science* (Blackwell, 1986); J. Y. Grieg, *The Philosophy of David Hume* (Garland, 1983); Maurice Cranston, *John Locke* (Oxford Univ., 1985); J. W. Yolton, *John Locke* (Blackwell, 1985); Norman Hampson, *Montesquieu, Rousseau, and the French Revolution* (Univ. of Oklahoma, 1983); J. N. Shklar, *Montesquieu* (Oxford Univ., 1987); A. J. Ayer, *Voltaire* (Random House, 1986); Maurice Cranston, *Jean-Jacques* (Penguin, 1987); J. Starobinski, *Jean-Jacques Rousseau* (Univ. of Chicago, 1988); and James J. Hoecher, *Joseph Priestley and the Idea of Progress* (Garland, 1987).

Religious issues in the Enlightenment are discussed in Edwin M. Curley, *Descartes Against the Skeptics* (Harvard Univ. 1978). The opposite orientation is revealed in Joseph P. Wright, *The Skeptical Philosophy of David Hume* (Univ. of Minnesota, 1983) and in T. A. Mitchell, *David Hume's Anti-theistic Views* (Univ. Press of America, 1986). Margaret C. Jacob, *The Radical Enlightenment* (Allen and Unwin, 1981) also deals with religion, along with republicanism and the prevailing radical influence of Free Masonry in the eighteenth century.

For the French economic assault upon absolutism, see Elizabeth Fox-Genovese, *The Origins of Physiocracy* (Cornell Univ., 1976) and Henry Higgs, *The Physiocrats* (Kelley, 1989). Adam Smith's significance is analyzed in R. H. Campbell, *Adam Smith* (St. Martin's, 1985); R. Lamb, *Property, Markets, and the State in Adam Smith's System* (Garland, 1987); and Maurice Brown, *Adam Smith's Economics: Its Place in the Development of Economic Thought* (Routledge Chapman and Hall, 1988). See also Michael Perelman, *Classical Political Economy* (Rowman and Allanhild, 1983) and Karl Pribram, *A History of Economic Reasoning* (Johns Hopkins Univ., 1983).

For Locke's political theory, see John Dunn, *The Political Thought of John Locke* (Cambridge Univ., 1983); Ruth W. Grant, *John Locke's Liberalism* (Univ. of Chicago., 1987); and James Tully, *A Discourse on Property: John Locke and His Adversaries* (Cambridge Univ., 1980). Other examples of conservative liberalism may be seen in Thomas L. Pangle, *Montesquieu's Philosophy of Liberalism* (Univ. of Chicago, 1989) and Peter Gay, *Voltaire's Politics*, 2nd ed. (Yale Univ., 1988). For the radical liberal movement, see Donald Harvey Meyer, *The Democratic Enlightenment* (Putnam's, 1975); Jack Fruchtman, *The Apacalyptic Politics of Richard Price and Joseph Priestley* (American Philosophical Society, 1983); and Nancy L. Rosenblum, *Bentham's Theory of the Modern State* (Harvard Univ., 1978).

On Rousseau as a political thinker, see Ramon M. Lemos, *Rousseau's Political Philosophy* (Cornell Univ., 1976) and R. Wokler, *Social Thought of J. J. Rousseau* (Garland, 1987). Rousseau's ambiguous views on democracy are given special attention in James Miller, *Rousseau, Dreamer of Democracy* (Yale Univ., 1984); John B. Noone, *Rousseau's Social Contract* (Univ. of Georgia, 1980); and P. Coleman, *Rousseau's Political Imagination* (Droz, 1984).

The radical Enlightenment produced a trickle of feminism, which is described in the following works: Ruth Perry, *The Celebrated Mary Astell* (Univ. of Chicago, 1986); Alice Browne, *The Eighteenth-Century Feminist Mind* (Wayne State Univ., 1987); and Moira Fergusun and Janet Todd, *Mary Wollstonecraft* (Twayne, 1984).

Kant's reinterpretation of the Enlightenment is thoroughly covered in Ernest Cassirer, *Kant's Life and Thought* (Yale Univ., 1981). See also A. V. Gulyga, *Immanuel Kant* (Kirkhauser, 1988). For special emphases on aspects of Kant's thought, see Robert Hahn, *Kant's Newtonian Revolution in Philosophy* (St. Martin's, 1988); H. E. Allison, *Kant's Transcendental Idealism* (Yale Univ., 1986); Gordon C. Brittan, *Kant's Theory of Science* (Princeton Univ., 1978); James Booth, *Interpreting the World: Kant's Philosophy of History and Politics* (Univ. of Toronto, 1987); and H. L. Williams, *Kant's Political Philosophy* (St. Martin's, 1986).

David Sherman Lovejoy, *Religious Enthusiasm and the Great Awakening* (Prentice-Hall, 1969) captures the spirit of pietism and religious humanitarianism. Among recent works on Methodism, two excellent ones are V. H. Green, *John Wesley* (Univ. Press of America, 1987) and T. E. Dowley, *Through Wesley's England* (Abingdon, 1988). See also Samuel J. Rogal, *John and Charles Wesley* (Twayne, 1983) Stanley E. Ayling, *John Wesley* (Collins, 1979); and Frank Baker, *John Wesley and the Church of England* (Abingdon, 1970). John Charles Pollock, *Wilberforce* (St. Martin's, 1978) is an excellent recent biography of the great English emancipator.

Notes

1. Carl L. Becker, *The Heavenly City of the Eighteenth-Century Philosophers* (New Haven: Yale University Press, 1932), pp. 49, 129.
2. René Descartes, *Discourse on Method* (New York: Liberal Arts Press, 1956), pp. 20–26.
3. Francis Bacon, *Novum Organum* (London: William Pickering, 1844), pp. 13–17, 84–89.
4. Quoted in Stillman Drake, *Galileo at Work* (Chicago: University of Chicago Press, 1978), p. 41.
5. Quoted in G. K. Anderson and W. E. Buckler, eds., *The Literature of England*, 2 vols. (Glenview, IL: Scott, Foresman, 1958), vol. 1, p. 1568.
6. Jean Jacques Rousseau, *The Social Contract*, trans. by W. Kendall, (Chicago: Henry Regnery Co., 1954), p. 2.
7. Adam Smith, *Selections From the Wealth of Nations* (Chicago: Henry Regnery Co., 1953), p. 12.
8. See John Locke, *Second Essay on Civil Government* (Chicago: Henry Regnery, 1955), pp. 2, 63–65, 71, 127–128, 154–170; Baron de Montesquieu, *The Spirit of Laws* (New York: Hafner Publishing, 1949), pp. 151–158.
9. Jean-Jacqes Rousseau, *A Discourse on Political Economy* (Chicago: Henry Regnery, 1949), pp. 118–119; and Jean-Jacques Rousseau, *The Social Contract* (Chicago: Henry Regnery, 1954), pp. 19–20, 24–25, 39.
10. See Immanuel Kant, *The Critique of Pure Reason* (New York: Collier, 1902.)

The Rights of Man

Revolution in the Western World

The last four decades of the eighteenth century marked a decisive turning point in the history of Western Civilization. Before 1760, divine-right monarchy and aristocratic society were accepted as normal; after 1800, everstronger voices would speak for civil liberties and constitutions—political concepts that are basic to modern societies. The intervening era had seen a fundamental revolution in thought and political life.

This age of revolution was nevertheless a culmination of earlier trends. As we have seen, developing European capitalism, expanding population, growing cities, and a rising middle class had partially undermined traditional monarchies by 1750. The Enlightenment, particularly its more radical variation, was also approaching maturity. Each of these trends—economic, social, and intellectual—converged when colonial conflicts were plaguing the Western maritime states. The American Revolution, resulting from one such conflict, was first. It encouraged a much more comprehensive French upheaval, which had been brewing for more than a century. These were but the two most dramatic examples of the resulting revolutionary wave that rolled over much of western Europe and America during the late 1700s.

The American and French revolutions provided later generations with a new set of values. The two heroic struggles critically weakened the Old Regime, identifying freedom with progress in the popular mind and projecting democracy, as well as emotional nationalism, into the nineteenth century. For most Western societies before World War I, the revolutions provided a special heritage. This was particularly true for Americans, whose liberal ideals were deeply rooted in the developing traditions of a new land and assimilated in the folklore of a popular culture. Even in Europe and the rest of the world, however, the revolutionary dream of human liberty has lingered into the twentieth century, notably among the emerging nations of Asia and Africa.

Unfortunately, the revolutionary ideals were not all realized in their own time. The rights of "all men," proclaimed with such solemn dignity in 1776 and repeated with ringing appeal in 1789, were denied to women and most black people, many of whom had fought and died for liberty. This omission would have to be corrected later, at the price of great strife and hardship.

The Background of Revolution

Eighteenth-century revolutions can be explained by two sets of circumstances in their past. One of these was the momentous social change that outmoded institutions, disrupted traditional ways of life, and brought hardships or injustices. Such conditions became especially prevalent after the Seven Years' War in the 1760s. A second source of revolution can be found in ideas, some recently generated by the Enlightenment, and others, even older, derived from English precedents.

English Precedents

Eighteenth-century revolutionaries looked back with respect to the 1640s, when the English Parliament, after struggling to maintain its rights through two reigns, fought a civil war, executed a king, and established a republic. For one brief period, revolutionary soldiers had even proclaimed a democratic system, guaranteed by a written constitution. Although this effort failed and the republic ultimately produced an unpopular dictatorship, it could never destroy the traditional popular ideal of limited monarchy, functioning in cooperation with a representative Parliament.

After the monarchy was restored in 1660, Parliament continued its struggle against the last two Stuart kings. The Whig opposition party in Parliament forced the resignation of Charles II's first minister, imprisoned the second, excluded the king's Catholic supporters from public office, and provided individuals with legal security against arbitrary arrest and imprisonment. Such actions forced Charles to dismiss four Parliaments and face a serious political crisis during the last years of his reign. James II, who succeeded his brother in 1685, dismissed Parliament and attempted to rule as a despot, using a standing army, largely commanded by Catholics. His actions caused such universal opposition that James was forced to call a new Parliament, which he tried to pack with his supporters, but local officials would not cooperate. Finally, when his wife gave birth to a prince, who was widely regarded as a potential Catholic king, parliamentary leaders offered the English crown to William of Orange, the Protestant stadtholder of the Netherlands and husband of Mary, one of James' Protestant daughters by an earlier marriage.

William and his Dutch army, welcomed as deliverers, soon effected the so-called Glorious Revolution of 1688, and James fled to exile in France. Because he needed English support for his war with France, William was ready to accept Parliament's conditions, enacted as the famous "Bill of Rights." This declaration provided that

1. the king could not suspend laws.

2. no taxes would be levied or standing army maintained in peacetime without the consent of Parliament.

3. sessions of Parliament would be held frequently.

4. freedom of speech in Parliament would be assured.

5. subjects would have the right of petition and be free of excessive fines, bail, or cruel punishments.

6. the king would be a Protestant.

This document has exerted tremendous influence on developing constitutional governments, an influence that is seen in the first ten amendments to the U.S. Constitution.

Other parliamentary acts supplemented the Bill of Rights and consolidated the Revolution. In 1689, the Mutiny Act required parliamentary approval for extending martial law more than one year. Although Catholics were subjected to harsh new restrictions and non-Anglican Protestants were still excluded from public office, the Toleration Act (1689) gave all Protestants freedom of worship. In 1693, when Parliament failed to renew the customary Licensing Act, the country achieved practical freedom of the press. Finally, in the Act of Settlement in 1701, Parliament prescribed a Protestant succession to the throne and barred the monarch from declaring war, removing judges, or even leaving the country without parliamentary consent.

The Glorious Revolution permanently limited the English monarchy, guaranteed important legal rights, and helped popularize the ideal, if not the practice, of popular sovereignty. For these reasons it provided a model for Locke and hope for Voltaire and Montesquieu. In many respects, however, it was neither glorious nor revolutionary; it certainly did not establish democracy, for the country after 1688 continued to be governed by a minority of merchants and landowners.

Their control during the eighteenth century was exercised through the developing cabinet system. The first two Hanoverian kings, George I (1714–1727) and George II (1727–1760) were so ignorant of the English language and politics that they had to rely on chief advisors (prime ministers), who could maintain support in Parliament. Sir Robert Walpole (1676–1745) first held this post, managing a Whig political machine. Walpole insisted that the entire ministry (cabinet) should act as a body; single members who could not agree were expected to resign. Later, he learned the practicality of resigning with his whole cabinet, when he could not command a parliamentary majority. This pragmatically developed system of cabinet government and ministerial responsibility provided the constitutional machinery needed to apply the principles of 1689, permitting Parliament to assert its supremacy and still avoid awkward conflicts with royal authority.

Behind the cabinet was Parliament and behind Parliament was a tight aristocratic organization. Membership in the House of Commons after 1711 was confined to those with high incomes from land. It represented an electorate of about 6000 voters. Two representatives were elected from each county by the lesser freeholders, but most of these seats were filled by arrangements among the great land-owning families. Of more than 400 members from the boroughs, or towns, most were named by prominent political bosses. The Duke of Newcastle, for example, held estates in twelve counties, was Lord Lieutenant of three, and literally owned seven other seats in Commons. The system that filled the seats also determined votes in Parliament. Here the bases of loyalty were public offices, army commissions, and appointments in the church. Local magnates extracted all manner of concessions from the king's ministers, who framed policies in accordance with the system. English politics, which had been so dynamic in the 1600s, thus became stagnant by the end of George II's reign.

Conditions Favoring Revolution After 1760

While the English parliamentary system became increasingly conservative in the eighteenth century, converging economic, social, and intellectual forces pointed in an opposite direction. Sugar and slavery were transforming the European and American economies, encouraging the growth of cities and expanding populations. At the same time, the Enlightenment, with its emphasis upon reason and utopian expectations of progress, was reaching full maturity. Finally, and most importantly for the immediate future, the costs of imperial competition created serious problems for European maritime states. The most obvious source of such problems was the great Anglo-French colonial war, which ended with the Peace of Paris in 1763. The war left both France and Britain burdened with unprecedented debts. Since the international financial system was centered in the Netherlands, Dutch neutrality aroused more tensions. In addition, the elimination of a common French enemy in Canada generated new frictions between Britain and the American colonies. As the greatest world empire, Britain was suspicious of all its neighbors, particularly France. The fear was justified, because France, recently stripped of possessions in Canada and India, was determined on humbling Britain, not only to satisfy French pride but also to accommodate an expanding economy. Large objectives but limited resources encouraged the French and British governments, as well as other states such as Austria, to tighten administration and raise taxes. These policies naturally encouraged popular unrest.

Alignment with Britain after 1689 caused difficulties for the Dutch, whose trade in the eighteenth century declined while that of Britain increased. This ultimately forced the Dutch economy to specialize in financing foreign state debts, a policy which tied the Netherlands closer to Britain and increased the threat of French invasion. When this conflict actually occurred in the 1740s, the Dutch lower middle classes demanded better relations with France; in 1747, they even attempted revolution. The situation not only caused agitation in the Netherlands but also encouraged British and French meddling in Dutch internal politics.

A continuing French aggressive foreign policy against Britain after 1763 was a flagrant refusal to face fiscal realities and therefore a direct contribution to impending revolution. The steadily mounting French debt after 1740 reached a point in the 1760s when taxes failed to meet even the interest payments. Dutch bankers were reluctant to provide new loans because of declining French credit and the close official ties between the Netherlands and Britain. In 1769, following a struggle with the nobles in the provincial courts, Louis XV abandoned tax reform, which might have shifted more revenue burdens to the French upper classes. The country was thus almost bankrupt when it entered war against England on the side of the American colonies, a venture that led to the complete breakdown of French finances in the 1780s.

Britain faced similar problems. With a debt in 1763 roughly double that of 1756, the government had to manage an empire that had tripled

Purchasing a Seat in the Unreformed English Parliament

These selections are from the letters of Lord Chesterfield (1767) and the *Memoirs* of Sir Samuel Romilly (1807).

Bath, December 19, 1767.

My Dear Friend,

. . . In one of our conversations here, this time twelvemonth, I desired him to secure you a seat in the new Parliament; he assured me he would; and, I am convinced, very sincerely; he said even that he would make it his own affair; and desired I would give myself no more trouble about it. Since that, I have heard no more of it; which made me look out for some venal borough: and I spoke to a borough-jobber, and offered five-and-twenty hundred pounds for a secure seat in Parliament; but he laughed at my offer, and said, that there was no such thing as a borough to be had now; for that the rich East and West Indians had secured them all, at the rate of three thousand pounds at least; but many at four thousand; and two or three, that he knew, at five thousand. This, I confess, has vexed me a good deal; and made me the more impatient to know whether Lord Chatham had done anything in it; which I shall know when I go to town, as I propose to do in about a fortnight; and, as soon as I know it, you shall. To tell you truly what I think—I doubt, from all these *nervous disorders*, that Lord Chatham is *hors de combat*, as a Minister; but do not even hint this to anybody. God bless you!

(Signed)   Chesterfield.

[June 27th, 1807.] I shall procure myself a seat in the new Parliament, unless I find that it will cost so large a sum, as, in the state of my family, it would be very imprudent for me to devote to such an object, which I find is very likely to be the case. Tierney, who manages this business for the friends of the late administration, assures me that he can hear of no seats to be disposed of. After a Parliament which has lived little more than four months, one would naturally suppose, that those seats which are regularly sold by the proprietors of them would be very cheap; they are, however, in fact, sold now at a higher price than was ever given for them before. Tierney tells me that he has offered £10,000 for the two seats of Westbury, the property of the late Lord Abingdon, and which are to be made the most of by trustees for creditors, and has met with a refusal. £6000 and £5500 have been given for seats with no stipulation as to time, or against the event of a speedy dissolution by the King's death, or by any change of administration. The truth is, that the new Ministers have bought up all the seats that were to be disposed of, and at any prices. . . .

This buying of seats is detestable; and yet it is almost the way in which one in my situation, who is resolved to be an independent man, can get into Parliament. To come in by a popular election, in the present state of the representation, is quite impossible; to be placed there by some great lord, and to vote as he shall direct, is to be in a state of complete dependence; and nothing hardly remains but to owe a seat to the sacrifice of a part of one's fortune. It is true that many men who buy seats, do it as a matter of pecuniary speculation, as a profitable way of employing their money: they carry on a political trade; they buy their seats, and sell their votes. For myself, I can truly say that, by giving money for a seat, I shall make a sacrifice of my private property, merely that I may be enabled to serve the public. I know what danger there is of men's disguising from themselves the real motives of their actions; but it really does appear to me that it is from this motive alone that I act. . . .

Source: Elizabeth K. Kendall, ed., *A Source-Book of English History* (London: The Macmillan Company, 1912), pp. 302–305.

in size during those same years. The cost of administering the North American colonies alone rose to £135,000 a year in 1763—five times what it had cost in 1756. Colonials were determined to resist new taxation and were intent on occupying western lands held by former Indian allies of the French. The tribes were restless and difficult to pacify since many had fought on both sides and did not know what to expect from British rule; Pontiac's rebellion, between 1763 and 1766, kept the northwestern colonial frontier in a state of near-anarchy. Restoring order to this vast land promised to be a long and expensive process, involving many differences between the crown and its colonial subjects.

At the same time, the new king, George III (1760–1820), was causing a stir in English politics. He alienated many commercial and colonial interests by opposing an aggressive policy toward France. Moreover, he demonstrated a determined intention of wielding constitutional powers never claimed by his Hanoverian predecessors, who had been virtual captives of Whig politicians. It took George only a few years to destroy the power of the Whigs and gain control of Parliament. His ministers accomplished this by means of lavish bribery and patronage, using methods developed earlier by Walpole. By 1770, they had filled the House of Commons with their supporters, known as "the King's Friends." For twelve years, George was the effective head of government, but his policies made enemies and produced a determined opposition party.

Parliamentary opposition merged with popular agitation in the person of John Wilkes (1725–1797), a wealthy member of the Commons and publisher of a newspaper, *The North Briton*. Wilkes became an outspoken critic of the king's policies. When he was imprisoned by the government, Wilkes posed as the champion of civil liberties, becoming overnight the darling of the London populace; but despite preliminary victories in court, he was ultimately forced into exile. Returning from France in 1768, he was again elected to the Commons, again thrown into jail, and again became the center of a great public clamor. For a while, in the early 1770s, England experienced a mild threat of revolution, as people were killed in clashes between protestors and government troops.

This trouble at home was less serious, in the long run, than that provoked in the American colonies. George Grenville (1712–1770), the king's chief minister after 1763, devised a comprehensive plan to settle problems in North America. He forbade colonial settlement beyond the Appalachians, put Indian affairs under English superintendents, established permanent garrisons of English troops for maintenance of order on the frontiers, issued orders against smuggling, sent an English fleet to American waters, assigned English customs officials to American ports, and had Parliament impose new taxes on the colonies. The Sugar Act of 1764 increased duties on sugar, wines, coffee, silk, and linens. The Stamp Act of 1765 required that government stamps be placed on practically every kind of American document, from college diplomas to newspapers. Grenville's program aroused an almost universal colonial protest, immediately allied in spirit with Wilkes' movement in England.

In response to the Stamp Act, colonial assemblies passed resolutions and sent petitions to the king and Parliament protesting the new measure. In the streets the reaction was one of violent protests, riots, and mob actions.

The American Revolution

Within a decade after passage of the Stamp Act, Britain faced open rebellion in its American colonies. The resulting conflict was also a civil war, with many colonists remaining loyal to the crown. Indeed, one of Benjamin Franklin's sons was a Loyalist leader and the last royal governor of New Jersey. But a majority of the colonists, whether New England merchants, Pennsylvania farmers, or Virginia planters, formed a united opposition. Their outlook, combining Locke's political ideas with a spirit of rough frontier independence, was also nationalistic in its dawning awareness tht many English ways were foreign to American needs and values.

A Revolution in Minds and Hearts

John Adams (1735–1826), looking back on the Revolution, was well aware of this developing American nationalism when he wrote in 1818:

> But what do we mean by the American Revolution? Do we mean the American war? The Revolution was effected before the war commenced . . . in the minds and hearts of the people . . . This . . . was the real American Revolution.[1]

From almost the beginning, the American colonies had developed in a direction different from England's. Most Puritan settlers in New England opposed the Stuart kings; hundreds went to fight against Charles I in the 1640s. At the restoration of Charles II, rebels fled again to America. Catholics, who had been favored by the later Stuarts, were persecuted at home after the Glorious Revolution, and many came to the colonies, particularly to Maryland. By 1775, 40 percent of the colonial population had descended from non-English stock, mostly from Ireland and southern Germany. The resulting cultural mix fostered more toleration for differences than was typical of any place in Europe.

Experience in self-government conditioned colonial development. Except for an unsuccessful attempt under James II, England had allowed the colonies relative freedom in conducting their own affairs. This was particularly true during the early eighteenth century, under the corrupt and static Whig oligarchy. Radical political opinion, driven deep underground in England after 1649, ran much nearer the surface in America. Educated colonists remembered Locke's emphasis on the social contract and the right of revolution. These ideas appealed to people who had created their own governments in the wilderness and who were somewhat suspicious of a distant king. In contrast, the ruling Whig politicians forgot Locke's revolutionary implications as they gained power and became proponents of stability.

Colonial political thought was shaped as much by growth as by circumstances, as over 2 million discontented Europeans arrived in the eighteenth century. The Irish and Scotch-Irish, who pushed the frontier to the Appalachians, settled on free or cheap western land. Its easy availability popularized the idea that property was each individual's birthright. Grenville's restriction on westward migration after 1763 therefore aroused much colonial resentment. His policy was generally interpreted as an English effort to monopolize land for a privileged aristocracy. Land speculators, in condemning the English land policy by appealing to free enterprise, found common interests with craftsmen, merchants, and planters, who felt themselves exploited by trade restrictions and credit controls. Expanding American enterprises and profits could not be easily accommodated within British mercantilism.

The peace of 1763, followed by the Grenville program, brought all the major differences between Britain and the colonies into focus. With the French and Spanish out of Canada and Florida, colonists felt little need for British protection while yearning to settle the new lands. They were naturally angered by new taxes and controls over trade, which were required by the rising costs of the new stabilization program. British troops, under these circumstances, were regarded as oppressors rather than defenders or peacekeepers. The changes in British imperial policy came at just the time when they were least likely to be successful.

Confrontation, War, and Independence

Between 1763 and 1775, relations between England and the colonies grew steadily worse, eventually erupting into open hostilities. Neither the king's government nor the colonists had foreseen or planned this result. The few American radicals who may have dreamed of a new political order did not advocate such ideas in this period, when most Americans wanted reforms to restore rights and redress grievances within the British system. The idea of an open break—of war and revolution—became acceptable only as reform efforts failed.

The first colonial protests came with the Grenville program, when the Sugar Act sparked outcries against "taxation without representation" in colonial newspapers and pamphlets. These reactions were mild, however, in comparison with those following the Stamp Act. Colonial assemblies in Massachusetts and New York denounced the law as "tyranny," and a "Stamp Act Congress" meeting in New York petitioned the king to repeal the law. Mob actions occurred in a number of places, but they were less effective than boycotts of English goods, imposed by a thousand colonial merchants. Soon hundreds of British tradesmen were petitioning Parliament, pleading that the taxes be rescinded. This was done in 1766, although Parliament issued a declaration affirming its absolute right to legislate for the colonies.

Having repealed the Stamp Act, Parliament almost immediately enacted other revenue measures. Charles Townshend (1725–1767), chancellor of the exchequer in the next cabinet, had Parliament levy duties on paint, paper, lead, wine, and tea imported into the colonies from Britain. The returns were to pay colonial governors and maintain troops garrisoned in America. Other laws established admiralty courts at Halifax, Boston, Philadelphia, and Charleston, to sit without juries and enforce trade regulations. The decisions of these courts soon generated popular agitation. In Boston, this culminated on March 5, 1770, when soldiers fired into an unruly crowd, killing five people. Meanwhile, American merchants had entered nonimportation agreements that cut British imports by 50 percent. Again, commercial losses induced Parliament to repeal most of the duties, on the very day of the Boston massacre.

For a while, the colonies appeared angry but pacified, until Lord North (1732–1792), the king's new chief minister, blundered into another

Outrage over the Boston Massacre was fanned by propaganda like this etching by Paul Revere, which shows British redcoats firing on unarmed colonial citizens. Revere's view of the incident strayed from the truth.

crisis. He persuaded Parliament to grant a two-thirds cut in duties on East India Company tea delivered to American ports. Because the Company could thus undersell smugglers and legitimate traders, both of these groups quickly converted to political radicalism. The tea was turned away from most American ports. In Boston, at the famous tea party, townsmen in Indian garb dumped the tea into the harbor. The English government retaliated in the "Intolerable Acts," by closing the port of Boston, revoking the Massachusetts Charter, and providing that political offenders be tried in England.

By September 1794, the crisis in Boston had created a revolutionary climate. Representatives of twelve colonies, meeting in the First Continental Congress at Philadelphia, denounced British tyranny, proclaimed political representation to be a natural right, and made plans for armed resistance. By the next April, the explosive situation around Boston had led to a conflict between British regulars and the Massachusetts militia. In battles at Lexington and Concord, near Boston, 8 Americans and 293 British soldiers were killed. Those shots "heard 'round the world" marked the beginning of the American Revolution.

The war begun at Lexington and Concord lasted eight years. At first, the American cause appeared almost hopeless, because the king's government was not inclined to compromise, wishing to make an example of the rebels. The prospect encouraged radical colonial leaders to fight on desperately. It was a time, as Thomas Paine wrote, "to try men's souls,"[2] but it was also a time for dreams of new liberties, new opportunities, and a new social justice that might come with independence.

The turning point of the war came in October 1777. Already occupying New York and Philadelphia, the British attempted to split the colonies by moving an army south from Canada. This army was forced to surrender after suffering a crushing defeat at Saratoga in upper New York. France, which had been cautiously helping the Americans, then signed an alliance guaranteeing American independence. Ultimately, the French persuaded their Spanish ally to enter the war. The Dutch also joined the alliance in a desperate effort to save their American trade. With their sea power effectively countered, the British pulled their two main armies back to defensive positions in New York and on the Virginia coast. In the final campaigns of 1781, French and American troops, aided by the French fleet, forced the surrender of British commander Lord Cornwallis (1738–1805) to George Washington (1732–1799) at Yorktown in Virginia.

While the war continued, American radicals were creating a new nation. Thomas Paine's *Common Sense*, published early in 1776 as a spirited plea for liberty, heavily influenced popular opinion and helped convince the American Congress to break with England. In June, a special Congressional Committee drafted a formal statement of principles. The resulting Declaration of Independence, written by Thomas Jefferson, first announced the creation of the United States. In claiming for every individual "certain inalienable rights . . . to life, liberty, and the pursuit of happiness,"[3] it embodied typical radical appeals to natural law and the social contract.

Similar radical political principles, drawn from the Enlightenment, were espoused in the Articles of Confederation. This document, completed by the Congress in 1778 and ratified by the states three years later, established the new government as a loose league, much like the Dutch Republic. Taxation, control of trade, and issuance of money were all left to the sovereign states, each represented by one vote in Congress. Major decisions required the assent of nine states; amendments to the Articles had to be accepted by the states unanimously. Although Congress could make war and peace, maintain armies, and conduct Indian affairs, it was financially dependent on the states for these functions. The system was designed to protect liberties against a distant central government, dominated by the wealthy.

More obvious demonstrations of radical principles were provided by the new states, which were the real centers of political power. Their constitutions, often ratified in town meetings, manifested Locke's and Montesquieu's ideas concerning the separation of executive, judicial, and legislative function. "Bills of rights" typically guaranteed freedom of speech, press, and religion. Eleven of the thirteen states provided for separation of church and state. Many great loyalist estates were divided into small holdings, and property qualifications for voting were considerably lowered. These were but a few indications of applied radicalism during the war years.

The Conservative Reaction and the American Constitution

After the war ended in 1783, the Articles of Confederation provoked a strong conservative reaction. Some merchants wanted to send their goods to English ports. Others wanted a common stable currency and tariff protection against foreign goods. Wealthy people were frightened by popular uprisings, such as Shays' Rebellion in Massachusetts, and by inflation, caused by state issues of cheap paper currency. Moved by such concerns, prominent conservatives urged a reconsideration of the Articles. Their efforts led to the Constitutional Convention, which met at Philadelphia from May to September 1787. Since radicals, such as Patrick Henry (1736–1799), refused to attend the convention, delegates were united by their concerns for protecting property and maintaining order. Led by George Washington, Alexander Hamilton (1757–1804), Benjamin Franklin (1706–1790), James Madison (1751–1836), and Charles Pinckney (1746–1825), they successfully compromised differences between large and small states, as well as those between mercantile New England and the plantation south. In the end, they succeeded in producing a document that strengthened the national government.

Despite the conservative views of its drafters, the Constitution affirmed some popular principles. It limited the autonomy of public officials, delegated specific powers to the states, and provided for state participation in the amending process. It thus retained some of the states' rights which were so important to the radicals.

The separation of powers was another fundamental principle of the Constitution. It was also revealed in the Constitution's careful definition of the functions ascribed to the legislative, judicial, and executive brances of government. Congress was to make the laws, the president was to apply and enforce them, and the courts were to interpret them. Other provisions prevented any one of the branches from becoming too independent and powerful. The president, for example, could veto laws passed by Congress, but the legislature, by a two-thirds vote, could override a presidential veto. The Supreme Court later expanded its original charge of interpreting laws to interpreting the Constitution itself, thus acquiring the right to declare any law void as unconstitutional.

In recognizing the principle of popular sovereignty, the Constitution was similar to the Articles; it differed in its centralization of government and in its securities against disorder. Proclaiming itself as the supreme law of the land, it specifically prohibited the states from coining money, levying customs, or conducting foreign diplomacy. The president, as chief executive, commanded national military forces, an arrangement meant to protect against popular unrest and disorder. Most of the delegates at Philadelphia feared democracy and favored property qualifications on the franchise, a policy they abandoned only because it was politically impractical. They indicated their distrust of democracy, however, by avoiding the direct election of senators and presidents.

The process of ratifying the Constitution precipitated a great political debate. Congress, dominated by conservatives, ignored the amending provisions of the Articles and appealed directly to the states. Radicals everywhere were alarmed but were generally overwhelmed by arguments from the wealthier, more articulate, and better educated Federalists, who supported the Constitution. By promising written guarantees of individual liberties, the Federalists ultimately won the required nine states and the Constitution was formally adopted on July 2, 1788. Three years later, the first ten amendments guaranteed freedom of religion, speech, and the press, along with security against arbitrary government. Thus the radicals left a lasting legacy, despite the Federalist triumph.

After winning their greatest victory, the Federalists dominated American politics for more than a decade. George Washington was elected as the first president in 1789. His two administrations imposed a high tariff, chartered a national bank, paid public debts at face value, negotiated a commercial treaty with England, and opposed the French Revolution, which began in the year of Washington's election. Ironically, some French revolutionaries, such as Lafayette, who had helped win American independence, were bitterly denounced by American leaders a decade later.

Unfinished Business of the American Revolution

The war for American rights and liberties left much unfinished business. The right to vote did not extend to all male citizens for decades, until changes were made in state constitutions, particularly in the developing western states. An even more flagrant omission involved blacks and women, who were denied freedom and full civil equality after the Revolution, despite their many contributions to the American cause.

Many women helped promote the Revolution. A few, like Mercy Warren, wrote anti-British plays and pamphlets; some published newspapers; and others organized boycotts against British goods. Female patriots in Philadelphia, including Benjamin Franklin's daughter, raised funds to buy shirts for Washington's troops. Women were often involved in dangerous exploits as spies and couriers. Seventeen-year-old Emily Geiger of South Carolina ate the message she was carrying to General Nathanael Green when she was captured by the British. She later delivered it verbally, after riding a hundred miles.

The Franchise Issue in the American Constitutional Convention

Excerpts from the debate here reported arose from a motion to place a property qualification on voting in the Constitution. The proposal failed, leaving authority to decide this question with the states.

Mr. GOUVENEUR MORRIS. He had long learned not to be the dupe of words. The sound of aristocracy, therefore, had no effect on him. It was the thing, not the name, to which he was opposed, and one of his principal objections to the Constitution as it is now before us, is that it threatens this country with an aristocracy. The aristocracy will grow out of the House of Representatives. Give the votes to people who have no property, and they will sell them to the rich who will be able to buy them. We should not confine our attention to the present moment. The time is not distant when this country will abound with mechanics and manufacturers who will receive their bread from their employers. Will such men be the secure and faithful guardians of liberty? Will they be the impregnable barrier against aristocracy? He was as little duped by the association of the words 'taxation and representation'. The man who does not give his vote freely is not represented. It is the man who dictates the vote. . . .

Col. MASON. . . . The true idea in his opinion was that every man having evidence of attachment to and permanent common interest with the society ought to share in all its rights and privileges. . . .

Mr. MADISON. The right of suffrage is certainly one of the fundamental articles of republican government, and ought not to be left to be regulated by the Legislature. A gradual abridgement of this right has been the mode in which aristocracies have been built on the ruins of popular forms. . . . In future times a great majority of the people will not only be without landed, but any other sort of, property. These will either combine under the influence of their common situation; in which case, the rights of property and the public liberty will not be secure in their hands: or what is more probable, they will become the tools of opulence and ambition, in which case there will be equal danger on another side. . . .

Dr. FRANKLIN. It is of great consequence that we should not depress the virtue and public spirit of our common people; of which they displayed a great deal during the war, and which contributed principally to the favorable issue of it. . . . He did not think that the elected had any right in any case to narrow the privileges of the electors. He quoted as arbitrary the British statute setting forth the danger of tumultuous meetings, and under that pretext narrowing the right of suffrage to persons having freeholds of a certain value. . . .

Mr. MERCER [Md.]. . . . He objected to the footing on which the qualification was put, but particularly to the mode of election by the people. The people can not know and judge of the characters of candidates. The worse possible choice will be made.

Source: Samuel E. Morison, ed., *Sources and Documents Illustrating the American Revolution* (Oxford, England: Clarendon Press, 1929), pp. 276–278.

In addition to those who stayed home, some 20,000 women moved with the armies. Many were wives of Continental common soldiers, who marched on foot behind the troops, carrying their baggage and their children. In camp, they cooked, washed, and cared for their men, sometimes foraging after battles among enemy dead for clothing and ammunition. A few saw combat, like the legendary Mary Hayes (Molly Pitcher) and Margaret Corbin, who continued to fire their husbands' artillery pieces after the men fell in battles at Fort Washington (1776) and Monmouth

(1778). Corbin's husband was killed, and she was severely wounded in the arm and chest. The most famous female fighter in the Revolution was Deborah Sampson, an orphaned Connecticut schoolteacher, who donned men's clothes and served for more than a year in Washington's army, before she was discovered and honorably discharged.

Despite their sacrifices, American women gained few immediate improvements. They remained legally subordinated to their husbands in the disposition of property and practically denied the possibility of divorce. Reacting against these conditions, Abigail Adams and Mercy Warren both urged their husbands to promote legal and political equality for women during the Revolution. For a while, a mild feminism was publicly expressed. The New Jersey constitution of 1776 gave women the vote, and the same state's election law of 1790 permitted local boards to enfranchise women. But general indifference to the nascent women's movement led the New Jersey legislature to end female suffrage in 1807.

The conservative reaction was even stronger against blacks, who provided a major problem to leaders of the Revolution. Although slavery was already losing its practical value, it was still important in the southern plantation economy. Moreover, free northern blacks, including several hundred around Boston, were already becoming politically conscious. To many slaveholders, the situation promised violent black rebellion.

In response to this fear, blacks were at first banned from military service, despite the embarrassing facts that many free blacks had supported the Stamp Act protest. But when the British promised freedom to slave recruits and the supply of white American volunteers dwindled, Congress began enlisting blacks, promising slaves their freedom. Even before they could be legally recruited, black soldiers fought at Lexington, Concord, and Bunker Hill, and they participated in every major battle afterward. They also served at sea, even on Virginia ships; but they were never admitted to the Virginia militia or to any military forces of Georgia and the Carolinas, although a contingent of Santo Domingo blacks under French command fought the British at Savannah. The southern adherence to slavery divided the new country, providing a major controversial issue at the Constitutional Convention.

Outside of the Deep South, a strong black emancipation movement developed during and immediately after the Revolutionary era. While more than 100,000 former slaves escaped to Canada, to the Indians, or to British sanctuary ships, many blacks, both free and slave, exploited the rhetoric of the Revolution to petition for their freedom and equality. Such petitions were supported by a growing number of white dissidents among Quakers and political activists, such as James Otis (1724–1783), Thomas Paine, Benjamin Rush (1745–1813), and Benjamin Franklin. In response, every state limited or abolished the slave trade; many owners, even in the south, freed their slaves; six state constitutions (Vermont, Connecticut, Rhode Island, Pennsylvania, New York, and New Jersey) abolished slavery; and practical legal emancipation was achieved in New Hampshire and Massachusetts. Free Massachusetts blacks won the vote in 1783, a precedent slowly adopted by other free states.

Such gains, however, were offset by losses. Many blacks who had been promised their freedom were enslaved by their former masters and even by their new British friends. Laws against slavery were not always enforced. Even in the northern states, emancipation was often legally delayed for decades, so that in 1810 there were more than 35,000 slaves in New York, New Jersey, and Pennsylvania. The conservative reaction of the 1790s, stimulated by debates in the Constitutional Convention, and the invention of the cotton gin, which gave a new impetus to cotton planting, confirmed the south in its economic and emotional commitments to slavery. American slaves after the 1790s were further from "the rights of all men" than they had been before the Revolution. This injustice was the ultimate cause for a subsequent bloody and tragic civil war.

Impact of the American Revolution Abroad

Even with its shortcomings, the American Revolution exerted a tremendous influence elsewhere in the world. Americans were generally regarded as having returned to a "state of nature" and then established a new government by a written social contract. As their republic promised freedom, maintained order, and achieved moderate prosperity, it seemed to validate the principles of the Enlightenment for literate peoples of western Europe, generating a wave of revolutionary sentiment, from Ireland to Hungary.

The trend was evident, even in England. Before the Revolution, a number of influential Englishmen, notably Edmund Burke (1729–1797), championed the American cause in Parliament and English radical reformers, like Major John Cartwright (1740–1824), welcomed American independence. Pro-American enthusiasm languished after the war began, but it revived when American fortunes improved after Saratoga. In 1779, reform societies sprang up in London and in rural Yorkshire. The more radical London society grew into a National Association, with delegates drawn from county organizations, imitating the American town meetings, state conventions, and Congress. The Association welcomed American independence while calling for parliamentary reform.

Even more drastic changes occurred in Ireland. During the war, after centuries of religious persecution and economic exploitation under English rule, Henry Gratton (1746–1820) and Henry Flood (1732–1791), two leaders of the Irish Protestant gentry, exploited British weakness to obtain concessions. Having created an Irish militia, supposedly to protect the coasts against American or French attacks, they then followed American precedents. In February 1782 a convention at Dublin, representing 80,000 militiamen, demanded legislative independence. After the British Parliament subsequently agreed, a new Irish legislature could make its own laws, subject only to a veto by the British king. Ireland thus acquired a status denied the American colonies in 1774.

Ireland's response to the Revolution was almost matched in the Netherlands, where a popular movement, in sympathy with the Americans and the French, nearly ruined the Dutch economy. William V, the stadtholder and a relative of the English royal family, was unjustly blamed for the nation's misfortunes. Radical propaganda during the 1780s subjected his government to the most violent abuse, followed by uprisings in 1785 and 1787, which forced William to leave his capital. For a brief period, in the ensuing civil war, "patriots" held most of the country. The revolt was suppressed only when

William's brother-in-law, the king of Prussia, sent 20,000 troops.

In France, revolutionary refugees from Holland found a congenial atmosphere, decisively affected by American ideas. To French philosophical radicals, the American Revolution proved their principles; to Frenchmen in the establishment, it promised a new and favorable diplomatic alignment against Britain. Consequently, radical ideas were no longer confined to learned treatises but appeared everywhere in pamphlets, newspapers, and even in the theater. Aristocractic vanities and even royal formalities suddenly became subjects for humorous comment; but, as one French noble observed, no one "stopped to consider the dangers of the example which the new world set to the old."

The French Revolution

Beginning in 1789, France produced the most significant of the eighteenth-century revolutions. In some ways it was remarkably similar to the American movement that had preceded it. Both revolutions applied principles of the Enlightenment; both swept away traditional systems; both followed similar three-stage courses, moving from moderate to radical before a final conservative swing; and both helped set in motion modern constitutional government, along with democracy and nationalism. There were, however, striking differences. Unlike the American colonies, France had a classic Old Regime, with aristocratic privilege and monarchy. Instead of being far removed from the centers of civilization, it was the most populous and cultured state of western Europe. Its revolution, therefore, was more violent and more decisive.

The Explosive Summer of 1789

During the summer of 1789, France faced a financial crisis, caused primarily by military expenditures and a parasitic aristocracy, which resisted any cuts in its returns from the treasury and any taxes on its wealth. Louis XVI had succeeded his grandfather in 1774. The young king was intelligent but indolent and dominated by his frivolous wife, Marie Antoinette, whose limited political vision and influence over her husband increased his problems. The result of this lapse of leadership was a political near-breakdown, followed by a sudden explosion of popular unrest and agitation.

Between Louis' succession and 1789, his finance ministers continuously struggled with a rapidly rising debt. It had increased by 400 million livres during French participation in the American Revolution and had reached a total of 4 billion livres in 1789 (equivalent to $5.6 billion in 1980 dollars), when interest payments absorbed half of the national revenues. Robert Turgot (1727–1781), controller-general of finance, had proposed deep cuts in expenditure, but he was forced out by the nobles. His successor, Swiss banker Jacques Necker (1732–1804), after resorting to more exhaustive borrowing, was dismissed in 1781, and two succeeding ministers failed to deal with the problem. In 1788, Louis called an assembly of nobles, hoping that they might accept taxation and economy measures. They flatly rejected his requests, insisting that he call the Estates-General, which had not met since 1614. In this body, where the clergy and nobility traditionally voted separately, they hoped to dominate the Third Estate, including the middle-class majority of taxpayers.

Ultimately, Louis summoned the Estates-General, with more than 600 elected delegates representing the Third Estate. They were chosen during the spring of 1789, amid feverish excitement, and supplied by their constituents with lists of grievances, the famous *cahiers*, which involved a diverse mixture of reform proposals, including demands for a national legislature, a jury system, freedom of the press, and equitable taxes. Once the Estates-General had convened, the Third Estate insisted that voting should be by head rather than by chamber, because it had more members than the other two estates (clergy and nobles) combined. Six weeks of wrangling over this issue brought delegates from the Third Estate along with lesser numbers from the other two orders, to a meeting at an indoor tennis court. There, on June 20, 1789, they solemnly swore the historic tennis-court oath, agreeing not to disband until they had produced a French constitution. Later, after defying a royal order to reconvene separately, they declared themselves to be the National Constituent Assembly of France.

Within weeks, the king had completely lost control of the situation. Although grudgingly accepting the National Assembly, he had 18,000 troops moved to the vicinity of Versailles. Middle-class members of the Assembly, in near panic at the threat of military intervention, appealed for popular support. On July 14, an estimated 100,000 Parisian shopkeepers, workers, and women demolished the Bastille, liberating the prisoners. It had served as the most visible symbol of the Old Regime, and its fall clearly demonstrated the rapily growing popular defiance. The event also destroyed Louis' courage and his municipal Parisian government, which was replaced by a middle-class council, with its own "national guard." Meanwhile, other urban uprisings and peasant violence in the country consolidated the Assemby's position.

As emotional tensions ran high throughout the country, the government faced a serious problem involving blacks. Although illegal in France, slavery was a legal foundation of the economy in the French West Indies, that remaining valuable gem of the French empire. Many wealthy French aristocrats and businessmen who owned plantations in Santo Domingo and Martinique feared that revolutionary rhetoric would promote slave rebellion. Another complication was provided by mulattoes, many of whom were wealthy planters themselves, who supported the slave system but complained about infringement of their civil rights, both in France and in the islands. Their petitions were enforced and carried further by an organization known as the *Amis des Noirs* ("Friends of the Blacks"), which capitalized upon the revolutionary atmosphere during the summer of 1789 to spread abroad antiracist ideas from the Enlightenment.

Another unique aspect of the summer upheaval was the aggressive roles played by women. In the *cahiers* they had presented demands for legal equality, improved education, and better conditions in the markets. They were present in large numbers at the fall of the Bastille. Later, as bread prices rose, they organized street marches and protests. On August 7, hundreds went to Versailles and praised the king for accepting the Assembly. A climax in this drama came on October 5, when some 6000 women, many of them armed, marched to Versailles, accompanied by the National Guard. There a deputation of six women, led by a seventeen-year-old flower seller, Louison Chabray, met the king, who promised more bread for the city. Other women entered the hall where the Assembly was sitting, disrupted proceedings and forced an adjournment. The next day, after a mob stormed the palace and killed some guards, the king and his family returned to Paris as virtual prisoners, their carriage surrounded by women carrying pikes, upon which were impaled the heads of the murdered bodyguards.

The First Phase of Middle-Class Revolution

Shortly after the march on Versailles, the Assembly achieved some political stability by declaring martial law, to be enforced by the National Guard. During the next two years, its leaders followed the Enlightenment in attempting to reorganize the whole French political system. Because most came from the middle class, with a preponderance of lawyers and a sprinkling of nobles, they were committed to change but also determined to keep order, protect property, and further their special interests. Thus, as they achieved their goals, they became increasingly satisfied and conservative.

The most dramatic action of the Assembly occurred on the night of August 4, 1789. By then, order had been restored in the cities, but peasants all over France were still rising against their lords—burning, pillaging, and sometimes murdering—in desperate efforts to destroy records of their manorial obligations. Faced with this violence and at first undecided between force and concessions, the Assembly ultimately chose concessions. Consequently, on that fateful night, nobles and clergy rose in the Assembly to denounce tithes, serfdom, manorial dues, feudal privileges, unequal taxes, and the sale of offices. In a few hours between sunset and dawn, the Old Regime, which had evolved over a thousand years, was completely transformed.

To define its political principles and set its course, on August 26 the Assembly issued the *Declaration of the Rights of Man and the Citizen.* Intended as a preamble to a new constitution, it proclaimed human "inalienable rights" to liberty, property, security, and resistance to oppression. It also promised free speech, press, and religion, consistent with public order. Property was declared inviolate unless required for "public safety," in which case the owner was to receive "just compensation." All (male) citizens were to be equal before the law and eligible for public office on their qualifications. Taxes were to be levied only by common consent. With its emphases upon civil equality and property rights, the declaration was a typical middle-class statement.[4]

Understandably, the Assembly aimed its economic policies at freeing capitalistic enterprise. It assured payment to middle-class bondholders of government issues and financed this policy by sale of lands, confiscated from the church and from nobles who had fled the country. It sold to middle-class speculators much of this new public land; very little was ever acquired by peasants. The Assembly also abolished all internal tolls,

A contemporary print of Parisian women advancing on Versailles on October 5, 1789, shows the determined marchers carrying pikes and dragging an artillery piece. The following day the king and the royal family were returned to Paris, and the women were hailed as heroines of the Revolution.

The Declaration of the Rights of Man and Citizen

This moderate middle-class document of the French Revolution was inspired by the American Declaration of Independence. Notice, however, that it differs slightly in its precise mention of property rights.

The National Assembly recognizes and declares, in the presence and under the auspices of the Supreme Being, the following rights of man and citizen.

1. Men are born and remain free and equal in rights. Social distinctions can be based only upon the common good.

2. The aim of every political association is the preservation of the natural and imprescriptible rights of man. These rights are liberty, property, security, and resistance to oppression.

4. Liberty consists in the power to do anything that does not injure others; accordingly, the exercise of the natural rights of each man has no limits except those that assure to the other members of society the enjoyment of these same rights. These limits can be determined only by law.

5. The law can forbid only such actions as are injurious to society. Nothing can be forbidden that is not forbidden by the law, and no one can be constrained to do that which it does not decree.

6. Law is the expression of the general will. All citizens have the right to take part personally, or by their representatives, in its enactment. It must be the same for all, whether it protects or punishes.

7. No man can be accused, arrested, or detained, except in the cases determined by the law and according to the forms which it has prescribed. Those who call for, expedite, execute, or cause to be executed arbitrary orders should be punished; but every citizen summoned or seized by virtue of the law ought to obey instantly. . . .

8. The law ought to establish only punishments that are strictly and obviously necessary, and no one should be punished except by virtue of a law established and promulgated prior to the offence and legally applied.

9. Every man being presumed innocent until he has been declared guilty, if it is judged indispensable to arrest him, all severity that may not be necessary to secure his person ought to be severely suppressed by law.

10. No one should be disturbed on account of his opinions, even religious, provided their manifestation does not trouble the public order as established by law.

11. The free communication of thoughts and opinions is one of the most precious of the rights of man; every citizen can then speak, write, and print freely, save for the responsibility for the abuse of this liberty in the cases determined by law.

12. The guarantee of the rights of man and citizen necessitates a public force; this force is then instituted for the advantage of all and not for the particular use of those to whom it is entrusted.

13. For the maintenance of the public force and for the expenses of administration a general tax is indispensable; it should be equally apportioned among all the citizens according to their means.

14. All citizens have the right to ascertain, by themselves or through their representatives, the necessary amount of public taxation, to consent to it freely, to follow the use of it, and to determine the quota, the assessment, the collection, and the duration of it.

16. Any society in which the guarantee of the rights is not assured, or the separation of powers not determined, has no constitution.

17. Property being a sacred and inviolable right, no one can be deprived of it, unless a legally established public necessity evidently requires it, under the condition of a just and prior indemnity.

Source: George L. Mosse et al., eds., *Europe in Review* (Chicago: Rand McNally, 1962), pp. 162–164.

industrial regulations, and guilds, thus throwing open all arts and crafts. It banned trade unions, decreeing that wages be set by individual bargaining. Except for a few remaining controls on foreign trade, the Assembly applied the doctrines of Adam Smith and the physiocrats, substituting free competition for economic regulation.

The Assembly's land policies conditioned its approach to organized religion. Having taken church property and eliminated tithes, many members were reluctant to abolish the state church completely, believing the church, if controlled, would help to defend property. Consequently, the Assembly passed the Civil Constitution of the Clergy, which made the clergy salaried public servants but abolished all archbishoprics and reduced the number of bishoprics. Monastic orders were simply dissolved. Incumbent churchmen were required to swear first loyalty to the nation, but only seven bishops and half the clergy conformed. The remainder became bitterly hostile to the government, exerting great influence, particularly among the peasants.

Another serious problem involved the West Indian colonies, blacks, and free mulattoes. News from France in 1789 brought quick and sometimes violent political reactions in Santo Domingo and Martinique, as planters, merchants, poor whites, mulattoes, and slaves hoped that the Revolution would further their diverse interests. French absentee planters and island delegates in the Assembly differed on trade policies and local colonial autonomy, but they concurred in their fanatic defense of slavery and their opposition to civil rights for free mulattoes. Meanwhile, mulattoes in France spread their pamphlets and petitioned the Assembly, supported by the *Amis des Noirs*, whose spokesmen also angrily attacked slavery in the Assembly hall. The chamber was left divided and nearly powerless. It first gave the island governments complete control over their blacks and mulattoes. Then, yielding to the radicals, it granted political rights to mulattoes born of free parents. Finally, as civil war racked the islands, it bowed to the planters and repealed its last measure in September 1791.

The Assembly also dashed some high hopes for French women. The early Revolution enlisted many, not only from the poor rioting Parisians of the shops and markets, but also women of the middle class, whose salons were political centers. These hostesses included Theroigne de Méricourt (1762–1817), a Belgian courtesan who became a revolutionary street orator, Madame de Staël (1766–1817), Necker's daughter and a popular novelist, and Madame Roland (1754–1793), a successful party stategist. Women were already prominent in the political clubs of this era. Etta Palm d'Aelders, a Dutch activist, formed a woman's patriotic society, and even proposed a female militia. In addition, some women were involved in a strong feminist movement. Olympe de Gouges (see ch. 20), charged the Assembly with securing the "inalienable rights" of women. The cause was taken up by the *Amis de la Verité*, a women's organization which regularly lobbied the Assembly for free divorce, women's education, and women's civil rights. Its pleas, however, were ignored.

After two years of controversy, the Assembly produced the Constitution of 1791, which made France a limited monarchy. It assigned the lawmaking function to a single-chambered Legislative Assembly, which was to meet every two years. The king could select ministers and temporarily veto laws but could not dismiss the legislature. The Constitution also created an independent and elected judiciary. Local government was completely reorganized on three levels—departments, districts, and communes—with elected officials relatively free of supervision from Paris. Despite rights guaranteed in the Declaration, only those male citizens who paid a specified minimum of direct taxes acquired the vote. Property qualifications were even higher for deputies to the Assembly and national officials. Women were made "passive citizens," without the vote, but marriage became a civil contract, with divorce open to both parties. Other individual rights under a new law code were guaranteed according to the principles of the Declaration.

These provisions, and other acts of the Assembly involving the colonies, blacks, and women, indicated the conservative orientation of the early Revolution, before September 1791. This was particularly true of the property qualifications on voting and office-holding, which guaranteed that the new monarchy would be largely controlled by the upper middle classes. Their concern now was to retain their supremacy by blocking further changes.

The Drift Toward Radicalism

After June 1791, when the king and his family attempted to flee the country, the Revolution drifted steadily toward radicalism. Although the attempt failed, Louis' action as well as the suspicion that he was conspiring with enemies of the Revolution turned many French people into republicans.

When the Legislative Assembly met in September 1791, it was plagued with troubles. The lower classes distrusted the Assembly because they were not represented. Peasants, angry because their priests had been dispossessed, and urban workers, worried about inflation and unemployment, petitioned the Assembly with their grievances. Mulattoes on Santo Domingo denounced the recent denial of their civil rights and launched revolts against the governor. The Assembly also learned that many foreign governments were displeased with its treatment of the French royal family and the nobles.

Factionalism within the Assembly reflected divisions and differences of opinion in the country. About a third of the deputies supported the constitutional monarchy. Another large group wavered from issue to issue, and a vocal minority wanted to scrap the monarchy and establish a republic. These radical deputies generally expressed sentiments originating with the Jacobin Club, a highly vocal organization of political extremists who met regularly at a former Dominican monastery. Although most members were from the middle class, they ultimately depended upon support from Parisian artisans and workers.

Sterile debate gave way to enthusiasm as the country slipped into foreign war during the spring of 1792. Leopold of Austria, brother of the French queen, joined the king of Prussia in declaring publicly that restoration of French absolutism was "of common interest to all sovereigns."[5] In response, Theroigne Mérincourt, just released from Austrian custody, addressed the Jacobin Club, eloquently pleading for overthrow of the monarchy and war against the Habsburg enemy. Her call echoed all over France. At the same time, raging civil war in the West Indies, which drove up sugar prices and encouraged speculative hoarding, turned popular opinion against the planters. Angry mobs of men and women stormed the warehouses, seized the sugar, and sold it at reasonable prices. The Assembly responded to both challenges by restoring civil liberties to free black and mulatto citizens and declaring war on Austria. French citizens went mad with fanatic patriotism. Thousands of recruits enlisted, and Mérincourt organized a company of "Amazons," armed with pikes and muskets.

Despite their enthusiasm and dedication, French armies suffered early defeats when Prussia allied with Austria against France. These misfortunes aroused further suspicion of Louis, which intensified when the Prussian Duke of Brunswick, commanding the invading army, threatened in June to destroy Paris if the French royal family were harmed. The faction of the radicals known as the Girondists, who mainly represented the middle class outside of Paris, used the proclamation as propaganda. They relied on the support of paramilitary organizations of men and women in the provinces and used a mulatto legion in the army to arouse popular support.

The French nation, particularly Paris, responded to Brunswick's manifesto with fury maintained by the Jacobin leaders' impassioned oratory against the king and the moderates. The most effective of the Jacobins was Georges-Jacques Danton (1759–1794), the deputy prosecutor for the Paris Commune, an enormous brute of a man with a voice of commanding power, who mesmerized angry audiences as he denounced the king as a traitor. Supported by Paris mobs, the Commune seized power from the Legislative Assembly, deposed the king, and executed some 2000 suspected royalists in the notorious "September massacres." It then called for a national convention, with members elected by universal male suffrage, to draw up a new constitution. Jacobin hysteria spread throughout France, even after September 22 when the newly assembled National Convention declared France a republic.

Debate over the fate of the king and the nature of the new constitution intensified the contention between moderates and radicals. Danton shared leadership of the radicals in the Convention with Maximilien Robespierre (1758–1794), an idealistic and fanatic follower of Rousseau, and Jean-Paul Marat (1743–1793), publisher of *Ami du Peuple,* a newspaper which violently and consistently denounced traitors and counter-revolutionaries. Opposing Danton, Robespierre, and Marat were the Girondists, who also favored war but feared mob violence and democratic reforms. Most of them wanted to postpone the king's trial, but they lost ground during the fall. The Jacobins finally triumphed in the crucial debates that led to the king's execution in January 1793.

Imbued now with a new fighting spirit, French armies defeated the foreign invaders and went on the offensive, occupying the Rhineland, Belgium, Nice, and Savoy. These French victories so fired the hopes and imaginations of the Jacobins that they insisted on exporting the Revolution by force. The National Convention, which the Jacobins now controlled, announced that France would "grant fraternity to all peoples who wish to recover their liberty."[6] It then declared war on all tyrants and ordered the inhabitants of all countries to accept the principles of the Revolution. Alarmed by the execution of the king and this proclamation, England, Holland, Spain, and Sardinia joined Austria and Prussia in a general coalition against France. In the spring of 1793, four armies of the coalition crossed the French frontiers.

Louis' execution plus worsening conditions among the Paris poor widened the breach between Jacobins and Girondists and brought matters to a desperate crisis. When Girondists staged uprisings in Marseilles, Lyons, Bordeaux, and Toulon, Jacobins in the Paris Commune called a howling mob into the Convention hall on May 31, 1793 and purged the National Convention of any remaining Girondists. Other Girondists throughout France were placed under surveillance.

The Jacobin Republic

The Convention was now a council of the most extreme Jacobins, but the transition of power was not completed until after July 12, 1793, when Charlotte Corday, a young Girondist sympathizer, came to Paris from Caen and murdered Marat. He had been the revered leader of the extreme left, known as the *Enragés,* and his death

Jacques-Louis David, *The Death of Marat* (1793). David's painting extols the murdered Marat as a martyr of the Revolution.

infuriated the street people. The resulting wave of anti-Girondist hysteria brought the Convention under the domination of Robespierre, who remained in power until the late spring of 1794. During that time, revolutionary France reorganized itself, suppressed internal strife, and drove out foreign invaders, thus bringing to climax the success of the radical Jacobin party.

The regime achieved its success largely through rigid dictatorship and terror. The Convention created a twelve-member Committee of Public Safety, headed first by Danton and after July by Robespierre. Subordinate committees were established for the departments, districts, and communes. These bodies deliberately forced conformity by fear, using neighbors to inform on neighbors and children to testify against their parents. Suspects, once identified, were brought to trial before revolutionary tribunals, with most receiving quick death sentences. Between September 1793, and July 1794, some 25,000 victims were dragged to public squares in carts—the famous tumbrels—and delivered to the guillotine. Ultimately, the Terror swallowed most of the revolutionaries, including Danton in April 1794 and Robespierre himself in July 1794.

While it lasted, the Jacobin dictatorship was remarkably successful in its war efforts, mobilizing all of France to fight. The convention made all males between eighteen and forty eligible for military service, a policy which ultimately produced a force of 800,000, the largest standing army ever assembled in France. Officers were promoted on merit and encouraged to exercise initiative. The government also took over industries and directed them to produce large quantities of uniforms, arms, medical supplies, and equipment. In Paris alone, 258 forges made 1000 gun barrels a day. Between 1793 and 1795, the French citizen armies carried out a series of remarkably sucessful campaigns. They regained all French territory, annexed Belgium, and occupied other areas extending to the Rhine, the Alps, and the Pyrenees, thus gaining, in two years, the "natural frontiers" that Louis XIV had dreamed about. By 1794, Prussia and Spain had left the coalition and Holland had become a French ally. Only England, Austria, and Sardinia remained at war with France.

Flushed with their victories, the Jacobins enacted domestic reforms reflecting a peculiar combination of hysteria and reason. They abolished all symbols of status, such as knee breeches, powdered wigs, and jewelry. Titles were discarded, and people were addressed as "citizen" or "citizeness." Streets were renamed to commemorate revolutionary events or heroes. The calendar was reformed by dividing each month into three weeks of ten days each and giving the months new names; July, for example, became Thermidor (hot) to eliminate reference to the tyrant Julius Caesar. The Revolution took on a semireligious character in ceremonies and fêtes, which featured young attractive women as living symbols for reason, virtue, and duty. Along with these changes came a strong reaction against Christianity: churches were closed and religious images destroyed. For a while a "Worship of the Supreme Being" was substituted for Roman Catholicism, but finally in 1794 religion became a private matter.

Despite their stated beliefs in free enterprise as an ideal, the Jacobins imposed a number of economic controls. The government enacted emergency war measures such as rationing, fixed wages and prices, and currency controls. It also punished profiteers, used the property of emigrés to relieve poverty, sold land directly to peasants, and freed the peasants from all compensatory payments to their old lords.

Colonial problems, which had confounded the National and Legislative Assemblies, were met head-on by the Jacobin Convention. The grant of citizenship to free blacks and mulattoes of the islands in 1792 had drawn the mulattoes to the government side, but colonial armies, enlisted by the governors, faced determined insurrection from royalists and resentful escaped slaves. Sometimes the two forces were united, with support from Spain or the British. In the late spring of 1793, the harried governor of Santo Domingo issued a decree freeing all former slaves and calling upon them to join against foreign enemies. His strategy narrowly averted a British conquest. Subsequently, the Convention received a delegation from Santo Domingo and heard a plea for liberty from a 101-year-old former slave woman. The chamber responded by freeing all slaves in French territories, giving them full citizenship rights.

Unfortunately, the revolutionary women in France were not so successful. At first, the radicals welcomed women as supporters, but after the Jacobins gained power they regarded revolutionary women as troublemakers. By the spring of 1794, the Convention had suppressed all women's societies and imprisoned many, including Olympe de Gouges. She was soon sent to the guillotine for her alleged royalist sympathies. The Jacobin legislature continued to deny women the vote, although it did improve education, available medical care, and property rights for women.

Because they regulated the economy and showed concern for the lower classes, the Jacobins have often been considered socialists. The Constitution of 1793, which was developed by the Convention but suspended almost immediately because of the war, does not support this interpretation. The new constitution guaranteed private property, included a charter of individual liberties, confirmed the Constitution of 1791's accent on local autonomy, and provided for a Central Committee, appointed by the departments. The greatest difference, in comparison with the earlier constitution, was the franchise, which was now granted to all adult males. Although the Jacobin constitution indicated a concern for equality of opportunity, it also revealed its authors to be eighteenth-century radical liberals, who followed Rousseau rather than Locke.

End of the Terror and the Conservative Reaction

The summer of 1794 brought a conservative reaction against radical revolution. With French arms victorious everywhere, rigid discipline no longer seemed necessary, but Robespierre, still committed to Rousseau's "republic of virtue," was determined to continue the Terror. When he demanded voluntary submission to the "General Will" as necessary for achieving social equality, justice, and brotherly love, many practical politicians among his colleagues doubted his sanity. Others wondered if they would be among those next eliminated to purify society. They

In this satirical print, Robespierre, having executed all others during the Terror, guillotines the executioner. Robespierre himself was guillotined in the summer of 1794.

therefore cooperated to condemn him in the Convention. In July 1794 he was sent, with twenty of his supporters, to the guillotine, amid great celebration by his enemies.

Robespierre's fall ended the Terror and initiated a revival of the pre-Jacobin past. In 1794, the Convention eliminated the Committee of Public Safety; the next year it abolished the Revolutionary Tribunal and the radical political clubs, while freeing thousands of political prisoners. It also banned women from attendance in the Convention hall, an act which symbolized the return to a time when women's political influence was confined to the ballroom, the bedroom, or the salon. Indeed, as the formerly exiled Girondists, emigré royalists, and nonconforming priests returned to France, Parisian politics moved from the streets to private domiciles of the elite. Outside of Paris, by the summer of 1795, armed vigilantes roamed the countryside, seeking out and murdering former Jacobins. Everywhere, the earlier reforming zeal and patriotic fervor gave way to conservative cynicism.

There was to be one last gasp of idealism, although it was outside the revolutionary mainstream. Francois-Noël Babeuf (1760–1797) was a radical journalist and true believer in the spirit of the Enlightenment, who expected utopia from the Revolution. To its success, he sacrificed his worldly goods and his family; his wife and children went hungry while he moved into and out of jails before 1795. An earlier follower of Robespierre, he later condemned his former mentor as a traitor to the principle of equality. According to Babeuf, liberty was not possible while the rich exploited the poor; the solution had to be a "society of equals," where the republic would guarantee efficient production and equitable distribution of goods. Babeuf's nascent socialism, so out of tune with his times, was suppressed in May 1796, along with his attempted uprising against the government. At his trial, despite his heroic oratory, the support of his long-suffering wife, and his self-inflicted stab wound, he was condemned and sent to the guillotine.

Before it dissolved itself in 1795, the Convention proclaimed still another constitution and established a new political system known as the Directory, which governed France until 1799. Heading the new government was an executive council of five members (directors) appointed by the upper house of a bicameral (two-house) legislature. Deputies to the two chambers were selected by assemblies of electors in each department. These electors were chosen by adult male taxpayers, but the electors themselves had to be substantial property owners. Indeed, they numbered only some 20,000 in a total population of more than 25 million. Government was thus securely controlled by the upper middle classes, a condition also evident by the return to free trade.

The Directory was conspicuously conservative and antidemocratic, but it was also antiroyalist. A Bourbon restoration would have also restored church and royalist lands, which had been largely acquired by wealthy capitalists during the Revolution. Politicians who had participated in the Revolution or voted for the execution of Louis XVI had even greater reason to fear restoration of the monarchy.

In pursuing this antiroyalist path at a time when royalist principles were regaining popularity, the Directory had to depend on the recently developed professional military establishment. In 1797, for example, the army was used to prevent the seating of royalist deputies. The Directory encouraged further military expansion, hoping to revive the patriotic revolutionary fervor. Of three armies it sent into Austrian territory, two failed, but the one led by Napoleon Bonaparte (1769–1821) crossed the Alps in 1796 to crush the Austrians and Sardinians. After 1797, only England, protected by its fleet, remained at war with France. The French Revolution was over, but its momentous Napoleonic aftermath of military dictatorship was just beginning.

Significance of the French Revolution

The French Revolution, as evidenced by the Napoleonic dictatorship which it produced, was an immediate failure; for France at the turn of the nineteenth century, had secured neither liberty, nor equality, nor fraternity. Except for certain prosperous members of the middle classes, the French economy promised less for most people in 1796 than it had two decades earlier. Most discouraging was the realization that the Revolution had betrayed its own ideals, leaving the French people cynical and disillusioned.

The Revolution, nevertheless, had brought great changes. It had abolished serfdom and feudal privileges, created a uniform system of local government, laid the groundwork for a national education system, started legal reforms that would culminate in the great Napoleonic Code, abolished slavery in the colonies, and established the standardized metric system. The ideal, if not the practice, of constitutional government had been rooted in the French mind. Moreover, French armies, even before 1800, had scattered abroad the seeds of liberalism, constitutionalism, and even democracy. The most striking result of the Revolution in its own time was its violent disturbance of old orders; from Ireland to Poland, nothing would ever be the same again.

Long-term results of the Revolution may be evaluated much more positively than its immediate effects. During the first decade of the nineteenth century, many former idealists saw dark curtains drawn over windows through which the Enlightenment had once shone so brightly. This blackout, however, was only temporary. Even before Napoleon experienced his first major defeat at Leipzig in 1813, his enemies had adopted that philosophy of liberation which had fired French imagination in the early 1790s. The spirit of radicalism was revived again among English working-class rioters in 1817. Every other European liberal movement of the nineteenth century borrowed something from the French Revolution.

Another result was equally significant but less promising. The Jacobin republic spawned a fanatic and infectious patriotism, most effectively exploited by Napoleon. When this was combined with the self-righteous idealism of the Enlightenment, it produced a mass hysteria that seems common to most modern peoples as they first become aware of their national identities. A parallel development was French militarism, symbolized later by Napoleon. The concept of the nation in arms—military conscription and the marshalling of an economy for war—appears familiar today. This modern note was a forerunner of industrial society, with its complexities, interdependence, and mass conformity. France in 1800 was not yet industrialized, but it was ripe to be and was already populous enough to experience some tensions evident in modern industrial societies.

Conclusion

In the latter part of the eighteenth century, traditional governments in Europe were challenged by a wave of political revolutions, the most significant of which were the American and the French. These movements resulted from dynamic economies and drastically changing societies, but they were also products of the Enlightenment. In addition, they owed much to the English limited monarchy, with its cabinet system, which was initiated by the Glorious Revolution of the seventeenth century.

The American and French revolutions were similar to the earlier Dutch and English upheavals but they were conditioned more directly by an expanding capitalistic economy which gave them more of a middle-class orientation. They were also more secular in tone. Their impacts upon other societies were naturally more forceful; indeed, they nearly completely destroyed the credibility of absolutism and aristocracy by popularizing and applying the principles of the Enlightenment.

Despite their obvious similarities, the two revolutions also were significantly different. The American movement was more limited in scope and in direct political effects. It was unique in its own time as a demonstrable proof of the "return to nature" and the practicality of the "social contract." Its foreign influence was primarily indirect, through the emotional and intellectual appeal of its example. The French Revolution, on the other hand, was much broader in its economic, social, religious, and political results. It brought the violent overthrow of a social order that had lasted for centuries. Moreover, it launched military conquests that brought the same general upheaval to the whole of western Europe.

Both revolutions merit serious study today. They left a legacy of liberal and constitutional ideas for all peoples, as evidenced by the Latin American movements of the early nineteenth century and by many more recent ones in Asia and Africa. This heritage of the French Revolution has been partially obscured by another legacy of nationalism and war. In contrast, the American liberal heritage has been maintained, almost completely intact, into the twentieth century. Rural people in a vast land which continually beckoned the pioneer, stayed closer to the simple individualistic assumptions of the eighteenth century. That is why American individualism is dying so hard and with such contortions in our time.

Suggestions for Reading

Maurice Ashley, *A History of Europe, 1648–1815* (Prentice-Hall, 1973) is still among the best general surveys. See also G. R. Treasure, *The Making of Modern Europe, 1648–1780* (Methuen, 1985) and Michael S. Anderson, *Europe in the Eighteenth Century* (Longman, 1987). For internal political backgrounds in the revolutionary era, see William Doyle's comprehensive *The Old European Order* (Oxford Univ., 1978). Derek McKay and H. M. Scott, *The Rise of the Great Powers, 1648–1815* (Longman, 1983) provides excellent coverage of the international scene. Crane Brinton's classic *Anatomy of Revolution* (Vintage, 1957) is an interesting comparative study of the English, American, French, and Russian revolutions. An overview of a major social malaise of the era may be found in David B. Davis, *The Problem of Slavery in the Age of Revolution, 1770–1823* (Cornell Univ., 1975).

For English political developments under the later Stuarts, see Maurice Ashley, *England in the Seventeenth Century* (Penguin, 1975). Among the best treatments of Charles II and his problems are David Ogg, *England in the Reign of Charles II*, 2nd ed. (Oxford Univ., 1984); Kenneth H. D. Haley, *Politics in the Reign of Charles II* (Blackwell, 1985); and James R. Jones, *Charles II: Royal Politician* (Unwin Hyman, 1987). For James II and the Glorious Revolution, see Maurice Ashley, *James II* (Univ. of Minn., 1977); John Childs, *The Army, James II, and the Glorious Revolution* (St. Martin's, 1981); and K. M. Chacksfield, *The Glorious Revolution* (Wincanton Press, 1988). See also David Ogg, *England in the Reigns of James II and William III* (Oxford Univ., 1984) and D. S. Lovejoy, *The Glorious Revolution in America* (Wesleyan Univ., 1987).

Dorothy Marshall, *Eighteenth Century England* (Longman, 1974) presents excellent general background for the workings of the aristocratic parliamentary system. A sound biography of the first Hanoverian monarch is Ragnhild Hatton, *George I* (Harvard Univ., 1978). See also the following works dealing with Hanoverian society and politics: John Cannon, ed., *The Whig Ascendancy* (St. Martin's, 1981); Michael A. Reed, *The Georgian Triumph* (Routledge and Kegan Paul, 1983); Paul Langford, *Walpole and the Robinocracy* (Chadwyck-Healey, 1986); and S. Hopewell, *Walpole and the Georges* (Wayland, 1987).

The mid-eighteenth-century background for revolution is described in a number of pertinent studies. For England, see Peggy Liss, *Atlantic Empires: The Network of Trade and Revolution, 1713–1826* (Johns Hopkins Univ., 1983) and Alan Rogers, *Empire and Liberty* (Univ. of California, 1974). For biographical insights into both extremes of the English political spectrum see Reginald James White, *The Age of George III* (Walker, 1968); Richard Pares, *King George*

III and the Politicians (Oxford Univ., 1988); Louis Kronenberger, *The Extraordinary Mr. Wilkes* (Doubleday, 1974); and Audrey Williamson, *Wilkes, A Friend to Liberty* (Readers' Digest Press, 1974). Good perspectives on Dutch involvement are presented in M. C. Rady, *The Netherlands* (Arnold, 1987); in Alice Clare Carter, *Neutrality or Commitment: The Evolution of Dutch Foreign Policy, 1667–1795* (Arnold, 1975); and, by the same author, *The Dutch Republic in Europe in the Seven Years' War* (Univ. of Miami, 1971). For France, see Louis R. Gottschalk and Donald Lach, *Toward the French Revolution* (Scribner, 1973); Jacques Godechot, *France and the Atlantic Revolution of the Eighteenth Century* (Free Press, 1965); and Timothy Tacket, *Religion, Revolution, and Regional Culture in Eighteenth-century France* (Princeton Univ., 1986).

Page Smith, *A New Age Now Begins: A People's History of the American Revolution*, 2 vols. (Penguin, 1989) is a detailed and exciting narrative. Other good general histories of the American Revolution include Richard Ernest Dupoy, *The American Revolution: A Global War* (McKay, 1977); B. Lancaster, *The American Revolution* (Hill and Wang, 1985); E. Countryman, *The American Revolution* (Penguin, 1987); and John R. Alden, *A History of the American Revolution* (Da Capo Quality Paperbacks, 1989). For contrasting views on the nobility of the American struggle, see Robert Middlekauff, *The Glorious Cause* (Oxford Univ., 1985) and Norman Gelb, *Less Than Glory* (Putnam's, 1984). The revolution is evaluated in British terms by Robert W. Tucker and David C. Hendrickson in their *Fall of the First British Empire* (Johns Hopkins Univ., 1982).

Thomas Ladenburg, *The Causes of the American Revolution* (Social Sc. Education, 1989) is a useful study aid. Among the best other studies on the genesis of the Revolution are Cass Canfield, *Samuel Adams' Revolution, 1775–1776* (Harper and Row, 1976); Pauline Maier, *From Resistance to Revolution* (Knopf, 1972); R. B. Morris, *Founding of the Republic* (Lerner, 1985); D. E. Leach, *Roots of Conflict* (Univ. of North Carolina, 1986); and J. A. Henriatta, *Evolution and Revolution* (Heath, 1987).

The following works include the best studies on specific aspects of the Revolution. On economics and class interests, see T. H. Breen, *Tobacco Culture: The Mentality of the Great Tidewater Planters on the Eve of the Revolution* (Princeton Univ., 1985); Jack M. Sosin, *Agents and Merchants* (Univ. of Nebraska, 1965); John W. Tyler, *Smugglers and Patriots* (Northeastern Univ., 1986); and C. K. Wilbur, *Pirates and Patriots of the Revolution* (Globe Pequot Press, 1984). Ideological issues are probed in Thomas L. Pangle, *The Spirit of Modern Republicanism: The Moral Vision of American Founders and the Philosophy of John Locke* (Univ. of Chicago, 1988); J. P. Reid, *The Concept of Liberty in the Age of the American Revolution* (Univ. of Chicago, 1988); and Gordon S. Wood, *Social Radicalism and the Idea of Equality in the American Revolution* (Univ. of St. Thomas, 1976). Financial problems are given detailed attention in William G. Anderson, *The Price of Liberty, the Public Debt of the American Revolution* (Univ. of Virginia, 1982). For the very relevant constitutional results of the Revolution, see Charles A. Beard, *An Economic Interpretation of the Constitution of the United States* (Free Press, 1986) and Clinton L. Rossiter, *The Grand Convention* (Norton, 1987). James B. Perkins, *France in the American Revolution* (Corner House, 1970) throws light on revolutionary foreign policy.

For the hardships and heroics of women in the Revolution, see Anne Voth, *Women in the New Eden* (Univ. Press of America, 1983); Joseph J. Kelley and Sol Feinstone, *Courage and Candle Light* (Stackpole, 1974); Elizabeth Evans, *Weathering the Storm: Women of the American Revolution* (Scribners, 1975); Walter Hart Blumenthal, *(Women Camp Followers of the American Revolution* (Ayer, 1974); Robert Middlekauff, *The Glorious Cause* (Oxford Univ., 1985); Elizabeth Ellet, *The Women of the American Revolution*, 3 vols. (rev. ed., Corner House, 1980); Linda K. Kerber, *Women of the Republic* (Univ. of North Carolina, 1980); and Mary Beth Norton, *Liberty's Daughters* (Little, Brown, 1980).

For the roles played by blacks in the Revolution, see D. J. MacLeod, *Slavery, Race, and the American Revolution* (Gordon, 1975); Ira Berlin and Ronald Hoffman, *Slavery and Freedom in the Age of the American Revolution* (Univ. of Illinois, 1986); Philip S. Foner, *Blacks in the American Revolution* (Greenwood, 1976); John Hope Franklin, *From Freedom to Slavery*, 5th ed. (Knopf, 1980); Benjamin Quarles, *The Negro in the American Revolution* (Norton, 1973); and Sidney Kaplan and Emma Nogrady, *The Black Presence in the Era of the American Revolution*, rev. ed. (Univ. of Mass., 1989).

On effects of the American Revolution abroad, for Ireland, see Maurice R. O'Connell, *Irish Politics and Social Conflict in the Age of the American Revolution* (Greenwood, 1976); Robert B. McDowell, *Ireland in the Age of Imperialism and Revolution* (Oxford Univ., 1979); and Nicholas Canny, *Kingdom and Colony: Ireland in the Atlantic World, 1560–1800* (Johns Hopkins Univ., 1987). For England, see Colin Bonwick, *English Radicals and the American Revolution* (Univ. of North Carolina, 1977); Robert Toohey, *Liberty and Empire: British Radical Solutions to the American Problem* (Univ. of Kentucky, 1978); Bernard Peach, ed., *Richard Price and the Ethical Foundation of the American Revolution* (Duke Univ., 1979); Charles R. Ritcheson, *British Politics and the American Revolution* (Greenwood, 1981); and James E. Bradley, *Popular Politics and the American Revolution in England* (Mercer Univ., 1986). For the Netherlands, see Simon Schama, *Patriots and Liberators: Revolution in the Netherlands* (Knopf, 1977) and J. W. Schulte Nordhelt, *The Dutch Republic and American Independence* (Univ. of North Carolina, 1982). See also Horst Dippel, *Germany and the American Revolution* (Univ. of North Carolina, 1977) and Gwyn A. Williams, *The Search for Beulah Land: the Welsh and the Atlantic Revolution* (Holmes and Meier, 1980).

The following biographical studies of American revolutionary leaders are recommended: H. J. Merry, *The Founding Fathers* (McFarland, 1987); Pauline Maier, *The Old Revolutionaries* (Knopf, 1980); Richard R. Beeman, *Patrick Henry* (McGraw-Hill, 1974); Burke Davis, *George Washington and the American Revolution* (Random House, 1975); G. W. Nordham, *George Washington* (Adams Press, 1987); Forest McDonald, *Alexander Hamilton* (Norton, 1979); Henry Steele Commager, *Jefferson, Nationalist, and the Enlightenment* (Braziller, 1975); and Page Smith, *Jefferson* (American Heritage, 1976). Otto Vossler, *Jefferson and the Revolutionary Ideal* (Univ. Press of America, 1980) is a reinterpretation by a foreign scholar who sees Jefferson's revolutionary idealism as the result of a late conversion in France.

Robert Rosswell Palmer's classic *The World of the French Revolution* (Harper and Row, 1971) examines French eighteenth-century developments in broad perspective. The coming of the Revolution is described in a number of other thoughful works: William Doyle, *Origins of the French Revolution* (Oxford Univ., 1980); Jean Egret, *The French Pre-Revolution* (Univ. of Chicago, 1977); Michel Vovelle, *The Fall of the French Monarchy* (Cambridge Univ., 1984); and Georges Lefebvre, *The Coming of the French Revolution* (Princeton Univ., 1989). The first three volumes of Claude Manceron's massive study of the French Revolution deal with the pre-Revolutionary period: *Twilight of the Old Order, 1774–1778* (Knopf, 1977); *The Wind from America, 1779–1781* (Knopf, 1978); and *Their Gracious Pleasure, 1782–1785* (Knopf, 1980). These presentations, however, are so highly detailed and personalized that they blur the big picture for anyone not very familiar with the era.

Among the best recent general surveys of the French Revolution are William Doyle, *The Oxford History of the French Revolution* (Oxford Univ., 1989); J. F. Bosher, *The French Revolution* (Norton, 1988); T. C. W. Blanning, *The French Revolution* (Macmillan, 1987); M. J. Sydenham, *The French Revolution* (Greenwood, 1985); and J. M. Thompson, *The French Revolution* (Blackwell, 1985). See also R. J. Caldwell, *The Era of the French Revolution* (Garland, 1975); and Leo Gershoy, *The Era of the French Revolution* (Krieger, 1984). Christopher Hibbert, *The Days of the French Revolution* (Morrow, 1981) complements any survey with its colorful accounts of selected major events.

L. A. Hunt, *Politics, Culture, and Class in the French Revolution* (Methuen, 1986) focuses on the total dynamics of the great upheaval. For the significance of class hostilities and mob psychology, see Peter Jones, *The Peasantry in the French Revolution* (Cambridge Univ., 1988); Allan I. Forrest, *The French Revolution and the Poor* (St. Martin's, 1981); and G. F. E. Rude, *The Crowd in the French Revolution* (Greenwood, 1986). Lynn Avery Hunt turns attention to the cities in *Revolution and Urban Politics in Provincial France, 1786–1790* (Stanford Univ., 1978). For the marshalling of public opinion, see Hugh Gough, *The Newspaper Press in the French Revolution* (Lyceum, 1988) and M. L. Kennedy, *The Jacobin Clubs in the French Revolution* (Princeton Univ., 1988). The role of the revolutionary army is ably depicted in Samuel Scott, *The Response of the Royal Army to the French Revolution* (Clarendon, 1978); Jean-Paul Bertaud, *The Army of the French Revolution: From Citizen Soldiers to Instrument of Power* (Princeton Univ., 1989); and Alan Forrest, *Conscripts and Deserters: The Army and French Society During the Revolution and Empire* (Oxford Univ., 1989). For glimpses of the chronological development of the Revolution, see Georges Lefebvre, *The Great Fear* (Vintage, 1973); Marc Bouloiseau, *The Jacobin Republic, 1791–1794* (Cambridge Univ., 1984); C. Blum, *Rousseau and the Republic of Virtue* (Cornell Univ., 1986); S. Loomis, *Paris in the Terror* (Richardson and Slierman, 1986); and Martyn Lyons, *France Under the Directory* (Cambridge Univ., 1975).

On the part played by women in the Revolution, see Linda Kelley, *Women of the French Revolution* (David and Charles, 1988); Joan B. Landes, *Women and the Public Sphere in the Age of the French Revolution* (Cornell Univ., 1988); Samia I. Spencer, *French Women and the Age of the Enlightenment* (Indiana Univ., 1984); and Winifred Stephens, *Women of the French Revolution* (Dutton, 1922).

For issues relating to blacks, see Edward S. Seebes, *Antislavery Opinion in France During the Second Half of the Eighteenth Century* (Greenwood, 1969); Shelby McCloy, *The Negro in France* (Univ. of Kentucky, 1961): Mitchell Ganett, *The French Colonial Question, 1789–1791* (Negro Universities, 1970); and Anna J. Cooper, *Slavery and the French Revolutionists* (Edwin Milleau Press, 1988).

The following biographical studies of French personalities in the revolutionary era are recommended: Robert R. Palmer, *Twelve Who Ruled* (Princeton Univ., 1970); James M. Thompson, *Leaders of the French Revolution* (Blackwell, 1988); John Mills Whitham, *Men and Women of the French Revolution* (Ayer, 1982); Vincent Cronin, *Louis and Antoinette* (Morrow, 1975); Bernard Fay, *Louis XVI* (Regnery, 1968); Olivier Bernier, *Lafayette, Hero of Two Worlds* (Dutton, 1983); Norman Hampson, *Danton* (Holmes and Meier, 1978); Louis R. Gottschalk, *Jean Paul Marat* (Univ. of Chicago, 1967); D. P. Jordan, *The Revolutionary Career of Maximilen Robespierre* (Free Press, 1985); and James M. Thompson, *Robespierre and the French Revolution* (English Universities, 1970).

For short-term impacts of the Revolution, see Robert R. Dozier, *For King, Constitution, and Country* (Univ. of Kentucky, 1983), which shows the reaction of British conservatives. The radical reaction is revealed in H. T. Dickenson, *British Radicalism and the French Revolution, 1789–1814* (Blackwell, 1985) and S. Deane, *The French Revolution and Enlightenment in England, 1789–1832* (Harvard Univ., 1988). The long-term effects are recognized in Geoffrey Best, *The Permanent Revolution: the French Revolution and Its Legacy, 1789–1989* (Univ. of Chicago, 1989).

Notes

1. Quoted in Clinton Rossiter, *The First American Revolution* (New York: Harcourt, Brace, 1956), prefatory note.
2. Thomas Paine, *The Crisis*, first published in the *Pennsylvania Journal*, Dec. 19, 1776, and reprinted in Moncure D. Conway, ed., *The Writings of Thomas Paine* (New York: Ames Press, 1967), p. 168.
3. William Macdonald, ed., *Select Documents Illustrative of the History of the United States* (New York: Bart Franklin, 1968), p. 2.
4. For the text of the Declaration, see J. N. Larned, ed., *The New Larned History*, 12 vols. (Springfield, MA, 1923), vol. 4, pp. 3301–3302.
5. For the text of Leopold's Declaration of Pilnitz (August 27, 1791), see John Hall Stewart, *A Documentary Survey of the French Revolution* (New York: Macmillan, 1951), pp. 223–224.
6. *Ibid.*, p. 181. Quotation is from the Convention's decree of November 19, 1792.

The European Shadow over Africa and Asia

Developments in the Non-Western World, 1650–1815

Napoleon's occupation of Egypt (see ch. 23, p. 595) in 1798 was only one indication of a new European aggressiveness against Asia and Africa. Taking advantage of Iberian decline in the 1600s, northern Europeans eagerly sought to exploit the markets and influence the political affairs of people on other continents. This north European expansion was furthered by the Enlightenment, which encouraged interest in foreign lands; by European capitalism, which revolutionized native economies; and by increasing European, notably British, naval power.

Africans and Asians responded in various ways to these insistent challenges to their traditions and ways of life. The Japanese, fearful of contamination, attempted complete isolation of their country. Burma, Thailand, and Ethiopia tried similar policies, in defense against presumptuous Jesuit missionaries or unprincipled European soldiers of fortune. China cooperated with the Jesuits but cautiously kept them under strict controls. In other places, such as Vietnam, Persia, the Ottoman Empire, and parts of Africa and the Pacific, opinion and even official policy fluctuated between outraged rejection and enthusiastic acceptance of Western culture. Such divisiveness was most evident by 1800 in some regions of Indonesia and India, where Europeans were courted, and imitated, and treated as a new ruling class. Although some Asians and Africans were still openly scornful of European culture, all were now forced to take Europeans seriously.

At the end of the 18th century, large areas of the world were still free of European political domination, but their continued independence was becoming more doubtful. Even in East Asia, where China and Japan were strong states, with deep-rooted traditions and magnificent cultural achievements, changes brought by Europeans caused serious internal problems. Across southern Asia and along the African coasts, steady European penetration brought social disintegration while furthering civil and regional strife, results perhaps best illustrated by the African slave trade. Elsewhere, Europeans were already conquering and exploring less politically organized societies. The Russian movement across Siberia, the English and French forays into Polynesia, and Dutch advances in Indonesia and South Africa continued a process similar, if not identical, to earlier Spanish exploits in the Western hemisphere. The way was thus prepared for European mastery over Asia and Africa in the nineteenth century.

Sub-Sahara Africa

By 1800, the population of sub-Sahara Africa stood at more than forty million people, almost a third more than in 1650. Such expansion helps explain the continuing Bantu migrations, which reached the vicinity of the Cape of Good Hope by the late eighteenth century. Increasing population also contributed to great social and political changes, including the rise of new kingdoms, both in the interior and along the coasts. New inland states developed largely from native traditions, but along the West coast, from the Senegal beyond the Niger delta, European influences were growing rapidly with the rising Atlantic slave trade. For the most part, these European contacts did not yet threaten native authority; but farther south, the process of North European colonialism had already begun, with the Portuguese and the Dutch playing major roles.

The Dutch in South Africa

Established in 1652 as a supply post for Dutch East India Company ships, Cape Colony in South Africa developed very slowly at first but later grew rapidly, producing a dynamic society almost completely isolated from the outside world. The colony's white settlers, constantly at odds with the company and the home government, were even more antagonistic towards black Africans, some of whom made up a depressed majority of the Cape's population while others presented an imposing foreign obstacle to the colony's expansion.

During the first half century of its existence, the colony acquired its distinguishing characteristics. Although the first governor, Jan van Riebeeck, was given strict instructions to seek cooperation and avoid friction with Africans, the native Khoisans (Hottentots) and Bushmen were cattleherders and hunters who did not want to work for the Dutch or respect their property. After 1659, when nine company agents were permitted to occupy adjacent lands, the new settlers clashed with Hottentots over land rights and cattle raids. Such problems multiplied with the arrival of more settlers, including three hundred French Huguenots. Reluctantly, the company extended its lands, organizing the outlying provinces under appointed officials. By 1700, the colony had extended its domain a hundred miles beyong Cape Town, and the white population had expanded to more than sixteen hundred people.

This growth continued while the colony's distinctive culture developed to full maturity. Whites in Cape Town made up one distinct class among the elite; a second included the farmers within the colony's boundaries, which extended 300 miles north and 500 miles east by 1800. Twenty thousand whites lived there. Beyond the boundaries were more whites, already moving their families, wagons, and herds toward new pasturelands. Most free Hottentots and Bushmen had now been eliminated by wars or smallpox; some remained as servants and laborers, particularly at Cape Town, along with a large number of mixed-breed "colored peoples." Blacks from other parts of Africa and Malays from Southeast Asia made up a slave majority of the population. The typical colonist (*Afrikaner*) was an uneducated and narrow God-fearing Calvinist, who felt superior to all non-whites. Among ranchers on the frontier, these characteristics were augmented by fierce individualism, bravery, and aggressiveness.

While Afrikaners (also called Boers) were migrating toward the interior, a similar process was in progress among the Nguni, a Bantu people, ranging along the southeast coast. Like the Boers, the Nguni were cattle herders, looking for land as their population expanded. One of their numerous kinship groups, the Xosa, had reached the Fish River by 1700. Other Nguni groups were soon involved in wars leading toward political amalgamations. One of these groups, the Zulu, was a recognized formidable power among the Nguni. Around 1800, a Zulu chief named Dingiswayo developed mass infantry tactics and new weapons, such as the short stabbing spear, which were to be so effective in subsequent Zulu wars.

Although the major clash of cultures was yet to come, Boer and Bantu began a long series of wars when they first met along the Fish River. At first, the two sides traded cattle, horses, and even guns, but major violence erupted in 1779, when raiding blacks were driven back across the river. After another war ten years later, the provincial governor (*landrost*) prevented the white settlers from sending a punitive expedition into Xosa territory. The farmers, however, raised their own hard-riding commando forces and conducted their own campaigns. This was only one in a series of disagreements between the frontier farmers and the Cape government.

Discontent and political agitation increased markedly during the Napoleonic era. At first, the three major issues were the dictatorial policies of the government, the parent company's monopolistic trade policies, and the authorities' unwillingness to deal forcefully with the Xosa. In 1795, after another Xosa war, the provinces of Graaff Reinet and Swellendam rose against the Cape government and set up new republics.

These movements collapsed with British occupation of the Cape, which began in 1795 and was interrupted briefly between 1803 and 1806. The new regime restored order, affirmed the legal dependency of the Hottentots, freed trade, and erected garrisons on the eastern frontier; but it also forbade the importing of slaves and took legal action against those who abused their Hottentot servants. Moreover, the firm but essentially conciliatory British policy toward the Xosa continued to frustrate backcountry Boers. With the eastern frontier seething and recently-arrived English missionaries demanding human rights for slaves and Hottentots, the country faced a serious crisis in 1815.

Impact of the Atlantic Slave Trade

While Afrikaners were moving toward the Fish River, other Europeans were becoming increasingly active in the Atlantic slave trade, a great international complex of enterprises involving the economies of four continents. It had begun earlier with the Portuguese but reached its peak in the eighteenth century. Because it was conducted in parternerships between Africans and Europeans, the trade was a less obvious short-term danger to African interests than the migrating Dutch settlers, but it posed a more serious long-term threat.

The full historical significance of the trade can best be understood if it is viewed in its broader setting. Europe's economy at the time derived large profits from bulk plantation commodities like sugar, tobacco, and coffee. The most productive European plantations, in the West Indies, depended primarily upon slave labor from West Africa. Thus slaving ports like Liverpool in England and Bordeaux in France became thriving centers of a new prosperity. Other related industries, such as shipbuilding, sugar refining, distilling, textiles, and hardware also flourished. All contributed much to the development of European capitalism and ultimately to the Industrial Revolution.

Northern Europe's commercial impetus reached West Africa in the middle of the seventeenth century. The Portuguese, after losing the whole Atlantic coast to the Dutch, won back only Angola. For a while, the Dutch nearly monopolized the trade, operating from Elmina on the Gold Coast. The British subsequently established footholds there at Cormantin and Cape Castle; by 1700, they had seven other posts in the area. The French, meanwhile, acquired St. Louis on the Senegal, in the north, controlling most trade as far south as the Gambia River. In the resulting triangular competition, the Dutch faced constant pressure from their two rivals but maintained their dominance from a dozen strong Gold Coast forts.

By 1700, Britain was challenging this Dutch predominance. Having defeated the Dutch at sea in the late 1600s, England next defeated France in the War of the Spanish Succession. At the ensuing Peace of Utrecht in 1713, Britain obtained the right to sell 4800 slaves each year in Spanish ports. Another advantage after 1751 was the British shift from a monopolistic chartered company to an association of merchants, which increased incentives by opening opportunities for individual traders. Finally, in the continuing Anglo-French colonial wars of the eighteenth century, the British fleet consistently hampered French operations. For these reasons, the British by 1780 were transporting twice as many slaves from West Africa as all of their competitors.

Despite this regional competition among Europeans, they conducted the trade locally as a black-white partnership, largely on black terms. Native rulers, like Queen Auguina, a British ally on the Gold Coast in the eighteenth century, were not only able to enforce their authority but eagerly took profits from regular port fees, rents on the slave stockades, called *barracoons*, and a contracted percentage on the sale of slaves. Ordinary subjects also participated as partners in the slave trade. Some free native blacks conducted trading expeditions to the interior, while others found work as guides, clerks, or translators. Thus arose a middle class of semi-Europeanized blacks and mulattoes. Many adopted European dress, and a few were lionized in Europe or became Christian missionaries. For example, Betsy Heard, the mulatto daughter of a Liverpool slave factor on the Guinea Coast, was educated in England before returning to manage her father's post. She became wealthy, powerful, and respected, but most white traders were not so fortunate. Plagued by an unhealthy climate and surrounded by suspicious foreigners, they led short, dreary lives in their remote exiles.

Mungo Park, with a Slave Caravan to the Coast

This account of personal experiences is from the journal of Mungo Park, a great English pioneer of African exploration, who discovered the headwaters of the Niger. He died on the return journey down the river in 1805.

April 19th. The long wished-for day of our departure was at length arrived; and the Slatees [black slave traders] having taken the irons from their slaves, assembled with them at the door of Karfa's house, where the bundles were all tied up, and every one had his load assigned him. The coffle [caravan] on its departure from Kamalia, consisted of twenty-seven slaves for sale but we were afterwards joined by five at Maraboo and three at Bala, making in all thirty-five slaves.

When we depared from Kamalia, we were followed for about half a mile by most of the inhabitants of the town, some of them crying and other shaking hands with their relations, who were now about to leave them; and when we had gained a piece of rising ground, from which we had a view of Kamalia, all the people belonging to the coffle were ordered to sit down with their faces towards Kamalia. The schoolmaster, with two of the principal Slatees, pronounced a long and solemn prayer; after which they walked three times round the coffle, making an impression in the ground with the ends of their spears and muttering something by way of charm. When this ceremony was ended, all the people belonging to the coffle sprang up, and without taking a formal farewell of their friends set forward. As many of the slaves had remained for years in irons, the sudden exertion of walking quick with heavy loads upon their heads occasioned spasmodic contractions of their legs; and we had not proceeded above a mile before it was found necessary to take two of them from the rope, and allow them to walk more slowly until we reached a walled village, where some people were waiting to join the coffle.

. . . On the morning of the 21st we entered the woods. During this day's travel, two slaves, a woman and a girl, were so much fatigued that they could not keep up with the coffle; they were severely whipped, and dragged along until about three in the afternoon when they were both affected with vomiting, by which it was discovered that they had *eaten clay*. This practice is by no means uncommon amongst the Negroes; but whether it arises from a vitiated appetite, or from a settled intention to destroy themslves, I cannot affirm. They were permitted to lie down in the woods and three people remained with them until they had rested themselves; but they did not arrive at the town [where we were camping] until past midnight, and were then so much exhausted that the Slatees gave up all thought of taking them across the woods in their present condition. . . .

On the 30th we reached Jallacotta, a considerable town. Here one of the slaves belonging to the coffle, who had traveled with great difficulty for the last three days, was found unable to proceed any further: his master proposed therefore to exchange him for a young slave girl, belonging to one of the townspeople. The poor girl was ignorant of her fate until the bundles were all tied up in the morning, and the coffle ready to depart, when, coming with the other young women to see the coffle set out, her master took her by the hand, and delivered her to her new owner. Never was a face of serenity more suddenly changed into one of the deepest distress; the terror she manifested on having the load put upon her head, and the rope fastened around her neck, and the sorrow with which she bade adieu to her companions were truly affecting.

Source: Rhoda Hoff, ed., *Africa: Adventures in Eyewitness History* (New York: Henry Z. Walck, 1963), pp. 39–40, 42–44.

Most slaves awaiting shipment in West African *barracoons* had been taken in war, but some had been kidnapped or bought from their own people by profit-seeking black middlemen. Only a very few had been seized by white raiders. Slaves were usually forcibly marched to the coast in gangs, chained or roped together, and worn down by poor food, lack of water, unattended illnesses, and brutal beatings. Once in the *barracoons*, where they might stay for months, they were examined for physical defects by ship doctors and then displayed before captains, looking to buy their cargoes. The bargaining was hard and complex, as slaves were exchanged for trinkets, rum, cloth, and particularly firearms. Because the overseas demand was for plantation laborers, males brought the highest prices. Women were less valuable abroad and more desired for work in African villages, so they were less than half as frequently traded as men. Late in the eighteenth century, when slave prices rose, some efforts were made to use female slaves for breeding. Generally, however, such efforts failed, because most slave women regarded children as burdens and resisted pregnancy by every means possible to them.

Although relatively few African women were transported in the Atlantic trade, it hurt them in other ways. Slavery, as practiced earlier in African societies had been more humane than under white tutelage, but women had been customarily enslaved as concubines and used to produce offspring for rulers and wealthy men. As more black males were shipped abroad, this process was further encouraged. Thus more women lost the protection of their families, which they would have enjoyed as legal wives. But for females in the slaving ports, conditions were much worse. African rulers furnished women as favors to their European business partners, along with fresh fruit and flowers. Every white man had free access to black slave women, who could be used, abused, and discarded at will.

After the *barracoons*, slaves met a worse nightmare on the ships. Women were usually huddled together on an open deck; male slaves were packed together, side by side in lower decks, each being allotted a space sixteen inches wide by two and a half feet high. When some refused to eat, a special device, the "mouth opener" was used to force-feed them. Some slaves jumped into the sea while being exercised, and those who contracted diseases were frequently thrown overboard. Mutinies were common and were punished with savage brutality. One woman mutineer on a British ship in the early 1800s was hoisted by her thumbs, whipped, and slashed with knives, in view of other slaves, until she died. Understandably, the mortality rate on slave ships exceeded 12 percent, not counting those who died after landings. Yet these conditions did not shake the Christian faith of some captains. "This day," one confided to his journal in 1752, "I have reason . . . to beg a public blessing from Almighty God upon our voyage. . . . "[1]

The era after the Peace of Utrecht has been termed the slave century. Between 1600 and 1700, when the slave trading companies were mostly state-chartered monopolies, some 1.5 million slaves were carried across the Atlantic. In the next eleven decades, until 1810, when much more trade was being conducted by individual captains outside the forts, over 6 million slaves were actually landed in the Americas. In the decade after 1780, during which 750,000 blacks were taken from West Africa, the trade reached its peak.

In 1807, Britain outlawed the slave trade. The Enlightenment, plus the strong humanitarian movement in England, had prepared the way for this act, but even more decisive factors were Britains rapidly declining Caribbean plantations and pressure from British industrialists, whose primary concern was free foreign markets. With the British fleet patrolling the Atlantic after 1807, looking for slavers, many West Africans were confused by an economic future for which they were unprepared by two centuries of commerce with Europeans.

While it lasted, the Atlantic slave trade hurt emerging black states, but the results were not in themselves decisive. Even with the loss of ten to fifteen million people over three centuries, the population still expanded. Indeed, new foods bought from the West, such as cassava and sweet potatoes, may have increased population more than slaving diminished it. Other direct European influences failed to penetrate very far inland before 1800, but indirect influences were very significant. A native trend in the direction of political centralization was reoriented towards war, tyranny, and brutality. While concentrating upon European weapons and trinkets, West Africans failed to acquire the knowledge or capital for stimulating local productivity. Finally, the trade divided Africans and promoted racism, both in West Africa and abroad.

Native African States

While West Africa developed, under the influence of the slave trade, new states in the remote interior of the continent were forming and making contact with the outside world. In the process, royal powers, militarism, and male authority were all increasing. These trends, which were common among new inland states, were magnified in West Africa, where slave trading and war became the main activities.

The most Europeanized states of West Africa were the independent slave-market cities of the marshy Niger delta tributaries. Originally fishing villages under clan leaders, they developed with the trade after 1650 into wealthy republics like Brass and Calabar or autocratic monarchies, like Bonny, under Queen Kanbasa. Their old kinship wards became commercial "houses," each comprising a family, with an extended organization, including multiple laboring wives, servants, slaves, and sometimes, adopted white traders. These business organizations and secret societies combined African rites with European capitalism in conducting their slave trading. Using fleets of war canoes, armed with cannon and manned by musket-bearing paddlers, they acquired slaves from contacts in the interior. The most dependable source was a native religious order, which collected religious fines in slaves, using armed mercenaries to enforce its exactions.

West of the Niger and the declining empire of Benin, the period brought a political transition, as inland states were forced into slaving competition. The first of these was Oyo, inland on the savanna. It became a great military state, conquering an area along the coast near Bagdari and dominating the trade there. The *Alafins* (kings) of Oyo were autocrats, whose mothers were executed when their sons were crowned. A new official queen mother was given absolute authority over the king's conjugal wives and hundreds of other women who conducted palace business. But all were humble royal servants.

Of all the West African states, Dahomey, located west of Oyo, was perhaps most decisively affected by the slave trade. Constantly at war with Oyo and once nearly destroyed, it reoriented its whole culture toward discipline and military prowess, becoming an absolute monarchy, with every subject's life at the ruler's command. The slave trade and every aspect of the economy were rigidly controlled as royal business. Everyone was required to do military service, even women, who served in the famous "Amazon" contingents, fighting in major wars and providing an élite palace guard. Women comprised the inner government, centered in the palace. The king's first wife often shared real power in what was perhaps a carryover from an earlier day; but the appointed queen mother, her staff, which conducted all public affairs for the king, the royal harem, and a horde of female servants, were usually slaves. Despite such dangerous insecurity, they were considered safer than male subjects. This was all part of a ruthless, brutal realm, where human sacrifice was regularly performed and piles of freshly severed human heads adorned the royal chambers.

More successful in war than Dahomey was Assante (Ashanti), a state still farther west behind the Gold Coast, which was forced about 1680 to unite its clans and fight for its independence against a slave-seeking neighbor, Denkyra. This occurred under an *asantehene* (king) named Osei Tutu (1680–1717), who established control around his capital at Kumasi. His successor, Opoku Ware (1720–1750), extended Assante dominion into the Savannah. By 1800, Assante kings controlled most inland trade through European posts on the Gold Coast.

Although not a rigid military dictatorship like Dahomey, the Assante Empire was the most formidable military power in West Africa before 1815. It profited largely from the slave trade but also exported kola nuts, cloth, metalwork and gold to the Muslim north. This economic diversity allowed Assante to avoid complete dependence upon slave trading and preserve many of its rich traditions. Assante confidence, pride, and courage were also maintained without the brutal repression of Dahomey. Royal authority was shared locally by semiautonomous subkings; in the central government, the king was assisted by the official queen mother, who advised him on public decisions, sat in the council, presided over her own court, supervised affairs directly involving women, and, upon occasion, might participate in deposing a king. Such safeguards against absolutism did not prevent Assante from successfully opposing European imperialism into the nineteenth century.

The southwest coast, from the Bight of Biafra to the Cunene River, presented a contrasting picture, as it remained under disastrous Portuguese domination. In 1665, after years of friction, the Portuguese invaded Kongo, leaving the central government in a shambles and the country ruled by local nobles. By 1800, European influences there were hardly discernible, and the once-proud kingdom was only a distant memory. Angola suffered an even worse fate. Despite heroic efforts at defense by Queen Anna Nzinga (1623–1663), the Portuguese conquered the land and turned it into a vast slave-hunting preserve. In the eighteenth century a governing élite lived in luxury at the ports of Luanda and Benguela, while Portuguese captains ruled over native chiefs in outlying districts. The nearby kingdoms of Kasanje, Matamba, and Ovimbundu, having become Portuguese allies, acquired slaves for the coast by trading or raiding in remote inland areas.

Equally calamitous events followed Portuguese endeavors in southeast Africa. Soon after 1629, rebellion and wars ended Portuguese influence in the Rhodesian highlands. Portuguese puppet rulers, the Monomotapas, held only nominal control over the Zambezi hinterlands between Tete and Sena. In this unhappy country, the only effective authority was held by half-caste Portuguese, who occupied large estates (*prazos*), led armies, raised taxes, and took slaves where they could. Most of their slaves were laborers, but a few, including some women, became overseers or low-level managers on plantations. More ruthless and cruel than native African chiefs, *prazo* adventurers contributed most to the continuing turmoil of the region.

During the eighteenth century, strong new kingdoms arose in south central and eastern Africa. They included the Lunda Empire, east of Angola; Kazembe, one of Lunda's vassals and the strongest central African state just before 1800; the Shona state of Changamire, which drove out the Portuguese and ruled the upper Zambezi from the ancient capital of Great Zimbabwe; and

finally Buganda, after the late 1600s a new empire of banana-growing farmers in the north, between Lakes Albert and Victoria. Each of these states, while unique in its own traditions, created a large territorial monarchy, complete with military forces and provincial administrations. They were especially similar in their still-functioning matriarchial institutions, with queen mothers (sometimes actually king's sisters) exercising real political power, often in their own palaces or commanding their own armies. Such institutions began to change, however, as each kingdom developed trade with the east coast in the eighteenth century.

While new states were rising in East Africa, the oldest African polity, Ethiopia, was near collapse in the same region. Trouble began when the political intrigues of resident Jesuits caused Emperor Fasilidas (1632–1667) to expel them and sever all relations with Europeans. This nationalistic reaction brought temporary unity and cultural advance, but isolation from the Christian world, along with traditional Muslim hostility, soon led to new wars and internal rebellions. In their permanent capital at Gondar, most eighteenth-century Ethiopian monarchs lost touch with their people, although an eccentric folk hero, Emperor Asma Giorgis, with the counsel of this queen, Burgan Mugassa, restored order between 1719 and 1729. After her husband's death, Mugassa provided relative stability during her son's reign and into the 1750s, but her era was followed by harem intrigues, palace murders, army mutinies, and foreign invasions. By 1790 the country was a strange synthesis of savagery and decaying grandeur.

The Muslim World in Decline

Political problems facing black African states after the middle of the seventeenth century were minor compared with those of the Muslim world. From North Africa to Indonesia, Muslim polities were verging on collapse after 1700. Even in the great Islamic empires, vested interests, traditional orthodoxy, and overconfidence continually prevented necessary adjustments. Only in parts of Africa, where Islam was still beginning to put down roots, could Muslim societies generate new energies.

Muslim Africa

The Swahili city-states of East Africa almost had been destroyed by the Portuguese, and the black states of the western Sudan languished after the Moroccan conquest. In this era, however, conditions were changing. Omani Arabs first drove the Portuguese from the East African coast. Then a wave of Muslim religious zeal, rising on the Senegal, spread past the Niger and Hausaland to the borders of Guinea. By the nineteenth century, Muslim Africa was beginning to recover.

In East Africa this revival was more symbolic than real. Two centuries of Portuguese domination and Portuguese-Omani wars had conditioned the area to ruthless brutality and treachery. Once free of the Portuguese, the Swahili cities fought among themselves and, except for Zanzibar, against their new Muslim masters. Although confusion prevailed, population did grow, and commerce prospered sporadically. Most trade was in slaves, particularly with the French, who were developing plantations on their Indian Ocean islands of Mauritius and Bourbon. But increasing wealth brought no cultural or religious renaissance. Although the maturing Swahili language produced some excellent literature, the strikingly beautiful architecture, so evident in earlier mosques and palaces, was generally missing in this period.

A similar evaluation might be made about another African Muslim state, Morocco under the Alawite dynasty. Sultan Mulay Ismail (1672–1727), the most colorful Alawite ruler, corresponded with Louis XIV and sent an ambassador to the court of Charles II in England. His uncontested power was based upon a standing army of black slaves, recruited or captured in the Sudan as children and trained for specialized tasks. The sultan proved himself to be an exceptionally competent administrator, a wily military commander, and a patron of the arts. Yet Morocco was a pirate state, similar to Algeria or Tunis; its values were symbolized when Mulay received the French ambassador with his royal hands bloodied by his personal participation in a recent execution.[2] Under Mulay's successors, the country achieved stability but remained isolated and economically backward.

Even more isolated were the Muslim states of the Sudan, as the overland gold trade declined after 1650. The Moroccan conquest of 1590 had broken the Songhai Empire into a number of small kingdoms, which fought among themselves while resisting the degenerating regimes of Moroccan *pashas* in the commerical cities. For awhile, Kanem-Bornu exerted a stabilizing force in the region around Lake Chad, but its power steadily weakened during the eighteenth century. By that time, the Hausa city states, notably Kano, Katsina, and Gobir, were rising to prominence as they profited from the expanding trade now moving across the central Sahara to the Mediterranean coast. Meanwhile, new Muslim states were rising at the eastern and western extremities of the region; Fulani-Tukulor kingdoms along the Senegal in the west and the sultanates of Tonjur, Fur, and Funj in the Egyptian Sudan.

In these areas, so remote from the complex Middle Eastern world, Islam launched its one effective crusade during the period. Supporting the movement were Fulani religious leaders, who criticized the lax morality, heretical policies, and the religious subordination of women by West African Muslims, particularly the rulers. The Fulani, a seminomadic people, having established a number of theocratic regimes on the Senegal, spread their communities and their religious societies throughout the western Sudan. Between 1786 and 1809, an eloquent Fulani holy man named Usman dan Fodio (1754–1817) led a holy war (*jihad*), which overthrew the native governments and united most Hausa lands into a highly centralized state, with a capital at Sokoto on the lower Niger. Although failing to conquer Bornu, Sokoto did expand considerably while evoking Muslim enthusiasm as far as the eastern Sudan. This fervor continued through much of the nineteenth century, although its concern for female piety did little to check the decline of women's rights in the region.

Delayed Disintegration of the Ottoman Empire

The African Islamic revival encouraged already rising unrest throughout the Ottoman Empire, which, in its glory days, had stretched across North Africa, around the Red Sea, and through the Middle East (see map, p. 366). Now many of these areas were breaking away, while internal revenues dropped and civil turmoil spread. Ottoman collapse was generally anticipated, but this catastrophe was somehow mysteriously delayed. While the sultan's government broke down, local authorities still functioned, imperial pretenses remained in court formalities, and, at times, some intellectual vigor flourished. Even in this dream world, however, it was readily apparent that what had once been the fighting empire of the Ghazis could no longer defend its boundaries and existed only as a pawn for European nations. Only the competitive distrust among these foreign powers delayed the Ottoman demise.

Toward the middle of the seventeenth century, the empire experienced an abortive revival. For nearly a decade after the deposition of Sultan Ibrahim in 1648, the state was nearly destroyed by palace intrigues and general rebellion, reaching a climax when mutinous janissaries hanged thirty officials before a mosque in Istanbul. The *vizier*, a seventy-nine-year-old Albanian bureaucrat named Mehmet Köprülü (1656–1661), restored order by executing more than 35,000 dissidents within his five year term. His son, Ahmed, who served effectively from 1661 to 1676, could afford to be more humane than his father. Under the two Köprülüs, taxes were reformed, a cultural renaissance encouraged, and Ottoman forces defeated Poland and Austria. It was the last significant period of Ottoman expansion and achievement.

After this brief revival, the Ottoman polity weakened steadily, as special interests multiplied. The central bureaucracy and the janissary contingents, no longer consisting of trained slaves, became self-perpetuating elites, consistently pursuing their selfish objectives while opposing reforms. Another grasping hereditary aristocracy arose among tax-farmers in the country. Their selfishness was matched by the narrow Muslim prejudices of the *ulema*, a religious guild that stubbornly controlled the courts and education. Non-Turkish minorities, who conducted most industry and internal trade, felt increasingly alienated from a government without respect for commerce. Yet representatives of French and English companies, while often subject to public indignities, had to be granted special trade concessions so they would supply

necessary goods, such as military weapons and supplies. All of these problems reflected the Ottomans' inability to make necessary adjustments.

The most convincing evidence of the need for change was provided by continuing territorial losses. The Turks lost Hungary, part of Romania, and much of Serbia to Austria by the Peace of Carolowitz in 1699 and the Treaty of Passarowitz in 1718. In three wars with Russia, culminating in the Treaty of Kuchuk Kainarja (1774), they had to give up the Crimea, the right to protect Christians in Istanbul, and commercial access to the Black Sea. In the next two decades, as the Turks were pushed westward along the Black Sea coast, Russian plans for dismembering Turkey were abandoned only because of British and Prussian opposition. Meanwhile, the Ottomans were also losing territories to independence movements. Near home in European Rumelia and eastern Anatolia, native governors with popular backing established semi-independent dynasties, as did other nominal agents of the sultans in Kurdistan, Lebanon, and Arabia. In Iraq, Egypt, Tunis, Tripoli, and Algeria, *mamluk* or *janissary* garrisons created foreign military regimes amid native populations. A puritanical religious reaction against the Turkish caliphate, led by Abdul Wahhabi (1703–1792), laid foundations for the later Kingdom of Saudi Arabia. These new states sometimes nominally recognized Ottoman authority, but they were all practically independent by 1815.

Faced with so many serious problems, Ottoman policymakers alternated for more than a century between reform and reaction, as crises rose and abated. In the eighteenth century, two notable reform attempts occurred between 1713 and 1730 and again between 1774 and 1779. Each time, hopeful *viziers* attempted to reform the military along French lines and import new ideas from the West. Both efforts created mild initial enthusiasm, followed by violent reactions from the *ulema* and the janissaries. The classic example of such futility came during the reign of Selim III (1789–1807), who launched the most ambitious reform program yet attempted. He first conducted extensive investigations and then instituted sweeping changes in the whole Ottoman system, including administration, finance, and education. Most of his efforts and resources went to modernizing the navy and training a

Selim III's efforts to reform the Ottoman state were thwarted by the janissaries who deposed the sultan, imprisoned and later assassinated him.

"new model" army of 25,000 men, for which he used an enlarged corps of French officers. Unfortunately, Napoleon's invasion of Egypt in 1798 ruined everything. Caught in a squeeze between two sets of great European powers and accused at home of favoring the hated foreigners, Selim was deposed by a violent janissary uprising in 1807. His policies were all subsequently reversed or abandoned.

During the last years of the Napoleonic era, the Ottoman Empire endured still another serious crisis, barely surviving into the nineteenth century. The new sultan, Mahmud II (1807–1839), influenced by a strong-willed queen mother, was a progressive youth who was forced to hide his true intentions from the cabal of reactionary zealots surrounding him. Throughout the empire, local notables controlled the provinces; the Serbs were in revolt; the Wahhabi movement was sweeping through Arabia; and Egypt, under the Albanian strongman, Mehmet Ali, was rapidly becoming a new military power, capable of overthrowing Mahmud, despite Ali's assertions

of loyalty. Mahmud also faced a continuing war with Russia, which brought the loss of Bessarabia when the war finally ended in 1812. Under these circumstances, the only favorable prospect for the Muslim state was the British determination to exclude other great powers from the eastern Mediterranean.

Decline in Muslim Middle Eurasia

East of the weakening Ottoman realm, Muslim Middle Eurasia experienced its own dreary decadence. Central Asia, the earlier saviour of Islam, was now caught between the Russians and the Chinese, its nomad armies scattered and its bazaar cities languishing. Iran and Afghanistan, so prominent during the golden era of the Safavids and the Mughuls, now comprised a commercial and cultural backwater. Despite temporary military revivals and destructive forays into India, the area produced no lasting powerful states. Subject to rising pressure from Russia and increasing dependence upon Britain for protection and vital world trade, Iranians and Afghans had lost control of their destinies by 1815.

Much of Iran's degeneration resulted from a decree of 'Abbās I (1588–1629) stipulating that future princes be raised within the harem, isolated from affairs. Consequently, the four last Safavid shahs all lacked experience and leadership. The best of them, 'Abbās II (1642–1667), managed to take back Kandahar from the Mughuls and patronize the arts. Sulayman (1667–1694) left affairs to his vizier while pursuing his sensual pleasures. His son, Sultan Husayn (1694–1772), a meek man who let the *mullahs* make most decisions, finally abdicated his throne to a marauding Afghan chieftain, and for nearly a decade, the land was given over to civil war, massacre, and plunder. When the Turks and Russians attacked, the country survived only because the two invaders restrained each other.

Iran raised itself from such chaos twice during the eighteenth century, but in neither case was the recovery lasting. The first revival was effected by Nader Shah (1736–1747), an army officer of Turkish descent, who drove out the Afghans, reformed the government, reorganized the army, and assumed the imperial title. By 1747, he had regained territories lost to the Russians and the Turks, conquered western

Afghanistan, plundered the Mughul capital at Delhi, and extended Iranian hegemony over the Uzbegs to the north. But his plans for uniting Shi'ite and Sunni Muslims failed, and he ended his reign as a frustrated tyrant, struck down by his own officers. The second revival, a milder one, came under Karim Khan Zand, who ruled justly over a much smaller state in western Iran between 1750 and 1779. At his death the country lapsed again into savage feudal contention.

In the third quarter of the eighteenth century, a new Muslim empire arose between the faltering Iranian and Mughul states. It was created by a contingent of Nader Shah's Afghan cavalrymen, who chose Ahmad Shah Durrani to be their commander in 1747, thus establishing an Afghan dynasty that would last into the twentieth century. In twenty years, Ahmad united the Afghans and conquered a vast empire, which took in eastern Iran, present-day Afghanistan, the major part of Uzbeg Turkestan, and much of northwestern India, including Kashmir and the Punjab. During one campaign in India, Ahmad sacked Delhi, decisively defeating the Marathas, and opening the country to the British. Although brutal to his enemies, the Afghan monarch was very able, but his sprawling tribal-feudal state lapsed into continuous civil wars after he died in 1772.

As these states weakened, they faced increasing European pressures. Russia and Britain, particularly, had long competed for Iranian trade; in addition, the Russians continued to seek territories around the Caspian and actually forced substantial concessions from Iran after a long war, terminating in 1813. The British, fully occupied in India after Nader Shah's death, had about abandoned their commercial ventures in Iran, but their interests were aroused again by French designs on India during the Napoleonic period. An Anglo-Persian defense and commercial treaty of 1880 encouraged the Shah to expect aid against Afghanistan and Russia; when this was not forthcoming, he accepted a French military mission to train his troops. This entente collapsed when the French and Russians signed a temporary truce. The British now negotiated a military alliance, took over Iranian military tutelage, and agreed to pay the Shah an annual subsidy. Subsequently, the Persian Gulf became a British sphere of influence.

Collapse of the Mughul Empire

The decline of Muslim civilization in India was even more pronounced than in the Middle East. European advances had long been a problem in western Asia and the Persian Gulf, but the Mughul Empire had been one of the world's wealthiest and most powerful states, with rich traditions, art, and literature, affecting the whole subcontinent. Its sudden collapse in the eighteenth century was a major catastrophe.

This tragedy resulted largely from the empire's internal contradictions, but the speed of decline must be mainly attributed to the last emperor. Aurangzeb (1659–1707) defeated and eliminated his brothers before seizing the throne from his father, Shah Jahan. The old ruler died in captivity, attended by his daughter, Johanara. Later, Aurangzeb exiled or imprisoned all but one of his sons and confined his eldest daughter, the poetess Zeb-un-Nisa, for life, because she had aided a rebellious brother. Aurangzeb clamped the same ruthless tyranny upon the country. He was an effective military commander and an able administrator but utterly without humane concerns in pursuing his objectives. This rigid determination, arising from the most narrow-minded confidence, was both his greatest strength and weakness.

Aurangzeb's policies directly undermined the imperial order established by the great Akbar (see ch. 14, pp. 372–372). The new emperor destroyed Hindu temples and schools, reimposed the ancient poll tax on Hindus, and dismissed Hindus from government service. Until about 1679, while occupied in securing his northern frontiers, he did not push these policies vigorously; but his later reign brought unyielding persecution, along with a holy war against "infidels" and Muslim heretics in southern India. For the rest of his life, Aurangzeb stayed in the field, heading an unwieldy host of 500,000 servants, 50,000 camels, and 30,000 elephants, in addition to the fighting men. By 1690, after terrible losses, he had overcome most resistance, but the area could not be permanently pacified. Time and again the aging ruler, ailing and afraid of death because of his sins, was forced to undertake new campaigns. He died amid his failures in 1707.

Even during Aurangzeb's reign the empire showed unmistakable signs of degeneration.

Obsessed as he was by fanatic Muslim orthodoxy and determined to suppress all opposition, the grim ruler neglected architecture, ceased patronizing the arts, and discouraged literary activities, although he did sponsor various projects in law and theology. Hindus suffered terribly, particularly the women. Unlike their Muslim counterparts, many had been educated and active in public life; some among the Marathas even led armies. Most of this ended with Aurangzeb's wars. And as revenues declined, tax-farming raised quick government income but also enriched corrupt officials at the expense of both Hindu and Muslim peasants. When Aurangzeb died, the once flourishing empire faced a serious economic crisis.

For another half century, the system lingered on the verge of collapse. After a series of civil wars, Muhammad Shah (1719–1748) succeeded to the imperial throne. Described by one contemporary as "never without a mistress in his arms and a glass in his hand," this indolent monarch made some effort to placate Hindus, with little practical result. Local Muslim dynasties sprang up in the south and in Bengal; the Sikhs, a Hindu-Muslim sect, became autonomous in the northwest; the Hindu Rajputs, once Mughul allies, began to break away; and the fierce Hindu Marathas, whom Aurangzeb had fought thirty years to subdue, extended their sway over much of central India. The impotence of the empire was most effectively demonstrated in 1739, when an invading Persian army burned and looted the Mughul capital at Delhi, carrying away the imperial peacock throne.

The Persian invasion was but a prelude to a nearly complete anarchy known as the "Time of Troubles," which prevailed after Muhammad Shah's death in 1748. His two successors during the next ten years became prisoners of their ministers, who fought each other in alliance with any supporters available. The Maratha Confederacy soon emerged as the most powerful force. It was effectively opposed, however, by the Afghan ruler Ahmad Shah (see p. 580) who declared his independence of Persia and invaded Hindustan. He sacked Delhi for the first time in 1756 and returned two years later. At Panipat, in 1761, his Afghans crushed a huge Maratha army, with their north Indian Muslim allies. This disaster settled nothing because the Afghans soon left

India, and the country became a nearly lawless land of tyrants, greedy brigands, deserted cities, and famine-stricken villagers.

As the Mughul Empire disintegrated, the French and British were drawn into Indian politics as they competed against each other. Both spread their influence by using native troops, the famous *sepoys*, to protect native rulers, with whom they had negotiated trade agreements and alliances. For a time, France gained the advantage in this game, but British sea power during the Seven Years' War forced the French to abandon their political position in India. The British, meanwhile, at the battle of Plassy in 1757, had won outright control of Bengal from the local lord. Between 1806 and 1812 governors of the East India Company succeeded in forcing the emperor to accept British supremacy. With the Mughul emperors subsisting on British pensions, many Muslim rulers protected by garrisons under British officers, and the wealth of Bengal flowing through British hands, Mughul India was no longer a center of power in the Muslim world.

European Encroachments Around East Asia

The destructive European impact upon Africa and Muslim lands was matched by a similar process in the outlying areas of East Asia. On the mainland and among the islands of Southeast Asia, Europeans continued to intervene, with varying degrees of success, in the chaotic internal affairs of perpetually contending established states. Farther east, on hundreds of Pacific islands, European discovery and exploration resulted in quick revolutions, which tended to demoralize and destroy native cultures.

European Influences in Southeast Asia

The islands and the mainland in Southeast Asia showed contrasting reactions to European influences. The more flexible culture of the archipelago largely succumbed or remained inertly traditional. The stronger mainland states, aware of their vulnerability to China or their immediate neighbors, were sometimes compromised in seeking European aid. A more decisive factor, however, was their relatively sterile wars for survival and supremacy, in which Thailand and Vietnam were more successful than Burma, Cambodia, and Laos.

The late seventeenth century was a chaotic time for all the mainland states, with the possible exception of tiny Laos. Burma struggled under weak kings, corrupt ministers, local uprisings, Thai invasions, and Chinese-European competition for advantage. Thailand, meanwhile, faced internal turmoil, complicated by Dutch commercial and political pressure, which led first to British and then to French efforts to take over the country. Vietnam emerged from savage civil wars as two separate states, north and south. Both became tributaries of Ming China while trying to avoid granting special concessions to Europeans. These efforts were mainly successful, except in the case of French missionaries, who gained a strong foothold in the southern kingdom. Only Laos, during the long reign of Souligna-Vongsa (1637–1692) enjoyed sustained peace and good relations with its neighbors.

This situation changed drastically during the eighteenth century. Burma enjoyed a brief revival between 1752 and 1776, when two strong monarchs, Alaungpaya (1752–1759) and his son, Hsinbyushin (1763–1776), defeated the Thai, French, British, and Chinese. But this was the apex of Burmese power. In Thailand, after all Europeans were expelled in the early 1700s, a half-Chinese military commander, Paya Taksin, drove out the Burmese invaders, made himself king, and extended Thai influence over Laos, Cambodia, and Malaya. South Vietnam, meanwhile, doubled its territory by expanding into the Mekong Valley at the expense of Cambodia. Between 1786 and 1801, it united the country and began eliminating French control of affairs. On the surface, Southeast Asia seemed to be consolidating political power, buttressing traditional institutions, and ending foreign domination. But the stage was nevertheless set for the British conquest of Burma and French moves into Indochina, later in the nineteenth century.

Farther south, in Indonesia, the European presence was much more compelling and the native resistance much weaker. Of all Muslim societies, those in the Malay archipelago were less imbued with Islamic values and loyalties. Muslim and Malay traditions had been transformed by thousands of migrating Chinese. Most important of all, the Dutch, by the end of the period, had subordinated native dynasties in Malaya, Java, Sumatra, and the islands. Dutch plantation agriculture had brought an economic revolution that conditioned much of life and labor in the whole area within the limits set by European commercial capitalism.

For a time a Muslim Malay people known in history as the Bugis challenged Dutch supremacy. Originating on the island of Celebes, the Bugis first won fame as searovers and mercenary warriors, serving all sides in the competitive spice trade through the city of Macassar. When the Dutch took Macassar in 1667, the Bugis scattered from Borneo to the Malay Peninsula, where they concentrated at Selangor. Through conquest, intermarriage, and intrigue, they gained control of Jahore, Perak, and Kedah on the mainland, while extending their influence to Borneo and Sumatra. The Bugis fought two wars against Dutch Malacca in 1756 and 1784 but were ultimately forced to accept Dutch overlordship. In the end, they accomplished little beyond a further weakening of Malay power.

At the same time, the Dutch were losing ground to the British. With their East India Company facing internal corruption, increasing costs, and mounting competition, the Dutch could no longer maintain their independence amid the rising Anglo-French colonial rivalry. In Asia, this rivalry was centered primarily in India, but the British were also expanding their trade through the Malacca Straits and seeking a naval port to counter the French in the Bay of Bengal. In 1786, the British obtained Penang on the Malay coast. Later, when France dominated Holland during the Revolution and the Napoleonic era, the British temporarily took Malacca and Java. Penang then became a rapidly expanding center of British influence in Malaya.

Europeans on New Pacific Frontiers

Before 1650, the Pacific area was almost unknown to Europeans, but during the next century, they moved much closer. Some of this contact involved Russian ships cruising southward toward Japan from Kamchatka and French and

British penetration of the North Pacific from Polynesia. By the late eighteenth century, Western ships at Canton often operated from Hawaii or other Polynesian islands, as they conducted the developing maritime trade of the Pacific. For the first time, East Asians felt the Western world crowding in upon them.

Russians moved out toward the Pacific in 1632, when they established Yakutsk in eastern Siberia. From there, adventurers drifted down the Lena, first reaching the Arctic, and later sailing east to the open Pacific. Their discoveries were largely ignored until 1728, when Vitus Bering (1680–1741), a Danish navigator sailing for Peter the Great, charted the Bering Strait, which links the Arctic and Pacific Oceans. This opened the North Pacific to Russia during the eighteenth century. Meanwhile, the Russians founded Okhotsk on the Pacific coast opposite the Kamchatka peninsula. At Okhotsk and at other timbered forts in Siberia, Russian governors and their Cossack soldiers exacted tribute in furs from a society of nomadic hunters. Relations between the conquerers and their subjects were not particularly friendly; indeed local native populations around the forts were often wiped out by direct violence or European diseases.

Shortly after Bering's expeditions, French and English navigators began their own extensive explorations. The most significant were those of the French noble, Louis de Bougainville (1729–1811), and the English captain, James Cook (1729–1779). Bougainville visited much of southern Polynesia, the Sandwich (Hawaiian) Islands, Australia, New Guinea, and New Britain. Cook's three voyages between 1768 and 1779 went beyond the known waters of the South Pacific to Antarctica and north of Alaska to the Arctic coasts, where Cook made contact with the Russians. Although Cook was killed by natives in Hawaii on his last voyage, his journals fired European imaginations and encouraged European migration across the Pacific. Botany Bay in eastern Australia, established by the English as a penal colony in 1788, soon became a colony of settlement. Meanwhile a swarm of Western traders, whalers, missionaries, and beachcombers descended upon the South Pacific islands and the North Pacific coasts.

Perhaps the most typical feature of relations between Europeans and Pacific natives was the

Captain James Cook charted the coasts of New Zealand, Australia, and New Guinea, the Pacific coast of North America, and mapped nearly every island in the Pacific.

contrast in sexual roles and mores, which French and British sailors callously exploited. Male islanders, unlike European men, were used to female leadership, if not absolute domination; men were less ambitious and possessive; and sexual gratification was considered by both men and women as pleasurable but not immoral or even very significant. No wonder that Polynesian women in Tahiti or Hawaii, when they learned that their charms could be traded for European goods, swarmed over the ships at every anchoring. Their preference for iron nails almost caused the ships to be taken apart. In time, the crews became so conditioned that they initiated similar transactions in North America, where the Indian women were less interested but more subservient to their greedy husbands and fathers.

In Polynesia, after Cook's time, original cultures rapidly declined, as trade goods, rum, and guns stimulated avarice, status seeking, competition for power, violence, and war. With European help, native rulers, male and female, fought to dominate their islands. Such conflict was particularly true of Hawaii in the decade after 1790, where a Hawaiian chief, Kamehameha, used European ships and cannons to unite the three main islands. Sexual commerce with European also brought syphilis to the islands, blame for which was long disputed by the French and the English.

Captain James Cook, Departure from Tahiti

This selection is from Cook's journal on his second voyage into the South Pacific (1772–1775) in a major effort to explore Antarctica.

Thursday 16th. This Morning the Natives came off to the Sloops in their Canoes as usual, after breakfast Captain Furneaux and I paid the Chief a Viset, we found him at his house perfectly easy and satisfied in so much that he and some of his friends came a board and dined with us. . . . Having got a board a large supply of refreshments I determined to put to Sea in the morning and made the same known to the chief who promised to come and take leave of me on board the Ship.

‡Whilest I was with him [Oreo] yesterday, my Otaheite young man Porio took a sudden resolution to leave me, I have mentioned before that he was with me when I followed Oreo, and of his advising me not to go out of the boat, and was so much affraid at this time that he remaned in the boat till he heard all matters were reconciled, then he came out and presently after met with a young woman for whom he had contracted a friendship, he having my powder horn in keeping came and gave it to one of my people who was by me and then went away; I, who knew that he had found his female friend, took no notice thinking that he was only going to retire with her on some private buisness of their own, probably at this time he had no other intention, she however had prevailed upon him to remain with her for I saw him no more and to day I was told, that he was married. . . . In the after noon our boats returned from Otaha . . . they made the Circuit of the isle, conducted by one of the Aree's whose name was Boba, and were hospitably entertained by the people who provided them with victuals lodgeing and bed fellows according to the custom of the Country; the first night they were entertained with a Play, the second night their repast was disturbed by the Natives stealing their military Chest, which put them upon making reprisals by which means they recovered the most of what they had lost.

Friday 17th. At 4 o'Clock in Morning we began to unmoor and as soon as it was light Oreo and some of his friends came to take leave, many Canoes also came off with Hogs and fruit, the former they even beged of us to take from them, calling out, Tyu Boa Atoi which was as much as to say, I am your friend take my Hog and give me an ax, but our decks were already so full of them that we could hardly move, having on board the Resolution about 230 and on board the Adventure about 150. . . .

The Chief and his friends did not leave us till the Anchor was a weigh. At parting I made him a present of a Broad Ax and several other things with which he went away well satisfied. He was extremely desirous to know if, and when I would return, these were the last questions he asked me. After we were out of the Harbour and had made sail we discovered a Canoe conducted by two men following us, upon which I brought to and they presently came a long side with a present of fruit from Oreo, I made them some return for their trouble, dismissed them and made sail to the Westward with the Adventure in company. The young man I got at Otahiete left me at Ulietea two days before we saild being inticed away by a young Woman for whom he had contracted a friendship. I took no methods to recover him as there were Volanteers enough out of whome I took one, a youth about [17 or 18] years of age who says he is a relation of the great Opoony and . . . may be of use to us if we should fall in with and touch at any isles in our rout to the west. . . .

From *The Voyage of the* Resolution *and* Adventure, *1772–1755*, edited by J. G. Beaglehole. (Cambridge: Cambridge University Press, 1961), pp. 228–30.

Other European imports included cattle, small-pox, and missionaries. Amid sensual competition and Christian condemnation, the old religion was largely abandoned; whole communities became alcoholic; other evidences of psychological malaise, such as suicide, became prevalent; and population declined drastically.

European expansion in the Pacific brought significant changes for civilized East Asia, particularly in maritime commerce. After the middle of the eighteenth century, the British began replacing the Dutch as the major European traders, a trend climaxed by the collapse of the Dutch East India Company in 1794. At Canton, the number of British and American ships increased dramatically after 1790. Seeking a product which might be exchanged profitably for Chinese silk and tea, the British first concentrated on opium from India. When the opium trade created friction with Chinese officials, British merchants began seeking furs, particularly sea otter skins, which were obtained in the North Pacific. Hawaiian ports soon became busy centers for fitting ships and recruiting sailors. By 1815, European expansion into the Pacific had generated a dynamic commercial revolution.

East Asia on the Defensive

Among the great states of the East Asian mainland, the European impact was felt less than elsewhere, but it still figured largely in a strange composite of contradictions, typical of the area. Although China and Japan remained strongly attached to traditional values and were the most prosperous and stable of all non-European states, each felt forceful changes that conflicted with their ancient heritages. While struggling against these changes, both nations saw their problems magnified by the increasing European presence around the western Pacific.

The Rise and Decline of Manchu China

After 1644, when the Manchu armies took Peking, China was the most populous country on earth. Its society was more refined than most in Europe; and its literature, art, and philosophy evoked great admiration from European intellectuals. The Manchu emperors were generally efficient and conscientious; but, like many barbarian rulers of the past, they were so awed by Chinese institutions that they were incapable of promoting necessary change. The main problem was not that China was backward—it developed and prospered under the Manchus—but its progress was much slower than that of the West.

The Manchu system was a unique and highly successful modification of the traditional Chinese institutional structure. Although the conquerors sought to maintain their identity by avoiding intermarriage with Chinese, they retained the Chinese examination system and the privileged scholar-bureaucracy. Manchu and Chinese, working in pairs, conducted government above the provincial level. The most significant innovation was the "banner" system, comprising elite military units, both Manchu and Chinese. Because they were kept distinct from family, tribal, or even geographic identities, the banner companies proved reliable imperial troops. Augmented by Chinese conscripts and foreign tributaries, they extended China's control farther than ever before. Manchu armies subdued Sinkiang, Taiwan, Mongolia, Turkestan, and Tibet (see map, p. 379). The emperors also established tributary control over Korea, North Vietnam, and Burma.

One reason for the stability of Manchu China was the strength and durability of the rulers, particularly the K'ang-hsi emperor, who reigned longer (1661–1722) than any predecessor. Intelligent, hardworking, and devoted to duty, he was a brave soldier, an inquisitive scholar, and an able administrator. In six grand tours of the country, he sought to improve local government and promote justice. Always fascinated by learning, he encouraged scholarship by sponsoring great research projects. As a commander, he defeated the remaining Ming forces, then directed the long and arduous campaigns that ultimately conquered Mongolia. At the end of his reign, having experienced the bitter disappointment of having to disinherit his only legitimate son, the old monarch, in a final testament, revealed his human weaknesses and concerns.[3] Of all the world's rulers, K'ang-hsi was among the wisest, the most efficient, and the most respected.

The Manchu regime reached its climax during the next two reigns. Between 1723 and 1735, the Yung-cheng emperor, one of K'ang-shi's nineteen illegitimate sons, ruthlessly eliminated opposition groups formed around his brothers. His dictatorial methods set dangerous precedents but also lessened corruption and prepared the way for the reign of the Ch'ien-lung emperor (1735–1796), the fourth son of Yung-cheng. At first the new ruler was sincere, frugal, and industrious, like his famous grandfather. His early reign was marked by peace at home, victories abroad, expanding wealth, and noteworthy achievements in scholarship and the arts. Unfortunately, these conditions did not last. After about 1770, the expensive military campaigns began depleting the treasury. The emperor also instituted a rigorous policy of censorship and book burning. Ultimately, government fell into the hands of a royal favorite, whose corruption and inefficiency brought widespread rebellions as the eighteenth century ended.

The weakening of the Manchu regime was accompanied by increasing foreign problems. After years of fighting along the Manchurian and Mongolian frontiers, K'ang-hsi negotiated the treaty of Nerchinsk in 1689, which set the Siberian-Manchurian border and permitted limited Russian trade in Peking. The Chinese-Russian accord was made more specific by the Treaty of Kiakhta in 1727, when the Russians recognized Chinese sovereignty over Mongolia. As advisors to the Manchu emperors, Jesuits helped negotiate both of these treaties. They enjoyed considerable status at Kang-hsi's court, where they preached a version of Christianity consistent with traditional Chinese beliefs, such as ancestor worship. But at the opening of the eighteenth century the pope required Chinese Christians to renounce such paganism. The new policy brought disfavor to Catholics and to western Europeans generally. In 1757, the Chinese government confined all trade to Canton, where Europeans were forced to deal through a merchant monopoly and corrupt officials. Because of these conditions, Europeans, particularly the British, continually pressed for free trade and regular diplomatic relations.

China during Ch'ien-lung's reign was rapidly approaching the limits of its traditional system. Although Europeans were impressed by the country's order, wealth, and expanding population, which doubled between 1700 and 1800, they saw a façade rather than actual conditions. Chinese agriculture increased its productivity but not enough to provide for three hundred million people. Consequently, migrating Chinese moved into the southwestern provinces, into North Vietnam, and even across the seas to the Philippines and Java. At home, famine became prevalent as the soil wore out. Peasant uprisings were matched by growing unrest in the southern cities, which were also swelling in size, without increased economic resources. While a few Cantonese merchants, Yangtse salt monopolists, and favored government officials amassed great wealth, Chinese below the élite classes suffered great hardships and injustices.

Despite these problems, the late Manchu emperors held fast to their faith in China's ancient values. K'ang-hsi had been curious about Western medicine, astronomy, and mathematics, without conceding the validity of Western Science. After his time, European material advances were noted without awe or envy. Both K'ang-hsi and Ch'ien-lung fostered massive scholarly projects in history and philosophy, as their predecessors had done. Thousands of Chinese scholars, supported by the state, labored at these compilations while others, less favored, taught the Confucian classics in government schools or private academies. Their conservatism was demonstrated in a movement that, like its Japanese counterpart, opposed Ming neo-Confucianism in favor of Confucian principles expounded in the Han period. Thus, while China slipped inevitably toward the future, its intellectuals remained preoccupied with the distant past.

Such paralyzing conservatism is perhaps best illustrated by the Manchu espousal of classic Confucian doctrine on the social status of women. Early Manchu emperors forbade footbinding among their own females, but the practice was so fashionable and the Manchu women so eager to prove their acceptability that the prohibition was soon forgotten. In the eighteenth century, Chinese women suffered more than ever under a stifling Confucian double standard for female chastity and self-denial, in comparison with men. A famous heroine of the time, accused along with some companions of having sexual relations with

Father Ripa, Family Relations in Manchu China

Father Ripa, an Italian Jesuit missionary, was at the court of the great Manchu emperor, K'ang-Hsi, from 1711 to 1723.

One day as I was talking in my own house with a mandarin who had come to pay me a visit, his son arrived from a distant part of the empire upon some business relating to the family. When he came in we were seated, but he immediately went down on one knee before his father, and in this position continued to speak for about a quarter of an hour. I did not move from my chair till, by the course of the conversation, I discovered who the person was, when I suddenly arose, protesting to the mandarin that I would stand unless he allowed his son to sit down also. A lengthy contest ensued, the father saying that he would quit his seat if I continued to stand; I myself declaring that it was impossible for me to sit while his son was kneeling; and the son protesting that before his father he must remain on his knees. At last, however, I overcame every scruple, and the mandarin signified to his son by a sign that he might be seated. He instantly obeyed, but he retreated to a corner of the room, where he timidly seated himself upon the edge of a chest. . . .

Chinese women live entirely shut up by themselves in a remote apartment of their houses. Among persons of rank they are seldom allowed to go out, unless it be during the rejoicings of the new year, and even then they are shut up in sedans. They are indeed kept so strictly that they are not allowed to speak even with the father or the brother of their husbands, much less with their uncles, or any other man, however close may be the relationship. . . . And here I will not omit the description of a practice which, while it proves the excellent social order of the Chinese, caused me to smile when I heard of it. If a man, for careless conduct or any other fault, considers it his duty to correct his daughter-in-law, as he cannot, according to the custom of the country either enter her room or speak to her, and much less beat her, he summons his son before him, and after reproaching him with the faults of his wife, he bids him prostrate himself, and inflicts a severe flogging upon him. The son then rises upon his knees, and, touching the ground with his forehead, thanks his father for the castigation; after which he goes to his wife, and repeats the correction exactly, giving her the same number of blows that he received from his father.

From their inordinate jealousy arose the custom of crippling the feet of the women, in order to render walking a torment, and induce them to remain at home. I was informed by Chinese that the first who discovered this stratagem was one of their ancient emperors, who purposely hinted that nothing was more beautiful in a woman than to have the smallest feet possible. This imperial opinion being made public throughout China, every husband desired that his wife should be in the fashion, and mothers sought to secure to their daughters an imaginary beauty which it was found could be procured by art. Accordingly, at the tender age of three months, female infants have their feet bound so tightly that the growth of this part of their body is entirely stopped, and they cannot walk without hobbling and limping; and if upon any occasion they endeavour to quicken their pace, they are in danger of falling at every step. . . . In cases of marriage, the parties not being able to see each other, it is customary to send the exact dimensions of the lady's foot to her intended, instead of sending him her portrait as we do in Europe.

Source: Rhoda Hoff, ed., *China: Adventures in Eyewitness History* (New York: Henry Z. Walck, 1965), pp. 63–66.

a lecherous monk, saved the other girls by showing a mole on her body that the monk could not describe. Having thus dishonored her family by revealing her nakedness, she committed suicide and was praised as a model. Mao Ch'i-ling, a rare Chinese champion of women's rights in the eighteenth century, condemned unreasonable contemporary customs, which required engaged women to remain single, commit suicide, or be buried alive if their fiancés died.

This conservative myopia was typical but not quite universal among writers and artists. Most creative endeavors aimed to please the aristocratic urban classes, who lived artificial lives in their gardens, amid their books and paintings. Painters usually followed the classical Sung schools. Traditional drama, having emerged in the Yuan period, remained popular into the nineteenth century. There were, however, some links between Chinese art and the contemporary world. Lacquer and porcelain wares attained such popularity in Europe that they were produced in great quantities to suit foreign tastes. The same was true of some Chinese painting, which came to utilize European techniques in achieving perspective. Finally, Chinese literature showed some social concern and attempted realism. *The Dream of the Red Chamber*, an eighteenth-century depiction of a declining aristocratic family, has been widely acclaimed as China's greatest novel.

Korea, the reluctant Manchu vassal state, experienced more serious problems but came closer to devising solutions. Japanese and Chinese invasions in the early seventeenth century so weakened the scholarly bureaucracy and central government that they could barely function. In the resulting disorder and confusion, the economy developed rapidly when controls were not enforced, but population increased by 50 percent and many suffered, particularly the peasants. Such conditions encouraged new thinking, and by the eighteenth century, a movement among intellectuals, known as "practical learning," was advocating reforms in government, while showing some sympathy for Western Christianity and science. Some of this reform spirit was revealed in the policies of King Yungjo (1724–1776) and his grandson, Chongjo (1776–1800), who gradually restored some order and efficiency.

Tensions in Japan Under the Mature Tokugawa Shogunate

While the rest of Asia and Africa felt European influences, the Tokugawa regime in Japan seemed unaffected, in an immunity that was somewhat illusory. At first, after outlawing Christianity and expelling Europeans, the Japanese perfected an efficient bureaucratic system on the old feudal foundations. The economy flourished, cities grew, population stabilized, and the standard of living rose. But these favorable results also brought changes and great social tensions, which threatened the political order. At the same time, external stimuli caused some Japanese to advocate foreign ideas, while others reacted emotionally in defense of their sacred traditions.

The Tokugawa system, originally a rigid feudal order, became highly centralized during this era. Without the disruption of foreign wars, the shoguns consolidated their power by turning the *daimyo* into dependent courtiers and changing the *samurai* from vassals of their lords into state employees. This was largely accomplished by educating the warrior class in the Confucian classics, which emphasized civic duties over personal loyalties, as taught in the old *Bushido* code. Reorientation of the *samurai* was furthered by paying them fixed stipends and restricting some of their traditional violent practices, such as feuding or committing honorable suicide (*seppuku*). With its loyal *samurai* corps of soldiers, scholars, and bureaucrats, the shogunate became a highly efficient political organization.

Such bureaucratic order naturally lessened flexibility. Confucianism looked to the past, suspected the future, and resisted most proposed improvements. It was also narrowly male-oriented. This meant that female influence, particularly in politics, was often significant but limited largely to domination over shoguns by their mothers, plus other attendant intrigues and extravagances of court women. Among this elite group, practical affairs were hidden behind an artificial etiquette and old *samurai* standards, which demanded humble service and sacrifice, even unto death, by a wife for her husband and his family. Such principles, often ignored within families of the noble classes, were espoused by male *samurai* writers for public consumption.

Their efforts were at least partially successful in popularizing Confucian conservatism.

The official disciplinary tone was reflected in an outpouring of cultural expression during this era. While Buddhism declined generally, its temple schools fostered a rapid expansion of education. The intellectual climate was further improved by a phenomenal increase in book publishing. *Samurai* scholars produced national histories and Confucian philosophical works to honor Tokugawa accomplishments and provide a basic rationale for state and society. *Samurai* architects perpetuated traditional baroque grandeur in castles and public buildings. In painting, the *samurai* influence was represented by the Kano school's synthesis of classical Japanese and Chinese traditions, such as the literal pictoral essays of the "literati" (*nanga*) painters.

Although the Tokugawa government and society were supposedly prescribed within official limits, the economy underwent dynamic development and change. In agriculture, land reclamation, improved seeds, better fertilizers, and new tools brought a doubling of grain production between 1600 and 1730. Rising wealth in the villages was reflected in many new small industries and generally increased industrial output. A complex monetary and financial system gave rise to large capitalistic enterprises centered in the cities, which were rapidly expanding in number and size. With a population of nearly a million, Edo, capital of the shogunate, was among the largest cities of the world by 1750. The total Japanese population, meanwhile, peaked at approximately twenty-nine million, declining only slightly in the 1700s. This combination of increasing productivity and stable population, unmatched elsewhere in the world, produced a spirit of enterprise and optimism, most evident among the urban classes, especially among women, many of whom were actively involved in hand manufacturing or business.

Increasing wealth, rising expectations, and other changes subjected Japanese society to dangerous tensions after the late seventeenth century. Many peasants were alienated from the land and from the upper classes as they became hired laborers or free tenants. The new money economy, while stimulating a desire for luxuries among the *samurai*, diminished their economic independence and encouraged them to borrow heavily from merchant bankers. Even the *daimyo* were forced to engage in business enterprise to pay for their many social obligations at court. At the same time, their creditors among the urban middle classes were dissatisfied by numerous frivolous demands and penalties imposed by the government upon commerce and banking. As such dissatisfaction grew, frequent disorders in both the towns and villages had to be forcefully repressed.

Government met these problems with alternations between reform and inertia. The first four shoguns ruled wisely and forcefully, but later ones allowed their ministers to make policies, which brought increasing rigidity as often happens in bureaucracies. While revenues dropped, inflation increased, and respect for authority declined. Some partially successful efforts at reform were attempted by the scholar-minister, Arai Hakuseki (1709–1716). An even more determined reformer was the eighth shogun, Yoshimune (1716–1745). An honest, sincere, and just statesman, Yoshimune tried to restore traditional morality with the famous Kyoho reforms, which cut expenses, encouraged agriculture, regularized taxes, standardized the diverse feudal laws, and relaxed the ban on foreign technial books. He also ordered the dismissal of nearly half of the court women, a measure designed to save money and promote stability. With such policies, Yoshimune hoped to restore the efficiency of the past, but they were only temporary remedies rather than permanent solutions to his problems.

Yoshimune's successors pursued no consistent policies. His son, Ieshige (1745–1760), was a semi-invalid with a speech defect, who ushered in an era of definite political decline. The next shogun yielded to his chamberlain, an unscrupulous adventurer who courted the merchant-bankers, attempting to increase revenues and strengthen the regime. His extravagance and corrupt practices brought economic depression and frequent rice riots. This commercial policy was reversed by Matsudaira Sadanobu, who served as chief minister until 1793. A stern traditionalist, he tried to cut expenses and restore the *samurai* values. But after he retired, the government drifted aimlessly during the long reign of Shogun Ienari (1787–1837).

While the government floundered, a new urban subculture challenged official Confucian values. Prosperous urbanites, disillusioned with old-fashioned morality, idealized "the floating world" of irrational sensuality, featuring fine food, alcohol, gambling houses and brothels. Free love and sexual independence, illustrated by the lifestyles of adventurers, entertainers, and prostitutes, became subjects of a new literature, produced in the revolt against *samurai* morality. Other writings, rejecting artificial themes, evoked appreciation for the realistic or the esoteric. For example, *haiku* poetry, which won great popularity, used seventeen syllables in three lines and expressed pithy microcosmic observations on universal themes. A new pictoral art for the masses used woodblock printing and vivid colors to portray nature, street scenes, pretty women, and mild erotica. With or without conscious intent, such works weakened established values.

More threatening to the shogunate than the new urban alienation was the criticism from intellectuals. By the end of the eighteenth century, a growing number were questioning the shogun's authority and emphasizing loyalty to the emperor. Many of these "nationalists" were prejudiced militarists, who thought that the shogunate had betrayed Japanese traditions. A shade further to the left, Confucian proponents of "ancient learning" blamed all troubles on neo-Confucianists, who had strayed from the old texts. Others turned to practical subjects, such as economics, while rejecting the highly moralistic perspectives of official scholars. After Yoshimune relaxed the ban on foreign non-Christian writings in 1720, "Dutch studies" were pursued widely in medicine, astronomy, and various technical fields. The movement gained momentum as the century passed, indicating that Japanese society was torn by dissension and that European ideas were significantly involved.

Conclusion

Despite the near destruction of local cultures around the Cape, many African and Asian civilizations remained highly functional in 1815. Assante, Buganda, and Omani Zanzibar were all rising south of the Sahara without having yet reached their peaks. Sokoto was spreading its

Muslim orthodoxy throughout the Sudan; Morocco and the Barbary states continued to prey upon Mediterranean commerce; and the Egyptian ruler, Mehemet Ali, was apparently building a new Muslim empire. Along with the recently formed Sikh state, the Marathas posed serious military problems for British India. France had recently lost influence in a united Vietnam, which was now acutely aware of a revived Thailand. To the north, in East Asia, China persisted in rejecting regular diplomatic relations with European nations; Korea's "practical learning" was producing reforms; and Japan was a convincing example of prosperity and independence.

The non-European areas of Asia and Africa had nevertheless slipped considerably, in comparison with the West, since 1650. China and Japan were both seriously disturbed by internal tensions. Burma faced a military threat from the British in Bengal. A similar insecurity was felt by the tottering Muslim states of the Middle East and the slave-trading states of West Africa. In addition to South Africa, much of India, Indonesia, Polynesia, and Siberia had felt the direct shock of foreign conquest. One may conclude that much of sub-Sahara Africa had arrested its own development by accepting foreign ways, and that East Asia was so locked into its past that it could not effectively pursue its future.

All these cultures demonstrated a common connection between their misfortunes and the European presence. Indeed, the true significance of the period lies in the opportunities provided for European, particularly British, expansion. The Peace of Vienna in 1815 not only brought a decisive British victory over France in Europe, it also unofficialy ratified the recent rise in British power and influence around the globe—in China, Southeast Asia, India, the Persian Gulf, the eastern Mediterranean, and Africa. With other advantages derived from their phenomenal industrial development, the British were well prepared to lead the great European scramble for empire in the nineteenth century.

Suggestions for Reading

From the many good surveys of early South Africa, the following are recommended: Kevin Shillington, *A History of South Africa* (Longman, 1988); Christopher Saunders,

The Making of the South African Past (Barnes and Noble, 1988); T. R. Davanport, *South Africa: A Modern History* (Macmillan, 1987); and J.D. Omer-Cooper, *A History of South Africa* (Heinemann, 1987). For the beginning of the Xosa wars, see Donald R. Morris, *The Washing of the Spears: The Rise and Fall of the Zulu Nation* (Touchstone, 1986) and E. A. Ritter, *Shaka Zulu* (Penguin, 1985).

The best background treatments of black sub-Sahara Africa include Robert W. July, *A History of the African People* (Scribner 1980); Paul Bohannan and Philip Curtin, *Africa and Africans*, 3rd ed. (Waveland Press, 1988); Roland Oliver and J. D. Fage, *A Short History of Africa*, 6th rev. ed. (Penguin, 1989). See also Frank Willet, *African Art* (Thames and Hudson, 1985).

Philip Curtin, *The Atlantic Slave Trade* (Univ. of Wisconsin, 1972) is the classic work on the subject. See also James A. Rawley, *The Trans-Atlantic Slave Trade* (Norton, 1981); James Walvin, *Slavery and the Slave Trade* (Univ. of Minnesota, 1983); Edward Reynolds, *Stand the Storm* (Allison and Busby, 1985); Basil Davidson, *The African Slave Trade* (Little, Brown, 1988); and D. W. Galenson, *Traders, Planters, and Slavers* (Cambridge Univ., 1986). For the participation of Europeans, see Norman R. Bennet, *Africa and Europe*, 2nd ed. (Univ. of Calif., 1985); John C. Hatch, *The History of the British in Africa* (Praeger, 1969); Robert Stein, *The French Slave Trade in the Eighteenth Century* (Univ. of Wisconsin, 1980); Johannes M. Postma, *The Dutch in the Atlantic Slave Trade* (Cambridge Univ., 1989); and David Eltis, *Economic Growth and the Ending of the Trans-Atlantic Slave Trade* (Oxford Univ., 1987). For the effects of the trade on Africans, see J. E. Inikori, *Forced Migration: The Impact of the Export Slave Trade on African Societies* (Holmes and Meier, 1983); Paul E. Lovejoy, *Transformations in Slavery* (Cambridge Univ., 1983); and Paul E. Lovejoy, ed., *Africans in Bondage: Studies in Slavery and the Slave Trade* (Univ. of Wisconsin, 1987). The tragedy of African women in slavery is recounted in Claire C. Robertson and Martin A. Klein, eds., *Women and Slavery in Africa* (Univ. of Wisconsin, 1983); Marietta Morrissey, *Slave Women in the New World* (Kansas Univ., 1989); and Barbara Bush, *Slave Women in Caribbean Society, 1650–1832* (Indiana University, 1989).

Black African regions and states in the era are overviewed in John Stewart, *African States and Rulers* (McFarland, 1989) and David Sweetmen, *Women Leaders in African History* (Heinemann, 1984). For West Africa, see Basil Davidson, *A History of West Africa* (Longman, 1987); C. W. Newbury, *The Western Slave Coast and its Rulers* (Greenwood, 1983); Robin Law, *The Oyo Empire* (Oxford, 1977); Karl Polyani and Abraham Rotstein, *Dahomey and the Slave Trade* (AMS, 1988); Patrick Manning, *Slavery, Colonialism, and Economic Growth in Dahomey, 1640–1960* (Cambridge Univ., 1982); and J. K. Flynn, *Asante and Its Neighbors, 1700–1807* (Northwestern Univ., 1971). For Central Africa, see David Birmingham and Phyllis Martin, eds., *A History of Central Africa*, 2 vols. (Longman, 1983); John Thornton, *The Kingdom of Kongo, 1641–1718* (Univ. of Wisconsin, 1983); Anne Hilton, *The Kingdom of Kongo* (Oxford Univ., 1985); K. Somerville, *Angola* (Pinter, Rienner, 1986). For East Africa, see Gideon S. Were and Derek A. Wilson, *East Africa Through a Thousand Years* (Africana, 1970); Arnold H. Jones and Elizabeth Monroe, *A History of Ethiopia* (Oxford, 1966); and E. A. Budge, *A History of Ethiopia* (Methuen, 1966).

John S. Trimmingham, *The Influence of Islam Upon Africa* (Longman, 1980) is a well-researched treatment of a broad topic. For more limited studies, see the same author's *History of Islam in West Africa* (Oxford, 1959) and *Islam in East Africa* (Oxford, 1964). North Africa is covered in Jamil M. Abun-Nasir, *A History of the Maghrib* (Cambridge Univ., 1975) and Charles A. Julien, *A History of North Africa* (Praeger, 1970). The ambiguous role of women is described in Barbara Calloway, *Muslim Hausa Women in Nigeria* (Syracuse Univ., 1987).

The standard suvey of the declining Ottoman Empire is Lord Kinross, *The Ottoman Centuries* (Morrow, 1977). Useful special studies of Ottoman government and society are D. Nicolle, *Armies of the Ottoman Turks* (Osprey, 1985); Bruce McGowan, *Economic Life in the Ottoman Empire, 1600–1800* (Cambridge Univ., 1982); and H. Inalcik, *Studies in Ottoman Social and Economic History* (Variorum Reproductions, 1985). For interesting biographical sketches, see Noel Barber, *The Sultans* (Simon and Schuster, 1973). Ottoman relations with Europe are treated in Charles A. Frazee, *Catholics and Sultans* (Cambridge Univ., 1983); P. F. Sugar, *Southeastern Europe Under Ottoman Rule, 1354–1804* (Univ. of Washington, 1984); and Fatma M. Gocek, *East Encounters West* (Oxford Univ., 1987). A personalized look at English-Ottoman relations is provided in Sonia Anderson, *An English Consul in Turkey: Paul Rycaut at Smyrna, 1667–1678* (Oxford Univ., 1989).

For backgrounds on Muslim Middle-Eurasia in this period, see Arthur Goldschmidt, *A Concise History of the Middle East* (Westview, 1979) and E. H. Parker, *A Thousand Years of the Tartars* (Dorset, 1988). The classical work on Iran, still indispensable, is Percy M. Sykes, *A History of Persia* (Gordon, 1976). See also D. Morgan, *Medieval Persia, 1040–1797* (Longman, 1988) and Roger Savory, *Iran Under the Safavids* (Cambridge Univ., 1980). For eighteenth-century Iran, see L. Beck, *The Qashqu'i* of Iran (Yale Univ., 1986) and, for a readable biography, as well as a history of the period, see John R. Perry, *Harim Kahn Zand* (Univ. of Chicago, 1979). Yu. Gankovsky, *The History of Afghanistan* (Progress Pubs. [U.S.S.R.], 1985) throws welcome light on that obscure corner of Asia.

Stanley Wolpert's *A New History of India*, 3rd ed. (Oxford Univ., 1989) is a sound survey which puts the Mughul era in clear perspective. More concentrated attention is provided in Waldemar Hausen, *Peacock Throne: The Drama of Mughul India* (Orient Book Dist., 1986) and Stanley Lane-Poole, *The Triumph and Fall of the Mughul Empire*, 2 vols. (Found Class Reprints, 1987). Percival Spear, *Twilight of the Mughuls* (Cambridge Univ., 1951) is still valuable for its clear focus on Mughul decline. The following works present more specialized studies on varied aspects of the Mughul state and society: Neelan Chaudgary, *Socio-economic History of Mughal India* (South Asia Books, 1987); S. C. Dutta, *The North-east and the Mughuls, 1661–1714* (D. K. Pubs., 1984); Robert C. Hallissey, *The Rajput Rebellion Against Auranqzeb* (Univ. of Missouri, 1977) and O. Prakash, *The Dutch East India Company and the Economy of Bengal, 1630–1720* (Princeton Univ., 1985). For good biographical presentations, see Bamber Gascoigne, *The Great Mughuls*, rev. ed. (Cape, 1987); L. K. Agarwal, *Biographical Account of the Mughal Nobility, 1556–1707* (Coronet Books, 1985); and Muni Lal, *Aurangzeb* (Advent, 1988).

Among the best general surveys of Southeast Asia in this period are Steven Warshaw, *Southeast Asia Emerges*, rev. ed. (Diablo, 1987) and G. Coedes, *The Making of Southeast Asia*, 2nd ed. (Allen and Unwin, 1983). The Beginning of European encroachment is discussed in A. Reid, *Southeast Asia in the Age of Commerce, 1450–1680* (Yale Univ., 1988). Good special studies of individual states include, for Burma, M. Aung-Thwin, *Pagan, the Origins of Modern Burma* (Univ. of Hawaii, 1985); for Vietnam, Joseph Buttinger, *A Dragon Defiant* (Praeger, 1972); for Cambodia, Martin F. Herz, *A Short History of Cambodia* (Praeger, 1958); and for Indonesia, John D. Legge, *Indonesia* (Prentice Hall, 1965) and Joseph Kennedy, *A History of Malaya* (St. Martin's, 1962).

European expansion into the Pacific, in its Russian phases, is traced in John A. Harrison, *Founding of the Russian Empire in Asia and America* (Univ. of Miami, 1971) and Gerhard F. Muller, *Bering's Voyages: The Reports From Russia* (Univ. of Alaska, 1988). See also G. W. Steller, *Journal of a Voyage With Bering, 1741–1742* (Stanford Univ., 1988). For English exploration, see Lynne Withen, *Captain Cook and the Exploration of the Pacific* (Univ. of California, 1989) and D. Hoobler, *The Voyages of Captain Cook* (Putnam, 1983). More detailed accounts are presented in J. Elliott, *Captain Cook's Second Voyage* (Caliban, 1985) and S. A. Parkinson, *A Journal of a Voyage to the South Seas* (Caliban, 1984). A recent biography of the great English navigator is Alan Blackwood, *Captain Cook* (Watts, 1987). See also W. G. McClymount, *The Exploration of New Zealand* (Greenwood, 1986).

Traditional native Pacific cultures are ably depicted in the following works: Peter S. Brentwood, *The Polynesians* (Thames and Hudson, 1978); K. Sinclair, *A History of New Zealand*, rev. ed. (Penguin, 1985); David A. Howarth, *Tahiti* (Penguin, 1985); Edwin N. Ferdon, *Early Tahiti as the Explorers Saw it* (Univ. of Arizona, 1981); and Elizabeth Bott, *Tongan Society at the Time of Captian Cook's Visits* (Univ. of Hawaii, 1983).

Alan Moorehead, *The Fatal Impact* (Harper and Row, 1987) registers the disasters to native cultures which came with European "invasion of the South Pacific." See also O. H. Spate, *Paradise Found and Lost* (Univ. of Minnesota, 1988) and Ernest S. Dodge, *Islands and Empires* (Univ. of Minnesota, 1976). For specific results on one island, see David A. Howarth, *Tahiti, a Paradise Lost* (Viking, 1984) and E. H. Dodd, *The Rape of Tahiti* (Dodd, Mead, 1983). The Hawaiian reaction is evident in Richard Tregeskis's *The Warrior King: Hawaii's Kamehameha the Great* (C. E. Tuttle, 1973).

A general perspective on China under the Manchus can be gained from Wolfrom Eberhard, *A History of China* (Univ. of California, 1977); Charles O. Hucker, *China to 1850* (Stanford Uiv., 1978); and William S. Morton, *China, Its History and Its Culture* (McGraw Hill, 1982). Lynn Struve, *The Southern Ming, 1644–1662* (Yale Univ., 1984) records the pathetic last years of the old dynasty. J. D. Spence, *Ts'ao yin and the K'ang-hsi Emperor* (Yale Univ., 1988) provides an intimate glimpse of the greatest Manchu ruler. Social conditions under the Manchu are carefully examined in Susan Naquin and Evelyn S. Rawski,

Chinese Society in the Eighteenth Century (Yale Univ., 1989) and in Esther Yao, *Chinese Women, Past and Present* (Idle House, 1983). The deterioration arising from economic sources is evident in S. Arasaratram, *Merchants, Companies, and Commerce on the Coromandel Coast, 1650–1740* (Oxford Univ., 1987); Dean Murray, *Pirates of the South China Coast, 1790–1810* (Stanford Univ., 1987); and G. B. Souza, *The Survival of Empire: Portuguese Trade and Society in China and the South China Sea, 1630–1754* (Cambridge Univ., 1986).

Andrew C. Nahm, *Tradition and Transformation: A History of the Korean People* (Hollym International, 1988) gives a good account of major Korean developments during the period. See also Isabella Bird, *Korea and Its Neighbors* (Charles C. Tuttle, 1986); Ki-baik Lee, *A New History of Korea* (Harvard Univ., 1984); and William E. Griffis, *Korea* (AMS, 1971). For the roles of Korean women, see Yung-Chung Kim, *Women of Korea* (Ewha Women's Univ. [Seoul], 1979) and Laurel Kendall and Mark Peterson, eds. *Korean Women* (East Rock Press, 1983).

The mature Tokugawa era in Japan is given excellent coverage in Edwin O. Reischauer and Alfred M. Craig, *Japan, Story of a Nation*, 4th ed. (McGraw-Hill, 1989); Albert C. Danley, *Japan: A Short History* (Wayside, 1989); R. H. Mason, *A History of Japan* (Charles C. Tuttle, 1987); Mikiso Hane, *Modern Japan* (Westview, 1986); W. Scott Morton, *Japan, Its History and Culture* (McGraw-Hill, 1984); and Conrad Totman, *Japan Before Pery* (Univ. of California, 1981). John H. Wigmore, *Law and Justice in Tokugawa Japan* (Colorado Univ., 1986) reflects the lingering Japanese penchant for authority and discipline. Japanese social turmoil during the period is treated in Anne Walthall, *Social Protest and Popular Culture in Eighteenth-Century Japan* (Univ. of Arizona, 1986); S. Vlasos, *Peasant Protests and Uprisings in Tokugawa Japan* (Univ. of California, 1986); and H. P. Bix, *Peasant Revolt in Japan, 1590–1884* (Yale Univ., 1986). For Japanese intellectual developments, see R. N. Bellah, *Tokugawa Religion*, rev. ed. (Free Press, 1985); Herman Ooms, *Tokugawa Religion* (Princeton Univ., 1985); T. Najita, *Visions of Virtue in Tokugawa Japan* (Univ. of Chicago, 1987); and B. T. Wakaboyashi, *Anti-Foreignism and Western Learning in Early Modern Japan* (Harvard Univ., 1986).

Notes

1. Quoted in John Newton, *Journal of a Slave Trader*, edited by Catherine M. Bull (London: Epworth Press, 1962), p. 63.
2. This incident is cited in Charles André Julien, *A History of North Africa* (New York: Frederick A. Praeger, 1970), p. 79.
3. For the full text of this valedictory statement, see Jonathan Spence, *Emperor of China, a Self-Portrait of K'ang-hsi* (New York: Alfred A. Knopf, 1974), pp. 143–151.

Europe Transformed

The Napoleonic and Industrial Revolutions

Napoleon spread the values of the French Revolution throughout the continent, even as he stifled them in France, thus setting in motion the major social and political developments that dominated the century. By his military and foreign policies he inaugurated modern Latin American history and enabled the United States to double in size. Through rearranging the Holy Roman Empire he set in motion the development of "modern Germany." The breadth and nature of his conquests sparked the growth of modern nationalism throughout the continent (see map, p. 594). His economic policies changed the flow of capital and stimulated industrialization in Britian and economic reform throughout Europe.

Industrialization continued to bring new tools and power sources to do jobs formerly done by humans and animals. It brought about the biggest transformation of human life since the Neolithic Revolution. The economic strength generated by industrialization brought Europe global dominance during the nineteenth century.

Napoleon and the industrial inventors transformed Europe. The French leader broadcast the immense transformation that had occurred in his country to the world and made necessary a wholesale redrawing of political boundaries. The people who devised new tools and new ways to do old jobs set in process the transition from an agrarian to a modern, urbanized society. The monumental changes of this era engendered a new political vocabulary and a wide range of cultural responses.

Napoleon and France

Revolutions favor the bright, the ambitious, and the lucky. Napoleon Bonaparte (1769–1821) had all three qualities in abundance. He was born in Corsica to a lower-ranking Florentine or minor noble family in 1769—the year after control of that island passed from Genoa to France. At the age of ten his father placed him in the military academy at Brienne. Six years later he received his officer's commission. At the beginning of the French Revolution he was a twenty-year-old officer doomed by his family's modest standing and the restrictions of the Old Regime to a mediocre future. Ten years later, he ruled France. The revolution gave him the opportunity to use his brains, ability, charm, and daring to rise rapidly.

A potent mixture of eighteenth-century rationalism, romanticism, and revolutionary politics dominated his thought. He learned constantly, reading the classics, absorbing Enlightenment tracts, and constantly talking to people who could teach him. As an outsider from Corsica, he was tied to no particular faction in France and pursued his own interests with a fresh point of view. He drew close first to the men of 1789, then to the Jacobins, and later to the Directory (see ch. 21). Never did he allow control of his fate to escape from his own hands, pragmatically choosing whatever political, social, or religious option that could serve his goals.[1]

He never doubted that fate had chosen him to accomplish great things. Equipped with a vast

NAPOLEONIC EUROPE

- France in 1789
- Acquisitions of Napoleon to 1810
- Dependent States of Napoleon
- Allies of Napoleon
- → Napoleon's Campaigns

reserve of energy to match his enormous ego, Napoleon worked and studied ceaselessly, running on very little sleep. He was disciplined in his use of time and gifted in public relations skills. He pitched his messages and dreams to all levels of society, and had the ability to inspire and gain the maximum sacrifice from his nation and his armies.

The Opportunist

Napoleon came at the right time—a generation earlier or later and the situation would not have allowed him to gain power. He took advantage of the gutting of the old officer class by the revolutionary wars and the Jacobins to rise quickly to a prominent position from which he could appeal to the Directory. That self-

interested group of survivors asked the Corsican to break up a right-wing uprising in October 1795. The following year the Directory gave Napoleon command of the smallest of the three armies sent to do battle with the Austrians.

The two larger forces crossed the Rhine on their way to attack the Habsburgs while Napoleon's corps went over the Alps into Italy as a diversionary move. Contrary to plan, the main forces did little while Napoleon, who was supposed to be little more than bait, crushed the Sardinians and then the Austrians in a brilliant series of campaigns. As he marched across northern Italy he picked off Venice and was well on the road to Vienna where the Austrians approached him to make peace. Without instructions from his government, Napoleon negotiated the Treaty of Campo Formio (1797) and returned home a hero.

After considering an invasion of Britain in the first part of 1798—a cross-Channel task he deemed impossible—Napoleon set out with the Directory's blessing to strike at Britain's economy by attacking its colonial structure. He would invade Egypt, expose the weakness of the Ottoman Empire, and from there launch an attack on India. The politicians were as much impressed by this grand plan as they were relieved to get the increasingly popular Napoleon out of town. He successfully evaded the British fleet in the Mediterranean, landed in Egypt and took Alexandria and Cairo in July. The British Admiral Horatio Nelson (1758–1805) found the French fleet and sank it at Aboukir on August 1, 1798. Even though their supply lines and access to France were cut off, Napoleon's forces fought a number of successful battles against the Turks in Syria and Egypt.[2]

However, the fact remained that the French armies were stranded in Egypt and would be forced to remain there until 1801 when a truce allowed them to come home. This development would normally be regarded as a defeat, yet when Napoleon abandoned his army in August

This heroic portrait by Antoine Jean Gros shows the 27-year-old Napoleon leading his troops at the Battle of Arcola in northern Italy in November 1796.

1799, slipped by the British fleet, and returned to Paris, he was given a frenzied, triumphant homecoming. In public appearances, he adopted a modest pose and gave addresses on the scientific accomplishments of the expedition, such as the discovery of the Rosetta stone, a development that led to deciphering hieroglyphics (see ch. 1).

Napoleon, his brothers, and the Abbé Sieyès sought to take advantage of the political crisis surrounding the Directory. A coalition including Russia, Great Britain, Austria, Naples, Portugal, and the Ottoman Empire threatened France from the outside, while a feverlike inflation ravaged the economy internally. Various political factions courted Napoleon, whose charisma made him appear to be the likely savior of the country. In the meantime, he and his confederates planned their course. They launched a clumsy, though successful, coup in November 1799 and replaced the Directory with the Consulate. The plotters shared the cynical belief that "constitutions should be short and obscure" and that the nature of democracy consisted of the fact that the rulers rule and the people obey.

The takeover ended the revolutionary decade. France remained, in theory, a republic, but nearly all power rested with the thirty-one-year-old Napoleon, who ruled as first Consul. Still another constitution was written and submitted to a vote of the people. Only half of the eligible voters went to the polls, but an overwhelming majority voted in favor of the new constitution: 3,011,007 in favor versus 1,526 against.[3]

France to 1804: New Foundations

Ten years of radical change made France ready for one-man rule—but of a type much different from that exercised by the Bourbon monarchy. The events of 1789 had overturned the source of political power. It no longer came from God, but from the people. The social structure of the Old Regime was gone and with it the privileges of hereditary and created nobility. The Church no longer had financial or overt political power. The old struggles between kings and nobles, nobles and bourgeoisie, peasants and landlords, and Catholics and Protestants were replaced by the rather more universal confrontation between rich and poor.

Ten years of revolution had seen three attempts to rebuild the French system: the bourgeois-constitutional efforts to 1791; the radical programs to 1794; and the rule to 1799 by survivors who feared both the right and the left. Although each attempt had failed, each left valuable legacies to the new France. The first attempt established the power of the upper middle classes; the second showed the great power of the state to mobilize the population; and the third demonstrated the usefulness of employing former enemies in day-to-day politics.

Being the pragmatic tactician that he was, Napoleon used elements from the Old Regime and the various phases of the revolution to reconstruct France. He built an autocracy far more powerful than Louis XVI's government and took advantage of the absence of old forms of competition to central power from the nobility and the feudal structure, which were destroyed in the name of liberty, equality, and fraternity. He used the mercantile policies, military theories, and foreign policy goals of the *Old Regime*, the ambitions of the middle class, and the mobilization policies of the Jacobins. All he asked from those who wished to serve him was loyalty. Defrocked priests, renegade former nobles, reformed Jacobins, small businessmen, and ambitious soldiers all played a role. His acceptance of the ambitious brought him popularity because ten years of constant change had compromised most politically active people in some form of unprincipled, immoral, or illegal behavior.

Napoleon built his state on the *philosophes'* conception of a system in which all French men would be equal before the law. The revolution destroyed the sense of personal power of a sovereign and substituted what the British historian Lord Acton would later in the century call the "tyranny of the majority." The French state accordingly could intervene more effectively than ever before, limited only by distance and communications problems.[4]

The mass democratic army created by the total mobilization of both people and resources was one of the best examples of the new state system. A revolutionary society had fought a mass ideological war, and the experience changed the nature of combat forever. Because advancement and success were based on valor and victory, rather than bloodlines or privilege, the army profited from the new social structure and sought to preserve and extend it. The army best symbolized the great power of the French nation unleashed by the Revolution. Many of the economic and diplomatic problems that preceded the Revolution remained, but Napoleon's new state structure provided inspired solutions.

Taking advantage of his military supremacy, Napoleon gained a breathing space for his domestic reforms by making peace with the Second Coalition by March 1802. He then set about erecting the governing structure of France that remains with few changes to this day. He developed an administration that was effective in raising money, assembling an army, and exploiting the country's resources. His centralized government ruled through prefects, powerful agents in the provinces who had almost complete control of local affairs and were supported by a large police force. He then established a stable monetary policy based on an honest tax-collecting system, backed by up-to-date accounting procedures. The Bank of France that he created remains an institution regarded as a model of sound finance.

Napoleon knew that the country he ruled was overwhelmingly Catholic and that national interest dictated that he come to terms with the papacy. Through the Concordat of 1801 with Pope Pius VII the pope gained the right to approve the bishops whom the First Consul appointed to the re-established Catholic Church. The state permitted seminaries to be reopened and paid priests' salaries. Pius regained control of the Papal States and saw his church recognized as the "religion of the majority of Frenchmen." The Church thus resumed its position of prominence, but without its former power and wealth.

Napoleon viewed education as a way to train useful citizens to become good soldiers and bureaucrats, and he pursued the development of mass education by trying to increase the number of elementary schools, *lycées* (secondary schools), and special institutes for technical training. The schools were to be used to propagandize the young to serve the state through "directing political and moral opinion." Overarching the entire system was the University of France, more an administrative body to control education than a teaching institution.

Napoleon had neither the time nor the resources to put mass education in place during his lifetime, although he did gain immediate success in training the sons of the newly arrived middle classes to become state functionaries.[5]

Perhaps Napoleon's greatest accomplishment came in the field of law. Building on reforms begun ten years earlier, he put a talented team of lawyers to work to bring order to the chaotic state of French jurisprudence. At the time he took power the country was caught in the transition from the old legal system of 366 separate local systems to a uniform code. His staff compiled a comprehensive Civil Law Code by 1804 (called the Code Napoléon after 1807) that was a model of precision and equality, when compared to the old system. The Code ensured the continuation of the gains made by the middle classes in the previous decade and emphasized religious toleration and the abolition of the privileges held under the old order. Unfortunately, the Code perpetuated the inferior status of women in the areas of civil rights, financial activities, and divorce. Nonetheless it has influenced lawmaking in many other countries.

The price France paid for all of this was rule by police state that featured censorship, secret police, spies, and political trials that sent hundreds to their deaths and thousands into exile. Order did prevail, however, and for the first time in ten years it was safe to travel the country's roads. Napoleon also reduced the "representative assemblies" to meaningless rubber stamps. Liberty, equality, and fraternity meant little in a land where the First Consul and his police could deny a person's freedom and right of association because of a perceived intellectual or political conflict.

To consolidate all of the changes, Napoleon proclaimed himself emperor in December 1804. Fifteen years after the outbreak of the revolution, France had a new monarch. The nation approved the change in a plebiscite by 3,572,329 to 2,579. As Napoleon took the crown from Pope Pius VII, who had come from Rome for the occasion, and crowned himself, the First French Republic came to an end.

The artist Jacques Louis David, an ardent admirer of Napoleon, painted several pictures glorifying him. This is a preliminary sketch for David's coronation painting of the emperor.

Napoleon and the World

Since 1792, war had been France's primary occupation, and on the whole it had been a profitable one. The French had gained much land and money, as well as the opportunity to export the revolution. Napoleon's reforms helped make his country even stronger in battle. At the end of 1804 Napoleon embarked on a series of compaigns designed to show France's invincibility. A key to French success was the emperor himself, who brought his own remarkable genius to lead his strong and wealthy country.

Military Superiority

Napoleon brought equal parts of intellectual strength, sensitivity to mood and opportunity, and undoubted bravery to the task of making war. He had been trained in the most advanced methods of his day, and he had better, more mobile artillery and more potent powder to blow holes through the enemy's lines. He worked well with a talented command staff to which he gave much responsibility to wield their divisions as conditions dictated. Finally, he was the ultimate leader. Whether as lieutenant, general, first consul, or emperor, Napoleon inspired masses of soldiers in a dramatic way. At the same time he mobilized the home front through the use of the press and skillfully written despatches.

Beneath this image making, the supreme commander was extremely flexible in his use of resources, always changing his tactics. He was pragmatic, moved rapidly, and lived off the land—until the Russian campaign. He won the loyalty of his men by incentives and rewards, not brutal discipline. He set many military precedents, among them the use of ideological and economic warfare, and rapid simultaneous movement of a large number of columns which could quickly converse on a given point with devastating results, breaking the will of the enemy. Finally, he personally led his troops into battle, exposing himself to incredible dangers, with little regard for his own safety.[6]

His nemesis was Great Britain, and during 1803 and 1804 he prepared a cross-Channel invasion, but the inability of the French navy to control the Channel and the formation of the Third Coalition (Great Britain, Russia, Austria, and Sweden) forced him to march eastward. In October 1805 Admiral Nelson and the British ended Napoleon's hopes of dominating the seas by destroying the joint French-Spanish fleet at the Battle of Trafalgar.

France did far better on land, gaining mastery over the continent by the end of 1807. Napoleon totally demoralized the Third Coalition in the battles at Ulm (October 1805) and Austerlitz (December 1805). He then annihilated the Prussians who had entered the conflict in the battles at Jena and Auerstadt (October 1806). He occupied Berlin, where he established the Continental System, a blockade of the continent that was an effort to defeat Britain by depriving it of trade with the rest of Europe. Finally in June 1807 he defeated the Russians at the battle of Friedland, and forced Tsar Alexander I to sign the Tilsit Treaty in July. This treaty, signed on a raft anchored in the middle of the Nieman River, brought the two major land powers of Europe together in an alliance against Britain.

At the beginning of 1808 Napoleon stood supreme in Europe, leading France to dominance it had never experienced before or since. Several of his relatives occupied the thrones of nearby countries. The rest of the continent appeared to be mere satellites revolving around the Napoleonic sun.[7]

France's Revolution in Europe

In achieving his military goals, Napoleon set in motion a chain reaction of minirevolutions that had a profound impact on the rest of the century. British sea power stood in the way of France's total mastery of the continent. Safe behind its wall of ships, the British turned out increasing quantities of goods. Even though their economy suffered under the impact of the Continental System (exports dropped by 20 percent with a resultant cutback in production and rise in unemployment), the damage was not permanent. At the same time, Great Britain was in the midst of the early phases of industrialization (see p. 606), and in 1815 Britain stood generations ahead of the continent in economic development. Napoleon inadvertently contributed to Britain's development by forcing it to industrialize quickly as it sought new markets and methods.

Napoleon's armies carried French ideological baggage and institutional reforms with them as they fought across the continent. Even though the emperor consolidated the Revolution in a conservative way in France, he broke apart the old regime's fragile social and governmental structures when he marched across the Rhine. Napoleon consciously spread the messages of liberty, fraternity, and equality with all of the antifeudal, antiprivilege, and antirepressive themes inherent in the revolutionary triad. Where the French governed directly (see map, p. 594), they used the Code Napoléon and the reformed administrative practices. Although initially the changes were not always obvious, they became quite evident throughout most of Europe by 1848.

The French presence triggered a hostile wave. Many Europeans saw Napoleon as an imperialist, and the people he had "emancipated" began to realize that they had exchanged an old for a new form of despotism. By posing as the champion of the Revolution, Napoleon sowed the seeds of the opposition that would work against him later, especially in Prussia. With the exception of the Poles, who had labored under Russian dominance and now served Napoleon well, the rest of Europe reacted against the French yoke.

The most significant rebellion took place in Portugal and Spain. His entry into the countries to topple the passive Bourbons and strengthen the leaky Continental System was uncharacteristically shortsighted. Napoleon had a serious fight on his hands in the Peninsular War that followed. Guerrilla uprisings soon broke out, supported by a British expeditionary force and supplies. These bloody wars tied down from 200,000 to 300,000 French troops over a period of five years and drained the French treasury. The invasion of Spain also prompted a series of uprisings in the New World that gave birth to modern Latin American history (see p. 602).

The social and political changes the French triggered in Germany were equally profound. When he redrew the map of Europe after his victories, Napoleon destroyed the remnants of the Holy Roman Empire, and in so doing erased 112 states of that ancient league. Only six of the former fifty free cities retained their status. Further, by changing the territorial arrangements of other areas, he reduced the number of German political units from more than 300 to 39. The historial Hajo Holborn wrote that "it was the French invasion and the rule of Napoleon that finally led German intellectuals to the problem of the state." All over Germany a wave of nationalism stirred the politically conscious population and prepared the way for the liberation movement. Prussia in particular underwent a rebirth after 1806 to enable it to compete with France, and many German nationalists thereafter began to look to Berlin for strength and leadership.

Prussian Reform politicians such as Baron Heinrich vom und zum Stein (1757–1831) and Prince Karl von Hardenberg (1750–1822) initiated a program of social change that included abolition of serfdom—without turning land over to the peasants—a degree of self-government in the cities, and emancipation of the Jews. Although Napoleon had limited the Prussian army to 42,000 men, the Berlin authorities undermined this restriction by a subterfuge—as soon as one army was trained it was placed on reserve and a new army was called up for training. In this way Prussia managed to build a force of 270,000 men. These efforts gained the support of Prussian

intellectuals who used education as a means of nationalistic propaganda. The University of Berlin, founded in 1810, became a strong center for national movements.[8]

The Invasion of Russia

Opposition to Napoleon grew in both Austria and Russia. After the valiant but unsuccessful campaigns against the French in 1809, culminating in the bloody battle of Wagram, Vienna became a docile though not a dependable ally. Napoleon's marriage to Marie Louise, the daughter of Francis I of Austria, proved to be only a tenuous tie between the French emperor and the Habsburgs. In Russia, the Tilsit Treaty had never been popular, and the economic hardships brought on by the Continental System made a break in the alliance virtually inevitable. By the end of 1810 both France and Russia were preparing to go to war with each other.

Napoleon understood the shaky base on which his dominance rested. Involvement in Spain had drained France. The Continental System was not working against Britain. Alexander I proved to be an increasingly undependable ally. Finally, after two years of preparations, Napoleon launched a massive invasion of Russia in 1812 to put an end to at least one of his problems.

The emperor prepared carefully for his attack on Russia. Food supply would be a major problem for the 611,000 troops in the first and second lines of the invasion because his forces would be too large to live off the land. Furthermore the French troops took with them over 200,000 animals which required forage and water. The invasion force delayed its march until late June to ensure that the Russian plains would furnish sufficient grass to feed the animals. The well-thought-out, massive preparations for the invasion proved inadequate to the problems posed by the six-hundred-mile march from the Nieman River to Moscow.

Although Napoleon's twelve-nation army made almost constant headway, the Russian forces remained intact. Because they were outnumbered nearly three to one, the tsar's armies under the leadership of General Barclay de Tolly (1761–1818) and later General Mikhail Kutuzov (1745–1813) continually retreated into the vastness of their land, rather than face almost certain defeat in the hands of the invaders. The Russians destroyed everything of possible use to Napoleon's forces—the so-called scorched earth policy—continually harassed the advancing columns, and threatened the French supply lines. When the Russians finally stood their ground at Borodino (September 7, 1812), the effects of distance and disease had taken their toll among the French, and the numbers of the opposing forces were nearly equal. After a brutal conflict in which 75,000 of the total 200,000 combatants were left dead or wounded, the road to Moscow was open to the victorious French.

The Russian campaign was both a success and a failure for Napoleon. The French did gain their objective—the former capital city of Moscow—but the Russians refused to surrender. Shortly after the French occupied the city, fires broke out, destroying three-fourths of the ancient capital. After spending thirty-three days in the burned shell of the city waiting in vain for the tsar, who was 400 miles north in St. Petersburg, to agree to peace, Napoleon gave orders to retreat. He left the city on October 19. To remain would have meant having his lines cut by winter and being trapped with no supplies. His isolation in Moscow would have encouraged his enemies in Paris. Leaving the Russian capital, as it turned out, condemned most of his men to death.[9]

As the remnant of Napoleon's forces marched west in October and November, they were forced to retrace virtually the same route they had used in the summer. They suffered the attacks of the roving bands of partisans, starvation, and the continual pressure of Kutuzov's forces. Thousands perished daily, and by the end of November only about 100,000 of the original force had made their escape from Russia. Napoleon had thirteen years earlier abandoned an army in Egypt to return to Paris. In November 1812 he abandoned another army, this time in Russia, and returned to pursue his fortunes.

Napoleon's Defeat

Russia, which had stood alone against the French at the beginning of 1812, was soon joined by Prussia, Austria, and Britain in 1813 and 1814 in what came to be known as the "War of Liberation." While British armies under the Duke of Wellington (1769–1852) helped clear the French

forces out of Spain, the allied troops pushed Napoleon's forces westward. A combination of Napoleon's genius and the difficulties in coordinating the allied efforts prolonged the war, but in October 1813 the French suffered a decisive defeat at Leipzig in the Battle of the Nations, one year to the day after Napoleon had fled Moscow.

The allies sent peace offers to Napoleon, but he refused them, pointing out that "...you sovereigns who were born to the throne may get beaten twenty times, and yet return to your capitals. I cannot. For I rose to power through the camp."[10] After Leipzig the Napoleonic empire rapidly disintegrated, and by the beginning of 1814 the allies had crossed the Rhine and invaded France. At the end of March the Russians, Austrians, and Prussians took Paris. Two weeks later Napoleon abdicated his throne, receiving in return sovereignty over Elba, a small island between Corsica and Italy.

Napoleon arrived in Elba in May and established his rule over his 85-square-mile kingdom. He set up a mini-state, complete with an army, navy, and court. Boredom soon set in and in February 1815 he eluded the British fleet and returned to France. His former subjects, disillusioned with the restored Bourbon, Louis XVIII, gave him a tumultuous welcome. Napoleon entered Paris and raised an army of 300,000 men and sent a message to the allies gathered to make peace at Vienna (see ch. 24) that he desired to rule France and only France. The allies, who were on the verge of breaking up their alliance, united, condemned Napoleon as an enemy of peace, and sent forces to France to put him down once and for all.

At the Battle of Waterloo on June 18, 1815, the Duke of Wellington, supported by Prussian troops under Field Marshall Gebhard von Blücher (1749–1819), narrowly defeated Napoleon. The vanquished leader sought asylum with the British, hoping to live in exile either in England or the United States. But the allies, taking no chances, shipped him off to the bleak south Atlantic island of St. Helena, five thousand miles from Paris. Here he set about writing his autobiography. He died of cancer in 1821 at the age of 51.

Even with the brief flurry of the One Hundred Days, Napoleon had no hope of recreating the grandeur of his empire as it was in 1808. The reasons for this are not hard to find. Quite simply,

Napoleon on His Place in History

In his conversations with the Count de Las Cases, Napoleon clearly expressed *his* notion of his place in history.

"I closed the gulf of anarchy and cleared the chaos. I purified the Revolution, dignified Nations and established Kings. I excited every kind of emulation, rewarded every kind of merit, and extended the limits of glory! This is at least something! And on what point can I be assailed on which an historian could not defend me? Can it be for my intentions? But even here I can find absolution. Can it be for my despotism? It may be demonstrated that the Dictatorship was absolutely necessary. Will it be said that I restrained liberty? It can be proved that licentiousness, anarchy, and the greatest irregularities, still haunted the threshold of freedom. Shall I be accused of having been too fond of war? It can be shown that I always received the first attack. Will it be said that I aimed at universal monarchy? It can be proved that this was merely the result of fortuitous circumstances, and that our enemies themselves led me step by step to this determination. Lastly, shall I be blamed for my ambition? This passion I must doubtless be allowed to have possessed, and that in no small degree; but at the same time, my ambition was of the highest and noblest kind that ever, perhaps, existed—that of establishing and of consecrating the empire of reason, and the full exercise and complete enjoyment of all the human faculties! And here the historian will probably feel compelled to regret that such ambition should not have been fulfilled and gratified!" Then after a few moments of silent reflection: "This," said the Emperor, "is my whole history in a few words."

From the Count de Las Cases, *Memoirs of the Life, Exile, and Conversations of the Emperor Napoleon*, new ed. (New York: Eckler, 1900).

Napoleon was the heart and soul of the empire, and after 1808 his physical and intellectual vigor began to weaken. Administrative and military developments reflected this deterioration, as Napoleon began to appoint sycophants to positions of responsibility. Further, by 1812 the middle classes on whom he depended began suffering the economic consequences of his policies. The Continental System and continual warfare made their effects deeply felt through decreased trade and increased taxes. Even though some war contractors profited, the costs of Napoleon's ambitions began to make Frenchmen long for peace.

Outside of France, the growth of national resistance on the continent worked against the dictator who first stimulated it by exporting the call for liberty, equality, and fraternity. Equally important, the twenty-five years of French military superiority disappeared as other nations adopted and improved on the new methods of fighting. Finally, the balance of power principle made itself felt. France could not eternally take on the whole world.

Napoleon and the Americas

The forces generated by the French Revolution and Napoleon deeply affected the Americas in the fifty years after 1776. The former English colonies south of Canada had gained their independence with French assistance and the new government had close relations with Paris until the outbreak of the revolutionary wars, when President George Washington proclaimed neutrality. When relations with the British began to improve during the 1790s, the French waged a virtual war on American shipping, taking over 800 ships in the last three years of the century. The United States benefitted from one aspect of Napoleon's activities. In 1803, the emperor sold the region known as Louisiana for $15 million;

this Louisiana Purchase increased the land area of the new country by 200 percent. Unfortunately, the United States suffered considerable commercial losses as it became caught up in the French-British conflict.

The French overthrow of the Spanish Bourbons in 1808 encouraged the revolts that created thirteen republics in Spanish America by 1824 (see map, p. 603). The charismatic leader who stepped into the void was Simon Bolívar (1783–1830), hailed as "the Liberator " of South America. After completing his rationalist education in Paris during the last years of the Directory, he returned to his native Venezuela to exploit colonial resistance to the Napoleonic takeover of Spain in 1808. Convinced after the disaster at Trafalgar that transatlantic ambitions were pointless, Napoleon left the Spanish colonial empire to its own complex fate.[11]

Loyal at first to the deposed Spanish Bourbons and newly filled with refugees from the parent country, Spain's colonies soon began to entertain the idea that they had their own destinies to fulfill as new nations. The American-born elite of European blood, the creoles, were especially attracted to the prospect of expelling the controlling *peninsulares*, Spaniards of European birth who usually returned to Spain after a profitable term of colonial service.[12]

Bolívar stepped into this situation by issuing a series of inflammatory and visionary messages calling for the liberation of Venezuela and then of a larger unit called Gran Colombia (modern-day Colombia, Panama, Ecuador, and Venezuela) which he hoped would expand to include all of Spanish South America. He was frequently defeated by Spanish loyalist forces, yet he kept fighting, making use of skills as an orator and as a tactician. He eventually forced the remnants of the Spanish military and administrative personnel to go home. He proposed a constitution that favored the élite of the new nations, a document that was much like the one written by the Directory. He ran afoul of liberal critics and regional loyalties, and eventually died in exile in British Jamaica. He dreamed of continental state split into the nation-states of Venezuela, Colombia, Ecuador, Peru, and Bolivia.

Argentina, Uruguay, and Chile were liberated in comparable fashion by the stoic, Spanish-educated creole officer José de San Martín (1778–1850) who was as austere and reserved as Bolívar was flashy and outgoing. The two could never forge an alliance, partly because of personality differences and partly because of San Martín's preference for a constitutional monarchy like that of Britain or the French Constitution of 1791. His wishes were rejected by the Spanish

Simon Bolívar and his army battle the Spanish at Araure in Venezuela. Although the Spanish were better trained and equipped, Bolívar led his soldiers with such personal valor that he managed to liberate four countries.

colonies he had freed but were followed by the Portuguese in Brazil. King John VI of Portugal had fled his country in 1807 and ruled the Portuguese empire from Rio de Janeiro for the next fourteen years. Returning to Lisbon in 1821, the king left his son Dom Pedro as regent of Brazil. Impatient with the reactionary behavior of the Lisbon government, Pedro declared himself emperor of an independent Brazil, which he and his son Pedro II ruled as a constitutional monarchy for nearly seventy years.

The Mexican revolution began earlier and produced more extreme consequences than its South American counterpart. The Mexican middle class was even smaller than that of the rest of Spanish America and far more conservative. Between 1808 and 1810 anti-Bonapartist sentiment shifted to a general rejection of the European monarchy in creole circles throughout the vice-royalty of New Spain.

The revolution was actually begun by an enlightened provincial creole priest, Miguel Hidalgo (1753–1811), who issued a call for universal freedom on September 16, 1810 (the date is celebrated in Mexico today as the *Dia del Grito*, the Day of the Call). Hidalgo led his ragged army of Indians and idealists to the gates of Mexico City, but hesitated to take the city fearing the bloodbath that would follow. Although Hidalgo was condemned by the colonial bishops and executed for treason six months after his uprising began, his cause was taken up by others, including José Maria Morelos (1765–1815), a radical mestizo (mixed blood) parish priest who became an effective guerrilla leader. Finally, in August 1821, the last Spanish viceroy recognized the independence of Mexico, whose ruling classes promptly fell to squabbling over the constitution.

While men of ideas argued, military opportunists took power. Two would-be Napoleons, Augustín de Iturbide (1783–1824) and Antonio López de Santa Anna (1794–1876), dominated politics for the next quarter-century, at the end of which Mexico lost the northern half of its territory to the United States. Iturbide, a creole landowner and officer who had fought as a Spanish loyalist until 1816, became emperor of Mexico for a turbulent ten month reign in 1822–1823. Santa Anna, who emulated Napoleon's opportunism more successfully than many of his other qualities, became president or dictator of the

LATIN AMERICA 1826
European Colony

Mexican republic eleven times between 1833 and 1855. His career as a military leader included several disastrous incidents, notably his humiliating defeat and capture by Texan rebels at San Jacinto in April 1836 — six weeks after he had exterminated their comrades at the secularized Franciscan mission in San Antonio known as the Alamo and a month after he had mercilessly massacred Texan prisoners at Goliad (see p. 713).[13]

The social and economic consequences of the Latin American revolutions were far different from those in North America and Europe. The area was much poorer and more divided. The new nations of Latin America quickly fell to the commercial dominance of the British Empire. Their economies, exploited by speculators in North America and Europe, have been subject to drastic fluctuations ever since, based as they are on exportation of raw materials. The conditions of the Indian population declined as the new liberal regimes confiscated the large landholdings of the religious orders which had served to insulate the surviving Indians from direct confrontations with the Europeans' economic and technological dominance. As in every country since the Reformation where Church property was bought up by the monied classes, the local population was reorganized into a new labor force more profitable to the new owners. In this case, the owners simply reorganized the Indian communities into a labor force and drove those who were not productive and the mestizos off the land. This movement in some countries has continued in one form or another to the present day.

The Latin American Church, staffed largely by *peninsulares*, was shattered by the national revolution. When reconstituted with greatly reduced property and clerical personnel, the Church desperately sought to win the protection of the more conservative elements in the creole elite by opposing liberalism in any form. Since the Church had been the exclusive instrument of education and social welfare before liberation and since the ruling classes showed little interest in providing for the continuation of schools, orphanages, and relief for the lower classes, the misery of the Latin American poor grew more acute throughout the nineteenth century.

The position of women rose momentarily and then fell, as in France. Individual creole women such as Bolívar's astute mistress Manuela Sanches, made major contributions to the revolution, but the adoption of the Napoleonic Code in the 1820s had the same impact on women's legal status as in Europe at the same time.

It can be argued that in the wake of Napoleon's deposing the Spanish Bourbons Latin America suffered a decline in political stability and internal economic health. The peasants and urban laborers of Indian and mixed blood descent, the culture-shaping Church, and women of all classes paid a heavy price for liberation from the Spanish and Portuguese overlords. The single group that gained was the secular, male Creole leadership. Nevertheless, what Napoleon had destroyed was gone, and no serious attempt was made to restore the old colonial regime. The political independence of the new nations of Latin America was guaranteed, at least in theory, by the United States in the proclamation of the Monroe Doctrine in 1823 (see p. 710).

Industrialization: The First Phase

While Europe's "great men" plotted grand schemes to pursue their political and intellectual ambitions during the crisis of the Old Regime, French Revolution, and Napoleonic wars, obscure British inventors designed machines whose impact would dwarf their efforts. They industrialized textile making by using machines and new power sources to accomplish a task formerly done by human and animal power. They began what has been called by some the Industrial Revolution.

The huge increase in productivity made possible by using machines can be shown in the amount of raw cotton Britain imported in 1760 and 1850. In 1760 the British imported a bit over 1000 tons; in 1850 the number had risen to over 222,000 tons. The story behind the growth of the textile industry is one of a continual "catch-up" game between the spinners and weavers to respond to a growing market. After the 1707 Act of Union with Scotland, Britain possessed an expanding population with a larger per capita income than that of any other European state. The population growth stemmed from a gradual decline in death rates and an increase in the birth rate.[14] It provided more customers and workers.

The Revolution in Making Cloth

Practical people seeing the need for greater output solved the practical problems of production. In the many steps from the raw cotton to the finished cloth, there were bottlenecks—primarily in making yarn and weaving the strands together. In 1733, John Kay (1704–1764), a spinner and mechanic, patented the first of the great machines—the flying shuttle. This device made it possible for one person to weave wide bolts of cloth by using a spring mechanism that sent the shuttle across the loom. This invention upset the balance between the weavers of cloth and the spinners of yarn: ten spinners were required to produce enough yarn needed by one weaver. James Hargreaves (d. 1778), a weaver

Power looms in operation in an English mill in the 1820s.

Finally, the textile industry became so large that it outgrew the possibilities of its power source: water power. Steam came to drive the machines of industrializing Britain. In the first part of the eighteenth century a mechanic, Thomas Newcomen (1663–1729), made an "atmospheric engine" in which a piston was raised by injected steam. As the steam condensed, the piston returned to its original position. Newcomen's unwieldy and inefficient device was put to use pumping water out of mines. James Watt (1736–1819), a builder of scientific instruments at the University of Glasgow, perfected Newcomen's invention. Watt's steam engine also was first used to pump water out of mines. It saved the large amounts of energy lost by the Newcomen engine and led to an increase in coal productivity. After 1785 it was also used to make cloth and drive ships and locomotives. The application of steam to weaving made it possible to expand the use of cloth-making machines to new areas, and after 1815 hand looms began to disappear from commercial textile making, replaced by the undoubted superiority of the cloth-making machines.

These inventors made their contributions in response to the need to solve a particular problem. Their machines and the new power sources expanded productivity and transformed society in ways never before dreamed of. The transition from a rural agrarian to an urban lifestyle merits applying the term *revolutionary* to the process of industrialization. The steps in increasing textile production were repeated and continue to be repeated in other goods as well. The liberation from the productive limitation of human and animal power to satisfy essentially unlimited demand is the great gift of industrialization.

Britain's Dominance

Industrialization began in Britain in the eighteenth century for a number of reasons. Neither the richest nor the most populous country in western Europe, it did, nevertheless, possess at virtually all levels of society a hard-working, inventive, risk-taking private sector that received strong support from the government. Industrialization could not begin and grow without individual business owners who took a chance on something new. The British kept this close tie

and carpenter, eliminated that problem in 1764 with his spinning jenny, a mechanical spinning wheel that allowed the spinners to keep up with the weavers.

Five years later, a barber named Richard Arkwright (1732–1792) built the water frame that made it possible to spin many threads into yarn at the same time. Ten years after that Samuel Crompton (1753–1827), a spinner, combined the spinning jenny and water frame into the water mule, which, with some variations, is used today. By this time the makers of yarn were outpacing the weavers, but in 1785 Edmund Cartwright (1743–1823) invented the power loom that mechanized the weaving process. In two generations what had once been a home-based craft became an industry.

The appetite of the new machines outran the supply of cotton. Since most of the material came from the United States, the demand exceeded the capability of the slave-based southern economy to fill the supply. The best worker could not prepare more than five or six pounds of cotton a day because of the problems of the seeds. American inventor Eli Whitney (1765–1825), among others, devised the cotton gin, a machine that enabled a worker to clean more than fifty times as much cotton a day. This device coincidentally played a major role in the perpetuation of slavery in the United States.

between private initiative and creative governmental support throughout the eighteenth and nineteenth centuries.

Thanks to early governmental support of road improvements and canal construction, Britain had a better transportation network than any other country in Europe (see map at right). The British also had mastery of the seas, excellent ports, and a large merchant fleet. They enjoyed the advantage of living safely on their island, away from the carnage of war, even during the Napoleonic wars. The chance to industrialize in stable conditions gave them the opportunity to profit from war contracts between 1792 and 1815. They developed their industrial capacity without fear of battle damage or loss of life.

Probably the most important factor was the relative flexibility of the British social and political systems. Members of the élite, unlike their colleagues on the continent, pursued their wealth in the new industrial framework with great energy. They worked closely with the middle classes and workers, even to the point during the nineteenth century of sponsoring gradual reform efforts to stifle any chance of revolution from below.

The combination of inventiveness, growing markets, governmental support, and social flexibility made Britain the world's dominant economic power until the end of the nineteenth century. Napoleon's interference had hurt economic growth, but had also spurred the British to look for new manufacturing methods and markets. Once the wars were over, Britain flooded the continent and the Americas with high-quality, inexpensive goods. No nation could compete against British efficiency. When Britain began industrializing before 1789, there were isolated areas on the continent such as the French Le Creusot works that could have served as the base for a similar growth. Twenty-six years of revolution and mercantile policies made that competition impossible.[15]

Cotton production continued to increase and was supplemented by the arrival of the modern Iron Age. In 1800 Russia and Sweden had exported iron to Britain. By 1815 Britain exported more than five times as much iron as it imported. By 1848 the British produced more iron than the rest of the world combined. As in textile production, in ironmaking a number of inventions

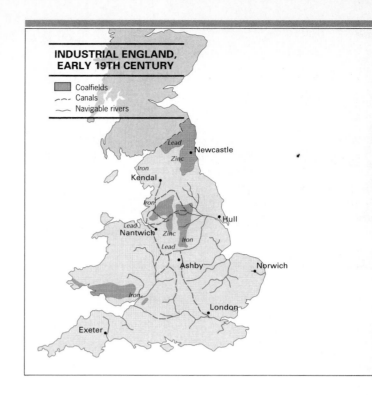

INDUSTRIAL ENGLAND, EARLY 19TH CENTURY

Coalfields
Canals
Navigable rivers

appeared to respond to problems. Refining of the brittle cast iron was improved to make it more malleable and tougher. At the same time more efficient mining processes for both coal and iron ore were used to ensure a constant supply of raw materials.

To further dominate the metals market, in the 1850s Henry Bessemer (1813–1898) developed a process to make steel, a harder and more malleable metal, quickly and cheaply. So effective was the process that between 1856 and 1870 the price of British steel fell to one half the amount formerly charged for the best grade of iron. The drastic reduction in price, a mark of industrialization, had a positive impact on all areas of the economy.

In the period after midcentury Britain produced more than two-thirds of the world's coal and more than half of the world's iron and cloth. Industrial development encouraged urbanization and by 1850 more than half of the population lived in cities and worked in industries. The British continued to enjoy the highest per capita income in the world, and the island nation stood head and shoulders above the world in terms of economic and material strength.

Industrialization: The Second Phase

The second phase of industrialization brought new products and power sources to the continent. Increased food production and improved health standards and diet led to a population explosion that promised both economic gains and bureaucratic burdens. The rapid and massive growth of cities brought with it the social problems of urbanization. Workers united to fight for their interests, while the middle classes extended their wealth and influence. Both groups changed the nature of social and political life.

Food and Population Increases

Liberated from many of the restraints of the past by the French, Napoleonic, and Industrial revolutions, most Europeans made the transition from a society based on agriculture to a modern urban society. The spectacular growth of the industrial sector makes it easy to overlook the great strides in food production during the nineteenth century. Because of the improved global transportation network and better farming methods, the expanding number of city dwellers had more and better food to eat in 1914 than they had had in 1815.

It is estimated that in 1815 around 60 percent of the money and 85 percent of the Europeans were tied to farming. These large quantities of capital and labor were not effectively used, because the advances made in Holland and Britain in the seventeenth and eighteenth centuries had not spread to the continent. However, progressive landowners gradually introduced these improved methods when they saw the money to be made feeding the growing population of the cities.

By the end of the nineteenth century farmers on the continent were plowing new lands and using higher yielding crop varieties to survive in the worldwide agricultural competition. Industrial nations such as Britain, in which only 10 percent of the population was engaged in farming, imported more than a fourth of their food. Farmers in the Americas, Australia, and New Zealand competed with each other in the cutthroat export market. The peasants of Ireland and southern and eastern Europe were unable to produce efficiently enough to prosper in this new setting. Russia, where the peasantry comprised 70 percent of the population, had to export to bring in foreign capital to finance industrialization. When the country had to compete with efficient foreign farmers, the tsarist minister of finance stated, "we may go hungry, but we will export."[16]

The expanded food supply supported the growth in European population from 175 million to 435 million.[17] This 130 percent increase between 1800 and 1910 partially disproved the views the British clergyman Thomas Robert Malthus (1766–1834) set forth in his *Essay on Population*. Malthus asserted that human reproduction could easily outrun the earth's ability to produce food.[18] In his own day he could point to the limited food supply and rapidly increasing population. From this evidence he concluded that the inevitable fate of humanity was misery and ruin, since the number of people would rise geometrically while food supply would grow only arithmetically. The experience of the next two centuries has at least temporarily disproved Malthus' thesis.

A gradual decline in mortality rates, slightly better medical care, more food, earlier marriages, and better sanitary conditions contributed to the population increase. The number of people grew so rapidly in Europe that although 40 million Europeans emigrated throughout the world, the continent still showed a population increase in one century that was greater than that of the previous two thousand years. Where the economies were advanced, such as in northern and western Europe, the population growth could be absorbed. But in the poorer countries of southern and eastern Europe, the masses faced the choices of overcrowding and starvation or emigration.

The Ties That Bind: New Networks

To bring the increased food supply to the growing population, to distribute new resources to larger markets, and to connect augmented capital with essential information, Europeans built the most complete and far-reaching transportation and communication networks ever known. Without rapid and dependable transport and contact the Industrial Revolution could not have occurred, cities would not have grown, factories could not have functioned, and the new millions of Europeans would not have been fed. The new networks became the arteries and nervous system of Europe.

The Duke of Bridgewater made a major step forward in water transportation in 1759 when he built a seven and one-half mile long canal from his mines to Manchester. Water transport cut the price of his coal in half and gave Britain a vivid lesson in the benefits of canals. Nearly four thousand miles of improved rivers and canals were built, with strong governmental support by the 1830s, making it possible to ship most of the country's products by water. Following the British example, canal building spread through Europe and North America and then to Egypt with the Suez Canal in 1869 and Latin America with the Panama Canal in 1914. The first project cut the sailing time between London and Bombay India by nearly half, while the second did away with the need to sail around South America to reach the Pacific Ocean.

Until 1815 most roads were muddy, rutted paths that were impassable during spring thaws and autumn rains. In that year a Scotsman, John McAdam, created the all-weather road by placing small stones in compact layers directly on the road bed. The pressure of the traffic moving over the highway packed the stones together to give a fairly smooth surface. This practical solution cut the stagecoach time for the 160 miles from London to Sheffield from four days in the 1750s to 28 hours.

Steam-powered vessels replaced the graceful though less dependable sailing ships in ocean commerce. Clipper ships are among the most beautiful objects ever built, but they could not move without wind. Sturdy, awkward-looking steamships carried larger cargo with greater regularity and revolutionized world trade. The price of American wheat on the European market dropped by three-fourths in the last part of the century, thanks to a considerable degree to the savings made possible by the large, reliable steam ships. Transatlantic passenger and mail services were also improved by the use of steam to power seagoing vessels.

The most important element in the European arterial network was the railroad. Between 1830 and 1860 rails linked every major market in Europe, and the United States. By 1903 the Russians had pushed the Trans-Siberian railroad to the Pacific Ocean. Railroads cheaply and efficiently carried large amounts of material and people long distances and knit countries and continents closer together. Within cities, urban rail lines and trolleys were widespread by the end of the century; these had an impressive effect on

Lavish ceremony celebrated the opening of the Suez Canal in 1869.

This English royal train was built in the early 1840s for the special use of Queen Victoria in her travels over the nation's rapidly expanding railway system.

housing and business patterns by permitting a wider diffusion of workers. London established subways first in the 1860s, followed by Budapest in 1896 and Paris in 1900.

Connected with the growth of the transportation networks and technological innovation, major improvements came in the area of communications. Postal agreements among the various countries made cheap and dependable mail service possible. The modern postage stamp and improved transportation brought astronomical increases in the amount of letters and packages mailed after 1850.[19] Starting in the 1840s the electric telegraph, undersea cable, telephone, wireless telegraph, and typewriter expanded humanity's ability to exchange ideas and information. No longer would distance be a critical obstacle after the transportation and communications revolutions. The world became a smaller, if not more unified, place.

The Continent Industrializes

The continent faced many hurdles to economic growth after 1815. Obstacles to mobility, communication, and cooperation among the classes prevented the social structures there from adapting as easily to change as had the British. The farther south and east the social system, the more repressive was the structure. In many parts of the continent, the restored nobilities reclaimed their power, and they were neither intellectually nor financially prepared to support industrial development. Fragmented political boundaries, geographical obstacles, and tolltakers along primary river and road systems hampered growth, especially in central Europe. In eastern Europe, the middle classes were weaker and more isolated than in the west.

At the end of the Napoleonic wars, the initial stages of industrialization could be found in Belgium, France, and Germany. In Sweden, Russia,

and Switzerland there were pockets of potential mechanized production, but the total of all of these activities was tiny compared to Britain's economy. In 1850 only Belgium could compete with British products in its own markets. There a combination of favorable governmental policies, good transportation, and stability brought some success.

Governments and businesses sent officials and representatives to Britain to try to discover the secrets of industrialization. The British tried to protect their advantage by banning the export of machines and processes and limiting foreign access to their factories. Industrial espionage existed then as now, and continental competitors did uncover some secrets. Britain's success could be studied, components of it stolen, and its experts hired, but no country on the continent could combine all the factors that permitted Britain to dominate.

After midcentury, a long period of peace, improved transportation, and strategic government assistance encouraged rapid economic growth in France and the German states. Population increased 25 percent in France and nearly 40 percent in the Germanies, providing a larger market and labor supply. Two generations of borrowed British technology began to be applied and improved upon; but the two most important developments came in banking and customs and toll reforms.

After 1815, aggressive new banking houses appeared across Europe, strengthened by the profits they had made extending loans to governments during the Napoleonic wars. They saw the money to be made investing in new industries such as railroads and worked with both governments and major capitalists. Firms such as Hope and Baring in London, the Rothschilds in Frankfurt, Paris, Vienna, and London, and numerous Swiss bankers were representative of the private financiers who had well-placed sources and contacts throughout the state and business communities.[20]

Banking changed radically during this period to satisfy the growing demands for money. Long-range capital needs were met by the formation of investment banks, while new institutions were created to fill the need for short-term credit. The ultimate source of financial liquidity was the middle classes—the thousand of little people who put their money in banks to make their own profits on interest earned. More money could be gained from the many small investors than from the few rich families who used to dominate banking.

The Germans led the way in the other major development, the *Zollverein* (customs union), that began under Prussian leadership in 1819. This arrangement helped break down the trade barriers erected by state boundaries and in the next twenty-three years came to include most of central and northern Germany. Instead of the more than 300 divisions fragmenting the Germans in 1800, there was a virtual free trade market, something Britain had enjoyed since the union of Scotland and England in 1707—and which the European Economic Community will create after 1992. The significance of the *Zollverein* was that it allowed goods to circulate free of tolls and tariffs, thus reducing prices and stimulating trade.

In the second half of the century, industrialization grew rapidly, aided by the increased flow of credit and elimination of many internal barriers. Tariff walls throughout the area fell to a degree not matched until after World War II. Major firms such as the German Krupp works and the French silk industries controlled portions of the European market and competed effectively with Britain throughout the world.

Technological Growth and Advances

Another reason for the continent's economic emergence was a wide range of new technologies using new materials, processes, and transportation. New competitors began with state-of-the-art factories that allowed them to outproduce Britain, whose older factories were less productive.

The basic change in the second phase of industrialization was the use of electricity in all aspects of life. Scientists had discovered electricity's basic principles a century earlier, but it was difficult to generate and transmit power across long distances. When the first dependable dynamo, a device that changed energy from mechanical into electrical form, was perfected in 1876, it became possible to generate electricity almost anywhere. Inventors such as the American Thomas A. Edison began to use the new resource in industry, transportation, entertainment, and the home. Humanity had finally found a source of power that could be easily transported and used. The British took the lead in bringing electricity to home use. The Germans made the most advanced application of electric technology to industry.

Another fundamental change came in the use of gas and oil in the newly devised internal combustion engine. Steam power's use was limited by its appetite for huge amounts of fuel and its sheer bulk. Gottleib Daimler perfected the internal combustion engine used in most automobiles today. In 1892 Rudolf Diesel invented the engine that bears his name. It burned fuel instead of harnessing the explosions that drove the Daimler engine.

These new developments led directly to the search for and use of petroleum and the beginning of the passenger car industry. By 1914 the making of cars was a key part of the Italian, Russian, German, French, and American economies. Automobile manufacturing called for a number of "spinoff" industries such as tires, ball bearings, windshields—the list extends to hundreds of items. Leaving aside the passenger car's economic contribution, the world's cities and people felt the complex impact of this new form of transportation, with consequences extending from the range of an individual's world to the increased noise level and pollution that changed the character of urban areas.

Other new machines changed life. Bicycles became commonplace in the 1890s, as did sewing machines, cameras, and typewriters, to name a few. Never had people had the ability to transform ideas almost instantly into products accessible to the average person. This was another dividend of industrialization and a symbol of a rapidly changing Europe.

The Human Costs of Industrialization

Industrialization drove society from an agricultural to an urban way of life. The old system, in which peasants worked the fields during the summer and did their cottage industry work in the winter to their own standards and at their own pace, slowly disappeared. In its place came urban life tied to the factory system. The factory was a place where people did repetitive tasks using machines over long hours to process large amounts of raw materials. This was an efficient way to make a lot of high-quality goods at cheap cost. But the factories were often dangerous places and the lifestyle connected to them had a terrible effect on the human condition.

In the factory system the workers worked and the owners made profits. The owners wanted to make the most they could from their investment and to get the most work they could from their employees. The workers, in turn, felt that they deserved more of the profits because their labor made production possible. This was a situation guaranteed to produce conflict, especially given the wretched conditions the workers faced in the first stages of industrialization.

The early factories were miserable places, featuring bad lighting, lack of ventilation, dangerous machines, and frequent breakdowns. Safety standards were practically nonexistent and workers in various industries could expect to contract serious diseases—workers with lead paint suffered lung problems, pewter workers fell ill to palsy, miners suffered black lung disease, and primitive machines claimed many fingers, hands, and even lives. Not until late in the century did health and disability insurance come into effect. In some factories workers who suffered accidents were deemed to be at fault, and since there was little job security, a worker could be fired for virtually any reason.

The demand for plentiful and cheap labor led to the widespread employment of women and children. Girls as young as six years old were used to haul carts of coal in Lancashire mines, and boys and girls of four and five years of age worked in textile mills—their nimble little fingers could easily untangle jammed machines. When they were not laboring, the working families lived in horrid conditions in such wretched industrial cities as Lille, France, and Manchester, England. There were no sanitary, water, or medical services for the workers and working families were crammed twelve and fifteen to a room in damp, dark cellars. Bad diet, alcoholism, cholera, and typhus led to a reduction of life span in the industrial cities. Simultaneous with, and perhaps part of, the industrialization process was the vast increase in illegitimate births. Up to midcentury, corresponding to the time of

Industrialization and Children

Early industrialization demanded huge sacrifices, especially from children.

Sarah Gooder, Aged 8 years

I'm a trapper in the Gawber pit. It does not tire me, but I have to trap without a light and I'm scared. I go at four and sometimes half past three in the morning, and come out at five and half past. I never go to sleep. Sometimes I sing when I've light, but not in the dark; I dare not sing then. I don't like being in the pit. I am very sleepy when I go sometimes in the morning. I go to Sunday-schools and read *Reading made Easy*. She knows her letters and can read little words. They teach me to pray. She repeated the Lord's Prayer, not very perfectly, and ran on with the following addition:—"God bless my father and mother, and sister and brother, uncles and aunts and cousins, and everybody else, and God bless me and make me a good servant. Amen. I have heard tell of Jesus many a time. I don't know why he came on earth, I'm sure, and I don't know why he died, but he had stones for his head to rest on. I would like to be at school far better than in the pit."

From *Parliamentary Papers* (London, 1842).

maximum upheaval, continent-wide figures indicate that at least one-third of all births were out of wedlock.[21]

Later generations profited from the sacrifices made by the first workers in the industrialization, and factory owners came to understand that they could make more profit from an efficient factory staffed by contented workers.

Urban Crises

Huge population increases and industrialization prompted a massive growth of European cities in the nineteenth century, as can be seen in the following table.[22]

CITY	1800	1910
London	831,000	4,521,000
Paris	547,000	2,888,000
Berlin	173,000	2,071,000
Vienna	247,000	2,030,000
St. Petersburg	220,000	1,907,000

In addition, new towns sprang up throughout the continent and soon reached the level of over 100,000 inhabitants. Even in agrarian Russia, where 70 percent of the population worked on the land, there were seventeen cities of more than 100,000 by the end of the century.

Political leaders faced serious problems dealing with mushrooming city growth. The factory system initially forced families to live and work in squalor, danger, and disease, a condition to be found today in countries undergoing the first stages of industrialization. City leaders had to maintain a clean environment, provide social and sanitation services, enforce the law, furnish transportation, and—most serious of all—build housing. They uniformly failed to meet the radical challenges of growth.

Until midcentury human waste disposal in some parts of Paris was taken care of by dumping excrement in the gutters or the Seine or through street-corner manure collections. Not until Haussman's urban renewal in the 1850s and 1860s did the city get an adequate garbage, water, and sewage system. Police protection remained inadequate or corrupt. Other cities shared Paris' problems to a greater or lesser degree. The new industrial towns were in even worse condition than the older centers.

The terrible life in the industrial towns touched observers like novelist Charles Dickens, who in his book *Hard Times* described a typical British factory town:

It was a town of red brick, or of brick that would have been red if the smoke and ashes had allowed it; but as matters stood, it was a town of unnatural red and black, like the painted face of a savage. It was a town of machinery and tall chimneys, out of which interminable serpents of smoke trailed themselves for ever and ever, and never got uncoiled. It had a black canal in it, and a river that ran purple with ill-smelling dye, and vast piles of building full of windows where there was a rattling and trembling all day long, and where the piston of the steam engine worked monotonously up and down, like the head of an elephant in a state of melancholy madness. It contained several large streets all very like one another, and many small streets still more like one another, inhabited by people equally like one another,

This illustration, *Over London—By Rail,* vividly depicts the problems that accompanied urbanization—cramped living spaces, crime, and air and water pollution.

who all went in and out at the same hours, with the same sound upon the same pavement, to do the same work, and to whom every day was the same as yesterday and tomorrow, and every year the counterpart of the last and the next.[23]

By the end of the century, however, governments began to deal effectively with urban problems. By 1914, most major European cities began to make clean running water, central heat, adequate street lighting, mass public education, dependable sewage systems, and minimal medical care available for their people.

Ideological Responses to an Age of Change

The terms that describe most of the world's political choices—nationalism, liberalism, conservatism, socialism, and communism—all came into common use in the first half of the nineteenth century. These "isms" describe European political theorists' responses to the great changes through which they were living. They built on the legacy of the Western tradition, especially the Enlightenment's exaltation of the power of reason to define "how man should live" in the wake of the French, Napoleonic, and Industrial revolutions.

In the half century after 1789 romantics made the first steps to define their relationship to the new world. As the world changed around them, they found little solace in socially approved standards. They preferred to look far to the past, to long-forgotten civilizations imprecisely recalled, and commemorated them in simulated ruins. They also paid serious attention to the hazy examples of the medieval world, especially myths and folklore. They rejected eighteenth century classicism and the cold logic of the Enlightenment. On the continent, romantics reacted against the French and Napoleonic dominance while their colleagues lashed out against the ugliness and de-humanization of industrialization.

Romantics wanted to break out of the rational, measured patterns, and rules of the classicists to respond to the emotional needs of the soul. They argued that one could not rationally define

beauty, love, friendship, or anger. Jean-Jacques Rousseau (1712–1778), for example, pointed out that a people must live more by their instincts and feelings than by society's scaffold of intellect and rationalization. He argued that the "noble savage" was to be admired because he was close to nature, uncontaminated by the false constraints of society. Lutheran Pietists also responded to this view and tried to replace the austerity and abstraction of their theology with the warmth, fervor, and emotion of religious sentiment.

By stressing an individual's past, uniqueness, emotions, and creativity, the romantics had a critical effect on the arts (see p. 618) and politics. The romantic movement opened the way for the rise of the modern age's most potent, enduring, and least-defined force—nationalism. By emphasizing the right of individuals to define their own standards instead of adhering to universal principles, the romantics contributed to the emergence of the one "ism" that cuts across class lines and intellectual divides, nationalism.

Nationalism

By emphasizing research into the past and the picturesque to find their own roots, the romantics helped give birth to nationalism. They investigated their own history, folklore, linguistic background, and myths to define their own uniqueness. They saw the world not as a cosmopolitan and rational unit, but as a place of natural variety. Scholars investigated myths and folklore ranging from the Scandinavian sagas to the French *Chanson de Roland* to the *Nibelungen* stories in Germany. During a time of uncertainty, change, and stress, looking to the past, even an imagined one, was both comforting and uplifting.

The persistence of nations and nationalities is not the same as nationalism, which involves pride in a common identity as well as loyalty to a state. After the events in France after 1789, this new ideological force dominated the cultural and political activities of the nation. The spirit of fraternity projected by the French Revolution united the French nation. Napoleon's domination over the continent had a similarly strong effect, bringing people together in opposition to him, especially in Germany, and this led to the belief in

The brothers Grimm are perhaps best known as collectors and publishers of German folk tales, known in English as *Grimm's Fairy Tales*.

George Wilhelm Friedrich Hegel (1770–1831), although not a romantic, built on the movement's contributions in his lectures and writings at the University of Berlin. For Hegel, history was a process of evolution in which the supremacy of primitive instincts would give way to the reign of clear reason and freedom—the "world spirit"—that would be manifested in the state. Hegel believed that the Prussia of his day offered the best example of the state as a spiritual organism, because in Prussia the individual had the greatest "freedom"—defined not as the individual escaping from society but as a condition in which there is no conflict between the individual and society. The Prussian state, in Hegel's eyes, blended the proper proportions of national identity and structure to enable its individuals to gain their greatest growth. His high regard for the state was not shared by most romantics, but his exaltation of the Prussian state at a time when Germany was still fragmented had a powerful unifying influence.

Romantic nationalism in Britain reacted strongly against the human costs of industrialization and the pretensions of the new merchant classes. It focused on the medieval roots of Britain, as well as on movements such as philhellenism (the love of ancient Greece). In France, Spain, Italy, Russia, and other parts of the continent the romantic movement made important contributions to the growth of national identity. In Italy, for example, Giuseppe Mazzini (1805–1872) and Alessandro Manzoni (1785–1873) played important roles in the unification struggle of the country (see ch. 24).[24]

Unique conditions in different parts of Europe produced different variants of nationalism. However, common to them all was a nation consciously embracing a common land, language, folklore, history, enemies, and religion. These elements are the ingredients of the nation's and the individual's identity and pull the members into an indivisible unity. Nationalism can exist where there is no state structure and can thrive in a state where the nation is repressed. Nationalism, unlike patriotism, does not need flags and uniforms. All that is needed is a historical and emotional unity around which the members of the nation can gather, a unity that entails the cultural and political loyalty to the nation and the prime element of each individual's identity.

the uniqueness and superiority of Germany that had such drastic consequences in the twentieth century.

The research and writings of the Germans Johann Gottfried von Herder (1744–1803) and Jakob (1785–1863) and Wilhelm Grimm (1786–1859) provided historical support and linguistic bases for the Slavic nationalist movements. Herder conceived of a world spirit *(Weltgeist)* made up of component parts of the various national spirits *(Volksgeist)*. Each of these national spirits was seen as playing an essential role in the world process, and Herder believed that the Slavs were soon to make an important contribution. The Grimm brothers' philological work aided the literary and linguistic revivals of many Slavic groups. Romantic nationalism was also found in the writings of history by Leopold von Ranke in Germany, Jules Michelet in France, František Palacky in Bohemia-Moravia, and George Bancroft in the United States.

Conservatism

The reaction to the French Revolution, especially as expressed by Edmund Burke, provided the basis of nineteenth-century European conservatism. There were many thinkers who did not believe in the revolutionary slogan of liberty, equality, and fraternity. They did not believe that liberation could be gained by destroying the historically evolved traditions of the Old Regime. Freedom could be found only in order and maintained solely by continual reference to precedents. A legitimate political and social life needed the framework of tradition to survive.

The conservatives did not have faith in the individual nor did they share the romantics' love of pure emotion and spontaneity. Beginning with Burke and continuing through the first part of the nineteenth century to the Frenchman Joseph de Maistre (1753–1821), the Russian Nicholas Karamzin (1766–1826), and the Spaniard Juan Donoso-Cortés (1809–1853) there was a body of intellectuals who found strength, not weakness, in the church and monarchy of the Old Regime; danger, not liberation, in the nationalistic movements; and degradation, not exaltation, in the new romantic art forms.

Conservatism took many forms during the nineteenth century, ranging from the romantic to the patriotic to the religious to the secular. Whatever their approach, conservatives stressed the need to maintain order through a constant reference to history. They believed that the welfare and happiness of humanity resided in the slowly evolving institutions of the past. Industrialization and the consequences of the French Revolution severed the connection with the past and were therefore dangerous. The conservatives were backward-looking, finding their standards and values in the proven events of the past, not in the untried reforms of the present.

Liberalism

The rising middle and commercial classes found their interests and ideals best expressed in the doctrine of liberalism. Liberalism affirmed the dignity of the individual and the "pursuit of happiness" as an inherent right. The ideology's roots were set firmly in the eighteenth-century soil of constitutionalism, laissez-faire economics, and representative government. Liberals thought in terms of individuals who shared basic rights, were equal before the law, and used parliament to gain power and carry out gradual reform. In addition, liberals believed that individuals should use their power to ensure that each person would be given the maximum amount of freedom from the state, or any other external authority.

In economics, liberals believed in the fair competition among individuals responding to the laws of supply and demand with a minimum of governmental regulation or interference. Scottish economist Adam Smith (1723–1790) best expressed this view in his *Wealth of Nations*. Liberals agreed with Smith that society benefited more from competition among individuals motivated by their self-interest than from governmental regulation. The most intelligent and efficient individuals would gain the greatest rewards, society would prosper, and the state would be kept in its proper place—that of protecting life and property.[25]

Liberals fought foes from above and below as they translated their ideas into public policy. Nobles and the landed gentry still controlled most countries in Europe, so throughout the century the middle classes fought to gain political power commensurate with their economic strength. While they were trying to increase their own influence, they sought to limit the political base of the emerging working classes. By the end of the century the middle classes had consolidated their control over the industrialized world. This was perhaps the major political achievement of the century.

Liberals were sufficiently liberated from the demands of manual labor and possessed enough wealth to spend their spare time in public pursuits. They had the time and leisure to work in government to control state policy to protect their own interests. They gained sufficient security that they undertook the enactment of social reform to head off revolution. They became the dominant voices in the press and universities and gained a commanding authority over public opinion. The liberals' most important contributions came in the areas of civil rights, promotion of the rule of law, government reform, and humanitarian enterprises.

Not surprisingly, the main interpreters of liberalism came from Britain, and during the

Adam Smith, The Wealth of Nations

The ideological mainstream of industrialization was Adam Smith's *Wealth of Nations*.

Every individual is continually exerting himself to find out the most advantageous employment for whatever capital he can command. It is his own advantage, indeed, and not that of the society, which he has in view. But the study of his own advantage naturally, or rather necessarily, leads him to prefer that employment which is most advantageous to the society.

. . . As every individual, therefore, endeavours as much as he can both to employ his capital in the support of domestic industry and so to direct that industry that its produce may be of the greatest value, every individual necessarily labours to render the annual revenue of the society as great as he can. He generally, indeed, neither intends to promote the public interest nor knows how much he is promoting it. By preferring the support of domestic to that of foreign industry, he intends only his own security; and by directing that industry in such a manner as its produce may be of the greatest value, he intends only his own gain, and he is in this, as in many other cases, led by an invisible hand to promote an end which was no part of his intention. Nor is it always the worse for the society that it was no part of it. By pursuing his own interest he frequently promotes that of the society more effectually than when he really intends to promote it. I have never known much good done by those who affected to trade for the public good. It is an affectation, indeed, not very common among merchants, and very few words need be employed in dissuading them from it.

From Adam Smith, *The Wealth of Nations* (Oxford: Clarendon Press, 1880).

---

first half of the century Jeremy Bentham (1748–1832) and John Stuart Mill (1806–1873) adapted some liberal theories to modern reality. Bentham devised the concept of utilitarianism, or philosophical radicalism, based on the two concepts of utility and happiness. He connected these two by noting that each individual knows what is best for himself or herself and that all human institutions should be measured according to the amount of happiness they give. Bentham built on these two eighteenth-century concepts to form the pain-and-pleasure principle. He believed that government's function was to gain as great a degree of individual freedom as possible, for freedom was the essential precondition of happiness. Utilitarianism in government was thus the securing of the "greatest happiness for the greatest number." If society could provide as much happiness and as little pain as possible it would be working at maximum efficiency. Bentham recognized what later liberals would eventually espouse—that the government would have to work at all levels—but he left no precise prescription as to how to proceed.

Mill spoke more to this issue. He began by noting that in industry the interests of the owners and workers did not necessarily coincide. He proposed the theory that government should, if necessary, pass legislation to remedy injustice, pointing out that when the actions of business owners harm the people, the state must step in to protect the citizenry. He challenged the liberal theory of minimal government interference in the economic life of the nation and pointed out that humanitarianism is more important than profit margin. He accepted that maximum freedom should be permitted in business and that natural law should dictate insofar as possible the relationship of citizens.

He also pointed out that the distribution of wealth depends on the laws and customs of society and that these can be changed by human will. The rights of property and free competition, therefore, should be upheld but within reasonable limits. Mill pointed out that the liberty of the individual is not absolute—it has to be placed under the wider interests of society. His ideas had within them the germ of the welfare state, but he had little effect on affairs in his own day.

In the late twentieth century the word *liberalism* has undergone some change in meaning. The term still implies reform, but liberals today advocate an active governmental role in minimizing the extremes of wealth, in balancing the great power enjoyed by business and labor, and in conserving natural resources. Today's liberals also advocate the state's intervention to help the individual by providing social security and in opposing racial, sexual, and age discrimination.

Socialism

The working classes of Europe, heartened by the French Revolution's call for equality and afflicted by the hardships inherent in the first phase of industrialization found that socialism best expressed their values and goals. Socialists attacked the system of laissez-faire capitalism as unplanned and unjust. They condemned the increasing concentration of wealth and called for public or worker ownership of business. The nature of the industrial system, dividing worker and owner, also raised serious problems, and socialists insisted that harmony and cooperation, not competition, should prevail.

Socialists believed that human beings are essentially good, and with the proper organization of society there would be a happy future with no wars, crimes, administration of justice, or government. In this perfectly balanced world there would also be perfect health and happiness. As one prophet foretold, "every man with ineffable ardor, will seek the good of all."[26] Karl Marx (see ch. 25) later derisively labeled socialists who sought such a world as "Utopians."

The first prominent Utopian socialist was the French noble Claude Henri de Rouvroy, Count de Saint-Simon (1760–1825). He defined a nation as "nothing but a great industrial society" and politics as "the science of production." He advocated that humanity should voluntarily place itself under the rule of the paternalistic despotism of scientists, technicians, and industrialists who would "undertake the most rapid amelioration possible of the lot of the poorest and most numerous class."[27]

Francois Marie Charles Fourier (1772–1837), another French utopian, believed that the future society must be cooperative and free. He worked out a communal living unit of 1620 people called a "phalanstery." The members of the group chose voluntarily those tasks that appealed to them to do the work needed to ensure the phalanstery's survival. Although his plan was endorsed by many prominent people, attempts made to found cooperative Fourierist communities were unsuccessful.

Plan for a model prison, called the Pantopicon, designed by Jeremy Bentham. The circular arrangement allowed a centrally located guard to monitor all outside cells. The Pantopicon was never built, but the plan influenced the design of later prisons.

PANOPTICON.

Artist's rendering of Robert Owen's utopian community at New Harmony, Indiana. Square, fortresslike buildings surround the community's interior gardens and exercise grounds. The community was established in 1825, but internal dissension forced its dissolution three years later.

The famous Brook Farm colony in Massachusetts was one such short-lived experiment.

Robert Owen (1771–1858), a successful mill owner in Scotland, was a more practical utopian socialist. His New Lanark, the site of his textile mills, was a model community. Here, between 1815 and 1825, thousands of visitors saw rows of neat, well-kept workers' home, a garbage collection system, schools for workers' children, and clean factories where workers were treated kindly and no children under eleven were employed. In 1825 Owen moved to the vicinity of Evansville, Indiana, where he established the short-lived community at New Harmony.

Their optimism blinded the utopians to the nature of humanity and the world in which they lived. Brook Farm and New Harmony were based on the notion that human beings naturally love one another or could be brought to that level. The basic impracticality of the experiments doomed them to failure. However, the notion that capitalism was inherently corrupt and that it was essential to remove the system remained an article of faith for subsequent socialists,

including Karl Marx, who had a far more comprehensive and hard-headed plan that will be examined in chapter 25.

Cultural Responses to an Age of Change

The romantic movement unleashed sensitivities that played a major role in forming the literary, artistic, and musical changes of the nineteenth century. The romantics' emphasis on the individual is apparent in the novels of Friedrich von Schiller (1759–1805) and Wolfgang von Goethe (1749–1832). Goethe's *The Sorrows of Young Werther* (1774) tells the story of a sensitive, feeling, outcast young man who kills himself with the pistol of his rival after failing to gain his true love. Schiller's *Wilhelm Tell* (1804) describes the heroic struggle of the Swiss patriots in their drive for independence against tyranny. Unlike the brittle wit and irony of

Enlightenment authors such as Voltaire, these stories were sentimental and emotional descriptions of people acting in response to that which their hearts told them was right. It was better to experience a moving young death or to rise up against impossible odds than to look dispassionately and rationally at life.

The romantic movement's emphasis on the individual created among some of its participants a truly picturesque lifestyle. For every Victor Hugo (1802–1885) who lived a long, full, and respectable life there were artists, writers, and musicians from London to Moscow who were deeply affected by the romanticism. To most romantics it was better to live briefly and intensely according to the commandments of the heart than to die old, fat, rich, bored, and bourgeois.

In Gustave Doré's illustration for Coleridge's *Rime of the Ancient Mariner,* the seaman bears the terrible burden of the albatross, hung around his neck as a curse for killing the bird of good luck.

Eugène Delacroix's illustration for the Prologue of Goethe's *Faust* portrays the archfiend Mephistopheles as a winged devil.

Literature

The novel form came into prominence in the eighteenth century, but it became the dominant literary form of the nineteenth. Writers such as Victor Hugo and Sir Walter Scott mined the myths and legends of France and Britain respectively to write vastly successful works for the ever-expanding middle-class audiences. Hugo's *Notre Dame de Paris* (1831) and Scott's *Ivanhoe* (1819) detailed their nations' past so effectively that both books were imitated and sequels and imitations appeared into the twentieth century. By midcentury a variety of social and psychological themes challenged the historical novel along with the gently critical works of William Makepeace Thackeray (1811–1863) who in works such as *Vanity Fair* (1848) poked deft characterizations at the *noveau riche* social climbers that dominated society.

Poets responded far more pointedly to the challenges thrown down by the Napoleonic and Industrial revolutions. The French poet Alphonse de Lamartine (1790–1869) led the way in making the transition from classicism to romanticism and had an impact across the continent.

In 1798, two young British poets, William Wordsworth (1770–1850) and Samuel Taylor Coleridge (1772–1834), published a volume of verse called *Lyrical Ballads*. Wordsworth wrote in the preface that poetry was "the spontaneous overflow of powerful feelings recollected in tranquility." Wordsworth sought to express "universal passions" and the "entire world of nature" through simple, unladen vocabulary. He stressed the intuitive and emotional contemplation of nature as a path to creativity. In an 1802 sonnet he expressed his love of nature and country.

... Oft have I looked round
With joy in Kent's green vales; but never found
Myself so satisfied in heart before.
Europe is yet in bonds; but let that pass
Thought for another moment. Thou are free,
My Country! and 'tis joy enough and pride
For one hour's perfect bliss, to tread the grass
Of England once again. ...

In his *Rime of the Ancient Mariner* (1798) and *Kubla Khan* (1816) Coleridge pursued the supernatural and exotic facets of life. His vivid descriptions of distant subjects and nonrational elements of human life served as the precedent for later artists as they examined the areas of fantasy, symbolism, dream states, and the supernatural.

The British poets George Gordon (Lord Byron) (1788–1824) and Percy Bysshe Shelley (1792–

Lord Byron in Greek dress. One of the leading romantic poets, Byron lived the life of the romantic hero he created in his writing. He lived passionately and died tragically of fever in 1824 while he was in Greece fighting with Greek insurgents.

1822) rebelled against the constraints of their society and expressed their contempt for the standards of their time through their lives and works. Byron gloried in the cult of freedom, and when the Greeks rose up against the Turks in 1821 he joined their cause, dying of fever soon after his arrival. Shelley believed passionately that human perfectibility was possible only through complete freedom of thought and action. On the continent, Heinrich Heine (1797–1856), who was like Byron a cutting satirist and like Shelley a splendid lyricist, shared their romantic ideals. Heine is best remembered today for his *lieder*, which were put to music by Franz Schubert (1797–1828) and Felix Mendelssohn (1809–1847).

John Keats (1795–1821) was neither social critic nor rebel; for him, the worship and pursuit of beauty were of prime importance. In *Ode on a Grecian Urn* (1821) he states:

Beauty is truth, truth beauty—that is all
Ye know on earth, and all ye need to know.

Keats advocated for art's sake and beauty in itself, instead of the classical formulas of an earlier age or the socialist realism of the latter part of the century.

Alexander Pushkin (1799–1837), Russia's greatest poet, liberated his nation's language from the foreign molds and traditions forced upon it in the eighteenth century. While serving as the transition between the classical and romantic ages, Pushkin helped create a truly Russian literature, one that expressed the profound depth of his love for his country.

Art and Architecture

The age of change brought new tendencies to painting as well as to other art forms. There is a great contrast between the precise draftsmanship and formal poses of the classical painters and the unrestrained use of color and new effects of the romantic artists. Some artists such as the French master Eugène Delacroix (1798–1863) received major critical resistance. Conservative critics panned his *Massacre of Chios*, a flamboyant work painted in 1824 under the direct impact of receiving the news of the Turks' slaying of Christians on Chios, as the "Massacre of painting."

This watercolor by the romantic artist Joseph M. W. Turner is of Tintern Abbey, a famous 12th-century Gothic ruin in Wales. In his later work, Turner was chiefly concerned with the painting of light, and the subject matter became almost incidental.

Less flashy but equally part of the romantic transition are the works of the British painter John Constable (1776–1837). Deeply influenced by romanticism's emphasis on nature, Constable was in some respects the originator of the modern school of landscape painting. His choice of colors was revolutionary, as he used greens freely in his landscape, an innovation considered radical by critics who favored brown tones. Constable's countryman, J. M. W. Turner (1775–1851), sparked controversy with his use of vivid colors and dramatic perspectives, which gave him the ability to portray powerful atmospheric effects.

In the hands of Beethoven, formal music, which had previously reflected the polished and artificial manners of the salon, became a vehicle for expressing deep human emotions.

Around 1830 romanticism's fascination with the medieval period led to a shift from Greek and Roman models to a Gothic revival, in which towers and arches became the chief architectural characteristics. Sir Walter Scott's romances played a major role in this development, and his house at Abbotsford was a model, designed as it was along Scottish baronial lines. In France Eugène Viollet-le-Duc (1814–1879) spearheaded the movement by writing, teaching, and restoring properties under the aegis of the Commission on Historical Monuments. Victor Hugo's *Notre Dame de Paris* popularized the revival with its discussion of fifteenth-century life. For the next few decades, architecture was dominated by styles that looked back especially to the Gothic and Rococo styles, which were sometimes combined in esthetically disastrous presentations.

Music

Ludwig van Beethoven (1770–1827) served as a bridge between the classical and romantic periods. The regularity of the minuet, the precision of the sonata, and the elegant but limited small chamber orchestra—all forms he mastered—were not sufficient to express the powerful forces of the age. A comparison of his relatively measured and restrained First Symphony with the compelling and driven Fifth or the lyrical, nature-dominated Sixth Symphonies dramatically reveals the changes that he underwent. Beethoven was the ultimate romantic—a lover of nature, passionate champion of human rights, and fighter for freedom. Beethoven spoke to the heart of humanity through his music.

The momentum of the forces that Beethoven set in motion carried through the entire century. Carl Maria von Weber (1786–1826), Hector Berlioz (1803–1869), Robert Schumann (1810–1856), and Felix Mendelssohn and Franz Schubert made major contributions in developing the musical repertoire of Europe by midcentury.

Conclusion

The French Revolution had a bulldozerlike effect on traditional French institutions. Napoleon's impact had a similar, if delayed, result. Whether through the force of his arms or his ideas, his actions or reactions to him, the old structures of Europe and the new nations of the Americas were deeply affected.

In Britain, artisans bringing practical solutions to bottlenecks in the making of cotton cloth successfully escaped the bounds of animal and human power to increase output. The island nation possessed the proper balance of population, money, governmental support, internal markets, and a risk-taking entrepreneurial class to accomplish the first revolution in industrialization. The results achieved in textiles were reproduced in iron and steel, as Britain came to dominate the world economically by midcentury.

The second phase of industrialization brought new wealth and a whole new range of products to the continent and carried the urban problems already experienced in Britain across the Channel. The rapid growth of cities strained the capabilities of local and national authorities to respond to the challenges of providing utilities, education, law enforcement, and social services.

Both the Napoleonic and the Industrial revolutions brought with them heavy prices to be paid. Napoleon changed the nature of warfare and increased state power. Industrialization drew great sacrifices from the first generation of workers caught up in it.

Europe's political theorists and artists gave graphic testimony through their works to the reality of change brought about by the Napoleonic and Industrial revolutions. They devised modern ideologies and created diverse cultural expressions to define the new world that they faced.

Suggestions for Reading

Napoleon has attracted the attention of a broad range of historians. See, for example, P. Geyl, *Napoleon: For and Against* (Humanities Press, 1974). F. Markham, *Napoleon and the Awakening of Europe* (Collier, 1965) is a convenient introduction to the period. The best surveys dealing with Napoleon's activities are R. B. Holtman, *The Napoleonic Revolution* (Lippincott, 1967) and Owen Connelly, *French Revolution/Napoleonic Era* (Holt, Rinehart & Winston, 1979). See also Jean Tulard, *Napoleon: The Myth of the Saviour* (Weidenfeld and Nicholson, 1984).

The military art of the era is well described in Gunther Rothenberg, *The Art of Warfare in the Age of Napoleon* (Indiana, 1978). David G. Chandler's *The Campaigns of Napoleon* (Macmillan, 1966) is comprehensive and well written. One of Napoleon's opponent's receives excellent coverage in E. Longford, *Wellington, the Years of the Sword* (Harper, 1969). Leo Tolstoy's *War and Peace* gives an incomparably vivid coverage of the 1812 campaign. For those wanting complete bibliographic reference, see Donald D. Howard, ed., *Napoleonic Military History* (Garland, 1986).

G. Brunn's *Europe and the French Imperium* (Harper, 1938) is a classic. See also essays in Hajo Holborn's *Germany and Europe: Historical Essays* (Doubleday, 1971) for insights into the French emperor's impact in central Europe. Hans Kohn's *Prelude to Nation-States: The French and the German Experience, 1789–1815* (Van Nostrand, 1967) is useful.

The French influence on the Americas is reviewed in Alexander de Conde, *The Quasi-War: The Politics and Diplomacy of the Undeclared War with France 1797–1801* (Scribner, 1966). R. A. Humphreys and John Lynch edited a useful series of essays and primary documents in *The Origins of the Latin American Revolutions, 1806–1826* (Knopf, 1967). See also Irene Nicholson, *The Liberators: A Study of Independence Movements in Spanish America* (Praeger, 1969) for an essential volume in understanding the revolutionary period. The first chapters of David Bushnell and Neill Macaulay, *The Emergence of Latin America in the Nineteenth Century* (Oxford, 1988) provide essential social, economic, and political background.

David Landes' *The Unbound Prometheus: Technological Change and Industrial Development in Western Europe*

from 1750 to the Present (Cambridge, 1969) is a well-written and excellent survey of the entire sweep of industrialization. For Britain specifically see T. Ashton, *The Industrial Revolution: 1760–1830* (Oxford, 1949). Also recommended is S. B. Clough, *Economic History of Europe* (Walker, 1968). C. Singer et al., eds., *The Late Nineteenth Century, 1850–1900*, vol. 5, in the series *A History of Technology* (Oxford, 1958) is lavishly illustrated and clearly written. See also W. O. Henderson, *The Industrialization of Europe: 1780–1914* (London, 1969) and J. C. Chambers and G. E. Mingay, *The Agricultural Revolution* (Schocken, 1966). Rondo E. Cameron's *France and the Economic Development of Europe: 1800–1914* (Octagon, 1961) gives another perspective along with A. S. Milward and S. B. Saul, *The Economic Development of Continental Europe 1780–1870* (Allen & Unwin, 1973). For a useful survey of German developments, see T. Hammerow, *Restoration, Revolution, Reaction: Economics and Politics in Germany* (Princeton, 1958). William Blackwell provides useful background on tsarist developments in his *Industrialization of Russia* (Crowell, 1970). A useful volume on international economic growth is Sidney Pollard, *European Economic Integration* (Harcourt Brace Jovanovich, 1974). Francis Sheppard's *London 1808–1970: The Internal War* (University of California, 1971) is a fine account of a city experiencing the challenge of growth.

The social impact of industrialization can be seen in the novels of Charles Dickens such as *Hard Times*. T. K. Rabb and R. I. Rotberg include several selections on the social impact of industrialization in *The Family in History* (Harper & Row, 1973). Asa Brigg's *Victorian Cities* (Harper & Row, 1968) and *Victorian People* (University of Chicago, 1959) are vivid portrayals. Peter Stearns, *European Society in Upheaval* (Macmillan, 1967), and W. L. Langer, *Political and Social Upheaval, 1832–1852* (Harper & Row, 1969) are valuable surveys.

H. D. Aiken, ed., *The Age of Ideology: The Nineteenth Century Philosophers* (Mentor, 1962) explores selections from the works of Hegel, Mill, and others. For a lively survey of the economic thinkers, see Robert L. Heilbroner's *The Worldly Philosophers* (Touchstone, 1970). One of the best surveys of nineteenth century European thought is G. L. Mosse, *The Culture of Western Europe: the Nineteenth and Twentieth Centuries* (Rand McNally, 1974).

Notes

1. Herbert Butterfield, *Napoleon* (New York: Collier Books, 1977), pp. 20–25.
2. Gunther E. Rothenberg, *The Art of Warfare in the Age of Napoleon* (Bloomington: Indiana University Press, 1980), pp. 31–45.
3. Alfred Cobban, *A History of Modern France*, vol. II (Harmondsworth: Penguin, 1970), pp. 9–13.
4. George LeFebvre, *The French Revolution: from 1793 to 1799*, vol. II, trans. by J. H. Steward and J. Friguglietti (New York: Columbia University Press, 1964), pp. 259–317.
5. Owen Connelly, *French Revolution/Napoleonic Era* (New York: Holt, Rinehart and Winston, 1979), pp. 236–237.

6. Robert B. Holtman, *The Napoleonic Revolution* (New York: J. B. Lippincott, 1967), pp 38–40.

7. Rothenberg, pp. 42–52.

8. Hajo Holborn, *Germany and Europe: Historical Essays* (New York: Doubleday, 1971), p. 9.

9. For a view from the Russian side, see Michael and Diana Josselson, *The Commander: A Life of Barclay de Tolly* (Oxford: Oxford Univ. Press, 1980).

10. H. A. L. Fisher, *A History of Europe*, vol. III (Boston: Houghton Mifflin, 1936), p. 891.

11. C. K. Webster, "British, French, and American Influences," in R. A. Humphreys and J. Lynch, eds., *The Origins of the Latin American Revolution, 1800–1826* (New York: Alfred A. Knopf, 1967), p. 78.

12. David Bushnell and Neill Macaulay, *The Emergence of Latin America in the Nineteenth Century* (New York: Oxford Univ. Press, 1988), pp. 3–9.

13. Bushnell and Macaulay, pp. 55–82.

14. J. D. Chambers, "Enclosures and the Labour Supply in the Industrial Revolution," *Economic History Review*, 2nd series, V, 1953, pp. 318–343, as cited in David Landes, *The Unbound Prometheus: Technological Change and Industrial Development in Western Europe from 1750 to the Present* (Cambridge: Cambridge University Press, 1969), p. 115.

15. E. J. Hobsbawm, *The Age of Revolution, 1789–1848* (New York: New American Library, 1964), pp. 44–73.

16. I. Vyshnegradsky, quoted in William L. Blackwell, *The Industrialization of Russia: An Historical Perspective* (New York: Thomas Y. Crowell, 1970), p. 24.

17. Fernand Braudel, *Capitalism and Material Life: 1400–1800* (New York: Harper & Row, 1975), p. 11; William Langer, "Checks on Population Growth: 1750–1850," *Scientific American* 226 (1972), pp. 92–99.

18. Thomas R. Malthus, "An Essay on Population," in *Introduction to Contemporary Civilization in the West*, vol. II (New York: Columbia University Press, 1955), p. 196.

19. Eugen Weber, *A Modern History of Europe* (New York: W. W. Norton, 1971), p. 988.

20. Sidney Pollard, *European Economic Integration: 1815–1970* (New York: Harcourt Brace Jovanovich, 1974), pp. 56–62.

21. Edward Shorter, "Illegitimacy, Sexual Revolution, and Social Change in Modern Europe," in Theodore K. Rabb and Robert I. Rotber, eds., *The Family in History* (New York: Harper & Row, 1973), pp. 48–84.

22. Heinz Gollwitzer, *Europe in the Age of Imperialism: 1880–1914* (New York: Harcourt Brace Jovanovich, 1969), p. 20.

23. Charles Dickens, *Hard Times* (London: Thomas Nelson and Sons, n.d.), p. 26.

24. Peter F. Sugar, "External and Domestic Roots of Eastern European Nationalism," in Peter F. Sugar and Ivo J. Lederer, eds., *Nationalism in Eastern Europe* (Seattle: University of Washington Press, 1969), pp. 3–21.

25. Robert L. Heilbroner, *The Worldly Philosophers* (New York: Simon and Schuster, 1972), pp. 40–72.

26. W. Godwin, "Political Justice," in Sidney Hook, *Marx and the Marxists: The Ambiguous Legacy* (Princeton: Van Nostrand, 1955), p. 28.

27. Quoted in E. R. A. Seligman, ed., *Encyclopedia of the Social Sciences*, vol. XIII (New York: The Macmillan Company, 1935), p. 510a.

Revolution, Reaction, and Reform

Political Change, 1815–1871

In the half century after Waterloo, many changes took place in the political boundaries and population distribution of Europe. The French and Napoleonic revolutions created new conditions that challenged the leaders of Europe gathered at the Congress of Vienna in 1814–1815. Delegates had to construct a peace settlement that digested the political and social transformations that had taken place in the previous quarter century and anticipate the new demands created by those changes. They redrew the state borders and redefined the spheres of influence. The geopolitical structure they created and the surface order that resulted endured until 1848.

A wave of revolutions spread across the continent in that year and put an end to the structure created at Vienna. The revolutionaries, because of their conflicting goals, failed to turn their ideals into state policy. After 1848, continental politics would be built on the basis of *realpolitik*, that is, realism in politics. *Realpolitik* disregards theory or idealism and emphasizes the practical application of power to gain state goals, no matter the damage to ethics or morality. The European map changed once again as Cavour consolidated Italy and Bismarck united Germany.

The Vienna Settlement: 1815

Once Napoleon was "safely" exiled to Elba, representatives of all the European powers, except the Ottoman Empire, gathered in September at Vienna. They had the imposing task of building a new political and diplomatic structure for Europe after a quarter century of wars and revolutions. The factor that had brought the British, Prussians, Austrians, and Russians together —Napoleon—was gone, and wartime unity dissolved into peacetime pursuit of self-interest.

Work went slowly during the ten-month span of the Congress of Vienna. The leaders who gathered at Vienna—Lord Castlereagh of Great Britain, Count von Hardenberg of Prussia, Prince Klemens von Metternich of Austria, Tsar Alexander I of Russia, and Prince Charles Maurice de Talleyrand of France—met in small secret conferences to decide the future of Europe. Metternich came to dominate the conference, as much by his diplomatic skills as by his ability to impress on the participants the need for stability.

The Congress dealt with numerous issues: the status of France, the new political boundaries, the response to liberal and national attitudes sweeping the continent, the fate of those powers who had lost territory during the previous twenty-five years, and the future of dispossessed dynasties. The solutions proposed were moderate ones. France was allowed to return to its 1792 boundaries; however, after Napoleon's return and the One Hundred Days, the allies cut back the boundaries and imposed penalties. They virtually ignored the democratic, liberal, and nationalistic forces in favor of a more traditional solution to the upheavals of the past twenty-five years.[1]

Allied Dilemmas

The events since 1789 had drastically altered the map of Europe. For example, the thousand-year-old Holy Roman Empire had disappeared. In an attempt to restore some balance, the

Congress followed four principles: legitimacy, encirclement of France, compensation, and balance of power. The Congress ruled that royal houses that had been expelled, such as the Bourbons in France, Spain, and Naples, the House of Savoy in Sardinia-Piedmont, and the House of Orange in Holland, would be replaced on their thrones. The redrawn map of Europe resembled the 1789 configuration, except that the Holy Roman Empire remained dissolved (see map below). In its place were the thirty-nine states of the German Confederation, dominated by Austria. The redrawing of boundaries created a protective belt of states around France to make future aggression more difficult. The principle of compensation assured that no important power suffered a loss as the result of the Congress' work. Austria was compensated for the loss of the Austrian Netherlands by gaining territory in Italy and along the Adriatic. Sweden received Norway in return for permitting Russia to keep Finland.

The desire to construct an effective balance of power remained at the center of the Congress' attention. Each power, however, had its own idea of what constituted a proper balance. Russia's ambitions in Poland almost broke up the conference: Britain believed that an enlarged Russia threatened peace. Prussia wanted all of Saxony: Austria feared a growing Prussia. While the four wartime allies split, the clever French

This cartoon, *La Balance Politique,* lampoons the balance of power politics played out at the Congress of Vienna. Here, Wellington places money on the scales opposite the king of Prussia and Metternich. At right, Tsar Alexander I confers with Talleyrand.

representative, Talleyrand, negotiated a secret treaty among the French, Austrians, and British that pledged mutual assistance to restrain the Russians and Prussians. Russia and Prussia eventually reduced their demands for land in Poland and Saxony, and the sought-after balance of power was achieved.

Although the Congress has received criticism for ignoring the growth of liberty, equality, and fraternity in Europe, it has received praise for finding a general settlement of a complex series of problems, especially from scholars who favorably compare its work to that of the victorious allies at Versailles after World War I (see p. 781).[2] The representatives were not totally, blindly reactionary: many of the changes of the previous twenty-five years were retained. The forty years of general peace that followed, flawed though they may have been, are testimony to the success of Metternich and his colleagues in gaining stability. But, by ignoring the forces of change, the representatives at Veinna ensured the ultimate failure of the system they created.

The Congress System and Revolution

The Vienna negotiators set out to coordinate their policies to maintain stability. The first proposal for postwar consultation was symbolic and quixotic. In the fall of 1815, Tsar Alexander I proposed the formation of a Holy Alliance to be based on "the precepts of justice, Christian charity, and peace." No one was quite sure what the tsar meant by this pact, but every ruler in Europe signed it, except the British king, the Turkish sultan, and the pope. Castlereagh dismissed the Holy Alliance as "a piece of sublime mysticism and nonsense." In November 1815 Austria, Prussia, Russia, and Britain signed the Quadruple Alliance—to become the Quintuple Alliance when France joined in 1818. Under this agreement the powers pursued their goals through what came to be known as the Congress System, a Europe-wide network to maintain order, peace, and stability. This was the first truly functional experiment in collective security.

The Congress System's dedication to the 1815 status quo was challenged in 1820 and 1821 by nationalistic and liberal revolts in the Germanies, Greece, Spain, Italy, and Latin America. The most violent revolutions occurred in Spain and Italy. Spanish liberals rebelled against the misgovernment of the restored Bourbon King Ferdinand VII, and their insurrection spread to the army, which mutinied. The general uprising that followed forced the king to give into the liberals' demands for a constitution and representative government. The Spaniards' success sparked rebellions in Naples and Sicily, governed by the Neapolitan Bourbon King Ferdinand I. The

Metternich on His Political Principles

In the aftermath of the Napoleonic age, waves of change threatened the structure erected at the Congress of Vienna. Metternich had a precise notion of what was happening.

Kings have to calculate the chances of their very existence in the immediate future; passions are let loose, and league together to overthrow everything which society respects as the basis of its existence; religion, public morality, laws, customs, rights, and duties, all are attacked, confounded, overthrown, or called in question. The great mass of the people are tranquil spectators of these attacks and revolutions, and of the absolute want of all means of defense. A few are carried off by the torrent, but the wishes of the immense majority are to maintain a repose which exists no longer, and of which even the first elements seem to be lost . . .

Having now thrown a rapid glance over the first causes of the present state of society, it is necessary to point out in a more particular manner the evil which threatens to deprive it, at one blow, of the real blessings, the fruits of genuine civilisation, and to disturb it in the midst of its enjoyments. This evil may be described in one word—presumption; the natural effect of the rapid progression of the human mind towards the perfecting of so many things. This it is which at the present day leads so many individuals astray, for it has become an almost universal sentiment.

Religion, morality, legislation, economy, politics, administration, all have become common and accessible to everyone. Knowledge seems to come by inspiration; experience has no value for the presumptuous man; faith is nothing to him; he substitutes for it a pretended individual conviction, and to arrive at this conviction dispenses with all inquiry and with all study; for these means appear too trivial to a mind which believes itself strong enough to embrace at one glance all questions and all facts. Laws have no value for him, because he has not contributed to make them, and it would be beneath a man of his parts to recognise the limits traced by rude and ignorant generations. Power resides in himself; why should he submit himself to that which was only useful for the man deprived of light and knowledge? That which, according to him, was required in an age of weakness cannot be suitable in an age of reason and vigour amounting to universal perfection, which the German innovators designate by the idea, absurd in itself, of the Emancipation of the People! Morality itself he does not attack openly, for without it he could not be sure for a single instant of his own existence; but he interprets its essence after his own fashion, and allows every other person to do so likewise, provided that other person neither kills nor robs him.

From Prince Richard Metternich, ed., *Memoirs of Prince Metternich, 1815–1829*, vol. III, Mrs. Alexander Napier, trans. (New York: Charles Scribner's Sons, 1881).

Italian revolt ran much the same path as that in Spain, and with much the same result—a constitution based on the Spanish model.

Metternich arranged for the Congress allies to meet at Troppau in 1820, Laibach in 1821, and Verona in 1822 to deal with the uprisings. Ferdinand I came to Laibach, supported Congress System intervention, and reneged on granting a constitution; Austrian troops invaded Italy and placed him back on his throne. In 1822 the Congress allies met to consider the Spanish problem, and the French volunteered to restore the status quo. They sent their armies in to crush the liberals. The repression of the revolts in Spain and Italy marked the high point of the Congress System's success.

Britain began its withdrawal from the continent into "splendid isolation" in 1820, and the ardent support of British liberals for the 1821 Greek revolt against the Turks further weakened London's interest in cooperating with its former allies. When the Congress System discussed restoring the Spanish king's authority in Latin America, the British objected. Further, U.S. President James Monroe in 1823 warned the Europeans that their intervention into the western hemisphere would be regarded as an unfriendly act. By the middle of the decade the Congress system had withered to an Austrian-Russian alliance in which Metternich set the agenda and the Russians acted as the "gendarme of Europe."

Restoration and Revolution: 1815–1848

The restored Bourbon monarch, Louis XVIII (1814, 1815–1824), was an unhappy choice for the French throne. The new king, a brother of the guillotined Louis XVI, was ill-equipped to lead France out of a quarter century of revolution and Napoleonic charisma. Dull and unpopular, he had been the target of a Talleyrand epigram that "the Bourbons have learned nothing and forgotten nothing." Nonetheless, he tried to hold the country together by blending elements of the revolutionary period with remnants of the old regime. Unfortunately, the mixture helped create the instability that plagued the country throughout the century.

Louis began by "granting" his subjects a charter that established a form of constitutional monarchy in which he kept all executive power, controlled lawmaking, and influenced the makeup of the legislature. The restored Bourbon made little attempt to return to the institutions of the old regime and accepted Napoleon's Civil Code, the Concordat with the papacy, and the governmental reforms. For nine years he suffered the fate of moderates trying to navigate between two extremes—he was attacked by both sides. The right wing assailed the charter for giving too much to the middle classes while the liberals and radicals said that he had not gone far enough in his policies. Louis was succeeded by his brother, Charles X (1824–1830), who cared nothing about maintaining political balance.

In the July Revolution of 1830, Parisians took to the streets to protest the restrictive laws of Charles X.

Charles did not accept any of the changes of the age. In 1829 he announced that he "would rather saw wood than be a king of the English type." So out of tune was he to the times that in July 1830 he drove the usually submissive legislature to the point that it refused to support his proposed ultraroyalist ministry. When elections went badly for him, he issued a set of laws censoring the press and further limiting the already heavily restricted right to vote. These repressive acts drove liberals, radicals, and their journalist allies to revolt. They barricaded the narrow streets of Paris with overturned carts, boxes, tables, and paving stones. Fighting behind these obstacles and from rooftops, they held off the army. Three days later a less reactionary faction took power after Charles fled across the Channel to exile in Great Britain.

The new government represented the upper middle classes and landed gentry, and represented a compromise between the French republicans—led by the aging Marquis de Lafayette, hero of the American Revolution—and the relatively liberal monarchist supporters of the Orléans branch of the Bourbons. The new king, Louis Philippe (1830–1848), who claimed the title of "the citizen king," resolutely supported the interests of the wealthy.

Louis Philippe took great pains to portray a "bourgeois" image. He received the crown from "the people" and replaced the white Bourbon flag with the revolutionary tricolor. However, Louis Philippe's policies consistently favored the upper bourgeoisie and gentry and shut the workers and middle classes out of the political arena. Of the 32 million French citizens, only 200,000 wealthy male property owners were allowed to vote.

Workers protested that the government was ignoring their interests. Louis Philippe and his advisers were more interested in pursuing a policy of divide-and-conquer and ignored most suggestions for reform. Restrictive legislation such as the "September Laws" were passed in 1835 to control the growing radical movement. The government kept control, but under the surface calm serious pressures were building. By 1848 France faced a serious crisis.

The French Influence in Belgium and Poland

Liberals across the continent were encouraged by the Paris uprising of 1830, but only in Belgium were there any lasting results. The Vienna Congress had placed the Belgians under the Dutch crown, but this settlement ignored the cultural, economic, religious,and linguistic differences between the two people. The Belgians were primarily French-speaking Catholic farmers and workers while the people of Holland were Dutch-speaking Protestant seafarers and traders.

Belgian liberals asked the Dutch King William I of Orange to grant them their own administration in August 1830. When he refused, rioting broke out in Brussels, which the Dutch troops were unable to put down. After expelling the

The citizen king, Louis Philippe, shown here strolling through Paris, attempted some reform, but it was not enough to stop the revolution of 1848.

troops, the Belgians declared their independence and drew up a liberal constitution. William asked in vain for help from Tsar Nichoas I. The principle of legitimacy as a pretext for intervention was dead. Stalemate ensued until the summer of 1831 when the Belgian national assembly met in Brussels and chose Prince Leopold of Saxe-Coburg-Gotha as king. Eight years later the international status of the new state was settled. Belgium was recognized to be a "perpetually neutral state."

The French rebellion had an impact in Poland, where Poles in and around Warsaw rose up in the name of liberal and national principles. After the Congress of Vienna, Poles in this region gained a special status. The area known as Congress Poland had its own constituion and substantial local autonomy. The winds of change and the repressive tendencies of Tsar Nicholas I combined to push the Poles into rebellion in the winter of 1830–1831. The rebels suffered from internal division and the numerically and militarily superior Russians crushed them. Their major accomplishment was to tie down the Russian troops, whom Nicholas wanted to send to help the Dutch king, for six months and perhaps save the Belgian revolution.[3]

German and Italian Nationalism

The forces of nationalism influenced central Europe from the tip of Italy through the Habsburg lands to the Baltic Sea. Napoleon had performed a great, though unwitting, service for the Germans and Italians through his direct governing in the area and also by his revising the European map. After 1815, the region knew the positive effects of a different style of governing and was divided into a much more rational set of political units.

Metternich had ensured that the Vienna Congress made Austria the dominant partner in the German Confederation. To preserve his country's dominance both in the Confederation and throughout the Habsburg monarchy he knew that he had to fight continually against nationalism. The currents of romanticism found forceful expression in the works of German poets and philosophers and in lectures in German classrooms. Nationalism and liberalism found many followers among the young. For example, in the great patriotic student festival that took place in Octber 1817 (the tercentenary of the Reformation) at Wartburg where Luther had taken refuge, liberal students burned reactionary books on the great bonfire to protest their discontent with the status quo. Protests spread both openly and secretly in the *Burschenschaften* (liberal societies). Metternich moved harshly against the students. He pushed through the Diet of the German Confederation the Carlsbad Decrees (1819). These acts dissolved student associations, censored the press, and restricted academic freedom. These decrees failed to stop the forces of liberalism and nationalism, and these forces grew during the next twenty years.

Italy, which Metternich saw as being only a "geographic expression" and not a nation, also posed special problems. The Congress of Vienna, in accord with the principles of legitimacy and compensation, had returned Italy to its geographic status of 1789, divided into areas dominated by the Bourbons, the Papal States, and the Austrians. This settlement ignored the fact that in the interim the Italians had experienced more liberty and better government than ever before. The return to the old systems was also a return to high taxes, corruption, favoritism, and banditry.

It was perhaps ironic that this fragmented, individualistic land should produce the most notable romantic nationalist in Europe, Giuseppe Mazzini (see p. 000). After the Austrians put down the Italian revolutionary movements in 1820 and 1821, Mazzini began to work actively for independence. In 1830 he was implicated in an unsuccessful revolution against the Sardinian royal government and thrown into jail for six months. Once released, he went to London and started a

Mazzini on the Duties of the Individual

Giuseppe Mazzini saw the individual's obligation to the human family to be transcendent.

Your first duties—first as regards importance—are, as I have already told you, towards Humanity. You are men before you are either citizens or fathers. If you do not embrace the whole human family in your affection, if you do not bear witness to your belief in the Unity of that family, consequent upon the Unity of God, and in the fraternity among the peoples which is destined to reduce that unit to action; if, wheresoever a fellow-creature suffers, or the dignity of human nature is violated by falsehood or tyranny—you are not ready, if able, to aid the unhappy, and do not feel called upon to combat, if able, for the redemption of the betrayed or oppressed— you violate your law of life, you comprehend not that Religion which will be the guide and blessing of the future.

From Emilie A. Venturi, *Joseph Mazzini: A Memoir* (London, 1875).

patriotic society that he called "Young Italy." This organization sent appeals to students and intellectuals to form an Italian nationalist movement. In the meantime, the reactionary forces weathered nationalist pressures.

Metternich also feared nationalism in the Habsburg realm, a mosaic composed of many different nationalities, languages, and religions. If nationalism and the desire for self-rule became strong among the Magyars, Czechs, southern Slavs, and Italians, the Habsburg Empire would fall apart. Nationalism threatened the Germans who controlled the Empire yet constituted only 20 percent of its population.

By understanding the complex and combustible nature of the region in which Metternich exercised his power, we can begin to appreciate his dread of democratic government and nationalism and his obsession with maintaining the status quo. Liberalism and nationalism would destroy his power. In a world that was rapidly industrializing, Metternich's power rested on a backward system. Except for Bohemia and the areas immediately around Vienna, there was no middle class. A great majority of the inhabitants were peasants, either powerless serfs, as in Hungary, or impoverished tenant farmers who owed one-half of their time and two-thirds of their crop to the landlord. Government was autocratic and the regional assemblies had little power and represented mainly the nobility. The social, political, and economic structures were extremely vulnerable to the winds of change that came in 1848.[4]

This painting, *24 Février 1848,* celebrates the revolutionary spirit of the mid-19th century. A young French hero encourages his fellow citizens to fight for liberty.

The Revolutionary Year of 1848

As it had before, France once again opened a revolutionary era, and the events there set a model for what was to occur throughout Europe in 1848. The overthrow of the old order came first in Paris in February and then spread to Berlin, Vienna, Prague, and Budapest in March. Never before had France—or Europe—seen such a fragmented variety of political and social pressures at work at the same time (see map at left). Romantics, socialists, nationalists, middle classes, peasants, and students could all agree that the old structure had to be abandoned, but each group had a different path to that goal and a separate view of what the new world should be Louis Philippe fled Paris, Metternich abandoned Vienna, and the Prussian King Frederick William IV gave in. But the movements in France and elsewhere fell apart as soon as they had won because of their diversity, lack of experience, and conflicting goals.

France and the Second Republic

The pressures building since 1830 and strengthened by economic depression in 1846 and 1847 erupted in Paris in February 1848 in a series of banquets. In this seemingly harmless arena, liberals and socialists pushed for an end to corruption and reforms of the electoral system. The government tried to block the banquet scheduled for February 22, and in response the opposition threw up more than 1500 barricades to block the streets of Paris. When violence broke out, republican leaders took the opportunity to set up a provisional revolutionary government and proclaimed the introduction of universal manhood suffrage. Louis Philippe fled to exile in England.

The new government, the Second Republic, had a brief (1848–1851) and dreary existence. Neither the new leaders nor the voters had any experience with representative government. The forces that united to overthrow the king soon split into moderate and radical wings. The first group wanted middle-class control within the existing social order, while the latter faction desired a social and economic revolution. By the summer the new government faced a major crisis over the issue of national workshops sponsored by the socialist Louis Blanc (1811–1882). The workshops were to be the state's means to guarantee every laborer's "right to work." The moderate-dominated government voiced its belief in Blanc's principle of full employment, but the leaders gave the plan's administration to men who wanted to ridicule it. As a result, the workshops became a national joke. Laborers were assigned "make-work" jobs such as carrying dirt from one end of a park to the other on one day, and then carrying it back the next.

The disbanding of the workshops incited a violent insurrection known as the "June Days." The unemployed workers raised a red flag as a sign of revolution—the first time that the red flag had been used as a symbol of the proletariat. With the cry of "bread or lead," the demonstrators rebuilt the barricades and tried to overthrow the government. The most bloody fighting Paris had seen since the Reign of Terror gave the insurgents far more lead than bread, and the movement was crushed. After that, the bourgeoisie and the workers would be on the opposite sides of political strife, and moderates would look elsewhere for their future.

Germany and the Frankfurt Assembly

The example of the French February revolution quickly crossed the Rhine River and spread to central Europe. At public assemblies throughout Germany patriotic liberals demanded unification. Rapid changes came with minimal casualties, thanks largely to the humane response of the Prussian king Frederick William IV. When his subjects erected barricades in Berlin on March 15, he decided to make concessions rather than unleash further violence and bloodshed. He ordered the regular army troops out of Berlin and tried to make peace with his "dear Berliners" by promising a parliament, a constitution, and a united Germany. Upon learning of this development, the rulers of the other German states agreed to establish constitutional governments and guarantee basic civil rights.

The Frankfurt Assembly opened its first session on May 18. Over 500 delegates attended, coming from the various German states, Austria, and Bohemia. The primarily middle-class membership of the assembly included about 200 lawyers, 100 professors, and many doctors and judges. Popular enthusiasm reached a peak when the assembly's president announced that "We are to create a constitution for Germany, for the whole Empire." The assembly deliberated at length over the issues of just what was meant by Germany and what form of government would be best for the new empire. Some debaters wanted a united Germany to include all Germans in central Europe, even Austria and Bohemia. Others did not want the Austrians included, for

a variety of religious and political reasons. Another issue of contention was whether the new imperial crown should be given to the Habsburgs in Vienna or the Hohenzollerns in Berlin.

Germany's history changed tragically when the Assembly failed to unite and bring a liberal solution to political problems. From May to December the Assembly wasted time in splendid debates over nonessential topics. As the participants talked they contributed to the failed dreams of 1848. Gradually, the conservatives recovered from the shocks of the spring revolts and began to rally around their rulers, exhorting them to undo the reformers' work. In Prussia, the king regained his confidence, as the army remained loyal and the peasants showed little interest in political affairs. The Berlin liberals soon found themselves isolated and the king was able to regain control.

Even though the anti-liberal forces were at full tide, the Frankfurt Assembly continued its work. It approved the Declaration of the Rights of the German People, an inspiring document that articulated the progressive political and social ideals of 1848. In April 1849, the Assembly approved a constitution for a united Germany that included an emperor advised by a ministry and a legislature elected by secret ballot. Austria was excluded when it refused to join the new union.

When the leadership of the new German Reich (nation) was offered to Frederick William, he refused to accept it, later declaring that he could not "pick up a crown from the gutter." After this contemptuous refusal, most of the Assembly's members returned home. Outbreaks against the conservative domination continued, but the Prussian army effectively put them down. Thousands of prominent middle-class liberals fled, many emigrating to the United States.

Italy

The news of the revolutions in Paris and Vienna triggered a rash of uprisings on the Italian peninsula. In Sicily, Venice, and Milan revolutionaries demanded an end to foreign domination and despotic rule. In response, King Charles Albert of Sardinia voluntarily granted a new liberal constitution. Other states such as Tuscany also issued constitutions. Absolute government

The artillery attempts to demolish a barricade in the scene of the street fighting during the Frankfurt insurrection of 1848.

The Habsburg Monarchy

The events of 1848 took a tragic toll in the Habsburg territories. When the news of the February uprising reached Vienna, Prague, and Budapest, reformers immediately called for change. In Budapest, the nationalist liberal Louis Kossuth (1802–1894) attacked the Habsburg ruler's "stagnant bureaucratic system" and spoke of the "pestilential air blowing from the Vienna charnel house and its deadening effect upon all phases of Hungarian life." He demanded parliamentary government for the whole of the empire.

In Vienna, Kossuth's speech inspired some Austrian students and workers to demonstrate in the streets. The movement soon gained the force of a rebellion and the frightened Austrian emperor forced Metternich, the symbol of European reaction, to resign. Meanwhile, the Hungarian

In this satiric cartoon, Pope Pius IX removes his liberal "saviour's" mask to reveal his true nature after his refusal to support the revolution in Italy.

in Italy almost disappeared. In the Papal States, meanwhile, reform had begun as early as 1846.

As in the rest of Europe, the liberal and nationalist triumphs and reforms were quickly swept away by the reactionary tide. The Austrians regained their mastery in the north of Italy in July when they defeated Charles Albert at the decisive battle of Custozza. Another defeat a year later forced him to abdicate in favor of his oldest son, Victor Emmanuel II. Austria helped restore the old rulers and systems of government in Italy to their pre-1848 conditions.

The final blow to the Italian movements came in November 1848 when Pope Pius IX, who had begun a program of reform, refused to join in the struggle against Catholic Austria for a united Italy. His subjects forced him to flee from Rome, and the papal lands were declared a republic, with Mazzini as the head. The pope's flight prompted a hostile reaction from conservative Europe, and the French sent in an army to crush the republic in July 1849. When the pope returned to Rome, he remained bitterly hostile to all liberal causes and ideas until his death in 1878.

Diet advocated a liberal, parliamentary government under a limited Habsburg monarchy. The Vienna-controlled Danubian region, that mosaic of nationalities, appeared to be on the verge of being transformed into a federation.

The empire's diversity soon became a characteristic of the revolutionary movements, as the various nationalities divided among themselves. The Hungarians wrote a new constitution that was quite liberal, calling for a guarantee of civil rights, an end to serfdom, and the destruction of special privileges. In theory, all political benefits guaranteed in the constitution were to extend to all citizens of Hungary, including non-Magyar minorities. The emperor accepted these reforms and promised, in addition, a constitution for Austria. He also promised the Czechs in Bohemia the same reforms granted the Hungarians.

By summer the mood suddenly shifted. German and Czech nationalists began to quarrel and the Magyars began to oppress the Slavic nationalities and Romanians after they, in their turn, demanded their own political independence. Divisions among the liberal and nationalistic forces gave the conservatives in Vienna time to regroup and suggested to them the obvious tactic to follow to regain their former dominance: divide and conquer the subject nationalities. In June demonstrations broke out in the streets of Prague, barricades were thrown up, and fighting began. The

Austrians lobbed a few shells, Prague surrendered, and any hope for an autonomous kingdom of Bohemia ended.

In Hungary, Kossuth announced that he would offer civil rights, but not national independence, to the minority nationalities under his control. In protest, the South Slavs under the Croat leader Joseph Jellachich (1801–1859) attacked the Magyars, and civil war broke out. The Austrians took advantage of the situation and made Jellachich an imperial general. Following his attack against the Magyars, he was ordered to Vienna where in October he forced the surrender of the liberals who controlled the capital.

By the end of the year the weak and incapable emperor Ferdinand I abdicated in favor of his nephew, Franz Joseph. The Austrians began to repeal their concessions to the Hungarians, arguing that their new emperor was not bound by the acts of his predecessor. The Magyars, outraged by this maneuver, declared complete independence for their country. The Austrians, aided by 100,000 Russian troops sent by Tsar Nicholas I, defeated the Hungarians in a bloody and one-sided struggle. By the summer 1849 Kossuth fled the country and the Hungarian revolution reached its tragic conclusion.[5]

New Political Forms in France, Italy, and Germany

In France, the violence of the June Days moved the conservatives in the countryside and the moderates in the cities to elect Louis Napoleon (1808–1873), nephew of Napoleon I, to the presidency of the Second Republic. Although he had failed miserably in his attempts to overthrow the king in 1836 and 1840, he was sure that destiny intended great things for him. When he came back to Paris after the revolution he was untainted by any involvement in the June Days and appeared to be a unifying force.

France's Second Empire

The republic's constitution gave strong powers to the president, but limited the office to only one term. Louis Napoleon took advantage of the

A French satirist's view of Jellachich, Radetzky, and Windischgrätz, the military leaders who crushed the 1848 revolts in the Austrian Empire.

One of the most outstanding achievements of Napoleon III's beautification program was the Operá in Paris. The baroque style of the building demonstrated the emphasis on recreating the grandeur of the past.

authority given him and his strong majority to fortify his position. He and his conservative allies dominated France for the next two years, becoming strong enough to overthrow the constitution in a coup d'état in December 1851. Louis Napoleon and his allies brutally put down the workers and peasants who opposed the coup and engineered a plebiscite that gave him virtually unanimous support. In 1852 he proclaimed himself Emperor Napoleon III, and the Second Empire replaced the Second Republic.

During its eighteen-year span the Second Empire accomplished a great deal. Industrialization brought prosperity to France. Production doubled. France supported the building of the Suez Canal and increased railway mileage by 500 percent. The partial legalization of labor unions and guarantee of the right to strike improved workers' conditions. Baron Georges Haussmann (1809–1891) transformed Paris in an ambitious urban renewal that featured broad boulevards, unified architecture, modern utilities, and improved traffic flow.

The price for the order and stability needed to build this prosperity came in the form of political control. The government remained, in theory, a parliamentary regime. The emperor's agents rigged the elections to ensure a majority in the powerless legislature for the emperor. The secret police hounded opponents—both real and potential—and the state censored the press, which accordingly rarely reported bad news.

At first the emperor brought glory to France through an interventionist and imperialist foreign policy. He continually claimed to be a man of peace, but he allied with Britain in the Crimean War (see ch. 26), supported Cavour—briefly—in Italy, expanded French influence to assure a foothold in Indochina, raised the French flag over Tahiti, and penetrated West Africa along the Senegal River. Foreign affairs soured for him in the 1860s when he made an ill-advised attempt to take advantage of the confusion caused by the U.S. Civil War to establish a foothold in the Americas. He placed Maximilian, a Habsburg prince, on the Mexican throne and sent 40,000 troops to support him. Mexican patriots expelled the forces and executed the prince. After 1866 Louis Napoleon met his match in the Prussian chancellor Otto von Bismarck (1815–1898), when his blundering ambition contributed to a quick Prussian victory over Austria. Finally, in 1870 he gambled on a successful war against Prussia and lost. With this defeat the Second Empire ended.[6]

Cavour Unites Italy

After 1848, the Italian unification movement came to be centered in the Kingdom of Sardinia,

Count Camillo Benso di Cavour, the leader of the movement for Italian unification.

declaring war. The French and Sardinians defeated them at Magenta and Solferino and drove them out of Lombardy. At the same time, revolts broke out in Tuscany, Modena, Parma, and Romagna. Napoleon received praise and was proclaimed the savior and liberator of Italy.

Upon receiving his share of the agreement, Napoleon III reversed himself and made peace with Austria, before the allies could invade Venetia. The massing of Prussian troops on French borders and second thoughts about the implications of a united Italy drove him to this move. The Sardinians were outraged, but there was little they could do but agree to a peace settlement. The agreement added Lombard to Sardinia; restored the exiled rulers of Parma, Modena, Tuscany, and Romagna; and set up an Italian confederation in which Austria was included.

where the young monarch Victor Emmanuel II refused to withdraw the liberal constitution granted by his father. The prime minister, Count Camillo Benso di Cavour (1810–1861), a liberal influenced by what he had seen in Switzerland, France, and Britain, assumed leadership of the drive to unify the peninsula.

From 1852, when he became prime minister, Cavour concentrated on freeing his country from Austrian domination. He knew, however, that Sardinia needed allies to take on the Habsburgs. To that end, in 1855 Sardinia joined Britain and France in their fight against Russia in the Crimean War (see p. 688). This step enabled Cavour to speak at the peace conference after the war, where he stated Italy's desire for unification.

Cavour's presentation won Napoleon III's support, and the two opportunists found that they could both make gains if they could draw the Austrians into war. They agreed that if Cavour could entice the Vienna government into war, France would come to Sardinia's aid and help eject the Austrians from Lombardy and Venetia. In return, France would receive Nice and Savoy from Sardinia. The plan worked to perfection. In April 1859, Cavour lured the Austrians into

THE UNIFICATION OF ITALY 1859–1870

- Kingdom of Sardinia to 1859
- To Kingdom of Sardinia 1860
- Annexed to Kingdom of Sardinia 1861; establishes Kingdom of Italy
- To Kingdom of Italy 1866
- To Kingdom of Italy 1870

France's duplicity did not stop Cavour. A year later, appealing to the British, he made major changes in the peace settlement. Plebiscites were held in Tuscany, Modena, and Parma, and they voted to join Sardinia. Even with the loss of Nice and Savoy to France, the addition of the three areas made Sardinia the dominant power in the peninsula (see map at left).

With the consolidation of power in the north, Giuseppe Garibaldi (1807–1882) became the major figure in the unification struggle. This follower of Mazzini, secretly financed by Cavour, led his 1000 tough adventurers — the Red Shirts — to conquer Sicily and Naples. He then prepared to take the Papal States. This move prompted Cavour, who feared that a march on the pope's holdings might provoke French intervention, to rush troops to Naples. He convinced Garibaldi to surrender his power to Victor Emmanuel II, thus ensuring Sardinian domination of the unification movement. By November 1860, Sardinia had annexed the former kingdom of Naples and Sicily, and all the papal lands, except Rome and its environs.

A meeting at Turin in March 1861 formally proclaimed the existence of the Kingdom of Italy, a new nation of 22 million people. But Austrian control of Venetia and the pope's jurisdiction over Rome, were problems that did not find solution before Cavour's death in 1861. In the decade that followed Italy gained Venetia in 1866, acting as Prussia's ally in the Austro-Prussian war. When the Franco-Prussian war broke out in 1870, the French could do little to help the pope. Italian forces took control of Rome, and in 1871 it became the capital of a unified Italy.

The opportunistic methods used by the Sardinians have been criticized. Cavour made no attempt to hide the true nature of his policies. He once said "if we did for ourselves what we do for our country, what rascals we should be."[7] He fully understood the rules of the *realpolitik* game in the post-1848 state system. His skill in playing that game and in gaining Italian unification cannot be doubted.

Germanic Competition

Conservative forces regained control in Vienna and Berlin after 1848, but the Austrian Habsburgs operated from a much weaker position

"Right Leg in the Boot at Last" was the caption on the British cartoon of 1860. Garibaldi is surrendering his power to Victor Emmanuel II, king of Sardinia and later king of the united Italy.

than did the Prussian Hohenzollerns. The Habsburg victory over the Hungarians brought only temporary comfort. The collapse of the liberal and nationalistic movements in the Habsburg empire was followed by a harsh repression that did little to address the basic political problems facing Vienna. Centralizing and Germanizing tendencies stimulated nationalist sentiments in the empire. After their losses to the French and Sardinians in 1859, the Austrians considered moving toward a federal system for their lands. The Hungarians, however, demanded equality with Vienna.

Prussia, on the other hand, went from strength to strength. Facing a different range of problems in a much more unified state, King Frederick William issued a constitution in 1850 that paid lip service to parliamentary democracy but kept real power in the hands of the king and upper classes. The Berlin court wanted to form a confederation of north German states, without Austria. This plan frightened the Austrians and made the Russians uneasy. A conference of the three powers meeting at Olmütz in 1850 forced the

Prussians to withdraw their plan. Instead, the 1815 German Confederation was affirmed, with Vienna recognized as the major German power (see map below). The embittered Prussians returned to Berlin, pledging revenge for the "humiliation of Olmütz."

Despite this diplomatic setback, Prussia gained success in other areas. Berlin kept the Austrians out of the *Zollverein*, the customs union of German states, and fought off their efforts to weaken it. The noble-dominated government was modern and efficient, especially when compared with that in Vienna. The Prussians extended public education to more of their citizenry than in any other European state. At the end of the 1850s, a new ruler, William I (1861–1888), came to power. He had a more permissive interpretation of the 1850 constitution and allowed liberals and moderates the chance to make their voices heard.

Bismarck and German Unification

A stalemate occurred in 1862 when the king wanted to strengthen his army, but the Chamber of Deputies would not vote the necessary funds. The liberals asserted the constitutional right to approve taxes, while the king equally strongly expressed his right to build up his forces. As the king struggled with this constitutional crisis, he called Otto von Bismarck (1815–1898) home from his post as Prussian ambassador in France and made him prime minister.

Bismarck advised the king to ignore the legislature and collect the needed taxes without the Chamber's approval. Bismarck knew the

THE UNIFICATION OF GERMANY
1815–1871

- Prussia 1815-1866
- Annexed by Prussia 1866
- Joined Prussia in forming the North German Confederation 1867
- Joined with Prussia to form the German Empire 1871
- Alsace-Lorraine ceded to German Empire by France 1871
- German Confederation 1815-1866

Otto von Bismarck, the "Iron Chancellor," was the shrewd and masterful prime minister of Prussia from 1862 and the first chancellor of the united Germany from 1871 to 1890.

necessity of armed strength in order to gain Prussia's diplomatic goals. Ironically, his later military victories would gain him the support of many of the liberals whom he had encouraged the king to defy.

Bismarck's arrival in Berlin strengthened not only the king but also the hopes of those who wanted a united German state. Unification appealed to virtually all segments of German society, from the liberals to the conservatives such as the historian Heinrich von Treitschke who stated "There is only one salvation! One state, one monarchic Germany under the Hohenzollern dynasty."[8] The Berlin government through its leadership of the *Zollverein*, sponsorship of the confederation of north German states, and efficient bureaucracy was the obvious choice for the capital of a unified German state. With the arrival of Bismarck, the Prussians gained the necessary leadership for unification.

The prime minister was a master of the art of *realpolitik*. He had the intelligence to assess accurately the actual state of conditions, the insight to gauge the character and goals of his opponents, and the talent to move skillfully and quickly.

Unlike most of his colleagues, he was a master image maker, so effective that historians have used his self-applied epithet "blood and iron" to describe his career. But in addition, few statesmen have ever accomplished so much change with such a comparatively small loss of life and controlled use of war. Bismarck was a master politician who knew that force was the final card to be played, to be used as the servant of diplomacy and not its master.[9]

Some historians have attributed his successes to mere luck, whereas others have deemed them products of genius. An example is his approach to Russia. Bismarck knew that he would have to solidify relations with Russia, and he achieved this in 1863 by promising the Russians that he would aid them in all Polish-related problems. Giving up virtually nothing, he gained a secure eastern flank and thus set up his three wars that brought about German unification.

The Danish and Austrian Wars

In 1864 Bismarck invited Austria to join Prussia and wage war on Denmark. The cause of the conflict was the disputed status of two duchies bordering on Prussia and Denmark. These two duchies of Schleswig and Holstein were claimed by both the Germans and the Danes. The two Germanic powers overwhelmed the modest Danish forces and split the duchies: Austria took Holstein, and Schleswig went to Prussia. With his eastern and northern flanks stabilized, Bismarck set out to isolate Austria.

Italy was already hostile to the Austrians and remained so when Bismarck promised it Venetia in return for its assistance in the future war. He encouraged the French to be neutral by intimating that Prussia might support France should it seek to widen its borders. Severe domestic crises with the Hungarians absorbed Austria, which soon found itself isolated. The Prussian leader provoked war with Vienna by piously expressing alarm at the manner in which the Austrians were ruling Holstein and sending troops into the province. Austria took the bait, entered the war, and was devastated by the

Prussians at the battle of Sadowa. In this Seven Weeks' War, the Prussians avenged the "humiliation of Olmütz."

Prussia offered a moderate peace settlement that ended the old German Confederation. In its place Bismarck formed the North German Confederation, with Austria and the south German states excluded. Prussia annexed several territories such as Hanover, Mecklenberg, and other states north of the Main River in this penultimate stage in the unification of Germany (see map, p. 640).

The War with France

After 1867 Bismarck turned his attention westward to France and Napoleon III. The French leader had allowed himself to be talked into neutrality in 1866 because he anticipated a long war between his German neighbors that would weaken both of them and because he hoped to expand into the neutral state of Belgium. In August 1866 he approached Bismarck for his share of the fruits of victory, but the German leader refused to agree to French demands. Frustrated and offended, Napoleon III insisted that Prussia approve France's annexation of Luxembourg and Belgium. In a crafty move Bismarck

asked the French envoy to Berlin to put these demands into writing but still avoided giving a definite response. Four years later Bismarck sent the document to the British in order to gain their sympathy for the upcoming war with the French. After France's active participation in the Crimean War, there was no chance that Russia would come to Napoleon's aid. Bismarck let the Austrians know about France's cooperation with the Prussians during the 1866 war, and Italy was not about to help Napoleon III after his activities in 1859. By 1870 France was isolated. It was simply a question now of Bismarck maneuvering the French into war.

The immediate controversy centered on the succession to the Spanish throne left vacant after a revolution had overthrown the reactionary queen Isabella. The Spaniards asked Leopold, a Hohenzollern prince, to become the constitutional king of their country. France saw this as an unacceptable extension of Prussian influence, and Leopold withdrew his candidacy. But this was not enough for Paris. The French sent their ambassador to Ems, where the Prussian king was vacationing, to gain from him a pledge that he would not again permit Leopold to seek the Spanish throne. This was not a reasonable request, and the king refused to agree to it. After

German troops march down the Champs-Elysées in Paris during the Franco-Prussian War. The better prepared German troops, outnumbering the French nearly two to one, quickly overwhelmed the French during the short-lived war of 1870–1871.

Bismarck and the Ems Despatch

Bismarck knew how to manipulate public opinion through press leaks and doctored documents. See how he altered the Ems despatch to achieve his goals vis-a-vis France.

I made use of the royal authorization communicated to me through Abeken, to publish the contents of the telegram; and in the presence of my two guests I reduced the telegram by striking out words, but without adding or altering, to the following form: "After the news of the renunciation of the hereditary Prince of Hohenzollern had been officially communicated to the imperial government of France by the royal government of Spain, the French ambassador at Ems further demanded of his Majesty the King that he would authorize him to telegraph to Paris that his Majesty the King bound himself for all future time never again to give his consent if the Hohenzollerns should renew their candidature. His Majesty the King thereupon decided not to receive the French ambassador again, and sent to tell him through the aide-de-camp on duty that his Majesty had nothing further to communicate to the ambassador." The difference in the effect of the abbreviated text of the Ems telegram as compared with that produced by the original was not the result of stronger words but of the form, which made this announcement appear decisive, while Abeken's version only would have been regarded as a fragment of a negotiation still pending, and to be continued at Berlin.

After I had read out the concentrated edition to my two guests, Moltke remarked: "Now it has a different ring; it sounded before like a parley; now it is like a flourish in answer to a challenge."

From *Bismarck, The Man and the Statement*, tr. A. J. Butler, 2 vol. (New York, 1899).

---

the interview he directed that a message be sent to Bismarck, describing the incident. Bismarck altered the message of this "Ems dispatch" to give the impression that the French ambassador had insulted the Prussian king and that the king had returned the insult. The rumor was leaked to the press and infuriated both the Germans and the French.

France declared war in July. The two countries' forces appeared to be evenly matched in equipment, but the Germans had a better trained and more experienced army. In two months the Prussians overwhelmed the French, delivering the crowning blow at the battle of Sedan, where the emperor and his army were surrounded and forced to surrender. Forces of the north and south German states besieged France for four months before the final French capitulation. By the Treaty of Frankfurt, France lost Alsace and a part of Lorraine to Germany and was required to pay a large indemnity. In the Hall of Mirrors at Versailles, the Second Reich was proclaimed and William I was crowned German emperor.

The call for revenge for France's defeat and humiliation became a major issue in French politics.

Russia and Britain: The Extremes of Europe

Russia avoided the revolutionary currents after 1815, but unlike Britain, Russia had neither the economic strength nor the social and political flexibility to change. Tsar Alexander I (1801–1825) understood the major problems facing his empire, especially those of serfdom and the need to reform the autocratic system. His grandmother, Catherine II, had educated him in the traditions and assumptions of the Enlightenment, and for the first four years of his reign he attempted major reforms in the areas of education, government, and social welfare.

Russia, however, possessed neither the inventive and flexible ruling classes nor the economic wealth of Britain. Its problems were far more harsh. Serfdom, a system that held millions of Russians in its grip, was socially repressive and economically inefficient. The autocratic system simply was inadequate to govern efficiently the world's largest state.

Obstacles to Reform in Russia

Alexander's experiments with limited serf emancipation, constitutionalism, and federalism proved his desire for change. The tsar was all-powerful in theory, but in reality he depended on the nobles who, in turn, gained their wealth from serfdom. Carrying out the necessary reforms would destroy the foundations of Alexander's power. The fact that his father and grandfather had been killed by nobles made him cautious. Further, it was his misfortune to rule during the Napoleonic wars, and for the first fifteen years of his reign he had to devote immense amounts of money and time to foreign affairs. His reform plans were never carried through to completion, and not until the 1850s, when it was almost too late, would there be another tsar willing to make the fundamental social and political reforms needed to make Russia competitive in the industrializing world.[10]

In the reactionary decade after 1815 reformers fell from favor. However, the open discussion of the need for change in the first part of Alexander's reign, the experiences of the soldiers returning from western Europe and the activities of the expanding number of secret societies kept the dream of change alive. When Alexander failed to respond, the intensity of the reformers' discussions increased. Alexander died in December 1825, and there was confusion over which of his two brothers would succeed to the throne. The days between his death and the confirmation of his younger brother Nicholas I (1825–1855) gave a small circle of liberal nobles and army officers the chance to advance their ill-defined demands for a constitution. The officers who led this revolt had been infected with liberal French thought. They sought to end serfdom and establish representative government and civil liberties in Russia. On December 26 these liberals led a small uprising in St. Petersburg. This Decembrist revolt, as it was called, lasted less than a day and could have been put down even earlier had Nicholas been more decisive. This abortive, ill-planned attempt doomed any chance of liberal or democratic reform in Russia for thirty years.

Nicholas I and Reaction

The Decembrist incident shook Nicholas badly, and throughout his reign he remained opposed to liberal and revolutionary movements. He sponsored "Official Nationalism," whose foundations were "Autocracy, Orthodoxy, and Nationalism"—the Romanov dynasty, the Orthodox

This 1854 engraving by Gustave Doré satirizes the callous indifference of Russian serf owners. Masters hard-pressed for cash were occasionally known to bet their serfs as stakes in card games.

church, and a glorification of a putative Russian spirit. He carried out a thorough censorship that included the screening of foreign visitors, publications, even musical compositions. The government closely monitored both students' activities and curricula in schools and universities. Finally, some 150,000 "dangerous" people were exiled to Siberia. Millions of non-Russians in the empire began to experience a limitation of their identity through a forced adherence to Russian customs called "Russification." These activities strengthened Nicholas' immediate control and stopped potential upheaval, but he failed to address adequately the important social and political reforms Russia so badly needed.

Despite his efforts to control intellectual and political currents, Nicholas failed. Reformist activity may have been repressed, but the Russian intellectual was fruitful, tuned as it was to the works of the German philosophers and poets. In the 1840s and 1850s a new breed of intellectuals appeared, thinkers devoted to achieving political goals. Although they would not make their strength felt until after the 1860s, these thinkers, known as the *intelligentsia*, established strong roots during Nicholas' reign. Alexander Herzen (1812–1870) and Michael Bakunin (1814–1876) were the pioneers of this peculiarly Russian movement. Herzen was a moderate socialist who advocated freeing the serfs, liberalizing the government, and freeing the press. In 1847 he went into exile in London where he founded his famous paper, the *Kolokol* (the *Bell*) ten years later. It was widely read in Russia, supposedly appearing mysteriously on the tsar's table. Bakunin, the father of Russian anarchism, was more radical. He felt reform of Russia was useless and advocated terrorism. He preached that anarchy—complete freedom—was the only cure for society's ills. He too went into exile in the west.

The Russian intellectuals debated many questions, most important of which was whether Russia should imitate Europe or pursue its own tradition. The question had been posed since the reign of Peter the Great. The Westerners argued that if Russia wished to survive it had to imitate basic aspects of the west and renounce much of its own past. The Slavophiles, on the other side of the dialogue, renounced Europe and the west, regarding it as materialistic, pagan, and anarchic.

Michael Bakunin, the leading spokesman for anarchism, advocated destruction of the state through acts of violence and terrorism to achieve liberation.

Nicholas was able to maintain control to the extent that the 1830 and 1848 revolutions had little influence or impact on Russia. Some aspects of industrialization were introduced, as the first Moscow-to-St. Petersburg rail line was put into operation. The government appointed commissions to examine the questions of serfdom and reform, but these were extremely secret considerations.[11] Still basic doubts about Russia's future remained. Dissident intellectuals, economic and social weakness, and autocratic stagnation were indicators that difficult times were in store for the country.

Alexander II and the Great Reforms

Russia's inept performance in the Crimean war (see p. 687) spotlighted the country's weaknesses and the need for reform. When Alexander II (1855–1881) came to the throne, even the conservatives among his subjects acknowledged the need for major change. The new tsar moved quickly to transform the basis of the autocratic structure—the institution of serfdom—but ran into delay from the nobility. After five years of deliberation a committee appointed by Alexander drew up the Emancipation Proclamations, issued in March 1861. By this reform, 32 million state peasants and 20 million serfs who had no civil rights and could not own property and who owed heavy dues and services began the transition to landownership and citizenship.

The government paid the landlords a handsome price for the land that was to be turned over to the peasants. In return, the peasants had to pay the government for the land over a period of forty-nine years by making payments through their village commune, the *mir*. The drawn-out nature of the land transfer disappointed the former serfs, who had expected a portion of the lords' lands to be turned over to them without charge. Instead, the peasants were trapped in their village community, which received and allocated all of the land—much of it poor—and divided it among the various families and paid taxes. Even though they were granted ownership of their cottages, farm buildings, garden plots, domestic animals, and implements, the restrictions placed on the peasants by confining them to their villages constituted a serious problem. New generations of peasants would bring a large population increase, with no corresponding increase in their amount of land.

The emancipation of the serfs was the single most important event in the domestic history of nineteenth-century Russia. In its wake it brought about thoroughgoing reforms of the army, judiciary, municipal government, and system of local self-government. One of the most important reforms came in 1864 when local government was transformed by the *Zemstvo* Law. In the countryside the gentry, middle classes, and peasants elected representatives to local boards *(zemstvos)*. These boards collected taxes for and maintained roads, asylums, hospitals, and schools. The *zemstvos* became one of the most successful governmental organizations in Russia.[12]

British Flexibility

Like Russia, Britain did not directly experience the revolutionary upheaval that afflicted the continent, even though the island nation felt many of the same pressures as did France during the same period. The postwar period was the most difficult time for Britain, as the transition back to a peacetime economy and the wrenching changes caused by industrialization made their effects felt. Some handskilled workers lost their jobs due to the increasing use of machines, and in response, workers smashed the machines and destroyed some factories. Violence broke out when some working-class groups and radicals pushed for rapid reforms. The worst incident took place in August 1819 in what became known as the Peterloo Massacre. In Manchester, a crowd of 60,000 gathered at St. Peter's Fields to push for parliamentary reforms. When the army was sent to disband the meeting, several people were killed and hundreds injured.

Britain's ruling class, in power since the 1770s, were conservatives who were blind to the hardships of their workers. They continued to respond to the long-departed excesses of the French Revolution. Instead of dealing with the misfortunes of the poor and unemployed, they declared that the doctrine of "peace, law, order, and discipline" should be their guide. To that end, they pushed through a series of repressive acts after 1815 that suspended the Habeas Corpus Act, restricted public meetings, repressed liberal newspapers, and placed heavy fines on literature considered to be dangerous. Massive conflict between the rich and poor appeared inevitable.

The Duke of Wellington's failure to acknowledge the need for reforms in the 1830s so aroused the public that the "Iron Duke" and the Tories (Conservatives) were forced to resign. They were replaced by a more liberal group, the Whigs. The drive toward self-interested reform by the upper classes had begun in the 1820s, led by Robert Peel (1788–1850) and George Canning (1770–1827), who started the modern British reform tradition that continued to 1914. When Wellington was voted out of office, Lord Charles Grey (1764–1845), leader of the Whig party, became head of government. In 1832 Grey pushed immediately to reform Parliament.[13]

Britain's political abuses were plain for all to see. Representation in the House of Commons had no relation to the population. Three percent of the people dictated the election of members. The rapidly growing industrial towns such as Manchester and Birmingham—each with over

100,000 citizens—had no representatives, while other areas, virtually without population, had delegates. After being blocked by aristocratic interests, first in the House of Commons and then in the House of Lords, reform bills responding to these electoral abuses were finally passed. But this occurred only because King William IV threatened to create enough new members of the House of Lords who would vote for the bills in order to pass them. Grey's reform bills did not bring absolute democracy, but they pointed the way toward a more equitable political system.

The Reformist Tide

Beginning in the 1820s reformers pushed through laws that ended capital punishment for over one hundred offenses, created a modern police force for London, recognized labor unions, and repealed old laws that kept non-Anglican Protestants from sitting in Parliament. They also passed the Catholic Emancipation Act that gave Roman Catholics voting rights and the right to serve in Parliament and most public offices. The reform tide increased in the 1830s and 1840s. Abolitionist pressures brought about the ending of slavery in the British empire in 1833. Parliament passed laws initiating regulation of working conditions and hours. In 1835 the Municipal Corporations Bill introduced a uniform system of town government by popular elections.

Britain's government was far from being a democracy, and in the 1830s and 1840s a strong, popular movement known as Chartism developed. Its leaders summarized the country's needs in six demands: universal manhood suffrage, secret voting, no property qualifications for members of Parliament, payment of Parliament members so that the poor could seek election, annual elections, and equal districts. In 1839, 1842, and 1848 the Chartists presented their demands, backed by over a million signatures on their petitions. But, each time they failed to gain their goals, and the movement declined after 1848. By the end of the century, however, all of their demands, exept that for annual parliamentary elections, had been put into law.

Mirroring the ascendancy of the middle classes, economic liberalism became dominant. A policy of free trade came to be favored because, given Britain's overwhelming economic superiority,

the country could best profit from that approach. The Corn Laws' protective duties on imported grain, which had favored the gentry since 1815, no longer suited the industrializing British economy. These laws had been designed to encourage exports`and to protect the British landowners from foreign competition. By the middle of the century the population had grown to such an extent that British farmers could no longer feed the country and the price of bread rose alarmingly. The potato crop famine in Ireland in 1845 that led to the death of perhaps one-half million people spotlighted the situation and the need for low-priced food from abroad. Repeal of the Corn Laws made possible the import of cheaper food for the masses. Soon Britain abandoned customs duties of every kind. The economy boomed under the stimulus of cheap imports of raw materials and food.

For the next twenty years an alliance of the landed gentry and the middle classes worked together to dominate the government and to keep the lower classes "in their stations." The newly ascendant middle classes believed that political reforms had gone far enough, and the Whig government of Lord Palmerston who served as prime minister from 1855 to 1865 reflected this view.

Conclusion

The French seeds of individualism, freedom of thought, pride in nation, and equality under the law that had appeared after 1789 and were spread by Napoleon began to take root across the map of Europe. The middle classes and underprivileged throughout the continent demanded change and pursued rights and liberties inherent in these ideals. The Congress of Vienna failed to stop these currents and revolutions broke out in the 1820s, 1830s, and 1840s.

The 1848 outbreaks dealt a deadly blow to the idealistic liberals, nationalists, and romantics who failed to achieve their goals. In France, some moderates learned that a revolution in the name of liberal principles could unleash forces that would threaten the middle classes. They turned to Louis Napoleon, who destroyed the Second Republic and, as Napoleon III, installed a new empire. In the Habsburg realm the various nationalities who tried to free themselves from Vienna's control found that the nationalism that motivated each of them also doomed their struggle for freedom by making a unified attack impossible. The Habsburgs took advantage of this lack of unity and imposed twenty years of sterile repression, before they were defeated by the Prussians. By the end of 1848, the leaders of Germany and Italy discarded most of the liberal demands of the revolutionaries, but they retained the potent nationalistic forces that would eventually lead to unification.

Russia and Britain avoided the revolutionary upheavals: the first through a policy of repression that failed to respond effectively to its overwhelming problems and the second because of an improving standard of living and a flexible, self-interested political leadership. Throughout the half century after Waterloo, however, the advanced nations of Europe underwent the traumas of industrialization, which had as devastating an effect on the old idealism as had the political upheavals of 1848.

Suggestions for Reading

H. Nicolson, *The Congress of Vienna: A Study of Allied Unity, 1812–1822* (Compass, 1961) is a civilized analysis of diplomatic interaction and a good companion to Henry A. Kissinger, *A World Restored: Metternich, Castlereagh, and the Problems of Peace, 1812–1822* (Sentry, 1957). The following are excellent on the general background to the period: A. J. May, *The Age of Metternich, 1814–1848* (Holt, Rinehart, and Winston, 1967), E. Hobsbawm, *The Age of Revolution, Europe 1789–1848* (Mentor, 1969), J. Talmon, *Romanticism and Revolt: Europe 1815–1948* (Harcourt Brace Jovanovich, 1967), P. Stearns, *European Society in Upheaval* (Macmillan, 1967), R. C. Binkley, *Realism and Nationalism: 1852–1871* (Torchbooks, 1935), W. E. Mosse, *Liberal Europe* (Harcourt Brace Jovanovich, 1974), John Weiss, *Conservatism in Europe* (Harcourt Brace Jovanovich, 1977).

Vol. 4 of A. Cobban's *A History of Modern France* (Penguin, 1970) is a useful survey. For greater detail see F. Artz *France Under the Bourbon Restoration, 1814–1830* (Russell, 1931); T. Howarth, *Citizen King: The Life of Louis-Philippe, King of the French* (Verry, 1961); G. Duveau, *1848: The Making of a Revolution* (Vintage, 1967), and F. A. Simpson, *Louis Napoleon and the Recovery of France* (Greenwood, 1975).

Two valuable surveys on Britain are Asa Briggs, *The Making of Modern England, 1783–1867: The Age of Improvement* (Torchbooks, 1959) and E. L. Woodward, *The Age of Reform, 1815–1870* (Oxford, 1962).

A. J. P. Taylor, *The Course of German History* (Capricorn, 1962) is a short, controversial essay on German national history since the French Revolution. T. Hamerow, *Restoration, Revolution, Reaction: Economics and Politics in Germany, 1815–1871* (Princeton, 1966) is highly praised. L. Namier's *1848: The Revolution of the Intellectuals* (Anchor, 1946) is critical of the liberals at Frankfurt. E. Eyck's balanced *Bismarck and the German Empire* (Norton, 1964) is offset by Taylor's hostile *Bismarck: The Man and the Statesman* (Alfred A. Knopf, 1955). O. Pflanze's *Bismarck and the Development of Germany: The Period of Unification, 1815–1871* (Princeton, 1963) is first-rate. Barbara Jelavich's *The Habsburg Empire in European Affairs* (Rand McNally, 1969) is an excellent, brief history. C. A. Macartney's *The Habsburg Empire: 1790–1918* (Weidenfeld and Nicholson, 1968) is thorough, but pro-Hungarian.

J. N. Westwood's *Endurance and Endeavour: Russian History 1812–1986* (Oxford, 1988) is the best new survey, replacing Hugh Seton-Watson's *The Russian Empire 1801–1917* (Oxford, 1967). Allen McConnell's *Tsar Alexander I* (Crowell, 1970) remains the best short biography. W. Bruce Lincoln's *In the Vanguard of Reform* (Northern Illinois, 1982) sets the standard for scholarship on Nicholas I. Deep insights into Russian intellectual development are to be found in N. Berdyaev's *The Russian Idea* (Beacon, 1962). The best introductory book on nineteenth-century Russia is Marc Raeff's *Understanding Imperial Russia* (Columbia, 1984).

Notes

1. Geoffrey Bruun, *Europe and the French Imperium* (New York: Harper & Row, 1938), p. 38.
2. L. C. B. Seaman, *From Vienna to Versailles* (New York: Harper and Row, 1963), p. 8.
3. Norman Davies, *Heart of Europe: A Short History of Poland* (Oxford: Oxford University Press, 1987), pp. 166–167.
4. Barbara Jelavich, *The Habsburg Empire in European Affairs: 1814–1918* (Chicago: Rand McNally & Co., 1969), pp. 21–39.
5. Jorg K. Hoensch, *A History of Modern Hungary: 1867–1986* (London: Longman, 1988), pp. 4–10.
6. For vivid characterizations of this period see Roger L. Williams, *The World Of Napoleon III: 1851–1870* (New York: Collier Books, 1962).
7. Quoted in J. S. Schapiro, *Modern and Contemporary European History: 1815–1940* (Boston: Houghton Mifflin Co., 1940), p. 222.
8. Quoted in K. S. Pinson, *Modern Germany* (New York: The Macmillan Company, 1954), p. 116.
9. Seaman, pp. 96–129.
10. See Allen McConnell's biography *Tsar Alexander I: Paternalistic Reformer* (New York: Crowell, 1970), for a clear treatment of this most complex personality.
11. W. Bruce Lincoln, *In the Vanguard of Reform* (DeKalb: Northern Illinois University Press, 1982), pp. 139–167.
12. J. N. Westwood, *Endurance and Endeavour: Russian History 1812–1986* (Oxford: Oxford University Press, 1987), pp. 79–103.
13. G. Bingham Powell, Jr., "Incremental Democratization: The British Reform Act of 1832," in G. A. Almond, S. C. Flanagan, and R. J. Mundt, eds., *Crisis, Choice, and Change* (Boston: Little, Brown, 1973), p. 149.

Chapter 25

Society, Politics, and Culture, 1871–1914

Since 1500 the European state system had been going through a process of competition and concentration; in the four centuries after 1500 the number of political units declined from around 500 to roughly 25.[1] The six largest survivors—Britain, Germany, France, Rusia, Italy, and the Austro-Hungarian monarchy—took advantage of their new material and economic power and adjusted more or less successfully to the challenges and opportunities presented by the times.

Industrialization gave some of these states immense material strength, economic power, and technology to affect the every day lives of their citizens. The states vastly expanded their activities in building up their armed forces, controlling the food supply, overseeing the economy, training technical personnel, increasing the police functions, and compiling statistical records.

During the second half of the nineteenth century, major European states turned their full attention to education. The increase in literacy and the corresponding growth of the mass circulation press during the latter part of the era brought politics to the common people and changed the nature of political life.

In the cultural realm, as in the areas of politics and economic growth, Europe experienced revolutionary changes by the end of the nineteenth century. "High culture" became more and more specialized, while increasing literacy created a wide market for popular novels and the sensationalist press among the lower middle class. Technology introduced new forms of popular entertainment, such as home photography, the cinema, and recorded music.

Modern, mass participation Europe came into existence between 1871 and 1914, built on the foundations of economic and demographic growth and dominated by astute politicians. By the end of the period, those states that had demonstrated the greatest flexibility in adapting to the new conditions—Britain, France, and Germany—would stand as Europe's most powerful countries.

Economic and Social Challenges: Political Responses

The Marxian Analysis

The middle of the nineteenth century did not in any way mark the arrival of workers as a major political force in Europe, but it was then that Karl Marx (1818–1883) made a major contribution to their cause through his ideological work. Marx and his colleague, Friedrich Engels (1820–1895) wrote the *Communist Manifesto* in late 1847. In it they outlined the theory of scientific socialism, sketched a wide-ranging program that advocated violent revolution, preached the inevitable conflict of the classes, rejected traditional morality and religion, and condemned contemporary governments. In so doing, they made the transition from a philosophical approach to social problems to a basis for modern socialist and communist movements. In the next three decades Marx conceptualized the framework he and Engels erected in the *Manifesto*.

Marx was born in Trier to middle-class Jewish parents who had converted to Protestantism.

Karl Marx and Friedrich Engels, Manifesto of the Communist Party

The Manifesto by Marx and Engels had little impact on 1848 Europe. However, it became one of the most widely read tracts in world history in the twentieth century.

A spectre is haunting Europe—the spectre of Communism. All the Powers of old Europe have entered into a holy alliance to exorcise this spectre; Pope and Czar, Metternich and Guizot, French Radicals and German police-spies.

. . . The first step in the revolution by the working class is to raise the proletariat to the position of ruling class, to win the battle of democracy.

The proletariat will use its political supremacy to wrest, by degrees, all capital from the bourgeoisie, to centralise all instruments of production in the hands of the State, i.e., of the proletariat organized by the ruling class; and to increase the total of productive forces as rapidly as possible.

. . . In the most advanced countries the following will be pretty generally applicable:

1. Abolition of property in land and application of all rents of land to public purposes.
2. A heavy progressive or graduated income tax.
3. Abolition of all right of inheritance.
4. Confiscation of the property of all emigrants and rebels.
5. Centralisation of credit in the hands of the State, by means of a national bank with State capital and an exclusive monopoly.
6. Centralisation of the means of communication and transport in the hands of the State.
7. Extension of factories and instruments of production owned by the State; the bringing into cultivation of waste lands, and the improvement of the soil generally in accordance with a common plan.
8. Equal liability of all to labour. Establishment of industrial armies, especially for agriculture.
9. Combination of agriculture with manufacturing industries; gradual abolition of the distinction between town and country, by a more equable distribution of the population over the country.
10. Free education for all children in public schools. Abolition of children's factory labour in its present form. Combination of education with industrial production, etc., etc.

When, in the course of development, class distinctions have disappeared, and all production has been concentrated in the hands of a vast association of the whole nation, the public power will lose its political character. Political power, properly so called, is merely the organised power of one class for oppressing another. If the proletariat during its contest with the bourgeoisie is compelled, by the force of circumstances, to organise itself as a class, if, by means of a revolution, it makes itself the ruling class, and, as such, sweeps away by force the old conditions of production, then it will, along with these conditions, have swept away the conditions for the existence of class antagonisms, and of classes generally, and will thereby have abolished its own supremacy as a class.

In place of the old bourgeois society, with its classes and class antagonisms, we shall have an association in which the free development of each is the condition for the free development of all.

From Karl Marx and Friedrich Engels, *Manifesto of the Communist Party* (International Press, 1911).

He attended the University of Berlin as a doctoral candidate in philosophy, instead of law as his father desired, and there joined a circle that followed some aspects of Hegel's thought. After finishing his degree, he could not find a university position, so he returned to the Rhineland where he began writing for a local liberal newspaper. The injustices he saw around him and his reading of the French Socialists Henri de Saint-Simon and Pierre Joseph Proudhon led him to concentrate on the economic factors in history. He went to Paris to continue his studies, met Engels, and was expelled by the authorities in 1845. From there he went first to Belgium and finally to England where, after 1848, he spent most of the rest of his life.

Marx was uncompromising in his hostility to capitalism, stating in the *Manifesto* that communists "openly declare that their ends can be attained only by the forcible overthrow of all existing social conditions." Virtually every day he made his way to the British Museum where he waged intellectual war on capitalism by doing research for his major works, especially *Das Kapital.*

At night he returned home to write, enduring difficult living conditions and the death of three of his children in the 1850s. He wrote prolifically, although suffering from boils, asthma, spleen and liver problems, and eye strain. His constant inability to handle money drove him into fits of rage against his creditors. He was increasingly intolerant of those who disagreed with him and became an embittered recluse; yet his vision and theories inspired reformers for the next century. Marx gave the oppressed an explanation for their difficult position and a hope for their future.

Marx held a materialistic view of history, stating that economic forces drove history. He did not deny the existence or importance of spiritual or philosophical values; nor did he doubt that the occasional genius could alter the flow of events. However, the material aspects of life were much more important. Marx believed that "it is not the consciousness of men which determines their existence, but on the contrary, it is the existence which determines their consciousness." As an economic determinist he believed that when the means of production of a given era changed, the whole social and ideological structure was transformed.

Karl Marx with his daughter. After being expelled from several European countries, Marx settled in England where he devoted himself to the development of his theory of scientific socialism.

Marx saw the productive forces of society as the key factor in history. The world was driven by class conflict between those who controlled the means of production and those who did not, whether master against slave in ancient Greece, patrician against plebeian in Rome, lord against serf in the middle ages, noble against bourgeois in the early modern times, or capitalist against the proletarian in the modern world. The world's history moved in this zigzag pattern through class struggle, a reflection of the Hegelian dialectic.

Hegel had written that history is made up of a number of cultural periods, each one the expression of a dominant spirit or idea. After fulfilling its purpose, a given period is replaced by a period of contradictory ideas or set of values. The original thesis is negated, and that negation in turn is also negated after it has run its course. Where Hegel saw history driven through a historical dialectic in cultural terms to a final phase, Marx saw history moving to its conclusion of the workers controlling the means of production.

The bourgeoisie, which had erected the new capitalist society by gaining control of the means of production through organizing trade and industry, created its opposition in the proletariat, the class-conscious workers. This group would be according to Marx, "the seeds of the bourgeoisie's own destruction." According to the dialectic, when the workers recognized their true power, they would overthrow the bourgeoisie. Out of this conflict would come the final act of the dialectical process, the classless society in which "each person would work according to his ability and receive according to his need." An interim dictatorship might have to occur, because a number of features of the old order would remain and the proletariat would have to be protected. However, as the classless society evolved, the state would wither away.

Through his research, Marx identified a number of defects that foretold the inevitable overthrow of the bourgeoisie, among them alienation and surplus value. The factory system turned workers into cogs in the larger machine, and deprived them of satisfaction in their work. In addition, Marx charged that owners did not pay workers for the value they created. A worker could, for example, produce in seven hours the necessary economic value to supply one individual's needs, but the owner would keep the worker laboring for twelve hours. The owner thereby took the "surplus value" of five working hours stolen from workers, thus robbing them of the fruits of their work.

Finally, Marx noted that in the capitalist system the rich got richer and fewer and the poor got poorer and more numerous. This produced huge discontent and increased the chance of revolution. Further, the masses would be unable to buy all of the goods they produced and economic crises of overproduction and unemployment would become the rule. In time, once the bourgeois phase of dominance had run its course, the contradictions between the classes would become so great that the proletariat would rise up and take over the means of production.

Marx was the last of the great universal theorists. As is the case with other ideologists in the rationalist eighteenth-century tradition he built on the foundations erected by others, making a creative synthesis that has had worldwide appeal. As was also the case with other major thinkers, his thoughts, which were often hypotheses, have been frozen in dogma or revised in various countries to take forms he would have trouble recognizing. It is not surprising that the rapidly changing age in which he lived would outrun many of his projections, especially those concerning the rigidity of the capitalists.

Labor Movements

Well before Marx conceived his theories, the British economy suffered through a difficult time after the end of the Napoleonic wars. High unemployment struck skilled workers, especially hand loom weavers. In frustration, some of them fought back and destroyed textile machines, the symbol of the forces oppressing them. Strikes, demonstrations, and incidents such as the tragedy at St. Peter's Fields (see p. 646) vividly expressed the workers' rage. Not until the British reformers came forward in the 1820s did the laborers begin to gain some relief.

Their efforts to form labor unions received an important boost in 1825 when the Combination Acts, passed in 1799 against the formation of workers' associations, were repealed. The first unions, such as the half-million strong Grand National Consolidated Trades Union, were weak

This plate commemorates a protest meeting of the Trades Union Congress held April 21, 1834, to present a petition to the king.

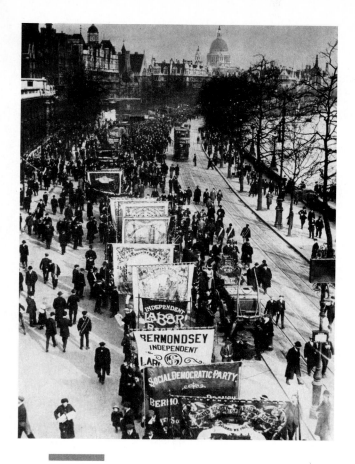

Socialist parties in the second half of the century helped the workers' movements by providing a theoretical basis and an agressive public statement of their case. Karl Marx, who spent his life researching and writing in the defense of the proletariat—even though he had precious little contact with them, organized the International Organization of Workers, the First International, in London in 1864. The First International included labor activists ranging from English trades unions to East European refugees to anarchists to German theorists.

Not much came of the First International's efforts because of constant arguments among the factions and Marx's vindictiveness towards other major figures such as the Russian anarchist Bakunin. Defeat of the Paris Commune in 1871 (see p. 660) delivered a devastating blow to the French socialist movement. However, the Social Democrats—Marxian socialists—made important gains in Germany, forcing Bismarck to make concessions (see p. 662). It became the largest party in the country and the strongest socialist

This 1848 lithograph by Honoré Daumier contrasts the gluttonous bourgeois in his frock coat and top hat with the shabbily dressed workingman.

In this workers' demonstration in London, the banners of trade unions follow the standard of the Social Democratic party. Workers banded together to protect themselves from powerful business corporations.

and disorganized, split by the gulf between skilled workers and common laborers. Nonetheless, the workers laid the foundations for the powerful unions that defended them by the end of the century.

As industry became more sophisticated and centralized, so too did the labor movement. Across Europe the workers could choose anarchist, socialist, or conservative paths to follow. Some unions centered on a particular occupation—the trade or the craft unions. Others found their focus in the various productive stages of an industry, while still others, such as the English Trade Unions Congress, were nationwide and all-encompasing, wielding great power. Whatever the choice, by 1900 unions had made important advances through their solidarity in launching paralyzing strikes.

party in Europe under the leadership of its founder, Ferdinand Lassalle. In 1871 there were two socialists in the *Reichstag;* by 1912 the number had risen to 110.

In the three decades after Marx's death in 1883 his theories dominated the European workers' movements, even if those movements themselves were not united. The French split into three distinct socialist groups. Some British socialists were greatly influenced by the maxims of Christianity, while the Fabian Society—among whose members were George Bernard Shaw, H. G. Wells, and Sidney and Beatrice Webb—pursued a more prosaic political path. With the spread of industrialization, workers and their leaders found important support in Marx's work even in places such as Russia, where Marx had never foreseen his thoughts having any influence. Because of the widespread impact of Marx's ideas in the social sciences and the labor movement, "the period of the Second International (1889–1914) may be called without any exaggeration the golden age of Marxism."[2] A broad spectrum of thinkers among the twelve million members of the Second International claimed Marx as their inspiration, even though they might differ on the role of the state, the functions of unions, the crisis of capitalism, or the role of the proletariat. There was not a single, monolithic Marxist movement in Europe. Yet despite their philosophical difference, the Social Democrats in all countries could agree on essential needs for the workers: an eight-hour day, the need to replace standing armies with militias, and the welfare state buttressed by universal suffrage.

The socialist movement strengthened labor unions, and the workers achieved substantial progress by 1914. Whether by working within the various states' legislatures or by raising the specter of revolution, the unions and their socialist allies helped bring about substantial reforms in the economy, labor practices, civil rights, the courts, and education. They pushed the capitalists to reform, thus avoiding the apocalyptic revolution forecast by Marx.

By 1914, although the workers could not negotiate on an equal basis with the owners, they had vastly improved their position over that endured by their grandparents. The British movement had four million members and was a powerful force, while German unions benefited members in a broad number of areas from life insurance to travel. The income gap between rich and poor began to narrow by 1914. Working hours were shortened and living conditions improved. The real wages of workers, that is, the amount of goods that their income could actually buy, increased by 50 perecent in the industrial nations in the last thirty years of the nineteenth century.

The Middle Classes

The greatest beneficiaries of industrialization were the *bourgeoisie,* the middle classes. They profited directly from the new industrial economy. Their newfound wealth, harnessed to the social and legal changes that resulted from the French Revolution on the continent and the reform movement in Britain, allowed them to dominate all aspects of European life.

While it is difficult to give a strict definition of the bourgeoisie, it is easier to say who was *not* middle class. Neither factory workers and peasants nor the aristocracy were included. Those closer to the laboring classes were called the lower middle classes, or the *petite bourgeoisie* while those near the élite were the upper middle classes, or the *haute bourgeoisie.* Included in the lower middle classes were skilled artisans, bureaucrats, clerks, teachers, shopkeepers, and the clergy. They realized how little separated them from the laboring masses and were constantly trying to climb socially. Later in the century they benefitted most from the compulsory education laws and were avid consumers of the books written by the new wave of authors, the penny-press newspapers, and state propaganda. Both literate and numerous, they played a key role in political affairs.

The *haute bourgeoisie* controlled most of the wealth created by industrialization. In fact, they were often much richer than the nobles. It was not easy to gain admittance to this level of society, but money, taste, and aggressiveness could open the doors for the bankers, factory owners, lawyers, architects, occasional professors, doctors, or high governmental officials who tried. Once admitted, they gained access to many of the benefits of the aritocracy such as the best

Queen Victoria's sitting room at Osborne House, her personal residence. The room, with its clutter of photographs, sentimental paintings, and heavy furniture, epitomizes the Victorian style.

schools, shops, restaurants, and cultural life. Because of their wealth and leisure time they dominated politics, the press, and the universities.

The British upper middle class was a group riddled with contradictions. The age in which they lived has come to be labeled the Victorian period, after Victoria (1837–1901), the long-reigning English queen. On the surface the Victorians had little doubt about what was right and wrong, moral and immoral, and most importantly, proper and improper. Underneath this surface propriety the middle classes pursued—as recent research indicates—a life marked by sexuality, perverted passion, and drug addiction. The prime minister of the era, William Gladstone, devoted considerable attention to reforming prostitutes. The Victorian literary establishment concentrated on "cleaning up" Shakespeare's plays and toning down some parts of Gibbon's *Decline and Fall of the Roman Empire.*

The British upper middle class employed more than two and a half million servants at century's end—nearly a million people more than farmed the land—and led crusades against slavery, alcohol, pornography, and child labor. Their efforts led to the passage of a series of reforms limiting the employment of young children, setting maximum working hours for teenagers, and regulating working conditions for women—even when the factory owners argued that such changes were bad for the country because they

violated the freedom of contract between the worker and the employer. The British upper middle class set the tone to be imitated by their peers across the continent.[3]

The Leninist Critique

Western Europe responded successfully to the changes brought on by industrialization during the nineteenth century, but Russia presented an entirely different picture. The Russians did not experience the most demanding parts of industrialization until the end of the century and then on a different basis from that of the western European countries. Russia remained an overwhelmingly agrarian society in which the state paid for building factories by using grain produced by the peasants for export on the depressed world market. The government did little to aid the transition from an agrarian to an industrial society and crushed opposition political movements. In 1900 Russia lacked a tradition of gradual reform and the habits of compromise such as existed in England. The government controlled its populace through the use of force.

In this troubled environment, the solutions proposed by Karl Marx attracted a number of supporters. Marx himself did not believe that Russia would be a favorable laboratory for his theories, and he expressed surprise when *Das*

Lenin, the main force of the Russian Revolution from which emerged the Soviet Union, spent years studying Marx's theories and adapting them to conditions in Russia.

Kapital was translated into Russian in 1872 and pleasure when he learned of the broad impact of his theories there. Not until 1898, however, was there an attempt to establish a Russian Social Democratic party.

The nature of Marx's theories sparked debate over the way in which they applied to Russia. The thinker and actor who would eventually apply and implement Marxist theory was Vladimir Ilich Ulyanov (1870–1924), who later took the name of Lenin. Born in Ulyanovsk, formerly Simbirsk, a small city along the Volga river, Lenin grew up in the moderate and respectable circumstances provided by his father, a school administrator and teacher. In 1887, the government arrested and executed Lenin's brother, Alexander, in St. Petersburg for plotting against the life of the tsar.

Shortly thereafter Lenin began to master the writings of Marx and to study the situation in which Russia found itself. He overcame major obstacles from tsarist officials and passed his law exams at St. Petersburg University without formally attending classes.

After 1893 he began to compile his theories of tactics and strategy that continue to form the bulk of twentieth-century dogma. In 1895 a court sentenced him to exile in Siberia for his political activities. Although in exile, he enjoyed complete liberty of movement in the district and could hunt, fish, swim, study, read, and keep up a large correspondence. His comrade, Nadezhda Krupskaia, joined him and they were married. Later they translated Sidney and Beatrice Webb's *The History of Trade Unionism*. Lenin's exile ended in 1900 when he and Krupskaia went to Switzerland where they joined other Russian Social Democrats in exile in founding the newspaper *Iskra* ("*Spark*," whose motto was "From the Spark—the conflagration").

In applying Marx to Russian conditions, Lenin found it necessary to sketch in several blank spots. Lenin's methods differed greatly from those of western European Marxists, as did his theories. Lenin advocated the formation of a small élite of professional revolutionaries, the vanguard of the proletariat. These professionals, subject to strict party discipline, would anticipate the proletariat's needs and best interests and lead them . . . to the oxymoronic theory of "democratic centralism." After 1903 Lenin had little success in changing the political conditions of Russia, beyond affecting the most sophisticated part of the workers' movement. However, he continued to make significant doctrinal contributions. Lenin recommended a socialism whose weapon was violence and whose tactics allowed little long-range compromise with the bourgeoisie. However, he also saw the advantages of flexibility and encouraged temporary deviations that might serve the goals of the working class. He took little for granted and reasoned that the development of class unity to destroy the capitalists among the Russian workers might require some assistance. To that end he refined his notion of the way in which the élite party would function. In revolution the élite party would infiltrate the government, police, and army while participating in legal workers' movements; in government the party would enforce its dictates on the populace with iron discipline.

The Romantic spirit often expressed itself in architecture in Gothic revival, a style best represented by London's Houses of Parliament, designed by Sir Charles Barry (1795–1860), with details designed by A. W. N. Pugin (1812–52). The horizontal symmetry of the buildings is broken by tall, irregularly spaced towers. At the west end is the elaborate Victoria tower and at the east, the smaller clock tower, probably designed by Pugin.

Two leading Romantic painters were the English landscape painter John Constable and the French artist Eugène Delacroix. In *Salisbury Cathedral from the Bishop's Garden* (c. 1826), left, Constable is less concerned with details of the scene than with conditions of light, atmosphere, and sky, which he regarded as "the chief organ of sentiment." Delacroix' sensuous use of color and his love of exotic settings are evident in *Women of Algiers* (1834), below, inspired by the artist's 1832 trip to Morocco.

Rejecting the historical, religious, and mythological themes of the painters who preceded him, Gustave Courbet chose to portray what he saw—the contemporary life of the world around him. For this he was soundly criticized by his contemporaries. Critics attacked *Young Ladies from the Village Giving Alms to a Cowherd* (1851—52) for its "ugliness," vulgarity, lack of perspective, and violation of tradition. Yet it is these same attributes that made Courbet a revolutionary figure in the history of art.

Portfolio Seven

A concern for the effects of light and color united the impressionists, yet each also developed a personal style. Often regarded as the boldest innovator was Claude Monet, who did series of paintings of the same subject, such as *Water Lilies* (1906), opposite page. Mary Cassatt specialized in paintings of mothers and children, as in *The Bath* (1891–92), above left. With its vibrant color and shimmering light, *On the Terrace* (1881), above right, is a typical work of Auguste Renoir. Careful control of line, calculated design, and off-center composition are hallmarks of Edgar Degas, evident in *A Woman with Chrysanthemums* (completed in 1865), left.

Originally associated with the impressionists, Paul Cézanne became dissatisfied with the limitations of impressionist style and began a relentless search for the structure and form beneath the color. *Montagne Sainte-Victoire* (1904) is one of a long series Cézanne painted of a mountain scene near his home in Aix-en-Provence. It was works like this that had such a profound influence on the cubists and expressionists who followed Cézanne.

Vincent van Gogh was less interested in the photographic reproduction of nature than in the recreation of his vision of what he saw, expressed through his use of brilliant, intense, unmodulated color and dynamic brush strokes. The swirling, exploding stars in *The Starry Night* (1889), painted at the sanatorium at St.-Rémy during one of van Gogh's lucid periods, seem to express the artist's turbulent emotions.

A growing disenchantment with the values and traditions of Western civilization led Paul Gauguin (1848–1903) to Tahiti, where he spent a number of years living in accord with the local life-style. In its carved look, bold pattern, tropical colors, and subject matter drawn from primitive life, *The Red Dog* (1892) is typical of Gauguin's later works in which the origins of modern primitivism can be found.

Portfolio Seven

Lenin looked out at the undoubted strength of the advanced technological nation state and marveled at its extension of power. In his *Imperialism, the Highest Stage of Capitalism* (1916) he forecast that the modern capitalist states would destroy themselves. He argued that the wages of the workers did not represent enough purchasing power to absorb the output of the capitalists' factories, and that the vast amounts of capital that were accumulated could not be invested profitably in the home country. Therefore, the states would engage in an inevitable competition for markets, resources, and capitals that would drive them from cutthroat competition to outright war and their ultimate destruction. At that point, he reasoned his élite party would be ready to pick up the pieces from the blindly selfish powers.

The Modern State

By the end of the 19th century the major European states had transformed themselves to head off "inevitable" class conflict and to tap into the forces that raised the general level of prosperity. The states became unprecedentedly richer, more powerful, and more effective. New technology enabled them to touch the everyday lives of their citizens. They formed huge conscript armies, increased taxation, established universal education, improved medical and social support services, and installed communications networks. The states generated so much energy that they fueled Europe's imperialist expansion across the globe (see ch. 26) while improving the material lives of citizens at home.

The Committee of Public Safety during the French Revolution and then Napoleon Bonaparte had recognized the essential need for mass public education.[4] The state could not use illiterates for their jobs or as citizens. By 1900 all of the major states had invested heavily in education, and the evolution of the popular press to accommodate mass literacy helped change the nature of political life. Politics went from the reasoned discourse of the drawing rooms of the élite to the crude rhetoric of mass movements that reflected working class and middle class values.

With the increased effectiveness of communications brought by the railroads, the telephone, and the telegraph, nations became much more unified and governments intervened directly in each individual's life. The kept statistics and records of each citizen's life and exercised control over such matters as food supply and public order. As wealth and population grew, so did the number of bureaucracies. In two areas in Germany, the postal service and railroads, the number of employees soared from 245,000 in 1880 to nearly 700,000 in 1910.[5] Further, military conscription touched the lives of most young men, except in Britain. By 1897 France and Germany each had nearly 3,500,000 men in the field or on reserve, and these soldiers were better and more expensively armed than ever before.

The states tapped an increasing tax base to finance their augmented functions. The German empire's income grew from 263 million marks in 1873 to over 1200 million marks in 1909.[6] Other governments, even the poorest, registered comparable increases. By 1914, the states that were the most flexible—Britain, Germany, and France—were the most powerful. Russia, Italy, and the Austro-Hungarian monarchy struggled to remain great powers.

Britain and Democracy

Blessed by its wealth and adaptability, Britain built a truly democratic political structure by 1914. The state continued to support business even as it became more intimately involved in matters affecting the welfare of its citizens. Two great statesmen, William Ewart Gladstone (1809–1898), a Liberal, and Benjamin Disraeli (1804–1881), a Conservative, dominated the first part of this period with their policies of gradual reform. They alternated as prime minister from 1867 to 1880. After Disraeli's death, Gladstone prevailed until he retired in 1894.

Gladstone and Disraeli

The two leaders came from sharply contrasting backgrounds. The son of a rich Liverpool merchant, Gladstone had every advantage that wealth and good social position could give him. He entered Parliament in 1833 and quickly became one of the greatest orators of his day. He began as a Conservative, working in the tradition

In this *Punch* cartoon, political rivals William Gladstone (left) and Benjamin Disraeli (right) are ready to sling mud at each other. The cartoon's caption reads, "A Bad Example."

of the Tory reformer, Robert Peel. Gradually he shifted his alliance to the newly formed Liberal party in the 1850s and became a strong supporter of laissez-faire economics and worked to keep government from interfering in business. He was a far more effective political than social or economic reformer.

Disraeli had few of Gladstone's advantages. The son of a Jew who became a naturalized British subject in 1801, Disraeli was baptized an Anglican. He first made a name for himself as the author of the novel *Vivian Grey* (1826). In contrast to Gladstone, Disraeli went from liberalism to conservatism in his philosophy. He stood for office as a Conservative throughout his career and became the leader of the party.

Both Liberals and Conservatives had to face the fact that the complacency of government during the "Victorian Compromise" from 1850 to 1865 could not continue. The alliance of landed gentry and middle classes may have successfully kept the lower classes "in their stations" but serious problems plagued the country. Only one adult male in six was entitled to vote. Both parties felt the pressure to make the political

system more representative. Both parties also knew that reform must come, and each hoped to gain the credit and resultant strength for extending the vote.

The Liberals' turn came first. In 1866 they introduced a moderate reform bill enfranchising city workers. Some conservatives opposed it, fearful that increasing the franchise would bring the day of revolution closer. When the proposal failed to pass, political agitation and riots rocked the country. The outbreaks evidently impressed the members of Parliament and when the Conservatives came to power in 1867, Disraeli successfully sponsored the Second Reform Bill that added more than a million city workers to the voting rolls. The measure increased the electorate by 88 percent, although women and farm laborers were still denied the vote.

Even though the Conservatives passed the voter reform, the new elections in 1868 brought the Liberals back to power and Gladstone began his so-called Glorious Ministry, which lasted until 1874. With the granting of the vote to the urban masses it became imperative to educate their children. The Education Act of 1870 promoted the establishment of local school boards to build and maintain state schools. Private schools received governmental subsidies if they could meet certain minimal standards. Elementary school attendance, which was compulsory between the ages of five and fourteen, jumped from 1 to 4 million in ten years.

Other reforms included a complete overhaul of the civil service system. Previously, in both the government and military, appointments and promotions depended on patronage and favoritism. But in 1870, this method was replaced by open examinations. The government also improved the military by shortening enlistment terms, abolishing flogging, and stopping the sale of officers' rank. Gladstone's government successfully revamped the justice system and introduced the secret ballot. Finally, some restrictions on labor unions' activities were removed. By 1872 the Glorious Ministry had exhausted itself, and Disraeli referred to Gladstone and his colleagues in the House of Commons as a "range of exhausted volcanoes."

Disraeli's government succeeded the Glorious Ministry in 1874, and he stated that he was going to "give the country a rest." He was no stand-pat conservative, however. He supported an approach known as Tory democracy that attempted to weld an alliance between the landed gentry and the workers against the middle class. Even during this "time of rest" Disraeli's government pushed through important reforms in public housing, food and drug legislation, and union rights to strike and picket peacefully.

Gladstone returned to power in 1880 and continued the stream of reforms with the Third Reform Bill that extended the vote to agricultural workers. This act brought Britain to the verge of universal male suffrage. Gladstone also secured passage of the Employers' Liability Act, which gave workers rights of compensation in case of accidents on the job.

The Irish Problem

One dilemma escaped and continues to escape the solutions of well-meaning reformers in Britain, that of British rule in Ireland. The present-day crisis in Northern Ireland originated in the seventeenth century. The British placed large numbers of Scottish emigrants in the province of Ulster, in northern Ireland, building a strong colony of Protestants—the so-called Orangemen, or Scotch-Irish. In the eighteenth century the British passed a number of oppressive laws against the Irish Catholics, restricting their political, economic, and religious freedom and effectively taking their lands. Passage of the Act

of Union in 1801 forced the Irish to send their representatives to the Parliament in London. A large part of the Irish farmland passed into the hands of parasitic landlords who leased their newly gained lands in increasingly smaller plots to more and more people. Many peasants could not pay their rent and were evicted from the land. The Irish lost both their representation and their livelihood.

In 1845 the potato crop, the main staple of diet, failed and a terrible famine ensued, which led to a tremendous decline in population. Hundreds of thousands emigrated to the United States; perhaps as many as 500,000 people died. Between 1841 and 1891 the population fell by more than 40 percent, from 8,770,000 to less than 5,000,000.

The Irish gained a few concessions from the British during the century in the form of the Catholic Emancipation Act (1829) and protection from arbitrary eviction for tenants, during the Glorious Ministry. The Irish Anglican Church lost its favored position when Roman Catholics were freed of the obligation to pay tax support to a church they did not attend. In 1881 Gladstone pushed through an act that allowed the Irish peasants the chance gradually to regain land that had once been theirs.

None of these concessions made up for the lack of home rule and in 1874 the Irish patriot Charles Stewart Parnell (1846–1891) began to work actively to force the issue through Parliament.

Wracked by poverty and famine, Ireland was further tormented during the 1840s by the mass eviction of tenant farmers. After the evictions, cottages were burned down at once to prevent other homeless farmers from occupying them.

Gladstone introduced home rule bills in 1886 and 1893, but both were defeated. A home rule bill was finally passed in 1914, but by this time the Ulsterites strongly opposed the measure and prepared to resist by force incorporation into Catholic Ireland. The outbreak of war with Germany postponed civil strife, but this was only a two-year delay until the Easter Uprising of 1916. Not until 1921 did southern Ireland finally gain the status of a British dominion. The home rule bill never went into effect.

The New Liberals

Gladstone's fight for Irish home rule split his party and paved the way for a decade of Conservative rule in Britain (1895–1905). Partly because of foreign and imperial affairs, the Conservatives departed from the reformist traditions of Tory democracy. By 1905 the need for social and political reform again claimed the attention of the parties.

Over 30 percent of the adult male laborers made the unacceptably low wage of less than seven dollars a week. It was impossible to save for periods of unemployment and emergencies. Workers demonstrated their discontent in a number of strikes. Partially in response to the workers' needs and at the prompting of the Fabian Socialists the Labour party was founded in 1900, under the leadership of J. Ramsay MacDonald (1866–1937), a self-made intellectual who had risen from humble status, and the Scottish miner Keir Hardie (1856–1915). The liberals found themselves threatened on both their left and right flanks. They decided to abandon their laissez-faire economic concepts and embrace a bold program of social legislation. The radical Welsh lawyer Lloyd George portrayed their program. "Four spectres haunt the poor: Old Age, Accident, Sickness, and Unemployment. We are going to exorcise them."[7]

Led by prime minister Herbert Asquith, Lloyd George, and the young Winston Churchill who had defected from the Conservatives, the Liberal party—with the aid of the Labour bloc—put through a broad program. It provided for old-age pensions, national employment bureaus, workers' compensation protection, and sickness, accident, and unemployment insurance. In addition, labor unions were relieved of financial responsibility for losses caused by strikes. Members of the House of Commons, until that time unpaid, were granted a moderate salary. This last act allowed an individual without independent wealth to pursue a political career.

The House of Lords tried to block the Liberal reform plan by not passing the 1909–1910 budget, which laid new tax burdens, including an income tax, on the richer classes in order to pay for the new programs. The Liberals and Labour fought back by directly attacking the rationale for the Lords' existence. They argued that a hereditary, irresponsible upper house was an anachronism in a democracy. The result was the Parliament Bill of 1911 that took away the Lords' power of absolute veto. Asquith announced that the king had promised to create enough new peers to pass the bill if needed (a tactic used with the 1832 Reform Bill). The Lords had to approve and thereafter could only delay and force reconsideration of legislation.

By 1914 the evolutionary path to democracy and a modern democratic state structure had been largely completed, except for women's suffrage. In the previous generation some effort had been put in to gain the vote for women, but by and large the effort had been unsuccessful. Women's suffrage was not a major concern for the major parties, most of whom felt that women's proper place was in the home. At the turn of the century the most effective group to work for women's rights was the Women's Social and Political Union (WSPU), whose members were the first to be known as suffragettes. Its founder, Emmeline Pankhurst (1858–1928), first agitated, then disturbed, and then challenged the order and stability of England in the decade before World War I. Pankhurst and her colleagues traveled and worked constantly to make the case for the vote for women, and to 1910 the WPSU abandoned traditional rhetoric in favor of mass marches, hunger strikes, and property damage. In 1913 a young suffragette martyred herself by running in front of the king's horse at the Derby.[8] With the outbreak of the war, the WPSU backed the national effort against the Germans, and finally in 1918 women age thirty and over were granted the vote. Ten years later, they gained equal voting rights with men.

Emmeline Pankhurst, in white scarf, at a rally protesting a government unresponsive to women's issues. After 1910, the women's suffrage movement turned increasingly militant.

The Second Reich to 1914

Within the brief span of one lifetime, the fragmented German areas of central Europe successfully united under Prussian, that is, Hohenzollern, leadership to challenge Britain for world leadership. Bismarck provided the initial genius to bring about unification, but the source of German strength was found in its rapid economic growth, population increase, and efficient political structure. Prussia's success drew the enthusiastic support of prominent businessmen, intellectuals, and artists and the increasing concern of its neighbors.

The Second Reich came into existence at a ceremony in January 1871 in the Hall of Mirrors at the Palace of Versailles. There King William I became emperor of a federal union of twenty-six states with a population of 41 million. The bicameral (two-house) legislature of the new empire consisted of a *Bundesrat*, representing the ruling houses of the various states, and a *Reichstag*, representing the people through its 397 members elected by male suffrage. The dominant power rested with the emperor, who controlled military and foreign affairs and the seventeen votes in the *Bundesrat* needed to veto any constitutional change.

Bismarck as Chancellor

The actual head of government was the chancellor who was appointed by the kaiser and responsible to him only. This arrangement allowed the chancellor to defy or ignore the legislature if it served his purpose. However, he had to operate within the constraints of the federal state structure in which large powers of local government were given to the member states. Bismarck was more constrained in domestic than in foreign affairs. It is not surprising, therefore, that he fared better in foreign matters. As chancellor, Bismarck built modern Germany on his belief in the inherent efficiency of a state based on one faith, one law, and one ruler. He distrusted those institutions that did not fit that tripartite formula: specifically the Catholic church and the Socialist party.

The Catholic political party had sent a large bloc of representatives to the *Reichstag* in 1871, and these members supported the complete independence of the church from state control, denounced divorce, objected to secular education, and questioned freedom of conscience. Many Catholics strongly supported the new dogma of papal infallibility (see p. 682). Within the Protestant Prussian part of Germany Bismarck introduced anti-Catholic policies that triggered a conflict known as the *Kulturkampf* (the struggle for civilization). These so-called May laws made it an offense for the clergy to criticize the government, regulated the educational activities of the religious orders, and expelled the Jesuits from the country. The state also required civil marriages and dictated that all priests study theology at state universities. Pope Pius IX declared these acts null and void and told loyal Catholics to refuse to obey them. Many of the chancellor's laws applied equally to Protestants, who actively protested them.

As opposition spread, Bismarck struck hard at the Catholics, imprisoning priests, confiscating church property, and closing down pulpits. When the tide did not turn in his favor, he realized that he could not afford to create millions of martyrs. Showing his shrewd sense of power, he cut his losses, retreated, and repealed most of the anti-Catholic laws.

The Social Democratic (Marxist) movement posed a greater challenge to Bismarck's rule. The party's founder, Ferdinand Lassalle (1825–1864) rejected violence as a means to gain power and instead advocated working within the existing political structure. After his death the movement retained its nonviolent nature. The party's popularity soared when it was officially established in 1875 and its leaders pushed for true parliamentary democracy and wideranging social programs.

In 1878 Bismarck used two attempts on the emperor's life as an excuse to launch an all-out campaign to weaken the Social Democrats, even though they had no connection with the acts. He dissolved extralegal socialist organizations, suppressed their publications, and threw their leaders in jail. Despite these measures the socialists continued to gain support.

When he failed to weaken the socialists by direct confrontation, the chancellor changed tactics. He decided to undercut them by taking over their program. Through the 1880s he implemented important social legislation that provided wage earners with sickness, accident, and old-age insurance. He sponsored other laws that responded to many of the abuses workers encountered. The Social Democrats continued to grow in size and influence. However, by creating the first welfare state, the pragmatic Prussian chancellor defused a potential revolution.

Kaiser William II

In 1888 William II, the grandson of the emperor, became head of the Reich. Just as Bismarck had dominated European affairs since 1862, the new emperor would play a key role until 1918. Here was a person who, without Bismarck's finesse, advocated a policy of "blood and iron." Where Bismarck knew the limits and uses of force and appreciated the nuances of public statements, William was a militarist and a bully. Serving in a modern age, the new emperor still believed in the divine right of kings and constantly reminded his entourage that "he and God" worked together for the good of the state. With such a contrast in styles, it is not surprising that William saw Bismarck not as a guide but as a threat. He once stated that "it was a question of whether the Bismarck dynasty or the Hohenzollern dynasty should rule."[9] Finally, in March 1890 Bismarck resigned.

At the beginning of the twentieth century Germany presented a puzzling picture to the world. On the one hand the blustering kaiser made fiery and warlike statements. He encouraged militarism and the belief that *Alles kommt von oben* ("Everything comes down from above"). On the other hand his thoroughly advanced country made great scientific and cultural strides. Observers of German affairs noted that one-third of the voters supported the Social Democrats, an indication of a healthy parliamentary system. A commonly held pride in Germany's accomplishments knit the country together.

More important than William's behavior was the fact that by the beginning of the new century the Germans competed actively in all areas with the British. Although Germany did not

Kaiser William II's Naval Ambitions

Kaiser William knew Germany had a grand future, an expanding future. He wanted Germans to travel on the high seas, to the dismay of the British.

In spite of the fact that we have no such fleet as we should have, we have conquered for ourselves a place in the sun. It will now be my task to see to it that this place in the sun shall remain our undisputed possession, in order that the sun's rays may fall fruitfully upon our activity and trade in foreign parts, that our industry and agriculture may develop within the state and our sailing sports upon the water, for our future lies upon the water. The more Germans go out upon the waters, whether it be in the races of regattas, whether it be in journeys across the ocean, or in the service of the battle-flag, so much the better will it be for us. For when the German has once learned to direct his glance upon what is distant and great, the pettiness which surrounds him in daily life on all sides will disappear.

From C. Gauss, *The German Kaiser as Shown in His Public Utterances* (New York: Charles Scribner's Sons, 1915).

---

outproduce Britain, long-term projections showed that the island nation's growth had leveled out and that in the next generation the Reich would surpass it. The Germans dominated the world market in the chemical and electrical industries and were making strides in other areas. They boasted a more efficient organization of their industries, a higher literacy rate for their workers, better vocational training, and a more aggressive corps of businessmen. German labor unions were less combative than the British, while the government gave more support to industry than did Parliament.

The French Third Republic to 1914

The defeat of France's Second Empire at the battle of Sedan in 1870 gave birth to the Third Republic. The humiliating peace terms that stripped France of a part of Lorraine and all of Alsace and imposed a huge indemnity on the country created a desire for revenge. The spectacle of the Germans crowning their emperor and proclaiming the Second Reich at Versailles, the symbol of French greatness, left a bitter taste.

Persistent class conflicts, covered over during Louis Napoleon's reign, also contributed to many years of shaky existence before the republic gained a firm footing. A new, overwhelmingly royalist national assembly was elected to construct a new, conservative government after the signing of the peace. This added to the shock of the defeat touched off a revolutionary outburst that led to the Paris Commune (1871).

Shaky Beginnings

Parisians had suffered such severe food shortages during the seige of the city that some had been forced to eat rats and zoo animals. When it turned out that their sacrifices had been in vain, republican and radical Parisians joined forces in part of the city to form a commune, in the tradition of the 1792 Paris Commune (see p. 562), to save the republic. The Communards advocated government control of prices, wages, and working conditions (including stopping night work in the bakeries). After several weeks of civil strife, the commune was savagely put down. Class hatred split France further yet.

Because the two monarchist factions that constituted a majority could not agree on an acceptable candidate for the monarchy, they finally settled on a republic as the least disagreeable form of government. The national assembly approved the new republican constitution in 1875. Unde the new system, members of the influential lower house—the Chamber of Deputies—was elected by direct suffrage. There was also a

Senate, whose members were elected indirectly by electoral colleges in the departments. The constitution established a weak executive, elected by the legislature. The ministry exercised real power, but its authority depended on whatever coalition of parties could be assembled to form a tenuous majority in the legislature.

The Boulanger and Dreyfus Affairs

The stormy tenure of the Third Republic was marked by a series of crises such as increased anarchist violence leading up to a series of bombings in 1893, financial scandals such as the notorious Panama Canal venture that implicated a wide range of leading figures, and lesser scandals. The two most serious threats were the Boulanger and Dreyfus affairs.

The weak and traumatized republic was both threatened and embarrassed by the public cries for vengeance uttered in 1886 by General Georges Boulanger (1837–1891), the minister of war. This charismatic, warmongering figure made a series of speeches which he ended by emotionally proclaiming: "Remember, they are waiting for us in Alsace." The considerable number of anti-republicans saw him as a man on horseback who would sweep away the republic in a *coup d'état*, much as Louis Napoleon had done in 1851 and bring back French grandeur. The government finally ordered Boulanger's arrest on a charge of conspiracy, and he fled the country. Later, he committed suicide.

The Dreyfus case was far more serious because it polarized the entire country, divided and embittered French opinion by the anti-Semitic fervor it unleashed and challenged the fundamental ideals of French democracy. Captain Alfred Dreyfus (1859–1935), the first Jewish officer on the French general staff, was accused in 1894 of selling military secrets to Germany. His fellow officers tried him, found him guilty, stripped him of his commission, and condemned him to solitary confinement on Devil's Island, a dreadful convict settlement off the northeast coast of South America. Even with the case supposedly settled, military secrets continued to leak to the Germans, and subsequently a royalist, spendthrift officer named Major Esterhazy was accused, tried, and acquitted.

Captain Alfred Dreyfus had to pass through this "Guard of Dishonor" each day on his way to the courtroom during his second trial in 1899.

The case became a *cause célèbre* in 1898 when the French writer Emile Zola (1840–1902) wrote his famous letter *J'accuse* ("I accuse"), in which he attacked the judge for knowingly allowing the guilty party to go free while Dreyfus remained in jail. The next year Esterhazy admitted his guilt, but by that time the entire country had split into two camps. On the one side were the anti-Dreyfusards—the army, church, and royalists; on the other side were the pro-Dreyfusards—the intellectuals, socialists, and republicans. The case was once again placed under review in the military courts, and even though Esterhazy had confessed, the court continued to find Dreyfus guilty. Finally, the French president pardoned him and in 1906 the highest civil court in France found him innocent.

The case had greater significance than just the fate of one man. Those who had worked against Dreyfus, especially the church, would pay dearly for their stand. Many republicans believed that the church, a consistent ally of the monarchists, was the natural enemy of democratic government. They demanded an end to the church's official ties to the state. In 1904 and 1905 the government closed all church schools and repudiated the Napoleonic Concordat. All ties between church and state were formally ended.

After weathering forty difficult years, by 1914 the Third Republic had gained prosperity and stability. Workers had gained their voice in the country as the various trade and local union groups came together in the *Confédération Générale du Travail*, the General Confederation of Labor. Monarchists and other right-wing parties still had considerable influence, although the Dreyfus affair had weakened them.

French republicanism had wide support across the political spectrum. Most French citizens had basic democratic rights which were pursued through the extremely complex multiparty political system of the republic. The various ministries that were constructed from the fragile coalitions came and went with bewildering rapidity. Yet France was strong, prosperous, and one of only two republics among the world's great powers.

Russia: Reformers, Reactionaries, Revolutionaries

While Alexander II pushed through the "Great Reforms," the revolutionary movement grew stronger. In the 1850s the nihilist movement developed, questioning all old values, championing the freedom of the individual, and shocking the older generation. At first the nihilists tried to convert the aristocracy to the cause of reform. Failing there, they turned to the peasants in an almost missionary frenzy. Some of the idealistic young men and women joined the movement to work in the fields with the peasants, while others went to the villages as doctors and teachers to preach the message of reform. This "go to the people" campaign was known as the populist, or *narodnik*, movement. Not surprisingly, the peasants largely ignored the outsiders' message.

Revolutionary Response

Frustrated by this rejection, the idealistic young people turned more and more to terrorism. The radical branch of the nihilists, under

the influence of Bakunin's protege Sergei Nechaev (1847–1882), pursued a program of the total destruction of the status quo, to be accomplished by the revolutionary élite. In his *Revolutionary Catechism* Nechaev stated that "everything that promotes the success of the revolution is moral and everything that hinders it is immoral." The soldiers in the battle, the revolutionaries, were "doomed men," having "no interests, no affairs, no feelings, no habits, no property, not even a name."[10] The revolution dominated all thoughts and actions of these individuals.

For the twenty years after his emancipation of the serfs, Alexander suffered under increasing revolutionary attack. It was as though the opposition saw each reform not as an improvement but as a weakness to be exploited. In Poland the tsar had tried to reverse the Russification program of his father and in return saw the Polish revolt of 1863. Would-be assassins made a number of attempts on him, and the violence expanded throughout the 1870s as a number of his officials were attacked by young terrorists such as Vera Zasulich (1851–1919). Finally Alexander was assassinated in 1881, on the very day he had approved a proposal to call a representative assembly to consider new reforms.

Reaction: 1881–1905

The slain tsar's son, Alexander III (1881–1894) could see only that his father's reforms had resulted in increased opposition and, eventually, death. During his reign he tried to turn the clock back and reinstate the policy of "Autocracy, Orthodoxy, and Nationalism." Under the guidance of his chief adviser, Constantine Pobedonostsev (1827–1907), Alexander pursued a policy of censorship, regulation of schools and universities, and increased secret police activities. Along with renewing Russification among the minorities, he permitted the persecution of Jews, who were bullied and sometimes massacred in attacks called pogroms. Alexander may have been successful in driving the revolutionaries underground or executing them and the nationalities may have been kept in their place, but under Alexander III Russia lost thirteen valuable years in its attempt to become competitive with western Europe.

Alexander was succeeded by his son, Nicholas II (1894–1917), a decent but weak man. He inherited and retained both his father's advisers and policies. Larger forces overwhelmed him. Industrialization and rural overpopulation spawned a wide range of political pressures that the autocratic structure could not deal with.

To fill the vacuum, different political movements, all illegal, developed. The Liberal party (Constitutional Democrats, or *Kadets*) wanted a constitutional monarchy and peaceful reform on the British model. The Social Revolutionaries combined non-Marxian socialism with the narodnik tradition and simplistically called for "the whole land for the whole people." These agrarian socialists wanted to give the land to the peasants. The Social Democrats, Marxian socialists in a Russian framework, attracted radical intellectuals and politically active city workers. They advocated complete social, economic, and political revolution.

The Social Democrats met in 1903 in London and split into two wings—the Bolsheviks and the Mensheviks—over the questions of the timing of the revolution and the nature of the party. (In Russian, Bolshevik means "majority" and Menshevik means "minority," the names stemming from a vote on party policies in 1903 when the Bolsheviks did prevail. On most occasions, however, the Bolsheviks were in fact in the minority.)

The two factions differed sharply on strategy and tactics. The Bolsheviks, led by Vladimir Ilich Lenin (see p. 656) were prepared to move the pace of history along through "democratic centralism" (see p. 656). The Mensheviks believed that Russian socialism should grow gradually and peacefully in accord with Marxist principles of development and historical evolution, and they were prepared to work within a framework dominated by bourgeois political parties. They knew that their victory was inevitable, given the historical dialectic, and that the proletariat would play the lead role, assisted by the party.

The tsarist regime worked energetically to eliminate the oppostion by placing secret agents among them to act as spies. The government continued to launch violent assaults on opponents and to carry on the diversionary anti-Semitic activities with bands of thugs called the Black Hundreds. By attacking the opposition, Nicholas'

government concentrated on a symptom of Russia's problems, rather than their causes—the repeated failures to carry out effective reform.

The Revolution of 1905 and Its Aftermath

Once again, a failure in war—this time a "splendid little war" against Japan—exposed the weaknesses of the autocratic tsarist regime. Strikes and protests spread throughout the land in response to the military failure in the last days of 1904. On January 22, 1905, the Cossacks opened fire on a peaceful crowd of workers who had advanced on the Winter Palace in St. Petersburg carrying a petition asking for the tsar's help. In response, a general strike broke out with the strikers demanding a democratic republic, freedom for political prisoners, and the disarming of the police. Soviets—councils of workers—appeared in the cities to direct revolutionary activities. Most business and government offices closed and the whole machinery of Russian economic life creaked to a halt. The country was virtually paralyzed.

After a series of half-measures and stalling in response to strikes and revolutionary activities, the tsar found himself pushed to the wall. Unable to find a dictator to impose order, he was forced to issue the October Manifesto of 1905 which promised "freedom of person, conscience, assembly, and union." A national Duma (legislature) was to be called without delay. The right to vote would be extended, and once in session, no law could be enacted without the Duma's approval. The Manifesto split the moderate from the socialist opposition and kept Nicholas on the throne, although he was heartbroken for having made the compromise. The socialists tried to start new strikes, but the opposition was now totally split apart.

Most radical forces boycotted the first Duma meeting in the spring of 1906. As a result, the *Kadets* became the dominant force. Even with this watered-down representation, the tsar was upset by the criticism of the government's handling of the Russo-Japanese war, treatment of minorities, handling of political prisoners, and economic policies. Claiming that the representatives "would not cooperate" with the government, Nicholas dissolved the first Duma. The Russian people turned a cold shoulder to the Kadets' appeals for support. Sensing the decline of political fervor, Nicholas appointed a law-and-order conservative, Peter Stolypin (1862–1911) as prime minister. He cracked down on a number of the radicals, ruling under the emergency article #87.

Unlike previous tsarist appointees, Stolypin knew that changes had to be made, especially in the area of agriculture. Stolypin created the process to develop a class of small farmers, even without Nicholas' full support. He pushed through reforms that abolished all payments still owed by the peasants under the emancipation law and permitted peasants to withdraw from the commune and claim their shares of the land and other wealth as private property. He also opened lands east of the Urals to the peasants and extended financial aid from the state. He was well on the way to finding a solution to that most enduring of Russian problems, the peasant problem, before he was assassinated in 1911 by a Social Revolutionary, who was also an agent of the secret police.[11]

In spite of a reactionary tsar and unprogressive nobility, Russia made major gains in the nine years after 1905 toward becoming a constitutional monarchy. The nation made great economic and social progress in that time. Industrialization increased and generated new wealth. Increased political and civil rights spawned an active public life. Stolypin's death, however, deprived the country of needed leadership. The coming First World War gave Russia a test it could not pass.

The Lesser Great Powers

Italy, united in 1861 and territorially completed by 1870, and the Austro-Hungarian monarchy, set in motion by the 1867 *Ausgleich*, faced overwhelming problems. The Italians had to deal with north-south differences, relations with the papacy, a lack of natural resources, and a politically inexperienced population. The Austro-Hungarian monarchy had to work through a cumbersome structure to govern a mosaic of nationalities.

Italy

This newly unified country faced serious problems. It had few natural resources and too many people. The political goals of the industrialized north and impoverished south rarely coincided. Most troubling was the question of the papacy, which seriously weakened the state. The pope, the spiritual father of most Italians, refused to accept the incorporation of Rome into the new nation. He called himself the "prisoner of the Vatican," and encouraged—with little effect—his Italian flock not to vote. In an attempt to satisfy the pope, the government passed the Law of Papal Guarantees (1871) that created the Vatican as a sovereign state and allocated the pope an annual sum of $600,000 (roughly the amount of money he had received from his previously held lands). Pius IX rejected the offer, but the state refused to repeal the law.

Despite conflicting and unstable political parties, the new state carried on an impressive program of railroad building, naval construction, and attempts at social and welfare legislation. But major problems remained, especially with the peasantry in the south. Radical political parties made their presence felt after the turn of the century in the form of widespread strikes. In 1900 an anarchist assassin killed King Umberto, who had taken the throne in 1878. Change proceeded slowly after that, and not until 1912 did the country gain universal manhood suffrage, a time when there was still widespread illiteracy.

The Italian leaders' ambition to make Italy a world power placed a great burden on the nation. Money spent on the army came at the expense of needed investments in education and social services. National resources were squandered in an unsuccessful attempt to build an empire in Africa.

Up to the beginning of World War I, Italy faced severe economic crises and labor unrest. In June 1914 a general strike spread through the central part of the peninsula. Benito Mussolini, editor of a socialist journal, played a key role in this movement. Attempts to achieve compulsory education, freedom of the press, and better working conditions did little to improve the economic hardships and high taxes that had driven thousands to emigrate to the United States. The south especially suffered, because it had not shared in the industrial gains of the northern part of the country.

The Austro-Hungarian Monarchy

After the Austrians' disastrous defeat by Prussia, Franz Joseph was forced to offer the Hungarians an equal partnership with Vienna in ruling the empire. The offer was accepted and in 1867 the constitution known as the *Ausgleich*

(compromise) was enacted. Under this document the Dual Monarchy came into existence in which the Habsburg ruler was both the king of Hungary and the emperor of Austria—that is, the area that was not a part of Hungary. Each country had its own constitution, language, flag, and parliament. Ministers common to both countries handled finance, defense, and foreign affairs, but they were supervised by "Delegations" which consisted of sixty members from each parliament who did not meet together, except in emergency circumstances. The *Ausgleich* was to be renegotiated every ten years.

The Dual Monarchy contained 12 million Germans, 10 million Hungarians, over 24 million Slavs, and 4 million Romanians, among other nationalities (see map, p. 669). Although the Germans of Austria had recognized the equality of the Hungarians, the rest of the nationalities continued to live under alien rule. Now, instead of having to deal with one dominant national group, they had to cope with two. In some cases, such as in the prospering, cosmopolitan, and sophisticated area of Bohemia-Moravia, the people wanted an independent state or, at the very least, more rights within the Habsburg realm. Others, such as the Serbs, sought the goal of joining their countrymen living in adjacent national states. The nationalities question remained an explosive problem for the authorities in Vienna and Budapest.

The functioning of the Dual Monarchy was best symbolized by the official bank notes which were printed in eight languages on one side and in Hungarian on the other. In the Hungarian part of the Dual Monarchy the aristocracy governed under the Kossuth constitution of 1848 (see p. 635). The Magyars refused to share rule with the minorities in their kingdom. A small, powerful landed oligarchy dominated the mass of backward, landless peasants. The conservative leadership carried out a virtual process of Magyarization with their minorities, while they continually squabbled with the Austrians.

In the Austrian portion, wealthy German businessmen and the landed aristocracy dominated political life. But even with this concentration of power, the government was much more democratic, especially after 1907 when the two-house legislature was elected by universal manhood suffrage. Here, too, nationalism was a

THE NATIONALITIES OF
AUSTRIA-HUNGARY

- Germans
- Italians
- Magyars
- Poles

serious problem, and political parties came to be based not on principle but on nationality. Each nationality had to work with the Germans, even though it might detest them. The nationalities frequently disliked one another, and this prevented the formation of any coalitions among them. By 1914 the Austrians had extended their subject nationalities substantial local self-government, but this concession did little to quiet discontent.

The *Ausgleich* functioned poorly, yet its defenders could still tell themselves that they were, after all, citizens of a "great" empire. The Dual Monarchy occupied a strategic geographical location and had enough military strength to be very influential in the Balkans. In addition, the area had great economic potential with Hungarian wheat, Croatian and Slovenian livestock, Prague banks and industry, and Vienna commerce. But Franz Joseph ruled over a disjointed conglomeration of peoples whose economic and political strength could not compare with that of Germany or even France.

Modern Cultural Responses

After the middle of the nineteenth century, artists and writers reponded to the new age in the realist movement. Artists, especially the French, who were among the most notable early proponents of realism, focused on the concrete aspects of life. From the end of the century until and beyond 1914 the artistic community experimented with a range of new forms and structures in the modernist movement. At the same time that these movements were developing, a huge new group of consumers, the lower and middle classes, were becoming participants in the new mass culture. They might find little to admire in the fine arts, but through their buying power and their numbers, they would come to have a great effect on some parts of the creative community.

Realism

In literature and art as in politics, realism replaced romanticism after midcentury. To the realists it was no longer enough to be true to one's instincts and emotions. Now they must faithfully observe and graphically report all aspects of life in a dispassionate, precise manner in order to depict individuals in their proper setting. In this age of change, there was much for writers and artists to portray, and a much larger public now had the leisure time and political interests to respond to their works.

The trend towards the realistic novel had been foreshadowed in the work of Honoré de Balzac (1799–1850), the author of the ninety-volume *La Comédie Humaine (The Human Comedy)*, which depicts French life in the first half of the nineteenth century. Balzac, a master of characterization, described life in such detail that his work is a valuable reference on social history for twentieth-century scholars. Gustave Flaubert (1821–1880) was the first French realist writer. His masterpiece, *Madame Bovary* (1856), exhaustively described how the boredom of a young romantic provincial wife led her into adultery, excess, and ultimately, suicide.

British novelist Charles Dickens (1812–1870) protested social conditions in his works characterizing the everyday life of the middle classes and poor. In such works as *Oliver Twist* (1838), *Dombey and Son* (1847–1848), and *Hard Times* (1854), he describes some of the worst excesses of industrial expansion and social injustice. Later, in novels such as *Far from the Madding Crowd* (1874) Thomas Hardy (1840–1928) dealt with the struggle — almost always a losing one — of the individual against the impersonal, pitiless forces of the natural and social environment.

American writers such as Henry James (1843–1916), Samuel Clemens (1835–1910), and Harriet Beecher Stowe (1811–1896) made important contributions to the realist tradition. James tried to catch the "atmosphere of the mind" through an almost clinical examination of the most subtle details. Clemens, perhaps better known as Mark Twain, used humor and accurate descriptions of the midwest and far west to underscore social injustice. Stowe, through her detailed work in *Uncle Tom's Cabin* (1852), captured the American public's attention and strongly influenced the antislavery movement.

The Russian novelists Leo Tolstoy (1828–1910) and Feodor Dostoevski (1821–1881) produced the most developed presentation of the realistic novel. Tolstoy stripped every shred of glory and glamor from war in his *War and Peace* (1869) and gave an analytical description of the different levels of society. Dostoevski devised a chilling, detailed view of life in St. Petersburg in *Crime and Punishment* (1866), and his *Brothers Karamazov* (1880) offered a painstaking analysis of Russian life during a period of change.

Drama was deeply influenced by realism, as could be seen in the works of the Norwegian Henrik Isben (1828–1906), the Irishman George Bernard Shaw (1856–1950), and the Russian Anton Chekhov (1860–1904). In his *Doll's House* (1879) Ibsen through his exhausting, quiet, tension-filled work assailed marriage without love as being immoral. Though his characters are not heroic in their dimensions, Ibsen captures the quiet desperation of normal life. Shaw used satire and nuance to shock the British public into reassessing their conventional attitudes. Finally, Chekhov's *Cherry Orchard* (1904) showed the changes wrought by emancipation of the serfs on the lives of a gentry family. Lacking obvious plot and action, the play depends on portrayal of detail to build a subtle, exhausting tension.

Modernism

Romanticism broke the classical forms and opened the way for diversity in forms, styles, and themes. Romantics followed their emotions, while realists advocated a more objective way of portraying the world by stressing accuracy and precision. By the end of the century a new movement — modernism — fragmented, disorganized, and united only in its reaction to the past came to dominate Europe's writers, artists, and musicians.

Modernism freed the writer from all rules of composition and form and obligations to communicate to a large audience. Poetry was especially affected by this new tendency. Toward the end of the century, in reaction to the demands of realism, French poets Stéphane Mallarmé (1842–1898) and Paul Verlaine (1844–1896) inaugurated the symbolist movement. Poetry rather than prose best fit the symbolists' goal of conveying ideas by suggestion rather than by precise, photographic word-pictures.

In a sense, all modern literature stems from the symbolist movement. By increasing the power of the poet to reach the readers' imagination through expanded combinations of allusions, symbols, and double meanings, symbolism gave new life to the written word. But in exploring new poetic realms and possibilities, the symbolists left behind the majority of readers who had been trained to see clarity, precision, simplicity, and definition as positive aspects of literature.

Modernism freed painters from the need to communicate surface, photographic reality. Gustave Courbet (1819–1877) consciously dropped all useless adornments and instead boldly painted the life of the world in which he lived. He was soon surpassed by his countrymen who became preoccupied with problems of color, light, and atmosphere. Artists such as Claude Monet (1840–1926), Edouard Manet (1832–1882), Edgar Degas (1834–1917), Mary Cassatt (1845–1926), and Pierre Auguste Renoir (1841–1919) tried to catch the first impression made by a scene or an object on the eye, undistorted by intellect or any subjective attitude. They were called impressionists and worked in terms of light and color rather than solidity of form.

The impressionists found that they could achieve a more striking effect of light by placing one bright area of color next to another without any transitional tones. The also found that shadows could be shown not as gray but as colors complementary to those of the objects casting the shadow. At close range an impressionist painting may seem little more than a splotch of unmixed colors, but at a proper distance the eye mixes the colors and allows a vibrating effect of light and emotion to emerge. The impresssionists' techniques helped revolutionize art.

One of the weaknesses of the impressionists' work was that they sacrificed much of the clarity of the classical tradition to gain their effects. Paul Cezanne (1839–1903) addressed that problem. He tried to simplify all natural objects by stressing their essential geometric structure. He believed that everything in nature corresponded to the shape of a cone, cylinder, or sphere. Proceeding from this theory, he was able to get below the surface and give his objects the solidity that had eluded the impressionists, yet he kept the impressionists' striking use of color.

The Dutch artist Vincent van Gogh (1853–1890) pursued his own style of using short strokes of heavy pigment, which accentuated the underlying forms and rhythms of his subjects. He achieved intensely emotional results, as he was willing to distort what he saw to communicate the sensations he felt. His short life of poverty and loneliness was climaxed by insanity and suicide.

Before 1914 other modernist inspired forms emerged. French artist Henri Matisse (1869–1954) painted what he felt about an object, rather than just the object itself. He had learned to simplify form partly from his study of African primitive art and the color schemes of oriental carpets. The Spanish artist Pablo Picasso (1881–1974) and others helped develop the school called cubism. Cubists would choose an object, then construct an abstract pattern from it, giving the opportunity to view it simultaneously from several points. Such a pattern is evident in Picasso's *Three Musicians* (1921).

Pablo Picasso painted *Three Musicians* in the summer of 1921.

Music

After midcentury, Johannes Brahms (1833–1897), Anton Bruckner (1824–1896), and Gustav Mahler (1860–1911) built on the momentum of forces that Beethoven had set in motion and made lyrical advances in composition and presentation. Each made unique use of the large symphony orchestra, and Brahms also composed three exquisite string quartets.

In addition, many composers turned to their native folk music and dances for inspiration. Beethoven had used native themes as had Schubert and Schumann in Austria and Germany. Frederick Chopin (1810–1849), even though he did most of his work in France, drew heavily on Polish folk themes for his mazurkas and polonaises. Jean Sibelius (1865–1957) in Finland, Anton Dvořák (1841–1904) and Bedrich Smetana (1824–1884) in Bohemia-Moravia, and Russians Peter Ilich Tchaikovsky (1840–1893), Modest Moussorgsky (1835–1881), and Sergei Rachmaninov (1873–1943) all incorporated folk music in their work. This use of folk themes was aesthetically satisfying and pleasing to the audiences.

Romanticism and nationalism, plus the increasing number of enthusiasts, sparked developments in operas during the century. In his fervid Germanic works, Richard Wagner (1813–1883) infused old Teutonic myths and German folklore with typically romantic characteristics such as emphasis on the supernatural and the mystical. Wagner's *Ring* cycle was the culmination of a long and productive career. His descendants still manage the *Festspielhaus*, a theater in Bayreuth, Germany, that he designed and his admirers financed.

The greatest operatic composer of the century was Giuseppi Verdi (1813–1901) who composed such masterpieces as *Aida, Rigoletto, Il Trovatore, La Forza del Destino*, and many others. His operas, along with those of Wagner, form the core of most of today's major opera house repertoires.

Modernism affected music, such as it had affected poetry and art. The French composer Claude Debussy (1862–1918) tried in his music to imitate what he read in poetry and saw in impressionist paintings. He engaged in "tone painting" to achieve a special mood or atmosphere. This device can be seen in his *Prélude à l'aprésmidi d'un faune (Prelude to the Afternoon of a Faun)*, which shocked the musical world when it was first performed in 1892. The impressionist painters had gained their effects by juxtaposing widely different colors. The composers juxtaposed widely separate chords to create similarly brilliant, shimmering effects.

The music world rarely dealt with social problems or harsh realism. Its supporters were by and large the newly ascendant middle classes who had benefitted from the economic growth triggered by industrialization. They used the wealth derived from their commercial prosperity to finace the building of new opera and symphony halls and maintain the composers and orchestras. Major soloists were the idols of their day, as they showed their virtuosity in compositions that made use of romantic subject matter infused with sentiment and, not infrequently, showmanship. The drew capacity audiences of contented listeners.

Popular Culture

The urban working and lower middle classes began to be important consumers of the popular cultural products of their countries. With increasing literacy these classes provided a huge audience for publishers. More leisure time and money enabled them to fill the music halls and public sporting arenas. They would rarely be found in the concert halls, art galleries, or in serious bookstores. Rather they read the penny press and the "dime novel," both of which featured simple vocabulary and easy to follow information and plots. The penny press served many functions: to inform, entertain, and sell goods. Sensationalism, whether the confessions of a "fallen woman" or the account of some adventurer, was the main attraction of the "dime novel." Comic strips first appeared in central Europe in the 1890s.

There was a level of literature between "great" novels and the penny press, and that was the comforting literature such as the works of Scottish author Samuel Smiles (1812–1904). Smiles' *Self Help* (1859) sold 20,000 copies its first year and 130,000 in the following thirty years. Titles of Smiles' other works—*Thrift, Character*, and *Duty*—form a catalog of Victorian virtues. In the

United States, Horatio Alger (1834–1899) wrote over a hundred novels following similar themes: virtue is rewarded, the good life will win out in the struggle with temptation, and the heroes—usually poor but purehearted youths—will come to enjoy wealth and high honor.

A number of technological advances—coated celluloid film, improved shutter mechanisms, reliable projectors, and a safe source of illumination—were combined to introduce the cinema, or the movies, to the world. These developments seem to have come together almost simultaneously in France, Britain, and the United States. The first public moving picture performances took place in Paris in 1895 and soon after in London and New York. Even though another twenty years passed before feature-length films were produced, movies proved to be an immediate success, attracting an infinitely larger audience than live performances could ever reach.

Sports, including football—in its North American and European forms—bicycle racing, cricket, baseball, and boxing, captured the popular imagination. Pierre de Coubertin (1863–1937) revived the Olympic games of ancient Greece in 1896 in Athens. Thirteen nations took part in an event that instantly caught the international public's imagination.[12]

In the new society of early twentieth-century Europe, the popular culture of mass literature, movies, and sports played as important a role as did high culture. In a simpler way, purveyors of popular culture communicated values and lessons that bound a nation together much more than did the serious writers and artists of the age. The gulf between "high" and "popular" culture has yet to be bridged.

Conclusion

In the latter half of the nineteenth century, workers and the middle classes entered the public arena, the first group struggling, with the help of the socialist parties, for just treatment in the modern, industrial world and the second profiting from their advantaged positions in society. Both groups pressed the state structures to respond to their demands. Strengthened by increased tax revenues and improved technology, the governments of Europe expanded their scope and influence, while providing an outlet for public opinion.

By the beginning of the twentieth century, Britain and Germany were the most powerful states in Europe. Both countries made the necessary adjustments to the new economic and social forces generated by industrialization to build state structures based on mass democratic participation. France and Russia recovered from defeats in wars in 1871 and 1856 to reform and rebuild their state structures. Emerging from the ruins of the Franco-Prussian War, the French Third Republic endured serious class conflict and the Boulanger and Dreyfus affairs to become the strongest republic in Europe. Russia tried reform, but after the assassination of Alexander II reverted to its traditional reactionary stance until the 1905 Revolution. Despite the unfortunate Nicholas II, the country made considerable strides by 1914. Both Italy and Austria-Hungary faced overwhelming problems, and neither state could compete with the four largest powers.

At all levels of European society, life-styles, aesthetic standards, and the means for self-expression changed dramatically by the end of the nineteenth century. Cultural activities were no longer the sole preserve of the élite and elect, all of whom shared a common classical conception of "good" and "bad." At the end of the century, cultural activities were as fragmented and diverse as was the European world. The classicism of the eighteenth century at least had the advantage of unifying the participants in cultural activities. By 1900, in art, music, poetry, prose, and architecture it would have been difficult to gain a consensus between the artist and the audience on what was "good" and "bad."

Never before had the creators of poetry, art, prose, music, and architecture had a greater opportunity to communicate to such a large audience. The cinema and vastly increased publishing facilities held out great opportunity to artists and writers. Unfortunately, by the end of the century the modernist writers, artists, and musicians were seemingly able to communicate only with a finely trained élite. In a sense, what was needed was a new series of classical definitions, forms, and functions upon which all could agree. But the romantic drive to individualism, which came to full flower in the century, made that impossible. Even today, the vast gulf between "mass culture" and the "fine arts" continues to grow.

Suggestions for Reading

In the immense number of works dealing with Karl Marx, the following are clear and valuable introductions for the student: I. Berlin, *Karl Marx: His Life and Environment* (Oxford, 1963); George Lichtheim, *Marxism* (Praeger, 1961); and Alexander Balinky, *Marx's Economics* (Heath, 1970). A well-written and penetrating biography of Lenin is L. Fischer, *The Life of Lenin* (Harper & Row, 1965).

D. Thomson, *England in the Nineteenth Century, 1815–1914* (Penguin, 1964) and J. Conacher, ed., *The Emergence of Parliamentary Democracy in Britain in the Nineteenth Century* (Wiley, 1971) are valuable brief accounts. See also F. Ensor, *England, 1870–1914* (Oxford, 1936); G. Kitson Clark, *The Making of Victorian England* (Atheneum, 1967); George M. Young, *Victorian England, Portrait of an Age* (Galaxy, 1954); P. Magnus, *Gladstone* (Dutton, 1954); and Robert Blake *Disraeli* (Anchor, 1969). G. Dangerfield's *The Strange Death of Liberal England 1910–1914* (Capricorn, 1935) describes the inability of the Liberals to deal with major problems.

D. W. Brogan, *The French Nation: From Napoleon to Pétain* (Colophon, 1957) is a good survey. See also B. Gooch, *The Reign of Napoleon III* (Rand McNally, 1970); D. Thomson, *Democracy in France Since 1870* (Oxford, 1946); Stewart Edwards, *The Paris Commune, 1871* (Quadrangle, 1970); and Douglas Johnson, *France and the Dreyfus Affair* (Walker). See also John McManners, *Church and State in France, 1870–1914* (Harper & Row, 1972). Eugen Weber, *Peasants into Frenchmen* (Univ. of California, 1976) and T. Zeldin, *France: 1848–1945* (Oxford, 1973–1975) are two brilliant, conflicting social surveys.

Michael Balfour, *The Kaiser and His Times* (Houghton Mifflin, 1964) describes the impact of William II on Germany and Europe. See also A. Rosenberg, *Imperial Germany: The Birth of the German Republic, 1871–1918* (Oxford, 1970). F. Stern's *Gold and Iron* (Vintage, 1979) is a fascinating study of the interaction of capital and politics.

Events in Russia have been thoroughly studied in L. H. Haimson, ed., *The Politics of Rural Russia: 1905–1914* (Indiana, 1979); Philip Pomper, *Sergei Nechaev* (Rutgers, 1979); D. W. Treadgold, *The Great Siberian Migration* (Princeton, 1957); Paul Avrich, *The Russian Anarchists* (Norton, 1978); A. Yarmolinsko, *The Road to Revolution* (Collier, 1962); and B. D. Wolfe, *Three Who Made a Revolution* (Beacon, 1974). A fine collection of translation documents giving a first-hand view of the huge changes Russia underwent at this time is G. L. Freeze, *From Supplication to Revolution* (Oxford, 1988).

A notion of the complexity of the nationalities question in the Habsburg realm can be found in the chapters of P.

F. Sugar and I. Lederer, eds., *Nationalism in Eastern Europe* (Univ. of Washington, 1969). C. E.Shorske's *Fin de Siècle Vienna: Politics and Culture* (Vintage, 1981) is a classical intellectual history of the Dual Monarchy in its decline. Jorg K. Hoensch discusses Hungary's motivations and programs in chapter 2 of *A History of Modern Hungary* (Longman, 1988). Christopher Seton-Watson's *Italy from Liberalism to Fascism: 1870–1925* (Methuen, 1967) is clear and concise.

Useful guides to nineteenth-century cultural developments are D. S. Mirsky, *A History of Russian Literature* (Vintage, 1958); H. L. C. Jaffe, *The Nineteenth and Twentieth Centuries*, Vol. 5, *The Dolphin History of Painting* (Thames and Hudson, 1969); C. Edward Gauss, *The Aesthetic Theories of French Artists: From Realism to Surrealism* (Johns Hopkins, 1949); and H. C. Colles, *Ideals of the Nineteenth and Twentieth Century*, Vol. 3, *The Growth of Music* (Oxford, 1956).

Notes

1. Charles Tilly, "Reflections on the History of European State-Making," in Charles Tilly, ed., *The Formation of National States in Western Europe* (Princeton: Princeton Univ. Press, 1975), p. 15.
2. Leszek Kolakowski, *Main Currents of Marxism*, Vol. 2., P. S. Falla, trans. (Oxford: Oxford Univ. Press, 1978), p. 1.
3. J. H. Plumb, "The Victorians Unbuttoned," *Horizon*, XI, n. 4, 1969, pp. 16–25. See also S. Marcus, *The Other Victorians: A Study of Sexuality and Pornography in Mid-Nineteenth Century England*, (New York: Basic Books, 1966.)
4. Edward H. Reisner, *Nationalism and Education Since 1789* (New York: Macmillan, 1923), pp. 35, 145, 211.
5. Robert Schnerb, "Le XIXe Siècle: L'Apogée de L'Expansion Européene (1815–1914)," *Histoire Générale des Civilisations*, Vol. 6 (Paris: Presses Universitaires de France, 1955), p. 235.
6. Gabriel Ardant, "Financial Policy and Economic Infrastructure of Modern States and Nations," in Charles Tilly, ed., *The Formation of National States in Western Europe* (Princeton: Princeton Univ. Press, 1975), pp. 219–222.
7. Quoted in F. Owen, *Tempestuous Journey: Lloyd George, His Life and Times* (London: Hutchinson, 1954), p. 186.
8. Emmeline Pankhurst, *My Own Story* (New York: Source Book Press, 1970), *passim*.
9. Quoted in C. G. Robinson, *Bismarck* (London: Constable, 1918), p. 472.
10. Quoted in Basil Dmystryshyn, ed., *Imperial Russia: A Source Book, 1700–1917* (New York: Holt, Rinehart, & Winston, 1967), p. 241.
11. Hans Rogger, *Russia in the Age of Modernisation and Revolution: 1881–1917* (London: Longman, 1988), pp. 243–247.
12. Schnerb, pp. 468–469.

The Foundations of European Global Dominance

The word *imperialism* has come to mean many things to many people. Broadly speaking, the term refers to the extension of authority or control, whether direct or indirect, of one nation over another. But we use the term *imperialism* in a more restricted sense to refer to the period from 1870 to 1914 when western Europe, which controlled much of the world's finance, commerce, military power, and intellectual life, extended its power over many of the peoples of the world.

As we will see in the next three chapters, Europeans gained control over most of Asia, Africa, and the Americas in the nineteenth century. They achieved their domination by sending their people to settle, their armies to conquer, or their merchants to trade.

Scientific and economic superiority harnessed to efficient state structures provided the strength for the European expansion and domination. The nations of western Europe justified their imperialism with a number of rationalizations. Imperialism was variously defended as an attempt to spread civilization, to bring Christianity to the "heathen," and to introduce progress to the "less fortunate." Some inventive thinkers distorted scientific discoveries and theories to devise self-serving arguments for the supposed inevitability and eternal nature of their dominance.

Not all Europeans approved. Some observers saw in Europe's inability to deal with the rivalry surrounding the exploitation of the Ottoman empire a portent of approaching disaster. Some critics warned that the imperialistic rush was the prelude to the capitalist world's death struggle.

Scientific Superiority

Europe's world dominance in basic scientific research began with Copernicus in the 1500s and extended through the nineteenth century. The major difference between sixteenth-century work and modern discoveries was that the effects of the latter research had almost immediate and widespread economic and intellectual implications.

Darwin and Evolution

In the mid-nineteenth century Charles Darwin (1809–1892) formulated a major scientific theory in *On the Origin of Species by Means of Natural Selection* (1859). This theory of evolution, stating that all complex organisms developed from simple forms through the operation of natural causes, challenged traditionalist Christian beliefs on creation and altered views on life on earth. The theory contended that no species is fixed and changeless. Classical thinkers first stated this view, and contemporary philosophers such as Hegel had used the concept of evolutionary change. In the century before Darwin, other research supported the concept of change, both biological and social.

Darwin built on the work of Sir Charles Lyell (1797–1875) and Jean Baptiste Lamarck (1744–1829) when he began his investigations. Lyell's three-volume *Principles of Geology* (1830–1833) confirmed the views of the Scottish geologist James Hutton (1726–1797), who stated that the earth developed through natural rather than supernatural causes. Lyell helped popularize the notion of geological time operating over a vast span of years. This understanding is essential to the acceptance of any theory of biological evolution, based as it is on changes in species over many thousands of generations. Lamarck, a naturalist, argued that every organism tends to develop new organs to adapt to the changing conditions of its environment. He theorized that these changes are transmitted by heredity to the descendants, which are thereafter changed in structural form.

Though he had originally studied medicine at Edinburgh and prepared for the ministry at Cambridge University, Darwin lost interest in both professions and became a naturalist in his twenties. From 1831 to 1836 he studied the specimens he had collected while on a five-year surveying expedition aboard the ship *Beagle*, which had sailed along the coast of South America and among the Galapagos Islands. The works of his predecessors, plus questions that he had about the theories of Thomas Robert Malthus, as presented in Malthus' *Essay on Population*, helped him define the problem he studied. When Darwin's book finally appeared, it changed many basic scientific and social assumptions.

In his revolutionary work, Darwin constructed an explanantion of how life evolves that upset the literal interpretation of the Bible taught in most Christian churches.

> *... Species have been modified, during a long course of descent ... chiefly through the natural selection of numerous successive, slight, favorable variations; aided in an important manner ... by the direct action of external conditions, and by variations which seem to us in our ignorance to arise spontaneously.*[1]

His explanation radically affected the views of the scientific community about the origin and

THE MODERN THEORY OF THE DESCENT OF MAN.

In *The Descent of Man* (1871), Charles Darwin theorized that humans evolved from lower life forms. Using Darwin's theory, Ernst Haeckel prepared this schematic history of the process of evolution showing the progression from the simplest single-cell organisms to present-day human beings.

Gregor Johann Mendel. Mendel's experiments on the formation and development of hybrids laid the foundation for modern biological research.

scientific breeding of plants and animals and demonstrated that the evolution of different species was more complex than Darwin had concluded. Based on their work, biologists hypothesized that there are chromosomes that carry the characteristics of an organism. Darwin had hinted at and now further research supported the mutation theory, which states that sudden and un-predictable changes within a chromosome can be transmitted by heredity to produce new species. Scientists began to work with the very fundamental building blocks of life, establishing the groundwork of contemporary biotechnical research.

Darwin and his colleagues carefully researched and cautiously stated their findings. Unlike earlier discoveries however, their work came to be widely reported in popular journals and applied by commentators and politicians. The newly ascendant middle classes responded enthusiastically to their understanding of evolutionary theory, finding in it a comfortable reassurance of their own upward mobility and Europe's dominance in the world.

Medicine, Chemistry, and Physics

Important advances in medicine, chemistry, and physics contributed to a population explosion on the continent and had significant economic implications, further strengthening the bases of Europe's dominance. At the beginning of the nineteenth century, medical practices were making the slow transition from the use of leeches and bleeding. By 1900, fairly sophisticated and much safer surgical procedures were available. In the 1840's, physicians began to use ether and chloroform to reduce pain during operations. The Scottish surgeon Joseph Lister (1827–1912) developed new antiseptic practices that made major advances against the spread of infection. Probably the most important single advance came with the substantiation of the germ theory of disease by Louis Pasteur (1822–1895) and Robert Koch (1843–1910). During his search for a cure to anthrax—a disease that in the late 1870s destroyed over 20 percent of the sheep in France—pasteur established the principle that the injection of a mild form of disease bacterium will cause the body to form antibodies that will prevent the vaccinated individual from

evolution of life on the planet. The hypothesis, in its simplified form, states that all existing plant and animal species are descended from earlier and, generally speaking, more primitive forms. The direct effects of the environment causes species to develop through the inheritance of minute differences in individual structures. As the centuries passed, the more adaptable, stronger species lived on, while the weaker, less flexible species died out. Additionally, a species may also be changed by the cumulative working of sexual selection, which Darwin saw to be the "most powerful means of changing the races of man."

After the announcement of Darwin's theories, others, such as the German biologist August Weismann (1834–1914) and the Austrian priest Gregor Mendel (1822–1884), worked along similar lines to explore the genetic relationships among living organisms. Weismann proved that acquired characteristics cannot be inherited. Mendel's investigations into the laws of heredity, based on his experiments with the crossing of garden peas, proved to be invaluable in the

This 1882 engraving shows the Lister carbolic spray being used as an antiseptic as the surgeons perform an operation.

getting the severe form of the particular disease. Koch discovered the specific organisms that caused eleven diseases, including tuberculosis. The work of Pasteur and Koch placed the sciences of bacteriology and immunology on a firm footing and gave promise that the end of such deadly diseases as typhoid and smallpox might be in sight.

Modern chemistry gained its foundations during the ninteenth century, founded on the atomic theory advanced by an English Quaker schoolmaster, John Dalton (1766–1844). In 1869 the Russian chemist Dmitri Mendeleev (1834–1907) drew up a periodic table in which all known elements were classified according to their weights and properties. From gaps in this table, chemists were able to deduce the existence of undiscovered elements. Other researchers made advances in the field of nutrition, discovering significance of vitamins. Biochemical research threw light on the presence and function of the ductless glands. Chemotherapy advanced with the discovery of a chemical that could destroy the syphilis bacteria and of procedures that woud lead to the discovery of sulfa drugs, penicillin, and other antibiotics.

Revolutionary strides in physics came in the areas of electricity and thermodynamics, of which the First Law was formulated in 1847. Michael Farady (1791–1867) prepared the way for the dynamo, a device that made possible changes in communications, the transmission of current over long distances, and the development of the electric motor. The Scottish scientist James Clerk Maxwell (1831–1879) and the German Heinrich Hertz (1857–1894) conducted basic research into the nature of electromagnetic phenomena such as light, radiant heat, and ultraviolet radiation.

Pierre (1859–1906) and Marie (1867–1934) Curie made major strides toward the discovery of the X-ray and radioactivity. When they extracted radium from uranium ore in 1896 the scientific world became aware of the strength of radioactivity. Marie Curie was the first person to be awarded two Nobel prizes, one in physics and one in chemistry.

At the beginning of the twentieth century, the British physicist Ernest Rutherford (1871–1937) helped develop the electron theory. It had been postulated that the atom contains particles known as electrons. Rutherford contributed the idea that each atom has a central particle, or nucleus, that is positively charged and separate from the negatively charged electrons. These discoveries destroyed one of the foundations of traditional physics—that matter is indivisible and continuous.

New Certainties

The territory opened up by the scientists seemed to complement the global claims of the imperialists. The optimism generated by science in the laboratory and Europe's advance across the globe supported the commonly-held belief in inevitable progress. It also buttressed the theories of a new breed of social scientists known as the positivists. Positivism is a mechanistic way of though that uses the methods and principles of science to define the laws of a strictly material world that presumably may be scientifically verified.

Auguste Comte (1798–1857), an engineer who was formerly secretary to Saint-Simon (see p. 651), established the foundations for the philosophical approach known as positivism in a series of lectures and publications in the 1830s and 1840s. He stated that one could find and verify the laws that controlled society in the same way that a scientist discovered physical laws. For Comte humanity was a part of a machine, possessing neither free will nor a divinely infused spark of life. Comte's goal was to understand the machine and to devise a science to discover the laws of history and society. He developed the social science of sociology and stated that once humanity could base itself on science, and not on opinion, harmony would arise.

Darwin's hypotheses were very attractive to the positivists, who, along with their imitators, distorted the British scientist's findings by applying them to areas Darwin never dreamed of discussing—human social, economic, and political activities—to justify the fantasies of eternal progress, the dominance of science, the perfectibility of humanity through obedience to the supposedly unchanging laws of society, and the assumption of Anglo-Saxon racial dominance. The Social Darwinists, positivists, and others of their kind followed a simplistic approach to the world based on their comforting belief that humanity is a cog in a machine and that the possibilities of individuals are predetermined by their place in the larger scheme of things.

Auguste Comte. Comte developed the theory of positivism, according to which science is totally objective and value-free.

William Graham Sumner on Socialism

The nineteenth century was the prime age of the "fit." Darwin's scientific theories were applied to, among other things, political theory. William Graham Sumner saw socialism as retrograde.

The origin of socialism, which is the extreme development of the sentimental philosophy, lies in the undisputed facts which I described at the outset. The socialist regards this misery as the fault of society. He thinks that we can organize society as we like and that an organization can be devised in which poverty and misery shall disappear. He goes further even than this. He assumes that men have artificially organized society as it now exists. Hence if anything is disagreeable or hard in the present state of society, it follows, on that view, that the task of organizing society has been imperfectly and badly performed, and that it needs to be done over again. These are the assumptions with which the socialist starts, and many socialists seem also to believe that if they can destroy belief in an Almighty God who is supposed to have made the world such as it is, they will then have overthrown the belief that there is a fixed order in human nature and human life which man can scarcely alter at all, and, if at all, only infinitesimally.

The truth is that the social order is fixed by laws of nature precisely analogous to those of the physical order. The most that man can do is by ignorance and self-conceit to mar the operation of social laws.

From William Graham Sumner, *The Challenge of Facts*, 1914.

The most popular Social Darwinist was the English philosopher Herbert Spencer (1820–1903), who applied Darwin's theories to all aspects of human social and political life. Spencer had a deep influence in both Europe and the United States. As a convenient doctrine to justify the actions and philosophies of those newly arrived at the top of the social and political structure, Social Darwinism dominated Western social thought in the late nineteenth century.

Stressing the role of change and chance in nature, the broadly applied Darwinian theory reinforced the trend away from absolute standards and procedures. The American physicist Charles Sanders Peirce (1839–1914) broke new philosophical ground in this area. In the late 1890s, William James (1842–1910) popularized Peirce's approaches in his philosophy of pragmatism. James stated that "an idea is true so long as to believe it is profitable to our lives." In effect, the pragmatists rejected any concept of truth or reality as an absolute and favored a more flexible, result-oriented approach.

New Identities

The rapid political, social, economic, and intellectual changes that shook Europe and the world led to new ways of defining individuals and groups. Even before Darwin publicized his theory of evolution, pseudoscientists such as Joseph Arthur de Gobineau (1816–1882) laid the foundations of modern racism, justifying the domination of one group over another for "scientific" reasons. Gobineau applied biological theory to politics, regarding nations as organisms. He argued that different races are innately unequal in ability and worth and that the genius of a race depended upon heredity, not external factors. Gobineau stated a widely held belief among Europeans that white peoples alone were capable of cultural creativity and that intermixture with other races would destroy that creativity. Social Darwinist arguments and Gobineau's theories in support of white superiority gave "rational" justifications to blatant bigotry and provided a reassuring sanction for European domination over Asians and Africans.

Supported by the new pseudoscience and the belief that Europeans alone bore the burdens of progress, European nationalism took on a more

William James. In 1875, at Harvard University, James established the first laboratory of experimental psychology in the United States.

blatant and bellicose form. Aggressive nationalism was adhered to almost as a religion; it served as a powerful vehicle for politicians to mobilize their constituents. Nationalistic pressures became especially strong in eastern Europe and the Balkans, where political instability and economic underdevelopment created insecure conditions.

One of the manifestations of the identities was the Anglo-Saxon movement. In Britain and Germany writers and speakers presented the case for the superiority of northern Europeans. They stated that world leadership should naturally reside in London and Berlin because the people living there possessed the proper combination of religion, racial qualities, and culture to dictate the world's future. People as diverse as Kaiser William II and U.S. president Woodrow Wilson were affected by this outlook.

Another manifestation of a regrouping on the basis of new principles came with the so-called pan-cultural movements. Pan-Slavic movements had begun before 1850. These were based either around the Orthodox Slavs' foundation in Moscow or the Catholic Slavs' center at Prague.

Houston Stewart Chamberlain on the Characteristics of the German Race

Houston Stewart Chamberlain had no doubts about the superiority of the Germans. His views found their way into Hitler's beliefs.

Let us attempt a glance into the depths of the soul. What are the specific intellectual and moral characteristics of this Germanic race? Certain anthropologists would fain teach us that all races are equally gifted; we point to history and answer: that is a lie! The races of mankind are markedly different in the nature and also in the extent of their gift, and the Germanic races belong to the most highly gifted group, the group usually termed Aryan. Is this human family united and uniform by bonds of blood? Do these stems really all spring from the same root? I do not know and I do not much care; no affinity binds more closely than elective affinity, and in this sense the Indo-European Aryans certainly form a family. . . .

Physically and mentally the Aryans are pre-eminent among all peoples; for that reason they are by right, as the Stagirite expresses it, the lords of the world. Aristotle puts the matter still more concisely when he says, "Some men are by nature free, others slaves"; this perfectly expresses the moral aspect. For freedom is by no means an abstract thing, to which every human being has fundamentally a claim; a right to freedom must evidently depend upon capacity for it, and this again presupposes physical and intellectual power. One may make the assertion, that even the mere conception of freedom is quite unknown to most men. Do we not see the *homo syriacus* develop just as well and as happily in the position of slave as of master? Do the Chinese not show us another example of the same nature? Do not all historians tell us that the Semites and half-Semites, in spite of their great intelligence, never succeeded in founding a State that lasted, and that because every one always endeavoured to grasp all power for himself, thus showing that their capabilities were limited to despotism and anarchy, the two opposites of freedom?

From Houston Stewart Chamberlain, *Foundations of the Ninteenth Century*, 1900.

In the latter part of the century the Russians would use their Pan-Slavic movement to expand their influence into the Balkans in pursuit of their "destiny" to create and rule a great Slavic empire. The Pan-Germanic League was organized in Berlin in the 1890s to spread the belief in the superiority of the German race and culture.

Anti-Semitism—hatred of the Jews—had been a part of European history since the legalization of Christianity. But the movement attained a new strength and vigor in the last part of the nineteenth century. In Germany, the historian Heinrich von Treitschke (1834–1896) stated that "the Jews are our calamity." In France, anti-Semitism played a significant role in the Dreyfus affair (see p. 664). In eastern Europe, the Jews suffered many injustices, while in Russia many Jews died in organized pogroms. Anti-Semitism became stronger because of the economic dislocation that modernization introduced and of the work of bigoted cranks who turned out pseudo-scientific tracts and forgeries such as the *Protocols of the Elders of Zion*.

In response, a desire for a homeland grew among the Jews. In 1896 Theodor Herzl (1860–1904) came forward with the program of Zionism, which had as its purpose the creation of an independent state within Palestine. The first general congress of Zionists was held in Switzerland in 1896 and a small-scale emigration to Palestine, which had been settled for centuries by Arabs, began. In the first decade of the twentieth century, the election of Karl Leuger (1844–1910), who ran and stayed in power on an anti-Semitic platform, as mayor of Vienna, foretold the tragic genocide that would occur later in the century. It was in this atmosphere that the young Adolf Hitler spent some of his formative years, reading racist, Social Darwinist, and Pan-Germanic tracts.

Christianity and the Modern Age

Europe's drive to dominate the globe came from a variety of sources. The belief in scientific superiority and the arguments of the pseudo-scientists and racists provided some of the motivation for expansion. Another motivator was the Christian churches, which were themselves experiencing the challenges posed by industrialization and urbanization.

After the Reformation, Christianity endured serious intellectual, political, and social challenges. The Scientific Revolution and the Enlightenment ate away at the authority of the traditional church. Darwin's theories challenged the traditional Christian view of the origins of the world as presented in the Bible. The population increases that resulted from urbanization forced the church to respond to different audiences facing more difficult problems than those of an earlier, simpler age. Yet Christianity endured and adapted.

The Missionary Thrust

During the age of imperialism, European missionaries went forth in their centuries-old function as self-proclaimed messengers of the word of God. Once the European states began competing for land around the globe, the churches often complemented national policy in their religious work. Buttressed by Social Darwinism and the notion of progress, missionaries felt justified in altering the cultures of the peoples with whom they came in contact if that was the price to be paid for eternal salvation.

Changes in the Catholic Church

In 1864 Pope Pius IX (1846–1878), who had become extraordinarily reactionary after having been expelled from Rome in 1848 and in the wake of the Italian unification movement (see p. 635), issued the *Syllabus of Errors*, a document that attacked the critical examination of faith and doctrine. In 1870 he called a general council of the church to proclaim the doctrine of papal infallibility, which states that when speaking *ex cathedra* (from the chair) on issues concerning religion and moral behavior, the pope cannot err.

Pius' successor, Leo XIII (1879–1903) was more flexible and less combative and helped bring the church into the modern age. In his *Rerum novarum* (Concerning new things) issued in 1891, Leo condemned Marxism and upheld capitalism but

This 1895 cartoon satirizes the missionary mania of the age of imperialism. According to the caption, "The Chinaman *must* be converted even if it takes the whole military and naval forces of the two greatest nations of the world [Great Britain and the United States] to do it."

Pope Leo XIII, Rerum Novarum

Pope Leo XIII responded to the radical changes affecting Europe in his encyclical *Rerum Novarum*, issued May 15, 1891. The document addressed the challenges facing Christians and advised them how to respond. See, for example, Leo's advice on unions.

Associations in immense variety and especially unions of workers are now more common than they have ever been. This is not the place to enquire into the origins of most of them, their aims or the methods they employ. There is plenty of evidence to confirm the opinion that many are in the hands of secret leaders and are used for purposes which are inconsistent with both Christian principles and the social good. They do all that they can to ensure that those who will not join them shall not eat. In this state of affairs Christian workers have but two alternatives: they can join these associations and greatly endanger their religion; or they can form their own and, with united strength, free themselves courageously from such injustice and intolerable oppression. That the second alternative must be chosen cannot be doubted by those who have no desire to see men's highest good put into extreme danger. . . .

High praise is due to the many Catholics who have informed themselves, seen what is needed and tried to learn from experience by what honourable means they might be able to lead unpropertied workers to a better standard of living. They have taken up the workers' cause, seeking to raise the incomes of families and individuals, introduce equity into the relations between workers and employers and strengthen among both groups regard for duty and the teaching of the Gospel—teaching which inculcates moderation, forbids excess and safeguards harmony in the state between very differently situated men and organizations. We see eminent men coming together to learn from each other about these things and unite their forces to deal with them as effectively as possible. Others encourage different groups of workers to form useful associations, advise them, give them practical help and enable them to find suitable and well-paid employment. The bishops offer their goodwill and support. . . .

From Leo XIII, *Rerum Novarum*, translated by Joseph Kirwan (London: Catholic Society, 1983).

---

severely criticized the evils affecting the working classes. By pointing out some of the Christian elements of socialism, Leo placed the church on the side of the workers who were suffering the greatest ills resulting from industrialization. Leo worked to improve relations with Germany, encouraged the passage of social welfare legislation, and supported the formation of Catholic labor unions and political parties.

A New Spirit

Spiritual life in England received a powerful stimulus from the Oxford Movement. At the beginning of the nineteenth century, a core of spiritual activists at Oxford, including the future Cardinal, John Henry Newman (1801–1890), met to defend the church from the various secular and political forces that were besieging it. During the 1830s the group split, some members remaining within the Anglican church, and others—including Newman—joining the Catholic church. During the rest of the century, the Oxford Movement brought new life to the church in England through its missionary work, participation in social concerns, and improvement of the intellectual level of the faith. Similar developments occurred across the continent.

Economic Bases for Imperialism

The nineteenth century's economic growth brought with it demands for more money and better management. Industrialists came to live or die by their efficiency, and efficiency often meant consolidation. Large firms could make more products at a cheaper cost than small firms, because they could raise the money to buy the resources, install the newest technology, and train and employ more workers. Large firms carried more political clout than did small ones and lobbied for state policies and regulations that favored them. Some firms, such as that of Alfred Nobel (1833–1896), the Swedish industrialist and inventor of dynamite, set up branches in many different countries. Others tried to control an entire market in one country as did the Standard Oil firm of John D. Rockefeller (1839–1937) in the United States. Whatever the strategy, the gigantic firm became the dominant industrial force.

With the need for more capital, firms began to sell stock to the middle classes. Joint stock companies were not new, but they had not been favored, because if an enterprise failed the investors were liable for its debts. Britain, followed by other industrial states, adopted statutes—limited liability laws—that protected investors from business failure. As wealth increased more people began to "play" the stock market.

New Structures

Businesses developed new strategies to gain control of discrete segments of the market. One new development was the *trust,* an arrangement in which a body of trustees held a majority of stock in a given industry and can control wages, prices, and merchandising policies of several companies. Another tactic was the *holding company,* in which a corporation was incorporated to gain the same control as with the less formal trust. In Europe these alliances took the form of huge industrial combinations known as *cartels.* The cartel, often secret, controlled prices and markets in fundamentally important goods such as rubber or steel. The ultimate way to dominate an area of business was the *monopoly,* in which one firm gains control of the total economic cycle of a product.

The new generations of industrialists developed more efficient management methods. American engineer Frederick W. Taylor (1856–1912) devised the scientific management system, which recommended breaking down each stage of the industrial process to its most

Assembling magnetos on the assembly line at the Ford Motor Company plant in Highland Park, Michigan. One worker could assemble a magneto in 29 minutes; 29 workers, properly arranged, could assemble one in 5 minutes.

minute segment and studying the efficiency of each step of work to establish the optimum speed of productivity. New methods such as the use of interchangeable parts and the introduction of the assembly line brought productivity to a high level by 1914. The new structures could satisfy the infinite desires of a world market.

The New World Economy

From the fifteenth through the eighteenth centuries, a large part of Europe had expansionist ambitions. Prevailing mercantilist theories encouraged the seeking of colonies and monopolies in overseas trade. A combination of political and economic factors, however, slowed down the imperialistic drive in the half century after 1815. Britain's desire for empire had been diminished after the loss of the thirteen American colonies in 1783, and France had lost nearly all of its overseas possessions by the end of the Napoleonic wars. In addition, the laissez-faire school of economics argued against the possession of colonies.

France reignited the drive for world empire during Louis Napoleon's reign, and the scramble for colonies heated up after 1870. In his six years as British prime minister, Disraeli annexed Fiji and Cyprus, fought a war against the Zulus in southeastern Africa, purchased controlling interest in the Suez canal shares, and proclaimed Queen Victoria empress of India. The other major powers in greater or lesser degree followed Britain's lead and the race to carve up the globe began in earnest. It has been estimated that in 1800 fully half of the world was not known to Europeans. By 1900 more land had been explored and acquired by them than in the previous four centuries. The nations of the small, northwest peninsula of the Eurasian landmass claimed control of 60 percent of the earth's surface.

In 1914 Great Britain with its far-flung empire was the world's richest nation. Even though it imported more goods than it exported, it earned nearly a billion dollars a year from overseas investments, shipping fees, and banking and insurance services. Germany had become the continent's economic giant. Its population had risen from 41 million to 65 million between 1871 and 1910. Close cooperation between government and private industry paid dividends. The state established protectionist tariffs after 1879, supported technical education, and encouraged industrial cartels. France lagged behind Germany in both population and industrial output, but it was still an economic power.

In the fifty years before World War I, international trade rose from $7 billion to $42 billion. European nations were by and large their own best customers, even with the tariff barriers that were erected on the continent after 1879. Europe became the chief supplier of world capital: Britain invested heavily in its empire and the United States, France made huge loans to Russia, and Germany and England extended large loans to the Ottoman Empire. The European economic primacy was felt in the far corners of the world. Soon the Argentinean *gaucho*, the Australian sheep man, and the American cowboy—each a symbol of the *free man* in the mythology of his own country—were cogs in the global economic machine of constantly circulating raw materials and finished goods.

The international economy tied the world to the rhythms of the booms and busts of Europe. Economic historians differ in their interpretations of the frequency and causes of the stages of economic expansion and contraction in the business cycle. Whether one believes in a ten-year, twenty-year, or century-long cycle, the fact remains that the world became increasingly an extension of Europe's economic changes.[2] The depression that lasted from 1873 to 1896 is symbolic of the impact of economic events in Europe on the world. Overall, prices fell by roughly 30 percent in all products. Around the world, suffering was severe, especially in those areas that depended on shipping raw materials to cities or abroad and that had no control over the price their products could demand. But by 1896, there had been a readjustment, and the period to 1914 was generally prosperous.

Political Implications

The internationalization of the economy placed diplomacy and finances into common harness.

In this 1876 cartoon from *Punch,* Queen Victoria exchanges her royal crown for a new imperial crown proclaiming her empress of India.

"NEW CROWNS FOR OLD ONES!"

The developing countries needed money to compete in the new world economic system. The industrialized countries looked on the rest of the world as a supplier of labor and raw materials, a market for finished goods, and a place for capital investments.

For the creditor, the investments abroad broke into three logical groupings. The lenders could purchase the bonds of strong nations—a safe investment but with a low rate of return. They could make loans to underdeveloped countries—a riskier venture but with a much higher rate of return. Finally, the financial powers could put their money into stable countries that needed capital in specialized areas. This would ensure a good return on a safe investment. Within these categories were many variations, all of which held the promise of a handsome payoff, usually in financial and political terms.

For the debtor, however, loans could be helpful or devastating, depending on the circumstances. The United States was able to get needed capital with a minimum infringement on its sovereignty. The opposite extreme was the case of the Ottoman empire, which received its first loan in 1854. Twenty-two years later the Turks were so deeply in debt that they had to put a major portion of their tax base in foreign hands just to pay the interest. Unlike the Americans, the Turks put just 10 percent of the borrowed funds to productive use. Other countries had similar results. Russia by 1914 had a funded debt of 9 billion rubles, half of which was owed to foreigners. Hungary had to use 10 percent of its gross national product to pay to foreign investors to cover loans and interest in the pre-war period.[3] Foreign investments of this type were just one facet of Europe's financial dominance. Economic control implied a profound political impact on the debtor country and represented the most efficient form of imperialism.

The Failed Test: The Eastern Question

One of the key geopolitical questions facing the Europeans was the Eastern Question: What was to be done about the disintegrating Ottoman Empire. At the beginning of the nineteenth century, the Turks had sovereignty over the strategic eastern Mediterranean and North African regions. However, they did not possess the power to rule this broad realm effectively, and parts of the area were virtual power vacuums. The Eastern Question would test whether Europe's political wisdom had kept pace with its increase in material strength.

The Balkans Awaken

By the end of the eighteenth century, Ottoman power had substantially declined in the Balkans, just at a time when the various peoples began to experience the waves of nationalism. In 1799, Sultan Selim III acknowledged the independence of the mountainous nation of Montenegro, after its long and heroic defense of its liberty. Further proof of Ottoman weakness came in 1804 when some renegade Turkish troops in Belgrade went on a rampage, disobeyed the sultan's orders, and forced the Serbian people to defend themselves. This initial act of self-protection blossomed into a rebellion that culminated, after eleven difficult years, with the Serbs gaining an autonomous position under the Turks.

Turkish weakness attracted both Russian and British interests. Russia had made a substantial advance toward the Mediterranean during the reign of Catherine II. By the Treaty of Küchük Kainarji (1774) the Russians gained the rights of navigation in Turkish waters and the right to intervene in favor of Eastern Orthodox Christians in the Ottoman Empire. The British protested these gains, and in 1791 Prime Minister William Pitt the Younger denounced Russia for its supposed ambitions to dismember Turkey. Only the common threat of Napoleon from 1798 to 1815 diverted Great Britain and Russia from their competition in the eastern Mediterranean.

The forces of nationalism in Greece took advantage of the chaotic administration of the Turks in 1821. Unlike the Serbian rebellion, the Greek revolution gained substantial outside support from Philhellenic societies of Great Britain. Even though Metternich hoped the revolt would burn itself out, the Greeks were able to take advantage of intervention by the great powers to gain their independence.

During the Greek revolt, the British feared that Russia would use the Greek independence movement as an excuse for further expansion at Turkish expense. The British intervened skillfully, and the Greeks were able to gain their independence without a major Russian advance toward the Straits. Tsar Nicholas I wanted to weaken Turkey in order to pave the way for Russia to gain control over the Dardanelles and the Bosporous. So much did he want this expansion of his realm that he set aside his obligations to support the European balance of power. Britain became alarmed at this policy, and the upshot was an agreement in 1827 in which Britain, France, and Russia pledged themselves to secure Greek independence. Russia eventually defeated the Turks, and in 1829 the Treaty of

THE TREATY OF ADRIANOPLE 1829

Adrianople gave the Greeks the basis for their independence while Serbia received autonomy (see map below left). The Danubian Principalities of Moldavia and Wallachia, the basis of the future state of Romania, became Russian protectorates.

By the 1830s it became apparent that the Turks were to be an object of, rather than a subject in, European diplomacy. The sultan's government had few admirers in Europe, but the European powers agreed—at least for the present—to prop up the decaying Ottoman Empire rather than allow one nation to gain dominance in the strategic area.

In 1832 Mehemet Ali, the virtually independent governor of Egypt, attacked the sultan, easily putting down the forces of the empire. To prevent the establishment of a new and probably stronger government at the Straits, Nicholas I sent an army to protect Constantinople. The Treaty of Unkiar Skelessi (1833) made Turkey a virtual protectorate of Russia.

Britain could not tolerate Russia's advantage, and for the next ten years worked diplomatically to force the tsar to renounce the treaty and sign a general agreement of Turkish independence. This diplomatic game did little to improve the Ottoman Empire's condition. In 1844, while visiting Britain, Nicholas referred to Turkey as a "dying man" and proposed that the British join in a dissection of the body.

The Crimean War

The Crimean War, which lasted from 1853 to 1856, was a major turning point in the course of the Eastern Question. The immediate origins of the war were to be found in a quarrel over the management and protection of the holy places in Palestine. Napoleon III upheld the Roman Catholics' right to perform the housekeeping duties, in a move to gain support from Catholics and the military in France. On the other side, acting under the terms of the treaty signed to Küchük Kainarji in 1774, Nicholas stated that the Orthodox faithful should look after the holy places.

From this obscure argument the Crimean War eventually emerged, as the great powers all intervened in the discussions to protect their interests. The tsarist ambassador to the Turks tried to use the dispute to improve Russia's position in the empire while the British told the sultan to stand firm against the Russians. After the Russians occupied the Danubian Principalities in an attempt to show the Turks the seriousness of their demands, the Turks declared war on the Russians in October 1853. By the next summer the French, Sardinians, and British and joined the Turks. Napoleon III saw the war as a chance to enhance his dynasty's reputation, and the Sardinians found an opportunity to gain allies in their drive for Italian unification. Under the impact of anti-tsarist public opinion the British took steps to stop the Russians. The stated aim of all the allies was, of course, the defense of the Sultan.

A combination of the allies' military strength and the tsarist forces' inefficiency stalemated the Russians. Austria, a former close ally of Russia, took advantage of Russia's difficulties to extend Austrian influence into the Balkans.

The Russians sued for peace and the Treaty of Paris (1856) once again attempted to resolve the Eastern Question. The treaty affirmed the integrity of the Ottoman Empire. The Black Sea was to be a neutral body of water, and the Straits were closed to foreign warships. The treaty declared that no power had the right to intervene on behalf of the sultan's Christian subjects. Russian control of the Principalities was ended. The Crimean War momentarily stopped the Russian advance into the Balkans, but the problems posed by the "sick man of Europe" remained. Further, the various Balkans nations became even more inflamed with the desire for self-rule.

The Unanswered Question

In the generation after the Crimean War the problems posed by the disintegrating Ottoman Empire became more severe. To the north, the Russians, who could do little militarily in the Balkans during this period of intense internal reforms, broadcast the message of Pan-Slavic solidarity to their "Orthodox" brothers in the Balkans. The Austrians, appetites whetted by their part in the Crimean War, kept a wary and opportunistic eye on developments in the Balkans. British loans to the Turks cut into the Turkish tax base and led to the destruction of the indigenous Ottoman textile industry. In addition,

with the completion of the Suez Canal in 1869, the eastern Mediterranean came to be even more essential to British interests. Finally, the Germans began to increase their influence in the area after 1871.

Nationalism further inflamed the unresolved Eastern Question. The Bulgarians, who had been under the Turkish yoke since the fourteenth century, started their national revival in the late eighteenth century. By the 1860s they had formed a liberation movement, which was strengthened in 1870 by the founding of the Bulgarian Exarchate, a Bulgarian wing of the Greek Orthodox faith. The Bulgarians took strength from the example of the Romanians, who after centuries of Turkish dominance and a quarter century as a Russian protectorate had gained their independence in 1861, largely as a result of great power influence. Also, during the 1860s the Serbian leader Michael Obrenovich had worked toward a Balkan union against the Turks. Amid this maneuvering and ferment, the Turks were unable to strengthen their rule over areas theoretically under their control.

The crisis came to a head in 1875, when peasants revolted in the district of Bosnia, a Turkish-governed province populated by a religiously diverse group of Slavs. Following this insurrection Serbia and Montenegro declared war on the Turks. In the summer of 1876, the Bulgarians revolted, but the Ottoman forces forcefully put down the rebellion. When highly emotional accounts of the Turkish massacres were published in western Europe, the incident became known as the "Bulgarian horrors" and drew British attention to the Balkans. The Pan-Slav faithful in Moscow and St. Petersburg were naturally thrilled at the exploits of their "little brothers," and money and "volunteers" flowed southward.

The series of nationalistic uprisings in the improperly governed Ottoman provinces had captured the attention of the great powers, and by the end of 1875 the Eastern Question was once again the main focus of international diplomacy. The "sick man of Europe" was still strong enough to devastate the Serbs and Montenegrins in the field. The insurgents were forced to sue for peace, which drew Tsar Alexander II and the Russians into war with Turkey in 1877. After a hard-fought campaign the Russians broke through early in 1878 and were close to achieving their final goal of taking Constantinople, when the sultan sued for peace.

The resulting Treaty of San Stefano in March 1878 recognized the complete independence of Serbia and Romania from the theoretical Ottoman sovereignty and reaffirmed Montenegro's independence. A large Bulgarian state was set up, nominally tributary to Turkey but actually dominated by Russia. The Straits were effectively under Russian control, as the Bulgarian state would have a coast on the Aegean (see map below). The Eastern Question was almost solved.

Britain and Austria, however, correctly perceived a major shift of the balance of power in Russia's favor, and the two of them forced a reconsideration of the San Stefano treaty at the Congress of Berlin in June and July of 1878. Held

under the supervision of Bismarck, the self-styled "honest broker," the congress compelled Russia to agree to a revision of Bulgaria's status. The large state created in March was broken into three parts: the northernmost would be independent, paying tribute to the Turks, while the other two parts would be Turkish controlled. Austria got the right to "occupy and administer" the provinces of Herzegovina and Bosnia (see map below).

The congress turned back the Russian advance, stymied the national independence movement, and did little to impel Turkey to put its house in order. The Austrian gains caused great bitterness among the Serbs and Russians, a mood that added to the tension in the Balkans. The Eastern Question remained unanswered, and the Balkans remained an arena of local

THE TREATY OF SAN STEFANO 1878

Bulgaria as proposed by the Treaty

THE CONGRESS OF BERLIN 1878

Bulgaria as amended by the Congress of Berlin

The Foundations of European Global Dominance **689**

nationalistic conflicts that would appeal to the imperialistic designs of the great powers, especially the Russians and Austro-Hungarian monarchy.[4]

Conclusion

By 1914 Europe had brought together the material strength, intellectual vitality, and governmental flexibility to dominate the planet. The explosive increase in productivity made possible by industrialization and Europe's massive population growth contributed to the power and personnel to extend economic and political control from the western tip of the Eurasian landmass to the entire world.

In the fields of biology, chemistry, physics, and medicine, European scientists made fundamental discoveries that greatly expanded the frontiers of knowledge. Charles Darwin's work not only upset the understanding of the development of organisms, its popularization had immense, if misdirected social implications. The progress made in economics and science encouraged some Europeans to believe their own superiority and gave them sanction to pursue their destiny. A range of pseudoscientific and racist theories came to be espoused, with terrible consequences.

The Christian faith endured attacks from a number of different quarters during the nineteenth century and made significant changes to respond to new constituents and to play a role in missionary work to the world.

Running like a thread through the century, the Eastern Question, the fate of the disintegrating Ottoman Empire, was transformed from a balance-of-power question to one of small power nationalism and great power expansion. The failure to resolve this question would lead to World War I.

Suggestions for Reading

See Stephen F. Mason, *A History of the Sciences* (Collier, 1962) and Rupert Hall and Marie Boas Hall *A Brief History of Science* (Signet, 1964) for clear and concise surveys of the development of science. The literature on Darwin and his times in voluminous. Darwin's *Origin of Species* and *Voyage of the Beagle* are available in a number of editions. C. C. Gillespie nicely sets the stage for the period in *Genesis and Geology* (Harvard, 1951). G. Himmelfarb's *Darwin and the Darwinian Revolution* (Norton, 1968) and W. Irvine's *Ape, Angels & Victorians: The Story of Darwin, Huxley, & Evolution* (McGraw-Hill, 1955) are excellent studies. R. Hofstadter's *Social Darwinism in Amercian Thought* (Beacon, 1955) is a fascinating study of how a subtle theory can be misapplied. Dubois' *Louis Pasteur: Free Lance of Science* (Little Brown) 1950 is an example of a biography that is sound both as history and literature. J. Bronowski's *The Ascent of Man* (Little, Brown, 1974) is a humane, wise overview of the development of science through the ages.

George F. Mosse provides a valuable overview of intellectual developments during the nineteenth century in *The Culture of Western Europe, the Nineteenth and Twentieth Centuries: An Introduction* (Rand McNally, 1974). Franklin L. Baumer's *Modern European Thought, Continuity and Change in Ideas: 1600–1950* (Macmillan, 1977) is a classic analysis of the development of Western thought and a helpful guide through the nineteenth century.

For background on the factors aiding Europe's expansion abroad, see in addition to suggestions provided in chapter 23; Carl Cipolla, *The Economic History of World Population* (Penguin, 1962); Thomas McKeown, *The Modern Rise of Population* (Academic, 1976); George Lichtheim, *Imperialism* (Praeger, 1971); Heinz Gollwitzer, *Europe in the Age of Imperialism: 1880–1914* (Harcourt Brace Jovanovich, 1979); Roger Price, *The Economic Modernisation of France* (John Wiley, 1975); Sidney Pollard, *European Economic Integration: 1815–1970* (Harcourt, Brace Jovanovich, 1974); D. Fieldhouse, *Colonialism: 1870–1945*; (London, 1981); W. J. Mossman, *Theories of Imperialism*; (London, 1981); Alan Hodgart, *The Economics of European Imperialism* (Norton, 1978); G. H. Nadela nd P. Curtis, eds., *Imperialism and Colonialism* (Macmillan, 1965).

M. S. Anderson's *The Eastern Question, 1774–1923* (St. Martin's, 1966) is the best treatment of the Balkans dilemma. For the nationalities conflicts in the region see Barbara Jelavich, *History of the Balkans*, I (Cambridge, 1983).

Notes

1. C. Darwin, "The Origin of Species," in *Introduction to Contemporary Civilization in the West*, II (New York: Columbia Univ. Press, 1955), pp. 453–454.
2. David S. Landes, *The Unbound Prometheus: Technological Change and Industrial Development in Western Europe from 1750 to the Present* (Cambridge: Cambridge Univ. Pres, 1969), p. 233.
3. Sidney Pollard, *European Economic Integration: 1815–1970* (New York: Harcourt Brace Jovanovich, 1974), pp. 74–78.
4. See M. S. Anderson, *The Eastern Question, 1774–1923* (New York: St. Martin's Press, 1966), *passim*.

Chapter 27

Europe Transplanted

The British Dominions, the United States, and Latin America

The greatest population movement in history took place between 1500 and 1914, when millions of Europeans crossed the oceans and made new homes for themselves (see map below). At the same time, the slave trade brought vast numbers of Africans to the Americas. These immigrants, whether voluntary or forced, brought with them their languages, religions, cultures, political institutions, and laws.

No matter where they settled—the Americas, South Africa, Australia, and New Zealand—the Europeans faced the same challenges of unexplored lands, racial diversity, isolation, and the search for new identities. The newly ascendant

WORLD POPULATION MOVEMENTS

- European
- Japanese
- Chinese
- Indian
- European Russian

middle classes with their generally liberal politics dominated, usually at the expense of the indigenous population or the African slaves.

Although the challenges were the same, the results were unique to each region. Canada, Australia, New Zealand, and the Union of South Africa illustrate the transplantation of British culture to the far corners of the globe. The United States developed the political stability and strong economy that allowed it to grow and prosper, though not without the tragedies of the Civil War, the oppression of its black population, and the devastation of native American culture. Latin America faced fundamental challenges of racial and social diversity, economic exploitation, and political instability.

Common Denominators

In various ways, each of the new lands reflected nineteenth-century movements that had originated in western Europe—nationalism, democracy, and imperialism. In addition, they had problems and opportunities which sprang from conditions specific to their environments. One was the assimilation of the tremendous tide of immigrants entering the new lands. But before the settlers and slaves came, vast spaces had to be explored, paths to the interior mapped, and natural resources located.

Exploration

In what is now Canada, Alexander Mackenzie in 1789 traveled to the Great Slave Lake, then down the river that now bears his name to the shores of the Arctic. Four years later he crossed the Rocky Mountains to the Pacific and thereby became the first European to cross North America at its greatest width.

In the United States, Meriwether Lewis and William Clark started from St. Louis in the winter of 1803–1804, blazed a trail through the unknown Northwest, and reached the Pacific two years later. For a half century the process of exploration and mapping continued, reaching its climax in John Frémont's expeditions to Oregon and California.

The most famous figure in the exploration of South America was the German naturalist Alexander von Humboldt, who from 1799 to 1804 explored Mexico, Cuba, and South America. He investigated the valley of the Orinoco, crossed the Andes, and studied the sources of the Amazon.

The continent of Australia was not crossed from north to south until the middle of the nineteenth century. Between 1860 and 1862 John McDouall Stuart made three attempts before he successfully completed the journey from Adelaide to Van Diemen's Gulf. The penetration of the interior of South Africa differed from explorations in the other new lands. It was achieved by the gradual expansion of white settlement in such movements as the Great Trek rather than by exploratory expeditions.

Immigration

The poor and landless people of Europe settled the vast and often fertile lands found by the explorers. The increase in European population from 200 million to 460 million during the nineteenth century provided the pool of 40 million immigrants who crossed the oceans. By 1914, the number of people of European background living abroad totaled 200 million—a figure almost equal to Europe's population in 1815.

For some 350 years this movement from Europe was accompanied by an equally significant forced migration from West Africa to the Americas. The number transported in the slave trade ran into the millions, and many died from ill treatment at the time of capture and during the forty-day voyage across the Atlantic. This trade cost Africa perhaps 15 million people, not including the Arab slave trade from the East African coast.

Black Africans in the New Lands

In general, the liberal and egalitarian trends in western Europe took root in the new lands. However, the millions of Africans seized and forcibly transplanted to the Americas had little chance to benefit from those ideals.

The slave trade in Latin America began shortly after 1502. Because many native Indians died

A Slave's Memoir

Olaudah Equiano captured the misery of transported slaves in his *Travels*.

One day, when all our people were gone out to their works as usual and only I and my dear sister were left to mind the house, two men and a woman got over our walls, and in a moment seized us both, and without giving us time to cry out or make resistance they stopped our mouths and ran off with us into the nearest wood. Here they tied our hands and continued to carry us as far as they could till night came on, when we reached a small house where the robbers halted for refreshment and spent the night. . . .

The first object which saluted my eyes when I arrived on the coast was the sea, and a slave ship which was then riding at anchor and waiting for its cargo. These filled me with astonishment, which was soon converted into terror when I was carried on board. I was immediately handled and tossed up to see if I were sound by some of the crew, and I was now persuaded that I had gotten into a world of bad spirits and that they were going to kill me. Their complexions too differing so much from ours, their long hair and the language they spoke (which was very different from any I had ever heard) united to confirm me in this belief. Indeed such were the horrors of my views and fears at the moment that, if ten thousand worlds had been my own, I would have freely parted with them all to have exchanged my condition with that of the meanest slave in my own country. When I looked round the ship too and saw a large furnace or copper boiling and a multitude of black people of every description chained together, every one of their countenances expressing dejection and sorrow, I no longer doubted my fate; and quite overpowered with horror and anguish, I fell motionless on the deck and fainted. When I recovered a little I found some black people about me, who I believed were some of those who had brought me on board and had been receiving their pay; they talked to me in order to cheer me, but all in vain. I asked them if we were not to be eaten by those white men with horrible looks, red faces, and loose hair. They told me I was not, and one of the crew brought me a small portion of spirituous liquor in a wine glass, but being afraid of him I would not take it out of his hand. . . .

The stench of the hold while we were on the coast was so intolerably loathsome that it was dangerous to remain there for any time, and some of us had been permitted to stay on the deck for the fresh air; but now that the whole ship's cargo were confined together it became absolutely pestilential. The closeness of the place and the heat of the climate, added to the number in the ship, which was so crowded that each had scarcely room to run himself, almost suffocated us. This produced copious perspirations, so that the air soon became unfit for respiration from a variety of loathsome smells, and brought on a sickness among the slaves, of which many died, thus falling victims to the improvident avarice, as I may call it, of their purchasers. This wretched situation was again aggravated by the galling of the chains, now become insupportable, and the filth of the necessary tubs, into which the children often fell and were almost suffocated. The shrieks of the women and the groans of the dying rendered the whole a scene of horror almost inconceivable. Happily perhaps for myself I was soon reduced so low here that it was thought necessary to keep me almost always on deck, and from my extreme youth I was not put in fetters. . . .

At last we came in sight of the island of Barbados, at which the whites on board gave a great shout and made many signs of joy to us.

From Paul Edwards, ed., *Equiano's Travels: His Autobiography, The Interesting Narrative of the Life of Olaudah Equiano or Gustavus Vassa the African* (London: Heinemann Educational Books, 1967).

from European diseases such as smallpox and measles, the local population could not fill the mounting demand for labor on the plantations. To meet that demand, the influx of black slaves increased geometrically. The first slaves imported into Brazil arrived in 1538. By 1600 they formed the basis of the economy there, along the Peruvian coast, in Mexico's hot lands, in Santo Domingo, in Cuba, and in the mines of Colombia. By 1800 the population of Haiti was predominantly black or mulatto, and the African element was substantial in Brazil and Cuba. There were smaller, though still significant, black populations in the Dominican Republic, Panama, Venezuela, and Colombia.

A century after Africans were brought to Latin America, they appeared in the English colonies to the north. The first blacks landed in Jamestown in 1619, but their status was uncertain for some fifty years. Between 1640 and 1660 there is evidence of slavery, and after the latter date the slave system was defined by law in several of the colonies. White indentured servants, at first an important part of the work force, were soon replaced by African slaves, who provided a lifetime of work to the plantation owner. In 1790 when the white population was just over 3 million, there were some 750,000 blacks in the United States.

During the American Revolution, serious questions arose about the morality of slavery. Some people saw an embarrassing contradiction between human bondage and the ideals of the Declaration of Independence. This antislavery sentiment temporarily weakened as fear grew over a bloody slave insurrection in Santo Domingo, unrest among American slaves, and the unsettling economic and social consequences of the French Revolution. Slave rebellions in the early 1800s shocked many Americans.

The Industrial Revolution played a large role in harnessing slavery to the economy of the southern states. English textile mills required an increased supply of cotton. New technology and new lands made the plantation system more profitable, creating an additional demand for slaves even as their importation ended in 1808.

Race Problems in the New Lands

The imposition of European hegemony over native inhabitants in the far corners of the globe

This 1856 engraving shows slaves pressing cotton on a Louisiana plantation. Slaves often labored 14 hours a day and even as many as 18 hours during harvest time.

COTTON PRESSING IN LOUISIANA

Slaves rose up against the French in Saint Domingue in 1791. Napoleon sent an army to restore slavery in 1799, but many of the French soldiers died of yellow fever, and the rebels defeated the decimated French army in 1803.

and the slave trade created tragic racial conflicts. It is difficult to gain an accurate estimate of the number of Indians in North America, but it is generally held that before European settlement there were around 200,000 in Canada and 850,000 in the United States. Since the arrival of white settlers, the number of Indians in the two North American areas has been reduced by approximately half, largely through disease and extermination. While in modern time attempts have been made to help native Americans make a place for themselves in urban society, these efforts have generally been inadequate. Even though in the past two centuries Canada has compiled a much more humane record dealing with native Americans than the United States, Indians remain the most neglected and isolated minority in North America.

The aborigines of Australia and Tasmania—numbering possibly 300,000 at the time of the arrival of the Europeans—were decimated by the diseases and liquors brought by the white settlers. The native inhabitants could not adjust to the new ways of life brought about by the disappearance of their hunting grounds. At times they were treated brutally: in some places they were rounded up in gangs and shot; sometimes the Europeans encouraged drunkenness among the natives, then gave them clubs to fight each other

for the entertainment of the "civilized" spectators. The natives of Tasmania are now extinct, and the aborigines of Australia are a declining race.

In New Zealand the native Maoris were better able to stand up to the whites. After serious wars in the 1860s peace was finally secured and the Maoris slowly accommodated themselves to the new world created by the whites. Since 1900 the Maoris have shared the same political rights and privileges as the white settlers and have obtained the benefits of advanced education. The Maoris now constitute about 9 percent of the population and their numbers are increasing.

In two areas colonized by Europeans, Latin America and South Africa, the indigenous peoples greatly outnumbered the white settlers. Some authorities, for example, estimate that the population of Latin America in pre-Columbian days was at least 25 million. While a large percentage of these people died following the initial

This 1816 pictograph was meant to demonstrate to Australian aborigines the evenhandedness of British justice.

This family picture of a mestizo father, a Spanish mother, and their daughter, known as a castiza, was part of a racial chart of Mexican peoples.

European impact because of disease, war, and famine, in the long run their numbers substantially increased. There was much racial mixing between the Indians and the Europeans, giving rise to the *mestizo*. This mixed strain together with the Indians outnumbered the white population. In the early twentieth century population there were estimated to be 20 million Indian, 30 million *mestizos*, 26 million black and mulatto, and 34 million white. Only in Argentina, Chile, and a few smaller states such as Costa Rica, Cuba, and Uruguay have European stocks overwhelmed the Indians.

The thousand years of contact between the Spanish and Portuguese with the dark-skinned Moorish people and their early African explorations helped prevent the development of the virulent form of racism found in North America. There was also a difference in the status of the slave in North and South America. In the north the slave was regarded as a piece of property, with no legal or moral rights. In the south, because of the traditions of Roman law and the Catholic church, slaves had a legal personality and moral standing.

Even though slave status was generally considered to be perpetual, gaining freedom was not as difficult in Latin America as in the north. By 1860 free blacks outnumbered slaves 2 to 1 in Brazil while slaves outnumbered free blacks 8 to 1 in the United States. Finally, there has been greater racial mixing in Latin America. The greatest meld of races—red, white, and black—in the history of the world has taken place there. This intermingling has gone a long way to ease racial tensions.[1]

In South Africa the indigenous people were not exterminated, but they were denied the opportunity to share in European civilization. The fierce fighting between the European frontier people (mainly the Dutch) and the Africans caused constant misunderstanding and fear. Despite many political and economic disabilities, in the nineteenth century the South African natives showed a substantial increase in numbers. By 1904 the population breakdown of the roughly 8 million people showed 21.6 percent European, 67.4 percent African, 2.4 percent Asiatic, and 8.6 percent "coloured." Unlike the situation in Latin America, the European minority resolutely opposed any mixing with the nonwhites and enforced unyielding segregation—*apartheid*.

The Search for a New Nationality

The transplanted Europeans generally focused their energies on domestic matters and left world affairs to the European states. Those under the British flag generally accepted British leadership in world affairs and depended on London's fleet for protection. The United States devoted considerable energy to exploiting its vast natural resources and Americanizing the millions of immigrants who flocked to its shores. Latin America was politically unstable but rich in natural resources. The region managed to avoid the cruder imperialistic partitions and outright annexations so evident in Africa, China, and Southeast Asia. This lack of total exploitation owed more to luck rather than to the virtue of the outside powers. The economic interests of the United States—and to some extent of Britain—coincided with the preservation of the status quo in Latin Ameria.

Among all the transplanted Europeans, the United States found the quest for independence the easiest. Its power, size, resources, and heritage of freedom and the rule of law contributed to a distinctive and recognizable national ideal that survived the threat of the Civil War. The search for national unity has not been as successful in Canada, given the split between the closely knit French Canadian minority and the majority English-speaking population.

Nationalism has burned brightly in each of the Latin American nations, sometimes at the expense of political stability. The eight major administrative divisions in the late colonial era have fragmented into nineteen states—a process frequently accompanied by insurrection, rebellion, and war.

Australia and New Zealand have found the search for a new nationality difficult. Remote from Europe, inhabitants of these islands have clung to the traditions and life of their ancestors, even to the point that the New Zealanders claim to be more British than the British. More difficult is the situation in South Africa where the white majority are the Boers rather than the British. These Afrikaners have developed a distinctive, unbending culture based on rigid Calvinism and the Dutch tongue. The dislike of the British segment may have lessened recently because of a common fear of black domination and resentment of the outside world for its criticism of *apartheid*.

The British Dominions

The British Dominions became self-governing without breaking their political ties to Great Britain. With the exception of South Africa, these new nations were predominantly British in stock, language, culture, and governmental traditions. In the case of Canada, however, a strong French Canadian minority in Quebec, inherited from the original French regime, persisted and preserved its French heritage. In South Africa, following a confused history of rivalry and war between the British and Dutch settlers, a shaky union was achieved. There were no complications of rival Europeans in Australia and New Zealand, which were settled by the British in the beginning and did not have to adjust to an influx of other Europeans. Both Australia and Canada attained political unity by merging a number of colonies into a single government.

South Africa

The first European contact in the area later known as the Union of South Africa, located at the southern tip of Africa, occurred in 1487 when Bartholomew Diaz reached the Cape of Good Hope. Ten years later Vasco da Gama rounded the Cape on his way to the Indies. Two centuries later, large fleets of Dutch ships made their way around Africa to the Indies to trade for spices and oriental wares. The cape became a strategic place to get fresh water and replenish supplies.

In 1651 the Dutch established a settlement at the Cape of Good Hope, named Cape Town, which grew slowly. As the Dutch settlers pushed inland, they came into conflict with the Bantu-speaking Africans, who strongly resisted white expansion. The Dutch period of South African history came to an end in 1814 when the Dutch ceded the colony to Great Britain.

Friction between the British and the Boers, or Dutch burghers, quickly developed over the treatment of the native peoples. The Dutch had many slaves and resented the attitudes of the missionaries, who continually accused the Dutch of abusing the natives. Britain's emancipation of all slaves in the empire in 1833 exacerbated ill feeling.

Two years later 12,000 Boers undertook an epic journey in their ox-drawn wagons to a new country where they could pursue their way of life without interference. This Great Trek was a folk movement comparable to the covered wagon epic of the American West.[2] Finally on the high plateau, or *veld*, the Boers established two little republics, the Orange Free State and the Transvaal. The British, in the meantime, extended their settlement along the eastern coast north of the Cape and founded the colony of Natal (see map, p. 698).

The Great Trek did little to resolve the difficulties of the Boers. In the mid-nineteenth century there was much fighting with the Africans, who resisted the incursions of both Boers and British. In 1852 the British government made treaties with the Boers, acknowledging the independence of the Organge Free State and the Transvaal but

UNION OF SOUTH AFRICA

RHODESIA

RMAN

THWEST

FRICA

BECHUANALAND
(British Prot. 1885)

Limpopo R.

PORT.

EAST

AFRICA

TRANSVAAL

•Pretoria

Mafeking•

•Johannesburg

BRITISH BECH.
(Annexed 1885)

ORANGE
FREE
STATE

Kimberley•

Bloemfontein•

Great Trek 1835-1848

•Ladysmith

NATAL

BASUTO-
LAND

•Durban

Orange R.

CAPE COLONY

•Graaff Reinet

•East London

•Cape Town

•Port Elizabeth

INDIAN OCEAN

British imperial interests. Born in 1853, he had a frail constitution and as a young man emigrated to South Africa to improve his health. He became fabulously wealthy in the diamond fields, the leading figure in the DeBeers diamond syndicate and the owner of many goldmining properties in the Transvaal. Rhodes was determined to thwart Kruger by uniting a self-governing South Africa within the British Empire.

To forestall Kruger's plans, Rhodes persuaded Britain to annex territory on the Transvaal's eastern and western borders. He prevented Boer expansion to the north by gaining extensive settlement and mining right in the high and fertile plateau through which flowed the Zambezi River. In 1890 the town of Salisbury was founded, becoming the capital of the region named Rhodesia.

Meanwhile, the *Uitlanders* began to plot an insurrection. At the close of 1895, a group of Rhodesian mounted police invaded the Transvaal, but they were quickly forced to surrender

Cecil Rhodes. He once declared that his lifelong dream was to "bring the whole civilized world under British rule, to make the Anglo-Saxon race into an empire."

retaining a shadowy right to have a voice in the foreign affairs of the two republics.

The Boer War. The discovery of diamonds in 1868 on the borders of the Cape and of gold in 1885 in the Transvaal attracted thousands of Englishmen and people of other nations to the mines. The president of the Transvaal, Paul Kruger, was determined that these newcomers would not gain control. He was passionately devoted to the Boer way of life, which was simple, mainly rural, and uncomplicated. To curb the growing power of the *Uitlanders* (outlanders), Kruger began to impose heavy taxes on them, while the Boers paid practically nothing. English was banned in the courts and public schools. It was almost impossible for the *Uitlanders* to become naturalized citizens of the Transvaal.

Kruger's main adversary was Cecil Rhodes, a man of driving ambition both for himself and for

Sidney Low on Cecil Rhodes

During his time, Cecil Rhodes stood as the foremost European imperialist in Africa. The journalist Sidney Low captured Rhodes' philosophical essence.

Whatever inconsistency there may have been in his actions, his opinions, so far as I could perceive, did not vary. In fact, he repeated himself a good deal, having a kind of apostolic fervour in expatiating on the broad simple tenets of the Rhodesian religion. His cardinal doctrines I should say were these: First, that insular England was quite insufficient to maintain, or even to protect, itself without the assistance of the Anglo-Saxon peoples beyond the seas of Europe. Secondly, that the first and greatest aim of British statesmanship should be to find new areas of settlement, and new markets for the products that would, in due course, be penalised in the territories and dependencies of all our rivals by discriminating tariffs. Thirdly, that the largest tracts of unoccupied or undeveloped lands remaining on the globe were in Africa, and therefore that the most strenuous efforts should be made to keep open a great part of that continent to British commerce and colonisation. Fourthly, that as the key to the African position lay in the various Anglo-Dutch States and provinces, it was imperative to convert the whole region into a united, self-governing, federation, exempt from meddlesome interference by the home authorities, but loyal to the Empire, and welcoming British enterprise and progress. Fifthly, that the world was made for the service of man, and more particularly of civilised, white, European men, who were most capable of utilising the crude resources of nature for the promotion of wealth and prosperity. And, finally, that the British Constitution was an absurd anachronism, and that it should be remodelled on the lines of the American Union, with federal self-governing Colonies as the constituent States. . . .

From Sidney Low, *Contemporary Recollections,"* in *The Nineteenth Century and After,* 1902.

to a force of Boer commandos. This incident alienated the Dutch population in the Cape, pushed the Orange Free State into an alliance with the Transvaal, and strengthened Kruger's policies.

The South African crisis now moved from the area of covert *Uitlander* plots to British diplomacy. Britain did not want totally independent Boer states. British statesmen also feared that a hostile Transvaal, with its immense mining wealth and consequent economic power, would be able to dominate all South Africa. From 1896 to the spring of 1899 continuous efforts were made to reconcile Boer and British differences but without success. Britain began to send troops, and the Transvaal and the Orange Free State prepared for war. Hostilities began in the fall of 1899.

The world was amazed at the war that followed. The Boers were crack shots and expert horsemen. Knowing every inch of ground on which they fought, they frequently outmaneuvered the British troops. But the tide turned in 1900 when the British inflicted several disastrous defeats on the Boers.

The Union of South Africa. After the Boers surrendered in 1902, the British treated them magnanimously. They gave them loans to rebuild burned farmhouses and buy cattle, and more significantly, they extended the right of self-government to the Transvaal in 1906 and to the Orange Free State two years later. The Liberal government in Great Britain permitted the Boer and English states to unite and form the Union of South Africa in 1909. Only seven years after the war, Boer and Briton joined hands to create a new self-governing dominion. The first prime minister of the Union was Louis Botha (1863–1919), who had been a Boer general in the war. Botha's primary purpose was to create neither an English nor a Boer nationality but a blend of the two in a new South African patriotism.

Australia

The discovery of Australia dates back to the seventeenth century, when Dutch explorers sighted its shores. Captain Cook's South Seas voyage in 1769, however, paved the way for British settlement. In 1788 Britain transported a group of convicts to Australia and settled them at Sydney. From the parent colony of Sydney, later called New South Wales, five other settlements were founded.

Although a majority of the first Europeans in Australia were prisoners, most of them were political prisoners and debtors, rather than hardened criminals. After seven years of servitude many were liberated and as "emancipists" became citizens. Quite early in the ninteenth century, many free settlers also came to Australia. They began to protest the dumping of convicts in their new home, and Britain took the first steps to end the practice in 1840. By 1850 the Australian colonies were enjoying a liberal form of self-government.

The Australian colonies grew slowly during the first half of the nineteenth century. Sheep raising became the basis of the economy. The discovery of gold in 1851 quickened the tempo of development, but agriculture continued to be the mainstay of Australia's economy. Railway mileage was expanded, and large investments of foreign capital helped the young nation to develop its resources. In 1850 the population of the country was about 400,000; a decade later it had nearly doubled. In the decade before 1914 the population increased from just under 4 million to 5 million people.

In 1901 the six Australian colonies formed a federal union known as the Commonwealth of Australia, which bears many resemblances to the American system of government. The legislature is composed of a House of Representatives and a Senate. Each state elects six senators, while the lower house is made up of members elected by each state in accordance with its population. In the Commonwealth government the chief executive, the prime minister, is responsible to the legislature, and thus does not prossess the fixed term guaranteed the American president.

New Zealand

About a thousand miles from the Australian mainland is a group of islands, two of which are of particular importance. These lonely projections of British influence in the South Pacific constitute the self-governing Dominion of New Zealand. The total population of this country, which has an area five-sixths the size of Great Britain, is just over 3.3 million. The earliest white

Because it was considered too far from England to be attractive to free settlers, Australia was first used as a penal colony for English convicts. Although many of the convicts were sentenced to deportation for relatively minor offenses, they often suffered great cruelty and hardships in the prison camps. Here, English convicts plow an Australian field while the guard cracks the whip over their heads.

settlers were desperate convicts who had escaped from penal settlements in Australia. The activity of other colonizers forced the British government to assume protection of the islands in 1840, and British agents signed a treaty guaranteeing certain rights, especially land rights, to the Maoris.

New Zealand gradually became a rich pastoral, farming, and fruit-raising country. The chief export, then as now, was wool. Later the development of refrigeration enabled large quantities of meat and dairy products to be shipped to foreign markets, especially to Great Britain.

Both New Zealand and Australia have been seen as sociological laboratories because of their pioneering activities in democratic government and social welfare legislation. As early as 1855, the state of Victoria in Australia introduced the secret ballot in elections. The "Australian ballot" was later adopted in Great Britain, the United States, and other parts of the world. Woman suffrage was introduced in New Zealand in 1893 and in Australia nine years later. In New Zealand a program of "land for the people" was implemented through the imposition of heavy taxes on large tracts of land held by absentee landlords. New Zealand also led the world in the adoption of noncontributory old-age pensions in 1878 and the establishment of a national infant welfare system in 1907. Before 1914 Australia had passed similar measures.

Canada

From 1534, when Jacques Cartier sailed up the Saint Lawrence River and claimed the area for France, until 1763, Canada was part of the French empire. Unlike the English colonies in the New World, the French colony of Canada was rigidly supervised by Paris. The home government supervised all trade activities, and the Catholic church monopolized education. Few Protestants were allowed to settle in New France. The French king granted huge tracts of land to nobles, who in turn parceled out their estates to peasant farmers. This introduction of a version of European feudalism seriously hampered development in Canada. It limited expansion by denying free land to pioneers, and it also subjected the population to restrictive control by royal officials, priests, and nobles.

Canada became caught up in the worldwide French-British competition. In addition to Britain's interest in its Atlantic seaboard colonies, its fishermen frequently landed at Newfoundland. In 1670 the Company of Gentlemen Adventurers of England Trading into Hudson's Bay was chartered to carry on fur trading with the Indians. When war broke out in Europe between France and Britain, their colonies in the New World also went to war. Britain's ultimate victory was anticipated in the Treaty of Utrecht (1713) in which France gave up Acadia (later known as Nova Scotia), surrendered claims to Newfoundland, and recognized the Hudson's Bay Company territory as English.

The last of the four colonial wars ended in a complete victory for Britain. In 1763, by the Treaty of Paris, the British gained all of Canada. London tried to ensure the loyalty of the French Canadians by issuing a royal proclamation guaranteeing the inhabitants' political rights and their freedom to worship as Roman Catholics. These guarantees were strengthened in 1774 when the British government passed the Quebec Act, called the "Magna Carta of the French Canadian race." This act reconfirmed the position of the Catholic church and perpetuated French laws and customs. However, there was no provision for a representative assembly, such as existed in English-speaking colonies. At that time the French lacked both the interest and experience in self-government.

Canada's Formative Stage. The period from 1763 to 1867 is known as the formative stage of Canada. A number of developments took place during this period; the growth of the English-speaking population, the defeat of an attempted conquest by the United States, the grant of local self-government, and finally the confederation of Canada into a dominion.

The major source of growth of the English-speaking population was the American Revolution. Although the rebellious colonists tried to conquer Canada, the Canadians remained loyal to Britain, largely because of the liberal provisions of the Quebec Act, and the invasion failed. Those inhabitants of the thirteen colonies not in favor of separation from Great Britain suffered at the hands of the victorious patriots, and a large number of them went to Canada. The

The Loyalist encampment at Johnston, a settlement on the banks of the St. Lawrence River in Canada, founded on June 6, 1784.

immigrants, known as United Empire Loyalists, settled in Nova Scotia, along the Saint Lawrence River, and north of the Great Lakes.

The newcomers resented the absence of political representation in their new home and pushed for a measure of self-government. Numerous struggles arose between the French Canadians and the newly arrived Loyalists. To meet this situation the British in 1791 divided British North America into two separate provinces called Upper and Lower Canada and granted each of them a representative assembly. The quarrel between the English- and French-speaking populations has continued to the present day.

Open rebellion in 1837 was put down militarily, and in response, the British government sent a special commissioner, Lord Durham (1792–1840), to study the Canadian situation and make recommendations. A statesman with vision, Durham realized that a much larger degree of self-government had to be granted if the home country wished to keep the loyalty of its colonies. He recommended that certain matters of imperial concern, such as foreign relations, should be directed from London, but that Canada alone should control its own domestic affairs. By the mid-nineteenth century London granted self-government to Canada. Unlike the thirteen colonies that severed their connection with the parent country by revolution, Canada achieved virtual independence peacefully and remained loyal to Britain.

Fear of the United States, the need for a common tariff policy, and a concerted effort to develop natural resources led Canadians into confederation. A plan of union, the British North American Act, was drawn up, approved by the British government, and passed by the Parliament in London in 1867. This act united Canada—until then divided into the provinces of Quebec and Ontario, Nova Scotia, and New Brunswick—into a federal union of four provinces. The new government had some similarities to the political organization of the United States, but it adopted the British cabinet system, with its principle of ministerial responsibility. As a symbol of its connection with Great Britain, provision was made for a governor-general who was to act as the British monarch's person representative to Canada.

Modern Canada. The new nation encountered many problems from the first. Its vast size caused communications problems, which became even more acute in 1869 when the dominion purchased the territories of the Hudson's Bay Company extending from present-day Ontario to the Pacific coast, south to the Columbia River (see map, p. 703). In 1871 the new colony of British

Columbia joined the dominion on the promise of early construction of a transcontinental railroad to link the west coast with eastern Canada.

Another disturbing problem was the lack of good relations with the United States. After the Civil War, Irish patriots in the United States, seeking revenge against the British for their treatment of Ireland, launched armed incursions over the border. However, in 1871 the major differences between the two countries were ironed out in the Treaty of Washington, a landmark in the use of arbitration.

The country developed rapidly under the leadership of the dominion's first prime minister, Sir John A. Macdonald (1815–1891), who served from 1867 to 1873 and again from 1878 to 1891. Canadians developed their country through encouraging new industry, putting a railroad across the country in 1885, and attracting immigrants. Sir Wilfrid Laurier (1841–1919), who served as prime minister from 1896 to 1911, continued Macdonald's work. Between 1897 and 1912, Canada received 2,250,000 new citizens, bringing the total population to over 7 million. Internal restructuring created new provinces out of the former Hudson's Bay Company holdings, so that in 1914 the dominion consisted of nine provinces. At the same time, the country had to deal with the consequences of its rapid growth: labor discontent, corruption, and agrarian unrest. Canada was becoming a mature nation, with all of the accompanying problems of depressions, maldistribution of wealth, and the need for governmental restraint of business.

A more long-lasting challenge has been the bicultural nature of the country. In 1761, the entire country was French, but a momentous change began with the American Revolution, when English-speaking American Loyalists wishing to keep their British allegiance fled to Canada. In 1761 there were only 65,000 people in New France; by 1815 the population of all the British North American colonies had increased to 600,000, of whom only 250,000 were French. Between 1815 and 1850 a second wave of immigrants from Britain brought the entire population to 2,400,000, of whom fewer than one-third were French. During the nineteenth century, and indeed down to the present, the population of French origin has remained between 28 and 31 percent of the total.

From the first arrival of significant numbers of British to the latter part of the twentieth century, the relations between the French and English speakers have been strained. Lord Durham saw this clearly in 1837 when he wrote "I found two nations warring in the bosom of a single state; I found a struggle not of principles but of races." Durham singled out the most persistent and disturbing problem facing Canada.

This cultural conflict is based on the French resentment of the British victory two centuries ago and the British pride in that accomplishment. There was also a clash in the field of religion. New France was highly conservative, ruled by an authoritarian regime. When this political authority was removed, the Catholic church in Quebec became the main defender and citadel of French Catholic culture. The English-speaking Canadians, however, tended to be antagonistic to the church's role. Further complicating relations was the fact that the French portion remained largely agricultural with a high rate of illiteracy. The British were more urban and technologically educated, and consequently the English-speaking part became richer and dominant. Although the federal constitution sought to create a bilingual society and a dual school system, the French continued to be bitter over the progressive erosion of this guaranteed equality in the western provinces, where no appreciable French population developed. The English-speaking Canadians assumed a pose of superiority and ridiculed French culture, while making little effort to learn the French language.

At the end of the nineteenth century, while Canada was a united federation in political structure, a common Canadianism had not been achieved. The French had no intention of being absorbed by the culture of the majority. At the end of the twentieth century how to create a single nationality comprised of two separate but offically equal cultures remained Canada's major problem.

The United States

The revolutionary movements in Europe during the nineteenth century fought aristocratic domination or foreign rule—or both. The nineteenth-century struggles in the United States were not quite the same. Instead, there were two major related problems. One was the annexation, settlement, and development of the continent; the other was slavery. Free land and unfree people were the sources of the many political confrontations that culminated in the Civil War, the greatest struggle of nineteenth-century America.

At the conclusion of its successful revolution in 1783, the United States was not a democracy. At the time of the ratification of the Constitution only one male in seven had the vote. Religious requirements and property qualifications ensured that only a small elite participated in government. These restrictions allowed patricians from established families in the south and men of wealth and substance in the north to control the country for nearly half a century.

Democratic Influences

The influence of the western frontier helped make America more democratic. Even before the Constitution was ratified, thousands of pioneers crossed the Appalachian Mountains into the new "western country." In the west, land was to be had for the asking, social caste did not exist, one person was as good as another. Vigor, courage, self-reliance, and competence counted, not birth or wealth. Throughout the nineteenth century the west was the source of new and liberal movements that challenged the conservative ideas prevalent in the east.

Until the War of 1812, democracy grew slowly. In 1791 Vermont had been admitted as a manhood suffrage state, and the following year

Armed members of the White League guard the ballot box to prevent newly enfranchised black citizens from depositing their ballots.

Kentucky followed suit; but Tennessee, Ohio, and Louisiana entered the Union with property and tax qualifications for the vote. After 1817 no new state entered the Union with restrictions on male suffrage except for slaves. Most appointive offices became elective, and requirements for holding office were liberalized.

Andrew Jackson changed the tone and emphasis of American politics. In 1828 he was elected to the presidency following a campaign that featured the slogan "down with the aristocrats." He was the first president produced by the west; the first since George Washington not to have a college education; and the first to have been born in poverty. He owed his election to no congressional clique, but to the will of the people, who idolized "Old Hickory" as their spokesman and leader.

The triumph of the democratic principle in the 1830s set the direction for political development. With Jackson's election came the idea that any man, by virtue of being an American citizen, could hold any office in the land. Governments widened educational opportunities by enlarging the public school system. With increased access to learning, class barriers became less important. The gaining and keeping of political power came more and more to be tied to satisfying the needs of the people who voted.

Simultaneous with the growth of democracy came the territorial expansion of the country. The Louisiana territory, purchased from France for about $15 million in 1803, doubled the size of the United States (see map, p. 706). In 1844, Americans influenced by "manifest destiny," the belief that their domination of the continent was God's will, demanded "All of Oregon or none." The claim led to a boundary dispute with Great Britain over land between the Columbia River and 54′ 40″ north latitude. In 1846 the two countries accepted a boundary at the 49th parallel, and the Oregon territory was settled. The annexation of Texas in 1845 was followed by war with Mexico in 1846. In the peace agreement signed two years later Mexico ceded California, all title to Texas, and the land between California and Texas to the United States. As a result of these acquisitions, by 1860 the area of the United States had increased by two-thirds over what it had been in 1840.

The addition of the new territories forced the issue of whether slavery should be allowed in those areas. Parallelling developments in Great Britain, abolitionists in the United States, particularly New England, vigorously condemned slavery. Henry Clay's Missouri Compromise of 1820 permitted slavery in Missouri but forbade it in the rest of the Louisiana Purchase. This settlement satisfied both sides for only a short time. The antislavery forces grew more insistent. In the senatorial campaigns of 1858, candidate Abraham Lincoln declared:

A house divided against itself cannot stand. I believe this government cannot endure permanently half slave and half free. I do not expect the Union to be dissolved—I do not expect the house to fall—but I do expect it will cease to be divided. It will become all one thing, or all the other.[3]

Slavery was an important issue; it served as a focus for the differences and tensions separating the North from the South. However, a more

TERRITORIAL EXPANSION OF
THE UNITED STATES 1783-1853

fundamental cause of conflict was that, in a sense, the two sections had become separate societies. The former was industrial, urban, and democratic; the latter was mainly agricultural, rural, and dominated by a planter aristocracy. The South strongly opposed the North's desire for higher tariffs, government aid for new railroads, and generous terms for land settlement in the West. These fundamental differences brought North and South to war. Slavery served as a moral irritant.

The Civil War and Its Results

Soon after Abraham Lincoln was inaugurated as president, the southern states seceded from the Union and formed the Confederate States of America. The first shot of the Civil War was fired at Fort Sumter, South Carolina, in 1861, initiating the bloodiest war experienced by any western nation to that time. Four agonizing years of conflict, in which more than one-half million men died, ended when General Robert E. Lee surrendered to General Ulysses S. Grant at Appomattox Courthouse in Virginia in April 1865. A few days later, the nation was stunned by assassination of President Lincoln, who had just begun his second term.

With the final collapse of the Confederacy before the overwhelming superiority of the Union in manpower, industrial resources, and wealth, the Civil War became the grand epic of American history in its heroism, romance, and tragedy. The victorious North used military occupation to try to force the south to extend voting and property rights to the former slaves. Eventually, this so-called Reconstruction period (1865–1877) was ended by a tacit agreement between the northern industrial and the southern white leaders that enabled the latter to regain political control and to deprive blacks of their newly won rights. Southerners invoked Social Darwinist arguments to justify their actions in denying full "blessings of freedom" to the former slaves.

Southern politicians deprived blacks of their voting rights by enacting state laws or employing devices such as poll taxes, literacy tests, property qualifications, and physical threats. Racial segregation in schools, restaurants, parks, and hotels was effectively applied. Laws prohibiting interracial marriage were enacted, and blacks were generally excluded from unions. Between 1885 and 1918, more than 2500 blacks were lynched in the United States. As second-class citizens, freed but landless, the former slaves essentially formed a sharecropping class,

American artist Henry Ossawa Tanner demonstrated remarkable talent to create a strong and memorable mood, as is evident in *The Banjo Lesson* (1893).

George Washington Carver. As director of agricultural research at Tuskegee Institute, he derived many new products from southern crops.

mired in poverty and deprived of equal educational opportunity.[4]

It took more than a century after the Civil War for black Americans to gain a politically equal footing. Despite all of the obstacles they encountered in the half century after the Emancipation Proclamation, by 1914 black Americans made some substantial achievements: the creation of a professional class estimated at 47,000; a 70 percent literacy rate; ownership of 550,000 homes, 40,000 businesses, and savings of some $700 million. Black churches, banks, and insurance companies evoled into substantial institutions. In addition black individuals made major contributions to a number of different fields: Henry Ossawa Tanner (1859–1937) was recognized as a distinguished painter; George Washington Carver (1865–1943) made substantial contributions in the field of agricultural chemistry; and W. E. B. DuBois (1868–1963), a social scientist of national stature, began the first effective black political protest early in the century.

If the causes and consequences of the American Civil War are complex, the all-important result was simple. It settled the issue of whether the United States was an indivisible sovereign nation or a collection of sovereign states. The sacrifice of hundreds of thousands of lives preserved the Union, but the inhuman treatment of blacks remained.

Development, Abuse, and Reform

The North's victory was a boost for industrialization as well as a result of it—and the economic revolution in the United States that followed was more significant than the conflict itself. Railroads were built across broad prairies and the first transcontinental line, the Union Pacific, was completed in 1869.

Settlers swarmed west. Between 1850 and 1880 the number of cities with a population of 50,000 or more doubled. The number of men employed in industry increased 50 percent. In 1865 there were 35,000 miles of railroads in the country. By 1900 the trackage was estimated to be about 200,000—more than in all of Europe. In 1860 a little more than a billion dollars was invested in manufacturing; by 1900 this figure had risen to 12 billion. The value of manufactured products increased proportionately. In 1870 the total production of iron and steel in the United States was far below that of France and Britain. Twenty years later the United States had outstripped them and was producing about one-third of the world's iron and steel.

In the age of rapid industrialism and materialistic expansion, many who pursued profits lost sight of ethical principles both in business and government. In five years, between 1865 and 1870, the notorious Tweed Ring cost the city of New York at least $100 million. Ruthless financiers, such as Jay Gould and Jim Fisk, tampered with the basic financial stability of the nation. The administration of President Ulysses Grant was tainted by scandals and frauds. A new rich class failed to appreciate its responsibilities to society. Corruption was a blatant feature of the new order.

Railroad companies distributed elaborately illustrated brochures and broadsides to lure people to the West, where they would settle on land owned by the railroad.

For roughly a century the gospel for the new nation of America had been rugged individualism. As in Europe, governmental interference in business was unwelcome because of the strong belief that individuals should be free to follow their own inclinations, run their own businesses, and enjoy the profits of their labors. In an expanding nation where land, jobs, and opportunity beckoned, there was little to indicate that the system would not work indefinitely. By 1880, however, the end of the frontier was in sight. Free land of good quality was scarce, and the frontier could no longer serve as a safety valve to release the economic and social pressures of an expanding population.

Between 1850 and 1900 the United States became the most powerful state in the western hemisphere, increased its national wealth from $7 billion to $88 billion, established an excellent system of public education, and fostered the spread of civil liberties. But there were many disturbing factors in the picture. Unemployment, child labor, and industrial accidents were common in the rapidly growing cities. Slums grew and served as breeding places for disease and crime. Strikes, often accompanied by violence, brought to a head the tension between labor and capital.

In response, the wide-ranging Progressive reform movement developed between 1890 to 1914. This movement was rooted partly in the agrarian protests against big business sparked by the Populists of the Midwest and South. The Progressives effectively mobilized the middle classes to work to eliminate sweatshops, the exploitation of labor, and the abuse of natural resources.

The success of the Progressive movement was reflected in the constitutions of the new states admitted to the Union and in their introduction of the direct primary, the initiative and referendum, and the direct election of senators. All these measures tended to give the common people more effective control of the government. After the enactment of the Interstate Commerce Act in 1887, which had introduced federal regulation over railroads, a steady expansion of governmental regulation of industry began.

As president of the United States from 1901 to 1909, Theodore Roosevelt launched an aggressive campaign to break up the trusts, conserve natural resources, and regulate railroads, food, and drugs. In 1913 President Woodrow Wilson started ed a militant campaign of reform called the "New Freedom." His administration reduced the tariff because it was too much the instrument of special economic privilege, enacted banking reform with the Federal Reserve Act of 1913, and regulated businesses in the public interest through the Clayton Antitrust Act and the establishment of the Federal Trade Commission, both in 1914.

In 1914 the United States was the richest, most populous, and most influential nation in the West. The country's first census, taken in 1790, counted a population of just under 4 million; by 1910 the number was 99 million. During the nineteenth century more than 25 million immigrants had made their way to America. Since the days of George Washington, the national wealth had increased at least a hundredfold. Once the producer of raw materials only, the United States by 1914 was the world's greatest industrial power, producing more steel than Britain and Germany combined. A single company—United States Steel—was capitalized for $1.460 billion, a sum greater than the total estimated wealth of the country in 1790.

The United States and the World

From the first, U. S. foreign policy pursued three goals: national security, trade, and the

THE BOSSES OF THE SENATE.

This cartoon, "The Bosses of the Senate," appeared in *Puck* in 1889, shortly before the Senate began debate on the Sherman Antitrust Bill. Public uproar over the proliferation of gigantic trusts eventually led to passage of the Antitrust Act in 1890.

spread of democracy. During its first quarter-century, The United States fought a brief naval war with France, became embroiled with Britain in the War of 1812, and sent two expeditions to the Mediterranean to deal with the Barbary pirates. These complications notwithstanding, Americans spent the next century developing their country. Thomas Jefferson summarized the country's foreign policy with these words: "Peace, commerce, and honest friendship with all nations—entangling alliances with none."[5]

Early in the 1820s the policy of noninvolvement was seriously challenged when conservative members of the Quadruple Alliance offered to help the Spanish king regain control of Latin America. Both Britain and the United States viewed this possibility with alarm. George Canning, the British foreign secretary, suggested that his government and the United States make a joint declaration warning against European intervention in South America. U. S. President James Monroe seriously considered the invitation, but decided against it.

Instead Monroe offered a unilateral doctrine in his message to Congress in December 1823. He warned the European powers against any attempt to impose their system in the Western Hemisphere and also declared that the United States had no intention of interfering in European affairs. In 1823 the United States could "have its cake and eat it too." The shield of the British fleet stood behind the Monroe Doctrine, with or without a formal alliance between Washington and London, and the United States avoided the complications and dangers inherent in European intervention.

It was sometimes difficult to reconcile the desire for isolation with the country's stated love of freedom—for example, much sympathy was expressed for the Greeks as they fought against Turkish tyranny in the 1820s, but there was little active support. When the country established new foreign contacts, it went across the Pacific. In 1844 the United States made its first treaty with China, opening certain ports to American trade and securing the rights of American merchants and sailors to be tried in American tribunals in China. In 1853 Commodore Matthew Perry visited Japan, and by his show of force, persuaded the Japanese to open some of their harbors to American ships. By 1854 the United

A LITTLE MONROE DOCTORING MIGHT BE GOOD FOR HIM.

American cartoonist Thomas Nast satirized British imperialism with this cartoon; the caption reads, "A Little Monroe Doctoring Might Be Good For Him."

States was considering the annexation of the Hawaiian Islands, and in 1867 it purchased Alaska from Russia for the amazingly low price of $7.2 million.

Emperor Napoleon III tested the Monroe Doctrine during the Civil War by sending over Maximilian to establish the Mexican empire (see ch. 24). While the war raged, U. S. protests did little to sway the French. But after 1865, the 900,000 veterans backing up the protests plus the actions of the Mexican patriots forced Napoleon to withdraw his military and financial support. In 1867 a Mexican firing squad executed Maximilian.

Foreign affairs were virtually forgotten for the next generation, and one New York newspaper recommended the abolition of the foreign service. However, as productivity increased, the United States was forced to seek new outlets for its goods, especially now that the frontier had disappeared. Foreign trade increased from $393 million in 1870 to more than $1.333 billion in 1900. Investments abroad in the same period went from virtually nothing to $500 million. At the same time American missionary activity greatly expanded in Africa, the Middle East, and Asia. Like their European counterparts, many American leaders were influenced by Darwinism, especially when it was applied to foreign affairs. The slogan "survival of the fittest" had its followers in the U. S. Congress as well as in the British Parliament, French Chamber of Deputies, and German Reichstag. In order to be truly great, many argued, the United States must expand and assume a vital role in world politics. This argument was instrumental in the United States, acquisition of a global empire.

Roosevelt the Activist

The United States began building a modern navy in 1883, and by 1890 the buildup had accelerated greatly. Care was taken not to alarm the country, however, and the new ships were officially known as "seagoing coastline battleships," a handy nautical contradiction. When this naval program was initiated, the U. S. Navy ranked twelfth among the powers; by 1900 it had advanced to third place.

The growing international stature of the United States received startling confirmation in the border dispute between Britain and Venezuela in 1895. When Britain delayed before agreeing to submit the issue to arbitration, the State Department of the United States took the initiative and drafted a blunt note to London. The note warned the British that grave consequences would follow their refusal to accept arbitration. The State Department noted U. S. dominance in the western hemisphere and boasted that America's "infinite resources combined with its isolated position render it master of the situation and practically invulnerable against any or all other powers." Britain was preoccupied with the Boers in South Africa, the Germans on the continent, and the French in the Sudan and thus could not argue too strenuously against the message. The British agreed to resolve the dispute through arbitration.

There were signs of the new dynamism in American foreign policy in Asia as well. In 1899 U. S. Secretary of State John Hay initiated a policy for maintaining equal commercial rights in China for the traders of all nations, and the Open Door Policy in China became a reality. In the melodrama of the Boxer Rebellion (see p. 751), the United States again was a leader rather than a follower.

This heightened activity of the United States is best symbolized by the ideas and actions of Theodore Roosevelt. In his terms as president he was one of the leading figures on the world stage. At the request of the Japanese he assumed the role of peacemaker in the Russo-Japanese War. The peace conference, which met at Portsmouth,

The execution of Maximilian by firing squad in 1867. The protests of the United States against France's violation of the Monroe Doctrine helped convince Napoleon III to withdraw French military support of Maximilian's empire in Mexico. Without this support the empire soon collapsed.

President Theodore Roosevelt visited the Culebra Cut at the Panama Canal in November 1916. Here he is shown sitting on a 95-ton steam shovel.

from banker and financier John Pierpont Morgan. Panama, the new republic that seceded from Colombia in 1903, concluded a canal treaty with the United States, and in 1914 the canal was opened. The United States had moved far from its traditional place on the periphery of world affairs.

Latin America

The new nations of Latin America faced a complex of dilemmas that bequeathed a frustrating century of political instability and foreign economic domination. Civil wars, revolutions, and regimes came and went with alarming and costly regularity. Progressive leaders who tried to modernize their countries had to face the opposition of powerful, traditional institutions and massive and complex social problems.

The Creation of the Latin American States

In the first decades of the nineteenth century, the Latin American colonies pursued an irresistible movement for independence (see ch. 23). By 1825, Spanish and Portuguese power was broken in the Western Hemisphere, and nine new political units emerged in Latin America. Mexico, Guatemala, Great Colombia, Peru, Bolivia, Paraguay, Argentina, and Chile were free of Spain, and Brazil had gained its independence from Portugal. Once free of those powers, however, the new nations of Latin America were hampered by European and North American dominance over their economic and political affairs.

For most of the new Latin American nations their first half century was a time of decline and disappointment. The great liberators could not maintain control of the nations they had freed. The liberal, urban Creoles who had begun the independence movements were inexperienced and unable to make the political compromises necessary to govern new countries. They soon lost power to crude military leaders, or *caudillos*, whose armed gangs struggled for power in a confusing series of upheavals. A growing sectionalism accompanied these coups. Mammoth states

New Hampshire, in 1905 successfully concluded a treaty, and in 1910 Roosevelt received the Nobel Peace Prize.

Roosevelt was not always a man of peace, however. When he believed the legitimate interests of the United States to be threatened, he did not hesitate to threaten or use force, as could be seen in Panama. In 1901 the British conceded to the United States the exclusive right to control any Isthmian canal that might be dug. For $40 million the United States bought the rights of a private French company that had already begun work on the canal. A lease was negotiated with Colombia, through whose territory the canal would be built, but that country's senate refused to ratify the treaty, claiming the compensation was too small. Roosevelt is reputed to have responded, "I did not intend that any set of bandits should hold up Uncle Sam." The upshot was a revolution, financed with money borrowed broke up into tiny republics, which in turn were threatened by localism.

In part, Latin America's problems resulted from the Spanish colonial system that had offered native-born whites little opportunity or responsibility in government. The tradition of autocracy and paternalism was a poor precedent for would-be democratic republics. The emphasis on executive power inspired presidents, generals, landowners, and church officials to wield authority with arrogant disregard for public opinion and representative government.

The colonial economic system, based on raw materials rather than industry, encouraged concentration of land and other forms of wealth in a few hands. The church with its vast properties, monopoly on education and welfare agencies, and command over cultural life complicated the politics of every new nation.

In addition, the new states were cursed by problems associated with the wars of independence. Some of the most productive areas were devastated. Hatred and division remained. Many men who had fought the royalists remained armed, predisposed to a life of violence and pillage and likely to group themselves about the *caudillos*, who promised adventure or profit in revolutions.

The final problem facing the new states was that of racial disunity. In 1825 there were from 15 to 18 million people in the former Spanish empire. About 3 million of them were whites, the wealthiest and most educated population. That figure remained constant until the last third of the century, when immigration from Europe increased drastically. There were about the same number of *mestizos*, who scorned the Indians, but were not accepted by whites. Their numbers steadily increased, as did their ambition. During the nineteenth century at least half of the population in some states was Indian. Deprived of the small protection once offered by the Spanish crown, they either sank into peonage or lived in semi-independence under their tribal rulers. Finally, in Brazil and most of the Caribbean island, blacks were in a large majority. Conflicts of interest quickly developed between these broad racial groups, particularly between the Creoles and the *mestizos*. The pernicious effects of these divisive factors can be seen in the experiences of each nation.

Mexico

Despite its promising beginning in 1821, Mexico suffered a half-century of turmoil. The empire of Iturbide (see p. 603) lasted only a few months, and was replaced by a federal republic. In less than ten years, however, a coup enabled a preposterous military leader name Antonio Lopez de Santa Anna (1795–1876) to become dictator. His notorious rule witnessed the massacre of the defenders of the Alamo in 1836 and the general debasement of Mexico's political life. His conduct of the war with the United States (1846–1848) humiliated Mexico. The overthrow of this corrupt, incompetent *caudillo* in 1855 brought more thoughtful and circumspect men into politics.

The liberals, under the leadership of Benito Juarez (1806–1872) set out to implement a reform program known as the *Reforma*. They planned to establish a more democratic republic, destroy the political and economic force of the church, and include the *mestizos* and Indians in political life. A terrible civil war followed their anticlerical measures; it ended in 1861 with the apparent victory of Juarez, but inability to meet payments on debts owed to foreigners brought an invasion of Mexico by European powers and the establishment of a French puppet regime. By 1867 popular uprisings and pressure from the United States had driven French troops from Mexican soil.

Juarez again set out to institute the *Reforma*, but the poverty of the country hampered progress. After he died, one of his adherents, Porfirio Diaz (1830–1915), took power. Under Diaz, who served as president from 1877 to 1880 and again from 1884 to 1911, Mexican politics stabilized. Foreign capital entered in large amounts. Factories, railroads, mines, trading houses, plantations, and enormous ranches flourished, and Mexico City became one of the most impressive capitals in Latin America.

Diaz's rule, though outwardly conforming to the constitution, was a dictatorship. If there was much encouragement of arts and letters, there was no liberty. The Indians sank lower and lower into peonage or outright slavery. In spite of the anticlerical laws of the Juarez period, the church was quietly permitted to acquire great wealth, and foreign investors exploited Mexico, creating a long-lasting hatred of foreigners.

In 1910 the critics of Diaz found a spokesman in a frail, eccentric man named Francisco Madero (1873–1913) who undertook to lead a revolutionary movement and surprised the world by succeeding. Madero was murdered in 1913, and Mexico endured another period of turmoil during which the country was controlled mainly by self-styled local rulers. Still, a determined group was able to organize a revolutionary party and to bring about the only genuine social revolution that Latin America experienced until the First World War.

Argentina

Until the 1970s, Argentina was probably the most advanced Spanish-speaking country in the world. It attained this position in a period of sudden growth that followed a half century of sluggishness. Its beginning as a free nation was promising. Soon, however, the bustling port city of Buenos Aires, whose energetic population sought to encourage European capital and commerce, found itself overawed by the *caudillos*, the great ranchers of the interior, and their retainers, the *guachos*—colorful, nomadic, cowboys and bandits whose way of life has been romanticized in literature and folklore. The *caudillos* intimidated the supporters of constitutional government in Buenos Aires, and until midcentury, Argentina was not a republic, but rather a *gaucho* paradise, isolated and ruled by men who wanted to keep European influences out.

In 1852 a combination of progressive elements overthew the *gaucho* leader. Commerce with Europe was revived and within ten years Argentina had become a united republic of admirable stability. The constitution was usually observed and individual rights were respected to a high degree. Immigrants poured in, and soon the population of Argentina became the most European of the New World republics, for it contained few Indians or blacks.

Foreign capital, especially British, brought about amazing developments; port facilities, railroads, light industry, and urban conveniences were among the most advanced in the world. Buenos Aires became by far the largest and most beautiful city in Latin America, despite its location on a monotonous, flat plain beside a muddy estuary.

The flat plain, or pampas, is perhaps the richest land in the world for grass and wheat, and livestock have been multiplying there for centuries. The introduction of refrigerated ships around 1880 made it feasible to transport enormous quantities of fresh beef to Britain in exchange for capital and finished goods. About 1900 wheat joined beef as a major Argentine export. This intimate commercial relationship with Britain, which lasted until after World War II, affected nearly every aspect of Argentine life.

Nevertheless, although elite society was dominated by leaders who were pro-British in business and pro-French in culture, a true Argentine nationalism was developing. Along with the growth of this powerful sentiment came demands for more democracy and a wider distribution of wealth.

Brazil

For many years this former Portuguese colony escaped the turbulence and disorders that befell its Spanish-speaking neighbors, probably because it had achieved independence without years of warfare and military dominance and because it enjoyed the continuity and legitimacy afforded by a respected monarchy. The first emperor, Pedro I (1822–1831), promulgated a constitution in 1824, and the accession to the throne of Pedro II in 1840 initiated a period of political liberty and economic and cultural progress that lasted throughout his fifty-year reign.

Immigrants were attracted to this peaceful land, and foreign investments were heavy, but without the massive exploitation that Mexico experienced under Diaz. Economic growth tended to favor the southeastern part of the country at the expense of the great sugar plantations in the tropical north. The abolition of slavery in 1888 hurt the sugar lords economically, and they rose up against the emperor. Joining them were army officers, who resented the civilian nature of Pedro's regime, and a small number of ideological republicans. In 1889 the aging emperor was forced to abdicate.

For nearly ten years the new federal republic of Brazil underwent civil wars and military upheavals, much like those experienced by other Latin American countries. Finally, the republic

Francisco Madero, The Plan of San Luis Potosí

The Mexican revolutionary movement received its most eloquent definition in the plan of San Luis Potosí, written by Francisco Madero from his exile in San Antonio, Texas.

Peoples, in their constant efforts for the triumph of the ideal of liberty and justice, are forced, at precise historical moments, to make their greatest sacrifices.

Our beloved country has reached one of those moments. A force of tyranny which we Mexicans were not accustomed to suffer after we won our independence oppresses us in such a manner that it has become intolerable. In exchange for that tyranny we are offered peace, but peace full of shame for the Mexican nation. . . .

It may almost be said that martial law constantly exists in Mexico; the administration of justice, instead of imparting protection to the weak, merely serves to legalize the plunderings committed by the strong; the judges instead of being the representatives of justice, are the agents of the executive, whose interests they faithfully serve; the chambers of the union have no other will than that of the dictator; the governors of the States are designated by him and they in their turn designate and impose in like manner the municipal authorities.

From this it results that the whole administrative, judicial, and legislative machinery obeys a single will, the caprice of General Porfirio Díaz, who during his long administration has shown that the principal motive that guides him is to maintain himself in power and at any cost. . . .

For this reason the Mexican people have protested against the illegality of the last election and, desiring to use successively all the recourses offered by the laws of the Republic, in due form asked for the nullification of the election by the Chamber of Deputies, notwithstanding they recognized no legal origin in said body and knew beforehand that, as its members were not the representatives of the people, they would carry out the will of General Díaz, to whom exclusively they owe their investiture.

In such a state of affairs the people, who are the only sovereign, also protested energetically against the election in imposing manifestations in different parts of the Republic; and if the latter were not general throughout the national territory, it was due to the terrible pressure exercised by the Government, which always quenches in blood any democratic manifestation, as happened in Puebla, Vera Cruz, Tlaxcala, and in other places.

But this violent and illegal system can no longer subsist.

I have very well realized that if the people have designated me as their candidate for the Presidency it is not because they have had an opportunity to discover in me the qualities of a statesman or of a ruler, but the virility of the patriot determined to sacrifice himself, if need be, to obtain liberty and to help the people free themselves from the odious tyranny that oppresses them. . . .

Therefore, and in echo of the national will, I declare the late election illegal and, the Republic being accordingly without rulers, provisionally assume the Presidency of the Republic until the people designate their rulers pursuant to the law. In order to attain this end, it is necessary to eject from power the audacious usurpers whose only title of legality involves a scandalous and immoral fraud.

From United States Congress, Senate Subcommittee on Foreign Relations, *Revolutions in Mexico*, 62nd Congress, 2nd Session (Washington, D.C.; Government Printing Office, 1913).

was stabilized with the army in control, and Brazil resumed its progressive course. Foreign capital continued to enter, and immigration from Europe remained heavy. By 1914 Brazil was generally stable and prosperous, with a growing tradition of responsible government.

Other Latin American Nations

Political turmoil, geographical handicaps, and racial disunity all played a part in the development of the other new nations in Latin America. Bolivia, named so hopefully for the Liberator Simon Bolívar, underwent countless revolutions. Peru's course was almost as futile. The state of Great Colombia dissolved by 1830, and its successors—Colombia, Venezuela, and Ecuador—were plagued by instability and civil wars. Paraguay endured a series of dictatorships and Uruguay, created in 1828 as a buffer between Argentina and Brazil, long suffered from interventions by those two countries.

An exception to the prevailing pattern of political chaos was the steady growth of the republic of Chile. in 1830 Chile came under the control of a conservative oligarchy. Although this regime proved to be generally enlightened, the country was kept under tight control for a century and was ruled for the benefit of the large landlords and big business.

Central America narrowly escaped becoming part of Mexico in 1822. After a fifteen-year effort to create a Central American confederation, Guatemala, San Salvador, Honduras, Nicaragua, and Costa Rica asserted their independence. Except for Costa Rica, where whites comprised the bulk of the population, racial disunity delayed the development of national feeling. In the Caribbean the Dominican Republic, after decades of submission to more populous but equally underdeveloped Haiti, maintained a precarious independence.

Foreign Dominance

The Industrial Revolution came into full stride just after the Latin American republics were born. The great industries of western Europe and the United States demanded more and more raw materials and new markets in which to sell finished products. Capital accumulated, and investors eagerly sought opportunities to place their money where they could obtain high rates of interest. This drive for markets, raw materials, and outlets for surplus capital led to classic examples of economic imperialism.

The continual disorder and the lack of strong governments in Latin America gave businesses the opportunity to obtain rich concessions and float huge loans. Many of the Latin American government leaders, brought to power through revolution and interested only in personal gain, often resorted to the vicious practice of selling concessions to foreign corporations for ready cash. Political bosses bartered away the economic heritage of their lands, for Latin America was rich in minerals, oil, and other important resources. Foreign investors sometimes acted in good faith, providing capital at a reasonable rate of interest to Latin American regimes which, it became apparent, had no intention of fulfilling the contract. On other occasions unscrupulous capitalists took full advantage of officials in ignorant or helpless governments.

Injured foreign investors usually appealed to their government to intercede in their behalf, and an unending stream of diplomatic correspondence over debt claims was begun. The United States, Great Britain, Germany, France, Italy, Spain—the chief investor states—would not permit their citizens to be mistreated in their ventures into foreign investments.

In 1902–1903 a dispute between Venezuela and a coalition formed by Germany, Great Britain, and Italy provoked the three European powers into blockading the Latin American country and even firing on some of the coastal fortifications to remind the Venezuelan dictator of his obligations to some of their nationals. U. S. President Theodore Roosevelt at first stood by, watching Venezuela take its punishment. Then he became suspicious of German motives and began to match threat with threat, forcing the Europeans to back down and place the issue into international arbitration.

In 1904 Roosevelt issued the Roosevelt Corollary to the Monroe Doctrine, an addition that was a frank statement that chronic wrongdoing on the part of Latin American governments might force the United States to exercise an international police power. Picturesquely described as the policy of speaking softly but carrying a big stick, the Roosevelt pronouncement launched the era of the Big Stick. The United States established a customs receivership in the Dominican Republic and exercised similar control in Nicaragua and Haiti. The Roosevelt Corollary expanded the Monroe Doctrine from its original purpose of keeping out European political interference in Latin America to enlarging the commercial interests of the United States.

In 1898 the United States had gone to war with Spain over the way the Spaniards ruled Cuba: the mistreatment of the Cubans also affected American commercial interests. Victory in the brief, dramatic, and well-publicized Spanish-American War brought the United States recognition as a world power and a conglomeration of islands in the Pacific Ocean as well as in the Caribbean. The United States annexed Puerto Rico and placed the Philippines, halfway around the world, under American rule. Sensitive to accusations of imperialism in Cuba, the U. S. government offered Cuba an imperfect, closely tutored independence in which the Cubans were obliged by law to acknowledge the right of the United States to intervene for the "preservation of Cuban independence" and the "maintenance of a government adequate for the protection of life,

President William McKinley on Imperialism

Even the Americans joined the imperialistic race. Unlike the Europeans, who propounded intellectually sophisticated rationalizations, the Americans moved for different, often celestial, reasons. McKinley noted:

I have been criticized a good deal about the Philippines, but I don't deserve it. The truth is, I didn't want the Philippines, and when they came to us, as a gift from the gods, I did not know what to do with them. When the Spanish war broke out, Dewey was at Hongkong, and I ordered him to go to Manila, and he had to; because, if defeated, he had no place to refit on that side of the globe, and if the Dons were victorious they would likely cross the Pacific and ravage our Oregon and California coasts. And so he had to destroy the Spanish fleet, and did it. But that was as far as I thought then. When next I realized that the Philippines had dropped into our lap, I confess that I did not know what to do with them. I sought counsel from all sides—Democrats as well as Republicans—but got little help. I thought first we would take only Manila; then Luzon; then other islands, perhaps all. I walked the floor of the White House night after night until midnight; and I am not ashamed to tell you, gentlemen, that I went down on my knees and prayed Almighty God for light and guidance more than one night.

And one night late it came to me this way—I don't know how it was, but it came:

(1) That we could not give them back to Spain—that would be cowardly and dishonorable; (2) that we could not turn them over to France or Germany—that would be bad business and discreditable; (3) that we could not leave them to themselves—they were unfit for self-government—and they would soon have anarchy and misrule over there worse than Spain's was; and (4) that there was nothing left for us to do but to take them all, and to educate the Filipinos, and uplift and civilize and Christianize them, and, by God's grace, do the very best we could by them, as our fellowmen for whom Christ also died. And then I went to bed, and went to sleep, and slept soundly, and next morning I sent for the chief engineer of the War Department (our map-maker), and told him to put the Philippines on the map of the United States (pointing to a large map on the wall of his office); "and there they are, and there they will stay while I am president!"

From G. A. Malcolm and M. M. Kalw, *Philippine Government* (Boston, 1932).

A Critic of Imperialism

Francisco Garcia Calderón saw not only the great powers' political impact but also the debilitating cultural problems.

Interventions have become more frequent with the expansion of frontiers. The United States have recently intervened in the territory of Acre, there to found a republic of rubber gatherers; at Panama, there to develop a province and construct a canal: in Cuba, under cover of the Platt Amendment, to maintain order in the interior; in Santo Domingo, to support the civilising revolution and overthrow the tyrants; in Venezuela, and in Central America, to enforce upon these nations, torn by intestine disorders, the political and financial tutelage of the imperial democracy. In Guatemala and Honduras the loans concluded with the monarchs of North American finance have reduced the people to a new slavery. Supervision of the customs and the dispatch of pacificatory squadrons to defend the interests of the Anglo-Saxon have enforced peace and tranquility: such are the means employed. The New York American announces that Mr. Pierpont Morgan proposes to encompass the finances of Latin America by a vast network of Yankee banks. Chicago merchants and Wall Street financiers created the Meat Trust in the Argentine. The United States offer millions for the purpose of converting into Yankee loans the moneys raised in London during the last century by the Latin American States; they wish to obtain a monopoly of credit. It has even been announced, although the news hardly appears probable, that a North American syndicate wished to buy enormous belts of land in Guatemala, where the English tongue is the obligatory language. The fortification of the Panama Canal, and the possible acquisition of the Galapagos Island in the Pacific, are fresh manifestations of imperialistic progress. . . .

Warnings, advice, distrust, invasion of capital, plans of financial hegemony all these justify the anxiety of the southern peoples. . . . Neither irony nor grace nor scepticism, gifts of the old civilizations, can make way against the plebeian brutality, the excessive optimism, the violent individualism of the [North American] people.

All these things contribute to the triumph of mediocrity; the multitude of primary schools, the vices of utilitarianism, the cult of the average citizen, the transatlantic M. Homais, and the tyranny of opinion noted by Tocqueville; and in this vulgarity, which is devoid of traditions and has no leading aristocracy, a return to the primitive type of the redskin, which has already been noted by close observers, is threatening the proud democracy. From the excessive tensions of wills, from the elementary state of culture, from the perpetual unrest of life, from the harshness of the industrial struggle, anarchy and violence will be born in the future. In a hundred years men will seek in vain for the "American soul," the "genius of America," elsewhere than in the undisciplined force or the violence which ignores moral laws. . . .

Essential points of difference separate the two Americas. Differences of language and therefore of spirit; the difference between Spanish Catholicism and multiform Protestantism of the Anglo-Saxons; between the Yankee individualism and the omnipotence of the State natural to the nations of the South. In their origin, as in their race, we find fundamental antagonism; the evolution of the North is slow and obedient to the lessons of time, to the influences of custom; the history of the southern peoples is full of revolutions, rich with dreams of an unattainable perfection.

From Francisco Garcia Calderón, *Latin America: Its Rise and Progress* (London: T. F. Unwin, 1913).

Nearly one-quarter of the invasion force that sailed for Cuba was made up of black troops. This illustration of the Battle of Quasimas near Santiago, Cuba, June 24, 1898, shows the 9th and 10th Colored Cavalry supporting the Rough Riders in the battle against the Spanish. Black soldiers also helped the Rough Riders take San Juan Hill.

property, and individual liberty." These and other restrictions on Cuban independence were embodied in the Platt Amendment (1901) to the new Cuban constitution. Thus the United States established its first American protectorate. Panama soon became another protectorate of the United States. Generally both American business and the local population profited.

Roosevelt oversaw the introduction of what has been called Dollar Diplomacy—the coordinated activites of American foreign investors and the U. S. State Department to obtain and protect concessions for the investors. From 1890 this policy won concessions for Americans in Latin American products such as sugar, bananas, and oil from more than a dozen Latin American republics.

In the face of such activities, the pious assertions of those espousing the Pan-American philosophy—that the nations of the western hemisphere were bound by common geography and democratic political ideals—gained little acceptance. The "Colossus of the North," as the Latin American nations referred to the United States clearly acted in its own self-interest. Sarcastic observers referred to the Pan-American Union, founded in 1889, as "the Colonial Division of the Department of State." By 1914 Latin America's relations with the rest of the world were neither healthy nor comforting. After a century of independence, Latin America still lingered on the margins of international life. Left to shift for itself in the face of a future shaded by U.S. imperialism, Latin America saw only a hard road ahead in its relations with the outside world.

Conclusion

From the seventeenth through the nineteenth centuries the greatest human migration from the smallest continent, Europe, had taken place. This migration surpassed in scope such momentous human wanderings of the past as those of the Indo-Europeans into India and southern Europe and the incursions of the Germanic tribes into the Roman Empire. Transoceanic in character, this mass movement originated in Europe, which during this period, forged ahead of the rest of the world in industry, technology and science, wealth, and military power.

This dispersal of Europeans has been treated mainly in the history of the British Dominions, the United States, and Latin America. However, equally affected were the African peoples, shipped by the million in a vicious slave trade to develop the vast natural resources of the new lands. They contributed substantially to the cultures and economies of their new societies, especially in Latin America and the United States, but paid an incredible cost—especially in the United States.

The United States with its profound varieties of development, despite a common European heritage, was by far the most important of the new lands of the nineteenth century. The frontier and slavery both influenced the formation of a distinctive society, and the latter bequeathed to the country the most intractable of its twentieth century domestic problems. The Civil War had more "revolutionary" consequences—socially, economially, and politically—than any other event occurring in the new lands.

Suggestions for Reading

R. W. Logan, *The Negro in the United States* (Anvil, 1954). . . . *The Nadir, 1877–1901.* traces the plight of blacks in post-reconstruction America. See also C. Vann Woodward, *The Strange Career of Jim Crow* (Oxford, 1974); J. Forbes Munroe, *Africa and the International Economy* (London, 1976). and E. D. Genovese, *Roll Jordan, Roll: The world the Slaves Made* (Random House, 1976). See H. E. Driver, *Indians of North America* (Chicago, 1969) for an overview of the Native Americans' contact with and overwhelming by the whites and Basil Davidson, *Black Mother: The Years of the African Slave Trade* (Little, Brown, 1961).

A. R. M. Lower's *Colony to Nation: a History of Canada,* (Toronto, 1946) a history of Canada from the British conquest to 1850. For two important aspects of Canadian history see Bruce Hutchinson, *The Struggle for the Border* (Longman, 1955), and D. M. L. Faar, *The Colonial Office and Canada* (Toronto, 1948). See L. Lipson, *Politics of Equality,* (Chicago, 1948). For provocative studies of history and society, see O. H. K. Spate, *Australia* (Praeger, 1968) and Douglas Pike, *Australia* (Cambridge, 1969). See M. Wilson and L. Thompson, eds., *The Oxford History of South Africa* (1969). Also recommended is E. Roux, *Time Longer than Rope, A History of the Blackman's Struggle for Freedom in South Africa* (Wisconsin, 1964).

For a brief and stimulating survey of the first half of U. S. history, see M. Cunliffe, *The Nation Takes Shape: 1789–1837* (Univ. of Chicago, 1959), Also recommended is A. M. Schlesinger's classic *The Age of Jackson* (Mentor, 1945). Paul H. Buck's *The Road to Reunion 1865–1900* is a good survey of the consequences of the Civil War (Little, Brown, 1937), A good chance to read great literature and fine biography is Carl Sandburg's three-volume biography of Lincoln. (Many editions)

A critique of the American scene that has become a classic is Alexis de Tocqueville's *Democracy in America* (Mentor). George E. Mowry skillfully characterized *The Era of Theodore Roosevelt* (Torchbook, 1958). See also Arthur S. Link, *Woodrow Wilson and the Progressive Era* (Torchbooks, 1963).

Some useful studies of Latin America in the nineteeth and early twentieth centuries are Miron Burgin, *The Economic Aspects of Argentinian Federalism, 1820–1852* (Harvard, 1946); J. R. Scobie, *Revolution on the Pampas: A Social History of Argentine Wheat* (Texas, 1964); R. L. Gilmore, *Caudillism and Militarism in Venezuela 1810–1910* (Ohio Univ., 1964); T. L. Karnes, *The Failure of Union: Central America 1824–1960* (Univ. of North Carolina, 1961); and M. C. Meyer and W. L. Sherman, *The Course of Mexican History* (Oxford, 1979). See also D. Bushnell and N. Macauley, *The Emergence of Latin America in the Nineteenth Century,* (Oxford, 1988)

Notes

1. Hubert Herring, *History of Latin America* (New York: Alfred A. Knopf, 1956), p. 97.
2. Alfred L. Burt, *The British Empire and Commonwealth* (Boston: D. C. Heath, 1956), p. 286.
3. C. Van Doren, ed., *The Literary Works of Abraham Lincoln* (New York: Limited Editions Club, 1941), p. 65.
4. S. E. Morison, *The Oxford History of the American People* (London: Oxford Univ. Press, 1965), p. 793.
5. Quoted in F. R. Dulles, *America's Rise to World Power* (New York: Harper & Row, 1955), p. 4.

Chapter 28

The Middle East and Africa, 1800–1914

I n the eigthteenth and nineteenth centuries, Europeans steadily advanced into the Middle East and Africa. Europe's economic, technological, and military superiority overwhelmed the diverse civilizations and made them targets in the competition for empire.

The Islamic world retained its religious strength in the face of the European onslaught, but the disintegration of the Ottoman Empire brought about massive change. In Central Asia, the Persians and Afghans were caught up in the great power rivalry between the British and the Russians. In Africa the diversity of tribes made a unified political response to the Europeans impossible. By the beginning of the nineteenth century the Africans had begun a slow and painful process of adapting to the industrialized world.

The Middle East

In 1800 the Islamic world stretched from the Atlantic Ocean to the Pacific, in a broad band that reached across North Africa, the Middle East, Central Asia, and down to Indonesia. The Islamic religion retained its original vigor, and the Islamic world followed similar religious and cultural forms. This came from a way of life based on the Koran emphasizing daily prayers, fasting, and pilgrimages to Mecca. By the late nineteenth century, more than 175 million Muslims performed daily religious duties. Whatever their race or nationality, Muslims shared the same sacred language, law, morality, social structure, and institutions. Every year the number of believers traveling to Mecca grew. It is estimated

that by 1900 more than 50,000 Indians and 20,000 Malays were making the trip each year.

The Islamic world mirrored the great diversity of peoples, environments, and external pressures that affected the faithful from Ceuta in Morocco to Djakarta in Indonesia. Even in religious matters, doctrinal differences split devout Muslims into rival sects, and these differences were as devastating as those afflicting Christianity.

Fragmentation made the Islamic world vulnerable, especially before the material strength of the industrialized Western world. The diverse populations with the Islamic world, including Arabs, Indians, Berbers, and Egyptians, had little in common except in matters of religion, culture, and language. The absence of political unity made the region militarily vulnerable.

An equally serious problem was economic weakness. Consisting principally of deserts and arid lands, the Islamic world clung to outdated agricultural techniques long abandoned by the West. Islam's prohibition of usury hampered the growth of modern capitalist institutions (banks, for example) and the evolution of a middle class. Despite the fact that Muslims occupied such strategic locations as areas around the Bosporus and the Dardanelles, the Suez, the overland route to India, and the Persian Gulf region, the Islamic world suffered from a poor communications and transportation system.

During the nineteenth century, the Ottoman Empire, Persia, and Afghanistan could not build an adequate political or economic base from which to defend themselves against Britain or Russia. The modern state structure—with its professional bureaucrats, broadly based nationalism and patriotism, ideologies, mass literacy, and civil law structure—did not exist in the Islamic world.

To a large degree the major occupations of nineteenth-century western Europe—research scientist, party politician, state functionary, technologist, and industrial worker—and the social flexibility for men and women were not present among the Muslim nations either. Instead, the function of warrior remained primary, and political life fluctuated between the despotic and the nonchalant. Corruption, social decay, lack of education and literacy also blocked effective government. In short, the Middle Eastern states could not effectively mobilize their resources or move their citizens. The Europeans moved in to take advantage of the Islamic world's vulnerability.[1]

The Disintegrating Ottoman Empire

Even though the Ottoman Empire had been in a state of decline since the end of the seventeenth century, two hundred years later it was still the largest and most prestigious realm in the Islamic world (see map below). The Sultan ruled territory extending from North Africa to the Indian Ocean. But the sultan's control over forty million people living there was often weak and sporadic.

The lines of power and communication to the empire's far corners were not dependable. The farther one went from Constantinople the less secure was Turkish control. At its inception in the sixteenth century the Ottoman administration had been a picture of effectiveness. In the next two centuries it declined as the merit basis for administration came to be replaced by bribery and favoritism. The armed forces, once the most feared in all Europe, also weakened and they came to be as much a threat to the sultan as to foreign enemies.

More than most, the Ottoman state was based on war, and to ensure its stability the Turks needed the momentum of continuous victory. However, their very success as fighters doomed them. They had pushed the Ottoman control to its extreme limits of the Atlas and Caucasus mountains. Short-range wars of conquest were no longer possible, and the warrior class became complacent. In addition, by the late seventeenth century the Europeans had become stronger and for the first time were able to defeat the Turks. Europe profited from the Scientific Revolution,

THE OTTOMAN EMPIRE c. 1900

— Ottoman Empire about 1878
☐ Territory lost 1878-1912
▨ Ottoman Empire in 1914

Enlightenment, and industrialization. The Ottoman Empire chose not to pursue these developments, nor did it look to take advantage of the forces of nationalism and patriotism to mobilize its diverse populations. As the western states improved their positions, the Turks could not change to keep up.[2]

Discontent with the Turks' rule resulted in revolts in the 1630s (the Druse), the 1740s (the Wahhabi), and 1769 (the revolt led by Ali Bey Al-Kabir). Instead of addressing the causes of these major rebellions, the Turks rededicated themselves to the defense of their foundation of life and law—Islam.[3] In the nineteenth century this was not a sufficiently flexible basis for competition in the international arena.

From the 1790s on, there were attempts made to reform the Turkish system. The Koran was the foundation for Islam, and although it was the most important basis for a Muslim's daily existence, it did not contain all of the answers to the questions of technological change. Firearms and artillery had been accepted from the infidel for centuries because they could be used in defense of the faith. The clock and the printing press, two symbols of Western advance, were not allowed. Bernard Lewis tells us that no printing was allowed in Istanbul in either Turkish or Arabic until 1729, and then the publication of books was sporadic until the end of the century.

After the 1780s, foreign influences were increasingly felt in the Ottoman empire: military advisers and diplomats entered more and more and the sultans began establishing permanent diplomatic posts in Europe. As is the case with developing states today, the military in the empire came to be the most advanced element in society. The training it received in modern technology necessitated the learning of foreign languages and political theory. A whole new group emerged, trained to look beyond the Koran for their information, and even their inspiration.[4]

The power of tradition and the faith made the drive for reform a hesitant one at best. Those who went too fast, such as Sultan Selim III (1789–1807) were overthrown. Later in the nineteenth century, sultans concerned with becoming more competitive with the Europeans were hampered in their reform attempts by the administrative chaos of the empire. Reforms rarely had reached further than a day's ride from Istanbul.

Eugène Delacroix, *Massacre of Chios* (1824). European liberals and romantics like Delacroix supported the Greeks in their struggle for independence from the Turks, who were seen as cruel oppressors.

Perhaps sensing the weakening at the center and taking advantage of the changes brought by the Napoleonic era, the peoples of the Balkans began to work for independence. The Montenegrins, who never acknowledged Ottoman domination, received recognition of their independent status in 1799. In response to a breakdown of Ottoman administration, the Serbs rose in revolt in 1804, followed by the Greeks in 1821, Romania in the 1850s, and Bulgaria in the 1870s. Russia continued to pressure the Turks while the other powers intruded more and more on the sultan's affairs. Vassals in Albania, Egypt, and Macedonia rebelled. Particularly serious was Mehmet Ali's challenge in the 1820s and '30s when he took Crete and Syria. Not only did he threaten Istanbul, he pushed his gains to the Persian Gulf and Indian Ocean. By the 1840s a combination of the great powers pushed him back to Egypt, where he remained as a viceroy.

The empire's weakness was especially exposed in the prelude to the Crimean War when Russia and France squabbled over the holy places of Christianity. Istanbul served merely as an arena in which Europe's diplomats debated the Turks' fate. Even though the Turks emerged from the turmoil with their great power status guaranteed, it was apparent to all that the empire was kept alive only because the Europeans could think of no other alternative for the strategic state. In 1860 France gained the right to intervene in Syria. In 1874 the Ottoman financial structure collapsed under the pressure of huge foreign loans, just at the time of renewed uprisings in the Balkans.

Young Turks

In 1876 Midhat Pasha, a dedicated reformer and provincial Governor, unveiled a plan for a new, western-style political structure in the Ottoman empire. Under his scheme the empire was declared to be a unitary state with the guarantees of free press, freedom of conscience, equality under the law, and equal taxation. In addition, he proposed the creation of an Ottoman citizenship, a step away from the traditional theocratic basis of power. The plan was proclaimed in Istanbul in December 1876 and Midhat Pasha became grand vizir. Unfortunately for the empire, Abdul Hamid II—the new sultan who came to the throne soon after—destroyed the reform plans, dismissed Midhat Pasha as grand vizir, and suspended the parliament.

By the spring of 1877, Abdul Hamid was trying to rule as his predecessors four centuries earlier had—absolutely. Spies spread throughout the country to track down liberals and other opponents. Censorship was applied and those who had worked for reforms disappeared mysteriously or were forced into exile. At a time when he needed unity and change to preserve his crumbling holdings, Abdul Hamid chose to split up potential opponents and destroy them. The sultan's basic problem was not the reform movement, but the reactionary nature of his policies.

The sultan faced severe challenges on all fronts. Throughout his realm nationalist movements threatened his rule. The European powers continued their economic and political pressures on his holdings: France annexed Tunis in 1881, Britain occupied Egypt in 1882, and

Abdul Hamid II. Widespread discontent with his oppressive rule lent strength to the reform movement of the Young Turks, who ultimately deposed the sultan in 1909.

in 1900 Italy reached for Tripoli. Remaining under Turkish rule were the Arabs of the Middle East, primarily Muslim in religion, with significant Christian minorities in some areas. They were beginning to be affected by the same nationalistic spirit that had spread through nineteenth-century Europe. They joined the Balkans nations in pushing for concessions from the weak Ottoman structure. By the beginning of the twentieth century, opposition to the sultan's tyranny and misrule was widespread among his many subjects.

A nucleus of opposition formed among a group of exciled reformers who had been educated in western European universities. In 1902 these opponents—the Young Turks—and other national groups oppressed by the sultan met in Paris to form a united opposition to Abdul Hamid. They advocated a modernized, western state with a professional police force, a sound economic policy, and substantial social reforms. They adopted the European clock and recommended broad-ranging educational opportunities and revised dress codes to bring women out of seclusion.

At the same time a number of young army officers joined the Young Turks, giving the movement the military power and coordination it needed for a successful rebellion. In 1908 the Young Turks told the sultan to put the 1876 constitution into effect or else face an armed uprising. Abdul Hamid saw the weakness of his position and agreed to the demands. But after gaining their initial goals, the revolutionaries split deeply over the question of the status of non-Turks in the new regime. Some of the Young Turks wanted to grant full political rights to the minorities, while others advocated severe restrictions. The new parliament that came into existence after the restoration immediately bogged down over the rights of subject nationalities. Encouraged by the division within the parliament, the sultan attempted a counterrevolution to regain power. When he turned against the Young Turks—who by this time had gained substantial popular support—he was overthrown in 1909.

Arabs in Syria, Lebanon, and the vast Arabian peninsula were not happy with the new regime. Along with the Albanians in the Balkans, they were repelled by the Young Turks' program of Turkish supremacy and their policy of centralization, which would obviously leave no hopes for Arab home rule. When World War I broke out in 1914, the British, once an Allied victory was assured, had little difficulty in turning the Arab nations against the Turkish sultan.

Other parts of the empire fell away during and after the Young Turk revolt. Between 1908 and 1913, Austria-Hungary annexed Bosnia and Herzegovina, Greece annexed Crete, and Italy—in the course of a short but difficult war—seized Tripoli and Cyrenaica. Finally, in 1912 and 1913, the Balkan nations fought two wars, which resulted in the partitioning of Macedonia. The once mighty Ottoman empire was finally destroyed.

The "Great Game"

The area between the Caspian Sea and the Persian Gulf served as the focus of conflict between Britain and Russia during the nineteenth century. The attention of these two major powers could not have been welcomed by the two nations caught in the crossfire, Persia and Afghanistan (see map, p. 726).

Persia (now Iran), one of the more strategically located areas of the Islamic world, contained many different peoples (Turks, Arabs, Persians, Kurds, Jews, and Armenians) and religions (Islam, Zoroastrianism, Judaism, and Armenian Christianity). Ruling over this crossroads area was the Kajar Dynasty, which had to deal with the Russians to the north and the British to the south.

Afghanistan, which lay to the east of Persia, controlled the Khyber Pass, the most direct land

Young Turks march in triumph after their successful coup and overthrow of the despot Abdul Hamid II and his reactionary government.

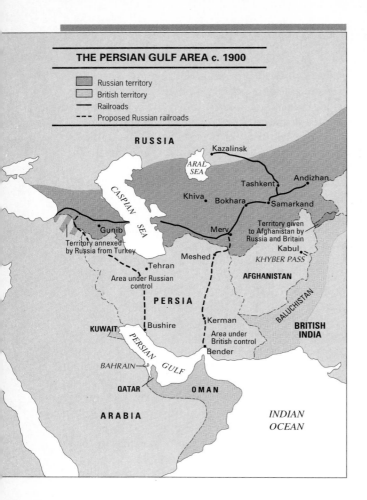

THE PERSIAN GULF AREA c. 1900

- ▨ Russian territory
- ▢ British territory
- — Railroads
- --- Proposed Russian railroads

RUSSIA

Kazalinsk

ARAL SEA

CASPIAN SEA

Tashkent   Andizhan

Khiva   Bokhara   Samarkand

Gunib   Merv   Territory given to Afghanistan by Russia and Britain

Territory annexed by Russia from Turkey

Meshed   Kabul   KHYBER PASS

Tehran

Area under Russian control   AFGHANISTAN

PERSIA

BALUCHISTAN

KUWAIT   Bushire   Kerman

Area under British control   BRITISH INDIA

Bender

BAHRAIN   PERSIAN GULF

QATAR   OMAN

ARABIA   INDIAN OCEAN

route from Russia to British-controlled India. The mountainous country had been divided previously between the Mongols and Persians. By the nineteenth century the shah in Kabul, Afghanistan's capital city, ruled over the tribal confederations that roamed the country.

Russia had begun its advance toward the region in the middle of the sixteenth century. From that time to the present, the Russians have had a deep and abiding interest in the Islamic world to the south. Russia had several motives in pursuing control of this region: it needed a warm-water port, a direct trade route to India, and a defensive buffer zone between European Russia and Asia. Throughout the eighteenth and nineteenth centuries the Russians extended their control across the Black Sea, the Caucasus, and into central Asia to the frontiers of Persia and Afghanistan. Their advance drew the worried attention of the British.

Britain wanted to maintain control of the sea lanes of the eastern Mediterranean, and after 1869 it sought sole access to the Suez Canal. European power politics in the 1840s, 1850s, and 1870s had helped the British thwart the Russian drive to control the Straits, Constantinople, and the eastern Mediterranean. But Russia's expansion across the Urals threatened the British from another flank—through central Asia. British foreign policy in the nineteenth

This 1885 cartoon from *Punch* shows the British lion and the Indian tiger watching apprehensively as the Russian bear attacks the Afghan wolf.

A contemporary Russian drawing of a construction train on the Trans-Caspian Railway. Completion of this railway allowed Russia to transport and supply troops to central Asia and extend its economic influence in that area.

century focused equally on defense of India's land frontiers to the north and protection of the Suez Canal, Red Sea, and the Persian Gulf.

During the first half of the century, Persia and Afghanistan were caught up in armed conflicts with the Russians and the British. The Persians, defeated in two wars by the Russians, lost large amounts of territory and had to pay substantial indemnities. In an attempt to gain control of the Khyber Pass, the British fought the Afghans from 1839 to 1842. In the first part of the conflict a 3,000-man British force was massacred. Later, British troops from India took control of the region. Britain's advances were gained by a strong army and controlled by a well-trained colonial government. Persia and Afghanistan weakened as the two major European forces extended their power from north and south.

While the British consolidated their hold on India, Russia expanded toward the southeast. Many indigenous peoples, such as the Mongols, Afghans, Turkomans, and Tatars, came within Russia's sphere of influence. Their cities—Samarkand, Tashkent, and Bokhara—became tsarist administrative centers.

Russia's advance was won not only by its army, but also by the construction of the Trans-Caspian Railway which, at its completion in 1888, reached 1064 miles into the heart of Asia. The Orenburg-Tashkent railway, completed in 1905, stretched 1185 miles farther. Both lines vastly increased Russia's ability to maintain military pressure on and economic superiority over the area. Inspired by the feats of both the army and the engineers, some Russian imperialists

dreamed of conquering Afghanistan and penetrating India itself. The central Asian thrust was part of the "Great Game" between Britain and Russia—Russian pressure against India was designed primarily as a counter against Britain in other areas.[5]

At the end of the nineteenth century Afghanistan and Tibet continued to be serious areas of tension. Effective British pressure blocked Russia's design on Afghanistan and a British military expedition to Lhasa in 1904 countered Russian influence in Tibet. Persia, however, remained a more difficult problem.

The Persian Dilemma

Britain made economic inroads into Persia during the nineteenth century, gaining control of most of the area's mineral wealth and banking operations. The British completed a telegraph line from London to Persia in 1870, symbolizing the direct tie between Britain and that far-off land.

During the last part of the century, the Persians attempted a program of westernization, complete with a new capital at Tehran. They made major investments to establish hospitals, a school system, as well as an army. But all of this cost money, which the Persians borrowed from the British and the Russians. The great powers, in their turn, gained control of a large part of the country's economy.

The British may have blocked the Russians in other areas, but Persia remained an area of competition. The Royal Navy, based at Aden, was charged with keeping communications routes open from India to the Suez and with protecting the entry to the Red Sea. Along the Arabian coast the British gained control, through treaties with a number of friendly, minuscule sheikdoms such as Muscat, Oman, Bahrain, and Kuwait. The maintenance of this sphere of influence effectively blocked German and French efforts to gain footholds along the Persian Gulf.

Germany had tried unsuccessfully to build a terminus on the Persian Gulf for its projected Berlin-to-Baghdad railroad. In 1903 the British foreign secretary issued what has been called a British Monroe Doctrine over the area: "I say it without hesitation, we should regard the establishment of a naval base or a fortified port in the Persian Gulf by any other power as a very grave menace to British interests, and we should certainly resist it by all means at our disposal."[6]

Although Britain had discouraged German attempts to build a railroad to Persia, there was still the possibility that the Russian Trans-Caucasian Railway might be extended south through Persia to the warm waters of the Persian Gulf. In this event the tsar's government might not only profit commercially but might also build a naval base that would threaten the British sea route to India.

Persia was in no position to resist Russian pressure. Its government was corrupt and inefficient, and Russia took advantage of its weakness. By the beginning of the twentieth century parts of northern Persia were in the control of the Russians. Tsarist forces trained the Persian army, put up telegraph lines, established a postal system, and developed trade. Some Persian workers crossed into Russia to work in the Caucasus oil fields. The Russian ministry of finance even set up a bank—The Discount and Loan Bank of Persia—with branches in many parts of the nation. This bank loaned the Persian government 60 million rubles and provided 120 million rubles to Persian merchants to enable them to buy Russian goods.

The British government had no desire to see Russia gain power along the Persian Gulf. To counter this threat to the British-Indian lifeline, the British set up the Imperial Bank of Persia in southeastern Persia. At the same they gained a profitable tobacco monopoly.

Persian patriotic reformers carried out a successful revolution in 1906. The established a parliament and initiated reforms, aided by American advisers. This development, plus the changing diplomatic situation in western Europe brought on by the increase in tensions with the Germans brought the two competitors—Britain and Russia—together in 1907 to sign an agreement to end their rivalry in central Asia.

By the terms of the Anglo-Russian entente, Russia agreed to deal with the sovereign of Afghanistan only through the British government. Great Britain agreed to refrain from occupying or annexing Afghanistan so long as it fulfilled its treaty obligations. Persia became an Anglo-Russian holding, split up into three zones: the northern part was a Russian sphere of influence, the middle section was a neutral zone, and the southern portion was under British control.

The partnership was, however, only a marriage of convenience brought on by larger pressures in Europe. Russia continued intervening in Persian domestic politics, throwing its support to the shah, who was willing to do its bidding. Though upset by the Russians' activities, the British chose not to alienate them because they needed to build an alliance to counter Germany. Britain needed Russia's help and abided by the compromise arrangement in Persia.

The nineteenth-century extension of European state power over the Middle East reflected each great power's views of its own trade and defense needs. But the colonial powers ignored the desires, goals, and legitimate demands of the indigenous population.

North Africa

At the beginning of the nineteenth century, the Ottoman empire controlled—albeit tenuously—all of the African coast along the Mediterranean, with the exception of Morocco. The weakening of Turkish power, however, made the area virtually self-governing or subject to foreign pressures. By 1914 all of North Africa from Casablanca to Cairo had come under direct European control.

Egypt

Europe had long been fascinated by Egypt, and Napoleon's invasion of that country had increased interest in both its historic sights and its economic potential. As the Turkish control weakened in the first quarter of the century, Mehmet Ali came to be the dominant figure in the country. He was able to increase his authority in the theoretically Turkish-controlled land and carry out economic and agricultural changes. By the 1830s he had expanded his power (see p. 723) to the point where the great powers had to step in to save the Turks from his forces.

The dynamism of Mehmet Ali, however, did not touch the life of the Egyptian *fellah* (peasant), who lived amid poverty, disease, and ignorance. Most Egyptians continued to depend on the narrow green strip along the Nile River for survival, just as they had for thousands of years. Mehmet Ali's successes did not bring Egypt prosperity.

In the 1850s the government had to borrow a substantial amount of money from Great Britain to provide basic services. Dependence on foreign finance increased as the Egyptians tried to build railroads, schools, and factories to improve their economy. One of the foremost projects undertaken was that of the Suez Canal, built in cooperation with the French from 1859 to 1869. The more the Egyptians built, the more their debts increased. By 1875 financial difficulties forced Ismail, ruler of Egypt, to sell his block of 175,000 shares in the Suez Canal. The stock was snapped up by Disraeli, the astute prime minister of Great Britain. This maneuver gave Britain virtual control of this essential water link between Europe and the East.

When Ismail tried to repudiate his debts in 1879, Great Britain and France took over financial control of Egypt. The British and French forced Ismail to abdicate in favor of his son. The Egyptian ruling classes and officer corps did not relish foreign control, and violence broke out in 1881 and 1882. The worst outbreak came at Alexandria, where many Europeans lost their lives during rioting. The British, acting unilaterally, then routed the Egyptians at Tell el-Kebir. After that, the British took responsibility for the running of the country.

To reorganize Egyptian finances, eliminate corruption from the administration, and improve the all-important (for the British) cotton industry, Sir Evelyn Baring, later Lord Cromer, was

British troops rest near the pyramids after the British bombardment and occupation of Alexandria, Egypt, in 1882.

The Earl of Cromer on Egypt

The Earl of Cromer looked back after his career in Egypt and claimed the following benefits of European domination.

No one can fully realise the extent of the change which has come over Egypt since the British occupation took place unless he is in some degree familiar with the system under with the country was governed in the days of Ismail Pasha. The contrast between now and then is, indeed, remarkable. A new spirit has been instilled into the population of Egypt. Even the peasant has learnt to scan his rights. Even the Pasha has learnt that others besides himself have rights which must be respected. The courbash may hang on the walls of the Moudirieh, but the Moudir no longer dares to employ it on the backs of the fellaheen. For all practical purposes, it may be said that the hateful corvée system has disappeared. Slavery has virtually ceased to exist. The halcyon days of the adventurer and the usurer are past. Fiscal burthens have been greatly relieved. Everywhere law reigns supreme. Justice is no longer bought and sold. Nature, instead of being spurned and neglected, has been wooed to bestow her gifts on mankind. She has responded to the appeal. The waters of the Nile are now utilised in an intelligent manner. Means of locomotion have been improved and extended. The soldier has acquired some pride in the uniform which he wears. He has fought as he never fought before. The sick man can be nursed in a well-managed hospital. The lunatic is no longer treated like a wild beast. The punishment awarded to the worst criminal is no longer barbarous. Lastly, the schoolmaster is abroad, with results which are as yet uncertain, but which cannot fail to be important.

All these things have been accomplished by the small body of Englishmen who, in various capacities, and with but little direct support or assistance from their Government or its representative, have of late years devoted their energies to the work of Egyptian regeneration. They have had many obstacles to encounter. Internationalism and Pashadom have stood in the path at every turn. But these forces, though they could retard, have failed to arrest the progress of the British reformer. The opposition which he has had to encounter, albeit very embarrassing, merely acted on his system as a healthy tonic. An eminent French literary critic has said that the end of a book should recall its commencement to the mind of the reader. Acting on this principle, I may remind those who have perused these pages that I began this work by stating that, although possibly counterparts to all the abuses which existed, and which to some extent still exist in Egypt, may be found in other countries, the conditions under which the work of Egyptian reform has been undertaken were very peculiar. The special difficulties which have resulted from those conditions have but served to bring out in strong relief one of the main characteristics of the Anglo-Saxon race. Other nations might have equally well conceived the reforms which were necessary. It required the singular political adaptability of Englishmen to execute them. A country and a nation have been partially regenerated, in spite of a perverse system of government which might well have seemed to render regeneration almost impossible.

From Earl of Cromer, *Modern Egypt,* vol. 2 (New York: Macmillan, 1908).

sent to Egypt to oversee the country's affairs from 1883 to 1907. He overhauled the system of government, curbed the use of forced labor, and carried out substantial public works projects. Some authorities have maintained that the best record of British imperialism is to be found in Egypt. European technology, governmental expertise, and financial practices aided the country's development. Despite this, in the first years of the twentieth century, Egyptians were voicing a growing demand for self-government.

Other States of North Africa

In Tripoli, Tunis, Algeria, and Morocco, the Europeans also made steady inroads during the nineteenth century. These four areas lacked the fertile green belt along a river such as Egypt possessed along the Nile. They also lacked both the economic basis and political leaders to attempt such grandiose projects as those pursued by the Egyptians. By the end of the century the rest of the north coast of Africa came under the control of the Italians and the French.

The area around Tripoli had gained its independence from the Turks in the first part of the eighteenth century. For the rest of the century the area served as a base for Mediterranean pirates. In 1835 it once again came under Turkish control where it remained until the Italians focused their attention on the area at the end of the century. The Italians declared war on the Turks, after having gained the consent of the great powers, and after a more difficult campaign than they had expected, Italy forced the Turks to cede the area to them in 1912.

The Ottomans had taken control of Tunis in 1575 and held on to it until the French established a protectorate there in 1881. As in the case with Tripoli, the power of the local government was weak, and the coastline harbored pirates and thieves. As had been the case in Egypt, the Tunisian government became indebted financially to European lenders, even before the French took over. After 1881 most of the country's wealth went abroad, and most of the population lived in desperate poverty.

Algeria's coastline also served as a base for piracy from the sixteenth to the nineteenth century. In the 1820s the French complained forcefully of the pirates' activities along the French coast. When in 1827 the Algerian ruler insulted the French consul in public by hitting him with a flyswatter, France used the incident as a suitable pretext to enter the country. Paris sent down a large army to occupy Algeria, but it took seventeen years to put down the fierce Berber tribesmen. Algeria was then incorporated as an integral part of the French state.

From the 1840s to the end of the century French interests also dominated in Morocco, the first country to experience overseas expansion

Seventeen years of intermittent military clashes followed France's invasion of Algeria in 1830 until the country was finally subjugated and integrated into the French state in 1847.

"Dr. Livingstone, I presume." When the famous Scottish missionary and explorer David Livingstone vanished in the interior of Africa after three decades of travel on that continent, the *New York Herald* commissioned Henry Stanley to locate him.

by Europe. But European states contested the area until 1911, and the Moroccan question increased tensions between Germany and France up to the beginning of World War I.

In general, the North African countries west of Egypt lacked the vigorous leadership, strong economies, and unified populations needed to stand off the European advances. Geographical obstacles were perhaps the major issue, as a nomadic population had to search continuously for the scarce means of existence.

Sub-Sahara Africa

Until the nineteenth century the great continent of Africa, many times the size of Europe, was virtually unknown to most Europeans. Still less was known about the 150 million people living there. But this state of affairs changed rapidly thanks to the intrepid investigations of some European explorers. The most successful representative of this group was David Livingstone (1813–1873), a Scottish missionary who crossed the vast barren wastes and jungles from the Cape of Good Hope to Lake Tanganyika. He began his explorations in 1853 and discovered Victoria Falls and the Zambezi River for the Europeans. After his death in 1873, his work in the

interior was carried on by Henry M. Stanley (1841–1904), the British explorer and journalist who had located Livingstone in 1871 and had with classic British understatement greeted him, "Dr. Livingstone, I presume."

The Europeans Arrive

African tribes and nations were too disunited to mount an effective resistance to the Europeans. The comparative ease with which the whites took and divided the continent may give the impression that there were few effective leaders among the Africans. There were many, especially among the Bantu people of southeastern Africa. Toward the end of the eighteenth century they made contact with the white civilization that spread from the Cape. After 1820, as black populations increased and room for expansion lessened, 2 million people became engulfed in a vast, bloody terror. In this fiery crucible, newly emerging black rulers forged many scattered clans into a few powerful states. The mightiest of these strong men was Shaka, king of the Zulus.

Born in 1787, an illegitimate son of a minor chief, Shaka spent a miserable childhood as an outcast among his mother's relatives. As a youth he became a warrior in the army of Dingiswayo, a powerful chief, who had learned some military tactics from the English and traded with the

Portuguese. In his first battle Shaka distinguished himself and was promoted to captain. Shaka soon became supreme commander, succeeded his father as chief, and later supreme commander of northern Natal. By 1824 he governed 250,000 people along the coast between the Pongola and Umzimbubu rivers.

Shaka was a complex and magnetic personality. He dabbled in magic and witchcraft as well as capricious statecraft. He was customarily attended by executioners who were casually ordered to dispose of those who displeased him. He also was responsible for incidents of mass murder. Yet Zulu traditions have always portrayed him as a folk hero, one who cared for his soldiers and his people and who could cover eighty miles a day and dance all night. Whites who encountered him were appalled by his cruelty and amazed by his dignity, honesty, and intelligence.

CHAKA KING OF THE ZOOLUS.

London, Published by E. Churton, 26 Holles St.

Shaka, Zulu chief and military and political leader, holds the traditional Zulu assagai, or spear.

Zulu warriors under Cetshwayo, Shaka's nephew and king of the Zulus from 1873 to 1879, attacked and destroyed the British garrison at Isandlwana in 1879.

Shaka's power attracted hundreds of isolated clans into his nation. Shaka revolutionized the Zulu army by introducing the "stabbing spear," using mass, disciplined infantry tactics, and perfecting the regimental organization begun under Dingiswayo. He tried to transform the ancient pattern of his society, based on kinship, into a territorial state under one absolute ruler, whose subchiefs lost most of their power. He was well on the way to leading his people beyond family and clan loyalty to national consciousness when he was assassinated in 1828. His empire successfully resisted expanding white civilization for half a century after his death, and his legacy lived on to enable his successors to wage the most successful wars ever fought by blacks against Europeans. In 1879 the Zulus under King Cetshwayo defeated a British force, killing 700 soldiers, 130 colonists, and hundreds of their African allies, at Isandlwana.

However, there were neither enough Shakas nor Zulus after 1870. In that year the Europeans controlled only 10 percent of the continent. The two most important foreign holdings were French-administered Algeria and the Cape Colony, governed by Great Britain. Most of the other European holdings were mere coastal ports along West Africa. There were also strong political forces in Africa. In present-day Nigeria there was the Muslim Fulani Empire, created by Usman dan Fodio (1754–1817). In Ethiopia, Theodore II and Menelik II built a united state.

After 1870 the tempo of European intervention in Africa increased rapidly. One of the first European leaders to act was King Leopold II of Belgium. In 1876 he organized the International Africa Association and brought the explorer Stanley into his service. The association, composed of scientists and explorers from all nations, ostensibly was intended to serve humanitarian purposes. But the crafty king had other motives. As an agent of the association, Stanley went to the Congo where he made treaties with several African chiefs and, by 1882, obtained over 900,000 square miles of territory.[7]

Britain's occupation of Egypt and the Belgian acquisition of the Congo moved Bismarck in 1884 to call a conference of major European powers to discuss potential problems of unregulated African colonization. The assembly, meeting in Berlin, paid lip service to humanitarianism by condemning the slave trade, prohibiting the sale of liquor and firearms in certain areas, and expressing concern for proper religious instruction for the Africans. Then the participants moved to matters that they considered to be much more important.

They set down the rules of competition by which the great powers were to be guided in their search for colonies. They agreed that the area along the Congo River was to be administered by Leopold of Belgium, but that it was to be a neutral territory with free trade and navigation. No nation was to stake out claims in Africa without first notifying the other powers of its intention. No territory could be claimed unless it was effectively occupied, and all disputes were to be settled by arbitration.

In spite of these declarations, the competitors often ignored the rules. On several occasions, war was barely avoided. The humanitarian rules were generally ignored. The methods Europeans used to acquire lands continued in many cases to involve the deception of the Africans. European colonists got huge land grants by giving uneducated chiefs treaties they could not read and

Representatives of fourteen nations including the United States met in Berlin in 1884 to set new rules to govern their "scramble for Africa." The conference included no representatives from Africa.

Lord Lugard Justifies European Imperialism in Africa

Lord Lugard gave as effective a rationale for European imperialism in Africa as one can find. His argument is a model of elevated self-serving.

The "Scramble for Africa" by the nations of Europe—an incident without parallel in the history of the world—was due to the growing commercial rivalry, which brought home to civilised nations the vital necessity of securing the only remaining fields for industrial enterprise and expansion. It is well, then, to realise that it is for our *advantage*—and not alone at the dictates of duty—that we have undertaken responsibilities in East Africa. It is in order to foster the growth of the trade of this country, and to find an outlet for our manufactures and our surplus energy, that our far-seeing statesmen and our commercial men advocate colonial expansion . . . .

There are some who say we have no *right* in Africa at all, that "it belongs to the natives." I hold that our right is the necessity that is upon us to provide for our ever-growing population—either by opening new fields for emigration, or by providing work and employment which the development of over-sea extension entails—and to stimulate trade by finding new markets, since we know what misery trade depression brings at home.

While thus serving our own interests as a nation, we may, by selecting men of the right stamp for the control of new territories, bring at the same time many advantages to Africa. Nor do we deprive the natives of their birthright of freedom, to place them under a foreign yoke. It has ever been the key-note of British colonial method to rule through and by the natives, and it is this method, in contrast to the arbitrary and uncompromising rule of Germany, France, Portugal, and Spain, which has been the secret of our success as a colonising nation, and has made us welcomed by tribes and peoples in Africa, who ever rose in revolt against the other nations named. In Africa, moreover, there is among the people a natural inclination to submit to a higher authority. That intense detestation of control which animates our Teutonic races does not exist among the tribes of Africa, and if there is any authority that we replace, it is the authority of the Slavers and Arabs, or the intolerable tyranny of the "dominant tribe." . . .

From Captain F. D. Lugard, *The Rise of Our East African Empire*, vol. I (London: William Blackwood and Sons, 1893).

whose contents they were not permitted to understand. In return, the natives were rewarded with bottles of gin, red handkerchiefs, and fancy dress costumes. The comparison between the European treaty methods and those of the Americans in the negotiations with the Indians is all too apparent.

The ethical and cultural differences between the Africans and the Europeans were especially vast regarding the subject of land ownership. Since in many cases native customs reserved ownership of the land to tribes, allowing individuals only the use of it, chiefs granted land to European settlers with no idea that they were disposing of more than its temporary use. When the settlers later claimed ownership of the land,

the natives were indignant, feeling that the tribe had been robbed of land, contrary to tribal law.

The Division of Africa

By 1914 European imperialists divided Africa among themselves, with two exceptions. Only Liberia and Ethiopia remained independent (see map, p. 736).

Shortly after the Berlin conference, King Leopold organized his African territories into the African Free State, subject to his control alone. He began to exploit the colony's economic resources by granting concessions to private companies, reserving for his own administration an extensive rubber-producing area ten times as

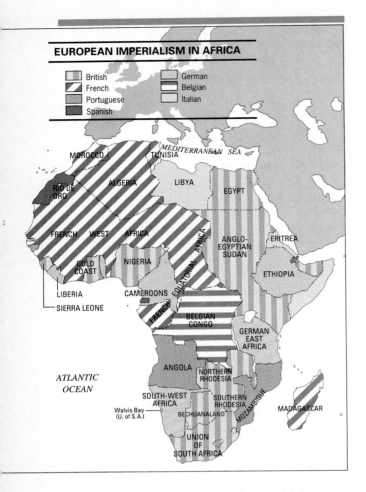

EUROPEAN IMPERIALISM IN AFRICA

British
French
Portuguese
Spanish
German
Belgian
Italian

MEDITERRANEAN SEA
MOROCCO
TUNISIA
RIO DE ORO
ALGERIA
LIBYA
EGYPT
FRENCH WEST AFRICA
ANGLO-EGYPTIAN SUDAN
ERITREA
GOLD COAST
NIGERIA
ETHIOPIA
LIBERIA
CAMEROONS
SIERRA LEONE
FRENCH EQUATORIAL AFRICA
BELGIAN CONGO
GERMAN EAST AFRICA
ATLANTIC OCEAN
ANGOLA
NORTHERN RHODESIA
SOUTH-WEST AFRICA
SOUTHERN RHODESIA
MOZAMBIQUE
MADAGASCAR
Walvis Bay (U. of S.A.)
BECHUANALAND
UNION OF SOUTH AFRICA

mission to eastern Africa. Peters succeeded in obtaining treaties from local chiefs giving him control of 60,000 square miles. The next year, Bismarck proclaimed the region to be German East Africa.

The British had been laying claims to the region directly north of Peters' concessions. Contradictory German and British claims were settled amicably in 1886 and 1890. After the agreements, which included the British concession of the strategic Helgoland Island in the North Sea, the British held Uganda along the shores of Lake Victoria, British East Africa (later known as Kenya), the rich spice island of Zanzibar, and the area of Nyasaland. Germany's claim to its protectorate in East Africa (later called Tanganyika, now Tanzania) was recognized by the British.

Meanwhile, by 1884 the British had gained control over a stretch of African coast fronting on the Gulf of Aden. This protectorate (British Somaliland) was of great strategic value since it guarded the lower approach to the Suez Canal. Equally important were the headwaters of the Nile, situated in the area known later as the Anglo-Egyptian Sudan. In 1898 the British gained control of this area. Among the British acquisitions on the west coast of Africa, the most important were the territories around the mouth of the Niger, stretching back toward the Sudan. These British possessions included Gambia, Sierra Leone, the Gold Coast, and Nigeria.

During this same period British influence in southern Africa had expanded northward from Cape Colony to German East Africa. The main force behind this drive came from the capitalist Cecil Rhodes, who dreamed of an uninterrupted corridor of British territory from the Cape of Good Hope to Cairo (see p. 698).

If overpopulation, lack of trade, and widespread poverty had been the most compelling reasons for gaining colonies, Italy should have obtained the most extensive areas in Africa. But Italy emerged from the scramble for colonies with very little territory. The Italians gained a piece of the Red Sea coast and a slice of barren and desolate land on the Indian Ocean. But these areas were of little value without the rich plateau of Abyssinia (Ethiopia) in the hinterland. An attempt to take the ancient empire in 1896 ended in the humiliating destruction of a 20,000-man Italian army.

large as Belgium. A system of forced labor was introduced, and soon stories of filthy work camps, horrible whippings, and other atrocities leaked out of the "Free State," which was undergoing the process of "civilization" as the Belgians referred to it. In the face of a rising tide of international outrage, Leopold was forced to turn the "Free State" over to the Belgian government in 1908. The conditions of the colony, renamed the Belgian Congo, improved under the direct administration of the government.

In the 1880s Germany acquired three colonies on the west coast of Africa: German Southwest Africa, Togoland, and Cameroons. They made their most important gains, however, on the east coast of the continent. German penetration there was largely the work of one man, Carl Peters, a student of British colonization methods. In 1884 he and three other colonial enthusiasts, disguised as British workers, set out on a secret

THE RHODES COLOSSUS
STRIDING FROM CAPE TOWN TO CAIRO.

An 1892 cartoon from *Punch* captures the dream of empire builder Cecil Rhodes for British domination of Africa from "Cape to Cairo."

Building on Louis Napoleon's ambitions, France continued in 1884 developing a colonial program by acquiring a large section of equatorial Africa along the right bank of the Congo River. From trading posts along the west coast of the continent, France pushed into the interior and obtained most of the basins of the Senegal and Niger rivers. Expeditions from France's north African holdings penetrated the Sahara. Although France did not succeed in getting to the Nile, by 1900 it controlled the largest empire in Africa, one which stretched eastward from the Atlantic to the western Sudan and soutward to the Congo River. The French also took control of the large island of Madagascar in the south Indian Ocean. They completed their colonial gains in 1911—over German protests—by making Morocco a French protectorate.

Costs and Benefits

Africa's wealth surpassed the hopes of the most avid imperialist. By the first decade of this century the continent was the world's greatest producer of gold and diamonds. Rich resources of tin, phosphates, and copper had also been discovered. Africa supplied large amounts of rubber, coffee, and cotton. European imperialists gained not only huge territories and vast reserves of raw materials; they also gained the labor of millions of Africans.

The Africans who came under European domination had to make severe adjustments. The impact of European imperialism was profound and widespread. European imperialists divided Africa by drawing lines on a map with total disregard for traditional political and social structures. For the first time, many villagers were forced to pay money taxes to a distant central authority. In most cases, Africans had lived within a small tribal area of law and political affiliation. With the advent of imperial rule, dozens of formerly distinct—and often antagonistic—tribes were

An Ethiopian painting of the Battle of Adowa in 1896 in which the army of Emperor Menelik II defeated the invading Italians. At the top of the painting, Saint George intercedes for the Ethiopians.

brought together, as in the case of Nigeria, into one colony. In other cases of imperialism, large tribes were split into two or three European colonial segments. Colonies were not usually unified nations, a fact that would have bloody consequences as they became independent after World War II.

The colonization process in Africa, undertaken by a dynamic, self-confident, and technologically advanced civilization, severely disrupted cultures that had been isolated from the mainstream of world affairs. Kinship and family ties were weakened when villagers sought jobs in distant towns and mines. In some areas as many as 50 percent of the young males sought employment in order to pay the new hut taxes or to buy cheap but enticing European wares.

Their mothers, wives, and sisters left behind received a double shock. They had to carry on the increased work load and maintain the family unit single-handedly, with an enormous increase in their hours per week of labor to feed their families. However, they also saw their roles diminished as European notions of the "woman's place" displaced them from their traditional positions of social influence. In the new export markets, men monopolized the raising of cash crops, cutting women out of economic opportunities. Undoubtedly, wages from absent husbands did help raise standards of living, but the effect on family ties and tribal loyalties was destructive.

The old ways of life were most disrupted in colonies that attracted European settlement, such as Kenya and Southern Rhodesia. In such areas, Africans were confined to "native reserves" or to segregated areas in the towns. On occasion large tracts of land were allocated exclusively for European use. It was in these plural societies that racial tensions most rapidly developed.

For a half century after the scramble for colonies began, the incidence of social change was uneven. In some remote areas, Africans may never have seen white persons, let alone worked for them. But tribal life was gradually transformed by the introduction of new forms of land tenure, enforcement of alien systems of law, and the growth of the money economy. In an attempt to imitate the technologically and militarily superior Europeans, many Africans tried to adopt the ways of their new rulers. As a result, some

of them became "detribalized" and often bewildered, as they were also alienated from much of their traditional culture but unable to understand fully and be part of the new. Although the transformation of Africa was probably inevitable at some point, it was unfortunate that this revolutionary change occurred so quickly, and at the hands of intruders, whose motives were so selfish. Much too frequently the imperialists disparaged all African culture, dismissing the Africans as barbarous and uncivilized.

Colonialism may have been an abrupt and rude awakening to the new day of the industrialized world, but it did bring several benefits. The arrival of Europeans introduced more peace between the tribes by imposing more efficient law enforcement methods. The international slave trade ended. The Europeans brought in material and technological advances, such as telegraph and telephone communications, railroads, improved harbors, and improved medical standards. European organizational and educational techniques were introduced in the form of better administrative systems, widespread schools, and a money economy. All of these things may have been necessary to enable Africa to enter the modern age, but they came at a very high price.

Conclusion

By 1914 the European states had established their primacy over the Middle East and Africa. There was no doubting the nature and extent of Europe's material and technological dominance over southwest Asia and Africa. While thousands of Persians crossed into Russia to work in tsarist oil fields, thousands more Africans worked in European-owned mines. Both groups were begrudgingly witnesses to Europe's economic strength. While financiers in London, Berlin, and Paris skimmed the profits off the top of their newly controlled areas, European officials and diplomats dictated policy for most of the region.

Even before 1914, however, the forces that would eventually remove European dominance in the next half century were at work. These forces gained strength from European ideals. All of the apologists in Europe who spoke of carrying the "white man's burden" or of spreading "civilization" to the "lesser peoples" had a major blind spot in their world view. They confused technological and material strength with cultural strength. There could, of course, be no doubting the European material superiority over the Middle East and Africa. There was no military, economic, or technological arena in which the non-Europeans could claim superiority by 1914. Yet the identities of the peoples caught under European dominance did not disappear. Rather, under the influence of the European ideologies and political structures that accompanied the diplomats and industrialists, their identities became more sharply defined.

The rapid expansion of European primacy over the Middle East and Africa failed to establish firm roots. Europeanization remained a surface phenomenon, affecting mainly the material aspects of life. Islam retained its strength and the African peoples the essence of their identities. The contact of both areas with European state systems was immediately tragic, but not fatal. Armed with the technological, intellectual, and political lessons they learned from the Europeans, the Middle East and Africa could hope, someday, to compete on an equal basis.

Suggestions for Reading

R. H. Davison, *Turkey* (Prentice-Hall, 1968) is a brief, well-written survey. Bernard Lewis provides excellent analyses in *The Emergence of Modern Turkey*, 2nd ed. (Oxford, 1968). William Miller, *The Ottoman Empire and Its Successors, 1801–1927* (Octagon, 1966) and L. S. Stavrianos, *The Balkans Since 1453* (Holt, Rinehart & Winston, 1961) provide thorough treatment of the multi-ethnic challenge facing the Turks. P. Coles, *The Ottoman Impact on Europe* (Harcourt Brace Jovanovich, 1968) is a wise survey.

Kenneth Ingham, *A History of East Africa* (Longman, 1962) and J. D. Fage, *An Introduction to the History of West Africa* (Cambridge, 1969) are useful studies, as is J. B. Webster and A. A. Boahen, *History of West Africa* (Praeger, 1967). See also R. Hallett, *Africa to 1975* (Michigan, 1974); J. D. Fage, *History of West Africa*, (Cambridge, 1969). Ronald Robinson and J. Gallagher, *Africa and the Victorians* (St. Martin's, 1969); and Peter Duignan and L. H. Gann, eds., *Colonialism in Africa* (Cambridge, 1969) which contains perceptive essays on the motivations for imperialism. The nature of Britain's imperial mission in Africa is shown in the lives of three men: F. Gross, *Rhodes of Africa* (Praeger, 1957); Lord Elton, *Gordon of Khartoum* (Knopf, 1955); and M. Perham, *Lugard, The Years of Adventure* (Archon, 1968).

Notes

1. Robert Schnerb, "Le XIXe Siècle: L'Apogée de L'Expansion Européene (1815–1914)," *Histoire Générale des Civilisations*, VI (Paris: Presses Universitaires de France, 1955), pp. 347–352.
2. L. S. Stavrianos, *The Balkans Since 1453* (New York: Holt, Rinehart & Winston, 1961), pp. 135–136.
3. Bernard Lewis, *The Emergence of Modern Turkey* (Oxford: Oxford Univ. Press, 1968), pp. 1–17.
4. Ibid., pp. 41–64.
5. Peter Fleming, *Bayonets to Lhasa* (New York: Harper & Row, 1961), p. 21.
6. Quoted in N. D. Harris, *Europe and the East* (Boston, Houghton Mifflin, 1926), p. 285.
7. L. H. Gann and P. Duignan, *Burden of Empire* (New York: Praeger, 1967), p. 286.

South and East Asia, 1815–1914

The large countries of south and east Asia—India, China, and Japan—and their smaller neighbors faced decisive challenges from the western powers in the nineteenth century. Only Japan possessed the adaptability to meet the Europeans on their own terms before 1914. As for the rest, their religious, cultural, and political characteristics combined with technological and economic underdevelopment doomed their efforts to resist the western advance. Mughul rule was extremely weak in the Indian subcontinent; the Indochinese peninsula and the islands of the Pacific and Indian oceans had long been subjected to European influence; and China with its unbending sense of superiority refused to recognize a changing world.

All of south and east Asia shared similar geographic problems and challenges. The area contained many regions of densely populated territory that made large-scale agriculture impossible. The people, on the whole, lived in villages, with the exception of a few large cities. In nineteenth-century India, for example, roughly 80 percent of the people lived in communities of less than 2000 inhabitants. The area was and still is vulnerable to natural disasters such as tidal waves, earthquakes, and occasional droughts. These conditions produced a population suffering poor living conditions, high infant mortality rates, endemic diseases, and a lack of adequate nutrition.

India to 1914

Dual Control Under the British

The decline of Mughul power (see chapter 22) proved to be a great opportunity for the British and French, who through the late seventeenth and most of the eighteenth centuries competed for dominance in India. They fought through their trading companies and agents who sought local allies. India, like North America, was part of the world struggle for empire between the two European powers. The British victory over Bengal in the battle of Plassey (1757) ushered in the British phase of Indian history. Britain's naval supremacy and the superior discipline of its European-led armies enabled Britain to defeat France in 1760. French influence in India soon disappeared.

The traders became rulers, assuming the dual roles of businessmen and representatives of a sovereign state. Anarchy spread until 1818 when the British East India Company stepped in to become the subcontinents's police force. Some local rulers accepted the company's rule but others who resisted lost their land. The subcontinent was divided into two sections. British India was ruled directly by London, while in Indian India the local dynasties ruled under British supervision. The British Parliament, concerned that a profit-seeking company controlled the lives of millions of people, enacted legislation in 1773 and 1784 that gave it power to control company policies and appoint the governor-general, the highest company official in India.

The system of dual control lasted until 1858 and brought several benefits to the peninsula, especially to women. The practice of *suttee* in which widows burned themselves on the funeral pyres of their deceased husbands was prohibited. The company worked against the practice of killing female infants. Further, steps were taken to end the seclusion of women from society. A secret police force broke up the brutal system

This drawing by a British officer of a Bengal regiment shows a British magistrate settling a court case in 1853, during the period of dual control when the British East India Company and the British government shared authority over India.

of banditry and murder called *thuggee* (hence our word *thug*). In addition the British introduced a multilevel educational system.

Rebellion and Reform

In the spring of 1857 a serious rebellion interrupted the flow of liberal reforms. Indian troops who formed the bulk of the company's armed forces, called *sepoys*, started the uprising when they complained that a new cartridge issued to them was smeared with the fat of cows and pigs. This outraged both the Hindus, for whom the cow was a sacred animal, and the Muslims, who considered the pig unclean. Fortunately for the British, many areas remained loyal or at least calm. But in the affected areas there was fierce fighting and many lives were lost.

The Sepoy rebellion marked the final collapse of the Mughuls. The mutineers had proclaimed as their leader the last of the Mughul emperors permitted to maintain a court at Delhi. After the British put down the revolt, they exiled him to Burma. The rebellion also put an end to the system of dual control under which the British government and the East India Company shared authority. Parliament removed the company's political role, and after 258 years, the East India Company ended its rule.

Under the new system, the governor-general gained additional duties and a new title—viceroy. The viceroy was responsible to the secretary of state for India in the British cabinet. In the subcontinent, the British maintained direct control of most of the high positions in government, while Indians were trained to carry out administrative responsibilities in the provincial and subordinate systems. London reorganized the courts and law codes, along with the army and public services. English became the administrative language of the country. Only on rare occasions could native civil officials rise to higher positions in the bureaucracy.

India was governed by and for the British, who viewed themselves as the only people able to rule. By 1900, there was still 90 percent illiteracy

The storming of the Kashmir Gate at Delhi during the Sepoy Rebellion of 1857.

among native men and 99 percent for the women. Few schools existed at the village level to remedy that situation. The masses of the rural poor paid for the government through taxes on beverages and salt. India provided rich resources and vast markets for the British. In return the British introduced improved health standards, better water systems, and political stability.

The English language and British railroads introduced more unity to the country than it had ever known. But the imperial rulers took advantage of the subcontinent's diversity of religions, castes, and principalities (over 700 separate political units) to rule by a policy of divide and conquer. The British justified their political policies and economic dominance over India by pointing out that they were improving the lives of nearly one-fifth of the human race—almost 300 million people. This rationale could not remove the fact that the contrasts between the European and Asiatic ways of life in cities like Bombay, Delhi, and Calcutta were as great as the difference between night and day.

Resentment against British rule led to the rapid growth of the Indian nationalist movement. In 1885, with the help of several Englishmen who had Indian political ambitions, the Indian National Congress was formed. The British educational system, although it touched only a minority of the people, served as one of the most potent forces behind the new movement, as the

Indians embraced many of the liberal causes popular in England. Especially strong was the drive for women's equality and freedom, away from their traditional position of dependence, in which the only position and power women had was in relation to men.

As Indians learned the history of the rise of self-government in England, their desire for political freedom in their own land grew. The system of British control prevented Indians from rising above a certain level. At the same time, newly educated Indian youths, for social and cultural reasons, disdained manual labor. The result was a pool of thousands of frustrated and unemployed educated Indian youths who turned angrily against the government.

The British responded to the spread of violence with a major shift in policy between 1907 and 1909. They allowed the various provincial legislatures to elect Indian majorities, and an

Indian was seated in the executive council of the governor-general. The central government's legislature, however, remained under British control (see map, p. 742). These concessions satisfied moderates, for the time being, but did not appease the more radical protestors. In the twentieth century the spirit of nationalism would become even more insistent.

Southeast Asia to 1914

Southeast Asia includes the lands wedged between India and China and the multitude of islands in the Indian and Pacific oceans (see map below). It is a complex, diverse area whose fragmentation rendered it unable to resist the entry of the Europeans, which had begun in the sixteenth century.

European Incursions

Throughout the area European investors established a plantation economy to develop the coffee, tea, pepper, and other products demanded by the world market. Europeans discovered and exploited important mineral deposits. The Europeans attempted to introduce law and order for the purpose of limiting the chronic civil war and banditry that plagued the area. As was the case in India, the impact of European ways of life, especially western education, created a new generation of nationalists. In the Dutch East Indies, French Indochina, and the Philippines, young intellectuals aspired to complete independence for themselves and their countries.

In the eighteenth and nineteenth centuries Great Britain gained control of Ceylon, Malaya, and Burma. The first colony, taken from the Dutch in 1796, became one of the most valuable British holdings, producing such prized commodities as tea, rubber, lead, and sapphires. The Malayan peninsula, with the important island of Singapore, provided a vantage point from which Britain could dominate the seas surrounding southern Asia and export valuable supplies of tin and rubber. The British conquered Burma in three wars between 1823 and 1885 and annexed it to India.

France returned to the southeastern Asian area in the nineteenth century. French commercial and religious interests were established as

IMPERIALISM IN SOUTHEAST ASIA ABOUT 1914

In 1859, on the pretext of preserving Catholicism in Indochina, a French and Spanish expeditionary force stormed and captured the fortress of Saigon.

early as the seventeenth century, but British power in the Indian Ocean prevented France from stabilizing its position at that time. Not until the mid-nineteenth century did France increase its presence in Indochina. Anti-Christian persecutions in the area in 1856 and the fear that Catholicism would be eliminated if France did not go to its aid moved the French to join the British against China and Vietnam.

France took Saigon in 1860 and from that base expanded its influence and power through treaties, exploration, and outright annexation. The French took Hanoi in 1882, governed Cochin China as a direct colony, and held Annam (central Vietnam), Tonkin, and Cambodia as protectorates in one degree or another. Laos too was soon brought under French "protection." By the beginning of the twentieth century France had created an empire in Indochina nearly 50 percent larger than the parent country. Only Siam (Thailand) managed to hold off the French advance and keep its independence.

Late in the sixteenth century the Dutch had taken most of the East Indies from the Portuguese, and in 1602 the Dutch East India Company was organized to exploit the resources of

the Spice Islands. In 1798 the company's holdings were transferred to the Dutch crown. For some time the spice trade had been declining, and early in the nineteenth century the Dutch set about raising new products.

In the 1830s the so-called culture system was introduced, under which one-fifth of all native land was set aside to raise crops for the government. One-fifth of all the natives' time was also required to work the lands. As a result, the production of sugar, tobacco, coffee, tea, and other products increased tremendously. In the long run, the culture system gave the islands a prosperous system of raising crops, but it also often deprived the natives of sufficient land for their own use. Conditions for the natives improved in 1900 when the Dutch abandoned the culture system. Less favorable for the local population was the Dutch neglect of higher education and the failure to prepare them for eventual self-government.

American Imperialism

While the Europeans were pursuing their interests in the far east, a new imperial power was emerging in the Pacific—the United States. In 1867 the Americans occupied the Midway Islands and purchased Alaska from the Russians. The next step was in the Hawaiian Islands.

During the nineteenth century, Americans and Europeans had developed large sugar plantations on the mid-Pacific islands. The United States poured capital into them and by 1881 the U.S. secretary of state referred to the islands as part of the "American system." To ensure United States' control, a revolt in 1893, engineered with the assistance of the Marines, deposed the Hawaiian queen and set up a republic. Five years later the islands were annexed by a joint declaration of both houses of Congress.

The United States' successful war against Spain in 1898 (see chapter 27) affected both Cuba and the Philippines. In May of that year Admiral George Dewey destroyed the Spanish fleet at Manila and the first American soldiers began operations in the Philippines. In the treaty of December 1898 Spain ceded the Phillippines, Guam, and Puerto Rico to the United States. One year

Filipino guerrilla fighters at an outpost. When the United States refused to support Filipino claims of independence, fighting broke out between the Americans and the Filipino insurgents and lasted for three years.

Sugar clippers and inter-island steamers crowd Honolulu Harbor in 1892. In 1900, President McKinley defended the U.S. annexation of Hawaii as "manifest destiny."

later the Americans occupied the small Pacific outpost of Wake island.

Some of the liberal Filipino patriots who had rebelled against the Spanish in 1896 had assisted the Americans, but they had no wish to exchange one master for another. When it became evident that they would not quickly gain self-rule, fighting broke out. The hostilities that began in 1899 lasted for three years. The ironic spectacle of American forces being used in a second conquest of the Philippines brought about a strong revulsion against imperialism in many quarters of the United States. A New York newspaper addressed Rudyard Kipling, an apologist for imperialism, in this way:

> We've taken up the white man's burden
> Of ebony and brown:
>
> Now will you kindly tell us, Rudyard,
> How we may put it down.[1]

American colonial administration in the Philippines proved to be liberal and well-intentioned for the most part. In 1913 the legislature became dominantly native, although final authority in the most important matters was still reserved to the U.S. Congress. The Philippine tariff was shaped to favor American trade, and large amounts of capital from the United States were invested in the islands. Increased educational facilities produced an increasingly strong desire for independence among many Filipinos. In their eyes, American government in the Philippines, no matter how efficient or humanitarian, was no substitute for self-government.

There could be no doubt that by 1900 the United States sat astride the Pacific basin as did no other power. The consequences of this Pacific imperial posture were to become a major and costly constituent of American life in the twentieth century. A massive conflict with Japan, another in Korea, and the tragic war in Vietnam lay in the future. Whether such involvement was essential for American basic interests was to become a crucial and painful question.

The Central Kingdom

At the end of the 1800s China's four million square miles held 450 million people, up from 200 million a century earlier. The ruling dynasty was the Ch'ing, established by Manchus from Manchuria, who in 1644 had superseded the Ming. These descendants of the Tatars appreciated Chinese civilization and adopted a conciliatory attitude toward their subjects. They refused, however, to allow intermarriage with the Chinese, for they realized that only their blood difference kept them from being assimilated and conquered. By and large, however, the Manchus gradually became Chinese in their attitudes and habits.

The Manchu emperors were remarkably successful. The reign of Ch'ien-lung (1736–1795) was a time of great expansion. The Manchus gained Turkestan, Burma, and Tibet. By the end of the eighteenth century Manchu power extended even into Nepal, and the territory under the Ch'ing control was as extensive as under any previous dynasty.

The Perils of Superiority

The prevailing attitude of superiority to the cultures of all other peoples was an obstacle to China's leaders. They regarded with contempt rather than admiration advances in other parts of the world. Evidence of China's problems could be found in the eighteenth-century revolts in Formosa, Kansu, Hunan, Kueichou, and Shantung. All of them were suppressed, but clearly China was not functioning effectively.

In the first part of the nineteenth century, China continued to act imperiously toward foreigners. Merchants from western Europe came to China in increasing numbers, pursuing their trade in the face of great difficulties. Trade restrictions confined the foreign merchants to Canton and the Portuguese colony of Macao. In Canton, the Chinese controlled both trade and taxes. In spite of these obstacles, the foreigners made enough profit to compensate for their being treated as inferiors by the Chinese government.[2]

China knew that the foreigners needed Asian products more than the Chinese required European goods. In addition, the Manchus would neither recognize nor receive diplomatic representatives of foreign powers. In 1793 the imperial court responded to the British request for a permanent trade representative in Peking in this manner:

The Canton waterfront in a 19th-century painting. Canton was the first Chinese port regularly visited by European traders. The Portuguese arrived in 1511, followed by the British in the 17th century, and the French and the Dutch in the 18th.

... to send one of your nationals to stay at the Celestial Court to take care of your country's trade with China ... is not in harmony with the state system of our dynasty and will definitely not be permitted ... there is nothing we lack, as your principal envoy and others have themselves observed. We have never set such store on strange or ingenious objects, nor do we have need of any more of your country's manufactures.[3]

The Western Response

The foreigners were especially irritated by the high customs duties the Chinese forced them to pay and by the attempts of Chinese authorities to stop the growing import trade in opium. The drug had long been used to stop diarrhea, but in the seventeenth and eighteenth century people in all classes began to use it recreationally. Most opium came from Turkey or India, and in 1800 its import was forbidden by the imperial government. Despite this restriction, the opium trade continued to flourish. Privately owned vessels of many countries, including the United States, made huge profits from the growing number of Chinese addicts. The government in Peking noted that the foreigners seemed intent on dragging down the Chinese through the encouragement of opium addiction.

In the meantime, the empire faced other problems. The army became corrupt and the tax farmers defrauded the people. The central bureaucracy declined in efficiency, and the generally weak emperors were unable to meet the challenges of the time. The balance of trade turned against the Chinese in the 1830s, and the British decided to force the issue of increased trade rights. The point of conflict was the opium trade. By the late 1830s more than 30,000 chests, each of which held about 150 pounds of the extract, were being brought in annually by the

The stacking room at an opium factory in Patna, India. Opium smuggling upset the balance of trade and destroyed China's economy.

Lin Tse-hsu on the Opium Trade

Lin Tse-hsu saw that the opium trade, which gave Europe such huge profits, undermined his country. He asked Queen Victoria to put a stop to the trade.

After a long period of commerical intercourse, there appear among the crowd of barbarians both good persons and bad, unevenly. Consequently there are those who smuggle opium to seduce the Chinese people and so cause the spread of the poison to all provinces. Such persons who only care to profit themselves, and disregard their harm to others, are not tolerated by the laws of heaven and are unanimously hated by human beings. His Majesty the Emperor, upon hearing of this, is in a towering rage. He has especially sent me, his commissioner, to come to Kwangtung, and together with the governor-general and governor jointly to investigate and settle this matter.

All those people in China who sell opium or smoke opium should receive the death penalty. If we trace the crime of those barbarians who through the years have been selling opium, then the deep harm they have wrought and the great profit they have usurped should fundamentally justify their execution according to law. We take into consideration, howver, the fact that the various barbarians have still known how to repent their crimes and return to their allegiance to us by taking the 20,183 chests of opium from their storeships and petitioning us, through their consular officer [superintendent of trade], Elliot, to receive it. It has been entirely destroyed and this has been faithfully reported to the Throne in several memorials by this commissioner and his colleagues.

Fortunately we have received a specially extended favor from His Majesty the Emperor, who considers that for those who voluntarily surrender there are still some circumstances to palliate their crime, and so for the time being he has magnanimously excused them from punishment. But as for those who again violate the opium prohibition, it is difficult for the law to pardon them repeatedly. Having established new regulations, we presume that the ruler of your honorable country, who takes delight in our culture and whose disposition is inclined towards us, must be able to instruct the various barbarians to observe the law with care. It is only necessary to explain to them the advantages and disadvantages and then they will know that the legal code of the Celestial Court must be absolutely obeyed with awe.

We find that your country is sixty or seventy thousand *li* [three *li* make one mile] from China. Yet there are barbarian ships that strive to come here for trade for the purpose of making a great profit. The wealth of China is used to profit the barbarians. That is to say, the great profit made by barbarians is all taken from the rightful share of China. By what right do they then in return use the poisonous drug to injure the Chinese people? Even though the barbarians may not necessarily intend to do us harm, yet in coveting profit to an extreme, they have no regard for injuring others. Let us ask, where is your conscience? I have heard that the smoking of opium is very strictly forbidden by your country; that is because the harm caused by opium is clearly understood. Since it is not permitted to do harm to your own country, then even less should you let it be passed on to the harm of other countries—how much less to China!

From Lin Tse-hsu, Letter to Queen Victoria, 1839.

various foreign powers. Some authorities assert that the trade in opium alone reversed China's formerly favorable balance of trade. In the spring of 1839 Chinese authorities at Canton confiscated and burned the opium. In response, the British occupied positions around Canton.

In the war that followed, the Chinese could not match the technological and tactical superiority of the British forces. In 1842 China agreed to the provisions of the Treaty of Nanking. Hong Kong was ceded to Great Britain, and other ports, including Canton, were opened to British residence and trade. It would be a mistake to view the conflict between the two countries simply as a matter of drug control; it was instead the acting out of deep cultural conflicts between east and west.[4]

The French and Americans approached the Chinese after the Nanking Treaty's provisions became known, and in 1844 gained the same trading rights as the British. The advantages granted the three nations by the Chinese set a precedent that would dominate China's relations with the world for the next century. The "most favored nation" treatment came to be extended so far that China's right to rule in its own territory was limited. This began the period referred to by the Chinese as the time of unequal treaties—a time of unprecedented degradation for China. The humiliation the Central Kingdom suffered is still remembered and strongly affects important aspects of its foreign policy. Meanwhile, the opium trade continued to thrive.

The British and French again defeated China in a second opium war in 1856. By the terms of the Treaty of Tientsin (1858) the Chinese opened new ports to trading and allowed foreigners with passports to travel in the interior. Christians gained the right to spread their faith and hold property, thus opening up another means of western penetration. The United States and Russia gained the same privileges in separate treaties.

The Manchu empire appeared to be well on the way to total physical dismemberment and economic collapse. Three provisions of these treaties caused long-lasting bitterness among the Chinese: extraterritoriality, customs regulations, and the right to station foreign warships in Chinese waters. Extraterritoriality meant that in a dispute with the Chinese, westerners had the right to be tried in their own country's consular court. Europeans argued that Chinese concepts of justice were more rigid and harsh than those in the west. But the Chinese viewed extraterritoriality as not only humiliating to China's sovereignty, but also discriminatory in favor of western nations. The other two provisions greatly weakened China's fiscal and military structure. After 1860 China was a helpless giant.

China's Response

The Chinese competition with the westerners had been carried on in military and economic terms. But the basic conflict was in the realm of civilization and values. The Chinese could note the obvious—that the Europeans possessed technological and military superiority. The question they faced was how to adapt the strength of Europe to the core of Chinese civilization. In Chinese terms, this was the t'i-yung concept. T'i means "substance" and yung means use. Under this concept, China should make use of western advances in order to become able to compete effectively with the west.

Combining the two elements presented the severe problem of gaining a proper balance. Those who wanted to keep the old culture opposed those who wanted to modernize the country. In 1860 the T'ung ch'ih Restoration movement attempted to strengthen the Manchus. Serious attempts were made to preserve Chinese culture while trying to make use of western technology. If these attempts at adaptation could have been carried out in a time of peace, perhaps the Chinese could have adjusted but China did not enjoy the luxury of tranquility. The concessions to the "foreign devils" resulted in a great loss of prestige for the Manchus.

More dangerous for the Manchus than the west was the spate of revolts in the north, west, and south of the country. The most tragic was the Taiping rebellion that lasted from 1850 to 1864. The uprising, fought to attain the Heavenly Kingdom of Great Peace (T'ai-p'ing t'ien-kuo) stemmed from widespread discontent with the social and economic conditions of Manchu rule and the perception of the lack of authority in Peking. The revolt began near Canton and centered on the plans of Hung Hsiu-ch'uan, a person who was driven to desperation by consistently failing the lowest examination to gain entry into the civil service. After contact with American missionaries and some reading of Christian tracts, he came to identify himself as a son of God, Jesus' little brother. His task was to bring salvation to China. He accumulated followers, especially from the poor, and prepared to fight. He and his forces controlled the southern part of China for ten years from Nanking, and he set out to create a new society, totally detached from the traditional Chinese fabric. Hung struck out at vice, Confucianism, private property, and the landlords. By taking on all that was established in China, he ensured his defeat. The Taiping rebellion was one of the most costly movements in history. It was felt in seventeen of China's eighteen provinces. Estimates of the number of deaths range between 20 and 30 million.[5]

After the external buffeting from the west and the internal uprising, the Manchu dynasty limped along for another half century, led by a conservative coalition of Manchu and Chinese officials who advised the empress dowager, Tzu-hsi, who served from 1861 until her death in 1908. Known first as Orchid, then as Yehonala, then as the Yi Concubine, then as Tzu-hsi, and finally as the Old Buddha, she followed the most direct path for a bright and ambitious Manchu female—she entered court circles as a concubine. After receiving the traditional training in court, she honed her political skills. She understood the intricate ceremonial life and mastered the intrigue of palace politics. When the senior concubine failed to give birth to a healthy heir to the throne, Tzu-hsi bore the emperor a strong and healthy child.

Her position as mother of the heir-apparent opened the door to power, and during the reigns of the next three emperors she was a dominant power, either as co-regent or regent. She built a network of powerful allies and informers that helped her to crush internal revolts and restore a measure of prestige to China during a brief period of tranquility from 1870 to 1895. She and her circle were so removed from the world that she used funds earmarked for the navy to rebuild her summer house, in honor of her sixtieth birthday. At a time when the Japanese were rapidly modernizing and foreign powers introduced

Tzu-hsi, the Empress Dowager or Old Buddha. The Boxer Rebellion near the end of her reign indicated the degree to which the central government had lost power in China.

many forms of their technology in their factories, railroads, and communications, China held to the policies based on tradition and custom.

Carving Up China

During the first wars against the Europeans, the Chinese began the process of ceding territory and spheres of influence to foreigners. By 1860, as a result of the Treaty of Peking, Russia gained the entire area north of the Amur River and founded the strategic city of Vladivostok. In 1885 France took Indochina and Britain seized Burma. In 1887 Macao was ceded to Portugal. China was too weak to resist these encroachments on its borders. But the crowning blow came not from the western nations, but from Japan—a land the Chinese had long regarded with amused contempt.

Trouble had long brewed between China and Japan, especially over the control of Formosa and Korea. War broke out in 1894 in a dispute over China's claims on Korea. The brief Sino-Japanese struggle resulted in a humiliating defeat for China. By the treaty of Shimonoseki (1895), China was forced to recognize the independence of Korea and hand over the rich Liaotung peninsula and Formosa to Japan (see map below).

The Chinese defeat was the signal for the renewal of aggressive actions by western powers, who forced Japan to return the strategic Liaotung peninsula to China. Shortly thereafter, the European powers made their demands of China. Germany demanded a ninety-nine-year lease to Kiaochow Bay and was also given exclusive mining and railroad rights throughout Shantung province. Russia obtained a twenty-five-year lease to Dairen and Port Arthur and gained the right to build a railroad across Manchuria, thereby achieving complete domination of that vast territory. In 1898 Britain obtained the lease of Weihaiwei, a naval base, and France leased Kwangchowan in southern China.

The United States, acting not from any high-minded desires but rather from the fear that American business was being excluded from China, brought a halt — or at least a hesitation to the

The imperialist contenders line up for the race to acquire territory in China in this 19th-century cartoon entitled "The China Cup Race."

process of dismemberment. In 1899 Secretary of State John Hay asked the major powers to agree to a policy of equal trading privileges. In 1900 several powers did so, and the Open Door policy was born.

The humiliation of the defeat by Japan had incensed the younger Chinese intellectuals who agitated for liberation from foreign dominance. Led by enlightened and concerned patriots such as K'ang yu-wei, the liberals proposed a wide-ranging series of economic, social, political, and educational reforms, and the young emperor, Tzu-hsi's nephew, approved them. What followed came to be known as the "hundred days of reform."

Tzu-hsi and her advisers encouraged antiforeign sentiment and opposed the patriots' attempts to bring about basic democratic reforms on a Confucianist basis. The reform attempts threatened the interests of the Tzu-hsi's supporters, and she came out of retirement in 1898, imprisoned her nephew, and revoked all of the proposed reforms.

After the suppression of the reform movement, a group of secret societies united in an organization known as the Righteous Harmony Fists, whose members were called Boxers by the westerners. At first they were strongly anti-Manchu, but by 1899 the chief object of their hatred had become the foreign nations who were stripping China of land and power. The Boxers started a campaign to rid China of all "foreign devils." Many Europeans were killed and the legations at Peking were besieged. In August 1900

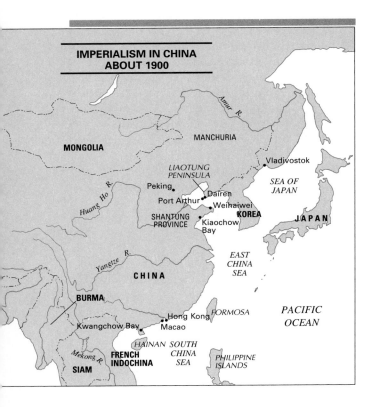

IMPERIALISM IN CHINA
ABOUT 1900

MONGOLIA
MANCHURIA
Amur R.
LIAOTUNG PENINSULA
Vladivostok
Peking
SEA OF JAPAN
Port Arthur Dairen
Huang Ho R.
Weihaiwei
SHANTUNG PROVINCE
KOREA
Kiaochow Bay
JAPAN
Yangtze R.
EAST CHINA SEA
CHINA
BURMA
Hong Kong FORMOSA
PACIFIC OCEAN
Kwangchow Bay Macao
HAINAN SOUTH CHINA SEA
Mekong R.
FRENCH INDOCHINA
PHILIPPINE ISLANDS
SIAM

The Benefits of Imperialism

Imperialism provided a previously unattainable standard of living for Europeans, as a letter from Miss Eden proves.

I wish you could see my passage sometimes. The other day when I set off to pay George a visit I could not help thinking how strange it would have seemed at home. It was a rainy day, so all the servants were at home. The two tailors were sitting in one window, making a new gown for me, and Rosina by them chopping up her betel-nut; at the opposite window were my two Dacca embroiderers working at a large frame, and the sentry, in an ecstasy of admiration mounting guard over them. There was the bearer standing upright, in a sweet sleep, pulling away at my punkah. My own five servants were sitting in a circle, with an English spelling-book, which they were learning by heart; and my jemadar, who, out of compliment to me, has taken to draw, was sketching a bird. Chance's (Miss Eden's dog) servant was waiting at the end of the passage for his "little excellency" to go out walking, and a Chinese was waiting with some rolls of satin that he had brought to show.

From *The Sahibs*, ed. Hilton Brown (London: Willam Hodge & Company Limited, 1948).

an international army forced its way to Peking and released the prisoners. China was forced to apologize for the murder of foreign officials and pay a large indemnity.

By this time, even the Old Buddha acknowledged the need for change. After 1901 she sanctioned reforms in the state examination system, education, and governmental structure, and economic life; she even approved of the drive to end the binding of girls' feet—all to no avail.

Only a decade after the conclusion of the Boxer rebellion, a revolution broke out all over China, and in 1912 the Republic of China was proclaimed with Sun Yat-Sen as president. The revolutionary Chinese leaders knew that there had to be radically different approaches taken in China to allow it to survive and compete. As one official wrote in the 1890s:

> Western nations rely on intelligence and energy to compete with one another. To come abreast of them China should plan to promote commerce and open mines; unless we change, the westerners will be rich and we poor. We should excel in technology and the manufacture of machinery; unless we change, they will be skillful and we clumsy.... Unless we change, the westerners will cooperate with each other and we shall stand isolated; they will be strong and we shall be weak.[6]

The Japanese Alternative

Western powers gained effective control of India, southeast Asia, and China by the end of the nineteenth century. Japan, however, responded in an alert and united manner, successfully adapting elements of strength from the west to the core of its own structures and ways of life.

At the beginning of the eighteenth century Japna was ruled from Edo (now Tokyo), the largest city in the country, by the head of the Tokugawa clan, whose leaders had declared themselves *shogun* since 1603. As the military dictator with a retinue of feudal lords and warriors, the *shogun* kept the country united and at peace. The Tokugawa strengthened the feudal framework of unity and stability that helped give Japan the basis for a successful response to the European challenge.

The Japanese emperor, in residence at Kyoto, served as a figurehead with no real function other than as a symbol around which the nation could rally. The Tokugawa ruled the country through their feudal lords, the *daimyo*. These officials in turn governed their regions with the aid of the *samurai*, the soldiers who also acted as administrators and governed and taxed the peasants.

Below the peasants on the social scale were the artisans and merchants who lived in the cities, a reflection of the fact that the Tokugawa saw agriculture as the foundation of politics and society.

The stratified society may well have ensured the power of the Tokugawa, but over a period of two centuries it was tested by peasant uprisings in the countryside and discontent in the cities. The peasant rebellions could be put down by force. But in the cities in the late eighteenth and early nineteenth centuries there was remarkable economic growth accompanied by rapid urbanization. New social and political forces posed difficulties for the Tokugawa structure. The spread of education and the increase in wealth helped spur the growth of the new urban classes drawn from young, aggressive merchants and intellectuals. The lower end of the social scale became wealthier than many of the *samurai*. These social forces could not be dealt with so easily by the Tokugawa governmental structure.

By the nineteenth century the shogunate lost much of its force and authority. The once-efficient government had become lax, especially in the realm of tax collection. Changing conditions in the cities and the flow of western information from the open port of Nagasaki worked to undermine the traditional system.

The Western Advance

Both European and American merchants and diplomats tried to open relations with Japan during the first part of the nineteenth century, but by 1850 foreign traders and missionaries still found their ability to move throughout the country greatly limited. Within the country the question of how and when to open up to the west was discussed. European inventions such as the daguerreotype and new manufacturing techniques had already made their appearance, but in response to Japanese policy towards foreigners would not be defined until 1853. On July 7 of that year the United States under the command of Commander Matthew Perry sailed into Edo Bay.

Perry, commanding a force of two steam frigates and two sloops-of-war, had been sent by the American government to convince the Japanese that a treaty opening trade relations between the two countries would be of mutual interest. He had been instructed to be tactful and to use force only if necessary. After delivering

Westerners and Japanese gather at the Foreign Merchants' Building in Yokohama, a major trading port.

Commodore Perry meeting the imperial commissioners at Yokohama. In 1854 Perry secured a treaty in which Japan agreed to permit foreign vessels to obtain provisions within Japanese territory and to allow U.S. ships to anchor in the ports at Shimoda and Hakodate.

a letter from the U.S. president, he remained in port ten days. When he departed, he told the authorities in Edo that he would return in a year for an answer. He actually came back eight months later, in February 1854. The Americans returned with more ships and before the deadline because they feared that the French or the Russians might gain concessions sooner from the Japanese.

The *shogun*, after a period of intense debate within his country, agreed to Perry's requests. The Treaty of Kanagawa, the first formal agreement between Japan and a western nation, was signed. By its terms, shipwrecked sailors were to be well treated and two ports were to be opened for provisioning ships and a limited amount of trade. European traders soon obtained similar privileges, plus the right of extraterritoriality.

The entry of the west placed a severe strain on the already weakened Japanese political structure. Antiforeign sentiment grew, even as many Japanese recognized that accommodation with the west was bound to come. The western representatives in Japan were caught in the middle, and there were a number of attacks against them. By 1867, after a time of strife and confusion, Japan reached the point of revolution. European and American fleets had illustrated their military superiority in 1863 and 1864 by bombarding Kagoshima and Shimonoseki, and thereby convinced some of the antiforeign elements

of the hopelessness of their position. In 1867 the system of dual government, with the emperor at Kyoto and the shogun at Edo, was abandoned. The capital was moved from Kyoto to Edo, which was renamed Tokyo (eastern capital).

The Meiji Restoration

The next generation of Japanese accomplished what no other non-western leaders were able to do—they adapted the Europeans' strengths to their own situation and successfully competed against the west. The new leaders who oversaw the ending of the dual power system were young and most were of *samurai* origin. They understood the nature of western power and the threat it posed to their country. They proposed as Japan's best defense the forming of a "rich country and strong military," based on western technology and institutions adapted to their country's needs. The young emperor, whose rule was known as the *Meiji* (enlightened government), reigned from 1868 to 1912. During that time Japan became a dynamic, modern power the west had to recognize as an equal.

Centuries earlier the Japanese had gained a great deal from China. Now they set out to learn from the west the lessons of how to construct an industrialized, bureaucratized state. For the next generation, the results of those lessons would be applied in a broad variety of areas. The voluntary abolition of feudal rights accompanied and facilitated the restoration of the emperor's supreme authority. In 1871 the end of the feudal system was officially announced, although it was far from actual fact. At the same time the government established a new territorial division and reformed the education and mail systems.

In 1882 a commission went out to study the world's various governmental systems in order to write a new constitution for Japan. The committee members were particularly impressed by Bismarck's German system, and the new constitution proclaimed in 1889 gave the premier a postion analogous to that held by the chancellor in Germany. Under the new system the cabinet was responsible to the emperor alone. Only the army and the navy could appoint their respective ministers. Since no statesman could form a cabinet without a war minister, and the army could overthrow any cabinet by simply withdrawing its

During the Meiji period, Japan undertook a successful program of industrialization, as is evident in this 1905 photo of a Japanese silk-weaving factory.

This 1905 photo illustrates the coming together of traditional and modern Japan. Farmers pull their carts through the streets while, above them, workers install electric power lines.

minister, ultimate control of policies rested with military interests. The constitution provided for a Diet, which wielded financial influence through its refusal power over unpopular budgets in peacetime. Under the new system the emperor, who held sovereign power, was considered "sacred and inviolable."

The Japanese adapted the lessons they learned from the west in other areas. In 1876 national conscription went into effect, and a modern military machine was created. German and French advisers trained army officers while naval officers received their instructions from the British. The government initiated the founding of banks, factories, and business concerns. Later, when they became successful, these establishments were turned over to private ownership and management. Japan also changed to the modern calendar, symbolizing its entry into the modern age.

Although the Japanese went to the west to find the best ways to modernize their country, they themselves, and not foreigners, made the major changes. The railways, telegraphs, lighthouses, and dockyards may have been constructed by foreigners and the warships may have been made in Britain, but the authorities in Tokyo kept their control.

Ito Hirobumi on the New Japanese Constitution

The Japanese were the only non-Europeans to adopt, choose, and use European concepts successfully for their own purpose. Ito Hirobumi's thoughts on drafting the new Japanese constitution represent one instance of how this system worked.

It was in the month of March, 1882, that His Majesty ordered me to work out a draft of a constitution to be submitted to his approval. No time was to be lost, so I started on the 15th of the same month for an extended journey to different constitutional countries to make as thorough a study as possible of the actual workings of different systems of constitutional government, of their various provisions, as well as of theories and opinions actually entertained by influential persons on the actual stage itself of constitutional life. . . . I sojourned about a year and a half in Europe, and having gathered the necessary materials, in so far as it was possible in so short a space of time, I returned home in September, 1883. Immediately after my return I set to work to draw up the Constitution . . . .

It was evident from the outset that mere imitation of foreign models would not suffice, for there were historical peculiarities of our country which had to be taken into consideration. For example, the Crown was, with us, an institution far more deeply rooted in the national sentiment and in our history than in other countries. It was indeed the very essence of a once theocratic State, so that in formulating the restrictions on its prerogatives in the new Constitution, we had to take care to safeguard the future realness or vitality of these prerogatives, and not to let the institution degenerate into an ornamental crowning piece of the edifice. At the same time, it was also evident that any form of constitutional régime was impossible without full and extended protection of honor, liberty, property, and personal security of citizens, entailing necessarily many important restrictions on the powers of the Crown. . . .

Another difficulty equally grave had to be taken into consideration. We were just then in an age of transition. The opinions prevailing in the country were extremely heterogeneous, and often diametrically opposed to each other. We had survivors of former generations who were still full of theocratic ideas, and who believed that any attempt to restrict an imperial prerogative amounted to something like high treason. On the other hand there was a large and powerful body of the younger generation educated at the time when the Manchester theory was in vogue, and who in consequence were ultra-radical in their ideas of freedom. Members of the bureaucracy were prone to lend willing ears to the German doctrinaires of the reactionary period, while, on the other hand, the educated politicians among the people having not yet tasted the bitter significance of administrative responsibility, were liable to be more influenced by the dazzling words and lucid theories of Montesquieu, Rousseau, and other similar French writers. A work entitled *History of Civilization*, by Buckle, which denounced every form of government as an unnecessary evil, became the great favorite of students of all the higher schools, including the Imperial University. On the other hand, these same students would not have dared to expound the theories of Buckle before their own conservative fathers. At that time we had not yet arrived at the stage of distinguishing clearly between political opposition on the one hand, and treason to the established order of things on the other. The virtues necessary for the smooth working of any constitution, such as love of freedom of speech, love of publicity of proceedings, the spirit of tolerance for opinions opposed to one's own, etc., had yet to be learned by long experience.

From Rusaku Tsunoda et al., eds., *Sources of Japanese Tradition* (New York: Columbia University Press, 1958), pp. 673– 676. © 1958, Columbia University Press. Reprinted by permission of Columbia University Press.

Japan's Success

On the surface the Japanese government was liberal and parliamentary. In reality it was ultraconservative, giving the emperor and the cabinet dominant power. Though Japan was the first Asian nation to achieve a high degree of literacy, education remained the tool of the government, and one of its chief functions was to produce docile servants of the state. The press was subjected to wide control and censorship. The army was used as a means of instilling conscripts with unquestioning loyalty and obedience to the emperor. In army barracks young soldiers learned that the noblest fate was death on the battlefield. Unlike the Chinese, who revered the scholar most of all, the Japanese admired the soldier—warfare was the supreme vocation.

The Japanese were ready to seize the new methods and ideas of the west to serve their own military ends. It should not be forgotten, however, that ultimately it was through a display of military power that the west forced home the notion of its own superiority on Asia.

In adopting many of the aspects of the western state system—universal conscription, professional bureaucracy, mass literacy, state ideology—some Japanese institutions were forced to change. The *samurai*, who had formerly made their living as warriors or by serving their feudal lords, had to change their life styles. Many of them made the transition to the new system effortlessly. The conservative *samurai* were upset when the government passed a law in 1876 that diminished their financial advantages and also forbade the carrying of swords in public. Civil war broke out in some districts, and the government's forces put down the stubborn *samurai* and their armies.

The oligarchy that carried out the revolution through which Japan passed was able to keep a fair amount of control. They brought all of the people into the new system in one form or another. They could accomplish such a major revolution with a minimum of turmoil because all the changes were done within the traditional reverence for the emperor.

Through Shintoism, virtually the state religion, the restoration leaders devised the ultimate political and religious ideology. In Shinto the emperor, directly descended from the Sun Goddess, can demand unlimited loyalty to himself. He expresses the gods' will. As a former president of the privy council, Baron Hozumi, wrote:

> *The Emperor holds the sovereign power, not as his own inherent right, but as an inheritance from his Divine Ancestor. The government is, therefore, theocratical. The Emperor rules over his country as the supreme head of the vast family of the Japanese nation. The government is, therefore patriarchal. The Emperor exercises the sovereign power according to the Constitution, which is based on the most advanced principles of modern constitutionalism. The government is, therefore, constitutional. In other words, the fundamental principle of the Japanese government is theocratic-patriarchal-constitutionalism.*[7]

This cartoon, "A Dangerous Venture," pictures the Russo-Japanese War as a contest between a small but clever acrobat and a large but stupid bear. The acrobat, representing Japan, lures the Russian bear onto a fragile bamboo pole stretched over a chasm.

The process of industrialization coincided with this fundamental social and political revolution. In its rapid economic growth, Japan faced the same problems of demographic and urban growth the west faced. Social and cultural discontent naturally followed from such a rapid transformation. But the ideological and political structure constructed in the Meiji restoration was enough to hold the country together while at the same time repelling the Europeans and the Americans.

In the eyes of western diplomats, Japanese prestige had begun to increase soon after the conclusion of the Sino-Japanese war of 1894–1895. In 1902 Japan scored a diplomatic triumph in allying itself with Great Britain, an alliance viewed by both nations as a deterrent to Russian expansion. When a year later the Russians rebuffed Japanese attempts to negotiate a sphere-of-influence agreement over Korea and Manchuria, the Tokyo government attacked Port Arthur and bottled up Russia's fleet, without a formal declaration of war. The quick series of Japanese victories that followed forced the Russians to agree to the Treaty of Portsmouth in September 1905. Japan gained half the island of Sakhalin, the leaseholds on the Liaotung peninsula and Port Arthur, and various Russian railway and mining rights in southern Manchuria. Japan's paramount position in Korea was also conceded, paving the way for its annexation of that nation in 1910.

Japan's victory in the war with Russia in 1904–1905 astounded the world. Japan had successfully met the challenge of European primacy and was now accepted as a first-class power in its own right.

Conclusion

In the Indian subcontinent, southeast Asia, China, and Japan there were a variety of reactions to the European advance during the eighteenth and nineteenth centuries. In India the Mughul Dynasty was unable to control the myriad of peoples and religions over which it ruled, and the resulting instability furnished a convenient pretext for the ultimate imposition of British control. Only Siam (Thailand) maintained its independence in southeast Asia, and that only because the French and British wanted a buffer state between their holdings in the region. China suffered a distressing decline in the nineteenth century from its position as Central Kingdom to a helpless giant split into spheres of influence. Japan alone was able to adapt and successfully compete with the western nations.

Japan had a number of advantages, compared to its neighbors. The Confucian base of Japanese culture promoted a rational consideration of western technological and intellectual advantages that might be useful. It also emphasized hard work, self-sacrifice, loyalty, and the role of the family. Japan's island location helped it resist direct foreign rule. Its leadership was in the hands of a group of aggressive young officials who embraced the theories and practices of a modern economy. The Japanese brought back from the west the best and most useful elements of a modern economy and applied them to their cultural and social base. The speed with which they accomplished this transformation, barely forty years after the fall of the *shogun*, is an impressive indication of the strength of Japanese society.

The Japanese defeat of the Russians in 1905 did not alter any basic power relationships. Yet it was the first step in a new direction. The nineteenth century, by and large, saw the west expand its holdings over colonies worldwide, building on sheer technological and economic superiority. At the same time the foreigners' successes did not fundamentally change the cultural basis of the native peoples. The Japanese showed one example the non-western world could follow, by adapting the strong technology of the west to its own strong culture. They paved the way for other countries during the course of the twentieth century who would find their own paths to reassert their self-rule, after they too had mastered some of the western tools.

Suggestions for Reading

For valuable insights into British rule and its consequences see M. Edwards, *British India* (Taplinger, 1968) and S. Gopal, *British Policy in India* (Cambridge, 1965).

P. Speare provides a good short history in *The Oxford History of Modern India: 1740–1795* (Oxford, 1979). Two good studies of British imperial rule are P. Woodruff, *The Men Who Ruled India*, 2 vols. (St. Martins, 1954) and J. Morris, *Pax Britannica* (Harcourt, Brace, Jovanovich, 1980).

Li Chien-nung, *The Political History of China* (Van Nostrand, 1956), is a fine history of nineteenth-century China. For a good discussion of the transition China faced, see A. Feuerwerker, ed., *Modern China* (Prentice-Hall, 1964). Another useful study of China is Immanuel Hsu, *The Rise of Modern China* (Oxford, 1975). A key study on China's greatest rebellion is Franz Michael, *The Taiping Rebellion* (Univ. of Washington, 1972). P. W. Fay's *The Opium War, 1840–1842* (Norton, 1976) is a fine study. For views on the stresses of the late imperial period, see D. H. Bays, *China Enters the Twentieth Century . . .* (Michigan, 1978).

W. B. Beasley, *The Modern History of Japan* (Holt, Rinehart, Winston, 1973) is a useful overview. For an investigation into the early contacts between Europe and Asia see George B. Sansom, *The Western World and Japan* (Knopf, 1974) and *Japan: A Short Cultural History* (Stanford, 1952). Thomas Haber, *The Revolutionary Origins of Modern Japan* (Stanford, 1981) and G. M. Beckmann, *The Modernization of China and Japan* (Harper & Row, 1962) are essential to an understanding of the Meiji programs.

The Americans' entry into the Pacific is outlined in F. R. Dulles, *America's Rise to World Power* (Harper & Row, 1955). Recommended surveys of Southeast Asia are D. G. E. Hall, *A History of Southeast Asia* (St. Martin's, 1968); and H. J. Benda and J. A. Larkin, *The World of Southeast Asia* (Harper & Row, 1967).

Notes

1. Quoted in T. A. Bailey, *The American Pageant* (Lexington: D. C. Heath, 1956), p. 630.
2. K. S. Latourette, *A Short History of the Far East* (New York: Macmillan, 1947), p. 184.
3. Quoted in F. H. Michael and G. E. Taylor, *The Far East in the Modern World* (New York: Holt, Rinehart & Winston, 1956), p. 122.
4. Li-Chien-nung, *The Political History of China, 1840–1928*, trans. by Sau-yu Teng and J. Ingalls (Princeton: D. Van Nostrand Co., 1956), p. 29.
5. Michael and Taylor, *The Far East in the Modern World*, p. 183.
6. Quoted in Ch'u Chai and Winberg Chai, *The Changing Society of China* (New York: Mentor Books, 1962), p. 189.
7. Michael and Taylor, *The Far East in the Modern World*, pp. 253–256.

Chapter 30

Tragic War and Futile Peace: World War I

In 1914 Europeans had many reasons to be optimistic about the future. The growth produced by the previous three generations was supported by a sturdy belief in progress. Business and labor leaders had avoided the explosive class conflicts that Marx had forecast. Statesmen made serious efforts toward international cooperation.

There were, however, danger signs for the continent. Revolutionaries around the globe challenged Europe's stability. Within Europe the competitive energies generated by the states came to be harnessed in two conflicting alliance systems. The nagging Eastern Question eventually dragged the alliances into war.

In the four years of bloodshed that began in 1914, over 13 million Europeans died. Europe lost a generation of the best and bravest of its sons. The world economy lost what little equilibrium remained. Four empires—the German, the Austro-Hungarian, the Russian, and the Ottoman—either disappeared or were in the process of disappearing. In Russia Lenin gained power largely due to the impact of the war on the tsarist empire. In Germany Adolf Hitler took advantage of postwar conditions to make a bid for power. Europe's golden age was brought to an end by a combination of tragic forces: militarism, rival alliances, economic imperialism, secret diplomacy, and narrow, bellicose nationalism.

Forces of Progress and Signs of Danger

At the beginning of the twentieth century, Europe was Christian, Caucasian, capitalist, in-

dustrialized; and it dominated the world. Europeans shared the same vibrant Western tradition; the rulers of the various European states were all related to one another. With all that the Europeans had in common, there was little reason to expect the outbreak of the First World War.

International Cooperation

Europeans devised new ways to organize international communication, defuse conflicts, and maintain peace. As early as 1865 a meeting was held in Paris to coordinate the use of telegraph lines and to establish a unified rate structure. The International Telegraph Union made up of twenty nations was formed. Ten years later a Universal Postal Union was set up to handle the world's mail. To protect the rights of authors, an agreement was drawn up in 1886 for an international copyright union.

International cooperation could be found in a number of other areas. In 1896 Baron de Coubertin revived the ancient Greek Olympic games. The organized world peace movement gained a foothold and increased influence throughout the nineteenth century. The Christian-based British Society for the Promotion of Permanent and Universal Peace was formed in 1816. Thirty years later workers for peace began the League for Universal Brotherhood in the United States.

Scholars and statesmen worked to strengthen international law, the rules of warfare, and the use of arbitration. A significant example of this was the opening of the Hague Conference in 1899. The Russian foreign minister invited the great powers to the Dutch city to discuss arms reductions. Although no progress was made on disarmament, the conference did reform the rules of war by improving the treatment of prisoners, outlawing the use of poisonous gas, and defining the conditions of a state of war. An international court of arbitration, the Hague Tribunal, was established. A list of jurists from which nations could select judges was drawn up. Appearance before the court was voluntary, as was acceptance of its decisions. The effectiveness of arbitration as a means to solve problems could be seen the ten years before the war. Various powers signed 162 arbitration treaties that pledged the signatories to arbitrate disagreements such as boundary disputes and conflicts over fishing rights.

Alfred Nobel, the Swedish manufacturer of dynamite, personified the contradictions of the age. This international producer of explosives established a Peace prize two weeks before his death in November 1896. The first prizes were awarded in 1901. Andrew Carnegie, the steel

maker, founded the Carnegie Endowment for International Peace and built a peace palace at the Hague to be used for international conferences. Ironically, the building was finished just weeks before the outbreak of the First World War.

All of these developments encouraged believers in progress to see a peaceful future. They pointed out that wars during the nineteenth century were generally local and short. They believed that if war should break out in the future, the murderous new technology would ensure that it would not be lengthy or costly. Some Social Darwinists asserted that humanity might well evolve from the stage of fighting wars altogether. These optimists conveniently ignored the brutal, lengthy, and costly American Civil war, in many ways the first modern war.

Social Compromises

In 1848, it had looked as though Marx's predictions in the *Communist Manifesto* about the inevitability of class conflict, the destruction of capitalism and the *bourgeoisie*, and revolution might come true. But capitalism proved to be stronger and more flexible and labor unions more effective than Marx had predicted. Europe industrialized so successfully that a communist revolution, contrary to Marx's forecast, had never occurred in an industrialized country.

In the late nineteenth century, Europe moved toward the modern welfare-state concept. Some governments provided unemployment insurance, old-age pensions, and accident compensation. Because these social programs were often paid for out of tax revenues, some states, such as Britain, introduced the graduated income tax, by which individuals paid an amount relative to their earnings. The gulf between the rich and the poor did not disappear—the poor got less poor as the rich got richer. It has been estimated that "real wages" of workers (calculated as the amount of goods their take-home pay could actually buy) went up 50 percent between 1870 and 1900.

Business managers began to work more closely with the better organized unions. Bosses realized that a contented and healthy work force would be more productive. At the same time they knew that the unions could inflict damaging, costly strikes. In addition, business adapted to the constantly changing conditions to guard

The futility of disarmament agreements is the subject of this British cartoon in which heavily armed Germany, France, Russia, and Great Britain politely invite one another into the Hague "Temple of Disarmament."

itself against government regulation of its activities, such as was occurring in the United States.

Workers also tried to make business decisions more democratic and products less expensive by establishing cooperatives. Capital was secured by selling stock, goods were sold at prevailing prices, and profits were distributed annually in proportion to the amount of goods each consumer had purchased. By 1913 at least half of the British population was buying some of its purchases from cooperatives.

Mass education also contributed to the reduction of social tensions before 1914. As the common people were granted suffrage, it became apparent that they needed at least the basics of education to vote intelligently. As a result of the education bill passed in 1870, school attendance in Great Britain jumped from 1 to 4 million in ten years. Similar acts were passed in France, Germany, the Low Countries (Holland and Belgium), and Scandinavia. By 1914 southern and eastern Europe pursued a similar course to educate all of their people.

By 1900 international and domestic conflicts were well on their way to being defused. Political and business leaders learned that it was in their own best interest to guarantee a decent standard of living. This relative tranquility, along with the progress in international cooperation, justified much of the optimism held by many Europeans before 1914.

Portents of Change

As strong as the case for optimism might have been, observant critics could point to several signs of danger. The United States was beginning to overtake Europe economically. The Japanese victory over Russia in 1904–1905 suggested that the tide of western domination might be turning. Non-Europeans could master the west's skills and apply them to their own culture for their own ends.

Independence and revolutionary movements erupted around the globe. In South Africa, Mohandas K. Gandhi (1869–1948) developed his strategy of passive resistance that would later lead to liberation in India. The Chinese revolutionary movement was under way by 1914, laying the foundation for the return of the world's most populous nation to major power status by mid-century. In Vienna, Adolf Hitler was formulating his racial philosophy that would have such tragic results in the 1930s and 1940s. In Mexico the forces that carried out the successful revolutionary movement gained strength. In Africa, led by Ethiopia, forces that would culminate in the expulsion of the Europeans began to grow. In Russia, Lenin formed a cadre and developed a plan to bring about revolution.

In France, a new form of radicalism took root. It opposed the gradual improvement of relations between labor and capitalism and refused to

This cartoon portrays international power politics as a deadly billiard game in which the players use rifles and swords as cue sticks to strike the cannonballs. Bombs are stacked beneath the table, which is covered with a map of Europe. The snake-haired figure at center is identified as Diplomacy.

The U.S.S. *New Jersey* leads the Great White Fleet of 16 warships in a show of American naval strength. The fleet sailed world sea lanes from 1907 to 1909.

abandon the use of violence. Starting in Paris in the 1890s, the syndicalists argued that labor leaders were becoming capitalist tools. The syndicalists' goal was to overthrow the bourgeois state and replace it with a society consisting of "cells," each one representing an industrial union. Although they lacked disciplined leadership and a rigorous program of action, they were a disruptive and potentially dangerous element of society.

State Competition

Europe's greatest danger came not from critics or the occasional radical group, but from competition among the great powers. Europe's militarism, rival alliances, secret diplomacy, imperialism, and nationalism were the underlying, long-range causes of the First World War. These elements had long been present on the European scene, but at the turn of the century they were made even more explosive by the ambitions and policies of Germany.

At the beginning of the twentieth century, European politics remained much the same as it had in the previous three centuries—a competition among states. The main difference in 1900 was that there were some twenty-five independent political units instead of about five hundred. The laws were the same as those

established at Westphalia in 1648. The states recognized no authority above themselves and followed international law only when it suited their interests. They were ready to take advantage of a neighbor's weakness and threaten war if the prize to be won was substantial enough. War, whether the threat or the reality, remained the prime instrument of national policy. This "extension of politics" was frequently used whenever peaceful methods did not work.

Military force was the ultimate arbiter in international affairs. By the end of the 1870s, five of the six major powers had introduced compulsory military training. Although the British had not done so, they were in the process of expanding their fleet. By the first decade of this century the great powers had nearly 4.5 million men in the military and spent annually more than $2 billion on arms. The weapons industry became an important part of the European economy.

Economic rivalry and tariff restrictions heightened the competitions between states. In the new mercantilism, states acted as aggressive champions for their own businesses. In some cases economic rivalry led to fighting: Japanese designs on the Asian mainland caused war with China in 1894; Great Britain fought the Boer War in South Africa from 1899 to 1902; Japan and Russia fought over Manchuria in 1904–1905; and Italy took Tripoli from Turkey in 1912.

Friedrich von Bernhardi Summarizes Germany's Intentions

Friedrich von Bernhardi stated German dreams and frustrations a full two years before the outbreak of World War I.

Duties of the greatest importance for the whole advance of human civilization have thus been transmitted to the German nation, as heir of a great and glorious past. It is faced with problems of no less significance in the sphere of its international relations. These problems are of special importance, since they affect most deeply the intellectual development, and on their solution depends the position of Germany in the world.

The German people has always been incapable of great acts for the common interest except under the irresistible pressure of external conditions, as in the rising of 1813, or under the leadership of powerful personalities, who knew how to arouse the enthusiasm of the masses, to stir the German spirit to its depths, to vivify the idea of nationality, and force conflicting aspirations into concentration and union.

We must therefore take care that such men are assured the possibility of acting with a confident and free hand in order to accomplish great ends through and for our people.

Within these limits, it is in harmony with the national German character to allow personality to have a free course for the fullest development of all individual forces and capacities, of all spiritual, scientific, and artistic aims. "Every extension of the activities of the State is beneficial and wise, if it arouses, promotes, and purifies the independence of free and reasoning men; it is evil when it kills and stunts the independence of free men." This independence of the individual, within the limits marked out by the interests of the State, forms the necessary complement of the wide expansion of the central power, and assures an ample scope to a liberal development of all our social conditions.

We must rouse in our people the unanimous wish for power in this sense, together with the determination to sacrifice on the altar of patriotism, not only life and property, but also private views and preferences in the interests of the common welfare. Then alone shall we discharge our great duties of the future, grow into a World Power, and stamp a great part of humanity with the impress of the German spirit. If, on the contrary, we persist in that dissipation of energy which now marks our political life, there is imminent fear that in the great contest of the nations, which we must inevitably face, we shall be dishonourably beaten; that days of disaster await us in the future, and that once again, as in the days of our former degradation, the poet's lament will be heard:

O Germany, the oaks still stand,
But thou art fallen, glorious land!
                                    Körner

From Friedrich von Bernhardi, *Germany and the Next War,* translated by Allen H. Powles (New York: Longmans, Green, and Co., 1914).

Nationalism was the greatest force fueling the rise in tensions on the continent. As used by Europe's politicians, the spirit of nationalism took on narrow, blatant, and warlike qualities to unite the populations of Europe behind the policies of their leaders. Among both ruling groups and state minorities, nationalism became a new religion and an essential tool of power politics.

The greatest danger to peace came in the nationalistic ambitions of the Balkan nations. Proud of their new freedom, they were determined to extend it to their compatriots still under the Turks or Austrians. Serbia in particular was ready to liberate the other Slavs. However, there was no reason that this local problem should have plunged the Europe into war.

In this atmosphere of international anarchy, most states did not feel strong enough to rely solely on their own resources for defense. Nations whose interests ran along parallel lines joined together. In response, nations outside an alliance formed unions to match their competitors. The creation of the two major rival alliances—the Triple Alliance (Germany, Austria-Hungrary, and Italy) and the Triple Entente (Britain, France, and Russia)—was the key fact in European diplomacy before 1914. However the alliances brought no assured peace. Rather, they increased the possibility of major war, because it was impossible now to localize a problem such as that of the Balkan Slavs.

Closely tied to the system of alliances was the practice of secret diplomacy. Some diplomats threatened, intimidated, and jockeyed for power. The traditional activities of spies with their secret reports and unscrupulous methods poisoned the atmosphere even further. The increase in tension overwhelmed the efforts of decent and honorable statesmen to keep peace.

Diplomatic Failure

From 1870 to 1890 the German chancellor Otto von Bismarck dominated European diplomacy. He built a foreign policy devoted to the diplomatic isolation of France by depriving it of potential allies. He reasoned that the French would try to take revenge on Germany and regain Alsace and Lorraine, but he knew they could do little without aid from the Austrians or Russians. In 1873 Bismarck made an alliance, known as the Three Emperors' League *(Dreikaiserbund)*, with Russia and Austria-Hungary.

The System of Shifting Alliances

The conflicts between the Austrians and Russians in the Balkans soon put a strain on the League, and at the Congress of Berlin (1878) Bismarck was forced to choose between the conflicting claims of Vienna and St. Petersburg. He chose to support Austria-Hungary for a number of reasons, including fear of alienating Great Britain if he backed the Russians. In addition, he felt that he could probably dominate Austria

more easily than Russia. This momentous shift paved the way for a new arrangement. In 1879 Bismarck negotiated the Dual Alliance with the Austro-Hungarian monarchy; in 1882 a new partner—Italy—joined the group, now called the Triple Alliance.

The choice of Austria over Russia did not mean that Bismarck abandoned his ties with the tsars. In 1881 the Three Emperor's League was renewed. Rivalries between the Dual Monarchy and Russia in the Balkans put an effective end to the arrangement, and the *Dreikaiserbund* collapsed for good in 1887. Bismarck negotiated a separate agreement with Russia called the Reinsurance Treaty, in which both sides pledged neutrality—except if Germany attacked France or Russia attacked Austria—and support of the status quo.

Under Bismarck's shrewd hand, Germany kept diplomatic control for twenty years. Bismarck chose his goals carefully and understood the states with which he worked. He made every effort to avoid challenging Britain's interests and to continue isolating France. As a result, Germany was not surrounded by enemies. The chancellor kept from alienating Russia while maintaining his ties with Austria.

In the 1890s, however, the rash actions of the new kaiser, William II, destroyed Germany's favorable position. He dismissed Bismarck in 1890, took foreign policy in his own hands, and frittered away the diplomatic advantages the chancellor had built up. France had been attempting to escape from its isolation for some time, and through its loans had begun to make important inroads into Russia, even before Bismarck retired. When the kaiser allowed the Reinsurance Treaty to lapse, the Russians sought new allies. By 1894 France got what it had wanted for twenty years—a strong ally. The Triple Alliance of Germany, Italy, and Austria-Hungary was now confronted by the Dual Alliance of Russia and France. Germany's worst fears had come to pass as it was now encircled by enemies.

Britain Ends Its Isolation

At the end of the nineteenth century Britain found itself involved in bitter rivalries with Russia—both in the Balkans and in the Middle East—and with France in Africa. During the Boer

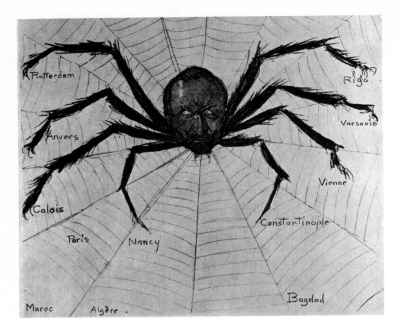

War, all of the great powers in Europe were anti-British. However, the supremacy of the British fleet helped discourage intervention. As the new century began, London became concerned that its policy of splendid isolation might need to be abandoned. In these circumstances, the most normal place for Britain to turn would be to Germany.

On the surface, nothing seemed more natural than that these two dominant European powers should adjust their national interests to avoid conflict. From the 1880s to 1901 both sides made several approaches to investigate an "understanding" between the major sea power, Britain, and the strongest land power, Germany. Tradition and dynastic relations spoke in favor of a closer tie between the two. By 1900, Berlin and London may have competed in economic and imperialistic terms, but they were far from any major strife in any either area.

The two countries could not, however, come together in an alliance. Even though important figures on both sides could see the advantages of an alliance, strong forces worked against this development. German and British interests did not match sufficiently to permit equal gain from an alliance. The kaiser's numerous bellicose statements and clumsy actions—such as his meddling in British colonial affairs with his telegram to South African President Paul Kruger in 1896—offended many British leaders. Germany's expanding influence in the Middle East and the Balkans worried the British as did Germany's tremendous economic progress.

Most threatening for London was Germany's plan to build a fleet that would compete with Britain's. In 1900, Germany initiated a huge naval program providing for, within a twenty-year timetable, a fleet strong enough to keep Britain from interfering with German international goals. The British knew that the German program was aimed directly at them. For the island nation, the supremacy of the Royal Navy was a life-or-death matter. Since food and raw materials had to come by sea, it was crucial that the navy be able to protect British shipping.

Challenged by Germany, Britain looked elsewhere for allies. In 1904 officials from London and Paris began to settle their outstanding differences and proclaimed the *Entente Cordiale* ("friendly understanding") setting aside a tradition of hostility going back to the fourteenth century. The *Entente*, and an alliance with Japan in 1902, ended Britain's policy of diplomatic isolation and brought it into the combination that would be pitted against Germany's Triple Alliance. In 1907 London settled its problems with Russia, thereby establishing the Triple Entente.

The British made no definite military commitments in the agreements with France and Russia. Theoretically they retained freedom of action, but they were now part of the alliance system.

The Moroccan Crises

In the decade before the First World War Europe experienced a series of crises on its peripheries, none of which vitally threatened the great powers' survival. However, because of the alliance systems, these incidents increased tensions and brought Europe ever closer to war.

The first serious test came in 1905 over Morocco (see map below). France sought control of this territory in order to establish a continuous line of dependencies from the Atlantic across the North African coast to Tunisia. Carefully timing their moves, the Germans arranged for the kaiser to visit the Moroccan port of Tangier, where he declared that all powers must respect the independence of the country. The French were forced to give up their immediate plans for taking over Morocco and agree to Germany's suggestion that an international conference be called at Algeciras (1906) to discuss the matter.

At this meeting the Germans hoped for a split between the British and French. This did not occur. On the contrary, all but one of the nations in attendance—even Italy—supported France rather than Germany. Only Austria-Hungary remained on the kaiser's side. The conference agreed that Morocco should still enjoy its sovereignty, but that France and Spain should be given certain rights to police the area.

DIPLOMATIC CRISES
1905-1914

In 1911 a second Moroccan crisis escalated tensions. When France sent an army into the disputed territory, ostensibly to maintain order, Germany responded by sending the gunboat *Panther* to the Moroccan port of Agadir. Great Britain came out with a blunt warning that all of its power was at the disposal of France in this affair. A diplomatic bargain was finally struck in which France got a free hand in Morocco and Germany gained a small area in Equatorial Africa. The two rival alliance systems managed to avoid war over Morocco. Feelings were soothed when the imperial powers compensated each other with pieces of the African landscape.

The Balkan Crises

The two rival alliances came to blows over the Balkans, where the interests of Austria-Hungary and Russia directly collided. In that complex area, the forces of local nationalism drew the great powers into a military showdown.

Austria and Russia had long kept a wary eye on each other's policies in southeastern Europe. During the nineteenth century each country had had an obsessive interest in the Balkan holdings of the Ottoman Empire. Neither side could afford for the other to gain too great an advantage in the area. Throughout the last part of the nineteenth century the two had occasionally disagreed over issues involving Macedonia, railroads, and boundary revisions. In 1908 a crisis erupted that threatened to draw Europe into war. The issue that increased hostility was the Dual Monarchy's annexation of Bosnia and Herzegovina.

The Austro-Hungarian monarchy had administered the two areas since the 1878 Congress of Berlin, so the annexation actually changed very little. But the Slavs perceived the annexation as humiliating to them and their "protector," Russia. The fact that the Russians, through an ill-considered plan, had initiated the train of events that led to the annexation made the whole affair doubly frustrating for the Slavs.

A tsarist diplomat Count Izvolskii had initiated discussions whereby the Russians would approve the annexation in return for increased Black Sea rights for the Russians. Bosnia and Herzegovina were annexed, but the Russians

THE BOILING POINT.

In this *Punch* cartoon, European leaders are barely able to keep the lid on the boiling kettle of Balkan crises.

never got their part of the bargain. Serbia was outraged by the incorporation of more Slavs into the Habsburg domain and expected its Slavic, Orthodox protector, Russia, to do something about it. The Russians had been badly bruised in their war with Japan and the Revolution of 1905. Aside from making threatening noises, they could do little, especially in the face of Germany's support for Austria-Hungary.

Austro-Hungarian interests in the Balkans were primarily concerned with defense and keeping Serbia under control. The Dual Monarchy was experiencing serious domestic strains as the multinational empire limped along under the terms of the renegotiated *Ausgleich*. Austro-Hungarian pretensions to great power status increasingly outdistanced its ability to play that role.

Germany's motives in the Balkans were largely strategic in the long term and diplomatic in the short term. The Germans envisioned a Berlin-based political and economic zone stretching from the Baltic Sea to the Persian Gulf. Berlin could not afford to alienate its Austrian ally through lukewarm support.

After 1908 tensions remained high in the Balkans. The Austrians looked to increase their advantage, knowing they had the full support of Germany. Serbia searched for revenge, while Russia found itself backed into a corner. The Russians in the future would be forced to act strongly and encourage aggressive policies on the part of their Balkan allies or lose forever their position of prestige. The 1908 crisis changed relatively few of the major features of the competition for influence in the Balkans, except to limit further the major powers' options.

In 1912 Serbia and its neighbors, especially Greece and Bulgaria, formed an alliance with the objective of expelling Turkey from Europe. The First Balkan War began later in the year and came to a quick end with the defeat of the Turks. Each of the Balkan allies had its own particular goals in mind in fighting the Ottomans. When the great powers stepped in to maintain the balance, problems arose.

Serbia had fought for a seaport and thought it had gained one with the defeat of the Turks. However, the Italians and Austrians blocked Serbia's access to the Adriatic by overseeing the creation of Albania in the Treaty of London of 1913. Denied their goals, the Serbs turned on their former ally, the Bulgarians, and demanded a part of their spoils from the first war. Bulgaria refused and, emboldened by its successes in the first war, attacked its former allies, starting the Second Balkan War. The Serbs were in turn joined by the Romanians and the Turks. The Bulgarians were no match for the rest of the Balkans and signed a peace which turned over most of the territory that they had earlier gained. The Turks retained only a precarious toehold in Europe, the small pocket from Adrianople to Constantinople (see maps, p. 771).

Had the great powers found a way to place a fence around the Balkans and allow the squabbling nations to fight their miniwars in isolation, then the two Balkan wars of 1912 and 1913 would have had little significance. As it was, however, they added to the prevailing state of tension. The

two competing alliances effectively tied their policies to the narrow constraints of the Balkans. In effect, the tail wagged the dog, as the alliances reacted to every flareup in the turbulent peninsula.

By the end of 1913 no permanent solution had been found to the Balkan problems. Austria was more fearful than ever of Serbia's expansionist desires. Serbian ambitions had grown larger since its territory had doubled as a result of the recent wars. The Serbian prime inister declared: "The first round is won: now we must prepare the second against Austria." Russia's dreams of Balkan grandeur had not been blocked but only interrupted. The rest of Europe lay divided.

Assassination at Sarajevo

The spark that set off World War I was struck on June 28, 1914 with the assassination of the heir to the Austrian throne, Archduke Francis Ferdinand. The archduke and his wife were visiting the Bosnian town of Sarajevo which his realm had recently annexed. While they were driving through the narrow streets in their huge touring car, a nineteen-year-old Bosnian student named Gavrilo Princip, one of seven youthful terrorists along the route, shot them.

Princip had been inspired by propaganda advocating the creation of a greater Serbia and assisted by Serbian officers serving in a secret organization. The direct participation of the Serbian government was not proved; even so, the Belgrade authorities were likely to have been involved, at least indirectly.

The legal details of the case were lost in Vienna's rush to put an end to the problem of Serbia. Count Leopold von Berchtold, the foreign minister, believed that the assassination in Bosnia justified crushing the anti-Austrian propaganda and terrorism coming from the Serbs. The kaiser felt that everything possible must be done to prevent Germany's only reliable ally from being weakened, and so he assured the Austrians of his full support. Berchtold received a blank check from Germany. Vienna wanted a quick, local Austro-Serbian war, and Germany favored quick action to forestall Russian intervention.

On July 23 the Austro-Hungarian foreign ministry presented an ultimatum to the Serbs.

Expecting the list of demands to be turned down, Berchtold demanded unconditional acceptance within forty-eight hours. On July 25 the Austro-Hungarian government announced that Serbia's reply, which was conciliatory, was not satisfactory. The Austrian authorities immediately mobilized their armed forces.

The Alliances' Inevitable War

The Germans, having second thoughts, urged their ally to negotiate with Russia, which was anxiously following developments. Russia realized that if the Austrians succeeded in humbling the Serbs, Russia's position in the Balkans would suffer irreparably. The French, in the meantime, assured the Russians of their full cooperation and urged full support for Serbia. The British unsuccessfully advised negotiation.

Europe had reached a point of no return: the Austrians had committed themselves to the task of removing a serious opponent, and the Russians could not permit this removal to happen. Neither side would back down, and each had allies ready to come to its aid. Fearful that Serbia would escape from his clutches, Berchtold succeeded on July 27 — thanks in part to deception —

in convincing the Habsburg emperor that war was the only way out. On the following day the Austro-Hungarian empire declared war against Serbia.

As the possibilities of a general European war loomed, Berlin sent several frantic telegrams to Vienna. The German ambassador was instructed to tell Berchtold that "as an ally we must refuse to be drawn into a world conflagration because Austria does not respect our advice."[1] Had the Germans spoken to their ally in such tones a month earlier, war might have been avoided. But Austria's belligerence moved the Russians to act. The tsar ordered mobilization on July 30.

Germany was caught in a dilemma that Bismarck would never have allowed. Surrounded by potential enemies, the Germans had to move decisively or face defeat. The Russian mobilization threatened them, because in the event of war on the eastern front, there would also be war on the western front. The best plan to Berlin, one that had been worked out since 1905, seemed to be to launch a lightning attack against France — which could mobilize faster that Russia — crush France, and then return to meet Russia, which would be slower to mobilize. To allow Russian

Archduke Francis Ferdinand and his wife Sophie leave the Senate House in Sarajevo on June 28, 1914. Five minutes after this photograph was taken, Serbian terrorist Gavrilo Princip assassinated them both, helping to touch off World War I.

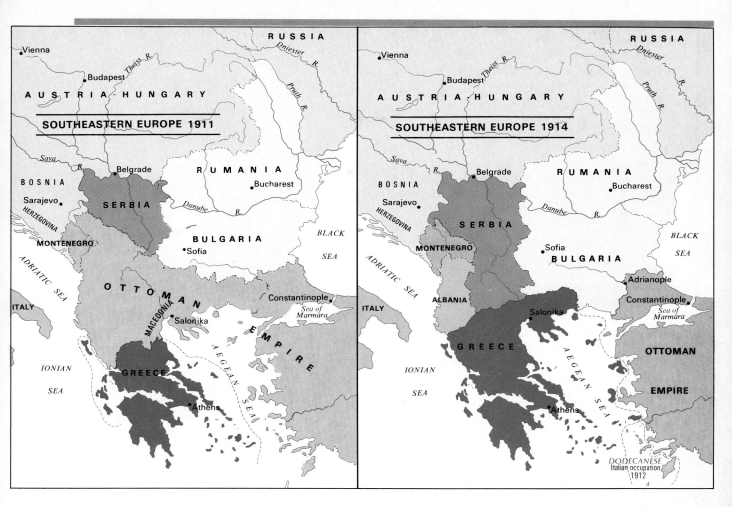

Southeastern Europe 1911

Southeastern Europe 1914

mobilization to proceed without action would jeopardize this plan. In the wake of the crisis, the Germans set into effect their long-planned strategy to gain European dominance.

On July 31 Germany sent ultimata to Russia and France, demanding cessation of mobilization from the former and a pledge of neutrality from the latter. Failing to receive satisfactory replies, Germany declared war on Russia on August 1 and on France two days later. On August 2, the German ambassador in Brussels delivered an ultimatum to the Belgian government announcing his country's intention to send troops through Belgium, in violation of the 1839 Neutrality Treaty. The Belgian cabinet refused to grant permission and appealed to the Triple Entente for help.

A majority of the British cabinet did not want war, but with the news of the German ultimatum

to Belgium, the tide turned. Sir Edward Grey, the British foreign secretary, sent an ultimatum to Germany demanding that Belgian neutrality be respected. Germany refused, and on August 4, Great Britain declared war.

Because Germany and Austria-Hungary were not waging a defensive war, Italy declined to carry out its obligations under the Triple Alliance and for a time remained neutral. In the latter part of August, Japan joined the allies. Turkey, fearing Russia, threw in its lot with the Central Powers.

In the last days of peace, diplomats tried desperately to avert general war. Through confusion, fear, and loss of sleep, the nervous strain among them was almost unbearable. Many broke down and wept when it became apparent they had failed. Grey himself noted in his autobiography that one evening, just before the outbreak of the war, he watched the streetlights being lit from his office window and remarked: "The lamps are going out all over Europe; we shall not see them lit again in our lifetime."[2]

World War I

Although the terrible struggle that racked the world from 1914 to 1918 was fought mainly in Europe, it is rightly called the First World War. In the sixteenth and seventeenth centuries European powers had competed across the globe; however, never had so many fighters and such enormous resources been brought together in a single conflict. Altogether twenty-seven nations became belligerents, ranging the globe from Japan to Canada and from Argentina to South Africa to Australia. The Central Powers—German, Austria-Hungary, Bulgaria, and Turkey—mobilized 21 million men. The Allies eventually called 40 million men to arms, including 12 million Russians (see map, p. 773). The two sides were more equally matched than the numbers would indicate, however. Since the Russian divisions were often poorly equipped and ineffectively used, the Allies' apparent advantage was not so great as numbers would indicate. In addition, in the German army the Central Powers boasted superb generalship and discipline. Another advantage was that the Central Powers fought from a central position and were able to transfer troops quickly and efficiently to various fronts.

The Allies had the advantages of greater resources of finance and raw materials. Britain maintained its naval dominance and could draw on its empire for support. In addition, because Germany was effectively blockaded, the United States, even though officially neutral for most of the war, served as a major source of supplies for the Allies.

The warring nations went into battle in a confident mood. Each side was sure of its strength and felt it had prepared carefully. Each nation's propaganda machine delivered reassuring messages of guaranteed victory. All expected that the war would soon be over, concluded in a few decisive battles. It was generally believed that the war would be over by Christmas.

The First Two Years of War

All of the general staffs had been refining their war plans for years. The Germans knew that Allied naval supremacy would cut them off from needed sources abroad. They realized that they were potentially surrounded and that they should strike a quick knockout blow to end the war. Following the plan devised by Chief of the General Staff Alfred von Schlieffen, the Germans aimed to push the Belgians aside and drive rapidly south into France. The plan then called for the German forces to wheel west of Paris, outflank the French forces, and drive them toward Alsace-Lorraine, where they would be met by another German army. Within six weeks, the French would be destroyed, caught between the western hammer and the eastern anvil. Meanwhile, a small German force would be holding the presumably slow-moving Russians on the eastern front, awaiting the arrival via the excellent German rail system of the victorious western forces. The plan nearly worked.

The Germans marched according to the plan until they got so close to Paris that they could see the top of the Eiffel Tower. They were hurled back by a bold French offensive through a gap that opened between their armies in the First Battle of the Marne, fought between September 5 and 12. With the assistance of a small British

The Queen's Lancers pass a detachment of French mounted troops during the advance from the Marne to the Aisne in September 1914. This Aisne Valley was the site of four major battles of World War I.

WORLD WAR I

- ▨ Triple Entente
- ▨ Central Powers
- ▨ Allies of Triple Entente
- ☐ Neutral nations
- → Allied thrust
- → Central Powers' thrust

Battles:
- × Allied victory
- ⊗ Central Powers' victory

expeditionary force and Parisian taxi drivers providing transportation, the French then marched north in a race with the Germans to reach and control the vital ports along the English Channel. After much desperate fighting, the enemies established battle positions that stabilized, creating the "western front." This solid line of opposing trenches, which stretched from the Channel to near Nancy, was the scene for a grisly new war of attrition.

The other part of the German scheme that did not go according to plan was the unexpected speed with which the Russians mobilized. They penetrated deeply into East Prussia and overran the Austrian province of Galicia. However, confused leadership resulted in two catastrophic Russian defeats in East Prussia, and Germany never again faced a serious threat on its eastern frontier.

By the end of 1914 all sides knew that they were trapped in a new type of war, one of

Soldiers manning a Vickers machine gun at the Somme in July 1916 wear gas masks as protection against phosgene. The new technology of World War I included increased use of the machine gun and poison gas.

horrible consequences. Single battles claimed hundreds of thousands of lives, and the toll during the first few months of the conflict ran as high as one and one-half million dead and wounded.

In 1915 the British attempted a major campaign to force open the Dardanelles, closed by Turkey when it joined the Central Powers. This plan, attributed to Winston Churchill, then first lord of the admiralty, was designed to open up the sea route to Russia, which was badly in need of war supplies, and to take the pressure off the western front. After heroic and costly attacks, Allied Australian and New Zealand troops, known as Anzacs, were forced to withdraw from their landing positions on the Gallipoli peninsula in European Turkey.

Another major Allied setback in 1915 was the defeat of the Russian forces in Poland. More than 1,200,000 Russians were killed and wounded, and the Germans took nearly 900,000 prisoners. Although Russia somehow remained in the war, fighting well against the Dual Monarchy, it was no longer a concern for the Germans. These defeats generated rising criticism against the tsar's government, and Russian morale deteriorated.

Serbia was the next Allied victim. In September 1915, Bulgaria, still aching from its defeat in the Second Balkan War, entered the war on the side of the Central Powers. Surrounded by enemies, Serbia was helpless, and resistance was quickly crushed. The Austrians had finally gained their goal of the previous summer, but in the context of the continental tragedy, this achievement no longer seemed significant.

The Allies' only bright spot in 1915 was Italy's entry into their ranks. Italy had remained neutral in August 1914 when it had defected from the Triple Alliance, of which it had been at best a token member. Italy joined the Allies following promises made in a secret treaty in London promising the Italians huge concessions of territory once victory had been attained.

Stalemate

The Allies' strategy on the western front was to restrict attacks in France to intermittent nibbling, thus saving manpower and at the same time concentrating on their naval blockade. Denied badly needed imports, it was assumed, the German war effort would be seriously weakened. Countering this tactic, the German high command launched a massive offensive against the strategic fortress of Verdun in the spring of 1916. This forced the Allies to throw hundreds of thousands of men into battle. The slaughter brought

The Battle of Verdun

The initial euphoria accompanying World War I soon dissolved in the face of disasters such as the Battle of Verdun.

There are slopes on Hill 304 where the level of the ground is raised several meters by mounds of German corpses. Sometimes it happens that the third German wave uses the dead of the second wave as ramparts and shelters. It was behind ramparts of the dead left by the first five attacks, on May 24th, that we saw the Boches take shelter while they organized their next rush.

We make prisoners among these dead during our counterattacks. They are men who have received no hurt, but have been knocked down by the falling of the human wall of their killed and wounded neighbors. They say very little. They are for the most part dazed with fear and alcohol, and it is several days before they recover.

From Charles F. Horne, ed., *Source Records of the Great War*, vol. 4 (New York: National Alumni, 1923).

Unlike previous wars, World War I became a war of position and defense rather than one of movement and territorial conquest. Soldiers on both sides dug trenches, piled sandbags, and stretched barbed wire to protect their positions.

on by massed artillery and infantry charges between the trenches was horrible. The total loss of wounded and dead from this battle came to some 700,000 men.

To ease the pressure against Verdun, the British army began an offensive along the Somme River along the western front. The attackers' losses were catastrophic: 60 percent of the officers and 40 percent of the men became casualties the first day of the battle. Despite these awesome figures—which included the British firing 2 million shells at the first battle of the Somme—the attacks continued for three months without any substantial gains. Total German losses at the Somme were about 450,000, while the British and French lost about 600,000 men.

The only major naval engagement of the war, the Battle of Jutland (May 31–June 1, 1916), reaffirmed British control of the seas. The Germans maneuvered brilliantly and took risks. They could afford to gamble, because defeat would in no way worsen their existing position. The British fleet, on the other hand, had to act cautiously and absorbed greater losses. However the Germans retreated to their base and remained there for the rest of the war.[3]

On the eastern front in 1916 the Russians continued their generally successful campaigns against the Austro-Hungarian forces. But the Germans were always there to save their allies from destruction. Romania, impressed by the Russian victories, finally joined the Allies and launched an attack on the Hungarians. After an initial success, the Romanians were soon knocked out of the war by a joint German-Bulgarian invasion.

Total War and the Home Front

At the close of 1916, after more than two years of fighting, neither side was close to victory. Instead, the war had turned into a dreary contest of stamina, a far cry from the glories promised by the propaganda of 1914. War was no longer fought between armies, it was fought between states and every component within the state participated.[4]

On the home front, rationing was instituted to ensure sufficient supplies for soldiers at the front. As men went off to fight, women took over their jobs in the workplace. Intensive propaganda campaigns encouraged civilians to buy more bonds and make more weapons. Nations unleashed a barrage of propaganda inciting total hatred of the enemy, belief in the righteousness of the cause, and unquestioned support for the war effort.

Civil liberties suffered, and in some cases distinguished citizens were thrown into prison for opposing the war effort. In Britain, for example, the philosopher and mathematician Bertrand Russell was imprisoned for a short time for his pacifist views. Governments took over control of their national economies, gambling everything on a victory in which the loser would pay all the expenses incurred in the war. The various states outlawed strikes and rigidly controlled currencies and foreign trade.

At the beginning of the war, all was flag-waving and enthusiasm. The international socialist movement, whose policy it was to promote international proletarian unity, fell victim to the

Traditional warfare mixed with new technology in World War I; here, French cavalry officers watch a scout fighter plane.

Battle of the Somme

The "glories of war" were exposed for what they were—pain and suffering. These diary extracts show what war was like.

Diary of Private Tom Easton

A beautiful summer morning, though we'd had a bit of rain earlier. The skylarks were just singing away. Then the grand mine went up, it shook the earth for nearly a minute, and we had to wait for the fallout. The whistles blew and we stepped off one yard apart going straight forward. We were under orders not to stop or look or help the wounded. Carry on if you're fit, it was. . . .

Men began to fall one by one. . . . One officer said we were OK, all the machine-guns were firing over our heads. This was so until we passed our own front line and started to cross No Man's Land. Then trench machine-guns began the slaughter from the La Boiselle salient [German positions]. Men fell on every side screaming. Those who were un-wounded dare not attend to them, we must press on regardless. Hundreds lay on the Ger-man barbed wire which was not all destroyed and their bodies formed a bridge for others to pass over and into the German front line.

There were few Germans, mainly in machine-gun posts. These were bombed out, and there were fewer still of us, but we con-solidated the lines we had taken by preparing firing positions on the rear of the trenches gained, and fighting went on all morning and gradually died down as men and munitions on both sides became exhausted.

When we got to the German trenches we'd lost all our officers. They were all dead, there was no question of wounded. About 25 of us made it there. . . .

. . . Yes, as we made our way over the lat-ter stages of the charge, men dropped all around like ninepins. Apart from machine-guns, the German artillery was also very ac-tive, great sheets of earth rose up before one. Every man had to fend for himself as we still had to face the Germans in their trenches when we got there.

I kept shouting for my **MOTHER** to guide me, strange as it may seem. Mother help me. Not the Virgin Mother but my own maternal Mother, for I was then only 20 years of age.

Diary of Captain Reginald Leetham

I got to my position and looked over the top. The first thing I saw in the space of a tennis court in front of me was the bodies of 100 dead or severely wounded men lying there in our own wire. . . .

The dead were stretched out on one side [of the trench] one on top of the other six high. . . . To do one's duty was continually climbing over corpses in every position. . . . Of the hundred of corpses I saw I only saw one pretty one—a handsome boy called Schnyder of the Berkshires who lay on our firestep shot through the heart. There he lay with a sandbag over his face: I uncovered it as I knew he was an officer. I wish his Mother could have seen him—one of the few whose faces had not been mutilated.

Diary of Subaltern Edward G. D. Liveing

There was the freshness and splendor of a summer morning over everything. . . .

A hare jumped up and rushed towards me through the dry yellowish grass, its eyes bulg-ing with fear. . . .

Suddenly I cursed. I had been scalded in the left hip. A shell, I thought, had blown up in a water logged crump hole and sprayed me with boiling water. Letting go of my rifle, I dropped forward full length on the ground. My hip began to smart unpleasantly, and I felt a curious warmth stealing down my left leg. I thought it was the boiling water that had scalded me. Certainly my breeches looked as if they were saturated with water. I did not know they were saturated with blood.

From Michael Kernan. "Day of Slaughter on the Somme," *The Washington Post*, June 27, 1976, pp. C1, C5, passim. Reprinted by permission.

As the men marched off to war, women left their homes to work in munitions plants. Here, women workers operate cranes in a British shell-filling factory.

rabid patriotism that infected the continent. Workers of one country were encouraged to go out and kill workers of the enemy country in the name of the state. There was much idealism, sense of sacrifice, and love of country. At first there was no understanding of the horror, death, and disaster that comes with modern, industrialized war. British poet Rupert Brooke caught the spirit in his poem "The Soldier":

If I should die, think only this of me:
That there's some corner of a foreign field
That is forever England. There shall be
In that rich earth a richer dust concealed;
A dust whom England bore, shaped, made aware,
Gave, once, her flowers to love, her ways to roam,
A body of England's breathing English air,
Washed by the rivers, blest by suns of home.[5]

But this early idealism, this romantic conception of death in battle, gradually changed to one of war weariness and total futility. This growing

mood is best seen in the poetry of the young British officer and poet Wilfrid Owen, himself a victim on the western front:

What passing-bells for those who die as cattle?
Only the monstrous anger of the guns. . . .
No mockeries for them; no prayers nor bells,
Nor any voice of mourning save the choirs,—
The shrill, demented choirs of wailing shells;
And bugles calling for them from sad shires.[6]

By the end of 1916 a deep yearning for peace dominated Europe. Sensing this mood, leaders on both sides put forth peace feelers. But these half-hearted overtures achieved nothing. Propaganda was used effectively to continue the war and support for it. The populations of the warring states were made to believe that their crusade was somehow divinely inspired. In reality, the Dual Monarchy and France fought for survival; Russia, German, and Italy all fought to

The face of a battle-weary corporal in the Argonne Forest reflects the disillusionment of many who set out to fight what they believed would be a short-lived, "glorious war."

Wilfrid Owen, "Dulce et Decorum Est"

Leading antiwar poet Wilfrid Owen, who was killed in action in 1918, expressed the bitterness of
the war's victims.

Bent double, like old beggars under
    sacks, Knock-kneed, coughing like
    hags, we cursed through sludge,
Till on the haunting flares we turned our
    backs
And towards our distant rest began to trudge.
Men marched asleep. Many had lost their
    boots
But limped on, blood-shod. All went lame; all
    blind;
Drunk with fatigue; deaf even to the hoots
Of tired, outstripped Five-Nines that dropped
    behind.

Gas! Gas! Quick, boys!—an Ecstasy of
    fumbling,
Fitting the clumsy helmets just in time;
But someone still was yelling out and
    stumbling
And flound'ring like a man in fire or lime . . .
Dim, through the misty panes and thick green
    light,
As under a green sea, I saw him drowning.

In all my dreams, before my helpless sight,
He plunges at me, guttering, choking,
    drowning.

If in some smothering dreams you too could
    pace
Behind the wagon that we flung him in,
And watch the white eyes writhing in his
    face,
His hanging face, like a devil's sick of sin;
If you could hear, at every jolt, the blood
Come gargling from the froth-corrupted
    lungs,
Obscene as cancer, bitter as the cud
Of vile, incurable sores on innocent tongues,—
My friend, you would not tell with such high
    zest
To children ardent for some desperate glory,
The old Lie: Dulce et decorum est
Pro patria mori.

From C. Day Lewis, *Collected Poems of Wilfred Owen.*
Reprinted by permission of New Directions and Chatto
& Windus, p. 55. Copyright © Chatto & Windus, Ltd., 1946,
1963, and The Owen Estate.

improve their respective positions in Europe;
while Britain fought for Belgium and a renewed
balance of power on the continent.

Allied Fatigue and American Entry

In 1917 British and French military strength
reached its highest point, only to fall precipitous-
ly. Allied commanders were hopeful that the
long-planned breakthrough might be accomplished, but a large-scale French attack was beat-
en back, with huge losses. Some French
regiments mutinied rather than return to the inferno of "no-man's land" between the trenches.
The British sacrificed hundreds of thousands of
men without any decisive results in several massive offensives into German machine guns. The
Allies also launched unsuccessful campaigns in
Italy. Aided by the Germans, the Austrians
smashed the Italian front at the battle of
Caporetto (1917), an event vividly described by
Ernest Hemingway in *A Farewell to Arms.* Italian
resistance finally hardened, and collapse was
barely averted.

The growing effectiveness of the German submarine menace deepened Allied frustration. By
1917 Allied shipping losses had reached dangerous proportions. In three months 470 British
ships fell victim to torpedoes. Britain had no
more than six weeks' supply of food on hand, and
the supply situation became critical for the Allies. As it turned out, the very weapon that
seemed to doom their cause, the submarine, was
the source of the Allies' salvation: Germany's decision to use unrestricted submarine warfare
brought the United States openly into the war.

The Americans had declared their neutrality in 1914 when President Woodrow Wilson announced that the American people "must be impartial in thought as well as in action." The events of the next two years showed that this would not be the case. American sentiment was overwhelmingly with the Allies from the first. France's help to the colonies in the American Revolution was warmly recalled. Britain and America were closely tied by language, literature, and democratic institutions. Because Britain cut off communications between Germany and the United States, British propaganda and management of the war news dominated public opinion. Another factor predisposing the United States to the Allied cause was Germany's violation of international law in the invasion of Belgium. This buttressed the widely-held view created by the kaiser's saber-rattling speeches that the Germans were undemocratic, unpredictable, and unstable.

These attitudes were reinforced by the fact that the United States had made a substantial investment in the Allied war effort. As the war progressed it became apparent that the British blockade would permit American trade to be carried on only with the Allies. Before long, American factories and farmers were producing weapons and food solely for Great Britain and France. Industry expanded and began to enjoy a prosperity dependent on continued Allied purchases. Between 1914 and 1916 American exports to the Allies quadrupled. Allied bonds totaling about $1.5 billion were sold in the United States in 1915 and 1916. It was quite apparent to the Germans that there was little neutrality on the economic front in the United States.

The immediate cause of the U.S. entry into the war on the Allied side was the German submarine campaign. Blockaded by the British, Germany decided to retaliate by halting all shipping to the Allies. Its submarine campaign began in February 1915, and one of the first victims was the luxury liner *Lusitania*, torpedoed with the loss of more than a thousand lives, including one hundred Americans. This tragedy aroused public opinion in the United States. In the fall of 1916 Wilson, campaigning with the slogan "he kept us out of war," was reelected to the presidency. Discovery of German plots to involve Mexico in the war against the United States and more

submarine sinkings finally drove Wilson to ask Congress to declare war against Germany on April 6, 1917.

Submarine warfare and a wide range of other causes brought the president to the point of entering the war. Once in the conflict, however, he was intent on making the American sacrifice one "to make the world safe for democracy." Wilson's lofty principles caused a great surge of idealism among Americans.

Germany's Last Drive

The United States mobilized its tremendous resources of men and materiel more rapidly than the Germans had believed possible when they made their calculated risk to increase submarine warfare. Nonetheless the Central Powers moved to try to gain a decisive victory before U.S. aid could help the Allies.

The fruitless offensives of 1917 had bled the British army white, and the French had barely recovered from their mutinies. The eastern front collapsed with the February/March revolution in Russia. Eight months later, Lenin and the Bolsheviks took power in Russia and began to negotiate for peace. By the Treaty of Brest-Litovsk early in 1918, Russia made peace with Germany, giving up 1,300,000 square miles of territory and 62 million people.[7]

Freed from the necessity of fighting on the east, the Germans unleashed a series of major offensives against the west in the spring of 1918. During one of these attacks, a brigade of American marines symbolized the importance of U.S. support when they stopped a German charge at Chateau-Thierry. The Germans made a final effort to knock out the French in July 1918. It was called the *Friedensturm*, the peace offensive. The Germans made substantial gains, but did not score the decisive breakthrough. By this time the German momentum was slowing down, and more than a million American "doughboys" had landed in France. The final German offensive was thrown back after a slight advance.

With the aid of U.S. troops, Marshal Ferdinand Foch, the supreme Allied commander, began a counterattack. The badly beaten and continually harassed German troops fell back in rapid retreat. By the end of October, German

German assault troops attack the French in the Montdidier-Noyon area in June 1918. The Germans tried to force the Allies to sue for peace before Allied reinforcements arrived from the United States.

forces had been driven out of France and Allied armies were advancing into Belgium. The war of fixed positions separated by "no man's land" was over. The Allies had smashed the trench defenses and were now in open country.

Already on October 1 the German high command urged the kaiser to sue for peace, and three days later the German chancellor sent a note to President Wilson seeking an end to hostilities. Wilson responded that peace was not possible as long as Germany was ruled by an autocratic regime. The German chancellor tried to keep the monarchy by instituting certain liberal reforms, but it was too late. Revolution broke out in may parts of Germany. The kaiser abdicated and a republic was proclaimed.

While Germany was staggering under the continual pounding of Foch's armies, the German allies were suffering even greater misfortunes. Bulgaria surrendered on September 30 and Turkey a month later. Austria stopped its fighting with Italy on November 3. Nine days later the Habsburg empire collapsed when Emperor Charles I fled Vienna to seek sanctuary in Switzerland.

At five o'clock on the morning of November 11, 1918, in a dining car in the Compiegne Forest, the German delegates signed the peace terms presented by Marshal Foch. At eleven o'clock the same day hostilities were halted. Everywhere except in Germany, the news was received with an outburst of joy. The world was once more at peace, confronted now with the task of binding up its wounds and removing the scars of combat. Delegates from the Allied nations were soon to meet in Paris, where the peace conference was to be held.

The Allied Peace Settlement

In November 1918 the Allies stood triumphant, after the costliest war in history. But the Germans could also feel well pleased in 1918. They had fought well, avoided being overrun, and escaped being occupied by the Allies. They could acknowledge they had lost the war but hoped that U.S. President Wilson could help them. In February 1918 Wilson had stated that "there shall be no annexations, no contributions, no punitive damages," and on July 4 he affirmed that every question must be settled "upon the basis of the free acceptance of that settlement by the people immediately concerned."[8] As events transpired, the losers were refused seats at the peace conference and were the recipients of a dictated settlement.

Idealism and Realities

The destructive nature of World War I made a fair peace settlement impossible. The war had been fought on a winner-take-all basis, and now it was time for the Central Powers to pay. At the peace conference, the winning side was dominated by a French realist, a British politician, and an American idealist. The French representative was the aged French Premier Georges Clemenceau, representing Britain was the British Prime Minister David Lloyd George, and the U.S. representative was President Woodrow Wilson. The three were joined by the Italian Prime Minister Vittorio Orlando, who attended to make sure his country gained adequate compensation for its large sacrifices. These four men made most of the key decisions, even though most of the interested nations and factions in the world were represented in Paris, except for the Soviet Union.

Clemenceau had played a colorful and important role in French politics for half a century. He had fought continuously for his political beliefs, opposing corruption, racism, and antidemocratic forces. He wanted to ensure French security in the future by pursuing restitution, reparations, and guarantees. Precise programs, not idealistic statements, would protect France.

The two English-speaking members of the big three represented the extremes in dealing with the Germans. Lloyd George had been reelected in December on a program of "squeezing the German lemon until the pips are squeaked." He wanted to destroy Berlin's naval, commercial, and colonial position and to ensure his own political future at home. In January 1918 U.S. President Wilson had issued to Congress the Fourteen Points describing his plan for peace. Wilson wanted to break the world out of its tradition of armed anarchy and establish a framework for peace that would favor America's traditions of democracy and trade. At the peace conference he communicated his beliefs with a coldness and an imperiousness that masked his shy and sensitive nature and offended his colleagues.

The World War had not been a "war to end all wars" or a "war to make the world safe for democracy," as Wilson had portrayed it. The United States had hardly been neutral in its loans and shipments of supplies to the Allies before 1917. In fact, during the war, the financial and political center of balance for the world had crossed the ocean. The Americans made a rather abrupt shift from debtor to creditor status. The United States had entered the war late and had profited from it, and Wilson could afford to wear a rather more idealistic mantle.

The Europeans had paid for the war with the blood of their young and the coin of their realms.[9] The Allies now looked forward to a healthy return on their investment. The extent of that harvest had long been mapped out in secret treaties, copies of which the Bolsheviks released for the world to see.

Open Covenants, Secret Treaties

Wilson wanted to use his Fourteen Points as the base for a lasting peace. He wanted to place morality and justice ahead of power and revenge as considerations in international affairs. The first five points were general in nature and guaranteed: "open covenants openly arrived at," freedom of the seas in war and peace alike, removal of all economic barriers and establishment of an equality of trade among all nations, reductions in national armaments, and readjustment of all colonial claims, giving the interests of the population concerned equal weight with the claim of the government whose title was to be determined. The next eight points dealt with specific issues involving the evacuation and

John Maynard Keynes on Clemenceau

John Maynard Keynes caught the spirit of the peacemakers at Versailles in his work, *The Economic Consequences of the Peace*. His portrait of Clemenceau is especially revealing.

He felt about France what Pericles felt of Athens—unique value in her, nothing else mattering; but his theory of politics was Bismarck's. He had one illusion—France; and one disillusion—mankind, including Frenchmen, and his colleagues not least. His principles for the peace can be expressed simply. In the first place, he was a foremost believer in the view of German psychology that the German understands and can understand nothing but intimidation, that he is without generosity or remorse in negotiation, that there is no advantage he will not take of you, and no extent to which he will not demean himself for profit, that he is without honor, pride, or mercy. Therefore you must never negotiate with a German or conciliate him; you must dictate to him. On no other terms will he respect you, or will you prevent him from cheating you. But it is doubtful how far he thought these characteristics peculiar to Germany, or whether his candid view of some other nations was fundamentally different. His philosophy had, therefore, no place for "sentimentality" in international relations. Nations are real things, of whom you love one and feel for the rest indifference—or hatred. The glory of the nation you love is a desirable end,—but generally to be obtained at your neighbor's expense. The politics of power are inevitable, and there is nothing very new to learn about this war or the end it was fought for; England had destroyed, as in each preceding century, a trade rival; a mighty chapter had been closed in the secular struggle between the glories of Germany and of France. Prudence required some measure of lip service to the "ideals" of foolish Americans and hypocritial Englishmen; but it would be stupid to believe that there is much room in the world, as it really is, for such affairs as the League of Nations, or any sense in the principle of self-determination except as an ingenious formula for rearranging the balance of power in one's own interest.

From John Maynard Keynes, *The Economic Consequences of the Peace* (New York: Harcourt Brace Jovanovich, 1920).

---

restoration of Allied territory, self-determination for minority nationalities, and the redrawing of European boundaries along national lines.

The fourteenth point contained the germ of the League of Nations—a general association of all nations, whose purpose was to guarantee political independence and territorial integrity to great and small states alike. When Wilson arrived in Europe, the crowds on the streets and the victorious and the defeated nations alike greeted him as a messiah. His program had received great publicity, and its general, optimistic nature had earned him great praise.

The victorious Allies came to Paris to gain the concrete rewards promised them in the various secret treaties. Under these pacts, which would not come to public knowledge until the beginning of 1919, the Allies had promised the Italians concessions that would turn the Adriatic into an Italian sea, the Russians the right to take over the Straits and Constantinople, the Romanians the right to take over large amounts of Austro-Hungarian territory, and the Japanese the right to keep the German territory of Kiaochow in China. In addition, the British and French divided what was formerly Ottoman-controlled Iraq and Syria into their respective spheres of influence. An international administrative organization would govern Palestine. In 1917 Great Britain pledged its support of "the establishment in Palestine of a national home for the Jewish people."

Wilson refused to consider these agreements, which many of the victors regarded as IOUs now

The "Big Four" at the Versailles Peace Conference were, left to right, British prime minister Lloyd George, Italian prime minister Vittorio Orlando, French premier Georges Clemenceau, and President Woodrow Wilson of the United States. Representatives from Germany were excluded from the negotiating tables. The Big Four became the Big Three when Orlando withdrew abruptly because the conference refused to grant Italy all it demanded.

due to be paid in return for their role in the war; but the contracting parties in the treaties would not easily set aside their deals to satisfy Wilson's ideals. Even before formal talks—negotiations that would be unprecedented in their complexity—began, the Allies were split. Lloyd George and Clemenceau discovered early that Wilson had his price, and that was the League of Nations. They played on his desire for this organization to water down most of the thirteen other points. They were also aware that Wilson's party had suffered a crushing defeat in the 1918 elections and that strong factions in the United States were drumming up opposition to his program.

The League of Nations

When the diplomats began their first full meetings, the first issue was the formation of the League of Nations. Wilson insisted that the first work of the conference must be to provide for a league of nations as part of the peace treaty. After much negotiation, the covenant was approved by the full conference in April 1919. In order to gain support for the League, however, Wilson had to compromise on other matters. His Fourteen Points were partially repudiated, but he believed that an imperfect treaty incorporating the League was better than a perfect one without it.

The Covenant of the League of Nations specified its aims "to guarantee international cooperation and to achieve international peace and security." To achieve this goal, Article X, the key section of the document, provided that

> The Members of the League undertake to respect and preserve against external aggression the territorial integrity and existing political independence of all Members of the League. In case of any such aggression or in case of any threat or danger of such aggression, the Council shall advise upon the means by which this obligation shall be fulfilled.[10]

The League of Nations was the first systematic and thorough attempt to create an organization designed to prevent war and promote peace. It was a valiant effort to curb the abuses of the state system while maintaining the individual sovereignty of each member of the community of nations.

The League's main organs were the Council, the Assembly, and the Secretariat. Dominated by the great powers, the Council was the most important body. It dealt with most of the emergencies arising in international affairs. The Assembly served as a platform from which all League members could express their views. It could make recommendations to the Council on specific issues, but all important decisions required the unanimous consent of its members, and every nation in the Assembly had one vote.

The Secretariat, which had fifteen departments, represented the bureaucracy of the League. Numbering about 700, the personnel of the Secretariat constituted the first example in history of an international civil service whose loyalty was pledged to no single nation but to the interests of the world community. All treaties made by members of the League had to be registered with the Secretariat. It handled routine administrative matters relating to such League concerns as disarmament, health problems, the administration of former German colonies, and the protection of oppressed minorities.

Two other important bodies created by the Covenant of the League were the Permanent Court of International Justice and the International Labor Organization (ILO). The first was commonly referred to as the World Court. Its main purpose was to "interpret any disputed point in international law and determine when treaty obligations had been violated." It could also give advisory opinions to the Council or Assembly when asked for them. By 1937 forty-one nations had agreed to place before the World Court most basic international disputes to which they were a party. The ILO was established to "secure and maintain fair and humane conditions of labor for men, women, and children." The organization consisted of three divisions: a general conference, a governing body, and the International Labor Office.

Redrawing German Boundaries

After establishing the League, the diplomats got down to the business of dealing with Germany. France reclaimed Alsace-Lorraine, and plebiscites gave part of the former German empire to Denmark and Belgium (see map, p. 787). The French wanted to build a buffer state made up of former German territory west of the Rhine to be dominated by France. The Americans and the British proposed a compromise to Clemenceau which he accepted. The territory in question would be occupied by Allied troops for a period of from five to fifteen years, and a zone extending 50 kilometers east of the Rhine was to be demilitarized.

In addition, the French claimed the Saar basin, a rich coal area. Although they did not take outright control of the area—it reverted to the League administration—they did gain ownership of the mines, in compensation for the destruction of their own installations in northern France. It was agreed that after fifteen years a plebiscite would be held in the area. Finally Wilson and Lloyd George agreed that the United States and Great Britain by treaty would guarantee France against aggression.

To the east, the conference created the Polish Corridor, which separated East Prussia from the rest of Germany, in order to give the newly created state of Poland access to the sea. This creation raised grave problems, as it included territory in which there were not only Polish majorities but also large numbers of Germans. The land in question had been taken from Poland by Prussia in the eighteenth century. A section of Silesia was also ceded to Poland, but Danzig, a German city, was placed under Leage jurisdiction. All in all, Germany lost 25,000 square miles inhabited by 6 million people, a fact seized upon by German nationalist leaders in the 1920s.

The Mandate System and Reparations

A curious mixture of idealism and revenge determined the allocation of the German colonies and certain territories belonging to Turkey. Because outright annexation would look too much like unvarnished imperialism, it was suggested that the colonies be turned over to the League,

When Wilson arrived in Europe in December 1918, cheering crowds hailed him as the "peacemaker from America."
This photograph is from the parade in Paris.

which in turn would give them to certain of its members to administer. The colonies were to be known as mandates, and precautions were taken to ensure that they would be administered for the well-being and development of the inhabitants. Once a year the mandatory powers were to present a detailed account of their administration of the territories of the League. The mandate system was a step forward in colonial administration, but Germany nevertheless was deprived of all colonies, with the excuse that it could not rule them justly or efficiently.

As the Treaty of Versailles took shape, the central concept was that Germany had been responsible for the war. Article 231 of the treaty stated explicitly:

> The Allied and Associated Governments affirm and Germany accepts the responsibility of Germany and her allies for causing all the loss and damage to which the Allied and Associated Governments and their nationals have been subjected as a consequence of the war imposed upon them by the aggression of Germany and her Allies.[11]

Britain and France demanded that Germany pay the total cost of the war, including pensions. The United States protested this demand, and eventually a compromise emerged in which, with the exception of Belgium, Germany had to pay only war damages, including those suffered by civilians, and the cost of pensions. These payments, called reparations (implying repair) were exacted on the ground that Germany should bear the responsibility for the war.

Although the Allies agreed that Germany should pay reparations, they could not agree on how much should be paid. Some demands ran as high as $200 billion. Finally, it was decided that a committee should fix the amount; in the meantime Germany was to begin making payments. By the time the committee report appeared in May 1921, the payments totaled nearly $2 billion. The final bill came to $32.5 billion, to be paid off by Germany by 1963.

The Allies required Germany, as part of "in kind" reparations payments, to hand over most of its merchant fleet, construct one million tons of new shipping for the Allies, and deliver vast amounts of coal, equipment, and machinery to them. The conference permitted Germany a standing army of only 100,000 men, a greatly reduced fleet, and no military aircraft. Munitions plants were also to be closely supervised.

The treaty also called for the kaiser to be tried for a "supreme offense against international morality and the sanctity of treaties," thus setting a precedent for the Nuremberg tribunals after World War II. Nothing came of this demand, however, as the kaiser remained in his Dutch haven.

THE PEACE SETTLEMENT IN EUROPE

Newly Created States
Ceded Territories

Dictated Treaties

Before coming to Paris in April 1919 to receive the Treaty of Versailles, the German delegation was given no official information about its terms. Even though the German foreign minister denied that "Germany and its people . . . were alone guilty . . . ,"[12] he had no alternative but to sign. The continued blockade created great hardships in Germany, and the Allies threatened an invasion if the Germans did not accept the peace. The treaty was signed on June 28, the fifth anniversary of the assassination of the Archduke Francis Ferdinand, in the Hall of Mirrors at Versailles, the same room where the German empire had been proclaimed. As one American wrote, "The affair was elaborately staged and made as humiliating to the enemy as it well could be."[13]

The Allies imposed equally harsh treaties on Germany's supporters. The Treaty of St. Germain (1919) with Austria recognized the nationalist movements of the Czechs, Poles, and South Slavs. These groups had already formed states and reduced the remnants of the former Dual Monarchy into the separate states of Austria and Hungary. Austria became a landlocked country of 32,000 square miles and 6 million people. It was forbidden to seek *Anschluss*—union with Germany. Italy acquired sections of Austria, South Tyrol, Trentino (with its 250,000 Austrian Germans), and the northeastern coast of the Adriatic, with its large numbers of Slavs.

To complete their control of the Adriatic, the Italians wanted a slice of the Dalmatian coast and the port of Fiume. Fiume, however, was the natural port for the newly created state of Yugoslavia, and it had not been promised to the Italians in 1915. Wilson declared the Italian claim to be a contradiction of the principle of self-determination, and the ensuing controversy almost wrecked the peace conference. The issue was not settled until 1920, when Italy renounced its claim to Dalmatia and Fiume became an independent state. Four years later it was ceded to Italy.

By the Treaty of Sèvres (1920), the Ottoman empire was placed on the operating table of power politics and divided among Greece, Britain, and France. An upheaval in August 1920 in Constantinople led to the emergence of the

This German cartoon, "The Mask Falls," expresses German reaction to the terms of the Treaty of Versailles, which held Germany and its allies totally responsible for the war and demanded huge reparations.

Nationalists under Mustapha Kemal, who refused to accept the treaty. Not until July 1923 did Turkey's postwar status become clear in the milder Treaty of Lausanne, which guaranteed Turkish control of Anatolia.

Hungary (Treaty of Trianon, 1920) and Bulgaria (Treaty of Neuilly, 1919) did not fare as well as Turkey in dealing with the Allies. The Hungarians lost territory to Czechoslovakia, Yugoslavia, and Romania. Bulgaria lost access to the Aegean Sea and territory populated by nearly one million people, had to pay a huge indemnity, and underwent demilitarization.

Those eastern European states that profited from the settlements proved to be useful allies for France in the first fifteen years of the interwar period. Those that suffered were easy prey for the Nazis in the 1930s.

Evaluating the Peacemakers

The treaties ending the First World War have received heavy criticism from diplomatic historians, especially when compared with the work of the Congress of Vienna. The peace that emerged brought only weariness, new disagreements, and inflation.

There was a complete disregard of Russia. Lenin's government, in it weak position, indicated a willingness to deal with the west on the issue of prewar debts and border conflicts, if the west would extend financial aid and withdraw its expeditionary forces. The anti-Bolshevik forces in Paris did not take the offer seriously.[14] By missing this opportunity the Allies, in the view of a major American observer, took a course that had tremendous consequences for "the long-term future of both the Russian and the American people and indeed of mankind generally."[15]

Many commentators have laid the genesis of the Second World War just one generation later at the feet of the Paris peacemakers. The opportunism of Orlando and the chauvinism and revenge-seeking nature of both Clemenceau and Lloyd George appear short-sighted. Other critics point that the United States' reversion to isolationism doomed the work of the conference. Furthermore, never were there any broad plans for European economic recovery.

Considering the difficult conditions under which it was negotiated, the peace settlement was as good as could be expected. The delegates were the prisoners of their own constituents, who had themselves been heavily influenced by wartime propaganda. In addition, the diplomats had to deal with the nationalistic pressures and territorial conflicts of the newly formed eastern European nations. Given the costs of the war and the hopes for the peace, it is not surprising that the treaties left a legacy of disappointment for those who won and bitterness for those who lost. Symbolic of the obstacles faced by the statesmen was the fact that while they worked to return order, the globe reeled under the blows of a Spanish influenza outbreak that, when the costs were added up, was shown to have killed twice as many as had died in the war. The influenza outbreak was both a tragic conclusion to the war years and a sign for the future.

Conclusion

For more than four years, the science, wealth, and power of Europe had been concentrated on the business of destruction. Germany's rapid economic growth, military buildup, ambitious foreign policy, and inability to control its Austro-Hungarian ally helped bring the normally competitive European economic arena to a crisis in the summer of 1914. By violating Belgian neutrality and declaring war on Russia and France, Germany stood clearly as the aggressor in the First World War, a fact for which it was severely punished in the Treaty of Versailles.

When the victorious Allies gathered at Paris in 1919 to settle the peace, they did not have the luxury of time, distance, and power the leaders at the Congress of Vienna had enjoyed in 1815. The 1919 peacemakers had endured the most destructive war in history. In this total war, psychological methods were used to motivate all the people of each of the states to hate the enemy, during and after the war. In these conditions, the treaty settled at Versailles produced a mere break in the hostilities. Some observers have referred to the period from 1914 to 1945 as the "New Thirty Years' War."

With all that the Europeans shared, World War I was a conflict that need never have been fought. The Europeans threw away the advantages they had gained since 1815 and set in motion a series of disasters from which they did not recover until the second half of the twentieth century.

Suggestions for Reading

The standard account on the causes of the war is F. Fischer, *Germany's Aims in the First World War* (Norton, 1968). Classic views on the war are to be found in W. L. Langer, *European Alliances and Alignments, 1871–1890* (Vintage, 1931) and the *Diplomacy of Imperialism, 1890–1902* (Knopf, 1935) and S. B. Fay, *The Origins of the World War* (Macmillan, 1928). Bernadotte Schmidt, *Triple Alliance and*

Triple Entente (Fertig, Holt, 1934) is a good introduction. See also R. Albrecht-Carrié, *A Diplomatic History of Europe Since the Congress of Vienna* (Harper, 1973). A good overview of the war's origins is L. Lafore's *The Long Fuse: An Interpretation of the Origins of World War I* (Lippincott, 1971).

Specific topics are dealt with by Oron J. Hale, *The Great Illusion, 1900–1914* (Torchbooks, 1971); V. Dedijer, *The Road to Sarajevo* (Simon & Schuster, 1966); Colin Simpson, *The Lusitania* (Harper, 1976); A. Moorehead, *Gallipoli: Account of the 1915 Campaign* (Harper, 1956); A. Horne, *The Price of Glory: Verdun 1916* (St. Martin's, 1979); E. Coffman, *The War to End all Wars: The American Military Experience in World War I* (Oxford, 1968); G. Ritter, *The Schlieffen Plan* (Praeger, 1958); G. Feldman, *Army Industry, and Labor in Germany, 1914–1918* (Princeton, 1966).

Alexander Solzhenitsyn's *August 1914* (Bantam, 1974) is a fine piece of literature describing Russia's entry into the war. Barbara Tuchman's *The Guns of August* (many eds.) (Dell) is a fine history that is beautifully written. Paul Fassell brutally portrays the nature and impact of the war in *The Great War and Modern Memory* (Oxford, 1977).

See A. S. Link, *Wilson the Diplomatist* (Hopkins, 1957) regarding the U.S. president's participation at Paris. Charles L. Mee, Jr., captures the aura of Paris during the negotiations in *The End of Order, Versailles, 1919* (Dutton, 1980). Harold Nicolson's beautifully written *Peacemaking, 1919* (Houghton Mifflin, 1939) is a fine firsthand account, as is J. M. Keynes, *The Economic Consequences of the Peace* (Macmillan, 1924).

Notes

1. Quoted by C. J. H. Hayes, *A Political and Cultural History of Modern Europe*, II (New York: The Macmillan Co., 1939), p. 572.

2. Viscount Grey of Fallodon, *Twenty-Five Years*, II (New York: Frederick A. Stokes Co., 1925), p. 20.

3. *The New Cambridge Modern History*, 2nd ed., XII (Cambridge: Cambridge Univ. Press, 1968), p. 191.

4. Quoted in F. P. Chambers, *The War Behind the War, 1914–1918* (New York: Harcourt Brace Jovanovich) p. 473.

5. "The Soldier," *The Collected Poems of Rupert Brooke* (Canada: Dodd, Mead, & Co., 1915).

6. Wilfred Owen, "Anthem for a Doomed Youth," *Collected Poems* (Chatto & Windus, Ltd., 1946).

7. D. W. Treadgold, *Twentieth Century Russia* (Chicago: Rand McNally & Co., 1959), p. 154.

8. Quoted in L. M. Hacker and B. B. Kendrick, *The United States Since 1865* (New York: F. S. Crofts and Co., 1939), p. 520.

9. A. J. Ryder, *Twentieth Century Germany: From Bismarck to Brandt* (New York: Columbia Univ. Press, 1973), pp. 132–141.

10. Quoted in F. P. Walters, *A History of the League of Nations*, I (London: Oxford Univ. Press, 1952), p. 48.

11. Quoted in R. J. Sontag, *European Diplomatic History, 1871–1932* (New York: Century Co., 1933), p. 275.

12. Quoted in E. Achorn, *European Civilization and Politics Since 1815* (New York: Harcourt Brace Jovanovich, 1938), p. 470.

13. Quoted in Sontag, *European Diplomatic History, 1871–1932*, p. 392.

14. Louis Fischer, *The Soviets in World Affairs* (New York: Vintage Books, 1960), p. 116.

15. George F. Kennan, *The Decision to Intervene* (Princeton: Princeton Univ. Press, 1958), p. 471.

The Eclipse of the Democracies

Economic Crises and Political Retreat, 1918–1939

World War I, the war that was to make the world "safe for democracy," left a legacy of physical damage, economic disruption, and doubt that endangered the hard-won liberal victories of the nineteenth century. The twenty years between the first and second global wars was a perilous time for democracy (see map, p. 792). The horrible costs of the war made the victory a hollow one for the European victors, and after the initial taste for revenge had been satisfied, revulsion for war became widespread. The economic dislocation caused by inflation and depression sapped the strength of the middle classes, the traditional supporters of democracy. The certainty and belief in progress that had helped fuel Europe's dominance in the nineteenth century was replaced by doubt and cynicism.[1]

Economic Disasters

One of the most serious problems facing the survivors of World War I was the confused and desperate situation of the European economy. Much of the direct and indirect cost of the war had been covered by borrowing, and now the bills had come due in a world unable to pay them. The lasting results of the war touched many areas. The conflict altered world trading patterns, reduced shipping, and weakened Europe's former economic dominance. The various peace treaties multiplied the number of European boundaries, which soon became obstacles to the flow of goods, especially in the successor states of the Habsburg monarchy and in Poland.

The Costs of the War

It is impossible to give a true accounting of the costs of any war, because there is no way to calculate the contributions that might have been made by those killed in battle. From 2 to 3 million Russians died, and more perished in the civil war. Among the other major participants, almost 2 million Germans, over 1.5 million French, close to a million English, a half-million Italians, 1.2 million from Austria-Hungary, and 325,000 from Turkey died in battle. These figures do not count the wounded whose lives may have been shortened as a result of their injuries. Put another way, the young paid the highest price; it is estimated that Germany and France each lost over 15 percent of its young men.

Estimates of the financial drain of the war range between $250 billion and $300 billion, figuring the dollar at its early 1920s level. These figures do not bring home the depth of the war's impact on trade, shipping, and monetary stability. Belgium, for example, lost over 300,000 houses and thousands of factories, and 15,000 square miles of northeastern France were in ruins.

There is no balance sheet or set of figures to measure the psychological expense of the conflict. How does one calculate the cost of taking 75 million men who were mobilized away from their jobs and their homes? How can the mental carnage inflicted on the participants be measured?

Political institutions felt the effects of the war in different ways. The German, Habsburg, Russian, and Ottoman empires crumbled and disappeared from the historical stage. Replacing them

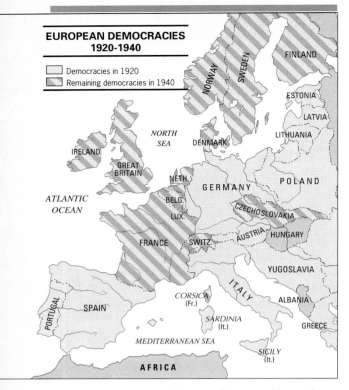

NORWAY
SWEDEN
FINLAND
ESTONIA
LATVIA
LITHUANIA
NORTH SEA
DENMARK
IRELAND
GREAT BRITAIN
NETH.
GERMANY
POLAND
BELG.
LUX.
CZECHOSLOVAKIA
ATLANTIC OCEAN
FRANCE
SWITZ.
AUSTRIA
HUNGARY
YUGOSLAVIA
ITALY
CORSICA (Fr.)
ALBANIA
PORTUGAL
SPAIN
SARDINIA (It.)
GREECE
MEDITERRANEAN SEA
SICILY (It.)
AFRICA

being able to deal with the Germans, blocking further profits, but by 1919 Europeans owed the United States more than $10 billion. This tremendous debt posed what economists call a transfer problem. The international obligations could be paid only by the actual transfer of gold or by the sale of goods.

To complicate the picture, Allied powers in Europe had also lent each other funds, with the British acting as the chief banker, lending more than £1.7 billion. When their credit dried up, they turned to the United States for financial help. Even though Britain owed huge sums to U.S. financiers, it remained a net creditor of $4 billion because of its own European debtors. France, on the other hand, stood as a net debtor of $3.5 billion. In addition to war debts, the French government suffered greatly when the Bolsheviks renounced the tsarist debt of some 12 billion francs—one quarter of France's foreign holdings.

Some of the Allies argued that the inter-Allied debts were political, that all of them had, in effect, been poured into a common pool for victory. These people wondered how France's

were uncertain republics or dictatorships. Those colonial empires that remained were weakened and indigenous nationalist movements made substantial progress. Rail and communications lines had to be reconfigured to reflect the interests of newly created states.

The roots of the economic problems that plagued Europe after the war—agricultural overproduction, bureaucratic regulations, and protectionism—could be seen before 1914. Compounding these factors were the traditional challenges encountered in shifting from a wartime to a peacetime economy—especially that of demobilizing millions of soldiers and bringing them back into the labor market.

The Debt Problem

A radical change had taken place during the war in Europe's economic relationship with the United States. In 1914 the United States had been a debtor nation, mostly to Europe, for the amount of $3.75 billion. The war totally reversed this situation. The United States lent billions of dollars and sold tons of supplies to the Allies. British blockades kept the United States from

A British cartoonist's view of the debt and reparation problems following World War I. Germany's inability to pay reparations meant that the Allies were unable to pay their inter-Allied war debts.

PASSING THE BUCK.

contribution in the lives of its young men could be figured into the equation in terms of francs, dollars, or pounds. They proposed that, with victory, all debts should be cancelled. The United States, which had gone to Paris with a conciliatory spirit toward Germany in the treaty negotiations, changed its tune when dollars and cents were involved. This attitude was best expressed in a remark attributed to Calvin Coolidge, who expected full repayment, when he said: "They hired the money, didn't they?"[2] Beneath the extremes of these positions was understandable motives of getting out of paying a huge debt. The German side resorted to financial mismanagement. In the first three years after the war, the German government, in a policy of deliberate inflation, spent much more than its income. This policy was masked by "floating debts . . . in other words, by the printing press."[3]

The situation became so serious in the summer of 1922 that Great Britain proposed that it collect no more from its debtors—Allied and German alike—than the United States collected from Britain itself. Such statesmanship was prompted by the fact that London had gained what it wanted from the peace settlement: Germany's navy was destroyed; Germany's merchant ships were transferred as reparations; Germany's empire was gone. No more could be squeezed out. Britain saw that Germany would not be able to meet its reparations payments, and without them, the payments of the inter-Allied debts, especially debts owed to the United States, would be extremely difficult, if not impossible, to make.

Although the United States insisted that there was no connection between the inter-Allied debts and German reparations, negotiations were carried on, and debt payment plans were set up with thirteen nations. No reductions were made in principal, but in every case the interest rate was radically decreased. The total amount owed came to more than $22 billion.

Germany's debt problem was complicated by the additional problem of reparations. Although reparations constituted a drain of major proportions on the German economy, they were far more significant as a political factor.

The German government's calculated inflationary policies contributed far more to the economic disaster that occurred in 1923 than did reparations. Between May and September 1921 the value of the German mark fell some 80 percent. A year and a half later, after Germany defaulted on some payments, French troops, supported by Belgian and Italian contingents, marched into the rich industrial district of the Ruhr, undeterred by American and British objections. This shortsighted French move contributed nothing to the solution of Europe's problems and indeed played into the hands of radical German politicians.

Encouraged by the Berlin government, German workers defied the French army and went on strike, many ending up in jail. The French toyed for a while with the idea of establishing a separate state in the Rhineland to act as a buffer between Germany and France. Chaotic conditions in the Ruhr encouraged the catastrophic

In January 1923, after Germany defaulted on reparations payments, French and Belgian troops occupied the Ruhr district to collect reparations in kind, mainly coal. The German workers responded by calling a general strike, and the occupation accomplished nothing, except to exacerbate Europe's already catastrophic economic problems. Here, French soldiers guard a German locomotive during the Ruhr district strike.

inflation of the German currency to make up for the loss of exports and to support the striking workers. The French, in return, gained very little benefit from the occupation.

Inflation and Stabilization

All European nations encountered a rocky path as they attempted to gain equilibrium after the war. Britain had minimal price increases and returned to prewar levels within two years after the signing of the Versailles treaty. On the continent, price and monetary stability came less easily. Only Czechoslovakia seemed to have its economic affairs well in hand.

France did not stabilize its currency until 1926, when the franc was worth fifty to the dollar (as contrasted to five to the dollar in 1914). In Austria prices rose to 14,000 times their prewar level until stability of sorts came in 1922. Hungary's prices went to 23,000 times prewar level, but this increase is dwarfed by Poland's (2.5 million times prewar level) and Russia's (4 billion times prewar level).

But Germany served as the laboratory of the horrible impact of inflation on society. Germany's prices went up a trillion times (a thousand billion) what they were in 1914. The German mark had been worth four to the dollar in prewar times. At its weakest point in November 1923, after the French occupation of the Ruhr, the German mark reached the exchange rate of 4.2 trillion to the dollar. During the worst part of the inflation, the Reichsbank had 150 firms using 2000 presses running day and night to print Reichnotes. To get out of their dilemma, the Germans made an effective transition to a more stable currency by simply forgetting the old one.[4]

The millions of middle-class Germans, small property owners who would be the hoped-for base of the new Weimar Republic, found themselves caught in the wage-price squeeze. Prices for the necessities of life rose far faster than did income or savings. As mothers wheeled baby carriages full of money to bakeries to buy bread, fathers watched a lifetime of savings dwindle to insignificance. Pensioners on fixed incomes suffered doubly under this crisis. The bourgeoisie, the historical basis for liberal politics throughout Europe, suffered blows more devastating than those of war, for inflation stole

Inflation in Germany during the 1920s grew so drastic that the German mark became nearly worthless. It was cheaper, for example, to burn the marks for fuel than to use them to purchase kindling.

not only the value of their labor, but the worth of their savings and insurance.

Where the middle classes and liberal traditions were strong, democracy could weather the storm. But in central Europe, especially in Germany where the inflation was the worst, the cause of future totalitarianism received an immense boost. Alan Bullock, a biographer of Adolf Hitler, has written that "the result of inflation was to undermine the foundations of German society in a way which neither the war nor the revolution of 1918, nor the Treaty of Versailles had ever done."[5]

Temporary Improvements

After 1923 the liberal application of U.S. funds brought some calm to the economic storm. Business was more difficult to conduct because protectionism became more and more the dominant

Alex de Jonge on Inflation in Weimar Germany

Alex de Jonge captured the truly devastating impact of inflation in Weimar Germany.

Hyperinflation created social chaos on an extraordinary scale. As soon as one was paid, one rushed off to the shops and bought absolutely anything in exchange for paper about to become worthless. If a woman had the misfortune to have a husband working away from home and sending money through the post, the money was virtually without value by the time it arrived. Workers were paid once, then twice, then five times a week with an ever-depreciating currency. By November 1923 real wages were down 25 percent compared with 1913, and envelopes were not big enough to accommodate all the stamps needed to mail them; the excess stamps were stuck to separate sheets affixed to the letter. Normal commercial transactions became virtually impossible. One luckless author received a sizable advance on

a work only to find that within a week it was just enough to pay the postage on the manuscript. By late 1923 it was not unusual to find 100,000 mark notes in the gutter, tossed there by contemptuous beggars at a time when $50 could buy a row of houses in Berlin's smartest street.

A Berlin couple who were about to celebrate their golden wedding received an official letter advising them that the mayor, in accordance with Prussian custom, would call and present them with a donation of money.

Next morning the mayor, accompanied by several aldermen in picturesque robes, arrived at the aged couple's house, and solemnly handed over in the name of the Prussian State 1,000,000,000,000 marks or one half-penny.

From Alex de Jonge, *The Weimar Chronicle, Prelude to Hitler* (New York: New American Library, 1978).

---

trait of international trade. *Autarky*, the goal of gaining total economic self-sufficiency and freedom from reliance on any other nation increasingly became the unstated policy of many governments.

Nonetheless, production soon reached 1913 levels, currencies began to stabilize by mid-decade, and the French finally recalled their troops from the Ruhr. Most significantly, in September 1924 a commission under the leadership of U.S. banker Charles Dawes formulated a more liberal reparations policy in order to get the entire repayment cycle back into motion. Dawes' plan, replaced in 1929 by the Young plan (named for its principal formulator, U.S. businessman Owen Young), reduced installments and extended them over a longer period. A loan of $200 million, mostly from the United States, was floated to aid German recovery. The Berlin government resumed payments to the Allies, and the Allies paid their debt installments to the United States—which in effect received its own money back again.

Prosperity of a sort returned to Europe. As long as the circular flow of cash from the United States to Germany to the Allies to the United States continued, the international monetary system functioned. The moment the cycle broke down, the world economy headed for the rocks of depression. One economic historian has written:

In 1924–31 Germany drew some one thousand million pounds from abroad and the irony was that Germany, in fact, received far more in loans, including loans to enable her to pay interest on earlier loans than she paid out in reparations, thus gaining in the circular flow and re-equipping her industries and her public utilities with American funds in the processes in the 1920s before repudiating her debts in the 1930s.[6]

The system broke down in 1928 and 1929 when U.S. and British creditors needed their capital for investments in their own countries. Extensions on loans, readily granted a year earlier, were refused. Even before the U.S. stock market crash on October 29, 1929, disaster was on the horizon.

Few people in America could admit such a possibility during the decade, however. The United States had become the commercial center of the world, and its policies were central to the world's financial health. The United States still had an internal market in the 1920s with a seemingly inexhaustible appetite for new products such as radios, refrigerators, electrical appliances, and automobiles. This expansion, based on consumer goods and supported by a seemingly limitless supply of natural resources, gave the impression of solid and endless growth.

Tragically, the contradictions of the postwar economic structure were making themselves felt. The cornerstones of pre-1914 prosperity—multilateral trade, the gold standard, interchangeable currencies—were crumbling. The policies of autarky, with their high tariff barriers to protect home products against foreign competition, worked against international economic health. Ironically, the United States led the way toward higher tariffs, and other nations quickly retaliated. American foreign trade seriously declined, and the volume of world trade decreased.

There were other danger signals. Europe suffered a population decline. There were 22 million fewer people in the 1920s in the western part of the continent than had been expected.[7] The decrease in internal markets affected trade, as did the higher external barriers. Around the globe, the agricultural sector suffered from declining prices during the 1920s. At the same time that farmers received less for their products, they had to pay more to live—a condition that afflicted peasants in Europe and Asia and farmers and ranchers in the United States.

In the hopes of reaching an expanding market, many food raisers around the world borrowed money to expand production at the beginning of the decade. Many farmers went bankrupt as they could not keep up with payments on their debts. The food surplus benefited consumers, but across the world agricultural interests suffered. Tariff barriers prevented foodstuffs from circulating to the countries where hunger existed. By the end of the decade, people in the Orient were starving, while wheat farmers in Whitman County, Washington, dumped their grain into the Snake River and coffee growers in Brazil saw their product burned to fuel steam locomotives. The countryside preceded the cities into the economic tragedy.[8]

The Great Crash

Because of America's central position in the world economy, any development, positive or negative, on Wall Street reverberated across the globe. The United States, with roughly 3 percent of the world's population, produced 46 percent of the globe's industrial output. The country was ill-equipped to use its new-found power. Its financial life in the 1920s was dominated by the activities of daring and sometimes unscrupulous speculators who made the arena of high finance a precarious and exciting world of its own. This world, however, was not dominated by businessmen pursuing long-term stability. Their blind rush for profit led to America's crash, which in turn sparked a world disaster.[9]

Even before the stock market crash, Wall Street had been showing signs of distress such as capital shortfalls, overly large inventories, and agricultural bankruptcies. But nothing prepared financiers for the disaster that struck on October 29, 1929—Black Thursday. By noon, Wall Street was caught in a momentum of chaotic fear. The initial hemorrhage of stock values stopped by the end of the trading session, but the damage was done.

John Kenneth Galbraith has written: "On the whole, the great stock market crash can be much more readily explained than the depression that followed it."[10] Overspeculation, loose controls, dishonest investors, and a loss of confidence in the "ever-upward" market trend can be identified as causes for the crash. Further causes can be traced to the inequitable distribution of wealth, with the farmers and workers left out—while the top 3 percent grew incredibly rich and irresponsible. Industrial overexpansion was fueled by speculators buying stock on the margin, with insufficient cash backing for the investments. In addition, the government's hands-off policies permitted massive abuses to take place unchecked.

The international impact of the crash can be explained by the involvement of investors and

Anxious crowds throng the street in front of the New York Stock Exchange during the crash of October 1929 that touched off a worldwide economic depression.

bankers from a number of countries in the U.S. market, the interdependent world economic structure, the peculiar Allied debt and reparations structure, the growing agricultural crisis, and the inadequate banking systems of the world.

Some economic historians believe that the cycle of highs and lows hit a particularly vicious low point in 1929. Crashes had occurred before, but never with such widespread repercussions over such a long period of time. In the United States, stock prices declined one-third overall within a few weeks, wiping out fortunes, shattering confidence in business, and destroying consumer demand. The disaster spread worldwide as American interests demanded payment on foreign loans and imports decreased. The Kredit-Anstalt of Vienna did not have enough money to fill demands for funds from French

banks and failed in 1931. This set in motion a domino-like banking crisis throughout Europe. Forecasts by Washington politicians and New York financiers that the worst was over and that the world economy was fundamentally sound after a "technical readjustment" convinced nobody. There would be no easy recovery.

The World Depression

By 1932 the value of industrial shares had fallen close to 60 percent on the New York and Berlin markets. Unemployment doubled in Germany, and 25 percent of the labor force was out of work in the United States. In nation after nations, industry declined, prices fell, banks collapsed, and economies stagnated. In the western democracies the depression contributed even more to the feelings of uneasiness that had

Nationwide bankruptcy forced Germany to close all its banks in 1931. The smiling faces of the guards surrounding the crowd belie the grim economic reality that resulted in the bank closures.

existed since 1918. In other countries, the tendency to seek authoritarian solutions became even more pronounced. Throughout the world people suffered from lowered standards of living, unemployment, hunger, and fear of the future.

The middle classes on the continent, which had suffered from inflation during the 1920s, became caught in a whiplash effect during the depression. Adherence to old liberal principles collapsed in the face of economic insecurity, and state control of the economies increased. Governments raised tariffs to restrict imports and used command economies, an expedient usually reserved for wartime. As conditions deteriorated, fear caused most governments to look no farther than their own boundaries. Under the competing systems of autarky, each nation tried to increase exports and decrease imports.

After almost a century of free trade, modified by a comparative few protective duties levied during and after World War I, Great Britain finally enacted a high tariff in 1932 with provisions to protect members of its empire. In the United States the Hawley-Smoot Act of 1930 increased the value added duty to 50 percent on a wide variety of agricultural and manufactured imports.

Another technique to increase exports at the expense of others was to depreciate a nation's currency—reduce the value of its money. When Japan depreciated the yen, for example, U.S. dollar or British pound could buy more Japanese goods. In effect, lowering the yen reduced the price of Japanese exports. In most cases, however, devaluation brought only a temporary trade advantage. Other nations could play the same game, as the United States did in 1934 when it reduced the amount of gold backing for the dollar by 40 percent, thus going off the gold standard.

The debt problem that grew out of the war worsened during the depression. In 1931, U.S. president Herbert Hoover gained a one-year moratorium on all intergovernmental debts. The next year at the Lausanne Conference, German reparations payments were practically canceled in the hope that the United States would make corresponding concessions in reducing war debts. The Americans, for a variety of domestic financial and political reasons, refused to concede that there was a logical connection between reparations and war debts. As the depression deepened, the debtors could not continue their payments. France refused outright in 1932; Germany after 1933 completely stopped paying reparations; Britain and four other nations made token payments for a time and then stopped entirely in 1934. Only Finland continued to meet its schedule of payments.

Individual families had as many, or more, problems in paying their bills as did the governments of the world. Factories closed down and laid off their workers. Harvests rotted in the fields as the price of wheat fell to its lowest figure in 300 years. The lives of the cacao grower in the African Gold Coast, the coffee grower in Brazil, and the plantation worker in the Dutch East Indies were as affected as those of the factory worker in Pittsburgh, Lille, or Frankfurt.

The 1929 crash occurred in an economic framework still suffering from the dislocations of World War I. It began a downturn in the world economy that would not end until the world armed for another global conflict. Whether the depression ended because of World War II or whether the world would have eventually come out of the low part of the cycle is a question that will always be debated. The weaknesses in American stock market operations were by and large addressed in a series of reforms.

From the major banks to the soup lines in villages, the depression had profound implications for politics. The combination of inflation and depression threatened representative government. Unemployed and starving masses were tempted to turn to dictators who promised jobs and bread. The hardships of economic stability, even in those countries where the democratic tradition was strongest, led to a massive increase in state participation in the daily life of the individual.

Politics in the European Democracies

During the interwar period, the belief in the genius of big business and free-market capitalism received a death blow in most quarters, as business itself had to turn more and more to the powers of the state to survive. After 1918 parliamentary government, the basis of all that the liberals of the nineteenth century had wanted, came under attack everywhere.

For the most part, only in the Scandinavian countries—Norway, Sweden, and Denmark—did representative government operate smoothly throughout the interwar period. Economic prosperity was the general rule here throughout the 1920s, and during the depression these countries suffered comparatively less than did Britain, France, or the United States. Switzerland,

Germans line up for bread and soup during the Great Depression. Similar scenes were common in many other countries, including the United States.

Friedrich A. Hayek

Friedrich A. Hayek deftly portrayed the malaise affecting liberal Europe in the interwar period. His judgement is deeply controversial.

The crucial point of which our people are still so little aware is, however, not merely the magnitude of the changes which have taken place during the last generation but the fact that they mean a complete change in the direction of the evolution of our ideas and social order. For at least twenty-five years before the specter of totalitarianism became a real threat, we had progressively been moving away from the basic ideas on which Western civilization has been built. That this movement on which we have entered with such high hopes and ambitions should have brought us face to face with the totalitarian horror has come as a profound shock to this generation, which still refuses to connect the two facts. Yet this development merely confirms the warnings of the fathers of the liberal philosophy which we still profess. We have progressively abandoned that freedom in economic affairs without which personal and political freedom has never existed in the past. Although we had been warned by some of the greatest political thinkers of the nineteenth century, by De Tocqueville and Lord Acton, that socialism means slavery, we have steadily moved in the direction of socialism. And now that we have seen a new form of slavery arise before our eyes, we have so completely forgotten the warning that it scarcely occurs to us that the two things may be connected.

From Friedrich A. Hayek, *The Road to Serfdom* (Chicago: University of Chicago Press, 1944).

---

the Netherlands, and Belgium also maintained relatively high standards of living and kept their governments on the democratic road. But in the twenty years after peace came to Europe, Britain, France, and most of the other democracies exhibited lethargy and short-sightedness in the face of crisis.

Britain, 1919–1939

The 1920s was not a tranquil decade for Great Britain. The country endured a number of social and political crises that were tied to the bitter labor disputes and unemployment that disrupted the nation. Neither Liberals nor Conservatives could do little to alter the flow of events immediately after the war. From 1919 to 1922 David Lloyd George led a coalition, but it broke apart, leading to the division and decline of the Liberals. From May 1923 to January 1924 Stanley Baldwin led an unsuccessful Conservative government.

Ramsay MacDonald formed the first Labour government and became the first socialist prime minister. For ten months he and his party pursued a program to introduce socialism slowly and within the democratic framework. His move to recognize the Soviet Union was controversial. When the London *Times* published the so-called Zinoviev letter, a document in which the Communist Third International supposedly laid out the program for revolution in Britain, the public backlash defeated the Labour government in the October 1924 elections.

For the next five years the Conservatives under Baldwin held power. After renouncing the treaties the Labour cabinet had made with Russia, the Conservatives set out on a generally unsuccessful and stormy tenure. Britain returned its currency to the gold standard in 1925, a policy that led indirectly to an increase in labor unrest. The government struggled through a coal strike and a general strike in which more than 2.5 million of the nation's more than 6 million workers walked out. Baldwin reduced taxes on business, but this did little to remedy the deflationary effect of a return to the gold standard.

In May 1929 Labour under MacDonald won another victory. Once again the Labourites

The democratic genre art of the 1830s in the United States expressed the romantic adventure of the rapidly expanding frontier of Jacksonian America. George Caleb Bingham (1811–79) graphically portrayed lively images of frontier life in his paintings of riverboatmen, local politicians, and domestic scenes. *The Jolly Flatboatmen* (c. 1848) is one of a series of paintings of the same subject.

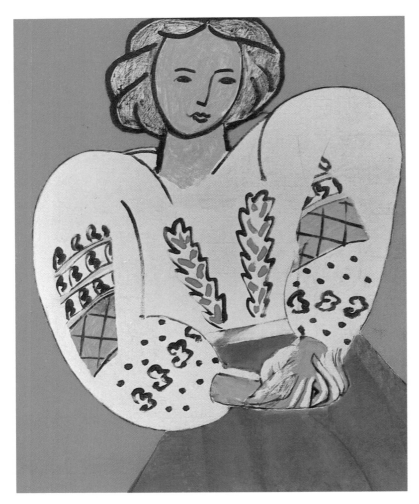

Leader of the expressionists, Henri Matisse emphasized the arrangement of simple, rhythmic forms and vivid areas of color. *Roumanian Blouse* (1940), left, is a late work. The experience of European imperialism affected all aspects of African life, including art. In the car below, an early twentieth-century work from the Congo, a Belgian magnate reclines in the back seat while the African chauffer drives.

Although Pablo Picasso is considered a founder of cubism, the range of his works extends over most of the significant trends in twentieth-century art. With its clearly defined shapes and boldly curved outlines, *Girl Before a Mirror* (1932) is an example of what has been described as curvilinear cubism.

The most famous surrealist painter is Salvador Dali (b. 1904), who sought to express the subjective world of dreams through disturbing and bizarre images like those in *The Persistence of Memory* (1931), below. The paintings of Marc Chagall (1887–1985), a forerunner of surrealism, also have a dreamlike quality, but the images are light and whimsical, as in *Birthday* (1915–23), right.

A master of twentieth-century art who, like Picasso, transcends any one movement or style is Paul Klee (1879–1940). *Senecio* (1922) combines elements of primitive art, cubism, surrealism, and children's drawings. In Klee's works, it is not only the subject, color, and spaces that give meaning to the picture; it is also the process of creation through which these elements are placed on the canvas that contributes to the total impression.

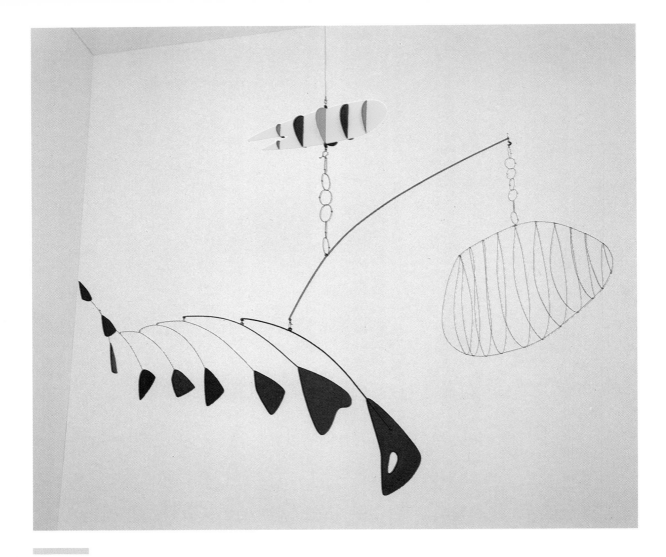

The American Alexander Calder (1898–1976) pioneered in the construction of kinetic, or mobile, sculptures in which physical motion is an essential part of the piece. Calder's mobiles are constructions of sheet metal and wire hinged together and so delicately balanced that the slightest breath of air sets the pieces in graceful motion. One of the largest hanging mobiles, *Lobster Trap and Fish Tail* (1939), is more than 8½ feet high and over 9½ feet in diameter.

Portfolio Eight

The great American architect of the twentieth century, Frank Lloyd Wright adapted the structure, materials, and plan of a building to its natural setting so that the land and the building become a unified whole. In the Kaufman House, *Falling Water,* at Bear Run, Pa. (1936), the overhanging concrete slabs blend harmoniously with the rocky ledges, while the interior of the house is a continuous flow of interrelated and interpenetrating areas.

Uninfluenced by twentieth-century trends in art, Edward Hopper (1882–1967) pursued his own course, using bold patterns of light, shadow, and color to convey the loneliness and isolation of modern urban life. The absence of distracting details and the geometric arrangement of strong verticals and horizontals contribute to the mood of haunting loneliness of the *Automat* (1927), in which a solitary woman sits in a deserted cafeteria, brooding over a cup of coffee.

A campaign poster for the British general election of 1931 urges voters to support the new national coalition government rather than the labour party with its failed socialist program.

resumed relations with the Soviet Union and attempted their measured socialist program. The effects of the depression, however, condemned MacDonald and his government to failure. In two years, exports and imports declined 35 percent and close to 3 million unemployed people roamed the streets. Labour could do little to address the basic causes of the disaster; in fact, no single party could. When MacDonald's government fell in 1931, it was replaced by a national coalition government which was dominated primarily by the Conservatives.

The coalition government initiated a recovery program featuring a balanced budget, limited social spending, and encouragement of private enterprise. By 1933, a substantial measure of prosperity had been regained, and productivity increased by 23 percent over that of 1929.

To achieve this comeback, some of what remained of laissez-faire policy was discarded. The

During the general strike of 1926 in England, armored cars equipped with machine guns patrolled London to suppress riots.

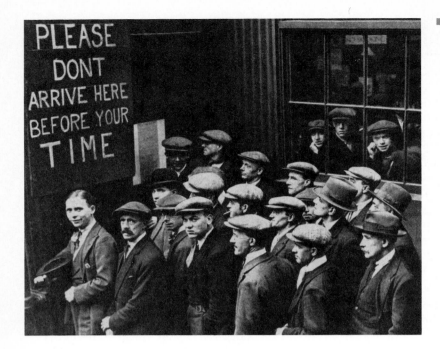

government regulated the currency, levied high tariffs, gave farmers subsidies, and imposed a heavy burden of taxation. The taxes went to expanded educational and health facilities, better accident and unemployment insurance, and more adequate pensions as a prelude to post World War II legislation that attempted to ensure security from "the cradle to the grave." As for the rich, they had a large portion of their income taxed away, and what might be left at death was decimated by inheritance taxes. It was ruefully declared that the rich could hardly afford to live, much less to die.

During the twenty years between the wars, with the decline of the Liberals, there was an absence of forward-looking programs by the political parties. The parties seemed unable to measure up to the demands of a difficult new age. To many people, unemployed and maintained on a government pittance, the interwar period was aptly symbolized by a popular play of the time, *Love on the Dole*.

Interwar France

France suffered the most of any of the democracies from World War I; loss of lives as a proportion of the population and direct property damage were enormous. More than two out of every ten young Frenchmen died. Years later, the nation, which had not experienced as rapid a population growth in the nineteenth century as other European states, still felt the war's heavy losses.

Victory did not address any of France's basic political problems. The French labored under much the same political stalemate and social stagnation after 1918 as it had before 1914. The economic impact of the war and the social disruptions that occurred during and after the conflict exacerbated these conditions. A dangerous inflation that threatened the franc plagued the country and undermined the rather shallow prosperity. The multiparty system hampered the parliamentary system of the Third Republic, and the brief tenure of governments formed from shaky coalitions. The exhausted country lacked vitality and a sense of national purpose after gaining revenge against the Germans.

After 1919, the British wished to withdraw from Europe to look after their imperial interests, and the United States withdrew into isolationism. Working from a dispirited domestic base, France had to bear the burden of overseeing international affairs on the continent. Overall, with the exception of the counterproductive occupation of the Ruhr, the French carried their duties well in the 1920s. In the next decade, however, France retreated into the so-called Maginot mentality, after the construction of the Maginot Line, a supposedly impenetrable line of fortresses to the east.

The depression struck France later than other countries, but in some ways the damage was greater. French leadership was no more astute than those of the other democracies before and during the depression. France managed to maintain a false prosperity from the 1920s for a while, partially because of its large gold holdings, but by the early 1930s it suffered much the same fate as the other countries. Tourism dried up, contributing to the already rising unemployment rate and budget deficits. In the face of these problems, the French carried the additional financial burden of rearming to face the renewed German threat.

Ministry after ministry took power, then collapsed a few months later. Citizens became impatient with the government, especially when the press exposed corruption in high places. One of the more shocking scandals was that surrounding the schemes of Alexander Stavisky, a rogue who had bribed officials and cheated French investors out of some 600 million francs. When the ministry in power in December 1933 refused to authorize an investigation after Stavisky's assumed suicide, thousands of angry citizens took to the streets of Paris in protest. In February 1934, mobs tried to storm the Chamber of Deputies.

The outcome of this affair was a new government, the National Union, a rightist coalition that endured strikes and avoided civil war for the next two years. France was becalmed. The leftists were unable to reorganize their forces quickly to gain control, and the rightists failed to deal with either domestic or foreign problems. In the spring of 1936 the leftist Popular Front took power.

This coalition, under the leadership of Léon Blum (1872–1950), won a national election and set in motion a program to bring socialist reforms to France's struggling economy. Blum's government tried to reduce the domination of the traditional ruling elite over the finances of the country on the one hand, and on the other work with the communists to block the growing fascist influences. The cooperation with the communists caused serious problems, including the usual one of how to work with the Moscow-dominated party without being captured by it. Many French voters refused to support the Popular Front from fear that it might commit France to fight against Germany for the benefit of the Soviet Union.

In foreign affairs the Popular Front worked closely with Great Britain and supported the

A Popular Front demonstration in Paris against the Nationalists in Spain who were seeking to overthrow the Spanish Republic. Despite this show of support for the Spanish Republicans, Blum's Popular Front government remained officially neutral during the Spanish Civil War.

work of the League of Nations. It also attempted to appease Germany, though it remained hostile to Italy. During the Spanish civil war (1936–1939), Blum's government, along with the British, declared neutrality in the face of fascist aggression, out of fear of a potential civil war.

In this atmosphere of social, economic, and international turmoil, Blum was unable to govern successfully. Further, an epidemic of sit-down strikes involving some 300,000 workers embarrassed the government. Gradually, laws introducing a forty-hour work week, higher wages, collective bargaining, and paid vacations were enacted to satisfy many of labor's demands. In addition, the government extended its control over the Bank of France and instituted a public works program. Blum navigated as best he could, favoring the worker against monopoly and big business while avoiding the totalitarian extremes of fascism and communism. After only a year in office, however, he was forced to resign. The unfavorable trade balance, huge public debt, and unbalanced budget brought down the Popular Front government. France swung back to the right with a government that ended the forty-hour week and put down strikes.

The National Union and the Popular Front mirrored the widening split between the upper and lower classes. The workers believed that the Popular Front's reforms had been sabotaged and that a France ruled by a wealthy clique deserved little or no allegiance. On the other hand, some business owners and financiers were horrified at the prospect of communism and openly admired Hitler's fascism. Soviet and German propagandists subtly encouraged the widening of the gulf.

While the French quarrelled and France's economic strength declined, Germany—regimented and feverishly working—outstripped France in the manufacture of armaments. There were no leaders to bring France together, and the ingredients for the easy and tragic fall of the country in the spring of 1940 were in place.

Eastern Europe

With the exception of Finland and Czechoslovakia, democratic governments fared poorly in eastern Europe in the interwar period. By 1939, most of the states retained only the false front of parliamentary forms. Real power was exercised by varying combinations of secret police, official censors, armed forces, and corrupt politicians.

Most of these countries had an unhappy legacy of oppression by powerful neighbors, minority problems, economic weakness, and backward peasant societies. Poland, the Baltic States, Finland, Czechoslovakia, Yugoslavia, and Albania had not existed as states before 1913. Hungary, Bulgaria, and Austria had been on the losing side in World War I and paid dearly for that alliance in the treaties ending the war. Romania, which had been among the victors, gained large amounts of land and also a number of non-Romanian minorities.

For the first decade after the war, the small countries of eastern Europe had the opportunity to develop without undue external influence or interference. However, the exclusivist, aggressive, perhaps paranoid nationalism that dominated each nation thwarted any possibility of regional cooperation. The peace treaties had settled few of the problems plaguing the area and instead constructed a series of arbitrary political boundaries that brought far more conflict than accord. The countries in the region all sought autarkist solutions to their economic problems by erecting huge tariff barriers, which only served to emphasize the states' weaknesses.

Czechoslovakia With its combination of a strong middle class, accumulation of capital, technology base, and high literacy rate, Czechoslovakia possessed the greatest possibility among the eastern European states for successful democratic government. Four hundred years of Austrian domination had not crushed Czech national spirit. After the collapse of the Dual Monarchy in November 1918, the Czechs joined with the Slovaks, who had been under Hungarian domination for a thousand years, to establish a republic.

The new state possessed a literate and well-trained citizenry and a solid economic base and managed to avoid the roller coaster ride of inflation in the immediate postwar period. The country was an island of prosperity, boasting solid financial institutions, advanced industry,

In 1918, Czechs turned out to welcome back from exile Edvard Beneš, who was named foreign minister of the new Czech republic.

and a small-farm-based agricultural sector. As in the other eastern European successor states, there were serious minority problems. But of all the new states Czechoslovakia extended the most liberal policies toward minorities. By the time of the depression, Czechoslovakia showed every indication of growing into a mature democratic country. The depression, however, heavily affected the country's export trade and hit especially hard in the textile industry, which was centered in the German-populated Sudetenland. By 1935 the economic blows had made the area ripe for Nazi agitation and infiltration.

Poland Aside from Czechoslovakia, Poland had the best chance of the successor states to form a democratic government. The Poles, however, had to overcome several problems: a border conflict with the Soviet Union, the dilemma of the Polish Corridor to Danzig, minority issues, and the fact that Poland had been partitioned for over a century. When the country was reunited after the war, the Poles chose to imitate the constitutional system of the French Third Republic. The multiplicity of parties, a weak executive, and the resultant succession of governments led to a political paralysis until 1926 when Marshal Josef Pilsudski (1867–1935) led a military revolt against the Warsaw government. For the next nine years Pilsudski imposed his generally positive, benevolent rule on the country. After his death in 1935, a group of colonels ruled Poland, and they permitted the formtion of several proto-fascist organizations. By the time the Poles turned back toward a more liberal government in 1938, it was too late. For three years, they had played up to the Nazis and now they stood isolated before Hitler's advance.

The Baltic and Balkan States Problems of geography plagued the Balkan states of Latvia, Lithuania, and Estonia, which came into existence in 1918. The democratic governments of these countries endured much political and economic strife before they eventually gave way to dictatorial forms of government to defend themselves against the Nazis.

Yugoslavia, Albania, and Greece were buffeted by the ambitions of Italian imperialism, economic upheaval, and political corruption. Disintegration seemed a real possibility for Yugoslavia in the 1920s, but the conglomerate state stubbornly attempted to hold together the six major ethnic groups within its boundaries. King Alexander established himself as dictator in 1929 and ruled until 1934, when he was assassinated by Croatian separatists. Thereafter, the rising Nazi state drew parts of economically depressed Yugoslavia into its orbit, deeply splitting the country. By the end of the 1930s, both Greece and Albania were ruled by dictators.

Romania gained greatly from the First World War, doubling its area and its population. Although the state had great economic potential, the government was unable to impose a stable rule during the interwar period. Severe problems with minorities and peasants and foreign control of the economy foiled the attempts of moderate politicians to rule, so by the 1930s fascist groups wielded a large amount of influence. In 1938 King Carol tried unsuccessfully to counter the pro-Nazi forces in Romania. Two years later the country lost one-third of its territory and population to the Bulgarians, Russians, and Hungarians, and Carol fled to Spain.

The Iberian Peninsula

During the interwar period, economic problems, aristocratic privilege, and peasant misery worked against successful democratic or parliamentary government in the Iberian peninsula. After the end of World War I, Portugal endured ten years of political indecision until Oliveira Salazar (1889–1970), a professor of economics, became minister of finance in 1928. After helping straighten out some of the country's financial problems, Salazar became Portugal's premier and virtual dictator. He maintained Portugal's close ties with Britain while lending assistance to right-wing elements in Spain.

None of the political parties could deal adequately with Spain's problems in the 1920s.

Revolts and strikes plagued the country until 1931, when the king abdicated and left the country. At the end of the year, a new liberal constitution was adopted, and a republic was proclaimed. The new constitution was extremely liberal, but it had the support of neither the left nor the right. Mob violence and the threat of military coups continually harassed the republic. By 1936 the peasants and workers were beginning to take matters into their own hands, while the military pursued its own political ends. In July, the army made its move and attacked the republican government. Even without Generalissimo Francisco Franco (see p. 881), there would have been a civil war in Spain. It would have come from the country's purely indigenous social antagonisms.[11]

Democracy Overseas

The United States emerged from World War I as the strongest country in the world. But while other states looked to Washington to play its proper role in the world, the U.S. government turned inward, away from the international scene. Americans shelved Wilson's wartime idealism, ignored the League of Nations, and returned to isolationism.

The United States in the 1920s

During the 1920s, three Republican presidents, Warren G. Harding, Calvin Coolidge, and Herbert Hoover, profited from the well-being of the country and presided over a generally carefree time. Although refusing to join the League of Nations, the United States did participate in the Washington Naval Conference in 1921–1922 to limit the race in warship construction, the Dawes and Young plans for economic stabilization (see p. 795), and the Kellogg-Briand pact (1928) to outlaw war.

Harding's domestic policies were marked by protectionist economics, probusiness legislation, and scandal. After Harding died suddenly in 1923, the widespread corruption of his administration was exposed. His vice-president, Coolidge, easily weathered the storm and after his 1924 election advocated high tariffs, tax

Throngs of unemployed line up in front of New York City's Municipal Lodging House for Sunday dinner in 1930.

reduction, and a hands-off policy on federal regulation of business. Only nagging problems in the agricultural sphere detracted from the dazzling prosperity and honest government that marked his administration.

In the 1928 elections, Herbert Hoover, a successful mining engineer who had directed Belgian relief during the war, been present at the

President Hoover's inability to solve the problems of the Great Depression helped Franklin D. Roosevelt win a landslide victory in the 1932 presidential election. Roosevelt is shown here at a political parade in Indianapolis, Indiana.

Versailles negotiations, and overseen the Russian relief plan in the early 1920s, overwhelmed the governor of New York, Alfred E. Smith—the first Catholic to be nominated for president. When he took office in 1929, Hoover had the support of a Republican Congress and a nation enjoying unbounded industrial prosperity. It would be his incredibly bad luck to have to deal with, and be given the blame for, the worst depression the United States has ever experienced.

The United States in the Depression

By 1932 Americans felt the tragic blows of the depression—25 percent unemployment, 30,000 business failures, numerous bank collapses, and a huge number of foreclosed mortgages. Hoover tried unprecedented measures to prop up faltering businesses with government money, devise new strategies to deal with the farm problem, and build confidence among the shaken citizenry. He failed to shift the tide of the depression. Indeed, some observers note that the only force that brought an end to the crisis was the arrival of the Second World War.

In the 1932 elections, Franklin D. Roosevelt, only the third Democrat elected to the presidency since 1860, overwhelmed Hoover by assembling a coalition of labor, intellectuals, minorities, and farmers—a coalition the Democratic party could count on for nearly a half century. The country had reached a crisis point by the time Roosevelt was inaugurated in 1933 and quick action had to be taken in the face of a wave of bank closings.

Under Roosevelt's leadership the New Deal, a sweeping, pragmatic, often hit-or-miss program, was developed to cope with the emergency. The New Deal's three objectives were relief, recovery, and reform. Millions of dollars flowed from the federal treasury to feed the hungry, create jobs for the unemployed through public works, and provide for the sick and elderly through such reforms as the Social Security Act. In addition, Roosevelt's administration substantially reformed the banking and stock systems, greatly increased the rights of labor unions, invested in massive public power and conservation projects, and supported families who were in danger of losing their homes or who simply needed homes.

The Democrats' programs created much controversy among those who believed that they went too far toward creating a socialistic government and those who believed that they did not go far enough toward attacking the depression. Hated or loved, Roosevelt was in control, and the strength and leadership he provided were unparalleled in the interwar democracies.

Interwar Latin America

The huge wartime demand for Latin American products resulted in an economic boom which, with a minor contraction, continued on into the 1920s. However, the area's crucial weakness remained—its economic dependence on only a few products. Among Latin America's twenty republics, Brazil based its prosperity on coffee, Cuba depended on sugar, Venezuela on oil, Bolivia on tin, Mexico on oil and silver, Argentina on wheat and meat, and the various Central American countries on bananas.

Another problem was that of land distribution. On many large estates, conditions resembled medieval serfdom. Because the Catholic church was a great landowner, certain churchmen combined with the landed interests to oppose land reforms.

During the 1920s, Mexico spearheaded the movement for social reform in Latin America. A series of governments, each claiming to be faithful to the spirit of the 1910 revolt, sought to gain more control over the vast oil properties run by foreign investors. The government solved the agrarian problem at the expense of the large landowners. These changes were accompanied by a wave of anticlericalism. Under these attacks, the Catholic church lost much property, saw many churches destroyed, and had to work through an underground priesthood for a time.

Mexico exerted a strong influence over other Latin American countries. Between 1919 and 1929 seven nations adopted new, liberal constitutions. In addition, there were growing demands for better economic and social opportunities, a breakdown of the barriers that divided the few extremely rich from the many abysmally poor, and improvement in health, education, and the status of women. Above all there was an increasing desire for more stable conditions.

Because of their dependence on raw material exports, the Latin American countries suffered a serious economic crisis during the depression. Largely as a result of the disaster, six South American countries had revolutions in 1930.

During the 1930s the "colossus of the north," the United States, attempted to improve its relations with Latin America and to stimulate trade. The Good Neighbor Policy, originated in Hoover's administration and begun in 1933, asserted that "no state has the right to intervene in the internal or external affairs of another." Less pious, but more effective, was the $560 million worth of inter-American trade that the new policy encouraged.

Rivalries among industrialized nations for the Latin American market became very intense during the 1930s. Nazi Germany concluded many barter agreements with Latin American customers and at the same time penetrated the countries politically by organizing German immigrants into pro-Nazi groups, supporting fascist politicians, and developing powerful propaganda networks. When war came, however, most of Latin America lined up with the democracies.

The British Empire

Demands for home rule grew during the interwar period in the British Empire, especially in

José Ortega y Gasset on the Rise of the Masses

José Ortega y Gasset captured the fear of the tyranny of the majority in his *Revolt of the Masses.*

There is one fact which, whether for good or ill, is of utmost importance in the public life of Europe at the present moment. This fact is the accession of the masses to complete social power. As the masses, by definition, neither should nor can direct their own personal existence, and still less rule society in general, this fact means that actually Europe is suffering from the greatest crisis that can afflict peoples, nations, and civilisation. Such a crisis has occurred more than once in history. Its characteristics and its consequences are well known. So also its name. It is called the rebellion of the masses. . . .

There exist, then, in society, operations, activities, and functions of the most diverse order, which are of their very nature special, and which consequently cannot be properly carried out without special gifts. For example: certain pleasures of an artistic and refined character, or again the the functions of government and of political judgment in public affairs. Previously these special activities were exercised by qualified minorities, or at least by those who claimed such qualification. The mass asserted no right to intervene

in them; they realised that if they wished to intervene they would necessarily have to acquire those special qualities and cease being mere mass. They recognised their place in a healthy dynamic social system. . . .

The characteristic of the hour is that the commonplace mind: knowing itself to be commonplace, has the assurance to proclaim the rights of the commonplace and to impose them wherever it will. As they say in the United States: "to be different is to be indecent." The mass crushes beneath it everything that is different, everything that is excellent, individual, qualified and select. Anybody who is not like everybody, who does not think like everybody, runs the risk of being eliminated. And it is clear, of course, that this "everybody" is not "everybody." "Everybody" was normally the complex unity of the the mass and the divergent, specialised minorities. Nowadays, "everybody" is the mass alone. Here we have the formidable fact of our times, described without any concealment of the brutality of its features.

From José Ortega y Gasset, *The Revolt of the Masses.* Reprinted by permission of W. W. Norton & Co., Inc. (New York, 1932), pp. 11, 16, 18.

India, Ceylon, Burma, and Egypt. An ominous trend was the growing antagonism between the Arab inhabitants of mandated Palestine and the Jewish Zionist immigrants. Yet, these issues would not come to a crisis until after the Second World War.

Happier developments could be seen in the attainment of home rule by the Irish Free State (the southern part of Ireland) in 1921 and Britain's recognition in the Statute of Westminster (1931) of a new national status for the dominions (Canada, Australia, New Zealand, and South Africa). Collectively, the four states were then known as the British Commonwealth of Nations and would be held together henceforth only by loyalty to the

crown and by common language, legal principles, traditions, and economic interests. Democratic traditions in the dominions did not succumb to the pressures of the depression, even though they were painfully susceptible to the effects of the world slump.

The Western Tradition in Transition

In the first two decades of the twentieth century, science made great strides, and such figures as Max Planck, Albert Einstein, Ivan

Pavlov, and Sigmund Freud, enlarged understanding of the universe and the individual. Even before the war, which had dealt a death blow to the nineteenth-century legacy of optimism, these physicists and psychologists pointed out that the old foundations and beliefs on which the European world rested had to be rethought. They and others like them opened new scientific vistas, and after 1918 their work began to have a much wider impact.

In the interwar period, artists too served as observant witnesses and penetrating critics of the difficult age in which they lived. After 1918, questioning of the accepted values and traditions of Western civilization increased.

Science and Society

As we saw in chapter 26, the British physicist Ernest Rutherford advanced the theory in 1911 that each atom has a central particle, or nucleus, which is positively charged. This did away with the belief that the atom was indivisible. On the continent, even greater discoveries were being made.

Max Planck (1858–1947), studied radiant heat, which comes from the sun and is identical in nature with light. He found that the energy emitted from a vibrating electron proceeds not in a steady wave—as traditionally believed—but discontinuously in the form of calculable "energy packages." To such a package, Planck gave the name *quantum*, hence the term *quantum theory*. This jolt to traditional physics was to prove invaluable in the rapidly growing study of atomic physics.

The scientific giant of the first half of the twentieth century, Albert Einstein (1879–1955), supported Planck's findings. In 1905 Einstein contended that light is propagated through space in the form of particles, which he called photons. Moreover, the energy contained in any particle of matter, such as the photon, is equal to the mass of that body multiplied by the square of the velocity of light (approximately 186,300 miles per second). This theory, expressed in the equation $E = mc^2$ provided the answer to many mysteries of physics. For example, questions such as how radioactive substances such as radium and uranium are able to eject particles at enormous velocities and to go on doing so for millions of years

could be examined in a new light. The magnitude of energy contained in the nuclei of atoms could be revealed. Above all, $E = mc^2$ showed that mass and energy are equatable.

That same year, Einstein formulated his special theory of relativity, which called for a radically new approach to explain the concepts of time, space, and velocity. For example, he maintained that time and distance are interrelated and that the mass of a body increases with its velocity. Again, he showed that mass and energy are equatable by $E = mc^2$.

In 1915 Einstein proposed his general theory, in which he incorporated gravitation into relativity. He showed that gravitation is identical to acceleration and that light rays would be deflected in passing through a gravitational field—a prediction confirmed by observation of an eclipse in 1919 and by various experiments carried out in the American space programs in the 1960s and 1970s. The theory of relativity has been subsequently confirmed in other ways as well. The interconversion of mass and energy was dramatically demonstrated in the atomic bomb, which obtains its energy by the annihilation of part of the matter of which it is composed.

Einstein's theories upset the Newtonian views of the universe. Einstein's universe is not Newton's three-dimensional figure of length, breadth, and thickness. It is, instead, a four-dimensional space-time continuum in which time itself varies with velocity. Such a cosmic model calls for the use of non-Euclidean geometry. Einstein's theory changed scientists' attitude toward the structure and mechanics of the universe. On a broader scale, his relativistic implications have penetrated philosophical, moral, and esthetic concepts of the twentieth century.

Planck and Einstein investigated the infinite extent of the external universe, with a massive impact on the state of knowledge. At the same time, the equally infinite extent of that universe known as the mind also began to be studied in greater depth than ever before.

The Russian scientist Ivan Pavlov (1849–1936) gave the study of psychology a new impetus. In 1900 he carried out a series of experiments in which food was given to a dog at the same time that a bell was rung. After a time, the dog identified the sound of the bell with food. Henceforth, the sound of the bell alone conditioned the dog to salivate, just as if food had been presented. Pavlov demonstrated the influence of physical stimuli on an involuntary process.

The psychology of "conditioned reflexes," based on Pavlov's work, achieved a wide popularity, especially in the United States, as the basis for behaviorism, which considered the human as analogous to a machine responding mechanically to stimuli. Behaviorism stressed experimentation and observational techniques and did much to create relatively valid intelligence and aptitude tests. It also served to strengthen the materialist philosophies of the period.

Probably the most famous and controversial name associated with psychology is that of Sigmund Freud (1856–1939). Placing far greater stress than any predecessor on the role of the unconscious, Freud pioneered the theory and methods of psychoanalysis. This theory is based on the idea that human beings are born with unconscious drives that from the very beginning seek some sort of outlet or expression. Young children often express their drives in ways that violate social conventions for proper behavior. Parents typically forbid these behaviors and punish children for performing them. As a result, many innate drives are repressed, that is, pushed out of conscious awareness. Repressed drives, however, continue to demand some kind of expression. Freud believed that many repressed drives were sublimated, that is, channeled into some kind of tolerated or even highly praised behavior.

Freud was particularly interested in psychological disorders, and he treated emotional disturbances by encouraging patients to bring back to the surface deeply repressed drives and memories. By making patients aware of their unconscious feelings, Freud hoped that patients would understand themselves better and be able to respond more effectively to the problems they faced. Freud used the techniques of free association and dream interpretation to explore how unconscious feelings might be related to patients' symptoms. He believed that many of his patients' symptoms resulted from repressed sexual and aggressive drives. Freud's theories not only have had tremendous influence in the science of psychology, they have also had a profound impact on our culture as a whole.

Sigmund Freud. Freud's theory of psychoanalysis gave people a new way of understanding and interpreting human behavior and new methods for treating mental disorders.

The Testimony of Artists

Even before the war, many of Europe's writers, and artists, and musicians had begun to question the generally held faith in European progress. The barbarism and tragedy of the war and its aftermath merely confirmed their perceptions. A whole generation of artists and thinkers cast doubts on their society and the worth of individuals caught in civilization's web. The war had shown to many the fallacies of the old order. Some artists sought release in drugs, oriental religions, or bohemian lifestyles. Other found comfort in ideas drawn from Einstein's relativity theory, which held that nothing was "fixed" in the universe, or in Freud's notions of the overwhelming power of the unconscious.

Franz Kafka (1883–1924) perhaps best captured the nightmarish world of the twentieth century. In works such as *Metamorphosis* and *The Trial*, he portrayed a ritualistic society in which a well-organized insanity prevails. Rational, well-meaning individuals run a constant maze from which there is no exit, only more structures. Many sensitive artists and writers cast serious doubt on the Renaissance notion that "man is the measure of all things." The western world had gone very far off course, and the best that could be hoped for was survival.

Historians worked under the profound influence of Oswald Spengler's *Decline of the West*. The book, finished one year before the defeat of the Central Powers, was more widely quoted than read. In it, the German historian traced the life span of cultures—from birth through maturity to death—and identified the symptoms of the west's demise. Other writers expressed a similar fascination with the death of their civilization, but perhaps more significant was that people in the west knew Spengler's name, just as earlier they had known the names of Freud, Einstein, and Darwin and their general messages.

Since before 1914, a number of composers had been rebelling strongly against lyrical romanticism and engaged in striking experimentation. Breaking with the "major-minor" system of tonality, which had been the musical tradition since the Renaissance, some of them used several different keys simultaneously, a device known as polytonality. Outstanding among such composers was Igor Stravinsky (1882–1971). He was less concerned with melody than with achieving effects by means of polytonality, dissonant harmonies, and percussive rhythms. Other composers, such as Arnold Schoenberg (1874–1951), experimented with atonality, the absence of any fixed key. Schoenberg developed the twelve-tone system, an approach in which compositions depart from all tonality and harmonic progressions, while at the same time stressing extreme dissonances. Stravinsky's and Schoenberg's music may strike the first-time listener as harsh and unpleasant, yet it must be acknowledged that these experiments with polytonality and atonality had validity for a time in which the old absolute values were crumbling, a time of clashing dissonance.

Young artists all over the world took up abstract, nonrepresentational painting. During the interwar period (1881–1973) Pablo Picasso modified his cubist style and became a public figure

Franz Kafka. In his visionary, psychological, and metaphorical fiction, Kafka expressed the anxiety and alienation of 20th-century Western society.

through paintings such as *Guernica*, a mural that vividly depicts the destruction of a small town in Spain by fascist air forces during that country's civil war. Henri Matisse (1869–1954) continued to exercise a major influence on young painters through his abstract works. Less significant, but a useful example of artistic response to the times was the Dada schools, which viewed World War I as proof that rationality did not exist, and that therefore, neither did artistic standards. Salvador Dali (1904–1989) perhaps indicated his convictions about the artistic establishment and the society it represented when he gave a lecture on art while wearing a diver's helmet.[12]

A more lasting movement that came out of the 1920s was surrealism. The proponents of this approach saw the subconscious mind as the vehicle that could free people from the shackles of modern society and lead them to total creative freedom. They felt an affinity with "primitive art" and its close associations with magical and mythological themes. They exalted the irrational, the violent and the absurd in human experience. French writer André Breton (1896–1966) wrote a manifesto of surrealism in 1924, but the movement had its greatest impact in the visual arts, in the works of such artists as Dali, Georgio de Chirico (1888–1978) and René Magritte (1898–1967).

Sculpture and Architecture

These two most substantial forms of art went through radical changes during the generation before and after the war. Auguste Rodin (1840–1917) has been called the father of modern sculpture. The realistic honesty and vitality of his work made him the object of stormy controversy during his career. He shared the impressionist painters' dislike of finality in art and preferred to let the viewers' imagination play on his work. Rodin's technique of "rough" finish can best be seen in his bronze works, which feature a glittering surface of light and shadow and convey a feeling of immediacy and incompleteness that emphasizes their spontaneous character.

While Rodin was making major contributions in sculpture, architects in Europe were taking advantage of new materials and technologies developed through industrialization to make major improvements in construction. With new resources and methods, architects were able to span greater distances and enclose greater areas than had hitherto been possible.

The Great Chicago fire of 1871 may have leveled much of the city, but it had the beneficial effect of permitting new building on a large scale. A new form of structure emerged—the steel-skeleton skyscraper, which enabled builders to erect much taller structures. Before, high buildings had required immensely thick masonry walls or buttresses. Now a metal frame allowed the weight of the structure to be distributed on an entirely different principle. Also, the metal frame permitted a far more extensive use of glass than ever before.

Outstanding among the pioneers in this new approach was American architect Louis Sullivan (1856–1924), who did most of his important work in Chicago. Like others, Sullivan saw the value of the skyscraper in providing a large amount of useful space on a small plot of expensive land.

He rejected all attempts to disguise the skeleton of the skyscraper behind a false front and boldly proclaimed it by a clean sweep of line. Sullivan's influence on function had a far-reaching influence.

In Europe, the French engineer Alexandre Gustave Eiffel (1832–1923) planned and erected a 984-foot tower for the Paris International Exposition in 1889. Delicately formed from an iron framework, the tower rests on four masonry piers on a base 330 feet square.

In the decade prior to World War I, an "international" style of architecture, which broke sharply with tradition, developed in Germany. This style, which stressed the use of different techniques from the machine age, was particularly well suited to early twentieth-century industrialization. In 1914 one of the outstanding leaders of this movement, Walter Gropius (1888–1969) designed an exhibition hall in Cologne that emphasized horizontal lines, used glass, exposed staircases, and did not hide its

Louis Sullivan, Carson Pirie Scott & Co. Building, Chicago (1899–1904). Sullivan influenced the development of the skyscraper, the dominant architectural form of the 20th century.

functionalism. Even at the end of the twentieth century this hall is still regarded as contemporary. Proponents of this new movement in architecture established a highly influential school of functional art and architecture, the *Bauhaus*, in 1918.

One of Louis Sullivan's pupils, Frank Lloyd Wright (1869–1959), originated revolutionary designs for houses. One feature of Wright's structures was the interweaving of interiors and exteriors through the use of terraces and cantilevered roofs. He felt that a building should look appropriate on its site; it should "grow out of the land." His "prairie houses," with their long, low lines, were designed to blend in with the flat land of the Midwest. Much of what is today taken for granted in domestic architecture stems directly from Wright's experiments at the beginning of the century.

Mass Culture

While the creative geniuses of high culture responded in their own ways to the era, purveyors of mass culture made amazing strides to please and entertain a widening audience. Movies became the most popular, most universal art form of the twentieth century. Movie newsreels brought home to millions the immediacy of the rise of Adolf Hitler, the drama of Franklin D. Roosevelt, or the home run power of Babe Ruth.

From the theaters of Main Street, U.S.A., to the private projection rooms of the Kremlin, artists such as Charlie Chaplin became universal favorites. Chaplin's favorite character, the Little Tramp, was an archetypal figure that communicated across all cultures. The tramp's struggle for food and shelter was universal, as was his appeal for freedom and dignity. Despite the odds, he always struggled against the forces of inhumanity, whether the soulless mechanization of the assembly line, as brilliantly shown in *Modern Times* (1935) or jackboot tyranny, as in *The Great Dictator* (1940) where the ranting "Furore" is ironically juxtaposed with the little Jewish barber who pleads for decency and predicts that "so long as men die, liberty will never perish."

Technology touched the common people in many ways and vastly expanded mass culture. Henry Ford's Model T made cars widely accessible and opened up the world to those who cared to drive. In cities, virtually every home had electricity, which powered bright lights, refrigeration, and other conveniences. Radio brought music, drama, and news into millions of living rooms. Politicians quickly learned the usefulness of the new medium; Stanley Baldwin in Britain, Franklin D. Roosevelt in the United States, and Adolf Hitler in Germany became masters at projecting their personalities and their ideas over the airwaves. The three great networks in the United States and organizations such as the British Broadcasting Corporation (BBC) in Europe got their start during these years.

The combination of increased leisure time, greater mobility, and improved communications led to the development of the modern "star" system in sports and entertainment. As times became more difficult and while front-page news was grim, Americans, Germans, and French citizens could find some diversion in reading about their boxers—Jack Dempsey, Max Schmeling, and Georges Carpentier. In the United States golfers and baseball stars became better known and better paid than presidents.

Through radio and phonograph records the mass audience discovered jazz, formerly the special preserve of black musicians and their audiences. Louis Armstrong and his trumpet and Paul Whiteman and his band became known worldwide. At the same time, Rosa Ponselle, Arturo Toscanini, and other figures from the opera and concert world became celebrities known to millions more than could ever have seen them perform in person.

Mass culture, with its movie stars, athletic heroes, and musical favorites, provided a diversion for many, even if it drew criticism from the élite. While intellectuals struggled to comprehend and express the changes occurring around them, mass culture provided release and relief from the stresses of the interwar period.

Conclusion

The democracies won World War I, and they dictated the peace at Paris, but the peace did not bring them the fruits of victory they so ardently desired. In the west, the vanguard of progress since the Middle Ages had been the middle classes. This group, originally small property owners, pursued private enterprise in an urban setting and favored an economy based on minimal governmental interference and free markets. After the war, the economic disasters of inflation and the depression strongly attacked the middle classes' economic strength and weakened the democracies.

Other basic institutions and assumptions also came under attack. The total mobilization for victory during the war laid the foundations for increased state dominance over society. By the end of the 1930s, Bismarck's welfare state had been copied in almost every country in the west. The family's innate obligation to care for its own people soon passed to the society and the state. Whether in the identification card of the French citizen or the social security number of the United States, every adult came to find a tentacle of the state reaching out to him or her to insure, support, and protect, while at the same time taxing and restricting.

Suggestions for Reading

E. H. Carr, *The Twenty Years' Crisis* (Torchbooks, 1964) and A. J. P. Taylor, *From Sarajevo to Potsdam* (Brace Jovanovich, 1966) give compelling and eloquent coverage of the malaise of the democracies in the interwar period. The problems of peacemaking and the aftermath of Versailles are discussed by J. M. Keynes, *The Economic Consequences of the Peace* (Macmillan, 1921) and F. P. Walters, *A History of the League of Nations* (Oxford, 1952). Harold Nicolson's thoughtful *Peacemaking* (Houghton Mifflin, 1939) is an essential introduction to the era.

The economic situation is well treated in David Landes, *The Unbound Prometheus* (Cambridge, 1969) and Sidney Pollard, *European Economic Integration, 1815–1870* (Harcourt Brace Jovanovich, 1974). See Fritz Ringer, ed., *The German Inflation of 1923* (Oxford, 1969) and Gustav Stolper, *et al., The German Economy 1870 to the Present* (Harcourt Brace Jovanovich, 1967) for the view from Berlin.

J. K. Galbraith's *The Great Crash 1929* (Houghton Mifflin, 1965) is wise and beautifully written. The global perspective of the thirties is found in C. P. Kindelberger, *The World in Depression* (California, 1975). C. Maier surveys the social and political consequences of the difficult interwar period in *Recasting Bourgeois Europe* (Princeton, 1975).

Two first-rate biographies of interwar British leaders are David Marquand, *Ramsay MacDonald* (Jonathan Cape, 1977) and Keith Midlemas, *Baldwin, A Biography* (Macmillan, 1970). J. Stevenson and C. Cook provide a good survey of British life between the wars in *Social Conditions in Britain Between the Wars* (Penguin, 1977). For France, John T. Marcus, *French Socialism in the Crisis Years, 1933–1936* (Praeger, 1963) and Peter Larmour, *The French Radical Party in the 1830s* (Stanford, 1964).

Notes

1. E. H. Carr, *The Twenty Years' Crisis* (New York: Harper & Row, 1964), p. 224.
2. T. Harry Williams, Richard N. Current, and Frank Friedel, *A History of the United States Since 1865* (New York: Alfred A. Knopf, 1960), p. 426.
3. A. J. Ryder, *Twentieth Century Germany: From Bismarck to Brandt* (New York: Columbia Univ. Press, 1973), p. 216.
4. David S. Landes, *The Unbound Prometheus* (Cambridge: Cambridge Univ. Press, 1969), pp. 361–362. Gustav Stolper, Karl Hauser, and Knut Borchardt, *The German Economy: 1870 to the Present*, trans. Toni Stolper (New York: Harcourt Brace Jovanovich, 1967), p. 83.
5. Alan Bullock, *Hitler, A Study in Tyranny* (New York: Torchbooks, 1964), p. 91.
6. Sidney Pollard, *European Economic Integration, 1815–1970* (New York: Harcourt Brace Jovanovich, 1974), p. 138.
7. Landes, *The Unbound Prometheus*, p. 365.
8. Pollard, *European Economic Integration, 1815–1970*, pp. 140–142.
9. William R. Keylor, *The Twentieth Century World* (Oxford: Oxford Univ. Press, 1984), p. 133.
10. John Kenneth Galbraith, *The Great Crash 1929* (Boston: Houghton Mifflin Co., 1961), p. 173.
11. Brian Crozier, *Franco* (London: Eyre & Spottiswoode, 1967), p. 13.
12. A. J. P. Taylor, *From Sarajevo to Potsdam* (New York: Harcourt Brace Jovanovich, 1965), p. 116.

The Quest for Total Power

The USSR, Italy, and Germany

World War I and its aftershocks prepared the way for authoritarian rule in Europe. By 1939, dictators ruled Russia, Italy, and Germany. Using modern technology, they tried to form a new kind of state, described as *totalitarian* by Benito Mussolini in 1925.

Totalitarian regimes, such as those led by Josef Stalin and Adolf Hitler, are at an opposite pole from democratic governments, which respect laws, representative assemblies, and civil and human rights. Totalitarianism exalts the leader of the state, who uses the law and society for personal ends. It invades and controls all areas of an individual's life, using propaganda to manipulate the masses. It orchestrates elections to achieve the "democratic fiction" of popular support. When totalitarian rule is perfected, society is atomized so there is no obstacle between the might of the leader and the individual.[1]

The costs of war and the incompetence of dual power destroyed the Provisional Government in Russia. The disappointments of the peace and unsettled economic conditions undermined the Italian government and the German Weimar Republic. Even before the war and the economic upheaval, the political soil in these countries had not been conducive to the development of liberal government. The postwar conditions combined with the exhaustion of the democracies led to the authoritarian alternative.

The Russian Revolution, 1917–1939

The Russians who survived World War I, revolution, civil war, and the 1930s endured one of the cruelest epochs in history. In passing from the rule of the inept tsar Nicholas II to the tyrannical Josef Stalin, they experienced the transformation of every aspect of their lives.

The enormous costs of the war set the stage for the revolution.[2] Nicholas and his subjects entered the war in a buoyant and patriotic mood.[3] It took only two months to dampen the initial optimism and to expose the army's weakness and the government's corruption. By the middle of 1915 the drastic losses (more than 2 million in that year alone) and food and fuel shortages lowered morale. Strikes increased among the factory workers during 1916, and the peasants, whose sons were dying in large numbers and whose desire for land reform were being ignored, became discontented.

The tsar and his government did little. Nicholas came more under the influence of his wife, Alexandra. She, in turn, had fallen under the control of the outrageous "holy man" Rasputin, the man who professed to be able to stop the bleeding of the tsar's hemophiliac son. Rasputin scandalized Petrograd by his influence over Alexandra and by his well-known seductions—he believed that "great sins made possible great repentances"[4] and in pursuit of that goal became one of history's notable sexual athletes.

When Nicholas took the symbolic act of assuming command of his armies in the field—a move that did nothing to help the Russian forces—Alexandra and Rasputin seized the opportunity to increase their power. The two capriciously dismissed capable generals and officials, making the government and army even less efficient. In December 1916 a group of Russian nobles tried to kill Rasputin by luring him to an

Tsar Nicholas and Tsarina Alexandra surrounded by their daughters (left to right) Marya, Tatiana, Olga, and Anastasia. The young tsarovitch sits below his parents. Nicholas and his entire family were executed by the Bolsheviks in July 1918.

apartment and poisoning him. When the massive amounts of poison had no effect, they shot him and then threw him into the Neva River. According to the autopsy, he finally died by drowning.

Alexandra's and Rasputin's roles in the capital reflected the sad state of the tsarist government in 1917. Under the pressure of war, the Russian economic and political bases dissolved. The tsarina and her associate did not cause the outbreak of the revolution. Rather, "the complex revolutionary situation of 1917 was the accumulated deposit of Russian history, detonated by the explosion of war."[5]

The February/March Revolutions of 1917

While politicians, ideologists, and generals acted out their parts in the drama, a spontaneous event from below sparked the 1917 Russian revolution. In the first part of March (late February in the Julian calendar in use in Russia at the time, all dates will be given in the new style), a strike broke out in a Petrograd (known in the west as St. Petersburg and in modern times as Leningrad) factory. By March 8 sympathy strikes had virtually paralyzed the city. At the same time, a bread shortage occurred, which brought more people into the streets. Scattered fighting broke out between the strikers and protesters on one side and the police on the other.

The tsar ordered the strikers back to work and dismissed the Duma (parliament) on March 11. These orders touched off the revolutionary crisis. The Duma refused to go home and the strikers held mass meetings in defiance of the government. The next day the army and police openly sided with the workers.

Three events occurred between March 12 and March 15 that marked the end of the old regime. On March 12 the Duma declared the formation of a provisional committee (renamed the Provisional Government on March 15) to serve as a caretaker administration until a constituent assembly could be elected to write a constitution for the future Russian republic. On the same day Marxist socialists in Petrograd formed the Soviet (council) of Workers' Deputies (renamed three days later the Soviet of Workers' and Soldiers' Deputies). Nicholas abdicated on March 15 to his brother Michael, who turned down the throne the next day in favor of the Provisional Government. After more than three centuries in power, the Romanov dynasty ceased to rule.

For the next six months, Russia proceeded under a system Leon Trotsky, the great Marxist theoretician and revolutionary, described as dual power—the Provisional Government and the Soviet. The moderates and liberals in the Provisional Government quickly produced a program of civil rights and liberties that gave Russia a

The Program of the Provisional Government

The freedom enjoyed by Russia from March to November 1917 was the most ever experienced in that country. A major reason for the freedom was the program of the Provisional Government.

Citizens, the Provisional Executive Committee of the members of the Duma, with the aid and support of the garrison of the capital and its inhabitants, has triumphed over the dark forces of the Old Regime to such an extent as to enable it to organize a more stable executive power.

The cabinet will be guided in its actions by the following principles:

1. An immediate general amnesty for all political and religious offenses, including terrorist acts, military revolts, agrarian offenses, etc.
2. Freedom of speech and press; freedom to form labor unions and to strike. These political liberties should be extended to the army in so far as war conditions permit.
3. The abolition of all social, religious and national restrictions.
4. Immediate preparation for the calling of a Constituent Assembly, elected by universal and secret vote, which shall determine the form of government and draw up the Constitution for the country.
5. In place of the police, to organize a national militia with elective officers, and subject to the local self-governing body.
6. Elections to be carried out on the basis of universal, direct, equal, and secret suffrage.
7. The troops that have taken part in the revolutionary movement shall not be disarmed or removed from Petrograd.
8. On duty and in war service, strict military discipline should be maintained, but when off duty, soldiers should have the same public rights as are enjoyed by other citizens.

The Provisional Government wishes to add that it has no intention of taking advantage of the existence of war conditions to delay the realization of the above-mentioned measures of reform.

President of the Duma, M. Rodzianko
President of the Council of Ministers,
*   Prince Lvov*
Ministers Miliukov, Nekrasov, Manuilov,
*   Konovalov, Tereschenko, Vl. Lvov,*
*   Shingarev, Kerenski.*
*   March 16, 1917.*

From *Documents of Russian History, 1914–1917*, ed. F. A. Golder, tr. E. Aronsberg (New York: Appleton-Century-Crofts, Inc. 1927).

springtime of freedom in 1917 the likes of which the country had never known before and would not experience again for seventy years. From the first, however, the Provisional Government was hampered by its temporary nature: it refused to take permanent action on major issues until the constitutent assembly, elected by all Russians, could convene.

The Soviet was dominated by the Menshevik wing of the Russian Social Democratic party. The Mensheviks believed, in accord with Marx' teachings, that a liberal, bourgeois revolution had to run its course. Even though they had greater popular support than the Provisional Government, they refused to take power until what they deemed to be the historically proper moment as defined by Marx's theories. After the fall of the tsar, power passed to those who could not rule or would not rule.

From the first, the dual power system functioned in a contradictory and ineffective way. On March 14 the Soviet issued its first law, Order No. 1, which placed the running of the army on a democratic basis, through a committee structure. Soldiers were to obey only those orders that agreed with the official position of the Soviet, which wanted peace. At the same time, the Provisional Government insisted on carrying out the war, in hopes of gaining the Bosporous, Constantinople, and the Dardanelles.

As the months wore on, the position of moderates in both parts of the system weakened, and all the parties involved became discredited. The Provisional Government put off calling the constituent assembly and thereby deferred any possibility of finding solutions to the problems facing Russia. It continued to pursue the war to "honor its commitments" and to gain the prizes promised in the secret treaties. The Mensheviks refused to take control, reasoning that the liberal, bourgeois phase of history had not run its course in Russia.[6] The masses who suffered from economic hardships or fought and died on the front lines could find little consolation in either branch of dual power.

By July, the liberals and moderates had given up the reins of power. Alexander Kerensky (1881–1970), who was further to the left and who had been the only real revolutionary in the original cabinet, became the head of the Provisional Government. He was in an impossible situation. Leftists accused Provisional Government of heartlessly pursuing the war, while rightists condemned it for tolerating too may leftists. In the meantime the Soviet extended its organization throughout Russia by setting up local affiliates. Through the summer, however, the Soviets lacked the forceful leadership to take control of the country.

Lenin's Opportunity, October/November 1917

In 1917 Lenin returned to Russia from exile in Switzerland, (see ch. 25), intent on giving the revolution the leadership it lacked. He had spelled out his tactics and ideas in the previous decade, and his disciples in Russia, the Bolsheviks, had built up a core of supporters in the factories and the army. As late as December 1916 he had stated that the revolution would not occur within his lifetime. Four months later, working through Swiss contacts and with German assistance, he returned to Russia. The Germans gave him transportation and financial support in the hope that he would cause widespread chaos that would force Russia to withdraw from the war.

From the moment he stepped off the train at the Finland station on the evening of April 16,

Lenin speaks to a crowd in Petrograd. The city was renamed Leningrad in 1924, but in 1991 residents voted to restore the original name of the city, St. Petersburg.

Lenin tried to control the revolution. He proposed immediately stopping the war against Germany and starting one against "social oppressors." He called for giving all power to the Soviets and nationalizing all land. He also pushed for calling all Social Democrats, of whatever persuasion, communists. Lenin badly misjudged his audience, and the Mensheviks and Social Revolutionaries rejected his program.

During the summer and fall of 1917 the Provisional Government and the Soviet continued their misgovernment. Kerenski tried to rule through a series of coalitions in which the political balance continually shifted to the left. By the middle of July, after a moderately successful offensive against the Austrians, soldiers began to desert in large numbers rather than face a useless death. The Russian front, along with the army, disintegrated. In the capital, the Mensheviks continued their refusal to take power through the Soviet: the historical time was not right.[7] As if to match the ineptness of dual power, the Bolsheviks made an ill-conceived attempt to take power. The move backfired, and Lenin was forced to flee in disguise to Finland.

After surviving the Bolshevik crisis, Kerensky faced a new threat from the right when General Lavr Kornilov tried to "help" the government by sending his troops to the capital. Kerensky and the Soviet interpreted this action as a right-wing counterrevolutionary move and mobilized to head it off. Kornilov's ill-advised manuever failed and, ironically, he weakened the people he wanted to help.

Between March and October 1917, the force of the revolution ground to bits all of Russia's structures and parties, from monarchist to Menshevik. The economic system fell apart as the rhythms of planting and commerce were disrupted by the uproar. To the people caught in this chaos, the moderates' political dreams, the Mensheviks' revolutionary timing, and the Bolshevik's schemes for the seizure of power were all totally irrelevant.

The actual revolution took place far away from the politicians and "great men." The army withered away as mass desertions and the execution of officers became commonplace. In the countryside the peasants began carrying out land reform on their own, expelling landowners and killing those who would not leave. In the cities, workers began to take over factories. The Russian empire broke apart from internal conflicts, the continued pressure of war, and the rising spirits of the nationalities who had been oppressed for centuries.

Only the Bolsheviks seemed to have an answer to Russia's crisis; even their slogans, such as "Peace, Land, and Bread," reflected what was already happening. Furthermore, they had the discipline and adaptability to take advantage of events. The Mensheviks clung to brittle intellectual formulas, while the Provisional Government continued to dream of Russian control of the Bosporous and Constantinople. Lenin and his colleagues took advantage of the Kornilov debacle and the failure of dual power to form their own revolution.

By October 1917 the Bolsheviks had discarded their slogan of "All Power to the Soviets." Frankly, Lenin, the unchallenged Bolshevik leader, no longer needed these local organizations. After much hesitation, he decided to move on November 6 (October 24 in the Russian calendar). The Bolshevik Military Revolutionary Committee led by Leon Trotsky, and supported by the communist-dominated crew of the battleship *Aurora*, took control of the communications and police centers in Petrograd. With the exception of sporadic fighting around the Winter Palace, Trotsky's military forces had little trouble. They arrested those members of the Provisional Government who could be found. Kerensky escaped from the capital in a car flying the U.S. flag.

Lenin suddenly found himself leading a party of over 200,000 people (an increase from 23,600 in February), which claimed control of a state of more than 170 million people. It was not his

Soldiers gathered in Petrograd's Admiralty Square in April 1917 and held banners reading (from left): "Long Wave the Democratic Republic," "Land and Freedom," and "Let Us Reject the Old World."

The Bolshevik attack on the Winter Palace in Petrograd, November 1917. The next day Lenin announced that the Bolsheviks had taken power.

individual genius or his plans but rather his discipline and opportunism that enabled him to gain power. He endured the mistakes of April and July to take power. He did not make the revolution, but he did pick up the pieces and profit from the changes brought about by the breakdown of the tsarist government under the pressure of war.

Power, Allied Intervention, Civil War

The Bolsheviks assumed power over a war-weakened, revolution-ravaged state that was in terrible condition. Lenin's takeover split the Soviet itself when the Mensheviks and the Social Revolutionaries refused to participate. Lenin had a bare majority at the Soviet's first postrevolutionary meeting. In the free elections held in December to form a constituent assembly, the Bolsheviks received just one fourth of the votes.

Yet such details as democratic representation did not stop Lenin. He proceeded to rule Russia. The Bolsheviks immediately put through decrees to declare peace and settle the land question. In the meantime, his cadres imposed their control over Moscow and the other cities in the country.

Lenin then began to lay the foundations for the single-party dictatorship that characterized Russia until 1989. When the constituent assembly convened in Petrograd on January 18, 1918 and proved that it would not be a tool for Lenin, the Bolsheviks closed it down at bayonet point the next day. By dissolving the constituent assemble, Lenin crushed all remnants of the briefly flowering democracy. This indecisive step sealed the fate of the Mensheviks and most other opposition leftist parties. Not for seventy-one years would there be contested elections, open criticism of the central power, and the possibility of a potential democratic opposition.

Lenin faced the need to make peace with Germany by concluding, after two months of negotiations, the Treaty of Brest-Litovsk. This agreement (see pg. 780) drastically reduced the territory under Russian control and made the centers of government much more exposed to attack. In reality, Lenin sacrificed territory over which he had no control and took his country out of a war it could not fight.

In the late spring the revolutionary government came under attack from the White forces and the Allies. The Whites, a powerful but fragmented group of anti-Bolsheviks began a civil war that would claim as many casualties in its three years as the country had lost in World War I. The Allied Powers sent several expeditionary armies to Russia for the stated purpose of controlling material they had sent the former tsarist army. In reality, they helped the Whites. The Allies, still at war with Germany, feared that the Bolsheviks were in a conspiracy with the Germans, especially after the terms of the Brest-Litovsk treaty became known. They also hoped that if Lenin could be overthrown, the Whites might reopen fighting against the Central Powers. By the fall of 1918, the Bolsheviks were besieged.

From its new capital at Moscow, the Red (Bolshevik) government took all means to defend the revolution. Lenin's forces reimposed the death penalty (it had been abolished by the Provisional Government) and unleased a ghastly reign of terror. The Red Army and the Cheka (secret police) systematically destroyed the enemies of the revolution as well as those who were only lukewarm in their support of the new regime. Prison camps and repressive terror harsher than any since Ivan IV dominated life in the Russian state. In July 1918, the former tsar and his family, under house arrest since the outbreak of the revolution, were herded into the cellar of the house in which they were being held and executed.

After the Central Powers surrendered in November 1918, Allied intervention in Russia ceased, and the Bolsheviks concentrated their energies against the Whites. Trotsky turned the Red Army into a disciplined, centralized force. The disorganized and dispersed White opposition, whose units ranged from Siberia to the Caucasus to Europe, could not match the Red forces. Taking advantage of their shorter supply lines, ideological unity, and dislike of Allied intervention, the Bolsheviks put an end to White resistance by 1920. The Whites were united on few issues besides their hatred of the Bolsheviks. After their defeat, nearly a million of them scattered across the globe, eternal émigrés grieving the loss of their country and their dreams.

Theory, Reality, and the State

Lenin had no hesitation about revising Marx' doctrines to fit Russian conditions. He had long opposed all democratic parliamentary procedures, especially the concept of an officially recognized opposition party. He advocated instead a revolutionary "dictatorship of the proletariat" under Bolshevik leadership. The new order would rule in accord with "democratic centralism," in which the vanguard party would anticipate the best interests of the masses and rule for them.

Lenin altered certain aspects of the Marxist concept of the historical process.[8] He accepted the view that the proletarian-socialist revolution must be preceded by a bourgeois-democratic revolution. He interpreted the March 1917 events as the first democratic revolution and his own coup d'état in November as the second, or proletarian-socialist, revolution. This approach drastically shortened the historical process by which the bourgeois stage was to run its course. Lenin justified dissolving the constituent assembly on the grounds that a higher form of democratic principle had now been achieved, making the constituent assembly superfluous. The November revolution had vested all power

This photograph of Lenin with Josef Stalin was taken in 1922, shortly after Stalin had been appointed general secretary of the Central Committee of the Communist Party.

in the Russian republic in the people themselves, as expressed in their revolutionary committees, or soviets.

Many orthodox Marxists believed that the state would "wither away" once the dictatorship of the proletariat had eliminated the bourgeoisie. Once in power, however, Lenin found that he had to create a far stronger, more efficient state to govern Russia. The Bolsheviks, as the ultimate democratic centralists, ruled with an iron hand and prepared the way for the totalitarianism of Josef Stalin.

The state acted in many spheres. In policies reminiscent of Robespierre's tenure during the French Revolution, the new government attacked the church, changed the calendar (adopting the Gregorian and rejecting the Julian system), and simplified the alphabet. The Cheka enforced ideological unity with a level of terror that set a standard for later Soviet secret police organizations. The individual came to be ground down by the all-encompassing power of the state.

In the first six years after Lenin seized power, there were three major developments relating to the Communist party, the name adopted by the Bolsheviks in 1918. First, all other parties were suppressed. Second, the function of the party itself was changed from that of carrying out the revolution to that of governing the country.[9] Third, within the party itself, a small elite group, the Politburo, consolidated power in its hands. The first Politburo included Lenin, Trotsky, Stalin, Zinoviev, Kamenev, Bubnov, and Sokolnikov. The second major organ of the party was the Secretariat for the Central Committee which oversaw the implementation of policy into practice.

The state, itself, came to be known as the Russian Socialist Federated Soviet Republic (RSFSR). As the Moscow-based communist government extended its authority after the civil war, the jurisdiction of the RSFSR grew. In 1922, the Union of Soviet Socialist Republics (USSR) was formed consisting of the four constituent socialist republics: the RSFSR, the Ukraine, White Russia (Belorussia), and Transcaucasia.

The communists had established the first constitution for their government in 1918, but events and growth soon led to the need for a new one, which was adopted in 1924. It set up a system based on a succession of soviets in villages, factories, and cities. This pyramid of soviets in each constituent republic culminated in the All-Union Congress of Soviets at the apex of the federal government. But, while it appeared that the congress exercised sovereign power, this body was actually governed by the Communist party, which was controlled in turn by the Politburo.

So great did the authority of the Communist party become over the formation and administration of policy that before Lenin's death in early 1924 it could be said without exaggeration that party and state were one. Consequently, whoever controlled the party controlled the state, and in the new Soviet state the key person would be Josef Stalin.

War Communism and the NEP

Lenin's ability as a politician can be seen in his flexibility between 1917 and 1924. From 1918 to 1921 he tried to apply undiluted Marxist principles to eliminate private ownership of land, nationalize banks, railways, and shipping, and restrict the money economy. This policy, known as war communism, was widely unpopular. The

peasants who had just attained their centuries-long goal of controlling their own land did not like the prospects of collectivization and the surrender of their surplus grain to the state. Many workers did not want to be forced to work in factories. Former managers showed little enthusiasm for running enterprises for the state's benefit.

In the early months of 1920 the new government faced its most dangerous crisis to date. Six years of war and civil strife had left Russia exhausted. Industrial production was 13 percent of what it had been 1914. Crop failures, poor management, and transportation breakdowns contributed to the disaster. Famine brought more than 20 million people to the brink of starvation. The government was forced to ask for help, and organizations such as Herbert Hoover's American aid project helped Russia through the crisis, but not before about 5 million people died.[10]

Internal chaos plus controversy with Poland over disputed borders further plagued Lenin's government. From 1918–1921 other areas of the former Russian empire—Finland, Estonia, Latvia, Lithuania, and Bessarabia—chose to go their own way. In February 1921 sailors at Kronstadt, formerly supporters of the regime, rebelled against the Bolsheviks and were massacred by the Red Army. Lenin said that the revolt "illuminated reality like a flash of lightning,"[11] and chose to make an ideological retreat.

War Communism was a total failure. Lenin decided that it was necessary to take "one step backwards in order to go two steps forward." He explained that Russia had tried to do too much too soon in attempting to change everything at once. He also noted that there had not been a firestorm of complementary communist revolutions sweeping the globe. The outbreaks in Germany and Hungary had been brutally squashed. Russia stood alone. Compromise was necessary to survive, and besides altering his diplomatic front abroad, he recommended a return to certain practices of capitalism, the so-called new Economic Policy, or NEP.

This retreat from War Communism lasted from 1921 to 1928 and allowed the Russian state to get on its feet. Peasants were relieved from the wholesale appropriation of grain. After paying a fixed tax, they were permitted to sell their surplus produce in the open market. Private management could once again run firms and factories employing less than twenty employees. Workers in state industries received a graduated wage scale. Foreign commerce and technology were actively sought. These compromises proved to be highly beneficial, and the Soviet economy revived.

Ideological purists criticized the policy and pointed out that the kulaks, as those ambitious peasants who accumulated property were called, and private businesses profited greatly. Lenin's concessions and compromises gave the communists time to regroup and recover, and the Russian people gained much-needed breathing space. Lenin emphasized the absolute necessity for the party to "control the commanding heights of the economy." The state continued to manage banking, transportation, heavy industry, and public utilities.

The NEP was Lenin's last major contribution. In broken health since he survived an assassin's bullet in 1918, he worked as much as he was able until his death in January 1924. In his fifty-four years Lenin deeply changed the world's history. He bequeathed to the globe its first Marxist state and provided the base from which his variant of Marxism could spread. He changed the tone and tactics of Marxism, stripping it of much that was humane and tolerant. His defenders argue that such steps were needed to apply a theory intended for industrialized society to an agrarian state. His critics argue that his methods and ideas were merely the reflection of his own ego. His tomb in Moscow's Red Square in which his embalmed body was placed on display became a Mecca for thousands of followers to come to pay homage to the creator of the Soviet state. Ironically, this secular, atheistic man who led a spartan existence was made by Stalin into a cult figure at the center of a new religion.

Trotsky vs. Stalin

A weakness of all dictatorships is that there is no well-defined mechanism to pass power from one leader to the next. Lenin was the one person in the party who possessed unchallenged authority and whose decrees were binding. After his death, Leon Trotsky and Joseph Stalin, rivals with conflicting policies and personalities, fought for power.

Leon Trotsky (1879–1940), born Lev Davidovich Bronstein, was a star in the political arena. He was a magnificent, charismatic orator, and energetic and magnetic leader in all areas, and a first-rate intellectual and theoretician. He turned to Marxism as a teenager and, like Lenin, had been exiled to Siberia for his revolutionary activities. He participated in the major events of Russian Social Democracy. Trotsky was a member of the *Iskra* group, had been present in London in 1903 for the Bolshevik-Menshevik split (see p. 666), played a key role in the 1905 Russian revolution, and was an essential figure in the 1917 revolutions and the Civil War. He had an ego and arrogance that contrasted with the shrewd and cunning nature of his less colorful, but more calculating rival.

Joseph Stalin (1879–1953), born in Georgia as Joseph Vissarionovich Dzhugashvili, labored for the revolution in obscurity. Where Trotsky was a star, Stalin worked behind the scenes. Trotsky was a crowd-pleasing orator; Stalin, when he spoke in his second language, Russian—Georgian was his first—was not an inspiring speaker. Admitted to a seminary to be trained for the priesthood, the young Stalin was later expelled for radical opinions. In the years before the revolutions, Stalin served the Bolsheviks by robbery to gain funds for the party's organization and propaganda activities. In all ways he faithfully supported Lenin, unlike Trotsky, who had not been a uniformly obedient disciple. Stalin was exiled a number of times east of the Urals before he returned to Petrograd in 1917 to play an active role in the events of that year. He knew his own strengths and weaknesses. He also formed his opinion of Trotsky rather early on, characterizing him in 1907 as being "beautifully useless."[12]

After the 1917 revolutions Stalin did a lot of the less glamorous organizational work of the party, along with being responsible for dealing with the various nationalities. While others in the Politburo dealt with ideological questions or fought the civil war, Stalin built up his own network of associates and gained control of the bureaucracy. In 1922, *Pravda*, the official party newspaper, carried a brief announcement that the Central Committee had confirmed Stalin as general secretary of the secretariat, a position that became the most powerful in the Soviet Union.

After Lenin's death, Stalin moved to construct a new secular religion for the Soviet Union. Leninism—complete with the renaming of Petrograd to Leningrad—formed in 1924, remained powerful for more than sixty years. The mark of faith came to be unquestioning loyalty to Lenin. Stalin became Lenin's St. Peter, even though Lenin had criticized both Trotsky and him in his so-called last will and testament, which, although written in 1922, was not widely published until the 1950s.[13]

In the competition with Trotsky, Stalin won because he was the better organizer and the more skillful manipulator of people. Staying in the background, the modest "helper," Stalin played the game of divide and conquer as members of the Politburo fought among themselves. By 1926 party members realized that Stalin had consolidated his position and had the full support of the party apparatus. By the end of that year, Trotsky and other opponents were removed from the Politburo. By 1929, Stalin was referred to as the "Lenin of today." Stalin's supporters occupied the key posts in both government and party, and he became the chairman of the Politburo. By 1940 he had eliminated all of the old Bolsheviks, including Trotsky, who was exiled and finally struck down by an assassin's ice axe in Mexico, on Stalin's orders.

More than just an opportunist or a superbureaucrat, Stalin too had ideological views on the future of the country. Trotsky and others had believed along with Lenin that the USSR could not survive indefinitely as a socialist island in a capitalist ocean. It was the duty, they held, of Russian communists to push for revolution elsewhere. Stalin, less a theorist than a political realist, viewed the idea of a world revolution as premature. He correctly noted that Marxism had made little headway outside the USSR, despite the existence of what, from the Marxist standpoint, were advantageous conditions for revolution in Germany and Italy. Stalin called for a new policy—"building up socialism in a single state." (Lenin had once hinted at that alternative in 1921.) He put an end to the NEP, and began taking "two steps forward"—with results that were both brutal and far-reaching.

Economics and Totalitarianism

Russia had begun industrialization at a late date, and from the 1890s on was continuously aware of its backwardness. The drastic impact of the war and civil war destroyed much of the progress that had been made, and by the late 1920s Stalin was deeply concerned with the country's economic weakness. He ordered a radical overhaul of the entire country and society to make fifty years progress in ten.

The NEP was scrapped in 1928 and Stalin imposed a series of five-year plans calling for heavy industrialization and collectivization of agriculture. Long working hours and a six-day week were instituted in the attempt to revolutionize Russia's economic structure. For the first time in history, a government truly controlled all significant economic activity through a central planning apparatus.

In the struggle to achieve its goals, the USSR went through what one scholar has called the "totalitarian breakthrough," in which there was "an all-out effort to destroy the basic institutions of the old order and to construct at least the framework of the new."[14] To drive the entire population along, Stalin strengthened his secret police so they could force the nation through what would be a decade of convulsive internal struggle. By 1939 Stalin had consolidated his personal dictatorship, at the cost of between 10 and 20 million lives.

War on the Peasants

Stalin wanted to transform the peasants into a rural proletariat, raising food on state and collective farms, not on their own plots. He had little doctrinal help from Marx, who had not considered that the revolution he forecast could take place in a peasant-dominated society. Marx left little guidance about what to do with the peasants, beyond mention of collectivized agriculture. He had assumed that capitalism would convert peasants into day laborers before the socialist revolution took place. Hence farming would continue, except now the state would own the farms.

Lenin's War Communism programs had failed, yet Stalin went back to them as he drew up his guidelines to transform agriculture. The major problem he faced was to convince the peasants to surrender their private lands, which they had finally got in 1917, to the state and collective farms.

Under Stalin's program, the state farms (*sovkhoz*) would be owned outright by the government, which would pay the workers' wages. The collective farms (*kolkhoz*) would be created from land taken from the *kulaks*—that hazily defined group of farmers who owned implements or employed others—and from the peasants who would voluntarily accept the government's decree to merge their own holdings. The *kolkhoz* members would work the land under the management of a board of directors. At the end of the year, the farm's net earnings would be totaled in cash and in kind, and the members would be paid on the basis of the amount and skill of their labor.

The theoretical advantages of large-scale mechanized farming over small-scale peasant agriculture were obvious. In addition, the government intended the reforms to permit the more efficient political education of the peasants. Further, the new programs would liquidate the *kulaks*, successful capitalist farmers who owned more property than their neighbors and who represented a disturbing element on the socialist landscape.

In actual practice, Stalin's collectivization program was a disaster. The vast majority of the peasants disagreed violently with Stalin's program. They did not want to give up their land. When the peasants did not flock to the government's banners, Stalin ordered harsher methods. When the class war between the poor peasants and the *kulaks* did not take place, he sent the secret police and the army to the villages. The transition to collectivization was carried out under some of the most barbarous and brutal measures ever enacted by a government against its own people.

In the butchery that followed, millions of people, especially in the Ukraine, died either from direct attack or starvation or in work camps. By a decree of February 1930, the state forced about one million *kulaks* off their land and took their possessions. Many peasants opposed these measures and slaughtered their herds and destroyed their crops rather than hand them over to the state. The number of horses in 1933 fell to below 50 percent of the 1928 number and there were 40 percent fewer cattle and half as many sheep and goats.[15]

In some sections the peasants rebelled en masse, and thousands were executed by firing squads. Villages that failed to capitulate were surrounded by army units which opened fire with machine guns. Official policy resulted in dislocation, destruction of animals and crops, and famine that claimed millions of lives. After nine years of war on the peasants, 90 percent of the land and 100 million peasants were in the collective and state farms.

Stalin's plan for economic revitalization of Russia called for collectivization of agriculture and heavy industrial development. The introduction of new machinery, like tractors, was intended to increase agricultural output and at the same time allow the state to remove agricultural laborers from the land and put them to work in factories.

Stalin and State Terror

Stalin's totalitarianism brought the development of state terror to unparalleled heights. Nadezhda Mandelstam defined the nature of the terror.

When I used to read about the French Revolution as a child, I often wondered whether it was possible to survive during a reign of terror. I now know beyond doubt that it is impossible. Anybody who breathes the air of terror is doomed, even if nominally he manages to save his life. Everybody is a victim—not only those who die, but also all the killers, ideologists, accomplices and sycophants who close their eyes and wash their hands—even if they are secretly consumed with remorse at night. Every section of the population has been through the terrible sickness caused by terror, and none has so far recovered, or become fit again for normal civic life. It is an illness that is passed on to the next generation, so that the sons pay for the sins of the fathers and perhaps only the grandchildren begin to get over it—or at least it takes on a different form with them. . . .

The principles and aims of mass terror have nothing in common with ordinary police work or with security. The only purpose of terror is intimidation. To plunge the whole country into a state of chronic fear, the number of victims must be raised to astronomical levels, and on every floor of every building there must always be several apartments from which the tenants have suddenly been taken away. The remaining inhabitants will be model citizens for the rest of their lives—this will be true for every street and every city through which the broom has swept. The only essential thing for those who rule by terror is not to overlook the new generations growing up without faith in their elders, and to keep on repeating the process in systematic fashion. Stalin ruled for a long time and saw to it that the waves of terror recurred from time to time, always on an even greater scale than before. But the champions of terror invariably leave one thing out of account—namely, that they can't kill everyone, and among their cowed, half-demented subjects there are always witnesses who survive to tell the tale. . . .

Excerpted from *Hope Against Hope: A Memoir* by Nadezhda Mandelstam, pp. 297–298, 304–305, 316–317, 369–371. Translated from the Russian by Max Hayward with introduction by Clarence Brown. Copyright © 1970 Atheneum Publishers. English translation copyright © 1970 Atheneum Publishers. Introduction copyright © 1970 Atheneum Publishers. Reprinted with the permission of Atheneum Publishers and Collins Publishers.

At the time, the atrocities accompanying Stalin's programs were largely overlooked or unknown in the west. Not until World War II was a casualty figure given, and then only casually when Stalin mentioned to British Prime Minister Winston Churchill a loss of life totalling around 10 million people. Only now are Soviet authorities telling the story of the massive suffering inflicted on the Soviet peasantry.[16]

The Five-Year Plans

Stalin introduced the system of central planning in 1928. He and his advisers assumed that by centralizing all aspects of the allocation of resources and removing market forces from the economy they could ensure a swift buildup of capital goods and heavy industries. The five-year plans, which began in 1929, restricted the manufacture of consumer goods and abolished capitalism in the forms permitted under the NEP. Citizens were allowed to own certain types of private property, houses, furniture, clothes, and personal effects. They could not own property that could be used to make profits by hiring workers. The state was to be the only employer.

The first five-year plan called for a 250 percent increase in overall industrial productivity. The state and police turned their entire effort to this goal. Even in the chaos that occurred—when buildings were erected for no machines and machines were shipped to where there were no buildings—growth did take place.

Whether the statistics the party cited to prove that the plan had been achieved in four- and one-half years were accurate—and they have been vigorously challenged—Soviet industry and society were totally transformed. The costs were disastrous, but Stalin portrayed Russia as being in a form of war with the world, and without strength, he pointed out, Russia would be crushed.

The second five-year plan began in 1933 and sought to resolve some of the mistakes of the first. The government placed greater emphasis on improving the quality of industrial products and on making more consumer goods. The third plan, begun in 1938, emphasized national defense. State strategies called for industrial plants to be shifted east of the Urals, and efforts were made to develop new sources of oil and other important commodities. Gigantism was the key, as the world's largest tractor factory was built in Chelyabinsk, the greatest power station in Dnepropetrovsk, and the largest automobile plant in Gorki.

The plans achieved remarkable results. In 1932 Soviet authorities claimed an increase in industrial output of 334 percent over 1914; 1937 output was 180 percent over 1932. But the high volume of production was often tied to mediocre quality, and the achievements were gained only with an enormous cost in human life and suffering. At first the burdensome cost of importing heavy machinery, tools, equipment, and finished steel from abroad forced a subsistence scale of living on the people. These purchases were paid for by the sale of food and raw material in the world's markets at a time when the prices for such goods had drastically fallen.

In the rush to industrialize, basic aspects of Marxism were set aside. The dictatorship *of* the proletariat increasingly became the dictatorship *over* the proletariat. Another ideological casualty was the basic concept of economic egalitarianism. In 1931 Stalin declared that equality of wages was "alien and detrimental to Soviet production" and a "petit-bourgeois deviation." So much propaganda was used to implant this twist that the masses came to accept the doctrine of inequality of wages as a fundamental communist principle. Piecework in industry became more prevalent, and bonuses and incentives were used to speed up production. It is ironic that capitalist practices were used to stimulate the growth of the communist economy. Stalin and Russia had deviated far from the Marxist maxim of "from

Economic activity in Stalinist Russia was carefully regulated by Stalin's five-year plans. Here, workers operate an oil rig.

This scene from a purge trial in Moscow in 1930 shows one of the eight defendants, all accused of treason, giving testimony. All eight were convicted; five were accorded the death penalty, the other three were given ten-year sentences.

each according to his ability, to each according to his need." Until the 1950s centralized planning enabled Russia to build a powerful industrial base and survive Hitler's assault. However, in the past four decades, as the Soviet economy has had to become more flexible, the system has proven to be counterproductive.

The Great Purges

During the 1930s Stalin consolidated his hold over the communist party and created the political system that would last until the ascent to power of Mikhail Gorbachev. Stalin established an all-powerful, personal totalitarian rule by doing away with all of his rivals, real and potential, in the purges. He also took the opportunity to remove all scientific, cultural, and educational figures who did not fit in with his plans for the future. By the end of the decade, Russians marched to Stalin's tune, or they did not march.[17]

The long arm of the secret police gathered in thousands of Soviet citizens to face the kangaroo

court and the firing squad. All six original members of the 1920 Politburo who survived Lenin were purged by Stalin. Old Bolsheviks who had been loyal comrades of Lenin, high officers of the Red Army, directors of industry, and rank-and-file party members were liquidated. Millions more were sent to forced labor camps. It has been estimated that between 5 and 6 percent of the population spent time in the pretrial prisons of the secret police.

Party discipline prevented party members from turning against Stalin, who controlled the party. The world watched a series of show trials in which loyal communists confessed to an amazing array of charges, generally tied after 1934 to the assassination—probably at Stalin's orders—of Sergei Kirov, Leningrad party chief and one of Stalin's chief aides. Western journalists reported news of the trials to the world, while the drugged, tortured, and intimidated defendants confessed to crimes they had not committed. A large portion of the leadership of the USSR was destroyed. By 1939, 70 pecent of the members of the central committee elected in

1934 had been purged. In the armed forces officer corps, the purges claimed 3 of 5 army marshals, 14 of 16 army commanders, 8 of 8 admirals, 60 of 67 corps commanders, 136 of 199 divisional commanders, 221 of 397 brigade commanders, and roughly one-half of the remaining officer corps, or some 35,000 men.[18] In a sense, the purges culminated in Mexico with Trotsky's assassination in 1940.

The lessons of the purges were chilling and effective. The way to succeed, to survive, was to be a dependable member of the apparatus—an *apparatchik.*

Changes in Soviet Society

In the twenty years after 1917, all aspects of Soviet society came under the purview of the party. The atomization of society, a prime characteristic of totalitarian government, did not permit such secret and trustful groups as the family to exist at ease. The party dealt in contradictory terms with various aspects of social life, but by and large the government worked to weaken the importance of the family. Initially after the revolution, divorces required no court proceedings, abortions were legalized, women were encouraged to take jobs outside the home, and communist nurseries were set up to care for children while their mothers worked. Pressure on the family continued under Stalin, but in different ways. Children were encouraged to report to the authorities "antirevolutionary" statements made by their parents.

The party did work to upgrade medical care, improve the treatment of the nationalities—at least initially—and extend educational opportunities. But even here political goals outweighed humanitarian objectives. Education existed primarily to indoctrinate pupils with communist precepts and values. Religious persecution was widespread. The church lost most of its power in education, and religious training was prohibited, except in the home.

The constitution of 1936 declared, "All power in the USSR belongs to the workers of town and country as represented by the Soviet of workers' deputies." Ironically, this document did not mention the Soviet Union's official ideology of Marxism-Leninism and referred only once to the communist party. On the surface, the 1936 constitution affirmed many basic rights, such as free speech, secret ballot, and universal suffrage, but it was mere window-dressing with no relationship to reality. Secret ballots meant little in a one-party state, and the parliament of the people, the Supreme Soviet, had no power. The Communist party, with a membership of less than 1.5 percent of the total population, dictated the life of each individual.

In the first decade after the revolution, intellectuals and artists experienced much more freedom than they would in the 1930s. The party emphasized the tenets of social realism but permitted some innovation. The Bolsheviks initially tolerated and even encouraged writers of independent leanings. Even though a large number of artists and writers fled the country after the revolution, others, including the poet Alexander Blok (1880–1921) and Vladimir Mayakovsky (1893–1930), remained and continued to write. During the NEP, Russia's cultural life bloomed in many areas, especially the cinema as can be seen in the works of the great director Sergei Eisenstein (1898–1948). In music, composers Sergei Prokofiev (1891–1953) and Dmitri Shostakovich (1906–1975) contributed works that added to the world's musical treasury.

Once Stalin gained control, he dictated that all art, science, and thought should serve the party's program and philosophy. Artists and thinkers were to become, in Stalin's words, "engineers of the mind." Art for art's sake was counterrevolutionary. Socialist realism in its narrowest sense was to be pursued. History became a means to prove the correctness of Stalin's policies.

Under Stalin's totalitarian rule, critics and censors tightened their control over artists and scholars. Artists and intellectuals found it safer to investigate, write, and perform according to the party line. Literary hacks and propagandists gained official favor, churning out what western critics referred to as "tractor novels."

Italy and Mussolini

After entering the war on the Allied side in 1915, Italy entered the peace negotiations with great expectations. The Italians had joined the

Allies with the understanding that with victory they would gain a part of Albania, Trieste, Dalmatia, Trentino, and some territory in Asia Minor. They came away from Versailles with minor gains, not nearly enough to justify the deaths of 700,000 of their youth.

Postwar Italy suffered social and economic damage similar to that of the other combatants. Inflation—the lira fell to one-third of its prewar value—and disrupted trade patterns hampered recovery. These ailments exacerbated the domestic crises the country had been struggling with before the war.[19] There were not enough jobs for the returning soldiers, and unemployed veterans were ripe targets for the growing extremist parties. In some cities residents refused to pay their rent in protest over poor living conditions.

Benito Mussolini, shown here speaking to a crowd in 1934, promised that a strong state could cure Italy's postwar ills, strengthen its economy, and rebuild national pride.

In the countryside, peasants took land from landlords. Everywhere food was in short supply.

In the four years after the armistice, five premiers came and went, either because of their own incompetence or because of the insolubility of the problems they faced. The situation favored the appearance of "a man on a white horse," a dictator. Such a man was a blacksmith's son named Mussolini, who bore the Christian name of Benito, in honor of the Mexican revolutionary hero Benito Juarez.

Benito Mussolini (1883–1945) grew up in and around left-wing political circles. Although he became editor of the influential socialist newspaper *Avanti* ("*Forward*") in 1912, he was far from consistent in his views and early on demonstrated his opportunism and pragmatism. When a majority of the Italian Socialist party called for neutrality in World War I, Mussolini came out for intervention. Party officials removed *Avanti* from his control and expelled him from the party. He then proceeded to put out his own paper, *Il Popolo d'Italia* ("*The People of Italy*"), in which he continued to call for Italian entry into the war on the Allied side.

To carry out his interventionist campaign, Mussolini organized formerly leftist groups into bands called *fasci*, a named derived from the Latin *fasces*, the bundle of rods bound around an axe, which was the symbol of authority in ancient Rome. When Italy entered the war, Mussolini volunteered for the army, saw active service at the front, and suffered a wound. When he returned to civilian life, he reorganized the *fasci* into the *fasci di combattimento* ("fighting groups") to attract war veterans and try to gain control of Italy.

The Path to Power

In the 1919 elections, the freest until 1946, the Socialists capitalized on the mass unemployment and hardship to become the strongest party. But the party lacked effective leadership and failed to take advantage of its position.

The extreme right-wing groups did not elect a single candidate to the Chamber of Deputies, but they pursued power in other ways. The fiery writer and nationalist leader, Gabriele D'Annunzio (1863–1938), had occupied the disputed city of Fiume with his corps of followers, in direct

Mussolini on Fascism

Benito Mussolini laid out his definition of fascism in the *Enciclopedia Italiana* in 1932.

He noted that fascism like every sound political conception . . . is both practice and thought; action in which a doctrine is immanent, and a doctrine which, arising out of a given system of historical forces, remains embedded in them and works there from within. . . .

The nation as the State is an ethical reality which exists and lives in so far as it develops. To arrest its development is to kill it. Therefore the State is not only the authority which governs and gives the form of laws and the value of spiritual life to the wills of individuals, but it is also a power that makes its will felt abroad, making it known and respected, in other words, demonstrating the fact of its universality in all the necessary directions of its development. It is consequently organized and expansion, at least virtually. Thus it can be likened to the human will which knows no limits to its development and realizes itself in testing its own limitlessness.

The Fascist State, the highest and most powerful form of personality, is a force, but a spiritual force, which takes over all the forms of the moral and intellectual life of man. It cannot therefore confine itself simply to the functions of order and supervision as Liberalism desired. It is not simply a mechanism which limits the sphere of the supposed liberties of the individual. It is the form, the inner standard and the discipline of the whole person; it saturates the will as well as the intelligence. Its principle, the central inspiration of the human personality living in the civil community, pierces into the depths and makes its home in the heart of the man of action as well as of the thinker, of the artist as well as of the scientist: it is the soul of the soul.

Fascism, in short, is not only the giver of laws and the founder of institutions, but the educator and promoter of spiritual life. It wants to remake, not the forms of human life, but its content, man, character, faith. And to this end it requires discipline and authority that can enter into the spirits of men and there govern unopposed. Its sign, therefore, is the Lictors' rods, the symbol of unity, of strength and justice.

---

violation of the directives of the Paris peace conference. This defiance of international authority appealed to the fascist movement. D'Annunzio provided lessons for the observant Mussolini, who copied many of the writer's methods and programs.[20]

The fascists gained the backing of landowning and industrial groups, who feared the victory of Marxist socialism in Italy. Mussolini's toughs beat up opponents, broke strikes, and disrupted opposition meetings in 1919 and 1920 while the government did nothing. Despite these activities, the extreme right-wing politicians still failed to dominate the 1921 elections. Only thirty-five fascists, Mussolini among them, gained seats in the Chamber of Deputies while the liberal and democratic parties gained a plurality. Failing to succeed through the existing system, Mussolini established the National Fascist party in November.

The Liberal-Democratic government of 1922 proved to be as ineffective as its predecessors, and the socialists continued to bicker among themselves. Mussolini's party however, attracted thousands of disaffected middle-class people, cynical and opportunistic intellectuals, and workers. Frustration with the central government's incompetence, not fear of the left, fueled the fascist rise. One historian has noted," . . . it was not on political ideas that fascism thrived, but on the yearning for action and the opportunities it provided for satisfying this yearning."[21]

In August 1922 the trade unions called a general strike to protest the rise of fascism. Mussolini's forces smashed their efforts. In October, after a huge rally in Naples, 50,000 fascists swarmed into Rome and soon thereafter king Victor Emmanuel III invited Mussolini to form a new government. During the next month Mussolini constructed a cabinet composed of his party members and nationalists and gained dictatorial powers to bring stability to the country. The fascists remained a distinct minority in Italy, but by gaining control of the central government they could place their members and allies in positions of power. The October "March on Rome" ushered in Mussolini's twenty-year reign.

Building the Fascist State

Mussolini followed no strict ideology as he consolidated his dictatorial rule. He threw out all the democratic procedures of the postwar years and dissolved rival political parties. He and his colleagues ruthlessly crushed free expression and banished critics of their government to prison settlements off Italy's southern coast. They censored the press and set-up tribunals for the defense of the state (not the citizens). Although he retained the shell of the old system, Mussolini established a totally new state.

Mussolini controlled all real power through the Fascist Grand Council, whose members occupied the government's ministerial posts. At one

The Fascists, dressed in their characteristic black shirts, began their march on Rome in October 1922. On October 29, the king telegraphed Mussolini in Milan to ask him to form a new government. The next day Mussolini arrived in triumph in Rome.

One of the most ominous acts of Mussolini's fascist regime was the burning of books and other literature considered "subversive."

time, Mussolini himself held no fewer than eight offices. All this activity and centralization of power provided a striking contrast to the lethargy of the four years immediately after the war. Encouraged by the popular support for his regime, Mussolini passed a series of laws in 1925 and 1926 in which the Italian cities lost their freely elected self-governments, and all units of local and provincial government were welded into a unified structure controlled from Rome.

Once he centralized Italian political life, Mussolini pursued the development of his ideology in a pragmatic manner. As one scholar noted, "If he had any principle or prejudice it was against the capitalists, the Church, and the monarchy; all of his life he abused the bourgeoisie."[22] But he would learn to work with all of those elements in his flexible pursuit of power. He once stated in an interview, "I am all for motion."[23] Movement, not consistency and science, marked his ideology.

Early in the 1920s Mussolini, a former atheist, began to tie the church into the structure of his new society. In 1928 he negotiated the Lateran Treaty with church representatives in order to settle the longstanding controversy between Rome and the Vatican. The new pact required compulsory religious instruction and recognized Catholicism as the state religion. Vatican City, a new state of 108 acres located within Rome itself, was declared to be fully sovereign and independent. In addition the state promised the Vatican $91 million. Mussolini gained a measure of approval from devout Italians and the Vatican's support for his fascist government.

Mussolini's economic system, which has come to be known as state capitalism, aimed to abolish class conflict through cooperation between labor and capital, by state force if necessary. In communist theory, labor is the basis of society. In fascism, labor and capital are both instruments of the state. The fascists constructed a corporate state, in which the country was divided into syndicates, or corporations: thirteen at first, later twenty-two. Initially six of these came from labor and an equal number represented capital or management. The thirteenth group was established for the professions. Under state supervision, these bodies were to deal with labor disputes, guarantee adequate wage scales, control prices, and supervise working conditions. After 1926 strikes by workers and lockouts by employers were prohibited.

The pragmatic Mussolini believed that private enterprise was the "most efficient method" of production. "The state intervenes in economic production only when private enterprise fails or is insufficient or when the political interests of the state are involved."[24] Mussolini liked to claim that his structure embodied a classless economic system that stood as one of fascism's greatest contributions to political theory.

Reflecting the practice of the time, the Italians sought economic self-sufficiency, especially in the areas of food supply, power resources, and foreign trade. Wheat production and hydroelectric generating capacity both increased, but the drive for self-sufficiency was carried to an extreme and unprofitable degree. The state, in its quest for economic independence, launched many projects to provide for a home supply of products that could be obtained much more cheaply from other nations.

State and Struggle

Mussolini's ideology built in a haphazard way on the cult of the leader, or "great man." The Italian dictator asserted that "life for the Fascist is a continuous, ceaseless fight . . . ," and "struggle is at the origin of all things."[25] Aside from statements of this type and his economic theories, it is difficult to determine exactly what Mussolini intended fascism to be, beyond being nationalistic, anti-communist, anti-democratic, expansionist, and statist. The lack of a theoretical base for his programs and policies did not concern Mussolini. He simply believed that his corporate state offered a solution to the basic social questions of the twentieth century.[26]

In his speeches, Mussolini referred constantly to the legacy of the Roman empire. He encouraged a high birth rate, but noted that individuals were significant only in so far as they were part of the state. Children were indoctrinated "to believe, to obey, and to fight."

Beneath the talk of struggle and the trappings of grandeur was the reality of Italy. Mussolini was no Stalin or Hitler, and his fascism was a far milder form of totalitarianism than that seen in the USSR or Nazi Germany. The Italian people simply defused many of the potentially atrocious elements of fascist rule. There was no class destruction or genocide in Italy.[27] The Italians, who had endured control by Goths, Normans, French, and Austrians before unification, were survivors.

As in the case of the other dictatorships, Mussolini's programs had some worthwhile features such as slum clearance, rural modernization, and campaigns against illiteracy and malaria. The trains *did* run on time, as Mussolini boasted, and the omnipresent Mafia was temporarily dispersed, with many of its more notable figures fleeing to the United States. But these positive achievements were more than outweighed by the ruinous drives into Ethiopia (see p. 879), excessive military spending, and special benefits to large landowners and industrialists. In 1930 real wages remained low in comparison to the rest of industrialized Europe.

The depression hit Italy later than other countries, but it lasted longer and its effects were devastating to Mussolini's economy. The 33 percent increase in gross national product over that of 1914 was soon wiped out and the old problems of inadequate natural resources, unfavorable balance of trade, and expanding population made the country vulnerable to economic disaster. In 1933 the number of unemployed reached one million and the public debt soared to an alarming level.

Despite a reorganization of the nation in 1934 into twenty-two government controlled corporations, a massive public works program, and agricultural reforms, Italy continued to suffer. In the 1930s Italy's fate and future came to be closely tied to that of Germany.

The German Tragedy

In the first week of Novemver 1918, revolutions broke out all over Germany. Sailors stationed at Kiel rebelled; leftists in Munich revolted. The kaiser fled to Holland after the authority of his government crumbled. On November 9 the chancellor transferred his power to Friedrich Ebert, the leader of the majority party, the Social Democrats, and the new leader announced the establishment of a republic.

Violence spread quickly. The Spartacists, led by Karl Liebknecht and Rosa Luxemburg, who formed the German Communist party at the end of 1918, wanted a complete social and political revolution. Ebert's Social Democrats favored a democratic system in which the property rights would be maintained. At the beginning of 1919 the radical and moderate socialists clashed violently. Experiments in revolutionary government in Bavaria and Berlin horrified traditionalists and even the Social Democrats. In the spring a coalition of forces ranging from moderate

Military training began early in Mussolini's fascist state. There were youth organizations for every age group over the age of four.

Rosa Luxemburg. A radical Marxist and one of the leaders of the Spartacist insurrection in Germany, she was arrested and murdered while being taken to prison.

socialists to right-wing bands of unemployed veterans crushed the leftists and murdered Liebknecht and Luxemburg.

By the end of the year, Germany had weathered the threat of a leftist revolution. Meanwhile, the moderate parties triumphed in elections to select a constitutional convention, with the Social Democrats winning the most votes. The constitution they wrote at Weimar, adopted in mid-1919, created some of the problems that would plague the new government.

The liberal document provided for a president, a chancellor who was responsible to the Reichstag, and national referenda. In addition, the constitution guaranteed the rights of labor, personal liberty, and compulsory education for everyone up to the age of eighteen. Once the new system was put into operation, its weaknesses were readily apparent. The multitude of parties permitted by the constitution condemned the government to function solely by shaky coalitions that often broke apart and forced the president to rule by emergency decree—thus bypassing legal constitutional procedures.

Failure of the Weimar Republic

The Weimar Republic faced overwhelming obstacles. First, the new republic had to live with the stigma of having accepted the Versailles treaty, with its infamous war guilt clause. The defeatist image, combined with opposition from both right- and left-wing extremists, plagued the Weimar moderates. The myth of betrayal in accepting the Versailles treaty helped Field Marshal Paul von Hindenburg, a stalwart Prussian and war hero, win election to the presidency in 1925. In 1927 he formally renounced the theory of war guilt, a politically popular move but one with little effect on the obligation to pay reparations. Although these payments did not noticeably affect the standard of living after 1925, they continued to be a visible sign of defeat—especially insofar as the money used to pay the victorious Allies had to come from foreign loans.[28]

The Weimar government ruled during an economically chaotic period. The government caused inflation, wiped out savings, and destroyed much of the middle classes' confidence, shaking the resolve of the group on whom the fate of the republic rested. Even after 1923, when the economy took a turn for the better, perceptive observers noted that the new prosperity rested on shaky foundations.

During the five years before the depression, Germany rebuilt its industrial plant with the most up-to-date equipment and techniques available to become the second-ranking industrial nation in the world. Rebuilding, however, was financed largely with foreign loans, including some $800 million from the United States.[29] In fact, the Germans borrowed almost twice as much money as they paid out. When the short-term loans came due, the economic bubble burst.

In addition to these economic difficulties, other problems plagued the Weimar government. Many people in Germany still idealized the authoritarian Prussian state. The German General Staff and its numerous and powerful supporters were not placed under effective civilian control. Disregarding the Versailles restrictions on military growth, Germany, in cooperation with the Soviet Union, the other European outcast, increased its armed forces in the 1920s. Probably more dangerous to the Weimar republic's existence was that group of individuals described by Peter Gay as the *Vernunftrepublikaner*, "rational republicans from intellectual choice rather than passionate conviction." These intellectuals, politicians, and businessmen who should have been the strength of Weimar, "learned to live with the Republic . . . but they

George Grosz, *The Pillars of Society*. The satirical painting captures the artist's contempt for militarism, capitalism, the complacent bourgeoisie, and the corrupt society of the Weimar Republic.

never learned to love it and never believed in its future."[30]

The insecurity of the middle classes was the factor most responsible for the failure of the Weimar republic. After the war and inflation, what professionals, white-collar workers, and skilled tradespeople feared most was being dragged down to the level of the masses. Right-wing orators played on such fears and warned that the Weimar republic could not stop the growth of communism. After 1929, the insecurity and discontent of the middle classes crystallized around their children, who blamed their parents for the catastrophe of 1918 and the humiliations that followed. German youth, many of them unemployed after 1929, repudiated the Weimar republic and sought a new savior for their country and themselves. In their rise to power, the Nazis skillfully exploited the fears and hopes of German middle-class youth.

Adolf Hitler

The man who was to "save the fatherland" came from outside its borders. Adolf Hitler (1889–1945) was born in Austria, the son of minor customs official in the Austro-Hungarian monarchy. A mediocre student and something of a loner during his school days, he went to Vienna in 1908 hoping to become an architect or artist. When he failed to gain acceptance to the art institute, his hopes of pursuing a career in art came to an early end.

In the cosmopolitan capital of Vienna, surrounded by a rich diversity of nationalities and religions, Hitler, always the loner, formed his political philosophy. He avidly read pamphlets written by racists who advocated the leader concept and variations of social Darwinism. Hajo Holborn has written that it was on the basis of such "popular and often cranky and murky writings that Hitler formed his original racist and anti-Semitic ideas . . . [He] derived his ideology from few sources, all of them of a rather low type."[31] Anti-Semitism was a popular political platform, and the city's mayor openly espoused it. Hitler also dabbled in Pan-Germanism and Marxian socialism. The swirl of ideas and theories percolated in the brain of the impoverished young man and furnished him with the motivations and ambitions that drove him forward.

Hitler's ability to communicate effectively and persuasively with a majority of the German population was a major asset in his rise to power and popularity. Here he is shown speaking with young members of the Nazi party.

A year before World War I, Hitler moved to Munich where he earned a meager living by selling his drawings. When the conflict erupted in 1914 he joined a German regiment and was sent to France where he fought well and bravely.[32] At the time of the armistice in 1918 he was in a hospital recovering from being blinded in a gas attack. He later said that news of Germany's defeat caused him to turn his face to the wall and weep bitterly.

Following his recovery, Hitler returned to Munich where he was hired by city authorities to act as a special agent to investigate extremists. In the line of duty he checked on a small organization called the German Workers' party. Hitler became attracted to the group's fervently nationalistic doctrine and agreed with their anti-democratic, anti-communist, and anti-Semitic beliefs. He joined the party and soon dominated it.

In 1920, the party took the name National Socialist German Workers' Party, and the words National Socialists (*Nationalsozialistiche*) became abbreviated to Nazi. That same year the party founded a newspaper to spread its views, formed a paramilitary organization from out-of-work veterans—the Storm Troops (SA), and adopted a symbol—the swastika set on a red background. The swastika has been used by many cultures to express the unending cycle of life. The red background symbolized the community of German blood.

More important than the party or its symbol was Hitler, who became widely known for his remarkable powers as a speaker. His ability to arouse and move mass audiences drew large crowds in Munich. Even those who hated all that he stood for were fascinated by his performances. In the early days he would hire a number of beer halls for his adherents and speed from one to the next delivering his emotion-filled message. He called for land reform, the nationalization of trusts, the abolition of all unearned incomes, expansion to include all German-speaking peoples in Europe, and the cancellation of the Versailles treaty. The points of his arguments were less important than the way he delivered them. As the ultimate demagogue he could package his concepts to fit whatever audience he addressed, and his popularity soared.

In November 1923, at the depth of Germany's crisis, Hitler staged his *Putsch*, or revolt, in Munich. Poorly planned and premature, the attempt failed. Hitler was sent to prison after his arrest and there, in comparatively luxurious conditions, he dictated his statement of principles in *Mein Kampf* (*My Struggle*). This work, far from a literary masterpiece, was both an autobiography and a long-winded exposition of Nazi philosophy and objectives.

In *Mein Kampf* Hitler wrote that history is fashioned by great races, of which the Aryan is the finest. The noblest Aryans, according to Hitler, are the Germans, who should rule the world. He charged that the Jews are the archcriminals of all time, that democracy is decadent, and communism is criminal. He stated that expansion into the Soviet Ukraine and the destruction of France are rightful courses for the Germans, who will use war and force, the proper instruments of the "strong," to achieve their goals.

The book, which was initially dismissed as the ravings of a wild man, was widely read in the 1930s. Its sales made Hitler a wealthy man.

Hitler's Chance

Hitler's first attempt to take advantage of economic disaster failed, but he would not fail the second time. After 1930 the *Führer* ("leader") took advantage of the desperate conditions resulting from closed banks, 6 million unemployed, and people roaming the streets for food. Night after night police and military police battled mobs of rioting communists and Nazis. The depression was "the last ingredient in a complicated witches' brew" that led to Hitler's takeover.[33]

The depression brought on the collapse of the moderates' position in the Weimar goverment. In the 1930 elections the Nazis increased their number of seats in the Reichstag from 12 to 107. As conditions grew worse, the hungry and frightened as well as rich and powerful turned to Hitler. The latter groups feared the communists and saw the *Führer* as a useful shield against a proletarian revolution.

As the Nazi movement grew in popularity, Hitler's brilliant propaganda chief, Joseph Goebbels, used every communications device available to convert the masses to Nazism. He staged huge spectacles all over Germany in which thousands of Storm Troopers and the audiences themselves all became supporting players to the "star" of the drama, Adolf Hitler. Such controlled hysteria was more important than the message Hitler continued to repeat.

In March 1932 presidential elections, Hitler lost to Hindenburg. However, after a strong showing by the Nazis in the July Reichstag elections, Hindenburg asked Hitler to join a coalition government. The *Führer* refused, demanding instead the equivalent of dictatorial power. The stalemate led to the dissolution of the Reichstag in September, and for the next two months the government limped along, until a second general election was held. This costly campaign nearly emptied the Nazis' treasury. It was also politically costly in that they lost some of their seats in the Reichstag.

Some observers believed that the Nazis had passed the crest of their power. At this critical point, however, a clique of aristocratic nationalists and powerful industrialists, fearing a leftist revolution, offered Hitler the chancellorship. In January 1933 a mixed cabinet was created with Hitler at the head. Because he did not have a clear majority in the Reichstag, Hitler called another general election for March 5.

The Nazis used all the muscle at their disposal during this campaign. They monopolized the radio broadcasts and the press and their Storm Troopers bullied and beat the voters. Many Germans became disgusted with the strong-arm methods, and the tide definitely swung against the Nazis. Hitler needed a dramatic incident to gain a clear majority in the election.

On the evening of February 27, a fire gutted the Reichstag building. The blaze had been set by a twenty-four-year-old Dutchman, Marinus van der Lubbe, as a statement against capitalism. Apparently acting alone, van de Lubbe gave the Nazis the issue they needed to mobilize their support. Goebbels propaganda machine went into action to blame the fire on the international communist movement. Uncharacteristically, the propaganda minister overplayed the story, and most of the outside world came to believe that the Nazis themselves had set the fire.[34]

Hitler may not have made much profit from the incident internationally, but he did use it to win the election. The Nazis captured 44 percent of the deputies which, with the 8 percent controlled by the Nationalist party, gave them a bare

The Nazis attributed the burning of the Reichstag building to the Communists and used the incident to mobilize support for Hitler.

expressed resentment against the rapid industrialization that had cut many of the people away from their traditional values. But it was primarily the racist elements of Aryan supremacy and hatred of the Jews that set Nazism apart.

War on the Jews

An essential part of the Nazi ideology was an absolute hatred of the Jews, an element of society the Nazi's considered unfit to continue in the new world. After crushing all opposition, real and potential, Hitler began to destroy the Jews. When he took power, he ruled over 500,000 Jews and 66 million Germans. Since 1880 the number of Jews in the population had been declining and would continue to do so through assimilation.[35] Hitler, however, proclaimed that Jews were everywhere and pledged to destroy the Jewish plot to gain control of the world. He based his policy on his own contempt for the Jews, not on the demographic reality.

All Jewish officials in the government lost their jobs, Jews were forbidden to pursue their business and industrial activities, and Jewish businesses were boycotted. Non-Jews snatched up at bargain prices valuable properties formerly owned by Jews. Non-Jewish doctors and

The banners proclaim the Nazis' message to Jews: "The Jews Are Our Ruin." "The Jews Are Our Disaster."

majority. Quickly, Hitler's forces put through the Enabling Act, which gave the *Führer* the right to rule by decree for the next four years.

Every aspect of the Weimar government was overturned, legally. The Nazis crushed all opposition parties and put aside the Weimar constitution, a document that was never formally abolished. Germany for the first time became national, not a federal, state. When Hindenburg died in 1934, Hitler became both chancellor and president. As if to put the world on notice that a renewed German force was rising in central Europe, he withdrew Germany from the League of Nations in 1933. Two years later, he introduced conscription, in defiance of the Versailles treaty.

Hitler proclaimed his regime to be the Third Reich, succeeding the First Reich of Otto the Great, which had lasted from 962 until 1806 and Bismarck's Second Reich, which lasted from 1871 to 1918. Hitler quickly introduced aspects of his Nazi variant of fascism, which was much more pernicious than Mussolini's. Hitler's ideology united the diverse German peoples and lawyers profited when Jewish professionals were forced from their practices. Hitler gained solid supporters among the business and professional classes as he pursued his racist policies.[36] Germans willingly believed that the Jews deserved their fate as the price they had to pay for the Versailles treaty, for the harmful aspects of capitalism, and for internationalism.

Half-hearted international protests failed to limit the anti-Semitic policies. Hitler had many fervent supporters both inside and outside Germany.

The Nazis built concentration camps immediately, but it was some time before they turned into death camps. In the meantime, the immediate pressures of government policies pushed many Jews into committing suicide. It has been estimated that in 1933 alone, 19,000 German citizens killed themselves and 16,000 more died from unexplained causes.

In 1935 the so-called Nuremberg laws came into force. Aryans and non-Aryans were forbid-

Nazi propaganda against the Jews was everywhere. This beer coaster reads, "Who buys from Jews is a traitor."

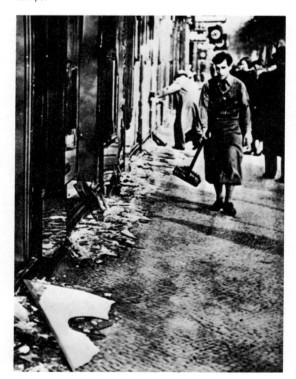

On *Kristallnacht,* thousands of shops owned by Jews were vandalized. Synagogues were set afire, valuables were confiscated, and many Jews were killed or sent to concentration camps.

den to marry. Jews (defined as any person of one-fourth or more Jewish blood) lost their citizenship, and anti-Semitic signs were posted in all public places. (During the 1936 Berlin Olympic games, these notices were taken down in order not to upset visitors.) Increasingly, there was public mention of the "inferior blood" of the Jews. As the state came to need more and more money for armaments, the Jews would be made to pay. This enterprise reached a climax on the evening of November 9, 1938, "the *Kristallnacht* or night of broken glass . . . [when] above the loss of life and heavy property damage, a fine of a billion marks was imposed on the Jewish community in retaliation for the murder of a German diplomat in Paris."[37]

Attacked, deprived of their citizenship and economic opportunities, barred from public service, the Jews of Germany, most of whom considered themselves to be good German citizens, bore the barbaric blows with remarkable resilience. Some, including a number of Germany's best scientific minds, were able to flee the country—a loss that may well have doomed Hitler's war effort. Most stayed. They, and the outside world which showed little concern, did not realize that Hitler's true goal was the "final solution," which would lead to the deaths of at least

6 million Jews throughout central and eastern Europe and the Soviet Union and 3 million others not "lucky" enough to be Aryan.

Nazi Propaganda and Education

Hitler and Goebbels controlled all of the media in the totalitarian Third Reich. A Reich culture cabinet was set up to instill a single pattern of thought in literature, the press, broadcasting, drama, music, art, and the cinema. Forbidden books, including works of some of Germany's most distinguished writers, were seized and destroyed in huge bonfires. The cultural vitality of the Weimar Republic, represented by the likes of Thomas Mann, Erich Maria Remarque, Kurt Weill, and Bertolt Brecht, was replaced by the sterile social realism of the third Reich.

The state used mass popular education, integrated with the German Youth Movement, to drill and regiment boys and girls to be good Nazis. Boys learned above all else to be ready to fight and die for their *Führer*. The girls were prepared for their ultimate task, bearing and rearing the many babies to be needed by the Third Reich.

German universities, once renowned for their academic freedom, became agencies for propagating the racial myths of Nazism and for carrying out far-fetched experiments in human genetic engineering on selected concentration camp inmates. Only good Nazis could go to universities, and professors who did not cooperate with the regime were fired. As Jacob Bronowski wrote, "When Hitler arrived in 1933 the tradition of scholarship in Germany was destroyed, almost overnight."[38]

Religion became entrapped in the totalitarian mechanism. Since Nazism elevated the state above all else, a movement was started to subordinated religion to the Hitler regime. The organized churches originally backed the Nazis warmly, until it became apparent that they were to serve the larger aim of the Aryan cause. The Protestant churches suffered under the Nazi attempt to make them an arm of the state, and several dissident ministers were imprisoned. By

Nazi persecution of Jews sometimes included humiliation. Here, a Nazi officer stops a Jewish businessman and orders him to sweep the gutter.

The Nazi message to women proclaimed that "German girls must be strong, to bear more children for the armies, for death in the victorious battles of the Fatherland."

the end of the decade, the Catholic church too came under constant and subtle attack.

Economic Policies

As in Italy, fascism in Germany revolved around a form of state capitalism. In theory and practice, Nazism retained capitalism and private property. The state, however, rigidly controlled both business and labor. The Nazis dissolved labor unions and enrolled workers and employers in a new organization, the Labor Front. As in Mussolini's corporate state, the right of the workers to strike or of management to call a lockout was denied. The Nazis took compulsory dues from the workers' wages to support Nazi organizations. As a sop, the state set up the "Strength Through Joy" movement, which provided sports events, musical festivals, plays, movies, and vacations at low cost.

The Nazis' ultimate goal was self-sufficiency—autarky, which they would try to reach through complete state control of the economy. They assumed, as did the Fascists in Italy, that only the state could ensure the social harmony needed to attain the maximum productive potential for the state's benefit.

The government tried to solve the nation's very serious economic problems by confiscating valuable Jewish property, laying a huge tax load on the middle class, and increasing the national debt by a third to provide work for the unemployed. To create jobs, the first four-year plan, established in 1933, undertook an extensive program of public works and rearmament. The unemployed were put to work on public projects (especially noteworthy was the system of superhighways, the *Autobahnen*), in munitions factories, and in the army.

Overlapping the first program, the second four-year plan was initiated in 1936. The objective of this plan was to set up an autarkist state. In pursuit of self-sufficiency, substitute commodities—frequently inferior in quality and more costly than similar goods available on the world market—were produced by German laboratories, factories, and mills. The gross national product increased by 68 percent by 1938, but the standard of living did not rise to meet the improved economic growth rate. As of the beginning of World War II, the industrial plant still produced insufficient munitions, even after Germany's appropriation of the Czech Skoda works. Germany's war economy did not hit its stride until 1942.[39]

Conclusion

The Soviet Union, Italy, and Germany each had separate and distinct cultural, social, and political roots which gave unique qualities to the authoritarian governments that developed in them. However, each of the states shared similar circumstances. Each faced economic upheavals, had weak traditions of middle-class dominance and liberal rule, and ambitious individuals ready to take command. In the absence of dynamic democratic forces in the world, these circumstances produced the interwar government structures of the totalitarian states.

To be sure, the communists and the fascists differed in theory: the fascists used capitalism while the communists opposed it; fascism emphasized nationalism while communism preached internationalism; fascism had a weak dogmatic basis while communism was based on Marx's scientific socialism; fascism made use of religion while communism attacked it. But by 1939 the common interests of the totalitarian states, whether fascist or communist, were much more important than theoretical differences. Although they may have been philosophically separate, in their impact on the individual, the totalitarian states were remarkably similar.

In the face of economic chaos and hardship, communism promised a society of well-being and peace, in which each person could work at full potential. In the face of governments marked either by weakness or a desperate pragmatism, the certainty and effectiveness of the fascists was especially attractive.

The ultimate figure symbolizing totalitarian rule was Adolf Hitler. How an advanced "civilized" nation such as Germany could have thrown itself willingly under Hitler's control is one of history's great questions. Other nations had stronger authoritarian traditions, greater economic problems, and more extreme psychological strain. Some observers maintain that there could have been no Third Reich without this unparalleled demagogue, that in fact the reason why Germany erupted as it did is due solely to the happenstance of his personality mixing with the disruptive elements of the postwar world.

Suggestions for Reading

Attempts to analyze the new forms of government in the twentieth century have occupied H. Arendt in *The Origins of Totalitarianism* (Brace Jovanovich, 1968); E. Weber in *Varieties of Fascism* (Anvil, 1973), and C. J. Friedrich and Z. K. Brzezinski in *Totalitarianism, Dictatorship and Autocracy* (Praeger, 1966). Novelist A. Koestler has perhaps best captured the essence of the diminution of the individual in *Darkness at Noon* (Signet, 1961).

Michael Florinsky's analysis of the forces destroying the tsarist regime, *The End of the Russian Empire* (Collier, 1961) is still useful. Alexander Solzhenitsyn beautifully sketches the shifting moods of Russia on the entry into the war in *August 1914* (Bantam, 1974). The best overall survey of Russian history in this century is Donald W. Treadgold, *Twentieth Century Russia* (Houghton Mifflin, 1981) Alec Nove, *The Soviet Economic System* (Allen & Unwin, 1977) is an essential study.

B. Wolfe's classic *Three Who Made a Revolution* (Delta, 1974) is a fine study of Lenin, Trotsky, and Stalin. Adam Ulam's *The Bolsheviks* (Macmillan, 1964) gives a clear discussion of the party's development, while S. Cohen in *Bukharin and the Bolshevik Revolution* (Random House, 1974) provides another perspective. J. L. H. Keep dissects the multifaceted and complex actions of the various elements in Petrograd in *The Russian Revolution: A Study in Mass Mobilization* (Norton, 1977). R. Daniels in *Red October* (Scribner, 1969) gives scholarly depth to the journalistic enthusiasm of John Reed in *Ten Days That Shook the World* (Vintage, 1960).

The most detailed analysis of the Russian revolutions and their aftermath is the multivolumed work of E. H. Carr, *The Russian Revolution* (Pelican, 1966). A discussion of the revolutionary aftermath in the outlying areas is in R. Pipes, *The Formation of the Soviet Union* (Atheneum, 1968). The Civil War is nicely outlined in J. F. N. Bradley's *Civil War in Russia 1917–1920* (Batsford, 1975). George F. Kennan has written the best analysis of Western relations with the young Soviet regime in *Decision to Intervene* (Princeton, 1958) and *Russia and the West Under Lenin and Stalin* (Mentor, 1961). Louis Fischer's *The Soviets in World Affairs* (Vintage, 1960) is a thorough discussion of east-west relations in the 1920s.

Isaac Deutscher has written sharply drawn biographies of *Stalin* (Vintage, 1961) and *Trotsky*, 3 vols. (Vintage, 1965). Placed in the context of A. Rabinowitch's *The Bolsheviks Come to Power* (Norton, 1978), Deutscher's two works provide a compelling description of the generation after 1917. Robert C. Tucker has compiled the most complete set of analyses of the influence of this century's most powerful man in *Stalinism* (Norton, 1977). Important social changes that occurred in the Soviet Union are discussed in H.

Geiger, *The Family in Soviet Russia* (Harvard, 1968). The relationship between the Marxist ideals and the peasantry is discussed in David Mitrany, *Marx Against the Peasant* (Collier, 1961). Stalin's purges are thoroughly analyzed in Robert Conquest, *The Great Terror* (Penguin, 1971). Conquest details the campaign against the peasantry in *Harvest of Sorrow* (Oxford, 1986) and the prison camp system in *Kolyma, the Arctic Death Camps* (Viking, 1978). The most passionate description of the labor camps is Alexander Solzhenitsyn's *The Gulag Archipelago*, 3 vols. (Harper, 1973). R. Medvedev approaches the same subject from another perspective in *Let History Judge* (Random House, 1973). The response of some western intellectuals to events in the Soviet Union is covered in David Caute, *The Fellow Travelers* (MacMillan, 1973).

Events in Italy have been concisely and clearly detailed by C. Seton-Watson in *Italy from Liberalism to Fascism: 1870–1925* (Methuen, 1967). A collection of Musolini's ideas has been compiled in Benito Mussolini, *Fascism: Doctrine and Institution* (Fertig, 1968). A clear and concise study of Italy under Mussolini is Elizabeth Wiskemann, *Fascism in Italy: Its Development and Influence* (St. Martin's, 1969). A more detailed discussion of the Fascist advance can be found in A. Lyttelton, *The Seizure of Power: Fascism in Italy 1919–1929* (Scribner, 1973).

Weimar Germany's brief time in the sun can be studied in A. J. Ryder, *Twentieth Century Germany: From Bismarck to Brandt* (Columbia, 1973) and Erich Eyck, *History of the Weimar Republic*, 2 vols. (Atheneum, 1962). Peter Gay's *Weimar Culture* (Torchbooks, 1968) and *Freud, Jews, and Other Germans* (Oxford, 1979) are penetrating studies of a turbulent time. Fritz Stern, *The Politics of Cultural Despair* (California, 1974) and G. Mosse, *The Crisis of German Ideology* (Grosset and Dunlap, 1964) are essential to understand the mental underpinnings supporting the rise of Hitler. A. Dorpalen, *Hindenburg and the Weimar Republic* (Princeton, 1964) is fine study of the dilemma faced by liberals in the 1920s. J. P. Nettl, *Rosa Luxemburg*, 2 vols. (Oxford, 1966) is a fine study of the socialists' dilemma in Germany.

Alan Bullock, *Hitler: A Study in Tyranny* (Torchbooks, 1964) remains the best biography. John Toland, *Adolf Hitler* (Ballantine Books, 1977) is more readable. William S. Allen, *Nazi Seizure of Power: The Experience of a Single Town 1930–1935* (New Viewpoints, 1969) makes Hitler's takeover more comprehensible. A. Schweitzer, *Big Business and the Third Reich* (Indiana, 1977) details the collaboration between capitalism and fascism. A Beyerchen, *Scientists under Hitler* (Yale, 1977) shows institutional responses to the Führer. K. D. Bracher gives a good structural analysis of fascism in operation in *The German Dictatorship* (Praeger, 1970). D. Schoenbaum discusses the social effects of the Nazi in *Hitler's Social Revolution: Class and Status in Nazi Germany* (Anchor, 1967).

Notes

1. Leonard Schapiro, "Totalitarianism," *Survey*, Autumn, 1969.
2. Michael T. Florinsky, *The End of the Russian Empire* (New York: Collier Books, 1961), pp. 246–248

3. Novelist Alexander Solzhenitsyn captures the mood in chapter 7 of *August 1914*, trans. Michael Glenny (New York: Bantam Books, 1974).

4. Sir Bernard Pares, "Rasputin and the Empress, Authors of the Russian Collapse," *Foreign Affairs*, VI, no. 1 (October 1927), p. 140.

5. *The New Cambridge Modern History*, XII, (Cambridge: Cambridge University Press, 1960), p. 9.

6. Donald W. Treadgold, *Twentieth-Century Russia* (Chicago: Rand McNally & Co., 1959), p. 127.

7. Treadgold, *Twentieth-Century Russia*, p. 133.

8. Alfred G. Meyer, *Leninism* (New York: Frederick A. Praeger, 1957), p. 276.

9. Zbigniew Brzezinski, "The Nature of the Soviet System," in Donald W. Treadgold, ed., *The Development of the USSR* (Seattle: University of Washington Press, 1964), p. 6.

10. J. N. Westwood, *Endurance and Endeavour: Russian History 1812–1986*, 3rd ed. (Oxford: Oxford University Press, 1987), p. 278.

11. Westwood, *Endurance and Endeavor*, p. 276.

12. Isaac Deutscher, *Stalin: A Political Biography*, (New York: Vintage Books, 1961), p. 91.

13. Harry Schwartz, "The Lenin Cult and Its Uses," in *Lenin and Leninism*, ed., Bernard Eissenstat, (Lexington, Mass.: Lexington Books, 1971), p. 238.

14. Brzezinski, "The Nature of the Soviet System," pp. 6–8.

15. See Robert Conquest, *The Harvest of Sorrow: Soviet Collectivization and the Terror-Famine*, (New York: Oxford University Press, 1986).

16. Winston S. Churchill, *The Second World War: The Hinge of Fate*, IV, (New York: Bantam Books, 1962), pp. 434–435.

17. Robert Conquest, *The Great Terror*, (New York: Macmillan Co., 1973), pp. 450–475.

18. Conquest, *The Great Terror*, p. 485.

19. Christopher Seton-Watson, *Italy from Liberalism to Fascism: 1870–1925*, (London: Methuen & Co., 1967), p. 503.

20. Elizabeth Wiskemann, *Fascism in Italy: Its Development and Influence* (New York: St. Martin's Press, 1969), pp. 6–10.

21. Seton-Watson, *Italy from Liberalism to Fascism*, p. 518.

22. Wiskemann, *Fascism in Italy*, p. 12.

23. Benito Mussolini, *Fascism: Doctrine and Institutions*, (New York: Howard Fertig, 1968), p. 38.

24. Wiskemann, *Fascism in Italy*, p. 23.

25. Mussolini, *Fascism*, pp. 35–38.

26. Wiskemann, *Fascism in Italy*, p. 35.

27. Seton-Watson, *Italy from Liberalism to Fascism*, pp. 702–703.

28. Hajo Holborn, *Germany and Europe: Historical Essays* (New York: Anchor Books, 1971), p. 173.

29. A. J. Ryder, *Twentieth-Century Germany: From Bismarck to Brandt* (New York: Columbia University Press, 1973), pp. 245–246.

30. Peter Gay, *Weimar Culture*, (New York: Torchbooks, 1968), p. 23.

31. Holborn, *Germany and Europe*, pp. 221–224.

32. John Toland, *Adolf Hitler* (New York: Ballantine Books, 1977), pp. 79–97.

33. David S. Landes, *The Unbound Prometheus* (Cambridge: Cambridge University Press, 1969), p. 398.

34. Toland, *Adolf Hitler*, p. 406.

35. Karl A. Schleunes, *The Twisted Road to Auschwitz: Nazi Policy toward German Jews: 1933–1939*, (Urbana: University of Illinois Press, 1970), pp. 37–38.

36. Landes, *The Unbound Prometheus*, pp. 416–417

37. Ryder, *Twentieth-Century Germany*, p. 348.

38. J. Bronowski, *The Ascent of Man* (Boston: Little, Brown and Co., 1973), p. 367.

39. Landes, *The Unbound Prometheus*, pp. 400, 406, 413.

Chapter 33

Asia and Africa in the Interwar World

Fifty years of aggressive expansion by the West had spread a veneer of Europeanization on its holdings. At the same time, the imperialists also exported Western social and political ideas to their colonies. The explosive concepts of nationalism and self-rule, tied to Western science and technology, revitalized the societies of Asia and Africa.

World War I and its aftershocks strengthened independence movements in Africa and Asia. Nationalist campaigns, present in embryonic form in most of the colonies before the war, grew rapidly in virtually all of the European possessions and mandates.

Japan emerged as a world power, but by the late 1920s the impact of the depression and a population crisis threatened its weakly rooted democratic institutions. China endured revolution and civil strife as the areas of Southeast Asia pursued independence. India's independence movement strengthened under the leadership of Mohandas Gandhi. Across the Islamic world and Africa, indigenous peoples emerged from under the shadow of European domination, which was in full retreat by the end of the 1930s.

Japan

Japan's victory over Russia in the 1904–1905 Russo-Japanese War served notice of the success of Japan's Meiji era reforms. In two generations, the island nation had changed from a static, mostly agricultural nation into a modern, highly industrialized state. There were, however, serious problems. The rapidly increasing population strained the nation's limited size and resources.

In the government, liberal statesmen tried to strengthen democratic practices in a hostile social and political setting. Ten years after World War I, population and economic pressures combined with a revival of militarism to launch the Japanese toward war and dictatorship.

The Asian Great Power

Japan's expansionist goals in China remained remarkably consistent after the Meiji restoration. In 1914 the Japanese ordered the Germans to remove their warships from the Far East and to surrender Kiaochow territory in China to Japan. When the Germans refused to reply to this order, Japan declared war on Germany and seized the territory without consulting China. In 1915, Japan presented China with the Twenty-one Demands, a document whose frank statement of Japan's aims on the Asian continent startled the world.

The Chinese government, weakened by a half century of decline and revolution, could do little but give in to the first sixteen demands, reserving the final five for further consideration. By leaking news of the demands to the press, the Chinese attracted the attention of the United States. Washington kept China from falling totally under Japan's domination. Nevertheless, the Chinese had no choice but to recognize Japan's authority in Shantung province and extend Japanese land and rail concessions in southern Manchuria. In 1917 the Allies secretly agreed to support Japanese claims against China, in return for Japan's respecting the Open Door policy.

Japan's sphere of economic dominance expanded during the 1920s in Shantung, Manchuria, and south Mongolia: It also occupied the

Kita Ikki's Plan for Japan

While liberal Europe struggled with the burdens of victory, Japan experimented with a variety of governmental approaches. A radical social and economic concept was enunciated by Kita Ikki, who was executed in 1937.

Suspension of the Constitution: In order to establish a firm base for national reorganization, the Emperor, with the aid of the entire Japanese nation and by invoking his imperial prerogatives, shall suspend the Constitution for a period of three years, dissolve the two houses of the Diet, and place the entire country under martial law.

The true significance of the Emperor: We must make clear the fundamental principle that the Emperor is the sole representative of the people and the pillar of the state. . . .

Abolition of the peerage system: By abolishing the peerage system, we shall be able to remove the feudal aristocracy which constitutes a barrier between the Emperor and the people. In this way the spirit of the Meiji Restoration shall be proclaimed. . . .

The members of the Deliberative Council shall consist of men distinguished in various fields of activities, elected by each other or appointed by the Emperor.

Limitation on private property: No Japanese family shall possess property in excess of one million yen. A similar limitation shall apply to Japanese citizens holding property overseas. No one shall be permitted to make a gift of property to those related by blood or to others, or to transfer his property by other means with the intent of circumventing this limitation.

Nationalization of excess amount over limitation on private property: Any amount which exceeds the limitation on private property shall revert to the state without compensation. No one shall be permitted to resort to the protection of present laws in order to avoid remitting such excess amount. Anyone who violates these provisions shall be deemed a person thinking lightly of the example set by the Emperor and endangering the basis of national reorganization. As such, during the time martial law is in effect, he shall be charged with the crimes of endangering the person of the Emperor and engaging in internal revolt and shall be punished by death.

Limitation on private landholding: No Japanese family shall hold land in excess of 100,000 yen in current market value. . . .

. . . Lands held in excess of the limitation on private landholding shall revert to the state. . . .

Distribution of profits to workers: One half of the net profits of private industries shall be distributed to workers employed in such industries. . . .

Continuation of the conscript system: The state, having rights to existence and development among the nations of the world, shall maintain the present conscript system in perpetuity. . . .

Positive right to start war: In addition to the right to self-defense, the state shall have the right to start a war on behalf of other nations and races unjustly oppressed by a third power. (As a matter of real concern today, the state shall have the right to start a war to aid the independence of India and preservation of China's integrity.)

As a result of its own development, the state shall also have the right to start a war against those nations who occupy large colonies illegally and ignore the heavenly way of the co-existence of all humanity. (As a matter of real concern today, the state shall have the right to start a war against those nations which occupy Australia and Far Eastern Siberia for the purpose of acquiring them.)

From David John Lu, *Sources of Japanese History*, vol. 2 (New York: McGraw-Hill, 1974), pp. 131–136. Reprinted by permission.

former German islands north of the equator (see map below). The Washington Conference of 1921 acknowledged the Japanese navy as the third most powerful in the world. The signatories (United States, Great Britain, France, Italy, Japan, Belgium, Netherlands, Portugal, and China) of the Nine-Power Treaty, signed in Washington in 1922, agreed to respect the independence, sovereignty, territoriality, and administrative integrity of China and to respect the Open Door policy.

The United States and Britain, however, were alarmed by the growth of Japanese power. By 1931, Japanese investments in China were second only to those of Great Britain, constituting around 35 percent of all foreign investment in China. That same year, responding to population pressures and resource needs, the Japanese disregarded international treaties and opinions and invaded China.

Authoritarian Victory

From 1889 to 1918 an aristocratic oligarchy of elder statesmen called the *Genro* controlled

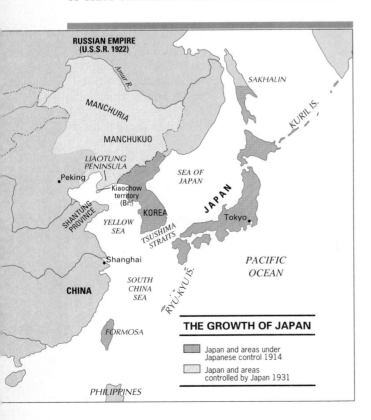

THE GROWTH OF JAPAN

- ■ Japan and areas under Japanese control 1914
- □ Japan and areas controlled by Japan 1931

the Japanese government. By the 1920s most of the patriarchs had passed away and the field of politics was open to new blood. Hara Takashi, the first commoner to hold the post of prime minister, was elected to the office in 1918.

Over the next twelve years, Japan seemed to be moving toward the establishment of a democratic, parliamentary government under its new political leaders. However, the liberals faced serious obstacles. There was no widespread tradition of democratic or parliamentary practices in Japan. Japanese society had concentrated wealth and power in the hands of a few families, while the traditional culture encouraged a militaristic system of values. The secret societies and the cult of Shintoism favored authoritarianism over liberalism.

Despite these obstacles, liberals in the Japanese parliament, the Diet, showed great promise and courage as they tried to lead the nation away from militant nationalism. They pressed for reforms at home while criticizing the imperialistic intervention of the Japanese army in Siberia during the Russian Civil War. Although the democratic cause suffered a serious setback in 1921 with the assassination of Prime Minister Hara, the liberals continued their work. Passage of the Universal Manhood Suffrage Bill in 1925 strengthened the liberal base. By 1930, after a reactionary interlude, Prime Minister Hamaguchi Yuko established the most liberal government Japan had ever had.

As was the case in Europe, as long as the economy remained strong, the liberals did well. In the 1920s the Japanese built thousands of factories that turned out products that enabled Japan to claim a major share of the world textile market and to flood the world with mass-produced, cheap, low-quality goods. Japanese industrialists were quick to adopt modern machine techniques and slow to raise wages A few giant concerns working together controlled the greater part of the country's wealth.

Prosperity—and by implication the liberals' position—rested on fragile foundations. Japan lacked natural resources, and its population grew at a rapid rate. In 1920 there were more than 55 million inhabitants. Eleven years later there were 65 million people, crowded into a land area smaller than the state of California. By 1932 the average annual population increase was

Japan's invasion of Manchuria in September 1931 violated a number of treaties, covenants, agreements, and promises that were made after World War I in the hope of creating a worldwide and lasting peace.

1 million. The Japanese economy had to create 250,000 jobs yearly and find the food to feed the growing population. Up to 1930 Japan paid its way by expanding its exports. But between 1929 and 1931, the effects of the great depression cut export trade in half. Unemployment soared, leading to wage cuts and strikes. As in Germany on the eve of Adolf Hitler's rise to power, frustration became widespread among the younger generation.

In response to the economic crisis, Prime Minister Hamaguchi adopted measured fiscal reforms and a moderate foreign policy. The first approach failed to satisfy the workers and the second approach offended the militarists. Hamaguchi was shot in November 1930 and died the following spring. The assassin's bullets dealt a blow to Japanese liberalism which was not overcome until after World War II.

A new group of ultranationalistic and militaristic leaders came to power, ruling not through a charismatic leader as in Germany and Italy but through a military clique. The members of the clique, who had nothing but contempt for democracy and peaceful policies, terrorized the civilian members of the government, plotted to shelve parliamentary government, and planned to use force on the mainland of China. Their goals were to gain resources for the economy, living space for the population, markets for Japanese goods, and cultural domination throughout Asia. They referred to their program as a "beneficial mission" and called it the "New Order in Asia." The military clique took its first step with the invasion of Manchuria in 1931, setting off the sequence of aggression that would lead to World War II (see ch. 34).

China: Revolution and Republic

During the nineteenth century China endured one of the darkest periods in its four thousand years. The old Confucianist, imperial government failed as China lost territory, suffered under the imposition of extraterritoriality, and witnessed its customs and tariffs come under foreign control. The 1898 reform movement and the Boxer Uprising of 1899–1900 were, in effect, two attempts to remove the Manchu dynasty. Thereafter, there were two approaches to change: the constitutionalist attempt to set up representative government and the revolutionary program to overthrow the dynasty.

Sun Yat-sen and Revolution

Sun Yat-sen (1867–1925) proved to be the key figure in the transition from the old to the new China. The son of a tenant farmer born near Canton, he received a western education in Hawaii. He converted to Christianity and in 1892 earned a diploma in medicine in Hong Kong. Soon, he became a leader in the Chinese nationalist movement, directing his energies toward the overthrow of the Manchus and the formation of a republic. For his activities, he was forced into exile in 1895 and thereafter traveled widely throughout the world seeking political and financial aid from Chinese living abroad. During that

Statesman and revolutionary leader Sun Yat-sen, the organizer of the *Kuomintang,* is known as the father of modern China.

period he organized the movement that eventually became the *Kuomintang,* or Nationalist party.[1]

In 1911 a revolt broke out in China over a foreign loan to finance railways. The outbreak spread like wildfire throughout the country. Yuan Shih-kai (1859–1916), an outstanding north Chinese military leader with modern ideas, persuaded the imperial clan that the Manchu dynasty was doomed. In 1912 the child emperor abdicated, and Yuan was asked to form a republican government. Although a few months earlier a revolutionary assembly in Nanking had elected Sun president of the new republic, he stepped aside in the interest of national unity and the Nanking assembly elected Yuan.

During the next fifteen years China went through a period quite similar to the dynastic interregnums that had punctuated its previous history. Trouble broke out in 1913 when Yuan negotiated a large loan with bankers from Britain, France, Germany, and Russia that gave these powers substantial influence in the government of the republic. Resentment over this agreement led to a new rebellion, backed by Sun. Yuan still had control of the army and put down the revolt, forcing Sun to flee to Japan until 1917. Overestimating his strength, Yuan dismissed parliament and proclaimed the restoration of the monarchy with himself as emperor. This act sparked another rebellion, and this time Yuan's prestige evaporated. In June 1916 the now discredited dictator died.

China then entered a period of political anarchy. Warlords heading armies based on local power centers marched across the country seeking control of Peking. Possession of the city apparently was seen as conferring legitimacy on its occupier. For a time, China was divided between two would-be governments, one in the north at Peking and the other in the south at Canton. The southern force was composed largely of those who had engineered the revolution of 1911–1912. The Canton government elected Sun president in 1921, and he remained there until his death in 1925, unable to unify the country.

Sun's genius was in making revolution, not in governing. His social ideology, however, provided some key elements for twentieth-century Chinese political theory. Sun's *The Three Principles of the People,* developed from a series of

Chiang Kai-shek, successor to Sun Yat-sen as leader of the *Kuomintang,* broke with the Communists in 1927 and set up a new government at Nanking.

lectures, became the political manual of the *Kuomintang.* The three principles are: nationalism, the liberation of China from foreign domination and the creation of a Chinese nation-state; democracy, "government by the people and for the people"; and livelihood, economic security for all the people.

In 1923, after failing to obtain from the West aid to overthrow the Peking government, Sun turned to the Soviet Union for advice and assistance. A military and political advisory group arrived, led by Michael Borodin. Under Borodin's guidance, the *Kuomintang* adopted many of the planks of the program subscribed to by the Soviet Communist Party as well as the party's organizational structure.

Chiang Kai-shek "Unites" China

Sun's successor as leader of the *Kuomintang* was Chiang Kai-shek (1886–1975), the son of a minor landlord. Chiang studied at a military academy in Japan before becoming caught up with Sun's vision for a new China. He returned home to take an active part in the revolution. His obvious abilities and loyalty attracted Sun's attention, and in 1923 he was sent to Russia for a brief period of training. Before establishing himself as leader of the *Kuomintang*, he formed a united force and began to drive northward in 1926. Chiang's group encountered little

opposition, and by the early spring of the following year they reached the Yangtze valley. However, dissension broke out between the radical and the conservative elements of the *Kuomintang*, and Chiang crushed the communists in his ranks when he occupied Shanghai. He went on to create a moderate government at Nanking, and before the end of 1927, public opinion had swung behind his regime.

Chiang continued to purge the leftist elements. The end of the *Kuomintang* alliance with the communists was written in blood, when a proletarian uprising in Canton was crushed, with the loss of 5,000 lives. The Soviet advisers returned to Moscow and many radicals, including the widow of Sun Yat-sen, were driven into exile. The Chinese communists fled to the hills and mountains of China.

The 1927 split of the *Kuomintang* is a major event in modern Chinese history. Not only were Marxist radicals ousted, but many moderate liberals also began to be eliminated. Chiang built his strength on the urban professional, banking, and merchant classes. His government depended for financial support on the foreign bankers of Shanghai. The regime took on a conservative, urban character, far removed from the huge mass of the Chinese people, the peasantry in the countryside.

With his government established at Nanking, Chiang, his armies, and his warlord allies again

THE KUOMINTANG REGIME

☐ Kuomintang regime 1928-1937
☐ Warlords' spheres of influence
■ Areas under Japanese control 1933
← Route of the Long March

U.S.S.R.

MONGOLIA

Amur R.

Peking

Huang Ho R.

Yenan

SEA OF JAPAN

KOREA

CHINA

JAPAN

Nanking

Yangtze R.

EAST CHINA SEA

Juichin

PACIFIC OCEAN

BURMA

Mekong R.

FORMOSA

SIAM FRENCH INDOCHINA

HAINAN SOUTH CHINA SEA

PHILIPPINE ISLANDS

more colloquial written language, while scholars labored for the adoption of Mandarin (a standardized version of the Peking dialect, used in government affairs) so that people from all parts of China could speak together. Social customs changed and western dress and folkways appeared. Large cities installed telephones, electric lights, modern water systems, and movie palaces. Much of the import of western conveniences was paid for by the foreign entrepreneurs who controlled most of Chinese industry. Despite all the changes, civil war, a weak currency, inadequate transportation, and grinding poverty kept China an underdeveloped nation.

A fervent patriot, Chiang unfortunately had little appreciation for the social and economic problems of his nation. The people were still tyrannized by bandits while famine in the northwest of the country claimed the lives of millions. Instead of responding to the plight of his nation, Chiang, a Christian whose faith incorporated much from Confucian principles, pursued the moral regeneration of his people through a combination of his religion and his culture–the New Life Movement which he established in the mid-1930s. He would have done better to appreciate the intellectual changes taking place and the social and economic hopes of the peasants.

The New Culture Movement and Chinese Communism

A Chinese intellectual revolution began at Peking University during World War I and spread from there to students all over the country.[2] The first influential voice for this intellectual group was the magazine *New Youth*. This journal transmitted the ideas of students who had returned from universities in the United States and Europe on subjects ranging from western science to liberalism to socialism. These students wanted to establish a new order and a new set of values to replace much of the old Confucian tradition.

The students became disillusioned with the west after the Versailles peace treaty, which gave Chinese Shantung to Japan. A violent student demonstration on May 4, 1919, featured virulent anti-western sentiment. A new ideological orientation began in the New Culture Movement. Study groups were formed, especially at Peking university where professors and students began

moved north and occupied Peking. China once again appeared to be united, but it was a unity more in appearance than in fact (see map above). While large areas of the country had been conquered by Chiang's forces, other regions came under the *Kuomintang* by agreement between Chiang and local warlords. In theory the warlords were subordinate to Chiang, but they maintained power in their spheres of influence.

Chinese foreign relations improved during the 1920s. The Nine-Power Treaty guaranteed China's territorial integrity, and China was a member of the League of Nations. The government regained the right to set its own tariffs in 1929, when ten foreign powers gave up or lost the right of extraterritoriality. Partially in response to the development foreign trade was seven times as great in 1929 as in 1894. In addition, while the liberals were in power in Japan, Tokyo was relatively conciliatory toward China.

Chiang engineered substantial changes in Chinese urban life. More Chinese received education. Linguists championed the use of a new, to read Marx and Lenin and to apply their thoughts to China. Lenin's analysis of and attack on imperialism struck a responsive chord.

With some guidance from Russian Comintern agents, the First Congress of the Chinese Communist Party was held in July 1921. A young student at Peking University named Mao Tse-tung was a delegate. About the same time, Chinese worker-students in France established the Young China Communist party in Paris. One of its leaders was Chou En-lai, later premier of Chinese People's Republic.

Mao Tse-tung (1893–1976) was born in Hunan province, a traditional center of Chinese revolutionary activity.[3] In 1918 he went to Peking University where he worked as library assistant under Li Ta-chao, the founder of an important Marxist study group and one of the founders of the Chinese Communist Party. Mao began to

Mao Tse-tung has been called the "Stalin" of Chinese communism.

emerge as a distinctive leader with a new program for revolution when he wrote a report for the Communist party in 1927 about the peasant movement in Hunan. In that document Mao expressed his belief that the revolution must base itself on peasant uprisings, a view that was condemned by the Central Committee of the Chinese Communist party, which closely adhered to the Russian policy of basing the revolution on the urban proletariat.

Mao led a Hunanese peasant uprising that became known as the Autumn Harvest Uprising. It was crushed, and in May 1928 Mao and other Communist leaders joined forces in the border region of Hunan and Kiangsi provinces. Acutely conscious of peasant needs, Mao organized the peasants in his region into a Chinese "soviet." Other Communist leaders did the same in other regions, and in 1931 delegates from the various local soviets in China met and proclaimed the birth of the Chinese Soviet Republic. Even though Chiang Kai-shek destroyed the Shanghai apparatus of the Communist party, Mao and his colleagues could still claim control of regions containing 9 million people.

Mao's success as a Communist leader stemmed from his observation that it was the Chinese peasant, not the urban worker, who could be made the agent of the revolution. In pursuit of this objective, Mao encouraged the establishment of farmers' cooperatives and equitable tax systems. He also redistributed land in the areas he controlled. Mao's achievements worried Chiang, who between 1931 and 1934 launched five military campaigns against the Communists—the last one using one million men and a German military staff. To avoid annihilation, the communists made their famous Long March 2000 miles to the northwest. Only a remnant of the original force reached Yenan, in Shensi province, where in 1935 a new Communist stronghold was set up.

Nationalism in Southeast Asia

The drive for independence became stronger in Southeast Asia between the two world wars. Taking advantage of the war-weakened colonialists, local leaders adapted the ideologies of the day—whether Wilson's "self-determination of peoples" or socialism, or a combination of the two—to their campaigns for freedom. The example of Japan's rise to the status of a great power showed that the west had no monopoly on technology and organization.

Populations grew dramatically in Southeast Asia during the interwar period. From 1930 to 1960 the number of people in Siam, Malaya, and the Philippines increased more than 100 percent; in Indonesia, Burma, and Indochina the number increased more than 50 percent. Population pressures naturally contributed to unrest.

Certain economic trends also characterized most of the region. The imperialist powers continued to exploit their colonies, ignoring the democratic rhetoric they had mouthed during the First World War. Europe's draining of the area's resources coupled with an irregular world market which crashed in 1929 led to increased hardship in much of the region. The Chinese played an increasingly important role as merchants and middlemen in the local economies. In Burma, Indians played the same role. European and Chinese capital investment encouraged a rapid growth in exports of minerals and forest products. In Siam, Indochina, and a few other countries rice production grew more rapidly than population, and as a result the economies became based on rice exports.

Throughout the area the élite became assimilated to European culture as more and more young people went to the "parent countries" to be educated. The masses, however, were barely touched by this process. The result was a growing cultural and social divide between the local leadership and the people at large. With the exception of the United States in the Philippines and Great Britain in Burma and Ceylon, none of the imperialist powers undertook to prepare their colonies for eventual self-government, as they had no intention of letting them go.

Indochina

French rule in Indochina was in some ways the least enlightened of all the colonial regimes in Southeast Asia. In 1941, for example, the colonial government had the highest proportion of Europeans in its service of any in the region—some 5100 French officials to 27,000

Indochinese.[4] Four fifths of the population was illiterate, and of the more than 21 million people, only about 500,000 children received any higher education. French rule was characterized by politial oppression, severe economic exploitation, and a rigid and stagnant traditional culture.

Revolution seemed the answer to Vietnam's problems. During World War I over 100,000 Vietnamese laborers and soldiers were sent to France, where many of them came in contact with liberal and radical thinking, which they then brought home. The Vietnam Nationalist party, patterned organizationally and intellectually on the Chinese *Kuomintang*, was officially outlawed, and by the late 1920s resorted to terrorism as the only form of political expression open to it.

Communism rapidly became the major revolutionary ideology in the French colony. In 1920 a young Vietnamese calling himself Nguyen Ai Quoc ("Nguyen, the Patriot"), and later known to

Ho Chi Minh found in Communist ideology a road to his ultimate goal: the liberation of his native Vietnam.

the world as Ho Chi Minh (1890–1969), participated actively in the formation of the communist party in France. In 1930 he organized in Hong Kong what eventually became the Vietnamese (later Indochinese) Communist party. Communist ideas and organization spread throughout Vietnam in the 1930s while the colonial government answered Vietnamese uprisings against French oppression with strong repressive measures. As a result, when World War II began, the communist party was the major vehicle for the expression of Vietnamese nationalism.

The Philippines

The United States established its form of government in the Philippines on July 4, 1901, under William H. Taft as civil governor of the area. President McKinley declared that the primary aim was to prepare the Filipinos for self-government. The first elections were held in 1907 and by 1913 Filipinos dominated both houses of the legislature, while an American remained as governor-general. By 1935, when the Philippine Commonwealth was inaugurated with a new constitution and the promise of independence within ten years, the islands had developed a complex governmental structure and a sophisticated political life.

Economic developments, however, constricted Philippine independence at the same time that the islands were being prepared for self-rule. Before the outbreak of World War II, four-fifths of Philippine exports went to the United States and three-fifths of its imports came from America. Like most underdeveloped economies, the export trade was dominated by a very few products: hemp, sugar, coconuts, and tobacco. Independence, with its accompanying imposition of tariffs would have been economically difficult. The United States had prevented the development of a colonial-type plantation economy by forbidding non-Filipinos to own plantation lands, but native landlordism was rampant, and the oppressed peasants launched a brief uprising in the mid-1930s.

Dutch East Indies

Unlike other western imperial powers which loosened their controls over their colonies, either through domestic weakness or planned decolonization, the Dutch increased their control in the East Indies. Stretched over 3100 miles of water, the numerous islands of Indonesia were integrated into a communications and political system by the Dutch. At the same time, the strict limits put on the power and advancement of native élites led to bitterness and resentment. Dutch imperialism strengthened Indonesian self-consciousness and nationalism.

A communist party, organized in 1920, attempted unsuccessful uprisings in Java and Sumatra in late 1926 and early 1927. Police repression increased. In 1930 the Dutch attempted to crush the Nationalist party and arrested one of its leaders, Achmed Sukarno (1901–1970), the man who after World War II became the first president of independent Indonesia. The Dutch banned all discussions of any subject that might involve the concept of national independence. Even the name Indonesia was censored from official publications.

Siam/Thailand

In the interwar period, Siam, which changed its name to Thailand in 1939, continued to modernize. Educational improvements, economic growth, and increased political sophistication contrasted sharply, however, with the political and administrative domination of the country by the rather extensive royal family. In 1932 a French-trained law professor led a bloodless coup d'état, and a new constitution was promulgated with the agreement of the king, turning him into a reigning, not ruling, monarch. Since then the country has been ruled by an alliance of army and oligarchy.

Burma and Malaya

The Burmese independence movement modeled itself on the tactics practiced by the Indian National Congress, but Buddhism provided the focus for organizational activity. A Young Men's Buddhist Association, formed in 1906, organized a General Council of Burmese Associations in 1921. The General Council brought nationalism to the village level.

British promises to promote Indian self-government created a similar demand in Burma, and in 1937 Burma was administratively split off from India. A parliamentary sytem was begun-with a Burmese prime minister under a British governor who held responsibility for foreign relations, defense, and finance.

No strong nationalist movement developed in Malaya, perhaps because the large ethnic groups living there distrusted one another more than they felt the need to make common cause against the British. The Malays feared Chinese ethnic domination; eventually, the Chinese came to outnumber the Malays themselves. The Chinese were primarily interested in commerce and in developments in China. The Indians, for the most part workers on plantations and in mines, were loyal to India as their homeland.

India: The Drive for Independence

Before 1914, many observers had predicted that in the event of war, Great Britain would find India a serious liability. When hostilities began, however, nearly all anti-British activity against Britain in India ceased.

Gradual Steps Toward Self-Rule

By 1917 Indian nationalists expected immediate compensation for their loyalty in terms of more self-government. The British, however, pursued a policy stressing gradual development of self-government within the British Empire. To this end, in 1918, a British commission was sent to India to study the question of self-government within the British Empire. To this end, in 1918, a British commission was sent to India to study the question of self-government and recommended a new constitution. The Government of India Act provided for a system of double government in the provinces by which certain powers were reserved to the British while the provincial legislatures were granted other, generally lesser, powers.

To Indian nationalists, this act represented only a small step toward self-rule. Their frustrations led to the outbreak of a struggle with the British in 1919. In an ill-advised move the British passed the Rowlatt Act (1919), which allowed the police and other officials extraordinary powers in searching out subversive activity. Although the act was never enforced, it was deeply resented as a symbol of repression.

Disgruntled and disheartened by the Government of India Act and the violence that followed, many nationalists demanded sweeping changes. Britain, however, lacked a comprehensive plan to grant independence, and a large segment of British public opinion strongly opposed any threat to the breakup of the empire, such as Indian independence.

Gandhi and Civil Disobedience

The foremost nationalist leader in India was Mohandas K. Gandhi (1869–1948). Born of middle-class parents, Gandhi had been sent to London to study law; later he went to South Africa, where he built up a lucrative practice. During these years his standard of values changed completely. The new Gandhi repudiated wealth, practiced ascetic self-denial, condemned violence, and believed firmly that true happiness could be achieved only by service to others.

Gandhi began his career as a reformer and champion of his people in South Africa. The Indians there were subject to numerous legal restrictions which hampered their freedom of movement, prevented them from buying property, and imposed added taxes on them. Disdaining the use of violence, Gandhi believed that a just cause will triumph if its supporters attempt to convince those in power of injustices by practicing "civil disobedience." With Gandhi as their leader, the Indians in South Africa carried out various protests, including hunger strikes. They refused to work, held mass demonstrations, and marched into areas where their presence was forbidden by law. By the use of such passive resistance, or noncooperation, Gandhi forced the government to remove some restrictions.

When he returned to his native land shortly after the outbreak of World War I, Gandhi was welcomed as a hero. During the war he cooperated with the British government, but the disappointing concessions in the new constitution and the Rowlatt Act led him to announce his determination to force the British to give India self-rule.

Mohandas Gandhi used the weapons of nonviolent protest and noncooperation in his struggle to win independence for India. An immensely popular and beloved leader, Gandhi was given the title Mahatma, or "Great Soul," by the people.

Gandhi introduced his campaign in 1919. A mass strike was declared in which all work was to cease and the population was to pray and fast. Contrary to Gandhi's plan, however, riots took place. After Europeans were killed soldiers came in to restore order. Although the British forbade public gatherings, a large body of unarmed Indians assembled at Amritsar. British troops broke up the meeting, killing hundreds.

This incident put a temporary end to all hope of cooperation between Indians and Britons. Many British colonials supported the bloody suppression of the Amritsar demonstrators. Arrested in 1922, Gandhi seemed to welcome being placed on trial; he assured the British magistrate that the only alternative to permitting him to continue his opposition was to imprison him. Sentenced to six years imprisonment, Gandhi suffered a temporary eclipse.

Road to Reform

A promising road to conciliation opened in 1930 when a series of round-table conferences was arranged in London. A new scheme of government was hammered out, providing for a federal union, which would bring the British provinces and the states of the princes into a central government. In the provinces the double government system was displaced by full autonomy, while in the federal government all powers were transferred to the Indians except defense and foreign affairs, which remained in the control of the British viceroy. From 1937, when this new Government of India Act came into operation, until 1939 the scheme of self-government worked smoothly. The possibility of federation, however, faded when the native princes refused to enter the central government.

The new system of government failed to satisfy the demands of the Indian nationalists, who continued to push for complete independence through demonstrations and articles in the popular press. The chief element in the independence movement was the powerful Indian National Congress, which had become the organ of the militant nationalists. The membership of several million was predominantly Hindu but also included many Muslims and members of other religious groups. Soon after the First World War, the congress had come under the leadership of Gandhi, whose personal following among the people was the chief source of the party's tremendous influence.

Gandhi transformed the congress, which had been primarily a middle-class organization, into a mass movement that included the peasants. Gandhi had other goals besides freeing India. He sought to end all drinking, raise the status of women, remove the stigma attached to the untouchables, and bring about cooperation between Hindus and Muslims. Permeating all of Gandhi's ideas and actions was his belief in nonviolence; he was convinced that injustices could be destroyed only through the forces of love, unselfishness, and patience.

In the 1930s Gandhi shared his leadership with Jawaharlal Nehru (1889–1964), who came from a Brahmin family of ancient lineage. In his youth Nehru had all of the advantages of wealth:

Jawaharlal Nehru, along with Gandhi a leader of Indian nationalism, served as prime minister of independent India.

English tutors, enrollment in the English public schools of Harrow and later Trinity College, Cambridge, where he obtained his B.A. in 1910. Two years later he was admitted to the bar. On his return to India, he showed little interest in the law and gradually became completely absorbed in his country's fight for freedom.

A devoted friend and disciple of Gandhi, Nehru could not agree with the older leader's mystical rejection of much of the modern world. At heart, Nehru was a rationalist, an agnostic, an ardent believer in science and a foe of all supernaturalism. Above all, he was a blend of the cultures of both East and West, perhaps with the latter predominating. As he himself said: "I have become a queer mixture of the East and the West, out of place everywhere, at home nowhere. Perhaps my thoughts and approach to life are more akin to what is called Western than Eastern, but India calls me."[5]

The Hindu-Muslim Clash

India is the classic example of a fragmented society. The major division in India was between the Hindus and Muslims, who were poles apart in culture and values. As Britain's imperial control over India began to show signs of ending, hostility between the two communities surfaced. Many Muslims believed that with independence they would become a powerless minority. Thus the conflict was a struggle for political survival.

In the early 1930s the Muslim League, a political party, began to challenge the claim of the Indian National Congress to represent all of India. The leader of the Muslim League, Muhammad Ali Jinnah (1876–1948), originally a member of the congress and once dubbed by Indian nationalists the "ambassador of Hindu-Muslim unity," had become alienated by what he considered the Hindu domination of the congress and its claim to be the sole agent of Indian nationalism.

The Muslim League began to advance the "two-nation" theory, and in 1933 a group of Muslim students at Cambridge Uniersity circulated a pamphlet for the establishment of a new state to be known as Pakistan. This leaflet was the opening act of a bloody drama. In 1939 the Muslim League emphatically denounced any scheme of self-government of India that would mean majority Hindu rule.[6]

Changes in the Muslim World

The Ottoman empire clung to a shaky dominance over the Muslim world of the Middle East and North Africa at the beginning of the nineteenth century. With the exception of Morocco, North Africa was nominally ruled by the Turkish sultan. By the end of the century, however, Europeans dominated North Africa, while the Middle East discontentedly remained under the sultan. World War I and its aftershocks fundamentally changed this situation.

The Arab Revolt

In 1913 an Arab Congress meeting in Paris demanded home rule and equality with the Turks in the Ottoman Empire. Because the Middle East was so important to Britain, the London government followed the Arab movement with great interest, especially after Turkey joined the Central Powers in the war. In the latter half of 1915, the British High Commissioner in Cairo carried on an extensive correspondence with Sherif Husein of Mecca (Husein ibn-Ali, 1856–1931), guardian of Islam's holy places. The British told Husein that in the event of an Arab revolt against the Turks, Great Britain would recognize Arab independence except in those regions of coastal Syria that were not wholly Arab—presumably excluding Palestine—and in those places that might be claimed by France.

In addition to the British alliance with the Arab nationalist movement, the desert warrior Abdul ibn-Saud (1880–1953), sultan of Nejd in south-central Arabia, agreed to adopt a policy of benevolent neutrality towards Britain. The wooing of the Arabs blocked the Turkish attempt to rouse the Muslim Middle East by preaching *jihad,* or holy war, against the British.

The Arab revolt began in late 1916. Husein raised the standard of rebellion in Hejaz, proclaimed independence from the Turks, and captured Mecca. In the fighting that followed, the Arab forces were commanded by the third son of Sherif Husein, Emir Faisal (1885–1933), who was assisted by a charismatic English officer, Colonel T. E. Lawrence (1888–1935), later known as Lawrence of Arabia.

Faisal al Husein cooperated with T. E. Lawrence in the campaign which captured Jerusalem and Damascus from the Ottomans in 1917 and 1918.

Under Lawrence, the Arabs played a decisive role in the last battle against the main Turkish forces in September 1918. When World War I ended, Syria was occupied by the victorious Allied forces; a small French force was located along the coast of Lebanon; emir Faisal and his Arab forces were in the interior, grouped around Damascus; and the British controlled Palestine.

A Flawed Peace

With Turkey defeated, the Arab leaders sought the independence they thought the British had promised in their correspondence with Husein. When the peace conference met in Paris, it became painfully clear that the problem of political settlement in the Middle East was a jumble of conflicting promises and rivalries.

A number of important commitments had been made during World War I, beginning with Britain's pledge to Sherif Husein in 1915. Britain, France, and Russia signed the secret Sykes-Picot Agreement in 1916. Under this pact, Syria and

Iraq were divided into four zones with London and Paris each controlling two and Russia gained parts of Asiatic Turkey. Palestine was to be placed under an international administration. The most important commitment bearing on the postwar history of the Middle East was Britain's declaration to the Jewish Zionist organization in 1917.

Jewish hopes to create a national home in Palestine grew rapidly after 1900. In 1903 a sympathetic British government had offered Theodore Herzl, the creator of the Zionist idea of a Jewish state, land in East Africa for a Jewish settlement. This proposal, however, had not been accepted. Following Herzl's death in 1904, the leadership of the Zionist movement had been assumed by Dr. Chaim Weizmann (1874–1952), a Russian Jew who had become a British subject. An intimate intellectual friendship developed between Weizmann and the English statesman Arthur James Balfour (1848–1930), who came to support the Zionist program. Balfour held a deep admiration for Jewish religious and cultural contributions. He believed that "Christian religion and civilization owed to Judaism a great debt and [one] shamefully repaid."[7]

During the course of World War I, the British government, strongly influenced by Balfour, then foreign secretary, became convinced that its support of a Zionist program in Palestine would not only be a humanitarian gesture but would also serve British imperial interests in the Middle East. Thus in November 1917 Britain issued the Balfour Declaration:

> *His Majesty's Government views with favour the establishment in Palestine of a national home for the Jewish people, and will use their best endeavors to facilitate the achievements of that object, it being clearly understood that nothing shall be done which may prejudice the civil and religious rights of existing non-Jewish communities in Palestine or the rights and political status enjoyed by Jews in any other country.*

Zionists were disappointed that the declaration did not unequivocally state that Palestine should be *the* national home for the Jewish people. In 1918 Great Britain made several declarations recognizing Palestinian national aspirations, and an Anglo-French pronouncement pledged the establishment of national governments "deriving their authority from the initiative and free choice of the indigenous populations."

At the Paris Peace Conference Emir Faisal, aided by Lawrence, pleaded the cause of Arab independence, but in vain. Faisal was still ruler in Damascus, and in March 1920, while the statesmen in Paris argued, a congress of Syrian leaders met and resolved that he should be king of a united Syria, including Palestine and Lebanon. But in April the San Remo Conference decided to turn over all Arab territories formerly in the Ottoman empire to the Allied powers to be administered as mandates. Syria and Lebanon were mandated to France; Iraq and Palestine to Britain (see map below).

Mandated Areas

The Arabs saw the mandate system as a poor substitute for independence and a flimsy disguise for imperialism. The great powers were caught up in their web of conflicting aims and promises. Apologists for Britain and France pointed out that Britain made promises to France during the war because the British could hardly deny the requests of their most important

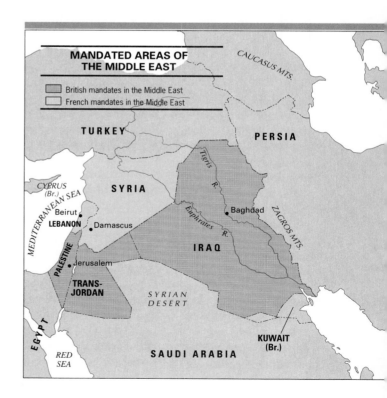

Memorandum of the General Syrian Congress

World War I and its destruction of the old empires paved the way for the rise of Arab nationalism. The memorandum of the General Syrian Congress sounded themes that would be heard throughout the twentieth century.

We the undersigned members of the General Syrian Congress, meeting in Damascus on Wednesday, July 2nd, 1919, made up of representatives from the three Zones, viz., The Southern, Eastern, and Western, provided with credentials and authorizations by the inhabitants of our various districts, Moslems, Christians, and Jews, have agreed upon the following statement of the desires of the people of the country who have elected us. . . .

1. We ask absolutely complete political independence for Syria. . . .
2. We ask that the Government of this Syrian country should be a democratic civil constitutional Monarchy on broad decentralization principles, safeguarding the rights of minorities, and that the King be the Emir Feisal, who carried on a glorious struggle in the cause of our liberation and merited our full confidence and entire reliance.
3. Considering the fact that the Arabs inhabiting the Syrian area are not naturally less gifted than other more advanced races and that they are by no means less developed than the Bulgarians, Serbians, Greeks, and Roumanians at the beginning of their independence, we protest against Article 22 of the Covenant of the League of Nations, placing us among the nations in their middle stage of development which stand in need of a mandatory power.
4. In the event of the rejection of the Peace Conference of this just protest for certain considerations that we may not understand, we, relying on the declarations of President Wilson that his object in waging war was to put an end to the ambition of conquest and colonization, can only regard the mandate mentioned in the Covenant of the League of Nations as equivalent to the rendering of economical and technical assistance that does not prejudice our complete independence. And desiring that our country should not fall a prey to colonization and believing that the American Nation is farthest from any thought of colonization and has no political ambition in our country, we will seek the technical and economic assistance from the United States of America, provided that such assistance does not exceed 20 years.
5. In the event of America not finding herself in a position to accept our desire for assistance, we will seek this assistance from Great Britain, also provided that such does not prejudice our complete independence and unity of our country and that the duration of such assistance does not exceed that mentioned in the previous article.
6. We do not acknowledge any right claimed by the French Government in any part whatever of our Syrian country and refuse that she should assist us or have a hand in our country under any circumstances and in any place.
7. We oppose the pretensions of the Zionists to create a Jewish commonwealth in the southern part of Syria, known as Palestine, and oppose Zionist migration to any part of our country; for we do not acknowledge their title but consider them a grave peril to our people from the national, economical, and political points of view. Our Jewish compatriots shall enjoy our common rights and assume the common responsibilities.

From *Foreign Relations of the United States: Paris Peace Conference*, vol. 12 (Washington, D.C.: Government Printing Office, 1919), pp. 780–781.

ally, which had close missionary and educational ties to Syria. In 1915 Britain made its ambiguous pledge to Husein because of its desperate need for Arab friendship. In the Balfour Declaration, Britain acted according to short-range interests — to swing the support of the world's Jewish community to the Allied cause and to maintain communications in the Middle East.

It should be kept in mind that British statesmen sincerely believed that a Jewish national home could be reconciled with Palestinian interests. They had no idea of the massive influx of Jewish immigration that would come in the 1930s. The fact remains, however, that the Allied statesmen during the war and at the peace conference were profoundly unaware of the intensity of Arab nationalism.

Against strong Arab opposition, France took control of both Syria and neighboring Lebanon, which it separated into two mandates. Its regime harshly suppressed political liberties but did construct new roads, public buildings, and irrigation works. The Lebanese situation was especially complex. While its population was predominantly Arab, it was divided by many religious groups. Among the Christians there were ten different sects, the Maronites being the largest. There were also various Muslim groups, including the ultra-orthodox Druze. Rivalries between these faiths plagued the life and politics of the country.

In Iraq, Arab rebellion immediately confronted British mandatory rule, and the British moved rapidly to try to satisfy Iraqi nationalism. In 1920 Faisal was recognized as king, with Britain retaining control of the finances and military control of the new state. Ten years later Iraq gained its full independence. By these concessions, Britain avoided the conflict that France experienced with Arab nationalism in Syria and Lebanon.

Arab-Jewish Conflict

Between the two world wars, Palestine was the most complex area in the Middle East. Britain tried to protect its imperial interests and at the same time reconcile them with Zionist and Palestinian nationalism. Almost as soon as the mandate was set up, the Palestinians rioted.

In 1919 the population of Palestine was estimated to be 700,000, of which 568,000 were Palestinians. Of the remaining about 58,000 were Jews and 74,000 were others, mainly Christians. Recognizing the concerns of the Arabs, the British sought to define the Balfour Declaration more precisely. While not repudiating Palestine as a national home for the Jews, the British government declared that it "would never impose upon them [the Palestinians] a policy which that people had reason to think was contrary to their religious, their political, and their economic interests."[8]

Such pronouncements and the fact that Jewish immigration was not large made possible a period of peace and progress from 1922 to 1929. As the Zionists reclaimed land, set up collective farms, harnessed the Jordan River for power, and established many new factories, a veritable economic revolution took place. Unfortunately, this brought little benefit to the Palestinian majority. Tel-Aviv grew into a thriving modern city, an excellent university was founded at Jerusalem, and Palestine became the center of a Hebrew renaissance.

The era of peace ended in 1929 when serious disorders broke out, mainly Palestinian attacks on Jews. Violence continued in the early 1930s as the Nazi persecution of the Jews brought about a steep rise in immigration to Palestine and threatened the Palestinians' predominant position in the area. In 1937 a British commission of inquiry recommended a tripartite division: Palestine would be divided into two independent states, one controlled by the Palestinians and one by the Jews, with Britain holding a third portion, a small mandated area containing Jerusalem and Bethlehem. This recommendation satisfied no one and was not accepted.

Throughout the 1930s the "Palestine question" provoked heated discussion in many parts of the world. Zionists argued that Jews had a historic right to the Holy Land, their original home. They stated that Palestine had been promised to them in the Balfour Declaration and that promise had been legalized by the League of Nations. They also pointed out that Jewish colonization constituted a democratic and progressive influence in the Middle East and Palestinian hostility was mainly the work of a few wealthy *effendis*, since the mass of Palestinians were profiting from the wealth being brought into the area.

The Palestinians responded that Palestine had been their country for more than a thousand years and declared that the Balfour Declaration did not bind them because they had not been consulted in its formulation. They further insisted that much of Zionist economic development was not healthy because it depended on subsidization by huge amounts of outside capital. Finally, they asked how any people could be expected to stand idly by and watch an alien immigrant group be transformed from a minority into a majority.

With the threat of war looming in 1939, Britain sought desperately to strengthen its position in the Middle East by attempts to regain Arab goodwill. A white paper was issued declaring that it was Britain's aim to have as an ally an independent Palestine, to be established at the end of ten years, with guarantees for both Palestinian and Jewish populations. During this ten-year period land sales were to be restricted. After the admission of 50,000 Jews, with the possibility of another 25,000 refugees from Nazi Germany, no more immigration would take place without the consent of the Palestinians. War between the two groups erupted in 1938, but the greater conflict of World War II shelved the quarrel in Palestine. The controversy would break out again with dire consequences.[9]

Saudi Arabia, Iran, and North Africa

The defeat of Turkey in 1918 left several rival states contending for supremacy in the Arabian peninsula. Following some hostilities, ibn-Saud welded all tribal groups into the new kingdom of Saudi Arabia. The discovery of vast oil reserves gave it enormous wealth.

Persia (or Iran as it came to be known in the 1920s), a land Muslim in religion, but not Arabic in culture, came under the rule of Riza Shah Pahlavi (1878–1944) following World War I. The new shah rapidly followed the path of modernization, especially in the military and in industry, and pursued an independent path. Iran became caught up in the events surrounding World War II, and in August 1941 Riza Shah Pahlavi was forced out by the British and Russians and replaced by his more cooperative son, Mohamed Riza Pahlavi (1919–1980).

While the Muslims in the Asian part of the Islamic band of countries struggled for the right of self-determination, a parallel development was taking place in North Africa. After three

Riza Shah Pahlavi. As shah of Iran from 1925 to 1941, he modernized the country by strengthening its infrastructure.

years of disorder in Egypt, the British government announced that Egypt would no longer be a protectorate of Britain. It was to be a sovereign state. However, Britain remained responsible for defense of the country, protection of foreign interests, and the Suez Canal, an essential link in the British Empire's communcations. Egypt grudgingly accepted this declaration, made its sultan a king, and proclaimed a constitution in 1923. Anglo-Egyptian relations remained unsettled, however, until 1936 when common fear of Mussolini's Italy brought the two nations together in a defense treaty.

In North Africa, the economy prospered and living standards advanced under French colonial rule. Algeria had become politically integrated with France, long before World War I. Tunisia had prospered under French rule and had maintained its native ruler, the bey, In the French Moroccan protectorate, the native sultan had been retained. Nevertheless, the storm signals of bitter nationalism appeared in North Africa, particularly in Morocco. A fundamental split existed between the privileged French Christian minority and the overwhelming Muslim majority.[10]

Mustafa Kemal and the New Turkey

Forty years before the war, the Young Turks had sought to establish a modern secular state. In 1908 they began to implement their dreams. However, defeat in the war and the Arab revolt convinced some Turkish patriots that only the most drastic measures, such as the massacre of more than 700,000 Armenians in 1915, could save their country. In addition, they bitterly rejected the Treaty of Sèvres (1920). It was bad enough to lose their empire, but it was much worse to see their homeland—namely Anatolia—partitioned and the city of Smyrna (Izmir) invaded by the Greeks.

As president of the Turkish republic from its beginning until his death in 1938, Mustafa Kemal instituted many civil and cultural reforms. In 1934 he was given the name Atatürk ("father of Turks").

The patriots rallied around the military hero Mustafa Kemal (1880–1938), who had a brilliant record against the British imperial forces at Gallipoli in World War I. An important figure in the Young Turks movement, Kemal was a born leader, thoroughly western in outlook and education. After the defeat of Turkey, he had been sent by the sultan to demobilize the Turkish troops in Asia Minor. Disregarding instructions, he reorganized the troops and successfully defied the Allies. A new government was set up in Ankara and Kemal was selected as president and commander in chief. The National Pact, a declaration of principles supported by Kemal, galvanized Turkish patriotism. This document upheld self-determination for all peoples, including the Turks, and proclaimed the abolition of the special rights previously enjoyed by foreigners in Turkey.

In 1921 Kemal's armies blocked Greek designs on Turkish land. The following year, the sultanate was abolished and a republic was established. The Allies agreed to a revision of the Treaty of Sèvres, and the Treaty of Lausanne, signed in 1923, returned to Turkey some Aegean islands and territory adjoining Constantinople (Istanbul). The Turkish heartland, Anatolia, remained intact, and no reparations were demanded.

The new constitution was democratic in form, but in reality, Kemal was a dictator who tolerated no interference with his plans. In the new Turkey there was little of the cult of the superior race and no concentration camps or purges. There was just the rule of a single individual in a situation where rough, efficient power was seen to be superior to that of the more lengthy processes of parliamentary rule. Kemal saw his dictatorial rule as a necessary state in raising his people to that level of education and social well-being that democratic government and parliamentary rule requires. Under his rule the old institutions and customs of a backward state were transformed or replaced within a few years.

Africa: From Colonialism to Nationalism

After 1890 the Europeans organized and consolidated their colonial possessions in sub-Saharan Africa. They mapped previously unknown areas, defined boundaries, and set up railroads and communications systems. The improvement of indigenous products such as rubber and palm oil, the introduction of new cash crops such as cotton and cocoa, and the importation of better breeds of cattle enriched the African economies. The colonialists placed forestry on a scientific basis, opened diamond, gold, and tin mines, and rapidly increased trade throughout Africa. European settlement also increased, especially in the highland areas.

The Europeans exported their systems of bureaucracy and tried to stamp out intertribal warfare, cannibalism, and dangerous secret societies. They opened educational facilities, primarily through the churches, and began the laborious task of transcribing the native tongues so that they could become written languages. The colonial governments introduced clinics, hospitals, and sanitation campaigns to improve public health. Meanwhile, agricultural and veterinary officers taught the Africans methods of fighting erosion, securing better seed, using fertilizers, and managing their herds more efficiently.

In the two decades following World War I European culture and technology spread throughout Africa, affecting all parts of the continent in varying degrees. While in some isolated bush areas tribes lived in Neolithic isolation, in the new cities, many Africans led lives almost wholly European, at least in externals. Under colonial rule, Africans had to obey the laws and regulations of white administrators as well as those of their tribal councils and chiefs. To pay for better roads, public buildings, health and agricultural departments, taxes now had to be paid in cash, forcing many Africans to seek employment outside of their tribal areas in the towns, mines, menial domestic or governmental service, or on plantations. Habits of living changed, new styles of dress were adopted, and new farming methods designed to produce cash crops were introduced. The desire to buy imported goods grew.

Contacts with European modes of life rapidly undermined old faiths, customs, tribal loyalties, and social institutions—a process known as detribalization. The Africans belonged neither to their old tribal world nor to the white world. No longer bound by tribal laws, they were uneasy about the courts and the law of the Europeans.

While accepting Christian doctrine, they retained their belief in the powers of tribal deities. No matter what the benefits of imperial rule might be, it was paternal at its best and exploitative at its worst. Perhaps it was necessary and perhaps desirable that Africa be brought into the mainstream of the modern world, but it was a profoundly disruptive experience.

Colonial Rule

While colonial systems of administration varied, few Africans were allowed to participate in the important aspects of colonial government. In British and French colonies, a modicum of training in self-government was available to a small minority. In British Nigeria, one of the most advanced colonies in terms of potilical participation, the Legislative Council of forty-six members in 1922 included ten Africans, four of whom were elected. These were the first elected Africans in the legislatures of British tropical Africa.

The colonial policies of Portugal and Belgium between 1914 and 1939 differed from those of Britain and France in important ways.[11] Belgium had virtually no colonial policy in the Congo, a territory more than three time the size of Texas with vast mineral wealth. Belgian officials ran a day-to-day, efficient economic system with little thought of ultimate objectives. Race relations were relatively harmonious, and the color bar was generally mild. The main emphasis was placed on the material improvement of the Africans and the development of valuable exports. Excellent medical services were provided together with the best system of elementary education in tropical Africa. There was, however, little secondary training, and university education was nonexistent. White settlement was not encouraged and the few thousand nonofficials who worked in the Congo were denied any voice in its political affairs. During the two decades after 1919, Belgium prided itself on the success of this paternal rule. It had created a population of artisans, mechanics, medical assistants, and clerks devoid of any dangerous thoughts of self-government.

The territories of Angola and Mozambique were constitutionally part of Portugal, so any ideas of separation and self-determination were unthinkable. The most backward in Africa, these territories stagnated in part because of Portugal's poverty and an exploitative administration. In early years, the territories were poorly staffed and badly governed. Their officials were described as "spending their time collecting taxes and mistresses."[12]

In theory, Portugal's objective was to develop an integrated society. Once Africans became assimilated, they would become Portuguese citizens with full voting rights. To become assimilated, they had to become Christian (Roman Catholic), practice monogamy, and learn to speak and write Portuguese. Above all, they had to learn "the dignity of labor." While this colonial system often referred to its "civilizing mission" in Africa, reality and practice fell far short. In Mozambique, for example, out of a population of 6 million, only some 5000 had become legally assimilated. The white population grew slowly, in the 1930s numbering only about 30,000 in Angola and some 18,000 in Mozambique. Many of the immigrants were poor and untrained, and a goodly number "went native"—ending up in African bush villages. The most admirable feature

was the absence of any color bar. The most deplorable aspect of Portuguese colonial rule was its extensive use of forced labor, frequently accompanied by cruel punishments, for the benefit of private business.

Mandate Administration

As a result of growing liberal sentiments and opposition to imperialism, all territories conquered by the Allies in World War I were declared to be mandates. Article XXII of the League of Nations Covenant stated that the "well-being and development" of backward colonial lands was a "sacred trust of civilization." In essence, the mandate system was a compromise between annexation of the spoils of war by the victors (although the mandatory powers were never accorded any sovereign rights over the mandates) and establishment of an international trusteeship. Parts of the Cameroons, Togoland, and German East Africa (Tanganyika) were to be administered by Great Britain. The remaining portions of the Cameroons and Togoland became French-administered mandates. Belgium

THE MANDATE SYSTEM IN AFRICA, 1926

- Belgian possessions
- British possessions
- French possessions
- Italian possessions
- Portuguese possessions
- Spanish possessions
- Independent nations
- Mandates (former German possessions)

After World War I, a new wave of liberal thinking and the League of Nations mandate system produced new efforts to improve the standard of living (by European standards) for Africans by building hospitals, libraries, and schools. The schools, like that shown here in the Congo, were run by Europeans and taught European, rather than African, history and culture.

received the mandate of Ruanda-Urundi (also a part of German East Africa), while the former German colony of Southwest Africa was allotted to the Union of South Africa (see map at left).

The Permanent Mandates Commission inspected the annual reports the mandatory governments submitted. While the commission had no effective power to improve unsatisfactory conditions in a mandate, it could place the matter before the eyes of the world. On numerous occasions the mandatory powers accepted the criticisms and heeded the suggestions and criticisms of the commission.

Judgments of the mandate system, a radically new concept in colonial administration, have differed widely. To many critics, international supervision was a unique invasion of national sovereignty. To others, the Permanent Mandate Commission did not have enough power, especially the right to send its own observers into the mandated areas.

"New Britains" Kenya and Rhodesia

Few Europeans lived in the French and British colonies of West Africa, and even they did not think of themselves as permanent settlers. Most returned home for retirement to escape the inhospitable climate. Such was not the case in British East and Central Africa, however, where Kenya and Rhodesia experienced the last thrust of European colonialism.

In the rich gold mines of South Africa, whites held relatively high-paying, skilled jobs while native workers received miserable wages for the grueling tasks they performed, like drilling veins in the cramped tunnels of the mines.

Although located on the equator, Kenya's highland area, which ranges from 6000 to 9000 feet above sea level, has a cool and bracing climate. With the British government's encouragement, the first settlers arrived in 1903, securing rich farmland in the interior. They attempted to make Kenya a white country, although the majority of the population was African. That was the goal of Lord Delamere, the leader of the white settlers, who wrote:

> In East Africa, England has possessed herself of a miniature new dominion, a little New Zealand tucked away between deserts and tropics and lakes, where yet another cutting from the British parent stock could be planted and would grow and flourish.[13]

Nairobi, the capital, became a modern city. New methods of agriculture and stock raising were introduced, which were later to form the basis of prosperity for a new black African nation. White settlement lagged, however, and by 1939 there were only 18,000 Europeans as compared with 3 million Africans. The rapid development of black nationalism in the 1930s made it obvious that Kenya would ultimately obtain self-government, not for the white settlers, but for the Africans.

To the south, in central Africa, another attempt to establish a British outpost was in the making. With the support of Cecil Rhodes, white immigrants began entering the region known as Rhodesia in the 1890's. The country had rich mineral and agricultural resources, and its white population increased more rapidly than in Kenya. Britain granted self-government to the area in 1923, subject to British retention of certain powers relating to the rights of the African majority.

By 1931 the population of Rhodesia consisted of 50,000 whites and 1 million Africans. The European community, whose numbers were growing slowly, controlled the country's best land and resources as well as its government. As the country developed economically and race relations remained calm, Europeans in the late 1930s were optimistic about their dominant role. The stormy days of the 1970s, with their militant rise of African nationalism, lay ahead.

White Exploitation in the Union of South Africa

South Africa was the most explosive area in the interwar period. Here African discontent was the deepest and the breakdown of traditional ways of life was the most widespread. Within the white population, the Dutch (called Boers) were rivals of the British settlers. Since 1902 when Britain defeated the two Boer republics, there had been tension between victors and vanquished.

United in 1909, the country had become a self-governing dominion in the British Commonwealth. But this union did not bring cooperation between the two dominant white groups, beyond enshrining segregation in law in a series of enactments between 1910 and 1913. In 1914 one Boer faction staged an unsuccessful rebellion against South Africa's participation in "England's war." Partnership between Boers and Britons continued to be strained into the 1930s. Even though the Boers gained official recognition of their language, Afrikaans (developed mainly from seventeenth-century Dutch), they continued to insist on their own flag and national anthem. Constantly they discussed secession from the Commonwealth.

Although the rift between Britons and Boers was serious, even more dangerous was the increasing numerical gap between all Europeans on the one hand and the native population on the other. After World War I, the Europeans began to eye the statistics nervously. There were 5.5 million Africans in the Union and 1.8 million whites—just under 50 percent of them of British stock. In addition, there were 200,000 Asians and 600,000 "coloured." Fearful of being overwhelmed by sheer numbers, many whites became convinced that the blacks had to be kept separate from the European community socially and politically and that all political control must remain in the hands of the Europeans.

Segregation and the color bar continued to spread rapidly in the 1920s and 1930s. Africans were restricted to their tribal reserves. Only those who obtained special permission could work on farms owned by Europeans or in the cities, and in urban areas they were obliged to live in squalid, segregated "locations." If found without their passes and identity cards, they were subject to arrest and fine or imprisonment. Native labor unions were discouraged and strikes forbidden. In addition, governmental regulations of the white labor unions excluded Africans from certain skilled trades.

Uneducated Europeans, the so-called poor whites, found it hard to make a living, competing, as they did, with the black majority which would work for pathetically low wages for limited jobs. To support the "poor whites" the white government passed laws allocating to them certain jobs with inflated wages on the railroads and in city services. Special subsidies, drawn from taxes on the entire population, paid for these jobs. This discriminatory practice resulted in huge wage disparities, the average wage for Europeans being just under four dollars a *day*,

while that for the African was just over three dollars a *week*. Africans were also excluded from politics. They could not vote or hold office in any influential elective body or parliament outside their own tribal reserves.

The pressures of increasing population in the reserves forced Africans to seek their livelihood outside. By 1936 more than 1 million Africans worked in white urban areas; another 2 million worked on European farms. About 3.5 million remained on the tribal reserves, which were neglected or impoverished. African unrest manifested itself in the increasing crime rate in the cities, in the formation of underground organizations, and in efforts to work for political rights. In the back alleys and cellars of Johannesburg and other cities, young Africans ran mimeograph machines, turning out handbills and papers advertising their grievances.

In spite of the political and social unrest, the country experienced substantial economic progress, as did much of sub-Saharan Africa, where by the early 1930s outside investments totaled nearly $5 billion. In South Africa agricultural production soared, together with mining products such as gold and diamonds. Africans, however, had little share in this economic progress.

Pan-Africanism and African Nationalism

All over Africa, opposition to imperialism grew throughout the war years. The fact that Europeans were killing one another on the battlefields did much to weaken white prestige. At the Paris Peace Conference, Wilson's ideology with its message of self-determination found a ready response among African intellectuals. Black leaders in the United States demanded greater recognition of rights for blacks, especially in Africa, and argued that the peace conference should help form an internationalized, free Africa. Dr. W. E. B. Du Bois (1868–1963), one of the organizers of the National Association for the Advancement of Colored People (NAACP) and editor of the influential newspaper *Crisis*, proposed the nucleus for a state of some 20 million people, guided by an international organization.

In 1919 Du Bois and other black leaders from the United States traveled to Paris to present

W. E. B. Du Bois shown here (standing at far right) in the editorial offices of the *Crisis,* was the pioneer advocate of the Pan-African movement.

their ideas in person to the delegates at the peace conference. While there, Du Bois was instrumental in convening a Pan-African Congress with representatives from fifteen countries. The gathering urged that the former German colonies be placed under an international agency, rather than under the rule of one of the victorious colonial powers, such as Britain.

Complementing the sentiments expressed at the Pan-African Congress were the ideals of black nationalism. In a convention held in New York in 1920, the members issued the Declaration of Rights of the Negro Peoples of the World. This document protested race discrimination in the United States and the "inhuman, unchristian, and uncivilized treatment" of Africans in the colonial empires. Frustrated by the patronizing attitudes of Christian missionaries, many Africans

founded their own churches, based on the doctrine of the "fatherhood of God and the brotherhood of man regardless of color or creed."[14]

Africans in most colonies formed nationalist groups, but they were largely ineffectual. The most important center for nationalist aspirations was in London, where a group of Nigerian students organized. African rights groups existed in South Africa, but the white government there was already perfecting its method of police repression that were to be so effective throughout the twentieth century.

Closely connected with Pan-Africanism and black nationalism was the movement among black intellectuals to recover and rediscover the African past. Relatively little was known about the religious systems, tribal organization, and agriculture of sub-Saharan Africa. Students of social anthropology, a new branch of the social sciences, took field trips to Africa as the interest in African life and culture spread among anthropologists, missionaries, and learned societies. New discoveries made it clear that Africa's comparative backwardness was due in large part to disease and isolation. The International Institute of African Languages and Cultures was organized in 1926. It was claimed with some justification that this project opened up a new era of international cooperation in the service of Africa. New departments in African studies were set up in various universities, and a small number of Africanists began to be trained in the United States.

Perhaps the most significant consequence of colonialism was the emergence of a small nucleus of African intellectuals, who took advantage of scattered educational opportunities and rare chances for study abroad, mainly in Britain, France, and the United States. The most prominent among this group of indigenous African leaders included Jomo Kenyatta (c. 1894–1978) of Kenya, Leopold Sedar Senghor (b. 1906) of Senegal, Kwame Nkrumah (1909–1972) of the Gold Coast (Ghana), and Benjamin Azikwe from Nigeria. It was largely from their ranks that the future leaders of independent Africa were recruited.[15]

Conclusion

Between the two world wars, imperialism went on the defensive before the rise of nationalism in the non-Western world. In the opening decades of the twentieth century, Japan made amazing progress in industrialization and attempted to introduce a democratic system of government. By 1919 the island nation had become one of the world's leading powers. Its spectacular rise to power was accompanied by serious demographic and resource problems that endangered the weakly rooted democratic forces.

Although China was not, strictly speaking, part of the colonial world, in many ways this vast land was under the indirect influence of the great powers. Chinese Nationalists, under the leadership of Sun Yat-sen, overthrew the Manchu Dynasty and established a republic. After years of confusion and conflict among rival factions, Chiang Kai-shek consolidated power in the Kuomintang regime. A nascent Chinese Communist movement, under Mao Tse-tung, survived efforts of the Chinese Nationalists to destroy it.

The strongest nationalist movement was that in India, under the leadership of Mohandas Gandhi. He preached a message of nonviolence and civil disobedience to force Britain to grant a substantial measure of self-government to the Indians. In the lands formerly controlled by the Ottomans, Arab nationalists bitterly contested European control in the mandated areas. Outbreaks of violence occurred in Palestine, where the Arabs resented the British attempt to set up a national home for the Jews.

In Africa, black nationalists sought to replace colonial rule with self-government and to bring about the cultural resurgence of a people whose way of life was slowly disintegrating in the face of western imperialism. The Pan-African movement did not affect the masses of the people in most areas; only in the troubled multiracial society of South Africa was there widespread unrest among Africans.

Suggestions for Reading

P. Welty, *The Asians: Their Heritage and Their Destiny* (Lippincott, 1973). A thorough coverage of Japan is E. O. Reischauer, *Japan: The Story of a Nation* (Knopf, 1974) and Takashi Fuktake, *The Japanese Social Structure: Its Evolution in the Modern Century* (Univ. of Tokyo, 1982). For a detailed description of how the military extremists undermined parliamentary government in Japan, see Richard Storry, *The Double Patriots: A Story of Japanese Nationalism* (Greenwood, 1973). Economic pressures in internal Japan are discussed in James Morley, Ed, *Dilemmas of Growth in Prewar Japan* (Princeton, 1971).

J. K. Fairbank and K. C. Liu, *The Cambridge History of China*, XII, "Republican China 1912–1949," (Cambridge, 1983) is the essential starting point for pre-Mao China. For a solid analysis of the four decades of revolution in China see Lucien Bianco, *Origins of the Chinese Revolution* (Stanford, 1971). See also Edward Friedman's study on Sun Yat-sen, *Backward Toward Revolution* (California, 1974). Stuart Schram, ed. *Mao Tse-Tung Unrehearsed* (London Penguin, 1974) is a good selection of the Chairman's thoughts. D. G. E. Hall, *A History of Southeast Asia*, (St. Martin's, 1968) and H. J. Berda and J. A. Larkin, *The World of Southeast Asia* (Harper and Row, 1967) provide good general coverage of the area.

For invaluable studies of the architects of Indian nationalism see K. Kripalani, *Gandhi: A Life* (Verry, 1968); E.

Thomson, *Rabindranath Tagore* (Greenwood, 1975) and M. C. Rau, *Jawaharlal Nehru* (Interculture, 1975). See also B. R. Nanda, *Gokhale, Gandhi, and the Nehrus: Studies in Indian Nationalism* (St. Martin's, 1975). T. W. Wallbank, *India in the New Era* (Scott, Foresman) is a useful and authoritative survey.

See S. N. Fisher, *The Middle East: A History* (Knopf, 1968) for a comprehensive outline of forces and events. A short history of the Jewish people is Abba Eban, *My Country* (Random House, 1972). See also B. Halpern, *The Idea of the Jewish State* (Harvard, 1969). An analysis of Arab changes is presented in M. Halpern, *The Politics of Social Charge in the Middle East and North Africa* (Princeton, 1967). On the impact of westernization in Turkey see Bernard Lewis, *The Emergence of Modern Turkey* (Oxford, 1968). See also studies by S. H. Longrigg: *Syria and Lebanon under French Mandate* (Octagon, 1972) and *Iraq, 1900 to 1950* (Verry, 1972)

An astute observer surveying Africa as it was before World War II is John Hatch, *Africa Emergent* (Regnery, 1974). See also C. G. Segre, *Fourth Shore: The Italian Colonization of Libya* (Univ. of Chicago, 1975); Michael Crowder, *West Africa Under Colonial Rule* (Northwestern, 1968); and W. Cartey and M. Kilson, eds., *The Africa Reader* I, *Colonial Africa* (Vintage, 1970). Robin Mallett gives a solid survey in *Africa Since 1875* (Michigan, 1974).

Notes

1. Harold Z. Scheffrin, *Sun Yat-sen and the Origins of The Chinese Revolution* (Berkeley: University of California Press, 1968).

2. Michael Gasster, *Chinese Intellectuals and the Revolution of 1911* (Seattle: University of Washington Press, 1969).

3. Stuart Schram, *Mao Tse-tung* (Baltimore: Penguin Books, 1967).

4. E. O. Reischauer, J. K. Fairbank, and A. M. Craig, *East Asia: The Modern Transformation* (Boston: Houghton Mifflin, 1965).

5. J. Nehru, *Toward Freedom* (New York: John Day, 1942), p. 353.

6. T. Walter Wallbank, *The Partition of India: Causes and Responsibilities* (Boston: D. C. Heath, 1966).

7. Blanche E. C. Dugdale, *Arthur James Balfour* (G. P. Putnam's Sons, 1937), p. 325.

8. Quoted in Hans Kohn, *Nationalism and Imperialism in the Hither East* (G. Routledge and Sons, 1932), pp. 132–133.

9. Walter Laqueur, *A History of Zionism* (New York: Holt, Rinehart, and Winston, 1972).

10. Edward Behr, *The Algerian Problem* (London: Hodder and Stoughton, 1961), pp. 13–54.

11. Raymond L. Buell, *The Native Problem in Africa*, 2 vols. (New York: Macmillan Co., 1928), a pioneer and classic study.

12. Robin Hallett, *Africa since Eighteen Seventy-five* (Ann Arbor: University of Michigan, 1974) p. 51.

13. T. Walter Wallbank, "British East Africa—A Case Study in Modern Imperialism," *World Affairs Interpreter*, Autumn 1983, p. 293.

14. Robert I. Rotberg, *A Political History of Tropical Africa* (New York: Harcourt Brace Jovanovich, 1965), p. 341.

15. Ronald Segal, *Political Africa: A Who's Who of Personalities and Parties* (New York: Praeger, 1961).

Chapter 34

Troubled Peace and World War II, 1920–1945

In the first decade after World War I, statesmen with global vision made serious attempts to control conflict through international organizations and treaties limiting arms and outlawing war. In the 1930s, however, the competition among states resumed its traditionally violent course. Ambitious dictators in Asia, Africa, and Europe made war, while representatives from the democracies tried to reason with them.

From 1939 to 1945 the Second World War, with its new and horrible technologies, ravaged the globe. Large bombers took the war to civilians hundreds of miles behind what used to be known as the front lines. Hitler made use of industrial technology to try to destroy an entire people. Only a massive counterattack by the Allied powers, capped by the use of the atomic bomb in Japan, brought an end to the fighting.

The Troubled Calm: The 1920s

The aftershocks of the First World War totally dominated the interwar period. The horror, expense, and exhaustion of the tragedy dominated the losers and winners alike. The better part of a young generation had died. Political leadership fell either to the old who had gained authority before 1914 or to the untried young. It was in this uncertain environment that the League of Nations began its work.

The League of Nations

The League's record from 1919 to 1929 was one neither of dismal failure nor of complete triumph.

Such threats to peace as disputes between Sweden and Finland and between Britain and Turkey were resolved. When a state defied the League, however, as in the case of Italy's quarrel with Greece over Corfu, the organization could do nothing. The refusal of the United States, the world's strongest democracy, to join weakened the League's peacekeeping possibilities.[1]

Through no fault of the League's, little progress was made in the field of disarmament. On one occasion, perhaps because of its relative weakness, Russia proposed complete disarmament. The British delegates, among others, were suspicious of Russia's sincerity in wanting to surround the world in a "loving embrace."[2] The member-states' firmly rooted feelings of mutual distrust and fear of losing sovereignty hurt the League's ability to keep the peace.

However, the League had a distinguished list of accomplishments in other areas. It supervised the exchange and repatriation of prisoners of war and saved thousands of refugees from starvation. It helped Austria, Bulgaria, and Hungary to secure badly needed loans. The League also provided valuable service in administering the region of the Saar Basin and the Free City of Danzig. It investigated the existence of slavery in certain parts of the world, sought to control traffic in dangerous drugs, and stood ready to offer assistance when disasters brought suffering and destruction to the globe.

In the intellectual and cultural realm the League published books and periodicals dealing with national and international problems of all kinds and from its own radio station broadcast important information, particularly in the field of health. Unfortunately, the League's excellent

The Senate's refusal to ratify the Treaty of Versailles meant that the United States would not join the League of Nations.

armistice the French wanted to impose maximum financial penalties on the Germans. In 1923, assisted by the Belgians, they occupied the Ruhr region in a move that had immense short- and long-range implications. Some historians have seen in this act the first step toward World War II because it hardened the German desire for revenge. Even though the Dawes Plan (see p. 795) eased the situation, the French attitude divided the former Allies and provided ammunition to the German ultranationalists.

The rift between the French and Germans was papered over in Locarno, Switzerland, in 1925. In the Locarno Pact, Germany, Great Britain, France, and Italy agreed to guarantee the existing frontiers along the Rhine, to establish a demilitarized zone 50 kilometers deep along the east bank of the Rhine, and to refrain from attacking one another. The problems along France's eastern frontier would be dealt with by international guarantee (although the British dominions stated their disagreement) and U.S. money. Germany received, and accepted, an invitation to join the League of Nations, a symbolic act that seemed to indicate its return to the international community. Still, the Locarno Pact

record in these areas has been obscured by its failure to maintain a lasting peace.

France Seeks Security

Because the United States chose to play a limited role in international affairs and Great Britain returned to its traditional focus on the empire and Commonwealth, France assumed the leadership of postwar Europe. In 1919 the French pursued a very simple, but difficult, foreign policy goal—absolute security. Since the Napoleonic heights a century earlier, the French had seen their power and authority diminish while German economic and military strength had increased. Twice in fifty years Germany had invaded France with terrible results. The obsession with security could be easily understood.

France spent much of the postwar decade trying to guarantee its own safety by keeping Germany weak. In the first five years after the

The artist of this hopeful cartoon pictured the 1925 Locarno Pact as the agreement that would put an end to a thousand years of war and bloodshed.

addressed only the western frontier of Germany and left unresolved the controversial issues of the territories of the newly formed and contentious nations of eastern Europe. Another well-meaning but ultimately ineffectual agreement was the Kellogg-Briand Pact (1928), developed by U.S. Secretary of State Frank Kellogg and French Foreign Minister Aristide Briand. This pact, which was eventually signed by sixty-two nations, outlawed war as an instrument of national policy, but omitted provisions to enforce the agreement.

The Paris government had little faith in the Covenant of the League of Nations as a guarantee of France's survival. The French, instead, depended more and more on their own diplomats. They tried to construct a wall of allies along Germany's eastern frontier that would simultaneously surround the Germans and isolate the Soviet Union. While Germany was weak and dependent on western loans, France could stand as the strongest diplomatic power on the continent. But even in the 1920's, France lacked the strength to serve as the leader of Europe. When Germany and Italy began to flex their muscles in the 1930s, France—even with British help—faced fascist aggression from a position of weakness.

Soviet and German Cooperation

The Soviet Union and Germany, the two diplomatic outcasts of the 1920s, quickly forged a working relationship that was useful to both of them. The USSR had isolated itself by signing the Treaty of Brest-Litovsk, nationalizing foreign property, and repudiating foreign debts as well as by its communist ideology. Probably the greatest barrier was the ideological one, as expressed through the activities of the Third Communist International, or Comintern. That body, organized in 1919, was dedicated to the overthrow of capitalism throughout the world.

In the 1920s the Comintern spread communist propaganda, established communist parties throughout the world, and infiltrated labor unions and other working class groups. Even after Lenin had given up hope for an immediate world revolution and started to normalize relations with the west, the Comintern encouraged radicals who had broken off from moderate socialist groups to organize Communist parties. Communists of all countries became members of the Comintern, meeting in congresses held in Moscow and setting up committees to coordinate their activities. Communist parties were different from other national political groups because they owed their allegiance to an international organization rather than to the nations in which they resided.

By 1922 the Soviet Union was pursuing a two-pronged foreign policy—one through the Communist parties to further the spread of communism, as in China, where the communists were active until defeated by Chiang-Kai-shek,

U.S. secretary of state Frank Kellogg signs the Kellogg-Briand Pact, which renounced war as an instrument of national policy. The agreement included no provisions for enforcement of this noble sentiment and thus was powerless to prevent war or punish aggressors.

and the other through normal international channels for traditional economic and diplomatic goals, generally in Europe.

From the time Lenin left Switzerland to return to Petrograd the Soviet Union enjoyed a mutually advantageous relationship with Germany. At the beginning of the 1920s the two nations carried on secret agreements allowing for joint military training enterprises. Their first major open diplomatic contact came at Rapallo, Italy, in 1922, where they renounced the concept of reparations. In the Rapallo pact, the Germans and Russians agreed to cooperate in a number of areas. Germany was extremely bitter about the treatment it had received at Versailles; the Soviets had faced Allied intervention during the civil war. It naturally followed that a main feature of the foreign policies of both countries would be either to ignore the Versailles settlement or to escape from its consequences. Both countries shared a common interest to dominate Poland, against whom the USSR had fought at the beginning of the decade.

Although, as Lenin perceptively noted, Russia wanted revolution while Germany sought revenge, the two nations cooperated closely until 1934. Then after a five-year gap they cooperated again in the Nazi-Soviet nonaggression pact.

The Weimar government under Gustav Stresemann wanted to rearm but was forbidden to do so by the Versailles treaty. Stresemann backed the cooperation between his government and the Soviet Union to build up both Russian and German military might. Berlin supplied technical aid while German pilots and specialists went on maneuver in Russia. Even after the proclamation of the so-called spirit of Locarno, the two nations worked with each other. In 1926 the Rapallo pact was renewed for another five years.[3]

The Epoch of the Aggressors

The world found little peace or stability after the First World War. Economic and social discontent, buttressed by widespread disillusionment with the peace treaties, posed grave problems for the victorious Allies. Almost as weak as the defeated powers, the Allies had to take on the responsibility for maintaining the peace. The awful toll taken by World War I convinced the democracies that never again should humanity have to endure such a tragedy. From the point of view of the new aggressors, however, this attitude reflected weakness and cowardice—and opportunity.

Japan Invades Manchuria

The first challenge to the fragile peace occurred in September 1931 when Japan moved into the traditional Chinese buffer zone of Manchuria. In occupying this region, Tokyo pursued centuries-old goals made more urgent by present-day pressures of resource scarcity and overpopulation. The Japanese invasion of Manchuria was the first step on the road to World War II.

Unable to cope with the invader, the Chinese appealed to the League of Nations, which appointed a committee of inquiry in 1933. The committee's report condemned the aggression, but at the same time tried not to provoke Japan. The outcome was that the League neither put an end to the aggression nor kept Japan as a member—two years later Tokyo withdrew from the organization.

The 1920s "Locarno spirit" of international conciliation and hope for peace ended with the aggressive acts of the 1930s, including Japan's invasion of Manchuria in 1931. The photo below shows Japanese soldiers in a street in Peking in 1937.

Erich Maria Remarque, The Road Back

Erich Maria Remarque, who wrote so eloquently of the horrors of war in *All Quiet on the Western Front,* compellingly expressed the despair and frustration of German veterans in *The Road Back.* He captures the mood that helped Hitler gain power.

Demonstrations in the streets have been called for this afternoon. Prices have been soaring everywhere for months past, and the poverty is greater even than it was during the war. Wages are insufficient to buy the bare necessities of life, and even though one may have the money it is often impossible to buy anything with it. But ever more and more gin palaces and dance halls go up, and ever more and more blatant is the profiteering and swindling.

Scattered groups of workers on strike march through the streets. Now and again there is a disturbance. A rumour is going about that troops have been concentrated at the barracks. But there is no sign of it as yet.

Here and there one hears cries and counter-cries. Somebody is haranguing at a street corner. Then suddenly everywhere is silence.

A procession of men in the faded uniforms of the front-line trenches is moving slowly toward us.

It was formed up by sections, marching in fours. Big white placards are carried before: *Where is the Fatherland's gratitude? — The War Cripples are starving. . . .*

It was no good to go on assuming that a common basis for all the different groups and classes in Germany could be found. The break between them became daily wider and more irreparable. The plebiscite of the Right "against the Young Plan and the war-guilt lie" proved just as unsuccessful as those arranged in former years by the Left, but the poison of the defamatory agitation remained in the body of the community, and we watched its effects with anxiety.

In my own family the political antagonism was growing past endurance. In October Fritz had finished his apprenticeship in an old-established export house, at the precise moment when the firm went bankrupt — a minor incident compared with such events as the breakdown of the Frankfurt General Insurance Company and the Civil Servants' Bank or the enforced reorganization and amalgamation of the Deutsche Bank and the Disconto-Gesellschaft, which all happened in the course of the year and dangerously damaged the whole economic life of Germany. Yet for my brother the bankruptcy of his firm overshadowed all other happenings, since it meant that he lost his job. His three years' training was in vain — there was not a single export firm which was not forced to dismiss as many of its employees as possible. . . .

"Yes, that's just it — millions! If it isn't my fault, whose fault is it? I tell you — your friends, the French, the English, the Americans, all those damnable nations who inflict on us one dishonorable penalty after the other — they are to blame for all this. Before the war the whole world bought German goods. My firm exported to Africa, to the German colonies. Hundreds of thousands we turned over every year. But they have robbed us of our colonies, of all our foreign markets. They have stolen the coalmines in the Saar and in Upper Silesia, they squeeze millions of marks out of our bleeding country. We'll never rise again unless we free ourselves by another war."

"Don't be foolish, Fritz. Things are bad in the whole world."

"I don't care about the world, I care only about Germany, which you and your pacifists have delivered into the hands of our enemies. I despise you, you are not worthy to call yourself a German."

From *The Road Back* by Erich Maria Remarque. "Der Weg Zurück." Copyright © 1931 by Ullstein, A. G.: Copyright renewed 1958 by Erich Maria Remarque.

Japan's war with China began with the invasion of Manchuria in 1931, escalated with the spread to Peking and Shanghai in 1937, and continued until 1945, even though there was never any formal declaration of hostility. Between 1937 and 1945, more than 20 million Chinese died—many of them civilians killed in bombing attacks. The photo here is one of the attack on Chucheng in 1939.

When the Chinese resorted to an effective nationwide boycott of Japanese goods, the invaders attacked Shanghai in 1932 and began to push deeper into northern China. To slow down the invasion and give themselves a chance in the inevitable struggle, the Chinese agreed to a truce in May 1933 that recognized Tokyo's conquests in Manchuria and northern China.

Despite virtual civil war between Chiang Kai-shek's nationalist forces and the communist movement led by Mao Tse-tung, China strengthened its position in the face of the Japanese threat. Following Soviet directions, Mao stated that the first objective of all China should be wholehearted resistance against foreign imperialists. A united front between Chiang and Mao was difficult, but in December 1936–January 1937 the communists and nationalists put aside their conflicts, proclaimed a truce, and established a united front against the Japanese. Neither of the parties in the front trusted the other, but both feared the Japanese more.

In 1937 the Japanese, with no official declaration of hostility, renewed their advance and began what would be an eight-year period of war. Tokyo's forces advanced rapidly up the Yangtze River to Nanking where they committed atrocities, captured Peking, and proclaimed the "New Order" in eastern Asia. The New Order's objectives were to destroy Chiang Kai-shek's regime, expel western interests from east Asia, and establish a self-sufficient economic bloc to include Japan, Manchuria, and China.

The outbreak of war in Europe in 1939 gave Japan a golden opportunity to expand the New Order in China and into the Asian colonies of the western powers. The Japanese took the island of Hainan in 1939 and after the fall of France in June 1940, built naval and air bases in Indochina. From there they put pressure on the Dutch East Indies and the British outposts at Hong Kong and Singapore.

None of the three great powers that might have halted the Japanese advance in the 1930s did anything. Britain was in the depths of an economic crisis. France was suffering from political and economic paralysis. The United States was totally absorbed in fighting the depression.

Italy Attacks Ethiopia

While Japan pursued old goals in new ways, Italy set out to claim a prize it had failed to take in 1896—Ethiopia, the only important independent native state left in Africa. Late in 1934 fighting broke out between the Ethiopians and the Italians, and in the following year, Mussolini's forces invaded the country.

Emperor Haile Selassie made a dramatic appearance before the League to appeal for help. The League tried to arrange for arbitration. Unconvinced by the shameless Italian argument that Ethiopia, not Italy, was the aggressor, the League voted to prohibit shipment of certain goods to Italy and to deny it credit. But the effect of the sanctions was minor because oil—without which no modern army can fight—was not included in the list of prohibited articles. France and Britain gave only lukewarm support to the sanctions because they did not want to alienate Italy. The United States, which had not joined the League, and Germany, which had left it by that time, largely ignored the prohibitions. Only outraged public opinion, moved by newspaper photographs showing barefooted Ethiopians fighting the modern Italian army drove the governments to even the pretense of action.

Using bombs, mustard gas, and tanks the Italians advanced swiftly into Ethiopia and crushed Haile Selassie's valiant but poorly armed soldiers. Meanwhile, the German reoccupation of the Rhineland in March helped shift international attention away from the conflict in Africa. The whole, sorry story ended in July 1936 when sanctions were removed. Haile Selassie, an emperor without a country, went to live in Britain, the first of several royal exiles who would be forced from their countries in the next decade.

The Rhineland and the Axis

Soon after taking power, Hitler carried out the revisions the Germans wanted in the Versailles treaty. He also won his country's support by seeking revenge against the Allies. As George F. Kennan noted at the time, "The man is acting in the best traditions of German nationalism, and his conception of his own mission is perhaps clearer that that of his predecessors because it is uncomplicated by any sense of responsibility to European culture as a whole."[4] During his first two years in power Hitler paid lip service to peace while increasing the tempo of rearmament. In March 1935 he negated the disarmament clauses of the Versailles treaty, and a year later reoccupied the Rhineland.

The move, which Hitler described as producing the most nerve-wracking moments of his life, sent German troops marching boldly into the Rhineland in defiance of the Versailles treaty and the Locarno agreements. The Germans could not have resisted had the British and French moved in response. London did nothing and Paris mobilized 150,000 troops behind the Maginot line—but did no more. Hitler later confessed that had the French advanced against him, "We would

Veteran Ethiopian soldiers and young boys barely into their teens march together to the front to battle the Italians who had invaded Ethiopia in 1935.

General Francisco Franco addresses a crowd shortly after he announced establishment of Spain's rebel Nationalist government in October 1936. The Spanish Civil War, which pitted the Loyalist defenders of the Spanish Republic against the rebel fascist Nationalists, served as a bloody and tragic prelude to World War II.

have had to withdraw with our tails between our legs, for the military resources at our disposal would have been totally inadequate for even a moderate resistance."[5]

The League's weak response to the Japanese invasion of China and the Italian attack on Ethiopia combined with the feeble British and French reaction to German reoccupation of the Rhineland encouraged the aggressors and served as the prelude to the forming of the Axis alliance. Until Hitler gained power, Germany had been without close allies. After the Ethiopian crisis and the League sanctions, Italy and Germany began to work more closely together. In 1936 they formalized the friendship in the Rome-Berlin Axis, and one year later, Mussolini followed Hitler's lead by withdrawing from the League of Nations.

Japan, the third major member of the Axis joined forces with Germany in 1936 in the Anti-Comintern pact. A year later, Italy also joined in that agreement, which effectively ringed the Soviet Union. Relations between Moscow and Berlin had cooled after 1934, and the Soviet Union now became the object of anti-Communist rhetoric. Many right-wing leaders in the west hoped that the "Red menace" would be taken care of by the *Führer* and his allies.

All in all, 1936 was a banner year for Hitler. He had gained allies, pleased his own people by remilitarizing the Rhineland, learned the weakness of the democratic powers and the League, and gained international prestige from his successful staging of the Olympic games. Finally, he found a successful device to distract potential opponents' attention in the Spanish Civil War.

The Spanish Tragedy

By 1936 the Spanish republic was disintegrating. It had brought neither prosperity nor stability to Spain. Reactionary forces had tried to gain control of the government while left-wing groups had resorted to terrorism. The liberal approach had failed, and in the summer of 1936 the army revolted against the legal government in Madrid.

General Francisco Franco (1892–1975) commanded the insurgents, who included in their ranks most of the regular army troops. Mussolini strongly backed Franco, and the rightist forces expected a quick victory. However, many groups stood by the republic, and they put up a strong resistance against the insurgents, stopping them at the outskirts of Madrid.

By the end of 1936 each side had gained the backing of a complicated alliance of forces. Franco had the support of the Italians, who sent large numbers of planes, troops, and weapons, and the Germans, who tested their latest military technology against the republicans. The republic gained the support of the Soviet Union, which sent arms, "advisers," and other supplies and large numbers of disorganized but idealistic antifascist fighters, including a number from Britain and the United States.

The insurgents capitalized on the Soviet support for the republic, and Franco pronounced his cause to be strictly an anti-communist crusade—a cunning oversimplification that would not have any validity except "for a few months (in 1938) the communists were in firm control of a remnant of republican Spain," until Stalin decided to pull out his support.[6] While Spain bled, suffering more than 700,000 deaths, outside forces took advantage of the tragic situation for their own selfish purposes.

The democratic powers—Great Britain, France, and the United States—attempted to stay officially out of the conflict. Britain did not want to risk a continental war. France suffered from internal divisions that made its leaders fear that their country, too, might have a civil war. The United States declared its official neutrality. Instead of permitting arms to be sent to the recognized, legally constituted republican government which had the right under international law to purchase weapons for self-defense, Great Britain

After the fall of Barcelona in 1939, which marked the end of the Spanish Republic, thousands of Spanish refugees streamed to the French frontier to escape the fascists.

and France set up a nonintervention system by which the nations of Europe agreed not to send arms to either side. This arrangement, meant to limit the scope of the conflict, was adhered to only by the democracies. The various dictators continued to send their support to their respective sides.

Madrid fell in March 1939, and the Spanish republic was no more. Franco, at the head of the new state, gained absolute power, which he held until his death. The Spanish civil war was a national catastrophe that left permanent scars on a proud and gallant people.

Appeasement and Weakness

In 1937, Neville Chamberlain (1869–1940) became prime minister of Great Britain. Years before he took office, the British had tried to build a detente with the Germans backed by "an efficient bomber air force." Chamberlain tried a new strategy: a defense policy based on a fighter air force and centered solely on protecting Britain. He wanted to make "more positive overtures to Germany to appease her grievances and reach a settlement on the basis not of fear by deterrence but of mutual interests and separate spheres of influence." Chamberlain's name came to symbolize the policy of appeasement, "the policy of meeting German demands and grievances without asking firm reciprocal advantages; asking instead only for future 'mutual understandings.'"[7]

Chamberlain took the direction of foreign policy on his own shoulders in his attempt to explore every possibility for reaching an understanding with the dictators. He dedicated himself to an effort to ease international tensions despite snubs from those he wished to placate and warnings from his military and foreign policy advisers. He

Hitler accomplished his goal of *Anschluss,* or union of Germany and Austria, in March 1938. Cheering Nazi supporters greeted Hitler's triumphant march into Vienna.

based his policy on the most humane of motives—peace—and on the most civilized of assumptions—that Hitler could be reasonable and fair minded. By showing good faith—by withdrawing from any possibility of being able to wage war on the continent—Chamberlain froze himself into a position of having to avoid war at any cost.[8] His policies were strongly supported in Great Britain and throughout most of the British Commonwealth.

France had shown that it would not move militarily without British backing, and under Chamberlain the entente with France was put on the back burner, a development that hurt French resolve. The democratic world became uneasily aware of its growing weakness in comparison with the dictators. As the European balance of power shifted, the small states began to draw away from the impotent League of Nations.

The Axis' prestige blossomed. Some nations tried to make deals with Germany and Italy, while others, including the Scandinavian countries and Holland, withdrew into the shelter of neutrality and "innocent isolation." In eastern Europe semi-fascist regimes came to be the order of the day, as the states in that unhappy region, with the exception of Czechoslovakia, lined up to get in Germany's good graces. In 1934 Poland had signed a nonaggression pact with Germany. Belgium gave up its alliance with France. In eastern Europe, only Czechoslovakia remained loyal to Paris.

Hitler became increasingly aware of the opportunity presented by Britain's "peace at any price" policy and the decline of the French alliance system. On November 5, 1937 in a meeting at the Reich Chancellery in Berlin that lasted for more than four hours, Hitler laid out his plans and ideas for the future. According to the notes of the meeting taken by Colonel Hossbach, the *Führer* gave a statement that was to be regarded "in the event of his death, as his last will and testament."

"The aim of German policy," Hitler noted, "was to make secure and to preserve the racial community and to enlarge it. It was therefore a question of space. . . . Germany's future was wholly conditional upon the need for space." The answer to that question was "force" which was to be applied in the next six years, because after 1943 German technological and military superiority would be lost. Hossbach noted that "the *Führer* believed that almost certainly Britain, and probably France as well, had already tacitly written off the Czechs."[9]

Historians still debate the importance of the Chancellery meeting. Hitler's message was not favorably received by the military staff present, for they knew full well that Germany was in no shape to fight. Yet the significance of the message can be found in the wholesale changes in personnel Hitler introduced at the end of 1937 and in the contrast it affords to the views of Chamberlain. The prime minister wanted peace at any price. The *Führer* wanted space at any price.

Toward Austria and the Sudetenland

When Hitler announced the military reoccupation of the Rhineland in the spring of 1936 he stated, "We have no territorial demands to make in Europe." He lied. By 1938, with the German army growing in strength and the air force becoming a powerful unit, the *Führer* began to implement one of his foreign policy goals—placing the German-speaking peoples under one Reich. The first step on that path was to unite Austria and Germany in the *Anschluss* (literally, a joining).

In 1934 the Nazis had badly bungled an attempt to annex Austria. Two years later, softening up operations began again, and by 1938 intense pressure had been levied against Austrian chancellor Kurt von Schuschnigg to cooperate with Berlin. After a stormy meeting with Hitler in February, Schuschnigg restated his country's desire to be independent, although concessions would be made to Germany. He called for a plebiscite in March to prove his point. Outraged at this independent action, Hitler ordered Schuschnigg to resign and to cancel the vote. Both actions were taken, but Hitler sent his forces into Austria anyway.

By March 13, 1938 a new chancellor, approved by Hitler, announced the union of Austria and Germany. After a month in which all opposition was silenced, Hitler held his own plebiscite and gained a majority of 99.75 percent in favor of union. The democratic powers did not intervene

The Hossbach Memorandum

Two years before the outbreak of World War II, Adolf Hitler recapitulated his goals in a secret meeting. Colonel Friedrich Hossbach took down Hitler's comments.

The aim of German policy was to make secure and to preserve the racial community and to enlarge it. It was therefore a question of space.

The German racial community comprised over 85 million people and, because of their number and the narrow limits of habitable space in Europe, constituted a tightly packed racial core such as was not to be met in any other country and such as implied the right to a greater living space than in the case of other peoples. . . .

Germany's future was therefore wholly conditional upon the solving of the need for space, and such a solution could be sought, of course, only for a foreseeable period of about one to three generations. . . .

The question for Germany ran: where could she achieve the greatest gain at the lowest cost. . . .

Case 1: Period 1943–1945

After this date only a change for the worse, from our point of view, could be expected.

The equipment of the army, navy, and Luftwaffe, as well as the formation of the officer corps, was nearly completed. Equipment and armament were modern; in further delay there lay the danger of their obsolescence. In particular, the secrecy of "special weapons" could not be preserved forever. The recruiting of reserves was limited to current age groups; further drafts from older untrained age groups were no longer available.

Our relative strength would decrease in relation to the rearmament which would by then have been carried out by the rest of the world. If we did not act by 1943–45, any year could, in consequence of a lack of reserves, produce the food crisis, to cope with which the necessary foreign exchange was not available, and this must be regarded as a "waning point of the regime." Besides, the world was expecting our attack and was increasing its counter-measures from year to year. It was while the rest of the world was still preparing its defenses that we were obliged to take the offensive. . . .

Case 2

If internal strife in France should develop into such a domestic crisis as to absorb the French Army completely and render it incapable of use for war against Germany, then the time for action against the Czechs had come.

Case 3

If France is so embroiled by a war with another state that she cannot "proceed" against Germany.

For the improvement of our politico-military position our first objective, in the event of our being embroiled in war, must be to overthrow Czechoslovakia and Austria simultaneously in order to remove the threat to our flank in any possible operation against the West. In a conflict with France it was hardly to be regarded as likely that the Czechs would declare war on us on the very same day as France. The desire to join in the war would, however, increase among the Czechs in proportion to any weakening on our part and then her participation could clearly take the form of an attack toward Silesia, toward the north or toward the west. . . .

The Fuehrer saw case 3 coming definitely nearer; it might emerge from the present tensions in the Mediterranean, and he was resolved to take advantage of it whenever it happened, even as early as 1938.

From *Auswartiges Amt: Documents on German Foreign Policy*, Series D (Washington, D.C.: Government Printing Office, 1949), vol. 1. pp. 29–49, passim.

At the Munich Conference in September 1938, British prime minister Neville Chamberlain (left) and French premier Edouard Daladier (next to him) capitulated to Hitler's demands regarding Czechoslovakia. Italian dictator Benito Mussolini stands to the right of Hitler.

to help Austria. "Indeed, Neville Henderson (the British ambassador to Berlin) had indicated only too clearly that Britain would welcome alteration in Austria's status, if it were done peaceably."[10]

Following his success in Austria, Hitler moved on to his next objective, the annexation of the Sudetenland. This area along the western border of Czechoslovakia was populated mainly by German textile workers who had suffered economically during the depression. The Sudetenland was also the site of the extremely well-fortified Czech defenses. In September 1938 the *Führer* bluntly informed Chamberlain that he was determined to gain self-determination for the Sudeten Germans. He charged, falsely, that the Czechs had mistreated the German minorities. In fact, among the eastern European states Czechoslovakia had the best record in dealing with minority nationalities. But in this affair, Great Britain and France consistently overlooked both the record of the Prague government and the Czech statesmen themselves.

Chamberlain persuaded French premier Edouard Daladier that the sacrifice of Czechoslovakia would save the peace. When the French joined the British to press the Czechs to accept the Nazi demands, the Prague government had little choice but to agree. Chamberlain informed Hitler of the Czech willingness to compromise, only to find that the German demands had increased considerably. Angered by the *Führer's* duplicity, Chamberlain refused to accept the new terms, which included Czech evacuation of some areas and the cession of large amounts of material and agricultural goods.

Munich and Democratic Betrayal

The crisis over Czechoslovakia would be the last major international issue decided only by European powers.[11] Symbolically it would be viewed as a failure that would affect diplomatic decisions for generations to come. On September 28, 1938, Chamberlain received a note from Hitler inviting him to attend a conference at

THE PARTITION OF CZECHOSLOVAKIA

— Czechoslovakia boundary 1937

ESTONIA

LITHUANIA

EAST PRUSSIA

G E R M A N Y

Elbe R.

Oder R.

Vistula R.

Warsaw

POLAND

To Germany Oct. 1938

Teschen To Poland Oct. 1938

ORE MTS.

SUDETENLAND

BOHEMIAN FOREST

Prague

Krakow

PROTECTORATE OF BOHEMIA-MORAVIA

SLOVAKIA

To Hungary Nov. 1938

CARPATHIAN MTS.

Danube R.

CARPATHO-UKRAINE

Munich

Vienna

AUSTRIA To Germany Mar. 1938

Budapest

HUNGARY

ROMANIA

ALPS

ITALY

Po R.

Danube R.

YUGOSLAVIA

Munich. The following day, Chamberlain flew to Germany to meet with Hitler, Mussolini, and Daladier at Nazi headquarters. They worked for thirteen hours on the details of the surrender of the Sudetenland. No Czech representative was present, nor were the Russians—outspoken allies of the Czechs—consulted.

The conference accepted all of Hitler's demands and, in addition, rewarded Poland and Hungary with slices of unfortunate Czechoslovakia (see map above). The tragedy for the Czechs brought relief for millions of Europeans, half-crazed with fear of war. But thoughtful individuals pondered whether this settlement would be followed by another crisis. Winston Churchill, who was then in political eclipse in Britain, solemnly warned: "And do not suppose that this is the end. This is only the beginning of the reckoning."[12]

The mounting fears of French and British statesmen were confirmed in 1939. Deprived of its military perimeter, the Czech government stood unprotected against the Nazi pressure that came in March. Hitler summoned Czech president Emil Hacha to Berlin. Subjected to all kinds of threats during an all-night session, Hacha finally capitulated and signed a document placing his country under the "protection" of Germany. His signature was a mere formality, however, for German troops were already crossing the Czech frontier. Not to be outdone, Mussolini took Albania the following month. The two dictators then celebrated by signing a military alliance, the so-called Pact of Steel.

In response to the taking of Czechoslovakia and violation of the Munich pledges, Britain ended its appeasement policy and for the first time in its history authorized a peacetime draft. In Paris, Daladier gained special emergency powers to push forward national defense.

In the United States, isolationism reigned supreme. Between 1935 and 1937, in response to feelings of revulsion stemming from World War I, the U.S. Congress passed neutrality acts that made it unlawful for any nation at war to obtain munitions from the United States. At the same time, in response to events in Ethiopia, Spain, and along the Rhine, President Franklin D. Roosevelt and the State Department worked quietly to alert the American people to the dangers of the world situation. In October 1937 Roosevelt pointed out that "the peace, the freedom, and the security of 90 percent of the population of the world is being jeopardized by the remaining 10 percent who are threatening a breakdown of all international order and law." The president's call, in this so-called quarantine speech, for "positive endeavors to preserve peace brought forth a hostile reaction from the press and public."[13] Two years later Roosevelt told political leaders that the Germans and Italians could win the next war. His warnings went unheeded, as a significant portion of the American public hoped that the Nazis could do away with the communists in Russia.

The Nazi-Soviet Pact

The final step on the road to World War II was Germany's attack on Poland. The treaty of Versailles had turned over West Prussia to Poland as a Polish corridor to the sea. While 90 percent of the corridor's population was Polish, the Baltic city of Danzig—a free city under a League of

Nations high commissioner—was nearly all German. Late in March 1939 Hitler proposed to Poland that Danzig be ceded to Germany and that the Nazis be allowed to occupy the narrow strip of land connecting Germany with East Prussia. Chamberlain, with French concurrence, warned the Nazis that "in the event of any action that clearly threatens Polish independence," the British, "[will] at once lend the Polish government all support in their power." This was an essentially symbolic gesture, as Poland's geography made any useful western aid impossible.

In the months that followed the Allied warnings, France and Britain competed with Germany for an alliance with Russia. Stalin had closely observed the actions of the democratic powers since Hitler's rise to power. He was aware of the hope expressed in some western conservative circles that Hitler might effectively put an end to the Soviet regime. Further, he pledged to stay out of a war between "imperialists." He had to make a closely reasoned choice between the two sets of suitors competing for Soviet partnership.

Chamberlain and Daladier had ignored Moscow at Munich, and generally British relations with the communists were quite cool. Now, with the Polish question of paramount importance, the French and British approaches struck Stalin as being opportunistic. In May, Vyacheslav Molotov became the Soviet foreign minister. While Molotov negotiated publicly with the British and French, who sent negotiators not empowered to make agreements, he was also in secret contact with the highest levels of the Third Reich.

For centuries, Germany and Russia had shared a common concern with the fate of Poland. They had been able to reach agreement at Poland's expense in the eighteenth and nineteenth centuries. From late 1938 on, Moscow and Berlin pondered yet another division of the country. Negotiations between the two proceeded intensely from June through August 1939. While top-ranking German and Soviet diplomats flew between the two capitals, the lower-ranking mission sent to Moscow by Britain traveled leisurely by boat.

By 1939 Stalin had to choose wisely between the western democracies with their spotty record of defending their friends and Nazi Germany which could offer him concrete advantages in eastern Europe. On August 21, to the world's great amazement, the Soviet Union and Germany signed a nonaggression pact.

In retrospect, it is not at all surprising that Stalin chose to work with the Nazis. Through this agreement, Stalin gave Hitler a free hand in Poland and the assurance of not having to fight a two-front war. After the British and French guarantees to the Poles in March, Hitler knew that his attack on Poland would precipitate a general European war. The *Führer* had prepared plans that called for the invasion to begin in August 1939, and with the nonaggression pact, Hitler could attack without fear of Moscow's intervention. Furthermore, he did not believe that Britain and France would dare oppose him.

The nonaggression pact gave Russia time to build up its strength while the imperialists weakened themselves in war. In addition, through secret agreements, Russia would gain Finland, Estonia, Latvia, eastern Poland, and Bessarabia. Germany would get everything to the west including Lithuania. In addition, the Nazis got guarantees of valuable raw materials and grain from the Soviets. Ideological differences could be set aside for such a mutually profitable pact.

World War II

When Nazi forces crossed the Polish border early on the morning of September 1, 1939, they started World War II, the conflict that killed more people more efficiently than any previous war. In all areas, the latest scientific and technological advances were placed in the service of war. New techniques and attitudes revolutionized the field of intelligence. Scientists made major advances in both codemaking and codebreaking. Intelligence gathering no longer depended on the old cloak-and-dagger stealing of messages and secrets. Now high altitude aerial reconnaissance aircraft, radar, the first computers, and radio intercepts allowed enemies to find out each others' plans. Among the major advances on the Allied side were the breaking of the Japanese code and the discovery of the German code mechanism. Less than a decade before the war an American statesman had noted that "gentlemen do not read other gentlemens' mail."

In the new style of warfare, information meant victory, and the cultured assumptions of an earlier age had to be discarded.

A New Way of War

Tactics and weaponry changed greatly between the two world wars. Tanks and planes had been used in World War I, but the concept of the *Blitzkrieg*, massive mobile mechanized movements and saturation bombings behind the lines, made the weapons far more lethal. The trench warfare of the First World War and the concept of fixed, fortified positions such as the Maginot line proved to be useless.

Mobility was the key—even more so that superior numbers of men and weapons. Better communications, provided by improved radio systems, increased mobility. To strike quickly, in great force, and then to exploit the advantage proved to be the main characteristics of the German successes in 1939 and 1940. The Germans broke through enemy lines by using a large number of tanks, followed by the infantry. Rarely, since Napoleon, had speed and concentrated force been used so effectively.

Complementing increased mobility on the ground was the expanded use of air power, which could spread devastating firepower across continents. The new forms of war, however, sparked the inventive genius of the scientists as each technological advance elicited a response— long-range German bombers brought the need for improved radar; improved propeller-driven

The new technology of World War II meant that fighting took place in the air as well as on the sea and on the ground.

A German motorized detachment rides through a Polish town badly damaged by *Luftwaffe* bombs. Poland was unable to withstand Hitler's *Blitzkrieg* of a combined air and ground attack and fell to the Germans within a month.

aircraft set off the development of jet-powered airplanes. No matter how sophisticated the aerial technology became, however, the war proved that, with the exception of nuclear weapons, air power alone could not bring an enemy to its knees.

Other innovations appeared during the wars—paratroopers, advanced landing crafts, flying bombs such as the V-1, rockets such as the V-2 used by the Germans. Aircraft carriers and amphibious forces played an important part in the war in the Pacific. The Japanese used carriers in their attack on Pearl Harbor and the Americans used amphibious forces in "island hopping" across the Pacific.

As in World War I, however, military success lay in the ability of the states to mobilize their populations and resources. During World War II, states came to control all aspects of life. But the final, deciding factor was the ability of the individual soldier, following the directions of such brilliant commanders as Rommel or Eisenhower, to apply all of these resources.

In the end, all of these factors were overwhelmed by the ultimate scientific and technological accomplishment, the atomic bomb. Ironically, although created to protect state interests, this ultimate weapon could destroy civilization.[14]

Blitzkrieg and Sitzkrieg

After staging an "incident" on the morning of September 1, 1939, Nazi troops crossed the Polish frontier without a declaration of war. At the same time the *Luftwaffe* began to bomb Polish cities. On the morning of September 3 Chamberlain sent an ultimatum to Germany demanding that the invasion be halted. The time limit was given as 11 A.M. the same day. At 11:15 Chamberlain announced on a radio broadcast that Britain was now at war. France also soon declared war. After twenty-one years, Europe was once again immersed in war.

The world now had the chance to see the awesome speed and power of Nazi arms. The Polish forces collapsed, crushed between the German advance from the west and, two weeks later, the Russian invasion from the east. By the end of the month, after a brave but hopeless resistance, the Poles once again saw their country partitioned between the Germans and the Russians.

Britain and France did not try to breach Germany's western defensive line—the Siegfried line along the Rhine. With their blockade and mastery of the seas, they hoped to defeat Hitler by attrition. During the winter of 1939–1940 there was little fighting along the Franco-German frontier. The lull in action came to be referred to as the phony war, or *Sitzkrieg*.

Russia took advantage of the lull to attack Finland in November. This campaign revealed to Moscow's embarrassment the Finns' toughness and the Soviet Union's military unpreparedness in the wake of the purges. After an unexpectedly difficult four-month-long campaign, the immense Soviet Union forced tiny Finland to cede substantial amounts of territory.

Forced to retreat by onrushing German tank units and nearly continuous bombing, British, French, and Belgian soldiers wait on the beaches of Dunkirk to be taken across the English Channel to England.

"Blood, Toil, Tears, and Sweat"

In the spring of 1940 the Nazi high command launched its attack on western Europe. In its scope, complexity, and accomplishments it would be one of the most successful military campaigns ever carried out. In April, Nazi forces invaded Norway and Denmark. The Norwegians fought back fiercely for three weeks before being vanquished, while Denmark was taken in even less time. In the second week of May the German armies overran neutral Holland, Belgium, and Luxemburg. The next week they went into northern France and to the English Channel. In the process they trapped an Anglo-French army of nearly 400,000 on the beach at Dunkirk.

The reversals in Norway and the Low Countries and the military crisis in France led to Chamberlain's resignation. Winston Churchill (1874–1965) became prime minister of Great Britain. Churchill had uneven success in both his political and military careers. In the 1930s his warnings against Hitler and Mussolini had been largely ignored. He was viewed as a "might-have-been; a potentially great man flawed by flashiness, irresponsibility, unreliability, and inconsistency."[15] Yet in 1940, at the age of sixty-six, Churchill offered qualities of leadership equal to the nation's peril. For the next five years he was the voice and symbol of a defiant and indomitable Britain.

Faced with the prospect of the destruction of the British army at Dunkirk, Churchill refused to be publicly dismayed. Appearing before Parliament as the new prime minister he announced, "I have nothing to offer but blood, toil, tears, and sweat." He prepared his people for a long and desperate conflict, knowing full well that only the Channel, a thin screen of fighter aircraft, and an untried device called radar protected Britain. Churchill's example inspired his people. Hitler had found his match in the area of charismatic leadership.

Hitler hesitated to squash the forces trapped at Dunkirk, thereby allowing time for hundreds of small craft protected by the Royal Air Force to evacuate 335,000 soldiers across the Channel, including more than 100,000 French troops. At first, military leaders had hoped to save 30,000 of the trapped men; now they had eleven times that number. An army had been saved, even though it had lost all of its heavy equipment.

After Dunkirk, the fall of France was inevitable. Eager to be in on the kill, Mussolini declared war on France on June 10. Designated as an open city by the French to spare it destruction, Paris fell on June 14. As the German advance continued, the members of the French government who wanted to continue resistance were voted down. Marshal Philippe Pétain (1856–1951), the eighty-four-year-old hero of Verdun in the First World War, became premier. He immediately asked Hitler for an armistice, and in the same dining car in which the French had imposed armistice terms on the Germans in 1918, the Nazis and French on June 22, 1940 signed another peace agreement. The Germans had gained revenge for their shame in 1918.

France was split into two zones, occupied and unoccupied (see map below). In unoccupied France, Pétain's government at Vichy was supposedly free from interference, but in reality it became a puppet of the Nazis. The Third Republic, created in 1871 from the debris of defeat suffered at Germany's hands, now came to an end because of a new blow from the same country.

A remarkable patriot, Brigadier-General Charles de Gaulle (1890–1970), fled to London and organized the Free French Government, which adopted as its symbol the red cross of Lorraine, flown by Joan of Arc in her fight to liberate France five centuries earlier. De Gaulle worked to keep alive the idea of France as a great power and continued to aid the Allied cause in his sometimes quixotic way throughout the war.

Only Britain remained in opposition to Hitler, and the odds against the British seemed overwhelming. The Nazis planned a cross-Channel assault, while in Buckingham Palace, the Queen, the present Queen mother, took pistol lessons saying, "I shall not go down like the others."[16] Britain possessed an army that left its best equipment at Dunkirk, radar, and fast fighter aircraft flown by brave pilots. Churchill had his eloquence to inspire his people:

> We shall go on to the end. . . . we shall defend our island, whatever the cost may be, we shall fight on the beaches, we shall fight on the landing grounds, we shall fight in the fields and in the streets, we shall fight in the hills; we shall never surrender. . . .[17]

THE DIVISION OF FRANCE

☐ German-occupied France
☐ Unoccupied Vichy France

ENGLISH CHANNEL
NETHERLANDS
BELGIUM
GERMANY
Seine R.
Paris
LUXEMBOURG
Rhine R.
Loire R.
BAY OF BISCAY
FRANCE
SWITZERLAND
Vichy
Rhône R.
ITALY
Garonne R.
SPAIN
CORSICA
MEDITERRANEAN SEA

The Germans sent an average of 200 bombers over London every night for nearly two months in the summer and fall of 1940. They suffered heavy losses to the Royal Air Force which profited from a combination of superior aircraft, pilots, radar sightings, and visual detection. Yet, all through the fall and winter of 1940–1941 Britain continued to be racked by terrible raids. Night bombing destroyed block after block of British cities. Evacuating their children and old people to the north, going to work by day and sleeping in air raid shelters and underground stations at night, Britain's people stood firm—proof that bombing civilians would not break their will.

Mastery of Europe

During the fall and winter of 1940–1941 Hitler strengthened his position in the Balkans, but not without some difficulty. By March 1941 Hungary, Bulgaria, and Romania joined the Axis. Hitler had to control the Hungarians and Bulgarians, who were pursuing ancient ambitions for Romanian land. In the process Romania lost a third of its population and territory to its two neighbors. The Romanians emerged, however, as helpful allies for the Germans.

Mussolini, eager to gain some glory for his forces, invaded neutral Greece in October 1940. This thrust proved to be a costly failure when in December, the Greeks successfully counterattacked. The Italians met other defeats in North Africa and Ethiopia, which the British recaptured.

Partially in an attempt to pull Mussolini out of a humiliating position, the Germans in the first four months of 1941 overran Yugoslavia and Greece. Two months of intense aerial and infantry attacks were needed to defeat the Yugoslavs and Greeks, forcing Hitler to spend considerable amounts of men and resources. But, by the end of that time, the *Führer* had secured his right flank prior to his invasion of Russia.

The results of these forays into the Balkans may have been positive for the Axis in the short run. But by going into the Balkans, Hitler delayed his attack on Russia by six to eight weeks. This delay plus inadequate intelligence and bad planning may have cost him victory on the Russian front. In addition, the Germans and the Italians controlled only the major cities of Yugoslavia. Large bands of resistance fighters and partisans, among them communist forces led by Joseph Tito, roamed the area. Hitler had to leave behind German troops formerly committed to the Russian invasion and replace them with lesser Bulgarian and Hungarian forces.[18]

By the spring of 1941 nearly all of Europe had come under German control (see map at right). Only Portugal, Switzerland, Sweden, Ireland, and Turkey remained neutral. While ostensibly neutral, Spain under Franco was pro-Nazi. Britain, though still dangerous, could do little to interfere on the continent. The United States became more disturbed over the Nazi successes, but not enough to take action.

The Nazi air attacks on London in the Battle of Britain caused widespread devastation but failed to bring the city to a halt or destroy the morale of its people.

War with Russia

Hitler and Stalin had signed the nonaggression pact for their own specific, short-term advantages. From the first there was tension and mistrust between the two, and neither side had any illusions about a long-lasting friendship. Stalin had hoped for a much more difficult war in the west among the "imperialists" and had not expected that Hitler would so quickly be the master of Europe.

As early as July 1940 Hitler resolved to attack Russia in an operation code name Barbarossa. In the fall of the year he decided not to invade Britain, but instead to pursue his original goal of obtaining living space. During 1941 British and American intelligence experts told Stalin of

THE CREST OF AXIS POWER

- Allies and areas they controlled
- Axis nations
- Area occupied by the Axis
- Vichy France
- Neutral nations

Battles: Allied victory ×   Axis victory ⊗

Thrusts: → →

ARCTIC OCEAN

ATLANTIC OCEAN

FAEROE IS. (Den.)

SHETLAND IS. (Br.)

ORKNEY IS.

Scapa Flow

NORTH SEA

Murmansk

WHITE SEA

Arkhangelsk

N. Dvina R.

Narvik

NORWAY

Trondheim 1940 Apr.

Bergen

Oslo

SWEDEN

GULF OF BOTHNIA

Goteborg

Stockholm

Copenhagen

DENMARK Apr. 1940

Hamburg

Hanover

Berlin

Elbe R.

FINLAND

Lake Onega

Lake Ladoga

Helsinki

Leningrad

Tallinn

ESTONIA

Pskov

LATVIA

Riga

W. Dvina R.

LITHUANIA

Kaunas

Danzig

Germany invaded Poland Sept. 1, 1939

Warsaw

SOVIET UNION

Kazan

Gorki

Moscow

Smolensk

Volga R.

Saratov

Minsk

Voronezh

Don R.

Glasgow
GREAT

IRELAND

Dublin

Liverpool

BRITAIN

Birmingham

Air battle for Britain July–Oct. 1940

London

Southampton

Dunkirk May–June 1940

NETHERLANDS May 1940

BELGIUM 1940

La Havre

Paris

Nantes

Loire R.

FRANCE

Vichy

Bordeaux

Lyons

VICHY FRANCE

Marseilles

Cologne

Lux.

Frankfurt

Rhine R.

GERMANY

Munich

Prague

CZECHOSLOVAKIA Mar. 1939

Dresden

POLAND

Krakow

Lvov

Kiev

Dnieper R.

Kharkov

Dniester R.

Rostov

Sea of Azov

Odessa

Sevastopol

BLACK SEA

Trabzon

Vienna

AUSTRIA Mar. 1938

Budapest

HUNGARY Oct. 1940

RUMANIA Nov. 1940

Bucharest

Danube

YUGOSLAVIA Apr. 1941

Belgrade

BULGARIA Mar. 1941

Sofia

Salonika

SWITZERLAND

Milan

Venice

Trieste

Genoa

ADRIATIC SEA

ITALY

Rome

Naples

Palermo

SICILY

ALBANIA Apr. 1939

GREECE Apr. 1941

Athens

AEGEAN SEA

Smyrna

TURKEY

Istanbul

Ankara

Kizil R.

Adana

Aleppo

SYRIA

Beirut

Damascus

CYPRUS (Br.)

CRETE

IONIAN SEA

S P A I N

Madrid

Barcelona

Valencia

BALEARIC IS.

CORSICA

SARDINIA

TYRRHENIAN SEA

MEDITERRANEAN SEA

MALTA (Br.)

Oran

Algiers

Bône

Tunis

TUNISIA

ALGERIA

Tripoli

LIBYA

Bengasi

Alexandria

Cairo

Nile R.

Suez Canal

EGYPT

Jerusalem

PALESTINE

TRANSJORDAN

SAUDI ARABIA

RED SEA

German troops at the Kharkov front in Russia pass a burning farmhouse. The same factors that had halted Napoleon and his army more than a hundred years earlier—bitter cold and inadequate protection against it—helped stop the German advance. Russia paid a heavy price for stopping the Germans, losing nearly 10 percent of its population in the war.

Hitler's intentions to attack, but the Soviet dictator clung to his obligations under the nonaggression pact. Even while the Nazis were invading Russia in June 1941, shipments of Soviet grain were headed to Germany.

Operation Barbarossa required far more effort and resources than were expended later against the British and Americans in North Africa. Along a battlefront 1800 miles long, 9 million men became locked in struggle. At the outset, the Nazi panzer units were unstoppable, as they killed or captured enormous numbers of Russian troops. In October Hitler's army neared the center of Moscow (a monument today between the city's Sheremetevo Airport and the Kremlin marks the farthest advance of the German army). A month earlier, the Nazis had besieged Leningrad, beginning a two-year struggle in which over one million civilians died. Russia appeared to be on the verge of collapse.

When winter came earlier, and more severely, than usual, the Nazi offensive broke down. Weapons froze, troops were inadequately clothed, and heavy snows blocked the roads. The German attack halted and in the spring of 1942 the Russian army recovered some territory. One reason the Russians could bounce back was the

success of the five-year plans in relocating industry behind the Urals. Another reason was the sheer bravery and tenacity of the Soviet people. Also, the United States and Britain had begun sending lend-lease supplies to Russia.

The United States Enters the War

Following the collapse of France and during the Battle of Britain, the American people had begun to comprehend the implications of an Axis victory. After Dunkirk, the United States sent arms to Britain, set forth on a rearmament program, and introduced the peacetime draft. The Lend-Lease Act of 1941 empowered the president to make arms available to any country whose defense was thought to be vital to the U.S. national interest. Despite ideological differences, America sent more than $11 billion worth of munitions to Russia.

To define the moral purpose and principles of the struggle, Roosevelt and Churchill drafted the Atlantic Charter in August 1941. Meeting "somewhere in the Atlantic," the two pledged that "after the final destruction of Nazi tyranny," they hoped to see a peace in which "men in all the lands may live out their lives in freedom from fear and want." If the United States had not yet declared itself at war in the fall of 1941, it was certainly not neutral.

One event on December 7, 1941, brought the full energies of the American people into the war against the dictators—the Japanese attack on Pearl Harbor. Even though Hitler was seen as the most important enemy, it was Japan's expansionist policy that brought the United States into the war.

Confronted with Tokyo's ambitions for the New Order in Asia and widely published accounts of Japanese atrocities, the United States had failed to renew trade treaties, frozen Japanese funds, and refused to sell Japan war materiel. Despite these measures Japan decided to continue its expansion. In October 1941 General Hideki Tojo (1884–1948), a militarist, became premier of Japan. On Sunday, December 7, while special "peace" envoys from Tokyo were negotiating in Washington, ostensibly to restore harmony in Japanese-American relations, Japanese planes launched from aircraft carriers attacked the American bases at Pearl Harbor, Hawaii. The stunningly successful attack wiped out many American aircraft on the ground and crippled one-half of the United States Pacific fleet.

On the following day the United States declared war on Japan, as did Britain. The British dominions, the refugee governments of Europe, and many Latin American nations soon followed the Americans and British. Four days later, Germany declared war on the United States. On January 2, 1942, the twenty-six nations that stood against Germany, Italy, and Japan solemnly pledged themselves to uphold the principles of the Atlantic Charter and declared themselves united for the duration of the war.

The Apogee of the Axis

After Pearl Harbor, Japanese power expanded over the Pacific and into Southeast Asia. Tokyo conquered Hong Kong, Singapore, the Dutch East Indies, Malaya, Burma, and Indochina. The Philippines fell when an American force surrendered at Bataan. The Chinese, however, from their remote inland fortress capital of Chungking, still managed to hold off the Japanese (see map, p. 896).

The summer of 1942 was an agonizing period for the nations allied against the Axis. A new German offensive pushed deeper into Russia, threatening the important city of Stalingrad. The forces

A Navy launch rescues a sailor from the blazing U.S.S. *West Virginia* during the Japanese attack on Pearl Harbor. The attack on Pearl Harbor brought the United States formally into the war.

FARTHEST LIMITS OF
JAPANESE CONQUESTS

	Area occupied by Japan
→	Japanese thrusts
→	Allied thrusts
×	Battle

of the gifted German general Rommel menaced
Egypt and inflicted a decisive defeat on the British army in Libya. All over the globe the Axis
powers were in the ascendancy. But their advantage was to be short-lived.

Further Japanese expansion in the Pacific was
halted by two major American naval victories,
the Coral Sea in May and Midway in June. In the
first the Americans sank more than 100,000 tons
of Japanese shipping and stopped the Japanese
advance toward Australia. In the second the
Americans turned back the advance toward
Hawaii by devastating the Japanese carrier
force. In both cases the American forces benefited by having broken the Japanese code and in-
tercepting key messages. After these spectacular
victories, U.S. marines began the tortuous rooting out of the Japanese at Guadalcanal and driving them back, island by island. In November
1942 British and American troops landed in

The British victory over Axis troops at El Alamein, Egypt, in
1942 helped turn the tide of the war in favor of the Allies.

North Africa and the British defeated Axis troops at El Alamein in Egypt. By May 1943 all Axis troops in North Africa had been destroyed or captured.

In July 1943 the Allied forces invaded and captured Sicily. On the twenty-fifth of that month, the whole edifice of Italian fascism collapsed, as Mussolini was stripped of his office and held captive. (He was rescued by Nazi agents in September.) In the meantime, the Allies began their slow and bitter advance up the Italian boot. The new Italian government signed an armistice in September 1943, months before Rome was taken in June 1944. German resistance in northern Italy continued until the end of the war.

The Russian Turning Point

As important as the victories in the Pacific, North Africa, and Italy were, the decisive campaign took place in Russia. Hitler threw the bulk of his men and resources against the Soviet troops in the hope of knocking them out of the war and of gaining badly needed resources and food supplies. Hitler's strategy and operations along the Russian front were one mistake after another.

The Nazis lost a great opportunity to further the disintegration of the Soviet Union in 1941, because they treated the peoples they encountered as *Untermenschen,* or subhumans. Often the Nazis, far from encountering resistance, would be treated as liberators by the villages they entered and given the traditional gifts of bread and salt. Often peasants dissolved the unpopular collective farms in the hope that private ownership would be restored. The separatist Ukrainians looked forward to German support for reinstituting their state. The Nazi occupation negated all of these potential advantages. The Nazis carried their mobile killing operations of genocide with them, conscripted Slavs for slave labor in Germany, and generally mistreated the population in areas that they occupied.

Hitler's campaign gave Stalin the opportunity to wrap himself in the flag of Russian patriotism. He replaced the ideological standards with those of nationalism and orthodoxy. He even went so far as to announce the end of the Comintern in 1943, an act more symbolic than real. For the first and perhaps the only time, the communist party and the Soviet people were truly united in a joint enterprise.

The long (September 14, 1942–February 2, 1943) and bloody battle between the Germans and the Russians was focused on the strategic, industrial city of Stalingrad on the Volga River. Hitler had fanatically sought to take the city, which under the constant pounding of artillery had little of importance left in it. His generals advised him to stop the attempt and retreat to a more defensible line. Hitler refused, and the German Sixth Army of 270,000 men was surrounded and finally captured in February 1943. A German soldier trapped at Stalingrad wrote in a letter:

> Around me everything is collapsing, a whole army is dying, day and night are on fire, and four men busy themselves with daily reports on temperatures and cloud ceilings. I don't know much about war. No human being has died by my hand. I haven't even fired live ammunition from my pistol. But I know this much: the other side would never show such a lack of understanding for its men.[19]

Along the long front 500,000 German and affiliated troops were killed or taken prisoner. By the autumn of 1943 an army of 2.5 million Germans faced a Soviet force of 5.5 million.

The initiative had definitely passed to the Allies in the European theater. The Germans lost their air dominance and the American industrial machine was cranking up to full production. By the beginning of 1944 the Germans were being pushed out of the Soviet Union, and in August Soviet troops accepted the surrender of Romania. Bulgaria was next to be "liberated" by the Soviet Union, while the Allies continued doggedly fighting their way north in Italy. But whereas the western Allies were—in their fashion—fighting the war to its military end, Stalin placed the postwar political objectives in the forefront of his advance into Europe.

An example of the Soviet use of military tactics to gain political goals could be seen in the action around Warsaw in August–September 1944, when the Red Army deferred the capture of the Polish capital to allow the Nazis to destroy potential opponents. The Polish resistance, which was centered in Warsaw and in contact with the exile government in London, had noted the arrival of Soviet forces in Warsaw's eastern suburbs. When the Nazis prepared to evacuate the city, the resistance rose up to claim control of the capital. As these were non-communist Poles, Stalin's forces refused to advance to the city, choosing instead to withdraw back across the Vistula.

During the next five months, the Soviets refused to permit the British and the Americans, who wanted to airdrop supplies to the resistance, to land and refuel in the Ukraine. Because the flight to Warsaw from London was too far to make in a round trip, the Allies could not supply the resistance. The Nazis stopped their retreat, returned to Warsaw, and totally destroyed the resistance. Russian forces then advanced and took the capital in January. Poland was now deprived of many of its potential postwar, non-communist leaders. When the Soviets advanced, they brought with them their own properly prepared Polish forces, both military and political, to control the country.[20]

Axis Collapse

Following months of intense planning and days of difficult decision making, the Allies on June 6, 1944 launched a vast armada of ships that landed half a million men on the beaches of Normandy. The Allied armies broke through the German defenses and liberated Paris at the end of August and Brussels at beginning of September. The combined forces wheeled toward Germany. After fending off a major German offensive in the Battle of the Bulge in December, the Allies were ready to march on Germany.

It took four more months for the Allies from the west and the Russians from the east to crush the Third Reich. By May 1, the Battle of Berlin had reached a decisive point, and the Russians were about to take the city. Unlike in the First World War, German civilians suffered greatly in the Second. The Allies gained total command of the skies and for every ton of bombs that fell on English cities, more than 300 tons fell on German settlements.

With victory in sight, Stalin, Roosevelt, and Churchill met at Yalta in the Crimea in February 1945 to discuss the peace arrangements. They agreed the Soviet Union should have a preponderant influence in eastern Europe, decided that Germany should be divided into four occupation zones, discussed the makeup and functioning of the United Nations, and confirmed that Russia

Supplies and reinforcements for the D-Day (June 6, 1944) invasion of Normandy pour onto the beach to be loaded onto trucks and funneled inland.

Churchill, Roosevelt, and Stalin at the Yalta Conference. The discussions at the conference, especially those concerning the establishment of new governments in liberated countries, exposed the mounting tensions that would divide the Allies after the war.

would enter the war against Japan after the defeat of Germany, which they did—two days after the atomic bomb was dropped on Hiroshima. Yalta was the high point of the alliance. After this conference, relations between the western powers and the Soviets rapidly deteriorated.

The European Axis leaders did not live to see defeat. Mussolini was seized by anti-fascist partisan fighters and shot to death, and his mutilated body, and that of his mistress, was hung by the heels in a public square in Milan on April 28, 1945. Hitler committed suicide two days later. His body and that of his mistress, Eva Braun, whom he had just married, were soaked in gasoline and set afire.

President Roosevelt also did not live to see the end of the war. He died suddenly on April 12, 1945, less than a month before the German armies capitulated. The final surrender in Europe took place in Berlin on May 8, 1945, named by the newly installed president, Harry Truman, as V-E Day, Victory in Europe Day.

The Unspeakable Holocaust

As the Allied armies liberated Europe and marched through Germany and Poland they came on sites that testified to the depths to which human beings can sink—the Nazi death camps.

Nazi Propaganda Minister Joseph Goebbels wrote in his diary on March 14, 1945 that "it's necessary to exterminate these Jews like rats, once and for all. . . . In Germany, thank God, we've taken care of that. I hope the world will follow this example."[21]

He was only too accurate in his assessment: Germany had "already taken care of that." In Belsen, Buchenwald, Dachau, Auschwitz, and other permanent camps and in mobile killing operations that moved with the armies, Hitler's forces sought to "purify the German race" and to "remove the lesser breeds as a source of biological infection." Working under the efficient efforts of the Gestapo, led by Chief Heinrich Himmler, and with the aid of hardworking Deputy Chief Reinhard Heydrich, the Nazis set out to gain the "final solution" of the Jewish question.

Although preparations had been under way for ten years, the completed plan for the final solution came in 1942. More than 3 million men, women, and children were put to death at Auschwitz, where more than 2000 people at a time could be gassed in half an hour; the operation could be repeated four times a day. The able-bodied worked until they could work no more, and then they were gassed. Millions more died from starvation, on diets that averaged from 600 to 700 calories a day. Torture, medical experimentation, and executions all claimed a large toll. The victims' eyeglasses were collected, their hair shaved off, their gold fillings were removed, and their bodies were either burned or buried.

Thus the captured Jews and assorted *Untermenschen* served a "biological necessity" by being destroyed and made an economic contribution on the way. The Nazis did not act alone, as they were aided by anti-Semitic citizens in Poland, Romania, France, Hungary, and the Soviet Union. Few of the more than 3 million Polish Jews survived the war, and similar devastation occurred among the Romanian Jewry.

With the exception of a few human beasts, all of this was done with bureaucratic efficiency, coldness, discipline, and professionalism. Himmler believed that his new variety of knights must make "this people disappear from the face of the earth." Had this been done in a fit of insanity and

madness by savages, it perhaps could be comprehended. But that it was done by educated bureaucrats and responsible officials from a civilized nation made the act all the more chilling and incredible.

Between 1939 and 1945 the Jewish population in Nazi-occupied Europe decreased from 9,739,200 to 3,505,800. Six million were killed directly in Nazi gas chambers or in executions. In addition, another 6 million people—Slavs, Gypsies, and others—also fell victim to direct Nazi slaughter.[22]

The Atomic Bomb

While the Allied armies finished off the Germans, the Americans from the summer of 1943 advanced toward Japan, capturing on the way the islands of Tarawa, Kwajalein, and Saipan

The Nazi Death Camps

Henry Friedlander gave a dispassionate description of the functioning of the Nazi death camps.

The largest killing operation took place in Auschwitz, a regular concentration camp. There Auschwitz Commandant Rudolf Hoess improved the method used by Christian Wirth, substituting crystalized prussic acid—known by the trade name Zyklon B—for carbon monoxide. In September, 1941, an experimental gassing, killing about 250 ill prisoners and about 600 Russian POWs, proved the value of Zyklon B. In January, 1942, systematic killing operations, using Zyklon B, commenced with the arrival of Jewish transports from Upper Silesia. These were soon followed without interruption by transports of Jews from all occupied countries of Europe.

The Auschwitz killing center was the most modern of its kind. The SS built the camp at Birkenau, also known as Auschwitz II. There, they murdered their victims in newly constructed gas chambers, and burned their bodies in crematoria constructed for this

purpose. A postwar court described the killing process:

Prussic acid fumes developed as soon as Zyklon B pellets seeped through the opening into the gas chamber and came into contact with the air. Within a few minutes, these fumes agonizingly asphyxiated the human beings in the gas chamber. During these minutes horrible scenes took place. The people who now realized that they were to die an agonizing death screamed and raged and beat their fists against the locked doors and against the walls. Since the gas spread from the floor of the gas chamber upward, small and weak people were the first to die. The others, in their death agony, climbed on top of the dead bodies on the floor, in order to get a little more air before they too painfully choked to death.

From Henry Friedlander, "The Nazi Camps," in *Genocide: Critical Issues of the Holocaust*, ed. Alex Grobman and David Landes (Los Angeles: The Simon Wiesenthal Center, 1983), 222–231.

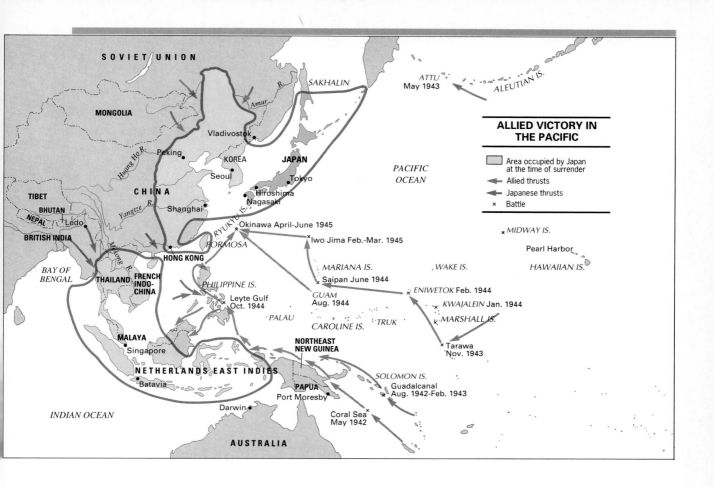

ALLIED VICTORY IN THE PACIFIC

Area occupied by Japan at the time of surrender
Allied thrusts
Japanese thrusts
× Battle

(Map labels:) SOVIET UNION, MONGOLIA, Vladivostok, Peking, KOREA, Seoul, JAPAN, Tokyo, Hiroshima, Nagasaki, SAKHALIN, ATTU May 1943, ALEUTIAN IS., PACIFIC OCEAN, CHINA, TIBET, BHUTAN, NEPAL, Ledo, BRITISH INDIA, Huang Ho R., Yangtze R., Shanghai, RYUKYUS, Okinawa April-June 1945, FORMOSA, Iwo Jima Feb.-Mar. 1945, MIDWAY IS., Pearl Harbor, HAWAIIAN IS., BAY OF BENGAL, THAILAND, FRENCH INDO-CHINA, HONG KONG, Mekong R., PHILIPPINE IS., MARIANA IS., Saipan June 1944, WAKE IS., Leyte Gulf Oct. 1944, GUAM Aug. 1944, ENIWETOK Feb. 1944, KWAJALEIN Jan. 1944, MARSHALL IS., MALAYA, Singapore, PALAU, CAROLINE IS., TRUK, NORTHEAST NEW GUINEA, Tarawa Nov. 1943, NETHERLANDS EAST INDIES, Batavia, PAPUA, Port Moresby, SOLOMON IS., Guadalcanal Aug. 1942-Feb. 1943, Darwin, Coral Sea May 1942, INDIAN OCEAN, AUSTRALIA

after bloody struggles on sandy beaches. In October 1944, with their victory in the battle of Leyte Gulf, the greatest naval engagement in history, the Allies ended the threat of the Japanese fleet.

The final phase of the war against Japan began to unfold. The Allies took Iwo Jima and Okinawa, only a few hundred miles from Japan. From these bases waves of American bombers rained destruction on Japanese cities. In the China-Burma-India theater, the Chinese with U.S. aid, made inroads on areas previously captured by Japan (see map above).

But the decisive developments took place across the Pacific in New Mexico, where by 1945 U.S. scientists, with the help of scientists who had fled central Europe to escape Hitler, invented a new and terrible weapon—the atomic bomb. Based on figures from the island-hopping campaigns, the projected casualty rate for the taking of the main island of Japan ran into the hundreds of thousands. When the Japanese refused to surrender, an American bomber on August 6 dropped the atomic bomb on the city of Hiroshima. As the mushroom-shaped cloud rose over the city, only charred ruins were left behind. An expanse of approximately three square miles, 60 percent of the city, was pulverized. The Japanese government estimated the bomb killed 60,000 people, wounded 100,000, and left 200,000 homeless. Three days later, a second bomb was dropped on the city of Nagasaki, with similar results.

The Japanese finally sued for peace. The surrender ceremony took place aboard the battleship *Missouri* on September 2, 1945, almost six years to the day after Hitler plunged the world into the Second World War.

The Bombing of Hiroshima

Nuclear weapons totally changed the nature and possibilities of warfare. The U.S. Strategic Bombing Survey gave a detached version of what happened at Hiroshima.

At about 0815 there was a blinding flash. Some described it as brighter than the sun, others likened it to a magnesium flash. Following the flash there was a blast of heat and wind. The large majority of people within 3,000 feet of ground zero were killed immediately. Within a radius of about 7,000 feet almost every Japanese house collapsed. Beyond this range and up to 15,000–20,000 feet many of them collapsed and others received serious structural damage. Persons in the open were burned on exposed surfaces, and within 3,000–5,000 feet many were burned to death while others received severe burns through their clothes. In many instances clothing burst into spontaneous flame and had to be beaten out. Thousands of people were pinned beneath collapsed buildings or injured by flying debris. Flying glass particularly produced many non-lethal injuries and the distances at which they occurred are discussed in the following chapter, but the foregoing presentation was necessary for one to appreciate the state of the population immediately after the bomb exploded.

Shortly after the blast fires began to spring up over the city. Those who were able made a mass exodus from the city into the outlying hills. There was no organized activity. The people appeared stunned by the catastrophe and rushed about as jungle animals suddenly released from a cage. Some few apparently attempted to help others from the wreckage, particularly members of their family or friends. Others assisted those who were unable to walk alone. However, many of the injured were left trapped beneath collapsed buildings as people fled by them in the streets. Pandemonium reigned as the uninjured and slightly injured fled the city in fearful panic.

From "The Effects of Atomic Bombs on Health and Medical Services in Hiroshima and Nagasaki," in *The United States Strategic Bombing Survey* (Washington, 1948).

Conclusion

When the war was finally over, the living counted the dead. The Germans lost 4.2 million military and civilian dead, while the western Allies lost 1.5 million. The Soviet Union suffered the greatest losses: close to 25 million citizens. Yugoslavia had the greatest per capita casualty rate—one in every ten. In Asia, the census for 1950 showed a loss of some 55 million people, even after a five-year period of recuperation.[23] A meaningful financial accounting for the six years of bloodshed is not possible.

The world went through this carnage to put an end to German, Italian, and Japanese aggression, which came frighteningly close to succeeding in its goal of world dominance. Unlike the First World War, which has spawned many historiographical controversies concerning its causes, there is no doubt that the key figure in the Second World War was Adolph Hitler. He was the essential link, the man whose policies and ideas welded together the dictators.

Unlike the Japanese and the Italians, whose global influence was limited by either geographical or internal problems, Hitler could build on Germany's industrial might and central location to forge a force for world conquest. Historians vary sharply on his goals and motivations. Some see him as a politician playing the traditional game of European power politics in a most skillful way while others view him as a single-minded fanatic pursuing the plans for conquest laid out in *Mein Kampf*. Between these two extremes are the scholars who believe that the *Führer* had deeply thought out, long-term goals but pursued them haphazardly, as opportunities presented themselves.

Hitler struck the spark that set off the world-wide conflagration. Aiding and abetting his ambitions was the obsessive desire of the democracies for peace. By 1939, the lesson had been learned that appeasement does not guarantee peace, and that it does not take two equally belligerent sides to make a war.

Suggestions for Reading

Two helpful introductions to the 1919–1945 period are Laurence Lafore, *The End of Glory* (Lippincott, 1970) and Joachim Remak, *The Origins of the Second World War* (Prentice-Hall, 1976).

The diplomacy leading up to and conducted during the war has received extensive study. Hans Gatzke, ed., *European Diplomacy between the Two Wars, 1919–1939* (Quadrangle, 1972) gives definition to some of the major problems involved in this period. His *Stressemann and the Rearmament of Germany* (Norton, 1969) emphasizes an interwar continuity. Jon Jacobson discusses a pivotal four years in *Locarno Diplomacy: Germany and the West 1925–1929* (Princeton, 1972). Gerhard Weinhard gives a penetrating analysis in *The Foreign Policy of Hitler's Germany: Diplomatic Revolution in Europe 1933–1936* (Chicago, 1970). Equally essential is Weinhard's follow-up study, *The Foreign Policy of Hitler's Germany . . . 1937–1939* (Chicago, 1980). Still one of the best studies of Soviet foreign policy is George Kennan's *Russia and the West Under Lenin and Stalin* (Mentor, 1961). W. L. Langer and S. E. Gleason discuss important aspects of U.S. foreign policy in *The Challenge to Isolation* (Harper, 1952). Herbert Feis' *Churchill, Roosevelt, Stalin* (Princeton, 1967) is a classic. René Albrecht-Carrié traces France's travail in *France, Europe, and the Two World Wars* (Harper, 1961). George Kennan's *Memoirs*, vol. I (Bantam, 1969) offers perceptive contemporary observations. Other fine studies on interwar affairs are Etienne Mantoux, *The Carthaginian Peace* (Ayer, 1978) and Sally Marks, *International Relations in Europe: 1918–1939* (St. Martin's, 1976). Robert Young's *In Command of France: French Foreign Policy and Military Planning, 1933–1940* (Harvard, 1978) gives needed perspective on France's dilemma.

One of the most discussed aspects of the interwar period is appeasement and the Munich Conference. Keith Middlemas, *The Strategy of Appeasement* (Quadrangle, 1972) gives a balanced survey of this very controversial issue. Francis L. Loewenheim, ed., *Peace or Appeasement* (Houghton Mifflin, 1965) provides a selection of documents, including the Hossbach Memorandum. Keith Eubank's study, *Munich* (Oklahoma, 1963) is a good summary.

The Spanish Civil War has also received much scholarly attention. John Coverdale discusses one aspect of the conflict in *Italian Intervention in the Spanish Civil War* (Princeton, 1975). Gabriel Jackson, *The Spanish Republic and the Civil War 1931–1939* (Princeton, 1965); Stanley G. Payne, *Spanish Revolution* (Norton, 1970); and Hugh Thomas, *The Spanish Civil War* (Harper & Row, 1977) are all first-rate studies. George Orwell, *Homage to Catalonia* (Harcourt) remains an invaluable contemporary description of that tragedy.

The war from the German perspective has to take into consideration the Führer himself, and Robert G. Waite's *The Psychopathic God: Adolf Hitler* (Mentor, 1983) offers fascinating insights into his personality. Harold C. Deutsch's *Hitler and His Germans: The Crisis of January–June 1938* (Minnesota, 1974) provides good insights into German planning and policies. David Irving's *Hitler's War* is a first-rate survey (Viking, 1977). Albert Speer gives an insider's point of view in *Inside the Third Reich* (Macmillan, 1970). Alexander Dallin's *German Rule in Russia 1941–1945* (St. Martin's, 1957) discusses occupation policies and problems. Albert Seaton's *The Russo-German War 1941–1945* (Praeger, 1970) is especially strong in its analysis of Soviet strategy.

The diplomacy surrounding Poland is well covered in Anna Cienciala, *Poland the the Western Powers 1938–1939* (Toronto, 1968). John A. Armstrong, *Soviet Partisans in World War II* (Wisconsin, 1964) is a deft analysis of a subtle theater of action. George Bruce gives thorough coverage of the 1944 Polish tragedies in *Warsaw Uprising 1 August 2 October* (Hart-Davis, 1972). Harrison Salisbury, *The Nine Hundred Days: The Siege of Leningrad* (Harper, 1975) is a heartbreaking story of heroism. The tragic story of repatriated Soviet citizens is told in Nikolai Tolstoy, *Victims of Yalta* (Hodder & Stoughton, 1978).

Three good books on the Pacific theater are Christopher Thorne, *Allies of a Kind: The United States, Britain, and the War Against Japan* (Oxford, 1978); Gordon W. Prange, *At Dawn We Slept: The Untold Story of Pearl Harbor* (McGraw-Hill, 1981); and Yoshiburo Ienaga, *The Pacific War, 1937–1945* (Pantheon, 1978), which views the war from Japan's perspective.

Other aspects of the war are covered in Anthony Adamthwaite, *France and the Coming of the Second World War 1936–1939* (Frank Cass, 1977); Maurice Cowling, *The Impact of Hitler: British Politics and British Foreign Policy 1933–1940* (Chicago, 1977); Henri Michel, *The Shadow War, European Resistance 1939–1945* (Harper, 1972); Leila J. Rupp, *Mobilizing Women for War, 1939–1945* (Princeton, 1977); Len Deighton, *Fighter: The True Story of the Battle of Britain* (Johnathan Cape, 1977). Three books dealing with intelligence activities are F. W. Winterbotham, *The Ultra Secret* (Dell, 1979); William Stevenson, *A Man Called Intrepid* (Ballantine, 1976); and R. V. Jones, *The Wizard War: British Scientific Intelligence 1939–1945* (Coward, McCann, 1978).

The Nazis' genocide policies have been analyzed by Raul Hilberg, *The Destruction of the European Jews* (Quadrangle, 1961); Karl A. Schleunes, *The Twisted Road to Auschwitz: Nazi Policy Toward German Jews 1933–1939* (Illinois, 1970); and Lucy S. Dawidowicz, ed., *A Holocaust Reader* (Behrman House, 1976). See also Dawidowicz's *The War Against the Jews: 1933–1945* (Bantam, 1976).

Just about all major participants who survived the war—on all sides—have produced memoirs. The classics among them are Churchill's *The Second World War*, 6 vols. (Bantam) and Charles De Gaulle, *Mémoires* (Plon).

Notes

1. Harold Nicolson, *Peacemaking 1919* (New York: Harcourt Brace, 1933), p. 207.
2. Quoted in A. G. Mazour, *Russia Past and Present* (New York: Van Nostrand Reinhold Co., 1951), p. 576.
3. A. J. Ryder, *Twentieth-Century Germany: From Bismarck to Brandt* (New York: Columbia Univ. Press, 1973), pp. 220–226.
4. George F. Kennan, *Memoirs* (New York: Bantam Books, 1969), p. 122.
5. John Toland, *Adolf Hitler* (New York: Ballantine Books, 1977), pp. 522–529.
6. Donald W. Treadgold, *Twentieth Century Russia* (Chicago: Rand McNally & Co., 1959), pp. 324–325.
7. Keith Middlemas, *The Strategy of Appeasement* (Chicago: Quadrangle Books, 1972), pp. 1–8.
8. Middlemas, *The Strategy of Appeasement*, pp. 410–412.
9. The minutes of the conference in the Reich Chancellery, as extracted and quoted in Francis L. Loewenheim, *Peace or Appeasement* (Boston: Houghton Mifflin, 1965), pp. 2–4.
10. Middlemas, *The Strategy of Appeasement*, p. 177.
11. Laurence Lafore, *The End of Glory* (Philadelphia and New York: J. B. Lippincott, 1970), p. 226.
12. W. S. Churchill, *Blood, Sweat, and Tears* (New York: G. P. Putnam's Sons, 1941), p. 66.
13. F. D. Roosevelt, "Address at Chicago, October 5, 1937," in *The Literature of the United States*, II, W. Blair, T. Hornberger, and R. Stewart, eds. (Chicago: Scott, Foresman, 1955), pp. 831–832.
14. Maurice Crouzet, "L'Epoque Contemporaine," *Histoire Générale des Civilisations*, VII (Paris: Presses Universitaires de France, 1957), pp. 303–349. F. W. Winterbotham, *The Ultra Secret* (New York: Harper & Row, 1974), pp. 1–55. William Stephenson, *A Man Called Intrepid* (New York: Ballantine Books, 1976), *passim*.
15. S. E. Ayling, *Portraits of Power* (New York: Barnes & Noble, 1963), p. 159.
16. Nigel Nicolson, ed., *Harold Nicolson, The War Years 1939–1945, Volume II of Diaries and Letters* (New York: Atheneum, 1967), p. 100.
17. Churchill, *Blood, Sweat, and Tears*, p. 297.
18. Albert Seaton, *The Russo-German War 1941–1945* (New York: Praeger, 1970), pp. 37–38.
19. *Last Letters From Stalingrad*, translated by Franz Schneider and Charles Gullas (New York: Signet Books, 1965), p. 20.
20. Seaton, *The Russo-German War*, pp. 453–456.
21. Quoted in John Vinocur, "Goebbels, in Published 1945 Diary Blames Goring for Nazis' Collapse," *New York Times*, January 3, 1978.
22. See Raul Hilberg, *The Destruction of the European Jews* (Chicago: Quadrangle Books, 1961), *passim*, and Crouzet, "L'Epoque Contemporaine," pp. 358–359.
23. Simon Kuznets, *Postwar Economic Growth: Four Lectures* (Cambridge, MA: Harvard Univ. Press, 1964), pp. 72–76, as cited in David Landes, *The Unbound Prometheus* (Cambridge: Cambridge Univ. Press, 1969), p. 487.

The Bipolar "North," 1945–1991

Soviet and American Spheres

The Cold War—the 44 years of great power tension after World War II—did not see a formal state of war between the U.S. and USSR. However, "proxy wars" fought by the clients of each superpower and conflicts occurring in the wake of decolonization killed millions in Asia, Africa, and Latin America. Ironically, Europe, caught in the stalemate between the United States and the Soviet Union enjoyed its longest time of peace in recorded history.

Washington and Moscow led their allies through the postwar decades with a mixture of aggressiveness and wisdom. From the first, the west's economic and social structures were more productive than those of the eastern bloc. Yet through a massive effort, the Soviet Union achieved military parity with the west by the mid-1970s. By the last decade of the twentieth century, economic exhaustion brought an end to the Cold War. Increased cooperation characterized the relations between Moscow and Washington, as both looked to a new era in which they would try to keep their dominant roles in the world.

The Elusive Peace

After World War II, many of the living had reason to envy the dead. Fire bombs and nuclear weapons depopulated and spread radiation to parts of Japan. One-fourth of Germany's cities were in rubble as were much of Italy and central Europe. The war claimed 10 percent of Yugoslavia's population. In China, after 15 years of fighting, the survivors faced hunger, disease, civil war,

and revolution. Twenty-five million people died in the Soviet Union, and the country lost one-third of its national wealth. Although casualty rates in Britain and France were lower than in World War I, both countries paid dearly in lives and in the ruin that took one-fourth of their national wealth. The allied countries such as the United States—which suffered 389,000 casualties—Canada, Australia, and New Zealand suffered no material damage but paid a heavy price in combat dead.

Postwar Problems

Postwar Europe faced two immediate problems: the fate of collaborators and millions of Nazi labor slaves. In countries that had been occupied by the Nazis, resistance groups began to take vigilante justice against those who had worked with the Germans. Across Europe they executed thousands of collaborators. In France alone 800 were sent to their deaths. After the war, courts sentenced thousands more to prison terms. Eight million foreign labor slaves who had been used by the Nazis remained to be dealt with. By the end of 1945, five million of them had been sent home, including many Soviet citizens who were forced to return. Some of them chose suicide rather than return to Stalin's rule.

In Germany, following the Yalta agreement, the Allies established four occupation zones—French, British, American, and Russian (see map, p. 906). They divided the capital, Berlin, located in the Soviet sector, into four parts. The Russians promised free access from the western zones to Berlin. The Allies then began to carry out a selective process of denazification. Some former Nazis

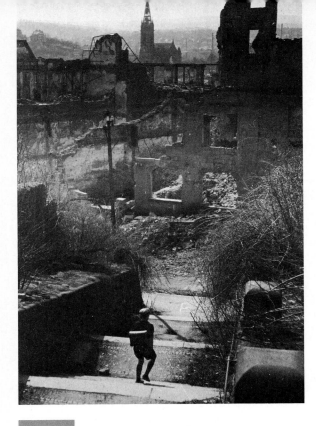

After World War II, the bombed-out cities of Europe seemed almost beyond hope. In 1947 Churchill described the Continent as "a rubble heap, a charnel house, a breeding ground of pestilence and hate."

were sent to prison while thousands received the benefits of large-scale declarations of amnesty. Many ex-Nazis were employed by the scientific and intelligence services of the Allies.

The most important denazification act came at the 1945–1946 trials of war criminals held at Nuremburg. An international panel of jurists conducted the proceedings and condemned 12 leading Nazis to be hanged and sent seven to prison for crimes against humanity. The panel acquitted three high officials. Critics condemned the trials as an act of vengeance, "a political act by the victors against the vanquished." The prosecution stated, however, the Nazi crimes were so terrible that "civilization cannot tolerate their being ignored because it cannot survive their being repeated."[1]

By the end of 1945, the growing tension between the Soviet Union and the United States made it impossible to construct a peace settlement. At the Potsdam Conference in the summer of 1945 a council of ministers was set up to draft peace treaties. After two years of difficult negotiations treaties were signed with Italy, Romania, Bulgaria, Hungary, and Finland. In 1951, an accord between the western powers and the Japanese reestablished Japan as a sovereign state. Austria's position remained uncertain until 1955 when a peace treaty was signed and occupation forces withdrawn. The western allies and the Soviets were completely at odds over the German peace settlement. Not until the signing of the Helsinki Accords in 1975 was a status quo for Europe acknowledged, and that agreement did not have the force of a binding legal treaty. Finally, in the summer of 1990 the diplomatic issues spawned by World War II were put to rest in a series of treaties signed by all European parties.

The United Nations

On only one issue, the establishment of an international peacekeeping organization, could the powers agree after the war. Great Britain and the United States laid the foundations for the United Nations in 1941 when they proposed "the establishment of a wider and permanent system of

THE DIVISION OF GERMANY

general security" so "that men in all lands may live out their lives in freedom from fear and want." Subsequent meetings at Moscow and Yalta led representatives of fifty governments meeting at San Francisco from April to June 1945 to draft the Charter of the United Nations.

To pursue its goals of peace and an improved standard of living for the world, the UN would work through six organizations: the Security Council, to maintain peace and order; the General Assembly, to function as a form of town meeting of the world; the Economic and Social Council, to improve living standards and extend human rights; the Trusteeship Council, to advance the interests of the colonial peoples; the International Court of Justice, to resolve disputes between nations; and the Secretariat, headed by the secretary-general, to serve the needs of other organizations. Much of the responsibility for improving the economic and social conditions of the world's people was entrusted to a dozen specialized agencies, such as the International Labor Organization, the Food and Agricultural and the World Health Organizations, and the UN Educational, Scientific, and Cultural Organization.

The greatest controversy at San Francisco arose over the right of veto in the Security Council. The smaller countries held that it was unjust for the big powers to be able to block the wishes of the majority. But the Big Five—the United States, the Soviet Union, China, France, and Great Britain—affirmed that singly and collectively they had special interests and responsibilities in maintaining world peace and security. The UN Charter, therefore, provided that the Security Council should consist of 11 members, five permanent members representing the great powers and six elected by the General Assembly for a term of two years. These numbers would be increased as the membership of the UN grew. On purely procedural matters a majority of seven votes was sufficient; on matters of substance, all permanent members had to agree.

The UN proved to be more effective than the League of Nations. The UN, like the League, lacks the sovereign power of its member states. However, as was shown in the Korean conflict in the 1950s and in the Gulf War in 1991 it has become more wide-reaching in its impact. In 1946 it had 51 members. At the beginning of the 1990s membership stood at more than 160. Over the years the UN's usefulness has repeatedly been demonstrated despite the difficulties of the Cold War, the strains of massive decolonization, and four Arab-Israeli wars—not to mention an interminable series of smaller crises. As was the case with the League, the UN cannot coerce the

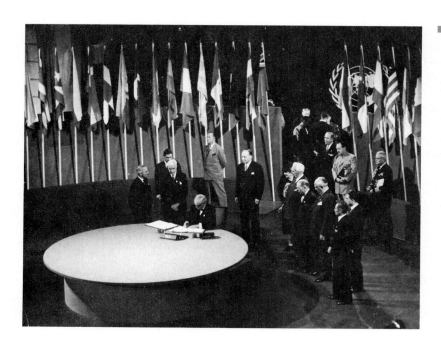

Nations put their hope in a new international organization, the United Nations, to rebuild the shattered world and preserve the peace. Here, U.S. senator Arthur Vandenberg signs the charter of the United Nations on June 16, 1945, as other members of the U.S. delegation wait for their turns. U.S. president Harry Truman and Secretary of State Edward Stettinius, Jr., watch from Vandenberg's right.

great powers when any of them decide a major national interest is involved.

The Cold War

The Cold War between Washington and Moscow dominated the world in the half century after World War II. When it began the United States held the advantage in nuclear weapons and world trade; when it ended each power had equal military power and dissimilar, but serious, economic crises. From 1945 to 1953 the struggle was centered in Europe. In the wake of decolonization the conflict shifted to Asia, Latin America, the Middle East, and Africa.

The Soviets and Americans have differed in their views on economics, politics, social organization, religion, and the role of the individual since 1917. The Nazi threat produced a temporary unity, but by 1943 Soviet frustration with the slowness of its allies to open the second front, discontent with being shut out of participation in the Italian campaign, and unhappiness with the amount of U.S. financial assistance increased tension. The western allies were suspicious of Soviet secrecy. London and Washington gave detailed data on strategy and weapons to Moscow, but got little information from the Soviets. Over $12 billion dollars in Lend-Lease aid was sent to the Soviet Union, but its extent and value were not publicly acknowledged for four decades in the Soviet Union.[2]

After the February 1945 Yalta Conference it soon became clear that Stalin had his view of the composition of postwar eastern Europe and Roosevelt and Churchill had theirs. As early as April 1, 1945, Roosevelt sent a telegram to Stalin protesting the violation of Yalta pledges. A month later Churchill sent a long message of protest to Stalin in which he concluded:

> There is not much comfort in looking into a future where you and the countries you dominate . . . are all on one side, and those who rally to the English speaking nations . . . are on the other . . . their quarrel would tear the world to pieces.[3]

From 1945 to 1948 Stalin expanded his control over the region carefully, working through coalition governments. He had a number of advantages. Most of the local élites had either been killed during the war or were condemned for collaborating with the Nazis. The communist parties, most of whom were underground during the interwar period, had gained public support by leading the resistance to the Nazis after June 1941. Further, the Red Army remained in place to intimidate eastern Europe.

The communists occupied the most powerful positions in the coalition governments; opposition parties gained largely symbolic posts. The communists soon used intimidation and outright force. The Czechs remained free longer than the other eastern European states. In the 1946 elections the communists had received only 38 percent of the vote, and they were losing support. In the spring of 1948 the Soviets forced Czechoslovakia to submit to communist control. By the end of 1948, when the Americans had totally withdrawn from Europe, the governments in Warsaw, East Berlin, Prague, Budapest, Bucharest, Sofia, and Tirana operated as satellites orbiting the political center of Moscow.

Stalin used the Soviet bloc as a four-hundred-mile-deep buffer against capitalist invasion and as a source to help the USSR rebuild. He blocked any political, economic, or cultural contact with the west. Once his allies gained control, he ordered a purge of the local parties, based on those in the Soviet Union in the 1930s. The main target for the purge was the national communists, those who were seen as being more loyal to their own nation than to Moscow or Stalin. Overall, the purge removed one in every four party members. Many of those eliminated had been loyal communists since the beginning of the century.

Meanwhile, in the three years after 1945, the four-power agreement on the governing of Germany soon broke apart. In the fall of 1946, Britain and America merged their zones into one economic unit, which came to be known as Bizonia. The French joined the union in 1948. Germany was now split into two parts, one administered by the western allies and the other by the Russians, and would remain divided until the line between the two powers—dubbed the Iron Curtain by Churchill—disappeared in 1990.

The Marshall Plan and Containment

The Soviets did not return their armies to a peacetime status after 1945. They and their allies challenged the west in Greece, Turkey, and Iran. Britain was too weak to play its former role in the region. The Americans, as they would subsequently do throughout the globe, filled the gap left by the British and French. President Harry Truman responded to Soviet pressure by announcing that the United States would support any country threatened by communist aggression. Soon after proclamation of the Truman Doctrine in 1947, the United States sent economic and military aid to Greece and Turkey, a move traditionally held to mark the American entry into the Cold War.

The United States' wartime goodwill toward the Soviet Union turned quickly to paranoid fear of international communism. The Americans, comfortable with their nuclear monopoly, had looked forward to a postwar peaceful world. They were angered by Soviet actions in the United Nations, Eastern Europe, China, and the growth of communist parties in western Europe. Conservatives attacked the Yalta agreement as a "sellout" and launched a new "Red Scare" campaign. A French observer noted the rapid change in attitude by pointing out that "a whole nation, optimistic and naive, placed its trust in a comrade in arms."[4] Now that comrade was the enemy.

The American diplomat, George F. Kennan, explained that the correct stance to take toward Stalin's policies was one of containment. In an article entitled "The Sources of Soviet Conduct," written under the byline of "Mr. X" in the July 1947 issue of *Foreign Affairs*, Keenan proposed a "realistic understanding of the profound and deep-rooted difference between the United States and the Soviet Union" and the exercise of "a long-term, patient but firm and vigilant containment

The Truman Doctrine

Once the Americans recovered from their post-1945 euphoria, President Truman spelled out his response to perceived Soviet aggression.

The peoples of a number of countries of the world have recently had totalitarian regimes forced upon them against their will. The Government of the United States has made frequent protests against coercion and intimidation, in violation of the Yalta agreement, in Poland, Rumania, and Bulgaria. I must also state that in a number of other countries there have been similar developments.

At the present moment in world history nearly every nation must choose between alternative ways of life. The choice is too often not a free one.

One way of life is based upon the will of the majority, and is distinguished by free institutions, representative government, free elections, guaranties of individual liberty, freedom of speech and religion, and freedom from political oppression.

The second way of life is based upon the will of a minority forcibly imposed upon the majority. It relies upon terror and oppression, a controlled press and radio, fixed elections, and the suppression of personal freedoms.

I believe that it must be the policy of the United States to support free peoples who are resisting attempted subjugation by armed minorities or by outside pressures.

I believe that we must assist free peoples to work out their own destinies in their own way.

I believe that our help should be primarily through economic and financial aid, which is essential to economic stability and orderly political processes.

From U.S. Congress *Congressional Record*, 80th Congress, 1st Session (Washington, D.C.: U.S. Government Printing Office, 1947), vol. 93, p. 1981; and U.S. Congress, Senate Committee on Foreign Relations, *A Decade of American Foreign Policy: Basic Documents. 1941–1949* (Washington, D.C.: U.S. Government Printing Office, 1950), pp. 1270–1271.

of Russian expansive tendencies."[5] This advice shaped U.S. policy throughout Europe.

The policy of containment was first used in Yugoslavia where a split between Joseph Broz Tito (1891–1980) and Stalin marked the first breach in the Soviet advance. The Yugoslavs initiated the ideological break known as national communism. Supported financially by the west, the Yugoslavs were able to survive Stalin's attacks.

The broad economic and political arms of containment came into play. Secretary of State George C. Marshall proposed a plan of economic aid to help Europe to solve its postwar financial problems. Western European nations eagerly accepted the Marshall Plan while the Soviet Union rejected American aid for itself and the bloc. Congress authorized the plan, known as the European Recovery Program, and within four years the industrial output of the recipients climbed to 64 percent over 1947 levels and 41 percent over prewar levels. The European Recovery Act stabilized conditions in western Europe and prevented the communists from taking advantage of postwar problems.

Rival Systems

In July 1948, after opposing a western series of currency and economic reforms, the Soviets blocked all land and water transport to Berlin from the west. For the next ten months the allies supplied West Berlin by air. They made over 277,000 flights to bring 2.3 million tons of food and other vital materials to the besieged city. Rather than risk war over the city and the use of American nuclear weapons, the Russians removed their blockade in May 1949. In the same month the Federal Republic of Germany, made up of the three western allied zones came into existence. Almost immediately, the Soviet Union established the German Democratic Republic in East Germany. Germany would remain divided for the next 41 years.

In the spring of 1949 Washington established the North Atlantic Treaty Organization (NATO), an alliance for mutual assistance. The initial members were Great Britain, France, Belgium, Luxembourg, the Netherlands, Norway, Denmark, Portugal, Italy, Iceland, the United States, and Canada. Greece and Turkey joined in 1952, followed by West Germany in 1955. In 1955 also the Soviets created the Warsaw Pact, which formalized the existing unified military command in Soviet-dominated eastern Europe, (see map at right). Warsaw Pact members included, in addition to the Soviet Union, Albania, Bulgaria, Romania, Czechoslovakia, Hungary, Poland, and East Germany. The alliance lasted until 1991.

The tension between the rival systems finally snapped in Korea. After Japan's surrender, Korea had been divided at the 38th parallel into

To try to force the Western powers out of Berlin, in July 1948 the Russians imposed a blockade on the city. In response, the allies organized an airlift to fly in supplies to the city and its beleaguered citizens. In May 1949, the Soviets lifted the blockade.

PACIFIC OCEAN

ALASKA (U.S.)

ARCTIC OCEAN

North Pole

CANADA

GREENLAND (DENMARK)

NORTH AMERICA

HUDSON BAY

ICELAND

UNITED STATES

ATLANTIC OCEAN

GULF OF MEXICO

ASIA

SOVIET UNION

EUROPE

NORWAY

POLAND

BLACK SEA

TURKEY

ROMANIA

BULG.

DEN.

E. GER.

CZECH.

HUN.

GREECE

NORTH SEA

W. GER.

ALBANIA

MEDITERRANEAN SEA

GREAT BRITAIN

NETH.

BELG.

LUX.

ITALY

FRANCE

PORTUGAL

AFRICA

American and Soviet zones of occupation. When the occupying troops left, they were replaced by two hostile forces, each claiming jurisdiction over the entire country. On June 25, 1950 North Korean troops crossed the 38th parallel into South Korea. Washington immediately called for a special meeting of the UN Security Council, whose members demanded a cease fire and withdrawal of the invaders. The Soviet delegate was boycotting the Council at the time and was not present to veto the action.

When North Korea ignored the UN's demand, the Security Council sent troops to help the South Korean government. Three years of costly fighting followed, in what the UN termed a "police action." UN forces led by the United States, which suffered over 140,000 casualties, repelled the invaders, who were supported by the USSR and the Chinese Peoples' Republic. An armistice was signed in July 1953, after Stalin's death in March and the U.S. threat to use nuclear weapons against China.[6] The border between the two parts of the country was established near the 38th parallel, and South Korea's independence was maintained. The peninsula remained a crisis point for the next 40 years.

The Cold War erupted into heated fighting in Korea in 1950, when North Korean troops crossed the border into South Korea in an attempt to force reunification of the country. The United States, with UN backing, rushed to South Korea's defense. Here, a U.S. soldier surveys the smoldering ruins of a village north of Chunchon, South Korea, near the 38th parallel.

By 1953 the first phase of the Cold War was over. Both the Soviet Union and the United States possessed terrifying arsenals of nuclear weapons, both competed in all aspects of the Cold War, and both constantly probed for weaknesses in the other's defenses. Varied forms of controlled conflict characterized the next four decades of relations between Moscow and Washington.

The Soviet Union in the Postwar Era

Stalin rewarded the Soviet people for their sacrifices in World War II with a return to the iron repression of the 1930s. In the city of Leningrad, which had lost one million people, streets had been renamed in honor of the war dead. Stalin's party ripped down these spontaneous tributes and restored the old, officially approved names.

Postwar Stalinism

Despite the immense destruction it had suffered the USSR emerged after the war as one of the world's two superpowers. Stalin took seriously his role to build communism and pursue world revolution. He used the secret police to rid Soviet society of any Western contamination. To achieve military equality with the United States, he launched the fourth Five-Year Plan in 1946 pushing growth in heavy industry and military goods. To increase Soviet output, he imposed double shifts on many workers.

Huge new factories producing an estimated 80 percent of industrial output sprang up east of a line from Leningrad to Moscow to Stalingrad (now Volgograd). The state lured workers to the new sites with salary increases and other benefits, but much of the need for workers was filled by mass deportation of people to labor camps. Those whose loyalty to Stalin was in the least suspect were sent to a network of camps spread from Siberia to central Asia to the Arctic region. "The economic demand for cheap labour [dictated] the supply of the guilty."[7] Thousands died in the camps from overwork, inadequate food, and the bitter cold.

To rebuild the devastated farming regions Stalin returned to his collectivization policies. Smaller farms became parts of larger units, and the ultimate goal remained to make peasants into members of the rural proletariat, working in a kind of food factory. After 1950 the effort was stepped up, but at the cost of discontent and low productivity.

The dictator continued to place his supporters in all important offices, combining "the supreme command of the party with the supreme administration of the state."[8] He made entry into the party more difficult and purged those people who had slipped in during the war. The party became a haven for the managerial elite rather than the ideologically pure. The 1946 Supreme Soviet elections illustrated Stalin's total control. The voters were given only one choice for each office. Officials reported that 99.7 percent of the citizens voted; of this total fewer than 1 percent crossed out the name of a candidate.

In the early 1950s Stalin lashed out more ruthlessly and unpredictably than ever before, as he came to suspect everyone. His half-million strong security police squashed any sign of dissent, criticism, or free expression. He ordered genocidal attacks on entire peoples such as the Crimean Tatars. The purges went beyond the functions of "élite self-renewal." Stalin removed and later executed the director of national economic planning. There were indications that Stalin was preparing a major purge in January 1953. The police announced that a "doctors' plot" had been uncovered and charged a group of physicians serving high military and governmental officials with planning to undermine their patients' health. Seven of the nine accused were Jewish, and in some quarters it was feared that an anti-Zionist purge was in the making. The purge did not occur because on March 5, 1953, Stalin died after a painful illness.

Thus passed one of the most powerful men in world history. He had taken Lenin's revolution and preserved it in Russia while exporting it to the world. In a quarter-century he remade his society, withstood Hitler's strongest attacks, and emerged from the Second World War as leader of one of the two superpowers. He built the Soviet economic and political systems that lasted until 1987 and cultivated a group of bureaucratic

The first major movement in painting to develop after World War II was abstract expressionism, sometimes called action painting because the activity of painting seems as important as the finished product. One of the leaders of abstract expressionism is Willem de Kooning (b. 1904), whose best-known works are his woman paintings, a series of female nudes, such as *Woman IV* (1952–53), executed in broad, violent brush strokes on large canvases.

The act of painting is as important as color-field painting as it is in abstract expressionism, although the technique is quite different. Morris Louis (1912–1962), for example, applied extremely thin acrylic paint to absorbent, unstretched canvas, allowing the paint to sink in and stain the fabric rather than lie on top of the surface. The technique produces shapes of rich, although subdued, colors and soft, fuzzy edges. A characteristic example is *Point of Tranquillity* (1959–1960).

Pop art, a movement of the 1960s, emphasizes the materialism of contemporary industrialized culture by focusing on the realistic presentation of commonplace items of popular culture, such as soup cans, comic strips, and drugstores. Andy Warhol (b. 1931) uses images of advertising in his paintings, producing facsimiles of familiar products, such as *Campbell's Soup* (1965). Roy Lichtenstein (b. 1923) is noted for his use of comic-strip techniques, flat surfaces, hard edges, and bright colors. In *Stepping Out* (1978), upper right, the female companion of the dapper young man is reminiscent of surrealist images of the 1920s. The most famous pop art sculptor is George Segal (b. 1924), who frequently uses white plaster casts of the human figure set in realistic environments. His works, such as *The Diner* (1964–66), lower right, with their mood of loneliness, have been compared to Edward Hopper's paintings.

The realistic portrayal of real objects and images reaches an extreme in photo, or super, realism, in which images are first photographed, then translated into meticulously realistic paintings. The result is a painting of a photograph, executed in a completely detached, impersonal, and objective manner. The devotion to detail and complete accuracy characteristic of photo realism are evident in the works of Richard Estes (b. 1936), such as *Drugstore* (1970).

Stalin's chief supporters surround his bier at his funeral, March 6, 1953. Left to right, they are Vyacheslav Molotov, Kliment Voroshilov, Lavrenti Beria, Georgi Malenkov, Nikolai Bulganin, Nikita Khrushchev, Lazar Kaganovich, and Anastas Mikoyan. Khrushchev was the victor in the power struggle to succeed Stalin.

survivors—*apparatchiki*—who ran the country until the advent of Mikhail Gorbachev. In doing all of this, he killed at least twice as many people as Hitler.

Khrushchev's Contribution

A committee made up of Lavrenti Beria (secret police), Georgi Malenkov (chief Stalin aid), and Vyacheslav Molotov (foreign affairs) succeeded Stalin. The new rulers issued orders urging the people to guard against enemies and prevent "any kind of disorder and panic." They placed Stalin's embalmed body in the tomb next to Lenin and then relaxed his policies. They dropped the doctors' plot charges, eased censorship, reduced terror, and released many from prison and the labor camps. Within three years, the initial triumvirate had disappeared, elbowed aside by the Ukrainian Nikita Sergeyevich Khrushchev (1894–1971).

Khruschchev was a self-made man who rose by his wits and ability. Born of peasant parents, he was a shepherd at seven and later a miner and factory worker. He joined the communist party and quickly rose through its ranks. Like so many of his colleagues, he came to power in the 1930s by taking the jobs of people killed by Stalin and ascended to the Politburo by 1939. By July 1953 he was the first secretary of the party; by 1955 he led the country. Educated Russians viewed Khrushchev as uncultured and uncouth. He delighted in shocking people by his blunt and frequently profane remarks. His crude behavior disguised a subtle, supple, and penetrating mind, which got rapidly to the center of a problem.

One of Khrushchev's main goals was to reform agriculture. He proposed increasing incentives for the peasants and enlarging the area under production in Soviet Siberia and central Asia—the virgin lands. Between 1953 and 1958 production rose by 50 percent. Thereafter farming in the

Khrushchev and Soviet foreign minister Andrei Gromyko pound the table to register their approval of the proceedings at a meeting of the UN General Assembly in 1960.

virgin lands proved to be economically wasteful and this, combined with other setbacks, ultimately undermined his position.

Khrushchev's greatest contribution was to begin the de-Stalinization campaign. In February 1956 at the Twentieth Party Congress he gave a speech entitled the "Crimes of the Stalin Era." He attacked his former patron as a bloodthirsty tyrant and revealed many of the cruelties of the purges and the mistakes of World War II. He carefully heaped full responsibility on the dead dictator for the excesses of the past twenty-five years, removing the blame from the *apparatchiki* such as himself who Stalin placed in power. Khrushchev blamed Stalin's crimes on the dictator's "cult of the personality." The speech hit like a bombshell and shocked every aspect of Soviet life from foreign policy to art and literature. In 1961 Stalin's body was removed from the Lenin mausoleum and placed in a grave by the Kremlin wall. His name disappeared from streets and cities; the "hero city" of Stalingrad was renamed Volgograd. Yet, the governing structure Stalin had built was carefully preserved, and his protégés remained in place until Gorbachev came to power in 1985.

Khrushchev's speech echoed throughout the communist world, helping to spark uprisings in Poland and Hungary and to widen the gulf between China and the Soviet Union. After 1956 Chinese-Soviet relations soured drastically and by 1960 Khrushchev had pulled all Soviet technicians and assistance out of China. During the next decade, the split grew still wider as Mao proclaimed himself to be Khrushchev's equal in ideological affairs.

Khrushchev survived an attempt to oust him from power in the summer of 1957, and from then until 1962, he dominated both Soviet and international affairs. During his rule, the standard of living in Russia gradually improved. Soviet scientists made remarkable strides, launching the first earth satellite, Sputnik, in the fall of 1957, and building a powerful fleet of intercontinental ballistic missiles. Khrushchev also relaxed, until 1959, the tensions of the Cold War and pursued "peaceful coexistence."

From 1959 to 1962 Khrushchev pursued aggressive policies in Asia, Africa, and Latin America. After drawing the world to the brink of catastrophe in the Cuban missile crisis in October 1962, he pulled back from the final step that would have resulted in nuclear war.

Khrushchev's blunders in Cuba and failures in agricultural policies led finally to his removal from power. While on vacation in October 1964 he received news from his colleagues that he had been "released from state duties" and that he had to return to Moscow. The fallen leader became a pensioned "un-person" under a mild form of house arrest in a comfortable compound outside of Moscow. He remained largely isolated from the public, writing his memoirs until his death in 1971.

The Last of Stalin's Protégés

After Khrushchev's "retirement" Leonid Brezhnev (1906–1982) and Aleksei Kosygin (1904–1980) strengthened the rule by Stalin's aging proteges. For the first ten years the two men split power: Brezhnev acted as General Secretary and Kosygin as premier, overseeing sporadic reform attempts. Brezhnev became president of the country under terms of the 1977 constitution.

Politics remained based on Stalin's foundations, as modified by Khrushchev. The central planners continued to emphasize industrial growth and slowly increase the supply of consumer goods. In foreign policy, the new team pursued peaceful coexistence at the same time that they greatly strengthened the Soviet armed forces. Brezhnev worked closely with military leaders to ensure that they had everything needed to gain equality with the United States in missiles, air, land, and sea forces. During the eighteen years of his rule, the Soviet Union built a powerful, global navy to support its foreign policies.

While the USSR gained military parity with the west, its civilian economy ground to a halt. The longstanding agricultural crisis grew worse. The Soviets spent huge amounts to import grain from abroad to cope with food shortages at home. Especially maddening to the Soviet leaders was the extraordinary amount of crops that rotted in the fields or en route to market. Private plots worked by peasants after hours for their own profit, which accounted for only 3 percent of sown land, provided 30 percent of all the table food in the Soviet Union.

The party leaders struggled to deal with low per capita output, poor quality, technological

Nikita Khrushchev, Address to the Twentieth Party Congress

After a quarter-century of Stalinist rule, the USSR badly needed a policy change. Khrushchev justified the change on the basis that Stalin had departed from Leninist norms and pursued the "cult of the personalities."

When we analyze the practice of Stalin in regard to the direction of the party and of the country, when we pause to consider everything which Stalin perpetrated, we must be convinced that Lenin's fears were justified. The negative characteristics of Stalin, which, in Lenin's time, were only incipient, transformed themselves during the last years into a grave abuse of power by Stalin, which caused untold harm to our party.

We have to consider seriously and analyze correctly this matter in order that we may preclude any possibility of a repetition in any form whatever of what took place during the life of Stalin, who absolutely did not tolerate collegiality in leadership and in work, and who practiced brutal violence, not only toward everything which opposed him, but also toward that which seemed to his capricious and despotic character, contrary to his concepts.

Stalin acted not through persuasion, explanation, and patient cooperation with people, but by imposing his concepts and demanding absolute submission to his opinion. Whoever opposed this concept or trend to prove his viewpoint, and the correctness of his position—was doomed to removal from the leading collective and to subsequent moral and physical annihilation. This was expecially true during the period following the 17th party congress, when many prominent party leaders and rank-and-file party workers, honest and dedicated to the cause of communism, fell victim to Stalin's despotism. . . .

. . . Lenin's traits—patient work with people; stubborn and painstaking education of them; the ability to induce people to follow him without using compulsion, but rather through the ideological influence on them of the whole collective—were entirely foreign to Stalin. He (Stalin) discarded the Leninist method of convincing and educating; he abandoned the method of ideological struggle for that of administrative violence, mass repressions, and terror. He acted on an increasingly larger scale and more stubbornly through punitive organs, at the same time often violating all existing norms of morality and of Soviet laws. . . .

During Lenin's life party congresses were convened regularly; always when a radical turn in the development of the party and the country took place Lenin considered it absolutely necessary that the party discuss at length all the basic matters pertaining to internal and foreign policy and to questions bearing on the development of party and government. . . .

Were our party's holy Leninist principles observed after the death of Vladimir Ilyich?

Whereas during the first few years after Lenin's death party congresses and central committee plenums took place more or less regularly; later, when Stalin began increasingly to abuse his power, these principles were brutally violated. This was expecially evident during the last 15 years of his life. Was it a normal situation when 13 years elapsed between the 18th and 19th party congresses, years during which our party and our country had experienced so many important events? These events demanded categorically that the party should have passed resolutions pertaining to the country's defense during the patriotic war and to peacetime construction after the war. Even after the end of the war a congress was not convened for over 7 years. . . .

In practice Stalin ignored the norms of party life and trampled on the Leninist principle of collective party leadership. . . .

From U.S. Congress, *Congressional Record*, 84th Congress, 2nd Session, 1956, CII, pp. 9389–9403, passim.

backwardness, transport breakdowns, and widespread corruption. Over the next twenty years, despite numerous reform attempts, the Soviet economy stagnated. The military sector absorbed most economic and technological improvements. Living standards slowly improved, but at a terrific cost. The Soviet Union exacerbated its economic problems by allowing political and ideological considerations to take precedence over productive efficiency.[9]

Until 1985 the Soviet Union plodded along under an aging, often ill, leadership. Brezhnev was succeeded by Yuri Andropov (1914–1984), a railway worker's son who worked his way up the ranks to become Soviet ambassador to Hungary from 1954 to 1957. After putting down the 1956 revolution in Hungary, Andropov returned to Moscow to take a number of increasingly important party and political jobs. In 1967 he became chief of the KGB, the organization which combined the powers and responsibilities of the U.S. FBI and CIA but without the legal restraints affecting those two groups. He remained in that post for the next fifteen years. He entered the Politburo in 1973 and seven months before Brezhnev's death Andropov became the secretary of the Central Committee. He rose to the top position in the Soviet Union the day after Brezhnev's death.

Andropov's jobs put him at the crossroads of all information. He knew the rotten condition of the USSR's infrastructure. He brought a large number of people from the provinces to work in high party positions in Moscow and set out immediately to increase output, fight corruption, and strengthen the military. He started campaigns to fight alcoholism and cheating and fired people who did not perform up to his standards. However, his own health problems caught up with him, and from the summer of 1983 until his announced death in February, 1984, Andropov was out of public view.

The last of the Stalin protégés was Konstantin Chernenko (1911–1985), who succeeded Andropov to the posts of first secretary and president. Chernenko had ridden Brezhnev's coattails since the 1950s but had been soundly defeated by Andropov for the top job in 1982. His age and poor health signified that he would be a transition figure between the old guard and a new generation. The strain of leadership almost immediately broke Chernenko's fragile health, and even before his death in March 1985, wholesale changes were taking place in the highest levels of the Soviet government.

The Gorbachev Revolution

Mikhail Gorbachev, representing a new college-educated generation of Soviet leaders, moved rapidly to take power, implementing a platform based on *glasnost* (openness) and *perestroika* (restructuring) to try to bring new life to the Soviet system. *Glasnost* was Gorbachev's way to motivate the Soviet people to be more creative and work harder. *Perestroika* attempted to remove the structural blocks to modernization. These two themes launched the final act in the de-Stalinization campaign begun by Khrushchev in 1956.

Gorbachev tried to mobilize the support of the cultural and scientific elite by encouraging them to participate in political life. As examples of the policy, he brought physicist Andrei Sakharov back from internal exile and permitted publication of the works of exiled author Aleksandr Solzhenitsyn. For the first time the party acknowledged mistakes, such as the Chernobyl nuclear disaster in April 1986. Past tragedies—especially from the 1930s—that had long been common knowledge were now openly discussed. Gorbachev permitted unprecedented criticism of party and political leaders by the press and television. He sponsored broad reforms in Soviet society, imposing the strongest anti-alcoholism campaign in history, making the force of the drive felt at the highest levels.

One of *glasnost's* unexpected results was a revival of separatist movements in the various Soviet republics. People in Estonia, Lithuania, Latvia, Armenia, Azerbaijan, the Ukraine, Moldavia, Kazakhstan, and Georgia declared the supremacy of their laws, institutions, and programs over those of the central government and claimed ownership of resources found within their borders.

Gorbachev originally sought to use *perestroika* to fine-tune the traditional central planning apparatus and party and state procedures, but the total failure of the Stalinist system has demanded a much more wide-ranging program. By 1990 the depth and severity of the Soviet

The coming to power of Soviet premier Mikhail Gorbachev and the election of U.S. president George Bush ushered in a new era of cooperation between rival superpowers the Soviet Union and the United States. In a White House ceremony on June 1, 1990, Gorbachev and Bush signed a series of accords between their two governments.

Union's problems drove Gorbachev to attempt to impose a market economy, reduce the role of the "vanguard party," and alter the governmental structure. The broader scope of *perestroika* has sought foreign capital, markets, and technology in order to make the USSR competitive. Gorbachev has had to rebuild most aspects of the Soviet economic structure, such as its banking system.

In politics until the summer of 1991, Gorbachev was the undisputed master of the party and the state, putting down rivals with great skill and using public opinion and free elections to neutralize opponents, while building a new power base. After being named president in October 1988, he set out to reform that most secret and powerful of all Soviet institutions, the KGB, urging its new leaders to imitate the structure of the U.S. CIA.

Until 1989 the Supreme Soviet was a carefully preselected, rubber-stamp body. Real power was concentrated in the Council of Ministers, headed by a prime minister. But after the elections of March and April 1989, in which many powerful officials were voted down, the Congress of People's Deputies replaced the old Supreme Soviet. The Congress is to be reelected every five years and meet annually. From its ranks comes the new Supreme Soviet. Unlike the old Supreme Soviet which never saw a no vote, the Congress and the new Supreme Soviet have proven to be outspoken and controversial bodies, even with the guaranteed positions for communist leaders.

The communist party posed a special problem for Gorbachev, a dedicated Leninist. He criticised the cumbersome and unresponsive functioning of the organization with its theoretical capstone, the Party Congress, which typically met once every five years and elected the 450-strong (300 voting, 150 nonvoting) Central Committee. The Committee, in turn, typically met at least once every six months to consider policies and elect the highest party body, the Politburo, with its 12 voting and 8 nonvoting members. From his post as General Secretary, he could see that the party and its special commissions would not attack the basic problems of the country.

The party had become corrupt and reactionary, concerned more with its privileges than its responsibilities. It was so inflexible that Gorbachev had to diminish its role after the July 1990 party congress. Thereafter, no major political figure sat on the Politburo, with the exception of the Soviet president. The party became subordinate to the state, losing its leading role. Millions gave up their party memberships after 1989, many of them going to work in city and republic governments where there was greater opportunity.

Gorbachev tried to deal with the USSR's systemic problems by firing large numbers of government, industry, military, and party officials, replacing them with younger, more aggressive people who could better implement his program. Unfortunately, he faced challenges that demanded more than just a change in personnel, and the longer he pursued his program, the smaller his constituency became. Nagging economic problems and resistance from the *apparatchiki* and party functionaries blocked Gorbachev's plans for reforms and forced him to make continual adjustments in order to hold power. In September, he abandoned a bold plan to bring a market economy to the Soviet Union within 500 days, dashing the hopes of progressives. For the next ten months his former liberal advisers and supporters either resigned or were dismissed from their positions.

As economic and social conditions deteriorated, Gorbachev increased concessions to party and bureaucratic hardliners, buying time to hold power and pursue his foreign policy objectives. In the spring hundreds of thousands of people marched in the streets of Moscow protesting the hardliners and Gorbachev's attempts to molify them. In the Baltic Republics, Georgia, the Ukraine, and Moldavia, separatist pressures increased. The economic system continued to decline, and standards of living plummeted along with productivity.

Although the revolution became mired in crisis domestically, it remained at high tide in the foreign policy arena. The Soviet president continued the policies begun in 1985. He had already renounced the Brezhnev doctrine permitting Soviet armed intervention into Socialist states. By doing so he allowed the Soviet bloc and its Warsaw Pact military strength to disintegrate, thereby opening the way for the revolutionary events of 1989 in Eastern Europe. He pulled Soviet troops out of Afghanistan in 1989 and worked to bring peace to several hot spots in Africa, including Angola. Most remarkably, he chose not to obstruct the reunification of Germany. He joined in the UN resolutions condemning Iraq's takeover of Kuwait in 1990 and cooperated in the alliance's military defeat of Saddam Hussein's forces in 1991. In July 1991 he initialed the Strategic Arms Reduction Treaty, continuing a process of working closely with U.S. presidents Ronald Reagan and George Bush at summits in Geneva, Iceland, Washington, Malta, and Moscow. The START treaty, which is yet to be ratified, took the disarmament campaign a major step ahead of the Intermediate Range Nuclear Forces agreeement signed in December 1987 (see ch. 37). Long running talks to reduce conventional forces in Europe began to produce results.

Domestic problems grew more severe during the summer of 1991. Agriculture faced an estimated grain shortfall of 77 million metric tons in the 1991 harvest, assuming the crop could even be brought in from the field. The tailspin in which the economy found itself continued to intensify. Economists who had predicted an 11 percent decline in Soviet GNP for 1991 were revising those figures to forecast an even greater decline. Boris N. Yeltsin, who had been popularly elected president of the Russian Republic in the spring, became an increasingly powerful figure as rudimentary public opinion polls gave Gorbachev a 7 percent approval rating.

In response to these crises, Gorbachev and Soviet Republic officials negotiated the Union Treaty that was to reallocate both authority and resources in the Soviet Union between the USSR government and the various republics. To be signed on August 20, it would have sharply reduced the authority of both the central power of the Soviet Union and the party.

In the face of this, an eight-man State Emergency Committee made up of leaders of the KGB, the military, the interior department, and other offices of the central government—all appointed by Gorbachev—launched an attempt to take power on August 19 while Gorbachev (like Khrushchev before him) was on vacation in the Crimea. Gorbachev's vice president announced that his leader was ill and that a state of emergency was to be imposed for six months.

The attempted coup was immediately denounced by Yeltsin, who barricaded himself inside the offices of the Russian parliament building in Moscow and instructed all army and KGB units not to obey the coup leaders' orders. The next day, 50,000 people turned out in Moscow to face down tanks sent by the central government. Larger groups mobilized in Leningrad and Kishinev. Several units of KGB and army forces refused to obey the central command's orders, and the coup began to unravel. By August 21, the crisis was over, and Yeltsin had emerged as the man of the hour.

When Gorbachev returned, he immediately attempted to resume power and to follow his old Leninist convictions. He soon found that he,

On August 19, 1991, president of the Russian Republic Boris Yeltsin stands atop an armored carrier in Moscow to read a statement urging people to resist the attempted hardline coup.

compared to Yeltsin, had little standing, especially after Gorbachev reiterated his belief that the party was the proper vehicle to carry out reform. Even as the coup leaders languished under arrest—or committed suicide—Gorbachev continued to defend the party. Finally, six days after the attempted coup, the reality of the situation became clear; Gorbachev resigned as leader of the Soviet Communist party and recommended dissolution of the Central Committee. Yeltsin claimed control of party archives and KGB records, and across the Soviet Union in a vast revolution the party—after 74 years of almost total power—was cut off from all its vanguard roles in running the country. In addition, the party had to surrender its wealth and property to the parliaments of the various republics. Gorbachev remained as president of the Soviet Union, at least until popular elections could be held.

But the future of the Soviet Union itself was in doubt. The Baltic republics of Lithuania, Latvia, and Estonia gained diplomatic recognition; and the Ukraine, Moldavia, Bielo-Russia, and Georgia declared independence. The Soviet Union as constituted before August 19, 1991, would not remain. Whether a loose economic federation or a series of squabbling successor states would emerge was a question debated both within and without the Soviet Union. The communist party of the Soviet Union and the Soviet Union itself faced possible extinction. Gorbachev had lost much of his political authority.

Where Peter the Great had overwhelmed his opposition with sheer power, and Stalin had sent his secret police, Gorbachev used *glasnost* and limited force to respond to his growing number of opponents. Ironically, it was the very people he chose who brought him down, and his defense of the party and the concepts he embraced that kept him down. His greatest gift to the Soviet people was that through *glasnost,* he had removed fear, and in the third week of August, people acted with great bravery. But the overwhelming problems of a nonfunctional infrastructure remained.

Eastern Europe

Eastern Germany

Since 1945 eastern Europe has reflected the changes that have taken place in the USSR. No place was this more evident than in East Germany from 1945 to 1991. Following the organization of the eastern zone of Germany into the German Democratic Republic, communist authorities broke up large private farms and expanded heavy industry. Thousands of discontented East Germans fled each week to West Germany through Berlin. In June 1953, severe food shortages coupled with new decrees establishing longer working hours touched off a workers' revolt, which was quickly put down. The westward flow of refugees continued, however, until 1961, when the Berlin Wall was constructed, in direct violation of the Four Power agreements.

The wall stopped the exodus of people, and East Germany stabilized. For the next 28 years the country had the highest density of armed men per square mile in the Soviet bloc and the communist world's highest economic growth rate. The country's athletes and businesses did well in world competition, and slowly and subtly under Erich Honecker and a new generation of *apparatchiki*, the German Democratic Republic improved relations with West Germany.

Gorbachev's program of liberalization threatened Honecker and his colleagues. After 1987 East German authorities stopped the circulation of Soviet periodicals that carried stories considered to be too liberal. At the same time, analysts noted the slowing economic growth rate of East Germany and the fact that the standard of living in West Germany was far higher. Old facilities, old managers, and old ideas eroded the economy of East Germany.

In September 1989, East Germans looking for a better life again fled in the thousands to the west, this time through Hungary and Czechoslovakia. This exodus, followed by Gorbachev's visit to Berlin in October, helped precipitate a crisis bringing hundreds of thousands of protestors to the streets of Berlin. Honecker was removed in October and on November 9 the Berlin Wall was opened. Once that symbolic act took place, both East and West Germans began to call for a unified Germany. Press exposés revealed the corruption and scandals among the communist élite. In the East German elections of March 1990 pro-western parties won an overwhelming triumph. By October 1990 Germany was reunited, with the first free all-German elections since Hitler took power.[10] Berlin was once again the capital of all Germany. Once the thrill of reunification had passed, Germans faced the difficult task of making the two parts of their country into one efficient unit.

In a scene that has come to symbolize the end of the Cold War, people dance atop the Berlin Wall, November 10, 1989.

Poland

In Poland, as in Yugoslavia, communism acquired a national character after a slow, subtle struggle that broke open in the fall of 1956 — following Khrushchev's "Crimes of the Stalin Era" speech. Polish leader Wladyslaw Gomulka set out on a difficult path to satisfy both Moscow and Warsaw — Soviet power and Polish nationalism. Gomulka governed skillfully through the 1960s until 1970, when he fell victim to the pressures caused by economic discontent on one hand and an increasingly corrupt party structure on the other.

Demonstrations and strikes broke out around the country and some, such as those at the Baltic port city Gdansk, were bloodily repressed. Gomulka was replaced by Edward Gierek, who throughout the 1970s walked the same narrow line as Gomulka between satisfying Moscow and Poland. Gierek borrowed extensively from the west and made several ill-advised economic decisions. By 1980 Poland was laboring to pay the interest on a foreign debt of $28 billion, and in the summer of 1980 the delicate compromise created by Gomulka and Gierek fell apart in a series of strikes caused by increases in food prices.

A nationwide labor movement came into being, *Solidarnosc*, or Solidarity. By October, around 10 million Poles from all segments of society had joined this movement, which stood for reform, equality, and workers' rights. In many ways, Solidarity's programs were protests against the Leninist concept of the party. It was Solidarity's proletarian base that made it so appealing to the world and so threatening to the other Marxist-Leninist leaders of the Soviet bloc.

At first the Polish government tried to work with the labor leaders, and Gierek made a symbolic purge of some of his less important associates. In September 1980 Gierek fell from power and in October Solidarity gained legal status — the first recognized union in a Soviet-dominated country. For the next ten months Solidarity pursued its goals. Workers won some concessions: a forty-hour, five-day work week and increased power in decision making in factories and offices.

Poland's economic problems did not disappear. Foreign debt increased. The currency, the

In Warsaw in 1965 Polish communist leader Gomulka (wearing glasses) stands between Soviet Communist party chief Leonid Brezhnev and Soviet premier Alexei Kosygin, viewing a medal representing a pledge of friendship, assistance, and cooperation between Poland and the Soviet Union.

zloty, inflated into meaninglessness with the pay increases and by the fall of 1981 the barter system was well on the way to replacing currency. Solidarity programs became increasingly radical. Conflict with the government, now headed by General Wojciech Jaruzelski, appeared inevitable. Solidarity's leader, Lech Walesa — an out-of-work electrician who had been fired for earlier attempts to organize a trade union in Gdansk — showed an instinctive genius for dealing effectively with every element of the Polish spectrum and the Soviet Union. He attempted to maintain a moderate position.

When Walesa's backers pushed him to call for a national vote to establish a noncommunist government, the Jaruzelski government responded with force, partially to maintain itself, partially to avoid Soviet intervention. Jaruzelski declared martial law and security forces rounded up Solidarity leaders. Outward shows of protest were squelched within two weeks.

Through the 1980s, communist party morale dipped as membership fell 20 percent. Although

Under the dynamic leadership of Lech Walesa, Solidarity, the Polish workers' union, grew into a nationwide social movement. In this photo from 1981, Solidarity members carry Walesa on their shoulders to celebrate a Polish Supreme Court decision upholding the workers' right to stage protest strikes throughout Poland.

In July Jaruzelski was elected president, though only with the minimum of votes, and Solidarity adviser Tadeusz Mazowiecki confirmed as prime minister. The party gave up its dominance, holding only four seats in the new cabinet. In January 1990, Poland decided to adopt a market economy. Even with substantial western financial support, the country faced rising unemployment and recession. The strains produced by this difficult step tested even the Solidarity movement, which split into two wings: that led by Mazowiecki and that led by Lech Walesa, who eventually emerged to be the Polish president.

Czechoslovakia

After the fall of the democratic government in 1948, the Czechoslovak communist party, the most Stalinist of the European parties, imposed harsh control for twenty years. However, in the spring of 1968, the country's liberal traditions came into the open. Under the influence of Marxist moderates, a new form of communism— "socialism with a human face"—was put into effect by the Slovak leader Alexander Dubček. As in Yugoslavia under Tito, the Czechoslovaks chose not to rebel against Moscow, but rather to adapt communism to their own conditions, but in August 1968 the Soviet Union and four Soviet bloc allies invaded Prague with more than 500,000 troops. Within 20 hours, the liberal regime, which advocated policies strikingly similar to those to be supported by Gorbachev twenty years later, was overthrown. The Soviets captured Dubček and took him to Moscow to confront Brezhnev.

The Soviets took their action against Czechoslovakia under the so-called Brezhnev Doctrine, under which communist states were obliged to aid their fraternal colleagues against "aggression," even when the fraternal colleague does not ask for aid, in order to safeguard the communal gains of the socialist movement. The Soviet-led forces crushed the Czechoslovak reforms to "protect the progress of socialism." Like that of East Germany, the Czech economy by the late 1980s was hampered by outmoded technology, timid leadership, and obsession with discredited ideology. The country suffered greatly from polluted

banned, Solidarity retained the genuine affection of the Poles and the support of the Roman Catholic Church, headed by Pope John Paul II, the former Polish Cardinal Wojtyla. To the embarrassment of the Polish state, Lech Walesa received the Nobel Peace prize in 1983. The economic situation deteriorated as inflation rates increased, the standard of living plummeted, and foreign debt soared to $40 billion. The party could not solve the problems it faced and in desperation, turned to Solidarity—which had been outlawed for eight years—in 1989. The June 1989 elections resulted in an overwhelming victory for the union, and in July it took its place in the Polish parliament, the *Sejm*, as the first opposition party to win free elections in eastern Europe since 1948. Solidarity won 99 out of 100 seats in the upper house and 161 seats (35 percent) in the lower house—all that was allotted to it in a preparatory round table.

On December 29, 1989, Czech playwright Vaclav Havel flashes the victory sign to thousands of Czechs after his election as president of Czechoslovakia.

air and acid rain, and the population suffered under a declining standard of living.

The wave of change from Moscow caught the Czech party out of place. Dissidents who in January 1989 had been thrown in jail for human rights protests, including president-to-be, writer Vaclav Havel, found themselves running the country by December. Events in East Germany precipitated the events in Prague in October, 1989, when a pro-democracy meeting by over 10,000 demonstrators was savagely broken up. Similar protests in November met similar results. Still the Czechoslovaks were not deterred. In the "Velvet Revolution" of November 1989 200,000 demonstrators demanded free elections and the resignation of the communist leaders. Alexander Dubček came out of internal exile, and in December Valclav Havel became president, a result confirmed in the June 1990 elections. As in the other Eastern European states, however, the high spirits of the 1989 revolution were soon replaced by the sober realities of repairing the effects of two generations of communist rule. By 1991 serious political and Slovak separatist demands were threatening progress of Czechoslovakia, now called the Czech and Slovak Federated Republic.

Hungary

After the Stalin purges, the Hungarian communist party became increasingly inept, until October 1956 when discontent with Soviet dominance erupted into revolution. For a week, a popular government existed, and Russian troops withdrew from Budapest. When the new government announced its intentions to leave the Warsaw Pact and be neutral, Soviet forces returned and crushed the rebellion. More than 200,000 refugees fled to the west.

Over the next thirty years, Janos Kadar (1912–1989) oversaw an initial bloody repression of the revolution and the execution of Imre Nagy, while he led a subtle pursuit of a Hungarian

In the 1956 Hungarian revolution, angry crowds burn Soviet propaganda—including photographs of Lenin—to protest Soviet domination of Hungary. Moscow responded by sending in tanks and troops to crush the uprising.

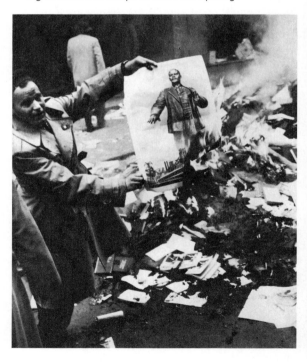

variant of communism. In the process, the Hungarians gained a higher standard of living than the Soviets, an active intellectual life, and a range of economic reforms. In the mid-1980s, however, the Hungarian economic system, which encouraged more private initiative and decentralization, experienced difficulties. Hungary's foreign debt increased and inflation rose. Gorbachev encouraged the Hungarians to pursue their reforms, sometimes at the discomfort of Kadar, who was gently moved from power in 1987.

In 1989 the Hungarians dismantled the barriers, fences, and mine fields between themselves and the Austrians. Hungary imposed the first income tax and value added tax in eastern Europe, allowed 100 percent foreign ownership of Hungarian firms, opened a stock market, and set up institutions to teach western management methods to Hungarian businessmen.

By March 1990 Hungary had installed a multi-party system and was holding free elections, which led to the election of a right-of-center government led by Joszef Antall and the overwhelming repudiation of the communists. The coming years may be difficult for Hungary, as the country makes the transition from a centrally planned to a market-oriented economy.

The Balkans

Bulgaria proved to be a loyal ally of Moscow after 1945, and its standard of living has greatly improved. The Bulgarian economy averaged a growth rate of close to 3 percent a year and became increasingly diversified. Todor Zhivkov skillfully followed the Soviet lead and showed flexibility in responding to the early Gorbachev programs, especially the agricultural reforms. Until the autumn of 1989 the party appeared to be conservative and nationalist, as shown in its campaign against the country's Turkish minority (nearly 8 percent of the population) to deprive them of their heritage.

The wave of freedom hit Bulgaria at the end of 1989. Zhivkov was ousted in a party-led coup and replaced by Peter Mladenov. It seemed in the free elections in May 1990 that Mladenov and his allies would be the only party group to make the transition and maintain power in east Europe. But even he was thrown out in July when his role as orchestrator of the Zhivkov Palace coup was

noticed, and the non-communist philosopher Zhelyu Zhelev became president.

Since the 1960s Romania under Nicolae Ceaucescu was the most independent of the Warsaw Pact countries in foreign policy. Domestically, the country labored under one of the most hardline and corrupt regimes in the bloc, whose economic policies of self-sufficiency plunged the standard of living to unprecedented depths. Ceaucescu achieved his goal to become free of the foreign debts by the summer of 1989, but at a cruel cost in human suffering.

Ceaucescu, accused by critics of desiring to achieve "socialism in one family," developed the "cult of the personality" to new heights. While imposing severe economic hardship on the nation, he built grandiose monuments to himself. Protected by his omnipresent secret police, the *Securitatea*, he seemed to be totally secure. But the 1989 wave of democracy spread even to Romania, which was the only country to experience widespread violence during that revolutionary year. Ceaucescu was captured and on Christmas day he and his wife were executed, thus bringing an end to their dreadful regime.

The Romanian pattern of political corruption continued, and Ion Iliescu manipulated the elections of May 1990 to keep power. The National Salvation Front made shameless use, later in the summer, of miners and ex-*Securitatea* officials to terrorize its critics. An uneasy equilibrium was attained, but little progress has been made to heal the devastating wounds inflicted by the Ceaucescu regime.

Albania under Enver Hoxha (d. 1985) worked closely with the Soviet Union until 1956. After Khrushchev's denunciation of Stalin, the country switched its allegiance to the Chinese until 1978. For the next decade Albania the poorest, most backward country in Europe, went its own way. Slowly, the Albanians entered into trade, diplomatic, and sporting relations with other nations. Even Albania felt the pressure of change in the summer of 1990, when people desperate to escape the country flooded foreign embassies. In early 1991 some 40,000 Albanians fled to Italy and Greece. Democratic elections were held in March in this last of the Stalinist states to enter the post-Cold War world. But even here, the Albanians marched to their own tune as the Communists carried two-thirds of the vote. However,

Marshal Tito, shown here delivering a speech while on an election campaign in Dalmatia, successfully pursued a policy of nonalignment with the Soviet Union and with the West.

as economic conditions worsened, the country suffered under increasing instability.

Yugoslavia

One of Stalin's major failures after 1945 was in his dealings with Marshal Josef Broz Tito of Yugoslavia. Tito had been a loyal communist and a good Stalinist in the 1930s. During the war he was an effective resistance leader, surviving attacks from Germans, Italians, and various right-wing factions in Yugoslavia. He had been in close contact with the western allies and after the war began to receive substantial assistance from them. Tito led the liberation of Yugoslavia from the Nazis and kept the country out of Moscow's orbit.

Stalin noted Tito's independence and from 1946 on sought measures to oppose him. Ethnically divided Yugoslavia overcame its internal divisions and a 10 percent casualty rate during the war to unite behind Tito. The Yugoslav leader's national backing, geographical distance from the Soviet Union, and support from the west enabled him to stand firm against increasing Soviet meddling in his country.

Tito became the first national communist—that is, a firm believer in Marxism who sought to apply the ideology within the context of his nation's objective conditions. This position placed him directly against Stalin, who believed that communists the world over must work for the greater glory and support of the Soviet Union. Tito believed that the setting in which ideology was found had to be taken into consideration, pointing out that Lenin had to adapt Marxist doctrine to conditions in Russia. Stalin insisted that Moscow's orders and examples must be slavishly followed. In 1948 Tito and Yugoslavia were expelled from the Soviet bloc. Successfully withstanding Stalin's pressures, including assassination attempts, Tito emerged as a key figure in the development of world communism.

Since 1948 the six republics containing ten ethnic groups that form Yugoslavia have survived the pressures of national diversity, the political stresses of the bipolar world, and serious economic difficulties. Many observers doubted that the country could survive Tito's death in 1980. However, Yugoslavia has remained tenuously united under its unique annually rotating head of state system despite an inflation rate of 80 percent and a 30 percent decline in the standard of living. The serious ethnic strife among Serbs and Croats and Albanians remains and continues to threaten the unity of the multinational state. Armed conflict broke out in the summer of 1991, as the Slovenes and Croats sought to break away from the Serbian-dominated coalition.

Life and Politics in the United States

The United States emerged from World War II with its landscape unscathed and its economy the most powerful in the world. This wealth enabled the United States over the next thirty years to assume vast global responsibilities, such as those mandated by the Marshall Plan, and to expand public services to improve health and education, provide unemployment, medical, and social security insurance, build housing, and launch anti-pollution campaigns. Until 1981 both Democratic and Republican administrations based their policies firmly on the legacy of Franklin D. Roosevelt's New Deal. Those who opposed the Roosevelt legacy suffered decisive defeats.

In addition to his foreign policy accomplishments after 1945, Harry Truman, who served as president from 1945 to 1953, continued to crusade for the rights of the "common man" and against the "fat cats" as he extended the New Deal. Republican Dwight David Eisenhower, the former supreme commander of Allied forces in Europe, was twice elected to the presidency with overwhelming victories. He continued, with somewhat less enthusiasm, to oversee the growth of federal programs. Eisenhower's successor, John F. Kennedy, was elected president in 1961 and promised a "New Frontier" spirit for America. While working actively for programs to aid the poor and minorities, he was unable to deal effectively with Congress. He captured the nation's idealism, especially with the Peace Corps, but his assassination in November 1963 cut short his presidency.

Johnson's Triumphs and Defeats

Kennedy's vice-president, Lyndon B. Johnson picked up the burden of the slain chief executive and completed a series of major domestic reforms. Johnson could claim credit for the Civil Rights Act of 1964, the war on poverty, Medicare, important environmental legislation, and the creation of the Department of Housing and Urban Development. However, major problems such as environmental pollution, decay of the urban "inner cores," and minority discontent — the crisis of rising expectations — remained unsolved.

Dr. Martin Luther King, Jr. (at left in front row) leads marchers on the historic trek from Selma to Montgomery, Alabama, to protest voting discrimination against blacks.

In foreign affairs, the increasingly unpopular Vietnam conflict plagued Johnson's presidency. The war alone cost upward of $30 billion annually, and that plus the expensive domestic programs fueled the inflation of the 1970s. Congress was slow to provide the massive funds needed to improve conditions for minorities and the inner cities and at the same time carry on the Vietnam war. In response, a powerful protest movement developed and many average Americans found themselves in deep and serious opposition to their government's policies. The political turmoil led in 1968 to the assassination of civil rights leader Dr. Martin Luther King, Jr. and of Senator Robert F. Kennedy, brother of the former president, who was close to gaining the Democratic presidential nomination before being shot in Los Angeles.

The Nixon Administration

The fragmentation of the liberal opposition led to the 1968 election by a razor-thin margin of Richard M. Nixon, Eisenhower's vice-president who had himself been narrowly defeated by John F. Kennedy in 1960. Nixon, re-elected by a landslide in 1972, shifted toward a more conservative philosophy of government. To fight inflation, caused in part by the costs of the Vietnam war and social programs, the administration imposed a wage-price freeze from August to November 1971 and wage-price controls from November 1971 to January 1973. These measures helped reduce the rate of inflation from 5 to about 3 percent. But when the administration returned to a free-market policy by the end of April 1974, prices began to rise. An oil embargo imposed by Arab nations opposed to American support of Israel contributed to the rise in inflation rates to 12 percent and a 6 percent unemployment rate.

The Nixon administration concentrated on foreign affairs during this time, especially those relating to ending the war in Vietnam, keeping peace in the Middle East, opening relations with China, and maintaining detente with the Soviet Union. In each area Nixon and his chief advisor, Henry Kissinger, compiled a substantial record of success. However, this record was overshadowed by the taint of scandal.

Nixon's vice-president, Spiro Agnew, resigned his office under the weight of charges of bribery, extortion, and kickbacks dating from his time as governor of Maryland. President Nixon himself resigned from office in the wake of the Watergate affairs. Men connected with the president's 1972 reelection campaign were arrested and charged with the break-in at the Democratic campaign headquarters. Nixon withheld information concerning these activities from a special prosecutor, a grand jury, and the public on the grounds of presidential confidentiality. After lengthy televised hearings and the conviction of his closest associates, Nixon lost the confidence of most of the nation. In May 1974 the Judiciary Committee of the House of Representatives began impeachment proceedings and in July the committee voted to recommend an impeachment trial in the Senate. Repudiated and disgraced, Nixon resigned in August. His appointed successor, Gerald R. Ford, who had also been appointed to the office of vice-president on Agnew's resignation, granted Nixon a full pardon.

The Carter Presidency

Economic problems, including high inflation, high unemployment, and a falling dollar, continued to plague the nation. In 1976 Ford ran against the relatively unknown Jimmy Carter, former governor of Georgia. Carter campaigned on promises to restore trust in government, extend social programs, and improve economic conditions. Carter won the close election, becoming

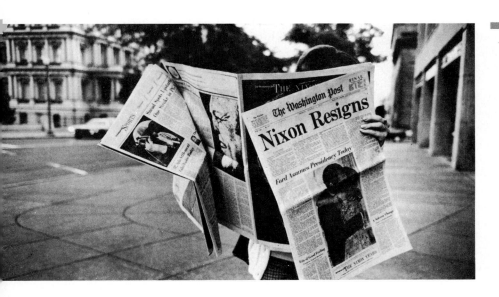

His attempt to cover up his personal involvement in the Watergate scandal brought President Richard Nixon into conflict with Congress. The House Judiciary Committee voted three articles of impeachment against Nixon, charging him with obstruction of justice, abuse of power, and contempt of Congress. On August 9, 1974, Nixon resigned the presidency.

Henry Kissinger, White House Years

Henry Kissinger, who served as Secretary of State under Presidents Nixon and Ford, advocated a balance-of-power approach to foreign relations and a policy of détente with the Soviet Union.

In my view, Vietnam was not the cause of our difficulties but a symptom. We were in a period of painful adjustment to a profound transformation of global politics; we were being forced to come to grips with the tension between our history and our new necessities. For two centuries America's participation in the world seemed to oscillate between overinvolvement and withdrawal, between expecting too much of our power and being ashamed of it, between optimistic exuberance and frustration with the ambiguities of an imperfect world. I was convinced that the deepest cause of our national unease was the realization—as yet dimly perceived—that we were becoming like other nations in the need to recognize that our power, while vast, had limits. Our resources were no longer infinite in relation to our problems; instead we had to set priorities, both intellectual and material. In the Fifties and Sixties we had attempted ultimate solutions to specific problems; now our challenge was to shape a world and an American role to which we were permanently committed, which could no longer be sustained by the illusion that our exertions had a terminal point. . . .

But in our deliberations at the Pierre Hotel the President-elect and I distilled a number of basic principles that were to characterize our approach to US-Soviet relations as long as we were in office:

The principle of concreteness. We would insist that any negotiations between the United States and the Soviet Union deal with specific causes of tensions rather than general atmospherics. Summit meetings, if they were to be meaningful, had to be well prepared and reflect negotiations that had already made major progress in diplomatic channels. We would take seriously the ideological commitment of Soviet leaders; we would not delude ourselves about the incompatible interests between our two countries in many areas. We would not pretend that good personal relations or sentimental rhetoric would end the tensions of the postwar period. But we were prepared to explore areas of common concern and to make precise agreements based on strict reciprocity.

The principle of restraint. Reasonable relations between the superpowers could not survive the constant attempt to pursue unilateral advantages and exploit areas of crisis. We were determined to resist Soviet adventures; at the same time we were prepared to negotiate about a genuine easing of tensions. We would not hold still for a détente designed to lull potential victims; we were prepared for a détente based on mutual restraint. We would pursue a carrot-and-stick approach, ready to impose penalties for adventurism, willing to expand relations in the context of responsible behavior.

The principle of linkage. We insisted that progress in superpower relations, to be real, had to be made on a broad front. Events in different parts of the world, in our view, were related to each other; even more so, Soviet conduct in different parts of the world. We proceeded from the premise that to separate issues into distinct compartments would encourage the Soviet leaders to believe that they could use cooperation in one area as a safety valve while striving for unilateral advantages elsewhere. . . .

We would have to learn to reconcile ourselves to imperfect choices, partial fulfillment, the unsatisfying tasks of balance and maneuver, given confidence by our moral values but recognizing that they could be achieved only in stages and over a long period of time.

It was a hard lesson to convey to a people who rarely read about the balance of power without seeing the adjective "outdated" precede it.

the first president from the Deep South since the civil war.

Carter inherited the same problems as his predecessors and incurred some new ones. To deal with the crisis in the Middle East he brought together at the presidential retreat of Camp David the leaders of Egypt and Israel. He continued to pursue limitations on nuclear arms, but for many his greatest accomplishment was that he made human rights considerations an operative part of American foreign policy. Domestically Carter attempted to enact an extremely ambitious program of social and economic benefits while maintaining sufficient military strength. Not surprisingly, spending increased despite the goal of a balanced budget.

Rising fuel prices and declining per capita output exacerbated economic difficulties. American helplessness and frustration grew when Iranian militants captured fifty-three hostages during a takeover of the U.S. embassy in Teheran. The combination of economic problems, the foreign policy crisis surrounding the Soviet invasion of Afghanistan, and the hostage dilemma led to Carter's defeat in November 1980 by former actor and Governor of California Ronald Reagan. Cruelly for Carter, the hostages were released just as Reagan took the oath of office in January 1981, after 444 days of captivity.

Ronald Reagan

Reagan won the presidency with an overwhelming victory, and he promised to set about reversing a half century of increasing federal involvement in American life by making drastic cuts in federal programs. This was part of his "New Federalism" program to reduce the budget, which went along with his program to make a 25 percent nominal cut in individual tax rates and a huge reduction in taxes paid by businesses. The administration planned, at the same time, substantially to increase military spending. The assumption underlying the policy was that the budget cuts and tax cuts would simultaneously cure inflation and bring about economic growth. However, the tax cuts were not matched by reduced federal spending, as the percentage of gross national product spent by government increased during Reagan's first term. The federal deficit had soared to unprecedented heights by the time he left office. Inflation rates fell significantly, although interest rates remained high.

The economic problems posed little obstacle to Reagan in the 1984 election, in which he took 49 states. Not even his most bitter critic could deny the effect of his will and personality on the office of president. Observers looked back to Franklin D. Roosevelt to find Reagan's equal as a communicator and master of the legislative process. Reagan won major tax and budget victories in the Democrat-controlled House of Representatives and gained backing in the Senate for such controversial diplomatic initiatives as the sale of sophisticated equipment to Saudi Arabia and the INF treaty (see ch. 37). He survived an assassination attempt in March 1981, and this, plus his considerable charm, gave him an aura of authority and respect—despite a sometimes shocking lack of mastery of the details of his own programs—that no president since Eisenhower had enjoyed.

Reagan faced a number of foreign policy challenges in the rapidly changing period of the latter part of the Cold War. He sent contingents of Marines to Lebanon in 1982 to act as part of an international peacekeeping force in that fragmented country. A bombing in October 1983 killed 241 of the Marines. This atrocity forced Reagan to withdraw U.S. troops from the area. Relations with Israel cooled when Israeli forces bombed an Iraqi nuclear facility, annexed the Golan heights, and invaded Lebanon. The aggressive policies of Libyan leader Muammar el-Kadaffi led to conflicts with the United States, which included U.S. air attacks on Libya in the spring of 1986. In another controversial move, Reagan sent U.S. naval forces to the Persian Gulf when the Iran-Iraq war threatened to disrupt international oil shipments.

Festering social and economic problems in Latin America erupted into revolutionary movements in El Salvador and Nicaragua. The Reagan administration sent in military advisers and millions of dollars to support those factions it considered to be democratic. When Congress withdrew support for efforts to support the Contra rebels against the Sandinista government of Nicaragua, officials in the Reagan administration conspired to carry out illegal maneuvers to gain financial support, including the shipping of weapons to supposed moderates in Iran. The

"Iran-Contra" controversy cast a pall over the last two years of the Reagan administration and led to felony convictions of high-ranking Reagan aides.

George Bush

The Republicans maintained their hold on the White House with the election of George Bush in 1988. Bush's first two years were marked by increasing fiscal problems, resulting from the budget deficit, productivity declines, balance of trade problems, and a domestic economy suffering from the excesses of the deregulated Reagan years—the failure of many Savings and Loan institutions and the fear of recession sparked by the rise in oil prices. However, Bush built on the improving relationship with the Soviet Union, and worked closely with allies and opponents alike to maintain stability during the massive changes in Eastern Europe and the Soviet Union during 1989. Makeshift solutions to the deficit crisis and other pressing domestic problems harmed the president's standing in the polls, until the Persian Gulf crisis of 1990–1991. Deftly working through the United Nations and mobilizing a broad coalition, Bush effectively stymied the Iraq government diplomatically and then sent U.S. troops to lead the UN coalition forces

General Norman Schwarzkopf, commander of the U.S.-led military victory over Iraq in 1991, and President Bush pose for photographers in the White House Rose Garden, April 23, 1991.

in a powerful bombing campaign against Iraq. A one hundred-hour ground offensive ultimately drove Saddam Hussein's Iraqi forces out of Kuwait. Even though Bush's popularity soared to unprecedented heights, the nagging economic problems plaguing the country remained unsolved.

The Western European Powers

Great Britain emerged from World War II at the height of its prestige in the twentieth century, but the glow of victory and the glory earned by its sacrifices served only to conceal Britain's dismal condition. The country was in a state of near-bankruptcy. As a result of the war, its investments had drastically declined and huge bills had been run up for the support of British armies overseas. In addition, the increase in welfare benefits drained the economy.

After 1945 the London government could not reinstate the delicately balanced formula under which Britain had paid for the massive imports of food and raw material through exports and income from foreign investments, banking, and insurance. The British people, who had paid dearly to defeat the Axis powers, did not produce the necessary export surplus to restore Britain's wealth. Over the next forty years they would watch their vanquished enemies become wealthy while they struggled with aging industrial facilities and extremely costly welfare programs.

Conservative Rule in Great Britain

Since 1945 the Conservatives have dominated politics, with interludes of Labour rule. The Conservatives oppose nationalization of industry, encourage private enterprise, and favor a reduced social welfare program. Labour supports nationalization of industry and a thoroughgoing welfare state. Neither party has been able to find a wholesale cure for the serious ailments afflicting the country.

After the wartime coalition government of Conservatives and Labour, the country held its first peacetime regular election in July 1945, and to the amazement of many, Labourite Clement Attlee defeated Churchill. Attlee was a low-key, hardworking, honest politician who came from a comfortable middle-class background. In foreign affairs the Labour government continued to work closely with the United States, while in domestic policy it set out to improve basic living standards while converting back to a peacetime economic base. Within two years most major industrial and financial functions had been nationalized. In Britain's "mixed economy," 80 percent remained employed by private enterprise. The Labour party suffered, as it would for the next forty years, from factionalism between its left wing, which was inclined to be anti-American and pro-Russian, and the mainstream. Weakened by this split, Labour lost the general election in 1951, and the Conservatives began a thirteen-year dominance.

Churchill returned as prime minister until 1955, when he resigned and was succeeded by Anthony Eden. Eden resigned in January 1957 following the Suez crisis, and Harold Macmillan took the party's leadership until July 1963. During the 1950s economic conditions slowly improved until 1959, when they rapidly deteriorated. Britain went deeply in the red in its balance of payments. By the end of 1960 the economic outlook was grim. The next year the government applied for membership in the European Economic Community (EEC), more popularly known as the Common Market, in the belief that a closer trading association with the continent would reverse the terrible economic condition. The issue of membership in the EEC split both the Conservative and Labour parties. Further, during the negotiations with the EEC, French president Charles de Gaulle moved successfully to block British membership.

The long period of Conservative rule ended in 1964 with the election of a small Labour majority headed by Harold Wilson, who had previously been the youngest cabinet minister in 150 years. Under his leadership Labour made important advances in education, slum clearance, and housing. But the old economic problems remained to plague the government. In 1967 Wilson was forced to devalue the pound. Labour's lackluster performance in the late 1960s led to a Conservative victory in the 1970 election under the leadership of Edward Heath. Heath's only significant achievement was bringing his country into the Common Market. Labor unrest in

Shortly after being named president of the new French Fifth Republic in 1958, Charles de Gaulle (left) met with West German Chancellor Konrad Adenauer. The two European leaders issued a joint communique in which they agreed to defend "with vigor the maintenance of the status of Berlin."

1973 and the Arab oil embargo dealt a crippling blow to the British economy, and Heath's bland leadership could not save his party from defeat in the 1974 elections. Labour returned once again, led by Wilson, who commanded a narrow majority. Continued industrial unrest, declining production, and alarming inflation led to major changes.

In 1975 Wilson resigned, to be succeeded by James Callaghan, a pragmatic moderate. He warned that "we are still not earning the standard of living we are enjoying. We are only keeping up our standards by borrowing, and this cannot go on indefinitely." During 1976, Britain had to borrow $5.3 billion from ten other countries. Massive cuts were proposed for social services and the armed forces. Many unions denounced this action, but it seemed imperative to all responsible leaders. Callaghan's inability to deal with what one authority called "the most serious challenge in [Britain's] recent history as a liberal democracy"[11] led to yet another change in the spring of 1979.

Margaret Thatcher led her Conservative forces to victory by proposing radical changes in Britain's economic and social programs.

Thatcher's success in carrying out her programs gave her overwhelming victories in 1983 and again in 1987. She demanded—and received—sacrifices from her own people, a more favorable treatment from the Common Market, and firm backing from the United States. She built a solid political base against a disorganized Labour opposition. From there she proceeded to change the nature of the Conservative party and to attempt to reform British society, until she was removed by her party in 1990 and replaced by John Major.

Slow economic growth and unemployment have been constant problems since 1945. Britain continues to try to find the difficult balance between making an industrial comeback without seriously sacrificing the extensive welfare services. Another serious dilemma is the stark contrast between the rich southeastern part of the country and the permanently depressed areas of the Midlands, Scotland, and Wales. The Irish problem remained, with violent incidents occurring almost daily in Northern Ireland. Racial problems generated by English resentment over the influx of "coloured" peoples from the Commonwealth defy solution.

France: Grandeur and Reality

While most of France agreed to do the "rational" thing and capitulate to the Nazis in June 1940, Charles de Gaulle urged the government to move to North Africa and continue the struggle. During the war he personified France as a great power, rather than a humiliated Nazi victim. In a famous broadcast to the French people from his exile in London de Gaulle declared:

> Whatever happens, the flame of French resistance must not and shall not die.... Must we abandon all hope? Is our defeat final and irremediable? To those questions I answer—No![12]

After the liberation of Paris in August 1944, de Gaulle was proclaimed provisional president and for fourteen months was a virtual dictator by consent. Elections held in October 1945 confirmed that the people wanted a new constitution. Sharp differences, however, developed between de Gaulle and members of the government. The general resigned in January 1946, occupying himself with the writing of his memoirs.

In the fall of that year, the Fourth Republic was established. Unfortunately, the old confusing patterns of the Third Republic were repeated. Too many parties and too much bickering precluded any significant action. The Fourth Republic had a mixed record during its dozen years of existence.

The Fourth Republic collapsed over the issue of Algeria. Revolt against the French colonial government there began in 1954 and for the next eight years drained French resources. The French population in Algeria, more than a million, insisted that Algeria be kept French. Army leaders supported them. Plots to overthrow the government in Paris were started. Faced with the prospects of a civil war, the ineffectual French government, which had been referred to as a "regime of mediocrity and chloroform," resigned in 1958, naming de Gaulle as president. His new government was granted full power for six months.

De Gaulle had been awaiting his nation's "call" in his country home. Eager to reenter the political arena, he returned to Paris and oversaw the drafting of a new constitution, this for the Fifth French Republic. The new code was overwhelmingly approved by referendum in September 1958. De Gaulle was named president for seven years and proceeded to make this office the most important in the government. In both the Third and Fourth Republics the legislature had been dominant, but now the president and his cabinet were the supreme power. During a crisis the executive could assume nearly total power. De Gaulle once commented, "The assemblies debate, the ministers govern, the constituent council thinks, the president of the Republic decides."

De Gaulle ended the Algerian war and shrugged off assassination plots and armed revolts. Then he set forth on his foremost objective—to make France a great power, to give it grandeur. He noted in his *Memoirs* that "France cannot be France without greatness." For the next seven years he worked to make France the dominant power in Europe, a third force free from domination by either the United States or the Soviet Union. To this end he persisted in making France an independent nuclear power. In 1966 he withdrew French military forces from active participation in NATO, although France remained a consultative member of the alliance.

Above all, de Gaulle was opposed to membership in any supranational agency. For this reason, while he tolerated the Common Market, he blocked any attempts to transform it into a political union. Even though he wielded great influence internationally, at home his position weakened.

A serious upheaval of university students and workers' strikes in 1968 further diminished de Gaulle's authority. A national referendum had been called to reorganize the government on a regional basis. De Gaulle unnecessarily made it a vote of confidence. When the referendum failed, he resigned his office and retired to his country estate, where he died eighteen months later.

His successor was Georges Pompidou, an able administrator who gave evidence of vision in his leadership. When Pompidou died prematurely in 1974, the country elected Valéry Giscard d'Estaing as president. A resistance hero and brilliant student, he had entered government service and became a high-ranking civil servant by the age of twenty-six. The new president initiated a series of important reforms relating to urban growth, real estate, and divorce. He also favored a voting age of eighteen.

Despite the generally high level of leadership in France, the country was also afflicted by the international economic difficulties relating to the energy crisis and American financial problems since 1973. Problems of inflation and housing shortages helped the rise to power of the communist and socialist parties, whose active participation in the wartime resistance had increased their popularity. There was a real possibility that a combined political program by the two parties might lead to a Marxist domination of the government. The March 1978 election, however, proved the alliance to be a weak one. Nevertheless the strength of the left was evident and continued to grow in the face of economic problems and discontent with Giscard's personal rule. In May 1981, Socialist leader François Mitterand was elected president, and twenty years of right-of-center government came to an end.

In June the Socialist party gained a majority in the National Assembly, and Mitterand set out to reverse two centuries of French tradition by decentralizing the governmental apparatus installed by Napoleon. In addition, he pursued a program to nationalize some of France's largest business and banking enterprises. Mitterand's "honeymoon" did not last long, as the parties to his right began to practice stalling tactics in the Assembly to block his programs. The communists, on the other hand, who had lost badly in the 1981 elections, received four relatively insignificant seats in the Cabinet, in return for which they promised cooperation with the new government.

Mitterand has had to deal with the economic problems of slow industrial growth, inflation, and unemployment, and he found these to be as resistant to solution as did Giscard. By the end of 1985 the economy began to improve. The president lost his majority in elections in March 1986 but regained it in 1988. Since then he has continued his policy of close cooperation with the United States and moderate domestic government.

West Germany: Recovery to Reunification

The most dramatic postwar European transformation has been that of West Germany. Recovering from the death, disaster, and destruction of World War II, the Bonn government accomplished political and economic miracles. When the Soviet bloc disintegrated in 1989, the Bonn government moved rapidly to extend economic aid and work for reunification. By October 1990, unification had been accomplished, justifying the dreams of postwar Germany's most important leader, Konrad Adenauer, who led his country from the status of despised outcast to that of valued western ally.

Adenauer was born in 1876 and entered politics in 1906 as a member of the city council of Cologne. In 1917 he became mayor of the city, holding office until 1933, when the Nazis dismissed him. During Hitler's regime he was imprisoned twice, but lived mostly in retirement at home, cultivating his rose garden. After 1945 he entered German national politics, becoming leader of the new Christian Democratic party. With the approval of the allied occupation authorities, German representatives drafted a constitution for the German Federal Republic, which was ratified in 1949. Adenauer, at the age of seventy-three, became chancellor of West Germany.

In the new democratic government, the presidency was made weak, while the real executive, the chancellor, was given specific authority to determine "the fundamental policies of the government." The chancellor was responsible to the Bundestag, a popularly elected legislative body. One of the weaknesses of the Weimar Republic had been the existence of many small parties, leading to unstable multiparty coalitions. In the new government, no party was recognized that did not win at least 5 percent of the total election votes.

Adenauer assumed power when Germany was still an outcast and its economy was in ruins. His one driving obsession was to get his people to work. Taking advantage of the tensions of the Cold War, he succeeded admirably. Under the force of his autocratic and sometimes domineering leadership, the Germans rebuilt their destroyed cities and factories using some $3 billion in Marshall Plan assistance. As early as 1955 West German national production exceeded prewar figures, with only 53 percent of former German territory. Providing the initial economic guidance for this recovery was Adenauer's minister of economics Dr. Ludwig Erhard, a professional economist and a firm believer in laissez-faire economics. Germany's economic growth was accompanied by little inflation, practically no unemployment, and few labor problems.

Adenauer's achievements in foreign affairs were as remarkable as his leadership in domestic affairs. The German Federal Republic gained full sovereignty in 1955. At that same time, West Germany was admitted into the NATO alliance. Adenauer decided to align closely with the west and cultivated close ties with the United States. In 1963 he signed a treaty of friendship with France, ending a century-long period of hostility. Adenauer expressed his attitude toward foreign affairs when he said "Today I regard myself primarily as a European and only in second place as a German." It was natural that he brought his nation into Europe's new institutions: the European Coal and Steel Community and the Common Market. Adenauer's great frustration in foreign affairs was his failure to achieve the reunification of West and East Germany.

In 1963, after fourteen years in office, Adenauer retired and was succeeded by Ludwig Erhard as chancellor, who was in turn succeeded by Kurt Kiesinger. The big change in German politics occurred in 1969 with the victory of the Social Democratic party. This moderate, nondoctrinaire socialist party was led by Willy Brandt, who became chancellor. A foe of the Nazis, Brandt had fled to Norway where he became a member of the resistance after Hitler's conquest. After the war he returned to Germany and became prominent in the Social Democratic party. In 1957 he became mayor of West Berlin, then in 1966 foreign minister in Bonn. Brandt was very active in setting West Germany's foreign policy. He was instrumental in getting Britain into the Common Market, he tried to improve relations with eastern Europe and the Soviet Union through *Ostpolitik*, a policy of cooperation with Warsaw Pact nations. In journeys to both Moscow and Warsaw in 1970 he negotiated a treaty with the USSR renouncing the use of force and an agreement with Poland recognizing its western border along the Oder and Neisse rivers. A treaty was also signed with East Germany for improving contacts and reducing tensions. These negotiations and others paved the way for the entry of the two Germanies into the United Nations.

Brandt's concentration on foreign affairs led to the appearance of neglect of domestic issues such as inflation and rising unemployment. Important segments of German public opinion attacked him on the policy of *Ostpolitik*. Finally a spy scandal rocked the government, and Brandt resigned in the spring of 1974. Helmut Schmidt, who succeeded him, paid closer attention to domestic affairs.

Under Schmidt's leadership Germany continued its strong economic growth in the wake of the oil embargo. German workers did not suffer the unemployment problems of other countries because of the practice of firing and sending home foreign workers when job cutbacks were needed. Germany's economy in the 1980s was not immune to issues such as foreign trade fluctuations and oil imports. Still, Schmidt, as head of the most powerful western European nation had the prestige and record to ensure his victory in the 1980 elections.

In the late 1970s Schmidt had asked the United States to counter the Soviet placement of SS-20 intermediate range missiles by placing intermediate range ballistic missiles in Europe, thereby setting off controversial debate that did not end until 1983. Schmidt faced both the disapproval of antinuclear demonstrators who did not want the missiles and the displeasure of conservatives in his country and the United States over German economic ties with the Soviet Union. In the autumn of 1982 political power passed again to the Christian Democratic Party, now led by Helmut Kohl.

For the rest of the decade Kohl's party proved to be a staunch supporter of the United States, in particular of its program to place U.S. intermediate range missiles in Europe. In the face of strident Soviet protests, Kohl guided a bill through the West German parliament in November 1983 to deploy the missiles. After that success, and a strong victory in 1987, Kohl—despite the reputation of being a plodding politician—came to play a strong role in European affairs and in relations with the Soviet Union. In the course of his tenure, Kohl changed with the times to deal with environmental issues brought forcefully to the public forum by the Green party. He masterfully took advantage of the breakdown of the German Democratic Republic in 1989 to claim the issue of reunification for himself and his party. By the end of 1990, Kohl had confounded those who had contempt for his intellect and those who thought him politically naive.

Italy: Political Instability, Economic Growth

Following the end of Mussolini's regime, Italy voted by a narrow margin to end the monarchy. A new constitution, adopted in 1947 provided for a premier and a ministry responsible to the legislature. The Christian Democratic party—strongly Catholic, pro-western, and anti-Communist—was the leading middle-of-the-road group. Its spokesman and leader was Alcide de Gasperi, whose ministry governed the country from 1947 to 1953. Like Adenauer, de Gasperi was a strong adherent of democracy and supported European unity. Italy joined NATO in 1949 and became a member of the Common Market in 1957.

Within little more than a decade the Italian economy changed from predominantly agricultural to industrial. For a time, in the late 1950s and early 1960s, industry advanced faster in Italy than in any other part of Europe. In 1960 the output of manufacturing tripled pre-1939 levels, and in 1961 steel production was more than one million tons. By the end of the 1980s Italy ranked among the world's leaders in high-tech industry, fashion, design, and banking. Most economic development occurred in northern Italy around the thriving cities of Turin, Milan, and Bologna.

Southern Italy has not progressed as rapidly. Too many people, too few schools, inadequate roads, landlordism, and inefficient, fragmented farms worked by poor peasants are among the problems besetting the area. The government has offered help in the form of subsidies, tax concessions, and programs for flood control and better highways, but southern Italy remains a challenge and an urgent problem.

While the Italian economy was a source of optimism, politics was another story. After de Gasperi's retirement in 1953, politics became increasingly characterized by a series of cabinet crises, shaky coalitions, and government turnovers. By 1990 there had been forty-nine governments since the end of World War II.

Corruption and inefficiency were widespread in the Christian Democratic-dominated system. In the 1970s labor unrest, unemployment, and inflation posed problems that politicians could not deal with, even in coalitions in which the Communist party joined with other factions. For a while terrorism dominated political life. In 1978 the anarchist Red Brigade kidnapped one of Italy's most prominent public figures, former premier Aldo Moro, and assassinated him nearly two months later, leaving his body in a car parked equidistant between the Christian Democratic and Communist Party headquarters in Rome. Terrorists spread chaos among business and political leaders. During the 1980s the government, dominated by Bettino Craxi and Ciriaco de Mita, improved conditions. The terrorist networks were broken and law enforcement agencies attacked the Mafia organization in southern Italy and Sicily.

Portugal, Spain, and Greece

In the western and eastern peninsulas of Europe, politics since 1945 has been marked by dictatorships and radicalism, but parliamentary forces have clung tenaciously to power. Portugal, Spain, and Greece have all experienced severe economic problems and traditions of instability.

Portugal was an incredibly corrupt monarchy until 1910. The country then became a republic, but its record of internal turmoil continued. Between 1910 and 1930 there were twenty-one uprisings and forty-three cabinets. Toward the end of that period the army ousted the politicians and took control of the government. In 1932 the generals called on Antonio de Oliveira Salazar to run the country. This former economics professor, a fervent and austere Catholic, shunned social life and was content to live on a very small salary. He devoted all of his time to running an authoritarian government. The press was censored and education—in a country in which two-thirds of the population was illiterate—was neglected. Some economic improvement did take place, but the people, who were frozen out of politics, remained poor. In 1955 a five-year program to stimulate the economy was launched, but its gains were cancelled by an increase in population and by huge financial drain of the national budget resulting from colonial wars in Portugal's African holdings.

Salazar retired in 1968 because of ill health, and six years later a group of junior army officers overthrew the government. Serious divisions appeared between the moderate liberal factions and the communists. In the summer of 1976, however, elections confirmed the victory of the moderate socialists. A new constitution was enacted, establishing a democratic system. The government faced difficult economic problems. Six hundred thousand refugees from Portuguese Africa had to be absorbed, adding to the high unemployment and runaway inflation. After the 1974 revolution workers had seized many businesses, large farms, and hotels. In most instances, private ownership had to be restored under efficient management. During the 1980s political and economic stability returned to the country, led in the latter part of the decade by Mario Soares, ruling through a socialist coalition. Compared with the rest of Europe, Portugal remained poor, with over 10 percent inflation and only 80 percent literacy, but in terms of the Iberian peninsula, much progress had been made.

In the four decades after the Second World War, Spain passed from the Franco dictatorship to a rapidly industrializing, modern European state. Franco ruled over an almost ruined country after taking control in 1939. Many of Spain's most talented and productive people had fled, and 700,000 people had died in the civil war. So horrible was the conflict and so great the losses, that Franco gained a grudging toleration from the majority of the exhausted population. Those who did not cooperate faced his secret police.

Cold War tensions eased Spain's reentry into the community of nations in the 1950s. The United States resumed diplomatic relations and Spain became a member of the UN in 1955. The following year the Pact of Madrid provided naval and air bases for the Americans, in return for which Spain received more than $2 billion a year in aid. In the 1960s and 1970s the widespread poverty and backwardness that had long characterized Spain began to diminish. Inspired by the Portuguese revolution of 1974, workers and students began to demonstrate and show their unrest. In the summer of 1975 Franco died. He had named Prince Juan Carlos as his successor, thereby indicating his wish that the monarchy be restored.

The young king was crowned in November 1975, and in his speech of acceptance he promised to represent all Spaniards, recognizing that the people were asking for "profound improvements." In 1976, the reformed government announced amnesty for political prisoners, freedom of assembly, and more rights for labor unions. An orderly general election took place in the spring of 1977. Post-Franco Spain began its parliamentary-monarchy phase with impressive stability. Underneath, deep ideological divisions remained, which decreased over time. The major crisis came in February 1981 when radical elements of the army invaded the parliament building to attempt a coup. It immediately became apparent that there was no support for the coup either in the military or among the public at large, and the attempt was brushed aside.

In May 1982 Spain joined NATO—still a controversial decision—and, later that year, elected the Socialist party led by Felipe Gonzales to run the country. Gonzales brought Spain into the Common Market and worked hard to diversify the country's economy. He strengthened his

Spanish prime minister Felipe Gonzales signs the treaty admitting Spain and Portugal to membership in the European Common Market in June 1985.

position in the 1986 elections and by 1990 was governing a country attractive to investors in high-tech industries. Spain looked forward to hosting the 1992 Olympic games.

Greece, since its modern creation in 1821, has rarely enjoyed political stability. From that year until 1945 there were fifteen different types of government with 176 premiers who obviously averaged less than one year in office. Inefficiency in government, economic backwardness, and political crises have continued to plague Greece since 1945. In the Greek civil war (1946–1949) pro-western forces, who controlled only the major cities, turned back a powerful communist surge for power and re-established the monarchy. Greek politicians ignored the complex economic issues affecting the peasants, preferring instead to attempt to regain control of various islands and territories controlled by Greeks in the long-distant past. In the spring of 1967 a group of army colonels seized power. A dictatorship was established which jailed many political figures and harshly punished any criticism of its rule. Many Greeks fled into exile. The military junta made a serious miscalculation in 1974 when it connived to increase Greek authority on

Cypress, a move that led to a Turkish invasion of the island. This mistake led to the junta's downfall.

Thereafter the Greeks created a republic, complete with a new constitution. They applied for membership into the Common Market in 1975, and were admitted in 1981. In its application, the government stated that its desire to join the European Community was "based on our earnest desire to consolidate democracy in Greece within the broader democratic institutions of the European Community to which Greece belongs." Since that time, Greek leaders have maintained their democratic traditions. In November 1981 the Socialist party led by Andreas Papandreou gained power and held it through 1989, gaining increased support in 1985. Papandreou ran on pledges to evict U.S. forces from Greek bases and to move Greek foreign policy away from western orientation. Yet the Greeks remained active participants in NATO and the Common Market. Like Portugal Greece is, by European standards, a poor country with a stagnant economy and an inflation rate of over 20 percent. In the 1989 elections, these factors plus scandals surrounding Papandreou's personal life led to the defeat of the Socialists and the forming of an unlikely coalition made up of the Communist and Conservative parties.

Conclusion

In the first decade after the war, Europe stood caught and divided between the superpowers of the United States and the Soviet Union. Only the most optimistic person would have believed that a tragic war between the two would *not* break out. But by the last decade of the twentieth century, the Cold War had ended, and the allies of Washington and Moscow looked ahead to a more independent and prosperous existence.

The Soviet Union and the United States both underwent profound social and economic changes in the postwar period. Suffering the losses from World War II and the effects of an unproductive economic system, the USSR faced a severe crisis. The United States, blessed with a productive industrial system, successfully weathered its economic difficulties.

The eastern European states paid the price for Soviet reconstruction and domination. Only East Germany showed any ability to compete economically during the postwar period, and that country had lost its edge in the 1980s. The Marxist-Leninist system, especially in its Stalinist variant, was widely acknowledged to have failed, and the transition to new systems promised to be difficult. The western European states had absorbed the changes more easily, but not without pain. A new age of dominance for the western European states loomed on the horizon in 1992.

Suggestions for Reading

Lynn E. Davis, *The Cold War Begins* (Princeton, 1974) is a thorough accounting of the origins of the conflict. Various points of view on American-Soviet relations can be found in Walter La Feber, *America, Russia, and the Cold War* (Wiley, 1976); P. Hammond, *Cold War and Détente: The American Foreign Policy Process Since 1945* (Harcourt Brace Jovanvich, 1975); and L. Wittner, *Cold War America: From Hiroshima to Watergate* (Praeger, 1974). Other studies of note on the Cold War are J. C. Donovan, *The Cold Warriors: A Policy Making Elite* (Heath, 1974) and H. S. Dinerstein, *Soviet Foreign Policy Since the Missile Crisis* (Johns Hopkins, 1976). Adam Ulam gives a good survey of Moscow's policies in *Expansion and Coexistence: Soviet Foreign Policy 1917–1973* (Holt, 1974) A penetrating study of the major figures in U.S. foreign policy formation is *The Wise Men* by W. Isaacson and E. Thomas (Touchstone, 1988). Robbin F. Laird and Erik P. Hoffman, eds., *Soviet Foreign Policy in a Changing World* (Aldine, 1986) is a solid collection of articles on the dilemmas facing the Soviets. Peter Zwick, *Soviet Foreign Relations: Process and Policy* (Prentice Hall, 1990) spells out the factors shaping Moscow's policies. The Committee on Foreign Affairs analysis of *Soviet Diplomacy and Negotiating Behavior—1979–1988: New Tests for U. S. Diplomacy* (Government Printing Office, 1988) gives good insights into Washington's understanding of Soviet diplomacy.

The Soviet world at the beginning of the 1990s still labored under the impact of Stalin's policies and accomplishments. R. C. Tucker, ed., presents the panorama of his life and policies in *Stalinism: Essays in Historical Interpretation* (Norton, 1977). M. Djilas, *Conversations with Stalin* (Harcourt Brace Jovanvich, 1962) gives a vivid, first-hand account of Stalin's personality. Khrushchev's tenure is competently covered in E. Crankshaw, *Khrushchev, a Career* (Viking, 1966) and in Khrushchev's own words in *Khrushchev Remembers* (Ballantine, 1976). Hedrick Smith, *The New Russians* (Random House, 1990) is an outstanding update of his classic introduction to the "way things really work." Martin McCauley, ed., presents an all-encompassing study of Khrushchev's time in power in *Khrushchev and Khrushchevism* (MacMillan, 1987).

Impressionistic and important is Roy Medvedev's *Khrushchev* (Doubleday, 1983). Elizabeth Valkenier discusses the problems of overextension in *The Soviet Union and the Third World: An Economic Bind* (Praeger, 1983). The Brezhnev years are examined by Archie Brown and Michael Kaser, eds., in *The Soviet Union Since the Fall of Khrushchev* (Free Press, 1976). Gail Lapidus examines the difficult lot of women in *Women, Work and Family in the Soviet Union* (M. E. Sharpe, 1982). Frederick Starr's splendid *Red and Hot: The Fate of Jazz in the Soviet Union, 1917–1980* (Oxford, 1983) gives a unique insight into cultural vitality in the "totalitarian" Soviet Union. A work anticipating the current crisis of the USSR is Paul Dibb, *The Soviet Union: The Incomplete Super Power* (Illinois, 1986). Martin Ebon gives essential background to the key figure in Soviet political change in the *The Andropov File . . .* (McGraw-Hill, 1983). Marshall Goldman's perceptive *Gorbachev's Challenge: Economic Reform in the Age of High Technology* (Norton, 1987) anticipates the Soviet crisis in the 1990s. A good primer on the "Balance of Terror" is Ray Perkins Jr. *The ABCs of the Soviet-American Nuclear Arms Race* (Brooks/Cole, 1991).

Eastern European developments through the 1960s can be studied in the surveys by Hugh Seton-Watson, *The East European Revolution* (Praeger, 1961), Ivan Volgyes, *Politics in Eastern Europe* (Dorsey, 1986), and Z. Brzezinski, *The Soviet Bloc: Unity and Conflict* (Harvard, 1971). F. Fejto, *History of the People's Democracies* (Pelican, 1973) is a solid survey of post-1945 Eastern Europe. Dennis Rusinow, *The Yugoslav Experiment, 1948–1974* (London, 1977) and Dusko Doder, *The Yugoslavs* (New York, 1976) give two views of the multinational state to the mid-1970s. Jorg K. Hoensch *A History of Modern Hungary: 1867–1986* (Longman, 1988) is an objective survey. The Czech crisis of 1968—and after—is well covered in G. Golan, *Reform Rule in Czechoslovakia* (Cambridge, 1971). Norman Davies, *Heart of Europe: A Short History of Poland* (Oxford, 1987) gives the best short survey of recent events in that country in chapters 1 and 7.

Post-1945 events in the United States are discussed in Jim Heath, *Decade of Disillusionment: The Kennedy-Johnson Years* (Indiana, 1984). Allen J. Matusow, *The Unraveling of America: A History of Liberalism in the 1960s* (Harper, 1984) traces the political results of that shocking decade. At the end of the 1980s, Joseph S. Nye, Jr., wrote a magisterial analysis of the changing nature of the United States's role in *Bound to Lead: The Changing Nature of American Power* (Basic Books, 1989). Most of the postwar presidents have produced their memoirs. Probably the best and most enjoyable are Truman's *Memoirs* (Doubleday, 1955–1956). See also Lyndon B. Johnson, *The Vantage Point*, (Holt, Rinehart and Winston, 1971) and Dwight D. Eisenhower, *The White House Years* (Doubleday, 1963). See also, Doris Kearns, *Lyndon Johnson and the American Dream* (Harper/Row, 1976).

The resurgence of Western Europe is dealt with in J. Robert Wegs, *Europe Since 1945* (St. Martins, 1991). See also Neil McInnes, *The Communist Parties of Western Europe* (Oxford, 1979) and T. Geiger, *The Fortunes of the West: The Future of the Atlantic Nations* (Indiana, 1973). Good accounts of the various western European countries are: David McKie and Chris Cook, eds., *The Decade of Disillusionment: Britain in the 1960s* (St. Martin's, 1973); C. J. A. Bartlett, *A History of Postwar Britain* (Longman, 1977);

John Darby, *Conflict in Northern Ireland* (Barnes and Noble, 1976); and George Dangerfield, *The Damnable Question* (Little, Brown, 1976). See also P. A. Allum, *Italy: Republic Without Government* (Norton, 1974) and Roy C. Macridis, *French Politics in Transition* (Winthrop, 1975). Max Gallo, *Spain under Franco* (Dutton, 1974) and Paul Preston, ed., *Spain in Crisis* (Barnes and Noble, 1976) study the evolution of that country under Franco. Neil Bruce, *Portugal: The Last Empire* (Halstad, 1975) presents the background of the 1974 revolution.

Notes

1. Max Radin, "Justice at Nuremberg," *Foreign Affairs,* April 1946, p. 371.
2. A useful guide to the historiography of the Cold War can be found in J. L. Black, *Origins, Evolution, and Nature of the Cold War: An Annotated Bibliographic Guide* (Santa Barbara, CA: ABC-Clio, 1986).
3. Winston Churchill, *Triumph and Tragedy* (Boston: Houghton Mifflin, 1953), p. 497.
4. Raymond Aron, "The Foundations of the Cold War," in *The Twentieth Century*, Norman F. Cantor and Michael S. Werthman, eds., (New York: Thomas Y. Crowell, 1967), p. 157.
5. David Rees, *The Age of Containment* (New York: St. Martin's Press, 1967), p. 23.
6. Joseph L. Nogee and John Spanier, *Peace Impossible—War Unlikely, The Cold War Between the United States and the Soviet Union* (Glenview: Scott, Foresman/Little, Brown, 1988), p. 67.
7. J. P. Nettl, *The Soviet Achievement* (New York: Harcourt Brace Jovanovich, 1967), p. 198.
8. Leonard Schapiro, *The Communist Party of the Soviet Union* (London: Methuen, 1963), pp. 534–535.
9. Alec Nove, *The Soviet Economic System* (London: George Allen & Unwin, 1977), p. 320.
10. Ferdinand Protzman, "East Germany Losing its Edge," *The New York Times,* May 15, 1989, D-1.
11. Michael R. Hodges, "Britain Tomorrow: Business as Usual," *Current History,* March 1975, p. 138.
12. Charles de Gaulle, *The Call to Honor* (New York: Viking Press, 1955), p. 33.

The Emerging "South" Since 1945

After 1945 the old European empires disappeared, replaced by over 80 new countries. These new states, primarily located to the south of the European powers, were born into a difficult environment, buffeted by the Cold War and economic upheavals. As of the last decade of the millennium, the "South" contained most of the world's expanding population and grim challenges.

In east Asia, Japan recovered from its postwar devastation to become a center of world finance. China participated in Cold War episodes from Korea to Vietnam and fought its own ideological battles before entering a period of rapid modernization after 1978. Indochina's fate was bound up in a series of bloody, devastating proxy wars.

In the rest of Asia and in Africa, nations freed themselves from the yoke of European dominance, but independence unleashed powerful ethnic and religious antagonisms, most of which remain unresolved. Great power intervention in the Middle East and in Africa exacerbated an already difficult situation and led to increased bloodshed.

More than Cold War tensions, economic upheavals have affected the Latin American states. The region's accumulation of massive debts and its dependence on the export of oil or agricultural products left it at the mercy of the North Atlantic powers. This economic domination provided a rich opportunity for revolutionaries in Cuba and Nicaragua who profited from the obvious exploitation of the population.

At the end of the twentieth century, Japan, South Korea, Hong Kong, and Singapore competed effectively in the world arena. Other countries, such as Brazil, India, China, and Zimbabwe, showed signs of potential strength. However, the vast majority of the nations of the "South" remain trapped by the cruel forces of poverty and overpopulation.

Japan: Conquered Nation to World Power

On August 28, 1945, nineteen days after the atomic bomb was dropped at Nagasaki, an advance party of 150 Americans, the lead group of a substantial army of occupation, landed on Japan. Supreme Commander General Douglas MacArthur soon arrived to preside over Japan's transition from one military authority to another.

Postwar Japan

The terms of armistice took all territory outside the four main islands away from Japan and imposed complete demilitarization on the Japanese. Key wartime military leaders were placed on trial, and General Tojo, along with six colleagues, was executed. Other militarist governmental and business leaders were blocked from postwar activities. For a while, industries were dismantled for reparations, but this practice was soon stopped.

In return, the allies gave aid to rebuild the shattered economy, while insisting on democratic institutions in the government and society. The new education system was based on the American pattern of decentralized public schools, with textbooks rewritten to delete militant nationalism. A land reform policy intended to reduce

Frantz Fanon, The Wretched of the Earth

Frantz Fanon noted the growing inequality between northern and southern parts of the globe—the industrialized and the nonindustrialized worlds.

The colonial world is a world cut in two. The dividing line, the frontiers are shown by barracks and police stations. In the colonies it is the policeman and the soldier who are the official, instituted go-betweens, the spokesmen of the settler and his rule of oppression. . . .

It is obvious here that the agents of government speak the language of pure force. The intermediary does not lighten the oppression, nor seek to hide the domination; he shows them up and puts them into practice with the clear conscience of an upholder of the peace; yet he is the bringer of violence into the home and into the mind of the native. . . .

The settlers' town is a strongly-built town, all made of stone and steel. It is a brightly-lit town; the streets are covered with asphalt, and the garbage-cans swallow all the leavings, unseen, unknown and hardly thought about. The settler's feet are never visible, except perhaps in the sea; but there you're never close enough to see them. His feet are protected by strong shoes although the streets of his town are clean and even, with no holes or stones. The settler's town is a well-fed town, an easy-going town; its belly is always full of good things. The settler's town is a town of white people, of foreigners.

The town belonging to the colonised people, or at least the native town, the negro village, the medina, the reservation, is a place of ill fame, peopled by men of evil repute. They are born there, it matters little where or how; they die there, it matters not where, nor how. It is a world without spaciousness; men live there on top of each other, and their huts are built one on top of the other. The native town is a hungry town, starved of bread, of meat, of shoes, of coal, of light. The native town is a crouching village, a town on its knees, a town wallowing in the mire. It is a town of niggers and dirty arabs. The look that the native turns on the settler's town is a look of lust, a look of envy; it expresses his dreams of possession—all manner of possession: to sit at the settler's table, to sleep in the settler's bed, with his wife if possible. The colonised man is an envious man. And this the settler knows very well; when their glances meet he ascertains bitterly, always on the defensive "They want to take our place." It is true, for there is no native who does not dream at least once a day of setting himself up in the settler's place.

This world divided into compartments, this world cut in two is inhabited by two different species. The originality of the colonial context is that economic reality, inequality and the immense difference of ways of life never come to mask the human realities. When you examine at close quarters the colonial context, it is evident that what parcels out the world is to begin with the fact of belonging to or not belonging to a given race, a given species. . . .

It is not enough for the settler to delimit physically, that is to say with the help of the army and the police force, the place of the native. As if to show the totalitarian character of colonial exploitation the settler paints the native as a sort of quintessence of evil. Native society is not simply described as a society lacking in values. It is not enough for the colonist to affirm that those values have disappeared from, or still better never existed in, the colonial world. The native is declared insensible to ethics; he represents not only the absence of values, but also the negation of values. . . .

The Church in the colonies is the white people's Church, the foreigner's Church. She does not call the native to God's ways but to the ways of the white man, of the master, of the oppressor. And as we know, in this matter many are called but few chosen.

From Frantz Fanon, *The Wretched of the Earth*, trans. by Constance Farrington. Copyright © 1963 by Presence Africaine. Used by permission of Grove Weidenfeld.

tenancy and absentee landlordism was introduced. Unions gained the right of collective bargaining, and their membership grew rapidly. American authorities tried with limited success to reduce the great concentration of wealth in the hands of monopolistic industries, the *zaibatsu*.

A new constitution, drafted in consultation with the occupation government, came into effect in May 1947. It set up a democratic, two-house parliamentary-cabinet system in which the majority party selected the prime minister. Sovereignty rested in the people; the emperor, forced to renounce his divinity, was referred to as "the symbol of state." No limitations were placed on voting because of income or sex. War was renounced as a sovereign right and "land, sea, and air forces, as well as other war potential will never be maintained."

As a result of the Cold War in Europe and the communist invasion of South Korea in 1950–1957, Japan became the United States' principal ally in the Pacific. Despite Soviet opposition and without the participation of the USSR, a peace treaty was signed in 1951 and went into effect the next year, giving Japan full sovereignty. A security pact between Japan and the United States allowed Americans to station troops in Japan.

Political and Social Change

Since 1945 conservatives have consistently, with the exception of two brief periods, controlled the Japanese government. In 1955 two conservative parties merged to form the Liberal Democratic party, which was friendly to the west, favored modest rearmament, and backed the alliance with the United States. Based on professional civil servants and business interests, it was sufficiently strong to endure periodic charges of corruption. The Socialist party, the major opposition, demanded nationalization of industry, opposed the 1947 security pact, and favored neutrality in foreign affairs. The small Communist party was vocal but weak.

The new system was flexible enough to absorb the radical transformation Japan has experienced in the past half century. Rapid urbanization posed the greatest challenges. Rural areas lost population while city populations—and consequent environmental problems—skyrocketed. With more than 11 million people, Tokyo became the largest urban area in the world. Three great concentrations of industry and population clustered around Tokyo, Osaka, and Nagoya occupy only 1 percent of the country's land area but contain over one-fourth of the country's population.

Two reflections of modern Japan. The influence of both the West and the media is reflected in the large group of Japanese teens dressed as Elvis impersonators. The presence of women at the welcoming ceremony for new railway employees reflects a 1985 equal opportunity law.

In the cities traditional values and attitudes have changed. Parental authority and family ties weakened as young married couples, forsaking the traditional three-generation household, set up their own homes. The stresses and strains of urbanization were reflected in student riots and in the appearance, for the first time in Japanese history, of juvenile delinquency. Western influence—seen in fashions, television, sports, and beauty contests and heard in rock music—clashed with the traditional culture.

Perhaps the greatest changes are those affecting women. Before World War II there was little opportunity for Japanese women outside the family. After 1945 they gained the right to own property, sue for divorce, and pursue educational opportunities. By the end of the 1980s, women constituted nearly 50 percent of the nation's work force, and more than 30 percent of women high school graduates attended post-secondary institutions.

Economic Dominance

Japan faced serious obstacles in its path to economic development. It had to import much of the food for its growing population (123 million by 1990) and most of the raw materials for its industries. The Korean war gave Japan an initial boost, as the American troops made large purchases. In 1950 the gross national product (GNP) was $10 billion; by 1973, it had risen to $300 billion. The 1973 oil embargo and subsequent price increases of more than 400 percent by all of the OPEC (Organization of Petroleum Exporting Countries) producers severely affected Japan. Inflation skyrocketed, economic growth plunged, and for a while the balance of trade was negative.

Japan's business managers made the necessary adjustments for recovery. By the end of the 1970s the Japanese built half the world's tonnage in shipping and had become the world's biggest producer of motorcycles, bicycles, transistor radios, and sewing machines. The Japanese soon outpaced the United States in automobile production and drove the American domestic television industry virtually out of business. By the 1990s, the Japanese boasted one of the world's strongest economies. Japan's per capita GNP was nearly $22,000—compared to the U.S. per capita GNP of $19,800. After the October 1987 stock market slide, Tokyo became the world financial center, dominating banking.

In the late 1980s the Japanese began to watch uneasily as South Korea, Taiwan, Hong Kong, and Singapore using the Japanese formula of a strong and disciplined work force and efficient use of new technology, became effective competitors in the world market. South Korea especially launched a direct challenge to Japan in high-technology and automotive markets.

Chinese Revolutions

Between 1927 and 1937 Chiang Kai-shek's Nationalist Chinese (Kuomintang) government initiated useful reforms in the cities which, had it not been for Japanese aggression in China, might have expanded to include the rest of the country. Unfortunately for Chiang, the Nationalists after 1937 lost many of their strongest supporters and most of their prosperous area to Japanese control. By the end of World War II, after eight years of combat, the Chinese Nationalist government of Chiang Kai-shek was a defeated and worn-out regime. In contrast, the communists came out of the war with great popularity, control of an area with 90 million people, and a disciplined and loyal army of 500,000.

Civil War in China

Following the victory over Japan, U.S. troops, cooperating with Chinese Nationalist forces, recaptured land taken by the Japanese. The Americans helped move Chinese troops to strategic areas such as Manchuria. At the same time, the Soviet Union reclaimed areas formerly controlled by the tsars. During this time Chiang tried unsuccessfully to negotiate a settlement with Mao Zedong (Mao Tse-tung). In October 1945 heavy fighting broke out between the Chinese Nationalist and Communist forces.

For the next three years the United States tried to end the conflict. In December 1945 President Truman defined American policy toward China: The United States regarded the Nationalist regime as the legal government of China, but since it was a one-party system, it was necessary that full opportunity be given to other groups to participate in a representative government. To that end, Truman urged an end to the fighting.

General George C. Marshall, U.S. army chief of staff, went to China to implement Truman's policy and to act as friendly mediator. Marshall, newly appointed as American secretary of state, returned home in January 1947, his mission a failure. In his final report, he blasted extremists on both sides for failing to make peace.

The Communist Victory

Chiang's army—poorly equipped, miserably paid, and suffering low morale—began to disintegrate. The communists captured city after city, frequently facing only token resistance. Economic problems added to Chiang's military dilemma. The Nationalists had been unable to rebuild the economy after 1945, and inflation soared: the U.S. dollar came to be worth 93,000 Chinese dollars on the black market. Serious riots broke out, and thousands of workers went on strike in Shanghai.

By the end of 1947 the Nationalist forces went into retreat. In 1948 the Nationalist presence in

Celebrating the first anniversary of Mao's government in 1950, Chinese workers, carrying giant placards of their leader, march through the streets of Peking.

Manchuria collapsed. The complete defeat of Chiang's armies occurred in 1949 when the "People's Liberation Army" captured the major cities in China. Mao proclaimed the establishment of his government on October 1, 1949, and by the middle of 1950 Mao ruled all of mainland China. Chiang's Nationalists sought refuge on Formosa (see map at right).

Mao and his forces imposed a tightly centralized administration extending to Manchuria, Inner Mongolia, and Chinese Turkestan. In 1950 his armies moved into Tibet. The Peking government continued to seek to regain the traditional holdings of the "Central Kingdom," especially those lands gained by Russia during the nineteenth century. Such a policy caused serious problems not only for the Soviet Union but also for Vietnam, Burma, and India.

Mao's policy attracted a large following, calling as it did for a mild program of reform, including the confiscation of large farms, state control of large businesses, protection of small private concerns, rapid industrialization under state control, and increased benefits to labor such as social insurance. The government that eventually appeared, however, was far more fierce and totalitarian.

Right-wing Americans, influenced by the demagoguery of Senator Joseph McCarthy, charged that liberals and "fellow travelers" (those who espoused social aims similar to the communists') lost China.[1] U.S. American military aid to China during World War II totaled $845 million; from 1945 to 1949 it came to slightly more than $2 billion. It is extremely doubtful whether additional American military aid poured into China would have changed the final outcome of the civil war. The bulk of the Nationalist forces had lost the will to fight. Large quantities of American arms sent to Chiang's army were turned over to the communists by apathetic Nationalist leaders.

Mao's Government

After 1949, Mao used his version of Marxism to change the whole order of society from its traditional patterns. Tolerating no opposition, he concentrated all power in the communist party, which was led by the People's Central Committee. This group held all major civil and military

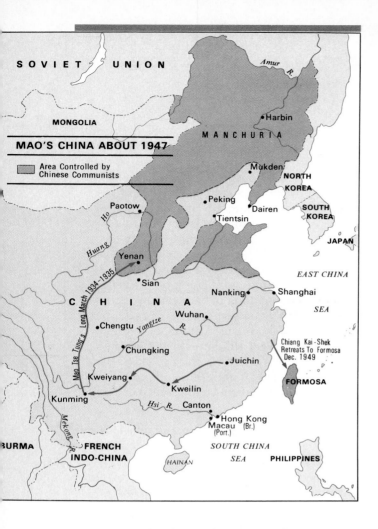

MAO'S CHINA ABOUT 1947

Area Controlled by Chinese Communists

SOVIET UNION

MONGOLIA

MANCHURIA

Harbin

Mukden

NORTH KOREA

Peking

Dairen

SOUTH KOREA

Paotow

Tientsin

JAPAN

Huang Ho

Yenan

EAST CHINA

Sian

C H I N A

Nanking

Shanghai

Wuhan

SEA

Chengtu

Yangtze R.

Chungking

Chiang Kai-Shek Retreats To Formosa Dec. 1949

Juichin

FORMOSA

Kweiyang

Mao Tse Tung's Long March 1934-1935

Kweilin

Kunming

Hsi R.

Canton

Hong Kong (Br.)
Macau (Port.)

BURMA

FRENCH INDO-CHINA

Mekong

HAINAN

SOUTH CHINA SEA

PHILIPPINES

in theory, all labor, farm equipment, and land were pooled.

In 1953 a Soviet-style Five-Year Plan for economic development in industry was begun. The Chinese made impressive advances in heavy industry, and the success of the first plan led to the second Five-Year Plan, the so-called Great Leap Forward. The Chinese built on their own experience, rejecting parts of the Soviet model. They launched the Great Leap Forward with a huge propaganda campaign and galvanized millions of urban and rural workers into a frezied effort to increase tremendously the production of steel, electricity, and coal. Thousands of small, backyard furnaces sprang up to produce steel. The Chinese boldly predicted that they would surpass British industrial capacity in fifteen years.

In the countryside Mao installed the People's Communes. The state created some 26,000 of these units, each averaging 5000 households, or about 25,000 people. The heads of the communes collected taxes and ran schools, child-care centers, dormitories, communal kitchens, and even cemeteries in this massive attempt at social experimentation. Mao tried to convert peasants into a rural proletariat paid in wages. All land, dwellings, and livestock reverted to the effective ownership of the communes until the late 1970s. During the two decades in which the People's Communes functioned, they helped produce improvements in medical care and literacy.

The Great Leap Forward ultimately proved to be disastrous for China. Central planners erred in allocating resources and capital, and farm production fell. The steel and iron produced in the backyard furnaces turned out to be unusable. At the same time the Great Leap was failing, the Soviet Union withdrew its technological and financial support. From 1959 to 1961 Chinese industry lacked essential raw materials and millions of people went without adequate food. Between 1960 and 1962 the combination of bad weather and chaos bequeathed by the failure of the Great Leap Forward resulted in malnutrition and the premature death of between 16 and 30 million people.

Faced with this crisis, the government radically changed its economic policy. In the communes social experimentation and centralized control were relaxed. Working conditions were

positions. The day-to-day work of the central committee fell to a smaller politburo, headed by Mao, the chairman of the republic.

The new government brought both inflation and corruption under control, and then began to apply the Soviet model of the 1930s to China. As more than 70 percent of farmland was owned by 10 percent of the rich landlords, the government proceeded to confiscate large holdings and redistribute them, temporarily, to landless peasants. Late in 1953 the party stripped the large landowners and even prosperous peasants of their holdings, executing an estimated 2 to 4 percent (from 2 to 5 million) of them in the process. The party then established huge farm collectives. Within three years, nearly all peasants had become members of rural collectives in which, although individual land ownership was retained

Mao Tse-tung on Communism in China

Mao Tse-tung adapted Marxism to China. After paying tribute to the Soviet Union in 1949, he stated his goals for the future.

Communists the world over are wiser than the bourgeoisie, they understand the laws governing the existence and development of things, they understand dialectics and they can see farther. The bourgeoisie does not welcome this truth because it does not want to be overthrown.

As everyone knows, our Party passed through these twenty-eight years not in peace but amid hardships, for we had to fight enemies, both foreign and domestic, both inside and outside the Party. We thank Marx, Engels, Lenin and Stalin for giving us a weapon. This weapon is not a machine-gun, but Marxism-Leninism. . . .

The Russians made the October Revolution and created the world's first socialist state. Under the leadership of Lenin and Stalin, the revolutionary energy of the great proletariat and labouring people of Russia, hitherto latent and unseen by foreigners, suddenly erupted like a volcano, and the Chinese and all mankind began to see the Russians in a new light. Then, and only then, did the Chinese enter an entirely new era in their thinking and their life. They found Marxism-Leninism, the universally applicable truth, and the face of China began to change. . . .

There are bourgeois republics in foreign lands, but China cannot have a bourgeois republic because she is a country suffering under imperialist oppression. The only way is through a people's republic led by the working class. . . .

Twenty-four years have passed since Sun Yat-sen's death, and the Chinese revolution, led by the Communist Party of China, has made tremendous advances both in theory and practice and has radically changed the face of China. Up to now the principal and fundamental experience the Chinese people have gained is twofold:

1. Internally, arouse the masses of the people. That is, unite the working class, the peasantry, the urban petty bourgeoisie and the national bourgeoisie, form a domestic united front under the leadership of the working class, and advance from this to the establishment of a state which is a people's democratic dictatorship under the leadership of the working class and based on the alliance of workers and peasants.
2. Externally, unite in a common struggle with those nations of the world which treat us as equals and unite with the peoples of all countries. That is, ally ourselves with the Soviet Union, with the People's Democracies and with the proletariat and the broad masses of the people in all other countries, and form an international united front.

To sum up our experience and concentrate it into one point, it is: the people's democratic dictatorship under the leadership of the working class (through the Communist Party) and based upon the alliance of workers and peasants. This dictatorship must unite as one with the international revolutionary forces. This is our formula, our principal experience, our main programme. . . .

The Communist Party of the Soviet Union is our best teacher and we must learn from it. The situation both at home and abroad is in our favor, we can rely fully on the weapon of the people's democratic dictatorship, unite the people throughout the country, the reactionaries excepted, and advance steadily to our goal.

From Mao Tse-tung, Speech "In Commemoration of the 28th Anniversary of the Communist Party of China, June 30, 1949," in *Selected Works*, vol. 5 (New York: International Publishers, n.d.), pp. 411–423.

improved and private plots in which peasants were allowed to keep or sell the crops and animals they raised were used as incentives to increase agricultural production. Between 1961 and 1964 industry also recovered, and the discovery of petroleum provided new energy sources. China made advances in light industry, especially in consumer goods and cotton production. Signs of technological progress included the detonation of a nuclear device in 1964 and a hydrogen bomb in 1967.

The Cultural Revolution and After

By the early 1960s an ideological schism widened between Mao and some of his longtime comrades. The moderates advocated gradual social change and economic development; the radicals sought to carry on immediately with the drastic restructuring of Chinese society. Mao believed, or so it seemed, that many in the party had lost their revolutionary zeal. He advocated a continuous revolution in which the masses should be kept in motion lest the revolution die.

In this photograph from the Cultural Revolution, members of the Red Guard display for public shame several Chinese students, wearing dunce caps, and denounce them as leaders of "antirevolutionary" groups.

In the mid-1960s Mao mobilized the Red Guards, a radical student militia. They attacked the moderates and forced Maoist orthodoxy on party members and populace alike. In all areas, from surgery to nuclear physics and beyond, Mao's words were law. Application of the wisdom of Chairman Mao, as contained in the little red book, *The Thoughts of Chairman Mao,* was to lead to miraculous achievements. Placing political purity above economic growth, the Red Guards hampered production and research. Their rallies and demonstrations disrupted the entire educational system.

The effects of this "Cultural Revolution" were dire. By 1967 industrial production had plummeted and basic education and research had ceased; some areas of the country were approaching anarchy. Into this void stepped the People's Liberation Army (PLA), which was the most important element in Chinese politics until 1985. The PLA brought the Red Guards under control, restored order, and put an end to the excesses of the Cultural Revolution.

Mao's long-time associate, Premier Chou Enlai (1898–1976) restored the country's industrial productivity. The return to political stability was more difficult, but Chou managed to hold the country together while rival factions intrigued for power. Chou removed China from the diplomatic isolation in which it had resided since 1958. He responded to a diplomatic initiative made by the Nixon administration in 1971 and moved closer to the United States, motivated perhaps by the armed border clashes with the USSR that occurred along the Amur River. In addition, China sought to develop its industrial capacity through the use of foreign technology and to bring in foreign currency through an expanded banking system based in the British crown colony of Hong Kong and the development of a tourist industry.

China Since 1976

After Chou's—and Mao's—death in 1976, the jockeying for control continued with varying intensity. Leading the more militant faction, the so-called Gang of Four, was Mao's widow, Jiang Xing (Chiang Ching), who was overthrown, disgraced, and brought to a televised show trial in

1980. Her demise paved the way for the advent of a more moderate, pragmatic group of officials led by Deng Xiaoping (Teng Hsiao-Ping).

Deng was a political survivor, whose roots in the party went back to the 1920s. He survived political exile and the cultural revolution to introduce his variant of reform Marxism in which the party kept control of the "commanding heights" of the economy. Aided by his liberal chief lieutenants, Hu Yaobang and Zhao Ziyang, Deng introduced a pragmatic series of economic reforms.

The first major move to introduce a more market-oriented economy came in the countryside in 1978. The party allowed greater personal profit for the peasants, and this resulted in a vast increase in productivity. China had a grain surplus in six of the next seven years. With more food in the cities, and a contented peasantry, Deng in 1985 encouraged the introduction of the free market economy in the cities, with the goal of gaining similar economic gains there. To foster the rapid transformation of the under-developed country, Deng permitted the entry of Western experts and technology. Western, especially American, influence grew in the cities in China during the 1980s, along with foreign trade and the influx of foreigners.

The government continued to keep the cost of medicine low and supplemented wages with accident insurance, medical coverge, day-care centers, and maternity benefits. The standard of living in China improved, but the removal of price controls on food and other staple items led to inflation. Even with economic progress, the standard of living in China remained far below the standards in industrialized countries.

The educational system changed drastically under the communists. In the 1930s only 20 percent of the people had been literate. By the end of the 1980s, the figure had risen to 75 percent. Across China, a crash program of schooling was initiated, and "spare-time" schools with work/study programs for those unable to attend school full-time were established. Thousands of Chinese students emigrated abroad to study, including some 40,000 who went to the United States.

Deng Xiaoping had worked for the economic liberalization of his country but had not sponsored similar reform on the political front. The students in 1987 were the first to express

In May 1989, Chinese students in Peking's Tiananmen Square rally around the 33-foot replica of the Statue of Liberty, which they had dubbed "The Goddess of Democracy."

discontent with inflation and corruption in China. In the spring of 1989, students across China demonstrated in honor of the liberal politician Hu Yaobang, who had died in March. The demonstrators went on to criticize the government of Deng Xiaopeng. The protest reached a climax in May and June when thousands of demonstrators calling for democracy occupied the ceremonial center of modern China, Tiananmen Square in Peking.

The party split over how to deal with the protestors and their supporters, sometimes numbering a million strong. Zhao advocated accommodation but Li Peng called for a crackdown. While the debate went on within the party, the students erected a tall replica of the Statue of Liberty to symbolize their demands for democracy and an end to corruption. By the end of May the students had won the enthusiastic support of the workers and citizens of Peking, Shanghai, and Chengdu. Finally, in June the party had decided what to do about the protestors. The People's Liberation Army, using tanks and machine guns, cleared the Square and the surrounding area of the student demonstrators. Over 3000 people were killed in the massacre.

By 1990, it was apparent that China would not retreat into another period of diplomatic isolation. Deng Xiaoping had integrated his country too firmly into the world economy for that. Chinese leaders worked skillfully to maintain their commercial relations and to regain two traditionally Chinese areas to help their struggling economy.

The leaders in Peking had already worked out an agreement with the British in which the rich crown colony of Hong Kong would come under Chinese authority in 1997. Peking saw a major potential source of economic strength across the Straits of Formosa in Taiwan, where Chiang and the remnant of his forces had fled in 1949. For the next quarter century, the United States recognized the Taipei government as the legitimate government of China. By 1989 Taiwan's GNP had reached $100 billion, and its 23 million people had an average annual per capita income of close to $5000. Mainland China, in contrast, had a GNP of $440 billion, and a per capita income of $360 for its 1.15 billion people.

Southeast Asia

One of the first indications that the whole structure of imperialism would quickly collapse came in the late 1940s when Indonesian nationalists demanded a complete break with the Netherlands. An ugly war ensued, and finally in 1948, through UN mediation, the Dutch East Indies became the nation of Indonesia. The biggest and potentially richest nation in Southeast Asia (see map below), Indonesia has enjoyed little tranquillity since it gained independence. The state is 88 percent Muslim but encompasses a mixture of many cultures in its 3000 islands, ranging from Stone Age people to urban professionals and intellectuals. Complicating the situation is the prominence of the Chinese minority, which dominates. There have been anti-Chinese riots and plots in various islands against the central government in Java.

For the first fifteen years after independence, Indonesia experienced declining exports, inflation, and food shortages. Its population increased while its economy declined. The main responsibility for this situation belonged to Indonesia's flamboyant president Achmed Sukarno (1901–1970). He contracted huge Russian loans for arms, fought a costly guerrilla campaign against Malaysia, confiscated foreign businesses, and wasted money on expensive, flashy enterprises.

Muslim students in Indonesia triggered the events that led to Sukarno's downfall. At the beginning of 1966 they launched attacks on Indonesians they believed to have communist connections. An estimated 300,000 to 500,000 were killed. The army's chief of staff, General T. N. J. Suharto became effective head of state, and in March 1967 became president officially.

Suharto brought stability to the country and initially installed a more west-leaning government. In return he got substantial American aid. In the next twenty-five years Suharto's essentially military regime faced serious problems. In 1971 and again in 1974 there were serious racial outbursts during which thousands of students went on rampages, looting and damaging Chinese shops and homes. During the 1970s some 30,000 political dissidents were imprisoned, while rampant corruption dominated government, the civil service, and business. Enormous wealth remained concentrated in the hands of a very few individuals.

Created out of former British holdings, the Federation of Malaysia was admitted into the British Commonwealth in 1957. In 1963 it became independent and immediately faced Sukarno-sponsored guerrilla attacks. As in Indonesia, a major problem in Malaysia is the country's racial mix and the resulting hostilities. The majority of the population is Malay, but the Chinese hold the majority of the wealth, and what they do not control is largely owned by the small Indian minority. In the late 1960s and early 1970s Malays attacked the other two groups.

One of the richest areas in Southeast Asia after the war was Singapore, a city-state roughly three times the size of Washington, DC. Singapore withdrew from the Federation of Malaysia in August 1965 and after that was dominated by the People's Action Party, run by Lee Kuan Yew. Taking advantage of its superb location at the Straits of Malacca, Singapore became one of the richest places in the world. At the end of the 1980s its 2.5 million people generated a GNP of more than $29 billion. What Lee Kuan Yew did not provide in terms of unfettered civil rights, he more than made up for in the efficiency and stability of his rule.

Vietnam: The Postwar French Phase

After World War II France was forced to grant a measure of autonomy to Cambodia and Laos, its former colonial possessions in Southeast Asia. The status of Vietnam posed a greater problem. In 1945 a nationalist and pro-communist movement led by Ho Chi Minh had established the independent Republic of Vietnam, usually referred to as the Vietminh regime.

Negotiations between the Vietminh and the French led nowhere, and war broke out in December 1946. The cruel and violent struggle, anticolonial as well as ideological, lasted for nearly eight years. In May 1950 the United States began sending substantial financial and military support to the French. The end came dramatically in 1954 when the French, despite U.S. assistance, surrendered their isolated outpost at Dien Bien Phu, along with 10,000 troops.

In a conference at Geneva later that year a truce line was established at the 17th parallel, to be regarded as a temporary boundary pending nationwide elections (see map below). These elections were never held, and instead a new group proclaimed the Republic of South Vietnam, based in Saigon, south of the truce line. Meanwhile, the division between the Vietminh regime in Hanoi and the Saigon government increased. Along with the movement of hundreds of thousands of Roman Catholic Vietnamese refugees from the north came a powerful infiltration of communist military personnel and materiel from Hanoi.

The United States shipped large numbers of men and weapons to Saigon in an attempt to create a South Vietnamese state capable of holding its own against the Vietminh and their allies in South Vietnam. The military activity on both sides violated the Geneva agreements, but it could be argued that since none of the governments had signed them, they simply were not binding. Washington sponsored the establishment of the Southeast Asia Treaty Organization (SEATO) to stop the spread of communism into Cambodia, Laos, and South Vietnam.

Increasing American Involvement

At first the Americans gave full support to Ngo Dinh Diem, the leading figure of the noncommunist south. He rejected Ho Chi Minh's requests to hold elections throughout all Vietnam under the Geneva agreements because he feared that his government would lose. He also refused to carry out comprehensive land reforms desired by Washington, choosing instead to rely for support on the landlord and the urban middle classes.

At the same time, the communists, thwarted in their aim to unite north and south by an election, began guerrilla operations against Diem's government. This so-called Second Vietnamese War began in 1957. Many peasants, disillusioned by Diem's failure to carry out land reform, tacitly or actively supported the communist guerrilla effort. In December, the National Liberation Front (NLF)—popularly known as the Viet Cong—was established in the south and gained full support from Hanoi.

Diem, in the face of a rising crisis, became even more autocratic and less inclined to make reforms, perhaps reflecting Washington's shift in policy from Eisenhower emphasis on "nation-building" to the Kennedy strategy of "counterinsurgency." The NLF threatened to take over the

THE VIETNAM WAR

Railroads to China bombed 1972
U.S. air raids 1966–1968, 1972
Dien Bien Phu 1954
Hanoi
Haiphong
Gulf of Tonkin
Gulf of Tonkin incident 1964
CHINA
LAOS
Vientiane
Mekong R.
NORTH VIETNAM
DEMILITARIZED ZONE (DMZ)
17th Parallel
Hue
Tet offensive 1968
Invasion of Laos 1971
Ho Chi Minh Trail
My Lai massacre 1968
THAILAND
SOUTH VIETNAM
CAMBODIA
Invasion of Cambodia 1970
Cam Ranh Bay
Phnom Penh
Gulf of Thailand
Saigon
Tet offensive 1968
Fall of Saigon 1975
Mekong Delta
SOUTH CHINA SEA

Major battles
Major U.S. air bases

0   100   200
MILES

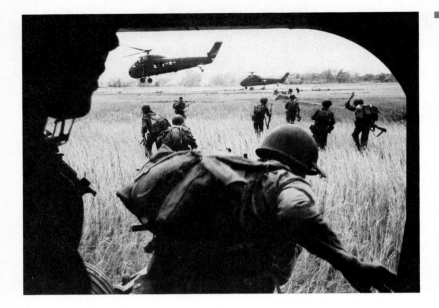

A marine helicopter drops off U.S. troops in Vietnam in 1965. In 1963, there were 16,000 U.S. combat forces in Vietnam; five years later, the number had increased to 500,000. More than 57,000 Americans were killed in action in Vietnam, making the Vietnam conflict the United States' fourth deadliest war—after the Civil War and World Wars I and II.

entire government by force, and a coup and Diem's assassination did little to improve the situation. Following a series of short-lived, essentially military governments, Nguyen van Thieu became president of South Vietnam in 1967.

In 1960 there were only 800 U.S. military advisers in the country. Four years later, this figure had risen to 23,000. In August 1964 Washington accused North Vietnam of attacking United States destroyers in the Gulf of Tonkin. Following President Johnson's request, Congress adopted—by a Senate vote of 88–2 and a House vote of 416–0—a joint resolution approving "all necessary measures . . . to prevent further aggression" and authorized the president to assist South Vietnam in its defense, using military force if required.

Thereafter, the war in all of its aspects became increasingly Americanized, and by 1968 there were more than 500,000 U.S. troops in the country. In 1965 the United States started an intensive air campaign against North Vietnam. The aerial campaign failed to intimidate the North Vietnamese and became a subject of bitter controversy in the United States.

Pulling Out

By 1968 many Americans had begun to question the U.S. role in Vietnam. Their doubts were sharpened in the early spring of 1968 when the

Viet Cong launched the Tet offensive against the Saigon forces and the Americans. Widely covered by television and print journalists, the offensive turned into a military disaster for the NLF and Hanoi, but the images of death and destruction communicated a notion of helplessness to the American people. The U.S. military victory became a political defeat for President Johnson.

As the number of Americans killed in Vietnam grew, the antiwar movement spread from a few score campus radicals to include moderate politicians, suburbanites, and mainstream clergy. The financial costs of the war were enormous, helping fuel an inflation that continued through the 1970s. The political cost for Lyndon Johnson was equally high, forcing him to step down after one term.

During the final months of Johnson's administration peace talks began in Paris with all interested parties represented. The Nixon administration continued the talks through three years of frustrating negotiations until, in January 1973, the Paris accord was signed. It provided for a cease-fire, the withdrawal of U.S. troops, and the release of all prisoners of war.

Pending elections to be arranged later, Nguyen van Thieu's South Vietnamese government was to remain in power. An international commission was to be established to investigate cease-fire violations. The Paris Accord contained no provision for the withdrawal of North

Vietnamese forces. Once the Americans withdrew, the North Vietnamese continued their advance, and the commission was predictably ineffectual. In early 1975, the Hanoi forces, soon to be the fifth strongest military in the world, began a massive offensive. Deprived of U.S. support, the southern forces fell apart once the northern frontiers were overrun. Saigon, now named Ho Chi Minh City, was captured in late April. Many South Vietnamese fled their homeland and some 140,000 gained sanctuary in the United States.

For the United States the legacy of the Vietnam conflict was 58,000 killed, a financial outlay of at least $146 billion, a society bitterly split, and a host of veterans who were rebuked or ignored. It took ten years for the United States to come to terms with the war. The legacy for Vietnam was a twenty-year delay in the Vietminh takeover and incalculable human and material losses. The country has barely begun to recover economically.

Indochina after 1975

The United States had expanded the fighting into neutral Cambodia in the spring of 1970, invading it with the goal of cutting North Vietnamese supply lines and driving the Hanoi army from its sanctuaries there. Following the North

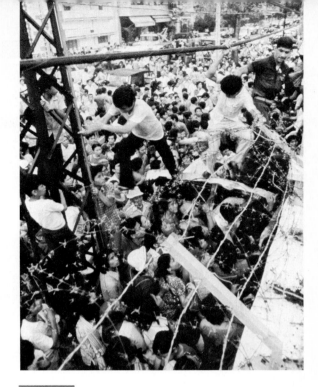

After the United States withdrew its troops from Vietnam in 1973, many South Vietnamese fled the country. Above, thousands of refugees crowd the U.S. embassy in Saigon. Below left, a mother and her children struggle across a river to escape aerial bombardment of their village.

Vietnamese victory in 1975, communists took control of Cambodia and Laos. The ruthless and brutal Khmer Rouge regime created a reign of terror in Cambodia, which was renamed Kampuchea. In Phnom Penh, the capital, nearly all the inhabitants—more than 2 million people—were driven into the countryside, regardless of age or infirmity. People in other cities suffered the same fate; many died from sickness or starvation. A new social system of farm units with labor brigades and communal kitchens was set up. The slightest sign of disobedience resulted in death.

The leader of the Chinese-supported Khmer Rouge regime was Pol Pot. His followers murdered thousands of innocent peasants along with "anyone who had been associated with the cities, with foreigners, or with intellectual, business, or technical activities."[2] The regime's goal seems to have been a self-sufficient agricultural society in which most people would have food and shelter but no pay. It is estimated that between 1975 and 1980 between 2 and 3 million Cambodians have died, "shot, beaten to death, starved, brutalized. Few people in modern times have been subjugated to such barbarism."[3] The Pol Pot regime was overthrown when Vietnamese armies invaded the country. The Cambodians now suffered the ravages of war in addition to continued, indiscriminate killings and massacres.

While China supported Pol Pot, the Soviet Union supported the Vietnamese invaders and a Cambodian faction opposed to Pol Pot. Early in 1979 Chinese armies invaded Vietnam, destroying several of its northern towns, but failed to draw Vietnamese armies out of Cambodia. After this brief sortie, the Chinese forces withdrew, and the world gained an appreciation of the military strength of the Vietnamese regime.

Although the situation in Laos was not so chaotic, yet there also the Vietnamese regime imposed some regimentation and abuse of the Laotians, some of whom were sent to "reeducation camps." Many professional people fled the country, and soon the lack of food and deplorable health conditions made Laos' standard of living nearly the lowest in the world.

Since the 1980s, much of Indochina has been a confused mass of fleeing refugees. Unwilling to accept North Vietnamese rule, thousands took to the sea in rickety boats. Many Chinese living in Vietnam were mistreated by the new regime and retreated across the border to China. Great numbers of refugees fled from Laos and Cambodia to Thailand, Malaysia, Indonesia, and Hong Kong. In addition, thousands of "boat people" have drowned at sea in their leaky craft, been attacked by pirates in the South China Sea, or died of thirst and starvation when refused permission to land.

The Subcontinent of India

In the Indian subcontinent, the western thrust of the Japanese armies induced the British government to make substantial concessions to Indian Nationalists leaders. In 1942 Britain offered India independence within or without the British Commonwealth following the war. Tragically, during and immediately after the war, antagonism between the Muslim and Hindu populations in India became acute. Britain,

represented by Lord Mountbatten, eased tensions by persuading both groups that partition of the country was inevitable. Thus, with the coming of independence in 1947, the fragile economic and geographical unity of the subcontinent was shattered (see map below).

Pakistan was an artificial creation, separated by about 1000 miles of intervening Indian territory. India itself is not a single nation but consists of numerous racial, linguistic, and cultural groups. "Nowhere do so many linguistically differentiated peoples, all of them so self-aware, all numbered in millions and tens of millions, confront each other within a single national body politic."[4] Once the British left, there was no longer an external force to bind together the ancient and conflicting cultural and regional loyalties.

The immediate aftermath of the partition was a rash of bloody riots between Hindus and Muslims. One of the victims of this violence was

Mahatma Gandhi, who because of his tolerance toward Muslims, was assassinated by a Hindu.

India: The Largest Democracy

In the long list of newly independent states after 1945, few have retained genuine liberal regimes. Until 1975, the only outstanding example was India, the world's largest democratically governed state.

After independence, India's parliament functioned with little friction. This success was due to Jawaharlal Nehru (1889–1964), the country's first prime minister and an ardent devotee of democratic government. Nehru sought to maintain close relations with both the Soviet Union and China, often to the discomfort of the United States. However, a border conflict that led to major military action between India and China in the first part of the 1960s drained India's economic growth.

After Nehru's death his daughter, Indira Gandhi (1917–1984), was elected prime minister in 1966. Her popularity reached a peak with the defeat of Pakistan in the 1971 war that led to the creation of the country of Bangladesh. Within two years, however, India's mildly socialist economy was battered by serious crop failures, food riots, strikes, and student unrest. In June 1975 Gandhi announced a state of emergency and assumed dictatorial powers. She jailed 10,000 of her critics, imposed a rigid press censorship, and suspended fundamental civil rights.

With all opposition muzzled, the people were exhorted to "work more and talk less." After a year, the new order claimed numerous gains, advances in productivity, a drop in inflation, curbs in the black market, and stepped-up birth control measures to alleviate India's population pressures. Although Gandhi declared that her drastic measures were only temporary, some critics observed that she was trying to move "from dictatorship to dynasty." Early in 1977, there was some relaxation of authoritarianism.

In that same year, the government released many political prisoners and announced that national elections would be held. In the elections Gandhi lost her seat in parliament and resigned her post as prime minister. A new government, led by aged politicians, tried with little success to solve India's problems. Caste tensions were on

Indira Gandhi was elected prime minister of India in 1966 and served until 1977, when she was defeated and imprisoned briefly for abuses while in power. Reelected in 1980, she held office until she was assassinated in 1984.

the rise, there was widespread violence, strikes increased, and student demonstrations closed universities. In addition, all the old economic problems remained. More than half of the population was illiterate and lived below the poverty level.

Disenchanted with the incompetent rule of bickering politicians, the Indian voters brought Gandhi back to power in the 1980 elections. She promised the country strong leadership, but with no more "excesses." For the next four years she pursued a neutral course, reflecting the geopolitical position in which India found itself. India's alliance with Russia served as a defensive shield against both Pakistan and China. The Soviet invasion of Afghanistan raised some disturbing questions, but Gandhi refrained from criticizing the action.

In October 1984 Gandhi was assassinated by Sikh bodyguards who were connected to the Sikh separatist movement. She was succeeded by her son Rajiv Gandhi, a former pilot and political novice who soon showed a surprising degree of confidence and competence in governing the world's largest democracy, containing over 800 million citizens. Continuing his mother's basic policies, he consolidated his political position. Still, the country's widespread poverty and vast diversity—especially the continuing Sikh separatist movement and the longstanding Kashmir border dispute with Pakistan posed great challenges that Rajiv Gandhi could not overcome. He was defeated in elections at the end of 1989 and was replaced by V. P. Singh of the National Front party, who similarly could not find solutions to India's overwhelming problems. The world's largest democracy balanced tenuously between sectarian fragmentation and unity in the elections of 1991, when Rajiv Gandhi was assassinated in May.

Pakistan

After its creation in 1947, Pakistan was plagued by feuds between its eastern and western wings. Shortly after independence the prime minister was assassinated, a number of short-lived governments followed, accompanied by intermittent rioting and states of emergency.

In 1958 General Mohammad Ayub Khan (1907–1974) gained power. His regime gave Pakistan reasonable stability and some relief from corrupt politicians. Under his tutelage, the country made economic progress. Ten years later, however, pent-up dissatisfaction against corruption in the government led to a new military dictatorship under General Yahya Khan. In the interim, regionalism continued to be a major problem. While Pakistan's population was predominantly Muslim, its two main provinces differed widely in race, economic interest, and language—not to mention the geographical separation. East Pakistan complained continually of being exploited by more prosperous West Pakistan, and these complaints escalated into riots and threats of secession.

In 1971 the Pakistani government sent troops into the eastern region and began a reign of terror. The influx of refugees into India created an intolerable burden, and in December the Indian army invaded East Pakistan, defeating the central government's forces. India encouraged the region to break away, and in 1972 East Pakistan became the new state of Bangladesh. Bangladesh, covering an area not much larger than the state of Arkansas, was an instantaneous economic disaster with twice the population density of Japan and nothing approaching the Japanese economic productivity. The Bangladesh population in 1990 was 121 million, while the per capita GNP was a mere $155.

A civilian government was reestablished in Pakistan, led by Zulkifar Ali Bhutto (1928–1979), who governed under a democratic constitution. Throughout the decade, Pakistan's economic problems persisted, along with its domestic instability. Bhutto, overthrown in 1977 by General Mohammad Zia al Haq, was executed in 1979. The new military dictator, who faced widespread opposition, invoked martial law and postponed elections indefinitely. Like his predecessors, he had to contend with both Indian hostility and potential Soviet intervention. Pakistan retained

Bengali guerrilla soldiers at Dacca, the site where Pakistani forces surrendered to Indian and rebel troops in 1971.

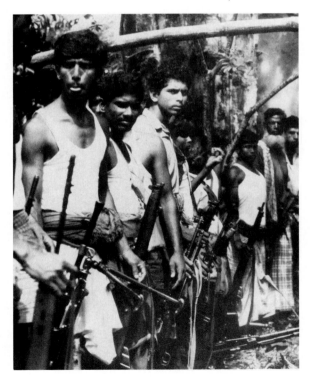

its traditional alignment with China, while India kept close ties with Moscow.

In 1979, events in Iran and Afghanistan posed particular threats to Pakistan. Thirty-six Islamic foreign ministers meeting in Pakistan condemned the Soviet aggression against the Afghan people. In 1981, however, a substantial American aid agreement was negotiated, providing for $3.2 billion in arms over a period of six years. Pakistan, thereafter, served as the American support base for the Afghan resistance.

In 1988 Zia al Haq was assassinated and succeeded by Bhutto's daughter Benazir, the first woman elected to govern a Muslim nation. She lasted twenty months, until, under pressure from the army she was dismissed under accusations of incompetence and corruption.

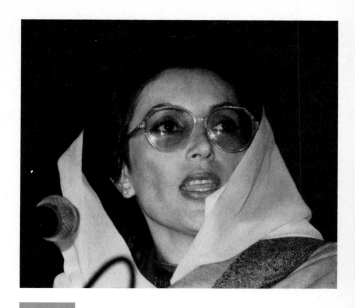

Prime Minister Benazir Bhutto of Pakistan, the first woman elected to govern a Muslim nation.

The Middle East

Decolonization in the Middle East began with British recognition of the independence of Jordan in 1946 and the end of the British mandate in Palestine in 1948. In the meantime, the arrival of European Jews seeking refuge in the area after the war, Zionist terrorist activities, and great power political pressure led to the creation of the state of Israel in May 1948. This touched off a bitter conflict between the new state and the Arab world that was intensified by the perennial statelessness of the more than million Palestinian Arab refugees represented by the Palestine Liberation Organization. Complicating this volatile situation were the Islamic fundamentalist revival, Iraqi aggression, and the overall great power competition between the Soviet Union and the United States.

At the end of World War II, Arab leaders joined forces to form the Arab League. Set up to advance common Arab interests and, in part, to counter Israel, it was used to further the pan-Arab ambitions of Egypt, a republic since 1953. The dominant figure in the Arab world was Colonel Abdul Gamel Nasser (1918–1970), leader of the Egyptian military junta, which had overthrown King Farouk in 1952. From his base in Cairo Nasser offered guidance and assistance to liberation movements in Sudan, Tunisia, Morocco, and Algeria.

The Arab-Israeli Conflict

Conscious of their hostile surroundings, the Israelis took steps to become militarily, economically, and politically strong. The success of their efforts became quite evident in 1956 when, as allies of the British and French, they overwhelmed the Egyptians in a war for control of the Suez Canal. International pressure applied by the United States, the USSR, and the United Nations forced the Israelis to withdraw from their territorial gains.

The conclusion of this crisis brought only a temporary reprieve from hostilities. In the next decade the issues of oil, Palestinian rights, the existence of the state of Israel, and free access to the Suez Canal monopolized the attention of foreign offices within the region, as well as in Moscow and Washington. As it became apparent that there were no simple solutions to the Middle Eastern problems, the Arabs sought to solve them in 1967 by mobilizing their forces. They requested the withdrawal of the UN peacekeeping forces and blockaded the Gulf of Aqaba, Israel's access to the Red Sea. War broke out on June 5. Within seventy-two hours an Israeli blitzkrieg completely overwhelmed and humiliated the combined Arab forces. When a cease-fire was arranged five days later, Israel occupied the Sinai peninsula, including the east bank of the Suez Canal, old Jerusalem, and border areas inside Syria commanding tactically important heights. This was no lasting solution to the conflict, however, and in 1973 the threat of war reappeared.

As in 1967, the opening of this chapter of hostility was preceded by a period of rising tension, characterized by attacks by Arab guerrillas and regular army detachments into Lebanon. The Soviet Union was a major supplier of arms and technicians to the Arabs. The United States committed itself to the existence of Israel, investing billions of dollars a year in foreign aid in the 1980s. Realizing the danger of a Russo-American confrontation in the Middle East should a new round of war explode, Britain, France, the United States, and the USSR explored ways to bring the contending parties to agreement.

The issues discussed were to the possibility of some return of captured Arab territory, the internationalization of Jerusalem, and a solution to the refugee problem. The Israelis, however, insisted on the Arabs' unequivocal recognition of Israel as a sovereign state with the right to exist. Acceptance of a cease-fire in the summer of 1970 gave some hope for a settlement, but the situation deteriorated a few months later when Israel charged Egypt with cease-fire violations and Nasser suddenly died.

On October 6, 1973 war broke out again when the Egyptians and Syrians launched a coordinated attack on Israel. For the first few days the Arabs held the initiative, but Israeli forces counterattacked, crossing the Suez Canal into Egypt and driving to within twenty-five miles of Damascus, the capital of Syria. In some of the most concentrated armored combat since World War II 1800 tanks and 200 aircraft were destroyed.

During the fighting, the United States organized a large airlift of arms to Israel, and the Russians responded with troop movements. Soviet and American leaders averted a possible showdown through consultations, and the danger passed when the UN arranged a cease-fire. In January 1974 Egypt and Israel signed a final pact, providing for mutual troop withdrawals, the occupation of the east bank of the canal by Egypt, a UN buffer zone, and the return of prisoners. Fighting continued between Israel and Syria in the strategic Golan Heights area. U.S. Secretary of State Henry Kissinger led the efforts for a cease-fire on that front in May 1974. This agreement provided for the return by Israel of some captured Syrian territory, a UN zone, and the return of prisoners.

The 1973 war and its spin-offs were costly for the world. Israel spent $5 billion and suffered 5000 casualties, plus an ever-increasing rate of inflation since that time generated by war expenses. Arab casualties were more than five times the Israeli losses. But where the Israelis came to a sober realization of their population and financial limitations, the Arabs came out of the second war with improved morale. After the 1967 war, Arab radicals, especially those in the Popular Front for the Liberation of Palestine, pushed the oil-producing countries to use the "oil weapon"—cutting or drastically reducing the export of petroleum—against Israel and its allies. Such a policy was following after the 1973 war, and this spread devastation throughout the economy of the industrial world.

Egyptian-Israeli Détente

In September 1975 Egypt and Israel reached a second pact in which additional territory in the Sinai peninsula was returned to Egypt and both sides agreed not to resort to force. The United States agreed to provide up to 200 civilian technicians to maintain a precautionary warning system between the two sides. Washington also committed additional arms and financial aid to Israel.

In late November 1977 President Anwar Sadat (1918–1981) initiated a dramatic shift in regional affairs when he flew to Jerusalem to conduct peace talks with Israeli leaders. He had already shown his ability to make controversial decisions in 1972 when he ordered the 18,000-member corps of Soviet military and technical advisers out of his country. Sadat faced serious problems at home brought on by a faltering economy and a rapidly increasing population. These problems had led to serious riots, sparked by runaway inflation. He understood his country's compelling need for peace and recovery.

Sadat, born of a peasant family, had excelled in school and entered the Royal Military

Academy. He had worked with other officers to rid Egypt of British domination and in the coup to expel King Farouk. He was a loyal follower of Abdul Nasser, and succeeded him as president in 1970. He showed his mettle in fighting off attempts Israel in 1973. Nothing he did was more courageous than making the trip to Jerusalem in 1977.

The United States strongly supported Sadat's venture and U.S. President Jimmy Carter invited Sadat to meet Israeli Prime Minister Menachem Begin, at Camp David in September 1978. After intense negotiations, the three leaders produced a framework for a permanent peace treaty. Israel agreed to return all the Sinai to Egypt, but no definite agreement was reached on the status of the west bank, where the one million displaced Palestinian Arabs lived. It was agreed, however, that negotiations should begin to set up an elected self-governing authority of Palestinians and also to end the Israeli military government. Following this step, there would be a transitional period of five years during which negotiations would take place on the final status of the west bank, an issue that remained in conflict at the end of the 1980s. Sadat and Begin received the Nobel Peace Prize in 1978.

The formal peace treaty signed in March 1979 ended the state of war between Egypt and Israel and began the process of returning all of the Sinai to Egypt. It also opened the Suez canal to Israeli ships. In 1980 the two nations opened their borders to each other, exchanged ambassadors, and began air service between the countries.

The Iranian Revolution

Iran, which had served as an area of competition between the British and the Russians since the nineteenth century, became a bone of contention between the United States and the Soviet Union after World War II. As a result of an agreement between the British and the Russians in 1941, Shah Mohammad Reza Pahlavi (1919–1980) gained the Iranian throne. After the war he asked foreign troops to withdraw from this country, but following the slow return of the Soviet army to its borders, aggressive activities of the Iranian communist party (Tudeh), and an assassination attempt on the Shah's life, Iran firmly tied itself to the west.

In 1953, Iranian premier Mohammad Mosaddeq advocated nationalization of Iran's oil fields and a comparatively radical tax program, and forced the Shah to flee the country. Mosaddeq was overthrown in 1954 in a CIA-supported military coup, and the Shah was restored to power. For the next twenty-five years, Iran rested firmly within the orbit of the United States, a valuable source of oil and an independent military force in a vitally strategic region.

Israeli Prime Minister Menachem Begin embraces U.S. president Jimmy Carter as Egyptian president Anwar Sadat looks on and applauds. Carter invited Begin and Sadat to a summit meeting at Camp David in September 1978 to work out a peace agreement between Israel and Egypt.

The Shah attempted a rapid modernization of his country, but the so-called White Revolution threatened the integrity of the Iranian cultural fabric. The presence of over 100,000 foreigners, including 47,000 Americans, alienated orthodox Muslim forces, who perceived the Shah as attacking the Muslim political and economic base. Opposition to the Shah's rule spread widely, from militant communists to Shi'ite clergy to discontented nationalities. In addition, inflation alienated some of the business classes and the laborers.

In the face of this growing opposition, the Shah began a reign of terror. After seven years, the storm broke in January 1978 when large numbers of students demonstrated against the absolute monarchy. Many were killed and wounded by the Shah's troops. Strikes and demonstrations paralyzed the country. The army and secret police proved helpless in the face of the national revolt. In January 1979 the Shah fled the country, seeking asylum first in the United States, then Panama, and finally in Egypt, where he died in 1980.

The diffuse and widespread revolution found its focus in the aged Ayatollah Ruhollah Khomeini, a Shi'ite holy man who had been in exile since 1963. From Iraq and then from Paris he had carried on an incessant propaganda effort against the "godless and materialistic" rule of the Shah. Khomeini was intensely opposed to western culture and once in power set to work to purge Iran of its "wickedness." Western music on radio and television was banned, as were "provocative" bathing suits, liquor, and a broad range of other items. The Ayatollah stamped out secular western political forms and instituted instead a theocratic state based on the Koran.

The Ayatollah viewed the United States as the "Great Satan" and encouraged Iranians to express anti-American sentiments. In November 1979 a mob of young Iranians stormed and seized the U.S. embassy and took fifty-three hostages, whom they held for over a year. Finally, the financial drain of the war with Iraq—begun when Iraqi leader Saddam Hussein attacked Iranian airfields and oil refineries in September 1980—forced the Iranians to release the hostages in return for the United States' release of Iranian assets frozen in response to the hostage taking.

The Iran-Iraq war lasted for the rest of the decade until an armistice—caused by exhaustion—in 1989. It had been a war of attrition in which both sides suffered enormous losses. The Iranians employed all of their resources including twelve- and thirteen-year-old children in human wave attacks against the well-ensconced but smaller Iraqi army. The Iraqis on their side violated the accepted rules of combat by using chemical weapons and poison gas.

The Soviet Invasion of Afghanistan

Armed coups and assassinations characterized the postwar political history of Afghanistan. Since 1945 the Soviet Union has extended its influence in the area, capping its overtures in 1978 with a "friendship treaty" between Kabul and Moscow. Postwar leaders have sought to introduce changes based either on Western or Marxist models such as nationalization and land redistribution, but they have encountered fierce

Iranian workers in Teheran, Iran, demonstrate their support for the Ayatollah Khomeini and for the Iranian students who seized and held hostage 53 Americans in the Ayatollah's name.

resistance. The strongly conservative Muslim tribes oppose modernization in almost any form, and civil war broke out in the late 1970s.

By 1979 it appeared that President Amin's government, which received support from the USSR, would be toppled by the rebellion. Earlier the Soviets had sent in 5000 military and civilian advisers to assist Amin and they could not now tolerate loss of their client state. In late December, thousands of Soviet troops crossed the border, captured the airport, and stormed the presidential palace in Kabul. They killed Amin and installed Babrak Karmal in his place. Karmal announced that Soviet troops had been invited in to save Afghanistan from imperialist plots fomented by the United States. Few nations accepted this fabrication. But, coming as it did during the U.S. dilemma with Iran, the invasion gave the USSR the opportunity to dominate this strategic region with little risk of armed opposition.

In the next year the USSR gained control of Afghan cities, while an assortment of tribal guerrilla forces roamed the countryside, but the Soviet advance sputtered during the 1980s. The Afghan resistance, supported by the United States, stalemated the Soviets and their puppets. The one advantage the USSR had in the battlefield, air power, was negated by the Afghans' use of U. S.-supplied Stinger anti-aircraft missile. As the decade wore on, Afghanistan became for the Soviet Union what Vietnam had been for the United States in the 1960s and 1970s—a costly, divisive conflict. The cost to the Afghan people was immense. Millions were uprooted, villages were destroyed, and many areas were littered with booby traps and mines. Finally, in the spring of 1989, the Soviet Union withdrew its forces from Afghanistan. The civil war continued, and to the surprise of many, the government did not collapse before a disjointed rebel offensive.

Toward a New Balance

Since the 1980s the four key elements in the Middle East have come to be Egypt, Israel, the United States, and Iraq. In 1990, an event occurred which cut across the traditional antipathies and its resolution gave a small opening for U.S. and Soviet diplomats to try to nudge the region onto a new path.

During the first part of the 1980s Egypt remained an outcast among Arab countries because of its détente with Israel. In October 1981, a small group of Islamic militants assassinated Sadat while he was reviewing a military parade. Shortly before his death, he had ordered a crackdown on the Muslim brotherhood, which opposed his reconciliation with Israel and Egypt's increasingly secular nature.

Sadat's successor, Hosni Mubarak, pledged continued support of Sadat's commitments and welcomed the support and friendship of the United States. During the 1980s Mubarak improved Egypt's relations with other moderate Arab states as he struggled with his country's overwhelming economic problems brought on by a mushrooming population along the Nile Valley and Delta. Mubarak solidified his position and maintained Sadat's foreign policies.

Huge outlays for defense drove Israel's inflation rate to average over 50 percent in the last part of the 1980s. The Israelis came to depend more and more on aid from the United States, whose annual announced subsidies exceeded $4 billion a year. Adding to Israel's concern was a shift in American public opinion as extreme Arab provocations in the Intifada—Palestinian active and passive resistance to Israeli policies—drew harsh Israeli police responses, which on American television almost uniformly cast them in a bad light.

While committed to Israel's security, the United States, especially in the administration of President George Bush, increased its interests in aiding friendly Arab states who opposed what they saw as Israeli aggression. This was particularly the case with Saudi Arabia, the main supplier of American oil imports. It was this concern that led the United States to sell the Saudis large quantities of sophisticated weapons and to send the U.S. Navy to keep the Persian Gulf oil shipment lanes open during the latter stages of the Iran-Iraq war.

Iraq, a country with immense oil and agricultural potential, had squandered much of its wealth on military strength. Under Saddam Hussein, the Iraqis had developed extensive capabilities in chemical and bacteriological warfare. Their nuclear facilities, destroyed by the Israelis in 1980, were rebuilt. Iraq had launched a war against Iranian airfields and oil refineries in

September 1980, and in the succeeding nine years, more than a million people died in fighting that saw the use of poison gas and chemical weapons. In August 1990, 100,000 Iraqi troops invaded and overran the oil-rich sheikdom of Kuwait in one day. This aggressive act, plus the implied threat to Saudi Arabia of Saddam Hussein's one million-man army produced an immediate response. The fear that Iraq, if it took the Saudi oil fields, would control one-third of the global oil reserves—moved the UN Security Council to impose a series of strict sanctions on Baghdad.

For the next six months the United Nations, led by a coalition assembled by U.S. President George Bush, increased the diplomatic pressure on Saddam Hussein by increasing sanctions and embargoes on his country. Hussein received the support of the Palestinians, and the young throughout much of the Arab world, and Jordan.

When sanctions and embargoes failed to move Iraq to withdraw from Kuwait, the American-led 26 nation coalition (including Egypt, Saudi Arabia, Syria, Turkey, France, Italy and United Kingdom) began heavy bombardment of Iraq beginning in January 1991. A month later, the allies launched a land offensive that in 100 hours evicted Iraq from Kuwait and left the coalition in possession of one-fifth of Iraq.

The successful smashing of Iraq's forces by the coalition opened the possibility that the Middle East might be able to break out of its entrenched and unchanging hostilities. Fervent diplomatic activity throughout the major capitals of the world prepared the way for conferences that could bring a lasting peace to the region.

A Tragic Stage

Few areas better illustrate the tragedy of the Middle East during the past half century than Beirut. Once the most beautiful and civilized city in the Middle East, a center for prosperity and a crossroads of cultures and religions, by 1991 Beirut had finally recovered from the tragic stage on which all of the competing factions of the Middle East waged virtually continuous warfare.

The problems were rooted in a number of causes. The Palestine Liberation Organization (PLO) led by Yasir Arafat from its headquarters in Lebanon stepped up demands for Israeli withdrawal from the west bank of the Jordan River and the Gaza Strip, both captured by Israel during the 1967 war. The PLO wanted an independent Palestinian state and in pursuit of that launched terrorist raids from its bases in southern Lebanon and encouraged riots to harass Israeli authorities. In response, beginning in 1978, Israel made repeated incursions during the next decade into Lebanese territory strike back at the PLO bases.

Civil war adds to Lebanon's dire situation. This small and racially mixed nation—its area is slightly less than that of Connecticut—is divided between Christian and Muslim factions. Before the influx of the Palestinians, the Christians held a slight majority, and the various factions maintained a delicately adjusted political balance. The influx of Palestinians in 1975 shattered that balance. The Christians—at first supported by the Syrians—and the Muslims with their Palestinian allies fought until the October 1976 cease-fire. The cost was 25,000 dead, thousands more wounded, and sections of the city gutted. The country's once flourishing economy was at a standstill.

A symbolic episode occurred in the summer of 1981 when PLO forces fired rockets into Israel, which responded with massive air attacks on Palestinian strongholds in Beirut. Hundreds of civilians were killed. In the summer of 1982 the

The allied coalition launched its war to drive Iraq out of Kuwait with a huge-scale air attack. Smoke pours out of the Defense Ministry in Baghdad, after its bombing by allied forces.

Israelis invaded Beirut, surrounding Muslim-held west Beirut. The PLO evacuated Beirut in September, under the direction of a French, Italian, and United States multinational contingent. After the multinational force departed, the newly elected president, the Phalange Christian Bashir Gemayel and 26 of his colleagues were killed by a bomb. In apparent response, Christian militiamen, allies of the Israelis, massacred hundreds of Palestinian men, women and children in two refugee camps.

In the succeeding decade the skeletal outlines of bombed buildings, shadowy videotapes of hostages, and pictures of young and old darting through streets to avoid gunfire have given the world an image of the total futility of violence. Beirut's tough citizens remained, hopeful that, perhaps finally, an equilibrium could once again be found in the Middle East.

Africa

In Africa, the European powers approached decolonization in a variety of ways. The British devised programs to provide financial and technical aid to prepare their colonies for independence within the Commonwealth. France also gave loans and grants, but the French wanted a political and economic structure dominated by Paris. Belgium showed no understanding of the need to prepare the Congo for the future and continued its paternalistic approach. Portugal had neither the resources nor the will to prepare its colonies for the future.

In the first decade after World War II, however, it was apparent that independence would come to Africa faster than anyone had anticipated. While on a visit to British Africa in 1960, Prime Minister Harold Macmillan declared:

The wind of change is blowing through this continent, and whether we like it or not, this growth of national consciousness is a political fact and our national policies must take account of it.[5]

Africans rightly think of 1960 as their year. Eighteen new nations emerged, the most important being Nigeria and the Congo.

The Challenges of State-Making

France had enacted various reforms to keep its African territories as autonomous republics within a French community. (Guinea, however, had elected to become completely independent in 1958.) This compromise did not satisfy African hopes. In 1960 all thirteen African republics within the French community proclaimed their independence. While the dream of a great French imperial structure had ended, France did retain a unique status in its former colonies. Its culture persisted in Africa, and France maintained its financial and technical dominance.

In 1945 there had been four independent African nations; by the end of the 1980s over fifty sovereign states could be identified. But independence did not bring a golden age. The optimism that accompanied the gaining of sovereign status did not last. State-building in the late twentieth century was a difficult process.

Each of the new states had to bear the heavy costs of creating a trained corps of bureaucrats, diplomats, and soldiers. All of the new states worked to build stable democratic governments led by just and strong executives. They wanted to work through responsible and freely elected legislatures and enjoy the benefits of incorruptible courts. But all of them, especially Kenya, which had emerged from revolutionary struggle, faced serious challenges.

The most pressing problem was how to build and maintain national unity among distinct and sometimes antagonistic religious, cultural, and ethnic groups. In most cases, the new African states were not the product of a long historical process such as took place in Europe where small feudal principalities were hammered into homogeneous nation-states. Most African boundaries were arbitrary creations of the imperialists and had little relationship to the people who lived there. Nigeria, for example, the result of British arms and the imagination of British geographers, encompassed many diverse and hostile ethnic and tribal segments. Throughout sub-Saharan Africa, tribal fragmentation worked against the development of nationalism.

These difficulties plus the economic problems—some produced by unwise investments in prestige-enhancing but economically wasteful enterprises—made the attainment of stable democratic governments difficult. Between 1960 and 1967 twenty-seven newly independent states experienced forceful takeovers. In four months in 1967 there were four military coups. In 1980 a dozen revolts took place, five of which successfully toppled the governments in power. Imitating some communist states, many of the leaders—including moderates such as Daniel Arap Moi of Kenya—discarded the two-party system in favor of a single party government, while insisting that their political systems were essentially democratic. In fact, in some countries, the one-party states did provide stability and progress. But this was not always the case; for example in Uganda under General Idi Amin from 1971 to 1979 thousands of people were killed and the country's economy went to ruin as the capricious and uneducated general pursued a quirky and unpredictable rule.

North Africa

France's two protectorates in North Africa, Tunisia and Morocco, gained independence in a relatively peaceful way in 1956. In sharp contrast stands the transfer of autonomy to Algeria. France had invested millions of dollars in the development of this territory, and by 1960 French immigrants constituted about one-tenth of the population. The French dominated Algeria's industry, agriculture, and government, while the Muslim majority remained hopelessly poor.

Although Algeria was an integral part of France and sent representatives to Paris, resentment against foreign control grew among the non-French majority. Following a mounting campaign of violence, revolution broke out in 1958. After four years of savage conflict, whose repercussions brought down the French Fourth Republic, Charles de Gaulle paved the way for Algeria's independence in 1962. Seventy percent of the Europeans left the scarred and battered country, emigrating to France. Well over 200,000 people had been killed and the number of seriously wounded was even higher.

Since its independence, Algeria has played an important diplomatic role in the world, serving as a crossroads in the Arab world. The economy has become more diversified, with important sectors in petroleum and agricultural exports. By 1990 Algeria's per capita gross national product reached $2400.

Libya made the transition from Italian colony to independent nation with help from the United Nations. The military led by Colonel Mu'ammar el-Kaddafi took power from the monarchy in 1969 and eight years later the country became known as the Socialist People's Libyan Arab Jamahiriya. Since that time the quixotic leader has pursued, generally unsuccessfully, military adventures against Egypt (1977), Uganda (1979), and Chad (1980). He has also supported international terrorism, drawing the anger of the United States which on three occasions in the 1980s shot down attacking Libyan jets in the Mediterranean and bombed Tripoli once. Revenues from the country's rich oil fields help finance Qaddafi's ventures and contribute to a per capita GNP of more than $5600 for the roughly 4 million Libyans.

Middle Africa

Ghana was the first nation south of the Sahara to gain independence. In 1957 Kwame Nkrumah, its prime minister, was the idol of African nationalists, and his newly freed nation was the symbol of liberalism and democracy in Africa. But almost immediately, Nkrumah began to muzzle the press and imprison the opposition. He quickly developed into an outright dictator while at the same time embarking on ruinous economic policies such as showy projects and a large military establishment. Nkrumah's controlled press called him the Great Redeemer and His Messianic Majesty, while his economy slid downhill under the impact of incompetence and corruption.

In 1966 a group of army officers seized control of the government. Anxious to speed economic recovery and to restore some semblance of political freedom, the army leaders permitted the return to parliamentary institutions in 1969. Ghana thus became the first African country to return to multiparty government after being a one-party state. During the 1970s another military junta carried off a coup, but by the end of the decade, civilian rule returned again. In 1981 the military under Flight Lieutenant Jerry Rawlings once again took control, and remained in control throughout the 1980s.

Jomo Kenyatta (center), flanked by his wife Njina and Chief Justice Sir John Ainley, is sworn in as president of the newly independent Republic of Kenya, December 12, 1964.

In contrast, the independent nation of Kenya gained stability and a sound economy under the sole political party, the Kenya African National Union, founded by the statesman Jomo Kenyatta. The state was able to mediate between the Kikuyu and Luo tribes and make its capital at Nairobi into a showplace for the continent. Kenya's history is not uniformly positive, however, as in 1972 Kenyatta expelled the East Indians, who had dominated trade.

Events were not so fortunate in the Belgian Congo (Zaire), a huge dependency as large as western Europe but lacking any ethnic or economic unity. In 1959 the Belgians, in the face of general unrest and serious rioting, promised independence. When self-government came the next year, civil war broke out among some of the seventy major groups. At the request of the Congolese government, UN forces intervened to restore order, which they did by 1964. By the mid-1970s a new regime under (Joseph) Mobutu Sese Seko succeeded in establishing the central government's uneasy authority over the tribal groups. The large, resource-rich country suffered from ineffective rule and terrible poverty among the general population. By the end of the 1980s the per capita GNP was only $172.

When it gained independence in 1960, Nigeria offered the most promise of the new African states of a prosperous and stable future. It had several thousand well-trained civil servants,

more than 500 doctors, an equal number of lawyers, and a substantial body of engineers and other professionals. It made rapid progress toward modernization, endowed as it was with a variety of important natural resources, especially oil. Unlike the Belgian Congo, it had some forty years of training in self-government. Its constitution was the result of a decade of constitutional experiments and discussion with British officials.

Nigeria, however, was similar to the Congo in its tribal and ethnic complexity. It had more than 200 tribes and a dozen important languages. Yet it appeared to have the forces of unity to overcome any fragmenting tendencies in its state structure. Nigeria was held up to be democracy's best hope in Africa; unfortunately this hope was not realized.

Between 1962 and 1966 a series of crises—disputed elections, corruption, and crime waves—threatened to tear the new nation apart. After witnessing these events, the Ibo tribal region proclaimed its independence as the state of Biafra. The Hausa and Yoruba encircled the Ibo, and crowded them into a small area without sufficient food or supplies. Thousands, especially children, died of starvation. In 1970 the Ibo surrendered and reconciled with the other tribes.

After thirteen years of military rule, civilian government was restored in 1979, along with a new constitution patterned after that of the

United States. Designed to prevent a return of the ethnic-regional feuds that had wrecked the first republic, the new constitution created a federal system providing for the allocation of powers between a central and nineteen state governments. However, Nigeria returned to military rule in 1983 and all political parties were banned, and it has thus remained.

The Eastern Horn of Africa, consisting of the Somali Republic and Ethiopia, became geopolitically significant after 1945 because of its proximity to the sea lanes of the Red Sea and the Persian Gulf. The British liberated Ethiopia from the Italians in 1941, and permitted Emperor Haile Selassie to return. While not an unenlightened ruler, he was unable to adapt to postwar conditions.

The crisis that led to his expulsion began with a famine in 1973 that killed 100,000 people. Strikes, student unrest, scandal among the royal family, and mismanagement all combined to bring success to the coup attempt that removed Haile Selassie. The new rulers were bitterly divided among moderates and radicals, and following two years of quarrels, the radicals gained control. Their governing council immediately set to work to abolish the country's traditional feudal system, transforming Ethiopia into a socialist state with a one-party system of a Stalinist type: collective farms, censorship, government control of all productive property, imprisonment, and mass execution of at least 10,000 opponents.

The council then turned to the problems in the Ethiopian provinces of Ogaden, adjacent to Somalia, and Eritrea on the Red Sea. Somalia took possession of Ogaden in 1977 but the next year the Ethiopians signed a treaty with the Soviet Union that gave them $1 billion in aid, 17,000 Cuban troops, and modern weapons. The Ethiopians launched a counter offensive and pushed the Somalis back. In the late 1970s the Ethiopians turned their attention on the Eritrean rebels and were able to expel them from some of their urban strongholds.

Overwhelming all of the political and diplomatic maneuvering was the series of massive famines that rocked the area during the 1980s. The government of Mengistu Haile-Mariam who ruled until May, 1991 either through intent or incompetence allowed thousands of Ethiopians to die, despite the massive outpour of aid from such

diverse groups as churches, charitable organizations, and rock musicians.

Southern Africa

Many significant events rocked the southern part of the continent. In 1974 the revolt of the Portuguese army in Lisbon ended nearly half a century of dictatorial rule. The military junta concluded thirteen years of costly revolt by black nationalists in Portugal's African territories—Angola, Mozambique, and Guinea-Bissau. The last two gained independence with little difficulty. Freedom for Angola was complicated by the presence of a half a million European inhabitants. Following the granting of independence in 1975, bloody strife between three rival nationalist groups broke out. Fighting continued until 1989 among the groups, which drew support from Cuba, the Soviet Union, and South Africa.

Zimbabwe, formerly Rhodesia, shares a common border with Mozambique. In the first part of the 1960s this colony contained some 250,000 whites and more than 5 million Africans. In 1963 the white minority-controlled colony declared its independence from Great Britain, which had insisted that such action could not be agreed to without the prior grant of full political rights to the African majority. Despite a crippling trade embargo imposed by Britain and economic sanctions levied by the United Nations, Rhodesia refused to compromise. In 1970 the final ties with Britain were severed when the former colony assumed the status of a republic.

During the 1970s violence increased as forces crossed over Mozambique and Zambia, while South African troops joined local forces in search-and-destroy missions against the guerrillas. By the end of the decade, the 250,000 Europeans voted to accept black-majority rule. Black factions led by Robert Mugabe boycotted the elections held in April 1979, and new elections were held in 1980. Mugabe, a Marxist, won and ruled Zimbabwe through the decade.

The country recovered quickly from the conflicts of the 1970s that left 25,000 dead and many more wounded and produced massive unemployment and food shortages. Mugabe proved to be a skilled leader, keeping the white infrastructure in place, and producing a per capita GNP of $540 by 1986. Tourism picked up and economic obstacles began to disappear. The de facto one-party state appeared to be one of the more stable and progressive on the continent.

Conditions in South Africa remained tense in the post-1945 period. With its booming cities, rapidly growing industries, and rich mining enterprises, South Africa was a thoroughly modern state, except for its racial policies. The Republic of South Africa, with a population was 70 percent black, 18 percent European, and the remainder "coloured," had to deal with the rising discontent of the African majority and with the censure of its racial policies of apartheid by the world community.

The South African government tried a program of territorial segregation, setting up ten distinct and partially self-governing African states known as Bantustans, which were aided by substantial economic grants (see map at left). First to be established was Transkei, with its Bantu population of 3.5 million people. This program did not satisfy the African populations, and strikes and political protests against apartheid continued through the 1980s. The government continued the program, granting partial independence to Transkei in 1976 and establishing two additional Bantustans three years later. The fact remains that the Homelands are generally poor and underdeveloped, forcing a constant exodus of blacks to find employment in white urban areas. Those who cannot find work and housing and meet other requirements are classed as illegal immigrants and shipped back to their Homelands.

In 1978, Prime Minister P. W. Botha, who retained that position until 1989, declared that the country "must adapt or die." Advocating a new program of race relations, he urged a lessening of race discrimination in the areas of loans and mortgage opportunities, jobs, working conditions, and wage disparities. In 1980 a new plan of government was announced. A President's Council was to be created, consisting of a white-nominated majority, coloured and East Indian members, and one Chinese representative. This body was to advise on constitutional proposals. Symbolically, this was the first time some political representation was given to non-Europeans. The plan denied Africans any such rights except in their tribal Homeland.

Botha oversaw some relaxation of apartheid: races began to mix freely in public places, areas reserved for whites only were reduced, and new black unions were legalized. Ultra-right wingers forced the prime minister to pull back. In effect apartheid remained intact. Meanwhile, the frustrations of the non-Europeans increased, fueled by the gain of independence in Angola and Zimbabwe. Militancy increased. When a new constitution was adopted in 1983, providing for a strong executive presidency and a three-part parliamentary body—whites, coloured, and Asians—blacks remained unrepresented and without rights except in their tribal "homelands." Only the white part of the parliament had any power.

F. W. DeKlerk, who replaced Botha in September 1989, moved to try to defuse the seemingly inevitable bloodshed between the races. In the face of death threats launched by extreme right-wing, proto-Nazi white parties, he opened negotiations with the African National Congress. He made the symbolically important step of releasing ANC founder and symbolic leader of many South African blacks, Nelson Mandela, from almost three decades of imprisonment and

In May 1990, South African president DeKlerk and deputy president of the African National Congress Nelson Mandela pose for photographers before beginning talks to end racial strife in South Africa.

whites. Namibia contained valuable mineral deposits, but more importantly to South Africa, it served as a buffer against potentially unfriendly black nations to the north. While South Africa reached an agreement with a coalition of blacks and whites for a form of self-rule, it refused to recognize the militant Southwest African Peoples' Organization (SWAPO), which was based in Angola and supplied by the Soviets. In the early 1980s a UN-sponsored plan for an election was blocked by the South Africans, who sent troops in to attack the guerrillas, killing hundreds and also killing Soviet advisers. At the end of the 1980s, the Namibia crisis was being negotiated once again.

began serious negotiations to pave the way for a multi-racial political structure. In response, the ANC suspended its twenty-nine-year declaration of war against the South African government.

DeKlerk's white opponents accused him of capitulation. Realistic observers noted that by the year 2000, whites will number a bare 13 percent of the population. South African industry will depend largely on black labor and expertise. Apartheid will be an unworkable anomaly in a black, hostile continent, a situation brought increasingly to world attention in 1985 and 1986 when the scale of violence steadily increased. Without wide-ranging reforms, the long-term prospects look bleak. At best the South African government will find itself increasingly isolated in the world community, and at worst a bloody civil war will result.

Another controversial area is Namibia. A German colony until 1919, the area was known as Southwest Africa and administered as a mandate under the supervision of the League of Nations. Following World War II, South Africa refused to transfer its jurisdiction to the United Nations, which formally ended South Africa's mandate in 1966. South Africa held on to control this huge area—half the size of Alaska—which is inhabited by a million blacks and one hundred thousand

Latin America: Reform or Revolt

After the war, Latin America shared many of the problems experienced by the developing countries of the non-European world. Formerly competitive economies such as those of Argentina, Mexico, and Brazil have fallen far behind rapidly advancing areas such as South Korea, Taiwan, and Singapore. Whether in countries of primarily European stock (Argentina, Uruguay, and Chile); dualistic Indian-Spanish societies (Peru, Bolivia, Ecuador, and Mexico); melting pot societies such as Brazil and Venezuela; or single crop economies such as those of Central America, Latin America faced serious problems at the end of the century.

The Perils of the Postwar Era

The period since 1945 witnessed much political instability and social unrest in the region. For example, the only countries with continuously elected governments after 1950 have been those dominated by a single major party. Between 1950 and 1966 fourteen governments were forcefully overthrown and dictatorial rule was imposed on more than half of the Latin American population. The political instability and the seeds of social upheaval spring from appalling socioeconomic disparities. Despite the region's great natural resources, the average citizen of Latin America is young and poor. Shanty towns on the edges of large cities house thousands amid filth, disease, hunger, and crime. Life expectancy for Latin American males is around 55 years—fifteen years less than in North America. Agricultural productivity is inefficient and low. The population increases by about 3 percent yearly. By 1990 the region's population topped 500 million, most in cities. Educational and health services are insufficient and literacy rates remain low.

Since 1948 the countries south of the Rio Grande have been aligned with the United States in the Organization of American States (OAS). Dominated by the United States, the OAS has sought to prevent communists from acquiring control in Latin American countries by well-meaning, if incomplete, social and economic aid. After 1959, when Fidel Castro rapidly transformed Cuba into a communist country, his attempts to export his revolution have been countered by an OAS boycott.

In Castro's Cuba, educational and health standards rose appreciably, as did living conditions among the peasants who comprised the great majority of the population. The professional and middle classes, however, suffered losses in both living standards and personal liberties and many hundreds of thousands fled to the United States. Cuba exported sugar to other communist countries in exchange for major economic subsidies from the Soviet Union. In 1975 sixteen members of the OAS voted to end the embargo and the United States intimated a desire for détente. This last possibility was made remote with the intervention of thousands of Cuban troops and advisers in Angola and other African countries.

By the end of the 1980s global political changes isolated Castro. Cuba's role overseas ended with peace talks in Africa. The Soviet Union could no longer afford the luxury of propping up Castro's failing economy. His version of Marxism-Leninism was shared only in North Korea and Albania.

Castro's rule in Cuba sharpened the United States' interest in the area south of its border. After the failure of the American invasion attempt at the Bay of Pigs in 1961, President John F. Kennedy initiated, with Latin American cooperation, the Alliance for Progress. The United States pledged $20 billion, to be matched by the other members of the alliance. After twenty years, the Alliance had done little to change basic

conditions. Oligarchic rule, paternalism, and incompetence hindered economic and political reform. By the end of the 1980s, the major Latin American countries such as Brazil and Mexico were deeply in debt, unable to pay even the interest on foreign loans. Rapidly increasing inflation also hampered economic growth. In Brazil there was substantial indication that a large percentage of the foreign loans were not being invested in needed industrialization and regional integration, but were instead being funneled to Swiss banks by top-ranking bureaucrats.

The Yankee Factor

A key element in Latin America is the relationship between the United States and its neighbors. American economic involvement in Latin America has remained massive. American companies continue to employ about 2 million people, pay 25 percent of the region's taxes and produce one-third of its exports. Softening the imperialist presence are the activities of humanitarian efforts from the Rockefeller foundation and churches, and federal programs of educational, agricultural, and social improvements.

At the same time, the U.S. Central Intelligence Agency (CIA) used large sums to support the opponents of President Salvador Allende of Chile. An avowed pro-Soviet Marxist, Allende had been elected to power. In his hasty efforts to nationalize industry, both domestic and foreign-owned, and to redistribute land holdings, he had antagonized many of his own people. Allende's regime came to a bloody end in a 1973 coup. Military leaders ousted the president, who died—perhaps by his own hand—during the fighting. The new repressive regime, under General Auguste Pinochet, imposed a harsh rule and acted aggressively to curb all opposition, which had been growing since the early 1980s. Pinochet stepped down in 1990 and was replaced by the moderate Patricio Aylwin.

One long-standing source of discord between the United States and Latin America was removed in 1978 when the United Senate approved the treaty that returned the Panama Canal Zone to the Republic of Panama, while safeguarding American interests in the area. This agreement, negotiated over a period of fourteen years under four American presidents, was a sign to some that the United States was eager to improve its relations with its neighbors. The American military invasion of Panama in December 1989, however, indicated that there were some excesses the United States would not tolerate. Allegations that Panamanian President Manuel Noriega cooperated in drug running and overturned democratic elections moved U.S. President Bush to order the preemptive strike to oust Noriega.

In the last decade the countries of Latin America dealt differently with the economic, social, and political challenges they faced. Many remained under military rule. Others, such as Nicaragua, carried out successful socialist revolutions, but faced the powerful overt and covert opposition of the United States, the economic effects of which drastically lowered the country's standard of living. Democratic elections in the spring of 1990 led to the defeat of the Sandinista party in Nicaragua, but economic and social problems remained to plague the new government. Tiny El Salvador struggled through a bloody civil war, in which death squads from both right and left brought terror to the countryside. Brazil made tentative economic progress before a series of poor policy decisions darkened that country's future. Out-of-control inflation destroyed Argentina's economy but Presidents Alfonsin and Salinas were able to restore normal democratic politics in the country. Mexico was stable under a single-party domination but faced a population rate that outstripped its economic progress. Colombia found its basic sovereignty undermined by drug lords, both foreign and domestic.

In the Caribbean, the British successfully ushered in independence in the West Indies — Jamaica, Tobago, Trinidad, and Barbados — but unrest continued in Haiti. President for Life Jean Claude Duvalier, "Baby Doc," was forced out of office and fled the country in February 1986. The Caribbean island of Grenada fell to a leftist government, before President Reagan sent the Marines to the island to overthrow the regime in 1983.

With the end of the Cold War, the United States began to take a longer-term, more economically focussed view of Latin America. Enhanced perceptions of stability moved Washington to policies that may well prove to be mutually beneficial to North and South.

Conclusion

The last half century has seen the emergence of the "south" as the major theater of action for the next century. This area, with the exception of Japan, Singapore, Hong Kong, Taiwan, and South Korea, has also been known as the "Third World," the "underdeveloped world," or the "less-developed world." It contains the fastest growing populations, the most essential resources, and the most politically explosive situations.

The countries range from the richest to the poorest. All of them have been affected by decolonization, the Cold War and its conclusion, and the technological revolution. All of them were brought into the modern age by forceful contact with the Europeans, but in the next century they will have to choose their own paths. All face major economic and demographic crises that are expressed in political instability. The North — the developed world — could find no comprehensive response to the needs of the South. The search for solution to the region's problems will form the opening chapter of the third millennium.

Suggestions for Reading

Edwin O. Reischauer, *Japan: The Story of a Nation* (Knopf, 1974) is the best general coverage. See also Reischauer's *The Japanese* (Harvard, 1977). K. Kawai, *Japan's American Interlude* (Chicago, 1960) discusses occupation policies and their impact. R. P. Dore traces one major problem in *Land Reform in Japan* (California, 1958). John K. Fairbank et al. discuss the challenges of change in *East Asia: Tradition and Transformation* (Boston, 1973).

Stuart Schram, *Mao Tse-tung* (Penguin, 1966) is good for the formative stages of the leader's life. R. H. Soloman, *Mao's Revolution and the Chinese Political Culture* (California, 1971) ties political change to social transformation. Edward F. Rice gives a good summation of Mao's theories in *Mao's Way* (California, 1975). Roderick Mac Farquar, *Origins of the Cultural Revolution* (Oxford, 1983) is first rate. Changes in the countryside are considered in Jan Myrdal, *Report from a Chinese Village* (Signet, 1969) discusses political change from a rural perspective. Thomas Raski gives an overall view of economic modernization in *China's Transition to Industrialism* (Michigan, 1980). See also I. K. Y. Hsu, *China Without Mao: The Search for the New Order* (Oxford, 1982).

For studies of Southeast Asia see Michael Leifer, *The Foreign Relations of the New States* (Longman, 1979); R. N. Kearney, *Politics and Modernization in South and*

Southeast Asia (Halstead, 1974); Robert Shaplan, *A Turning Wheel: The Long Revolution in Asia* (Random House, 1979). On Indonesia, see W. T. Neill, *Twentieth Century Indonesia* (Columbia, 1973) and A. M. Taylor, *Indonesian Independence and the United Nations* (Greenwood, 1975).

On the Vietnam War, see Stanley Kavnow, *Vietnam: A History* (Penguin, 1984). Thomas Powers, *The War at Home* (Grossman, 1973) and Paul Kattenberg, *The Vietnamese Trauma in American Foreign Policy* (Transaction, 1980) deal with the anti-Vietnam war movement. For personal assessments see J. Buttinger, *Vietnam: The Unforgettable Tragedy* (Horizon, 1976); A. M. Schlesinger, Jr., *The Bitter Heritage: Vietnam and American Democracy* (Premier, 1972); and F. Fitzgerald, *Fire in the Lake* (Vintage, 1973). Also, George C. Herring, *America's Longest War: The United States and Vietnam, 1950–1975* (Wiley, 1979).

Some valuable surveys of modern India include W. Norman Brown, *The United States and India, Pakistan, and Bangladesh* (Harvard, 1972) and Stanley Wolpert, *A New History of India* (Oxford, 1982). A solid biography of Indira Gandhi is Z. Masani, *Indira Gandhi* (Crowell, 1976). An informative guide to Indian politics is Richard L. Park and Bruce Bueno de Mesquita, *India's Political System* (Prentice Hall, 1979).

The Middle East's complexity is dealt with in M. Halpern, *The Politics of Social Change in the Middle East and North Africa* (Princeton, 1967) and W. R. Polk, *The Elusive Peace: The Middle East in the Twentieth Century* (St. Martin's, 1980). T. C. Bose gives a basic history of the international rivalry over the area since 1945 in *The Superpowers and the Middle East* (Asia, 1972). On the Arab point of view see W. R. Polk, *The United States and the Arab World* (Harvard, 1975). Two insightful books on Iran are R. K. Ramazani, *The Persian Gulf: Iran's Role* (Virginia, 1972) and Sepehr Zabih, *Iran's Revolutionary Upheaval* (Alchemy Books, 1979). David Pryce-Jones writes of the Arab victims in *The Face of Defeat: Palestinian Refugees and Guerrillas* (Holt Rinehart, Winston, 1973). Soviet participation in the area is spelled out in Jon D. Glassman, *Arms for Arabs: The Soviet Union and War in the Middle East* (Johns Hopkins, 1976). Two phases of Arab-Israeli war are studied in R. and W. Churchill, *The Six Day War* (Houghton Mifflin, 1967) and Chaim Herzog, *The War of Atonement, October 1973* (Little, Brown, 1975). See also H. M. Sachar, *A History of Israel* (Knopf, 1976) and W. Laqueur, *A History of Zionism* (MacMillan, 1968).

The difficulties of transition from white-dominated to black-dominated African states can be seen in the collection gathered on the former Rhodesia in George M. Daniels, ed., *Drums of War* (Third Press, 1974). See also Henry Wiseman and A. M. Taylor, *Rhodesia to Zimbabwe: The Politics of Transition* (Pergamon, 1981). A study of Ethiopia on the eve of Haile Selassie's fall is Patrick Gilkes, *The Dying Lion* (St. Martin's, 1975). Leonard Thompson and Jeffrey Butler, *Change in Contemporary South Africa* (California, 1975) is a superior collection of interpretive essays. L. H. Gann and Peter Duignan, *Africa South of the Sahara: The Challenge to Western Security* (Stanford, 1981) details this region's strategic importance to the West. See also Gwendolyn Carter and Patrick O'Meara, *Southern Africa: The Continuing Crisis* (Indiana, 1979). A solid collection of essays dealing with the global economic response to South Africa's racial policies is Robert E. Edgar, ed., *Sanctioning Apartheid* (Africa World Press). John Seiler's *Southern Africa Since the Portuguese Coup* (Westview, 1980) discusses some of the most contentious regions of the continent. For a fine overall view of politics since independence, see Basil Davidson, *Let Freedom Come: Africa in Modern History* (Little, Brown, 1978).

The following works help illuminate the complex developments in Latin America: Julio Cotler and Richard Fagen, eds., *Latin America and the United States: The Changing Political Realities* (Stanford, 1974); R. J. Shafer, *A History of Latin America* (Heath, 1978); Irwin Isenburg, ed., *South America: Problems and Prospects* (Wilson, 1975). See also R. E. Poppino, *Brazil: The Land and the People* (Oxford, 1973) and J. N. Goodsell, *Fidel Castro's Personal Revolution in Cuba* (Knopf, 1973).

Notes

1. Richard Rovere, *Senator McCarthy* (London: Methuen, 1959), p. 24.
2. Sheldon W. Simon, "Cambodia: Barbarism in a Small State Under Siege," *Current History*, December 1978, p. 197.
3. Robert A. Scalapino, "Asia at the End of the 1970s," *Foreign Affairs*, 1980, no. 3, p. 720.
4. Selig Harrison, *India: The Most Dangerous Decade* (Princeton, N.J.: Princeton Univ. Press, 1960), p. 4.
5. From Prime Minister Harold Macmillan's speech, 3 February 1960. *Vital Speeches*, 1 March 1960.

Chapter 37

Toward the Third Millennium: Integration and Diversity

I n the last half century scientific and technological advances have made the globe an ever more compact sphere. Common problems such as the nuclear threat, environmental crises, economic upheavals, and the population explosion have forced leaders to cooperate more closely.

While common interests and problems have brought leaders to work together, the world has maintained and extended its rich diversity. The dynamic and often tragic nature of the twentieth century has produced a variety of cultural and social responses. Television, radio, cinema, shared styles and music, and safe and easy travel broke down walls that formerly isolated nations one from the other. Far from producing a homogenized culture, however, greater understanding has refined nations' definitions and sharpened the diversity of the world's peoples.

Nuclear War or Survival?

By 1953, the United States and the Soviet Union had concluded the first phase of the Cold War. With the death of Stalin in March of that year, the USSR endured a three-year period of transition, and its foreign policy shifted from military probing to a more sophisticated approach. When Khrushchev gained control in 1956, he imposed his point of view that nuclear war would be suicidal for all concerned. He returned to the Leninist doctrine of peaceful coexistence and renounced the idea that war between the socialist and capitalist worlds was inevitable.

Varieties of Peaceful Coexistence

Peaceful coexistence ushered in temporarily better relations between Washington and Moscow and led to a summit meeting in Geneva in 1955 and Khrushchev's 1959 visit to the United States. Tensions increased in other parts of the globe, however. In Asia, Latin America, Africa, and the Middle East the rival systems competed to gain the support of the nonaligned nations. Two technological triumphs in 1957 escalated the tension between the United States and the USSR: Soviet scientists put the first artificial satellite into orbit and began producing intercontinental ballistic missiles (ICBMs). These achievements gave the Soviet Union the ability to deliver a nuclear weapon to U.S. territory in 25 minutes.

These developments made Cold War competition even more dangerous. Berlin, which had long been a thorn in the Soviet side, became the focal point of competition between the two major powers. West Berlin had become a showplace of freedom and affluence, compared with East Berlin and its drab surroundings and repressive police control. Thousands of the technical and intellectual élite from the east escaped to the west through Berlin. The Soviets, presumably seeking to bring the whole metropolis under communist control, demanded the withdrawal of all western forces and recognition of Berlin as a "free city." The allies refused to give in to this demand, strengthened in their resolve, partially at least, by the substantial advances in U.S. rocket power.

A series of events from 1960 to 1962 brought the superpowers closer to the brink of nuclear war. A summit convened in Paris in 1960 broke up angrily, the situation exacerbated by the shooting down of an American U-2 reconnaissance plane over the Soviet Union. In that same year, Khrushchev, speaking at the UN, demanded the resignation of Secretary-general Dag Hammarskjold, who, he believed, opposed the Soviet-backed force in the Congolese civil war. In 1961, with John F. Kennedy, a young and inexperienced president in office, Moscow stepped up its pressures around the world. The Soviets again demanded the withdrawal of allied forces from West Berlin. Once again the west refused to back down. In response, the USSR-backed East Germans erected a wall between the two halves of the city, thereby blocking the escape route formerly used by thousands. In Laos and Vietnam, tensions also increased. To a generation of leaders in the United States, students of the lessons of "appeasement" and the success of containment, it seemed evident that force had to be met by force.

In October 1962 the world came as close as it ever has to full-scale nuclear war. Three years earlier, Fidel Castro had wrested power from the right-wing Batista dictatorship in Cuba and had begun to transform the island into a communist state. During the early months of his administration in 1961, Kennedy had approved a previously developed plan to send an expedition of Cuban exiles to try to overthrow Castro. In a badly botched operation, the force was decisively defeated at the Bay of Pigs. The following year, the Soviet Union began to install missile sites in Cuba.

To the United States, these missiles represented a dangerous threat to the Cold War balance of power. Kennedy ordered what was, in effect, a naval blockade around Cuba and demanded that Moscow withdraw the offensive weapons. After a few days of "eyeball-to-eyeball" crisis in which one incident might possibly have triggered direct military action between the United States and the Soviet Union, Khrushchev ordered the missiles removed after having received assurance that the United States would respect Cuba's territory.

Creative Diplomacy

After 1962, the Soviet Union and the United States did not approach the brink of nuclear conflict, even though Moscow made significant advances in its military position vis-à-vis the United States. Close consultation between the two capitals, even during intense competition, helped avoid danger. The "hot line" in its increasingly sophisticated forms kept the Kremlin and the White House in minute-by-minute contact and helped avoid direct confrontations in Vietnam and the Middle East.

The Cuban crisis underscored the urgency of reducing the peril of nuclear war and ushered in a three-decade-long process of tortuous and complex negotiations. An immediate result was a limited nuclear test ban treaty negotiated in 1963 and signed on August 5 of that year by Great Britain, the Soviet Union, and the United States. The treaty outlawed the testing of nuclear devices in outer space, the atmosphere, or under water. Although France, China, and India—all of which became nuclear powers—refused to sign, over 100 other states did.

U.S. secretary of state Dean Rusk, Soviet foreign minister Andrei Gromyko, and Lord Home of Great Britain sign the nuclear test ban treaty of 1963. The treaty outlawed nuclear testing in the atmosphere, but it did not ban underground testing nor did it include provisions for on-site inspection. Still, the treaty was an important step forward on international agreement to halt the proliferation of nuclear weapons.

U.S. president Richard Nixon clinks glasses with presidential advisor Henry Kissinger to celebrate the signing of SALT I (the Strategic Arms Limitations Treaty) in May 1972.

This agreement was followed by the Latin American Nuclear-Free Zone Treaty (1968) and treaties and conventions dealing with the nonproliferation of nuclear weapons (1970, expanded 1978), a treaty to reduce the risk of nuclear war (1971), an updating of the "hot line" (1971), a convention dealing with biological weapons (1975), and other agreements dealing with the threat of catastrophic war. In addition, the Mutual Balanced Force Reduction talks between NATO and the Warsaw Pact to limit conventional forces in central Europe, which dragged on for over a decade, entered a new and vital phase in 1990.

The two most important treaties were the Strategic Arms Limitation Talks (SALT I and SALT II). In these negotiations the two superpowers acknowledged, in effect, an equivalence in kill power that led to the capacity for "mutual assured destruction" (MAD). After two years of complicated talks, SALT I was signed by President Richard M. Nixon in Moscow in 1972. SALT I limited the number of ICBMs that each side could deploy for five years and restricted the construction of antiballistic missile systems to two sites, to maintain MAD. Technological advances soon made the limits of SALT I obsolete, as both sides developed the ability to deploy multiple independently targeted reentry vehicles (MIRVs), which vastly expanded the kill power of each ballistic missile.

At a meeting in Vladivostok in November 1974, U.S. president Gerald Ford and Soviet general secretary Leonid Brezhnev established guidelines to deal with the addition of MIRVs, that led to the SALT II agreement. Even though considerations such as the Soviet invasion of Afghanistan and domestic politics in each country precluded the formal adoption of SALT II, the attempt to maintain parity continued. Each side charged the other at times with violating the agreement, which was eventually signed by President Jimmy Carter and Brezhnev in Vienna in 1979. Through the 1980s Moscow and Washington both adhered to the general framework, while maneuvering for strategic superiority.

The arms control talks were complex, difficult, and subject to frustration, as neither side could permit the other to gain an advantage. While the negotiations continued, so too did full-scale weapons research and espionage. In the first half of the 1980s, the Soviet Union upset the balance of force in Europe by placing SS-20 missiles in the Soviet bloc nations of Eastern Europe. The Americans responded by deploying Pershing II and ground-launched cruise missiles, a strategic necessity given NATO's military inferiority in conventional forces.

Both sides returned to yet another summit (the eighth in twenty-five years) in November 1985 in Geneva. President Ronald Reagan met with General Secretary Mikhail Gorbachev to discuss arms control issues as well as a range of other mutual concerns. The two nations agreed to further consultations, but in the interim both argued forcefully over Soviet violations of the 1972 SALT I agreement and the U.S. Strategic Defense Initiative (SDI), a space-deployed system employing the most advanced technologies against nuclear missiles. American negotiators asserted that SDI was an attempt to change the nature of arms control negotiations from assured destruction to assured defense. The Soviets saw SDI as a technological quantum leap that would upset the weapons parity between the two powers. Domestic opposition and Soviet flexibility defused the SDI issue to allow the two powers to sign the Intermediate Nuclear Forces agreement in Washington in 1987. The INF accord set up the destruction of all intermediate and shorter range missiles within three years.[1] Further, the treaty would be monitored by on-site verification, with Soviet and U.S. experts confirming the fulfillment of the treaty's provision.

At the end of the decade, new talks on strategic long-range weapons were resumed, as were negotiations to shut down plutonium production plants. Conventional force talks in Central Europe made more progress in two months than in ten years. Clearly, the combination of economic pressures, especially serious for the Soviet Union, and mutual interest brought the superpowers into close accord to control weapons that could destroy the planet. The need to survive and prosper brought the superpowers together on the nuclear weapons issue. The end of the Cold War removed the nightmare of bipolar nuclear annihilation from the world, as could be seen in the signing of the Strategic Arms Reduction Treaty (START) in July 1991. Even though it is not yet ratified, it makes the first step to cutting down the large stockpiles of nuclear warheads on both sides. However, nuclear proliferation continued, and analysts estimated that by the mid-1990s twenty countries would have the ability to build and deliver nuclear bombs. In addition, terrible new chemical and biological weapons threatened humanity. Perversely, some commentators had begun to look upon the period of the Cold War with some nostalgia, as a time when there was some dependable order.

Trade and Economics

Even before the defeat of the Axis in World War II, the Allies made plans to avoid the horrendous economic chaos that had followed World War I. Forty-four nations met in July 1944 at the New Hampshire resort town of Bretton Woods to put the peacetime world economy on a solid footing. Recalling the protectionist lesson of the 1930s, the financial leaders devised plans to ensure a free flow of international trade and capital.

Plans for a Global Economy

The Bretton Woods conference created the International Monetary Fund (IMF) to restore the money system that had collapsed in previous decades when countries abandoned the gold standard and embraced protectionist devices such as currency devaluations that seriously harmed world trade.

It established as system of fixed exchange rates, founded on the dollar, which could be easily

Soviet general secretary Mikhail Gorbachev and U.S. president Ronald Reagan met at a summit in Geneva, Switzerland, in November 1985. The two leaders announced several agreements on scientific and cultural issues but failed to come to terms on an arms control treaty.

exchanged for gold ($35.00 an ounce). The IMF was based on a foundation of currencies paid in by the member states that served as a world savings account from which a member could take money to handle debt payments without having to resort to the disruptive tactics of manipulating exchange rates or devaluation. The standard for the exchange rates among the various currencies was that in existence as of the first day of the Bretton Woods conference. Member countries could not change their currency's values without approval of the IMF. Although the system faced some problems based on the weaknesses of many of the member states' economies after the war, the Bretton Woods agreement set up a generation of monetary stability that allowed businesses to carry on their affairs with confidence.

Another economic development indicating the integration of the world was the establishment in 1947 of the General Agreement on Tariffs and Trade (GATT), under U.S. leadership. Again, having absorbed the lessons of the protectionist and autarchic 1930s, the allies put together an international institution to set up rules for business worldwide that would give nations the confidence to break down old barriers that blocked free trade. GATT operated through a series of meetings between nations to remove protectionist restrictions. The assurance a nation received for entering the GATT framework was the most-favored-nation-clause, which guaranteed that any trade advantage worked out on a nation-to-nation agreement would be automatically shared by all members of GATT. Over the next quarter century, thanks to the Bretton Woods agreement and GATT, world trade grew at a phenomenal annual rate of 7 percent—adjusted for inflation.

President Nixon's decision in 1971 to end the policy of the dollar's convertibility into gold dealt a fatal blow to the Bretton Woods framework. Yet the development of international organizations such as the International Bank for Reconstruction and Development—part of the Bretton Woods structure, established in 1956—the Organization for Economic Cooperation and Development, and many more organizations, helped to keep the international economy on track.

Ideological warfare between Moscow and Washington prevented the chance for the economic integration of Europe offered by the Marshall Plan. While the individual economies of the west prospered with the aid received through the plan, the economies of the Soviet bloc stagnated. By the 1980s, the economic gap between the two sides forced Moscow and its allies in the Council for Mutual Economic Assistance (COMECON) to seek admission to the IMF and GATT. In the postwar period it became evident that the global political economy was the most important factor in world relations. Nations such as the Soviet Union that allowed ideological considerations to determine economic policy did so with disastrous results.

After 1945 the world experienced incredible economic growth and change. Multinational firms, headquartered in one country but with operations throughout the world, spread rapidly. The United States lost its financial dominance as it faced competition from the European Common Market, Japan, and the "four tigers"—South Korea, Taiwan, Hong Kong, and Singapore. New technologies and cheaper labor overseas produced high-quality items that cost less than U.S. manufactured goods. Competition was especially severe in the high-tech and automobile markets. The resulting foreign trade deficits increased the desire for protectionist legislation in the 1980s. Many congressional members argued that EEC and Japanese trade restrictions and subsidies hampered U.S. agricultural and technological exports while American markets remained relatively open to foreign imports. The GATT mechanism was pushed to the breaking point. In 1989 the United States invoked Section 301 of the Trade Act of 1974 to levy sanctions against India, Brazil, and Japan for unfair trade practices.

The oil embargo of the 1970s imposed by the Organization of Petroleum Exporting Countries (see p. 981) dealt a serious blow to international stability, but even worse was the debt crisis of the 1980s. Banks in the United States, Europe, and Japan made substantial loans to eastern Europe, Latin America, and Africa—whose total debt by the end of the decade topped $1.3 trillion. Brazil had close to $100 billion in debt, Mexico close to $90 billion. To ensure their survival, nations such as Brazil, Hungary, and Poland allowed World Bank personnel to impose regulations on domestic economic policy in return for loans, an unprecedented sacrifice of national sovereignty to an international body. Nonetheless, nonpayment by the debtor nations threatened to topple the world's banking structure. The crisis pressed the International Monetary Fund to the limit. Debts continued to be rescheduled, but the largest debtors showed an ever-declining ability to pay.[2]

The world recession of 1978 to 1985 had different effects on different parts of the globe. Unemployment soared across the world, especially in the lesser developed countries, which were also plagued with soaring population. In the United States the recession contributed to the huge trade deficits and federal budget deficits. The United States was the first nation to recover from the recession, largely at the expense of generating a huge internal debt and borrowing heavily from foreigners. A creditor since 1917, the United States now became a debtor nation.

The Common Market and 1992

The most significant development in postwar Europe was the progress toward economic integration. The desire for cooperation came from the lessons learned during World War II, taught by visionaries such as the French statesmen Jean Monnet and Robert Schumann. In 1950 Monnet and Schumann put forth a program to create the European Coal and Steel Community to coordinate the supply of those two essential industrial commodities in West Germany, France, Italy, Belgium, the Netherlands, and Luxembourg. Five years later, the European Atomic Energy Community was created.

The same six nations that participated in these supranational organizations in 1957 established the European Economic Community, colloquially known as the Common Market. The organization's goal was to build "the foundations of an enduring the closer union between European peoples." To that end it reduced tariffs among its members and created a great free trade union that became the fastest growing area in the western free world.

From its headquarters in Brussels, a staff of some 3000 experts administered the affairs of the EEC. In the 1950s the income of its members

Jean Monnet on European Unity

Jean Monnet was a pioneer in building the foundations for a unified Europe. He expressed his hopes in a future—to be attained in 1992—in a 1953 speech.

Mr. President, Ladies and Gentlemen, on behalf of my colleagues of the High Authority and myself, I wish to say how very pleased we are to have this meeting to-day with the members of the Common Assembly and the members of the Consultative Assembly. The co-operation between the Council of Europe and the European Coal and Steel Community has now definitely entered a concrete phase. . . .

In respect of coal and steel, the community has set up a huge European market of more than 150 million consumers, *i.e.* equal in number to the population of the United States of America. Under the terms of the Treaty, customs duties and quota restrictions have been abolished between Germany, Belgium, France, Italy, Luxembourg and the Netherlands; the principal discriminations in respect of transport have been done away with. . . . the road along which the six countries of the Community have set out is the right road, but we must continue to seek even more zealously ways and means of achieving a more complete understanding with the other countries of Europe. When they have seen and understood, as we have done, what this new and living Europe means for them, they will, one of these day, I hope, themselves join in.

From the *Joint Meeting of the Members of the Consultative Assembly of the Council of Europe and of the Members of the Common Assembly of the European Community of Coal and Steel. Official Report of the Debate*, Strasbourg, 22 June 1953.

One indicator of a global economy in the 1980s and 1990s was the growth of multinational firms with operations throughout the world. Here, hundreds of Soviet citizens crowd around the first McDonald's in Russia, which opened in Moscow on January 31, 1990.

doubled. While the U.S. economy grew at a rate of 3.8 percent, that of France expanded 7.1 percent, Italy by 8.4 percent, and West Germany by 9.6 percent. During the rest of the decade trade nearly doubled among EEC members. As their factories and power plants hummed with activity, their work force was augmented by more than 10.5 million workers who migrated, many with their families, from southern Europe.

Lagging far behind these advances, Britain became a member of the Common Market in 1973; Ireland and Denmark also joined in that year. The admission of Spain and Portugal in 1986 brought the number to twelve. While the member nations jealously guarded their sovereignty, they made substantial strides toward total economic integration. Various advances have been made toward adopting a common passport, setting a basic work week and holiday policy for all workers and equalizing welfare benefits.

By the end of 1992 Europe will be a single market similar to that created by the 1707 Act of Union between England and Scotland, the Constitution of the United States, and the north German *Zollverein* of the first part of the nineteenth century. Reaching the goal of "Europe 1992" has not been easy. Serious controversies over agricultural policy, banking policies, and

tax differences had to be overcome. The European leaders worked hard to reassure the rest of the world that their twelve-nation market would not be protectionist, while they went about putting together the 300 directives that would form the laws for the commercial union. The program of the twelve nations involved the opening up of their union's boundaries so that there would be no restriction to stop the movement of goods and people and the establishment of the "social dimension" to define the "rights or ordinary people in the great market and to help the poorer among them . . . ." There was also a drive toward economic and monetary union including a single European currency and central bank. Economic union also included single standards on electricity, pressures, safety, and health.

Many obstacles, some born of a thousand years of nationalism, remain. The issues of a state's favoring its own industries in the purchase of supplies and equipment, protection of particular industries by sovereign states, and the value-added tax are unresolved. Japan and the United States feared they would by excluded from future economic possibilities and yet were excited by the promises of the largest market in the world. Members of the European Free Trade

Association—Finland, Austria, Iceland, Sweden, Switzerland, and Norway—were left to determine their relationship to the powerful group of twelve, as they approached 1992.[3]

The Soviet Bloc

After 1945, Moscow's consolidation of its power gave it control over an area that extended from Berlin to the Bering Straits and from the North Pole to the Black Sea and the Amur River. Soviet leaders imposed a centralized, Stalinist control over hundreds of millions of people in a way never before seen. By the end of the 1980s Moscow found itself caught between the forces of nationalism and Russian centralism, between inflation and Soviet economic demands, and between rising feelings of liberal democracy and a declining interest in Marxism.

Nowhere were the bloc's problems more effectively portrayed than in the dilemmas faced by COMECON. The Soviet Union set up COMECON in 1949 as a response to the Marshall Plan and other Western projects to promote economic growth. In its first decade, COMECON served Soviet postwar recovery needs, as Moscow worked a reverse system of mercantilism on the region: exporting raw materials at high prices, buying back finished goods at low cost. Eastern Europe suffered greatly under this system, as could be seen in the sharp contrast between West and East Berlin. In the 1960s and 1970s the Soviet bloc states primarily the Soviet Union, German Democratic Republic, Poland, Czechoslovakia, Hungary, Romania, and Bulgaria) began to profit from buying cheap energy supplies from the Soviet Union, in return for which they sent goods they could not market in the west, and their standards of living began to improve, along with their economic growth rates.

Soviet premier Yuri Andropov wanted to turn COMECON into a functioning and competitive trade bloc, but severe structural problems hampered the system's efficiency. The restrictive bilateral nature of the relationship between Moscow and its allies prohibited, for example, Prague and Budapest working directly to achieve production or trade—COMECON countries had far more barriers than the Common Market in 1967. The nonconvertibility of each country's currency meant that each bloc country's currency could be spent only within that country. The stagnant nature of each regime's central planning apparatus fostered an industrial plant that produced inferior goods wastefully. Central planning dictated the prices of resources and commodities, usually with no relation to their actual value. Shackled with these problems, COMECON could not compete with the Common Market.

Aggravating the situation for the Eastern Europeans was the fact that as world energy prices fell in the latter part of the 1980s, they were trapped into paying premium prices for Soviet oil and gas. Several eastern European states, including Poland, Hungary, and Romania, borrowed heavily from the west and invested the proceeds unwisely. Romania escaped the foreign debt problem only by slashing the standard of living for its people. Poland and Hungary in 1989 appealed openly to the United States for help. The COMECON plan announced in the mid-1980s to equal the west technologically by the year 2000 appeared to be little more than feeble rhetoric.

There was no doubt that the Soviet Union and eastern Europe had made great progress in recovering from the devastation of World War II. In basic industry, metals, chemicals, and armaments, the Soviets sometimes led the world. They trained more engineers, scientists, and technicians than any country in the world. Their nuclear arsenal and space explorations were testimony to their accomplishments. However, in other areas—computers, robotics, biogenetic engineering, superconductivity to name a few—the west far outpaced the Soviet Union. Western tourists visiting Moscow at the end of the 1980s were amazed to see clerks in major stores using abacuses to figure the cost of purchases.

As energy prices declined, the Soviet Union—the leading oil producer in the world, exporting 3 billion barrels a day for 60 percent of its hard currency earnings—saw its earnings cut by over 60 percent when oil dipped to $10 a barrel. By the end of the decade the price had gone back to $20, but the problems remained. The Soviets and their allies invested heavily in industrial espionage in the hope of gaining high-tech parity with the west.

Premier Mikhail Gorbachev launched a frontal attack on the Soviet Union's economic problems through his programs of *glasnost* and *perestroika.* Gorbachev attacked the Stalinist central planning system with its layers of bureaucracy and managerial ethic built around satisfying the plan and not on solving problems. His economists spoke of letting market forces set prices. The philosophy that justified the Marxist-Leninist system was rejected, at least in its economic components. Universities in eastern Europe dropped not only the compulsory study of Russian but also the works of Karl Marx, expecially *Das Kapital*. Westerners were amazed to hear communist officials in the Soviet bloc speaking the rhetoric of American neoconservatives, or nineteenth-century liberals. Leading spokesmen, up to and including Gorbachev, spoke of the fact that the welfare and happiness of the individual would be best served by economic individualism, the free operation of the marketplace, with the role of government severely reduced.

Merit and productivity were goals to be pursued, objectives that were anathema to the *apparatchiki*, who felt seriously threatened by Gorbachev's reforms. From the time of Stalin on, life was good for the managerial élite. They enjoyed the best apartments, summer houses, automobiles, access to the best schools, doctors, and hospitals, and the right to shop at special shops featuring foreign goods. The *apparatchiki* lived well while the workers had no right to strike and had to have permission to change jobs. For workers, housing and food were in short supply. Workers often had to wait in long lines to get what little was available, which frequently was of poor quality. In the countryside, life for the peasants was, if anything, worse. Despite Gorbachev's efforts, alcoholism remained a serious problem, as did the "unofficial" economy—an estimated 30 percent of the GNP—through which people could circumvent the system through bribes, corruption, and cheating.[4]

But the system endured because, even for the most oppressed, things were better than they had been. *Glasnost* and *perestroika* disturbed many traditionalists, but they gave the young some hope that conditions might improve. The nations of the Soviet bloc worked hard to join the market economies, and COMECON leaders tried frantic changes such as dealing with one another only in hard currency and decentralizing all aspects of the organizations' activities. By the beginning of the 1900s, critics pointed out that Gorbachev had to achieve rapid improvements in the face of figures that the infant mortality rate in the Soviet Union had fallen beneath that of the Barbados and that the average life span for a

The shift to a market economy could create hardships for Soviet citizens. Here, shoppers at the Kirovsky supermarket in the large industrial city of Sverdlovsk wait in line for food. Shoppers in the top line are waiting for meat; those in the bottom line are waiting for butter.

Soviet man had fallen more than five years in the past twenty. The general population was becoming increasingly aware of the relatively backward conditions.

The Nonindustrialized World

The newly independent states came into existence buffeted by the Cold War and the rapid economic and technological changes that dominated the past five decades. Their status ranged from the potentially wealthy, such as Indonesia and Nigeria to the miniscule and weak, such as the Republic of the Maldive Islands, with an area of 115 square miles and a population of 100,000. The new nations had to walk the thin line of gaining aid from the great powers while avoiding being dominated by them. The use of business managers, technicians, and capital from abroad made the less-developed countries (LDC) especially sensitive to the dangers of neocolonialism.

The LDCs tried to cooperate with one another in various conferences and regional associations. The first such effort, the Asian Relations Conference, held in New Delhi in 1947, pledged support for all national movements against colonial rule and explored the basic problems of Asian peoples. A more prominent meeting was the Afro-Asian conference at Bandung in 1955 attended by twenty-nine countries representing more than half the population of the world. In the Middle East the new states established the Arab League in 1945, with a permanent secretariat in Cairo. Africa witnessed the establishment of various regional organizations, the most prominent being the Organization of African Unity created at Addis Ababa in 1963. However, not until 1973 were the LDCs able to organize effectively to make their cause heard in the industrialized world.

In October of that year the Organization of Petroleum Exporting Countries (OPEC), a cartel that until that time had cooperated sporadically in setting a standard price for oil, drastically hurt the industrial world. Angered by U.S. support of Israel, ten Arab nations began cutting their oil production by 5 percent each month. Saudi Arabia cut production 10 percent and then banned all oil exports to the United States. Libya, Algeria, and Abu Dhabi joined the embargo that was eventually also applied to the Netherlands,

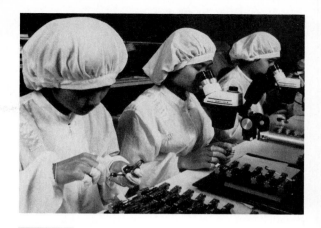

Industrialization and manufacturing have stimulated economic growth throughout the world. Here, Thai women assemble circuit boards at an electronics plant in Bangkok.

Portugal, Rhodesia, and South Africa. The United States, which imported only 11 percent of its oil supplies from the Arabs, was not as badly affected as Japan and the western Europeans, which imported 82 and 72 percent respectively of their oil from the Middle East (see map, p. 982). By March 1974 when the embargo was lifted, Arab oil production was 15 percent lower than in October.

The embargo caused economic and diplomatic dislocations throughout the world. It especially strained relations between Washington and its European allies who had refused to cooperate in the U.S. effort to supply arms to Israel. It also caused a number of nations friendly to Israel to change their policies in favor of the Arabs. However, in the next decade the west developed methods of oil conservation, while the united OPEC front fell apart, as could be seen in the Iraqi invasion of Kuwait and the U.S.-Saudi Arabian-Egyptian response in 1990.

By the end of the 1980s a few former LDCs, the so-called newly industrializing countries (NIC) mastered new technologies, gained sufficient capital, and developed domestic stability to become competitive with the traditional industrialized countries. In the 1980s South Korea, for example, was a major player in the high-tech world economy. Indonesia, Thailand, and India showed indications of putting together the necessary resources and capital to join the productive circle. Most of the other LDCs fell behind the developed world, however, and countries such as

Brazil, Mexico, and Argentina for which the future had once seemed promising, paid dearly for poor economic choices. These countries continued to run a tragic race between population explosion and financial collapse.

Less than 8 percent of the world's population lived in areas where the per capita GNP exceeded $3000. Two-thirds of the world's population lived in areas classified as underdeveloped, producing less than one-sixth of the world's income. Some observers feared that three consecutive crop failures in the grain-exporting nations could bring famine to one-third of the world's people. This widespread backwardness was due to dependence on a single export crop, the dominance of a peasant subsistence economy, lack of capital, lack of education, rising fuel prices, and inflation.

Women's Struggle for Economic Equality

In 1989 Switzerland extended the franchise to women, the last of the western nations to allow women the right to vote. This struggle still goes on throughout the nonindustrialized countries. Throughout the developed world women gained legal and political equality at varying rates, although progress once gained, was neither continuous nor consistent, as could be seen in the failure to pass the Equal Rights Amendment in the United States.

Even in countries where women had gained citizenship rights, they remained subject to wage and job discrimination and to commercial exploitation as sex objects. In the United States the National Organization of Women (NOW) and a number of other organizations worked to mobilize support to achieve economic equality and to gain adequate child care centers, legalization of abortion, and tax deductions by working parents for child-care expenses.

At the beginning of the 1990s the United States labor force was more than one-half female. However, the average woman earned only about 65 percent as much as the average man for comparable work. New patterns in work, marriage, and family had profound implications for

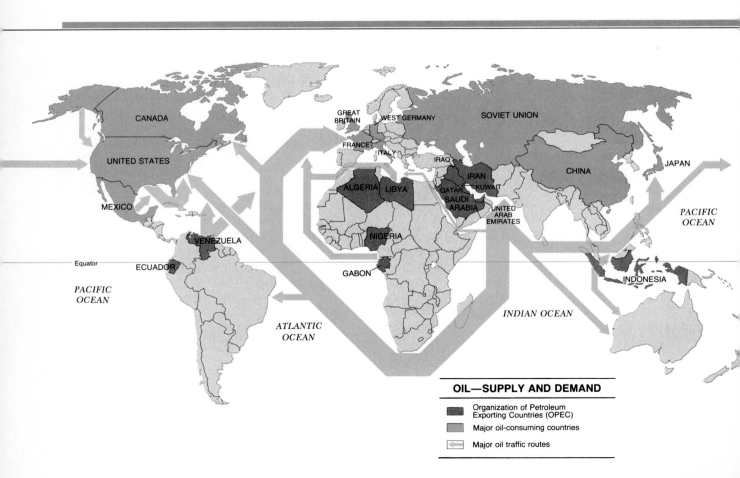

OIL—SUPPLY AND DEMAND

■ Organization of Petroleum Exporting Countries (OPEC)

■ Major oil-consuming countries

◁▭ Major oil traffic routes

The Feminist Movement

A profound, far-reaching postwar movement was the struggle undertaken to improve the status of women. Simone de Beauvoir compared women's status to that of other oppressed groups.

The parallel drawn . . . between women and the proletariat is valid in that neither ever formed a minority or a separate collective unit of mankind. And instead of a single historical event it is in both cases a historical development that explains their status as a class and accounts for the membership of *particular individuals* in that class. But proletarians have not always existed, whereas there have always been women. They are women in virtue of their anatomy and physiology. Throughout history they have always been subordinated to men, and hence their dependency is not the result of a historical event or a social change—it was not something that *occurred*.

From Simone de Beauvoir, *The Second Sex*, trans. H. M. Parshley (New York: Alfred A. Knopf, 1952).

society. Throughout the industrialized world birthrates declined, as much a result of women's new aspirations as of the availability of birth-control pills.

Precedent-making events occurred, despite the slow pace of progress. Britain became the first European country to elect a woman as head of its government with the election of Margaret Thatcher as prime minister in 1979. Norway followed suit in 1981. In 1988 Pakistan became the first Muslim country to elect a woman as head of its government and in 1991 Edith Cresson became Prime Minister of France. In the United States Sandra Day O'Connor became the first woman Supreme Court justice and in 1984 Geraldine Ferraro was the first woman to run for the office of vice-president. In societies throughout the world, women are gaining access to significant public responsibility, but they continue to suffer economic inequality.

One highly industrialized country where progress toward women's equality particularly lagged was Japan. Throughout the 1980s the cult of motherhood maintained its strength in Japan. What was most demanded of a Japanese woman was that once married, she deferred to her husband's career. Above all, the mother was to be devoted and self-sacrificing, an image widely reinforced by the media.

By contrast, since 1949 China made a fairly sustained attempt to change the deeply ingrained Confucian attitudes toward the roles of women. According to an old maxim, "As the Emperor should have a father's love for his people, so a father should have a sovereign's power over the family." With urbanization and the change away from a system of production centered in the household toward larger units of production the way was open for a concerted push for equal rights for women. The state passed laws changing patterns of inheritance and control over children, allowing young men and women to choose

The first woman to head a major British party (the Conservative party) and the first woman to be prime minister of Great Britain, Margaret Thatcher held that post for eleven-and-a-half years.

Women's Rights

This statement on women's rights was issued July 7, 1969, by Redstockings, a feminist organization.

I. After centuries of individual and preliminary political struggle, women are uniting to achieve their final liberation from male supremacy. Redstockings is dedicated to building their unity and winning our freedom.

II. Women are an oppressed class. Our oppression is total, affecting every facet of our lives. We are exploited as sex objects, breeders, domestic servants, and cheap labor. We are considered inferior beings, whose only purpose is to enhance men's lives. Our humanity is denied. Our prescribed behavior is enforced by the threat of physical violence.

Because we have lived so intimately with our oppressors, in isolation from each other, we have been kept from seeing our personal suffering as a political condition. This creates the illusion that a woman's relationship with her man is a matter of interplay between two unique personalities, and can be worked out individually. In reality, every such relationship is a *class* relationship, and the conflicts between individual men and women are *political* conflicts that can only be solved collectively.

III. We identify the agents of our oppression as men. Male supremacy is the oldest, most basic form of domination. All other forms of exploitation and oppression (racism, capitalism, imperialism, and the like) are extensions of male supremacy: men dominate women, a few men dominate the rest. All power structures throughout history have been male-dominated and male-oriented. Men have controlled all political, economic, and cultural institutions and backed up this control with physical force. They have used their power to keep women in an inferior position. *All men* receive economic, sexual, and psychological benefits from male supremacy. *All men* have oppressed women.

IV. Attempts have been made to shift the burden of responsibility from men to institutions or to women themselves. We condemn these arguments as evasions. Institutions alone do not oppress; they are merely tools of the oppressor. . . . .

We also reject the idea that women consent to or are to blame for their own oppression. Women's submission is not the result of brainwashing, stupidity, or mental illness but of continual, daily pressure from men. We do not need to change ourselves, but to change men. . . .

V. We regard our personal experience, and our feelings about that experience, as the basis for an analysis of our common situation. We cannot rely on existing ideologies as they are all products of male supremacist culture. We question every generalization and accept none that are not confirmed by our experience. . . .

The first requirement for raising class consciousness is honesty, in private and in public, with ourselves and other women.

VI. We identify with all women. We define our best interest as that of the poorest, most brutally exploited woman.

We repudiate all economic, racial, educational, or status privileges that divide us from other women. We are determined to recognize and eliminate any prejudices we may hold against other women.

We are committed to achieving internal democracy. We will do whatever is necessary to ensure that every woman in our movement has an equal chance to participate, assume responsibility, and develop her political potential.

VII. We call on all our sisters to unite with us in struggle.

We call on all men to give up their male privileges and support women's liberation in the interests of our humanity and their own.

In fighting for our liberation we will always take the side of women against their oppressors. We will not ask what is "revolutionary" or "reformist," only what is good for women.

The time for individual skirmishes has passed. This time we are going all the way.

Chief Justice Warren Burger administers the oath of office to Sandra Day O'Connor, the first woman named to sit on the U.S. Supreme Court, in September 1981.

their own marriage partners and giving women equal access as men to economic and political processes. Despite these advances, women lagged far behind in income and access to important offices in China.

In the years following the Russian revolution Lenin's government passed a series of laws establishing the formal equality of women with men in civic, political, economic, and family life in the USSR. During the 1920s and 1930s women played a major role in the economic reforms and Five-Year Plans. After World War II, they had to fill the gaps left by the war dead and entered all phases of the Soviet work force. Into the 1980s women constituted more than half of the labor force, including fields such as medicine—three-quarters of all Soviet physicians were women—and science and technology, where there was a larger percentage of women employed than in the west.

In the Soviet Union, as in the United States, women generally earned less than men for doing the same work. In any field of endeavor, the higher the level of authority, power, and prestige, the lower the percentage of women. The pattern of the Soviet economy and the nature of Soviet society forced an extra burden on private households and thus on women, who waited in long lines to do their shopping, performed most household tasks, and bore most of the responsibility for the rearing of children.

In most of Africa the bulk of agricultural labor was done by women, and it was common for African women to have to support a large number of children and older relatives. In Egypt about 80 percent of women were poor peasants who worked long hours in the fields and at home. They worked within the Arab-Islamic tradition that required female subordination in all areas. Even with a subordinate status, women played key roles in national liberation movements throughout Africa and the Arab countries.

Much remained to be done. In the 1980s close to three-fourths of women in Africa and the Arab countries were illiterate. Throughout wide areas of the African continent the ritual sexual mutilation of girls and young women—female circumcision to enhance the husband's sexual pleasure—was common. This physically and psychologically damaging practice drew the attention of the World Health Organization, which began a tentative discussion on ways to deal with the problem.

The word *machismo* continued to express the aggressive masculinity that played a key role in Latin cultures. Traditionally, women were totally subordinated to their husbands. In the latter part of the century, more women entered the job market, but with little improvement in their general status. In rural areas the role of women continued to be one of unceasing hard work with little opportunity for improvement. Some countries, such as Colombia, introduced reforms that promoted equal partnership in marriage. Cuba encouraged women to join the work force, providing them with child care facilities and paid maternity leaves. The Cuban family code made husbands and wives equally responsible for housework and rearing children. But even in Cuba, centuries-old attitudes did not change overnight.

Shared Concerns: Poverty, Famine, Racism, and the Environment

By the 1990s it appeared that the gap between the developed and the less-developed portions of the globe would continue to widen. However, nations such as Japan expressed increasing concern and in the summer of 1989 backed their concern with a $42 billion dollar program to help the LDCs. The major industrial powers worked through the 1980s to bring debt relief, reschedule loan repayments, provide technological assistance, and open markets to products from LDCs. The realization spread that as the world's population increased to 5.8 billion—increasingly poor and young—that the status quo could not be perpetuated. Competition continued, but with an eye to the common good that had not been present in an earlier age.

Another problem drawing the concern of the world was the severe and continuing food shortage throughout the 1980s in sub-Saharan Africa. This tragedy was brought on by a drought that lasted several years, wars and internal conflict, political instability, and rapid urbanization. Well-intentioned governments deepened the crisis by adhering to policies that favored industry or agriculture or by failing to diversify food production. Other governments used food supply as a weapon against political foes in civil wars. Several times nations crossed ideological barriers to join together in unprecedented shows of generosity to aid the victims of famine.

South Africa presented a special problem with its soundly condemned policy of apartheid. Outside of the Soviet Union, South Africa held the greatest supply of special metals, essential for the high-tech warfare of the era. South Africa's resources, as well as its location on the Cape, led

certain U.S. administrations to soften their opposition to the segregationist government, whose policies perpetuated black poverty. Ironically, Americans who advocated the withdrawal of U.S. investments in South Africa to punish the government unintentionally withdrew a major source of leverage for increased black rights that American firms represented.

Another general concern shared by the world's financial and political leaders was that of pollution and environmental deterioration. The UN Conference on the Human Environment held in Stockholm in 1972 produced no serious negotiations but did sound the call that environmental problems knew no national boundaries. This led to the creation of the UN Environmental Program (UNEP) based in Nairobi, Kenya, which unfortunately failed to live up to its expectations because of inadequate funding and jurisdictional disputes. However, in the 1970s and 1980s a series of conventions relating to the environment were signed, including agreements dealing with pollution from ships, prevention of marine pollution from land-based sources, transboundary air pollution, conservation of migratory species, protection of the Mediterranean Sea from land-based pollution, various regional pollution agreements, and in 1987 the convention for the protection of the ozone layer.

The international media brought to the world's attention serious accidents such as the 1986 fire in a Swiss chemical plant that poured 30 tons of toxic substances into the Rhine River, oil spills in France and Alaska, and the nuclear reactor disaster at Chernobyl in the Soviet Union in 1986. This concern and activity barely affected the rate at which modern industry and technology produced by-products that destroyed the environment and the equivalent pace of the destruction of the planet's forests.[5]

In the "Live Aid" concerts of July 1985, pop and rock stars from all over the world played to over 160,000 fans in London and Philadelphia. Broadcast by satellite to all corners of the globe, the concerts raised millions of dollars for African famine relief.

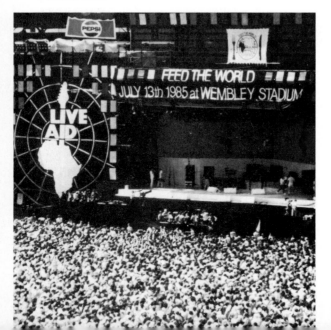

New Revolutions in Science and Technology

Technology and science and their by-products can affect any economic system or ideology. They cut across all political boundaries and ideological camps. The radioactive fallout from the

American tests in the Pacific poisoned entire coral reefs and islands just as surely as the radioactive discharge from the nuclear accident at Chernobyl poisoned the reindeer herds in Lapland. The technological dilemma of the modern age was best symbolized by the promises and perils of using atomic energy.

Energy Needs in the Atomic Age

The efficiency and productivity of societies depend largely on their access to and use of energy. Paleolithic people used their own muscles along with fire to get things done. Neolithic societies domesticated animals, while still later civilizations harnessed wind and water. Not until the eighteenth century was steam power effectively used and in the nineteenth century appeared the means to generate electricity and use the energy in petroleum. All of these sources, from muscle power to electricity, were limited and largely inefficient.

A technological revolution transformed society, making ever greater energy demands. The atom appeared to be a useful source. Before World War I, physicists studied the structure of the atom and the nature of its energy. They determined that the atom has a positively charged nucleus around which negatively charged electrons revolve. Einstein's relativity theory suggested that the nucleus must contain enormous energy. For example, a pound of coal, if converted entirely into energy, would release as much energy as the burning of 1.3 million tons of coal. But the atoms of radioactive elements such as radium and uranium disintegrated at their own speed, and physicists did not know how to speed up this process in order to release enough energy capable of being harnessed.

In the interwar years, however, the situation changed. In 1919 Ernest Rutherford was able to transmute one element into another by bombarding its nucleus with positively charged particles. The discovery in 1932 of the neutron in the nucleus enabled Enrico Fermi and his associates to produce nuclear reactions, but as in Rutherford's case, more energy had to be expended than was in turn released from the bombarded nuclei.

Just as a fire could continue to burn only because the combustion of each portion of fuel raised adjoining portions to the temperature of combustion, so an atomic "chain reaction" was required to split atoms in a way that produces more neutrons, which might then hit other atoms and cause them in turn to split and emit neutrons and so on. In January 1939, eight months before the outbreak of World War II, two German physicists found that the splitting of a uranium atom caused its nucleus to produce barium and also to emit large amounts of energy. Subsequent studies in the United States and elsewhere confirmed that the neutrons released during such fission made a chain reaction possible. Thus was born the atomic age, and the possibility of energy virtually without limits to fuel the future.

Just as in Greek mythology, when Prometheus paid a heavy price to acquire fire for humanity, so the atomic age ushered in both the promise of infinite energy and the peril of human self-destruction. The peril was evident in the fission bombs that pulverized Hiroshima and Nagasaki in 1945. The destructive power of these weapons was soon dwarfed by that of thermonuclear weapons using the principle of hydrogen fusion which is triggered by splitting uranium atoms, generating helium, and the resulting liberated energy creates enormous force: hundreds of times more powerful than fission weapons. These weapons could be sent to any point on the earth's surface by ICBMs, each of which could carry eight hydrogen bombs.

The promise could be seen by the use of the atom to generate energy cheaply and efficiently. Unfortunately atomic energy carried with it serious environmental hazards. Potentially lethal accidents occurred in numerous atomic installations. Another problem was the cost of providing suitable storage containers for radioactive waste and of maintaining them indefinitely. The use of atomic energy became a serious political issue throughout the world. In 1976 a Swedish government was toppled because of its plan to increase the use of nuclear power. The accident at Three Mile Island in Pennsylvania brought nuclear issues to the forefront, making them a major part of environmental protests. The massive nuclear accident at Chernobyl in the Soviet Union spread radioactivity across Europe.

The search for an efficient and safe energy source continues. Coal power creates serious problems in air pollution and acid rain. Oil supplies are finite. Solar energy is attractive but difficult to harness. Wind power has been explored and used in limited areas. Geothermal stations are used for energy supplies in New Zealand and Iceland. A number of alternate sources of power are available, awaiting research and development. The advent of superconductivity that promised virtually friction-free transmission of energy offers unprecedented possibilities, but much research is still required.

Biology and Biochemistry

As in the technological field, there has been an exciting revolution within the life sciences. By the second decade of the twentieth century, the concept that chance variations in organisms alone accounted for evolution had been replaced by an understanding of the ordered systems of genes and chromosomes. In the 1920s and 1930s scientists isolated enzymes. These comprised essential amino acids, of which proteins are built, and they directed the chemistry of the cell.

The average human body contained about a million billion cells, each of which had a complete copy of a fundamental genetic material known as DNA (deoxyribonucleic acid). In 1953 James D. Watson and Francis H. C. Crick revealed a model of the structure of the DNA molecule. It was built like a spiral staircase, in a double helix, and had four building blocks—small molecules called nucleotides. These four components were the same for all plants and animals. However, they were thematically programmed, so that their sequence along the double spiral not only made every species unique but in turn distinguished each member of that species.

> It is as though, in every room of a gigantic building, there was a book-case containing the architect's plans for the entire building. The "book-case" in a cell is called the nucleus. The architect's plans run to 46 volumes in man—the number is different in other species. The volumes are called chromosomes.[6]

Since DNA is a fundamental genetic material, analysis of its structures provided far-reaching insights into the processes of heredity and might lead to the possibility of shaping the future of numerous species, including our own.

This capability posed profound social and ethical issues. The ability to determine gender led to improvements in animal breeding and made food production more profitable. If "genetic engineering" could be employed to eradicate undesirable traits in our existing hereditary makeup, what should be the criteria for determining what was "undesirable," and who should make the determination?

Biological and biochemical advances have proved invaluable in medical research and treatment. During the interwar years, various new synthetic drugs based on sulfanilamide successfully treated diseases due to streptococcus and pneumococcus infections. There was similar success in developing bacterial products derived from molds. In 1928 Alexander Fleming discovered that a genus of fungus known as *penicillium* was toxic to staphylococcus. From his discovery came the development of the first antibiotic, penicillin, which with related drugs has proven the most effective means of treating certain types of pneumonia, syphilis, gonorrhea, and other infections. The result of such medical advances and improved diet lengthened life spans across the globe and contributed to a massive population increase.

Science and Technology

In the first phase of industrialization, which began in Britain in the latter part of the eighteenth century, machine power replaced animal and human power; productivity was thereby greatly increased. The early technical innovations were made by practical people with immediate problems to solve, rather than by scientists or teams of researchers. Later this situation changed. Increasingly science came to be involved in the production process. This development began in Germany in the last decades of the nineteenth century and has sometimes been called the scientific revolution in industry.

At the beginning of the century, the "scientific management" movement was applied to the industrial process to bring about profound changes not only in what society produced but in the nature of the work itself. Complex jobs were broken into a series of elementary steps, each performed by a different person according to a predetermined routine. This system enabled the rate of production to be increased, even by less-skilled workers hired at less cost, as can be seen in factory methods used to produce television sets, computers, and pocket calculators.

Since 1945 the organized application of science to industry has reached unprecedented levels. Scientific discoveries in laboratories rapidly reached the production lines in high-tech goods. Through the processes of mass production and distribution an incredible range of products were made available to a world market. Thus, while the post-1945 era marked a new stage in industry, it also was the latest chapter in the scientific revolution that began more than a century ago.

The potential for automation in industry was vastly enhanced by the development of the silicon chip. This was a complex miniature electric circuit etched onto a tiny wafer of silicon crystal. One type of chip, the microprocessor, is the "brain" of a computer. Besides being able to carry out computing functions in a very small space — no larger than a thumbnail — it was much cheaper than earlier technology and more reliable.

Microtechnology has markedly affected corporate structure and organization. Communications systems have become more sophisticated, inventories can be more effectively monitored, and financial operations have been simplified. Some manufacturers introduced robotic machines to their assembly lines. Everywhere industry was being organized by means of a systems approach that subdivided and then coordinated all activities to increase efficiency and productivity. Countries that adapted the new processes at the end of the century competed. Others, such as the Soviet Union, fell farther and farther behind.

The Worldwide Implications of Technology

Industrialization began in the west, where advanced economies exploited their indigenous resources and also imported raw materials from the rest of the world, thereby creating a global capitalist economy. By the end of the century all parts of the world were industrializing. There were petrochemical complexes in the Middle East, automated steel mills in India, computer factories in Brazil, and hydroelectric installations in Africa, All of Asia experienced technological transformation.

A vast network of highways, pipelines, railways, shipping and air lanes, fiber optic cables and communications satellites united the world. All of these served the needs of multinational firms and publicly owned enterprises. Technology in turn transformed agriculture and diet. Food canning and refrigeration, together with the bulk transport of grains, permitted the shipment of perishable goods to all parts of the world. Food production was increased by plant genetics, new managerial methods, and large-scale agribusinesses — with machines steadily reducing the number of workers doing menial labor.

As fewer people were required in agriculture, millions migrated from the countryside to the towns on every continent. In 1900 there were fourteen cities with a population of one million or more, six of them in Europe and three in Asia. By the 1980s there were more than seventy metropolitan areas with populations of over two million. Thirty of these were in Asia and nine in Latin America. It is projected that by the year 2000 there will be more than sixty cities with over 5 million people.

The impact of economic and technological change has integrated the human experience the world has become westernized. Although non-Western societies, in India, Mexico, and sub-Saharan Africa, for example, fought to rediscover and adapt their native cultures, there could be little doubt that every continent was marching to the drummer of the developed world.

Cultural Diversity

Throughout much of the nineteenth century, Europe enjoyed relative stability. People believed both in their ability to conquer their environment and in a concept of progress that was inevitable and unending. All this was shattered by a war intercontinental in scope and unprecedented in carnage. After 1918 there was widespread disillusionment with the old order; the world had not been made "safe for democracy." Social upheaval, economic depression, disillusionment, and experimentation marked the interwar years, which ended with the most distructive conflict in history, culminating with annihilation of Hiroshima and Nagasaki. Since 1945, the mushroom-shaped clouds of the atomic bomb have cast their shadow over the globe. Yet these atomic explosions were merely the first in a series of "explosions" that rocked the postwar world. We speak of the population explosion, the information explosion, and the urban explosion. World War II marked the end of the era of European hegemony and set the world on a new course: one of the global interaction of peoples, governments, economies, and resources.

European Transitions

Although the 1920s in the west have often been portrayed as an era of gaiety and triviality, the real picture was not quite so rosy. The prewar liberal complacency about the direction of society was shattered by the experiences of 1914–1918. Youths who had been promised that the war would save the world for democracy emerged from the trenches to become—if they were not already—bitterly disillusioned. The war did nothing to correct the inequalities of wealth and power in society, and labor unrest flared in numerous places.

This sense of disillusion was reflected in the arts. Writers clung to scientific notions such as the uncertainty theory of German physicist Werner Heisenberg (1901–1976) that nothing was "fixed" in the universe. Freud and the psychoanalytic psychologists were cited as authorities that society was little more than thinly veneered savagery, while behavioral psychology was seen to offer "proof" that the individual was little more than a set of conditioned reflexes. Perhaps the Anglo-American poet T. S. Eliot (1888–1965) captured the mood best in *The Waste Land* (1922). This long poem expressed weariness with the ugliness and sterility of industrialized civilization. It captured the skepticism and negation pervading the intellectual world in Britain and the United States.

A number of psychological studies appeared during the interwar period. English novelist D. H. Lawrence (1885–1930) emphasized the absolute significance of the sexual drive in such works as *Women in Love* (1920) and *Lady Chatterly's Lover* (1928). In the multivolumed *Remembrance of Things Past*, French writer Marcel Proust (1871–1922) explored psychological time, human relationships, and his own perceptions and mental processes. A writer who employed the stream of consciousness method was Irish writer James Joyce (1882–1941), who underscored the complexity and disorder of contemporary civilization in *Ulysses* (1922), a report on the experiences of a group of people during a single day in Dublin.

Truly vibrant, although only for a tragically short time, was cultural life in Weimar Germany. Disillusionment with old values along with new perspectives revealed by science and technology was evident in the painting of the expressionists. They employed distortion and clashing colors to break free from surface appearances and attempt to penetrate to the "essence" of their subjects. Wassily Kandinsky (1866–1944) devoted his talents to abstract art, allowing viewers to derive their own interpretation and significance from the artist's arrangement of colors and forms.

In his major work, *The Magic Mountain* (1924) novelist Thomas Mann (1875–1955) presented a realistic story of life in a tuberculosis sanitarium in the Alps that was also a symbolic evocation of European civilization on the eve of the war. In portraying the struggle between the promise of life and the lure of death, Mann was describing a conflict that occupied the spirit of many Germans. Playwright Bertolt Brecht (1898–1956), who with composer Kurt Weill (1900–1950) created *The Threepenny Opera* (1928), called for a theatre of political criticism and social protest. In his writings, Rainer Maria Rilke (1875–1926) used striking images and metaphorical language to create a universe in which life, death, and all things were celebrated as elements of a single organic whole.

The functionalism that became an internationally accepted style of architectural design in the interwar years had its most influential center in Germany's Bauhaus school. The school's staff included architect Ludwig Mies van der Rohe (1886–1969) and artist Paul Klee (1879–1940), as well as Kandinsky. Teachers and students worked together in programs aimed at joining artistic expression and industry in order to reconcile contemporary humanity with its technologically altered environment. From architecture to pottery, from typography to home furnishings, the Bauhaus design for living

Wassily Kandinsky, *In the Black Square* (1923). Kandinsky attempted to free painting from what he saw as the limitations of representational art.

reflected the belief that art and function should be synthesized. After Hitler closed down the school in 1933, many of its prominent members fled to other countries to carry on their work and to spread the Bauhaus philosophy.

Following the liveliness of Weimar German was the grotesqueness of Nazi culture. One of the roots of the Third Reich's beliefs came from the German Monist League. This group was hostile to the alienating and debilitating aspect of urban civilization and, instead, praised the virtues of rural life and called for a Germany rooted in strong peasant communities. This longing for roots and tradition was characteristic of the related folkism movement. Young people, in particular, were seeking an organic philosophy of life that emphasized a love of nature and an idealization of the German past. Such thinking opposed mechanical civilization in favor of *Kultur*, which meant a type of society joining the German people in an intimate union with the forces of nature. Houston Stewart Chamberlain (1855–1927), a leading racist ideologist who had considerable influence on Hitler, claimed that

the difference between *Kultur* and civilization could be summed up in the difference between the peasant and the factory worker: the peasant daily and subconsciously learned truth and living from nature while the worker lived in an essentially artificial urban environment. Nazi Minister for Propaganda Joseph Goebbels shared this point of view as he defined socialism. "We want socialism as the doctrine of the community. We want socialism as the ancient German idea of destiny."[7]

In this fuzzy philosophy there was no place for the sophistication of modern art and music or the critical role of the writer. Modern art, like the work of the Bauhaus artists, was condemned, as were cultural ideas of the "folkish" groups, which Hitler criticized as obsolete and backward. For the Nazis film, art, and writing were to exult Germans and Germany. A notable example was the film *The Triumph of the Will* by Leni Reifenstahl. The *Kultur* concept that was central to the Nazi world view was destroyed with Hitler in the Berlin bunker in 1945.

Characteristic of the literary works of postwar Germany were the novels of Günter Grass, such as the *Tin Drum*, which offered a dwarf's eye view of the events of the 1930s and 1940s. In his novel *1984*, published in 1949, George Orwell (1903–1950) created a society completely totalitarian in structure, methods, and values in which technology was employed to enslave people and destroy humanistic values. In *The Technological Society* (1954) Jacques Ellul painted a bleak picture of a world dominated by an "aristocracy of technicians," in which moral values were subordinated to the requirements of "technique," and human beings became mere appendages of technical processes.

One of the most widely read writers of the postwar period was the novelist, essayist, and dramatist Albert Camus (1913–1960). Camus, a liberal intellectual from French Algeria, combined a belief in the absurdity of human existence with the concept of self-esteem and a certain joy in living. This attitude was explicit in *The Myth of Sisyphus* (1942) in which he likened the human lot to that of the ancient Greek figure of Sisyphus, sentenced by the gods to push a rock to the top of a mountain, only to have it roll back down, and to have to repeat this task forever. Camus saw Sisyphus as not only accepting this task with dignity but finding satisfaction in his work. During the period of the Cold War and the struggles against colonialism Camus found himself caught between the dictates of his philosophy of rebellion and his allegiance to western cultures and values.

A more radical political position was adopted by Jean-Paul Sartre (1905–1980) in his existentialist philosophy. His belief that human beings are "condemned to be free" was expounded in *Being and Nothingness* (1943) and reflected in his plays and stories. After the war Sartre increasingly recognized the constraints and responsibilities imposed on individual freedom by social forces—a move evident in his three *Roads to Freedom* novels. Sartre became one of the leading advocates of *littérature engagée* (committed literature), which claimed that since all writing is bound up with social life, writers should be conscious of this fact and strive to help their readers understand the problems of society. In his massive philosophical work, *Critique of Dialectical Reason,* Sartre attempted to integrate existential insights into the situation of the individual with the historical perspective of Marxism. After the Soviet invasion of Czechoslovakia in 1968, Sartre, along with a number of other French Marxist adopted an increasingly critical tone toward communism.

The United States

Many of his fellow citizens shared the belief of Henry Luce, the co-founder of *Time* magazine, that the twentieth century was the American century. By the end of the century it was apparent that at least in the areas of life-style Luce was right. American popular culture, style, and attitudes had spread throughout the world.

The young country was thrust into world responsibilities in World War I, tried to avoid them in the interwar period, and became the "arsenal of democracy" during World War II. From the end of the war until the assassination of John F. Kennedy, the country basked in a period of innocence and power. Thereafter, the divisiveness of the Vietnam war and the upheavals of the civil rights and sexual revolutions shook the country to its foundations.

America's writers served as compelling witnesses for the century. Sinclair Lewis (1885–

1951) satirized the materialism and shallowness he saw in American life in a series of novels such as *Elmer Gantry.* Other Americans expatriated themselves to Paris. F. Scott Fitzgerald (1896–1940) is associated with the term *jazz age* and in his novels such as *The Great Gatsby* (1925) examined problems of wealth and violence on the American scene. Another expatriate, Ernest Hemingway (1899–1961), rocketed to fame with vivid stories glorifying manliness and action for its own sake. In the crisis-ridden 1930s Hemingway turned to the theme of the destructive impact of modern warfare, for example, in *For Whom the Bell Tolls* (1940). The depression spurred writers to social consciousness. William Faulkner (1897–1962) dealt with the poverty and ignorance of some parts of the U.S. south in such works as *The Sound and the Fury* (1929), while the plight of the "Okies" who trekked to California in search of survival was recounted by John

In his life F. Scott Fitzgerald embodied the "jazz age" that he described and criticized in his fiction.

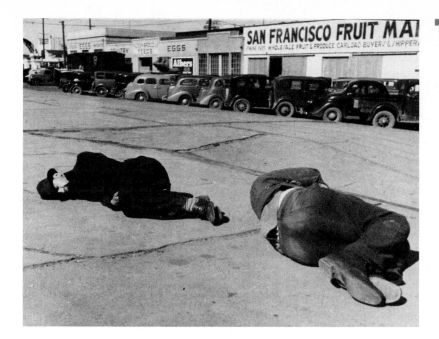

Our vision of the Great Depression owes much to the photographs of Dorothea Lange. Her 1937 photograph of this "Skid Row" scene on Howard Street in San Francisco captures the hopelessness of the urban unemployed during the 1930s.

Steinbeck (1902–1968) in his powerful novel *The Grapes of Wrath* (1939).

The revolt against traditional ways of thinking became especially apparent in the photographic arts. Still photography and motion pictures, whose basic principles had been developed in the nineteenth century, became major vehicles of expression following World War I. True photoreportage began in the mid-1920s when improved equipment and technical facilities enabled fleeting expressions and movements to be caught under varying light conditions. The movies became the most popular and universal art form of the century. While most movies were made and watched for entertainment, the medium lent itself to the visual depiction of relationships and issues in contemporary society. The best films, such as those of Charlie Chaplin (1899–1977), combined entertainment and social commentary.

As books and mass-circulation magazines replaced art exhibits as showcases for talented photographers, they helped spur a preoccupation with everyday people and situations. During the depression, Dorothea Lange (1895–1965) and other photographers working for federal agencies, notably the Farm Security Administration, employed their art as a powerful weapon to awaken Americans to the plight of their fellow citizens.

The depression also stimulated a new interest in folk songs of all kinds: regional, social, humorous, sad, but together projecting the vitality of a society determined to get on top of its problems. Perhaps the most significant interwar development in western popular music was jazz, an American form that originated with black musicians in New Orleans and in time spread over the continent and into Europe. Jazz musicians made use of both western and African cultural contributions, drawing on brass-band marches, French and Spanish songs and dances, and the spirituals and work songs of American blacks.

In the period from 1945 until the early 1960s J. D. Salinger (b. 1919) spoke to the "silent generation" of students in novels such as *Catcher in the Rye* (1951). Lawrence Ferlinghetti, Jack Kerouac, and Allen Ginsburg typified the writers of the "beat" generation of the 1950s. The film industry suffered the attacks of Senator Joseph McCarthy and his followers, who accused numerous actors, writers, and directors of being Communists and "blacklisted" them to prevent them from working. One of America's major contributions from this period was rock 'n roll. White musicians such as Elvis Presley, Jerry Lee Lewis,

Superstars of rock 'n roll in the 1950s and 1960s included Elvis Presley, "the King" (left), and the Beatles (right). Some members of the older generation cited the antics and lyrics of these rock performers as evidence of the decline of the younger generation.

and Buddy Holly took the work of black musicians and, adding their own interpretations, sang to a larger audience. Widely derided at the time by proponents of "high culture," rock n' roll in its various manifestations became popular throughout the world, inspiring such British groups as the Beatles and the Who in the 1960s.

Vietnam, the civil rights movement, and the sexual revolution set the 1960s and 1970s in vivid contrast to the rather more complacent 1950s. After the assassination of President John F. Kennedy, a number of factors came together to shake the foundations of American life: the large number of young people—the "baby boom"—the unprecedented amount of wealth they possessed, the impact of television's coverage of events, as well as the compelling nature of the issues themselves. Students and other young people challenged the right of those in power to rule. Demonstrations sometimes met with violence from authorities, such as the incident in 1970 at Kent State University in Ohio when National Guardsmen fired on and killed four students. Two students were killed in a similar incident a week later at Jackson State University in Mississippi.

Popular music provided one of the major means of communications during this turbulent period. The folk music revival of the 1960s went hand in hand with the civil rights and antiwar movements, where no rally was complete without its inspirational songs. In rock music the simple and somewhat naive themes of the music of the 1950s gave way to protests of rock musicians like Jimi Hendrix and Janis Joplin. Mindless disco music dominated for a while during the mid-1970s, as the idealism, selflessness, and fascination with abstractions that characterized an earlier generation were replaced with a desire for economic well-being, business success, and a thoroughgoing materialism.

The Soviet Union: Experiment and Debate

After the civil war and War Communism, the Soviet Union in the 1920s entered a vigorous debate over the kind of culture that should be encouraged for the Soviet masses. Should a specifically "proletarian" culture be arranged, or were "bourgeois" forms to be tolerated? Lenin himself, before his death in 1924, sided with those who advocated considerable freedom of expression in cultural fields and argued that there was much in prerevolutionary art and literature that could benefit the masses. "Culture" was not something that could be imposed from the top, but had to develop through the participation of everyone.

The early 1920s saw an explosion of creative endeavor in all fields of life. Some writers, including Maxim Gorky (1868–1936) and the poet Vladimir Mayakovsky (1893–1930) aligned their works specifically with the revolution. Others were less politically oriented, seeing in the revolution the opportunity for individual liberation and personal expression. The "constructivist" artists were interested in practical design and sought to integrate art with many aspects of everyday life. Soviet theater flourished under influential directors such as Vsevolod Meyerhold (1874–1940), while Sergei Eisenstein (1898–1948) and others produced notable documentary films.

The period of experimentation did not survive the 1920s, however. With the desperate and painful rush to industrialize that began once Stalin was firmly in power, restrictions were imposed in many areas. Experimental art and literature were discouraged, and things became difficult for those who did not conform. Yevgeny Zamyatin (1884–1937), who anticipated Orwell with his novel *We* (1920), felt it necessary to go into exile to pursue his literary career. Distinguished historians such as M. I. Pokrovsky found themselves trapped by Stalin's directive to shape their findings to agree with the "party line." Even scientists and linguists were forced to adhere to a predetermined order.

After 1945 the Soviet government strengthened the wall around its extended frontiers and attempted to isolate its citizens from contamination from the west by preventing outside books, periodicals, and radio signals from reaching the Soviet Union. The party took all these measures to aid the formation of the "new Soviet man." So that this superior individual could attain the necessary qualities, it was essential to control every aspect of life, expecially education.

As in the 1930s, Stalin continued to exercise harsh restrictions on both artists and intellectuals. The war had given a brief opportunity for the creation of spontaneous patriotic works. Afterwards, controls were even more firmly imposed. Stalin's word and tastes dominated both the arts and sciences, and the censors did their work thoroughly. In 1946 they launched an attack on artists and writers whose works did not

Through the masterful use of montage (the way a director arranges shots in order to assault the emotions of the viewer), Sergei Eisenstein created films of astounding impact. In this scene from *Potemkin* (1925), a horrified mother defies the tsarist troops who have killed her child.

sufficiently support the Soviet system. Distinguished composers such as Dmitri Shostakovich (1906–1975), Sergei Prokofiev (1891–1953), and Aram Khachatarian (1903–1978) felt the party's lash. Writers were controlled by an agency called *Glavlit* whose permission and approval were essential for any author or artist to publish, speak, or exhibit in any of the media. At the back of books and journals, the most important number was not that of the copies printed, but that noting the censors' approval. Artists who failed to meet the censors' standards were simply cut off from access to the public through the official media and also from contact with the Union of Soviet Writers. The automobiles, special stores, summer houses, preferred apartments, and other economic privileges that came with membership in the union were denied recalcitrant writers.

With Stalin's death, controls were relaxed and western readers gained the opportunity to read the works of Boris Pasternak (1890–1960) Alexander Solzhenitsyn (b. 1918), and Yevgeny Yevtushenko (b. 1933). Pasternak's *Doctor Zhivago* (1957) did not find favor with Soviet authorities, who refused Pasternak permission to accept his Nobel prize for literature. Solzhenitsyn, who had been imprisoned in the labor camp system of the Soviet Union, had been permitted to publish his book *One Day in the Life of Ivan Denisovich* by Khrushchev. Solzhenitsyn's later works, *Cancer Ward, August 1914*, and the *Gulag Archipelago*, did not bring him official favor, and he was exiled from the USSR in 1974. During the Brezhnev years Yevgeny Yevtushenko gave impassioned public readings of his work, expecially poems criticizing Stalin's regime. Other, more popular figures, such as Bulat Okudzhava, used satirical and antiwar songs to reach their audience.

Until Gorbachev came to power, many Soviet writers published their works in the underground

Charged with treason because of his dissident activities and writings critical of the Soviet Union, Alexander Solzhenitsyn was expelled from Russia before his case came to trial. The treason charges were officially dropped in 1991.

press, the *samizdat* (literally "self-publishing"). After 1985, under the tenets of *glasnost*, artists in the Soviet Union enjoyed the most creative freedom since 1917. Filmmakers led the way in producing works closely detailing the abuses of Stalin's era and the disappointments of contemporary society. Pasternak, Solzhenitsyn, and Zamyatin all were published. Solzhenitsyn, who had won the Nobel prize for literature in 1970, was readmitted to the Union of Soviet Writers in 1989. Plays and novels hidden on closet shelves for twenty years were produced and published. The Soviet Union, in the midst of its economic problems, experienced a cultural renaissance in the Gorbachev years.

China: Which Road Forward?

Classical Chinese culture was centered in the cities and was the preserve of a small sophisticated and literate ruling class. At the end of the First World War such scholars as Chen Tu-hsiu (1879–1942) and Hu Shih (1891–1962) broke with classical traditions, substituting vernacular for literary Chinese in their writings. They stressed the relation of contemporary thought to the life of the average Chinese, in contrast to the stereotyped and stilted subject matter of traditionalism. Vernacular literature spread rapidly during the interwar years and acquired a strongly social character. Lu Hsun (Lu Xun) (1881–1936), a writer much admired in China, used satire to expose social evils in the 1920s and 1930s and also translated many foreign works into Chinese.

In 1966 Mao Zedong and the more radical among the Chinese leadership, disenchanted with the Soviet model for building socialism, initiated the Cultural Revolution. The aim of the radicals, many of them students and young workers, was to reestablish the ideals of egalitarianism and encourage participation in political and cultural life among the masses. In particular, the objective was to break down the "three major differences" that they held to be retarding progress toward a just social order: between town and country, between worker and peasant, and between mental and manual labor. Even bureaucrats and intellectuals were now expected to engage in periodic stints of manual labor.

During the Cultural Revolution, the radical line was to "put politics in command" in all areas

A scene from "Red Detachment of Women" performed by the Peking Ballet. The ballet, which dates from China's Cultural Revolution era, tells the story of an early Communist uprising against the Nationalist government when it was still in power.

of life, whether in the factory or on the stage. Literary culture, which stresses individual creativity, was de-emphasized in favor of cooperative and visual art forms. Such operas as *Taking Tiger Mountain by Strategy* and such ballets as *Red Detachment of Women* were used to get political messages across to mass audiences. Artistic expression was stifled and the Chinese turned their backs on almost all foreign culture.

After Mao's death in 1976, a less dogmatic attitude to the arts began to emerge. Among the signs of this change was the reappearance of the traditional Peking Opera, which, with its acrobatics and dazzling costumes, provides one of the most entertaining spectacles in world theatre.

India's Cultural Revival

The centuries of British rule in India influenced both Indian institutions and values. The Indian intelligentsia was schooled in English educational forms and immersed in English literature and prepared itself for the professions and civil service, which in turn were English in structure and largely in content. Yet decades before independence, a cultural renaissance began.

While a number of European scholars, such as Max Müller (1823–1900) were studying the intellectual treasures of the ancient Indian classics, some outstanding Indian philosophers, including Swami Vivekenanda (1863–1902) and Sri Aurobindo (1872–1950) began not only to reinterpret the Vedanta and other classical schools of thought but to place their teachings in a new

relationship with western tradition as well. In addition, Indian culture produced a world-famous literary figure Rabindranath Tagore (1861–1914), a poet, author, painter, and dramatist. Steeped in India's literary and philosophical traditions, Tagore described the *Vedas*—the ancient Sanskrit collection of hymns, epic poems, and ritual formulas—as "the poetic testament of a people's collective reaction to the wonder and awe of existence." In his own works he sought in return to interpret afresh the contents of the *Vedas* and *Upanishads*, employing both English and Bengali as literary media.

Although primarily a nationalist leader and politician, Jawaharlal Nehru also encouraged the Indian cultural revival by his own rediscovery of the subcontinent's varied past. Nor was this national renaissance simply backward looking: by embodying the cultural heritage and ethos in twentieth-century forms of expression, it made Indian thought and art relevant to contemporary times and problems. In this connection, India developed one of the largest and most dynamic film industries in the world, and the government employed this art form for purposes of entertainment and education alike.

African Expression

Over the past century Africa absorbed the blows of colonialism and faced the challenges of developing new states. In his epic work *The Wretched of the Earth* (1961), Frantz Fanon (1925–1961) analyzed the psychological damage that resulted to the African peoples from the colonial experience and continued western dominance. According to Fanon, the colonizing force defined out of existence any reality in which black people could be accepted—by themselves or by others—as human beings with creative potential. Blacks were powerless because their experience had no validity in that realm, which both they and others accepted as "reality." Fanon took issue with the African cultural revolution epitomized in the *Négritude* movement, which rejected western history and culture and sought to describe a uniquely African culture and personality. *Négritude*, argued Fanon, was a reaction to the European challenge rather than a positive action to gain a true identity for blacks.

At the beginning of the 1960s a number of African leaders proclaimed socialism as the path their newly independent countries should take, because it was claimed that precolonial societies of sub-Saharan Africa exhibited a form of preindustrial socialism. What resulted was a socialism that could be described as African, but it was too broad and diverse to be described as a single ideology. Governments is Guinea, Mali, and Mozambique represented a more self-consciously revolutionary form of socialism, whereas Senegal's socialism had a more utopian character. No matter what the character of socialism, all variants rejected the view that African socialism must reflect socialist developments in other parts of the world. Julius Nyerere of Tanzania noted that "The differences between . . . societies will reflect both the manner of their development and their historical tradition."[8]

Latin America's Self-Discovery

For nearly 175 years, the countries of Latin America were politically independent, but only during the present century has their quest for cultural independence and a recognizable self-identity assumed major proportions. As a result, much Latin American art possessed a cultural character different from that of either Iberia or North America. In Brazil, which has a large black population, there was the growth of a black art style as well as the emergence of *Indianismo*, with its rediscovery of pre-Columbian America.

The National Museum of Anthropology in Mexico City was a monument to this search, as were the vivid frescoes of several brilliant Mexican painters, including Jose Clemente Orozco (1883–1949) and Diego Rivera (1886–1957).

The period since 1945 saw a flowering of Latin American literature, much of it rooted in the social and historical context of that part of the world. For example, in the works of Miguel Angel Asturias of Guatemala the special world view of the Mayan Indians is a central concern. In several of his other novels, he concerned himself with the plight of his compatriots under the yoke of local despots and foreign exploiters.

The Chilean poet and Nobel prize winner Pablo Neruda (1904–1973) expressed both his social commitment and an intense feeling for his landscape and history of Latin America. On the other hand, the surreal fantasies of Argentina's Jorge Luis Borges (b. 1899) could not be considered peculiarly Latin American, although they influenced the style of other regional writers. In *One Hundred Years of Solitude*, a tale that embodies much of the Latin American experience, Gabriel Garcia-Marques (b. 1928) of Colombia wove together fantasy and history in an epic tale about successive generations of a small-town family.

Conclusion

The postwar period witnessed the development of a number of concerns that brought the leaders of the world together: nuclear weapons, trade and economic policies, the environment, women's rights, and innovations in energy and technology. As the century came to an end, substantial international progress had been made in each area, although in none of the areas was there anything approaching a complete solution. Nuclear proliferation still concerned the globe even if the superpowers were on the path to arranging accords; the debt issue and the increasing gap between the developed and less-developed nations posed problems for the future; pollution problems frustrated nations' best efforts; women still suffered seriously from economic and other forms of discrimination; and technological innovations that increased efficiency also produced a jarring disruption of old patterns.

Throughout this century of war and upheaval, the artists and writers of the different regions of the world responded to changes in diverse ways. European artists and writers reflected the exhaustion of two world wars and the Cold War. America's mass culture tended to reflect society, not try to profoundly change it, as was the case in the Soviet Union. Chinese artists tried to turn the western influences to their own best advantages, while in India artists returned to their cultural roots. Africans struggled to gain some means to define their present and forecast their future, and in Latin America, the rich cultural heritage dominated contemporary creative expression.

Suggestions for Reading

For pioneering works of environmental concern see Barbara Ward and René Dubos, *Only One Earth: The Care and Maintenance of a Small Planet* (Penguin, 1973) and Barbara Ward, *The Home of Man* (Norton, 1976). On the profound transformation of women's roles in this century see Simone de Beauvoir, *The Second Sex* (Vintage, 1974) and Betty Friedan, *The Feminine Mystique* (Dell, 1977). For a worldwide survey see Kathleen Newland, *The Sisterhood of Man* (Norton, 1979). For poverty and north-south relations see Robert L. Rothstein, *The Weak in the World of the Strong* (Columbia, 1977) and Richard Critchfield, *Villages* (Anchor/Doubleday, 1981).

Christopher Lasch takes a provocative look at contemporary American society in *The Culture of Narcissism* (Norton, 1979). For lively accounts of two decades in American society, see Frederick Lewis Allen, *Only Yesterday: An Informal History of the 1920's* (Harper & Row, 1964) and Eric F. Goldman, *The Crucial Decade—and after: America, 1945–1960* (Vintage Books, 1960). A vivid portrait of the intellectual, artistic, and social life of France from the 1930s to the early 1970s can be found in three of the volumes of Simone de Beauvoir's autobiography: *The Prime of Life* (Penguin, 1965), *Force of Circumstance* (Penguin, 1968), and *All Said and Done* (Penguin, 1977). The problems of individual alienation within a German context, as depicted in the literature of Rilke, are analyzed in Erich Heller, *The Disinherited Mind: Essays in Modern German Literature and Thought* (Harcourt Brace Jovanovich, 1975) an Peter Gay, *Weimar Culture* (Torch-

books, 1970). Russian cultural trends are covered in J. P. Nettl, *The Soviet Achievement* (Harcourt Brace Jovanovich) and Hedrick Smith, *The Russians* (Quadrangle, 1976). V. S. Naipul examines a people's self-preoccupation in *India: A Wounded Civilization* (Vintage, 1978). Contemporary trends in life and culture in China are analyzed in the Committee of Concerned Asian Scholars, *China! Inside the People's Republic* (Bantam). Developments in Africa have been vividly portrayed in three novels. Chinua Achebe, *Things Fall Apart* (Fawcett, 1959), described as a "classic of modern African literature," dramatizes traditional Ibo life, the pre-Christian tribal life, and shows how the old ways were broken up by colonialism at the turn of the century. In *A Bend in the River* (Penguin, 1980), V. S. Naipul describes the problems of a postcolonial Africa that is losing touch with its past. Nadine Gordimer in *Burger's Daughter* (Viking, 1979) depicts contemporary South Africa and the lives of individuals caught in its maelstrom of historical and racial forces.

The relation of art to a society is explored in historical perspective by Ernst Fischer in *The Necessity of Art* (Penguin, 1978). For trends in painting and architecture, see Alan Bowness, *Modern European Art* (Thames and Hudson, 1980); E. H. Gombrich, *The Story of Art*, 12th ed. (Phaidon, 1974); and H. W. Janson, *History of Art*, 2nd ed. (Prentice-Hall, 1979), Part 4, "The Modern World." Directions in music are dealt with briefly in A. Einstein, *A Short History of Music* (Vintage) and Arthur Jacobs, *A Short History of Western Music* (Pelican, 1976)—see chapters 17–20 for twentieth-century developments.

Notes

1. Alvin Z. Rubinstein, *Soviet Foreign Policy Since World War II*, 3rd ed. (Glenview, IL: Scott, Foresman, 1989), p. 266.
2. For a cogent discussion of international economics and politics see Walter S. Jones, *The Logic of International Relations* (Glenview, IL: Scott, Foresman, 1988), chapters 12–14.
3. Nicholas Colchester, "Europe's Internal Market, A Survey," *The Economist*, 8–14 July 1989, after p. 48, insert, pp. 1–52.
4. Hedrick Smith, *The Russians* (New York: Ballantine Books, 1977), chapters 2, 3, 4, 9.
5. Seyom Brown, *New Forces, Old Forces, and the Future of World Politics*, (Glenview, IL: Scott, Foresman, 1988), pp. 278–281.
6. Richard Dawkins, *The Selfish Gene*, (Oxford: Oxford Univ. Press, 1976), p. 23.
7. Joseph Goebbels, from a 1926 speech, "Lenin or Hitler?" quoted in Z. A. Zeman, *Nazi Propaganda* (London: Oxford Univ. Press, 1973), p. 206.
8. Julius Nyerere, *Freedom and Socialism* (Dar es Salaam: Oxford Univ. Press, 1968), p. 3.

Toward the Twenty-First Century

*T*ime present and time past
 Are both present in time future . . .
 Time past and time future
What might have been and what has been
Point to one end, which is always time present.
 T. S. Eliot, "Burnt Norton" (Four Quartets)

Here one of the twentieth century's greatest poets wrestles with that mysterious dimension, time, which some have defined as a "flow" of distinguishable events. *Civilization Past & Present* has narrated the past-to-present flow of global events; but events can also be assessed in terms of a future which has yet to occur. In what way, if any, does that future "point" to our present situation?

The human species seems unique in that we can conceive of time in three phases: where and what we have been, where and what we are now, and where and what we might be tomorrow and beyond. To survive, corporations and governments alike have to be able to think ahead. This process is called *planning*, which, of course, is another way of speaking about "time future." Anyone familiar with systems concepts will understand the term *feedback*. In order to heat a room, for example, a furnace transforms an input of oil into an output of heat, which then raises the room's temperature to the desired level (say 72 degrees) set on the thermostat. When the level is reached, the thermostat will feed back that information to the furnace, which then discontinues its input of fuel. This simple example shows how the future environment we desire can set in motion activities affecting present behavior.

Nobel laureate Denis Gabor has stated that although we cannot prophesy the future, we can help invent it. Science and technology have already initiated actions of such potency that we must plan as intelligently and creatively as possible for the coming century if our global society is to endure and prosper. Casey Stengel, with his inimitable logic, put the matter succinctly: "If you don't know where you're going, you'll wind up somewhere else." So where do we want to go?

The Gulf War

On August 2, 1990, less than a year after the demolition of the Berlin Wall had marked the end of the Cold War between the superpowers, Iraqi troops poured across the border into Kuwait. A week later Iraq formally annexed Kuwait. Worldwide condemnation resulted in the UN Security Council enacting economic and other sanctions against Saddam Hussein's regime. In January 1991, Operation Desert Storm was launched by a coalition of governments, spearheaded by more than half a million U.S. air, sea, and land forces, to liberate Kuwait. Unrelenting high tech aerial bombing of Iraq, followed by a swift and overwhelming ground attack, settled the outcome within a month.

The Persian Gulf War would have long-range consequences, but its immediate effects were obvious. U.S. president George Bush spoke for a large majority of Americans in claiming that the victory had ended the "Vietnam syndrome" and restored the country's "credibility" in world affairs. The credibility of the United Nations was also restored, at least as that body exists as a useful mechanism for legitimizing collective security measures (but which it was never mandated to supervise). The economic consequences were bound to be momentous. Kuwait's infrastructure and oil fields had been devastated while Iraq, already impoverished after years of warfare with Iran, had now to repair vast wreckage in Basra and Baghdad and restore its own shattered oil industry to working order. Moreover, it could have to pay billions of dollars in reparations to Kuwait.

The social consequences were no less devasting. Many thousands in the region had been displaced, wounded, or killed. Only time will tell how many civilians had been permanently traumatized by the incessant bombings or how deeply humiliation and resentment runs in the Arab world. The political destabilization of the Middle East could make this area of the world more volatile than ever. Like nature itself, geopolitics abhors a vacuum. All in all, the war raised serious questions about Iraq's future as a country, to say nothing about a festering problem which the Gulf War had done nothing to resolve: Israeli-Palestinian relations and the occupation of the West Bank.

Conceivably, the most terrible immediate consequence of Desert Storm was the damage inflicted upon the region's environment. The largest oil spill in history covered vast regions of the Gulf, endangering species, fisheries, and coastal settlements. Hundreds of oil wells were set on fire, so that during the many months before the fires were extinguished, huge clouds of smoke poisoned the atmosphere of the region and beyond.

Ironically, the Gulf War occurred in the very region where (as we saw in chapter 1) the first civilization arose. During the conflict, archaeologists requested Washington to do everything possible to preserve priceless historical artifacts, but some destruction was inevitable. Their concerns raise a somber question: After 5000 years, how far has society progressed? We humans are still warring with one another and destroying the environment to an extent inconceivable to the men and women who built Ur with its ziggurat, crowned by a sanctuary or "high place." Have we demonstrated yet again a fixation to enlist science and technology to be ever more destructive in the "killing fields," or in this case, a "desert storm"?

North and South: Mutually Vulnerable

Our study of global civilization attests abundantly that societies everywhere have interacted and enriched one another. We can recall how the great riverine civilizations of North Africa

A Saudi Arabian government official examines a dead oil-coated cormorant. The massive oil slick that resulted from the war in the Persian Gulf is expected to devastate the Gulf's wildlife for years.

and Asia created mathematics, atronomy, irrigation systems, and a host of scientific discoveries and inventions which in time found their way to Europe. Europeans, utilizing inventions from China—printing, gunpowder, and the compass—embarked upon oceanic exploration and political expansion. From the resulting colonial empires came a cornucopia of raw resources which, with the advent of the Industrial Revolution, enabled the developed countries of the North to establish a global economy and to control the underdeveloped societies of the South.

Prosperous and complacent, the North's peoples have thought that they could insulate themselves from the South's poverty and problems; but such complacency is dangerously false because of developments that make the two segments of global society mutually vulnerable. We encounter this vulnerability in four areas.

1. Environmental. Scientists warn about the increasing pollution and heating of the earth's atmosphere, as well as the teratogenic consequences of weakening the ozone layer in the stratosphere. The burning of tropical forests in the South, notably in Brazil, and of fossil fuels, primarily in the North, might lead to a global temperature increase by one degree or more in 20 years. Such a trend, unless checked, will shift weather and rainfall patterns, global agriculture, and even raise sea levels (which could have disastrous consequences for, say, Florida and Bangladesh). The situation in the next century could become even more serious if China and India, whose combined population in A.D. 2000 will be double that of the North, continue to employ current technologies to increase energy production.

2. Economic. The economic gap between the North and South is huge. Some 70 percent of world income is produced and consumed by 15 percent of the world's population. Whereas the per capita annual income of developed market economies averges $14,500, in the 41 least developed countries the yearly average is under $300.[1] In Latin America, living standards are lower than they were in the 1970s, while those in Africa have fallen to the 1960s level. Each year in the South, 14 million children die before their fifth birthday, and another 150 million under five

This photograph of a shanty town slum in Brazil reveals the devastating poverty of the nonindustrial South. Scenes like this are common throughout Latin America.

are malnourished. The UN Economic Commission for Africa has described the 1980s as a "lost decade."

Much of the South's foreign exchange comes from the export of commodities—sugar, rubber, coffee, tea, cocoa—whose prices are controlled by the North's commodity exchanges, whereas manufactured goods come from the North at prices which it sets. For years developing countries have tried to work through the UN to make the global economy operate more equitably, and to this end call for a new international economic order. But without success. Meanwhile, in an effort to modernize and develop their economies, countries in the South have borrowed from the North well in excess of a trillion dollars. Although they receive considerable development assistance, this aid is less than the interest they have to pay on their loans. In 1988, interest amounted to $43 billion more than the amount of aid received: a situation described as "a perverse, unsustainable transfer of wealth from poor to rich."

But this imbalanced, inequitable relationship in the global economy has rendered the North vulnerable as well. Many developing economies are unable to pay back foreign loans, as U.S. and other banks have discovered. Take the case of Colombia. In 1989, the volume of its coffee exports increased by 14 percent, yet the country earned $192 million less because of falling prices (which were controlled elsewhere). Facing poverty conditions, many farmers in Colombia and other parts of the South shifted to raising illegal products—marijuana, cocaine, heroin—for which users in the North pay a high and ultimately tragic price.

3. Demographic. We face the following situation: the rich countries get richer, the poor countries get children—and lots of them. After millions of years of high birth and death rates, genus *Homo* reached the 1.7 billion mark in 1900. Half a century later, the figure rose to 2.5 billion, while after another 37 years there were 5 billion. Growth at this rate represents a net increase of some 9000 persons per hour, or 100 million a year for at least another 35 years. As of A.D. 2000, when it reaches 6.25 billion, global population will have almost quadrupled in one century, only to increase by billions more in the next. By A.D. 2000, too, more than three-fourths of the world's peoples will be in developing countries.

This population explosion is accompanied by yet another major phenomenon: the world is rapidly urbanizing. In 1960, only 3 of the world's 10 largest cities were in the South; in the year 2000, the South will have 45 of the 60 largest cities, 18 of them with more than 10 million inhabitants each. More than half—51.2 percent—of the world's population will be urban. And in the South, 35 percent will be under age 14. Lacking economic opportunity, all too many now find themselves abandoned, uneducated, and alienated from any societal norms. As many as a billion people may be living at or below "absolute poverty," which the United Nations defines as having caloric intake insufficient to supply energy to perform a day's work. Wretchedly poor people turn upon themselves and deplete their environment. More and more they seek relief by migrating, thereby placing immense pressures upon neighboring countries. As the South's population continues to expand, the North's rich countries will in turn be confronted by increasing pressures to relax immigration restrictions drastically, thereby risking new domestic tensions or conflicts.

4. Political. All of these problems exacerbate political instability in the South. But as the Gulf War proved, they can also draw the North into international political and military operations. Moreover, the industrialized countries have contributed to that instability. For example, the five permanent members of the UN Security Council which authorized force against Iraq had previously sold or transferred to that country and its neighbors hundreds of billions of dollars of sophisticated weapons, which those countries neither needed nor could afford. In a highly competitive international arms industry, the developing nations have been encouraged to forgo building their infrastructures, such as roads, schools, and irrigation systems, in favor of purchasing jet fighters, tanks, armored vehicles, and the gadgetry for operating them.

For millennia nations have armed in the attempt to be secure. But security is now taking on a new dimension. So long as people do not have equitable access to such necessities as food, health, education, and economic opportunity, no society can feel secure—as the apartheid regime in South Africa attests. This lack of equity is largely responsible for the South's political instability; and unless corrected, social turbulence could become an increasingly infectious phenomenon that will be immune to traditional, simplistic reliance on armed force.

The North and its political institutions are also being challenged. America's success in the Gulf War did nothing to address major problems at home: unemployment, homelessness, inner city crime, the drug crisis, polluted lakes and toxic waste dumps, and mounting governmental debt. All too often, minorities in the North feel that their governments treat them inequitably. In the United States, democratic institutions have existed for more than two centuries. Perhaps we need to take stock of their present health and effectiveness, as demonstrated, for example, by our presidential elections.

In 13 elections held between 1840 and 1900, 76.6 percent of entitled American voters went to the polls. Yet in our last 9 elections, the average percentage had fallen to 56.7. On three occasions in the nineteenth century, the turnout was above 80 percent; in two elections in this country, it was below 50 percent. In 1988, a bare half—50.2 percent—of voters exercised their right of ballot, with President Bush obtaining 54 percent of the votes cast. This means that while winning a large electoral vote, Bush had actually been endorsed by only 27.1 percent—scarcely more than a quarter—of all Americans entitled to vote.

This raises disturbing questions. Why has the percentage of voters exercising their ballot fallen so dramatically? Is the fall in voter participation due to apathy? Disillusionment? To a belief that one's vote does not count because "you can't change the system"? Can anything be done to reverse this trend? A feature of *Civilization Past & Present* throughout its many editions has been its continued interest in the genesis and prospects of democracy. We saw how Greek citizens participated directly in making political decisions, while Americans have made an invaluable contribution to representative government. can our democratic model be improved to make it as effective as its creators had envisaged?

"A New World Order": What It Might Involve

For over four decades following World War II, people everywhere had to live under the shadow of a nuclear holocaust while two superpowers were locked in a Cold War. But this ended with the demolition of the Berlin Wall, the collapse of Communist regimes in Eastern Europe, and desperate efforts by President Gorbachev and other Soviet leaders to restructure an overcentralized political structure and collapsing economy to prevent the fragmentation of the Soviet Union. A critical juncture in global affairs had been reached in the early 1990s. Would traditional international rivalries and power struggles continue to plague humanity, or had this crux presented a unique "window of opportunity," described by President Bush as "a new world order"? What might be required to bring about this novel dispensation?

1. Environmental Action. Our plant has been increasingly plundered and degraded throughout this century. In the late 1980s we heard warnings about global warming, accompanied by dire predictions of melting ice caps and ozone depletion.

Burned-out jungle vegetation in Jaru, Brazil. Among the disastrous effects of destruction of tropical rain forests, which absorb much of earth's carbon dioxide and produce much of its oxygen, are great climatic changes and the demise of thousands of species, some of which will be extinct before they are ever known.

Children display their environmental awareness and concern on Earth Day, April 21, 1990. Standing on the steps of the Museum of Natural History in New York, children hold a mile-long banner decorated with the handprints of children from across the country who have promised to honor the earth.

Satellites revealed for the first time the monumental scale of manmade fires destroying vast tracts of rainforest in the Amazon basin. These fires have created unprecedented amounts of carbon dioxide, a heat-trapping gas which warms the planet's atmosphere; they are wiping out the richest and most diverse region of natural life anywhere, together with a pharmaceutical treasury of incalculable value. These tragic events affect the future not just of Brazil but of every continent.[2] If we are to save our planet, concerted international remedial action is required—and there is no time to lose.

We need to begin by getting our priorities straight. We must acknowledge that while critical ecological problems may start in a given country, they do not respect national boundaries. Consequently, no government can logically claim that it has no responsibility to the world community for how its activities affect the environment. Further, as we saw in chapter 1 of *Civilization Past & Present*, our planet came into existence billions of years ago, while the biosphere with its multitude of faunal and floral species existed millions of years before genus *Homo* evolved. And the biosphere can continue to exist without us—arguably, it might be better off! But the converse does not hold: we cannot exist without the biosphere of which we are an integral part. In the final analysis, humankind's survival depends upon giving first priority to the continued well-being of our planet and its ecosystems. This means adopting a new attitude toward the environment. As far back as 1864, a remarkable American conservationist, George Perkins Marsh, warned that only a strong commitment to conserving the forest and other natural resources could save the nation from destroying its environmental endowment. "Man has too long forgotten that the earth was given to him for usufruct alone"—that is, to enjoy the benefits of someone else's property—"not for consumption, far less for profligate waste."[3]

The environment is not ours to destroy in the name of economic development, mistakenly called "progress." Instead, our role must be that of stewardship in order to preserve and enhance it for all species and future generations. An international conference on the global environment to be held in Brazil in 1992 will analyze ecological and related problems in depth, and set forth a strategy of action to save the planet's ecosystems. On the implementation of its recommendations could hinge humankind's survival.

2. Social and Economic Action. If global warming is the most critical environmental issue confronting us in the next century, the global population explosion might well be the most vexatious social problem. By 2025, the world's resources will have to support an estimated 8.2 billion people. But whereas the industrialized countries will have approached or reached zero growth, for a total of 1.4 billion, the Third World of the less-developed nations will have almost doubled its population to 6.8 billion.[4] In other words, the South will be then have almost five times as many people as the North. There can be no quick fix for getting the planet's population under control. In industrialized countries, rising incomes, urbanization, and improved education and social status for women have contributed to the decline in the birth rates. Developing countries will have to initiate mass programs aimed at health care, family planning, and eradicating urban slums and shanty towns.

Social instability and violence are bound to continue until the South's proliferating masses acquire new economic opportunities to allow escape from conditions of malnutrition, disease, ignorance, and ubiquitous poverty. That reality poses a fundamental challenge which *Our Common Future* (the report of the World Commission on Environment and Development) sums up in its term *sustainable development*. This means "development that meets the needs of the present without compromising the ability of future generations to meet their own needs."[5] It makes clear that societal development can only be based upon a viable global environment, which our excessive exploitation has been putting ever more at risk. *Our Common Future* remains committed to the concept of continued economic growth. However, environmental sustainability requires the industrialized nations to use less resource materials and become more energy efficient. The global economy must also ensure that developing countries grow fast enough to outpace their internal problems and so continue economic growth and diversification. At best, the planet's physical resources and its environment will be enormously taxed if such global development is to be possible. In the words of the report: "We do not pretend that the process is easy or straightforward. Painful choices have to be made. Thus, in the final analysis, sustainable development must rest on political will."[6]

3. Political Action. The Cold War reflected the realities of a division of political and military power within a bipolar world. The end of the cold War and the outcome of the Gulf War appeared to have created a unipolar world. But is this

assessment accurate? Some international analysis suggests that the victor emerging from the end of the Cold War is Japan. While the United States devoted huge amounts of technological resources to producing stealth bombers and Patriot missiles, Japan concentrated on robotics and automobiles, in the process becoming the dominant player in the global economic game. Meanwhile, the consolidation of the European Community in 1992 will create a powerful economic and political rival to North America.

As we saw in chapter 17, the Thirty Years' War ended with the creation of the modern nation-state system. This system recognized the sovereignty of individual states, giving to each an unrestricted right to act as it wished within its own borders, and free to pursue its interests abroad. *Independence*, with all its patriotic and nationalistic trappings, is the key concept of this system. But over the past hundred years, commerce, migration, tourism, science, technology, communications, and of course environmental problems have increasingly transcended national boundaries. Today as never before, the key word to express the reality of our world is *interdependence*.

The volatile situation which resulted in the Gulf War raises a critical question: how can independent states pursuing national interests ensure security for an interdependent world? Involved is the issue of arms control. The world's annual arms bill amounts to about $1 trillion, yet in this century reliance on weapons has resulted in two global wars as well as conflicts in Korea, Vietnam, the Gulf, and scores of other hot spots. Surely we need effective arms control, restraints on the world trade in weapons, and regional security arrangements which can be enforced.

Given the instability of the current era, marked by long-standing national rivalries, intense ethnic and religious turmoil, poverty and deep economic inequities, and population pressures, no one nation, or even a coalition of a few nations, can assume the role of global policeman. The United Nations, which the United States took the lead in creating but for two decades largely ignored, will have to be given a stronger role in securing international peace. The permanent membership of the Security Council should be expanded to include, say, Japan and Germany, as well as large Third World countries such as India and Brazil. Its peacekeeping machinery can be further strengthened, with units deployed in dangerous areas, where possible anticipating a crisis. The UN charter has always possessed a strong enforcement capacity, largely ignored during the Cold War. The Charter envisaged the gradual conversion of the existing military setup into a worldwide system of collective security, and the Council's Military Staff Committee could be instructed to study how this conversion might best be brought about. "Such a system would be a giant step forward from the belated and improvised efforts to which the United Nations has so far been limited. . . . Governments, if they want the United Nations to be respected and taken seriously, will also have to respect its decisions, and make decisions that can if necessary be enforced. Such changes in attitude would be the best practical test of a commitment to a 'new world order.'"[7]

The Continuing Relevance of History

In a widely publicized article, "The End of History," Francis Fukuyama argues that "What we may be witnessing is not just the end of the Cold War, or the passing of a particular period of postwar history, but the end of history as such: that is, the end point of mankind's ideological evolution and the universalization of Western liberal democracy as the final form of human government."[8] Fukuyama's central thesis is that history, which he defines as the record of human conflict, is determined by ideas—by "ideology," which provides a framework for choice and action, with each historical epoch developing its own internal contradictions and conflicts; but this process is ending because Western democracy has produced a socioeconomic and political system that contains no irresolvable internal contradictions. Since we have reached a point where "theoretical truth is absolute, and could not be improved upon," the need for new ideologies ends, and consequently history as defined by Fukuyama ends.

We reject such a reading of the historical record, and therefore the author's thesis. Far from one ideology triumphing over all others, the world remains a hodgepodge of conflicting beliefs.

Moreover, we regard history as much more than the conflict of ideas; it is also the record of human accomplishments among all our diverse cultures and societies, and humanity's endless challenge to live in harmony with its planetary environment. Finally, Fukuyama has failed to understand that the most basic characteristic of Western democracy is its own contradictions. It is precisely because democracy derives from the point of view that absolute truths are unreachable that it is necessary to consult majorities on a continuing basis over what they consider to be right.

The Gulf War demonstrated dramatically a unique interplay of human and impersonal forces: the megalomania of Saddam Hussein; the critical importance of oil to industrialized, energy-hungry economies; long-standing religious bitterness; and geopolitical rivalries in the Middle East. History is neither at an end, nor is it irrelevant. Its practitioners have meticulously documented the forces responsible for destabilizing the Middle East, which for decades was a powder keg waiting to explode. Despite history's proved relevance, governments failed to profit from its portents and take appropriate preventive measures in time. To paraphrase George Santayana, our failure to learn from past mistakes resulted in our repeating their tragic consequences.

History's role can be likened to Janus, the two-faced Roman god. History enables us to view the past as past and, in turn, to visualize the past and present as prologue. Past and present conjoin to alert us to the need not only to engage in new forms of planning for the turbulent years ahead but also to rethink our traditional social goals and value systems. The historical evolution of humanity is open-ended. Far from being immutable, humanity's beliefs and goals are continuously undergoing change. The historical record provides us with what we shall continue to require: as long and accurate a perspective as possible from our global experience, in order to safeguard our planetary inheritance and improve the quality of life for humans everywhere.

This edition of *Civilization Past & Present* has appeared in 1992, the 500th anniversary of Columbus' discovery of the New World. That event had incalculable consequences—societal, biological, and environmental—for global history.

It meant the expansion of European colonization and Christianity into the Western Hemisphere; it also meant the destruction of many indigenous societies and cultures as a result of imperialism and exposure to Old World diseases to which the native inhabitants had no immunity. The environment of the New World was permanently altered. Hundreds of millions of acres of forest were destroyed by trans-Atlantic settlers who brought with them new species of plants and animals in their desire to recreate the ecological conditions they had known in Europe. These hemispheric developments exemplify the vast changes which have occurred in the past half millennium, the most momentous epoch in all the hundreds of thousands of years in which our species has inhabited the earth.

The year 1992 also marks the anniversary of fifty years of existence for *Civilization Past & Present*. The half century immediately past has been the most dynamic and dramatic era in the past 500 years. Far more people have lived during these fifty years than in any previous half century. More physical resources have been consumed, and more damage has been inflicted upon the earth's environment than ever before. But also more inventions and scientific breakthroughs have occurred. So we move toward the twenty-first century with a dual heritage: unprecedented perils, and unprecedented promises. What will happen? To repeat Gabor's thought: the future is ours to invent.

Viewed from this perspective, our epilogue becomes a prologue to a new state of human experience and societal attainment. Our Paleolithic ancestors lived in a largely undifferentiated planet. Their descendants have spiraled through stages of ever-increasing complexity until we inhabit today a single but highly differentiated and interrelated planet. One species as ever, yet occupying innumerable ecological and cultural niches within a shared global ecosystem. It is true that, as Winston Churchill suggested, history often seems to be "one damn thing after another." But it is also the story of one achievement after another. And now a new chapter in our irreversible history is being written. We began this epilogue by quoting from Eliot's *Four Quartets*. Let us cite it again: "In our ending is our beginning."

Notes

1. Ivan L. Head, President, International Development Research Centre, "A World Turned Outside Down," Agricultural Institute of Canada, 1991, pp. 1–30.
2. See *World Resources, 1990–1991: A Guide to the Global Environment*, A Report by the World Resources Institute, Oxford University Press, 1991. See also Pearce Wright, *Environmental Damage and Climatic Change*, Ditchley Foundation Report Number D88/4, 1988.
3. George Perkins Marsh, *Man and Nature*, 1864.
4. United Nations, Department of International Economic and Social Affairs, *World Population Prospects Estimates* (New York: United Nations, 1986).
5. World Commission on Environment and Development, *Our Common Future* ("Brundtland Report") (Oxford: University Press, 1987).
6. Ibid., p. 9.
7. Brian Urquhart, former Undersecretary General of the United Nations, "Learning from the Gulf," *The New York Review of Books*, March 7, 1991, pp. 34–37.
8. Francis Fukuyama, "The End of History?" *The National Interest*; see *The Toronto Globe and Mail*, December 1 and 28, 1989.

Chronological Tables

Credits

Index

Reference Maps

	Near East and Egypt	India and China
	Neolithic revolution c. 7000 Sumerian city-states emerge c. 3500	
3000 B.C.	Menes unites Egypt c. 3100 Old Sumerian period c. 2800–2370 Old Kingdom in Egypt c. 2700–2200 Akkadian Empire c. 2370–2150 Neo-Sumerian period c. 2113–2006 Middle Kingdom in Egypt c. 2050–1800	Indus valley civilization c. 2500–1500—capitals at Mohenjo-Daro and Harappa
2000 B.C.	Hittites enter Asia Minor c. 2000 Hammurabi rules lower Mesopotamia 1760 Hittites sack Babylon 1595 New Kingdom or Empire in Egypt c. 1570–1090	
1500 B.C.	Thutmose III c. 1490–1436—the "Napoleon of Egypt" Hittite Empire c. 1450–1200 Akhenaton c. 1369–1353 Era of small states 1200–700 Phoenician and Aramean traders; the alphabet Period of Decadence in Egypt c. 1090–332	Invasion of India by Aryans from Black and Caspian seas c. 1500 Early Vedic Age c. 1500–1000—beginning of three pillars of Indian society: autonomous village, caste system, joint family. *Vedas*—oldest Sanskrit literature Shang Dynasty 1700–1122—China's first civilization Chou Dynasty 1122–221—China's "classical age"—Mandate of Heaven promulgated
1000 B.C.	United Hebrew kingdom 1020–922: Saul, David, Solomon Divided Hebrew kingdom: Israel 922–721; Judah 922–586 The great Hebrew prophets 750–550 Assyrian Empire 745–612 Lydians and Medes Chaldean Empire 604–539: Nebuchadnezzar Zoroaster, early sixth century Persian Empire 550–330: Cyrus; Darius 522–486 End of the Babylonian Exile of the Jews 538	Later Vedic Age in India c. 1000–500—caste system becomes more complex: priest, warrior, merchant, serf, "untouchable" *Upanishads* 800–600—foundation of Hinduism
500 B.C.		Gautama Buddha 563?–483—founder of Buddhism Confucius 551–479—most famous and influential Chinese philosopher Chinese poetry collected in *Shih Ching*, or *Book of Odes* Two greatest Indian epics composed: the *Mahabharata* (including the *Bhagavad-Gita*) and the *Ramayama*
400 B.C.	Conquests of Alexander the Great 334–331	Lao-tzu and Taoism—aim: intuitive approach to life: *Tao te Ching* Mencius c. 372–289 links theory of Mandate of Heaven to democratic concept of the will of the people in government Alexander the Great crosses Indus valley 326 Chandragupta Maurya founds Mauryan Dynasty in India 322–c. 185
300 B.C.	Death of Alexander 323; Ptolemy seizes Egypt; Seleucus rules Asia	Ashoka 273–232—"the first great royal patron of Buddhism" Period of Warring States in China—Ch'in defeat Chou 221 China reunited under First Emperor, Shih Huang-ti 221–210 Han Dynasty of China 202 B.C.–A.D. 220
200 B.C.	Maccabean revolt wins independence for Judea 142	Tamil kingdoms—Hindu states, chief trading area with the West Mauryan Empire falls 185; Bactrian rule extends to India and Punjab; Graeco-Bactrian kingdom created Han Emperor Wu Ti 141–187
100 B.C.	Dead Sea Scrolls Pompey annexes Syria and Palestine 63 Herod the Great, king of Judea 37–4 Jesus Christ c. 4 B.C.–A.D. 30 Paul d. c. 65	Kushan Empire in India first century B.C.–A.D. 220 Kanishka, Kushan ruler c. 78–128, sponsors *Mahayana* ("Great Vehicle") school of Buddhism spreads north and east; *Hinayana* ("Lesser Vehicle") Buddhism spreads south and east
A.D. 100	Jews revolt from Rome 66–70—end of the ancient Hebrew state	

Greece	Rome	
		3000 B.C.
Aegean civilization c. 2000–1200 Achaean Greeks invade Peloponnesus c. 2000 Zenith of Minoan culture 1700–1450	Indo-Europeans invade Italian peninsula 2000–1000; Latins settle in lower Tiber valley (Latium)	**2000 B.C.**
Mycenaean Age 1450–1200 Dorian invasion c. 1200		**1500 B.C.**
	Etruscans settle on Italy's west coast	
Greek Dark Ages c. 1150–750 and Homeric Age	Carthage founded in North Africa by Phoenicians c. 800 Rome founded 753 Greeks colonize southern Italy and Sicily Etruscans conquer Rome c. 600 Roman Republic established 509	**1000 B.C.**
Hellenic Age c. 750–338 Age of Oligarchy c. 750–500: Hesiod; colonization Athens—growth of democracy: Solon 594, Pisistratus 560, Cleisthenes 508 Sparta—militaristic totalitarian state, Spartan League	Plebeians vs. patricians 509–287—tribunes and *Concilium Plebis*	
Persian Wars 490–479: Marathon, Thermopylae Delian League 478 and Athenian imperialism Athens' Golden Age under Pericles 461–429 Peloponnesian War 431–404—Athens vs. Sparta	Laws of the Twelve Tables c. 450	**500 B.C.**
Philip II of Macedonia conquers Greece 338 Hellenic culture: Thales, Pythagoras, Democritus, Hippocrates, Socrates, Plato, Aristotle, Herodotus, Thucydides, Sappho, Aeschylus, Sophocles, Euripides, Aristophanes, Phidias, Praxiteles Alexander the Great conquers Persia 331 Hellenistic Age 323–31—Ptolemaic Egypt, Seleucid Asia, Macedonia; Greek federal leagues	Roman expansion in Italy 338–270: Latins, Etruscans, Samnites, Greeks	**400 B.C.**
Hellenistic culture: Epicurus, Zeno, Eratosthenes, Aristarchus, Euclid, Archimedes, Hipparchus, Polybius, Theocritus	Roman expansion in western Mediterranean 270–146—Punic wars: Hannibal	**300 B.C.**
	Roman expansion in eastern Mediterranean 200–133—wars with Macedonia and the Seleucids; Macedon and Greece annexed 146; first Roman province in Asia 133 Reform movement of the Gracchi 133–121	**200 B.C.**
	Marius vs. Sulla 88–82: dictatorship of Sulla 82–79 Pompey vs. Caesar 49–46: dictatorship of Julius Caesar 46–44 Antony vs. Octavian 32–30 Augustus' reconstruction—the Principate 30 B.C.–A.D. 180	**100 B.C.**
	Golden Age of literature: Cicero, Catullus, Lucretius, Virgil, Horace	**A.D. 100**

Europe

100 B.C.

A.D. 1

100
End of the *Pax Romana* 180–285—civil war, economic decline, invasions
Reconstruction by Diocletian 285–305—the Dominate

300
Constantine 306–337—Edict of Milan 313, Council of Nicaea 325, founding of Constantinople 330
Ulfilas d. 383, missionary to Goths

Theodosius divides Roman Empire 395
Battle of Adrianople 378—German invasions begin

400
Alaric sacks Rome 410
Attila crosses the Rhine—battle near Troyes 451
Pope Leo the Great 440–461

Odovacar deposes last Western emperor 476
Clovis 481–511 unites Franks and rules Gaul

500
Theodoric 493–526 rules Italy; Cassiodorus and Boethius
St. Benedict establishes Benedictine Order 529

Lombards invade Italy 568
Merovingian decline sixth–seventh centuries

600
Pope Gregory the Great 590–604
Isidore of Seville d. 636—the *Etymologies*

700
Charles Martel 714–741 rules the Franks; defeats Muslims at Tours 732
The Venerable Bede d. 735
St. Boniface d. 755, "apostle to the Germans"
Pepin the Short 741–768 ends rule of Merovingian kings; Donation of Pepin to pope
Charlemagne 768–814 revives Roman Empire in the West 800; fosters Carolingian Renaissance

800
Treaty of Verdun divides Carolingian Empire into West Frankland, East Frankland, and Lorraine 843
Magyar, Muslim, and Viking invasions terrorize Europe ninth–tenth centuries
Alfred the Great 871–899 establishes strong Anglo-Saxon kingdom in England
Kievan Russia emerges

900
Feudalism well established in France c. 900
Henry I, the Fowler 919–936, founds Saxon Dynasty in Germany
Otto I, the Great 936–973—alliance of crown and church; routs Magyars at battle of Lechfeld 955; crowned emperor by pope 962
Ethelred the Unready 978–1016—power of English government lags; invasion by Canute, Viking king Hugh Capet 987 founds Capetian Dynasty in France

1000
Peace and Truce of God eleventh century
Normans arrive in Italy 1016
Yaroslav the Wise 1019–1054—peak of Kievan Russia; Byzantine influences in art and literature
Salian House succeeds Saxon kings in Germany 1024
College of Cardinals formed to elect pope 1059
Pope Gregory VII 1073–1085 supports Cluniac religious reform; Investiture struggle

Norman Conquest of England 1066
Fall of Bari to Normans 1071—last Byzantine stronghold in Italy
Reconquista gains Toledo from Muslims 1085
First Crusade—Jerusalem captured; Latin kingdom of Jerusalem established 1099

1100
Renaissance of twelfth century; revival of trade and towns
Welf-Hohenstaufen rivalry 1106–1152 wrecks structure for strong German state
Louis the Fat 1108—first strong Capetian ruler in France
Concordat of Worms 1122
Second Crusade 1147
Frederick Barbarossa 1152–1190 centralizes feudal monarchy; struggle with popes and Lombard League

Henry II 1154–1189 reforms English judicial system; Thomas à Becket
St. Dominic 1170–1221; St. Francis of Assisi 1182?–1226
Philip II Augustus 1180–1223 extends royal power
Third Crusade, "Crusade of Kings," 1189
Frederick II 1194–1250—end of medieval German Empire

1200
Pope Innocent III 1198–1216—zenith of medieval papacy
Fourth Crusade 1202–1204—crusaders sack Constantinople
King John of England signs Magna Carta 1215
St. Thomas Aquinas 1225?–1274 reconciles faith and reason in *Summa Theologica*; zenith of scholasticism
Louis IX 1226–1270 brings dignity to French crown
Edward I 1272–1307—rise of Parliament in England; power of nobility curtailed
Philip IV, the Fair 1285–1314, centralizes French Government; humiliates Pope Boniface VIII
Acre, last Christian stronghold in Holy Land, conquered by Muslims 1291

1300
Dante d. 1321
Hundred Years' War between France and England 1337–1453

1400
Chaucer d. 1400

Near East and Byzantine Empire	*Far East*	
	Rule by Yamato clan in Japan	**100** B.C.
	Kanishka ruler in India c. 78–128	A.D. **1**
Christian missionaries	Expansion of Indian culture into Southeast Asia begins Fall of Han Dynasty in China 220	**100**
Eastern church Fathers: Clement of Alexandria Council of Nicaea 325—Nicene Creed Constantine established New Rome (Constantinople) 330	Buddhism gains popularity in China third century Chandra Gupta I founds Gupta Dynasty in India 320 Chandra Gupta II c. 380–c. 413—zenith of Gupta power	**300**
	Kalidasa c. 400–455, India's greatest poet and dramatist of Gupta age: *Shakuntala*	**400**
Justinian 527–565—reconquests; *Corpus Juris Civilis;* Hagia Sophia	Buddhism enters Japan sixth century Sui Dynasty in China 589–618	**500**
Muhammad 570–632—the Hijra 622 Heraclius 610–641—regains Syria, Palestine, Egypt	Harsha 606–647 rules northern India T'ang Dynasty founded 618	**600**
Umayyad Dynasty 661–750—expands in North Africa, Turkestan, Indus valley, Spain; defeated by Franks at Tours 732 Leo III 717–741 repulses Muslims 718; administrative and military reforms	T'ang poets: Li Po and Tu Fu Japanese imperial court established at Nara 710 New Japanese imperial court at Heian-kyo (Kyoto) 794 Heian period in Japan 794–1185	**700**
Abbasid Dynasty 750–1258—end of Arab predominance; Cyril and Methodius—missionaries to the Slavs	*Diamond Sutra* printed 868	**800**
Golden age of Muslim learning 900–1100—advances in medicine, mathematics, literature, philosophy, architecture, decorative arts; al-Razi, Avicenna, Alhazen, al-Khwarizmi, Omar Khayyám, Averroës, ibn-Khaldun	T'ang Dynasty falls 906 Expansion of Indian culture into Southern Asia ends tenth century Sung Dynasty founded in China 960	**900**
Basil II 976–1025 defeats Bulgars Final separation of the churches 1054 Seljuk Turks seize Persia and Iraq, conquer Bagdad 1055 Battle of Manzikert 1071—loss of Asia Minor to Seljuks	Vietnam achieves independence from China Wang An-shih 1021–1086, Chinese Socialist reformer Muslims invade India; Turks and Afghans annex Punjab 1022	**1000**
Kingdom of Jerusalem 1099–1291 and crusader states Saladin regains Jerusalem 1187	Angkor Wat built c. 1100 China divided between empires of Sung (south) and Chin (north) 1127 Yoritomo 1147–1199 rules Japan as shogun from Kamakura 1185 Temujin 1162–1227 unites Mongols; recognized as "Genghis Khan" 1206	**1100**
Fourth Crusade 1202–1204—Constantinople sacked Latin Empire 1204–1261 Fall of Abbasid Dynasty—Baghdad conquered by Mongols under Hulagu Khan 1258 *Michael Palaeologus regains Constantinople 1261*	Peak of Khmer Empire in Southeast Asia Delhi Sultanate established 1206; Indian culture divided into Hindu and Muslim Mongols conquer China, portions of Middle East and Southeast Asia 1241–1279; *Pax Tatarica* Kublai Khan 1260–1294 proclaims himself founder of Yuan Dynasty of China Marco Polo arrives at Kublai Khan's court c. 1275 Japan stops Mongol invasion 1281	**1200**
Ottoman Turks invade Europe 1356 Constantinople falls to Ottoman Turks 1453	Ashikaga shogunate replaces Kamakura 1336 Ming Dynasty established in China 1368	**1300**
		1400

	Europe
100 **900**	
1000	
1100	
1200	Mongols conquer Kiev 1240 Transitional period in Italian art c. 1250–c. 1400; Giotto d. 1336 Pope Boniface VIII 1294–1303 feuds with Philip IV
1300	Avignon papacy 1305–1377; Babylonian Captivity of the church Hundred Years' War 1337–1453 Black Death 1348 Golden Bull 1356 Classical revival, Humanism; Petrarch, Boccaccio Great Schism 1378–1417 John Wycliffe d. 1384 Grand Prince of Moscow defeats Mongols at Kulikovo 1380
1400	*Quattrocento* of Italian Renaissance; early Renaissance masters in Italy—Brunelleschi, Ghiberti, Donatello, Masaccio, Mantegana, Botticelli, Verrocchio Council of Constance 1414 Medici family rules Florence 1434–1494 Commercial Revolution 1450–1650 Gutenberg uses movable type to print Bible 1454 Wars of the Roses 1455–1485 Louis XI (the "universal spider") of France 1461–1483 Ivan III, the Great, of Russia 1462–1505 Ferdinand and Isabella begin joint rule in Spain 1479 Henry VII 1485–1509 founds Tudor Dynasty in England *Reconquista* ends with conquest of Granada 1492; unification of Spain completed Maximilian I 1493–1519, Holy Roman Emperor Italian wars 1494–1513 begin
1500	Northern Renaissance sixteenth century—Erasmus, More, Rabelais, von Hutten, Montaigne, van Eyck, Dürer, Holbein, Brueghel, Bosch High Renaissance in Italy c. 1500–1530—Bramante, Michelangelo, da Vinci, Raphael, Giorgione, Titian, Castiglione, Cellini Henry VIII of England 1509–1547; founds Anglican church 1534 Luther issues ninety-five theses 1517; excommunicated, declared heretic at Diet of Worms 1521 Charles V elected Holy Roman emperor 1519 Suleiman rules Turks 1520–1566 Machiavelli, *The Prince* 1532 Loyola establishes Jesuit order 1534 John Calvin publishes *Institutes of the Christian Religion* 1536 Council of Trent 1545–1563 Ivan IV, the Terrible, of Russia 1547–1584
1550	Mary Tudor reinstates Catholicism in England 1553–1558 Peace of Augsburg 1555 Philip II of Spain 1556–1598 Elizabeth I of England 1558–1603 Massacre of St. Bartholomew's Eve 1572 Shakespeare 1564–1616 Battle of Lepanto 1571 Dutch United Provinces declare independence 1581 Time of Trouble in Russia 1584–1613 Spanish Armada 1588 Henry IV 1589–1610 founds Bourbon Dynasty in France Edict of Nantes 1598
1600	James I 1603–1625 founds Stuart Dynasty in England Bank of Amsterdam founded 1609 Michael Romanov founds Romanov Dynasty in Russia 1613 Thirty Years' War 1618–1648—Peace of Westphalia 1648

Asia	Americas and Africa	
	Classical Period of Mesoamerican civilization 150–900	**100**
	Postclassical period of Mesoamerican civilization 900–1492	**900**
	Peak of development in Ghana	**1000**
	Incas settle Cuzco valley in Andes eleventh century	
		1100
	Fall of Ghana state 1203	**1200**
	Zenith of Great Zimbabwe 1250–1450	
	Peak of Swahili civilization 1200–1500	
	Aztec confederacy in Mexico fourteenth century	**1300**
	Reign of Mansa Musa of Mali 1312–1337	
Chinese naval expeditions to India, Near East, Africa fifteenth century		**1400**
Early Ming policy encourages foreign trade	Portuguese navigate West African coast	
Muslim commercial center at Malacca founded 1400	Atlantic slave trade begins fifteenth century	
	Reign of Montezuma I 1440–1468 of Aztec Empire	
	Reign of Zara Yakob of Ethiopia 1434–1468	
	Songhai Empire in the African Sudan c. 1468–1590	
	Zenith of Inca Empire 1438–1532	
	Arrival of Portuguese in Benin c. 1440	
	Diaz rounds Cape of Good Hope 1488	
	Columbus discovers New World 1492	
	Bull of Demarcation 1493; Treaty of Tordesillas 1494	
	North America claimed by Cabot for England 1497–1498	
	Da Gama reaches India 1498	
	Cabral sights east coast of Brazil	
Portuguese trade monopoly in Far East sixteenth century	Balboa sights Pacific Ocean 1513	**1500**
Malacca falls to Portuguese 1511	Cortés arrives in Mexico 1519; Aztec Empire falls 1521	
Peak of Ottoman power under Suleiman the Magnificent 1520–1566	Magellan rounds South America 1520	
	Pizarro reaches Peru 1531, conquers Incas	
Babur (the Tiger) defeats Delhi sultanate and Rajput Confederacy 1525–1527; founds Mughul Empire in India	Cartier explores St. Lawrence River for France 1534	
Waning of Ming power and effectiveness		
Portuguese traders in Japan		
Momoyama period in Japanese art		
Akbar 1556–1605 expands Mughul Empire; promotes religious tolerance	Bartolomé de las Casas 1474–1566 argues for Indian rights	**1550**
Portuguese granted right to trade with Chinese at Macao 1557	Saint Augustine, first colony in North America, founded 1565	
Spanish use Philippines as trading stop c. 1565	Coronado, de Sota explore North America	
Abbas the Great of Persia 1587–1629	Reignot Mai Idris Alooma of Kanem-Bornu 1580–1617	
Christian missionaries in Japan		
Hideyoshi 1536–1598 makes war against China and Korea, persecutes Christians in Japan		
Dutch East India Company formed 1602	Jamestown founded 1607; Champlain founds Quebec 1608	**1600**
English East India Company chartered 1609	Henry Hudson establishes Dutch claims in North America	
Tokugawa shogunate in Japan begins 1603		
Foundations for Dutch East Indies laid by Coen 1618	Plymouth founded 1620	
Shah Jahan 1628–1658; height of Mughul Empire in India	Dutch West India Company supplants Portuguese in West Africa, takes over Atlantic slave trade 1630	
Japan expels all Europeans 1637	Montreal established 1642	
Dutch expel Portuguese from Moluccas 1641, establish trade monopoly in Indonesia	Dutch settlement at Cape Town 1651	
Manchus establish Ch'ing Dynasty 1644	La Salle claims Louisiana for France 1683	

	Politics	Science and Technology, Thought and Art	
1500		Revolution in astronomy—Copernicus, *Concerning the Revolutions of Heavenly Spheres*, 1543; Brahe, Kepler, Galileo; heliocentric theory	**1500**
1600	James I 1603–1625 and Charles I 1625–1649 of England antagonize Parliament; Petition of Right 1628 Richelieu becomes real power behind French throne 1624–1642 Frederick William, the Great Elector 1640–1688, makes Brandenburg the most important Protestant state in Germany English Civil War 1642–1648; Charles I executed 1649; Oliver Cromwell takes control of government Louis XIV 1643–1715 transforms French state into absolute monarchy Colbert develops French mercantilist system—Colbertism; de Louvois revolutionizes French army House of Orange controls political regime in Holland c. 1640	William Gilbert describes magnetic force 1600 Bacon champions inductive method of philosophic inquiry; *Novum Organum*, 1620 Descartes proposes deductive method of philosophic inquiry; *Discource on Method*, 1627 Robert Boyle, father of modern chemistry, conceives crude atomic theory Neoclassical dramatists in France—Corneille, Racine, Molière Inventions of seventeenth century—telescope, microscope, thermometer, pendulum clock, micrometer, barometer, air pump Baroque style in art—Rubens, Velázquez, Vermeer, Hals, Rembrandt, Bernini; opera originates in Italy William Harvey describes human circulatory system	**1600**
1650	Restoration of Stuart monarchy in England 1660; Charles II 1660–1685 and James II 1685–1688 attempt to establish absolutist rule in England Leopold I 1657–1705 strengthens Austrian monarchy Peter the Great 1682–1725, absolutist tsar of Russia, attempts to Westernize realm Louis XIV revokes Edict of Nantes 1685 Glorious Revolution 1688 overthrows James II; William of Orange invited to rule England; William and Mary become joint sovereigns of England Aurangzeb 1658–1707 extends Mughul Empire over entire Indian subcontinent 1690	Hobbes of England (*Leviathan*, 1651) and Bossuet of France (*Politics Drawn from Scripture*) defend absolutism Scientific societies founded: Royal Society of London 1662; French Academy of Science 1664 Spinoza publicizes pantheistic philosophy (*Ethics*, 1663) Newton expounds theory of gravitation (Principia, 1687) Locke (*Essay Concerning Human Understanding*, 1690) advances doctrine of popular sovereignty as argument against absolutism; spreads ideas of Enlightenment	**1650**
1700	War of the Spanish Succession 1701–1713; Treaty of Utrecht 1713 Great Northern War 1709–1721; Charles XII of Sweden defeated by Peter the Great and allies Frederick William I of Prussia 1713–1740 creates powerful Prussian state George I 1714–1727 initiates Hanoverian Dynasty in England Robert Walpole becomes first prime minister of England 1721–1742 War of Jenkins' Ear 1739–1745; Peace of Aix-la-Chapelle 1745 Persian invaders sack Delhi 1739 Frederick II, the Great 1740–1786, makes Prussia important power in European politics	"Age of Reason" (eighteenth century); rococo style in art—Watteau, Boucher, Fragonard, Gainsborough, Reynolds Novel appears: Defoe (*Robinson Crusoe*, 1719); Swift (*Gulliver's Travels*, 1726); Richardson (*Pamela*, 1740–1741); Fielding (*Tom Jones*, 1749) Pope, foremost neoclassical English poet (*An Essay on Man*, 1733) Nonconformists in art: Hogarth (*The Rake's Progress*, 1735); Goya (*The Disasters of War*, 1810) Tull, Townshend, Bakewell develop improvements in agriculture Industrial Revolution begins in Britain Inventions revolutionize textile industry: flying shuttle, 1733; spinning jenny, 1764; water frame, 1769; spinning mule, 1779; power loom, 1785; cotton gin, 1793 Further experiments with electricity: Leyden Jar 1745; Franklin's experiment with kite 1752 Intellectual assault on absolutism led by *philosophes* Montesquieu (*The Spirit of Laws*, 1748), Rousseau (*Social Contract*, 1762)	**1700**

Politics	Science and Technology, Thought and Art
1750 Diplomatic revolution aligns Austria, Russia, France against England and Prussia Seven Years' War (in America, the French and Indian War) 1756–1763; Peace of Paris 1763 Catherine the Great 1762–1796 makes Russia a major European power George III of England 1770–1782 secures control of Parliament Poland partitioned in three stages among Russia, Prussia, and Austria 1772–1795 American Revolution 1775–1783; Declaration of Independence 1776 American Articles of Confederation 1781; Constitutional Convention 1787; U.S. Constitution adopted 1789; Washington first president of U.S. Pitt the Younger becomes prime minister 1783; restores cabinet government First phase of French Revolution 1789–1791; storming of Bastille; Declaration of the Rights of Man Second phase of French Revolution; Jacobin movement; Marat, Danton, Robespierre Louis XVI executed 1793; Reign of Terror begins under Robespierre 1793; Robespierre executed 1794; Directory governs France 1795–1799 Napoleon establishes Consulate 1799	**1750** Reaction on the Continent against baroque and rococo styles of architecture manifested in neoclassical style c. 1750 Formalism in music: Handel, Bach, Mozart, Haydn Voltaire, prince of *philosophes*, publishes *Candide* 1759; Diderot spreads doctrines of rationalism and Deism, edits *Encyclopédie* Great works of social science: Rousseau (*Emile*, 1762); Beccaria (*Essay on Crimes and Punishment*, 1764); Gibbon (*Decline and Fall of the Roman Empire*, 1776–1788); Condorcet (*Progress of the Human Mind*, 1794) Modern canal building in Britain begins 1759 Priestly isolates ammonia; discovers oxygen 1774; produces carbon monoxide gas 1799 Adam Smith (*An Inquiry into the Nature and Causes of the Wealth of Nations*, 1776) defends laissez-faire economics Lavoisier formulates law of the conservation of matter Kant (*Critique of Pure Reason*, 1781) sets forth doctrine of philosophic idealism James Watt's steam engine put to commercial use 1785 Hutton's *Theory of the Earth*, 1795, pioneer work in geology
1800 Napoleon proclaims himself emperor 1804; is defeated by British at Trafalgar; defeats Prussia 1805–1806; invasion of Russia fails 1812 British and allies defeat Napoleon at Leipzig 1813; Napoleon exiled to Elba 1814; returns to France and is defeated by Britain and Prussia at Waterloo; exiled to St. Helena 1815 Revolutions in Latin America—Miranda fails in attempt to establish independence of Venezuela; Simon Bolívar, José de San Martin win independence for Spanish colonies in South America; Augustin de Iturbide proclaims independence of Mexico; Pedro crowned emperor of independent Brazil 1822 Congress of Vienna 1814–1815; Metternich, Talleyrand, Alexander I, Lord Castlereagh; Quadruple Alliance formed—Austria, Prussia, Russia, Britain Louis XVIII of France establishes constitutional monarchy 1814–1824 Workers' rebellions in Britain 1816, 1819 Quintuple Alliance 1818—Austria, Russia, Prussia, Britain, France Carlsbad Decrees temporarily discourge German nationalist youth movement 1819	**1800** Romantic movement in art: preromantic writers—Rousseau, Schiller, Goethe Conservatives advocate return to old order—de Maistre, Karamzin, Donoso-Cortés Romantic writers: Wordsworth, Coleridge, Shelley, Byron, Keats, Scott Liberals: Bentham advocates utilitarianism; Mill, early proponent of welfare state Romantic painters: Delacroix, Constable, Turner Romanticism in music: Beethoven, Brahms, Tschaikovsky, Chopin, operas by Wagner and Verdi Romantic nationalist writers: Hugo, Pushkin, Hegel Michelet, Macauley, Bancroft write national histories McAdam develops new method of road construction 1815 Industrial Revolution spreads to Continent 1815–1870 Utopian socialists Saint-Simon, Fourier, Owen propose cooperative societies early 1800s

	Politics	Science and Technology, Thought and Art	
1820	Revolutions in Spain and Italy 1820–1821 Greeks rise against Turkish rule 1821–1827; Greek independence attained at Treaty of Andrianople 1829 Charles X, exponent of divine right, ascends French throne 1824 Tsar Nicholas I crushes Decembrist Revolt 1825; imposes reactionary repressive system Catholic Emancipation Act in Britain 1829	Philhellenic movement in Britain 1820s	**1820**
1830	Revolutions of 1830: July Revolution in Paris enthrones Louis Philippe; Belgians throw off Dutch rule; unsuccessful revolt in Poland Mazzini initiates Italian *Risorgimento* c. 1830 Whigs end reactionary Tory rule in Britain 1830; Reform Bill 1832; slavery abolished 1833 Treaty of Unikar Skelessi 1833 makes Turkey protectorate of Russia Victoria ascends British throne 1837 Chartist movement for reform in Britain fails 1839, 1842, 1848	Gothic revival in architecture c. 1830 Lyell's *Principles of Geology* 1830–1833 Faraday's electric dynamo 1831 *Zollverein* stimulates industry in German states	**1830**
1840	Famine devastates Ireland 1845 Corn Laws repealed 1846 Revolutions of 1848: France, Germany, Italy, Austria France—Second Republic, "June Days" insurrection crushed, Louis Napoleon becomes president Germany—Frederick William IV of Prussia grants constitutional government, Frankfort Assembly fails to establish new union Italy—revolution put down by Austria Austria—nationalist revolutions fail	First Law of thermodynamics stated 1847 Marx and Engels publish *Communist Manifesto* 1848 Victorian writers, poets: Thackeray, Tennyson, Browning Proudhon found anarchism Comte initiates science of sociology	**1840**
1850	Olmutz conference restores German Confederation, sets up Austria as major German power 1850 Cavour becomes prime minister of Italy 1852 Louis Napoleon proclaims himself Emperor Napoleon III 1852 Russia invades Turkey 1853; Crimean War 1854–1856; Russians defeated at Sevastopol; Treaty of Paris 1856 stops Russian advance in Ottoman Empire Italy united under Cavour; Austro-Italian War 1859; first Italian parliament 1861; Rome capital of united Italy 1871 Tsar Alexander II issues Emancipation Proclamation 1861; introduces reforms 1864–1874	Realist mvoement in literature: Balzac, Flaubert, Baudelaire, Dickens, Tolstoy, Dostoevski, Hardy, James, Clemens Social criticism: Arnold, Carlyle, Ruskin Realism in painting: Courbet, Daumier Bessemer improves smelting, refining of iron ore 1850s Great Exhibition, Crystal Palace, London 1851 Darwin publishes *Origin of Species* 1859 Lister introduces antiseptic surgical practices c. 1860 First International fails; anarchists under Bakunin oppose Marxist majority 1864–1873	**1850**
1860	Bismarck appointed Prussian prime minister 1862; advocates policy of *Realpolitik* Policy of repression reimposed by Alexander II 1863 Germany unified under Bismarck; Prussia defeats Denmark 1864, Austria 1866; wins Franco-Prussian War 1870–1871 *Ausgleich* establishes Dual Monarchy of Austria-Hungary 1867 Gladstone and Disraeli alternate as British prime minister 1867–1880; Reform Bill of 1867 extends vote; Gladstone's Glorious Ministry 1868–1874	International Telegraph Union formed 1865 Mendel explains laws of heredity 1866 Marx' scientific socialism expounded in *Das Kapital* 1867–1894 French impressionist painters: Monet, Degas, Renoir; sculptor: Rodin Spencer applies Darwin's theory to social, political, economic activities; Social Darwinism	**1860**

	Politics	Science and Technology, Thought and Art	
1870	Third Republic proclaimed in France 1870 German Second Reich proclaimed: William of Prussia emperor of united Germany Revolutionary Paris Commune suppressed 1871 Bismarck begins *Kulturkampf* 1872; forms Three Emperors' League with Russia and Austria-Hungary 1873; Triple Alliance with Austria and Italy 1882 Social Democratic party formed in Germany 1875; demands social legislation; wins popular support Turkey crushes Bosnian, Bulgarian revolts; defeats Serbia, Montenegro 1875 Russia defeats Turkey 1877–1878; Treaty of San Stefano 1878 Abdul Hamid II attempts to impose absolute rule over Ottoman Empire 1877 Congress of Berlin 1878	Mendeleev classifies all known elements in periodic table 1869 Suez Canal 1869 Darwin publishes *Descent of Man* 1871 Clerk-Maxwell advances electromagnetic theory of light 1873 Universal Postal Union set up 1875 Weismann distinguishes somatic and germ cells	**1870**
1880	Alexander II assassinated 1881; Alexander III revives system of repression; attempts policy of Russification 1881–1884 Three Emperors' League collapses 1887; Bismarck negotiates Reinsurance Treaty with Russia 1887 Spirit of internationalism and peace—annual Universal Peace Congresses begin 1889; Hague Conference 1899 establishes Hague Tribunal	Railroads link major markets in Britain, U.S. 1880 Naturalism in literature: Zola (*Nana*, 1880) Pasteur and Koch prove germ theory of disease 1881 Fabian Society organized in Britain 1883 Postimpressionist painters: Cézanne, van Gogh Realist dramatists: Ibsen, Chekhov, Shaw Symbolist movement: Mallarmé, Verlaine Hertz proves existence of electromagnetic waves 1886 Second International founded 1889; attracts socialists from many countries Pope Leo XIII endorses Christian democracy (*Rerum Novarum*, 1891)	**1880**
1890	Emperor William II dismisses Bismarck 1890; allows Reinsurance Treaty to lapse; France forms Dual Alliance with Russia 1894 Dreyfus case 1894–1906 Nicholas II becomes tsar of Russia 1894 Herzl introduces Zionism; first Zionist congress meets 1897	Freud pioneers psychoanalytic theory 1890s Syndicalists emerge in France 1890s Gobineau advances theory of "scientific racism" First moving picture performance, Paris 1895 X rays discovered 1895 Baron de Coubertin revives Olympic games 1896 Electron theory formulated c. 1897 Pierre and Marie Curie discover radium 1898	**1890**
1900	Labour party formed in Britain 1900: advocates social legislation Britain forms alliance with Japan 1902; proclaims Entente Cordiale with France 1904; establishes Triple Entente with Russia and France 1907 Social Democrats divide into moderate Mensheviks and radical Bolsheviks undere Lenin 1903; massacre of Bloody Sunday 1905; October Manifesto calls national Duma 1905 Anticlerical movement in France severs ties between church and state 1904–1905 Diplomatic crises (Morocco, Balkans) 1905–1914 Young Turks rebel 1908 Parliament Bill of 1911 curtails power of House of Lords Archduke Francis Ferdinand of Austria assassinated 1914; World War I begins	James develops philosophy of pragmatism from Darwinian theory Planck formulates quantum theory 1900 Pavlov advances study of conditioned reflexes 1900 First Nobel Prizes awarded 1901 Music: Richard Strauss (post-Wagnerian); Debussy (impressionism); Stravinski (polytonality); Schönberg (twelve-tone system) Architecture: Sullivan, Wright, Gropius, steel-skeleton skyscraper Expressionist (Matisse) and cubist (Picasso) movements in painting Trans-Siberian Railroad reaches Pacific 1903 Einstein proposes special theory of relativity 1905; general theory 1915 Ford's Model T 1909 Rutherford's theory of positively charged atomic nucleus 1911	**1900**

	United States and Latin America	British Dominions
1750	American Revolution 1775–1783 U.S. Constitution adopted 1789	Peace of Paris 1763; Canada becomes British possession Canada's formative period 1763–1867; Quebec Act 1774 guarantees French custom and Catholicism in Canada; division into Upper and Lower Canada 1791 Sydney, first English colony in Australia, established 1788
1800	Westward expansion of U.S. 1800–1860; Louisiana Purchase 1803; annexation of Texas 1845 War of 1812—U.S. vs. Britain and Canada 1812–1814 Missouri Compromise establishes boundaries of slave territory in U.S. 1820 Brazil achieves independence 1822 Monroe Doctrine 1823 Andrew Jackson president 1829–1837 New nations of Latin America—Bolivia, Peru, Columbia, Venezuela, Ecuador, Paraguay, Uruguay—experience revolutions, insurrections, dictatorships Chile controlled by conservative oligarchy 1830 Central American states—Guatemala, San Salvador, Honduras, Nicaragua, Costa Rica—assert independence c. 1840 Pedro II brings political liberty and economic and cultural progress to Brazil 1840–1899 U.S. signs first treaty with China 1844 U.S.-Mexican War 1846–1848; Mexico cedes California, Texas, territory in Southwest to U.S.	British government assumes protection of New Zealand, 1840
1850	Rapid industrial expansion in U.S. 1850–1880 Perry visits Japan 1853 Mexican dictator Santa Anna overthrown 1855; Juarez institutes anticlerical *Reforma*; civil war ensues U.S. Civil War 1861–1865; Union preserved, slavery abolished Argentina becomes united republic 1862 Napoleon III invades Mexico, establishes brief empire under Maximilian 1863–1867 Reconstruction period in U.S. 1865–1877 U.S. occupies Midway Islands 1867 U.S. buys Alaska from Russia 1867	Australian colonies achieve near self-government c.1850; secret ballot in Australia 1855 Province of Canada form federal union under British North America Act; Canada becomes Confederation 1867
1870	Porfirio Díaz, dictator, brings order without liberty to Mexico 1877–1880, 1884–1911 U.S. Interstate Commerce Act 1887 initiates expansion of government regulation of industry Slavery ends in Brazil 1888 First Pan-American Conference 1889 Ten years of civil war in Brazil 1889–1899 follows abdication of Pedro II Progressive movement in U.S. initiates economic reform c. 1890–1914 "Dollar diplomacy"—U.S. exercises indirect controls in Latin America to protect investments 1890–1920s Spanish-American War 1898; U.S. gains Philippines, Guam, Puerto Rico; Cuba becomes protectorate 1901 U.S. annexes Hawaii 1898	Treaty of Washington 1871; Canada and U.S. arbitrate major differences Woman suffrage introduced in New Zealand 1893
1900	Open Door Policy in China declared 1900 U.S. emerges as most powerful nation in Western Hemisphere c. 1900 Theodore Roosevelt 1901–1909 follows policy of trustbust- ing, conservation of resources, extended government regulation of railroads, foods, drugs	Commonwealth of Australia formed 1901

Asia	Africa	
Battle of Plassey 1757 begins domination of India by British East India Company and Britain; Parliament takes control of East India Company 1773; appoints its highest official, governor general of India 1784 English acquire Ceylon from Dutch 1796 Dutch government takes over East Indies; abolishes Dutch East India Company 1798		
	Britain acquires Cape Colony from France 1806 French army occupies Algeria 1830 Boer Great Trek 1836; Boers establish Orange Free State and the Transvaal	**1800**
China wars with Britain over opium and Western exploitation 1839–1842; Treaty of Nanking 1842; Hong Kong ceded to Britain, new ports opened to trade		
Taiping rebellion—revolt against the Manchu 1850–1864; Manchu Empress Tsu-hsi establishes national stability and furthers Chinese hatred of West 1861–1908 Japan opens first ports to West after Perry's visit 1854 British crush Indian mutiny 1857; relieve British East India Company of political responsibilities 1858 Russia penetrates land of the Caucasus, Turkestan c. 1860–1870 Meiji period in Japan 1868–1912; emperor made supreme authority; Japan modernized	Britain makes treaties with Boers acknowledging their independence 1852, 1854 Livingstone begins explorations in Central Africa 1853 Algeria incorporated into French state 1857 Increased friction between Britons and Boers 1860–1870 Suez Canal completed 1869	**1850**
Russia pushes south to Afghanistan and India c. 1870–1880 Indian National Congress formed 1885 Burma conquered by British c. 1885; Burma annexed to India French gain control over Indochina c. 1885 Macao ceded to Portugal 1887 New constitution promulgated in Japan 1889 Japan defeats China in Sino-Japanese War 1894–1895 Filipinos rebel against American forces 1899–1902	Europe's golden age of imperialism 1870–1914 Belgium—Leopold II acquires Congo region 1876–1882; Leopold forced to turn over Congo Free State to Belgian government 1908 France—Egypt under joint financial control of Britain and France 1879; French obtain Tunisia 1881; Morocco made a French protectorate 1912 Britain gains practical control of Suez Canal 1875; joint control of Egypt by Britain and France 1879; Lord Cromer assumes administration in Egypt 1883–1907; Somaliland is taken 1884; protectorate over Bechuanaland declared 1885; area developed for Britain by Rhodes' British South Africa Company named Rhodesia 1890; Anglo-Egyptian Sudan conquered 1898; Gambia, Sierra Leone, Gold Coast, Nigeria gained through Royal Niger Company 1900 Germany acquires Togoland, Cameroons, German East Africa, German Southwest Africa 1800s; British and Germans settle dispute over territories in East Africa 1886, 1890 Italy fails in attempted capture of Abyssinia (Ethiopia) 1896 Zulu war with British in South Africa 1879 Gold discovered in Transvaal 1885 Boer War 1899–1902; British defeat Dutch	**1870**
Anglo-Russian entente; Persia put under dual control of Britain and Russia 1907 Japan annexes Korea 1910; accepted as first-class power	Boers and Britons join states and form Union of South Africa 1909 Italy wrests Tripoli from Turks 1912	**1900**

International Politics	Western Democracies
1914 World War I—Germans invade Belgium, France, Poland 1914; Italy joins Allies 1915; Allies' Somme offensive 1916; Italian front smashed at Caporetto, U.S. enters war 1917; Russia signs Treaty of Brest Litovsk with Germany, armistice signed 1918	
Wilson presents Fourteen Points 1918	
Paris Peace Conference; League of Nations established 1919; Treaty of Versailles signed with Germany, Treaty of St.-Germain with Austria, Treaty of Neuilly with Bulgaria 1919; Treaty of Sèvres with Ottoman Empire, Treaty of Trianon with Hungary 1920	U.S. rejects membership in League of Nations 1919
	Irish Free State created in southern Ireland 1921
Little Entente (Czechoslovakia, Rumania, Yugoslavia) formed 1920–1921	Conservative Republican era in U.S. politics—Harding 1921–1923; Coolidge 1923–1929; Hoover 1929–1933
Washington Conference—limited naval disarmament 1921–1922	U.S. Hawley-Smoot (1930) Tariff Act levies high tariffs, jeopardizes war-debt payments, reparations
Nine-Power Treaty—signatories agree to respect sovereignty of China 1922	MacDonald, Britain's first Labour prime minister 1924; Conservatives in power 1924–1929; general strike 1926
Russia negotiates Treaty of Rapallo with Germany 1922	
Mussolini defies League of Nations in Corfu incident 1923	
France invades German Ruhr 1923–1924	
Dawes Plan eases German reparations. France evacuates Ruhr 1924	
Locarno Pact 1925	
Kellogg-Briand Pact renounces war 1928	
1929	Stock market crash in U.S. leads to world depression 1929
Young Plan scales down reparations payments 1930	Labour party regains power in Britain 1929–1931
	Revolutions in six South American nations 1930
Mussolini conquers Ethiopia 1936	Spain becomes republic 1931
	Statute of Westminster creates constitution for British Commonwealth of Nations (Canada, Australia, New Zealand, South Africa) 1931
Rome-Berlin Axis formed, Japan and Germany form Anti-Comintern Pact 1936; Italy joins Pact 1937	
Spanish civil war 1936–1939	U.S. inaugurates Good Neighbor Policy with Latin America 1933
	Franklin D. Roosevelt becomes president of U.S. 1933; inaugurates New Deal
Hitler engineers coup in Austria 1938	
Surrender of Sudetenland to Germany at Munich 1938; Hitler seizes Czechoslovakia, Mussolini seizes Albania 1939	Leftist Popular Front gains power in France 1936
	Conservatives regain control in France 1937
	Neville Chamberlain, advocate of appeasement, becomes prime minister of Britain 1937
1939 Russia, Germany sign nonaggression pact 1939	
World War II—Germany invades Poland; France, Britain declare war 1939; *Sitzkrieg*; Russia defeats Finland 1939–1940; Hitler seizes Denmark, Norway, Low Countries, France 1940; Battle of Britain; Italian invasion of Greece and Africa fails; Hitler seizes Hungary, Balkans 1940–1941; Germany attacks Russia; Atlantic Charter signed; Pearl Harbor attack brings U.S. into war 1941; Japanese victories in Pacific 1941–1942; battles of Midway and Coral Sea; Rommel victorious in Libya 1942; Soviets seize offensive in Russia; Axis surrender in Africa; Italy invaded; Teheran Conference 1943; Allies launch second front; battle of Leyte 1944; Yalta agreements; Germany surrenders; A-bomb dropped on Japan	Churchill becomes prime minister of Britain 1940 U.S. passes Lend-Lease Act 1941
1945 Japanese surrender 1945	

Rise of Totalitarianism	Asia and Africa	
Russian Revolution—Duma names provisional government, tsar abdicates, Bolsheviks under Lenin seize government 1917; Bolsheviks destroy White Russian resistance 1918–1920	Japan presents Twenty-one Demands to China 1915 Arabs revolt against Ottoman rule 1916–1918 Balfour Declaration 1917	**1914**
Period of war communism 1918–1921 German revolution 1918; Weimar Republic set up 1919 Third Communist International (Comintern) formed 1919	Mustafa Kemal Pasha of Turkey defies Allies 1918–1922 Government of India Act of 1919, Rowlatt Act passed, Gandhi begins campaign for independence 1919	
NEP—Lenin restores some capitalistic practices 1921–1928 Mussolini establishes National Fascist party 1921; seizes Italian government in march on Rome 1922; divides Italian economy into government-controlled syndicates Union of Soviet Socialist Republics established 1922 Hitler stages unsuccessful *Putsch* in Munich 1923; begins *Mein Kampf* 1925	French repress Arab nationalism in Morocco, Tunisia, Algeria, Syria, Lebanon 1919–1939 San Remo Conference—Allies overrule Arab nationalism, create mandates from Arab territories 1920 Communist party 1920, Indonesian Nationalist part 1927 oppose Dutch rule in East Indies Sun Yat-sen controls Canton government in China 1921–1925 Riza Shah Pahlavi seizes Iran government 1921–1925 British grant constitution to Burma 1922	
Election of Hindenburg as president underlines rising German ultranationalism 1925	Egypt becomes sovereign, with British restrictions 1923 Republic of Turkey set up, Teaty of Lausanne signed 1923 Ibn-Saud gains control of Arabian peninsula 1924–1925 Universal Manhood Suffrage Bill passed in Japan 1925 Chiang Kai-shek purges Communists 1927; conquers Peking, unites China 1928	
Dictatorships formed in Lithuania 1926; Yugoslavia 1929 Trotsky loses bid for power to Stalin 1927 Stalin purges rivals 1928–1931, 1934–1938 Stalin inaugurates first Five-Year Plan 1928 Mussolini negotiates Lateran Treaty with Catholic church 1928; Vatican City declared sovereign independent state	Hamaguchi's ministry peak of liberalism in Japan 1929; Hamaguchi assassinated, liberal setback 1930 Iraq gains full independence from Britain 1930 Round-table conferences in India 1930–1932 Arab violence in British mandate of Palestine 1930s Italian Fascists cement rule in Libya 1930s Segregation, unrest grow in Union of South Africa 1930s	**1929**
Russia begins second Five-Year Plan 1933 Hitler becomes dictator of Germany, proclaims Third Reich; Germany withdraws from League of Nations 1933; first Four-Year Plan established 1933, second 1936 Nuremberg laws enacted 1935 Germany reoccupies Rhineland 1936	Communists oppose French rule in Indochina 1930s British grant progressive constitution to Ceylon 1931 Japan invades Manchuria 1931 Chinese Communists proclaim Chinese Soviet Republic 1931; Chiang launches campaigns against Communists 1931–1934 Ibn-Saud's holdings renamed Saudi Arabia 1932 Japan attacks Shanghai 1932 Japan withdraws from League of Nations 1933	
Italy withdraws from League of Nations 1937 Russia initiates third Five-Year Plan 1938	Chinese-Japanese truce 1933 recognizes Japanese conquests in Manchuria, northern China Commonwealth of Philippines formed 1935 Government of India Act of 1935 goes into effect in British India 1937–1939; rejected by native princes 1939 British grant Burma restricted home rule 1937 War breaks out again between Japan and China 1937; Japan proclaims New Order in Asia 1938	
Fascist dictator Franco gains power, ends republic after Spanish civil war 1939		**1939**
	Tojo becomes premier of Japan 1941	
		1945

	International Politics	Asia and Africa
1945	Yalta Conference (Roosevelt, Churchill, Stalin) February 1945; Cold War begins Surrender of Nazi Germany May 1945 UN Charter signed June 1945 Hiroshima bombed August 1945 Surrender of Japan August 1945 Germany divided into four zones October 1946 Truman Doctrine enunciated March 1947 Berlin blockade and airlift June 1948–September 1949 Korean War begins 1950 Korean armistice signed at Panmunjon July 1953 French defeated at Dien Bien Phu May 1954; Vietnam divided July 1954	Civil war in China 1946–1949 Independence of India and Pakistan August 1947 Mahatma Gandhi assassinated January 1948 State of Israel established May 1948 Republic of Korea proclaimed August 1948 Communist victory in China; People's Republic of China established September 1949 Indonesia becomes independent December 1949 Mau Mau rebellion in Kenya 1952 Egypt declared a republic June 1953 Nassar becomes premier of Egypt February 1954 Beginning of nationalist revolt in Algeria 1954 Laos, Cambodia, Vietnam become independent states 1954 Suez crisis July 1956 Israelis invade Sinai peninsula October 1956 Beginning of decolonization in sub-Saharan Africa 1957 First conference of independent African states April 1958
1960	Big Four Paris summit meeting collapses May 1960 UN Security Council authorizes peacekeeping forces in Congo February 1961 Increasing U.S. involvement in Vietnam 1961 Berlin Wall constructed August 1961 U.S., Britain, USSR sign nuclear test ban treaty August 1963 U.S. begins bombing North Vietnam February 1965 Arab-Israeli Six-Day War June 5–10, 1967 Suez Canal closed 1967–1973 UN accepts nuclear nonproliferation treaty June 1968 U.S. bombing of North Vietnam ends October 1968	Many African states become independent; civil war in Belgian Congo 1960 Sino-Soviet dispute begins 1960 South Africa becomes independent republic 1961 Sino-Indian war 1962 Algeria becomes independent 1962 Communist China explodes its first atomic bomb October 1964 Indo-Pakistan war 1965 Military takeover in Indonesia 1965 Rhodesia declares its independence from Britain November 1965 Indira Gandhi becomes prime minister of India January 1966 Cultural Revolution in China 1966 Civil war in Nigeria; secession of Biafra 1967–1970
1970	U.S. detente with China, USSR 1971 People's Republic of China admitted to UN December 1971 SALT I treaty May 1972 Paris Accord ends U.S. fighting in Vietnam January 1973 U.S. troops withdraw from Vietnam 1973 Suez Canal reopened 1973 Arab oil embargo October 1973–April 1974 U.S., USSR sign five-year nuclear test treaty May 1976 UN orders arms embargo against South Africa November 1977 Camp David Accords between Sadat of Egypt and Begin of Israel September 1978 U.S., People's Republic of China establish full diplomatic relations January 1979 Egypt, Israel sign peace treaty March 1979 U.S. embassy seized, U.S. hostages taken in Iran November 1979	Rhodesia becomes republic March 1970 Nasser dies; Sadat becomes premier of Egypt September–October 1970 Bangladesh declares independence from Pakistan March 1971 Communist takeover of Vietnam, Laos, Cambodia April 1975 Fall of Shah of Iran; Ayatollah Khomeini takes over government January–February 1979 Vietnam invades Cambodia, expelling Khmer Rouge government 1979 South Korean president Park Chung Lee assassinated October 1979
1980	U.S. hostages freed by Iran January 1981 Argentina invades Falkland Islands April 1982 U.S., USSR open SALT talks June 1982 Britain reclaims Falkland Islands June 1982 U.S. President Reagan, USSR General Secretary Gorbachev meet at Geneva summit conference November 1985 U.S. bombs Libya 1986 U.S., USSR sign INF treaty providing for elimination of intermediate-range land-based nuclear weapons 1987 Berlin Wall opened November 1989	Zimbabwe wins independence April 1980 Shah of Iran dies July 1980 Iran-Iraq war breaks out September 1980 Mao's widow, nine others found guilty of counterrevolutionary crimes December 1980 Egyptian president Sadat assassinated; succeeded by Mubarak October 1981 Israel invades Lebanon June 1982 Massacre of Palestinian refugees in Beirut September 1982 Libya invades Chad August 1983 Famine in Ethiopia 1984 Indira Gandi assassinated October 1984 Civil unrest in South Africa 1985 Corazon Aquino replaces Marcos as Philippines president February 1986 South Africa declares national state of emergency in response to racial tensions June 1986 Palestinian uprising (*intifada*) against Israeli-occupied territories 1988 Ceasefire in Iran-Iraq war 1988 Emperor Hirohito of Japan dies; succeeded by son Akihito 1989 Ayatollah Khomeini dies 1989 Student demonstrators massacred at Tiananmen Square in China May–June 1989
1990	Germany reunited 1990 Multi-party elections throughout Eastern Europe 1990	Namibia becomes independent 1990 Nelson Mandela released from prison in South Africa 1990 Iraq invades Kuwait; announces annexation of Kuwait August 1990 Operation "Desert Storm" in Persian Gulf January– February 1991

Western Democracies	Soviet Bloc Nations	
New constitution establishes French Fourth Republic October 1946 Greek civil war 1947–1949 European Recovery Plan (Marshall Plan) introduced June 1947 Organization of American States (OAS) established 1948 Formation of NATO alliance April 1959 German Federal Republic (West Germany) established May 1949 Turkey and Greece join NATO September 1951 West Germany admitted to NATO May 1955 Creation of European Economic Community (Common Market) March 1957 Fifth Republic in France; de Gaulle becomes premier of France June 1958 Cuban Revolution 1959	Communist coup in Czechoslovakia February 1968 Communist takeover in Hungary 1968 Tito defects from Soviet bloc; Yugoslavia expelled from Cominform June 1968 German Democratic Republic (East Germany) formed May 1949 Explosion of first Soviet atomic bomb announced September 1949 USSR, People's Republic of China sign 30-year alliance February 1950 Stalin dies March 1953 USSR, Eastern European satellites sign Warsaw Pact May 1955 Revolution in Hungary crushed by Soviet army October–November 1956 USSR launches Sputnik; Space Age begins October 1957 Khrushchev becomes Soviet premier March 1958	**1945**
Cuban missile crisis October 1962 France vetoes British entry to Common Market January 1963 West German chancellor Adenauer resigns October 1963 U.S. President Kennedy assassinated November 1963 France announces withdrawal of French troops from NATO March 1966 De Gaulle resigns April 1969 Pompidou elected premier of France June 1969 U.S. astronauts land on moon July 1969 Willy Brandt elected chancellor of West Germany October 1969	Sino-Soviet rift splits Communist world 1963 Khrushchev ousted; replaced by Brezhnev and Kosygin October 1964 Soviet invasion of Czechoslovakia August 1968	**1960**
Britain, Ireland, Denmark join Common Market (EEC) 1973 Major recession in U.S. 1973 Brandt resigns; Schmidt becomes West German chancellor May 1974 Nixon resigns as U.S. president August 1974 Franco dies; succeeded by Juan Carlos I; end of dictatorship in Spain November 1975 Democratic elections in Spain 1977 Margaret Thatcher becomes British prime minister May 1979 Civil war in Nicaragua; Somoza overthrown 1979	Brezhnev named Soviet chief of state June 1977 USSR invades Afghanistan December 1979	**1970**
Mitterand elected president of France May 1981 Greece joins Common Market (EEC) 1981 Kohl elected West German chancellor October 1982 U.S., six Caribbean nations invade Grenada October 1983 Democracy restored in Brazil, Uruguay 1985 U.S. space shuttle Challenger explodes on takeoff January 1986 Soares sworn in as Portugal's first civilian president in 60 years March 1986 Spain and Portugal join Common Market (EEC) 1986 U.S. invades Panama December 1989	Tito dies May 1980 Independent Polish trade union Solidarity created October 1980 Brezhnev dies; succeeded by Andropov November 1982 Andropov dies; succeeded by Chernenko February 1984 Chernenko dies; Gorbachev comes to power in USSR March 1985 Nuclear reactor disaster at Chernobyl in USSR April–May 1986 Gorbachev announces policies of *glasnost* and *perestroika* 1988 Communist regimes in East Germany, Czechoslovakia, Bulgaria, Romania fall 1988 USSR withdraws troops from Afghanistan 1989 Spread of nationalism in USSR; Lithuania declares independence 1989	**1980**
Democratic elections in Nicaragua end Sandinista rule	Nationalist uprisings in Armenia and Azerbaijan result in communal massacres	**1990**

Credits

Color Photographs

Cover   The British Library

Portfolio One following p. 96
1   Alex Greely/Alpha/FPG
2   (both) Reproduced by Courtesy of the British Museum
3   Erich Lessing/Magnum
4   (l) Reproduced by Courtesy of the Trustees of the British Museum (r) Robert Frerck/Odyssey Productions, Chicago
5   (t) Hirmer Fotoarchiv, Munich (b) Staatliche Antikensammlungen und Glyptothek, Munich
6   Ray Garner/FPG
7   Scala/Art Resource, NY
8   Scala/Art Resource, NY

Portfolio Two following p. 160
1   Robert Frerck/Odyssey Productions, Chicago
2   V. Punjabi/Shostal/SuperStock
3   (t) Courtesy of The Cultural Relics Bureau, Beijing and The Metropolitan Museum of Art (b) Ma Yuan, *Bare Willows and Distant Mountains*, c. 1200. Chinese, Southern Song dynasty. Round album leaf: ink & colors on silk, 23.8 × 21.2 cm. Chinese and Japanese Special Fund, Courtesy, Museum of Fine Arts, Boston
4   The Seattle Art Museum, Eugene Fuller Memorial Collection, 48.173

Portfolio Three following p. 256
1   (l) The Board of Trinity College Dublin (r) Reproduced by Courtesy of the Trustees of the British Museum
2   The Pierpont Morgan Library, M. 1, Front cover
3   (t) The Pierpont Morgan Library, M. 736, f. 18v (b) Scala/Art Resource, NY
4   John Baker/Shostal/SuperStock

Portfolio Four following p. 400
1   Scala/Art Resource, NY
2   (t) Alinari/Art Resource, NY (b) Scala/Art Resource, NY
3   (both) Scala/Art Resource, NY
4   (t) Giraudon/Art Resource, NY (b) Saskia/Art Resource, NY

Portfolio Five following p. 464
1   (t) Courtesy of the Freer Gallery of Art, Smithsonian Institution, Washington, D. C. (45.9) (b) W. H. Purnell/Shostal/SuperStock
2   (t) The Cleveland Museum of Art, Bequest of John L. Severance (b) Tokyo National Museum
3   (both) Lee Boltin
4   Lee Boltin

Portfolio Six following p. 528
1   Dulwich Picture Gallery/Bridgeman/Art Resource, NY

2   Sir Joshua Reynolds, *Lady Elizabeth Delme and Her Children*. National Gallery of Art, Washington, Andrew W. Mellon Collection
3   The Metropolitan Museum of Art, Wolfe Fund, 1931. Catharine Lorillard Wolfe Collection (31.45)
4   Carle/Shostal/SuperStock

Portfolio Seven following p. 656
1   Jim Howard/Alpha/FPG
2   (t) The Metropolitan Museum of Art, Bequest of Mary Stillman Harkness, 1950 (50.145.8) (b) Scala/Art Resource, NY
3   The Metropolitan Museum of Art, Gift of Harry Payne Bingham, 1940 (40.175)
4   Claude Monet, *Water Lilies*, 1906, oil on canvas, 87.6 × 92.7 cm, Mr. and Mrs. Martin A. Ryerson Collection, 1933.1157. © 1992 The Art Institute of Chicago. All Rights Reserved.
5   (tl) Mary Cassatt, *The Bath*, 1891/92, oil on canvas, 39½ × 26″, Robert A. Waller Fund, 1910.2. ©1992 The Art Institute of Chicago. All Rights Reserved. (tr) Pierre Auguste Renoir, *Two Sisters (On the Terrace)*, 1881, oil on canvas, 100.5 × 81 cm, Mr. and Mrs. Lewis Larned Coburn Memorial Collection, 1933.455. © 1992 The Art Institute of Chicago. All Rights Reserved. (b) The Metropolitan Museum of Art, Bequest of Mrs. H. O. Havemeyer, 1929. The H. O. Havemeyer Collection (29.100.128)
6   Philadelphia Museum of Art, George W. Elkins Collection
7   Vincent van Gogh, *The Starry Night*, (1889). Oil on canvas, 29 × 36¼″. Collection, The Museum of Modern Art, New York. Acquired through the Lillie P. Bliss Bequest
8   Cliché des Musées Nationaux, Paris

Portfolio Eight following p. 800
1   The Saint Louis Art Museum, Museum purchase
2   (t) Art Resource, NY (b) Werner Forman Archive
3   Pablo Picasso, *Girl Before a Mirror*, 1932. Oil on canvas, 64 × 51¼″. Collection, The Museum of Modern Art, New York. Gift of Mrs. Simon Guggenheim
4   (t) Copyright 1992 ARS, N.Y./ADAGP (b) Salvador Dali, *The Persistence of Memory*, 1931. Oil on canvas, 9½ × 13″. Collection, The Museum of Modern Art, New York. Given anonymously
5   Kunstmuseum, Basel. © COSMOPRESS, Geneva/VAGA, New York
6   Alexander Calder, *Lobster Trap and Fish Tail* (1939). Hanging mobile: painted steel wire and sheet aluminum, about 8′ 6″ high × 9′ 6″ diameter. Collection, The Museum of Modern Art, New York. Commissioned by the Advisory Committee for the stairwell of the Museum
7   Michael Fedison
8   Des Moines Art Center, James D. Edmundson Fund, 1958

Portfolio Nine following p. 912
1   The Nelson-Atkins Museum of Art, Kansas City, Missouri. Gift of William Inge, 56–128

772 Imperial War Museum, London
774 Imperial War Museum, London
775 Imperial War Museum, London
776 Keystone-Mast Collection, California Museum of Photography, University of California, Riverside
778 (t) Imperial War Museum, London (b) U.S. Signal Corps/National Archives
781 Imperial War Museum, London
784 Brown Brothers
786 National Archives
788 *Illustrite Zeitung*, May 22, 1919
792 Historical Pictures Service, Chicago
793 UPI/Bettmann
794 UPI/Bettmann
797 New York Daily News Photo
798 UPI/Bettmann
799 UPI/Bettmann
801 (t) *Illustrated London News*, October 17, 1931 (b) AP/Wide World
802 AP/Wide World
803 David Seymour/Magnum
805 UPI/Bettmann
807 (t) UPI/Bettmann (b) The Franklin D. Roosevelt Library
811 Brown Brothers
812 Courtesy Schocken Books
813 Chicago Architectural Photo Co.
817 UPI/Bettmann
819 UPI/Bettmann
821 UPI/Bettmann
822 Sovfoto
826 Sovfoto
828 UPI/Bettmann
829 UPI/Bettmann
831 AP/Wide World
833 (both) UPI/Bettmann
835 UPI/Bettmann
836 UPI/Bettmann
837 Staatliche Museen Preussischer Kulturbesitz, Nationalgalerie, Berlin
838 Popperfoto
840 (t) UPI/Bettmann (b) AP/Wide World
841 (t) Wiener Library, London (b) Ullstein Bilderdienst
842 (l) U.S. Information Agency/National Archives (r) Pressefoto: E. Thaler, Berlin
849 Jerry Doyle, *Philadelphia Daily News*, 1931
851 Culver Pictures
853 UPI/Bettmann
854 UPI/Bettmann
857 Margaret Bourke-White, *Life* Magazine, © Time Warner Inc.
858 AP/Wide World
859 The Hulton Picture Company
863 The Hulton Picture Company
864 The Hulton Picture Company
867 Brown Brothers
868 AP/Wide World
870 NAACP
874 (t) Reprinted by permission: Triburn Media Services (b) William A. Ireland, *The Columbus Dispatch*
875 UPI/Bettmann
876 UPI/Bettmann
878 UPI/Bettmann
879 UPI/Bettmann
880 U.S. Information Agency/National Archives
881 UPI/Bettmann
882 Austrian National Library, Vienna

885 AP/Wide World
888 Photo by Kerlee/U.S. Navy/National Archives
889 UPI/Bettmann
890 Imperial War Museum, London
892 British Information Services, New York
894 AP/Wide World
895 AP/Wide World
896 Imperial War Museum, London
898 U.S. Coast Guard
899 The Franklin D. Roosevelt Library
906 Otto Hagel
907 United Nations
910 Consulate General of Germany
911 U.S. Army
913 (t) Sovfoto (b) AP/Wide World
917 AP/Wide World
919 AP/Wide World
920 AP/Wide World
921 AP/Wide World
922 UPI/Bettmann
923 (t) AP/Wide World (b) UPI/Bettmann
925 UPI/Bettmann
926 UPI/Bettmann
927 Alex Webb/Magnum
930 AP/Wide World
931 AP/Wide World
937 Contifoto/Sygma
942 (l) Nik Wheeler/Black Star (r) Asahi Shimbun Photo
944 Sovfoto/Eastfoto
947 AP/Wide World
948 AP/Wide World
950 UPI/Bettmann
952 Larry Burrows, *Life* Magazine, © Time Warner Inc.
953 (t) Nik Wheeler/Black Star (b) UPI/Bettmann
955 AP/Wide World
956 AP/Wide World
957 AP/Wide World
959 UPI/Bettmann
960 AP/Wide World
962 Reuters/Bettmann
965 UPI/Bettmann
968 AP/Wide World
973 UPI/Bettmann
974 UPI/Bettman
975 Pete Souza/The White House
978 AP/Wide World
980 Bill Swersey/NYT Pictures
981 Robert Nickelsberg/Gamma-Liaison
983 Peter Jordan/Gamma-Liaison
985 Michael Evans/The White House
986 Syndication International/Photo Trends
991 Wassily Kandinsky, *In the Black Square*, 1928. Collection, Solomon R. Guggenheim Museum, New York. Photo: Robert E. Mates
992 Jacket illustration by John Held, Jr. of F. Scott Fitzgerald's *Tales of the Jazz Age* is reproduced by permission of Charles Scribner's Sons
993 Dorothea Lange for FSA/Library of Congress
994 (l) Bob Verlin/Monkmeyer Press (r) AP/Wide World
995 The Museum of Modern Art/Film Stills Archive
996 Vyto Starinskas/Sygma
997 John Dominis/*Time* Magazine
E2 AP/Wide World
E3 Ken Heyman
E5 AP/Wide World
E6 AP/Wide World

Index

Suggested pronunciations for difficult or unusual words are respelled according to the table below. The local pronunciation of many foreign words are too unusual for persons untrained in linguistics, and pronunciations given here are those commonly acceptable in unaffected, educated American speech.

a	hat, cap	
ā	age, face	
ã	care, air	
ä	father, far	
b	bad, rob	
ch	child, much	
d	did, red	
e	let, best	
ē	equal, see	
ėr	term, learn	
f	fat, if	
g	go, bag	
h	he, how	
i	it, pin	
ī	ice, five	

j	jam, enjoy
k	kind, seek
l	land, coal
m	me, am
n	no, in
ng	long, bring
o	hot, rock
ō	open, go
ô	order, all
oi	oil, toy
ou	out, now
p	pet, cup
r	run, try
s	say, yes
sh	she, rush
t	tell, it
th	thin, both
TH	then, smooth

u	cup, son
ù	put, book
ü	rule, move
ū	use, music
v	very, save
w	will, woman
y	you, yet
z	zero, breeze
zh	measure, seizure

ə represents:
a in *about*
e in tak*e*n
i in penc*i*l
o in lem*o*n
u in circ*u*s

Foreign Sounds

Y as in French *lune*. Pronounce ē with the lips rounded as for English ü in *rule*.

Œ as in French *deux*. Pronounce ā with the lips rounded as for ō.

N as in French *bon*. The N is not pronounced, but shows that the vowel before it is nasal.

H as in German *ach*. Pronounce *k* without closing the breath passage.

Numbers preceded by PF refer to Portfolio pages E the Epilogue

Spice trade, 125, 264, 420, 425, 445
Spice Islands, 387, 441, 744
"spider king." See Louis XI
Spinoza, Baruch, 532, 535, 538
Srivijaya empire, 385
St. Augustine, settlement of, 428
St. Bartholomew's Eve massacre, 455
St. Helena, 131
St. Mark's Cathedral (Venice), 294
St. Peter's Basilica, 319, 321, 470
St. Peter's Fields, 646, 652
St. Petersburg, 490
Stadtholders, 485
  rise of, 465
Staël, Mme. de, 561
Stalin, Joseph, 816, 822, 823
  Cold War and, 908
  conduct of World War II, 892, 894, 897–898
  genocide by, 912
  international expansion by, 908
  protégés of, 915–916
  relations with Germany, 887
  relations with Tito, 925
  rise of, 824–825
  rule after World War II, 912
  totalitarian rule of, 825–830
Stalingrad, battle of, 897
Stamp Act (1765), 550, 551
Stanley, Henry M., 732
Star Chamber, court of, 466
START (Strategic Arms Reduction Treaty), 918, 975
Statute-petition duplication, 289
Stavisky, Alexander, 803
Stephen II, pope, alliance with Pepin, 174
Stephen, king of Hungary, 182
Stephen, nephew of Henry I, 248
Steppe frontier, and rise of Muslim empires, 364
Steppe nomads, 388
Steppe societies, 380
Stettinus, Edward, Jr., 907
Stock exchanges, growth of, 475, 503, 505
Stoicism, 64–65, 86, 92, 94, 135, 146
Stolypin, Peter, 667
Strabo, 126
Strafford, Earl of, 466
Strait of Gibraltar, 264
Strasbourg, in Reformation, 356
Strasbourg Oaths, 231
Strategic Arms Limitation treaty (SALT), 974
Strategic Defense Initiative, 975
Stravinsky, Igor, 812
Stresemann, Gustav, 876
Stuart, John, 692
Styria, 340
Sub-Sahara Africa, 421, M3
  hybrid civilizations, 396–417

native cultures, 390–396
European imperialism in, 732–735
native governments of, 575–576
rise of colonialism in, 570–575
Sudan, 17, 390, 391, 396, M5
Sudetenland, 805, 885
Sudra Strait, 386
Suffolk, Duchess of, 455
Suffrage movement, 555, 556, 600
Sufi Muslims, 387
Sugar Act (1764), 550, 552
Suharto, T. N. J., 950
Sui dynasty, 123, 200
Sukarno, Achmed, 950
Sulayman, 579
Suleiman I, the Magnificent, 366–368
Sulla, Cornelius, 81
Sullivan, Louis, 813
Sully, Duke of, 471
Sultanates, 365, 367, 396
Sumatra, 375, 385, 386, 441
Sumer, 8–11, 15, 26, 31, PF1
Sumner, William Grant, 679
Sun Yat-Sen, 752, 850–851
Sundiata dynasty, 402–403
Sung dynasty, 200, 375, 386
  art of, PF2
  culture in, 207–208
  economic and social conditions in, 205–208
  political system of, 204–205
  tributary status of Korea, 380
Sunni Islam, 155, 162, 368
  Akbar and, 372
Susenyos, emperor of Ethiopia, 438
Sutton Hoo treasure, PF3
Suzerainty, 249
Sviatoslav, Kievan hetman, 186
Swabian nobles, 256, 259
Swahili, 396, 399, 401
Swammerdam, Jan, 528
Sweden, 349
  in Great Northern War, 490
  interwar government in, 799
Swendenborg, Emanuel, 542
Swiss Reformation, 352–353
Switzerland, growth of Protestantism in, 352–353
Syene (Aswan), 15
Sykes-Picot Agreement, 859–860
Symeon, tsar of Bulgaria, 181
Synod of 1076, 268
Syracuse, 51
Syria, 9, 17, 24, 31, 109, 125, 126, 160, 163, 173, 261, 365, 783, 859
  Maunder Mamluk rule, 164
  Muslim conquest of, 174
  role in Middle East, 961
Szechwan, 379

T
Tabriz, 220
Tacitus, 85, 93, 133, 234
  writings of, 94
Tagore, Rabindranath, 997

Tahiti, European discovery of, 583, 584
Tahsmap, 368
Taika reforms, 210–212
Taiping rebellion, 749–750
Taiwan, 948, 976
Taj Mahal, 168, 373, PF5
Taklamakan desert, M2
Talleyrand, Charles Maurice de, prince, 625, 626–627
Tamerlane, 180, 199, 365
Tamil Land, 99, 109, 111
T'ang dynasty, 380, 386
  culture of, 203–204
  decline of, 204
  economy and society during, 202–203
  international affairs of, 215
  political system of, 201–202
  predecessors to, 200–201
  rise of, 201–202
Tanganyika, 736, 866, M4
  British rule over, 736
Tannenberg, battle of, 185
Tanner, Henry Ossawa, 707
Tanzania, 2, 998
Tao (the Way), 116
Taoism, 116–117, 200, 203
  popular (Chinese), 124
Tarawa, 900
Tarik, 160
Tarquin the Proud, 72
Tasmania, genocide in, 695
Taxation
  Akabar's reforms, 372
  class inequities, 453
  French, 341, 502
  and growth of towns, 267
  in late Mughul empire, 374
  by the medieval church, 282
  of the medieval church, 282
  Reformation spurred by, 338
  resistance by papacy and Lombard League, 259
  taille, 290, 499
  by Tudors, 341
Taylor, Frederick W., 684
Tehuacan Valley, 405
Temixtitan, 426
Templars, 254, 264
Temple at Jerusalem, 139, 140, 264
Temple of Good Harvest, 377
Temple of Heaven, 377
Ten, Council of, 294
Ten Kingdoms, 204
Tencin, Madame de, 532
Tenochtitlán, 411, 426, 427, 428, 429
Teotihuacan, 407, 408
Tepe, Vlad, 182
Terence, 311
Teresa of Avila, saint, 360
Tet offensive, 952
Tetzel, Johann, 344
Teutonic Knights, 264
Tezcatilipoca, 410
Thackeray, William Makepeace, 619
Thailand, 385, 387
  commercial alliance with Dutch, 386
  economic growth of, 981

industry in, 981
See also Siam
Thales of Miletus, 53, 54
Thatcher, Margaret, 931–932, 983
Theatines, 360
Thebes, 16, 22, 52, M1
Theocracy, in Old Sumerian period, 10–11
Theocratic socialism, 19
Theocritus, 66
Theodora, 171
Theodore II, Ethiopia, 734
Theodoric, 136, 242, 243
Theodosius I, 134, 135, 144, 147
Theophilus, 175
Thera (Santorini) eruption, 39
Thespis, 58
Thessalonica, 180
  Byzantine losses at, 176
Third estate, 255, 480, 497, 499
Third Rome (Moscow), 170
Thirty Years' War, 441, 443, 473, 479, 483, Map 5
  background of, 458–459, 470
  Bohemian and Danish phases, 459–460
  eyewitness account, 461
  Peace of Westphalia and aftermath, 458, 462–464, 470, 471
  Swedish and French phases, 460–462
Thomas Aquinas, saint, 167, 207, 276–277, 279, 298, 313, 341–342
Three Emperors' League, 765
Three Mile Island, 987
Thucydides, 49, 51, 57
Thutmose III, 17
Tiberius, 85
Tienanmen Square, 948
Tiepolo, Giovanni, 530
Tiepolo, Paolo, on Philip II, 452
Tihuanaco, 412
Tilsit Treaty, 598, 599
Timurid empire, 365
Tintoretto (Jacopo Robusti), 324, 326
Titian (Tiziano Vecellio), 322, 340
Tito, Joseph, 892, 910, 922, 925, M5
Titus (emperor), 85
Titus, son of Vespasian, 140
Tlaloc, 411
Tobago, independence of, 970
Togoland, 736, 866
Tojo, Hideki, 895, 940
Tokugawa period, 382, 383
Tokugawa Shogunate, 588–590
  political structure of, 382
Toleration Act, 547
Toltecs, 410, 411, 412, 413, 425
Tomb of the Reliefs, PF1
Tonjur, Sultanate of, 577
Topa Yupanqui, 413
Topiltzin, 411
Tordesillas, treaty of, 422, 424
Torun, Second Peace of, 185

The Reference Maps

History accounts for human activities in time, and maps depict them in space. Therefore, to understand humanity's experiences, knowledge of the planetary environment is essential. These reference maps show key areas at significant periods; they include basic physical features that affect human attempts to control the environment and their fellow beings.

Map 1: The Ancient Near East and Greece   In the area displayed, we can trace the progressive expansion of human environmental control resulting from the invention of new tools and social institutions. The transition from food collecting to farming occurred in well-watered sites bordering the Syrian, Arabian, and Iranian deserts—such as at Jarmo in uplands to the east of the Tigris. The breakthrough from Neolithic barbarism to civilization, that is, to societies sufficiently complex to permit the emergence of urban centers, occurred in two important river basins, the Tigris-Euphrates and the Nile—linked by a Fertile Crescent with minimal natural obstacles to impede the movement of peoples and goods.

Employing primitive craft, Neolithic seafarers hugged the Mediterranean coasts and slowly pushed westward—as attested by Neolithic sites in Cyprus, Rhodes, and Crete. Improvements in maritime technology permitted the emergence of a splendid Aegean civilization centering at Knossos in Crete, Pylos on the Greek mainland, and Troy in northwest Asia Minor. Civilization's center of gravity shifted progressively northward across the eastern basin of the Mediterranean, culminating in Hellas with its sea-oriented city-states: Corinth; Thebes; and, above all, Athens. Continued advances in maritime technology enabled the Greeks to master the eastern Mediterranean and Black seas and to establish colonies, while the Phoenicians carried their mercantile ventures from their port cities of Tyre and Sidon along the North African coast. What the Tigris-Euphrates had been to the Babylonians and the Nile to the Egyptians, the Mediterranean became to the Greeks, the Phoenicians, and eventually to the Romans—the "middle of the earth."

Map 2: The Roman Empire, c. A.D. 117   This map underscores the importance of physical features in the creation of the Roman world-state. From its east-west maritime axis, the Roman *imperium* stretched into the hinterland, which was linked by rivers and roads to strategically located ports that provided transshipment to other parts of the Empire.

The expansion of the Roman world began with the conquest of the Italian peninsula and Great Greece (including Sicily). The Punic Wars opened up the entire western basin of the Mediterranean, while subsequent intrusion into the eastern basin extended Roman dominion over the Hellenistic world. During the first century B.C., Rome consolidated its control in Asia Minor; conquered transalpine Gaul; and annexed Egypt, Numidia, and Cyrenaica. The territorial domain was rounded out later by the acquisition of Mauretania, Dacia, Armenia, and Mesopotamia.

In this map, we see the Roman world at its broadest expanse, encompassing almost 100 million people and linked by the greatest communications network then devised. However, the world-state soon entered its time of troubles, attended by declines in population, administrative efficiency, and military power. The Empire then found itself overextended and had to reduce its territorial perimeter. Armenia, Mesopotamia, and Dacia were abandoned, and eventually the Roman legions were recalled from Britain.

In the fourth century, the once majestic Roman Empire was polarized into two unequal segments. The western section, administered from Rome, had the weaker but spatially larger area; the eastern section, controlled from New Rome (Constantinople, formerly Byzantium), had a larger population, a more compact territory, and a stronger economy. When the two segments, each centering on one of the major basins of the Mediterranean, were split asunder by barbarian invasions, the classical world gave way to the medieval world.

Map 3: The Ancient East   Here we encounter the homelands of two major fluvial civilizations (societies originating in river basins) centering on the Indus-Gangetic and the Huang Ho (Yellow River) drainage basins. The remarkable longevity of Indian and Chinese societies owes much to physical factors that inhibited alien intrusion. The Indian triangle was protected by the Indian Ocean and the Himalayas, although invasion was possible through the western passes; as for China, the obstacles posed by the Pacific Ocean, the forbidding Taklamakan and Gobi deserts, and a series of mountain ranges effectively limited entrance into the Huang Ho valley.

The map also shows the boundaries of three empires: the Han in China, the Mauryan in India, and the Parthian in western Asia. Note that these empires were contemporary with the Roman world-state at its zenith. After centuries of feudal fragmentation, China was reunited, and under Shih Huang-ti (the First Emperor), the Great Wall was rebuilt and lengthened to keep the nomadic tribes in the north and west from pillaging the sedentary farmers in the south. The centuries marked by the Han Dynasty were stable and prosperous. So too were the centuries of Mauryan rule in India. Under Ashoka, a single administration extended from the Himalayas across the Narbada River and included the Deccan—leaving only the southernmost part of the subcontinent outside its rule. Meanwhile, to the northwest lay Bactria, where Hellenistic and Indian culture interfused, producing the Gandharan art found in Taxila.

This is the era, too, when the western and eastern segments of the Eurasian land mass were in commercial and cultural contact. Ships plied the Indian Ocean, taking advantage of the recently discovered monsoon mechanism, and a tenuous but profitable overland Silk Route stretched from Ch'ang-an to Kashgar and Samarkand and across Parthian lands to Ecbatana, Ctesiphon, and Seleucia.

Map 4: Medieval France, Spain, and the British Isles, 1328   We can perceive here the emerging outlines of the national state system in western Europe. For example, in 1328 Edward II had to recognize Scotland officially as independent, while across the Channel, the extinction of the Capetian line set the stage for a protracted struggle over the succession to the French throne. Known as the Hundred Years' War (1337–1453), it was marked by the loss of large English holdings obtained in Plantagenet days. Meanwhile, ambitious French kings enlarged their domain from the Ile de France around Paris southward to the Mediterranean and then sought to expand their territory eastward at the expense of the feudal-fregmented Holy Roman Empire. The Iberian peninsula was also fragmented, but here the Christian kingdoms were girding to clear the peninsula of the Moors in Granada.

Noteworthy for their economic importance during this era were the Low Countries, where the textile industry enriched such towns as Bruges, Lille, Ghent, Ypres, and Cambrai; Champagne in northeastern France, where the most famous medieval fairs in all Europe were held; and southern France, with its thriving commercial centers at Narbonne and Marseille.

Whereas in the classical era urban centers predominated on the coasts, in medieval Europe a large number of river-oriented towns were founded or acquired increasing importance. Roads were poor, and river transport was both economical and efficient. The Thames, Meuse, Seine, Loire, Rhone, Garonne, Tagus, Guadalquivir, and Po rivers were being constantly utilized, while the Rhine and the Danube—important as political and military boundaries in Roman times—were vital waterways throughout the medieval period.

Map 5: Europe, 1648   The year 1648 is a crucial one for it marks the end of the Thirty Years' War, which started as a religious conflict and concluded with the victory of the national state, which acknowledged no authority higher than its own sovereignty and interests. The map indicates the further territorial consolidation of the national state system (as compared with Map 4). Thus Scotland and England are now one political entity; the Iberian peninsula is demarcated as Spain and Portugal (although neither is any longer a first-class power); France has acquired bishoprics in Lorraine and a foothold in Alsace. The map also shows the emergence of Switzerland, the three Scandinavian countries, Poland, and Russia.

Germany and Italy remain territorially fragmented and politically unstable, as the Holy Roman Empire has vanished in everything but name and pretensions. The situation in the flat north European plain remains fluid as the boundaries of Brandenburg, Poland, and Russia are always shifting, reflecting the fluctuating balance of power in those states. Meanwhile, despite their defeat at Lepanto in 1571, the Ottoman Turks continue to threaten central Europe.

Map 6: Africa, A.D. 700–1500 The historical development and cultural evolution of Africa owe much to two physical features of the continent—the Sahara Desert and the Great Rift Valley. The valley runs from the Jordan Valley in Palestine to the Red Sea, through Ethiopia to form the basin containing Uganda and Lake Victoria, and southward through western Tanzania and Lake Tanganyika to Lake Nyasa. The Sahara cuts off northern Africa from the rest of the continent. Northwest Africa is largely oriented to the Mediterranean and to Europe; northeast Africa has long been linked with southwest Asia and the Arabian peninsula. Sub-Saharan Africa is drained by the Niger, Congo, Zambezi, and Limpopo rivers. In this huge region, the Sudanese savanna lands, equatorial rain forest, and steppes and deserts of southern Africa succeed one another from north to south. The map depicts the major cultures of the area and the various empires that flourished during the millenium under review, as well as trade routes across the Sahara, over which caravans carried Islamic proselytizers, ivory, slaves, and the wares of the marketplace and mind alike.

Map 7: European Empires, c. 1700 With the age of exploration, western Europeans set out for the unmapped portions of the globe, spreading their religion, cultures, and languages into new territories. In the wake of the explorer came the missionary, merchant, and musketeer so that in time

Europeans controlled most, or all, of the land surface of every other continent. The age of exploration both intensified and territorially expanded European national rivalries.

European states bordering the Atlantic attempted to explore and colonize lands in the New World in latitudes roughly comparable to their own. Thus, the Danes proceeded nortwestward to Iceland and Greenland, the English and French competed for lands north of the Gulf of Mexico, and Spain and Portugal staked their respective claims in more southerly latitudes. Following Portuguese initiative, other Europeans sought out—and fought over—islands, coastal strips, and spheres of interest on the African and Indian coasts and in the archipelagoes of Southeast Asia.

On the map, we can see clearly the contrasting depths of European penetration of the New and Old Worlds. In the Americas, Europeans encountered either Stone Age Amerinds or pre-Columbian civilizations incapable of assimilating, much less fighting off, the newcomers. Consequently, the European acquisition of North and South America—and later of Australia—was complete. In contrast, in sub-Saharan Africa as well as South and East Asia, the Europeans were invariably outnumbered. Hence, although they managed to establish trading settlements along the coast and eventually acquire political ascendancy in most of these regions, they did not succeed in replacing the indigenous culture patterns.

Map 8: Europe, August 1939 As a result of the defeat of the Central Powers in World War I, Germany was shorn of its overseas colonies, while in Europe it lost Alsace-Lorraine, half of Schleswig, three western districts to Belgium, the Polish Corridor, and a zone in the Rhineland, which was demilitarized. The Austrian Empire was dismembered: the nationalist movements of the Czechs, Poles, and Slavs achieved formal territorial recognition; the remnant of the Empire was converted into the separate states of Austria and Hungary; and further Austrian territories were awarded to Italy. The Ottoman Empire was also dissected: Greece obtained nearly all of European Turkey, Syria was mandated to France, and Palestine and Iraq went to Great Britain. After the Bolshevik Revolution, Russia lost much of its western territory, resulting in the establishment of Finland, Estonia, Latvia, and Lithuania, as well as the major portion of reconstituted Poland, while Bessarabia was ceded to Rumania.

In the interwar years, as the map shows, national appetites were whetted to gain new territory or reannex lost possessions. Under Hitler, Nazi Germany reoccupied the Rhineland in 1936, seized Austria and occupied Sudetenland in 1938, and the following year seized other Czech territory in addition to Memel. In 1939, too, Hungary annexed part of Slovakia, while Mussolini's Italy defeated and annexed Albania. The stage was also set for Russia to reannex territory lost after the Bolshevik Revolution.

Map 9: Africa, 1914 Africa possesses three major cultural environments, each with unique historical developments. Northeast Africa, partly cut off from the rest of the continent by the Sahara, has long been linked with southwest Asia. Africa east of the Great Rift Valley is oriented toward the Indian Ocean, toward the Arab trader, and since the last century, toward the European who has farmed the plateaus of Kenya, Uganda, and Tanzania. The lands in the southern section of the Great Rift Valley constitute a huge area drained by the Niger, Congo, Zambezi, and Limpopo rivers. In these lands occurred Europe's great scramble for empire in the nineteenth century. By 1914 all Africa had been partitioned among European powers except for Liberia (founded by ex-slaves from the United States) and Abyssinia, which successfully resisted Italian attempts at conquest in 1896.

Map 10: Africa Profound political and territorial changes have occurred in Africa since 1914—undoubtedly the most spectacular to be found in any continent during the past half century. From being a vast collection of colonial holdings, Africa has emerged as an agglomeration of national states, virtually all having minimal political stability or economic viability. During the interwar years, some major changes took place on the political landscape. German Togoland and the Cameroons were mandated to Great Britain and France; German East Africa was divided into two mandates: Ruanda-Urundi (Belgium) and Tanganyika (Great Britain); and German Southwest Africa was mandated to South Africa. Egypt became an independent kingdom but Italy's possessions in East Africa were enlarged by the conquest of Abyssinia. Since World War II, however,

a spectacular alteration has occurred. The entire continent has passed into indigenous political control, with the exception of South Africa where domination by the white minority, of European descent, remains entrenched.

Map 11: USSR and Asia Dominating Eurasia, the greatest land mass on earth, is the enormous area of the Soviet Union (more than 8 million square miles), extending along a west-east axis for nearly 5000 miles. European Russia, largely a continuation of the north European plain, is drained by the Dvina, Dnieper, Don, and Volga rivers, the last three flowing southward. East of the Urals, virtually all rivers flow north to the Arctic, except the Amur, which in its eastward journey also serves as a border with China. Soviet Asia is separated from middle- and low-latitude Asia by steppes, deserts, and mountains.

Russian eastward expansion reached the Pacific by 1649. In the next two centuries, the Russians penetrated east of the Caspian into what is now the Kazakh, Uzbek, and Turkmen Soviet Socialist Republics. In the process, they collided with the Chinese in Sinkiang, Mongolia, and Manchuria. These border regions today constitute areas of tension and jockeying between the two major Communist powers.

China has continued to develop south of the Great Wall and Gobi Desert and east and north of such massive mountain ranges as the Tien Shan, Pamirs, and Himalayas. Indian society occupies the subcontinent below the Himalyas and influences the culture patterns of neighboring lands to the east and south. Southeast Asia has long been subject to recurrent cultural and military intrusions. Its highly indented coastline and physical terrain have contributed to a fragmentation of cultures and languages. Offshore in East and Southeast Asia are three archipelagoes: Japan, the most highly industrialized and prosperous of non-Western countries; the Philippines; and Indonesia.

Map 12: Latin America Latin America was first colonized by southern Europeans, notably the Spaniards and Portuguese. Exploiting the mountain ranges that run the length of Central and South America for their precious metals, the Spaniards increased their holdings until the close of the eighteenth century. They created several vice-royalties: New Spain, including Mexico and

Central America; Peru, at first embracing all of Spanish South America; New Granada, in what is now Colombia and Venezuela; and La Plata, which subsequently became Bolivia, Paraguay, Uruguay, and Argentina. Brazil, discovered by the Portuguese Cabral in 1500, was made a vice-royalty in 1714.

In half a century (1776–1826) of colonial revolutions in the New World, Spanish and Portuguese America became independent (except for Cuba and Puerto Rico, which remained Spanish until 1898).

The tropical regions of Latin America—including Mexico; Central America; and the lands drained by the Magdalena, Orinoco, and Amazon rivers—have predominantly Amerind populations. In contrast, temperate South America, comprising southern Brazil, Uruguay, Argentina, and Chile, finds Europeans in the majority.

Map 13: The Middle East This region—segmented by deserts and seas but with the latter providing interconnecting routes of travel—has long permitted maximal movement of peoples, goods, and ideas in all directions. In this area, which is unique for the convergence of three continents, we find the birthplace of "civilization" and of three major religions, as well as a continuous succession of dynasties and empires. For centuries, Islamic political authority and cultural vitality were bound with the fortunes of the Ottoman Empire. When the Empire fell to the European powers, the Muslim people of the region were in turn subordinated in status and made to feel inferior. The twentieth century, however, has witnessed a resurgence of Islamic culture and political strength—attended by the creation of numerous independent states, including Morocco, Algeria, Libya, Egypt, Sudan, Syria, Lebanon, Jordan, Iraq, and Pakistan. This resurgence has capitalized on the strategic value of the region in the geopolitical programs of the superpowers, as well as on its massive oil resources.

The region has also been in a state of continuous tension and intermittent conflict since the end of World War II because of Arab-Israeli animosities. When the British mandate of Palestine was terminated in 1948, the area proclaimed itself the new state of Israel—a step sanctioned by the United Nations as well as by both the United States and the Soviet Union. But the Arab states remained opposed to any such recognition, and several campaigns were mounted in an effort to regain Palestine for the Muslim Arabs. Arab-Israeli hostilities erupted into war in 1967 and 1973. An Israeli victory resulted in occupation of the west bank of the Jordan River; the Sinai peninsula and the east bank of the Suez Canal have since been returned to Egypt. The Middle East in the 1980s is still the scence of violent and bloody conflicts. A revolution in Iran was followed by war between Iran and Iraq that continues with no apparent end in sight. Various factions in Lebanon are waging civil war. In addition, throughout the region, terrorist activities threaten both natives and visitors.

Map 14: Europe Compare this map with Map 8 to obtain a clearer picture of territorial changes resulting from the outcome of World War II. As after World War I, defeated Germany and its allies lost territory, and the Soviet Union emerged as the greatest single territorial beneficiary.

In 1945, Germany was stripped of East Prussia, while its eastern boundary was set at the Oder-Neisse rivers—the farthest line west achieved by the Slavs since the twelfth century. Moreover, postwar Germany was both ideologically and territorially split—its western segment associated in military and economic pacts with the Western world and its eastern section integrated in the Communist world and a member of the Warsaw Pact. Defeated Italy lost its overseas colonies and Albania.

The Soviet Union expanded westward, annexing part of Finland; all of Estonia, Latvia, and Lithuania; and the eastern portion of Poland, shifting that country's center of gravity westward at the expense of Germany. Stalinist policies and power created a series of "people's democracies" from the Baltic to the Black seas, resulting in the iron curtain. Yet, the region was to prove far from monolithic. Shortly after the war, Tito declared Yugoslavia an independent Communist state.

Tiny Albania was later to ally itself with China in the great split within the Communist world. In the 1980s, Soviet leader Mikhail Gorbachev introduced the new policies of *glasnost* (openness) and *perestroika* (restructuring) to encourage a freer economy. By the late 1980s, the Communist regimes in many Eastern European states had fallen, free multiparty elections had taken place, and democratic parties had come to power. All barriers between East and West Germany had been removed, and Germany was once more a unified state.

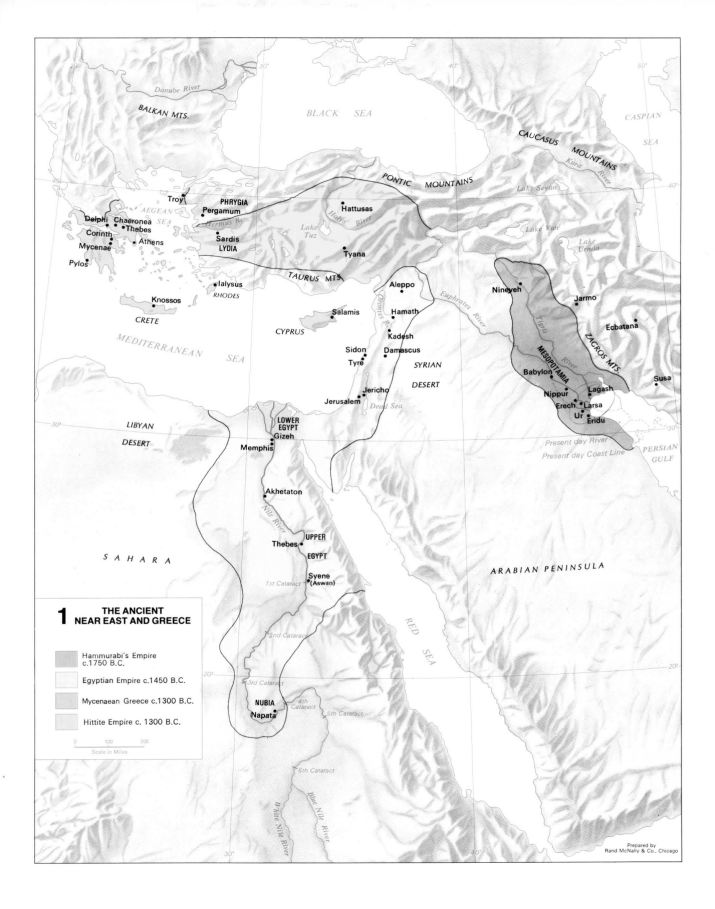

THE ANCIENT
NEAR EAST AND GREECE

Hammurabi's Empire
c.1750 B.C.

Egyptian Empire c.1450 B.C.

Mycenaean Greece c.1300 B.C.

Hittite Empire c. 1300 B.C.

0   100   200
Scale in Miles

Prepared by
Rand McNally & Co., Chicago

BALKAN MTS.   BLACK SEA   CASPIAN SEA

Danube River

PONTIC   MOUNTAINS   CAUCASUS   MOUNTAINS

Kura River

Lake Seyan

Troy   PHRYGIA   Hattusas   Lake Van
Pergamum   Halys River

Delphi   Chaeronea   AEGEAN   Lake Urmia
Corinth   Thebes   SEA   Tuz
Mycenae   Athens   Sardis   Tyana   Nineveh   Jarmo
Pylos   LYDIA   TAURUS MTS.   Ecbatana

Ialysus   Aleppo   ZAGROS MTS.
RHODES   Euphrates River   MESOPOTAMIA
Knossos   Salamis   Hamath   Tigris River
CRETE   CYPRUS   Kadesh   Babylon   Susa
Orontes R.   Damascus   Nippur   Lagash
MEDITERRANEAN   SEA   Sidon   SYRIAN   Erech   Larsa
Tyre   DESERT   Ur   Eridu

Jericho   Present day River
Jerusalem   Present day Coast Line   PERSIAN
Dead Sea   GULF

LIBYAN   LOWER
DESERT   EGYPT   Gizeh
Memphis

SAHARA   Akhetaton   ARABIAN PENINSULA

Nile River

Thebes   UPPER
EGYPT
Syene
(Aswan)
1st Cataract

RED   SEA

2nd Cataract

3rd Cataract

4th
Cataract
NUBIA   5th Cataract
Napata

6th Cataract

White Nile River   Blue Nile River

ATLANTIC
OCEAN

IRELAND

*IRISH
SEA*

Antoninus' Wall
(C. 140 A.D.)
Hadrian's Wall
(C. 122 A.D.)
York
Chester PENNINES Lincoln
BRITAIN
Colchester
Bath London
Thames R.

ENGLISH CHANNEL

NORTH
SEA

BALTIC

GERMANIA

Elbe River
Oder River
SUDETES

Cologne
BELGICA
Mainz
Seine River Rhine River
Paris
Loire River Meuse R.
GAUL
Saône R.
Bordeaux CENTRAL Danube
BAY OF MASSIF Lyons
BISCAY Garonne R. Rhône River ALPS
CISALPINE GAUL
CANTABRIAN MTS. PYRENEES Po River Genoa Ravenna
Douro River Ebro River Pisa APENNINES ADRIATIC
Segovia Salonae
Tagus River SPAIN Marseilles CORSICA ITALY SEA
Guadiana River Toledo Saguntum Rome
SIERRA MORENA Valencia SARDINIA Naples
Cordova BALEARIC Pompeii
Guadalquivir R. ISLANDS
Cádiz SIERRA NEVADA TYRRHENIAN
Strait of Gibraltar New SEA
Tangier Carthage Messina
Pillars of Hercules SICILY
M E D I T E R Syracuse
MADEIRA
ISLANDS R A MALTA
MAURETANIA N E A N
A T L A S M O U N T A I N S Utica
Moulouya R. Carthage
CANARY Cheliff Medjerda R.
ISLANDS

Chott
Djerid NUMIDIA Oea Leptis
Magna
GRAND ERG OCCIDENTAL

GRAND ERG ORIENTAL

2 **THE ROMAN EMPIRE**
C. A.D. 117

0   100   200   300
Scale in Miles

AHAGGAR
MOUNTAINS   SAHARA

50° 30° 20° 10° 0° 10°

30°

40°

20°

30°

20°

10°

0° 20° 10°

GOTHS

HUNS

SARMATIA

Lake Ladoga

Volga River

Kama River

URAL MOUNTAINS

Tobol R.

Western Dvina River

Bug River

Vistula R.

Dniester River

Dnieper River

Don River

Volga River

Ural River

ARAL SEA

CARPATHIANS

•Apulum

TRANSYLVANIAN ALPS

DACIA

River

BALKAN MTS.

•Naissus

Olbia•

SEA OF AZOV

BLACK SEA

CAUCASUS MOUNTAINS

Kura River

Aras River

Lake Sevan

•Artaxata

CASPIAN SEA

•Sinope

•Trapezus

PONTIC MOUNTAINS

ARMENIA

ELBURZ MTS.

Daryācheh-ye Namak

MACEDONIA

THRACE

Byzantium•

Sea of Marmara

PONTUS

River

Kizil

Lake Van

Lake Urmia

ASSYRIA

PLATEAU OF IRAN

PARTHIAN EMPIRE

Ecbatana•

PINDUS MTS.

EPIRUS MTS.

•Pergamum

ASIA

AEGEAN SEA

Lake Tuz

MESOPOTAMIA

Euphrates River

Tigris River

ZAGROS

•Thebes

•Ephesus

•Tarsus

CILICIA

•Ctesiphon

MTS.

Corinth• •Athens

•Sparta

RHODES

CYPRUS

•Palmyra

Dura Europos•

River

PERSIAN GULF

•Knossos

SYRIA

Sidon•

Tyre•

•Damascus

CRETE

SEA

PALESTINE Jerusalem•

Dead Sea

•Cyrene

Alexandria•

CYRENAICA

ARABIA

Memphis•

LIBYAN DESERT

EGYPT

Nile River

•Thebes

Berenice•

•Syene

RED SEA

Prepared by
Rand McNally & Co., Chicago

Prepared by
Rand McNally & Co., Chicago

3 THE ANCIENT EAST

Maurya Empire 320 B.C.—190 B.C.

Han Empire 200 B.C.—200 A.D.

Parthian Empire 200 B.C.—226 A.D.

Scale in Miles

0   200   400   600

MEDITERRANEAN SEA

RED SEA

BLACK SEA

CAUCASUS MTS.

Danube R.

Don R.

Volga River

Ural River

CASPIAN SEA

KIRGIZ STEPPE

URAL MTS.

Antioch

Jerusalem

Damascus

MESOPOTAMIA

PERSIA

PARTHIA

Persian Gulf

Euphrates River

Tigris River

Khorsabad

Ctesiphon

Seleucia

Babylon

Susa

ARABIAN PENINSULA

ARABIAN SEA

Pasargadae

Persepolis

ELBURZ MTS.

SISTAN DEPRESSION

BACTRIA

Bactra

Samarkand

Amu Darya (Oxus R.)

Syr Darya (Jaxartes R.)

Aral Sea

Ishim River

Irtysh River

Lake Balkash

Ob River

PAMIRS

HINDU KUSH

Tashkurgan

Yarkand

Kashgar

TIEN SHAN

ALTAI MOUNTAINS

SAYAN MOUNTAINS

Yenisei River

Angara River

Lake Baikal

THAR DESERT

Mohenjo-Daro

Indus River

Helmand R.

GANDHARA

Taxila

Harappa

Khotan

TAKLAMAKAN DESERT

Tarim River

KUNLUN MOUNTAINS

ALTYN TAGH

Loulan

PLATEAU OF TIBET

GOBI DESERT

YABLONOVY RANGE

Lena R.

Amur River

GREAT KHINGAN MTS.

SIKHOTE ALIN RANGE

WESTERN GHATS

EASTERN GHATS

ANDHRA

KALINGA

KOSALA

MAGADHA

Mathura

Indraprastha

Pataliputra

Champa

Ganges

Narbada

Godavari

Krishna

Brahmaputra River

HIMALAYAS

+ Mt. Everest

INDIAN OCEAN

BAY OF BENGAL

Irrawaddy River

Salween River

Mekong River

NAN LING

Shu

Pa

Ch'ang-an

YANG SHAO

LUNG SHAN

ORDOS DESERT

Great Wall

Taiyüan

Yen

GREAT KHINGAN MTS.

Lo-yang

Yüan

Chinan

+ Tai Mtn.

Tai Mtn.

Hsi River (West R.)

P'anyü

Yangtze River

Han R.

Wu

Hwang R.

Yellow River

SOUTH CHINA SEA

EAST CHINA SEA

SEA OF JAPAN

PHILIPPINE SEA

PACIFIC OCEAN

0°   20°   40°   60°   80°   100°   120°   140°

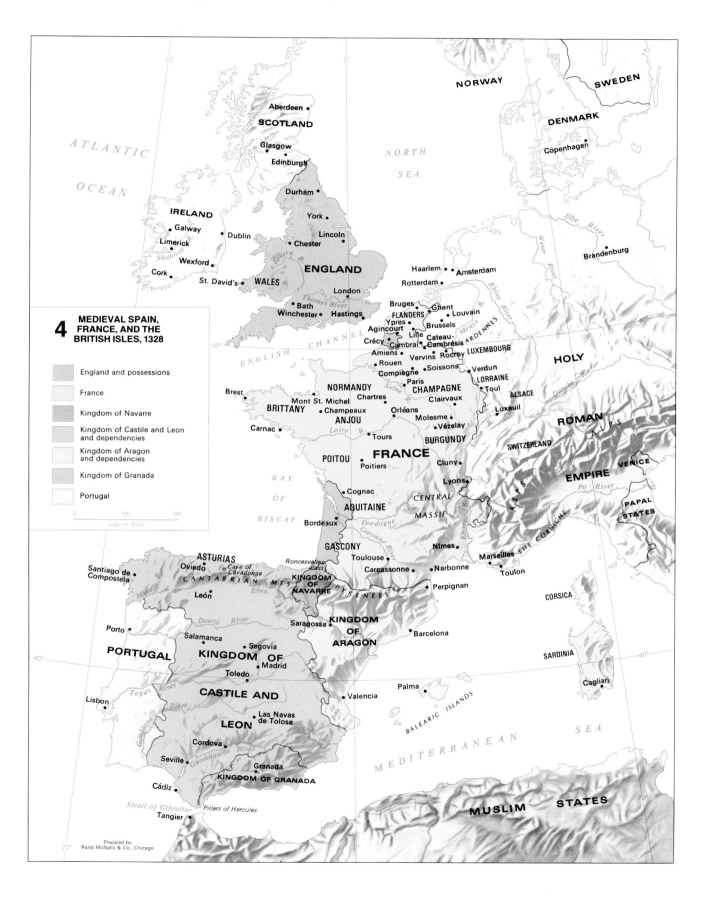

MEDIEVAL SPAIN, FRANCE, AND THE BRITISH ISLES, 1328

4

- England and possessions
- France
- Kingdom of Navarre
- Kingdom of Castile and Leon and dependencies
- Kingdom of Aragon and dependencies
- Kingdom of Granada
- Portugal

0   100   200
Scale in Miles

Prepared by
Rand McNally & Co., Chicago

NORWAY

SWEDEN

DENMARK

Copenhagen

ATLANTIC

OCEAN

Brandenburg

Elbe River

 SCOTLAND

Aberdeen

Glasgow

Edinburgh

NORTH

SEA

Durham

IRELAND

Galway

Dublin

York

Lincoln

Limerick

Chester

Wexford

Cork

St. David's

Shannon

WALES

ENGLAND

Severn R.

Bath

Winchester

London

Hastings

Thames River

Haarlem

Amsterdam

Rotterdam

Weser River

ENGLISH CHANNEL

Bruges

Ghent

Louvain

FLANDERS

Brussels

Ypres

Agincourt

Lille

Cateau-

Cambrésis

Rhine R.

ARDENNES

Meuse

LUXEMBOURG

HOLY

Crécy

Cambrai

Amiens

Vervins

Rocroy

Verdun

Rouen

Soissons

LORRAINE

Compiègne

Paris

Toul

ALSACE

Brest

NORMANDY

Chartres

CHAMPAGNE

Seine

Luxeuil

Danube River

ROMAN

Mont St. Michel

Clairvaux

BRITTANY

Champeaux

Orléans

Molesme

BURGUNDY

Carnac

ANJOU

Vézelay

SWITZERLAND

ALPS

Loire R.

Tours

FRANCE

Saône R.

VENICE

POITOU

Cluny

EMPIRE

Poitiers

Lyons

Po River

BAY

CENTRAL

PAPAL

OF

Cognac

MASSIF

STATES

BISCAY

AQUITAINE

Rhône R.

Bordeaux

Dordogne

Garonne River

Nîmes

THE CORNICHE

GASCONY

Toulouse

Marseilles

CORSICA

Roncesvalles Pass

Carcassonne

Narbonne

Santiago de

ASTURIAS

Toulon

Compostela

Oviedo

Cave of

Covadonga

CANTABRIAN MTS.

KINGDOM

Perpignan

PYRENEES

OF

Miño

León

Ebro R.

NAVARRE

SARDINIA

Porto

Douro River

Saragossa

KINGDOM

Barcelona

PORTUGAL

Salamanca

OF

Segovia

ARAGON

KINGDOM OF

Madrid

Cagliari

Toledo

Palma

CASTILE AND

Valencia

Lisbon

Tagus River

BALEARIC ISLANDS

Guadiana

Las Navas

de Tolosa

LEON

Cordova

Guadalquivir River

MEDITERRANEAN

SEA

Seville

Granada

KINGDOM OF GRANADA

Cádiz

Strait of Gibraltar

Pillars of Hercules

Tangier

MUSLIM   STATES

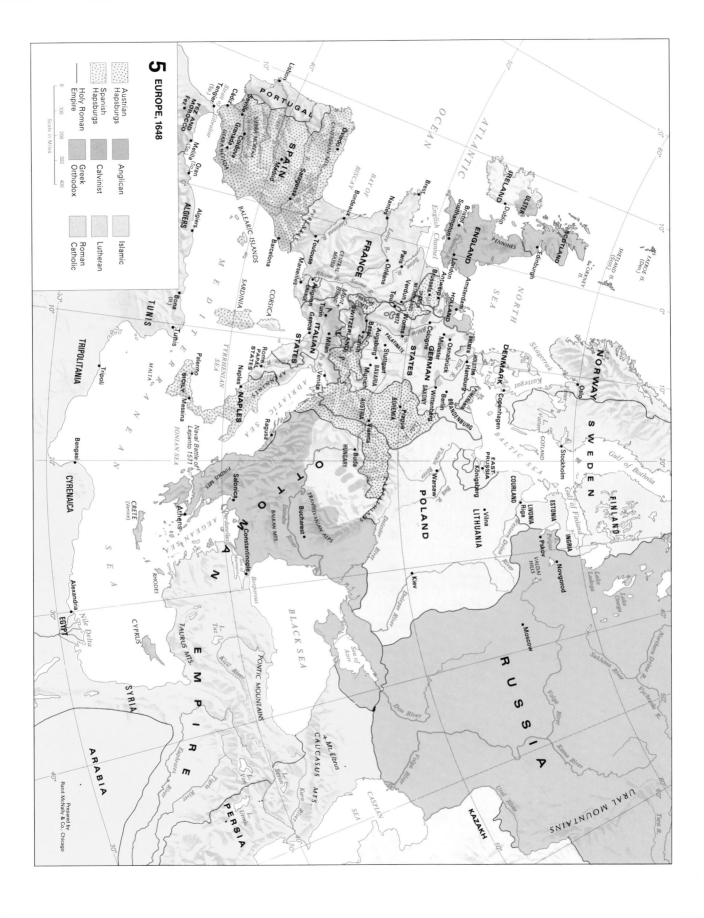

5 EUROPE, 1648

Austrian
Hapsburgs

Spanish
Hapsburgs

Holy Roman
Empire

Anglican

Calvinist

Greek
Orthodox

Islamic

Lutheran

Roman
Catholic

Scale in Miles

0   100   200   300   400

PORTUGAL

SPAIN

Lisbon

Oviedo

Seville

Cadiz

Tangier (Sp.)

Granada

Cordoba

SIERRA MORENA

SIERRA NEVADA

GUADALQUIVIR R.

Madrid

Saragossa

CANTABRIAN MTS.

PYRENEES

Barcelona

BALEARIC ISLANDS

FEZ AND MOROCCO

Fez

Melilla (Sp.)

Oran (Sp.)

ALGIERS

Algiers

SARDINIA

CORSICA

Bona (It.)

TUNIS

Tunis

TRIPOLITANIA

Tripoli

Bengasi

CYRENAICA

FRANCE

CENTRAL MASSIF

Bordeaux

Garonne R.

Toulouse

Marseilles

Avignon

Orange

Rhone R.

Saone R.

Nantes

Loire R.

Orleans

Paris

Seine R.

Brest

BAY OF BISCAY

ATLANTIC OCEAN

ENGLAND

London

Bristol

Southampton

Thames R.

IRELAND

Dublin

ULSTER

SCOTLAND

Edinburgh

PENNINES

SHETLAND IS. (Den.)

ORKNEY IS. (Scot.)

FAEROE IS. (Den.)

NORTH SEA

English Channel

HOLLAND

Amsterdam

Antwerp

Brussels

SPANISH NETHERLANDS

Lyon

Dijon

Besancon

FRANCHE COMTE

SWITZERLAND

Zurich

Basel

Geneva

Metz

Toul

Verdun

Worms

Cologne

Munster

Osnabruck

GERMAN STATES

Bremen

Hamburg

HOLSTEIN

MECKLENBURG

POMERANIA

DENMARK

Copenhagen

Stuttgart

Augsburg

Munich

BAVARIA

PALATINATE

SAXONY

Wittenberg

Berlin

BRANDENBURG

BOHEMIA

Prague

AUSTRIA

Vienna

HUNGARY

Buda

ITALIAN STATES

Milan

Turin

Genoa

Venice

PAPAL STATES

Rome

NAPLES

Naples

APENNINES

ADRIATIC SEA

TYRRHENIAN SEA

SICILY

Palermo

Messina

MALTA

Ragusa

MEDITERRANEAN SEA

IONIAN SEA

Naval Battle of Lepanto 1571

PINDUS MTS.

Salonica

Athens

CRETE (Venice)

AEGEAN SEA

RHODES

Dardanelles

OTTOMAN EMPIRE

Constantinople

Bosporus

BALKAN MTS.

Danube River

Bucharest

TRANSYLVANIAN ALPS

BLACK SEA

Sea of Azov

PONTIC MOUNTAINS

TAURUS MTS.

L. Tuz

Kizil River

CYPRUS

SYRIA

Euphrates River

Tigris River

ARABIA

PERSIA

EGYPT

Alexandria

Nile Delta

Nile River

CAUCASUS MTS.

Mt. Elbrus

Kura River

CASPIAN SEA

L. Urmia

L. Sevan

KAZAKH

URAL MOUNTAINS

Ural River

Volga River

Kama River

Sukhona River

Northern Dvina R.

Vychegda R.

Sura R.

Tura R.

RUSSIA

Moscow

Don River

Kiev

Dnieper River

Dniester River

Bug River

POLAND

Warsaw

Vistula River

LITHUANIA

Vilna

Novgorod

Pskov

VALDAI HILLS

Lake Ladoga

Lake Onega

INGRIA

ESTONIA

LIVONIA

Riga

COURLAND

Western Dvina River

EAST PRUSSIA

Konigsberg

BALTIC SEA

GOTLAND

Stockholm

SWEDEN

NORWAY

Oslo

Skagerrak

Kattegat

L. Vattern

L. Vanern

Gulf of Bothnia

FINLAND

Gulf of Finland

L. Peipus

Prepared by
Rand McNally & Co., Chicago

London

Paris

E U R O P E

Vienna

Belgrade

Danube

BLACK SEA

CAUCASUS MTS.

Dnieper R.

Don R.

Volga R.

Baku

CASPIAN SEA

Aral Sea

Syr Darya (Jaxartes R.)

Amu Darya (Oxus R.)

A T L A N T I C
O C E A N

Madrid

Lisbon

CORSICA

SARDINIA

M E D I T E R R A N E A N

Rome

SICILY

Athens

CRETE

Constantinople

BLACK SEA

Damascus

Baghdad

A S I A

MADEIRA IS.

CANARY IS.

Ceūta

Fez

Algiers

ATLAS MTS.

Tunis

Tripoli

S E A

Barqa

CYPRUS

Mecca

A R A B I A N

Agadir

Sijilmasa

Ghadames

S A H A R A

Aujila

LIBYAN DESERT

Cairo

MAMLUK EMPIRE 1260-1340

RED SEA

P E N I N S U L A

Adrar

Gat

Tamanrasset

KUFRA OASES

Kharga

DONGOLA

NUBIA

PERSIAN GULF

Sebka D'idjil

GHANA
4th–11th Centuries

Taudeni

Bilma

SONGHAI
15th–16th Centuries

Agades

KANEM

N'djimi

DARFUR

FUNG

Sennar

Axum

ETHIOPIA
L. Tana
AMHARA
PLATEAU

Blue Nile

Atbara R.

Tichitt

Walata

Timbuctu

S U D A N

BORNU

Abesehr

El Fasher

Nile R.

ADAL

Gulf of Aden

KRUR

Ghana

Gao

YATENGA

Sokoto

Kano

HAUSA BOKWOI STATES

Lake Chad

White Nile

Mali

MALI
13th–Mid 15th Centuries

DAGOMBA

MOSSI

NUPE

Gambia R.

YORUBA
Ife
BENIN

KWARARAFA

Benue R.

Bomu R.

Uele R.

Mountain Nile

NILOTES

L. Rudolf

Mogadishu

FERNANDO POO

GULF OF GUINEA

PRINCIPE

SÃO TOMÉ

CONGO

BASIN

Congo R.

L. Albert

BUNYORO-KITARA
13th–17th Centuries

Lake Victoria

+MT. KENYA

+MT. KILIMANJARO

Malindi

Mombasa

ZANZIBAR

ANNOBON

Kasai R.

L. Tanganyika

Kilwa

6 AFRICA, A.D. 700–1500

Caravan Routes

KONGO
15th–16th Centuries

LUNDA
16th–17th Centuries

LUBA
15th–16th Centuries

Ruvuma R.

COMORO IS.

L. Nyasa

0   200   400   600   800
Scale in Miles

Cunene R.

Mozambique

MOZAMBIQUE CHANNEL

A T L A N T I C

O C E A N

NAMIB DESERT

KALAHARI

DESERT

Orange R.

Zambezi R.

MONOMOTAPA

Zimbabwe

Sofala

DRAKENSBERG MTS.

MADAGASCAR

I N D I A N

O C E A N

CAPE OF GOOD HOPE

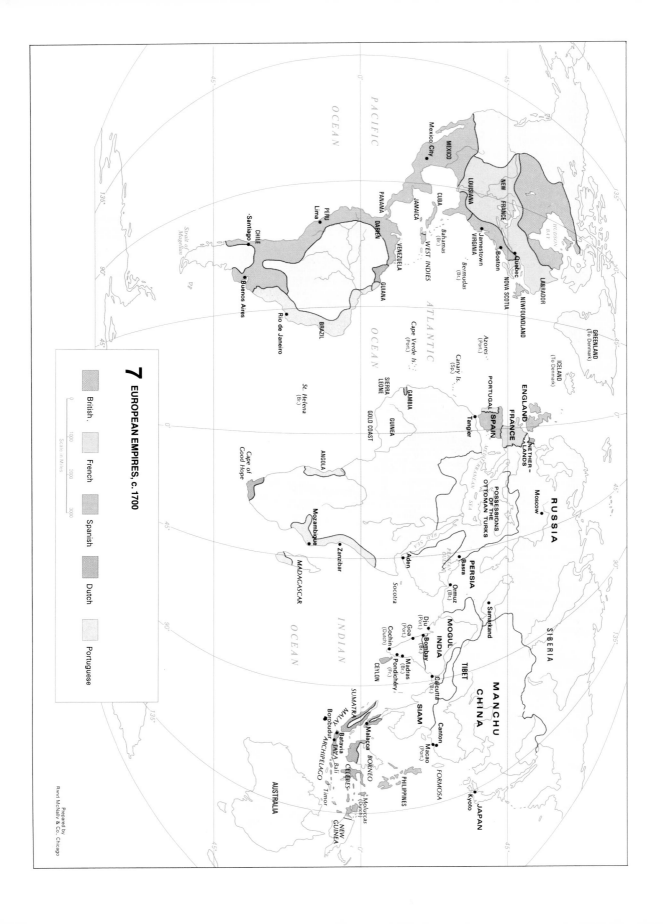

7
EUROPEAN EMPIRES, c. 1700

British

French

Spanish

Dutch

Portuguese

Scale in Miles

0   1000   2000   3000

Prepared by
Rand McNally & Co., Chicago

PACIFIC OCEAN

ATLANTIC OCEAN

INDIAN OCEAN

MEXICO
Mexico City

NEW FRANCE

LOUISIANA

PANAMA
DARIEN
PERU
Lima
CHILE
Santiago
Buenos Aires
BRAZIL
Rio de Janeiro
GUIANA
VENEZUELA
CUBA
JAMAICA
WEST INDIES
Bahamas (Br.)
Bermudas (Br.)
VIRGINIA
Jamestown
Boston
Quebec
NOVA SCOTIA
NEWFOUNDLAND
LABRADOR

HUDSON BAY

GREENLAND (To Denmark)

ICELAND (To Denmark)

Strait of Magellan

Cape Verde Is. (Port.)
Azores (Port.)
Canary Is. (Sp.)
St. Helena (Br.)
SIERRA LEONE
GAMBIA
GUINEA
GOLD COAST
ANGOLA
Cape of Good Hope
MOZAMBIQUE
Mozambique
Zanzibar
MADAGASCAR
Socotra

PORTUGAL
SPAIN
FRANCE
ENGLAND
NETHER-LANDS
Tangier

MEDITERRANEAN SEA

POSSESSIONS OF THE OTTOMAN TURKS

RED SEA
PERSIAN GULF
Aden
Basra
PERSIA
Ormuz (Br.)

RUSSIA
Moscow

SIBERIA

Samarkand

MOGUL INDIA
Diu (Port.)
Goa (Port.)
Bombay (Br.)
Cochin (Dutch)
Madras (Br.)
Pondichéry (Fr.)
CEYLON
Calcutta (Br.)
TIBET

MANCHU CHINA

Canton
Macao (Port.)
FORMOSA
Kyoto
JAPAN

SIAM

SUMATRA
MALAYA
Malacca
Batavia
JAVA
Borobudur
Bali
BORNEO
CELEBES
Moluccas (Dutch)
PHILIPPINES
Timor
ARCHIPELAGO
NEW GUINEA
AUSTRALIA

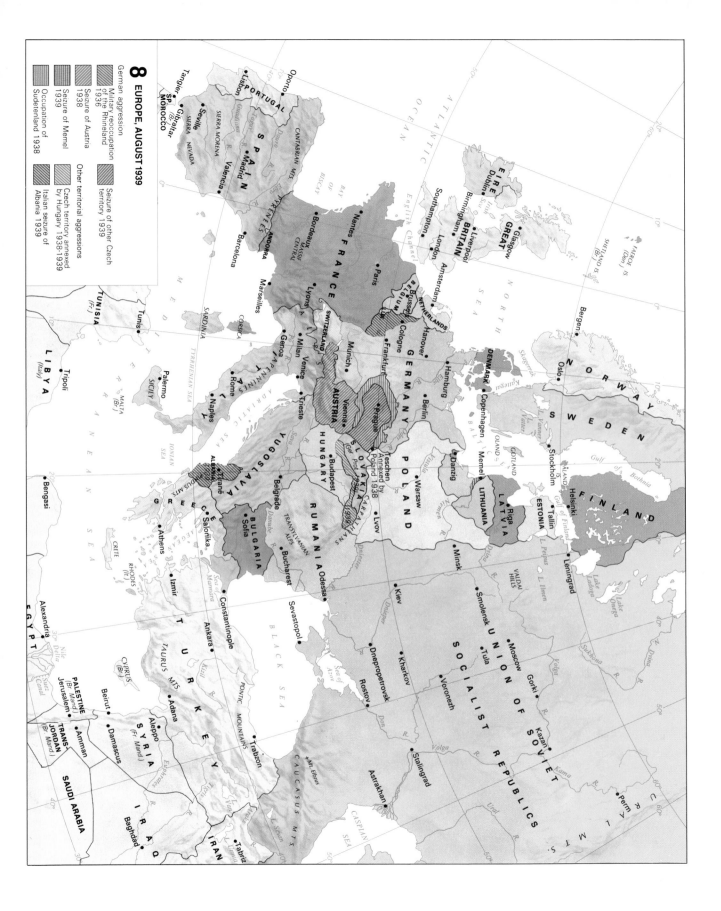

SP. MOROCCO
Tangier
Gibraltar (Br.)

PORTUGAL
Oporto
Lisbon
SIERRA MORENA
SIERRA NEVADA
Seville
Valencia
SPAIN
Madrid
Barcelona
Douro R.
CANTABRIAN MTS.
PYRENEES
ANDORRA

EIRE
Dublin
GREAT BRITAIN
Glasgow
Birmingham
Liverpool
London
Southampton

FRANCE
Nantes
Paris
Bordeaux
MASSIF CENTRAL
Lyons
Marseilles

Amsterdam
NETHERLANDS
Brussels
BELGIUM
LUX.
Hanover
Cologne
Frankfurt
Munich
SWITZERLAND

GERMANY
Hamburg
Berlin
AUSTRIA
Vienna
Prague
Teschen (Ger. Prot.) Annexed by Poland 1938
SLOVAKIA (1939)

POLAND
Danzig
Warsaw
Lvov
MEMEL
LITHUANIA
Riga
LATVIA
ESTONIA
Tallin

DENMARK
Copenhagen

NORWAY
Oslo
Bergen

SWEDEN
Stockholm
GOTLAND
OLAND

FINLAND
Helsinki
Leningrad

UNION OF SOVIET SOCIALIST REPUBLICS
Minsk
Smolensk
Moscow
Gorki
Kazan
Kiev
Kharkov
Dnepropetrovsk
Rostov
Voronezh
Tula
Astrakhan
Stalingrad
Perm
URAL MTS.
VALDAI HILLS

ITALY
Milan
Venice
Genoa
Trieste
APENNINES
Rome
Naples
CORSICA
SARDINIA
SICILY
Palermo

TUNISIA (Fr.)
Tunis

LIBYA (Italy)
Tripoli
Bengasi

YUGOSLAVIA
Belgrade
HUNGARY
Budapest
RUMANIA
Bucharest
Odessa
TRANSYLVANIAN ALPS
CARPATHIANS
BULGARIA
Sofia
ALBANIA (1939)
Tirané
PINDUS MTS.
GREECE
Salonika
Athens
CRETE
RHODES (It.)

TURKEY
Constantinople
Ankara
Izmir
Adana
Trabzon
TAURUS MTS.
PONTIC MOUNTAINS
CAUCASUS MTS.
Mt. Elbruz
Tabriz

Sevastopol
BLACK SEA
Sea of Azov
CASPIAN SEA

MALTA (Br.)
MEDITERRANEAN SEA
ADRIATIC SEA
IONIAN SEA
AEGEAN SEA
TYRRHENIAN SEA
BAY OF BISCAY
ATLANTIC OCEAN
NORTH SEA
BALTIC SEA
English Channel
Irish Sea
Gulf of Bothnia
Gulf of Finland
Skagerrak
Kattegat
FAROE IS. (Den.)
SHETLAND IS. (Br.)
Gulf of Riga
L. Ladoga
L. Onega
L. Ilmen
L. Peipus

EGYPT
Alexandria
Nile Delta
Suez Canal

PALESTINE (B. Mand)
Jerusalem
TRANS-JORDAN (Br. Mand.)
Amman
SYRIA (Fr. Mand.)
Beirut
Damascus
Aleppo
LEBANON
CYPRUS (Br.)

SAUDI ARABIA
IRAQ
Baghdad
IRAN
Euphrates
Tigris

Volga R.
Don R.
Dnieper R.
Dniester R.
Ural R.
Kama R.
Sukhona R.
N. Dvina R.
S. Dvina R.
Oka R.
Rhine R.
Elbe R.
Oder R.
Vistula R.
Niemen R.
Danube R.
Ebro R.

9 AFRICA, 1914

British
French
German
Belgian
Portuguese
Italian
Spanish

Scale in Miles
0   400   800

EUROPE

London
Amsterdam • Berlin
Brussels • Warsaw
Paris
Vienna
Budapest
Belgrade
Rome
Constantinople
Athens

ASIA

Tehran
BLACK SEA

Madrid
Lisbon

CASPIAN SEA
Aral Sea

Damascus • Baghdad
Jerusalem

ATLANTIC OCEAN

MADEIRA IS. (Port.)
CANARY IS. (Br.)

Tangier SP. MOROCCO
Casablanca
Algiers
Tunis

MOROCCO
IFNI

ALGERIA
ATLAS MOUNTAINS
TUNISIA
Tripoli
Bengasi
Alexandria
Cairo
Suez Canal

LIBYA

MEDITERRANEAN SEA

ARABIAN PENINSULA

Damascus
Jerusalem

PERSIAN GULF

Villa Cisneros
RIO DE ORO

LIBYAN DESERT
EGYPT
Aswan

S A H A R A

AHAGGAR MTS.

TIBESTI MASSIF

NUBIAN DESERT

Mecca

RED SEA

FRENCH WEST AFRICA

Timbuktu

S U D A N

ANGLO-EGYPTIAN SUDAN

Omdurman
Khartoum

ERITREA
Asmara
Aden
Gulf of Aden

Dakar
SENEGAL
GAMBIA
PORT. GUINEA
Bissau
FRENCH GUINEA
Bamako
Senegal R.
Niger R.

Kano
L. Chad
CHAD
Ft. Lamy
Shari

FR. SOM.
Djibouti
Berbera
BR. SOM.

Addis Ababa

Freetown
SIERRA LEONE
LIBERIA
Monrovia

IVORY COAST
GOLD COAST
TOGO
DAHOMEY
NIGERIA
Lagos
Lome
Accra
Benue R.

CAMEROONS
Douala

FRENCH EQUATORIAL AFRICA
UBANGI-SHARI

SUDAN

ABYSSINIA (ETHIOPIA)

ITALIAN SOMALILAND
Mogadishu

FERNANDO PO (Sp.)
PRINCIPE (Port.)
RIO MUNI
SAO TOME (Port.)
ANNOBÓN (Sp.)

GULF OF GUINEA

Libreville
GABON
Brazzaville
CABINDA
Léopoldville

CONGO
Congo R.
BELGIAN CONGO
CONGO BASIN
Uele R.
Bomu R.
Stanleyville
L. Albert
Entebbe
UGANDA
L. Rudolf

KENYA (BR. EAST AFR.)
Nairobi
Mombasa

Lake Victoria
Mt. Kilimanjaro ×
Tabora
GERMAN EAST AFRICA
ZANZIBAR (Br.)
Dar-es-Salaam

INDIAN OCEAN

Lake Tanganyika
Lake Nyasa

ALDABRA IS. (Br.)
COMORO IS. (Fr.)

ANGOLA (PORT. WEST AFR.)
Luanda
Benguela
Kwanza R.
Kwango R.
Cuanza R.

NORTHERN RHODESIA
SOUTHERN RHODESIA
Livingstone
Salisbury
Victoria Falls
Zambezi R.

NYASALAND
Blantyre

MOZAMBIQUE (PORT. EAST AFR.)
Beira

MADAGASCAR
Tamatave
Tananarive

GERMAN SOUTHWEST AFRICA
Windhoek
Walvis Bay
Lüderitz
NAMIB DESERT

BECHUANALAND
KALAHARI DESERT
Mafeking

UNION OF SOUTH AFRICA
Pretoria
Johannesburg
Lourenco Marques
SWAZILAND
Limpopo R.
Orange R.
BASUTOLAND
Durban

Cape Town
Cape of Good Hope
East London
Port Elizabeth

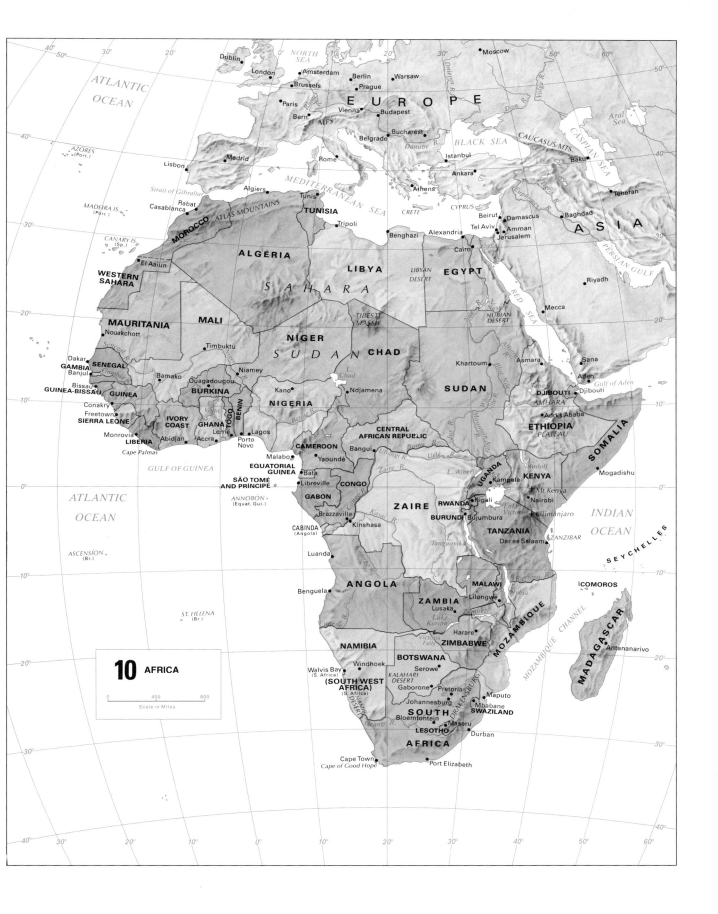

ATLANTIC OCEAN

NORTH SEA

Dublin
London
Amsterdam
Brussels
Berlin
Prague
Warsaw
Moscow

E U R O P E

Paris
Bern
Vienna
Budapest

ALPS

Belgrade
Bucharest
Danube R.
Don R.
Volga R.

AZORES (Port.)

Lisbon
Madrid
Rome
BLACK SEA
Istanbul
CAUCASUS MTS.
Baku
CASPIAN SEA
Aral Sea

Strait of Gibraltar
MEDITERRANEAN SEA
CRETE
Athens
Ankara
CYPRUS

A S I A

MADEIRA IS. (Port.)
Casablanca
Rabat
Algiers
Tunis
TUNISIA
Tripoli
Benghazi
Alexandria
Beirut
Tel Aviv
Jerusalem
Damascus
Amman
Baghdad

MOROCCO
ATLAS MOUNTAINS

CANARY IS. (Sp.)
El Aaiun

WESTERN SAHARA

ALGERIA

LIBYA

LIBYAN DESERT

EGYPT

Cairo
Suez

RED SEA

Riyadh

S A H A R A

Mecca

MAURITANIA
Nouakchott

MALI

TIBESTI MASSIF

NUBIAN DESERT

Timbuktu

NIGER

CHAD

Khartoum
Asmara
Sana
Aden
Gulf of Aden

Dakar
SENEGAL
GAMBIA
Banjul

S U D A N

Niamey

L. Chad

Ndjamena

SUDAN

Blue Nile R.
White Nile R.

DJIBOUTI
Djibouti

GUINEA-BISSAU
Bissau

Bamako
Ouagadougou
BURKINA

Kano

AMHARA

GUINEA

Conakry
Freetown
SIERRA LEONE
Monrovia
LIBERIA

IVORY COAST
GHANA
TOGO
BENIN
Lomé
Accra
Abidjan
Porto Novo
Lagos

NIGERIA

Volta R.
Benue R.

Bangui

CENTRAL AFRICAN REPUBLIC

Addis Ababa

ETHIOPIA

PLATEAU

Cape Palmas

GULF OF GUINEA

Malabo
Yaoundé

CAMEROON

Ubangi R.
Uele R.
Bomu R.

SOMALIA

EQUATORIAL GUINEA
Bata
Libreville

SÃO TOMÉ AND PRÍNCIPE

CONGO

Zaire R.

L. Albert
Rudolf

UGANDA
Kampala

Mogadishu

ANNOBÓN (Equat. Gui.)

GABON

ZAIRE

Kigali
RWANDA

Mt Kenya

KENYA

Nairobi
Kilimanjaro

ATLANTIC OCEAN

Brazzaville
Kinshasa

Kasai R.

BURUNDI
Bujumbura

Lake Victoria

INDIAN OCEAN

ASCENSION (Br.)

CABINDA (Angola)

Luanda

Lake Tanganyika

TANZANIA
Dar es Salaam
ZANZIBAR

SEYCHELLES

ST. HELENA (Br.)

ANGOLA

Benguela

ZAMBIA
Lusaka

Lake Kariba

MALAWI
Lilongwe
Lake Nyasa

Ruvuma R.

COMOROS

Zambezi R.

Harare
ZIMBABWE

MOZAMBIQUE

MOZAMBIQUE CHANNEL

MADAGASCAR

NAMIBIA

Victoria Falls

Windhoek

BOTSWANA
Serowe

KALAHARI DESERT

Antananarivo

Walvis Bay (S. Africa)

(SOUTH WEST AFRICA) (S. Africa)

Gaborone
Pretoria
Johannesburg
Maputo
Mbabane
SWAZILAND

NAMIB DESERT

Orange R.

SOUTH

Bloemfontein
LESOTHO
Maseru
Durban

AFRICA

Cape Town
Cape of Good Hope
Port Elizabeth

DRAKENSBERG

10 AFRICA

0   400   800
Scale in Miles

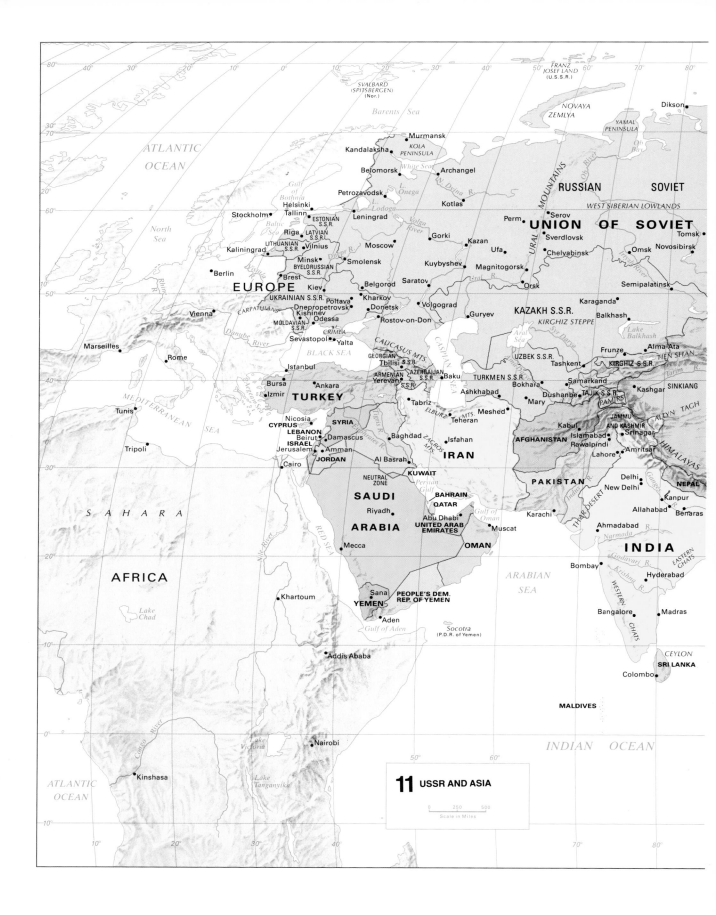

ATLANTIC
OCEAN

SVALBARD
(SPITSBERGEN)
(Nor.)

Barents Sea

FRANZ
JOSEF LAND
(U.S.S.R.)

NOVAYA
ZEMLYA

YAMAL
PENINSULA

Dikson

Murmansk

Kandalaksha

KOLA
PENINSULA

Belomorsk

White Sea

Archangel

RUSSIAN

SOVIET

L. Onega

Petrozavodsk

N. Dvina R.

Kotlas

URAL MOUNTAINS

WEST SIBERIAN LOWLANDS

Gulf of Bothnia

Helsinki

Serov

Perm

UNION   OF   SOVIET

Stockholm

Tallinn

ESTONIAN
S.S.R.

Leningrad

L. Ladoga

Volga River

Gorki

Kazan

Sverdlovsk

Tomsk

North Sea

Riga

LATVIAN
S.S.R.

Moscow

Ufa

Chelyabinsk

Omsk

Novosibirsk

Kaliningrad

LITHUANIAN
S.S.R.

Vilnius

Dnepr R.

Smolensk

Kuybyshev

Magnitogorsk

Ural R.

Orsk

Semipalatinsk

Berlin

Minsk

BYELORUSSIAN
S.S.R.

Brest

Vistula R.

EUROPE

Kiev

Belgorod

Saratov

Irtysh River

Volgograd

Karaganda

Vienna

Rhine R.

UKRAINIAN S.S.R.

Poltava

Kharkov

Donetsk

KAZAKH S.S.R.

Balkhash

CARPATHIANS

Dnepropetrovsk

Kishinev

Rostov-on-Don

Guryev

KIRGHIZ STEPPE

Lake Balkhash

MOLDAVIAN
S.S.R.

Odessa

Aral Sea

Syr Darya

Marseilles

Danube River

CRIMEA

Sevastopol

Yalta

Frunze

Alma-Ata

Rome

BLACK SEA

CAUCASUS MTS.

UZBEK S.S.R.

Tashkent

KIRGHIZ S.S.R.

TIEN SHAN

Istanbul

GEORGIAN S.S.R.

Tbilisi

CASPIAN SEA

Samarkand

SINKIANG

Bursa

Ankara

ARMENIAN
S.S.R.

AZERBAIJAN
S.S.R.

Baku

TURKMEN S.S.R.

Bokhara

Dushanbe

TAJIK S.S.R.

Kashgar

Tarim R.

Tunis

Izmir

TURKEY

Yerevan

Tabriz

ELBURZ MTS.

Ashkhabad

Mary

PAMIRS

ALTYN TAGH

MEDITERRANEAN   SEA

Nicosia

CYPRUS

SYRIA

Damascus

Tigris R.

Meshed

JAMMU
AND KASHMIR

HIMALAYAS

LEBANON

Beirut

Baghdad

ZAGROS MTS.

Teheran

Kabul

Srinagar

Tripoli

ISRAEL

Jerusalem

Amman

Al Basrah

Isfahan

IRAN

AFGHANISTAN

Islamabad

Rawalpindi

Amritsar

JORDAN

Cairo

KUWAIT

NEUTRAL
ZONE

Persian Gulf

Lahore

Indus R.

Delhi

NEPAL

Ganges R.

SAHARA

SAUDI

Riyadh

BAHRAIN

QATAR

PAKISTAN

New Delhi

THAR DESERT

Kanpur

Nile River

ARABIA

Red Sea

Abu Dhabi

UNITED ARAB
EMIRATES

Gulf of Oman

Muscat

Karachi

Allahabad

Benaras

Ahmadabad

Narmada R.

INDIA

AFRICA

Mecca

OMAN

ARABIAN
SEA

Bombay

Godavari R.

EASTERN GHATS

Hyderabad

WESTERN GHATS

Krishna R.

Khartoum

Lake Chad

Sana

YEMEN

PEOPLE'S DEM.
REP. OF YEMEN

Aden

Gulf of Aden

Socotra
(P.D.R. of Yemen)

Bangalore

Madras

CEYLON

SRI LANKA

Addis Ababa

Colombo

MALDIVES

INDIAN   OCEAN

Congo River

Lake Victoria

Nairobi

ATLANTIC
OCEAN

Kinshasa

Lake Tanganyika

11 USSR AND ASIA

0   250   500

Scale in Miles

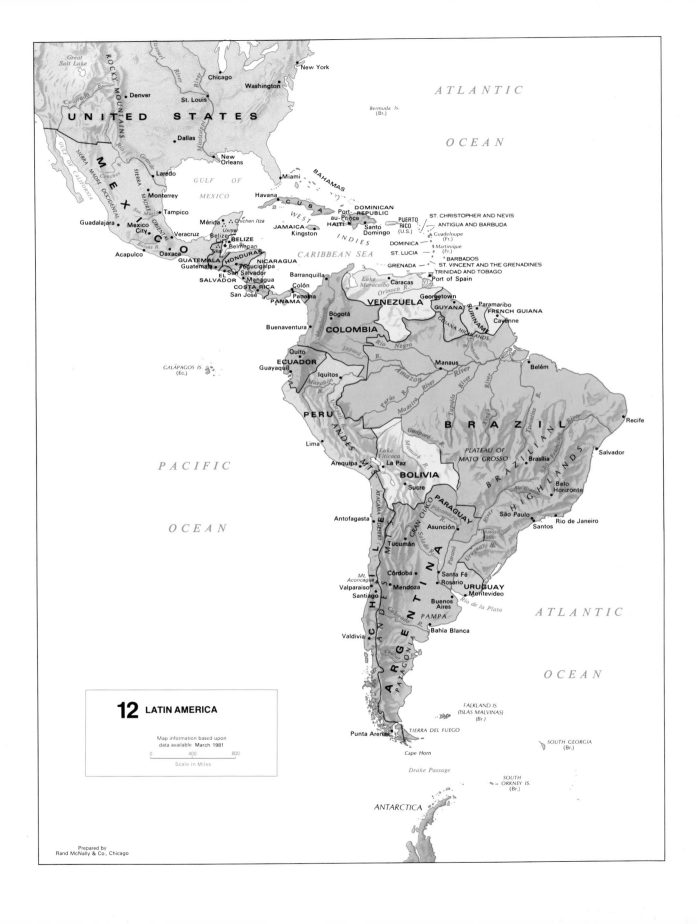

ATLANTIC

OCEAN

Bermuda Is.
(Br.)

New York
Chicago
Washington
St. Louis
Denver
*Great
Salt Lake*
Colorado
Missouri
River
River
River
Mississippi

UNITED   STATES

Dallas

GULF OF CALIFORNIA

MEXICO

SIERRA MADRE OCCIDENTAL

SIERRA MADRE ORIENTAL

Laredo

Monterrey
Tampico

Guadalajara
Mexico
City
Veracruz
Acapulco
Oaxaca

Mérida
Chichen Itza
Uxmal

GULF   OF
MEXICO

New
Orleans

Miami

BAHAMAS

Havana

CUBA

WEST

JAMAICA
Kingston

Port-
au-Prince
HAITI

DOMINICAN
REPUBLIC
Santo
Domingo

PUERTO
RICO
(U.S.)

ST. CHRISTOPHER AND NEVIS
ANTIGUA AND BARBUDA
Guadeloupe
(Fr.)
DOMINICA
Martinique
(Fr.)
ST. LUCIA
BARBADOS
ST. VINCENT AND THE GRENADINES
GRENADA
TRINIDAD AND TOBAGO
Port of Spain

INDIES

CARIBBEAN   SEA

Belize
City
BELIZE
Belmopan
GUATEMALA
Guatemala
HONDURAS
EL
SALVADOR
San Salvador
Tegucigalpa
NICARAGUA
Managua
COSTA RICA
San José
PANAMA
Colón
Panama

Barranquilla

Caracas

Lake
Maracaibo

VENEZUELA

Orinoco R.

Georgetown
GUYANA
Paramaribo
SURINAME
FRENCH GUIANA
Cayenne

Bogotá
Buenaventura

COLOMBIA

GUIANA HIGHLANDS

Magdalena R.

Río   Negro

Japurá
R.

Quito
ECUADOR
Guayaquil

GALÁPAGOS IS.
(Ec.)

Iquitos

Manaus

Belém

Amazon

River

Marañón R.

PERU

Ucayali R.

ANDES   MTS.

Lima

Paras R.

Madeira   River

Tapajós R.

Tocantins R.

Recife

BRAZIL

PACIFIC

Arequipa

Lake
Titicaca
La Paz

BOLIVIA

Sucre

Mamoré R.

Guaporé R.

PLATEAU OF
MATO GROSSO

Brasília

BRAZILIAN

HIGHLANDS

Salvador

Belo
Horizonte

OCEAN

Antofagasta

ATACAMA DESERT

GRAN CHACO

PARAGUAY

Asunción

Pilcomayo R.

Río Grande

São Francisco R.

São Paulo
Santos

Rio de Janeiro

Iguaçu
Falls

Iguaçu R.

Tucumán

Salado R.

Paraná

Santa Fé
Rosário

URUGUAY
Montevideo

Uruguay R.

Mt.
Aconcagua
Valparaiso
Santiago
Córdoba
Mendoza

ARGENTINA

Buenos
Aires

Río de la Plata

PAMPA

ANDES   MTS.

Colorado R.

Bahía Blanca

Valdivia

PATAGONIA

Chubut R.

ATLANTIC

OCEAN

12 LATIN AMERICA

Map information based upon
data available March 1981

0   400   800

Scale in Miles

FALKLAND IS.
(ISLAS MALVINAS)
(Br.)

SOUTH GEORGIA
(Br.)

Punta Arenas

TIERRA DEL FUEGO

Cape Horn

Drake Passage

SOUTH
ORKNEY IS.
(Br.)

ANTARCTICA

Prepared by
Rand McNally & Co., Chicago

GREECE
Tiranë
ALBANIA
Thessaloníki
Istanbul Üsküdar
Sea of Marmara
Bursa
Eskişehir
Izmir
AEGEAN SEA
Athens
CRETE
RHODES
MEDITERRANEAN SEA

T U R K E Y
Ankara
Konya
Kayseri
TAURUS MTS.
Adana
Gaziantep
Diyarbekir
Erzurum
Trabzon
Samsun
BLACK SEA
Kizil R.
Van L.
MT. ARARAT
Tiflis
Kura R.
Sevan L.
CAUCASUS MTS.
Baku
Araks R.
Resht
Tabriz
Urmia L.
KURDISTAN
Krasnovodsk

Benghazi
Tobruk
Siwa
El Alamein
Alexandria
El Faiyum
Cairo
SINAI
Port Said
Jerusalem
Tel-Aviv
ISRAEL
Elath
JORDAN
Amman
Beirut
LEBANON
Damascus
SYRIA
Homs
Hama
Aleppo
CYPRUS
Nicosia

LIBYA
LIBYAN DESERT

EGYPT
El Minya
Asyut
Kharga
Qena
Aswan
Wadi Halfa
Lake Nasser
Nile R.
Gulf of Suez
Suez Canal
Gulf of Aqaba

S U D A N
Dongola
El Obeid
Omdurman
Khartoum
Atbara
Kassala
Asmara
Port Sudan
White Nile
Blue Nile
Nile R.

ETHIOPIA

Jiddah
Mecca
Medina
Yanbú
Taima
Haii
HEJAZ
AN NAFUD
SYRIAN DESERT
Baghdad
Karbala
An Najaf
I R A Q
Mosul
Kirkuk
Kermanshah
Hamadan
ZAGROS MOUNTAINS
Isfahan
Teheran
ELBURZ MTS.

S A U D I A R A B I A
Buraida
Riyadh
Hofuf
Dhahran
NEUTRAL ZONE
KUWAIT
Kuwait
Basra
Abadan
Bushire
Shiraz
PERSIAN GULF
BAHRAIN
QATAR
Doha
Abu Dhabi
Sharja
UNITED ARAB EMIRATES
RUB' AL KHALI (EMPTY QUARTER)

I R A N
Kermanshah
Hamadan
Yezd
Birjand
Kerman
PLATEAU OF IRAN
DASHT-I-KAVIR (DESERT)
Meshed
KOPET MTS.
Ashkhabad
Chardzhou
Amu Darya R.
KARA KUM DESERT
KYZYL KUM DESERT

S O V I E T U N I O N

AFGHANISTAN
Herat
Maimana
Kandahar
Helmand R.

PAKISTAN

RED SEA
ASIR
Hodeida
San'a
YEMEN
Aden
PEOPLE'S DEM. REP. OF YEMEN
Mukalla
Sayhut
Undefined Boundary
KURIA MURIA IS.

OMAN
Masqat
Sur
GULF OF OMAN

ARABIAN SEA

---

13 **THE MIDDLE EAST**

Israeli occupied territory

0 100 200 300 400
Scale in Miles

Prepared by
Rand McNally & Co., Chicago

14 EUROPE

Map information based upon data available March 1981

Scale in Miles

0 100 200 300 400

ATLANTIC OCEAN

MOROCCO

ATLAS MOUNTAINS

ALGERIA

Rabat
Tangier
Ceuta (Sp.)
Gibraltar (Br.)
Strait of Gibraltar
Oran
Algiers

TUNISIA

Tunis

LIBYA

Tripoli

Benghazi

PORTUGAL

Lisbon
Porto

SPAIN

Madrid
Valencia
Bilbao
SIERRA MORENA
SIERRA NEVADA
CANTABRIAN MTS.
PYRENEES
Barcelona
BALEARIC IS.
Palma

ANDORRA

MEDITERRANEAN SEA

SARDINIA
Cagliari

CORSICA
Ajaccio

BALEARIC IS.

FRANCE

Brest
Paris
Lyon
CENTRAL MASSIF
Marseille
Nice
MONACO
Bordeaux
Loire R.
Seine R.
Rhône R.
Rhine R.

BAY OF BISCAY

ENGLISH CHANNEL

UNITED KINGDOM

IRELAND
Dublin
Belfast
NORTHERN IRELAND
SCOTLAND
Glasgow
Edinburgh
Aberdeen
WALES
ENGLAND
London
Liverpool
Manchester
Newcastle
IRISH SEA

NORTH SEA

Faeroe Is. (Den.)

Shetland Is.

NORWAY

Stavanger
Bergen
Oslo

SWEDEN

FINLAND

Luleå
Turku
Helsinki

GULF OF BOTHNIA

NETHERLANDS
Amsterdam
The Hague
Rotterdam

BELGIUM
Brussels
Antwerp

LUX.
Luxembourg

SWITZERLAND
Geneva
Bern
Zürich
Mont Blanc
ALPS

LIECHT.

ITALY
Turin
Milan
Venice
Genoa
Florence
Rome
Naples
APENNINES
SAN MARINO
Trieste

SICILY
Palermo

MALTA

TYRRHENIAN SEA

ADRIATIC SEA

IONIAN SEA

AEGEAN SEA

GREECE
Athens
Salonika
PINDUS MTS.

CRETE
Iraklion

RHODES

ALBANIA
Tirana

YUGOSLAVIA
Belgrade
Sarajevo

FED. REP. OF GERMANY
Cologne
Bonn
Frankfurt
Stuttgart
Munich
Hamburg
Bremen

GERMAN DEM. REP.
Berlin
Leipzig
Dresden
SUDETES

DENMARK
Copenhagen

Kattegat
Skagerrak

BALTIC SEA

Öland
Gotland

Stockholm

POLAND
Warsaw
Gdańsk
Szczecin
Wrocław
Kraków
Oder R.
Vistula R.

Kaliningrad

CZECHOSLOVAKIA
Prague
Bratislava

AUSTRIA
Vienna

HUNGARY
Budapest

Danube R.

ROMANIA
Bucharest
TRANSYLVANIAN ALPS
CARPATHIANS

BULGARIA
Sofia
Varna
BALKAN MTS.

TURKEY
Ankara
Istanbul
Bosporus
Dardanelles
TAURUS MTS.
PONTIC MOUNTAINS

CYPRUS
Nicosia

BLACK SEA

Odessa
Sevastopol
Yalta
CRIMEA
Sea of Azov

Riga
Vilna
Minsk
Smolensk

Leningrad
Lake Ladoga
Lake Onega

VALDAI HILLS

UNION OF SOVIET SOCIALIST REPUBLICS

Moscow
Orel
Kiev
Kharkov
Poltava
Rostov
Gorki
Penza
Kuybyshev
Volgograd
Astrakhan
Sverdlovsk
Perm
Ufa
Orenburg
Gurev
Kotlas
Arkhangelsk

URAL MOUNTAINS

Volga River
Don R.
Dnieper R.
Dniester R.

CAUCASUS MTS.
Mt. Elbrus
Tbilisi
Batumi
Sochi
Baku

CASPIAN SEA

White Sea

ISRAEL
Jerusalem

LEBANON
Beirut

SYRIA
Damascus
Amman
SYRIAN DESERT

IRAQ
Baghdad

IRAN
Tabriz

Suez Canal